D1515261

THE SOCIAL EXPERIENCE

*An Introduction
to Sociology*

THE SOCIAL EXPERIENCE

An Introduction to Sociology

James W. Vander Zanden

Ohio State University

Random House
New York

To today's students:
The citizens of the twenty-first century.

First Edition
987654321
Copyright © 1988 by Random House, Inc.

Library of Congress Cataloging-in-Publication Data

Vander Zanden, James Wilfrid.
    The social experience: an introduction to sociology /
James W. Vander Zanden.
        p.   cm.
    Bibliography: p.
    Includes index.
    ISBN 0-394-36579-8
    1. Sociology.   I. Title.
HM51.V347   1988   87-25651
301—dc19   CIP

ISBN 0-394-36579-8

Cover photo: Fukuhara/West Light

Manufactured in the United States of America

Preface

Today's students will be the citizens of the twenty-first century. The very best thing that colleges can do is to prepare them to live in an ever-changing world filled with countless choices and endless uncertainty. Sociology is uniquely poised to assist with this challenge. It is a discipline that illuminates the human experience. Sociology invites us to examine aspects of social life that we often ignore, neglect, or take for granted. As sociologists, then, we can provide our students with something special: A new vision of the social experience and a sharpening of their observational and analytical skills. After taking a course in introductory sociology, students should never again see social life in quite the same way.

Encouraging Students to Think Critically and Creatively

Like other instructors, I despair when students passively accept the information provided them without questioning and analyzing what they are taught. Our intention is not simply to fill the mental files of our students' brains with definitions and facts. We want to encourage them to think critically and strengthen their desire to recognize problems and attack them logically. *Cultivating a Sociological Consciousness* boxes show students how to focus the sociological perspective on a wide range of topics. The boxes also describe how sociologists have recognized and attacked problems in the past and how they are continuing their observations in the late 1980s.

Textbooks that are bereft of controversy and unanswered questions leave students believing that facts are the stuff of education. Students derive a false sense of security born of cramming their heads with information rather than refining their minds with analysis. *The Social Experience* offers students an opportunity to think critically about sociological information and its relationship to their personal lives and world. Many of the boxes are organized by the theme *Issues That Shape Our Lives.* The material in the boxes reveals sociology not as an ivory tower discipline but as one that informs about issues and policies that affect every day life. Controversies are presented in ways that students can ponder.

Fostering Student Interest and Motivation

The text seeks to inspire student motivation, curiosity, and interest so that students will want to explore its subject matter. Each chapter opens with a vignette portraying how our individual experiences are tied to the social world about us. The subject of sociology is everyday life and, even more significantly, the issues that confront us as we endeavor to lead fuller, richer, and more fruitful lives. A course in sociology should help students liberate their minds so that they become an integral part of a more truly human community. Not only should they learn about the social world in which they are immersed, but they should discover how they can contribute to the larger society. The first course in sociology can increase student awareness of social issues such as those related to race, gender, poverty, health care, and the environment. In the tradition of C. Wright Mills, then, the chapter introductions demonstrate that our personal fortunes and fates overlap with the larger structure and history of our society.

Creating Opportunities for Interactive Discussion

The *Thinking Through the Issues* inserts can be a powerful adjunct for discussion sessions. Instructors can use them to make sociology classes a time for intellectual enthusiasm—occasions to develop skills in reasoning and problem solving. Sociology, therefore, emerges not as the "light and the truth" but as a search for light and truth. It is curiosity, discovering things, and asking "Why? Why is it so?" Traditionally, social scientists conceived of thought as something that originates inside each person, and then comes to be expressed socially. But increasingly they are coming to realize that thought emerges primarily as a social process and becomes internalized as it is socially expressed. Because reflecting and working together with others is so important in our daily lives and because a substantial portion of our ability to think originates outside ourselves, it behooves us to see class discussion as more than just a peripheral part of an introductory course. One of the best ways instructors foster critical thinking is when they serve as facilitators, and simultaneously recognize, that they, too, are learners. Because individual differences abound, highly stylized procedures for promoting higher order thinking do not work for everyone. Students must ultimately find out what methods of problem finding and problem solving work best for them.

Affording Life-Long Career Preparation

In the past several years the narrow vocationalism of many programs in higher education has increasingly become the focus of critical reports and the subject of controversy (see Chapter 17). Indeed, many colleges and universities have undertaken a soul-searching revamping of their curriculums so that their graduates will be prepared to take a larger role in society. Students need to be more than technological mercenaries; they must not only be capable of solving problems but of framing them as well. Moreover, there are better ways of calculating the profit and loss associated with a bachelor's degree than merely looking at starting salaries. Few people stay in the same line of work over the life course; they switch jobs and even professions. Established jobs and occupations will also disappear and new ones will emerge. Given the difficulty of predicting which skills will be in demand in the years ahead, students' best career preparation is one that prepares them for lifelong learning. *The Social Experience* seeks to facilitate this process.

Providing a First-Rate College Education

Educating the citizens of the twenty-first century is an awesome task. But it is, nonetheless, our task. Sociology is a core discipline for preparing students to cope with the radically changing institutions and new and perplexing problems that await them in an uncertain future. Scientific inquiry is an essential response to the challenges brought about by change. Hopefully, this text can assist instructors in the development of those habits of mind that emphasize intellectual curiosity, logical thinking, and critical analysis, including abilities that permit thoughtful responses to problems and arguments that involve quantitative data. The educated person of the twenty-first century will be a person who is flexible, adaptable, creative, innovative, and comfortable with new and different things—not only a bearer of society's traditions but one who has the ability to integrate and apply knowledge wisely and so contribute to society's improvement.

Using the Text

Clearly, there is no one "right" way to teach introductory sociology. The chapters are sufficiently independent that they can be reordered in their assignment without posing problems for students. Users of this text should make it serve their unique teaching objectives and their students' needs. *The Social Experience* is meant to be a tool. Accordingly, instructors should feel free to omit chapters that do not meet their teaching needs. For those who would prefer a more compact text, I have written *Sociology: The Core* which contains 12 chapters and is published by Alfred A. Knopf. My experience and success with the core introductory text served as an inspiration in writing *The Social Experience*.

Supplements

The Social Experience is accompanied by a comprehensive package of learning and teaching aids that represent the combined efforts of a number of able sociology instructors.

The student *Study Guide with Classic Readings* and the *Test Bank* were prepared by Sherry Cable at the University of Tennessee, Gary Madsen at the University of Utah, Donald Hinrichs at Gettysburg College, Richard Dukes and Sandra Matthews at the University of Colorado at Colorado Springs, and Thomas Dunn at Western Kentucky University. The *Study Guide with Classic Readings* contains chapter outlines and objectives, along with key terms and review questions. The guide also offers classic statements from the sociology canon; each is prefaced by a sketch of the author and precis of the selection, followed by three or more questions that ask for analysis.

The *Test Bank* offers 75 multiple choice questions per chapter, arranged in pairs for duplicate testing. They are grouped by chapter topic and are categorized by type: factual or conceptual. Answers are keyed to the text. The *Test Bank* is available as a bound manual and on diskette for either IBM or Apple II computers.

The *Instructor's Manual* was prepared by Madeleine Adriance at Mount Ida College, Duane Dukes at John Carroll University, Joseph DeBolt at Central Michigan University, David Helm at Merrimac Education Center, Glenn Jacobs at the University of Massachusetts (Boston), Paul Leslie at University of North Carolina at Greensboro, and Ingram Parmley at Francis Marion College. The *Instructor's Manual* includes chapter summaries and goals, lecture outlines, and two to three lecture themes for each chapter. Along with these themes, come theme discussion questions and data and perspectives for analysis sections. The opening section of the manual provides teaching tips for the new instructor and the foreign TA, and suggests ways of assigning the text and using the supplement package.

Thanks and Appreciation

Authors do not write textbooks all by themselves. Countless scholars over the generations have contributed to our understanding of the social experience. And a multitude of reviewers helped me shape and reshape the manuscript at various stages. They appraised the clarity of expression, technical accuracy, and completeness of coverage. Their help was invaluable and I am indebted to them. They include:

Donald Alexander
Prarie State College

Tim Anderson
Bentley College

Bill Bailey
University of Wisconsin–Stout

George W. Barger
University of Nebraska

Kenneth Beausang
Black Hawk College

Donald Berg
South East Missouri University

Kendall Blanchard
Middle Tennessee State University

W.J. Brindle
Monroe Community College

Ben B. Bruggen
Junior College of Lake County

Edwina H. Byrd
Sinclair Community College

John Campbell
University of Wisconsin–Parkside

Walter F. Carroll
Bridgewater State College

Alfred L. Carter
Mercer County Community College

Mary Beth Collins
Central Piedmont Community College

Gerry R. Cox
Fort Hays State University

Lois C. Dilatush
Metropolitan State College

David A. Edwards
San Antonio College

David L. Ellison
Rensselaer Polytechnic Institute

Erwin H. Epstein
University of Missouri

Eugene Erickson
Cornell University

William Fairbanks
Cuesta College

Thomas J. Fararo
University of Pittsburgh

Mark A. Foster
Clinch Valley College of the University of Virginia

Theodore Fuller
Virginia Polytechnic Institute and State University

Michael J. Fuller
St. Louis Community College

Albeno P. Garbin
University of Georgia

Jurg Gerber
University of Idaho

John C. Gessner
College of St. Thomas

Norman Goldner
University of Detroit

Patricia Harvey
Colorado State University

Denny E. Hill
Georgia Southern College

Peter Hirschburg
Southeastern Missouri University

Kirk A. Johnson
Washburn University

Malcolm Kovacs
Montgomery College

Jerome Krase
Brooklyn College

Michael Kupersanin
Duquesne University

Don C. Larson
Utah State University

Charles Lawrence
Fashion Institute of Technology

Ellen L. Maher
Indiana University

Lou Maris
Milwaukee Area Technical College

Ruben Martinez
University of Colorado at Colorado Springs

Carol May
Illinois Central College

Roger McVannan
Broome Community College

J. Jack Melhorn
Emporia State University

W.D. Merchant
Thornton Community College

Al Miranne
University of Wisconsin, Eau Claire

Ray Ponte
Los Angeles Valley College

Kanwal D. Prashar
Rock Valley College

Richard Rettig
Central State University

J.D. Robson
University of Arkansas at Little Rock

Daniel J. Santoro
University of New Hampshire

Earl R. Schaeffer
Columbus Technical Institute

J. Scherer
Oakland University

William A. Schwab
University of Arkansas

Carol Slone
Calhoun Community College

Peter H. Smith
Ocean County College

Kevin B. Smith
Lamar University

W.E. Snizek
Virginia Polytechnic University

Gretta G. Stanger
Tennessee Technological University

Gerald Stott
South East Missouri University

Thomas J. Sullivan
Northern Michigan University

L. Alex Swan
Texas Southern University

Rance Thomas
Lewis and Clarke Community College

Jean H. Thoresen
Eastern Connecticut State University

Edgar L. Webster
Northeastern State University

William Jeremiah Wellisch
Red Rocks Community College

Kristen Wenzel
College of New Rochelle

Mary Whatley
Jefferson State Junior College

Sarah A. White
J. Sargeant Reynolds Community College

I thank everyone at Random House who helped to turn an ordinary manuscript into an attractive, stylish book. It truly has been a team undertaking: Carolyn Viola-John, the project editor; John Lennard, designer; Kathy Bendo, photo editor; Barbara Salz, photo researcher; and Lori Hatcher, marketing manager. Patricia Plunkett did a masterful job coordinating the review process and ancillaries. But most appreciated of all was her enthusiasm and dedication. My special thanks go once again to senior editor Bert Lummus. In the course of this and a number of other books he has become a good and valued friend. Bert is a person who cares: He cares about people and about books. Indeed, were one to fashion an ideal editor, Bert would be that editor.

Acknowledgments

I am especially obliged to the following people who reviewed large sections of the manuscript and saw the text through various drafts and phases:

Richard Anderson
University of Colorado at Denver

Robert Day
University of North Carolina at Charlotte

Gary Hampe
University of Wyoming

C. Allen Haney
University of Houston

Dean Harper
University of Rochester

John Hartman
Wichita State University

Beth Hartung
Southern Illinois University at Carbondale

Bradley Hertel
Virginia Polytechnic Institute and State University

Albert Higgins
State University of New York at Albany

Kathleen Kaleb
Western Kentucky University

Alice Kemp
University of New Orleans

Marvin Koller
Kent State University

Kenneth Mietus
Western Illinois University

Larry Perkins
Oklahoma State University

James Peterson
Western Michigan University

J. D. Robson
University of Arkansas at Little Rock

Dwayne Smith
Tulane University

James Smyth
San Joaquin Delta College

Jack Spencer
University of New Orleans

Ronald Stewart
William Rainey Harper College

Brad Stewart
Miami University

Sharon Timmerman
Indiana State University

William Tolone
Illinois State University

Eric Wagner
Ohio University

Ira Wasserman
Eastern Michigan University

James W. Vander Zanden

Contents

Boxes

PART ONE

Studying Social Life

1

Sociology: Illuminating The Social Experience

To him who devotes his life to science, nothing can give more happiness than increasing the number of his discoveries, but his cup of joy is full when the results of his studies immediately find practical application.

—Louis Pasteur

Exchange a glance with someone, then look away. Do you realize that you have made a statement? Hold the glance for a second longer, and you have made a different statement. Hold it for 3 seconds, and the meaning has changed again. For every social situation, there is a permissible time that you can hold a person's gaze without being intimate, rude, or aggressive.

If you are on an elevator, what gaze-time are you permitted? To answer this question, consider what you typically do. You very likely give other passengers a quick glance to size them up and to assure them that you pose no threat. Since being close to another person signals the possibility of interaction, you need to emit a signal telling others you want to be left alone. So you cut off eye contact, what sociologist Erving Goffman (1963) dubs "a dimming of the lights." You look down at the floor, at the indicator lights, anywhere but into another passenger's eyes. Should you violate the rule against staring at a stranger on an elevator, you will make the other person exceedingly uncomfortable, and you are likely to feel a bit strange yourself.

If you hold eye contact for more than 3 seconds, what are you telling another person? Much depends on the person *and* the situation. For instance, a man and a woman communicate interest in this manner. They typically gaze at each other for about 3 seconds at a time, then drop their eyes down for 3 seconds, before letting their eyes meet again. But if one man gives another man a 3-seconds-plus stare, he signals "I know you," "I am interested in you," or "You look peculiar and I am curious about you." This type of stare often produces hostile feelings. On the other hand, if your professor is talking to you, you would be well advised to listen intently, with your eyes riveted to the professor's face. To look around would signal disrespect. The professor, however, may look around while you are speaking; the higher-status person has this liberty (Mazur, 1985).

As these illustrations suggest, there is much in the social experience that you and others take for granted. Life contains many levels of meaning, and things are not always what they seem. Networks of invisible rules and social arrangements guide and influence your behavior. You continually evolve, negotiate, and rework subtle agreements with acquaintances, family members, friends, lovers, and work associates as you steer along the paths of everyday activity. Many of these understandings are outside the usual threshold of your awareness. As you look behind the outer structure of the world and scrutinize the hidden fabric, you encounter new levels of reality. It is this reality that sociologists investigate—the subject matter of the pages and chapters that follow.

PLANNING AHEAD: TARGETED READING

1. What unique insights do we gain about ourselves and society from a sociological perspective?

2. How are our private experiences and personal difficulties entwined with our society's structural arrangements and the historical times in which we live?

3. What are the social uses of sociological knowledge?

4. How are sociological ideas and theories shaped by the times in which sociologists live?

5. What major contributions did Auguste Comte, Herbert Spencer, Karl Marx, Emile Durkheim, and Max Weber make to our understanding of the social experience?

A Sociological Consciousness

More than 2300 years ago Aristotle wrote: "The human is by nature a social animal." Put another way, you may be many things, but above all you are a social creature destined to live your life with other people in society. Your relationships with others lie at the core of your existence. You were conceived within a relationship, were born into relationships, became genuinely human in relationships, and live your life within relationships. In brief, you cannot be human all by yourself. What you think, how you feel, and what you say and do is fashioned by your interaction with other people in group settings. It is the web of meanings, expectations, behavior, and institutional arrangements that result when people interact with one another in society that is the stuff of sociology. Let us define **sociology** as the scientific study of society, and more particularly, as the study of human organization.

Human beings have long had an interest in understanding themselves and their social arrangements. Judging by ancient folklore, myths, and archeological remains, they have pondered why people of other societies order their lives differently than themselves. They have wondered why some members of society violate social rules. They have questioned why some people should be wealthy and powerful and others poor and powerless. And they have been bewildered and troubled by episodes of mass hysteria, revolution, and war. It seems that our species wants to understand what life means, and how it has come about. At first human beings developed and applied the scientific method for the study of physical and biological phenomena. It has been only in the past hundred and fifty years or so that they have turned to science for an explanation of their behavior. This science—sociology—pursues the study of society through research governed by the rigorous and disciplined collection and analysis of facts.

The Sociological Challenge

Sociology illuminates the human experience. It invites us to examine aspects of the social environment that we often ignore, neglect, or take for granted. By studying sociology, we can achieve a better grasp of how our society is organized, where power lies, what beliefs channel our behavior, and how our society has come to be what it is. Sociology provides a unique perspective that encourages us to look behind the outer aspects of social life and discern its inner structure—to suspend the belief that things are simply as they seem. In other words, sociology equips us with a special form of consciousness. This consciousness helps us to better understand the social forces we confront, especially those that constrain us and free us. Thus sociology is a liberating science (Berger, 1963).

By looking at social arrangements in imaginative and fresh ways, we gain a new vision of the social experience. The old, familiar, and even comfortable ways we have for viewing life change. We find that the society into which we are born shapes our identities, personalities, emotions, thought processes, and fortunes in countless ways. Indeed, the structures of society become the structures of our own consciousness: "Society does not stop at the surface of our skins. Society penetrates us as much as it envelops us" (Berger, 1963:121). So the challenge of sociology is to go beyond appearances and peer behind the masks people and organizations wear.

A classic study carried out by the social scientist Elliot Liebow (1967) in Washington, D.C., helps to clarify these points. Liebow spent eighteen months studying the lives of some twenty black men who "hung out" on the streetcorner in front of the New Deal Carry-out Shop. The shop is located within walking distance of the White House in a blighted section of the city. Old, three-story, red-brick row houses occupy the neighborhood, most of them long since converted to rooming houses and tenements. Liquor shops, pawnbrokers, poolrooms, cleaners, barber shops, and related establishments predominate on the corners of most blocks. The New Deal Carry-out Shop is one of these businesses. It is open seven days a week, serving a diverse clientele coffee, hamburgers, french fries, hot dogs, and "submarines." Men in the area regularly come to the corner sidewalk in front of the shop to pass the time. Here they eat and drink, enjoy easy talk, banter with women who pass by, and "horse around."

If you were to happen on this Washington neighborhood on a typical weekday morning, you might witness the following scene (Liebow, 1967:29):

> A pickup truck drives slowly down the street. The truck stops as it comes abreast of a man sitting on a cast-iron porch and the white driver calls out, asking if the man wants a day's work. The man shakes his head and the truck moves on up the block, stopping again whenever idling men come within calling distance of the driver. At the Carry-out corner, five men debate the question briefly and shake their heads no to the truck. The truck

---

Black Streetcorner Men
Our work experiences leave few areas of our personal lives untouched. Elliot Liebow found that streetcorner men differ little from middle-class men in their attitudes and aspirations. Most of them also wanted stable marriages and jobs. But the work that was available to the streetcorner men was usually menial, seasonally variable, and low paying. The jobs offered little hope for advancement and often did not pay enough to support a family. *(Ethan Hoffman/Archive)*

turns the corner and repeats the same performance up the next street. In the distance, one can see one man, then another climb into the back of the truck and sit down.

The white truck driver is able to recruit only two or three men from the twenty to fifty he typically contacts. He interprets his experiences as confirming the stereotype that black streetcorner men are lazy and irresponsible, unwilling "to take a job even if it were handed to them on a platter." But Liebow discovered quite a different picture. In fact, most of the men on the corner that morning had jobs. Boley was a member of a trash-collection crew that worked on Saturdays and had this weekday off. Sweets worked nights mopping floors, cleaning toilets, and picking up trash in an office building. Tally had come back from his job after his employer had concluded that the weather was too cold for pouring concrete. Clarence had to attend an eleven o'clock funeral, and Sea Cat had to appear as a witness in a trial in answer to a court subpoena.

Others on the corner that morning had been laid off from work and were drawing unemployment compensation. They had nothing to gain by accepting a job that paid little more than they received in unemployment benefits. Still others like Bumdoodle, a numbers man, hustled money illegally. Yet others were disabled, like the man on the cast-iron steps, who turned out to be severely crippled by arthritis. Finally, there were a small number like Arthur, able-bodied men who had no visible means of support and who did not want a job.

The truck driver thought that the Arthurs do not work because they are shiftless and undependable. Liebow's research challenged these stereotyped images. He discovered that streetcorner men and middle-class men differ less in their attitudes toward the future than in the different futures they anticipate. Middle-class men command sufficient financial means to justify committing their resources to long-term goals in money-market funds, savings accounts, mutual funds, stocks, and bonds. They hold jobs that offer the promise of upward mobility in corporate or professional careers. They can reasonably expect their children to pursue a higher education. But for streetcorner men it is different: They must use all their resources to maintain themselves here-and-now. So when streetcorner men squander a week's pay in a day or two, it is not because they are unconcerned with the future. They do so precisely because they are aware of the bleakness of that future.

Like many privileged Americans, the white truck driver had located the job difficulties of ghetto men in the men themselves—or, more precisely, in their lack of willingness to work. Given this interpretation, government policy might best be directed toward changing the motivations of streetcorner men and encouraging them to develop the values and goals that lead to occupational achievement. But Liebow's research revealed something quite different. The streetcorner men and other American men did *not* differ in their fundamental values or goals, the men on the corner also wanted stable jobs and marriages. However, their experiences had taught them that jobs are only intermittently available, almost always menial, often hard, and invariably low-paying. Offered only routine jobs that present no challenge, they come to work feeling flat and stale. The jobs available to them as dishwashers, janitors, store clerks, and unskilled laborers lie outside the tracks leading to career advancement in the United States. The men are not going anywhere, and they know it. Moreover, earning too little money to support themselves, a wife, and children, they are uncertain of their ability to carry out their responsibilities as husbands and fathers.

In seeking to understand the lives of the streetcorner men, Liebow looked "beyond" the individuals themselves to the social fabric in which the men were enmeshed. He turned his investigative eye upon the social arrangements that are external to people, but that nonetheless *structure* their experiences and place constraints on their behavior. In any society some individuals must do the "dirty work," the tasks that are dead-end, seasonally variable, and at times dangerous (Gans, 1972; Ezekiel, 1984). As we will see in Chapter 10, the nation's institutions systematically discriminate against the members of minority groups, leading to the uneven distribution of society's benefits and burdens.

What we have been saying adds up to this: Society—and more particularly its groups and institutions—is the focus of sociology. The sociological perspective allows us to discern the unquestioned assumptions and expectations that obscure institutional life and to identify their social underpinnings. In brief, sociology brings previously inaccessible aspects of human life to awareness and provides a window on the social landscape that we often overlook or misunderstand.

The Sociological Imagination

A basic reason for studying sociology is that by understanding the society in which we live, we can gain fuller insights into ourselves. Sociologist C. Wright Mills (1959) termed this component **the sociological imagination**—the ability to see our lives, concerns, problems, and hopes as entwined within the larger social and historical context in which we live. He said we typically go about our daily activities bounded by a rather narrow orbit. Our viewpoint is limited to the close-up scenes of our school, job, family, and neighborhood. The sociological imagination allows us to break out from this limited vision and discern the relationship between our personal experiences and the social world about us.

Personal troubles/public issues Mills, an influential but controversial sociologist, pointed out that our personal troubles and public issues "overlap and interpenetrate to form the larger structure of social and historical life." Consider, for instance, the job difficulties experienced by the streetcorner men Liebow studied. In 1986, a "good economic year" in the United States, nearly one out of six black adults and one of two black teenagers were unemployed (in contrast to one out of seventeen white adults and one of five white teenagers). Moreover, between 1979 and 1984, some 11.5 million American workers lost jobs because of plant shutdowns or relocations and only 60 percent of them found new jobs. Most lost their jobs because of rapid changes in technology and foreign competition (see Chapters 15 and 22). A large proportion of the displaced workers were middle-aged people with long and stable job histories in manufacturing (Noble, 1986). Mills (1959:9) contended that we cannot look to the "personal character" of individuals to explain their employment problems under these circumstances: "The very structure of opportunities has collapsed. Both the correct statement of the problem and the range of possible solutions require us to consider the economic and political institutions of the society." (See Figure 1.1.)

Social and historical forces are currently imposing constraints on the career opportunities of many college students. Shifts in the age structure of the population are reshaping the social, economic, and political landscape. The graying of American society is posing particularly thorny problems in the workplace as younger and middle-aged workers jockey for advancement. A nearly 60 percent increase in the number of 35- to 44-year-olds will occur in the decade between 1985 and 1995. Consequently, while many people will be in line for promotions, there will be fewer open slots than there will be people hoping to fill them. In 1986, Americans between 21 and 39 years old were less satisfied with what they had been able to achieve than were the 40 to 64 age group (Lueck, 1986). Some baby boomers are reporting financial hardships their parents never faced. The job frustrations of many younger Americans must therefore be

Different Social Worlds
Children can live in the same city and nation, yet experience quite different social worlds. The attitudes and skills they acquire in their childhood years lay the foundations for the opportunities that will and will not be available to them in later life. Sociology demonstrates that social and historical forces impose constraints on who and what we are and what we can become. *(left, Rae Russel; right, C. Vergara/Photo Researchers)*

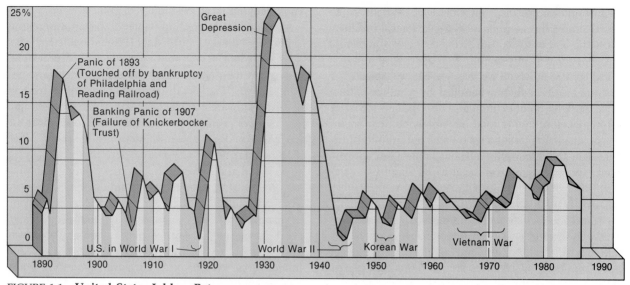

FIGURE 1.1   **United States Jobless Rates**
Average annual unemployment rate (unemployed as a percentage of the civilian labor force); shaded areas indicate recessions. *Source: U.S. Bureau of Labor Statistics.*

understood within the context of the structural factors operating in the larger society and the workplace.

What happens in the global arena similarly affects our lives. Mills (1959:9) also considered issues of war and peace:

> The personal problem of war, when it occurs, may be how to survive it or how to die in it with honor; how to make money out of it; how to climb into the higher safety of the military apparatus; or how to contribute to the war's termination. . . . But the structural issues of war have to do with its causes; with what types of men it throws up into command; with its effects upon economic and political, family and religious institutions, with the unorganized irresponsibility of a world of nation-states.

Mills saw the sociological imagination as a liberating tool that enables us to penetrate our social world and identify the links between our personal biographies and the larger social forces. In so doing, we recognize that what is happening to us is a point at which our personal lives and society intersect. Sociology can tell us why things happen in certain ways rather than in others. It has something to say, something that makes a difference, something that very likely we did not previously know (Collins, 1982).

Applying sociological knowledge   Mills contended that sociologists should not consider their sole mission to be

the development of abstract knowledge; they must also look at the structure of society and find ways in which human conditions can be improved and human freedom expanded. Many of the founders of sociology, including Auguste Comte, Karl Marx, and Lester F. Ward, hoped that the study of society would contribute to a more humane social order. Indeed, to call attention to some facts, however true, is to challenge moral or political views that ignore or distort them. So social science, even when conducted in the purest spirit, often becomes a kind of social criticism.

Like Mills, many sociologists are attracted to sociology because they would like to improve our world, to allow us to lead fuller, richer, and more fruitful lives. To do this, they need knowledge about the basic structures and processes of social life. Sociology can play a vital part in this enterprise by undertaking a search for the most effective ways to achieve particular ends. Put another way, knowledge must inform action. John Viscount Morley (1901:58) made a similar point at the turn of the century when he observed: "It is not enough to want to do good. One must do it the right way." Sociology provides a method of inquiry that enables us to probe the social world. For example, many governmental health, education, housing, and welfare programs depend on the collection of census and other statistical data based on sample, survey, and statistical techniques developed by sociologists.

Through its emphasis on observation and measurement, sociology allows us to be systematic in collecting information that bears on difficult questions associated with various social practices and choices. For instance, the U.S. Supreme Court relied on social science findings regarding the effects of segregation on children in reaching its historic 1954 decision declaring mandatory school segregation unconstitutional (Cook, 1984). Similarly, research on the nursery school experiences of children was influential in leading government officials to establish the Head Start Program in 1965. The purpose of Head Start is to provide preschool educational opportunities for economically disadvantaged children so that they may become financially independent adults. Later, sociologists and other social scientists designed studies to discover whether or not Head Start was achieving its goals. They found that children who participated in Head Start programs in the 1960s have performed in regular school as well as or better than their peers and have had fewer grade retentions and special-class placements. Additionally, youths who were in a Head Start program engage in less antisocial and delinquent behavior and are more likely to finish high school and get jobs or go to college than peers who were not in a program (Lazar and Darlington, 1982; Schweinhart and Weikart, 1985).

Social science research has dramatically changed our ideas about crime, aging, alcoholism, mental illness, foreigners, foreign cultures, and differences between men and women. As the box shows, the social sciences have debunked a good many myths. A particularly notable achievement was Gunnar Myrdal's 1944 landmark study, *An American Dilemma.* In it the Swedish sociologist documented how blacks were victimized by racism and discrimination. The report made a significant contribution toward changing American racial attitudes and practices. Because of sociological research, Americans today have a quite different view of human behavior and social institutions than did their parents only a generation ago (Sterba, 1982).

Sociology, then, can be a powerful tool both for acquiring knowledge about ourselves and for intervening in social affairs to achieve various goals. But a better understanding of social processes does not guarantee that our knowledge will be put to use in the formation of better social policies. What the sociological imagination promises is not easy to deliver. Knowledge can contribute to the improvement of the human condition only if it is used. Sociology is not a storehouse of facts and formulas to be applied mechanically to social problems, but a

way of looking at the human condition realistically. Sociological knowledge is everyone's property and responsibility—a set of tools not just for those with power, but also for those over whom power is exercised (Hewitt, 1979).

THINKING THROUGH THE ISSUES

Under what circumstances might policymakers be reluctant to use sociological findings? Why might privileged individuals and groups experience discomfort with a study such as that undertaken by Elliot Liebow in a Washington ghetto? Could Liebow's findings be seen as threatening their positions of privilege? In brief, might sociological findings run counter to the economic and political interests and goals of a society's power-holders? Why do policymakers typically resist sociological studies that evaluate the effectiveness of existing social programs (Rossi and Wright, 1984)? Might they be willing to support research to test programs they would like to have considered for future enactment and implementation? What implications do your answers have for sociology as a discipline and for sociological researchers?

Microsociology and Macrosociology

As we have seen in our discussion above, Mills emphasized that our personal troubles and public issues overlap and interpenetrate to form the larger structure of social life. We can extend his insight by distinguishing between the "micro" or small-scale aspects of the social enterprise and the "macro" or large-scale structural components. If we follow the first approach, we look at behavior close-up and see what happens as people interact on a face-to-face basis. We term this level **microsociology**—*micro* meaning "small," as in the word *microscope.* Microsociology involves the detailed study of what people say, do, and think moment by moment as they go about their daily lives. Elliot Liebow's study of the black men on the Washington streetcorner is a good example of microsociology. He examined how the men saw themselves, how they dealt with one another in face-to-face encounters, and how they balanced their hopes and aspirations with their real-world experiences. Microsociology, then, deals with everyday life—a man and a woman initiating a conversation at a singles bar, several teenagers playing basketball on a ghetto play-

CULTIVATING A SOCIOLOGICAL CONSCIOUSNESS

Sociology: Beyond Common Sense

Many of the sociological findings in this text will probably have already occurred to you. You should not be surprised, because the subject matter of sociology is everywhere around you. Should you conclude, therefore, that sociology is simply common sense dressed in new jargon? One problem with common sense explanations is that we usually invoke them *after* we know the facts. Social scientists find that our recollection of the outcomes we expect from some experiment or historical situation is instantly distorted once we know what actually happened. For instance, when we make predictions about future political events, we later mistakenly remember them as coinciding with what we now know happened (Myers, 1983).

Nor do we have much difficulty turning to a stockpile of ancient proverbs. Since nearly every possible outcome is conceivable, there are proverbs for virtually all occasions. But reflect. Does "Absence make the heart grow fonder"—or is it the reverse, "Out of sight, out of mind"? Do "Opposites attract"—or do "Birds of a feather flock together"? Or is it "Pennywise, pound foolish"—or "A penny saved is a penny earned"? As we will see in the chapters that follow, sociology has taken us a long way

beyond what is revealed by common sense. Common sense may apply under some circumstances, but it may also be wrong. Indeed, many of our common sense beliefs are myths. Consider the following:

Myth: Saturation bombing, such as that conducted against the Japanese and Germans during World War II, contributes to social disruption and leads to panic and societal disintegration.
Fact: Carpet bombing of civilian centers during World War II increased rather than diminished civilian morale and resistance by inducing a high degree of social bonding (Adams, 1982). See Chapter 5.

Myth: There is safety in numbers. You are more likely to receive help in an emergency if there is a large crowd of people about.
Fact: You are more likely to receive help if only one other bystander is present. When many people are present, both the obligation to assist and the potential blame for not helping are spread around. A "surplus" of helpers diffuses an individual's sense of responsibility (Latané and Darley, 1970; Latané and Nida, 1981). See Chapter 7.

Myth: The typical voter makes a rational decision based on candidates' records and positions on issues.
Fact: Most voters decide early, often even before they know who the candidates are (Adams, 1982). Moreover, a person's vote is strongly influenced by his or her family, ethnic, religious, class, and regional ties. See Chapter 16.

Myth: Among American blacks, those who are most deprived are much more likely to be militant than those who are better off.
Fact: During the 1960s and early 1970s, the better the education, the higher the prestige of the occupation, and the greater the income, the more likely an American black was to be militant (Marx, 1969). See Chapters 9, 10, and 21.

Myth: When the moon is full, there is a sharp increase in crime, suicide, alcoholism, and murder.
Fact: Data from thirty-seven studies reveal no relationship between the full moon and human behavior (Rotton and Kelly, 1985). The full moon does not make any difference in people's daily lives. However, social factors play a major part in deviance. See Chapter 8.

Myth: Most poor people prefer to live off government welfare.
Fact: Only about one-third of poor families received public assistance payments in 1984; 43 percent of poor households received food stamps; and 26 percent lived in publicly owned housing or received government rent subsidies (O'Hare, 1986). See Chapter 9.

ground, an office birthday party, a police officer directing traffic at a busy intersection, a barbershop quartet performing before an audience, an instructor fielding questions from a class of chemistry students, or a meeting of city officials.

Alternatively, we can turn our sociological eye upon the "big picture" and study social groups and societies. When we view life at this level, each person is simply one dot among many dots that comprise a larger picture, much in the manner of dots on a television screen. This approach is termed **macrosociology**—*macro* meaning "large." Macrosociology focuses upon large-scale and long-term social processes, including the "state," "class," the "family," the "economy," "culture," and "society." At this level we direct our attention to the interplay between economic and political processes in a

"Confound it, Merriwell! Do you mean that all this time you've been talking micro while we've been talking macro?"

Drawing by Lorenz; © 1982 The New Yorker Magazine, Inc.

society, changes in the structure of a religious sect, the impact of computer technologies on the workforce, shifts in the racial and ethnic composition of a community, modernization in a Third World nation, or the dynamics of intergroup rivalries. When we examine the lives of the streetcorner men from a macrosociological perspective, we gain a picture of the institutional constraints that minority men face and that limit their job opportunities. As we will see in Chapters 9 and 15, the American economy is structured so that millions of Americans are locked within dead-end jobs.

Clearly, the microsociological and macrosociological levels are not independent of one another. The circumstances of the streetcorner men testify to this fact (Ezekiel, 1984). Indeed, the distinction between micro and macro is one of degree. Larger structures are made up of repetitive patterns of interaction on the micro level. In turn, what people think, say, and do is influenced and shaped at the micro level by larger structures (Goode, 1986).

THINKING THROUGH THE ISSUES

Try to link your immediate classroom experiences—your experiences with your instructor and classmates—with the American higher educational system. Viewed at the microsociological level, you are immersed in a series of day-to-day activities. What motivates you to attend college and engage in these activities? Are you primarily interested in expanding your intellectual horizons, or in securing the credentials that you hope will lead to a good job? From the macrosociological level, how do various majors such as engineering, accounting, history, English literature, and psychology fit the dictates of the American job market? In what ways do your classroom experiences mirror the workplace and prepare you for a place in it? How has the class position of your parents influenced the academic skills and the educational goals you bring with you to the college environment?

The Development of Sociology

Just as we must seek an understanding of our private experiences and personal difficulties in the institutional arrangements and the historical period in which we live, so we must locate the origins of sociology in the social times in which it developed. In Europe, the political revolutions ushered in by the French Revolution in 1789 and carrying over through the nineteenth century provided a major impetus to sociological work. Many people, troubled by the chaos and disorder that character-

Sociology Arose in Turbulent Times
The French Revolution of 1789 and the Napoleonic Wars that followed in its wake severely disrupted European social and political life. Between 1800 and 1810, much of Europe was dominated by France under Napoleon Bonaparte. The disorder and chaos of the war years and the unsettled postwar social climate encouraged scholars like Auguste Comte to study society. They hoped to uncover insights that would allow humankind to achieve a more harmonious and prosperous social order. *(The Bettmann Archive)*

ized Europe, longed for more peaceful and orderly times. Many sophisticated thinkers also turned to questions of social order and progress, and an awareness of society as a distinctive object of study developed (Ritzer, 1983; Swingewood, 1984).

Simultaneously, another force was at work. A new industrial order was forming. The Industrial Revolution that swept many Western nations resulted in large numbers of people leaving a predominantly agricultural setting for work in factories. New social and economic arrangements arose to provide the many services required by emergent capitalism. The excesses of the industrial system led thinkers like Karl Marx to scrutinize the operation of social and economic institutions and to propose alternatives to them. Let us turn to a brief consideration of the contributions of five particularly influential sociologists and then to the emergence of sociology in the United States. You are asked to study these early sociologists not only for historical interest, but because their work remains of contemporary value. Table 1.1 provides a brief discussion of how sociology differs from psychology, economics, political science, and anthropology.

Auguste Comte

Auguste Comte (1798–1857) is commonly credited with being the "founder" of sociology and as having coined the name "sociology" for the new discipline. His main focus was the improvement of society. If we are to improve society, Comte reasoned, we need a special science to establish the laws of social life. On the basis of

these laws, we could then prescribe cures for societal ills. Since he believed that science is the foundation of all knowledge, Comte emphasized that the study of society must be scientific. So he urged sociologists to use systematic observation, experimentation, and comparative-historical analysis as methods (matters we will consider in Chapter 2).

Comte divided the study of society into social statics and social dynamics. **Social statics** involves those aspects of social life that have to do with order and stability and that allow societies to hold together and endure. **Social dynamics** refers to those aspects of social life that have to do with social change and institutional development. He thought that social order depended on the existence of a community of ideas—a *consensus*—shared by the members of a society. And he took an optimistic view of historical development, believing it resulted in long-term progress. Although the specifics of his work no longer govern contemporary sociology, Comte exerted enormous influence on the thinking of other sociologists, particularly Herbert Spencer and Emile Durkheim.

Herbert Spencer

Herbert Spencer (1820–1903), an English sociologist deemed by some to be the "second founder" of sociology, shared Comte's concern with social statics and social dynamics. Spencer viewed society as similar to the living body. Based on this organic analogy, Spencer depicted society as a *system*, a whole made up of interrelated parts. Just as the human body is made up of organs

Table 1.1   Sociology and the Other Social Sciences

In thinking about sociology's place in the social sciences, it is important that we avoid the tendency to view the various academic disciplines as somehow separated into "watertight" compartments. At best, academic disciplines are loosely defined—indeed, the border lines are so vaguely conceived that researchers following an interest often give little thought in practice to whether they are "invading" another discipline's field of study. The prevailing view has increasingly become one of welcoming aid and collaboration from any qualified persons, be they in the same discipline or not. Even so, broad, rough demarcation lines divide the social sciences.

Psychology. Psychology has traditionally focused upon *individual* behavior, considering such properties of personality as attitudes, needs, traits, and feelings, as well as such processes as learning and perception. Sociology, in contrast, has dealt primarily with relations among people—with social interaction and organization. Stated very simply, sociology has focused on what occurs *among* people; psychology has emphasized what occurs *within* people.

Economics. Economics arose primarily as a response to a practical concern with such matters as trade, taxation, pricing, manufacturing, and financing. Traditionally, economics has studied the production, distribution, and consumption of goods and services; for instance, the extent and nature of employment, income, welfare expenditures, and tax resources. Economists—in contrast with their sociological counterparts—have typically paid little attention to the actual interaction occurring between people in the economic sphere (to such things as the part values and preferences play in affecting the supply of labor or the influence of prestige or custom on the price of goods) or to the social structures (corporations and labor unions) that are the products of social life.

Political Science. Political science developed within the United States chiefly as a discipline having two main interests: political theory (the ideas of Plato, Machiavelli, Rousseau, Marx, and others) and government administration (the formal structure and functions of government agencies). In recent years, however, political scientists have become increasingly interested in political *behavior*, and have undertaken studies of community decision making, voting behavior, public opinion, power structures, political movements, and government bureaucracy. There is little that distinguishes these political scientists from sociologists with similar interests.

Anthropology. Anthropology has historically enjoyed considerable kinship with sociology. In recent decades, however, the fields have progressively separated, with sociologists and anthropologists going their separate ways. This development has gained momentum as prehistoric archeology, physical anthropology, psychological anthropology, and social anthropology have separated out of general anthropology. Social anthropology retains many of the same interests as sociology, except that anthropologists have traditionally studied preliterate groups, whereas sociologists have studied contemporary, complex, and literate societies. But even this distinction has broken down over the past two decades. In truth, there is little that distinguishes social anthropology and sociology other than the accidental and scientifically irrelevant differences in the routes by which the two fields have come to their current interests.

like the kidneys, lungs, and heart, so society is made up of institutions like the family, religion, education, the state, and the economy. Spencer's approach parallels that of biologists who portray an organism in terms of its structures and the functional contributions these structures make to its survival. Such an image of society is in line with what sociologists now call structural-functional theory, a perspective we will have more to say about in the next chapter.

Spencer handled social statics by means of the organic analogy, but he was even more concerned with social dynamics. He found ideas in Charles Darwin's evolutionary theory that were akin to his own and applied the concept of the "survival of the fittest" to the social world, an approach termed **social Darwinism.** He sought to demonstrate that government should not interfere with the natural processes of society, because only in this manner would people who were "fit" survive and

Auguste Comte

Karl Marx

W.I. Thomas

W. E. B. DuBois

Harriet Martineau

Emile Durkheim

Lester Ward

Charles Horton Cooley

Auguste Comte publishes *Course of Positive Philosophy* in six volumes (1830–1842).

Harriet Martineau publishes *How to Observe Manners and Morals* (1838), the first book on the methodology of social research; her mode of analysis is close to what is now known as the comparative analysis of social structure.

Karl Marx publishes the *Communist Manifesto* with Friedrich Engels (1848) and *Das Kapital* (1867).

Lester Ward publishes *Dynamic Sociology* (1883).

Emile Durkheim publishes *The Division of Labor in Society* (1893) and *Suicide* (1897).

American Journal of Sociology founded (1895).

W.E.B. DuBois publishes *The Philadelphia Negro* (1900).

Charles Horton Cooley publishes *Human Nature and the Social Order* (1902).

Max Weber publishes *The Protestant Ethic and the Spirit of Capitalism* (1904–1905).

American Sociological Society founded (1905).

W.I. Thomas coauthors with Florian Znaniecki *The Polish Peasant in Europe and America* (1918).

George Herbert Mead's lectures are published as *Mind, Self, and Society* (1934).

American Sociological Review founded (1935).

Talcott Parsons publishes *The Structure of Social Action* (1935) and *The Social System* (1951).

Robert K. Merton publishes *Social Theory and Social Structure* (1949).

C. Wright Mills publishes *The Sociological Imagination* (1959).

Hubert M. Blalock, Jr., publishes *Measurement in the Social Sciences* (1974) and *Causal Models in Experimental and Panel Designs* (1985).

Max Weber

Talcott Parsons

Robert K. Merton

C. Wright Mills

George Herbert Mead

FIGURE 1.2 **Milestones in Sociology**
(Comte and DuBois: Culver Pictures; Martineau, Ward, and Durkheim: The Bettmann Archive; Marx and Weber: courtesy of German Information Center; Cooley, Mead, Parsons, and Merton: courtesy of American Sociological Association; Thomas: Historical Picture Services; Mills: Library of Congress)

reproduce and those who were "unfit" die out. If this principle were allowed to operate freely, human beings and their institutions, like plants and animals, would progressively adapt themselves to the surrounding environment and reach higher levels of historical development. While Comte saw sociology as guiding humankind in the construction of a better society, Spencer wanted sociology to demonstrate that we should not interfere with societal processes.

Spencer's social Darwinist outlook shows that the ideas we hold about ourselves and the universe are shaped by the social age in which we live. Significantly, Spencer did much of his serious writing during the zenith of laissez-faire capitalism. So it is hardly surprising that he embraced the doctrine that rugged individualism, unbridled competition, and government restraint achieve the greatest positive good. Spencer's social Darwinist ideas were used extensively within England and the United States to justify unrestrained capitalism. John D. Rockefeller, the American oil tycoon, would echo Spencer and observe: "The growth of a large business is merely a survival of the fittest. . . . This is not an evil tendency in business. It is merely the working out of a law of nature" (quoted by Lewontin, Rose, and Kamin, 1984:26).

Karl Marx

Karl Marx (1818–1883) considered himself to be a political activist, not a sociologist. Yet his ideas have had a strong influence on sociology—and philosophy, history, social psychology, economics, and political science as well. He viewed science not only as a vehicle for understanding society, but also as a tool to transform it. Marx was especially anxious to change the structure of capitalist institutions and establish a more humane social order. Because of his activities as a political radical, he was exiled from his native Germany. In 1849, a year after the publication of *The Communist Manifesto*, he settled in London. Here he researched and wrote *Das Kapital* and other works that analyzed capitalism and its ills.

Marx has influenced sociological thinking both by his penetrating insights and by the fact that some sociologists have fashioned their work specifically *against* his theory (Giddens, 1971; Gurney, 1981; Zeitlin, 1981). Prior to the 1960s, most American theorists simply dismissed Marx as an ideologist whose partisan sympathies barred him from producing serious scientific work. But as young American sociologists were drawn into the civil rights and antiwar movements of the 1960s and early 1970s, they found a good deal that was relevant in Marx's ideas. In the intervening three decades, American sociologists have increasingly come to accord Marx his rightful place among the giants of sociological thought. Certainly without the work of Marx, sociology would not be what it is today (Mills, 1962; Ritzer, 1983).

Marx tried to discover the basic principles of history. He focused his search on the economic environments in which societies develop, particularly the current state of their technology and their method of organizing production (such as hunting and gathering, agriculture, or industry). At each stage of history, he said that these factors dictate the group that will dominate society and the groups that will be subjugated. He contended that society is divided into those who own the means of producing wealth and those who do not, giving rise to **class conflict** (see Chapters 9 and 15). All history, he asserted, is composed of struggles between classes. In ancient Rome, it was a conflict between patricians and

The Cruelty of the Early Industrial System
The abject misery and abuse of workers in the 19th century—many of them women and children—led Karl Marx to condemn capitalist arrangements. He believed workers were deprived of the fruits of their labor by capitalists. But Marx thought the working class was growing in numbers and discipline and would in time seize power from the capitalists. *(The Bettmann Archive)*

plebeians and between masters and slaves. In the Middle Ages, it was a struggle between guildmasters and journeymen and between lords and serfs. And in contemporary Western societies that sprouted from the ruins of the feudal order, class antagonisms revolve about the struggle between the oppressing capitalist class or bourgeoisie and the oppressed working class or proletariat. The former derive their income through their ownership of the means of production, primarily factories, which allows them to exploit the labor of workers. The latter own nothing except their labor and, because they are dependent for a living upon the jobs provided by capitalists, must sell their labor in order to exist. History is thus not simply a set of random happenings.

Marx's view of the world is known as **dialectical materialism.** It is based on the notion that development depends on the clash of contradictions and the creation of new, more advanced structures out of these clashes. Every economic order, he said, grows to a state of maximum efficiency, while it develops internal contradictions or weaknesses that contribute to its decay. Thus the roots of an opposing order already begin to appear in an old order. In time the new order displaces the old while simultaneously absorbing its most useful features. Society is propelled from one historical stage to another as each new order triumphs over the old. Marx depicted societies as advancing through a series of stages in which slavery was displaced by feudalism and feudalism by capitalism, and in turn in which capitalism would be dis-

placed by socialism and ultimately socialism by communism (the highest stage). History, then, proceeds by a series of conflicts and resolutions and not by minute and gradual changes. Since Marx thought that capitalism inevitably experiences one economic crisis after another, he was certain that one day it would reach its final crisis—a revolution mounted by the working class.

Marx portrayed political ideologies, law, religion, family organization, education, and government as making up the **superstructure** of society. The economic base of society—its mode of producing goods and its class structure—influences the forms its other institutions take. When one class controls the means whereby people derive their livelihood, they gain the leverage necessary to structure other aspects of institutional life—the superstructure—in ways that favor their class interests. Thus each historical stage or social order has its distinctive superstructure (see Figure 1.3).

We will have a good deal more to say about Marx in the chapters that follow. For our purposes here, suffice it to note that Marx is now recognized by most sociologists as a major figure in sociological theory. Today he is better known and understood, and more widely studied, than at any time since he began his career in the 1840s. His work has inspired hard, detailed examinations of the social order in which we live. Much of what is valuable in his work has now been incorporated in mainstream sociology, particularly as it finds expression in the conflict perspective we will consider in the next chapter.

Revolutionary Waves of 1830 and 1848
In 1830 and again in 1848 armed insurrections broke out in many European cities. The revolutionists called for democratic rights, including universal suffrage and individual liberty. Inspired by the revolutionary fervor of 1848, Karl Marx and Friedrich Engels issued The Communist Manifesto. It began with the words: ''A specter haunts Europe—the specter of communism.'' *(The Bettmann Archive)*

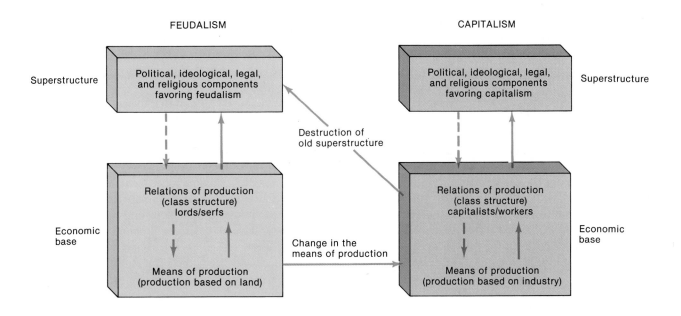

FIGURE 1.3 **The Marxian Model of Base and Superstructure**
The solid arrows represent a primary causal relation; the broken arrows depict a
secondary causal relation.

THINKING THROUGH THE ISSUES

**Are you a political radical? If you can answer
"yes" to most or all of the following questions,
you probably qualify as one. Do you believe that
piecemeal reforms (civil rights legislation, ERA,
antipollution laws) are like "the rearranging of
deck chairs on the *Titanic*"—too marginal to carry
out the fundamental restructuring society requires? Do you believe that "the Revolution" is
urgent if world war, world pollution, or some
similar catastrophe is to be avoided? Do you favor
mass demonstrations and "direct action" techniques, believing that the electoral process is too
slow, too heedless of public opinion, or too easily
thwarted by "the Establishment"? Do you think
that the present system is so bad there is no real
danger that its overthrow would lead to something worse? Do you have rather vague ideas of
what the "new society" would look like beyond
such concepts as "a planned society" or "more
equality"? Do you believe the intellectual basis
for your position has already been worked out by
some unusually gifted person—perhaps Marx,
Castro, or Ayatollah Khomeini (Bronfenbrenner,
Sichel, and Gardner, 1984)?**

Emile Durkheim

Marx was intrigued by the dynamics of class conflict and
historical forces that impel social change. In contrast,
the French sociologist Emile Durkheim (1858–1916)
was interested in how societies hold together and endure.
He thought Marx attributed too much importance to
economic factors and class struggle and too little to social
solidarity (Bottomore, 1981). Moreover, Marx operated
outside the established academic community. Durkheim
worked within it and sought to win acceptance of sociology as a rigorous scientific discipline. He had the distinction of being the first professional French sociologist to
be appointed to a faculty position in sociology.

Durkheim ascribed ultimate social reality to the
group, not to the individual. Accordingly, he contended
that social facts constitute the proper domain of sociological study. **Social facts** are aspects of social life that cannot be explained in terms of the biological or mental
characteristics of the individual. We experience a social
fact as external to ourselves. It takes on the qualities of a
"thing," something like an enormous rock. You come
up against it and cannot move it by simply wishing it out
of existence. In a similar sense society is real, something
you must reckon with (Berger, 1963). For instance, you
cannot flout moral and legal rules without encountering

social disapproval, perhaps even imprisonment or a death sentence. So the social fact serves to *constrain* your behavior. It surrounds and encompasses your life.

As viewed by Durkheim, society is a system formed by interacting people that comes to constitute a reality in its own right, one with distinctive properties. Society is more than the sum of its parts. In this sense, society is like a chemical compound such as sodium chloride, ordinary table salt. As an individual element, sodium is a soft solid; it reacts violently with water and ravages tissue if placed in the mouth. Chlorine is a greenish-yellow gas that was used in chemical warfare in World War I. When the two elements are brought together, a rapid reaction takes place that forms a white crystalline solid. The new substance is entirely—*qualitatively*—different from either sodium or chlorine. When tasted, nothing

unpleasant happens; in fact, it is a necessary food. Durkheim said that society too is not reducible to its individual members. It is an entity—a "thing"—in its own right. So he reasoned that the explanation of social life must be sought in society itself.

Durkheim emphasized that social facts are not only external to you; you typically incorporate your society's standards of behavior within your personality. Social rules become internalized and govern you "from within." Consequently, social facts are saturated with moral properties. This notion is central to Durkheim's work, because he distrusted human nature. He feared that left to themselves, people would pursue their individual advantage and as a result would find themselves engulfed in endless strife. In order to save people from social chaos and even suicide, a strong moral order is essential (Strasser, 1976). As we will see in Chapter 14, Durkheim thought that feelings of moral obligation fuse people together within a functioning social whole. He believed that a shared sense of right and wrong is inseparable from feelings of belonging to a group, be it the human race, a nation, a community, or a family.

In *The Division of Labor in Society* (1893/1964) Durkheim examined social solidarity. He distinguished between the solidarity found in early and modern societies. In early societies the social structure was relatively simple, with little division of labor. People engaged in essentially similar tasks as jacks-of-all-trades. Because as generalists they were alike, they experienced much the same social world. Their sense of oneness derived from this fact—they were so *alike*, what Durkheim called **mechanical solidarity**. Modern societies, in contrast, are characterized by much more complex social arrange-

Australian Aborigines Undertaking Totem Ceremonials
The religious practices of the Australian aborigines provided Emile Durkheim with a number of insights regarding social solidarity. The aborigines inhabit a semi-desert region and forage for food in small bands of two or three families. Given the long periods of separation from other bands, Durkheim wondered how the aborigines managed to retain their identities as members of a larger society. He believed he found the answer in religion. The small bands periodically assemble to worship their common totem ancestor. In this manner, the society harnesses the awesome force associated with the belief in the supernatural to create and intensify a sense of oneness and moral authority. *(Courtesy of the Department of Library Services, American Museum of Natural History)*

ments and by a sophisticated division of labor. People perform specialized tasks in factories, offices, and schools. Since each person performs a relatively narrow range of tasks, no one person can be self-sufficient—all must depend upon others in order to survive. Under these circumstances society "hangs together" because people are compelled to cooperate so that each may achieve goals that individually they cannot achieve, what Durkheim labeled **organic solidarity.**

Durkheim contended that social solidarity is necessary both for the maintenance of the social order and for the happiness of its individual members. He sought to demonstrate that the destruction of social bonds has negative consequences, and under some circumstances, can lead individuals to commit suicide. In his classic study entitled *Suicide* (1897/1951), Durkheim undertook the painstaking collection and analysis of data in order to test his theory. Whereas earlier sociologists were given to armchair speculation, he used population data gained from government records to refute theories that explained suicide in terms of climatic, geographic, biological, racial, or psychological factors. He proposed that suicide is a social fact and as such is explainable by social factors. Durkheim investigated suicide rates among various groups of Europeans and found that some groups had higher rates than others. For example, Protestants had higher rates than Catholics; the unmarried, higher rates than the married; and soldiers, higher rates than civilians. Additionally, suicide rates were higher in times of peace than in times of war and political turmoil, and in times of economic prosperity and recession than in times of economic stability. Based on these findings, he concluded that different suicide rates are the consequence of variations in social solidarity. People who are integrated in a web of social bonds are less inclined to suicide than those whose ties to group life are weak. Although critics have since faulted one or another aspect of Durkheim's work, *Suicide* remains a landmark study in the history of sociology.

Max Weber

Perhaps no sociologist other than Marx has had a greater impact upon sociology than the German sociologist Max Weber (pronounced "Vay-ber"; 1864–1920). Significantly, a good deal of Weber's work was a debate with "the ghost" of Marx. Although finding much of value in Marx's writings, Weber disagreed with Marx on a number of important matters. Over the course of his career, Weber left a legacy of rich insights for a variety of disci-

plines, including economics, political science, and history. Among sociologists he is known not only for his theoretical contributions, but for his insights regarding power, bureaucracies, social stratification, law, religion, capitalism, music, the city, and cross-cultural studies.

For Weber, the study of **social action**—behavior that involves the intervention of thought processes—is the heart of sociology. He concluded that a critical aspect of the sociological enterprise is the study of the intentions, values, beliefs, and attitudes that underlie our behavior. Weber believed sociologists can derive an *understanding* of social action in a manner that is unavailable to chemists and physicists. In investigating human behavior, sociologists are not limited to such objective criteria as weight and temperature; they can examine the "meanings" we bring to our interactions with one another. He used the German word **Verstehen**—meaning "understanding" or "insight"—in describing this approach to learning about the definitions we attach to our actions. In using this method, sociologists mentally imagine themselves in the shoes of other people and identify what those people think and how they feel. In this way sociologists grasp the *uniqueness* of the human experience.

Another notable contribution made by Weber is his concept of the ideal type. An **ideal type** is a concept constructed by a sociologist to portray the essential properties of a phenomenon. The term *ideal* has nothing to do with moral evaluations of any sort. Rather, it is an abstract portrait—a tool—that allows sociologists to generalize and "simplify" data by ignoring minor differences in order to emphasize major similarities. In the chapters that follow we will see how Weber employed the notion of the ideal type to devise a model of bureaucracy (Chapter 5), to examine the connection between Calvinism (the Protestant ethic) and capitalism (Chapter 14), and to distinguish types of authority (Chapter 16). Weber contended that if sociologists are to establish cause and effect relationships, they must use concepts that are defined precisely. The ideal type affords such a standard—it is a measuring rod against which sociologists can compare actual cases.

Weber did not share Marx's view of social theory. Marx believed that every social theory sustains or undermines specific class interests. Theory is not something sterile—ivory tower truisms lacking social meaning—but a class weapon. In the hands of the downtrodden and oppressed it becomes a tool to initiate fundamental social change. In contrast, Weber insisted that sociology must be **value-free,** owing allegiance to no flag or cause. He contended that sociologists must not allow their personal

The Protestant Ethic
Max Weber believed he identified the source of the capitalist ethos in the religious doctrines of John Calvin. The Puritans of colonial Massachusetts were followers of the Calvinistic tradition. The ethic encouraged hard work, sobriety, thrift, restraint, and the avoidance of earthly pleasures. Weber said these values are consistent with the spirit of capitalism and foster practices that lead people to amass capital and achieve economic success. (*North Wind Picture Archives*)

biases to affect the conduct of their scientific research. Weber recognized that sociologists, like everyone else, have individual biases and moral convictions regarding behavior. But he insisted that sociologists must rigorously cultivate a disciplined approach to the phenomena they study in order to determine facts as they are, not as they might wish them to be. By the same token, Weber recognized that objectivity is not neutrality. *Objectivity* is the pursuit of scientifically verifiable knowledge. *Neutrality* implies that a person does not take sides on an issue. Weber saw a role for values in certain specific aspects of the research process—namely, in selecting a topic for study and in determining the uses to which the knowledge is put. Clearly, data do not speak for themselves; they must be interpreted by scientists (Ritzer, 1983). For his part, Weber was a political liberal. He contributed numerous articles to newspapers and actively participated in politics.

American Sociology

The sociologists we have considered thus far have been European. Were sociologists to establish a Sociological Hall of Fame, Comte, Spencer, Marx, Durkheim, and Weber would unquestionably be among its first inductees. Yet as sociology entered the twentieth century, American sociologists assumed a central role in its development. In the period preceding World War I, a number of factors provided a favorable climate for sociology in the United States (Hinkle, 1980; Lantz, 1984). As in

Europe, industrialization and urbanization gave a major impetus to sociological study. An added factor was the massive immigration of foreigners to the United States and the problems their absorption and assimilation posed for Americans.

Lester F. Ward (1841–1913) played a role in the early development of sociology in the United States. Ward had an unusual career; he spent most of it as a paleontologist with the United States Geological Survey. He was influenced by the ideas of Spencer, but unlike Spencer, he was an advocate of social reform. Ward thought sociologists should identify the basic laws of social life, and then use this knowledge to improve human society. William Graham Sumner (1840–1910), who as a professor at Yale taught the first sociology course in the United States, was also influenced by Spencer. And like Spencer, he adopted a survival-of-the-fittest approach. Sumner gave sociology the distinction between we-groups and they-groups (see Chapter 5). Investigative field work was given impetus by W.E.B. DuBois (1868–1963), a leading black intellectual and one of the founders of the National Association for the Advancement of Colored People (NAACP). While an instructor at the University of Pennsylvania, DuBois gathered material on the black community of Philadelphia which appeared as *The Philadelphia Negro* in 1900. Between 1896 and 1914, DuBois led the annual Atlanta University Conferences on Negro Problems that produced the first real sociological research on the South.

Of particular significance in the development of American sociology was the work undertaken at the University of Chicago. Here the first American department of sociology was established in 1892, and until 1940 Chicago sociologists dominated the discipline (as late as 1971 half of all presidents of the American Sociological Association were Chicago faculty or former students at the department). Prominent in the scholarly enterprise of the Chicago sociologists was the study of Chicago itself. They viewed Chicago as a "social laboratory" and subjected it to intense and systematic study. Included in this research were investigations of juvenile gangs, immigrant ghettos, wealthy Gold Coast and slum life, dance halls, prostitution, and mental disorders (Kurtz, 1984; Bulmer, 1985). Influenced by Chicago researchers, such topics as marriage and family relations, crime, delinquency, and race relations attracted considerable sociological interest during the 1930s and 1940s. Many sociologists shared the conviction that a scientific sociology could provide both answers and solutions to the nation's social problems (Lantz, 1984).

From the mid-1940s and until the mid-1960s, sociologists at Columbia, Harvard, and the University of California at Berkeley took the lead and established the major directions for sociological research and theory. Paul L. Lazarsfeld and his colleagues crafted techniques for surveying public attitudes, while Talcott Parsons, Robert K. Merton, and Kingsley Davis refined models that portrayed society as a social system (see Chapter 2). The leaders of American sociology during these years insisted that the discipline should remain aloof from involvement with social problems and concern itself strictly with the enlargement of sociological knowledge.

The social turmoil of the 1960s and early 1970s brought to sociology many students who were student power, civil rights, and peace activists. These "new-breed" sociologists contended that much of traditional sociology promoted the interests of established authority. They saw the doctrine of sociological "neutrality" as a cloak concealing moral insensitivity—a crass disregard for such things as the suffering of the poor and minorities and the destructiveness of war. These sociologists looked to the writings of C. Wright Mills and other proponents of "the sociological imagination" for their inspiration. Many of them felt that sociological knowledge could not be advanced apart from efforts to transform the world (Gouldner, 1970). They also broke with established theory and sought new directions in both theory and research. In the process, critical sociology gained respectability. Thus sociology today is a much more diverse, and many would say richer, discipline than it was a few decades ago. But it is, of course, by no means complete. There are many areas of genuine disagreement, and much research remains to be done.

The Berkeley Student Revolt
Events at the Berkeley campus of the University of California in the fall of 1964 constituted a small-scale but genuine revolution. Through continuous violation of university regulations, sit-ins, daily demonstrations, and finally a student strike, the authority of both the administration and the faculty had become virtually nonexistent. "Berkeley" focused the attention of American college students on the issue of "student power"—the right of students to participate in decision-making processes affecting education and college life. It was a "revolt" that spread to campuses across the United States and drew many students to sociology. In this photo, Mario Savio addresses a mass Berkeley rally that led to Savio and other demonstrators being arrested. *(AP/Wide World Photos)*

CULTIVATING A SOCIOLOGICAL CONSCIOUSNESS

Sociology: Nobel Prizes and Careers

Swedish sociologist Alva Myrdal put her sociological background to work in service to her country and the cause of peace. In 1982 she was awarded the Nobel Peace Prize for her activities on behalf of world disarmament. Two years earlier, she had received the Albert Einstein Peace Prize. From 1962 to 1970 Myrdal was a member of Sweden's parliament and between 1962 and 1973 headed her nation's delegation to the disarmament talks in Geneva. During these years she became increasingly frustrated with how the Soviet Union and the United States were using the talks to prevent and delay progress on disarmament. She subsequently spelled out her thinking in *The Game of Disarmament* (1976). In it, she assessed the foolishness and expense of the arms race. She contended that the two superpowers were playing a "game"

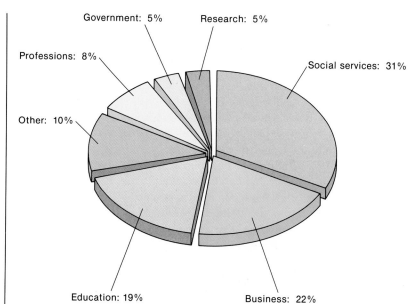

FIGURE A   Employment of Sociology Bachelor Graduates
Source: Adapted from R. Alan Hedley and Susan M. Adams. 1982. The job market for bachelor degree holders: A cumulation. The American Sociologist, 17:155–163.

with the people of the world, pretending to negotiate, when all that was really taking place was a kind of "occupational therapy." Her book re-

Chapter Highlights

1. Sociology equips us with a special form of consciousness. It encourages us to look behind the appearance of social life and discern its inner structure. This consciousness helps us to understand better the social forces we confront, especially those that constrain us and free us. Thus sociology illuminates the social experience.

2. The sociological imagination is the ability to see our private experiences and personal difficulties as entwined with our society's structural arrangements and the historical times in which we live. Sociology can tell us why things happen in certain ways rather than in others. It can play a vital part in the human enterprise by informing us as to the most effective ways for achieving beneficial ends.

3. We can take either a "small-scale" or a "big picture" approach to the study of social life. If we follow the first course, we look at behavior close up and see what happens as individuals interact on a face-to-face basis. We term this approach *microsociology*. Alternatively, we can turn our sociological eye on the "big picture" and study social groups and societies. This approach is termed *macrosociology*.

4. In Europe, the political revolutions ushered in by the French Revolution in 1789 and continuing through the nineteenth century provided a major impetus to sociological work. Simultaneously, an additional force was operating. A new industrial order was in the process of formation. The excesses of the industrial system led some thinkers to scrutinize the operation

counts many opportunities for disarmament that were either rejected or ignored. Her husband, Gunnar Myrdal, won the 1974 Nobel Prize in economics. He is also the author of *An American Dilemma* (1944), a landmark study of American race relations.

A career in sociology may not win you a Nobel Prize. Yet there are career payoffs for studying sociology. Sociology is a popular major and minor for students planning futures in such professions as law, politics, social work, public health, urban planning, community relations, and public administration, not to mention medicine and divinity school. You will likewise find that numerous courses in criminal justice, management, marketing, business organization, labor relations, communication, journalism, recreation, and nursing draw upon the principles, research techniques, and findings of sociology. Employers frequently look for potential employees with the specific skills that are acquired in sociology courses dealing with survey and research methods, statistics, population research, and urban studies. Students with a number of these latter courses may well find themselves at a competitive advantage with other liberal arts students who have majored in history, psychology, English, philosophy, and political science. Figure A shows that most students with bachelor degrees in sociology find employment in social services, followed by business and education.

Besides the specific knowledge gained in sociology courses, sociology majors have opportunities to develop interpersonal, analytical, problem-solving, and communication skills that are essential for success in today's competitive job market. According to *The Wall Street Journal,* after years of favoring job applicants with technical degrees, big employers are wooing social science and liberal arts graduates with growing fervor (Watkins, 1986:33). Employers find that these students can take a variety of problems and apply creative analysis to them.

In order to be hired specifically as a sociologist, it is often necessary to have a master's degree—an MA (Master of Arts) or an MS (Master of Science)—or a doctorate (Ph.D). The master's degree can be an end in its own right or a step toward the Ph.D. It typically requires from one to three years, depending on whether or not the particular department requires a thesis and the speed with which students work. The Ph.D. usually takes four to six years beyond the BA or BS and entails the completion of a dissertation that reveals original research and scholarship. In most situations, a Ph.D. is required for teaching and research at the college and university level and for higher-level employment with good promotion prospects in private industry or government.

of social and economic institutions and to propose alternatives to them.

5. Auguste Comte is commonly credited with being the "founder" of sociology and as having coined the name "sociology" for the new discipline. He divided the study of society into social statics and social dynamics.

6. Herbert Spencer viewed society as similar to the living body. Based on this organic analogy, he depicted society as a system, a whole made up of interrelated parts. Spencer found ideas in Charles Darwin's evolutionary theory that were akin to his own and applied Darwin's concept of the survival of the fittest to the social world, an approach termed Social Darwinism.

7. Karl Marx has influenced sociological thinking both by his penetrating insights and by the fact that some sociologists have fashioned their work specifically to disprove his theory. He tried to discover the basic principles of history. He focused his search upon the economic environments in which societies develop, particularly the current state of their technology and their method of organizing production. Marx contended that society is divided into those who own the means of producing wealth and those who do not, and that this division gives rise to class conflict.

8. Emile Durkheim was primarily interested in how societies hold together and endure. He ascribed ultimate social reality to the group, not to the individual. Accordingly, he contended that social facts constitute

the proper domain of sociological study. Durkheim believed that social solidarity is necessary both for the maintenance of the social order and for the happiness of its individual members. He investigated the social forces underlying suicide in order to test his theory.

9. Max Weber thought that the heart of sociology is the study of social action—behavior that involves the intervention of thought processes. He used the German word *Verstehen*—meaning "understanding" or "insight"—in describing his approach for learning about the subjective meanings we attach to our actions. In his writings, Weber insisted that sociology must be value-free.

10. As sociology entered the twentieth century, American sociologists assumed a central role in its development. As in Europe, the Industrial Revolution and urbanization gave a major impetus to sociological study. An added factor was the massive immigration of foreigners to the United States and the problems their absorption and assimilation posed for American life.

The Sociologist's Vocabulary

class conflict The notion advanced by Karl Marx that all history is composed of struggles between classes.

dialectical materialism The notion contained in the works of Karl Marx that development depends on the clash of contradictions and the creation of new, more advanced structures out of these clashes.

ideal type A concept constructed by a sociologist to portray the principal characteristics of a phenomenon.

macrosociology The study of large-scale and long-term social processes.

mechanical solidarity A form of social integration that characterized early societies in which a sense of oneness was derived from the fact that all the members of the society engaged in essentially similar tasks.

microsociology The detailed study of what individuals say, do, and think as they go about their daily lives.

organic solidarity A form of social integration that characterizes modern societies. A society is held together by the interdependence fostered by the differences among people.

social action Behavior that involves the intervention of thought processes.

social Darwinism The application of evolutionary notions and the concept of the survival of the fittest to the social world.

social dynamics Those aspects of social life that have to do with social change and that pattern institutional development.

social facts Those aspects of social life that cannot be explained in terms of the biological or mental characteristics of the individual. People experience the social fact as external to themselves in the sense that it has an independent reality and forms a part of their objective environment.

social statics Those aspects of social life that have to do with order and stability and that allow societies to hold together and endure.

the sociological imagination The ability to see our lives, concerns, problems, and hopes entwined within the larger social and historical context in which we live.

sociology The scientific study of society, particularly the study of human organization.

superstructure The notion of Karl Marx that political ideologies, religion, family organization, law, education, and government constitute a level of social life that is shaped primarily by the economic institution.

value-free sociology The view of Max Weber that sociologists must not allow their personal biases to affect the conduct of their scientific research.

Verstehen An approach to the study of social life developed by Max Weber in which sociologists mentally attempt to place themselves in the shoes of other people and identify what they think and how they feel.

2

Theoretical Perspectives and Research Methods

The most incomprehensible thing about the world is that it is comprehensible.

—Albert Einstein

Detective Albert E. Cachie is with the New York City Police Department. On a recent evening, an anonymous call came into the 71st Precinct shortly after 9 o'clock. A male voice said that there was a dead body in a black Mercedes parked on Rutland Road near Wingate High School. When Cachie got to the site he found an adult male in a leather jacket and jeans slumped forward in the front passenger seat. Blood from bullet wounds in the man's head, neck, and chest had soaked into the soft leather seat and drenched the double stack of cassettes next to the body. A little "fragrance tree" dangling from the dashboard mirror was still emitting a sweet-smelling cloud of strawberry scent. Cachie's task was to learn about the now-deceased owner of the Mercedes and to track down the killer (Rosenbaum, 1987).

As sociologist William B. Sanders (1974) points out, sociological research is very much like detective work. Both involve a problem, initial perplexity and conjecture, the search for evidence, perceptive reasoning, false leads, and ideally, a final sense of triumph. Detectives undertake to identify and locate criminals and collect evidence to convict them in a court of law. Sociologists develop concepts and theories to explain people's behavior. Even though their goals may differ, detectives and sociologists attempt to answer two types of question: "Why did something happen?" and "Under what circumstances is it likely to happen again?" In brief, both attempt to explain and predict.

Although television dramas have romanticized detectives as asking for "just the facts," in practice they necessarily work with and test theory. In homicide cases, detectives like Al Cachie typically begin their investigation by contacting friends, relatives, acquaintances, and associates of the victim, on the theory that most people are murdered by someone they know. They also use concepts like "motive" in their investigations, an idea that encourages them to look for those who would benefit from a crime. Cachie established that the murder victim was known by the street name "Halfback" and was a rising star in central Brooklyn cocaine-dealing circles. At first Cachie conjectured that Halfback was murdered by a rival drug syndicate or in the course of a robbery. But after tracking down countless leads, Cachie learned that a cocaine supplier had " 'beat Halfback' for a couple of hundred dollars—shorted him on a dope delivery." Halfback had decided to teach the supplier a lesson, a ploy that led to the shooting (Rosenbaum, 1987).

Like detectives, sociologists formulate theories that lead them to ask certain questions and pursue given lines of research. They use guiding concepts as starting points on which to build theory and conduct their investigations. And the questions they develop in turn draw their attention to certain "facts." These matters are the subject of this chapter. We will begin our discussion by considering three major sociological perspectives. Next we will appraise the nature of science. Finally, we will consider the techniques and methods sociologists use to test their theories.

PLANNING AHEAD: TARGETED READING

1. Why is theory necessary to the scientific enterprise?

2. What are the principal theoretical tools available to sociologists in the study of social life? What are the advantages and disadvantages of each?

3. Why is research essential to the scientific enterprise?

4. What assumptions and logic underlie the scientific enterprise?

5. Why do sociologists have the edge on amateurs in looking for answers to questions about social behavior?

6. How do sociologists go about investigating social life? What are the advantages and disadvantages of the various methods?

Perspectives in Sociology

Students in introductory sociology courses frequently complain, "Why do we have to bother with all these theories? Why not just let the facts speak for themselves!" College students, like Americans in general, pride themselves on being "practical." Theory seems irrelevant, little more than detached, ivory tower nonsense. Unfortunately, facts do not "speak for themselves." Facts are silent. Before facts can speak, we have to find relationships among them. For instance, you may baby-sit, care for younger brothers or sisters, have children of your own, or anticipate having children. What do you do when they misbehave? Do you reprimand them,

threaten them, spank them, bar them from a favorite activity, reason with them, or ignore them? What you do is based on a theory—whether explicit or not—about how children learn. Perhaps it is embodied in a proverb or maxim—"Spare the rod and spoil the child," "You got to toughen kids up so they can face the rough road of life," "Just give them security and a lot of love," or "Spanking youngsters produces emotional problems."

Theory is an attempt to make sense of our experiences. We must somehow "catch" fleeting events and find a way to describe and explain them. Only then can we predict and influence the world about us. Theory is the "net" we weave to accomplish these ends. **Theory** is a set of interrelated statements that provides an explanation for a class of events. It lets us bind together a multitude of facts so that we may comprehend them all at once. With theory, we can see relationships among events that are not evident in isolated bits of data. And it allows us to organize our search for knowledge about the many different, and often puzzling, aspects of our experience.

Through the years sociologists have evolved a number of theoretical perspectives. A **theoretical perspective** is a way of looking at various features of the world—an orientation that suggests methods for studying the social experience and finding explanations for it. The adherents of each perspective ask somewhat different questions about society and so provide us with different images of social life. You are not asked to accept one model and reject all the others. Rather, theoretical perspectives are aids—mental constructs—that allow you to visualize something. Any model necessarily limits experience and presents a tunnel image. But a good model also broadens the horizon of what you can see, much like a pair of binoculars. Within contemporary sociology there are three major perspectives: the functionalist, the conflict, and the symbolic interactionist. We will return to them repeatedly in the chapters that follow. For now, let us briefly examine each in turn.

The Functionalist Perspective

The structural-functional—or simply functionalist—perspective draws heavily upon the ideas of Auguste Comte, Herbert Spencer, and Emile Durkheim. Its theorists take a " big picture"—a macrosociological—view of social life. In the 1950s and early 1960s the functionalist theories of Talcott Parsons (1902–1979) and his students occupied the center stage of American sociology. By the 1970s, functionalism had fallen into disfavor among many sociologists. But in recent years interest in the work of Parsons and other functionalists has revived (Habermas, 1981; Alexander, 1984; Sciulli and Gerstein, 1985).

Society as a social system Functionalists take as their starting point the notion that society is a **system**, a combination of things or parts that form a larger whole. Functionalists attempt to do two things: relate the parts of society to the whole, and relate one part to another. Institutions—such as the family, religion, the economy, the state, and education—are among the crucial parts of any society. Functionalists appraise the structural properties of institutions much like biologists describe the

body's organs. They then identify the social functions performed by institutions. For instance, the family is said to have as its chief focus reproduction, socialization, and maintenance of children, and the personal fulfillment of its members.

One feature of a system is the interdependence of its parts. Change in one institution has implications for other institutions and for the society as a whole. For example, as women have been drawn into the wage economy, they have postponed marriage and have had fewer children. In turn, schools have seen their enrollments drop, and in some communities schools have had to be closed. Now military authorities foresee a shortage of young men and women for the armed services during the early 1990s.

Functionalists say that societies tend toward **equilibrium**—a self-maintaining order. A social system achieves some measure of stability by counterbalancing various forces. These compensating mechanisms enable a society to recover from a war or disaster. Such forces are also at work when a society's members attempt to bring deviants back into line. But every system changes, and a dynamic or moving equilibrium results as the parts continually alter and readjust their linkages. Social change occurs, but without major dislocations and upheaval.

Functions and dysfunctions Functionalists pay particular attention to the functions performed by a system's parts, including its values, norms, institutions, and groups. **Functions** are those consequences that permit the adaptation or adjustment of a system (Merton, 1968). If a system is to survive, certain essential tasks must be performed. If certain tasks are not performed, the system fails to maintain itself—it perishes. So if society is to exist, let alone flourish, its members must see to it that certain functions are performed. Goods and services need to be produced and distributed if the sustenance requirements of a people are to be met. Social control needs to be achieved if people are going to be protected in carrying out their daily tasks. Children need to be borne, socialized, maintained, and placed within social positions. Social consensus and solidarity, health and welfare, and a variety of other requirements have to be met. Institutions are the principal structures for organizing, directing, and executing these critical tasks. Each institution is built about a standardized solution to a set of problems.

Sociologist Robert K. Merton (1968) points out that just as institutions and the other parts of society can con-

The Functions and Dysfunctions of Poverty
Functionalist theorists say that poverty ensures that there is always a supply of workers ready to perform the unpleasant and poorly paid work essential to modern life.
New York City's garment industry is dependent on the cheap labor provided by
women of the city's ethnic minority communities. But the reverse side of poverty is
its enormous human costs. The ghetto neighborhoods of Spanish Harlem reflect this
social toll. *(Left, Ethan Hoffman/Archive; right, C. Vergara/Photo Researchers)*

tribute to the maintenance of the social system, they can
also do the opposite. Consequences that lessen the adaptation or adjustment of a system he terms **dysfunctions.**
Consider poverty. As shown by sociologist Herbert J.
Gans (1972), poverty is both functional and dysfunctional. In examining poverty, Gans was neither a social
apologist nor a social critic. Rather, he sought to identify
the part poverty plays within American life. In terms of
its functions, poverty ensures that the nation's "dirty
work" gets done—the jobs that are physically dirty, temporary, dead-end, poorly paid, and menial. Poverty also
creates jobs for those who serve the poor, or who "shield"
the rest of the population from them—police officers,
social workers, numbers runners, Pentecostal ministers,
loan sharks, and drug pushers. And the peacetime army
exists primarily because the poor are willing to serve in
it. Large numbers of poor people may also be dysfunctional for society. Poverty intensifies many social problems, including those associated with health, education,
crime, and drug addiction. Moreover, the poor often feel
alienated from society and consequently many withhold
their allegiance from the social system.

Manifest and latent functions　Merton (1968) also distinguishes between manifest functions and latent functions. **Manifest functions** are consequences that are intended and usually recognized by the participants in a
system; **latent functions** are consequences that are unin-

tended and often not recognized. In brief, people's *conscious* motivations for engaging in a behavior are not
necessarily identical with the behavior's *objective* consequences. Take the matter of spying. The manifest function of the American CIA and the Soviet KGB is to gain
access to the other nation's secrets and secure an advantage for the homeland. But spying also has latent functions. For deterrence to be effective, a nation's adversaries must be aware of its capabilities (for instance,
potential enemies must be able to photograph military
installations, intercept data from the testing of missiles,
and inspect selected equipment). Intelligence serves as a
form of de facto on-site inspection. In the last analysis,
intelligence may contribute less to victories than to the
prevention of failures; because it assures adversaries that
each has no surprises for the other, spies may actually
help to avert wars (Laqueur, 1986).

Social consensus　Functionalists believe it essential that
most members of a society agree on what is desirable,
worthwhile, and moral and what is undesirable, worth-
less, and evil. In other words, people need to share a
consensus regarding core values and beliefs. Most Americans accept the values and beliefs that inhere in the democratic creed, the doctrine of equal opportunity, and the
notion of personal achievement; most Russians agree on
the desirability of a society fashioned in accordance with
the Communist creed. Functionalists say that a high

degree of consensus binds society together as a cohesive unit and provides the foundation for social integration and stability. By virtue of a long socialization process, people come to accept the rules of their society, and for the most part they live by them.

Evaluation of the functionalist perspective   The functionalist perspective is a useful tool for describing society and identifying its structural parts and the functions of these parts. It provides a "big picture" of the social whole, particularly that of patterned, recurrent behavior and institutions. For some purposes, it is clearly helpful to "shut down" social processes and describe behavior at a given point in time. An anatomist does much the same thing when examining a cell under a microscope or a cadaver in a laboratory. From the functionalist perspective we gain primarily a static picture—a sort of snapshot—of social life at a particular time in history.

But functionalism does not tell us the entire story. It has difficulty dealing with history and the processes of social change. Critics say that a valid theory must ground itself in historical time and space (Tilly, 1986). With increasing frequency, sociologists are asking: "How did society and its institutions came to assume their contemporary form?" Critics also contend that functionalists exaggerate the extent of societal consensus, integration, and stability while disregarding conflict, dissensus, and instability. The problems that structural-functional theory has in dealing with change, history, and conflict have led critics to charge that it has a conservative bias—its ideas appeal to those who have a stake in existing social arrangements (Mills, 1959; Gouldner, 1970;

Abrahamson, 1978). Such is not the case with the conflict perspective; it paints quite a different picture of social life.

The Conflict Perspective

Like functionalists, conflict theorists focus their attention on the structural arrangements that characterize social life. Yet the two perspectives are at odds on many issues. While functionalists conceive of conflict as an indication of breakdown, conflict theorists see it as a source of change. While functionalists focus on social order and stability, conflict theorists scrutinize social life and find disorder and instability. While functionalists stress the common interests that the members of a society share, conflict theorists emphasize the interests that divide them. While functionalists view consensus as the basis of social unity, conflict theorists contend that social unity is an illusion resting on coercion. And while functionalists say that most existing arrangements are necessary and justified by the requirements of social life, conflict theorists insist that many of the arrangements are neither necessary nor justified (Dahrendorf, 1959; Lenski, 1966).

Diversity among conflict theorists   You may have concluded that conflict theory is the flip side of functionalism or functionalism turned on its head. In the hands of some sociologists, this may be true. But in the hands of radical social critics like Karl Marx, nothing could be farther from the truth (see Chapters 1, 9, and 15). And even though modern conflict theory derives much of its

Social Consensus
If a society is to survive, its members must be willing to pursue similar goals and be governed by similar values. Functionalists say that social integration and stability are fostered by social events that focus public attention on common interests and that arouse shared emotions. The return of the American hostages from Iran in early 1981 after 444 days of tension was this sort of event. It solidified national commitment to "the American way of life." (D. Goldberg/Sygma)

inspiration from Marx, it is not necessarily "Marxian." While class conflict is the centerpiece of Marxian theory, many contemporary sociologists emphasize that conflict characterizes a good many relationships—the young versus the old, taxpayers versus welfare recipients, Sunbelt versus Snowbelt states, consumers versus producers, central-city residents versus suburbanites, church versus church, race versus race, and so on. The conflict perspective draws upon many diverse currents, including the work of such sociologists as Georg Simmel (1908/1955, 1950), Lewis Coser (1956), and Randall Collins (1975).

Unlike Marx, the German sociologist Georg Simmel (1858–1918) was not politically involved, nor did he have a great passion for social reform. But like Marx, he was concerned with the existence of opposing tendencies within society. For Simmel, society was not so much a structure composed of domination and subjugation, but a whole made up of forces advancing, retreating, converging, and diverging in patterns of greater or lesser stability. And whereas Marx attempted to discern the causes of conflict, Simmel was content to note that conflict was inherent in social life. He focused instead on the consequences of conflict. Simmel contended that conflict is an essential element in group formation and the persistence of group life. He would view the conflict between pro-life and pro-abortion groups within the United States today as strengthening each group's consciousness and identity. Simultaneously, it ensures the stability of the American political system by bringing about a balance of claims by rival groups.

The American sociologist Lewis Coser (1956) has expanded upon Simmel's idea that conflict can be functional for a group. He shows that conflict quickens group allegiances and loyalties by functioning as a social glue that binds people together. For instance, the Roman Catholic Church has owed much of its doctrinal and organizational vigor to its struggles against early heresies and later conflicts with Protestant reformers. The civil rights and black power movements of the 1960s and early 1970s contributed to a sense of black unity, pride, self-worth, and dignity. Although these movements challenged established interests and racist patterns, they simultaneously contributed to the long-term stability of American institutions by bringing blacks into the "system." The more blacks and other minorities feel themselves integrated within society—as "Americans all"—the less likely they are to resort to violence. Their disputes find expression in conflict *within* the system, as opposed to conflict *about* the system. It is otherwise in contemporary Lebanon, where the number of people who think of themselves as Lebanese—as opposed to being Maronite Christians, Shiite Muslims, Sunni Muslims, Palestinians, or Druse—is becoming smaller and smaller.

Randall Collins (1975, 1982) is another American sociologist who has contributed to conflict theory. But unlike many other theorists who started, and stayed, at the macrosociological level, Collins also looks at conflict from the microsociological level. He believes that the overall structure of society can be best understood as the result of conflicting groups, some of which dominate

Abortion Controversies
Conflict theorists point out that people's interests and values are often at odds. The question then becomes, "Which group will prevail?" At the present time Americans are deeply divided on the issue of abortion. Here pro-life and pro-choice demonstrators exchange barbs. The issue is one that deeply touches the social experience, with consequences for the most intimate aspects of our lives. (*UPI/Bettmann Newsphotos*)

others. However, he emphasizes that conflict and domination are possible only because the groups are integrated on the microsociological level. He looks to Durkheim's theory as the best guide to how this is done (see Chapters 1 and 14). Among other things, Collins is interested in how some people have the power to affect, or even control, other people's social experiences, including their social interaction, conversation, and family relations. We will have more to say about Collins when we consider class and gender stratification (Chapters 9 and 12).

Society as conflict   Although the conflict perspective includes a variety of approaches, most of them share the view that society contains social forces that make conflict inevitable. For one thing, the existence of such scarce resources as wealth, prestige, and power generates a struggle over their distribution. For another, power differences ensure that some groups dominate and even exploit others. And finally, values and interests often diverge, so people vie with one another as they pursue different goals. Conflict theorists therefore ask how some groups acquire power, dominate other groups, apportion scarce resources to their advantage, and achieve their will in human affairs. More particularly, they look at who benefits and who loses from the way society is structured.

If conflict is an inescapable feature of social life, how is society possible? We have already noted how functionalists answer this question. They say that the members of a society have a consensus regarding core values and norms. Conflict theorists are dissatisfied with this answer. They contend that society holds together in one of two ways. Under one arrangement, one group enjoys sufficient power to dominate social life; it makes and enforces the rules and shapes institutional life so that its interests are served. Although the naked rule of force is most evident under totalitarian and colonial regimes, many conflict theorists extend the argument to include democratic and constitutional governments. They contend that the state—government and the rules it promulgates—is by its very nature an agency of oppression; it is an instrument by which ruling elites establish and maintain their positions of privilege. In contrast, functionalists depict the state as an organ of the total society that promotes social control and stability (see Chapter 16).

Under another arrangement, society holds together because there are so many overlapping and divided interest groups that people can win or lose only by joining together. People find that they can maximize rewards and minimize losses by entering into alliances against outsiders (Sprey, 1979). Viewed in this manner, society is a vehicle by which people regulate and order conflict so that civil anarchy does not result.

Evaluation of the conflict perspective   By now you may have concluded that the conflict perspective provides a welcome balance to functionalist theory. Since the strengths of the one perspective tend to be the weaknesses of the other, the two approaches do indeed complement one another. Where functionalists have difficulty dealing with history and social change, conflict theorists make these issues their strength. And where conflict theorists encounter difficulty dealing with some aspects of social consensus, integration, and stability, functionalists provide many penetrating insights. Additionally, both approaches have traditionally taken a macro view of social life, portraying societies as larger wholes or systems made up of interrelated parts (van den Berghe, 1963; Turner, 1982).

Some proponents of the functionalist and conflict schools find their differences so fundamental that they see no basis for reconciliation. Even so, a number of sociologists have undertaken the task. Sociologists like Ralf Dahrendorf (1959) and Gerhard E. Lenski (1966) depict society as "Janus-headed." They say that functionalist and conflict theorists are simply studying two faces of the *same* reality: one of stability, harmony, and consensus, and the other of change, conflict, and constraint. There is much to recommend efforts to integrate the two perspectives.

The Interactionist Perspective

The functionalist and conflict perspectives are primarily concerned with macrosociological or "big picture" issues. Yet some of the most intriguing questions confronting sociologists concern the relationship between the individual and society. How can the individual and society be separate and distinct and yet be interrelated—even incorporated, one within the other? How can people create, sustain, and change society and simultaneously be shaped by society? How can society persist past the lifetimes of its individual members if, at bottom, it rests on their actions?

These kinds of questions are addressed by the interactionist—also called the symbolic interactionist—perspective. Sociologist George Herbert Mead is considered its chief architect. His lectures at the University of Chicago between 1893 and 1931 were assembled from student notes into a book, *Mind, Self and Society*, first published in 1934. The two foremost exponents of interactionism following Mead's death were Herbert G. Blumer (1969) and Manford H. Kuhn (1964). Each of these took a somewhat different path, but a number of themes recur in the various formulations of interactionist thought.

Symbols   As their name implies, symbolic interactionists emphasize the capacity that human beings have to create and use symbols. Social insects—ants, bees, and termites—are able to live a group existence because they are genetically "prewired" to relate to one another in given ways. But for the most part humans lack such inborn mechanisms. Instead, we use symbols—arbitrary signs—to represent people, objects, events, and ideas. A **symbol** is anything that socially has come to stand for something else. Symbols take many forms, including spoken and written words, gestures, and such objects as flags, medallions, tattoos, and clothing.

Our ability to use symbols has revolutionary implications. Symbols allow us not only to name objects in our habitat, but also to designate one another: we give each person a name; we form age, occupational, and other categories for people; and we conceive of people as members of larger social units, including groups, families, tribes, communities, and nations. Moreover, because we can represent the world mentally, we are not limited to the "here and now." We can order our present behavior on the basis of a distant past and an anticipated future. Finally, symbols make it possible to communicate with one another. We can transmit information, attitudes, and sentiments to other people and so become "tuned" together with them. We will have more to say about symbols in Chapter 3.

Society as interaction   As portrayed by symbolic interactionists, society does not exist as something "out there"; rather, society is continually created and recreated moment-by-moment as we interact with one another. How do we accomplish this? As each of us "encounters" society, it is something independent of us. We give "it" a name—"The United States," "Ireland," or "South Africa," and we come to treat the United States, Ireland, and South Africa as *objects*. In large measure society derives from this fact. For example, we act as if the United States is real, and in doing so make it real. We recite the Pledge of Allegiance, talk about "America's" relations with the Soviet Union, debate with others "What is wrong with this country," and extol "the American way" in Fourth of July speeches. What holds for society as a whole also holds for smaller groups, organizations, and communities. In sum, by treating society and its parts as "things," we give them existence and continuity (Hewitt, 1979).

Simultaneously, through day-by-day interaction with others, each person—otherwise essentially vegetative—is fashioned into a social being with a distinctive personality. People relate to one another and integrate their activities *because* they acquire the capacity to do so as members of society. Society precedes its individual members—babies are born into families, students enter

The Symbolic Construction of Social Reality

Symbolic interactionists say that the modern nation "exists" only insofar as we create it in the course of our daily interactions. Since a nation-state is intangible—something we cannot see, hear, or touch—we must find some way to make it tangible. We achieve this outcome with symbolic "stand-ins." May Day parades contribute to the "making" of the Soviet Union through the symbolism of the event and the flags and banners that accompany the marchers. By acting as if the Soviet Union is real, the Russian people give an otherwise nebulous notion an existence and continuity. *(Erich Lessing/Magnum)*

colleges, and men and women get jobs in organizations. Society and the individual are reciprocally related in a fundamental way: Each presupposes the other, and neither exists except in relation to the other. They are two sides of the same coin (Cooley, 1902; Stryker and Statham, 1985).

Meaning: Constructing reality   Symbolic interactionists contend that we are creatures who strive to make sense out of our world. We do so by attributing *meanings* to people, objects, and events. Meaning is not something that inheres in things: It is a property that derives from, or arises out of, the interaction that takes place among us in the course of our daily lives (Blumer, 1969). As we noted in our discussion of society, interactionists say that reality is *manufactured* by us as we intervene in the world and interpret what is occurring there. Our experiences are senseless until our mind steps back and *makes* something out of them. The social philosopher Alfred Schutz (1971) points out that there are, strictly speaking, no such things as facts. We select facts from our universe of experience through the activities of the mind, and for this reason all "facts" are human creations. In brief, we *reify* social life. Put another way, we assume that the *humanly* created world of objects is in fact a world of *real* objects. Thus, symbolic interactionists say that our social world is a **constructed reality.**

The process by which we make our social creations into "real" and "necessary" objects is fundamental to social life. For example, we speak of a "career" as "making demands on us." In so doing, we imbue a humanly created abstraction with a life of its own. We credit it with "making demands." In truth, a "career" has no reality. By acting as if it has reality, we bring into being that very reality. For example, postal clerks and sales personnel in large stores find that established procedures make it difficult at times to meet customers' needs. "I'm sorry, but we can't do that" is a statement that imbues procedures with a finality they do not in fact possess. Humans have devised the procedures and humans can also change them. But having reified the procedures, clerks look upon them as necessarily and inevitably being what they are (Hewitt, 1979). All this leads symbolic interactionists to say that if sociologists are to understand social life, they must understand what people actually say and do from the viewpoint of the people themselves. This orientation is strongly influenced by Max Weber's concept of *Verstehen* (see Chapter 1).

Drawing by Stan Hunt; © 1986 The New Yorker Magazine, Inc.

Evaluation of the interactionist perspective   The interactionist perspective has the advantage of bringing "people" back into sociology. We come to see people as something more than robots who go through life mechanically enacting rules and roles. We encounter people as social beings endowed with the capacity for thought. Through interaction with one another, they acquire the symbols and meanings that permit them to intervene in events and shape their destinies. They can interpret situations, assess the advantages and disadvantages of given actions, and select among them. In sum, from interactionists we gain an image of humans as active beings who construct social reality, rather than as passive beings who merely respond to the dictates of societal constraints.

However, the interactionist perspective has its limitations. People do not enjoy total flexibility in fashioning their actions in their everyday lives. Although many interactionists acknowledge that much of our action is guided by systems of preestablished meanings—including culture and institutions—some like Herbert Blumer (1969) implicitly downgrade the part they play in our lives. Consequently critics contend that symbolic interactionism can lead to an overemphasis on the immediate situation and an "obsessive concern with the transient, episodic and fleeting" (Meltzer, Petras, and Reynolds, 1975:85). By focusing on the particulars of person-to-person interaction, interactionists often overlook the connections that outcomes have to one another, particularly the links that exist among episodes of interaction (Weinstein and Tanur, 1976). In brief, the perspective has difficulty dealing adequately with the large-

a

b

c

Contrasting Sociological Perspectives: Campus Greek Organizations
Fraternities and sororities have long been a fixture on many American college and university campuses. Each of the major sociological perspectives supplies us with a differing, but nonetheless useful, insight regarding this feature of campus life:
a. Functionalists portray Greek involvement in campus charity drives and support for intercollegiate athletic programs as fostering the esprit de corps so essential for college and university allegiances.
b. Conflict theorists depict Greek organizations as mirroring and reproducing the class, racial, and gender inequalities found in larger society. The social life provided by the Greeks reflects the "country-club" type of etiquette and interpersonal social skills that will be required of corporate officials and professionals.
c. Symbolic interactionists see the Greeks fashioning shared meanings through social interaction. Greek emblems and rituals facilitate a consciousness of oneness, symbolizing the reality of the group and the relationship of members to it.
(a, Bohdan Hrynewych/Southern Light; b, Hisham I. Youssef/The Picture Cube; c, Jeff Lowenthal/Woodfin Camp & Associates)

scale organizational aspects of society and with relations among societies. And since the framework focuses on the subjective aspects of human experience and the situational context in which it occurs, the objective realities of stratification—of the differential distribution of wealth, prestige, and power in society—are often neglected or taken for granted.

To correct some of these difficulties, a number of symbolic interactionists like Sheldon Stryker (1980; Stryker and Statham, 1985) have recently undertaken to introduce structural and large-scale components into interactionist thought. Stryker attempts to bridge societal structures and the individual with such concepts as "position" and "role." We will take a somewhat similar approach in Chapter 4 when we link the small-scale or micro components of status and role with the large-scale or macro components of groups and institutions. Such a

link was foreshadowed at the turn of the century by the sociology of Georg Simmel (1950). He said that society consists of individuals connected by interaction; institutions, such as the state, the family, religion, and economic organizations, are merely an extended version of the everyday interactions of men and women dealing with one another in stores and offices, on the street, or at a party.

THINKING THROUGH THE ISSUES

Try to discern ways for integrating the ideas from symbolic interactionist theory with those from conflict theory to arrive at additional insights concerning social life. For instance, if society is

primarily the product of our social definitions, will some interest groups have greater voice in shaping these definitions than other groups? If definitions differ, which groups or social classes will be able to make their definitions prevail for the society as a whole? How do some groups induce people to share their definitions of reality? If rules are reified, whose rules are most likely to be reified? What are the consequences for other members of society? Who determines which people are and which people are not deviant? Who has the power to make their definitions of deviance stick? (See Chapter 8.)

Using the Sociological Perspectives

The details of the theoretical perspectives will become clearer as we encounter them in the chapters to come. As we noted, all three have advantages and disadvan-

tages. Each affords a somewhat different view of reality and directs our attention to some dimension of social life that the others neglect or overlook (see Table 2.1). Consider poverty. Functionalism highlights poverty's functions and dysfunctions within the context of the maintenance and survival of society. Conflict theorists portray poverty as deriving from the inequalities embedded in society's institutions and show who gains and who loses from these arrangements. Interactionists say that the poor are people who have been so defined by society and evoke particular reactions from it (for instance, the modern observer might have discerned a great deal of misery, want, and deprivation in traditional Oriental societies, yet the members of these societies did not label the conditions as poverty and were oblivious to its prevalence).

Each sociological perspective affords a more effective approach, a better "fit," to some kinds of data— some aspects of social life—than the other perspectives. Consequently, each approach has merit and need not preclude the others in explaining given data or predicting particular outcomes. Indeed, each approach is valuable

Table 2.1 Major Theoretical Perspectives

	Functionalist	*Conflict*	*Interactionist*
Level of analysis	Macrosociological	Macrosociological	Microsociological
Nature of society	A social system made up of interdependent parts	A social order characterized by competing interest groups, each pursuing its own ends	A social reality created and recreated anew as people interact with one another
Basis of social interaction	Social consensus deriving from shared beliefs and values	Conflict, power, and coercion	Attribute meaning to people, objects, and events with symbols
Focus of study	Social order and the maintenance of the social system through the performance of essential functions	The interests that divide the members of a society and social change	The development of the self and the dynamic interplay between the individual and society
Advantages	Depicts the "big picture" of social life, particularly as it finds expression in patterned recurrent behavior and institutions	Has the ability to deal well with history and to handle institutional and societal change	Portrays people as active beings who have the capacity for thought and for fashioning social life
Disadvantages	Has difficulty dealing with history and processes of social change	Has difficulty dealing with social consensus, integration, and stability	Has difficulty dealing with the large-scale organizational aspects of society and with relations among societies

Top view   Side view   Three-dimensional
view

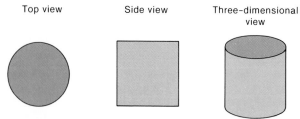

FIGURE 2.1 An Object from Three Perspectives
What do you think this object is? If you look down
from the top, it seems to be a circular disk. If you
look at it from the side, it looks like a square. Each
perspective tells a somewhat different story. Even
though the two perspectives at first seem contradictory, they actually complement one another. Their
respective images can be brought together in a more
complete three-dimensional image of the object,
which is a container. Likewise, the different perspectives in sociology provide us with complementary
images of society.

precisely because it provides us with an additional piece
of information regarding the exceedingly complex puzzle of social life. Different perspectives are like different
two-dimensional views of a three-dimensional object.
Each two-dimensional view is a useful perspective that
can be compatible with the others, yet none reveals the
entire picture (see Figure 2.1). Just as carpenters find
that a hammer, a plane, and a saw are useful tools that
complement one another as they go about building a
house, so we will use all three perspectives as sociological tools for describing and analyzing social behavior.

The Scientific Enterprise

The sociological perspectives we have considered provide important theoretical insights regarding the nature
and workings of society. However, theory that is not confirmed by facts is merely speculation. **Facts** are agreed-
upon statements about what we observe. As the French
mathematician Jules-Henri Poincaré (1854–1912) observed: "Science is built up with facts, as a house is with
stones, but a collection of facts is no more a science than
a heap of stones is a house." Clearly we require both
theoretical understanding and facts, and for this reason
both theory and research are essential components of the
sociological enterprise. A good theory organizes facts
into a coherent structure. Additionally, theory inspires
research that can be used to verify, disprove, or modify
it. So research continually challenges us to craft new and
better theories (see Figure 2.2).

The Assumptions of Science

Underlying the scientific enterprise are three basic assumptions. First, scientists assume that a real, external
world exists independent of our observation of it. In
other words, something is "out there" and this something is not simply a creation of our minds. For instance,
chemists accept the idea that a pure sample of ordinary
table salt—sodium chloride—contains 60.7 percent of
chlorine and 39.3 percent of sodium; all varieties of sodium chloride, regardless of their source, have identical
proportions of the two elements. The fixed composition
of sodium chloride is seen as a "law of nature"—one that

**FIGURE 2.2 The Relationship between
Theory, the Scientific
Method, and Observations
of the World**

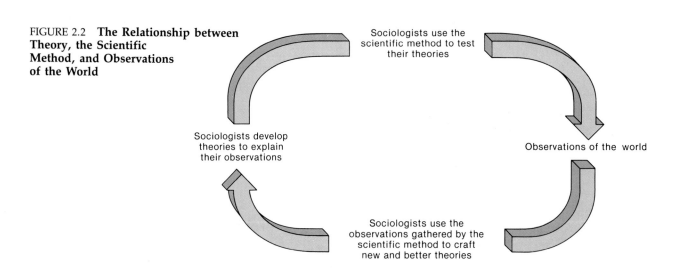

Science Is a Form of Social Behavior
Science is a human activity that occurs in social settings. Even the lone scientist finds that other scientists must accept and validate his or her findings. In recent decades, scientific research has increasingly become an undertaking funded by corporations and government and carried out in large organizations. Today, few scientists work in privately owned laboratories. Instead, they are employees of universities, institutes, and industrial concerns. *(Barbara Alper)*

is as true today as it was 800 million years ago. "Truth," then, exists independently of our experience of it and is the subject of scientific investigation.

Second, scientists take as their point of departure the **principle of determinism**—the notion that relations in the world are organized in terms of cause and effect. Every event or action is believed to result from a preceding cause. Put another way, sociologists, like other scientists, assume that when one event occurs, another event, one that ordinarily follows the first, will do so again. So sociologists operate on the assumption that crime, racism, social inequality, and marriage do not simply "happen"; they have causes. It follows that, under identical conditions, the same cause will always produce the same effect. If this were not the case, social life would be unintelligible because events would occur in a random or haphazard fashion and be utterly unpredictable.

Third, scientists assume that knowledge concerning the external world can be gained through objective observation. Since truth is not a matter of belief but of objective reality, it can be *empirically* tested—evidence can be gathered and analyzed by means of careful observation and meticulous measurement. Thus the reality established by science is believed to be the same for all

people regardless of what they think about it. It follows that facts discovered by one scientist can be verified by other scientists.

The goal of science, then, is to discover information about the world—about what *is*—so that predictions regarding events in the world become more accurate and hence more useful. Contrary to much popular opinion, science is not a collection of facts, science is a *process*, a form of social behavior. Science is what scientists do. And what scientists do is carried on in the context of other people and groups of people. It is this element that injects subjectivity into the scientific enterprise. All of us have values—conceptions of what is desirable, correct, and good. Even at our best, values subtly invade our work. Indeed, the very fact that we study human behavior reveals concern with it, and the decision to focus on social rather than biological, psychological, or other factors betrays an implicit belief that the social factor is somehow "more significant."

In sum, science, being a human activity, is not devoid of values. Rather, the key to science is to be found in its approach to data—the rigorous, disciplined attempt to look as objectively as is humanly possible on the phenomena studied. Sociologists are enjoined to avoid such emotional involvement in their work that they cannot adopt a new approach or reject an old answer when their findings indicate that this is required. At the heart of the scientific enterprise is a skepticism that dictates ideas be checked against observable evidence. Further, sociologists are expected not to distort their findings in order to support a particular point of view. In brief, sociologists, like other scientists, have an obligation not to turn their backs on facts or distort them simply because they do not like them. The box on pages 40–41 discusses how our notions of the world influence our attempts to understand it.

THINKING THROUGH THE ISSUES

How about trying your hand at sociological theorizing? Some symbolic interactionists, like Herbert Blumer (1969), contend that the "world of reality" exists only in human experience, appearing merely in the form in which human beings "see" events. Does this, then, shift "reality" from an observable world—a world "out there"—to the realm of mental activity—the world as we fashion it in our minds? Does symbolic interactionism make "science" impossible? How do you

think Blumer deals with these issues? Blumer holds that the world can "talk back" to our pictures and assertions by challenging or refusing to bend to them. He says that the ability of a world "out there" to resist our images and conceptions both calls for and justifies science. However, like Max Weber, he insists that sociologists should not limit themselves to the techniques of inquiry available to the physical sciences. Since human beings live in a world of meanings, no explanation of *human* conduct is possible except by understanding this world as the members of a society understand it. Blumer urges the use of *sympathetic introspection*—an examination of one's own mental and emotional states and processes—in order to study social life.

The Logic of Science

We have pointed out that a primary objective of science is to establish what causes what. Scientists approach the task of determining cause and effect relationships by testing for links among variables. A **variable** is the term scientists apply to a trait or characteristic that changes under different conditions. It usually occurs in different amounts, degrees, or forms. To explain why the water you left outside last evening in the cup froze, you say that the temperature fell below freezing or 32 degrees Fahrenheit. The statement that water solidifies—becomes ice—at 32 degrees is a statement of a relationship between two variables, something that varies. The variables sociologists typically study have to do with social conditions, attitudes, and behaviors. In studying people's attitudes on abortion, gun control, and taxes,

CULTIVATING A SOCIOLOGICAL CONSCIOUSNESS

The Sociology of Science

How does science develop? Many people think that science advances cumulatively through slow and steady additions to knowledge. Scientists formulate theories. They then confirm or refute them by experimentally testing predictions derived from the theories. In so doing, they are governed by a scientific ethos that dictates intellectual honesty, integrity, organized skepticism, disinterestedness, and impersonality (Merton, 1973). In sum, science is a logical, rational, and progressive enterprise. When old theories fail, new ones are proposed and adopted because of their greater explanatory power. In this fashion, science marches unrelentingly closer and closer to the truth.

Although the view that the scientific enterprise continually builds on itself is a popular one, many sociologists, historians, and philosophers say that it overlooks the human factor. A major force behind this change was the *Structure of Scientific Revolutions* by Thomas Kuhn (1962). Kuhn con-

Galileo before the Inquisition
Galileo (1564–1642) was an accomplished Italian scientist who in his lectures at the University of Padua demonstrated and popularized the Copernican view that the earth moved around the sun. This notion was contrary to ancient belief and religious dogma. As a result, at the age of 70, Galileo was brought before the Inquisition, a court set up by the Roman Catholic Church in the Middle Ages to seek out and punish heresy. While publicly recanting, he is said to have muttered: "Eppur si muove" (meaning "Even so the earth *does* move"). For his remaining years he was silenced by the Church. (*Painting by Robert Fleury/Culver Pictures*)

sociologists examine such variables as differences in sex, age, race, region, and socioeconomic class standing.

In investigating cause and effect relationships, scientists distinguish between the independent and the dependent variable. The **independent variable** is the variable that causes an effect. The **dependent variable** is the variable that is affected. The causal variable (the independent variable) precedes in time the phenomenon it causes (the dependent variable). For example, as the temperature of water is decreased, the motion of the molecules become slower. The temperature—a measure of hotness or coldness—is the independent variable and the vigor of the molecular movement is the dependent variable. Similarly, as the socioeconomic level of women (independent variable) rises, the mortality rate of their infants falls (the dependent variable). In their research, scientists typically attempt to hypothesize the re-

"*By God, for a minute there it suddenly all made sense!*"
Drawing by Gahan Wilson; © 1986 The New Yorker Magazine, Inc.

tends that even though science grows through increments, the truly major changes come as a result of revolutions. At any given time, the scientific community is dominated by a *paradigm*—a fundamental image or vision regarding the nature of the world; it is a world-view that opens some sights and closes others. A paradigm defines what should be studied, what questions should be asked, how they should be asked, and what rules should be followed in interpreting the answers research provides. Some sociologists see a paradigm as setting one scientific community apart from another—for instance, physics from chemistry or sociology from psychology. They also see the functionalist, conflict, and symbolic interactionist perspectives as different paradigms (Ritzer, 1983). But other sociologists disagree and visualize paradigms as providing totally different and incompatible conceptions of the world (Turner, 1982).

According to Kuhn, during a period of "normal science" when a particular paradigm is dominant,

teachers, textbook writers, and editors have a pretty good idea of what "counts" as a solution to a problem. But gradually a number of problems arise that are not solvable. As these problems mount, science goes into a state of crisis. The crisis is resolved when a new paradigm surfaces—a scientific revolution that breaks with past knowledge and so reorganizes our vision that we no longer see the world in old ways. For example, the sun replaced the earth as the center of the solar system as a result of the Copernican revolution, and natural selection and evolution replaced creation as the source of species as a result of the Darwinian revolution. An intellectual transformation involves putting on "a different thinking cap." As a result, adherents of differing paradigms "talk past each other" (Kuhn, 1977, 1986).

The philosopher Paul K. Feyerabend (1975) takes Kuhn's arguments much further. He contends that even "normal science" is a fairy tale. According to Feyerabend, history reveals science to be a political and propagandistic affair. Prestige,

power, age, and polemic determine which theories and theorists will triumph. The reason, he says, is that no theory, however good, ever agrees with all the facts. Facts that contradict the theory must be ignored, defused by a makeshift hypothesis, or nudged out of the picture. For example, rationalists see Galileo's ideas of the universe succeeding because he was able to show with the aid of a telescope that the moon was covered with mountains and so discredit his rivals. But Feyerabend says not so. Galileo's epoch-making sketches of the moon were so inaccurate that even naked-eye observation quickly exposed them as illusory. Galileo triumphed because he was a masterful propagandist. He wrote in Italian rather than in Latin, had a persuasive style, advertised his successes, hid his failures, and rewrote the life story of Copernicus to make it more acceptable to the Church. So there is considerable controversy as to how science develops—one school advancing an evolutionary and continualist view, the other a revolutionary or cataclysmic one.

lationship that they expect to find between the independent and dependent variables. Such a trial idea—called a **hypothesis**—is a testable statement that an expected outcome will result from particular conditions.

Scientists spend a good deal of their time attempting to figure out how one thing relates to another. Accordingly, they seek to determine the degree of association that exists between an independent and a dependent variable. If the variables are causally related, then they must be correlated with one another. A **correlation** exists if a change in one variable is associated with a change in the other variable. Since the mortality rate of infants falls as the socioeconomic level of women rises, the two variables are said to be correlated. Correlations are useful for making predictions about groups of people, but they do not provide accurate predictions for individuals (except in rare cases where there is a perfect correlation). For instance, correlations dealing with infant mortality do not tell us whether or not a particular infant will survive.

Knowing that two variables are correlated allows us to predict one, knowing the other. But correlation does not tell us what is causing what (Cole, 1972; Aronson, Brewer, and Carlsmith, 1985). For instance, the death rate is considerably higher among hospitalized individuals than among nonhospitalized individuals. Yet we would err were we to conclude that hospitals cause death. Likewise, the incidence of polio in children during the 1940s and 1950s was associated with the viscosity of road asphalt. Again, we would err were we to conclude that softer asphalt was the cause of polio (or that polio caused asphalt to become softer). In these cases the correlation is *spurious*—the apparent relationship between the two variables is produced by a third variable that influences the original variables (severe sickness is associated with admission to hospitals and with death; similarly, warm temperature caused the asphalt to become softer and also tended to increase children's exposure to the polio-causing virus). (See Figure 2.3.) In order to combat the likelihood that their research will be contaminated by third variables, scientists employ a *control* group (a group that remains as it is; no change is introduced into the group). We will consider this matter

FIGURE 2.3 **The Super Bowl and the Stock Market**
Does the Super Bowl winner portend the stock market? Between 1967 and 1986 it did so in nineteen of twenty Super Bowls. When the Super Bowl winner has been a team with NFL roots, the stock market has risen for the year. In all years, except 1984, an AFL victor has portended a market drop. Would you be willing to invest your money on the basis of this relationship? Why? *Source: USA Today, January 27, 1986, B-1.*

Year	Super Bowl winner	Team roots	Change in NYSE composite stock index
1967	Green Bay Packers	NFL	+ 23.1%
1968	Green Bay Packers	NFL	+ 9.4%
1969	New York Jets	AFL	− 12.5%
1970	Kansas City Chiefs	AFL	− 2.5%
1971	Baltimore Colts	NFL	+ 12.3%
1972	Dallas Cowboys	NFL	+ 14.3%
1973	Miami Dolphins	AFL	− 19.6%
1974	Miami Dolphins	AFL	− 30.3%
1975	Pittsburgh Steelers	NFL	+ 31.9%
1976	Pittsburgh Steelers	NFL	+ 21.5%
1977	Oakland Raiders	AFL	− 9.3%
1978	Dallas Cowboys	NFL	+ 2.1%
1979	Pittsburgh Steelers	NFL	+ 15.5%
1980	Pittsburgh Steelers	NFL	+ 25.7%
1981	Oakland Raiders	AFL	− 8.7%
1982	San Francisco 49ers	NFL	+ 14.0%
1983	Washington Redskins	NFL	+ 17.5%
1984	L.A. Raiders	AFL	+ 1.3%
1985	San Francisco 49ers	NFL	+ 26.2%
1986	Chicago Bears	NFL	+ 14.0%

at greater length a little later in the chapter when we deal with experimentation.

Steps in the Scientific Method

Albert Einstein once observed that "The whole of science is nothing more than a refinement of everyday thinking." In brief, people do science much the way that they do everything else. They make guesses and mistakes; they argue with one another; they try out their ideas to see what works and discard what does not. However, science differs from ordinary inquiry in that it relies on a systematic and formal process for gathering facts and searching for a logical explanation of them, what we call *the scientific method*. This method finds expression in a series of steps that seek to ensure maximum objectivity in investigating a problem. Ideally, sociological research follows this step-by-step procedure, although in practice it is not always possible to abide by every detail. Even so, the following steps provide useful guidelines for conducting research (see Figure 2.4 on page 44).

1. Selecting a researchable problem   The range of topics available for social research is as broad as the range of human behavior. We need to find a problem that merits study and that can be investigated by the methods of science. For example, two social scientists, Donald G. Dutton and Arthur P. Aron (1974), wished to explore how we experience emotion. More particularly, they were intrigued by the seeming connection between states of high anxiety and sexual attraction. This link was first noted by the first-century Roman poet Ovid. He had advised men that an excellent time to arouse romantic passion in women was while watching gladiators disembowel one another in the arena. Presumably the emotions of fear and repulsion excited by the grisly scene somehow translated themselves into romantic interest.

Dutton and Aron wondered about these matters. In the preceding two decades a number of scientists had said that no matter what emotion is aroused, you feel a kind of stirred-up set of internal reactions, including a more rapid pulse rate, shortness of breath, and perhaps trembling hands and sensations "in the pit of the stomach" (Schachter and Singer, 1962). Since the physiological reactions of anger, fear, and love are so similar, an interesting question is raised: How do you tell which emotion you are experiencing? According to one view, without being consciously aware that you are doing so, you use cues in the situation to interpret what you are feeling. If you feel all stirred up after someone has hit

you, you label the feelings anger; if you are on a roller-coaster ride, you label them fear; and if you are with an attractive person of the opposite sex, you label them love. This interpretation of emotion is consistent with the symbolic interactionist perspective. Recall that symbolic interactionists say we strive to make sense out of our experiences by attributing meanings to them. And by attributing meanings to our experience—interpreting what goes on about us—we manufacture "reality."

2. Reviewing the literature   Rather than plunging hastily into a research venture, Dutton and Aron surveyed the literature dealing with sexual attraction and states of strong emotion. This review told them about other research that had been undertaken, suggested a variety of leads, and saved them from unwittingly duplicating work others had already done. For instance, the ethologist Niko Tinbergen (1954) had found a connection between "aggression" and courting behaviors in some animal spe-

---

Does Danger Contribute to Sexual Arousal?
Researchers have undertaken experiments to determine whether or not situations of intense anxiety lead to increased sexual attraction. Much depends on the situation and the meaning people assign to their experiences. People who are unaware of the true cause of their physiological arousal can be induced to believe that romantic passion underlies their feelings. *(Georg Gerster/Photo Researchers)*

SELECTING A RESEARCHABLE PROBLEM

Finding a problem that merits study and that can be investigated by the methods of science

REVIEWING THE LITERATURE

Surveying the existing theory and research on the subject

FORMULATING A HYPOTHESIS

Arriving at a statement that specifies the relationship between the variables and developing an operational definition that states the variables in a form that permits their measurement

CHOOSING A RESEARCH DESIGN

Determining whether to test the hypothesis by designing an experiment, conducting interviews, observing the way people behave in particular situations, examining existing records and historical evidence, or combining these procedures

COLLECTING THE DATA

Gathering the data and recording it in accordance with the specifications of the research design

ANALYZING THE RESULTS

Searching for meaningful links between the facts that emerged in the course of the research

STATING CONCLUSIONS

Indicating the outcome of the study, extracting the broader meaning of the work for other knowledge and research, and suggesting future directions for future research

IDEAS FOR FUTURE RESEARCH

FIGURE 2.4   **The Steps in the Scientific Method**
The chart shows the steps researchers commonly follow in investigating a problem.

cies, and a number of psychologists had experimentally documented the existence of similar links in human behavior (Clark, 1952; Barclay and Haber, 1965). By following this procedure, each generation of scientists can begin where the last left off. As Isaac Newton observed: "If I have seen farther than others, it is because I have stood on the shoulders of giants."

3. Formulating a hypothesis   After reviewing the literature, researchers arrive at a tentative guess regarding the relationship they believe exists between two variables. They state this relationship in the form of a hypothesis. Dutton and Aron formulated the hypothesis that a state of high anxiety (the independent variable) heightens sexual attraction (the dependent variable). But before undertaking actual research, they had to develop operational definitions of their variables. In developing an **operational definition,** scientists take a concept and put it in a form that allows it to be measured. Dutton and Aron (1974:511) operationally defined their hypothesis as follows: "An attractive female is seen as more attractive by males who encounter her while they experience a strong emotion (fear) than by males not experiencing a strong emotion."

4. Choosing a research design   Once researchers have formulated and operationally defined their hypothesis, they have to determine how they will systematically collect the *data*—the information—that will provide a test of it. Depending on the nature of their hypothesis, they might design an experiment, conduct interviews, observe the way people behave in particular situations, examine existing records and historical evidence, or combine these procedures. Dutton and Aron undertook a field experiment in which they used the "real world" as their laboratory.

5. Collecting the data   The actual collection of data is a critical part of the research enterprise. Dutton and Aron collected their data near two footbridges hikers used to cross the Capilano River in North Vancouver, Canada. Imagine that you happened on the sites at the time of the experiments. It is a warm, sunny day, and you are on a hike. You come out of a forest, and before you is a bridge. It is 450 feet long and suspended 230 feet above a rock canyon and a surging mountain stream. The bridge looks unstable. It is 5 feet wide, has low wire handrails, and is made of boards attached to cables that span the gorge. As you cross the bridge, it tilts, sways, and wobbles. You realize that you could easily fall over the side. Chances are that by the time you reach the other side, you will be perceptibly aroused. This is the *experimental* bridge. The second or *control* bridge is a wide, solid wood bridge farther upriver that is only 10 feet above a small, shallow stream.

An attractive female interviewer approaches male hikers who cross either of the bridges. She explains that she is researching "the effects of scenic attraction on creative expression." The men are asked to complete a brief questionnaire and write a short dramatic story based on a picture of a young woman covering her face with one hand while reaching out with the other. When the men (termed *subjects*) complete their questionnaires, the woman gives each man her name and telephone number in case he wants to reach her later for more information about the study.

6. Analyzing the results   Once researchers have secured their data, they must analyze it to find answers to the questions posed by their research project. Analysis involves a search for meaningful links between the facts that have emerged in the course of the research. As revealed by the content of the stories, Dutton and Aron found that the men who crossed the wobbly suspension bridge wrote stories with far more sexual imagery than those who crossed the secure bridge (in a variation of the experiment, male hikers approached by an attractive male wrote stories with little sexual imagery). Additionally, half of the men on the high-fear bridge called the young woman, whereas only 13 percent of those on the low-fear bridge called her.

7. Stating Conclusions   After completing their analysis of the data, researchers are ready to state their conclusions. They typically accept, reject, or modify their hypothesis. Additionally, researchers usually seek to extract broader meaning from their work by linking it to other knowledge and theory. In this case, Dutton and Aron accepted the hypothesis that strong emotion associated with dangerous circumstances can lead to arousal and to increased sexual attraction. And they suggested that their findings offer support for the labeling theory of emotions.

More particularly, the two researchers concluded that love is a combination of physiological arousal and the application of the appropriate emotional label to the feelings. Presumably, the men on the high, wobbly bridge had defined their inner stirrings of fear as romantic attraction. This labeling is encouraged by the popular stereotype that depicts a pounding heart, shortness of breath, and trembling hands (also the physical symptoms of anger and fear) with falling in love. Viewed in this manner, love, or at least infatuation, arises when we define inner feelings of arousal as love. In our daily lives we find it easy to pick up on the romantic clues that abound in our environment and decide that we are "in love."

Of course, scientists are rarely convinced by one study. Perhaps the men who *chose* to cross the wobbly

bridge were more daring than those who chose to cross the sturdy control bridge. And if the men were more daring, they may have been more daring about calling a strange woman than were the possibly more timid control-bridge travelers. So Dutton and Aron undertook additional research. In another study, they found that men who expected to receive electric shocks were much more attracted to an attractive female confederate (a person in league with the experimenters) than were males who did not expect to be shocked (Dutton and Aron, 1974). The results provided further evidence for the idea that general arousal can lead to sexual arousal. Numerous studies have expanded these findings to include additional emotions. People who are unaware of the true cause of their physiological arousal can also be induced to view themselves as anxious, guilty, or amused (Dienstbier, 1978; Zillman, 1978; Kelley and Michela, 1980). These findings lend support to the symbolic interactionist perspective on how we go about giving meaning to our experiences.

Research Methods

Unlike a good many other scientific disciplines, sociology has over 5 billion amateur practitioners. Whereas we come to physics, chemistry, or genetics in almost total ignorance, we come to sociology with a good deal of everyday experience. Even so, professional sociologists have an edge on the amateurs, because the scientific method allows them to look for answers to their questions by gathering evidence in a systematic manner. In undertaking their research, sociologists use four primary data collection techniques: experiments, surveys, observation, and archival research.

Experiments

In life, a great many things happen all at once, and so we cannot always tell what caused what. Accordingly, scientists need some method for examining the different components of a situation separately—to control the relevant variables in order to eliminate other explanations for their findings. The **experiment** best meets this requirement. In a basic form of an experiment, researchers work with two groups that are identical in all relevant respects. They introduce a change in one group—the **experimental group**—but not in the other group—the **control group.** The two groups are identical, except for the independent variable that the researchers introduce in the experimental group. A control group is needed because we have to know what would have happened had the researchers not intervened. When the experiment is over, we compare the two outcomes. This procedure allows scientists to test the effects of an independent variable on a dependent variable. Ideally, then, researchers can either accept or reject a hypothesis (see Figure 2.5).

Experiments dealing with social behavior take place in two locations: the laboratory and the field. A good deal of the research undertaken by psychologists and social psychologists occurs in laboratories. But the kinds of questions sociologists ask often call for natural settings in which people normally interact with one another. The study conducted by Dutton and Aron was of this sort. Further, sociologists usually require more representative subject populations—people in the work-a-day world, youngsters quarreling on a playground, the infirm coping with illness in a nursing home, parents rearing children, parishioners preparing a church fund drive—than the college students usually available for laboratory studies. And finally, the subjects of field experiments are more likely to behave naturally and spontaneously and less likely to be distrustful and "on guard." Nor are they as likely to bias the results by seeking the experimenter's goodwill and doing what is "expected" of them. So, the major virtue of field experiments is that they are more realistic than laboratory experiments, and therefore allow the results to be generalized more readily to real life situations.

While the field experiment seemingly provides an ideal combination of the strict rules of experimentation with the realism of natural settings, it nonetheless does have disadvantages. For one thing, the nature of the setting and the activity restricts the manipulations and measurements researchers can undertake. So they have difficulty controlling the independent variable and getting a good "fix" on the dependent variable. And, in contrast to laboratory scientists, researchers in the field lack control over unexpected intrusions that may reduce or destroy the effectiveness of the changes they make in the independent variable. Then too, there is an ethical question. Is it reasonable for sociologists to involve people in an experiment without their knowledge or consent? Most social scientists believe that it is, provided people are protected from harm, undue embarrassment or distress, the setting is a public one, and the experiment does not alter people's daily lives in significant ways. We will have more to say on ethics later in the chapter.

Surveys

Often the quickest way to find out something we want to know about people is simply to ask them. This rationale underlies the survey. A **survey** involves gathering information by asking people a number of questions. Very likely, you or your friends have participated in a survey. And perhaps you may have conducted a simple survey of your own by asking your friends if they were contacted by a polling organization. There are two basic types of surveys, the interview and the questionnaire. In the *interview*, one person asks another person a series of questions and records each of the answers. In a *questionnaire*, the questions are printed and a person reads through and answers them at his or her own pace.

Since it is usually impossible to question everyone in a group, sociologists use a **sample**—they choose a few

FIGURE 2.5   **Sexual Attraction under Conditions of High Anxiety**
In the experiment undertaken by Donald G. Dutton and Arthur P. Aron, there was an experimental group and a control group. The independent variable was introduced in the experimental group but not in the control group. *Source: Donald G. Dutton and Arthur P. Aron, 1964. Some evidence for heightened sexual attraction under conditions of high anxiety.* Journal of Personality and Social Psychology, 30:513.

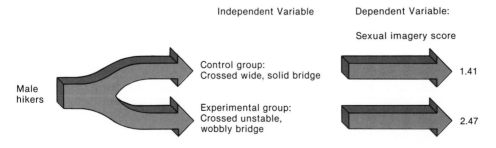

Market Research
How might the answers that the one woman supplies to the marketing survey be affected by the presence of the other woman? Researchers find that when other people are present, a person is more likely to cast his or her answers in a way that will win social acceptance. So it is important that a researcher interview a person in a private setting. *(Barbara Alper)*

individuals in such a way that the people are representative of the larger group. The best way to ensure representativeness is to use a **random sample**—the people are selected so that every individual in the population has an equal chance of being selected. Should sociologists prefer greater precision, they can use a **stratified random sample.** They group the population according to the characteristics they believe to be important—age, sex, socioeconomic level, race—and then select a random sample from each group. So if blacks constitute 12 percent of the population and Hispanics 7 percent, blacks will comprise 12 percent of the sample and Hispanics 7 percent.

Most surveys are conducted by telephone, since telephone surveys are relatively inexpensive to do and often yield data remarkably similar to door-to-door home interviews. However, using a telephone directory may introduce bias into the sample. People who are poor or who move frequently may not have telephones, and some individuals choose not to list their numbers in the directory. Mail surveys are not particularly reliable, because relatively few people return the questionnaires, and those who do are not representative of the general population.

One amazing fact is that whether we wish to study the attitudes of people in Manitowoc, Wisconsin, or the entire United States, we need to question only about 1200 randomly selected individuals. This number will allow us to be 95 percent confident of describing the entire population with an error margin of 3 percent or less. Put another way, imagine a huge jar filled with marbles, half of which are yellow and half green. If you

randomly sample 1200 of the marbles, you can be 95 percent certain of drawing out between 47 percent and 53 percent yellow marbles regardless of whether the jar contains 10,000 marbles or 230 million marbles. If you think of the yellow marbles as supporters of one presidential candidate and the green marbles as the other candidate's supporters, you can understand why polls provide a remarkably accurate snapshot of a nation's opinions.

Designing good questionnaires is hardly an easy task (see the box on how the Coca-Cola Company misread public sentiment in the case of the "new" Coke). The wording of the questions, their number, and the format

"How would you like me to answer that question? As a member of my ethnic group, educational class, income group, or religious category?"

Drawing by Dana Fradon; © 1969 The New Yorker Magazine, Inc.

CULTIVATING A SOCIOLOGICAL CONSCIOUSNESS

The "New Coke" Fiasco

There is much more to social research than simply asking a few questions or making a few observations. A good illustration of this is the Coca-Cola Company's experience with the "new" Coke (Oliver, 1986). A misreading of marketing information led the firm to make a major blunder in April 1985. The company—thinking it had a "big winner"—discontinued its 99-year-old product and brought out a new, sweeter Coke. The formula change was undertaken to break what for several years had been Pepsi's biggest advantage: its ability to beat Coke in consumer taste tests. But Coca-Cola had not counted on loyalty to the "old" Coke. By July 1985, a consumer revolt forced the company to bring back the old, familiar flavor.

When the firm had introduced the "new" Coke, its executives boasted it was the surest move they had ever made. Research showed that people liked the new, sweeter formula better than they did the old. The company had spent nearly $4 million

A San Francisco Rally against New Coke
The Coca-Cola Company underestimated the emotional stake Americans had in "old" Coke. The product had become a symbol of the American way of life. Many Americans felt threatened by the demise of a cherished item of Americana. *(Shahn Kermani/Gamma-Liason)*

to taste-test the new product on 190,000 consumers. Some were blind tests without the emotion-laden brand name attached to them. Others asked, "What if this were a new Coke taste?" But market researchers never disclosed that the product being tested would replace the old Coke.

In the first months after its introduction, the "new" Coke showed signs of fulfilling its promise. Shipments to bottlers rose substantially. A record number of people tried the new product, and more than three-quarters said they would eagerly buy it again. But then the mood of the public changed. In June, shipments fell 15 percent in some markets. And when in late June the company's researchers asked 900 consumers which Coke they liked better, 60 percent said the "old" and only 30 percent the "new." By early July the company felt it was losing control of how consumers saw its product. A retired Seattle real-estate investor had organized the Old Cola Drinkers of America, whose aim was to bring back the traditional drink (it mattered little that the

in which they appear influence the answers that people provide. To illustrate the point, answer the following two questions:

Question 1: Imagine that you have decided to see a play where admission is $10 per ticket. As you enter the theater you discover that you have lost a $10 bill. Would you still pay $10 for a ticket for the play?

Question 2: Imagine that you have decided to see a play and paid the admission price of $10 per ticket. As you enter the theater you discover that you have lost the ticket. The seat was not marked and the ticket cannot be recovered. Would you pay $10 for another ticket?

When students at Stanford University and the University of British Columbia were asked these questions,

88 percent answered "Yes" to the first question, while only 46 percent responded affirmatively to the second (Tversky and Kahneman, 1981). Why were so many students unwilling to spend $10 after losing a ticket but willing to spend it after losing the same amount of cash? The answer has to do with the way we go about "mental accounting." Most of us see going to the theater as a transaction in which we exchange the cost of the ticket for an opportunity to see a play. If we must buy a second ticket, it seems we have to pay $20 to see the show. In contrast, we do not associate the loss of $10 with the purchase of the ticket, so its effect on our decision is minimal.

Surveys allow researchers to sample the attitudes and behavior of large populations at moderate cost. Their principal disadvantage is that they must rely on people supplying accurate information. Unhappily, peo-

movement's founder expressed a preference for new Coke over old Coke in two blind tests). Coca-Cola's national headquarters was receiving more than 1500 angry phone calls and a barrage of furious letters daily. On July 10, in one of the most stunning flip-flops in marketing history, Coke publicly apologized for scrapping the 99-year-old product and announced it would once again make it available as "Coca-Cola Classic" (Koten and Kilman, 1985). "Classic Coke" jumped from No. 4 in 1985 to become the nation's No. 1 soft drink in 1986, with 18.9 percent of total soft-drink sales. "New Coke" plummeted to No. 9 (2.3 percent of sales) from No. 2 (Hillkirk, 1987).

What the Coca-Cola Company had failed to reckon with when it changed the Coke formula was brand loyalty (Fisher, 1985). When a branded product has been around for a long time and is heavily promoted, it often picks up emotional freight: It becomes associated with images that people have of themselves and summons fond memories of days gone by.

Many people felt that a symbol of America should not have been tampered with. President Donald R. Keough of Coca-Cola admitted, "The passion for original Coke was something that just flat caught us by surprise. The simple fact is that all of the time and money and skill poured into consumer research on the new Coca-Cola could not measure or reveal the depth and emotional attachment to the original Coca-Cola felt by so many people" (Greenwald, 1985:49). Other company executives labeled "new" Coke the "Edsel of the '80s." The firm conceded that its test marketing was flawed. Among other things, it neglected to inform consumers that choosing the new Coke meant they would never again be able to taste the original Coke. The company had also encountered difficulty in the mid-1950s when it first came out with 10-ounce, king-size bottles. Consumers were unhappy and said it did not taste the same as Coke in the traditional green 6-and-1/2-ounce bottles. But the difference between the 1950s and the 1980s was that the firm never took

the 6-and-1/2-ounce size off the market.

Researchers find that the more closely a brand is bound to people's images of themselves, the more likely they are to resist change in it (Fisher, 1985; Exter, 1986). The "I use this, this is me" principle applies to things like cigarettes, perfume, and beer. For instance, Marlboro is the American market leader in the high-loyalty cigarette category: the macho image of the Marlboro Man is one that many smokers would like to identify with. In the beer market, Budweiser is a high-loyalty market leader, tradition being a big part of its appeal. At the other extreme, with low loyalty, are products like cat litter, paper towels, and clothes pins. Coca-Cola learned not to tamper with Americana and a year later wrapped "Coke Classic" in a flag-waving image and the "Red, White and You" jingle (Kilman and Smith, 1986).

ple at times disguise their real feelings or activities when they believe them to be socially unacceptable, especially those having to do with race or sex. Further, many people lack the self-insight required to provide certain kinds of information. Finally, there is not a perfect correspondence between attitudes and behavior. For instance, much research shows that how people act in an interracial group situation bears little or no relation to how they feel or what they think. The *social context* in which people find themselves does much to determine their specific responses (Vander Zanden, 1983; 1987).

Observation

As baseball's Yogi Berra once noted, "You can observe a lot just by watching." Indeed, "people watching" is a

fairly common practice. It is also a major tool of sociological inquiry, one that involves watching and recording the behavior of people as they go about their activities. Sociologists usually observe people in one of two ways. They may observe what people do and say without intruding or participating in the activities, a technique called **unobtrusive observation.** Or sociologists may engage in activities with the people that they are studying, a procedure termed **participant observation.** Regardless of the approach, observation requires that a specific set of questions be formulated in advance of the study. Without such questions, observation becomes mired in a hopeless array of competing events.

Anthropologists have long used observation as the principal method for studying non-Western peoples. Sociologists have also applied it successfully to the study

Participation Observation Research
Anthropologist Margaret Mead studied a number of non-Western cultures by watching and observing people as they went about their activities. On occasion, she involved herself in some of the activities. Here she is shown playing with Manus children in the course of her 1928 study of the inhabitants of the Admiralty Islands. *(UPI/Bettmann Newsphotos)*

of Western society. A case in point is the field work undertaken by sociologist Erving Goffman (1961) in a large urban mental hospital. The declared purpose of mental hospitals is to cure mentally ill people. Goffman decided to take an inside look and so he secured employment as a recreation assistant. He blended into hospital life as he attempted to learn about the world of the inmates as they experienced it. In so doing, he used a **qualitative methodology,** an approach that seeks to understand behavior without undertaking a precise measurement of it. In contrast, experiments and surveys employ a **quantitative methodology,** an approach that seeks to understand behavior by counting instances of it.

Goffman came to see the mental hospital as a *total institution,* a place where large numbers of people are cut off from the wider society and compelled to lead tightly regimented lives (see Chapter 5). In this closely monitored world there are only two categories of people: patients, people who are viewed as basically flawed and incompetent, and staff, people who enjoy the freedoms denied patients and who exercise authority over them. On the basis of his observations, Goffman concluded that mental illness is a social role just like any other and that the mental hospital is a place where people learn the behaviors appropriate to this role (see Chapter 4). Deprived of dignity, privacy, and autonomy—permitted only an impoverished repertoire of actions—the inmates come to be the people of their roles. Their cursing, slobbering, fighting, defecating in clothing, and withdrawal

from social relationships are behaviors fostered by the way hospital life is organized. In fact, the hospital actually creates many of the symptoms it is supposed to cure.

Some sociologists, particularly symbolic interactionists, say that if we are to portray and understand the world as members of a social group experience it, we must become participants in their world. They maintain that total involvement with a group provides insights and understanding that can be gained in no other way. But these sociologists also acknowledge that observational field work can threaten a research project. Because field workers become closely involved with the people they are studying, they can develop personal feelings that distort their observations and bias their findings. And on occasion, researchers have teetered over the brink of membership in the worlds they study and become "natives," leaving their previous lives behind. For example, E. Burke Rochford, Jr., set out to study devotees of the Hare Krishna religious sect, and ended up a convert to Krishna Consciousness (Watkins, 1983).

At times observation is the only feasible way to gather data. People may be unable or unwilling to answer questions about their behavior: they may lack sufficient self-insight to report on it, or because what they do is illegal, taboo, or deviant, they may be reluctant to tell researchers about it. But observation presents many of the same limitations as does the field experiment. And there is the practical problem of using observational procedures to study phenomena that occur over a number of decades or even centuries. For these later types of investigation, researchers often turn to archival data.

Comparative and Historical Research

Much of what we take to be "facts" with respect to love, conformity, government, family life, work, and other matters are in truth bound up within the particular culture and environment in which we view them. So what is true in the United States and other Western societies may not be true in other parts of the world. And what is true for the 1990s may not have been true in the 1930s or the 1770s. If sociologists wish to determine whether or not their findings hold in general for social behavior, they have to look to other societies and other historical periods to test their ideas. This requires comparative and historical research.

In comparative research, sociologists formulate hypotheses by looking for differences between those societies having, and those lacking, some characteristic. Or they may use worldwide comparison to test their theoretical explanations. For example, sociologists might identify the conditions that they believe are associated with one another. They then might look at a worldwide sample of societies to see if the association they expect holds true. Take the question of sex roles. There are those who argue that the inborn biological and psychological differences between the sexes are the necessary and effective causes for the rights and duties assigned to men and women in all societies. And there are those who argue that women have been subject to oppression and discrimination because, on the assumption that their sex disqualifies them, they have not been permitted access to many valued positions and rewards of society. As we will see in Chapters 12 and 13, comparative research can help us assess the relative merits of each position.

A major goal of sociological study is to explain variation in cultural patterns or social arrangements. This requires that researchers specify the conditions that will favor one pattern or arrangement rather than another. In doing so, they assume that the supposed causal or favoring conditions preceded the phenomenon to be explained. Theoretical explanations, then, imply a *sequence* of changes over time—the stuff of history. Yet for a cause to be big enough to shape the behavior of thousands or millions of people, it has to grow to be that big—and it may take years and even decades to do so. It follows that if we wish to understand the factors that account for cultural and social variation, we should ex-

amine historical sequences to understand what caused what (Skocpol, 1984; Ember and Ember, 1985).

The greater the number of societies examined, the less likely it is that the sociologist will have detailed knowledge of the societies involved. And, of course, the sociologist lives in the present, and not the past. So if sociologists are to undertake comparative or historical studies, they must often undertake **archival research**—use existing records that have been produced or maintained by persons or organizations other than the researcher. Sources include census data, government statistics, newspaper reports, books, magazines, personal letters, speeches, folklore, court records, works of art, and the research data of other social scientists.

Theda Skocpol's *States and Social Revolutions* (1979) is a good illustration of a sociological work based on the use of comparative and historical materials. She took a Marxian concern—revolution—and reversed some of its basic notions. In undertaking her research, Skocpol looked for similarities in the societal conditions that underlay the French (1787–1800), Russian (1917–1921), and Chinese (1911–1949) revolutions. She then studied data from nations where revolutions failed or did not take place: Germany in 1848 and Russia in 1905 (where revolutions failed), England in the seventeenth century (where political reform occurred), and Prussia in the early 1800s and Japan in the late 1860s (where basic structural change was undertaken by a ruling elite). Rather than having economic causes, Skocpol found that revolutions have political ones. The three great revolutions she studied seem to have resulted from a military breakdown associated with defeat in a long-term international conflict, coupled with mass movements from below. Skocpol concludes that successful social revolutions pass through three stages: an old regime's state apparatus collapses; the peasantry mobilizes in class-based uprisings; and a new elite consolidates political power.

Archival research has the advantage of allowing researchers to test hypotheses over a wider range of societies and time than would otherwise be possible. However, the technique also has its disadvantages. The major problem is that missing or inaccurate records often prevent an adequate test of a hypothesis. And when material is available, it is frequently difficult to organize it within the categories that will provide a firm test of a hypothesis.

Providing Ethical Safeguards

Sociological knowledge can have positive and negative consequences for individuals and institutions. Accord-

Research Ethics
In the 1960s, the U.S. Army funded research in Latin America to identify actions pro-Western regimes could use in suppressing dissent. When news of the program ("Project Camelot") leaked, a public furor arose in Chile and other Latin American nations, and the Pentagon promptly cancelled it. The affair had far-reaching implications for American social scientists. It compelled them to take a closer look at the ethical issues involved in their research for their findings could have been used to reinforce repressive military dictatorships such as that of General Pinochet of Chile. Here demonstrators used the break in authoritarian restrictions associated with Pope John Paul II's 1987 visit to Chile to protest Pinochet's rule. *(G. Giansanti/Sygma)*

ingly, ethical considerations must govern sociological research. Yet in conducting research, sociologists confront a dilemma. On the one hand, they must not distort or manipulate their findings to serve untruthful, personal, or institutional ends. On the other hand, they are obligated to always consider people to be ends and not means. By virtue of the possible conflicts between their various responsibilities as sociologists, the American Sociological Association (1980) has provided a code of ethics to govern the behavior of its members. Among these principles are the following:

- Sociologists must not knowingly use their research roles as covers to obtain information for other than sociological research purposes.

- Research subjects are entitled to privacy and dignity of treatment.

- Research must not expose subjects to substantial risk or personal harm in the research process. Where risk or harm is anticipated, full informed consent must be obtained.

- Confidential information provided by research participants must be treated as such by sociologists, even when this information enjoys no legal protection or privilege.

Most universities and research institutes now have a committee that reviews all proposals for social science research before allowing the work to begin. The review process seeks to safeguard subjects from risk to health and from deceit. These procedures have been instituted because of questionable practices that have characterized some federally sponsored research projects. For instance, the Central Intelligence Agency, in its 25-year quest for control of the human mind, tested LSD and other psychochemicals on unsuspecting subjects, resulting in the death of at least one person. And the U.S. Public Health Service sponsored research in which a control group of poor and semi-literate blacks in Alabama went 40 years without treatment for syphilis, despite the fact that penicillin had become available 30 years earlier. In sum, because sociological knowledge can be a form of economic and political power, sociologists must exercise care to protect the people they study and teach, society, and their discipline from abuses that may stem from their professional work.

THINKING THROUGH THE ISSUES

Are sociologists responsible for the way their findings are used by politicians and other policymakers? Do the ways in which sociological research is financially supported—by government, corporations, foundations, or universities—mean that only certain kinds of research get funds? Does "he who pays the piper write the questions?" Does social research benefit only those in power? Does it give ammunition to those out of power? What measures can be taken to ensure the responsible use of social science?

Chapter Highlights

1. Theory is an attempt to make sense of our experience. The functionalist perspective takes as its starting point the notion that society is a system. One of the features of a system is the interdependence of the parts. Within system analysis, functionalists pay particular attention to the functions and dysfunctions performed by a system's parts. Functionalists believe it essential that most members of a society have a consensus regarding its core values and beliefs. The perspective has difficulty dealing with history and processes of change.

2. Although the conflict perspective encompasses a variety of approaches, most of them share the view that social forces within a society make conflict inevitable. Even so, society holds together in one of two ways. Under one arrangement, one group enjoys sufficient power to dominate social life. Under another arrangement, there are so many overlapping and divided interest groups that people join together to advance their collective interests against those of competing groups. The strengths of the conflict perspective tend to be the weaknesses of the functionalist perspective and vice versa. Accordingly, a number of sociologists have attempted to integrate the two perspectives.

3. Symbolic interactionists emphasize the capacity that human beings have to create and use symbols. As portrayed by these sociologists, society is continually created and re-created moment-by-moment as people interact with one another. Symbolic interactionists say that our social world is a constructed reality. By acting as if society is real, people make it real. We fashion reality by attributing meanings to people, objects, and events. Critics contend that symbolic interactionism overemphasizes the immediate situation and overlooks the links that exist among episodes of interaction.

4. Underlying the scientific enterprise are three basic assumptions. First, scientists assume that a real, external world exists independent of our observation of it. Second, scientists take as their point of departure the principle of determinism. Third, scientists assume that knowledge concerning the external world can be gained through objective observation.

5. Science differs from ordinary inquiry in that it relies on a systematic and formal process for gathering facts and searching for a logical explanation of them, what we call the scientific method. This method finds expression in a series of steps that seek to ensure maximum objectivity in investigating a problem.

6. In life, a great many things happen all at once, so we cannot always tell what caused what. Accordingly, scientists need some method for examining the different components of a situation separately—to control the relevant variables in order to eliminate other explanations for their findings. The experiment best meets this requirement.

7. Often the quickest way to find out something we want to know about people is simply to ask them. This rationale underlies the survey. There are two basic types of surveys, the interview and the questionnaire. Surveys allow researchers to sample the attitudes and behavior of large populations at moderate cost.

8. Observation is a major tool of sociological inquiry, one that involves watching and recording the behavior of people as they go about their activities. Some sociologists, particularly symbolic interactionists, say that if we are to portray and understand the world as members of a social group experience it, we must become participants in their world.

9. If sociologists wish to determine whether or not their findings hold in general for social behavior, they have to look to other societies and other historical periods to test their ideas. This requires comparative and historical research.

10. Because sociological knowledge can have positive and negative consequences for individuals and institutions, ethical considerations must govern sociological research. Sociologists must exercise care to protect their discipline, the people they study and teach, and society from abuses that may stem from their professional work.

The Sociologist's Vocabulary

archival research The use of existing records that have been produced or maintained by persons or organizations other than the researcher.

constructed reality Meaning is not something that inheres in things; it is a property that derives from, or arises out of, the interaction that takes place among people in the course of their daily lives.

control group In scientific research, the group that provides a neutral standard against which the changes in an experimental group can be measured.

correlation The term—or measurement—employed in scientific research referring to change in one variable that is associated with change in another variable.

dependent variable The variable that is affected in a scientific study; it is preceded in time by the independent variable.

dysfunctions Those consequences that lessen the adaptation or adjustment of a system.

equilibrium A self-maintaining order; the tendency for a system to achieve some sort of balance among contending forces.

experiment Researchers work with two groups that are identical in all relevant respects. They introduce a change in one group, but not in the other group. The procedure permits researchers to test the effects of an independent variable on a dependent variable.

experimental group The group in which researchers introduce a change in an experiment.

facts Agreed-upon statements about what we observe.

functions Those consequences that permit the adaptation or adjustment of a system.

hypothesis A trial idea; a testable statement that an expected outcome will result from particular conditions.

independent variable The variable that causes an effect in a scientific study; it precedes in time the phenomenon it causes, the dependent variable.

latent functions Those consequences that are unintended and often not recognized by the participants in a system.

manifest functions Those consequences that are intended and usually recognized by the participants in a system.

operational definition Taking an abstract concept and putting it in a form that permits its measurement.

paradigm A fundamental image or vision regarding the nature of the world.

participant observation A research technique in which investigators engage in activities with the people that they are observing.

principle of determinism The notion that relations in the world are organized in terms of cause and effect.

qualitative methodology An approach that seeks to understand behavior without undertaking a precise measurement of it.

quantitative methodology An approach that seeks to understand behavior by counting instances of it.

random sample Researchers select subjects on the basis of chance so that every individual in the population has the same opportunity to be chosen.

sample Researchers select subjects for study in such a way that they are representative of the larger group or population.

stratified random sample Researchers divide a population into relevant categories and draw a random sample from each of the categories.

survey The gathering of information by asking people a number of questions.

symbol Anything that socially has come to stand for something else; an arbitrary sign.

system A combination of things or parts that form a larger whole.

theoretical perspective A way of looking at various features of the world; an orientation that provides methods for studying various aspects of the social experience and finding explanations for them.

theory A set of interrelated statements that provides an explanation for a class of events.

unobtrusive observation A research technique in which investigators observe the activities of people without intruding or participating in the activities.

variable A trait or characteristic that changes under different conditions.

PART TWO

Macrosociological Foundations

3

Culture

*I have made a ceaseless effort not to ridicule, not to bewail,
nor to scorn human actions, but to understand them.*

—Baruch Spinoza, seventeenth-century Dutch philosopher

The peoples of our world differ in a good many ways, so anthropologists are not too surprised when they come across a group whose customs seem strange and exotic. Anthropologist Horace Miner (1956) studied one such people—the Nacirema—who have developed elaborate rituals about the care of their bodies. Indeed, the Nacirema are so preoccupied with their bodies that they seek to instill the rituals in youngsters as soon as they can. Miner notes that the Nacirema are quick to punish children and shun adults who violate the rituals.

It is very important to the Nacirema that each person give the appearance of being in robust health. Yet their culture defines the human body as naturally ugly and subject to debilitation and disease. Clearly, the Nacirema confront a difficult predicament. Their solution is to turn to magical practices and rituals in the hope of averting the ravages of ill health and aging. Every household has one or more shrines devoted to the care of the body. Although each family typically has at least one such shrine, the rituals that take place there are private and secret. For the most part, the ceremonies are discussed only with the children, and then merely to initiate them into the mysteries.

Some forty years ago, Miner established rapport with several natives, who described the rituals to him and allowed him to examine a few shrines. It seems that the focal point of a shrine is a chest built into the inside wall of a dwelling. In this chest the Nacirema keep the charms and magical potions that they secure from herbalists who provide the preparations to other members of the society for a gift. The curative potions are devised by powerful medicine men who write down the ingredients in an ancient and secret language. The medicine men are rewarded for their efforts with unusually large gifts.

Other priestlike practitioners play a role in Nacirema culture. Miner (1956:505) describes them as follows:

In the hierarchy of magical practitioners, and below the medicine men in prestige, are specialists whose designation is best translated "holy-mouth-men." The Nacirema have an almost pathological horror of and fascination with the mouth, the condition of which is believed to have a supernatural influence on all social relationships. Were it not for the rituals of the mouth, they believe that their teeth would fall out, their gums bleed, their jaws shrink, their friends desert them, and their lovers reject them.

As Miner's anthropological study makes clear, the Nacirema are a magic-ridden people. He finds it difficult to understand how they have managed to endure so long with such a burdensome culture. For our part, given our advanced civilization, we find it easy to discern the crudity and irrelevance of their magical practices.

Have you recognized the Nacirema? Miner wrote about the Nacirema—American spelled backwards—as a spoof on anthropologists. But as his commentary suggests, it helps to stand apart from our own culture and see it in a more objective light. In this chapter we turn our sociological eye upon culture and consider the part it plays in human life.

PLANNING AHEAD: TARGETED READING

1. Why is culture indispensable to human society?

2. Why do symbols and language underlie human culture?

3. What part do norms and values play in social life?

4. In what ways are all cultures similar? different?

5. How is culture affected by the manner in which people solve their subsistence problems?

6. How can we classify societies in terms of their subsistence strategies and their associated social arrangements?

The Significance of Culture

Culture refers to the social heritage of a people—the learned patterns for thinking, feeling and acting that characterize a population or society, including the expression of these patterns in material things. Culture is composed of **nonmaterial culture**—abstract creations like values, beliefs, symbols, norms, customs, and institutional arrangements—and **material culture**—physical artifacts or objects like clay pots, computers, football helmets, curtains, bathtubs, coins, and altars. In sum, culture reflects both the ideas we share and everything that we make. In ordinary speech, a person of culture is the individual who can speak another language—the person who is familiar with the fine arts, music, literature, philosophy, or history. But to sociologists, to be human is to be cultured, because culture is the common world of experience that we share with other members of our group.

A Social Blueprint

Culture is essential to our humanness. It contains a set of ready-made definitions each of us reshapes very little in dealing with social situations. Put another way, culture provides a kind of blueprint or map for relating to others. Consider how you find your way about social life. How do you know how to act in a classroom, a chapel, or a department store; at a Christmas banquet, a campus pep rally, or a funeral; or toward a person who smiles, leers, or swears at you? Your culture supplies you with broad, standardized, prefabricated answers—formulas or recipes—for dealing with each of these situations. Not surprisingly, if we know a person's culture, we can understand and even predict a good deal of his or her behavior (see Figure 3.1).

But although much of our behavior is channeled by culture, usually we are unaware of it. Anthropologist Ralph Linton (1945:125) notes:

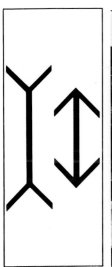

a   *b*

c

FIGURE 3.1   The Muller-Lyer Illusion and Culture
The vertical lines of the figures in the Muller-Lyer illusion *(a)* are exactly the same length, although they appear to be different. One explanation for this illusion is suggested by the two scenes shown in *b*. The arrow markings or fins on the lines in *a* lead us to perceive them as three-dimensional objects with corners. The corners activate the size-constancy effect. The center vertical line in the photograph on the left *(b)* seems to recede from us and hence appears to be further away. In contrast, the corresponding line in the photograph on the right seems to jut out toward us. Since the line on the left appears more distant, we perceive it as being larger. Some people like the Zulus of Africa live in a culture in which there are few straight lines and corners *(c)*. Since they are not accustomed to judging depths from these cues, they are less susceptible to the Muller-Lyer illusion than people who are raised in cultures with rectangular architecture. *(c, Hubertus Kanus/Rapho-Photo Researchers)*

It has been said that the last thing which a dweller in the deep sea would be likely to discover would be water. He would become conscious of its existence only if some accident brought him to the surface and introduced him to air. Man, throughout most of his history, has been only vaguely conscious of the existence of culture and has owed even this consciousness to contrasts between the customs of his own society and those of some other with which he happened to be brought into contact.

In brief, we typically take our culture for granted; it is more or less second nature to us.

Some social scientists use the term "society" interchangeably with "culture." But if we distinguish between them, each becomes a legitimate focus for study. Let us view **society** as a relatively independent, self-perpetuating group of people who occupy the same territory and participate in a common culture. Very simply, then, culture has to do with the customs of a people, and society with the people who are practicing the customs. Culture provides the blueprint that permits us to interpret our experience and guide our action; society represents the actual web of social relationships that evolve among a group. Culture lacks a life of its own. It comes into being only as the members of society follow its guidelines.

Society and culture are intertwined. Culture could not exist without people to enact it. And a human society requires culture to supply its members with a set of common guidelines telling them what to say and do. In so doing, culture binds separate lives into a larger whole. Only by sharing similar perspectives can people fit their actions together. So in "real life," neither society nor culture could exist without the other.

The Importance of Culture

The pervasive influence culture has on our lives is vividly captured in the following illustration by anthropologist Clyde Kluckhohn (1960:21–22):

Bororo nomad, Niger

Jalaja Kumar dancer, India

West Highland girl,
New Guinea

Punk, Western world

Yanomamo Indian, Brazil

The Power of Culture

Standards of beauty differ widely throughout the world. The members of different societies attempt to cultivate the highly stylized appearance set forth by their culture. Even those American college students who pride themselves on their individualism invariably, on most occasions, follow a pattern not of their own making. As we walk down Main Street in College Town, U.S.A., we observe that college students stand out unmistakably with the patterned, "regular" style currently in vogue. *(Clockwise from top left, Victor Englebert/Photo Researchers; Bettina Cirone/ Photo Researchers; Jack Fields/Photo Researchers; Harvey Stein; Claudia Andujar/Photo Researchers)*

Some years ago I met in New York City a young man who did not speak a word of English and was obviously bewildered by American ways. By "blood" he was as American as you and I, for his parents had gone from Indiana to China as missionaries. Orphaned in infancy, he was reared by a Chinese family in a remote village. All who met him found him more Chinese than American. The facts of his blue eyes and light hair were less impressive than a Chinese style of gait, Chinese arm and hand movements, Chinese facial expression, and Chinese modes of thought. The biological heritage was American, but the cultural training had been Chinese. He returned to China.

Unlike honeybees, ants, and other social insects, we cannot fall back on genetically programmed responses that permit us to exploit a special environmental niche. And we lack highly specialized appendages such as the elongated neck and front legs that allow the giraffe to reach vegetation inaccessible to other animals. A genetic straitjacket compels most other organisms to live out their lives within a limited habitat. Outside a zoo, penguins cannot survive the summers of Cleveland, Ohio—nor can lions survive the winters there. But we

can. Our ability to evolve and maintain culture—to learn and use symbols—gives us a mechanism for change that supersedes biological evolution as an adaptive mechanism. We can and do live all over the world, in the bleak heights of the Himalayas, in the frozen wastelands of the Arctic, in the deserts of Africa, in crowded cities all over the globe—even in outer space.

At best, nonhuman primates have only rudimentary or infrahuman culture (see the box on macaques). In evolutionary terms, our cultural repertoire gives us a tremendous advantage over all other organisms. Whereas genetic evolution proceeds slowly, cultural evolution is rapid and easily diffused from one community to another. Culture, then, is our social legacy—a "tool kit" of problem-solving strategies. Each one of us need not start from scratch and learn everything anew. Our ancestors met and found answers to many of the same problems that we confront. So when we use language, a computer, or mathematics, we "stand on the shoulders of giants." Of course, culture is a double-edged sword: We can benefit from what earlier generations learned, but we are also influenced by their superstitions and foibles.

CULTIVATING A SOCIOLOGICAL CONSCIOUSNESS

Infrahuman Culture: The Case of Imo

Culture provides a considerable evolutionary advantage: Its bearers' capabilities and habits are transmitted through social rather than biological heredity. Information is stored in the brains and neural circuits of organisms, rather than in their genes. Researchers at the Primate Research Institute of Kyoto University have carried out extensive studies of infrahuman—early or rudimentary—culture among Japanese macaques. Macaques are an unusually intelligent species of monkeys who have a complex social order (Eaton, 1976). Troops differ in their behaviors, suggesting that many of their customs are based on social learning. For example, males of some troops take turns looking after infants while their mothers are feeding. Troops also have different dietary preferences.

Researchers have observed the process by which behavioral innovations spread from individual to individual and become part of a troop's culture independently of genetic transmission. Consider the case of Imo, a 2-year-old female macaque. Imo and her troop of free-ranging monkeys live on the small Japanese island of Koshima, a high, wooded mountain with a surrounding beach (Itani, 1961; Miyadi, 1967). Researchers enticed Imo and a number of other younger monkeys out of the forest by leaving sweet potatoes on a stretch of open beach. In due course Imo began doing something that no other monkey had done. She would

Japanese Macaques
(C. R. Carpenter, The Pennsylvania State University)

carry her sweet potatoes to a fresh water pool, dip them in the water with one hand, and brush the sand off with the other. Soon her companions began copying her. The behavior spread to the playmates' siblings and mothers. However, adult males, who rarely participated in the group's behavior, did not acquire the habit. When the young females who engaged in potato-washing matured and had offspring of their own, all of the offspring learned to wash potatoes from their mothers. Then Imo undertook another new behavior. She took the potatoes that she had cleaned in the fresh water and washed them anew in the sea. Imo apparently liked the flavor of the salt water. Within ten years, the practice of washing sweet potatoes in the sea had spread to two-thirds of the monkeys.

For whatever reasons, Imo was an unusually innovative monkey. The researchers had wanted to keep the troop in an open area on the beach where they could be observed. Accordingly, when Imo was about 4 years old, they switched their offerings from sweet potatoes to unhusked rice. The researchers anticipated that it would take the monkeys a good deal of time to sift the rice grains out of the sand before eating them. But they had not reckoned with Imo. She quickly discovered that she could scoop up handfuls of rice and sand and throw the entire lot into the water. The sand sank, the rice floated, and Imo would quickly skim off her snack. Once more other members of the troop copied Imo, and the new eating practice was soon established in the macaque society. Moreover, the macaques have taken to swimming in the sea, something they had never been seen doing before the feeding program.

The notion of culture—the idea that human behavior varies from society to society over the globe—is a potentially liberating one. The discovery that each culture does things somewhat differently suggests that human beings make their own world. Even though alternative social arrangements often seem inconceivable to us, many people manage—and manage quite well—without our society's notions of religion, family life, or private property. This insight is not meant to pass judgment, favorably or unfavorably, on our cultural beliefs and practices. But it does say that culture is a humanly created adaptation to the world, one that we make and sustain in our day-to-day conduct. Cultural patterns exist only because we act consistently toward a set of people, events, or objects in recurrent ways. This recognition alerts us to our part in making the world what it is. We come to see that we shape the world by the way we live in it. And we can appreciate that our culture and society are not unchangeable cosmic products, but human creations that we can alter. Sociology, then, holds up a gigantic mirror to humankind and lets people look at themselves.

THINKING THROUGH THE ISSUES

Both insects and human beings live their lives in societies. However, the foundations of their social existences differ. The behavior of human beings is determined by open genetic programs. An *open genetic program* **is one that is subject to modification by experience during the life of the individual. In contrast, little or nothing can be inserted into a** *closed genetic program* **of the sort that characterizes insects. Under what circumstances would a closed genetic program be advantageous? an open genetic program? Biologists suggest the following answers. Closed genetic programs are most advantageous for organisms having short life spans and therefore little opportunity for environmental input. Open genetic programs are advantageous where an organism can gain something by storing more information via learning than can be transmitted by a genetic program. Organisms that depend primarily on open genetic programs typically require a considerable life span in which to acquire experience.**

Elements of Culture

As organisms go, we are rather unimpressive physical specimens. We cannot compete in strength with most other animals our size. We move awkwardly, at least in comparison with the graceful panther and antelope. Our senses of vision, hearing, and smell are inferior to those

of many other animals. Our skeleton is poorly suited to erect posture and for this reason we are probably the only animal that develops "lower back pain" in the course of normal activities. When we contemplate the evolutionary perfection of other organisms—the sheer efficiency of the swallow as it glides through the air or the trout as it slides through the water—we are left with an image of ourselves as rather clumsy and poorly designed creatures. It would seem that we could not compete with species that have perfected their adaptation within specific environmental niches (Asimov, 1972). But we have achieved dominance over other creatures. As we have stressed throughout the chapter, the explanation for our unusual accomplishment rests with culture. Let us take a closer look at a number of culture's components, beginning with symbols and language.

Symbols

You will recall from Chapter 2 that a **symbol** is anything that socially has come to stand for something else. As such, symbols are the vessels—the containers—of culture. In fact, one way to view culture is as a system of meaningful symbols. Symbols allow us to represent objects, events, and people to others and to ourselves. Consider rules for behavior. Since rules lack a physical existence, how can we know them? How can we talk to one another about "traffic regulations" or "proper modes of dress"? How can we think them over in our minds? And how can we size up people's behavior in terms of them? The answers have to do with symbols.

In Lewis Carroll's *Through the Looking Glass*, Humpty Dumpty says to Alice with finality: "When I use a word, it means just what I choose it to mean—neither more nor less." And so it is with symbols: we use them to stand for whatever it is we agree they should stand for. Consider the word "tulip," a symbol that when spoken or written stands for a physical object. It becomes a vehicle of communication because a community of users (Americans) "agree" that the symbol and the object are linked. So symbols are a powerful code or shorthand for representing and dealing with aspects of the world about us.

Symbols assume many forms. Take *gestures*—body postures or movements with social significance. To communicate "No," Americans shake their heads. The people of the Admiralty Islands accomplish the same end by quickly stroking the nose with a finger. Turks say "No" by throwing their heads back and making a clucking noise with their tongues. By virtue of our cultural rearing, we "read" these gestures differently. Objects such as flags, paintings, religious icons, badges, and uniforms also serve as social symbols.

Humans are creatures who live their lives in a symbolic environment. No other creatures have our capacity to create, manipulate, and use symbols to shape their behavior and influence that of others. Indeed, the symbol transformed our anthropoid ancestors into humans and made them social beings. Other organisms may communicate by means of gestures, sounds, touch, and chemical odors, but in large measure the meanings of these signals are genetically programmed (Colgan, 1983). Psychologists have trained chimpanzees and gorillas to use American Sign Language (used by deaf people), but human intervention was first necessary. Presumably some apes understand that meanings are attached to symbols. For instance, upon seeing a watermelon for the first time, the chimp Washoe invented the phrase *drink fruit* to refer to it and likewise labeled a swan a *water bird*. Similarly, the pygmy chimp Kanzi spontaneously began using symbols he apparently mastered by observing researchers teach them to his mother (Eckholm, 1985a, 1985b). And the gorilla Koko has learned to devise novel names for new objects, such as *finger bracelet* for a ring, *white tiger* for a zebra, and *eye hat* for a mask. But however impressive these feats may be, they pale when compared with the linguistic accomplishments of a normal 3-year-old child (Limber, 1977; Gould, 1983). Apes learn to deal with signs sluggishly and often only after being plied with bananas, cola, and M & Ms. Although the skills displayed by the chimps are related to human skills, they are clearly not equivalent to human skills (Terrace, 1979; de Luce and Wilder, 1983).

Language

The most important set of symbols we possess is language. **Language** is a socially structured system of sound patterns—words and sentences—with specific and arbitrary meanings. Language is perhaps our most distinctive and complex achievement as human beings. Consider its many uses. First, we use language to express everything from our physical needs to our spiritual wishes. Second, language allows us to create culture, to make our own experiences cumulative and permit us to transmit practices from one generation to the next. Third, speech is the vehicle we use to carry out complex social

activities; it is especially helpful in getting back on track when things do not go as we expect. Finally, language enables us to draw matters lying outside our immediate context into the larger social picture for our consideration. Language, then, is the "ticket" that admits us to social life and to full humanness.

How many words do you know for the term "camel"? for "rice"? for "snow"? The Arabs have 6,000 variations of the word "camel," but our only other term is "dromedary." The Hanunoo, a people of the Philippine Islands, have a name for each of ninety-two varieties of rice. And the Inuit (Eskimo) make minute distinctions among kinds of snow and snowfall. Do these differences in vocabulary mean that if people speak a certain language, they experience a different reality than people who speak another language? In other words, does our language determine the pattern of our thinking and our view of the world?

Benjamin Lee Whorf (1956) says "yes." Accordingly to Whorf's **linguistic relativity hypothesis,** each language "slices up" the world differently, drawing our attention to different facets of experience. For Whorf, we selectively screen sensory input in the way we are programmed by our language; we admit some things and filter out others. Put another way, the limits of our language are the limits of our world. So if a language lacks a particular expression, the thought to which the expression corresponds is unlikely to occur to speakers of that language. Recent efforts to make the English language less sexist (gender-biased) have built on the notion. Viewed in this manner, a language that uses masculine words to apply to both sexes ("mankind" and "political man") and that defines occupational titles by sex ("fireman," "foreman," "statesman," "maid," and "cleaning woman") encourages a stereotyped view of people and contributes to gender discrimination.

Few sociologists challenge the basic premise of the linguistic relativity hypothesis that the words people employ reflect their chief cultural concerns—camels, rice, snow, or whatever. But most sociologists contend that regardless of culture, people can make the same distinctions made by Arabs with regard to camels, the Hanunoo with regard to rice, and the Inuit with regard to snow. They may lack a word to name each distinction, but they are still capable of recognizing it. Rather than determining thought, language is viewed as simply helping or hindering certain kinds of thinking. Language, then, reflects the distinctions that are of practical importance in the life of a specific community. When new concepts are needed by a people, they develop them. The Inuit may need hundreds of words for snow because they encounter it so often in their daily lives and require precise distinctions. If we encountered snow every day, we would probably do the same thing. Indeed, Americans who ski have developed a specialized vocabulary for snow, including "powder," "corn," and "ice." In like fashion, the idioms and vernacular of sociologists, college students, surgeons, prostitutes, football players, gamblers, drug users, and antique collectors all reflect their special interests and concerns.

Language, then, is not simply a convenience. It is society's workhorse, allowing us to communicate with one another and to bind our separate lives together. Clearly, if we are going to live our lives in group settings, we must have common understandings about what each of us is expected to do. Language allows us to accomplish this. But what about these expectations? It is time we take a closer look at them.

Norms

We usually find that when we take the same things for granted, life works out better for us all. We are willing to wait in line at the supermarket, the bank, or the ticket office on the expectation that we too will be served when our turn comes. In so doing we are guided by the rule, "First come, first served." We accept for our work pieces of paper that have no inherent value on the expectation that we can exchange them later for the goods and services we want. Here we are guided by the rule, "Government-issued currency 'is legal tender for all debts, public and private.'" Thousands of such shared understandings characterize social life. They commonly take the form of social expectations embedded in norms. **Norms** are social rules or guidelines that specify the behavior that is and is not appropriate in given situations.

Some understandings may seem "better" than others in that they get the job done more effectively and efficiently. But the first requirement for organized social life is that there be some understandings, however arbitrary they may seem (Cohen, 1966). James S. Slotkin (1950:70–71) illustrates the point with an interesting case. Police officers had picked up a man on a hot summer day and brought him to a hospital for a diagnostic examination. All seemed to go fairly well, when the following dialogue took place between the man and an attending psychiatrist:

Q. How did you happen to come here?
A. I don't know. I was just minding my own business.
Q. Who brought you here?
A. The police.
Q. What had you been doing?
A. Nothing. Just minding my own business.
Q. What were you doing at the time?
A. Just walking along the street.
Q. What street?
A. [He gave the name of one of the busiest streets in the city.]
Q. What had you done just before that?
A. It was hot, so I took my clothes off.
Q. All your clothes?
A. No. Not my shoes and stockings.
Q. Why not those too?
A. The sidewalk was too hot.

In itself the man's behavior was more rational than that of any other man on the street at the time who sweltered in a suit. Yet we judge behavior by its conformity to norms rather than by how intuitively rational or irrational it may seem. On the basis of his answers and other information, the man was diagnosed as schizophrenic and hospitalized. For this man—and all of us—norms have social consequences.

Norms provide a *means* by which we orient ourselves within a world of people. They give us guidelines on how we should act so we can get on with our mutual activities. But norms are also *ends*. We attribute an independent quality to them; we make them "things" in their own right—constructed realities (Stokes and Hewitt, 1976). Consequently, they become standards by which we judge one another's actions and in turn reward or punish various behaviors. We attach a good deal of importance to some norms, which we call **mores** (pronounced MOR-ayz; singular mos), and we mete out harsh punishment to violators. Other norms, termed **folkways,** we consider less important, and violations typically bring only mild punishment (Sumner, 1906).

Folkways   Folkways are the customary and habitual ways by which the members of a group do things. American folkways include the expectation that we should bathe frequently and keep our teeth clean. We should show up on time for appointments. We should offer friends or neighbors a ride in our car if we are going in the same direction. We should not use foul language in the classroom. And we should dress nicely when we go to a formal occasion. We view people who violate folk-

Folkways

"How's Louise?" "Very well. And Eva?" "Say hello to Jill." "My best to Anne." "How's Mary?" "Give my regards to Michelle." "Love to Kate."
Drawing by Sempe; © 1986 The New Yorker Magazine, Inc.

ways, especially those who violate a good number of them, as "uncouth," "different," and perhaps even "strange." But ordinarily we do not consider them immoral, wicked, or criminal. For example, we may regard people who wear soiled clothing as crude but not as sinful, and people who are late for appointments as thoughtless but not evil. Gossip and ridicule are the principal mechanisms we use for enforcing folkways.

Mores We take a less benign approach to violators of mores. Murder, theft, rape, treason, and child molestation bring strong disapproval and severe punishment within the United States. We believe that mores are vital to society's well-being and survival. And we ordinarily attach moral significance to the mores, defining those who violate them as sinful, evil, and wicked. Offenders may be put to death, imprisoned, made outcasts, mutilated, or tortured. The violation of some mores is deemed so abhorrent—so loathsome—that they take on the properties of a **taboo**. This is true of incest and cannibalism in American life.

People typically act in a spontaneous and collective fashion in enforcing folkways and mores. Consider the Ibans, or Sea Dyaks, of Borneo. Ibans take care not to violate mores lest they antagonize or injure someone who in turn will place a supernatural curse or hex on them. Perhaps not surprisingly, theft is infrequent. They also have devised an ingenious way to punish liars.

Shortly after dishonesty is discovered, community members begin piling twigs and branches near the spot where the offense occurred. Thereafter all passersby add their contributions of twigs to the heap. Although some of the "liars' heaps" are very old, the name of the offender is not forgotten. The heap stands as a perpetual disgrace and a monument of shame (Davis, 1948).

Laws A society's mores are an important source of laws. **Laws** are rules that are enforced by a political body (the state) composed of people who enjoy the right to use force. The distinguishing property of law is the legitimate use of physical coercion. The members of a society typically allow the application of force, in threat or in fact, by a privileged party, "for a legitimate cause, in a legitimate way, and at a legitimate time" (Hoebel, 1958). In short, the people who administer laws may make use of physical coercion with a low probability of retaliation by a third party (Collins, 1975). For the most part, laws are the result of conscious thought, deliberate planning, and formal declaration. Accordingly, we can change laws more readily than we can change folkways and mores. (We will have more to say on these matters in Chapters 9 and 16.)

Values

Whereas norms are rules for behavior, **values** are abstract ideas of what is desirable, correct, and good that most members of a society share. Values are so general and encompassing that they do not explicitly specify which behaviors are and are not acceptable. Instead, values supply conceptions whereby we evaluate people, objects, and events as to their relative worth, merit, beauty, or morality. We appeal to values for the ultimate rationales for the choices we make in life. The principal value configurations within mainstream American culture include the assignment of high importance to achievement and success, work and activity, efficiency and practicality, material comfort, individuality, progress, rationality, patriotism, and democracy (Williams, 1970). Functionalist theorists say that values shared by a people have a cohesive, integrative function for society; they constitute a kind of societal glue that knits people together. Where values are shared, taken seriously, and invested with deep emotional significance, people are moved to make sacrifices, even to fight and die to preserve them (see Chapter 2).

Shared Values: Binding Us Together
Treasured documents like the Declaration of Independence and the Constitution embody values that Americans invest with deep emotional significance. These values afford a powerful force for national cohesiveness and oneness. *(Michael Evans/Sygma)*

At times different norms are based on the same values. For example, freedom is embodied in quite different norms in the United States than it is in the Soviet Union. Americans express the value in terms of legal rights associated with free speech, freedom of religion, and other Bill of Rights guarantees. The Soviets define freedom in terms of the right to receive a free education, free medical care, inexpensive housing, and material security in old age (Alexeyev, 1986:8A). Likewise, two Americans may both place a premium on social equality. However, one expresses it by supporting affirmative action programs, and the other by opposing these programs as "reverse discrimination."

Values are not etched in granite for all time. The advice columns of Ann Landers—full of readers' woes—mirror many of the changes that have taken place in American attitudes over the past thirty or so years (Hays, 1984). In 1955 Landers, despite the wisecracks, was a bit Victorian. Although many of the letters came from un-

happy wives, Landers was against divorce. And in contrast to the free couples of the later Me Decade, she portrayed the childless couple of 1955 as "a tragedy." Even in the early 1960s, we gain from her columns an image of a society guided by traditional values. But by 1970 many barriers had come down, and the columns dealt casually with homosexuality, runaway children, and marijuana. A decade later, Landers was even less likely to reply in a conservative tone. One letter of the 1980s thanked Ann for her "nonjudgmental" advice on what to do should a married lover suffer a heart attack in a hotel room. And in one of her spicier columns, Landers printed a piece by a physician who advocated masturbation as a means for dealing with sexual frustrations. The somewhat Victorian Ann had come to accept new ideas regarding what constitutes proper behavior, as had Americans in general.

THINKING THROUGH THE ISSUES

Do Americans value individualism over citizenship and self-interest above the common good of society? This question was asked by the French social philosopher Alexis de Tocqueville in his now famous book, *Democracy in America,* published in 1835. It is a question asked again 150 years later by sociologist Robert N. Bellah and his co-authors in *Habits of the Heart* (1985). The contemporary authors conclude that "the individualism that de Tocqueville described with a mixture of admiration and anxiety . . . may have grown cancerous." Many people, they say, marry not out of a sense of commitment or a belief in the value of marriage, but out of a sense of psychological fulfillment. And many people become involved in politics not out of any civic obligation, but in an effort to defend their own "special interests." But does individualism necessarily run counter to the public good or reduce the coherence of social life? Does the pursuit of individual interest prevent people from cooperating in the community, the political party, the university, or the corporation? Under what circumstances does the achievement of private goals require social cooperation and public harmony? If there were no overarching system of accepted values—if social anarchy were to reign—what would you stand to gain? to lose? Would your "triumphs" in material goods, prestige, or power necessarily be evaluated by others as "triumphs"?

Cultural Unity and Variation

We have talked about culture as though it were a whole—an integrated, unified way of life. And we have also said that societies differ in culture and implied that groups within a society may also have somewhat different cultures. How are we to make sense of these seeming contradictions? Some sociologists provide this answer: Social life is composed of tendencies that tug in opposite directions. It consists of an interplay of forces that advance, retreat, converge, and diverge in patterns of greater or lesser stability. In brief, within all societies there are tendencies that move toward integration—a state of being whole or entire—and those that move toward segmentation—a state of being separate or divided. Let us examine these tendencies more closely.

Cultural Universals

Sociologists (the author included) like to whet the appetites of their students for sociology by highlighting practices in other cultures that differ radically from our own. They point out that the "oughts" and "musts" of this society are the "ought nots" and "must nots" of that society; the "noble" and "moral" among this people, the "detestable" and "evil" among that people. Admittedly, this is powerful stuff—and, as we noted earlier, rather liberating as well. Should differences among societies lead us to conclude that cultures are dissimilar in all respects and hence not comparable? To put the question another way, can we realistically speak of **cultural universals**—patterned and recurrent aspects of social life that appear in all known societies?

We do indeed find common denominators or cultural constants. The reason is not hard to discover. At bottom all human beings are very much alike and must confront many of the same problems. Livelihoods must be earned, children reproduced and socialized, sickness confronted, deviance dealt with, sex regulated, and so on. Culture represents an accumulation of solutions to the problems posed by our biology and the common ingredients of the human experience.

Anthropologist George Peter Murdock (1950) has produced an itemized list of cultural traits that he claims has universal application. Included among the eighty-eight general categories of behavior are such practices as cleanliness training, food taboos, and funeral rites; such principles of social organization as property rights, religious practices, and kinship arrangements; and such practical knowledge as fire making, the use of tools, and names for different plants. It is important to keep in mind that at no point do cultural universals carry down to the actual details of what people say and do. It is the *forms*—the broad types of behavior—and not the specific *contents* of behavior that are found in all cultures.

Consider the influence of the weekly cycle on our experience of time and the organization of our lives. The seven-day week is so deeply embedded in Western life that the French Republicans of the late 1700s and the Stalinist Bolsheviks were unsuccessful in their efforts to abolish it. However, even though the categorization of time is a cultural universal, our specific approach for delimiting it is not. Other cultural arrangements include the Javanese six-day *sadwara*, the Nigerian four-day market week, and the Baha'i nineteen-day cycle. Such diversity reminds us that however natural the seven-day week may seem, none of these cycles is based on any physical or biological necessity. They are entirely cultural inventions that can serve many different functions (Zerubavel, 1985).

Cultural Integration

Culture is not an indiscriminate mixture of traits; the components of culture tend to form a consistent and cohesive whole. A stock market could not be a key feature of an economy like that of the Soviet Union, where the major industries are owned by the state. Nor could football be a central attraction among the nonviolent, nonaggressive Semai of Malaya (Kentan, 1968). Of course the complete integration of culture is impossible because historical events constantly exert a disturbing influence. Nor is it sufficient merely to know the traits of a people. Two cultures could have identical inventories of items, and yet the societies might be quite different (Kluckhohn, 1960). We need to know how the ingredients fit together. Perhaps an analogy may prove helpful. Take a musical sequence of three notes, C, E, and G. Knowing this information does not allow you to predict the type of sensation that the playing of these notes is likely to have. You need to know the relationship among the notes. In what order will you play them? What duration will each receive? How will you distribute the emphasis? And will you play the notes on a flute, a guitar, or a church organ?

Many early anthropologists erred in viewing culture as so loosely knit that all they had to do was disentangle the various elements and trace the manner in which each had been acquired from another society. Nowadays social scientists recognize that the parts of a culture are a

Culture: An Integrated Whole
Since culture is not an indiscriminate mixture of cultural traits, a change in one part has consequences for other parts and for the whole. These Maori children of New Zealand are examining a calculator. Should the calculator be defined as a toy, it is unlikely to have a significant impact on the lives of Polynesians. But should they incorporate it in their culture as a tool for computation, it has the potential for unleashing major currents of economic and technological change. (*J. Eastcott/Y. Monatiuk/The Image Works*)

carefully interwoven tapestry and that a change in one part has effects on other parts and on the whole. Culture is not a crazy-quilt of many unrelated patches and shreds that somehow are stitched together. An element undergoes modification in the process of being diffused from one society to another. Occasionally the modification of a cultural trait may take the form of *syncretism*—the blending or fusing of a cultural practice with a related element from another culture. Our Christmas and Easter holidays provide a good illustration of this. In pre-Christian times, many European groups had midwinter and spring rituals. Midwinter festivals often included games, dancing, the exchange of gifts, and general merrymaking. These elements have entered into the celebration of Christmas and are summed up in the traditional greeting, "Merry Christmas!" Early Christians merely found it advantageous to locate Christmas and Easter at the time of already existing festivals.

Ethnocentrism

Sociologists like to talk about "society in humankind." By this they mean that our society's ways become embodied in our consciousness. In fact, its patterns of cul-

ture typically become so deeply engrained within us that they seem to be second nature and we have difficulty conceiving of other ways of life. We judge the behavior of other groups by the standards of our own culture, a phenomenon termed **ethnocentrism**. By virtue of ethnocentrism, we operate on the premise that our society's ways are *the* ways—the *normal* and *proper* ways—for thinking, feeling, and acting. Our own group is the center or axis of everything, and we scale and rate all others with reference to it. When the Greenland Inuits (Eskimos) first had contact with Europeans, they concluded that the Europeans had been sent to Greenland to learn virtue and good manners from them. The highest form of praise an Inuit could give a European was that he was, or soon would be, as good as a Greenlander.

Ethnocentrism leads us to minimize our debt to other peoples. We point with pride to what other people have acquired from us, yet we often neglect to note what we have gained from them. Consider the following account of the cultural content of a "100 percent" American, written as satire by anthropologist Ralph Linton (1937:427–429):

> [D]awn finds the unsuspecting patriot garbed in pajamas, a garment of East Indian origin; and lying in a bed built on a pattern which originated in either Persia or Asia Minor. He is muffled to the ears in un-American materials; cotton, first domesticated in India; linen, domesticated in the Near East; wool from an animal native to Asia Minor; or silk whose uses were first discovered by the Chinese. . . .
>
> If our patriot is old-fashioned enough to adhere to the so-called American breakfast, his coffee will be accompanied by an orange, domesticated in the Mediterranean region. . . . He will follow this with a bowl of cereal made from grain domesticated in the Near East. . . . As a side dish he may have the egg of a bird domesticated in Southeastern Asia or strips of flesh of an animal domesticated in the same region.

Ethnocentrism is so prevalent and so embedded in us that even anthropologists have considerable difficulty avoiding it. Anthropologist Napoleon A. Chagnon (1983) recounts the "culture shock" he confronted when he studied the Yanomamo Indians of Brazil. After seven years of anthropological training at the University of Michigan, Chagnon had eagerly anticipated meeting the Yanomamo and becoming a "member" of their society. Yet he was aghast at his first encounter:

> I looked up and gasped when I saw a dozen burly, naked, sweaty, hideous men staring at us down the shafts

of their drawn arrows! Immense wads of green tobacco were stuck between their lower teeth and lips making them look even more hideous, and strands of dark-green slime dripped or hung from their nostrils. . . . We arrived at the village while the men were blowing a hallucinogenic drug up their noses. One of the side effects of the drug is a runny nose. The mucus is always saturated with the green powder and they usually let it run freely from their nostrils. . . . Then the stench of the decaying vegetation and filth hit me and I almost got sick. I was horrified. (1983:10)

Even more unsettling, Chagnon had arrived shortly after the Yanomamo men had returned from one of their intermittent skirmishes with neighboring tribes. The previous day a neighboring raiding party had abducted seven women. The Yanomamo had recovered five of them in a brutal club fight and were expecting a retaliatory raid. Chagnon says:

I pondered the wisdom of having decided to spend a year and a half with this tribe before I had even seen what they were like. I am not ashamed to admit that had there been a diplomatic way out, I would have ended my fieldwork then and there. . . . The whole situation was depressing, and I wondered why I ever decided to switch from physics and engineering in the first place. (1983:11)

Ethnocentrism is no stranger to nations, tribes, families, cliques, colleges, fraternities, businesses, churches, and political parties. The thought that we belong to the "best people" provides a sort of social glue that fastens us together. Feelings of group pride, belonging, and collective self-awareness promote social cohesion. But simultaneously these feelings generate intergroup ill-will. Ethnocentrism, then, is a double-edged feeling. It fosters a sense of oneness, overriding divisions within a group and knitting together people who otherwise are divided by economic tensions, social gradations, and political interests. At the same time it sets humans apart by promoting a longing not to belong to any other group. In sum, ethnocentrism has both social benefits and costs.

Cultural Relativism

Ethnocentric blinders get in the way of the scientific study of culture. We cannot grasp the behavior of other peoples if we interpret what they say and do in the light

of *our* values, beliefs, and motives. Instead, we need to examine their behavior as insiders, seeing it within the framework of *their* values, beliefs, and motives This approach, termed **cultural relativism,** suspends judgment and views the behavior of a people from the perspective of their own culture. We can appreciate the merits of cultural relativism when Soviet, Islamic, and foreign critics portray American life as they see it through the prism of their value systems. Outraged, we protest: "But that isn't the way it *really* is!" If we hope to understand another culture—including that of an adversary—we need to put ourselves in the shoes of its people and grasp reality as they perceive it.

An approach characterized by cultural relativism does not ask whether or not a trait is moral or immoral, but what part it plays in the life of a people. Consider cannibalism—eating members of one's own species. It is a behavior that has at once fascinated and repelled the members of virtually every known society, including groups alleged to have practiced it. Survival cannibalism is one type of cannibalism that has occurred and is well documented (Crossette, 1987). But evidence also suggests that cannibalism may involve the ceremonial consumption of flesh, particularly that of war captives. The ritualizing of what is otherwise seen as an inhuman, ghoulish act may be viewed as a social mechanism for imposing order on chaos, communicating with the supernatural, regenerating society, or capturing an enemy's power for oneself. Rather than condemning the practice, social scientists attempt to understand it. For instance, it seems that societies that have given religious meanings to cannibalism—the Fiji Islanders, the Aztecs, some New Guinea tribal societies, and others—have shared a physical, body-oriented view of the origins of human life. They see the vital essences of life and social renewal as symbolized by bodily fluids, food, and eating. Cultures with more abstract, metaphysical explanations for existence—for instance, the Navajo Indians who believe life comes from a wind spirit—do not appear prone to cannibalism (Eckholm, 1986; Shipman, 1987).

Cultural relativism does not call on us to abandon our moral standards. Like everyone else, sociologists make ethical judgments about different behaviors. Consider warfare, human sacrifice, wife beating, racism, child abuse, and poverty. One need not consider these behaviors worthy cultural achievements in order to study them objectively; one can dislike them intensely. The minimum requirement for social scientists is honesty, not ethical or political neutrality.

Variations within Cultures

Although we are members of the same society, this does not mean that we behave alike. Considerable cultural diversity characterizes large, complex societies like that of the United States. The world of the 45-year-old unemployed ghetto black in Harlem is light years away from that of the 45-year-old white corporate executive living only a few blocks away on Park Avenue. The 21-year-old Hispanic immigrant in Brownsville, Texas, manages with a somewhat different cultural script than does the fourth-generation Italian-American student at Cornell University. And the elderly widow living in a senior citizen complex encounters a different universe than does the upwardly mobile Yuppie residing in a singles' apartment across the street. In many modern nations, the members of some groups participate in the mainstream culture, while simultaneously sharing with one another a number of unique norms, values, traditions, and lifestyles. Sociologists term these distinctive cultural patterns a **subculture.** Religious, racial, ethnic, age, occupational, and regional subcultures abound in American life.

The Old Order Amish are a good example. The Amish are members of a religious sect that originated in Germany and Switzerland during the Reformation conflicts of the sixteenth century. Experiencing religious persecution in Europe, many Amish migrated to Pennsylvania in the early 1700s. Most live on farms, although some Amish work in skilled crafts like carpentry, furni-

ture making, and blacksmithing. They give a literal interpretation to biblical scriptures and reject modern standards of dress, "progressive" morality, "worldly" amusement, automobiles, and higher education. The Amish place a premium on hard physical work. They "rejoice" in their rejection of "worldly standards" and pride themselves on being a "peculiar people" who separate themselves from the world (Hostetler, 1980; Foster, 1980).

Subcultures are often adaptive in meeting people's needs and in helping them cope with special life situations. The youth subculture is a good illustration. The United States has postponed the entrance of teenagers into adulthood for economic and educational reasons. Simultaneously it segregates them in high schools and then in colleges. Suspended between childhood and adulthood—with diffuse, uncrystallized, and fluctuating roles in society—many adolescents look for social anchorage in "quick-fix" identities. "Who am I?" questions are answered by overidentifying with peer group fads: hit songs, entertainment idols, personal adornment, and distinctive jargon. The vogue in recent years for "punk" fashion, music, and behavior—the glorification of the "outrageous"—is a good example. And since boys are becoming men and girls women, standards of masculinity and femininity assume high priority. For boys, the critical signs of manhood are physical mastery, athletic skill, sexual prowess, risk taking, courage in the face of aggression, and a willingness to defend one's honor at all costs. For girls, the most admired qualities are physical

A Subculture: The Hasidic Jewish Community of Brooklyn
Hasidism is a Jewish sect founded in Eastern Europe in the eighteenth century. Now centered in Israel and the United States, it strongly supports Orthodox Judaism. The sect emphasizes religious zeal, mysticism, and prayer. *(A. Tannenbaum/ Sygma)*

attractiveness, personal vivaciousness, the ability to manipulate various sorts of interpersonal relationships, and skill in exercising control over sexual encounters.

Schools likewise have their own subcultures. Colleges have an "invisible quality"—a character, a certain style, a way of doing things. You noticed this when you made the transition from high school to college. And if you have transferred from one college to another, you readily appreciate the differences in campus subcultures. To understand the "soul" of a college requires that we travel below the rule books, organizational charts, classrooms, and dorms into the underground world of an often unspoken culture. Here we find colleges differ in the toughness of course work, departmental strengths and weaknesses, emphasis upon varsity sports, traditions of political activism, the importance assigned to research, the accessibility of senior faculty, attitudes toward student frolicking, and more.

At times the norms, values, and lifestyles of a subculture are substantially at odds with those of the larger society—what sociologists label a **counterculture**. Members of a countercultural group reject many of the standards and guideposts of the mainstream culture. The "hang-loose" orientation found among some youths in the early 1970s had a good many countercultural overtones. The young people questioned the legitimacy of the Establishment, rejected the hard-work ethic of their elders, repudiated modern technology, turned to drugs in a search for new experience, and dropped out of middle-class life. Delinquent gangs, revolutionary groups, "survivalists," and Satanic cults are other examples of countercultural groups.

Sociocultural Evolution

Societies differ culturally in a good many ways. How are we to make sense of the differences? And how do these differences come about? Such questions have long intrigued sociologists and anthropologists (White, 1949; Steward, 1955; Sahlins and Service, 1960; Parsons, 1966; Lenski and Nolan, 1984, 1986). In searching for answers to these questions, one feature stands out: There seems to be, over the long run, a trend for societies to change by becoming increasingly complex. This historical tendency is called **sociocultural evolution.** As reflected in Figure 3.2, about 10,000 or so years ago, some of our ancestors began taking new approaches to securing their livelihood. Other cultural and social changes rap-

idly followed. The specific pattern and form the changes took varied with the circumstances in which a people found themselves. Some societies evolved rapidly; others remained more or less on the same level; still others disintegrated and perished. No single prime agent seems to underlie sociocultural evolution. A great many processes, all interrelated in complex ways, seem to operate. Nor does evolution unfold in a continuous or necessarily linear manner. What insights can sociology provide on these matters?

Cultural Ecology

That an ecological crisis confronts humankind is now so central to our thinking that the notion that human beings adapt to their natural environment seems obvious. But ecological interpretations of world history are surprisingly recent. Sociologists, in attempting to classify societies, have looked increasingly to a people's relationship with their natural environment, and more particularly, to their mode of subsistence (Lenski and Lenski, 1982; Lenski and Nolan, 1984, 1986). All societies confront the problem of how they will provide food, clothing, and shelter. Human beings meet these needs in a wide variety of environments, including deserts, rain forests, savanna grasslands, scrub forests, arctic tundra, boreal-forests, and mountain lands. Such environments are part of an *ecosystem*, a complex web of interdependencies—networks of interlocking relationships and exchanges—among organisms, communities of organisms, and the natural habitat (see Chapter 19). Some societal variation derives from the different demands made by different ecosystems. Customs and ways of life that would be adaptive in one ecosystem would be maladaptive in another.

We confront a habitat and evolve a mode of subsistence not so much as lone individuals, but cooperatively as larger social units. Social organization and technology are our chief adaptive mechanisms. *Social organization* develops as we create stable, ordered relationships and become infused with common cultural traits. Much depends on whether or not our values, norms, beliefs, and institutions favor or foreclose new avenues of adaptation. Likewise, *technology*—the application of knowledge for practical ends—allows us to harness and change aspects of our environment. As technology has become more advanced, we have gained access to greater amounts of nonhuman energy (animal, water, fossil fuel, solar, and so on). In turn, new sources of energy have allowed our cultures to expand and change. Other

	Long accepted developments	New conclusions
10,000 BC	Small flint composite tools Stone-founded architecture	
		First permanent community
9,000 BC	Storage equipment Herding animals	Long distance trade
8,000 BC	Agriculture	Household crafts First building with communal purpose
7,000 BC	Pottery	Earliest metal working
		Full-time craft specialists
6,000 BC	Irrigation	View of town and volcano, wall painting, Çatal Hüyük, c. 6000 B.C. (Courtesy of James Mellaart, University of London, photo by Arlette Mellaart)
5,000 BC	Ranked society	
4,000 BC	Plow Wheel (pots and carts) Bronze metallurgy Writing	Fertility goddess from Cernavoda (Romania), c. 5000 B.C. National Museum, Bucharest. (Alexander Marshack)
3,000 BC	Cities Full-time armies Class society State bureaucracy	
2,000 BC	Written legal codes Chariots Iron metallurgy Alphabet	Ziggurat of King Urnammu. Ur, c. 2500 B.C. (Hirmer Fotoarchiv)
1,000 BC		

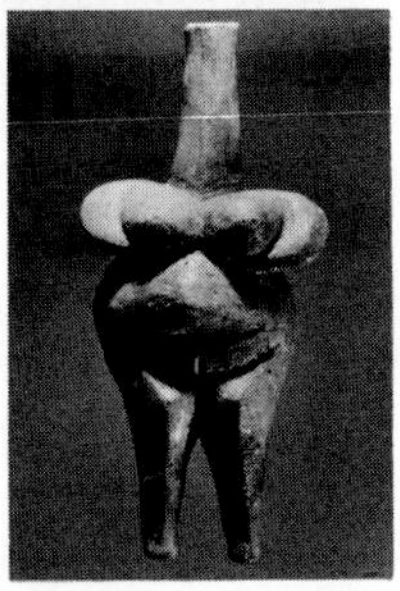

FIGURE 3.2 **Building on the Past**
Long accepted developments in the evolution of human cultures are described in the left column, along with corresponding dates. New conclusions, listed at right, date key social and economic systems earlier than had been thought. *Source: Dr. Mary Voight: "The Rise of Civilization" by Charles Redman; The New York Times, Dec. 15, 1986.*

changes follow as well. The box describes the changes that have occurred among the African !Kung San as they have altered their mode of subsistence.

Types of Societies

We have said that the way people solve their subsistence problems has vast implications for other aspects of their lives. A society's mode of subsistence depends on its environment, its social organization, and the kinds of technology available to it. Based on the subsistence strategies they follow, societies can be classified as hunting and gathering, horticultural, pastoral, agricultural, industrial, or postindustrial.

THINKING THROUGH THE ISSUES

Of considerable interest to social scientists is the question of why different societies have evolved different modes of subsistence. Archeological evidence suggests that new ways for securing one's livelihood—such as the domestication of plants and animals—have evolved independently in several areas of the world. How is this to be explained? And how are we to explain the various types of social organization that are associated with different modes of subsistence? (See Table 3.1 on pages 74–75). Reflect on these issues as you read the material that follows.

Hunting and gathering societies   **Hunting and gathering societies** represent the earliest form of organized social life. During the 2 to 5 million years that humans have been on earth, 99 percent of the time they have survived by foraging for edible foods, by fishing, and by hunting animals. Of the 80 billion or so people who have ever lived, 90 percent have been hunters and gatherers and 6 percent have been agriculturalists. People like us, who are members of an industrial society, are among the remaining 4 percent (Lee and DeVore, 1968). Today less than 300,000 people in a world population of nearly 5 billion are hunters and gatherers. They live mostly in marginal areas of the earth—the frozen wastes of Tierra del Fuego at the tip of South America; the shores of the Arctic; the deserts of Australia and southern Africa; and the jungles of Amazonia, Central Africa, and Malaysia.

The popular image of hunters and gatherers is of people who are unsettled, who wander far and wide, living a catch-as-catch-can existence. Yet in the real world, hunters and gatherers survive by taking a systematic approach to the exploitation of their environment. They live within a relatively circumscribed territory, and have remarkably detailed knowledge of their surroundings. Hunters and gatherers use this knowledge to extract the maximum resources at a given time for the least effort (Casteel, 1975; Gowlett, 1984). Indeed, they usually spend less time each day working to obtain food than do agriculturalists. For instance, anthropologist Richard Lee (1968, 1969) found that among the !Kung of the Kalahari Desert of southern Africa, each adult worker spent about 2 1/2 days at labor each week. This and related data have led anthropologist Marshall Sahlins (1972) to call the hunting and gathering economy "the original affluent society."

For the most part, hunters and gatherers live in small groups of about 50 to 100 members. This form of social organization allows them to respond flexibly to seasonal changes in resources and to maintain population levels in accordance with these resources. Large and complex forms of social organization are virtually impossible at this level of development. Kinship—blood and marriage ties—is the foundation for most relationships. The division of labor is based principally on age and sex. Specialized and enduring work groups, governments, and standing armies are unknown. Considerable equality prevails in the distribution of goods, with power, privilege, and prestige accorded on the basis of personal skills and ability (Lenski, 1966). A hunting and gathering way of life, then, is a rather successful existence. It may be less productive than other ways of life, but not necessarily less secure. If it were an unusually precarious mode of adaptation, our ancestors would hardly have survived as they did (Leakey and Lewin, 1977).

Horticultural societies   Some ten thousand or so years ago, human beings learned how to cultivate a number of the plants on which they depended for food. The penalty of the hunting and gathering way of life is that people are dependent on what nature provides. By cultivating plants, humans had an opportunity to become less dependent on the whims of nature. The digging stick, and later the hoe, provided the basis for **horticultural societies.** Horticulturalists clear the land by means of slash and burn technology, raise crops for two or three years, and then move on to new plots as the soil becomes exhausted. It is a technique carried on principally in tropi-

Table 3.1   Types of Societies

	Hunting and Gathering Societies	Horticultural Societies	Pastoral Societies	Agrarian Societies	Industrial Societies	Postindustrial Societies
Technology	Simple; primarily wood and stone	The digging stick/hoe; slash and burn agriculture	The raising and maintaining of domesticated animals	Plow; animal power; metallurgy; irrigation	Machines; energy from hydroelectric plants, petroleum and natural gas	Computerization and automation of many processes
Economy	Subsistence; trade minimal	Cultivate plants; trade minimal	Subsist on products of herds; trade with agriculturalists	Sedentary agriculture; market exchange and trade	Mass production; developed market economy	Tertiary industry centering on the provision of services
Settlements	Typically small, nomadic groups; low population density	Frequently move to new plots as soil becomes exhausted; occasionally large kingdoms as among the Inca	Nomadic camps; low population density	Permanent; urban centers; empires	Majority of population lives in urban areas; nation-states	Urban centers; nation-states
Social Inequality	Very little; division of labor based on sex and age	Social surplus provides basis for institutionalized inequality in the distribution of societal benefits and burdens	Institutionalized stratification; occasionally powerful chieftans	Pronounced institutionalized stratification; mass underclass of peasants	Considerable abundance contributes to a reduction in overall social inequality	A two-tier workforce—a small number of individuals performing spirit-enhancing and mind challenging jobs at the top and a large number of people with low job skills at the bottom
Social Organization	Kin ties form the foundation for most relationships; informal leadership patterns	Specialization of some economic, political, religious, and military roles	Kin relationships dominate; some craft specialists	Complex and elaborate division of labor; well-developed military, religious, and political institutions	Complex interdependence among institutions; family relinquishes many responsibilities to other institutions	Scientific and technological institutions based on the rational pursuit of knowledge assume ascendant roles

Table 3.1   Types of Societies (continued)

	Hunting and Gathering Societies	Horticultural Societies	Pastoral Societies	Agrarian Societies	Industrial Societies	Postindustrial Societies
Examples	The !Kung San prior to 1960; Australian aboriginal peoples; Mbuti of central Africa	Amahuaca Indians of Peru; New Guinea highland peoples	Tungus of Manchuria; Masai of Tanzania; Turkena of Kenya	Feudal Europe; Egyptian, Roman, and Chinese empires	United States and Japan	Emergent in the United States and Japan

cal forests and subtropical grasslands. The trees or underbrush are cut down and then burned on the spot, with the ash providing the only fertilizer.

Crop domestication appeared in several widely separated parts of the world at about the same time. The major early crops were cereals and legumes in the Middle East; rice, cereals, and root crops in the Far East; and a variety of beans, maize, squashes, and peppers in the Americas. The new methods of subsistence allowed societies to grow much larger. Sociologist Gerhard E. Lenski (1966) estimates that the population potential of simple horticultural societies is at least five times that of hunting and gathering communities. In a few cases, such as the Inca Empire and the West African state of Songhay, horticultural societies came to encompass populations of a million or more.

Horticulture permits the production of **social surplus**—goods and services over and above those necessary for survival. Now it is possible to sustain individuals who are themselves not directly engaged in agricultural tasks. This surplus becomes the basis for the specialization of some economic, political, and religious roles; growth in the importance of warfare; and the development of more complex forms of culture and social structure. Of equal significance, it contributes to large differences in social power and to institutionalized inequality in the distribution of societal benefits and burdens—in brief to *social stratification* (see Chapter 9). Land becomes a strategic productive resource and not merely a territory where the natural flora and fauna can be exploited. Overall, horticultural societies differ from those of hunters and gatherers in their more elaborate division of labor and in the increased opportunities that some people have to acquire power over other people and events.

Pastoral societies   **Pastoral societies** depend primarily on domesticated herds of animals for their livelihood. Beginning 6,000 or so years ago, a number of people

A Horticultural People: The Yanomamo Indians of Brazil
About 80 to 90 percent of the food eaten by the Yanomamo is from their gardens. Here they are shown harvesting cassava, a nutritious root crop. They look for tracts in the Amazon jungle that are relatively easy to clear by cutting down and burning the trees and brush. A Yanomamo garden lasts about three years, at which time the soil is depleted and weeds become a serious problem (Chagnon, 1983). *(Victor Englebert/Photo Researchers)*

CULTIVATING A SOCIOLOGICAL CONSCIOUSNESS

Changing Modes of Subsistence: The !Kung San

It took me all my youth to learn to hunt. Where has it taken me? I don't want my son to be a hunter. I want him to go to school and be a teacher or a farmer.

—An elder !Kung in Namibia

In Dobe Base Camp 12, occupied by a !Kung family in 1963 and 1964, all the huts faced toward the center. Close together and intimate, the huts still reflected the communal values of a people who ate together, listened to each other's arguments, and openly shared the details of their lives. This camp pictures the small grass huts, about six feet wide and five feet tall, of a father, his three sons and their wives, and a close relative.

FIGURE A   **Changing Patterns of Social Organization among the !Kung**
Source: John Yellen. 1985. Bushman. Science 85 *(May), pp. 44–45.*

A people's level of technology and the complexity of their social organization have profound consequences for how they respond to contact with Western industrial nations. Agrarian societies practicing plow agriculture bring to the modern era many of the cultural and social resources essential for economic growth and competing effectively in a world system. In comparison, hoe-horticultural societies have been severely handicapped (Lenski and Nolan, 1984, 1986). But the lot of hunting and gathering peoples has been much worse: They have experienced a relentless assault on their ways of life and land that imperils their very existence. Outnumbered and outgunned, lacking secure property rights and citizenship status, tribal peoples no longer retain mastery of their own fate. Many are subsisting on the margins of modern societies that have little respect for them, with growing numbers of their members becoming a demoralized and dependent underclass.

A case in point are the !Kung San, a foraging people of the Kalahari Desert in southern Africa. Today they find themselves engulfed in a torrent of social change. Their habitat con-

sists of tangled thickets of arrow grass, thorn bush, and mongongo trees. Here for thousands of years the !Kung lived, relatively insulated from outside forces. They evolved a hunting and gathering existence that provided a comfortable fit with the natural environment. Their foraging mode of subsistence afforded them a steady diet and considerable leisure. Indeed, the traditional !Kung needed to forage only a few hours a day to maintain themselves—hardly the nine-to-five hours the typical American office worker must put in. They valued the free time they had to cultivate fulfilling relationships with one another and

to celebrate their existence through ritual and dance. By no stretch of the imagination did the !Kung fit our stereotyped notions of "primitive" people, grubbing an existence from a stingy environment, beset by hungry predators, and living a mean, brutish, and short life (Lee, 1984).

Over the past fifteen years the !Kung's traditional nomadic life has given way to new patterns and social arrangements. Western consumer items—transistor radios, iron pots, blankets, mirrors, commercial infant milk preparations, skin lighteners, hair straighteners, alcohol, and tobacco—have made inroads on tradi-

Dobe Base Camp 36 was erected by the same extended family in 1978 and occupied until 1982. Fences of rail, thornbush, and barbed wire enclosing huts and goat and cattle *kraals* demonstrate their newly acquired ethic of privacy. The six huts clustered inside the large fence belonged to two of the sons and their grown and married children. Outside the group, a lone hut, unfenced, housed the third son. Another close relative occupied the last fenced hut. Now made of wattle and daub, the huts have doubled in size and spread apart. The family has even added wooden doors that can be closed and locked against intruders.

tional !Kung ways. Simultaneously, some !Kung have turned to farming and herding. Such critical changes in mode of subsistence have profound consequences for other institutional spheres. Take the base camp studied by Richard Lee (1984; Yellen, 1985). In 1963 it consisted of a circle of grass huts and a hearth in front of each. In 1969 the first *kraal*—a small thorn enclosure of acacia bushes—was constructed behind the circle of huts to contain a few goats. As the years passed, the huts changed from grass to mud. They now are larger and more solidly built. The !Kung also acquired more and more goats. To keep the goats away from the grass roofs, they began building fences around the houses. The *kraals* got larger and larger and in due course were incorporated within the circle of huts. All the while the !Kung spaced their huts farther and farther apart. And whereas their doorways formerly faced inward toward the other members of the group, they now turn them outward to look on the animals that represent an appreciable capital investment (see Figure A). These changes symbolize even deeper changes in their social bonds, as neighbors and extended-family members find themselves more and more emotionally distant from one another.

The South African government resettled some !Kung on a reservation at Chum!Kwe. Here the !Kung have been fed, housed, missionized, and schooled by the South Africans in a program of directed social change. Some of the men have found jobs in construction and on road gangs, but the majority remain unemployed. The women—no longer occupied with foraging activities—spend their days doing household chores and visiting. Still other !Kung have forsaken the hunter-gatherer way of life in order to farm and tend cattle for their Bantu and white neighbors. But per-

CULTIVATING A SOCIOLOGICAL CONSCIOUSNESS (Continued)

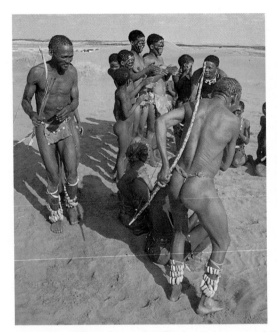

The !Kung: A Hunting and Gathering Existence and Today
For thousands of years the !Kung were a forging people. They once stalked giraffe, wildebeest, and other game with spears or bows and arrows. Their culture provided a comfortable fit with the semi-desert region they inhabited in southern Africa. They carried on their subsistence activities within a familiar environment that afforded ample leisure time. Since the !Kung produced little social surplus, there were no visible differences in prestige, power, or wealth. Today the animals in the mural at the Chum!kwe reservation, where !Kung wait for daily government rations, are silent reminders of the earlier hunting and gathering way of life. *(left, Marvin E. Newman/Woodfin Camp & Associates; right, Anthony Bannister)*

haps the most dramatic change has resulted from the wholesale recruitment of the !Kung as mercenaries by the South African Army. White South Africans have sought to exploit the !Kung's renowned tracking skills in their war against guerrilla units and infiltrators.

The !Kung use the wages they receive from soldiering and other jobs to buy great quantities of blankets and clothing, visible symbols of new wealth and status. Some !Kung purchase cattle, slaughter them, and sell the meat to other !Kung for cash. The introduction of a money economy is giving rise to sharp class differences among a people who previously were noted for their egalitarian ways. Much of the new wealth has also gone into purchasing alcohol. As a result, drunkenness and violence have become a troublesome feature of everyday life. Complicating matters, !Kung soldiers on weekend passes, armed with automatic weapons and new macho image, have begun killing each other in Saturday-night brawls. Had you visited the !Kung in 1950, you would have concluded that they were among the most peaceful people on earth. If you were to visit them today at Chum!kwe, you would say they are among the most violent (Lee, 1984).

So as the !Kung have altered their traditional modes of subsistence, other components of their lives have undergone fundamental change. All the while they have taken in great quantities of alien cultural material that their own social system has had difficulty ingesting and integrating into a whole. Yet a people's past is not dead history; it is the raw material out of which they fashion the present and shape their future. Change is a cumulative process. Earlier development influences the course of later development. Hence, as in the case of the !Kung, a people's technical and economic heritage affects current rates and patterns of development (Lenski and Nolan, 1984).

Pastoral Nomads: The Tuareg Nomads of Eastern Africa
In recent times, pastoralism has been practiced mainly in semi-arid habitats that are not suitable for the cultivation of crops. Since pastoral patterns permit the accumulation of a social surplus, stratification systems often evolve. Here members of a servant caste draw water from a well. *(Victor Englebert/Photo Researchers)*

began taming and using a variety of animals—including goats, sheep, cows, pigs, camels, and reindeer—as a food source. For the most part, pastoralists do not breed animals for meat. Rather, they take their protein from live animals in the form of milk and milk products and, occasionally, animal blood. Pastoralists also trade fur, hides, cheese, milk, and other animal products with agricultural peoples for plant foods and other necessities (Lee and Bates, 1974).

Pastoral societies emerge primarily in arid grasslands and steppes in which precipitation is too sparse or irregular to support rainfall agriculture. Pastoralists are usually nomadic peoples who move with their herds to new grazing pastures as necessary. Like horticultural systems, pastoral modes of subsistence permit the accumulation of a social surplus. This surplus allows some individuals to acquire greater wealth than others and to translate that wealth into social power. Physical prowess can also be turned into power. Over time, powerful chieftans emerge and pass their privileged positions to their descendants.

Trade with agriculturalists and townspeople often plays an important part in the life of pastoralists. For instance, among the Kurds of western Iran and the Gujars of northern Pakistan, only a small fraction of material items are produced by members of the community (Barth, 1960). At times pastoralists attempt to improve their position by plundering the villages of agriculturalists and carrying off grain and other booty. They can often do this because their horses or camels make them highly mobile. These traits, coupled with strong kinship ties and extraordinary fierceness, have made nomadic peoples into major military powers at critical historical

junctures. The Mongols and the Arabs are famous examples of relatively small groups of pastoral nomads who conquered huge civilizations. Even so, the conquerors were themselves absorbed in due course by the agricultural societies (Salzman, 1971; Lees and Bates, 1974).

Pastoralists have left their mark on modern life in a good many ways. Pastoral hordes from Central Asia doomed the Roman Empire. They led the emperors of the Chou dynasty in China to build the Great Wall. Perhaps even more significantly, major contemporary

Chinese Peasant Society
A Uygur man of western China threshes wheat with a horse as his ancestors did generations ago. The ancient ruins of Gaochang are in the background. The increased productivity of an agrarian economy provided the economic foundations for new social and political arrangements. *(George Holton/Photo Researchers)*

religions—including Judaism and its Christian and Islamic offshoots—originated among pastoral peoples (Lenski and Lenski, 1982).

Agrarian societies　Five to six thousand years ago, in fertile river valleys such as those of the Middle East, the plow heralded an agricultural revolution and the emergence of **agrarian societies** (Childe, 1936). Plowing stirs up the fertile elements in the soil that in semi-arid regions sink beneath the reach of plant roots. The harnessing of animal power (such as oxen) enhanced the value of the plow. In terms of technology and productivity, agrarian societies enjoy a clear advantage over the other three types of societies we have considered. The difference finds expression in the superior engineering achievements of highly developed agrarian societies. These achievements include the massive pyramids of Egypt, the cathedrals of medieval Europe, the countless palaces and temples of South and East Asia, the roads and aqueducts of Rome, the Great Wall of China, and the far-flung irrigation systems of the Middle East, India, and China.

At least 90 percent of the members of agrarian societies are peasants (Sjoberg, 1960). Peasants must produce enough to meet their family needs and to cover various ceremonial obligations associated with marriage, death, and village festivals. But they also have to produce extra crops to meet the requirements of landowners and church and state officials. These outsiders require that the peasants pay them rent or taxes, and the outsiders are capable of enforcing their expectations because they control the police and the military (Wolf, 1966). Government became a primary source of social inequality. To win control of the state was to win control of the most powerful instrument for self-aggrandizement. Consequently, the state became the supreme prize for those who coveted power, privilege, and prestige. In time sophisticated political institutions emerged, with power concentrated in the hands of hereditary monarchs.

Continuing advances in both productive and military technologies contributed to a substantial growth in the power of the state, the size of the territory it controlled, and the emergence of large capital cities. The great agrarian states of the past were all conquest states, social units formed through the forcible subjugation of one people by another. Few agrarian states emerged through peaceful political evolution and the expansion of a single people. From the standpoint of territory, the Russian Empire surpassed all others. By the time of Peter the Great (1689–1725), it embraced nearly 6 million square miles, and by 1858 had a population of 74 million. At its height, the Roman Empire had a land area of 2 million square miles and a population of 70 million people. The Chinese Empire of the Han dynasty (206 B.C.–A.D. 220) amassed a comparable territory and reached a population of several hundred million.

The availability of a social surplus permitted the emergence of a class of professional warriors. Some men were trained from childhood in the arts of warfare and outfitted with special armor. It took considerable wealth to provide a suit of armor, a lance, a sword, a powerful horse, and other essentials. Yet rulers found that the times required an army. The spiraling medieval arms race fostered expansionism. Rulers discovered that they could afford armies only by having them plunder and seize neighboring peoples and lands. Simultaneously, chronic warfare centralized power within a ruling elite, who found it militarily advantageous to vest ultimate authority in a king or an emperor (Lenski, 1966).

Industrial societies　**Industrial societies** are quite different from other types we have considered. Some 250 years ago, the Industrial Revolution gave birth to new productive and economic systems based on machines. Technology is used not to make work harder, but to "work smarter." The energy needed for production comes from hydroelectric plants, petroleum, and natural gas, rather than from people and animals. Impetus for industrial development came from mercantile navigation and commerce associated with the era of European expansionism. These forces contributed to the beginnings of a global market that could nourish industrial growth.

With the Industrial Revolution, humankind passed another threshold to a new level of social organization. Economic self-sufficiency and local market systems came to be displaced by complex divisions of labor, exchange relationships, and national and international market systems. In due course the changes transformed the world's peasants into social and economic appendages of the dominant nations of the Western world. Through new modes of transportation and communication and the marketing of standardized products, an industrial urban culture diffused far and wide to ensnare and transform the lifestyles of the most remote rural communities (Gamst, 1974). (See Chapters 15 and 22.)

In their earliest stages, industrial societies retained many of the features of agrarian societies. Social life was still dominated by landed aristocrats, and an individual's place was still largely determined by birth. But as increasing numbers of people migrated to the cities, traditional rural patterns were undermined. In the cities people were exposed to all the currents of economic, social, and political change that the Industrial Revolution fostered. Moreover, since they served as growing centers of industry and commerce, the cities gained in power. Monarchs who retained their thrones, like the kings of the Scandinavian nations, Belgium, Holland, Spain, and Portugal, did so only by making substantial concessions to the emerging business classes.

The emergence of an industrial order brought in its wake a good many other changes. The ability to read and write, limited to a small minority in agrarian societies, became an essential skill in advanced industrial societies and led to the growth of educational institutions. Many activities that were once the responsibility of families were relinquished to other institutions. Science and technology now assumed paramount roles in social life, and their development was rationally pursued by businesses and universities. Traditional religion lost some of its once unquestioned moral authority. Hastening these changes were the emergence of large-scale bureaucracies and formal organizations in both the private and public spheres, producing "big" businesses, unions, universities, hospitals, and government. Paralleling these developments were the rise of supersized cities such as London and New York, and in due course the burgeoning sprawl of strip cities or megalopolises (see Chapter 20). Not surprisingly, industrial societies are often very large societies, with populations of tens and hundreds of millions of people.

The changes associated with industrialization typically broadened the foundations of privilege, prestige, and power. With some exceptions, the overall trend in industrial societies has been toward a steady reduction in social inequalities (Lenski, 1966). More statuses are opened to achievement rather than ascription according to family of birth (see Chapter 9). People come to be divided primarily along class lines. Wealth consists not only of land, cattle, and dwellings, but also of money, interest-bearing notes, and socially recognized claims on the new means of production. Property could be acquired and accumulated within one person's life span. And the possession of special knowledge, competence, and talent opened additional avenues of opportunity.

As property became more broadly distributed among the population, the base of political power expanded. Eighteenth-century Enlightenment ideas of rationalism, universal suffrage, personal liberty, and equality of opportunity widened the scope of political participation to more groups. New conceptions of citizenship arose based on notions of fundamental rights to which all members of society were entitled (Marshall, 1964). Industrialization has tended to go hand in hand with the rise of democratic institutions (see Chapters 15 and 16).

Postindustrial societies   Some social analysts contend that the United States is currently moving in the direction of a **postindustrial society** (Bell, 1973). Other metaphors have been applied to the new and revolutionary

Thriving Commerce
The painting shows the busy drapers' market of Bologna in 1411. Brisk trade with other parts of the world made the cities of northern Italy thriving centers of world commerce. As merchants and bankers gained influence, the power of the landed aristocracy was diminished. Many of the social pieces already were being put in place for the new industrial order that was to arise several centuries later. *(Scala/Art Resource)*

patterns including Alvin Toffler's (1980) "third wave" and John Naisbitt's (1982) "megatrends." Two features characterize the postindustrial society. First, increasing numbers of workers find employment in tertiary industry, centering on the provision of services rather than the extracting of raw materials and the manufacturing of goods. Second, with the introduction of computers and complex feedback-regulation devices, new technologies permit the automation of many processes in the workplace. All these changes are accompanied by a knowledge explosion based on the creating, processing, and distributing of information.

The postindustrial society represents a fundamental change in economies comparable to that ushered in by the Industrial Revolution. Workers and the jobs they do are far different today from 25 years ago and will be different again 25 years from now. Today's workers are better educated, less likely to be union members, and more likely to be women. Throughout the American economy unskilled, blue-collar and manufacturing jobs are being replaced by white-collar, service, managerial, and professional positions (see Chapter 15). Already managers and professionals outnumber unskilled workers 5 to 1.

Chapter Highlights

1. One reason people differ in their behavior is that they have different cultures. Culture reflects the ideas and meanings we share and everything that is human-made. In evolutionary terms, culture gives us a tremendous advantage over all other organisms. It is our social legacy, a "tool kit" of problem-solving strategies.

2. By virtue of symbols, we can represent objects, events, and people to others and to ourselves. No other creatures have our capacity to create, manipulate, and use symbols to shape their behavior and influence that of others. The most important set of symbols we possess is language. Language makes our life experiences cumulative in that we can create culture and transmit it from one generation to the next.

3. Norms provide a means by which we orient ourselves within a world of people. They give us guidelines on how we should act so we can get on with our mutual activities. But norms are also ends. We attribute an independent quality to them, making them "things" in their own right. They become standards by which we judge one another's actions and in turn reward or punish behaviors.

4. Whereas norms are rules for behavior, values are ab-

In postindustrial societies service organizations—restaurants, banks, medical clinics, schools, and the like—are the principal source of employment. Accompanying these changes has been the rise of a "new class" of salaried professionals and technically trained managers (Brint, 1984). We will discuss postindustrial society at considerably greater length in Chapter 22, when we examine contemporary social change.

THINKING THROUGH THE ISSUES

Based on our survey of sociocultural evolution, identify the most important changes that have taken place since the earliest hunting and gathering societies. In doing this, you should note that societies have tended to become more differentiated in structure and function. The division of labor has intensified. More and more functions have moved away from the family and have been assumed by other institutions. Social inequalities and stratification have become institutionalized. And humankind has intensified its exploitation of the natural world (see Table 3.1).

---

stract ideas of the desirable, correct, and good that most members of a society share. Values are so general and encompassing that they do not explicitly specify which behaviors are and are not acceptable. Instead, values afford conceptions whereby we evaluate people, objects, and events as to their relative worth, merit, beauty, or morality.

5. At bottom all human beings are very much alike and must confront many of the same problems. Consequently, we encounter common denominators or cultural constants—cultural universals. Culture represents an accumulation of solutions to the problems posed by our biology and the common ingredients of the human experience.

6. Culture is not an indiscriminate mixture of cultural traits. The components of culture tend to form a consistent and cohesive whole.

7. Ethnocentrism gets in the way of the scientific study of culture. We cannot grasp the behavior of other people if we interpret what they say and do by our cultural standards. Instead, we need to examine their behavior as insiders, an approach termed cultural relativism.

8. Considerable cultural diversity characterizes large, complex societies like the United States. Religious, racial, ethnic, age, occupational, and regional subcultures abound in our society. At times the norms, values, and lifestyles of a subculture are substantially at odds with those of the larger society. Sociologists call this a counterculture.

9. In undertaking their subsistence activities, human beings encounter a wide variety of environments that are part of an ecosystem. Some aspects of societal variation derive from the different demands made by different ecosystems. Sociologists and anthropologists note a historical trend of sociocultural evolution in which societies become increasingly complex across time. The way in which people solve their subsistence problems has vast ramifications for other aspects of their lives. Based on the subsistence strategies they follow, societies can be classified as hunting and gathering, horticultural, pastoral, agricultural, industrial, or postindustrial.

The Sociologist's Vocabulary

agrarian societies Peasant societies based on plow agriculture that allow for the emergence of complex forms of social organization and stratification.

counterculture A subculture—norms, values, traditions, and a lifestyle—that is at odds with the ways of the larger society.

cultural relativism A value-free or neutral approach that views the behavior of a people from the perspective of their own culture.

cultural universals Patterned and recurrent aspects of social life that appear in all known societies.

culture The social heritage of a people; learned patterns for thinking, feeling, and acting that characterize a population or society, including the expression of these patterns in material and nonmaterial ways.

ethnocentrism Judging the behavior of other groups by the standards of our own culture.

folkways Norms people do not deem to be of great importance and to which they exact less stringent conformity.

horticultural societies Societies in which members clear the land by means of slash and burn technology, raise crops with the digging stick or hoe, and move on to new plots as the soil becomes exhausted.

hunting and gathering societies Societies in which individuals survive by foraging for edible foods, fishing, collecting shellfish, and hunting animals.

industrial societies Societies based on machine technologies in which the energy needed for work activities comes from hydroelectric plants, petroleum, and natural gas, rather than from people or animals.

language A socially structured system of sound patterns (words and sentences) with specific and arbitrary meanings.

laws Rules that are enforced by a political body (the state) composed of people who enjoy the right to employ force.

linguistic relativity hypothesis The view that each language "slices up" the world differently; the limits of our language become the limits of our world.

material culture Physical artifacts or objects that are made by humans.

mores Norms to which people attach a good deal of importance and exact strict conformity.

nonmaterial culture Abstract creations like values, beliefs, symbols, norms, customs, and institutional arrangements formed by the members of a society.

norms Social rules or guidelines that specify the behavior that is and is not appropriate in given situations.

pastoral societies Societies that depend primarily on domesticated herds of animals for their livelihood.

postindustrial societies Societies that center on the provision of services rather than the extracting of raw materials and the manufacturing of goods and that permit the automation of many processes in the workplace.

social surplus Goods and services over and above those necessary for a society's survival.

society A relatively independent, self-perpetuating group of people who occupy the same territory and participate in a common culture.

sociocultural evolution The long-run trend for societies to change by becoming increasingly complex.

subculture A group whose members participate in the mainstream culture of society while simultaneously sharing unique values, norms, traditions, and lifestyles.

symbol Anything that socially has come to stand for something else; an arbitrary sign.

taboo Prohibition against violating certain mores.

values Abstract ideas of the desirable, correct, and good that most members of a society share. Values are general and encompassing and do not explicitly specify which behaviors are and are not acceptable.

4

Social Structure

He who is unable to live in society, or who has no need because he is sufficient for himself, must be either a beast or a god.

—Aristotle, *Politics*, 1

Bars serve as gathering places for large numbers of Americans. Brady's, a college bar located in a large midwestern city, is such a place. Many of the cocktail waitresses at Brady's are young women attending nearby colleges. One of them is Denise. It is her first night on the job, and she admits that she is scared. When Denise introduces herself to the bartender, Mark Brady, he quips: "Haven't I seen you somewhere before?" Flustered, she shakes her head and thinks, "He's not going to be one of those, is he?"

After receiving some quick instructions, she begins her evening's work. Denise asks two girls who are clearly underage for identification. They do not have any. As she asks them to leave, Mark calls Denise over and tells her not to "card" the two girls. Embarrassed, Denise returns to their table, explains they can stay, and takes their order. A customer at the bar grabs at her each time she passes and attempts to engage her in conversation. Not knowing how to handle the situation, Denise smiles and tries to look occupied. An older man seated at the bar smiles and says, "Hello, Denise," as he places a dollar bill on her tray. Again she does not know what to say or do. She smiles and walks away, wondering what she has done or is supposed to do to make her worth the dollar.

As the weeks pass, Denise learns that the *bartender's* initial question, albeit a rather standard come-on, had been a sincere and friendly inquiry. The two girls were *friends of the Brady family* and were permitted to drink there despite their age. The grabby and talkative customer was Jerry, a *regular* and a harmless drinker. The dollar tip came from *Mr. Brady*, the patriarch of the bar. Denise soon discovered that different kinds of people frequent Brady's and all require different services and responses from her.

Denise finds that most of the people fall into three major categories: customers, employees, and managers (see Figure 4.1). When people enter the bar, she quickly sizes them up and places them in one or another category. The waitresses use these categories to identify people, anticipate their behavior, and plan strategies for carrying out their role. Although Denise often learns people's names and what they do for a living, it is not essential to her job. She merely needs to know the category to which each belongs. A critical distinction is that between a *real regular* and a *person off the street*. If a person is a *real regular*, she should know what he drinks and anticipate friendly bantering. A *person off the street*, in contrast, should receive minimal attention. Denise is aware of these distinctions and does not confuse the categories (Spradley and Mann, 1975). In capsule form, Denise's experiences at Brady's are the subject matter of this chapter, the interweaving of people's interactions and relationships in recurrent and stable patterns—what sociologists call *social structure*.

PLANNING AHEAD: TARGETED READING

1. What are the distinguishing properties of social structure?

2. What part do statuses play in locating us in social life?

3. How do we use roles to formulate our behavior mentally so that we can shape our actions in appropriate ways?

4. What difficulties do we encounter in carrying out the expectations associated with our roles?

5. Why are institutions and groups so critical to social life?

6. Can we account for social behavior primarily in biological terms?

7. Do we possess free will?

The Nature of Social Structure

Denise initially felt somewhat confused and awkward at Brady's because she was not attuned to its distinctive social routine and relationships. Soon she found much that was repetitious and predictable and acclimated herself to the bar's underlying order. In sociological terms, Denise had become incorporated into Brady's social structure. **Social structure** refers to the recurrent and patterned relationships that exist among the components of a social system. Because of social structure, human life gives the impression of organization and regularity. We find the notion of structure throughout the sciences: molecular structure, atomic structure, cellular structure, anatomical structure, and personality structure.

A good deal of what sociologists call social structure consists of subtle understandings and agreements—networks of invisible rules and institutional arrangements—that guide our behavior. Many issues are never raised and many institutional arrangements are never challenged because *we take them for granted*. Indeed, like Denise, we are rarely able to verbalize many of the rules that guide our behavior (Garfinkel, 1967; Cicourel, 1973). And in practice, it is not necessary that we do so. Nor is it even necessary that we have a mental map of the entire social structure. Typically all we need to do is manage a fairly limited routine in certain physical

places—primarily the home and workplace—and with the specific people we usually encounter there. We remember past situations and follow routines that worked for us. Certainly this approach is simpler than constantly devising new ones.

One way we structure our everyday lives is by linking certain experiences together and labeling them "Brady's," "the family," "the church," "government," "the neighborhood," and "the United States." However, strictly speaking, there are no such things; there are only collections of individual people acting in certain ways that we perceive as patterned and that we label with this kind of shorthand. In a somewhat similar manner, we perceive physical aspects of our experience as structures—parts organized into wholes—and not as isolated elements. For instance, when we look at a building, we do not simply see lumber, shingles, bricks, and glass, but a house. In brief, we mentally relate an experience to other experiences to make up a larger, more inclusive whole. Viewed in this fashion, social structure finds expression in a grouping of social positions and the distribution of people in them (Blau and Schwartz, 1984).

As we have said, social structure gives us the feeling that much of social life is routine and repetitive. Consider the social structure of your school. Each quarter or

Kinds of people at Brady's Bar		
Managers		
Employees	Bartender	Night bartenders
		Day bartenders
	Bouncers	
	Waitresses	Day waitresses
		Night waitresses
Customers	Regulars	Real regulars
		Regulars
	People off the street	Loners
		Couples
		Businessmen
		People off the street
		Drunks
	Female customers	

FIGURE 4.1 **Social Structure of Brady's Bar**
Source: James P. Spradley and Brenda J. Mann. 1975. The Cocktail Waitress. New York: Wiley, p. 62.

semester you enter new classes, yet you have little difficulty attuning yourself to new classmates and professors. Courses in sociology, philosophy, computer science, English literature, business management, and physical education are offered year after year. A new class enters college each fall and another class graduates each spring.

Football games are scheduled for Saturday afternoons in the autumn and basketball games for evenings and weekends during the winter months. Deans prepare budgets, allocate funds, and manage their academic domains. Students, professors, deans, secretaries, academic counselors, coaches, and players pass through the system and in due course make their exits. Yet even though the actual people that compose a college change over time, the college endures. In the same way, a clique, a family, a rock band, an army, a corporation, a religious denomination, and a nation endure—they are social structures.

Many sociologists view social structure as a *social fact* of the sort described by Emile Durkheim (see Chapter 1). We experience a social fact as external to ourselves—as an independent reality that forms a part of our objective environment. It is *there*, something that we cannot deny and that we must constantly deal with (Berger, 1963). Consequently, social structures constrain our behavior and channel our actions in certain directions. Beyond our characteristics as individuals are the characteristics of groups of which we are a part.

Although we use "motionless" terms as a convenient way to describe and analyze social life, we need to remember the dynamic and changing qualities of social structure. A college is not a fixed entity that, once created, continues to operate perpetually in the same manner. All social ordering must be continually created and re-created through the interweaving and stabilizing of social relationships. If social life seems to have a continuous reality to it, the reason lies in people repeating their individual behaviors many times. And if the "structures"

The Structuring of Social Life
If we are to live our lives as members of society, our actions must be guided and constrained by the requirements of the larger social enterprise. Much of human life is organized and focused rather than haphazard and random. The recurrent and patterned relationships we establish with one another find expression in our use of space. The way we lay out our buildings reflects our division of labor and our patterns of social inequality. *(Christopher Morrow/Photo Researchers)*

change, it is because the people who create them change their behaviors. As we will see in Chapter 22, organized social life is always undergoing modification and change (Blumer, 1969; Olsen, 1978; Collins, 1981). Let us take a closer look at social structure by examining two of its basic components, statuses and roles.

Statuses

In our daily conversations we use the word "status" to refer to a person's rank in wealth, prestige, and power. Sociologists use **status** to mean a position—an "empty slot"—in a social structure. It is by means of statuses that we locate one another in social life. As we noted above, student, professor, dean, secretary, academic counselor, coach, and football player are statuses in the social struc-

ture of a college. Other everyday examples of statuses include priest, friend, supervisor, male, child, customer, mother, and convict.

The Nature of Statuses

Statuses are marvelous human inventions that enable us to get along with one another and to determine where we "fit" in society. As we go about our everyday lives, we mentally attempt to place people in terms of their statuses. For example, we must judge whether the person in the library is a patron or a librarian, whether the telephone caller is a friend or a salesperson, whether the gregarious person at the party is a bartender or a guest, whether the intruder on our property is a thief or a meter reader, and so on.

The statuses we assume often vary with the people we encounter, and change throughout life. Most of us can, at very high speed, assume the statuses that various situations require. Much of social interaction consists of identifying and selecting among appropriate statuses and allowing other people to assume their statuses in relation to us. As we will see in Chapters 6 and 7, this means that we fit our actions to those of other people based on a constant mental process of appraisal and interpretation. Although some of us find the task more difficult than others, most of us perform it rather effortlessly.

A status has been compared to ready-made clothes (Newcomb, 1950). Within certain limits, the prospective buyer can choose style and fabric. But an American is not free to choose the costume of a Chinese peasant or that of a Hindu prince. We must choose from among the clothing presented by our society. Furthermore, our choice is limited to a size that will fit, as well as by our pocketbook. Having made a choice within these limits we can have certain alterations made, but apart from minor modifications, we tend to be limited to what retailers have on their racks. Statuses too come ready made, and the range of choice among them is limited.

Statuses: Placing People in Social Life
By locating people in various social structures, we can determine where they "fit" in society. As you go about your daily activities, you continually assess and monitor people in terms of their statuses. Consider the scene on the left. How many statuses can you identify that are ascribed? that are achieved? Which of these statuses are master statuses? (Joel Gordon)

Societies commonly limit the competition for statuses by sex, age, and social affiliations. For instance, realistically, not every American can be elected president; women, blacks, and members of lower classes suffer severe handicaps from the outset.

Ascribed and Achieved Statuses

All societies confront a constant stream of new babies who need to be placed in statuses. These infants cannot be ignored nor left to their own devices. Moreover, society needs these new babies to fill statuses left vacant by death and other causes. Only in this manner can the business of group living be accomplished. But every society is caught in a dilemma. On the one hand, the formation of attitudes and habits begins at birth. The earlier the training for a status can begin, the more complete it is likely to be. On the other hand, people differ greatly in abilities and talents. Yet short of actual experience over the years, there is no way of telling who the gifted will be. By postponing the allocation of statuses, society could better place each person in the status for which he or she is peculiarly fitted (Linton, 1936).

Every society must decide upon some sort of compromise between the two approaches. It can do this by assigning some positions to people independent of their unique qualities or abilities. Positions conferred on people arbitrarily by a group or society are called **ascribed statuses.** Age and sex are common reference points for ascription; race, religion, and family background are others. Society allocates still other statuses to people on the basis of unique abilities and talents. The positions they secure through choice and competition are called **achieved statuses.** Church deacon, plumber, actor, college student, artist, county sheriff, pickpocket, fullback, choir director, president of IBM, coach, and race car driver are illustrations of achieved statuses.

The impact of ascribed statuses is profound. Anthropologist Margaret Mead (1935:15) observes:

> If we hear that among the Mundugumor people of New Guinea children born with the umbilical cord wound around their necks are singled out as of native and indisputable right artists, we feel here is a culture . . . that has arbitrarily associated, in an artificial and imaginative way, two completely unrelated points: manner of birth and an ability to paint intricate designs upon pieces of bark. When we learn further that so firmly is this association insisted upon that only those who are so born can paint good pictures, while the man born without a strangulating cord labours humble and unarrogant, and never attains any virtuosity, we see the strength that lies in such irrelevant associations once they are firmly embedded in the culture.

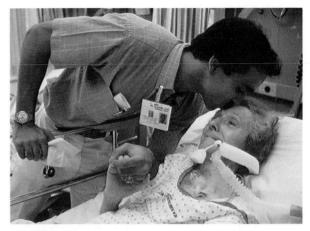

The Male Nurse
American society defines nursing as a "female" occupation, an extension of the traditional domestic role assigned women as caretakers of the young, old, and infirm. We attribute warmth, compassion, and tenderness to women, qualities often at odds with our stereotyped image of the virile, masculine man. The male nurse frequently finds himself in stressful circumstances because the behavior ascribed to him as a man runs counter to the caring behavior expected of him in his achieved status as a nurse. Recent changes in our society's definitions of masculinity and femininity allow men and women greater range in expressing their emotions and role preferences without regard to gender stereotypes. *(Eugene Richards/Magnum)*

Even so, no society ignores individual differences. All societies recognize individual acomplishment and failure, and apportion some statuses on the basis of individual achievement. In some cases, these statuses serve as bait for socially acceptable behavior or as escape hatches for "troublemakers." Societies often reserve certain achieved statuses as rewards for conformity. Simultaneously, they find it possible to channel what otherwise might be deviant impulses into socially acceptable channels: Individuals disposed to skeptical inquiry can become philosophers; to innovative tinkering, engineers; to aesthetic creativity, artists; and to religious inspiration, prophets.

Master Statuses

Some of our statuses overshadow others in our own minds and in those of other people. A **master status** is a key or core status that carries primary weight in our social interactions and relationships. Age and sex are master statuses in all societies. Race and occupation are also of central importance in American life. Master statuses lay the framework within which our goals are formulated and our training carried out.

By virtue of a master status, people hold rather specific expectations for our behavior, abilities, and traits (Martin and Greenstein, 1983). Consider age. It governs our entry to many other statuses and makes its own distinct imprint on them. The notion that you ought to "act your age" pervades many spheres. In the United States, for instance, a child of 6 is thought "too young" to babysit for other youngsters. A man of 80 is thought to be "too old" to dance the latest steps in a discotheque. Age operates *directly* as a criterion for driving a car (age 16 in some states, 17 in others), voting (age 18), becoming president (age 35), and receiving social security retirement benefits (age 62). Age also operates *indirectly* as a criterion for certain statuses through its links with other factors. For instance, age linked with reproductive capacity limits entry into the parental role; age linked with twelve years of elementary and secondary school usually limits entry into college. Consequently, age serves as a reference point that allows us to orient ourselves in terms of what and where we are within various social networks—school, family, church, and workplace. It is one ingredient that provides us with the answers to the question "Who am I?" Not surprisingly, the loss of a key master status can have devastating consequences for a person, as the box shows.

THINKING THROUGH THE ISSUES

Have you recently assumed or lost a master status? Have you made a vocational decision and embarked on a new occupation? Have you married, divorced, or become a parent? For some people, the status of college student assumes the properties of a master status. Has this been true for you? Identify the adjustments that have been required of you by virtue of assuming or losing a master status. Were the adjustments relatively easy or difficult? How have society's institutions assisted or failed you in making the adjustments?

Roles

A status carries with it a set of culturally defined rights and duties, what sociologists term a **role.** Expectations or *norms* specify what is appropriate and inappropriate behavior for the occupant of a status. The difference between a status and a role is that we *occupy* a status and *play* a role (Linton, 1936). One of the best ways to begin the study of social life is to examine people's roles. Few other concepts in the social sciences have commanded greater interest, not only in sociological work, but in psychology, social psychology, and anthropology as well.

The Nature of Roles

Sociologists took the notion of role from the theater. It is an analogy suggested by William Shakespeare in *As You Like It* (Act II, Scene 7):

> All the world's a stage,
> And all the men and women merely players.
> They have their exits and their entrances;
> And one man in his time plays many parts.

Actors perform their roles according to a script (which is analogous to culture), what the other actors say and do, and the reactions of the audience. But the theater analogy also has its limitations. Whereas the theater is a world of make-believe, in life our parts are *real*. And as we go about our daily activities, we are seldom aware of following a script. Moreover, in life we do a good deal of improvising; we continually test and revamp our actions according to what other people say and do.

Roles allow us to formulate our behavior mentally so that we can shape our actions in appropriate ways. We collect the details of an unfolding situation and identify *who does what, when, and where.* By means of roles, we order our social world into types or categories of people. We assume that we can ignore personal differences and for practical purposes treat the members of a given category as interchangeable. For example, every American "knows" that a physician is "a person who treats sick people" and a carpenter is "a person who uses lumber to build houses." Roles allow us to collapse or telescope a range of behaviors into manageable bundles. They are the primary link between a society's institutional arrangements and the private experiences of its members—the link between macrosociology and microsociology (see Chapter 1).

Role and Role Performance
For more than three decades the movie-going public flocked to see someone it knew as Rock Hudson. As created, packaged, and promoted by Hollywood, Hudson was a heroic, handsome, larger than life symbol of all-American virtue. Most of the public was unaware that his heterosexual persona was simply a role. Sociologists point out that a role is the expected behavior we associate with a status and that our actual behavior may not conform to these expectations. *(Memory Shop)*

A role is the *expected* behavior we associate with a status. **Role performance** is the *actual* behavior of the person who occupies a status. In real life a gap often exists between what people should do and what they actually do. And people vary in how they carry out the rights and duties associated with their roles. We are not carbon copies of one another. You take such differences into account when you select one professor over another for a course. One professor may have the reputation for coming late to class, lecturing in an informal manner, and assigning difficult term papers. Another professor may be a distinguished authority in the field, monitor class attendance, and assign take-home examinations. Regardless of which professor you select, you will still occupy the status of student and play its associated role. However, you will have to modify your behavior depending upon your selection. In sum, everyone's role performance is unique; it is not usually reproduced or re-created by another.

THINKING THROUGH THE ISSUES

Why do the statuses we occupy and the roles we play have major consequences for our personality? For one thing, we determine *who* and *what* we are primarily in a social context. As we will see in Chapter 6, we discover ourselves in our own actions and in the actions of others toward us. So the statuses we occupy and the roles we play tell us about ourselves. Moreover, as we discuss later in the chapter, we embrace many of our roles. As a result, we often *become* the role—*the* student, *the* banker, *the* president, and so on. This process is highlighted by the prison study undertaken by Philip G. Zimbardo and his associates and reported in the box on pp. 96–97. Identify a major role that you play that has important consequences for your personality. What are some of these consequences?

Role Set

A single status may have multiple roles attached to it, constituting a **role set.** Consider the status of a patient in a hospital. The status involves the sick role; another role as the peer of other patients; still another role as the "appreciative" recipient of the gifts and attentions of friends and family members; one role as a consumer of newspapers, magazines, and other small items purchased from a hospital attendant; and a role as acquaintance of a number of friendly hospital personnel (see Figure 4.2). Clearly, a role does not exist in a social vacuum; it is a bundle of activities that mesh with the activities of other people. For this reason there can be no professors without students, no husbands without wives,

CULTIVATING A SOCIOLOGICAL CONSCIOUSNESS

Loss of a Master Status: Farmer

Our master statuses locate us in the social world by establishing who and what we are, and they also anchor us in social networks. To be displaced from a key master status may set us socially adrift. Our identities can become confused and imperiled. Something of the sort is happening on many of the nation's family farms. For rural Americans, "farmer" is often a master status. There are no clear boundaries between job, family, and community roles. The farm economy's recent difficulties are forcing a growing number of farmers into bankruptcy and bringing emotional stresses that in some ways are more brutal than those of the Great Depression of the 1930s. The current agricultural problems have grown out of the boom and inflation of the 1970s and the deflation that followed. Around the clock through the year, 180 times a day now, another American farm disappears (Malcolm, 1987).

Small farmers have been most vulnerable to the economic downturn. Consider the case of Arlene and Norman Kunkle, who were forced off their Missouri farm around Thanksgiving 1983. Since then Mr. Kunkle has spent months in and out of hospi-

The Plight of American Farmers
More and more farmers are being forced to give up farming as their financial difficulties mount. Countless occupational, family, and community roles are entwined with the master status of farmer, making the loss all the more painful. In losing their farms, men and women find a way of life imperiled and they feel emotionally at sea—lost and abandoned. (*J.P. Laffont/Sygma*)

tals, under treatment for severe depression. And the children have mirrored the family's stress. Christopher, formerly an A and B student, started bringing home Ds. KiKi, then 11, would begin crying with little provocation. Carol, a junior in high school, had severe and recurrent headaches and stomachaches. Fifteen-year-old Kerri, angered by the adverse turn in his life, became subject to violent outbursts. He threatened his brother with a switchblade and stabbed his father in the arm with a paring knife. The family moved into a small trailer home, Mrs. Kunkle got a night job in

no whites without nonwhites, and no lawyers without clients.

Roles affect us as sets of norms that define our **duties**—the actions others can legitimately insist that we perform, and our **rights**—the actions we can legitimately insist that others perform (Goffman, 1961). Every role has at least one reciprocal role attached to it; the rights of one role are the duties of the other role. As we have noted, we have a social niche for the sick. Sick people have rights—our society says they do not have to function in usual ways until they get well. But sick people also have the duty to get well and "not enjoy themselves too much." Anything less is frowned upon as "malingering." The sick role also entails an appeal to another party—the physician. The physician must perceive the patient as trying to get well—this is the physician's right and the patient's duty. And the patient must see the doc-

tor as sincere and not as a quack or a money-gouger—the patient's right and the physician's duty.

One way that people are linked in groups is through networks of reciprocal roles. Role relationships tie us to one another because the rights of one end of the relationship are the duties of the other (see Figure 4.3). Groups consist of intricate complexes of interlocking roles, which their members sustain in the course of interacting. People experience these stable relationships as social structure—a hospital, a college, a family, a gang, an army, and so on (see Figure 4.4).

Role Strain

Role strain is the stress people experience when they encounter difficulties in meeting the requirements of a role. Consider the relationship physicians have with pa-

a nursing home, and Mr. Kunkle's condition seems to be improving. But the scars remain (Wall, 1985).

Suicide rates are on the rise throughout the farm belt. Mike Hrabe, a 41-year-old Kansas wheat grower, had written a suicide note telling a neighbor where to find his body when the sight of his son's baseball uniform, laid out for a Little League game, stopped him. Mr. Hrabe says: "A lot of people try to say this is no different from any other business failure. I tell you there is a great difference." The land he farms has been in his family and free of mortgages for 120 years. "Dad and Granddad had both been successful," Mr. Hrabe says. "And I was a member of the school board, member of the church board, a member of the board at the Farm Bureau, and I was a 4-H Club leader. I was pretty well thought of in the community. There is a certain pride in farming, and the shame of failure is just overwhelming. Death seemed better than facing it" (Robbins, 1986:9).

As century-old farms are threatened, marriages often crack and generations divide. Family abuse rates are rising as some farmers vent their frustration and anger in alcoholism or violence. Mental health workers say that couples under the stress of losing a farm sometimes find their self-confidence so undermined that they become ineffective parents. And the troubles of farm parents add tension to their children's lives. Jared Taylor, a sixth-grader from Dickens, Iowa, has had to use his savings and the bonds his grandparents gave him when he was born to help pay his family's electric, water, and telephone bills. Jared worries about his parents and fears they will have an accident or leave. One evening when his father was late returning home, Jared sat in the car and honked the horn until his mother agreed to go in search of her husband. "I was scared," he recalls. "I thought something might have happened" (Wall, 1985:1). Simultaneously, youngsters' participation in vocational agricultural classes, 4-H programs,

and Future Farmers of America has dropped sharply across the farm belt.

Social workers involved in retraining programs find that former farmers are in a bad position: They have few job-seeking skills, dismal credit records, and in many cases are older. An ex-Iowa farmer who enrolled in a job-training program had a résumé composed of just one sentence: "For twenty-seven years, hog farmer." Many former farmers still long for the farm lifestyle. Typical is Lloyd DeCourley, aged 50, forced into bankruptcy in 1981 and now a food-market vendor. He still subscribes to three farm magazines and regularly watches the evening farm news. Occasionally Mr. DeCourley dreams of the harvest: "I'll be sound asleep and I'm driving the tractor and you can see the dirt and the rows of soybeans. But you wake up at two or three in the morning and see nothing to relate to" (Kotlowitz, 1985:23). For many former farmers, the loss of the master status "farmer" has caused the collapse of a whole social world.

---

tients. Doctors are expected to be gentle healers—humanitarian, self-sacrificing saviors of the sick. Simultaneously, they are expected to be retailers of knowledge they have secured at considerable cost and sacrifice. While prescribing unnecessary services, tests, and X rays and aggressive bill collecting are consistent with the small-business/retailer aspects of the role, they are inconsistent with that of the gentle healer. And there are few well-defined or accepted answers to the dilemmas posed by these contradictory expectations.

Uncorrected role strain can lead to chronic frustration, a sense of failure, feelings of insecurity, and even ulcers, heart disease, and early death (Krantz, Grunberg, and Baum, 1985). Yet whether or not people will experience role strain depends in large measure on how they perceive their roles. Sociologist Ralph H. Turner (1978) points out that we put on and take off some roles like clothing—without lasting personal effect. Other roles we have difficulty putting aside even when the situation changes; these roles color the ways in which we think about ourselves and act in many circumstances. When the attitudes and behavior developed in the expression of one role carry over to many situations, Turner says there is "a merger of role with person." Take the case of the doctor, the judge, or the college professor who carries the bearing and air of authority of the professional role into family and community dealings. Such individuals are not merely incumbents of a status; they have fully embraced it. Each *is* the role—*the* doctor, *the* judge, or *the* professor.

The stress we experience with role strain may result from **role conflict**—a situation in which people are confronted with incompatible role requirements. There are countless sources of role conflict. We have already iden-

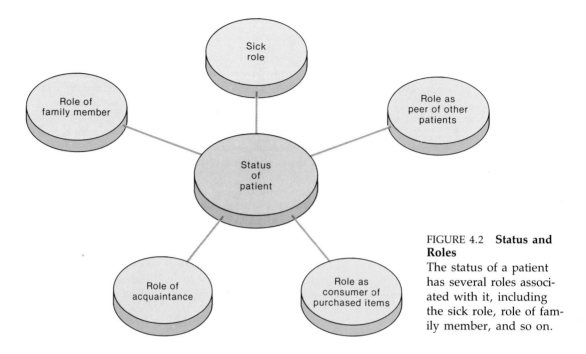

FIGURE 4.2 **Status and Roles**
The status of a patient has several roles associated with it, including the sick role, role of family member, and so on.

tified one source—namely, circumstances in which one expectation of a role clashes with another expectation. The clashing expectations of the physician as a gentle healer and an entrepreneur illustrate this type of difficulty. Some roles also conflict with other roles. A football coach whose son is a member of the team may expe-

rience role conflict when deciding whether to make his own son or another more talented player the starting quarterback. Some college students report they experience role conflict when their parents pay them a campus visit. They feel "on stage" before two audiences holding somewhat contradictory expectations of them. One way

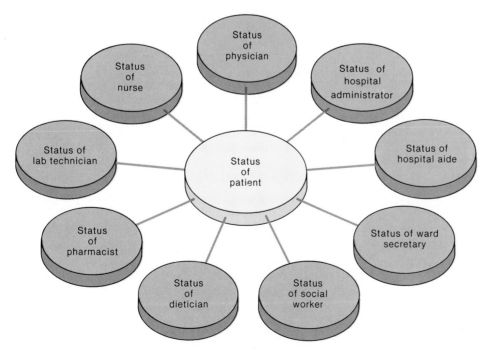

FIGURE 4.3 **A Role Set**
As occupants of statuses, we play roles with their associated rights and duties. The duties of the patient are the rights of the nurse and the rights of the patient are the duties of the nurse; the duties of the patient are also the rights of the social worker and the rights of the patient are the duties of the social worker. We are tied to one another within the same social arena through networks of reciprocal roles.

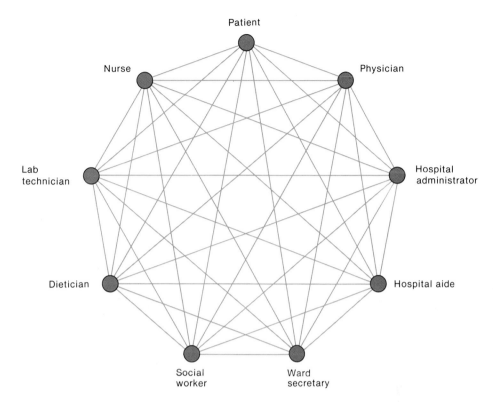

FIGURE 4.4 **The Hospital as a Social Structure** Groups consist of intricate complexes of interlocking roles that individuals sustain in their interactions with one another. We experience these recurrent and patterned relationships as social structure.

Embracing the Role

Some roles we put on and take off like clothing; they have little impact upon our attitudes and personalities. Other roles we fully embrace; the role becomes deeply merged with our sense of who and what we are. We literally become the person of the role. *(Comstock)*

to handle role conflict is to subdivide or compartmentalize one's life and assume only one of the incompatible roles at a time. For instance, college students may attempt to segregate their school and home experiences so that do not have to stage their behavior before their parents and peers simultaneously.

THINKING THROUGH THE ISSUES

Examine a recurrent source of friction in your relationship with a parent, friend, or employer. Does role conflict underlie some of the difficulties?

- **Are you confronted with contradictory expectations because you must play two or more conflicting roles simultaneously?**

- **Do some of the expectations associated with one role in a role set conflict with the expectations of another role in the same role set?**

- **Do you find that some of the demands of the role are incompatible with one or more of your personality characteristics?**

CULTIVATING A SOCIOLOGICAL CONSCIOUSNESS

Your Roles and Your Personality

Roles enhance as well as restrict behavior. They lubricate your relationships with others because you know what to say and do in many different situations. But your roles also influence and shape your personality. Philip G. Zimbardo and his colleagues (1973) have shown how this can happen. To investigate the consequences of being a prisoner or a prison guard, the researchers converted the basement of a Stanford University building into a mock prison. They recruited twenty-one emotionally stable, mature, well-adjusted, healthy, and law-abiding college students to take part in the study. Zimbardo randomly assigned eleven of the men to act as prison guards and the other ten to take the part of prisoners. To enhance the realism of the experiment, the "prisoners" were unexpectedly picked up at their homes by Palo Alto police. Each subject was charged with a felony, told of his constitutional rights, spread-eagled against the

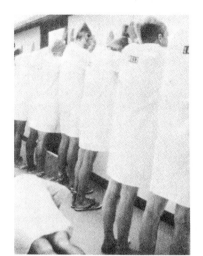

Zimbardo's Prison Study
The photos depict the mock prison in the basement of a Stanford University building. The research revealed that normal, healthy college men can be radically transformed under the institutional pressures of a prison environment. The bizarre social and personal reactions of the subjects cannot be attributed to preexisting personality differences or pathologies because these factors were eliminated by the careful selection processes and the random assignment. Instead, the guards' aggressive behavior and the prisoners' submissiveness arose out of situational factors in an institutional environment. Zimbardo suggests that we should not underestimate the power of an evil situation to overwhelm the personalities and good upbringing of even well-educated and bright people. *(courtesy of Philip G. Zimbardo)*

squad car, searched, handcuffed, and then delivered to the station for fingerprinting.

At the mock prison, the prisoners were stripped naked; skin-searched; sprayed for lice; issued a uniform, bedding, soap, and a towel; and placed in a 6 by 9 foot barred cell with

- **Are some of the role expectations ill-defined so that you do not know what is expected of you?**

- **Do you disagree with the other person as to what are the rights and duties of the role or in what ways the rights and duties should be performed?**

Having identified various sources of role conflict in your relationship, what actions might you take to reduce each role difficulty?

Role Taking and Role Making

Interaction usually has a tentative quality to it (Turner, 1962, 1968a, 1968b); we start or stop and implement or transform what we are saying or doing on the basis of

what other people say and do. The activities of others influence how we shape our actions. Consequently, we are involved in an ongoing process of **role taking**—we continually change our performance based on the feedback other people provide. In role taking we undertake to "get inside" another person and "observe" our own conduct from this person's point of view. As we will see in Chapter 5, this process entails "taking the role of the other toward ourselves."

Sometimes we do not know what we are supposed to say or do. We must innovate and improvise, create and modify our roles as we interact with other people. For these reasons, role taking also involves **role making**— a culture-creating process. Consider the school superintendent. Some constituents may call for new school programs and tax levies, while others insist that budgets and salaries are already high enough. Many pro-life and conservative religious organizations want teachers and books favorable to their views on abortion and evolution. Pro-

two other "convicts." The men were imprisoned around the clock and permitted out only for meals, exercise, toilet privileges, head-count lineups, and work details. Rules simulated the restrictiveness and depersonalization of prison life. Prisoners had to obtain permission to write a letter, smoke a cigarette, or go to the toilet. "Guards" worked on three 8-hour shifts and returned home when they were not on duty. Zimbardo instructed them to "maintain law and order" and not to take any nonsense from the prisoners. They wore khaki uniforms and carried billy clubs, whistles, and handcuffs.

Over the remarkably short period of 6 days, a "perverted" symbiotic relationship developed. As the guards became more aggressive, the prisoners became more passive. Each day, the guards escalated their aggressive behavior, insulting the prisoners, inventing petty rules for prisoner conduct, and improvising degrading and meaningless punishments. They made the prisoners sing songs, laugh or smile on command, and curse and vilify one another. One guard said later:

I was surprised at myself. . . .I made them call each other names and clean the toilets out with their bare hands. I practically considered the prisoners cattle, and I kept thinking: I have to watch out for them in case they try something. (Zimbardo, Haney, and Banks, 1973:42)

Although scheduled to run for 2 weeks, the study had to be discontinued after 6 days to prevent lasting harm to the subjects. Four of the ten prisoners had to be released within the first five days as a result of fits of rage, crying, acute anxiety, and symptoms of severe depression. A fifth had to be released when he developed a psychosomatic rash all over his body. It is not surprising that many individuals have raised ethical questions about the study (see Chapter 1).

The researchers were amazed by the surprising ease with which normal people could behave sadistically. Equally significant was the extent to which emotional disturbance developed in young men selected on the basis of their emotional stability. Zimbardo observes:

No personality test scores or other variables related to the subjects' past history were found to be related to the extreme differences in reaction observed between the prisoners and the guards. Thus the pathology witnessed here cannot be reasonably attributed to preexisting personality traits— such as those of "psychopathic" or "sadistic" guards, or of "criminal, weak impulse- controlled" prisoners. Rather, the abnormal personal and social behavior in both groups is best viewed as a product of transactions with an environment that supports such behavior. (Zimbardo and Ruch, 1975:561)

The study demonstrates how behavior that begins as a game can evolve into behavior that is real. Role playing often ceases to be "play" as we absorb the role within our personality.

fessional organizations, PTA groups, and teachers expect superintendents to make decisions on the basis of professional criteria and merit alone. In dealing with these conflicting pressures, superintendents must balance, adjust, and juggle the contradictory requirements. Typically, they give in to this interest group here and that interest group there, all the while maneuvering and negotiating. In the process, the contours of their role are hammered out, trimmed, and shaped. The role is defined through day-to-day activity. In sum, social structure is not a given—something fixed forever in human affairs.

Social Groups

Roles link us within social relationships. When these relationships are sustained across time, they take on the properties of a social group. A **social group** consists of two or more people who share a feeling of unity and who are bound together in relatively stable patterns of interaction. We acquire our humanness within a social group. Our first and most immediate experiences are small group experiences—families, childhood cliques, neighbors, teams. As adults, even though we may work in large organizations—firms, factories, colleges, or government departments—our immediate work experiences take place with only a few people.

Social groups have a number of characteristics. First, they have boundaries. We think of people as being either "inside" or "outside" a group. A group "encapsulates" us in a social membrane so that the flow and focus of our actions occur primarily within its confines. Second, social groups are products of social definitions. We attribute an "objective" existence to them, treating them *as if* they are real and exact things. In this sense, social groups are socially constructed realities (see Chapter 2). Third, we view a group as having a distinct subculture or

A Social Group Is More Than a Collection of People
The members of a social group not only interact with one another on a recurrent
basis; they share a sense that they belong together, what sociologists call a consciousness of kind. A family is a social group (left). Stable patterns of interaction and feelings of belonging together are absent in an aggregate, such as passersby who stop to
watch a street performer. They merely happen to be in the same place at the same
time (center). A social group also differs from a category, people who have something in common but do not enter sustained relationships with one another. However, the members of a category may occasionally get together for some purpose,
such as the MBA students who gathered for a conference at Duke University (right).
(left, Bruce Davidson/Magnum; center, Joan Liftin/Archive; right, McIntyre/Photo Researchers)

counterculture—a set of unique norms and values. And
fourth, we develop a sense of allegiance to a group that
leads us to feel we are a unit with a distinct identity.
We will examine these features at greater length in Chapter 5.

A social group is more than an **aggregate**—a collection of anonymous individuals who are merely in one
place at the same time. Shoppers in a mall, people waiting in line for football tickets, an audience at a concert,
and a crowd watching a hockey game are examples of
aggregates. Individuals shift in and out of an aggregate
rather easily and frequently. Since the people interact
only transiently and temporarily, patterns of social ordering are short-lived. This quality does not mean that aggregates are unimportant in social life. As we will see in
Chapter 21, they provide the foundation for many forms
of collective behavior.

A group also differs from a **category**—people who
share a characteristic deemed to have social significance.

Many categories are little more than statistical groupings, such as women, the labor force, preschool children, redheads, schizophrenics, left-handed persons,
people 65 years of age and older, and Vietnam veterans.
Information regarding categories of people can have
important uses. For instance, if we know the age distribution of a population, we can make projections at various future time intervals that anticipate the demand for
such social services as social security and Medicare benefits (see Chapter 19). Additionally, people who are aware
that they share certain traits may be motivated to interact. They may even establish organizations to advance
their common interests. Some women have banded together in the League of Women Voters and NOW (National Organization for Women) by virtue of an awareness that they are a social category and share certain
concerns (see Chapter 12). The same holds true for veterans organizations. Social groups that are deliberately
created for the achievement of specific objectives are

termed **formal organizations.** We will consider formal organizations in Chapter 5.

Institutions

A social group consists of people. In interacting with one another, people are governed by cultural patterns—norms, values, beliefs, and symbols—that define the behavior expected of them as occupants of various statuses. When we examine many of these relationships, we can discern an underlying order or pattern that is directed toward the fulfillment of important social goals. Because some social relationships are critical to a group or society, they are preserved as relatively lasting social arrangements called *institutions*. An **institution** is an enduring set of cultural patterns and social relationships organized to accomplish basic social tasks. Institutions provide established answers to recurring problems of living. Each institution is a sort of societal master plan—a kind of "grand design"—whereby essential activities are organized, directed, and executed. Because of institutions, we feel there is some measure of regularity, efficiency, and certainty in our daily activities. If we want to discover how a society "works," one of our first avenues of exploration must be institutions. Here we will take a brief look at institutions, saving for Chapters 13 through 18 a detailed discussion of contemporary American institutions.

Basic Institutions

Sociologists have traditionally viewed social life in terms of five major spheres or areas of societal functioning. Each institution is built around a standardized solution to the primary problems encountered in a particular sphere. The *family institution* has as its chief focus the reproduction, socialization, and maintenance of children and the meeting of our personal needs; the *economic institution*, the production and distribution of goods and services; the *political institution*, the protection of citizens from one another and from foreign enemies; the *religious institution*, the enhancement of social solidarity and consensus; and the *educational institution*, the transmission of the cultural heritage from one generation to the next. Admittedly this classification oversimplifies matters: An institution may perform more than one function, and several institutions may contribute to the performance of the same function.

An institution in one society often bears little resemblance to the same institution in another society. Consider the number of options available to a society in structuring sexual unions between men and women:

- A man and a woman could have sexual relations, then leave and never see one another again, as among some Americans.

- A man and a woman could marry and on the wedding night have intercourse for the first time, as has been the preferred practice among members of some Western religious groups.

- A man and a woman could ritually marry and after a few days separate forever, as among the Nayar of southern India (Schneider and Gough, 1961).

- A man and a woman could wait until a woman has her first child, marry, but expect the woman's brother to assume the primary responsibility for the child's upbringing, as among the Trobriand Islanders of the Pacific (Malinowski, 1922, 1929).

- A man could get together with his brothers and ask them whether they could jointly acquire a woman as their common wife, as among the Todas of India (Rivers, 1906).

- A man could take multiple wives, as among some privileged Arabs.

Even assuming young people have studied anthropology and know all these options, they would still have to decide which one to follow. Institutions have the social advantage of solving the problem for them. The institutional imperatives of their society will shut out all other options in favor of one or two. Indeed, their culture bars the other options from their consciousness. Accordingly, young people need simply retrace the steps outlined for them by their society's institutional script (Berger, 1963).

The Dynamic Nature of Institutions

Although we can examine each institution of a society independently, it never really stands by itself. The essence of life is the interrelatedness of various components and their ties to the larger whole. We cannot understand a plant simply by describing its size, color, texture, shape, root formation, and so on. We must see the relationships among the parts, the plant's connec-

Religious practitioners engaged in a ceremony in Soweto, South Africa. *(C. Steele-Perkins/Magnum)*

Hindu pilgrims bathing in the sacred waters of the Ganges River in India. *(Paolo Koch/Photo Researchers)*

Zen Buddhist monks meditating in Japan. *(Ethan Hoffman/Archive)*

A Russian Orthodox religious service in the Western world. *(Ethan Hoffman/Archive)*

The Religious Institution Varies Throughout the World

tions with its environment, and its development over time. In like fashion we cannot fully understand an institution without considering its internal dynamics, its relationships with the environment, and its developmental history. For example, the Nayar marriage patterns described above were an adaptation to life as a warrior caste. The men were frequently away from their home villages. The "men of the house"—the males who did the work and disciplined the children—were a woman's brothers and maternal uncles. Moreover, since the parts of a social system are interrelated, a change in one institution has consequences for the other institutions and for the society as a whole. As the Nayar's warrior lifestyle shifted to more peaceful pursuits, their marriage and family patterns also changed (Gough, 1959; Schneider and Gough, 1961).

The major sociological perspectives afford some-

what different images of institutions. Structural-functionalists depict institutions as social arrangements that accomplish for human beings what instincts do for lower forms of life. They "provide procedures through which human conduct is patterned, compelled to go, in grooves deemed desirable by society" (Berger, 1963:87). Conflict theorists do not necessarily disagree with this portrayal. But they emphasize that institutions constrain human behavior and reduce freedom. Of equal significance, they say that institutions serve the interests of some groups at the expense of others. For instance, the educational institution is seen as reproducing and legitimating capitalist economic and political arrangements (see Chapter 17).

Symbolic interactionists fault both functionalist and conflict theorists, who they contend depict humankind as little more than robots, blindly enacting institutionalized routines. Instead, interactionists portray institutions as existing only insofar as given arrangements are constructed anew in each situation. Social structure, then, is not something that is "out there" or that happens automatically. Rather, it must be constantly created and recreated as people repeat and reaffirm social acts. In interacting with one another, people arrive at agreements, subtle understandings, binding contracts, unhappy compromises, and coerced accommodations. Viewed in this manner, social structure is negotiated order. (We will elaborate on this image of institutional life in Chapter 7.)

Society

Societies represent the most comprehensive and complex type of social structure in today's world. The essence of a society is people, individuals engaged in a complex set of interrelated activities. If sociologists limited themselves to studying the imagined or real Robinson Crusoes of the world—solitary individuals washed ashore on some deserted island—there would be no need for the concept of society. A society emerges only as a multitude of people interact in patterned, recurrent ways and establish enduring relationships. By fitting their actions together, human beings are able to accomplish a great many things that they could not otherwise achieve. Society, then, is an adaptive mechanism, a social vehicle for adjusting to and transforming the environment and coping with the perennial problems of life. A society can be as small as a tribal community of several dozen people or as large as a modern nation-state with hundreds of millions of people.

Characteristics of Society

Sociologists see a **society** as a relatively independent, self-perpetuating group of people who occupy the same territory and participate in a common culture. Major cities like New York, London, Beijing, and Moscow are more populous than most societies of the world, but they are not societies because they are not self-sustaining social units. They depend on a larger social system, their respective nation-states, for defense and for their food and basic needs. The members of a society also typically occupy, or at least lay claim to, the same territory. Historically, people have maintained, marked, and defended what they consider to be their land and resources against intrusion by outsiders. Indeed, many contemporary tribal frictions and intergroup hatreds spring from

conflicting territorial aspirations: Arabs and Jews in the Middle East; Turks and Greeks on Cyprus; Protestants and Catholics in Northern Ireland; English and French in Quebec; Flemish and Walloons in Belgium; and blacks and whites in South Africa. Finally, the members of a society participate in a common culture. Where people have a common language, customs, norms, values, and beliefs, they are knit together by an all-encompassing, seamless web of shared experience.

The members of a society typically recognize their common ties, and this recognition affects their behavior. They are aware of something that they have in common with others like themselves. It is a sense that "I am one of

Societies Are Self-Sustaining Social Units
New York City, despite its size, is not a society because it is dependent upon the larger American social system for many of its needs. By contrast, these Sepik River villagers in eastern New Guinea comprise a society: a relatively independent, self-perpetuating group of people who occupy the same territory and participate in a common culture. *(above, Bill Aron/Jeroboam; below, Jen and Des Bartlett/Photo Researchers)*

these"—and by the same token, "I am not one of those." These shared sentiments form the basis of a social allegiance, an encompassing ingroup feeling or sense of *peoplehood*. Such ties produce a consciousness so that those charged with it feel that they are kin. A society, then, is the most inclusive organization to which individuals give their loyalty and which they defend against disruptive internal and external forces.

Society as Biology?

Sociologists stress that our uniqueness as human beings is rooted in a social existence made possible by culture. Yet we are also biological beings who are members of the animal world. Admittedly, we frequently find it convenient to overlook this fact; we have found it easy to focus upon our unique traits. Not too long ago, most members of the Western world thought of themselves as a special race that sprang, fully formed, onto the face of the earth. There is no denying that we are remarkable and unusual creatures. Even so, our biological heritage underlies our social experience. This premise is the basis for **sociobiology,** a new and controversial discipline that focuses on the biological foundations for social behavior in species ranging from amoeba colonies to human societies.

The novelist Samuel Butler once remarked that "the chicken is only an egg's way of making another egg." In the same vein, sociobiology views organisms as only the genes' way of making more genes. It depicts organisms primarily as survival machines for genes. Individual organisms may die, but their genes live on in future generations. The key to the entire process is survival, life's first order of business. To survive—and thus pass on their genes to offspring—organisms must be able to function in their habitat. And if they are to fit better in their environment, organisms must change across time—a process called *adaptation*.

The notion that organisms change and develop from earlier forms was detailed by the English naturalist Charles Darwin (1809–1882). Darwin proposed a specific mechanism by which adaptation occurs—**natural selection.** The idea behind natural selection is a remarkably simple one. The different organisms produce more offspring than the available resources can support. Since a habitat can support only a limited number of organisms, each must compete for a "place." Those that are best adapted to the environment survive, and pass on their genetic characteristics to their offspring. The others perish, with few or no offspring. Later generations re-

semble their better-adapted ancestors. The result is evolutionary change.

Sociobiologists apply the notion of natural selection to social life. They say that natural selection acts on *groups* as well as individuals. The entire group is constantly being tested for its capacity to survive and reproduce in a given environment. Individuals who possess behaviors consistent with group survival have an advantage in their own survival and reproduction. As a consequence, complex *group-oriented* patterns have evolved, and these patterns are encoded in the genes of each species.

The sociobiologist Edward O. Wilson (1975, 1984) suggests that a hereditary basis may underlie many kinds of social behavior, including "cannibalism" and "infanticide" among bees, "castes" and "slavery" among ants, "harem formation" in baboon societies, and "homosexuality," "male dominance," and "war" among human beings. Consider how he evaluates *altruism*—self-sacrificing behavior that helps to ensure the survival of other members of one's own species. Wilson notes that a honeybee worker will attack an intruder at the hive with its fishhook-shaped sting. The bee dies, but its sting remains embedded in the flesh of the enemy and continues to leak poison into the wound. The suicide of the individual bee supports the survival of the colony as a whole. Similarly, robins, thrushes, and titmice give warning signals to others of their kind should a hawk appear, thereby drawing the predator's attention to themselves. And during wars, human beings are known to throw themselves on top of grenades to shield comrades or aid the rescue of others at the price of certain death to themselves.

Altruistic behavior has long been a puzzle for classical Darwinian theorists. Why should altruism evolve if it entails surrendering one's own life? Individuals displaying self-sacrificing behavior would die out, while selfish ones would survive and prosper. Wilson provides this answer. In the course of evolution, natural selection has been broadened from individual selection to kin selection. **Kin selection** means that evolution favors genes which improve the chances of a *group's* survival. It is irrelevant whether an advantageous gene is passed on to the next generation by a particular individual or by a close relative who has an identical gene. Because all the members of the family or group *share* the gene for self-sacrificing behavior, the larger social unit survives even though a few individual members may not. These survivors in turn multiply and transmit altruistic genes to later generations.

Critics raise a number of objections to attempts by sociobiologists to explain human social behavior in biological terms. For one thing, since human beings have a common genetic heritage, how are we to explain the vast cultural differences among societies? And how are we to explain the rapid changes that occur in the behavior of the members of the same society across time? The answers to these questions, say critics, rest largely with *learning*. When a spider spins a web to catch flies, it acts primarily on instinct. When we weave nets to catch fish, we are acting primarily on learned skills transmitted culturally from one generation to another. Human evolution is unique in that our species gradually evolved biological capacities that have allowed us to create culture and society. Once cultural and social forces were set in motion, we were freed from many of the constraints posed by a fixed biological heritage (Kaye, 1986).

Critics also raise another point. They see sociobiology as a naive social philosophy fraught with political danger (Lewontin, Rose, and Kamin, 1984). In the past, people have used related notions of biological determinism as a justification for slavery, for the "final solution" of the Jewish "problem," and for the racism and sexism that persist today.

The Question of Free Will

Sociologists assume that human behavior is characterized by regularities and hence is in some measure predictable. The notion of social structure reflects this assumption. It draws our attention to the stable, recurrent, and patterned aspects of social life. But if social life is stable, recurrent, and patterned, are we not then simply puppets? Are not our actions programmed by culture and hence automatic? Are we not locked within a social order that constrains and even determines what we think, feel, say, and do? In sum, what becomes of the idea of free will—the ability to choose among alternatives?

In addressing these issues, we are tempted to take one of two positions. We can deny all external social influence and assert that we can do as we please. Or we can portray our existence as totally dominated and controlled by social structure. Both positions run counter to reality and experience. We do not live our lives in social vacuums; societal norms and institutional arrangements do constrain our options. Yet we are hardly robots. We do not always do what others expect us to do. Indeed, we *cannot* always live up to the expectations others hold of

us if for no other reason than we experience role conflict—incompatible role requirements. To fulfill one obligation is to fail to meet another. The woman who pursues a career, has family responsibilities, and renders regular help to her elderly parents may confront a role overload. Clearly, everyday life not only provides alternative options; it often *compels* us to choose among them.

In confronting such dilemmas, we possess the ability to reason and therefore to select among different lines of action. We are organisms capable of employing mental images and ideas. So there is not just the outer world, the world of social facts; there is also the inner world, the realm in which we interpret what goes on about us and devise actions. Regardless of the realm—our relationships with friends, work, parenting, or household management—we confront new circumstances, uncertainties, and difficulties that call for decision making and resourceful thought. Life dictates that we learn to identify problems, analyze them by breaking them down into their relevant components, and devise coping strategies.

Of course most of our choices take place in the context of other people. For the most part, we act together harmoniously and cooperatively because we share values that tell us which things are worth pursuing and norms that set the rules under which we pursue these ends. But we do not have to live up to the values and norms of our society. As we will see in Chapter 8 when we discuss deviance, the behavior of some people at times goes beyond that permitted by societal rules. Hence what some of us say and do may run counter to what other people judge to be acceptable. The question then is one of which individuals and groups will have the power to make their definitions of "proper" and "improper" behavior prevail. The issue often becomes "*Who* will enjoy freedom to do *what*?" In brief, the question of freedom is itself a social question, one that is continually answered on an ongoing basis as people interact with one another.

THINKING THROUGH THE ISSUES

Need social structure be an unalterable, eternal reality? How have blacks and women answered this question over the past several decades? How did Moses, Jesus Christ, and Mohammed answer this question? How can the findings of the social and behavioral sciences assist us in making choices and in changing social structure?

Chapter Highlights

1. Human life presents a picture of organization and regularity. A good deal of what sociologists label social structure consists of subtle understandings and agreements—networks of invisible rules and institutional arrangements—that guide our behavior. Many sociologists view social structure as a social fact of the sort described by Emile Durkheim.

2. It is by means of statuses that we locate one another in groups and society. We have greater control over some of our statuses than others. *Ascribed statuses* are assigned to us by our group or society. We secure *achieved statuses* on the basis of individual choice and competition. Some of our statuses overshadow others both in our own minds and in those of other people. A *master status* is a key or core status that carries primary weight in a person's interactions and relationships with others.

3. A status carries with it a set of culturally defined rights and duties, what sociologists term a *role*. These expectations define the behavior people view as appropriate and inappropriate for the occupant of a status. The difference between a status and a role is that we occupy a status and play a role. Roles allow us to formulate our behavior mentally so that we can shape our actions in socially defined ways. Whereas a role is the expected behavior we associate with a status, *role performance* is the actual behavior of the person who occupies a status. In real life a gap often exists between what people should do and what they actually do.

4. A single status may have multiple roles attached to it, constituting a *role set*. Roles impinge on us as sets of norms that define our *duties*—the actions others can legitimately insist that we perform, and our *rights*—the actions we can legitimately insist that others perform. Every role has at least one reciprocal role attached to it.

5. *Role strain* is the stress individuals experience when they encounter difficulties in meeting the requirements of a role. The stress often results from *role conflict*—a situation in which individuals are confronted with incompatible role requirements.

6. We are involved in an ongoing process of *role taking*—we continually create our performance based on the feedback other people provide. Role taking also involves *role making*—we innovate and improvise, creating, shaping, and modifying roles as we go about interacting with other people.

7. Roles link us within social relationships. When these relationships are sustained across time, they take on the properties of a social group. Groups have boundaries; are products of social definitions; possess a distinct subculture or counterculture; and stimulate a sense of loyalty.

8. Because some social relationships are so critical to a group or society, they are preserved as relatively lasting social arrangements called *institutions*. Institutions provide established answers to the recurring problems of social living. Although sociologists examine each institution of a society independently, they never really stand by themselves. The essence of life is the interrelatedness of various components and their ties to the larger whole.

9. Societies are the most comprehensive and complex type of social structure in today's world. The essence of a society is people, individuals engaged in a complex set of interrelated activities. By fitting their actions together, human beings are able to accomplish a great many things that they could not otherwise achieve. Society, then, is an adaptive mechanism, a social vehicle for adjusting to and transforming the environment and coping with the perennial problems of life.

10. Considerable controversy surrounds sociobiology and its claim that human social behavior can be explained in biological terms. Sociobiologists say that in the course of evolution, natural selection has been broadened from individual to kin selection.

11. Social structure is a necessary vehicle by which we meet our needs and reach our goals. But we are not its prisoners; we are creative participants. It is precisely because we can employ the social and behavioral sciences in making our choices that they are worthwhile.

The Sociologist's Vocabulary

achieved status A status people secure on the basis of choice and competition.

aggregate A collection of anonymous people who are in one place at the same time.

ascribed status A position arbitrarily assigned to an individual by a group or society.

category A collection of people who share a characteristic that is deemed to be of social significance.

duties Actions others can legitimately insist that we perform.

formal organization A social group that is deliberately created for the achievement of specific objectives.

institution An enduring set of cultural patterns and social relationships organized to accomplish basic social tasks.

kin selection Evolution favoring genes that improve the chances of the *group's* survival.

master status A key or core status that carries primary weight in a person's interactions and relationships with others.

natural selection A notion central to evolutionary theory that those organisms best adapted survive and pass on their genetic characteristics to their offspring. Consequently, later generations resemble their better-adapted ancestors.

rights The actions we can legitimately insist that others perform.

role Expectations (rights and duties) that define the behavior people view as appropriate and inappropriate for the occupant of a status.

role conflict A situation in which individuals are confronted with incompatible role requirements.

role making The process of improvising and innovating new features of a role; creating, shaping, and modifying a role as we go about interacting with others.

role performance The actual behavior of the person who occupies a status.

role set The multiple roles associated with a single status.

role strain The stress individuals experience when they encounter difficulties in meeting the requirements of a role.

role taking The process by which we devise our performance based on the feedback other people provide regarding their expectations of us and their assessments of our behavior.

social group Two or more people who share a feeling of unity and who are bound together in relatively stable patterns of social interaction.

social structure The recurrent and patterned relationships that exist among the components of a social system.

sociobiology A new and controversial discipline that focuses on the biological foundations for social behavior in species ranging from amoeba colonies to human societies.

society A relatively independent, self-perpetuating group of people who occupy the same territory and participate in a common culture.

status A position in a social structure.

5

Groups and Organizations

Man is a knot, a web, a mesh into which relationships are tied.

—Antoine de Saint-Exupery, *Flight to Arras, 1942*

On fall football Saturdays in Boulder, Colorado, Ralphie thunders onto Folsom Field as 50,000 University of Colorado loyalists break into "Glory, Glory, Colorado." Ralphie is a 1,000-pound bison and the nation's preeminent college mascot. It seems that when it comes to mascots, the fiercer, the better. Eagles predominate, followed, in order, by tigers, cougars, bulldogs, warriors, lions, panthers, Indians, wildcats, and bears (Brady, 1983).

But mascots are not always what they appear to be. North Carolina State students once sent $150 to an animal dealer for a wolf. Not until much later did State fans discover that their mascot was a coyote. Since then North Carolina State has dressed a sheepish student in wolf's clothing. Further complicating matters, animal mascots occasionally come to untimely ends. Once a Baylor bear choked to death when his collar and chain wrapped around his neck as he tried to climb a tree. Cynics labeled it a suicide, in view of Baylor's 0–10 record that season (Looney, 1979).

College mascots symbolize the group. American colleges and universities recruit students from a great many backgrounds and affiliations, allegiances, and interests. How are these colleges and universities to instill in each fall's new arrivals a consciousness of oneness and a sense of belonging to a common group? One especially powerful mechanism is a rivalry between the ingroup and an outgroup, particularly in the form of intercollegiate games. Such encounters provide a powerful mechanism for highlighting the boundaries of a group, cementing group ties, and fostering "we-group" sentiments.

On Sunday mornings that follow the Saturday contests, loyal alumni scan the sports section of local newspapers to locate an article on their alma mater's gridiron fate. "Football," says Ohio State University's athletic director, "is the rallying point for all those people out there. It is their tie to the university after they're gone." The benefits of football at Ohio State go far beyond the athletic department's budget. "Football Saturdays are when you have the reunions of grads from different colleges," says the athletic director. "The colleges (within the university) use the games to get people in here. Then they work on them for development fund contributions while they're here" (quoted by Baptist, 1984:C-1).

Intense intercollegiate rivalries such as that between Ohio State and Michigan provide an important source for creating, reinforcing, and maintaining social solidarity in a campus community. For instance, prior to the season-concluding Ohio State–Michigan game, Columbus radio and television stations carry special programs recalling previous games, presenting gridiron stars of earlier years, and interviewing current players and coaches. Campus-area stores display Ohio State slogans, souvenirs, and memorabilia. And students and alumni attend a gigantic pep rally the evening before the game.

At game time, the Ohio State football players, cheerleaders, and band members outfit themselves in distinctive uniforms, and fans wear the school's unique scarlet and gray colors. The university band plays rousing songs such as the "Buckeye Battle Cry" and "Carmen Ohio" to fire the enthusiasm of the crowd. Cheerleaders and the Brutus Buckeye mascot orchestrate chants that build collective excitement. On the field, the football players become the symbolic embodiment—a tangible expression—of the university and its community. What is otherwise rather ill-defined and indistinct—a gigantic university with over 50,000 students, thousands of faculty and staff, and countless alumni—becomes in the course of a Saturday football afternoon a living and profoundly meaningful social reality—indeed, a distinctive social entity. The subject matter of this chapter is such social entities—*social groups* and *formal organizations*—and the dynamic processes that they embody.

PLANNING AHEAD: TARGETED READING

1. How do various types of groups work?

2. How do group members contribute to carrying out joint transactions?

3. What part does leadership play in directing group activities?

4. How do we deal with situations in which we face a conflict between maximizing our personal interests and maximizing the collective welfare?

5. How do groups produce conformity among members?

6. Why are bureaucracies essential to contemporary life?

7. What problems do bureaucracies pose in getting organizational work accomplished?

8. How can bureaucracies be humanized?

Types of Social Groups

A **social group** consists of two or more people who share a feeling of unity and who are bound together in relatively stable patterns of social interaction. It is a human reality, a product of our social definitions. We bring social groups into existence by mentally clustering people in social units—families, teams, cliques, labor unions, sororities, clubs, and corporations. We then *act* on the basis of these notions, creating an existence *beyond* the people who are involved. In many cases, they extend beyond the life course of specific people. Put another way, we make groups real by treating them *as if* they are real. We attend "family" reunions, go to a "Green Bay Packer" game, hold a party for the "old high school gang," attend a "United Auto Workers" convention, pay

Primary and Secondary Groups
Primary groups are characterized by personal relationships; secondary groups, by impersonal relationships. In primary groups people are ends in their own right whereas in secondary groups people are a means to other ends. *(Left, Susan Lapides/ Design Conceptions; right, Ray Ellis/Photo Researchers)*

our dues to the "Weight Lifters Club," and write a check against our account at the "Huntington Bank."

Group life gives us advantages that we lack as solitary persons. More of us mature, reproduce, and reach old age because we receive group protection, nurturance, and cooperation. Moreover, group life provides a medium in which cultural adaptations can arise and benefit other community members. Equally significant, our humanness arises out of and is sustained through social relationships. Of course, some groups seem more important to us than others. This observation leads us to the distinction between primary and secondary groups.

Primary Groups and Secondary Groups

Sociologists distinguish between primary groups and secondary groups. A **primary group** consists of two or more people who enjoy a direct, intimate, cohesive relationship with one another (Cooley, 1909). We emotionally invest ourselves in and commit ourselves to a primary group. We view its members—friends, family members, and lovers—as worthwhile and important, and not simply as a means to other ends. A **secondary group** consists of two or more people who are involved in an impersonal relationship and have come together for a specific, practical purpose. We cooperate with other people to achieve some goal; the relationship is a means to an end, not an end in itself (see Table 5.1). Illustrations include our

relationships with a clerk in a clothing store and a cashier at a service station. At times, primary group relationships evolve out of secondary group relationships. This happens in many work settings. People on the job often develop camaraderie with their co-workers as they come to share gripes, jokes, gossip, and satisfactions.

A number of conditions enhance the likelihood that primary groups will arise. First, group size is important. We find it difficult to get to know people personally when they are milling about and dispersed in large groups. In small groups we stand a better chance of initiating contact and establishing rapport with them. Second, face-to-face contact allows us to size up others. Seeing and talking with one another in close physical proximity makes possible a subtle exchange of ideas and feelings. And third, the probability that we will develop primary group bonds increases as we have frequent and continuous contact. Our ties with people often deepen as we interact with them across time and gradually evolve interlocking habits and interests.

We use the word "primary" in our daily conversations to refer to things that are essential and important. Clearly the term is appropriately applied to primary groups, since they are fundamental both to us and to society. First, primary groups are critical to the socialization process. Within them, infants and children are introduced to the ways of their society. Such groups are the breeding grounds in which we acquire the norms and

Table 5.1   Primary and Secondary Groups

Characteristics of Primary Groups	*Characteristics of Secondary Groups*
Small number of people	Large number of people
Involves the whole individual	Involves segments of a person's life
Personal	Impersonal
Continuous interaction	Sporadic interaction
Long duration	Short duration
Informal expectations	Formal expectations
Informally imposed constraints	Formally imposed constraints
Expressive ties	Instrumental ties
Examples of Primary Groups	*Examples of Secondary Groups*
Family	Labor union
Clique	College
Work group	Corporation
Old-fashioned neighborhood	City
Friendship group	Army unit

values that equip us for social life. Sociologists view primary groups as bridges between individuals and the larger society because they transmit, mediate, and interpret a society's cultural patterns and provide the sense of oneness so critical for social solidarity.

Second, primary groups are fundamental because they provide the settings in which we meet most of our personal needs. Within them we experience companionship, love, security, and an overall sense of well-being.

Not surprisingly, sociologists find that the strength of a group's primary ties has implications for its functioning. For example, the stronger the primary group ties of troops fighting together, the better their combat record. During World War II, the success of German military units derived not from Nazi ideology, but from the ability of the Germany army to reproduce in the infantry company the intimacy and bonds found in civilian primary groups (Shils and Janowitz, 1948). What made the

Esprit de Corps among Israeli Troops
Strong primary group bonds that promote feelings of rapport and camaraderie are a key factor influencing the fighting effectiveness of military units. *(David Rubinger/ Archive)*

Wehrmacht so formidable was that, unlike the American army, German soldiers who trained together went into battle together. American fighting units were kept up to strength through individual replacement; German units were "fought down," then pulled back to be reconstituted as a new group (Van Creveld, 1982). The Israelis have found that combat units hastily thrown together without time to form an esprit de corps perform more poorly in battle and experience higher rates of psychiatric casualties than do units with close bonds (Cordes, 1984; Solomon, Mikulincer, and Hobfoll, 1986).

Third, primary groups are fundamental because they serve as powerful instruments for social control. Their members command and dispense many of the rewards that are so vital to us and that make our lives seem worthwhile. Should the use of rewards fail, their members can frequently win compliance by rejecting, or threatening to ostracize, those who deviate from its norms. Some religious cults, for instance, employ "shunning" as a device to bring into line individuals whose behavior goes beyond that allowed by the group's teachings—a truly devastating social experience. Even more important, primary groups define social reality for us by structuring our experiences. By providing us with definitions of situations, they elicit from us behavior that conforms to group-devised meanings. Primary groups, then, serve both as carriers of social norms and as enforcers of them.

Ingroups and Outgroups

It is not only the groups to which we immediately belong that have a powerful influence upon us. Often the same holds true for groups to which we do not belong. Accordingly, sociologists find it useful to distinguish between ingroups and outgroups. An **ingroup** is a group with which we identify and to which we belong. An **outgroup** is a group with which we do not identify and to which we do not belong. In our daily conversations we recognize the distinction between ingroups and outgroups when we use the personal pronouns "we" and "they." We can think of ingroups as "we groups" and outgroups as "they groups." As we become keenly conscious of who "they" are, we come to know who "we" are.

The concepts of ingroup and outgroup highlight the importance of *boundaries*—social demarcation lines that tell us where interaction begins and ends. Group boundaries do not represent physical barriers, but rather discontinuities in the flow of social interaction. To one degree or another, a group's boundaries encapsulate people

Intense Intergroup Rivalries Foster InGroup Bonds
Fighting among Lebanon's religious groups has heightened ingroup loyalties by promoting *us* against *them* feelings. *(C. Steele-Perkins/Magnum)*

in a social membrane so that the focus and flow of their actions are internally contained. Some boundaries are based on territorial location—neighborhoods, communities, nation-states. Others rest upon social distinctions—ethnic group, religious, political, occupational, language, kin, and socioeconomic class memberships. Whatever their source, social boundaries face in two directions. They prevent outsiders from entering a group's sphere, and they keep insiders within the sphere so that they do not even think of other possibilities for social interaction.

At times we experience feelings of indifference, disgust, competition, and even outright conflict when we think about or have dealings with outgroup members. An experiment undertaken by Muzafer Sherif and his associates (1966) has shown how our awareness of ingroup boundaries is heightened and antagonism toward

"I'm surprised, Marty. I thought you were one of us."

Drawing by Ziegler; © 1983 The New Yorker Magazine, Inc.

outgroups is generated by competitive situations. The subjects were 11- and 12-year-old boys, all of whom were healthy, socially well-adjusted youngsters from stable, middle-class homes. The setting was a summer camp, where the boys were divided into two groups.

During the first week at the camp the boys in each group got to know one another, evolved group norms, and arrived at an internal division of labor and leadership roles. During the second week, the experimenters brought the two groups into competitive contact through a tournament of baseball, touch football, tug-of-war, and treasure-hunt games. Although the contest opened in a spirit of good sportsmanship, positive feelings quickly evaporated. In fact, the conflict soon escalated to "garbage wars" in the dining hall, flag burnings, cabin ransackings, and scuffling encounters. Sherif observed that had you or I visited the camp at this point, we very likely would have concluded that these "were wicked, disturbed, and vicious bunches of youngsters" (p.85). In truth, however, the antisocial behavior was triggered by the antisocial situation in which the boys found themselves.

During the third week, the integration phase, Sherif brought the two groups of boys together for various events, including eating in the same mess hall, watching movies, and shooting off firecrackers. But far from reducing conflict, these setting merely afforded new opportunities for the two groups to challenge, berate, and harass one another. The experimenters then created a series of urgent and natural situations in which the two groups would have to work together to achieve their ends, such as the emergency repair of the conduit that delivered the camp's water supply. Whereas competition

had heightened the boys' awareness of group boundaries, the pursuit of common goals led to a lessening of hostilities and the lowering of intergroup barriers to cooperation. Research with adults has demonstrated that their reactions parallel those of Sherif's young subjects (Blake and Mouton, 1979).

THINKING THROUGH THE ISSUES

Countless sociologists have pointed out that by joining hands in opposition to an enemy "they," the members of a group cohere ever more closely together and develop a more secure and lasting sense of "we" (Erikson, 1986). In the chapter opening, we saw how colleges build on this principle to instill school spirit among students, staff, faculty, and alumni. Can you come up with other examples in which outgroup pressures foster ingroup solidarity? How does the principle help us to understand the survival of persecuted groups such as the perennial Jewish minority despite the horrors of organized massacres and the Holocaust? When political leaders find themselves in trouble with their citizenry, why may they find it to their advantage to provoke hostilities with a neighboring nation?

Reference Groups

More than a century ago the American writer Henry Thoreau observed: "If a man does not keep pace with his companions, perhaps it is because he hears a different drummer." Thoreau's observation contains an important sociological insight. We evaluate ourselves and guide our behavior by standards embedded within a group context. But since Americans are dispersed among a good many different groups—each with a somewhat unique subculture or counterculture—the frames of reference we use in assessing and fashioning our behavior differ. In brief, we have different **reference groups,** social units we use for appraising and shaping our attitudes, feelings, and actions.

A reference group may or may not be our membership group. We may think of a reference group as a base that we use for viewing the world, a source of psychological identification. It helps to account for seemingly contradictory behavior: the upper-class revolutionary, the renegade Catholic, the reactionary union member, the

Reference Groups as Agencies of Assimilation

A reference group need not be a membership group. Should people begin identifying with a non-membership group, they are likely to adopt some of its customs, norms, and language. Here Pennsylvania Amish farmers take part in a county horse auction. Pressure continuously operates upon members of the Amish community to compromise religious doctrine and accommodate religion to demands for excellence in agricultural pursuits. (*Cary Wolinsky/Stock, Boston*)

shabby gentleman, the quisling who collaborates with the enemy, the assimilated immigrant, and the social-climbing chambermaid. These individuals have simply taken as their reference group people other than those from their membership group (Hyman and Singer, 1968). Thus the concept helps to illuminate such central sociological concerns as socialization and social conformity (Singer, 1981).

Reference groups serve a number of functions (Kelley, 1952; Felson and Reed, 1986). First, they can serve a *normative* function in that they influence our standards. Since we would like to view ourselves as being members in good standing within a certain group—or we aspire to such membership—we take on the group's norms and values. We cultivate its lifestyles, political attitudes, musical tastes, food preferences, sexual practices, and drug-using behaviors. Our behavior is group-anchored. Second, a reference group also can have a *comparative* function. We employ the standards of our reference group to appraise ourselves—a comparison point against which we judge and evaluate our physical attractiveness, intelligence, health, ranking, and standard of living. When our membership group does not match our reference group, we may experience feelings of **relative deprivation**—discontent associated with the gap between what we have (the circumstances of our membership group) and what we believe we should have (the circumstances of our reference group). Feelings of relative deprivation often contribute to social alienation and provide fertile conditions for collective behavior and revolutionary social movements (see Chapter 21). Hence the reference group concept contains clues to processes

of social change. And finally, a reference group can have an *associative* function. By identifying with a group, we can "borrow" the status of the group and vicariously bask in its reflected glory. Fans of championship teams gloat over their team's accomplishment and proclaim their affiliation with buttons, bumper stickers, and banners.

However, not all reference groups are positive. We also make use of negative reference groups, social units with which we compare ourselves to emphasize the differences between ourselves and others. For Cuban-Americans in Miami, Florida, the Castro regime functions as a negative reference group (Carver and Humphries, 1981). A good many of them fled their homeland after Castro came to power in the 1959 revolution. Militant opposition to the Castro regime helps the Cuban-Americans determine their beliefs and identity. Of even greater significance, the negative reference group affords a mechanism of social solidarity, an instrument by which the exile community binds itself together. It provides a common denominator for acceptance and ensures for members of the "cause" the benefits that accrue to "true believers."

Group Dynamics

To understand groups is to understand much about human behavior. The reason is not difficult to come by, since groups are the wellsprings of our humanness. Although we think of groups as "things"—distinct and bounded entities—it is their dynamic qualities that make them the significant force they are within the human experience. Consequently, we need to examine what happens within groups. Let us turn our attention, then, to the processes that operate within group settings and invigorate social life.

Group Size

The size of a group is of considerable importance because, even though it is a structural component, it influences the nature of our interaction. The smaller the group, the more opportunities we have to get to know other people well and to establish close ties with them. The popular adage "Two's company, three's a crowd" captures an important difference between two-person and three-person groups. Two-person groups—**dyads**—provide many of our most intensive and influential relationships, including that between parent and child and that between husband and wife. Indeed, most of our social interactions take place on a one-to-one basis.

The sociologist John James (1951) and his students observed 7,405 informal interactions of pedestrians, playground users, swimmers, and shoppers, and 1,458 people in a variety of work situations. They found that 71 percent of both the informal and work interactions consisted of two people; 21 percent involved three people; 6 percent included four people; and only 2 percent entailed five or more people. Emotions and feelings tend to play a greater part in dyads than they do in larger groups (Hare, 1976). But this factor also contributes to their relatively fragile nature: A delicate balance exists between the parties so that if one of them becomes disenchanted, the relationship collapses. And contrary to what you might expect, two-person relationships tend to be more emotionally strained and less overtly aggressive than other relationships (Bales and Borgatta, 1955; O'Dell, 1968).

The addition of a third member to a group—forming a **triad**—fundamentally alters a social situation. Coalitions become possible, with two members joining forces against a third member (Hare, 1976). Under this arrangement, one person may be placed in the role of "intruder" or "outsider." However, under some circumstances, the third person may assume the role of "mediator," and function as a peacemaker between the other two.

One recurring question that has attracted the interest of sociologists is this: What is the optimum group size for problem solving? For instance, if you want to appoint a committee to make a recommendation, what would be an ideal size for the group? Small group research suggests that five persons usually constitutes the best size (Hare, 1976). With five members a strict deadlock is not possible, because there is an odd number of members. Further, since groups tend to split into a majority of three and a minority of two, being in a minority does not result in the isolation of one person, as it does in the triad. Additionally, the group is sufficiently large for the members to shift roles easily and for a person to withdraw from an awkward position without necessarily having to resolve the issue formally. Finally, five-person groups are large enough so that people feel they can express their feelings freely and even risk antagonizing each other, yet they are small enough so that the members show regard for one another's feelings and needs. As groups become larger, they become less manageable. People no longer carry on a conversation with the other members, but address them with formal vocabulary and grammar.

Leadership

Imagine football teams without quarterbacks; armies without officers; corporations without executives; universities without deans; orchestras without conductors; and youth gangs without bosses. Without overall direction, people typically have difficulty coordinating their activities. Consequently, some group members usually exert more influence than others. We call these individuals *leaders*. Small groups may be able to get along without a leader, but in larger groups a lack of leadership results in chaos.

Two types of leadership roles tend to evolve in small groups (Bales, 1970; Fiedler, 1981). One, a **task specialist,** is devoted to appraising the problem at hand and organizing activity to deal with it. The other, a **social-emotional specialist,** focuses on overcoming interpersonal problems in the group, defusing tensions, and promoting solidarity. The former type of leadership is *instrumental*, directed toward the achievement of group goals; the latter is *expressive*, oriented toward the creation of group harmony and unity. In some cases one person assumes both roles, but usually each role is played by a different person. Neither role is necessarily more important than the other, and the situation does much to dictate which is prominent.

Leaders differ in their styles for exercising influence. Through the years, the classic experiments in leadership by Kurt Lewin and his associates (Lewin, Lippitt, and White, 1939; White and Lippitt, 1960) have generated considerable interest. In these pioneering investigations, adult leaders working with groups of 11-year-old boys followed one of three leadership styles. In the *authoritarian* style, the leader determined the group's policies, gave step-by-step directions so that the boys were certain about their future tasks, assigned work partners, provided subjective praise and criticism, and remained aloof from group participation. In the *democratic* style, the leader allowed the boys to participate in decision-making processes, outlined only general goals, suggested alternative procedures, permitted the members to work with whomever they wished, evaluated the boys objectively, and participated in group activities. In the *laissez-faire* style, the leader adopted a passive, uninvolved stance, provided materials, suggestions, and help only when requested, and refrained from commenting on the boys' work (see Table 5.2).

The researchers found that authoritarian leadership produces high levels of frustration and hostile feelings toward the leader. Productivity remains high so long as the leader is present, but it appreciably slackens in the leader's absence. Under democratic leadership members are happier, feel more group-minded and friendlier, display independence (especially in the leader's absence), and exhibit low levels of interpersonal aggression. Laissez-faire leadership resulted in low group productivity and high levels of interpersonal aggression. However, it should be emphasized that the study was carried out

with American youngsters accustomed to democratic procedures. Under other circumstances and in different cultural settings, an authoritarian leader may be preferred. The frequency of authoritarian leaders in developing nations has suggested to some sociologists that people may prefer directed leadership styles under highly stressful conditions (Bass, 1960). Of course, an equally plausible explanation is that it is easier for authoritarian leaders to seize and maintain leadership under these circumstances. Practical experience also reveals that the democratic style does not always stimulate better performance or productivity. Some people prefer to be told what to do rather than to participate in decision making (Ridgeway, 1983).

THINKING THROUGH THE ISSUES

The role of the "great leader" in history has been debated many times. Writers like Thomas Carlyle (1795–1881) and Friedrich Nietzsche (1844–1900) never tired of praising the "hero" in the unfolding drama of human life. Indeed, we may ask, what would the world be like had there not been a Catherine the Great (Empress of Russia, 1762–1796), a Thomas Jefferson, a Karl Marx, a Marie

---

Table 5.2   Three Styles of Leadership

	Authoritarian	Democratic	Laissez-Faire
Nature of authority	The leader retain authority and responsibility.	The leader delegates a good deal of authority, with policies a matter of group discussion and decision.	The leader allows group members to do as they please and abdicates authority within the group.
Assignment of tasks	The leader assigns individuals to clearly defined tasks.	The members of the group divide tasks and assign responsibility on the basis of participatory decision making.	Group members work things out for themselves as they see fit.
Communication	Flows primarily one way in a downward direction to members.	Flows actively upward and downward.	Occurs primarily in a horizontal fashion among peers.
Strength	Resides in prompt, orderly, and predictable performance.	Promotes individual commitment through participation and cooperation.	Allows highly motivated and competent members to work without outside interference.
Weakness	Stifles individual initiative.	Procedures and processes are time-consuming and occasionally divisive.	The group often drifts aimlessly because it lacks direction.

Curie, or a William Shakespeare? This raises the intriguing question of whether a given person makes history or history makes the person. The most renowned presidents in American history—George Washington, Abraham Lincoln, and Franklin D. Roosevelt—were also identified as wartime leaders. Would they have been equally great if they had lived and governed during another period? Is the answer necessarily an either-or proposition? Does a dynamic interplay occur between society (history) and the person? Explain.

Social Loafing

An old saying has it that "Many hands make light the work." Yet the proverb falls short of the truth. For example, we might expect that three individuals can pull three times as much as one person and that eight can pull eight times as much. But research reveals that whereas persons individually average 130 pounds of pressure when tugging on a rope, in groups of three they average 352 pounds (only 2.5 times the solo rate) and in groups of eight only 546 pounds (less than 4 times the solo rate). One explanation is that faulty coordination produces group inefficiency. However, when subjects are blindfolded and *believe* they are pulling with others, they also slacken their effort (Ingham, 1974). Apparently when we work in groups, we cut down on our efforts, a process termed **social loafing** (Williams, Harkins, and Latané, 1981).

When undergraduate men are asked to make as much noise as possible by shouting or clapping in concert with others, they produce only twice as much noise in groups of four and 2.4 times as much in groups of six as when alone (Latané, Williams, and Harkins, 1979). Presumably we slack off in groups because we feel we are not achieving our fair share of credit or because we think that in a crowd we can get away with less work. And then too, when we work in groups, we often expect that others are also loafing (Jackson and Harkins, 1985). In comparable circumstances, Soviet peasants produce less when they work on collective farms than when they cultivate a small plot of land for their own use (although the private plots occupy less than 1 percent of Soviet agricultural land, some 27 percent of the total value of the nation's farm output is produced on them).

We should not conclude from these findings that we can do away with work groups. Groups are essential to social life, and they can accomplish many things that individuals cannot. Indeed, when we work on difficult tasks, our performance frequently improves when we work with other people (Jackson and Williams, 1985). And when social solidarity is high and we believe the group goal is compelling—as in the case of some team sports and Israeli collective farms—we may actually redouble our efforts. Moreover, such self-help groups as Alcoholics Anonymous, Parents Without Partners, and Weight Watchers testify to the desirable influences and outcomes that can be associated with group memberships.

Social Dilemmas

The social loafing effect suggests that in some group settings we are tempted to slacken our efforts. A closely

Social Loafing
People who work in groups tend to "free ride," exerting less effort than when they work individually to achieve a goal. (*Courtesy Henry Ford Museum, Dearborn, Michigan*)

related phenomenon is termed a **social dilemma** (also called a *social trap*)—a situation in which members of a group are faced with a conflict between maximizing their personal interests and maximizing the collective welfare (Komorita and Barth, 1985). Garrett J. Hardin's (1968) example of the tragedy of the commons is one type of social dilemma. Hardin explored the situation in which a number of herders share a common pasture. Each person may reason that by putting another cow to graze, he or she will realize a benefit from it. But if each person follows this course, the commons will be destroyed and each will ultimately lose. The "commons" could as well be clean air, water, electricity, gas, whales, or any jointly used but limited resource. Each person reasons that the personal gain associated with consuming more resources or polluting the environment outweighs the costs, because the costs are diffused among the entire population.

Social dilemmas appear in two basic forms: the *commons dilemma* in which we must decide whether to take from a common resource, and the *public goods problem* in which we must decide whether to contribute to a common resource (Brewer and Kramer, 1986). The public goods problem often arises in situations where a few members of the group can and will provide for the communal well-being. This "let George do it" approach is termed the **free-rider mechanism.** The problem is that, left to our own self-interest, we often are tempted to take unfair advantage of contributions others make to the community as a whole. Something of this sort occurred in the Three Mile Island area in 1979 following the serious nuclear accident in which radiation was leaked from the Unit 2 reactor. Although some residents became politically active, the vast majority, while agreeing with the goals of the citizen protest groups, never contributed any time or money to the movement. Instead, they became free riders on the efforts of their neighbors (Walsh and Warland, 1983). Free riding does not arise only from greed—a self-interested desire to benefit at the expense of others. It may also be fed by a fear that other people will free ride on our contributions—the *sucker effect* (Yamagishi and Sato, 1986). We are usually reluctant to "play the sucker" and instead reduce our own contributions to the group.

Given such problems, what ways are available to humankind to combat the attitude of "getting something for nothing, and everyone else be damned"? The box on page 118 discusses a number of mechanisms to encourage people in social dilemma situations to act cooperatively. Groupthink is another strategy, but it can have disastrous outcomes.

Groupthink

In 1961 the Kennedy administration undertook the ill-fated Bay of Pigs invasion of Cuba. Nothing went right for the 1,400 CIA-trained Cuban invaders, most of whom were killed or captured by Castro's forces. Not only did the invasion solidify Castro's leadership, it also consolidated the Cuban-Soviet alliance and led the Russian leadership to attempt to place atomic missiles in Cuba. And it contributed to the eagerness of American leaders to affirm their resolve by propelling the United States into the Vietnam quagmire. Later President Kennedy was to ask, "How could we have been so stupid?" Not only had the president and his advisers overlooked the size and strength of the Castro army, but in many instances they even had failed to seek relevant information.

The social psychologist Irving Janis (1982) suggests that the president and his advisers were the victims of **groupthink**—a decision-making process found in highly cohesive groups in which the members become so preoccupied with maintaining group consensus that they suppress critical inquiry. Under circumstances of groupthink, group members share an illusion of invulnerability that leads to overconfidence and a willingness to take risks. Its victims believe unquestioningly in the inherent righteousness of their cause—in this case, the need to overthrow the Castro regime, which the American leaders perceived to be the essence of evil. Members of the group demand conformity and apply pressure to

"All those in favor say 'Aye.'"
"Aye."   "Aye."   "Aye."
          "Aye."   "Aye."

Drawing by H. Martin; © 1979 The New Yorker Magazine, Inc.

ISSUES THAT SHAPE OUR LIVES

How Can the Public Good Be Promoted?

The eighteenth-century economist Adam Smith portrayed the common good as being served when people are motivated by self-interest. He said that an economy propelled by the pursuit of individual profit and regulated by competition would promote the wealth of a nation. Indeed, Smith contended that "by pursuing his own interest he [the producer] frequently promotes that of society more effectually than when he really intends to promote it." Yet Smith's plentiful society has more often been an ideal than a reality. In practice, we frequently confront social dilemma problems. Given this reality, what mechanisms are available to influence people to act cooperatively rather than selfishly? Researchers have identified a number of methods for promoting cooperation.

Instituting Social Regulation

Garrett J. Hardin (1968) sought a solution in social controls that restrict individual actions detrimental to the common good. Government often serves this function by regulating access to various resources. For example, the people of Los Angeles generated too much smog. They could not deal

Working for the Public Good
The photo shows Chinese students in the early days of the Chinese Revolution constructing a public sewer system. Inspired by the vision of building a new society, many Chinese youths volunteered for work on public projects. People can be impelled to work for the common good when they feel strong moral principles are at stake. *(Henri Cartier-Bresson/Magnum)*

with the problem by voluntary, market-type behavior because people sensed that individually they would achieve a minuscule share of the gains from installing pollution-abatement devices on cars or industrial plants. So the citizens of Los Angeles turned to government for assistance (see Chapter 20). Group norms frequently accomplish a similar end through informal sanctions (Messick et al., 1983). At times, however, norms may place heavier burdens on some group members than on others. For instance, parents are expected to contribute more to the maintenance of the family than are their children, and the wealthy are expected to contribute proportionally more of their earnings to the support of the state than are the poor (Kerr

those who express doubts about a proposed course of action. They then withhold dissent and exercise self-censorship. In fact, later evidence showed that the secretary of state (Dean Rusk) and the secretary of defense (Robert McNamara) held widely differing assumptions about the invasion plan even though they had participated in the same meetings.

Other historical fiascos associated with groupthink include the failure to anticipate the attack on Pearl Harbor, the escalation of the Vietnam war, the Watergate coverup, and the Iran-contra affair. In fact, based on his analysis of nineteen major international crises since

World War II, Janis concludes that American leaders used high-quality decision making in only 42 percent of them. In 37 percent of the crises, they were guilty of a high degree of groupthink behavior. Groupthink also pervades other realms of life. For instance, in making a marketing or product-development decision, a cozy group of corporate executives can make costly mistakes. All too often the questioning employee receives stares and frowns and the rolling of eyes. The failure of American automakers to build high-quality economy cars—and their subsequent loss of a large market share to the Japanese—is a good illustration of groupthink in the auto industry.

and MacCoun, 1985). In sum, a good deal of contemporary social life must be carried out in an explicitly organized, collective manner and not left to individual free choice. The free-rider problem, then, can be overcome by not leaving things free (Collins, 1982). However, this solution may require so many police and watchers that civil liberties and the quality of life are jeopardized.

Fostering Communication

People faced with a social dilemma have a better chance of resolving it if they communicate with one another. Admittedly, communication can degenerate into verbal abuse and threats. But it can also mean an opportunity for people to become acquainted and to deal with their common concern that the public good not be impaired. And by talking together they can assure one another of their good intentions, leading to greater trust and higher rates of cooperation (Dawes, McTavish, and Shaklee, 1977).

Decreasing Group Size

Decreasing group size seems to increase willingness to cooperate. Apparently, in a large group we feel our actions have little effect on the final outcome. And if the group fails to achieve a cooperative result, we can spread the blame for the failure over a good many people. But in a small group we are more likely to believe we can have an impact on policies and so we see that it is in our self-interest to cooperate and pursue the public good (Komorita and Lapworth, 1982). This finding suggests that neighborhood groups may be more effective than larger government units in achieving community beautification, sanitation, and law enforcement. However, it is not usually possible to manipulate the size of the groups facing actual social dilemmas.

Structuring Payoffs

Where we feel that we are rewarded for our cooperative behavior (for instance, sharing in the profits or benefits equally), we are less likely to switch to self-centered, individualistic behavior (Komorita and Barth, 1985). But this solution often requires using resources that might be used elsewhere. For instance, providing government financial incentives to keep farmers from overproducing certain crops prevents the use of these funds for other purposes. And cooperation achieved through material rewards and punishments soon ceases when the incentives are removed (Lynn and Oldenquist, 1986).

Promoting Prosocial Behaviors

There are also measures that induce people to act cooperatively and that elicit prosocial behaviors. Among them are those that highlight group boundaries and foster a superordinate group identity (Kramer and Brewer, 1984; Brewer and Kramer, 1986). The findings by Muzafer Sherif discussed earlier in the chapter provide a good illustration of circumstances in which the pursuit of common goals lowers barriers to cooperation. Where people have a strong sense of community and group loyalty, they are less likely to make sharp distinctions between their own welfare and that of other group members. Moral motives may also foster cooperative, nonselfish behavior (Lynn and Oldenquist, 1986).

Human history is replete with a good many episodes in which people were persuaded to make great personal sacrifices for the good of the group. War provides a good illustration of this. And in the 1960s many American civil rights workers willingly suffered harassment, beatings, and jail for the sake of a common cause. Even on the basketball court we witness cooperative behavior when a player passes up a good shot to offer a teammate a better one (Myers, 1983).

THINKING THROUGH THE ISSUES

Can you come up with a recent example of groupthink that occurred in a campus setting or on the job? What processes served to shut down a realistic appraisal of alternative courses of action? What techniques would you suggest for combating groupthink? When you have considered the matter, compare your ideas with those suggested by Janis and summarized in Table 5.3 on page 120.

Conformity

Groupthink research testifies to the powerful social pressures that operate in group settings and produce conformity. Although such pressures influence our behavior, we often are unaware of them. In a pioneering study Muzafer Sherif (1936) demonstrated this point with an optical illusion. If people view a small, fixed spot of light in a darkened room, they perceive it as moving about erratically in all directions. However, people differ in how far they think the light "moves." Accordingly, Sherif tested subjects alone and found their reference

Table 5.3   Techniques for Preventing Groupthink

1. Alert group members to the causes and consequences of groupthink.

2. The leader should remain impartial and not endorse any position.

3. Group members should be instructed to critically evaluate the issues and express their objections and doubts.

4. One or more members of the group should be assigned the role of "devil's advocate"—taking an opposing viewpoint.

5. The group occasionally should be subdivided into small groups that meet separately. Than the subgroups can be reassembled to air differences.

6. When the issue entails relations with a rival group, monitor closely the rival's warning signals and identify the rival's likely courses of action.

7. Once a preliminary decision is reached, hold a "second chance" meeting later to reevaluate the wisdom of the projected course of action.

8. Outside experts should be asked to attend meetings and challenge the group's views.

9. Group members should be encouraged to sound out the merits of the group's thought with trusted associates and report their reactions.

10. Several independent groups should work on the same question at the same time.

Source: Adapted from Irving L. Janis. 1982. Counteracting the adverse effects of concurrence-seeking in policy-planning groups: Theory and research perspectives. In I. H. Brandstatter, J. H. Davis, and G. Stocker-Kreichgauer, eds. *Group Decision Making.* New York: Academic Press, pp. 477–501.

point. He then brought together in group settings people with quite different perceptions and asked them to view the light again and report aloud on their observations. Under these circumstances, their perceptions *converged* toward a group standard. Later, in solitary sessions, they did not return to the standard they at first evolved but adhered to the standard of the group. Significantly, most subjects reported that they arrived at their assessment independently and that the group had *no* influence upon them.

Whereas Sherif presented subjects with an ambiguous situation, Solomon Asch (1952) asked subjects to match lines of the same length from two sets of cards displayed at the front of the room. He instructed the members of nine-person groups to give their answers aloud. However, all but one of the individuals were confederates of Asch, and they unanimously provided incorrect answers on certain trials. Despite the fact that the correct answer was obvious, nearly one-third of all the subjects' judgments contained errors identical with or in the direction of the rigged errors of the majority. Some three-fourths of the subjects conformed on at least one of the trials. Asch demonstrated that some individuals conform to the false consensus of a group, even though the consensus is contradicted by the evidence from their own eyes.

The case of Patricia Hearst provides a good illustration of group conformity. She was kidnapped in Berkeley, California, in 1974 by members of the Symbionese Liberation Army. Although she loathed her captors, was forced to have sex with all three of the men, and was abused by the women, she did not escape even when they left her alone. She participated in bank robberies with her captors, even on occasion driving the getaway van. In her autobiography (1981), Patricia Hearst says that she never believed in what the group was doing and that she was not indoctrinated by the Maoist lectures. Rather, she had been made a member of the "team" and wanted to perform as a "team" player. She asserts, "I felt I owed them something, something like loyalty." So where individuals become totally dependent upon a group, they may surrender their autonomy and relinquish control over their bodies and destinies. The case of Patricia Hearst highlights the critical part that groups play in our lives, particularly those groups from which we derive our identities and in which we embed ourselves in the course of our daily existence. As we will see shortly, such groups may function as total institutions.

Formal Organizations

As modern societies have become increasingly complex, so have the requirements of group life. As we noted in Chapter 3, the social organization of traditional societies revolves primarily about kin relations. The division of labor is simple; the people are culturally homogeneous; and formal law is lacking. But large societies, embracing millions of people, can no longer rely entirely upon primary group arrangements to accomplish the tasks of social life. Food has to be produced, preserved, and transported over considerable distances to support sizable

Group Conformity
Patricia Hearst, the daughter of a wealthy newspaper publisher, was kidnapped in February 1974 by members of the Symbionese Liberation Army. She was confined, abused, and sexually assaulted by her captors. The young woman took on a new identity as "Tania" and conformed to the norms of the terrorist organization, participating in bank robberies with them (left). Later she was arrested, convicted, and sentenced to a short prison term. Following her release from prison, Patricia Hearst returned to a conventional lifestyle and in 1979 married Bernard Shaw in a traditional ceremony (right). Her experiences vividly highlight the role the group plays in fashioning a person's attitudes and actions. *(left, UPI/Bettmann Newsphotos; right, AP/Wide World Photos)*

urban populations. Urban residents can no longer count upon family members and neighbors to enforce group norms and standards. Children can no longer be educated by the same "natural processes" by which parents teach their children to walk and talk. And longer life expectancies require sophisticated medical technologies for treating chronic illness. For these and many other tasks, people require groups they can deliberately create for the achievement of specific objectives. Such groups are termed **formal organizations.**

In recent decades the United States has increasingly become a society of large, semi-autonomous, and tightly knit formal organizations. Not only is there "big" government—extending from local municipal organizations to those of the federal government—but there are also "big" multinational corporations, "big" universities, "big" hospitals, "big" unions, and "big" farm organizations. Even organized crime has grown so large and become so entrenched that it requires administrative personnel. In sum, modern society is emerging as a web of formal organizations that appear, disappear, change, merge, and enter into countless relationships with one another. Although formal organizations have existed for thousands of years, dating back to ancient Mesopotamia, Egypt, and China, only in recent times has their scope become so pronounced. Not surprisingly, the sociologist Robert Presthus (1978) calls modern society "the organizational society."

Types of Formal Organizations

People enter formal organizations for a variety of reasons. Sociologist Amitai Etzioni (1964, 1975) classifies organizations on the basis of these reasons, and identifies three major types: voluntary, coercive, and utilitarian. **Voluntary organizations** are associations that members enter and leave freely. Examples include the PTA, a coin collectors club, the League of Women Voters, the Girl Scouts, the local chapter of the National Association for the Advancement of Colored People, the auxiliary of a neighborhood church, and a bowling league. Members are not paid for their participation. Rather, individuals join voluntary organizations to fill their leisure time, to enjoy the company of like-minded people, to perform some social service, or to advance some cause.

The proclivity of Americans for joining and supporting so many clubs and lodges has impressed foreign observers as one of the striking qualities of the nation's culture. Even in the 1830s, the French writer Count Alexis de Tocqueville noted: "Americans of all ages, all stations in life, and all types of disposition are forever forming associations." When voluntary organizations complete their goals, Americans often refashion them, finding new purposes to validate an enterprise. For example, once vaccines eliminated the scourge of infantile paralysis, the March of Dimes organization reformulated

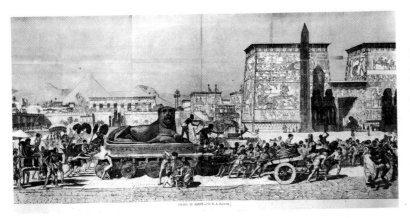

Formal Organization among the Ancient Egyptians
The building of the giant Egyptian pyramids required the labor of countless thousands of workers. The planning, direction, and coordination of their activities could not be left to chance. Formal organization was required—a group deliberately created to accomplish specific objectives. *(E. J. Poynter/ Culver Pictures)*

its goals to embrace new health missions (Shills, 1957). And in some cases, program failure is essential for many organizations because the effective solution of the problems they address would eliminate the purpose of their existence. Skid Row rescue missions provide a good illustration of this principle (Rooney, 1980).

People also become members of some organizations—**coercive organizations**—against their will. They may be committed to a mental hospital, sentenced to prison, or drafted into the armed forces. Sociologist Erving Goffman (1961) studied life in what he terms *total institutions*—places of residence where individuals are isolated from the rest of society for an appreciable period of time and where the members' behavior is tightly regimented. In these environments the "inmates" or "recruits" are exposed to jarring resocialization experiences that systematically seek to strip away their old roles and identities and fashion new ones. The induction process

often includes **mortification.** People are separated from families and friends who provide networks of support for old ways. They are rendered vulnerable to institutional control and discipline by being deprived of their personal items, clothing, and accessories and provided haircuts, uniforms, and standardized articles that establish an institutional identity. Often the new members are humiliated by being forced to assume demeaning postures, to engage in self-effacing tasks, and to endure insulting epithets (what sociologists term a *degradation ritual*). These procedures leave people psychologically and emotionally receptive to the roles and identities demanded of them by the total institution. As discussed in the box, elite prep schools function in many respects as total institutions.

People also enter formal organizations for practical reasons. These are called **utilitarian organizations.** Universities, corporations, farm organizations, unions, and government bureaus and agencies are among the organi-

Total Institutions: Degradation Rituals
Inmates of a Texas prison undergo full inspection before guards. The humiliation of such prison routines renders prisoners emotionally and mentally receptive to the roles and identities demanded of them by a total institution. *(Danny Lyon/Magnum)*

CULTIVATING A SOCIOLOGICAL CONSCIOUSNESS

Elite Prep Schools as Total Institutions

Like Eton and Harrow in England, America's elite boarding schools serve as educational country clubs for privileged children. Here they learn the social graces and acquire the academic skills that will allow them entry to positions of leadership in business and government. Each year more than a third of the graduating seniors at Phillips Exeter Academy, a leading New England preparatory school, make it into an Ivy League college. Indeed, Yale says it is "grateful" to have Exeter's graduates (Maeroff, 1986). Franklin D. Roosevelt, John F. Kennedy, George Bush, and James Baker III are examples of prep school graduates. Some 17 percent of those who are on the boards of two or more major American corporations graduated from an elite prep school. Prep schools, then, aim to train the nation's powerholders.

Sociologists Peter W. Cookson, Jr., and Caroline H. Persell (1986) have looked into fifty-five boarding schools throughout the United States. They find that attending an elite prep school is similar to joining an exclu-sive club. Not only must new members accept the rules by which the club operates, they must come to identify with and be loyal to it. In the process, the students are enmeshed in those webs of relationships and shared values that are so critical in creating a sense of solidarity among members of the upper class. In order to develop this "character" in their students, prep schools operate as total institutions. Like other total institutions, prep schools bar their "inmates" from outside influences, including parents. The transfer of attachment from parents to school to classmates is a central element in fusing a collective identity among the students.

Students enjoy very little personal freedom. School authorities and teachers minutely monitor what students do and say. Discipline is strict. In addition to prohibitions against stealing, cheating, and possessing alcohol and drugs, there are countless dormitory, dining-hall, bicycle, and other regulations. In exchange for their loss of freedom, preps earn the right to privileged positions—in short, "Present pain for future gain." But there is more than external discipline. Students are submerged in a system that represses the self and lim-its gratification. Nowhere is this more obvious than with eating. At home the youth had free access to food. But not at school. Indeed, the unconscious connection between nourishment and nurturing that contributes to the meaning of "home" in American life is severed immediately. In its place is substituted group "feeds." Meals are highly organized and ritualized affairs, based on the assumption that those who eat alike act and think alike.

Membership in an inmate clique is essential to survival in a total institution. Without a strong group, the student is doubly vulnerable: vulnerable to the impersonal force of the institution and to the antisocial, even cruel, behavior of classmates. Compelled to live day in and day out in forced intimacy with peers, many students form intense and lasting relations. All this contributes to a strong sense of psychological and social entitlement—the notion that one has earned authority and privilege. In sum, the elite prep school prepares students for life as members of the upper class and for leadership. They will go on to the right college, marry right, get the right job, join the right clubs, and travel to the right places.

---

zations people form to accomplish the vital tasks of everyday life. Utilitarian organizations fall between voluntary and coercive organizations in that membership in them is not entirely voluntary or entirely compulsory. For example, we may not be compelled to secure employment with a firm, but if we wish to support ourselves, it is an essential element of modern life.

Bureaucracy

So long as organizations are relatively small, they can often function reasonably well on the basis of face-to-face interaction. In contrast, if larger organizations are to attain their goals, they must establish formal operating and administrative procedures. Only as they standardize and routinize many of their operations can they function effectively. This requirement is met by a **bureaucracy,** a social structure made up of a hierarchy of statuses and roles that is prescribed by explicit rules and procedures and based on a division of function and authority. Sociologists employ the concept in a neutral way that differs sharply from the negative connotations that bureaucracy has in popular usage. For instance, in everyday life we often use the term to mean organizational inefficiency. The bureaucrat is typically stereotyped as an officious, rule-conscious, responsibility-dodging clerk entangled in red tape and preoccupied with busywork.

Bureaucracy has developed over many centuries in the Western world (Bendix, 1977). It grew slowly and erratically during the Middle Ages. In the twentieth century it has flowered in response to the dictates of modern life. As contemporary organizations have increased in size and complexity, more structural units and divisions have been required. In turn, some mechanism is needed for meshing their various activities. By providing for the performance of tasks on a regular and orderly basis, bureaucracies permit the efficient planning and coordinating of activities. Additionally, they aim to eliminate all unrelated influences on the behavior of their members so that people act primarily in the organization's interests. At the present time most large, complex organizations in the United States are organized as bureaucracies.

Weber's Analysis of Bureaucracies

The German sociologist Max Weber (1946, 1947) was impressed by the ability of bureaucracies to rationalize and control the process by which people collectively pursue their goals. Although he was concerned with some of the negative consequences of bureaucracy, Weber contended that the needs of mass administration made bureaucracy an essential feature of modern organizational life. Weber dealt with bureaucracy as an *ideal type*. As pointed out in Chapter 1, an ideal type is a concept constructed by sociologists to portray the principal characteristics of a phenomenon. For example, sociologists can abstract common elements from a government agency, the Roman Catholic Church, the Teamsters Union, IBM, and Yale University and arrive at a model for describing and analyzing organizational arrangements (see Figure 5.1). But the model should not be

FIGURE 5.1 **Bureaucratic Structure**
Bureaucratic offices are organized in a hierarchy, with officials accountable for their subordinates.

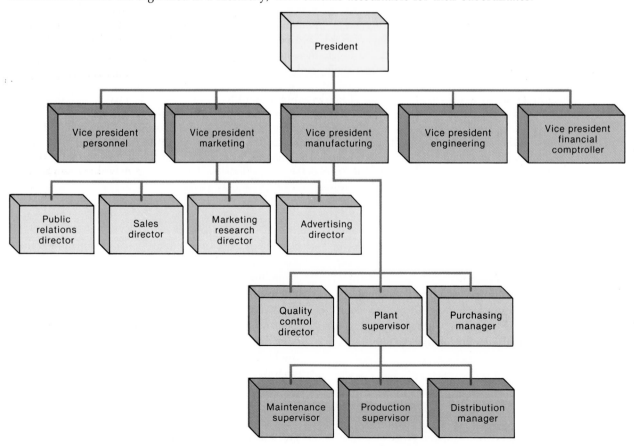

mistaken for a realistic depiction of how concrete bureaucracies actually operate in the contemporary world.

The following are the major components of Weber's ideal-type bureaucracy—a sketch of a completely *rationalized* organization centered on the selection of the most appropriate means available for the achievement of a given goal:

1. Each office or position has clearly defined duties and responsibilities. In this manner the regular activities of the organization are arranged within a clear-cut division of labor.

2. All offices are organized in a hierarchy of authority that takes the shape of a pyramid. Officials are held accountable to their superior for their subordinates' actions and decisions in addition to their own (see Figure 5.1).

3. All activities are governed by a consistent system of abstract rules and regulations. These rules and regulations define the responsibilities of the various offices and the relationships among them. They assure the coordination of essential tasks and uniformity in their performance regardless of changes in personnel.

4. All offices carry with them qualifications that are filled on the basis of technical competence, not personal considerations. Presumably trained individuals do better jobs than those who gain an office based on family ties, personal friendship, or political favor. Competence is established by certification (for instance, college degrees) or examination (for example, civil service tests).

5. Incumbents do not "own" their offices. Positions remain the property of the organization, and officeholders are supplied with the items they require to perform their work.

6. Employment by the organization is defined as a career. Promotion is based on seniority or merit, or both. After a probationary period, people gain the security of tenure and are protected against arbitrary dismissal. In principle this feature makes officials less susceptible to outside pressures.

7. Administrative decisions, rules, procedures, and activities are recorded on written documents, which are preserved in permanent files.

"I'd like to think of you as a person, David, but it's my job to think of you as personnel."

Drawing by Vietor; © 1986 The New Yorker Magazine, Inc.

Weber believed that bureaucracy is an inherent feature of modern capitalism. Yet he was equally insistent that a socialist society could not dispense with the arrangement. Indeed, Weber thought that socialism would see an increase, not a decrease, in bureaucratic structures. While recognizing the limitations of capitalism, he nonetheless felt it presented the best opportunity for the preservation of individual freedom and creative leadership in a world dominated by formal organizations (Ritzer, 1983). Some sociologists are not so optimistic. They have expressed concern that bureaucracies may pose an inherent challenge to human liberty by turning free people into "cogs" in organizational machines (Blau and Scott, 1962). Huge bureaucracies take control of our lives and follow their own logic of self-aggrandizement.

Disadvantages of Bureaucracy

As you are well aware, bureaucracies, while designed for maximal efficiency, are notorious for their inefficiencies. In practice, Weber's ideal form of bureaucracy is not achieved for a number of reasons (Perrow, 1979; Collins, 1982). First, human beings do not exist just for organizations. People track all sorts of mud from the rest of their lives with them into bureaucratic arrangements, and they have a great many interests that are independent of the organization. Second, bureaucracies are not immune to social change. When such changes are frequent and rapid, the pat answers supplied by bureaucratic regulations and rules interfere with a bureaucracy's rational operation. Third, bureaucracies are designed for the "average" person. However, in real life people differ in intelligence, energy, zeal, and dedication so that they are not in fact interchangeable in the day-to-day functioning of organizations. And fourth, since a bureaucracy consists of a network of specialists, each person considers anything that falls outside his or her province to be someone else's problem. Complaining to a bureaucracy is frustrating precisely because so many activities "fall between the cracks" and so bureaucrats find it is easy to evade responsibility.

It may have occurred to the reader that Weber's approach has a functionalist emphasis. He views the various components of his ideal type as a functional response to the requirements of large-scale organization. These properties permit a formal organization to achieve its goals in the most expeditious, efficient, and rational manner. But other sociologists have also pointed out that bureaucracies have disadvantages, termed *dysfunctions* (see Chapter 2). Let us consider a number of these problems.

Perverted rationality   Weber viewed bureaucracy as evolving rational procedures that coolly calculate how a result may be achieved most efficiently. However, functional rationality is concerned only with the means to an end, and not the end itself. Accordingly, bureaucratic machinery may run out of control. For example, programs designed to reduce unemployment may unleash rampant inflation; regulations designed to increase safety can contribute to skyrocketing costs and reduce industrial productivity. In short, because each bureaucrat concentrates on doing his or her own job, no one is looking

ahead to the larger ends. The purpose of a cog in a machine is to turn a particular wheel. But the person who acts as a cog becomes unable to form a judgment about why the wheel should turn in the first place or whether it might simply be better to replace the whole machine (Collins, 1982).

Trained incapacity   The social critic Thorstein Veblen (1921) pointed out that bureaucracies encourage their members to rely upon established rules and regulations and to apply them in an unimaginative and mechanical fashion, what he terms **trained incapacity.** Based upon the socialization provided by organizations, people develop a tunnel vision that limits their ability to respond in new ways when situations dictate that old ways are inapplicable. By virtue of trained incapacity, bureaucracies are often inflexible and inefficient in times of rapid change. For example, for more than a decade the American automobile industry was unresponsive and uncreative in meeting the changing tastes of the American public and in confronting the inroads of foreign competitors in the American market. Its managers continued to build the same size cars by the same manufacturing techniques despite the superior quality and appeal of the Japanese products.

Parkinson's law   Weber viewed bureaucracy as a mechanism for achieving organizational efficiency. We gain a quite different picture from C. Northcote Parkinson (1962), who has gained renown as the author of **Parkinson's law:** "Work expands so as to fill the time available

Bureaucratic Arrangements: Functions and Dysfunctions
Because American colleges and universities are typically large and complex organizations, they cannot carry out their functions without a specialized division of labor and a hierarchical chain of command. By providing for activities like student registration on a regular and orderly basis, bureaucracies process students in a relatively efficient manner. But the abstract system of rules and regulations and the well-defined duties and responsibilities of university personnel make for a rather rigid structure that does not take into account individual students needs, personal wishes, vocational requirements, or time demands. *(David Hurn/Magnum)*

for its completion." Despite the tongue-in-cheek tone of his writing, Parkinson undertakes to show that "the number of the officials and the quantity of the work are not related to each other." He contends that bureaucracy expands not because of an increasing workload, but because officials seek to have additional subordinates hired in order to multiply the number of people under them in the hierarchy. These subordinates in turn create work for one another while the coordination of their work requires a further burgeoning of officialdom.

The relentless growth of bureaucracy is reflected in American government. When George Washington was inaugurated as president in 1790, there were nine executive units and some 1,000 employees. A century later, over 150,000 civilians worked in the Harrison administration, a rate of growth 10 times as fast as the population. And by 1980 nearly 3 million civil servants were employed by the executive branch. Whereas only 1 in 4,000 Americans was employed by the executive branch in 1790, the figure stood at 1 in 463 in 1891 and 1 in 75 by 1980 (Porter, 1980). Of course, factors other than those associated with Parkinson's law contributed to the growth in American government, including the expansion of government services.

Oligarchy Organizations, like other groups, enjoy a formidable capacity for producing conformity. As we noted earlier in the chapter, groups not only control and dispense rewards and punishments, they also define social reality by structuring our experiences. Given the dominant role organizations have in contemporary life, some observers have expressed concern for the future of democratic institutions. They point out that all too often the needs of organizations take priority over those of individuals. Complicating matters, Robert Michels (1911/1966), a sociologist and friend of Weber, argues that bureaucracies contain a fundamental flaw that makes them undemocratic social arrangements. They invariably lead to **oligarchy**—the concentration of power in the hands of a few individuals who use their offices to advance their own fortunes and self-interests. He points to the developmental course of European socialist parties and labor unions as evidence in support of his thesis that leaders seldom reflect the democratic aspirations espoused by their organizations. Michels termed this tendency the **iron law of oligarchy**—"Whoever says organization, says oligarchy" (p. 365).

Michels cites a variety of reasons for the oligarchical tendencies found within formal organizations. First, they are structures with authority moving downward from the top. Even when final authority is vested in the membership, the dictates of leadership and administration make popular voting and related procedures merely rituals. Second, officials have a great many advantages over their members. They have access to information that is unavailable to others, and they usually possess superior political skills and experience. Additionally, they control such administrative resources as communication networks, offices, and a treasury that can be used to carry out their official tasks or to ward off would-be challengers. And third, ordinary members tend to be apathetic.

In sum, although the complexity of modern life requires large-scale formal organization, bureaucratic structures have their disadvantages and problems. There are limits to what large hierarchical organizations can accomplish. Yet as political scientist James Q. Wilson (1967:6) observes, we often lose sight of this fact:

If enough people don't like something, it becomes a problem; if the intellectuals agree with them it becomes a crisis; any crisis must be solved; if it must be solved, then it can be solved—and creating a new organization is the way to do it. If the organization fails to solve the problem (and when the problem is a fundamental one, it will almost surely fail), then the reason is "politics," or "mismanagement," or "incompetent people," or "meddling," or "inertia."

As Wilson points out, some problems cannot be solved and some organizational and governmental functions cannot be performed well.

THINKING THROUGH THE ISSUES

There are some organizations that have as their prime beneficiary the client—for instance, welfare, medical service, and library organizations. Other organizations, such as the police and fire departments, exist for the common welfare. Still other organizations benefit both their owners and their clients, for example, such profit-making organizations as banks and insurance companies. When dealing with organizations, in which of them does the client have the greatest clout? Why? Under what circumstances is the client in greater need of altruistic appeals ("Please help me!") and less in need of normative appeals ("I deserve this service")? Are the attitudes and behaviors of officials as undiscriminating and impersonal as that stipulated by the Weberian model?

Informal Organization

The realities of organizational life rarely correspond to the rules and procedures of a bureaucracy for another reason. Formal organization breeds **informal organization**—interpersonal networks and ties that arise in a formal organization but that are not defined or prescribed by it. Based on their common interests and relationships, people form primary groups. These informal structures provide patterns by which people bend and break rules, share "common knowledge," engage in secret behaviors, handle problems, and "cut corners." And when the members of a primary group oppose a policy, they may sabotage it. Consequently, work relationships are much more than the lifeless abstractions contained on an organizational chart that outline the official lines of communication and authority. These ideas are central to the *human relations model* of organizations (Roethlisberger and Dickson, 1939).

The roots of informal organization are embedded within formal organization and are nurtured by the formality of its arrangements. Official rules and regulations must be sufficiently general to cover a great many situations. In applying general rules to a particular situation, people must use their judgment, and so they evolve informal guidelines that provide them with workable solutions. Additionally, in order to avoid bureaucratic "red tape," employees often arrive at informal understandings with one another. Indeed, if formal organization is to operate smoothly, it *requires* informal organization for interpreting, translating, and supporting its goals and practices. So people are tied to the larger group by their membership in primary groups that mediate between them and the formal organization.

Factory workers typically evolve their own norms regarding what constitutes a "reasonable" amount of work, and these norms often do not conform with those of management. Sociologist Michael Burawoy (1979) studied informal organization among shop workers while working for a year as a machine operator at a large Chicago-area plant. He found that relations on the shop floor were dominated by "making out"—a competitive game the machine operators played by manipulating the rules and regulations governing their work. The workers did not passively conform to the dictates of management or the technical aspects of their work. They actively connived to put in place their own "shop-floor culture." The culture sought to maximize their payoff from the firm's piecework bonus system while simultaneously holding in place high rates through the restriction of output.

Research has also shown the strong influence of the work group in regulating deviance and theft among individual workers. For instance, Donald Horning (1970) studied blue-collar theft in a manufacturing plant and

Formal Organization Breeds Informal Organization
Bureaucratic and technological requirements determine formal organization. But within the larger formal structure, primary groups often arise. The roots of informal organization are embedded within formal organization and are nurtured by the very formality of its arrangements. Many workers long for congenial relations with others in which they may find warmth, rapport, and friendship. Here workers at a Chrysler upholstery plant "humanize" their work experience as members of a clique.
(Charles Harbutt/Archive)

concluded that informal norms regulate both the type and the amount of property that is taken. Employee pilferage was a group-supported activity even though the actual taking of property took place alone or in secret. And Gerald Mars (1974) reported in his study of dockworkers that materials in shipment were stolen according to the group-defined "value of the boat." In order for theft to go undetected by dock authorities, all members of a work group had to approve of and cooperate with the activity. In sum, no formal organization works strictly by "the book" because people continually inject a "human touch."

Alternative Perspectives

Until the past decade or so, Weber's approach to bureaucracy dominated American sociology. In large measure sociologists focused their attention on organizations as abstract social structures, while often neglecting the behavior of the people who compose them. Indeed, sociologists Peter M. Blau and Richard A. Schoenherr (1971:viii and 357) have championed such an approach, observing:

> Formal organizations, as well as other social structures, exhibit regularities that can be analyzed in their own right, independent of any knowledge about the individual behavior of their members. . . . it is time that we "push men [and women] out" to place proper emphasis on the study of social structure in sociology.

Many sociologists studied formal organizations without turning their sociological eye on the processes by which social structures are produced and reproduced in the course of people's daily interactions. But much has changed in recent years, as sociologists from the conflict and interactionist perspectives have looked at the ways by which organizational reality is generated through the actions of people and groups of people (Benson, 1977; Zey-Ferrell, 1981).

The conflict perspective Conflict theorists contend that organizational goals reflect the priorities of those who occupy the top bureaucratic positions. Viewed in this manner, organizations are not neutral social structures, but arenas for conflicting interests in which the social issues and power relations of society are played out (Collins, 1975). More particularly, Marxist social scientists, following in the tradition of Karl Marx (1970), have seen bureaucracy as an expression of the centralizing tendencies of capitalism and an instrument of class domination. They analyze organizations within the context of the broader inequalities that operate within society and find that the distribution of power and the allocation of rewards within them mirror the larger societal class structure (Edwards, 1979; Burawoy, 1983).

In *Capital* (1867/1967) Marx claimed that the modern factory is a despotic regime made necessary by the competitive pressures of the market. These pressures compel capitalists to seek a labor force that is both inexpensive and powerless. To achieve this goal, capitalists select technologies and administrative strategies that minimize worker skills in order to render workers interchangeable and susceptible to social control. But as we will see in Chapters 9 and 15, Marx also viewed the

The Factory System: A Despotic Regime?
Karl Marx portrayed the factory system under capitalism as a despotic regime. He thought it alienated workers from productive activity and deadened the human spirit. Marx envisaged new societies in which people would experience their work as a meaningful, creative, and self-actualizing process. Yet the bureaucratic organization of work persists in societies like contemporary China founded on principles inspired by Marx. Much in the manner of workers in capitalist nations, workers in China find their work regimented by the dictates of bureaucracy and technology.
(J. P. Laffont/Sygma)

factory as the crucible of revolution: The domination of the working class by capital would turn into its opposite, "the revolt of the working class."

More recent studies by Marxist social scientists suggest that bureaucratic mechanisms arose as much from the need of capitalists to impose labor discipline as from abstract notions of efficiency and rationality (Friedman, 1977; Edwards, 1978). Stephen Marglin (1974) shows that nineteenth-century British entrepreneurs established the hierarchical arrangement to guarantee themselves a central role in the production process. Katherine Stone (1974) also finds that turn-of-the-century steel magnates established top-to-bottom chains of command and job ladders to isolate individual workers, break the power of skilled craft workers, and combat growing labor militancy.

Marx thought that the bureaucratic structures inherited from capitalism would have to be altered and even eliminated by a revolutionary working class. He wrote (1966:64): "The working class cannot simply lay hold of the ready-made state machinery and wield it for its own purposes." Instead, the workers would have to create a transitional bureaucracy that was representative of and responsive to their needs and goals. However, as Marx's writing were interpreted and reformulated by Lenin and implemented by Stalin, the primary elements of Bolshevik policy in the Soviet Union centered on the expansion of bureaucratic offices and the dominance of the state apparatus by a "new class" of Communist Party officials (Djilas, 1957).

The symbolic interactionist perspective Critics of the structural or Weberian approach to organizations point out that people, not organizations, have motivations and goals. An organization's officers and managers can only offer incentives that they believe will motivate employees to conform to the goals they set forth (Zey-Ferrell, 1981). Critics, particularly symbolic interactionists, contend that human beings are not spongelike, malleable organisms who passively absorb and adapt to their environments. Instead, they portray people as active agents who shape and mold their destinies and continually refashion joint actions based upon their definitions of the situation (Blumer, 1969). Organizational constraints only provide the framework within which people forge their actions as they appraise, choose, and decide upon alternatives. In sum, symbolic interactionists portray organizational behavior as generated out of individual meanings that people then translate into social realities (see Chapter 2). As such, no one has ever seen an organi-

zation. We only see buildings (that we define as belonging to an organization) and organizational charts (that we say represent the relationships among the members).

Rather than depicting organizations in static terms, symbolic interactionists emphasize their dynamic and changing nature (Fine, 1984). This approach was taken by Anselm Strauss and his colleagues (1964) in their study of organizational behavior in two Chicago-area psychiatric hospitals. They treated formal organization as a **negotiated order**—the fluid, ongoing understandings and agreements people reach with one another as they go about their daily activities. To outsiders, the hospitals appear to be tightly structured organizations that function in accordance with strict bureaucratic rules and regulations. However, the researchers found that in practice the hospitals operate quite differently. The organizations are simply too complex for a single set of rigid rules to hold or for any one person to know all the rules, much less exactly what situations they apply, to whom, in what degree, and for how long. Matters are complicated by a constant turnover in staff and patients. Additionally, not only do people differ in their goals, they also differ in their ideas regarding the nature, causes, and treatment of mental illness. Given these circumstances, most "house rules" serve more as general understandings than as commands, and they are stretched, argued, reinterpreted, ignored, or applied as situations dictate. People reach agreements with one another that provide a consensus for a time, but the understandings are subject to periodic modification and revision.

Chaos does not reign in the hospitals because the negotiations follow patterns that permit some degree of predictability. Even so, Strauss and his colleagues concluded:

A skeptic, thinking in terms of relatively permanent or slowly changing structure, might remark that the hospital remains the same from week to week, that only the working arrangements change. . . . Practically, we maintain, no one knows what the hospital "is" on any given day unless he has a comprehensive grasp of the combinations of rules, policies, agreements, understandings, pacts, contracts, and other working arrangements that currently obtain. In a pragmatic sense, that combination "is" the hospital at the moment, its social order. Any changes that impinge upon this order—whether ordinary changes, like introduction of a new staff member or a betrayed contract or unusual changes, like the introduction of new technology or new theory—will necessitate renegotiation or reappraisal, with consequent changes in the organizational order. There will be a new order, not merely the re-establishment of an old order or reinstitution of a previous equilibrium. It is necessary continually to reconstitute the bases of concerted action, of social order. (p. 312)

Whether or not the negotiated-order model is applicable to other kinds of settings is a matter for future research. But negotiations apparently do occur in many kinds of organizations, including factories, symphony orchestras, and political organizations (Lauer and Handel, 1983).

A synthesis of alternative perspectives Sociologist Charles Perrow (1982) joins threads from the conflict and interactionist perspectives to argue that the notion of bureaucratic rationality masks the true nature of organizational life. He claims that our world is more "loosely coupled"—characterized by a substantial measure of redundancy, slack, and waste—than structural theories allow. Perrow says that organizations do not have goals, only constraints. Take the Sanitation Department of New York City:

> To say its goal is to pick up the garbage—even to pick it up frequently, pick it all up, and do it cheaply—does not tell us much. These are not goals of that department but merely loose constraints under which those who use the organization must operate, and these are not really any more important than the following constraints: The cushy top jobs in the department can be used to pay off political debts; some groups can use the Sanitation Department as an assured source of employment and keep others out; upper management can use its positions as political jumping-off places or training spots; equipment manufacturers use it as an easy mark for shoddy goods; and, finally, the workers are entitled to use it as a source of job security and pensions and an easy way of making a living. (p. 687)

Perrow contends that private, profit-making organizations are not much different. Punsters say that Lockheed is a pension plan that makes missiles and planes on the side so that its pension plan can be funded. Steel plants are closed even though they make a respectable profit because they are worth more as tax writeoffs. The goal of making steel or even a profit does not pose a significant obstacle. Countless other organizations continue to exist even though they fail to provide decent mail service, prepare students for careers, or offer acceptable medical care. But should the organizations fail to satisfy some special interest group that lives off of them, then the consequences are defined as a major social problem. Perrow concludes:

> Do organizations have goals, then, in the rational sense of organizational theory? I do not think so. In fact, when an executive says, "This is our goal," chances are that he is looking at what the organization happens to be doing at the time and saying, "Since we are all very rational here, and we are doing this, this must be our goal." Organizations, in this sense, run backward: The deed is father to the thought, not the other way around. (p. 687)

Perrow links the conflict perspective to his analysis by arguing that organizations serve elites much more than they serve other people. Organizations create a world in which inequality and profit making become legitimated.

Humanizing Bureaucracies

Since large organizations play such a critical part in our daily lives, it may be well to conclude the chapter by asking, "Can we make bureaucracies more humane instruments for modern living?" If we value freedom and independence—if we are disturbed by the conformity of attitudes, values, and behavior that bureaucracies often induce—then we may wish to set up conditions that foster uniqueness, self-direction, and human dignity. Although affording no panaceas, a number of programs have been proposed that allow people greater range for developing their full capacities and potentialities in the context of organizational life. Let us briefly consider a number of these.

Employee participation: Quality circles About the same time that Japanese manufacturers entered American markets in force, American academicians became intrigued by Japanese management methods (Serrin, 1984). They particularly touted quality circles, an arrangement where less than a dozen workers and one or two managers from the same department meet together on a regular basis to figure out ways of getting along better, making work easier, raising output, and improving the quality of their products.

Some 2,000 American companies, including General Motors, International Business Machines Corporation, and American Telephone and Telegraph, have instituted work reform programs. But not all firms like them. A University of Michigan survey found that 60 percent of the companies who had adopted quality circles were lukewarm or unhappy with what they were accomplishing, and 7 percent had dropped them entirely

Japanese Quality Circles
Many Japanese firms have sought to humanize the work experience by introducing quality circles that involve workers in managerial processes. Although the arrangement may make for more harmonious labor-management relations, the options available to managers and workers are still shaped and constrained by the dictates of a market economy. Products must reflect what consumers want and at prices consumers are prepared to pay. And since Japan is an exporting nation, the international community is a part of the Japanese market. *(Ernesto Bazam/Magnum)*

(Main, 1984). Many of the programs were established for their publicity value or because managers wanted employees to believe that they were being consulted, even though no real decision sharing actually occurred. Moreover, few workers participate in their companies' most important decisions, such as product choice, plant location, and investment. Conflict theorists contend that the relationship between management and labor is inherently adversarial, and they claim that worker-participation programs are simply cosmetic efforts that mask corporate attempts to scrap collective bargaining obligations. Union officials have also been distrustful of quality circles because they fear that the circles will assume some of their functions as workers' representatives.

Proponents of the programs say that where management and workers are committed to them, absenteeism, tardiness, grievances, strikes, and labor costs are reduced. Moreover, product quality improves and pilferage lessens. For instance, General Motors plants that have the most intensive programs have better performance than do automotive plants that lack programs. In practice, quality circles seem to buffer potential threats to the pleasantness of the workplace. But they do little to alter fundamentally or improve the core components of the work experience (Marks et al., 1986).

Overall, new management strategies in the 1980s have been emphasizing a lessening of hierarchy and authoritarianism. They mark a departure from the theories of Frederick Winslow Taylor (1911), which dominated management philosophies since the 1920s. Taylor's system of *scientific management* held that production could

be improved by rational, technology-centered organization and that workers could be pacified by providing them with adequate training and pay. But the changes should not be overestimated. Where managers must make tough decisions, they typically revert to the direct, authoritarian mode (Serrin, 1984).

Small work groups Some corporate officials say that small working groups are more productive for Americans than attempting to adopt Japanese management styles that depend on the worker's intense company loyalty (Larson and Dolan, 1983). The approach has proved beneficial within the computer industry, where small groups, given great freedom, can react quickly to abrupt technological change. Unlike other industries where change is typically gradual, computer firms must regularly come up with new products or enhancements of the old, and at constantly lower prices.

Apple Computer turned to small groups to develop its Lisa and Macintosh computers. And even giant IBM has recognized the need for small groups; it formed fourteen "independent" business units to capture the entrepreneurial spirit for a number of projects, including the development of factory robotic systems. IBM found that centralized organization interfered with innovation. One virtue of the small group approach is that responsibility rests with the employees doing the actual work. Additionally, small groups can focus their energies on a single goal, foster creativity, and reward employees commensurately with their contributions.

Employee-ownership plans By 1986 there were more than 8,000 firms in the United States that shared some ownership with more than 10 million employees. In about 1,000 companies, employees owned the majority of the stock (Rosen, Klein, and Young, 1986). Until recent years, most employee-ownership plans were management vehicles for sharing a piece of the pie and increasing worker productivity without fundamentally altering a company's structure. But more recent arrangements entail employees actually taking over a firm. In some cases, such as Hyatt Clark Industries, Weirton Steel, and Rath Packing Company, the companies were unprofitable and the buyouts were a last resort to save a business and jobs for workers.

In some cases employee-ownership has changed the way companies operate, including their labor-management relationships. Greater employee initiative in the workplace frequently cuts costs. Yet since most companies discourage shareholder participation, employees do not feel that owning stock gives them a greater voice in company decision making. And much depends on a firm's profitability. What workers like best about stock plans is the chance to make more money. When a company becomes profitable, differences tend to get smoothed over quickly. But when a firm continues to lose money, dissatisfaction mounts. Thus employee ownership does not guarantee labor peace. In sum, although there are no social panaceas, options are nonetheless available for humanizing the workplace (Russell, 1985).

Chapter Highlights

1. Groups are not tangible things that have actual substance in the real world. Rather, they are products of social definitions—sets of shared ideas. As such they constitute constructed realities. We make groups real by treating them as if they are real.

2. Primary groups are fundamental to the human enterprise: They are critical to the socialization process; they provide settings in which we meet most of our personal needs; and they are powerful instruments for social control. The concepts of ingroup and outgroup highlight the importance of boundaries—social demarcation lines that tell us where interaction begins and ends. Reference groups provide the models we use for appraising and shaping our attitudes, feelings, and actions.

3. The size of the group is of considerable importance because it influences the nature of our interaction. In group settings some members usually exert more influence than others, individuals we term leaders. Two types of leadership roles tend to evolve in small groups: a task specialist and a social-emotional specialist.

4. When individuals work in groups, they work less hard than they do when working individually, a process termed social loafing. A closely related phenomenon is termed a social dilemma—a situation in which members of a group are faced with a conflict between maximizing their personal interests and maximizing the collective welfare. Social dilemmas appear in two basic forms: the commons dilemma and the public goods problem.

5. Groups bring powerful pressures to bear that produce conformity among their members. Groupthink provides a good illustration of this. Although such pressures influence our behavior, we often are unaware of them.

6. For a good many tasks within modern societies, people require groups they can deliberately create for the achievement of specific goals. These groups are formal organizations. People enter formal organizations for a good many reasons. Amitai Etzioni classifies organizations on this basis by identifying three types: voluntary, coercive, and utilitarian.

7. Max Weber approached bureaucracy as an ideal type. He sketched the following characteristics of a completely rationalized organization centered on the selection of the most appropriate means available for the achievement of a given goal: Each office has clearly defined duties; all offices are organized in a hierarchy of authority; all activities are governed by a system of rules; all offices carry with them qualifications; incumbents do not own their positions; employment by the organization is defined as a career; and administrative decisions are recorded on written documents.

8. Bureaucracies also have disadvantages and limitations. These include perverted rationality, the principle of trained incapacity, Parkinson's law, and the iron law of oligarchy. Formal organization also breeds informal organization that may negate the policies and procedures of the formal organization.

9. Until recent years sociologists focused on organizations as abstract social structures while neglecting the behavior of the individuals who compose them.

But much has changed as sociologists from the conflict and interactionist perspectives have looked at the ways organizational reality is generated through the actions of people and groups of people.

10. Since large organizations play such a large role in our lives, we concluded the chapter by asking how they might be made more humane. Among the programs are those that allow for employee participation, small work groups, and employee ownership.

The Sociologist's Vocabulary

bureaucracy A social structure made up of a hierarchy of statuses and roles that is prescribed by explicit rules and procedures and based on a division of function and authority.

coercive organization A formal organization that people become members of against their will.

dyad A two-member group.

formal organization A group that people deliberately form for the achievement of specific objectives.

free-rider mechanism Left to our own rational self-interest, we often are tempted to take unfair advantage of contributions others make to the community as a whole.

groupthink A decision-making process found in highly cohesive groups in which the members become so preoccupied with maintaining group consensus that their critical faculties become impaired.

informal organization Interpersonal networks and ties that arise in a formal organization but that are not defined or prescribed by it.

ingroup A group with which we identify and to which we belong.

the iron law of oligarchy The principle set forth by Robert Michels that leaders seldom reflect the democratic aspirations espoused by their organizations. Instead, they use their offices to advance their own fortunes and self-interests.

mortification Rituals employed by coercive organizations that render individuals vulnerable to institutional control, discipline, and resocialization.

negotiated order The fluid, ongoing understandings and agreements that people reach with one another as they go about their daily activities.

oligarchy The concentration of power in the hands of a few individuals who use their offices to advance their own fortunes and self-interests.

outgroups Groups with which we do not identify and to which we do not belong.

Parkinson's law Work expands so as to fill the time available for its completion.

primary group Two or more people who enjoy a direct, intimate, cohesive relationship with one another.

reference group A social unit we use for appraising and shaping our attitudes, feelings, and actions.

relative deprivation Discontent associated with the gap between what we have and what we believe we should have.

secondary group Two or more people who are involved in an impersonal way and have come together for a specific, practical purpose.

social dilemma A situation in which members of a group are faced with a conflict between maximizing their personal interests and maximizing the collective welfare.

social-emotional specialist A leadership role that focuses on overcoming interpersonal problems in a group, defusing tensions, and promoting solidarity.

social group Two or more people who share a feeling of unity and who are bound together in relatively stable patterns of social interaction.

social loafing When individuals work in groups, they work less hard than they do when working individually.

task specialist A leadership role that focuses on appraising the problem at hand and organizing people's activity in dealing with it.

trained incapacity The term Thorstein Veblen applies to the tendency within bureaucracies for members to rely upon established rules and regulations and to apply them in an unimaginative and mechanical fashion.

triad A three-member group.

utilitarian organization A formal organization formed to achieve practical ends.

voluntary organization A formal organization that people enter and leave freely.

PART THREE

Microsociological Foundations

6

Socialization

Man is the only one that knows nothing,
that can learn nothing without being taught.
He can neither speak nor walk nor eat,
and in short he can do nothing at the prompting
of nature only, but weep.

—Pliny the Elder, _Natural History_, first century

They were hard years—the difficult years of the 1930s, of the Great Depression. Women who bore children out of wedlock were disgraced and their children shunned. So when Anna was born to his unwed daughter, the grandfather was deeply distressed. He hid Anna from outsiders in a small, dark attic. Anna's mother maintained the child physically, but otherwise neglected her. When local authorities "discovered" Anna at the age of 6, she was a gaunt, emaciated youngster who could not walk, talk, or do anything that showed intelligence. Physicians found her reflexes normal, but otherwise she was an apathetic, vegetable-like creature. Anna was placed in the county home and later in a school for retarded children.

Although she was to die of hemorrhagic jaundice at 10 years of age, Anna blossomed into a "human" being in the four years following her discovery. Her food habits became reasonably acceptable. Except for fastening her clothes, she was capable of dressing herself. She kept her clothing clean, habitually washed her hands and brushed her teeth, and used the toilet without fail. She could follow directions and would attempt to help other children. While easily excitable, she nonetheless had a pleasant disposition. Most remarkable of all, she learned to repeat words, could talk in phrases, and would attempt to carry on a conversation. Because of her early death, we do not know whether Anna would have developed into a fully functioning adult. Although medical specialists could not rule out mental retardation, her later development demonstrated that she was able to acquire skills and capabilities she could never have achieved in isolation.

Like Anna, Isabelle was a sequestered illegitimate youngster of about 6 years of age when social workers discovered her. However, Isabelle's circumstances differed from those of Anna in a number of respects. For one thing, Isabelle's mother, a deaf mute, spent much of her time with the girl in a dark room shut off from the rest of the family. For another, Isabelle was given prolonged, systematic, and expert training in speech and other skills by faculty members at Ohio State University. At first Isabelle made only strange croaking sounds and displayed fear and hostility in the presence of strangers. Specialists concluded she was deaf, retarded, and "uneducable."

Despite the pessimistic prognosis, the faculty members proceeded with their training program. Had you been one of them, what type of program would you have recommended? How would you find out what Isabelle already knew? What would you try to teach her first? How would you teach her? For their part, the Ohio State University professors undertook an intensive program of language training, and within a week Isabelle said her first word.

After Isabelle surmounted the early hurdles of language, a curious thing happened. She went through the usual stages of learning characteristic of children from 1 through 6 years of age not only in proper sequence, but far more rapidly than usual. Within two and a half months of saying her first word, she was using sentences. Nine months later, she could identify words and sentences in books, write well, add to ten, and retell a story after hearing it. Within two and a half years she attained the normal educational level for children her age. By 14, she had passed the sixth grade; appeared to be bright, cheerful, and energetic, and participated in school activities like other children. Isabelle is reported to have completed high school, to have married, and to have had her own normal family.

Cases like those of Anna and Isabelle raise a variety of questions concerning the processes by which we develop and learn to participate effectively in society. In this chapter, we explore these ideas and issues.

PLANNING AHEAD: TARGETED READING

1. Is there such a thing as "human nature"?

2. Are we born human, or do we become human through our experiences in society?

3. What makes each of us a unique individual?

4. What processes are involved in learning?

5. What stages do children pass through in the course of cognitive and moral development?

6. How do you go about answering the question "Who am I?"

7. What processes do you engage in when you undertake to fit your actions to those of other people?

8. How is socialization accomplished?

Processes of Socialization

Cases like Anna and Isabelle testify to the fact that we enter the world as amazingly "unfinished" beings. Deprived of significant contact with others, extremely neglected children have only their genetic endowments to draw upon. When found, they show only superficial signs of belonging to the human species. Clearly, we are not born human; we become human only in the course of interaction with other people. Our humanness is a social product that arises in the course of **socialization,** a lifetime process of social interaction by which we acquire the knowledge, attitudes, values, and behaviors essential for effective participation in society. Through socialization, a biological organism is transformed into a genuine social being capable of acting in concert with others.

Were it not for socialization, the renewal of culture could not occur from one generation to the next. As we pointed out in Chapter 3, we do not start life with a clean slate. Each of us is born into a world defined by already existing cultural patterns. Indeed, we are uniquely dependent upon this social heritage—this rich store of adaptations and innovations that countless generations of ancestors have developed over thousands of years. And in the absence of socialization, society could not perpetuate itself beyond a single generation. Just as individuals who have lost their memory are no longer "normal," so a society that is completely separate from its past culture is inconceivable. Individuals would lack the shared understandings necessary to align their actions and to bind their separate lives into a larger social whole (see the box on the Ik of Uganda). Both the individual and the society depend on socialization: It blends the sentiments and ideas of culture to the capacities and needs of the organism. Let us explore the processes by which this blending is achieved.

Nature and Nurture

Can you recall debating in a class or a bull session the question, "Which is more important, heredity or environment?" Phrasing the issue this way, as an either-or statement, has caused the scientific community, and society as a whole, untold difficulties. Carried to its logical conclusion, heredity would be defined as behavior that appears in the absence of environment, and environment as behavior that does not require an organism. This is like debating whether oxygen or hydrogen is more important to water or whether length or width is more important in determining the area of a rectangle. The point is that we cannot have water without both oxygen and hydrogen, and we cannot have a rectangle without both length and width.

A joint product   You are a joint product of your **nature,** your inherited traits, and your **nurture,** your experiences. None of the characteristics you display could occur in the absence of an appropriate heredity or an appropriate environment. Some of your behaviors may be primarily a product of nature and some of nurture, but all are shaped by both. Most contemporary scientists recognize the difficulty of ever completely separating the two influences, because they *interact* in various ways to provide you with a distinct **personality,** unique and enduring behavior patterns. Overall, it seems that heredity predisposes an individual toward and sets limits for certain behaviors. However, environment shapes their expression. For instance, intelligence is in part determined

by the genes received from parents. But the kind of home in which an individual was reared, the degree to which he or she was intellectually stimulated, the amount and quality of formal schooling, and his or her own decisions have all affected—and will continue to affect—the flowering of that person's intelligence.

Only in extreme cases does a specific genetic factor guarantee particular outcomes. For instance, no matter how enriched the environment, all individuals who at conception receive an extra chromosome 21 develop Down's syndrome. The disorder is characterized by mental retardation, neuromotor disabilities, and other physical anomalies. But even though a supportive environment cannot reverse the condition, it can make the

Studies of Family Resemblance
One way to find out about the relative influence of nature and nurture on human behavior is to conduct studies among family members. Identical twins like Jack Yufe (left) and Oksar Stohr (right) share the same genes. They were separated at six months of age, when their parents divorced. Yufe was raised as a Jew, joined an Israeli kibbutz in his youth, and served in the Israeli navy. Stohr was brought up as a Catholic and later became involved in the Hitler youth movement. Despite the differences in their backgrounds, when they first met at the airport, both sported mustaches and two-pocket shirts with epaulets, and each carried a pair of wire-rimmed glasses with him. Both read magazines from back to front. Both excel at sports and have difficulty with math. And both have similar personality profiles as measured by the Minnesota Multiphasic Personality Inventory. *(Courtesy of Thomas J. Bourchard, Jr., Department of Psychology, University of Minnesota)*

ISSUES THAT SHAPE OUR LIVES

Socialization Gone Awry: The Ik

Prior to World War II, the Ik were a cooperative, prosperous hunting and gathering people. They roamed in nomadic bands throughout a vast region that now makes up portions of three African nations—Kenya, Sudan, and Uganda. Today they are on the verge of extinction: They consist of scattered groups of hostile people, each of whom pursues individual survival at the expense of the others. This turnaround happened within three generations. As with other hunting and gathering peoples, life among the Ik had revolved about their traditional territory. From the land the Ik had derived not only their livelihood, but their sense of identity. After World War II, their lands were turned into a national park, and the Ik were barred from them. They moved eventually to the arid and barren mountains of northeast Uganda, and it was here that anthropologist Colin M. Turnbull (1972) found and studied them.

There is every reason to believe the Ik had at one time possessed those qualities most of us deem to be human virtues: kindness, generosity, consideration, affection, honesty, hospitality, compassion, and charity. For hunters in a tiny, close-knit society, these characteristics are essential for survival. Now the Ik are no longer hunters, but farmers. They exist in mountain villages that are far from livable and where famine prevails much of the time. A major source of their food comes from aiding and encouraging cattle raids and sheltering the raiders. These changes have produced an unfriendly, uncharitable, inhospitable, and overall "mean" people. Given their new circumstances, survival is the one and only governing principle for the Ik.

Cruelty and insensitivity dominate Ik life. Ik men sitting about a fire watch with eager anticipation as a child crawls toward the flames, then burst into gay and happy laughter when the child shrieks with pain as it plunges its hand into the coals. The elderly are abandoned by their relatives. Indeed, if Turnbull gave an aged Ik food, he would have to stand within arm's reach while the person ate. Otherwise, a younger Ik would snatch it. Because the Ik are on the verge of starvation, there simply does not seem to be room in their lives for warmth, sentiment, and love. Ik who cannot take care of themselves are considered burdens and hazards to the survival of others.

Children are thrown out of their parents' huts when they are 3 and survive by forming age bands. They enter into makeshift alliances that quickly disintegrate as allies become adversaries and former adversaries become allies. Children learn the wisdom of acting on their own, for their own good, while occasionally associating with others for some momentary gain. Nor can they count on their parents. When Giriko's son Lokol developed an intestinal blockage and was gravely ill, Giriko was amused and called others to look at the boy's distended belly. Although the 10-year-old could neither eat nor drink, he was the favorite topic for his father's jokes. Later, when Lokol was recovering, Turnbull had to force Giriko away to prevent him from stealing the boy's food.

Although the Ik still live in villages, people mistrust and fear one another in direct proportion to proximity and without regard to family and kinship. They still cling to only

---

difference between institutionalization and a measure of self-sufficiency.

Since nature and nurture interact in a dynamic relationship, what appears to be a hereditary contribution in one context can be seen as an environmental contribution in another. For instance, every February, as spring arrives, many children on the Mediterranean island of Sardinia suddenly become listless. Their schoolwork suffers; they fall asleep at their desks; and they complain of feeling dizzy and nauseated. In the United States, the behavior would be called "spring fever." Sardinian teachers know that children and adults can die of the affliction, especially after urinating quantities of blood. In 1959 scientists found that a hereditary condition, the lack of a single enzyme (glucose-6-phosphate dehydrogenase), underlies the disorder. However, since the disease appears only in spring, it seemed that an environmental factor was somehow implicated. Although the genetic defect was the gun, an environmental factor was pulling the trigger. Researchers soon identified the Italian fava bean as the culprit. Susceptible Sardinians can remain free of attacks by not eating the plant or its products. Viewed in this manner, the disorder is "environmental" in origin (Harsanyi and Hutton, 1979). Genes, then, determine the range of available possibilities, while the environment chooses among them (see Figure 6.1).

Shaping ourselves and our environments   The genes selected for us by evolution are a series of hedged bets as

one shared value—*ngag,* or food. Food is their rationale for action and thought. It is the one standard by which the Ik measure right and wrong. Their word for good, *marang,* is defined in terms of food. "Goodness," *marangik,* is defined as "food"—or more particularly, "individual possession of food." For the Ik, a "good person" is one who has a full stomach.

The family is incapable of holding itself together, much less serving as a model for a wider social network. Men may come back from a raid laden with meat, devour what they can, and sell the rest to a police post without giving as much as a bite to a starving wife or child. Economic interest is centered on as many individual stomachs as there are people. In this setting, socialization fails to provide rules for conduct. The prime maxim is that each person should do what he or she wants, and anything else only if forced to do so. The Ik no longer possess a sense of moral responsibility toward one another. And they lack any sense of social belonging. At first Turnbull was angry and upset by the ways of the Ik. But then, like the Ik, he found he needed to conserve energy to survive, and that survival was possible only through diligent attention to his own needs while ignoring those of others. When he returned to the Western world, Turnbull concluded that the Ik are beyond saving as a society— they are doomed because their members are no longer socialized to be truly social beings.

THINKING THROUGH THE ISSUES

Turnbull ends his report on the Ik by asking us to look at ourselves and determine just what *is* the difference between us and them: "If we grant, as the evidence indicates we should, that the Ik were not always as they are, and that they once possessed in full measure those values that we all hold to be basic to humanity, indispensable for both survival and sanity, then what the Ik are telling us is that these qualities are not inherent in humanity at all, they are not a necessary part of human nature" (p. 289). He says that their behavior is simply more extreme, "for we do not start throwing our children out until kindergarten" (and more recently even earlier in day care and nursery school). And he contends that we have shifted the responsibility for health, education, and welfare from the family to the state, whereas the Ik shifted it to the individual. He also criticizes our "cutthroat economics, where almost any kind of exploitation and degradation of others, impoverishment and ruin, is justified in terms of an expanding economy and the consequent confinement of the world's riches in the pockets of the few" (pp. 291–292). In sum, Turnbull fears that the fate of the Ik may also confront us in the future, given the direction of contemporary social change. What do you make of this argument?

to the environments we are likely to encounter and the behavioral strategies that will be successful in dealing with them. But the adaptations are essentially historical— what worked in the past. What is distinctive about human beings is our capacity for creating and using culture. It is undoubtedly true that if we had wings, like birds, or organs sensitive to electrical fields, like some fish, we would fashion a very different environment. Even so, although we lack genes for wings or for sensitivities to electrical fields, by virtue of culture we have acquired the ability to fly and to use sensitive equipment for detecting electrical fields. It may not be in "human nature" to fly or detect electrical fields, but it is "in" human nature to modify the environment so that these activities come well within our range.

What we have been saying adds up to this: We are not passive beings programmed by internal genetic forces, nor are we passive beings shaped by an external environment. We create, destroy, alter, and transform the external world by our activities. Nature and nurture mutually influence one another much like the processes in the baking of a cake. The taste of the final product is the result of a complex interaction among the components—the butter, sugar, flour, eggs, salt, and so on— exposed for a certain period to oven temperature. The outcome is not divisible into this or that percent of flour, butter, and the like, although each component makes a contribution, as does the oven heat.

The interactions between nature and nurture are even more complex for human beings than for other

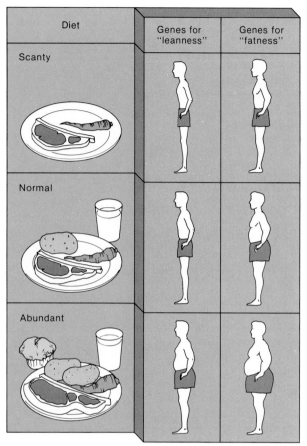

FIGURE 6.1 **Gene-Environment Interaction**
A person who has a gene for "fatness" may actually weigh less than a person with a gene for "leanness," if the former lives on a scanty diet and the latter on an overabundant one. *Source: Theodosius Dobzhansky.* Mankind Evolving. *New Haven: Yale University Press, 1962.*

organisms. As children develop, their behavior becomes less and less dependent on *maturation*—changes in an organism that unfold more or less automatically in a set, irreversible sequence due to physical and chemical processes—and more and more on *learning*. Significantly, in learning the human organism modifies itself by responding. So the mind is not *revealed* as children mature; it is *constructed*. For this reason, we are not locked into an unchangeable body or social system. We are active agents shaping both ourselves and our environments. We act on and modify the world in which we live, and in turn we are shaped and transformed by the consequences of our own actions. These transactions between us and the environment are the foundation of human intelli-

gence, knowledge, and culture. Learning is a good illustration of how these principles work.

THINKING THROUGH THE ISSUES

Is the debate regarding heredity and environment simply an academic squabble? Or does it have major policy implications for us all? Are crime, destructiveness, violence, hate, war, and stupidity genetically bred within the human animal, or are these vices bred by pathological social conditions? Are we all—black, white, Oriental, and American Indian—one big family, genetically identical except for the genes determining our different appearances? Or are we composed of a number of hereditary races endowed with different natural abilities? How does the manner in which we answer these questions influence our childrearing practices? our self-images? our attitudes toward compensatory education programs? our willingness to support programs for prisoner rehabilitation? governmental decisions regarding poverty issues?

Learning Theories

Learning is the more or less permanent modification in behavior that results from experiences in the environment. It occurs across the entire life span: in the family, among peers, at school, on the job, and in many other spheres as well. Learning allows you to adapt your behavior to changing conditions. It makes your behavior flexible. It also engenders hope: What is learnable is potentially teachable—an assumption that encourages parents, music teachers, athletic coaches, and educators. And what has been learned is potentially replaceable by new learning—an assumption that underlies psychotherapy, counseling, and rehabilitation. Learning occurs in two principal ways: conditioning and observing the behavior of others.

Conditioning Behavioral theorists, as their name suggests, are concerned with behavior—what people actually say and do. They contend that you learn by directly experiencing particular incidents or by acting and seeing the consequences of your actions. You establish an association or link between two events. For example, very likely you have formed an association between a hot stove and a painful, burning sensation, between studying for a test and passing a course, and between criticizing

Adaptations Made Possible by Culture
Although we lack wings for flying, we are able to fly by virtue of cultural improvisation. Hang gliding is one socially devised and transmitted means for achieving a goal otherwise barred to human beings by anatomical limitations. *(Steve Lissau/Rainbow)*

friends harshly and upsetting them. The process by which this linkage occurs is termed **conditioning**. The most prevalent type of associative learning among humans is **operant conditioning**, learning in which behavior is altered in strength by its consequences. It is called operant conditioning because you undertake actions that "operate" on the environment to gain something you want or to avoid something unpleasant.

The process whereby one event strengthens the probability of another event's occurring is **reinforcement**. Generally speaking, reinforcement is associated with pleasure, comfort, reward, or an end to discomfort. For example, consider how a researcher trains a pigeon to make a figure eight. She carefully watches a hungry pigeon strut about. When the bird makes a slight clockwise turn, the researcher instantly rewards it with a food pellet—a stimulus. Again the bird struts about, and when it makes another clockwise turn, the researcher repeats the procedure. In this manner, the pigeon can be

taught to respond by making a full circle in 2 to 3 minutes. Next, the researcher rewards the bird only when it moves in the opposite direction. Then she waits until it

Social Transmission of Attitudes and Behaviors
Children learn what is expected of them through socializing experiences. In the process they come to answer the question, "Who am I?" Answering this question, children also need to answer its corollary: "And who are all those?" The answers to these questions are already contained in the culture of the society and transmitted to children by parents and peers. Subcultural and countercultural roles are communicated and learned in much the same fashion as other roles. *(Contact Press Images)*

Drawing by Opie; © 1978 The New Yorker Magazine, Inc.

Underlying observational learning is our capacity to use symbols for comprehending and dealing with the environment. Verbal and mental symbols allow us to represent events; to analyze conscious experience; to communicate with others; to design, to create, to imagine, and to engage in planned action. Indeed, stimuli and reinforcements exert little impact on behavior unless we first represent them mentally with symbols. The reason is not hard to find: For associative learning to occur, we must *understand* the connection between two events (Rescorla and Holland, 1982; Carpenter, 1985). For instance, you may retrieve a volleyball from a bed of poison ivy. A few hours later, your skin becomes red and itchy; tiny blisters develop. It is quite unlikely that you will link the two events. But should a physician, friend,

Modeling: Observational Learning
Children of all cultures learn by watching others and imitating their behaviors. This mother, a Seminole Indian, is showing her daughter how to make embroidered horizontal designs on skirts and jackets.
(Michal Heron/Woodfin Camp & Associates)

makes a clockwise circle followed by a counterclockwise circle. In about 10 to 15 minutes, the pigeon is conditioned to do a perfect figure eight.

Much of life is structured through reinforcement. A business executive rewards appropriate work behavior by giving employees salary increases. A child stops whining to avoid further scolding from a parent. A doctor tries to make certain that a patient feels some benefit from an office visit to induce the patient to return for additional treatment. And a motorist slows down when noticing a police car so as not to be ticketed for speeding (Skinner, 1953).

Observational learning   You also learn from interaction with people in a social context. If you had to learn solely by direct experience—by the rewarding and punishing consequences of your behavior—you would probably not have survived to adulthood. If, for example, you depended upon direct conditioning to learn how to cross busy intersections, you probably would have been a traffic fatality. By watching other people, you learn new responses without first having had the opportunity to make the responses yourself, a process called **observational learning**. We avoid tedious, costly, trial and error experiment by imitating the behavior of socially competent models. This is how we learn how to put a light bulb in a lamp socket, kick a football, or use a hand calculator. We also learn how to show love, concern, or respect, as well as aggression and violence.

or co-worker alert you to the fact that you are allergic to poison ivy, you grasp the relationship between the blisters and the offending plant. You then take care to avoid contact with poison ivy in the future. You have learned!

Cognitive Developmental Theories

The processes underlying conditioning and observational learning are essentially the *same* for a child as they are for an elderly person. Learning is cumulative, building on itself. But the same cannot be said for all aspects of behavior. Clear-cut changes in behavior take place from one phase of life to the next, suggesting that *different* processes come into operation at various ages. Some theorists take this insight as the foundation for a stage approach to development. The **stage** concept implies that the course of development is divided into steplike levels. By way of analogy, consider the metamorphosis of a butterfly. Once a caterpillar hatches from an egg, it feeds on vegetation. After a time, it fastens itself to a twig and spins a cocoon within which the pupa develops. One day the pupal covering splits, and the butterfly emerges. In contrast, learning theories use the leaf metaphor. After a leaf sprouts from a seed, it grows by simply becoming larger; the change is gradual and continuous.

However, the learning and developmental stage models are not necessarily incompatible. Consider the butterfly metaphor again. If you first observe a caterpillar and later a butterfly, you are struck by dramatic change. But if you observe the developmental changes occurring within the cocoon, you gain a different impression. You see that butterfly characteristics are acquired gradually. You are then more likely to describe the process as continuous. Even so, learning and developmental theories focus on somewhat different dimensions. This is a topic worth pursuing. Here we will consider two types of development, cognitive and moral.

Cognitive development   Humans are thinking beings who receive raw sensory information that they in turn transform, elaborate, store, recover, and use. These mental processes, termed **cognition**, allow us to "make something" out of our perceptions. We use information from our environment and our memories to make decisions about what we say and do. It is this capacity for processing information intelligently and taking appropriate action that leads us to view our behavior as rational.

According to psychologists like Jean Piaget (1896–1980), normal children pass through a series of stages of cognitive development (see Table 6.1). Each period is

marked by discontinuities or abrupt changes from the previous one. Consequently, what is learned in one stage differs from what is learned in the preceding stage because the dominant *scheme* for handling information—the cognitive or thinking model—changes from one stage to the next. It follows, then, that the thought of infants and children is not a miniature version of adult thought. When children say that the sun follows them about when they go for a walk or that dreams come through the window, they are not being illogical. Rather, they are operating with a different mental framework.

Piaget distinguishes four stages in children's cognitive development. In the first, or *sensorimotor*, stage (birth to 2 years), youngsters are busy discovering the relationships between their sensations and their motor behavior (for example, their hands are a part of themselves, but a bottle, rattle, or rag is not). They also master the notion of object permanence—the idea that "things continue to exist even though I cannot see or touch them." The hallmark of the second, or *preoperational*, stage (2 to 6 years) is representational thought. Now children picture (represent) things in their minds. They do so with symbols, particularly language. The major milestone of the third, or *concrete operational*, stage (6 to 12 years) is the grasping of the conservation principle. Children learn that a given quantity does not change when its appearance is changed—for instance, a ball of clay can change to a sausage shape and still not contain more or less clay (see Figure 6.2 on page 149). Finally, in the fourth, or *formal operational*, stage (12 years to adulthood), adolescents become capable of logical thought. They achieve the ability to engage in abstract and hypothetical reasoning. (Table 6.1 summarizes the highlights of each stage).

Piaget says that children typically stretch a cognitive scheme as far as possible to accommodate new observations. But over time their experiences point up the limitations of the model and compel them to restructure their world view—to invent increasingly better schemes. In so doing, they pass from one cognitive stage to the next. In sum, Piaget viewed the individual and the environment as engaged in continuing interaction that leads to new perceptions of the world and to new ways for organizing knowledge. We cannot fully understand the socialization process by limiting ourselves to society and its childrearing practices. We must also take into account the child and the child's cognitive capabilities. In so doing, we once more see the interdependence of society and individual—both are part of the same process of social interaction.

Table 6.1   Piaget's Stages of Cognitive Development

Stage	Age	Characteristics
Sensorimotor	From birth to 2 years	Thinking is displayed in action, such as grasping, sucking, and looking. Children develop the capacity to coordinate motor activities with their perceptions. They also fashion a notion of object permanence: they come to view a thing as having a reality of its own that extends beyond their immediate perception of it.
Preoperational	2 to 6 years	Beginning of symbolic representation. Language appears; the child begins to draw pictures that represent things. The child cannot represent a series of actions in his or her head in order to solve problems.
Concrete operational	6 to 12 years	This stage marks the beginning of rational activity. Children master various logical operations, including arithmetic, class and set relationships, measurement, and conceptions of hierarchical structures. They also gain the ability to "conserve" mass, weight, number, length, area, and volume. Before this stage, for instance, children do not appreciate that a ball of clay can change to a sausage shape and still remain the same amount of clay.
Formal operational thought	12 years to adulthood	Thinking becomes more abstract and hypothetical. The individual can consider many alternative solutions to a problem, make deductions, contemplate the future, and formulate personal ideals and values.

Moral development   Developmental psychologist Lawrence Kohlberg (1981, 1984) has applied Piaget's cognitive stage approach to moral reasoning—how we decide what is right and what is wrong. He has studied children's development of moral judgment and finds three developmental levels in their conceptions of society's rules and expectations. The *preconventional level* is characteristic of most children under 9 years of age, some adolescents, and many criminal offenders. At this level rules and expectations are external to the person and are obeyed to avoid punishment or gain benefits. The *conventional level* is typical of most adolescents and adults. People incorporate the rules and expectations of the wider society within their personality. They conform to social rules to win the approval of others and because they believe it their "duty" to do so. The *postconventional level* is attained by less than 25 percent of all Americans. At this level, people differentiate between themselves and the rules and expectations of others. For instance, rather than blindly accepting the rules of society, they look to broad moral principles to guide their

behavior and to judge whether particular laws are just or unjust. These ethical tenets may include such abstract concepts as human equality, the Golden Rule, and respect for the dignity of each human being.

Kohlberg and his associates have tested people in the United States, the Bahamas, Great Britain, Israel, Mexico, Turkey, Taiwan, and Malaysia. He concludes that people in all cultures use the same basic moral concepts, including justice, equality, love, respect, and authority. Moreover, he says that all people, regardless of culture, go through the same stages of reasoning with respect to these concepts, and in the same order. It is Kohlberg's view that there is a universal morality: What we deem to be moral is not a matter of taste or opinion. For instance, when Taiwanese village boys are asked whether a man should steal food for his starving wife, a typical answer from a preadolescent is: "Yes, because otherwise he will have to pay for her funeral, and that costs a lot." A Malaysian of the same age is likely to say: "Yes, because he needs her to cook his food." Although the cultural content of the replies differs (funerals are less

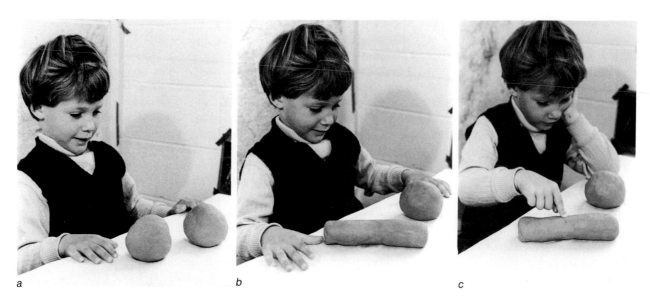

FIGURE 6.2   **A Piaget-type Conservation Experiment**
(*a*) Place two balls containing the same amount of clay before a four-year-old child
and ask if the balls are the same size. Invariably, the child responds affirmatively.
(*b*) As the child watches, roll one of the balls into a long sausagelike shape and again
ask the child if the objects are the same size. (*c*) The child will now assert that one of
the clay objects is larger than the other. In this case, the child has claimed that the
sausage-shaped clay is larger than the clay ball. Not until the child is several years
older will he or she recognize that the two different shapes contain the same quantity
of clay—the principle of conservation of quantity. (*Patrick Reddy*)

important in Malaysia than in Taiwan), the preconventional orientation (the evaluation of behavior in terms of one's own selfish needs) remains constant (Snarey, 1985). All this is not to say that moral development is not a social affair. At heart it is a process of restructuring the ways in which people engage in role taking. The social inputs from family, peer group, school, and the workplace provide role-taking opportunities. Participation in groups is therefore essential for stimulating the development of basic moral values (Gibbs and Schnell, 1985).

Some psychologists, like Carol Gilligan (1982), contend that there are gender differences in moral reasoning. Men typically define moral problems in terms of right and rules—the "justice approach." In contrast, women perceive morality as an obligation to exercise care and to avoid hurt—the "responsibility approach." Whereas men see autonomy and competition as central to life, women view life as a means for integrating themselves within the larger human enterprise. Thus men and women speak with somewhat different voices. But not all researchers find evidence that men and women

differ in their approaches to moral issues, suggesting that additional research is called for (Walker, 1984; Gibbs, Arnold, and Burkhart, 1984; Ford and Lowery, 1986). What is not in dispute, however, is that the *self* is central to moral development and the socialization process.

The Self

When you were very little, you learned to tell dolls, chairs, trees, and countless other things apart and to designate them symbolically by name. But you did even more. You came to use symbols to designate yourself. By naming yourself as others named you, you created another kind of object—the self. The **self** is the set of concepts you use in defining who you are. It is the human sense of "I"; the awareness you have of yourself as a separate being who is able to think and to initiate action. In everyday speech, you recognize the existence of the self in such phrases as "rewarding oneself," "proud of oneself," "talking to oneself," "losing control of oneself," "disgusted with oneself," "testing oneself," and "hating oneself." In brief, you not only interact with others; you also "interact" with yourself. The self is the core of our humanness; it provides us with the capacity to observe, to respond to, and to direct our own behavior. The sense of self distinguishes you as a unique person, different from all others. It gives you a feeling of place in the social and physical world and of continuity across time. And it provides the basis for identity—your answer to the question "Who am I?"

The emergence and gradual development of the self is a central part of the socialization process. Symbolic interactionists emphasize that the self is not a biological given, but arises in the course of social interaction. In orienting yourself to others, you size them up and anticipate what they are likely to say and do. You answer the questions "Who are those people?" and "What are they up to?" But you have to do more. You have to size yourself up, determine how other people are responding to you, and figure out what you are going to do next. So you have to supply answers to the questions "Who am I?" and "What am I to say and do?" Indeed, the two sets of questions are interrelated. For example, how do you respond if a person winks at you in class? You first define who the person is, classmate or instructor. But in defining who the other person is, you also define who you are, peer or student. And in defining what the other person is doing—flirting or showing rapport—you determine what you say and do. Consciousness, then, is built through relations with others. The mechanisms of social behavior and the mechanisms of self-awareness are the same. We are aware of ourselves because we are aware of others, and we come to know ourselves in the same manner that we come to know others. Sociologists like Charles Horton Cooley and George Herbert Mead have contributed a good deal to our understanding of these matters.

THINKING THROUGH THE ISSUES

Who are you—how do you define yourself? To answer this question, see Table 6.2. In the 1950s, when college students were asked to describe themselves as you did in the table, the majority gave responses in the B mode. These responses centered on group memberships and societal roles. Now students tend to use the C mode. How do you explain the change?

Charles Horton Cooley: The Looking-Glass Self

Early in this century, the sociologist Charles Horton Cooley (1864–1929) used the metaphor of a "looking glass" to describe how our consciousness arises in a social context. He called the **looking-glass self** that process by which we imaginatively assume the stance of other people and view ourselves as we believe they see us. Our ability to take the perspective of another person—to be an audience to our own actions—is a basic requirement for all social behavior. It is the foundation of role playing. As sociologist Albert K. Cohen (1966:98) observes: "We cannot really tell whether we are 'leaders,' 'glamour girls,' 'pool sharks,' or 'brains' without venturing into the icy waters of social interaction, trying our hand at the role, and seeing how others respond."

Self-awareness Cooley (1902) viewed the looking-glass self as a mental process characterized by three phases. First, we imagine how we appear to other people. For instance, we may believe that we have been putting on weight and have become "fat." Second, we imagine how others judge our appearance. We are aware, for example, that people typically think of obese people as unattractive. Third, we experience feelings such as pride or mortification on the basis of what we believe others' judgments to be. So we may be embarrassed because we are "fat." Note that the looking-glass self is a subjective process and does not necessarily accord with objective reality. Victims of anorexia nervosa deliberately starve themselves, denying that they are thin or ill, despite the fact that they are emaciated.

Cooley's notion of the looking-glass self does not imply that our self-concepts change radically every time we encounter a new person or a new situation. Sociologists distinguish between self-images and self-concepts (Turner, 1968; Swann and Hill, 1982). A **self-image** is a mental conception or picture that we have of ourselves which is relatively temporary; it changes as we move from one situation to another. For this reason, it is also called the *situated self*. A **self-concept** is a more overriding view, a sense of self through time—"the real me," or "I myself as I really am." The deposits of self-images—the ledger of positive and negative situated selves—typically cumulate over time and contribute to a relatively stable self-concept. For the most part, then, the succession of self-images *edits* rather than supplants our self-concepts. Life course research reveals that our self-

---

Table 6.2   Who Am I?

There are ten numbered blanks below. Please write 10 answers to the question, "Who am I?" in the blanks. Answer as if you are giving the answers to yourself, not to someone else. Do not worry about logic or importance.

_____ 1. I am _____

_____ 2. I am _____

_____ 3. I am _____

_____ 4. I am _____

_____ 5. I am _____

_____ 6. I am _____

_____ 7. I am _____

_____ 8. I am _____

_____ 9. I am _____

_____ 10. I am _____

When you have completed your list, analyze your responses as follows:

1. Place an *A* next to descriptions that refer to *physical characteristics* such as your build, height, gender, race, and appearance. The statements should be easily validated using a mirror, yardstick, or scale.

2. Place a *B* next to references to your *social status,* such as daughter, student, salesclerk, or manager of the baseball team. This category should contain descriptions that are socially defined and validated.

3. Put a *C* next to your descriptions of your *abstract characteristics* that transcend particular situations, for example, "I am friendly" or "I am a football fan." These are statements that pertain to qualities that differ from one situation to another but that characterize your personal style.

4. Finally, put a *D* next to statements that are relatively *vague* and *global,* for instance, as "I am a person" or "I am at one with the universe."

When you are finished add up the number of *A*'s, *B*'s, *C*'s, and *D*'s: Which category did you use most frequently? Which next, and least? Give the test to another person and see how your self-portrait compares to theirs.

Me		**Friend**	
_____ A mode		_____ A mode	
_____ B mode		_____ B mode	
_____ C mode		_____ C mode	
_____ D mode		_____ D mode	

Source: Adapted from Manford H. Kuhn and Thomas S. McPartland. 1954. An empirical investigation of self-attitudes. *American Sociological Review,* 19: 68–76.

---

concepts may remain stable for thirty-five years and longer (Costa and McCrae, 1980; Block, 1981).

Self-appraisals and self-esteem   Cooley's notion of the looking-glass self contains the idea that our self-appraisals are a reflection of how we think others view us. In short, our self-appraisals are in part "reflected appraisals." If children are approved, respected, and liked for what they are, they commonly acquire attitudes of self-acceptance and self-respect. Warm and accepting parenting tends to be associated with children who have high self-esteem. But if the significant people in their lives—especially family members—belittle, blame, and reject them, they are likely to develop unfavorable attitudes toward themselves (Coopersmith, 1967; Sears, 1970; Gecas and Schwalbe, 1986).

Moreover, our self-concepts influence our behavior. Consider "born losers." Some people seem to encounter failure after failure and misfortune after misfortune. Even when they are on the verge of a "sure thing," something always seems to go wrong and success eludes them. Apparently, these people set situations up in such a manner that they ensure failure. They define themselves as failures and then undertake to be "true to self" by failing. Only in this way can they maintain a consistent conception of themselves (Aronson and Carlsmith, 1962; Marecek and Mettee, 1972; Zautra, Guenther, and Chartier, 1985).

Shyness   Since we are "self-aware" or "self-conscious" beings, some of us experience shyness. *Shyness* is a mental attitude that predisposes us to be excessively concerned about others' evaluation of us (see Table 6.3). Surveys show that some 40 percent of adult Americans consider themselves shy, including such celebrities as Barbara Walters, Terry Bradshaw, Fred Lynn, Carol

Self-Concepts
Each of us arrives at definitions of who and what we are in the course of interaction with others. We evolve self-concepts—overriding notions and images that provide us with a sense of "the real me" or "I myself as I really am." These mental scripts allow us to bring to each new situation the generalizations about the self that we evolved from past experience. (*Guy Gillette/Photo Researchers*)

Burnett, and Warren Beatty (Zimbardo, 1978). Shy people often long for human contact, but they are prisoners of their own perceptions and feelings. The condition is similar to a person attempting to drive down the street with the brakes on. Shyness takes a heavy human toll because it creates barriers for people in school, in business, in love—in any arena of life where people meet their needs with and through others. Shy people seem to be too self-aware, too preoccupied with their own adequacy, and so their spontaneity is impaired.

Choking   At times we *choke*—we fail to perform up to our level of abilities and skills under social pressure (Baumeister, 1984). Like shyness, choking occurs when the selfhood process goes awry. You often become self-conscious when you are expected to provide an excellent performance. In athletic competition—a tennis match, a bowling tournament, a crucial football game—you may attempt to ensure the correctness of your execution by monitoring your performance. But by focusing on the coordination and precision of your muscle movements, you disrupt the automatic or overlearned nature of the activity. Consequently, you are susceptible to mistakes. This often happens to players in the final and decisive game of a championship series. The home team tends to choke and so is at a decided disadvantage. The crowd

Table 6.3   What Makes You Shy?

Situations	Percentage of Shy College Students
Where I am focus of attention—large group (as when giving a speech)	73%
Of lower status	56%
Social situations in general	55%
New situations in general	55%
Requiring assertiveness	54%
Where I am being evaluated	53%
Where I am focus of attention—small group	52%
One-to-one different-sex interactions	48%
Of vulnerability (need help)	48%
Small task-oriented groups	28%
One-to-one same-sex interactions	14%

Other People	
Strangers	70%
Opposite sex	64%
Authorities by virtue of their knowledge	55%
Authorities by virtue of their role	40%
Relatives	21%
Elderly people	12%
Friends	11%
Children	10%
Parents	8%

Source: Philip G. Zimbardo. *Shyness: What It Is, What to Do About It.* Reading, Mass.: Addison-Wesley, pp. 54–55.

Choking: World Series
Players are more self-conscious when they play before a home crowd in a crucial championship game and so become more prone to mistakes. Here Boston Red Sox rightfielder Dwight Evans hangs his head in dejection after he failed to hold on to a long fly ball hit by New York Mets Len Dykstra, resulting in two runs in the seventh inning of the fourth game of the 1986 World Series at Boston's Fenway Park. (*AP/Wide World Photos*)

typically claps, shouts, and moans in response to the performance of the home team players. It remains silent or jeers the visitors' exploits. During the regular season and in early games of the World Series, the crowd is usually a source of inspiration to the home team. But when a championship is imminent, home players become increasingly self-conscious and feel considerable pressure to win. This is when they make mistakes (Baumeister and Steinhilber, 1984).

Egocentric bias   At the core of shyness and choking seems to be an excessive preoccupation with self and a fear that other people will evaluate us unfavorably. An **egocentric bias** often complicates matters—the tendency to place oneself at the center of events. By virtue of the egocentric bias, you tend to see yourself as the victim or target of an event that in reality is not directed toward you (Greenwald, 1980). For instance, when a professor singles out a particularly good or poor exam for a few preliminary remarks before returning the papers to the class, you often assume that one of the papers belongs to you (Fenigstein, 1984). And if you play the lottery, you sense that your ticket has a far greater probability of being selected a winner than it in fact has. By virtue of the egocentric bias, you experience life through a self-centered filter. In group discussions you see yourself as attracting more attention, as having a greater impact on others' opinions, and as being more often the object of other people's comments than is the case. This bias carries over to memory. You find it far easier to remember

information 5, 10, or 20 years later if it somehow refers to you (Zuckerman et al., 1983; Goleman, 1984; Greenwald and Pratkanis, 1984).

George Herbert Mead: Mind, Self, and Society

The sociologist George Herbert Mead (1863–1931) elaborated on Cooley's ideas and contributed many insights of his own. Mead (1934) contended that we achieve a sense of self by acting toward ourselves in much the same manner that we act toward others. In our imagination, we step out of ourselves into the role of another person and attempt to view ourselves from that person's perspective. In so doing, we are said to "take the role of the other" toward ourselves.

The "I" and the "me"   For Mead, there are two parts to the self: the "I" or subject aspect and the "me" or object aspect. Consider what happens should you contemplate complaining to your instructor about an unusually long and difficult assignment. You think to yourself: "If I complain, she'll consider me lazy and shiftless. I better not do it." In this example, you imagine the attitude of the instructor. In so doing, you mentally take the role of the instructor and view yourself as an object or "me." It is you as the subject or "I" who decides that it would be unwise to complain. The use of the personal pronouns "I" and "me" in the statement illustrates the subject and object dimensions; the organized expecta-

Dual Perspectives
George Herbert Mead says that we mentally exchange roles with other people and so take a dual perspective. Simultaneously, we are the subject doing the viewing and the object being viewed. *(Van Bucher/Photo Researchers)*

tions of others is the "me," and your response to these expectations is the "I."

In settling on a course of action, you mentally assume a dual perspective, alternating between the "I" and the "me." Your behavior is the outcome of the internal tug and interplay between the two parts of the self. The "I" usually takes the "me" into account before acting, but at times your behavior is spontaneous, innovative, and unpredictable. This suggests that the "me" does not always keep the impulsive "I" in check. With respect to the self, then, the "I" propels behavior, while the "me" directs it.

Mind: Thought as inner conversation

Mead says that the key to the development of the self is the ability to use language. By carrying on an internal conversation—talking and responding to oneself—we arouse the same sentiments in ourselves that we do in others. Essentially we say to ourselves, "If I want to get this person to respond this way, what will it require? What would it take to get me to act in this fashion?" Consider what you do when you want a friend to accompany you to a movie. You say to yourself, "If this were me, I would go to a movie with a friend only if I did not have something better planned. So I had better find out what my friend is doing this evening and convince him (her) that it is a great movie." Next, you run through in your mind what you believe is a likely scenario. You may picture yourself talking with your friend and telling your friend why the movie is an especially good one. But then you recall, "My friend said he (she) was going to the library to study

this evening." You try to think up a convincing argument that will get around this obstacle ("This is the last day the movie is playing and you can study tomorrow evening instead!"). For Mead, then, thought is an internal conversation. Symbols—particularly vocal ones—allow us to re-create the external world internally in our minds.

Fashioning action

Sociologist Ralph Turner (1968) has clarified and extended Mead's ideas on the self. Turner points out that when speaking and acting, we typically adopt a state of *preparedness* for certain kinds of responses from the other person. If you complain to a co-worker about a headache, comment to a classmate about a professor's lecture, grimace at a child's misbehavior, or embrace a friend, you expect that the other person will respond with some action that will appropriately fit your own: The co-worker will offer sympathy, the classmate will agree with the comment, the child will stop the behavior, or the friend will return the embrace. As the other person responds, you enter a phase of *testing* and *revision*. You mentally appraise the other's behavior, and determine whether or not it accords with your expectations. To do so, you have to assign meaning to the behavior. For instance, you evaluate whether your co-worker's expression of sympathy was sincere or contained a note of sarcasm. You then plan your next course of action. If the person responds in an unanticipated manner, you might terminate the interaction, attempt to "go back" and reassert your original intention, disregard the other's response, or abandon your initial course of action and follow the other person's lead.

Genesis of the self   According to Mead, children typically pass through three stages in developing a self: an imitation stage, a play stage, and a game stage. In the first stage, children imitate other people without understanding what they are doing. They may "read" a book, but the behavior lacks meaning for them. Even so, such imitation is important because children are preparing themselves to take the stance of others and act as they do. In the play stage, children act such roles as mother, police officer, teacher, Mrs. Elliot, and so on. They take the role of only one other person at a time and "try on" the person's behavior. The model, typically a person central to the child's life, is termed by sociologists a **sig-**

nificant other. For instance, a 2-year-old child may examine a doll's pants, pretend to find them wet, and reprimand the doll. Presumably the child views the situation from the perspective of the parent and acts as the parent would act.

Whereas in the play stage children take the role of only one other person at a time, in the game stage they assume many roles. Much like a baseball game, a person must take into account the intentions and expectations of several people. For instance, if the batter bunts the ball down the third base line, the pitcher must know what the catcher, the shortstop, and the first, second, and, third basemen will do. In the game, children must assume the roles of numerous individuals in contrast to simply the role of one other person. To do so, they must abstract a "composite" role out of the concrete roles of particular

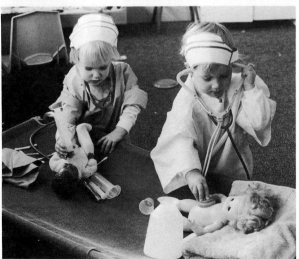

The Development of the Self
George Herbert Mead believed that children pass through three stages in fashioning a self. In the imitation stage (top left), they reenact what another person is doing without understanding the significance of the behavior. In the play stage (bottom left), children take on the role of another person and experiment with the behavior. In the game stage (bottom right), they broaden their perspective to encompass the points of view of many people at the same time; all the players must know the responses associated with the other positions and take these responses into account in devising their own behavior. *(clockwise from bottom: Martin Rogers/Woodfin Camp & Associates; Michael Siluk/EKM-Nepenthe; Joel Gordon)*

people. These notions are extended to embrace all people in similar situations—the "team." In other words,
children fashion a **generalized other**—they come to
view their behavior from the standpoint of the larger
group or community.

To think about our behavior, then, is to interact
mentally with ourselves from the viewpoint of an abstract
community of people. The generalized other is the
mechanism by which we become a society in miniature.
We incorporate—*internalize*—the organized attitudes
of our society within our own personalities. External social control becomes internal self-control. Without these
shared attitudes, there could be neither the self nor a
community life. Simultaneously, society is continuously
re-created through the dynamic interplay between the
"I" and the "me" and the behavior that results from it.
Society shapes the self and the self shapes society. Since
the person is the other side of the society coin, this view
leads to an image of the person as a structure of statuses
and roles that, when internalized, is the self. The basic
building blocks of social structure are the ingredients
from which the self is fashioned (Stryker, 1980).

Socialization across the Life Span

Socialization continues across the entire life span. Because the world about us changes, we also change. The
self is not carved in granite, somehow finalized for all
time in childhood. Life is adaptation—a process of constant renewing and remaking. Two-year-olds are socialized within the patterns of the day-care center, medical
students within their chosen profession, new employees
within an office or plant, a bride and groom within a
new family, the upwardly mobile to a new social class,
religious converts within a denomination, a new member to the League of Women Voters, and elderly patients
within a nursing home. Whenever we assume a new role
or join a new group, we learn new expectations and new
identities.

Types of Socialization

During the early years we are introduced to the basic
ways of our society—language, norms, values, and beliefs. We mastered the information and skills essential for
participating in the routines that compose daily life and
evolve a self, processes termed **primary socialization.**
Early socialization differs from later socialization in a

number of ways. For one thing, primary socialization is
directed chiefly toward such elementary matters as toilet
training and language competence. Adult socialization,
in contrast, requires a synthesis of existing elements, and
the addition of new ingredients. For another, later socialization focuses on realism rather than idealism. Children are taught to be honest and not to lie. Later they
learn that telling "little white lies" is appropriate behavior. And whereas primary socialization centers on imparting underlying societal values and motives, adult
socialization is usually considered satisfactory as long as
what a person says and does is acceptable (Brim, 1966).

As we move across the life course from infancy to
old age, we continually adopt new roles and shed old
ones, what sociologists term **role transition.** In the transitional periods, we commonly experience uncertainty
about what is expected of us and feel some measure of
strain between our inner self and the role. But in due
course we learn the role demands, and accept and redefine them to achieve a comfortable fit between the two.
In brief, we make adjustments in values, beliefs, behaviors, and self-image.

Role socialization frequently involves three phases
(Mortimer and Simmons, 1978). First, you think about,
experiment with, and try on the behaviors associated
with a new role—**anticipatory socialization.** For example, children informally acquaint themselves with such
adult roles as spouse and parent by "playing house."
Modern societies are also ordered in ways that formally
structure preparation for many new roles. Schools and
colleges are designed to transmit various skills, conferences and seminars to familiarize a firm's staff with its
operating procedures, apprenticeships to transmit specialized knowledge, and intern programs to acquaint
new physicians with medical procedures. Rehearsing
eases the transition into new statuses and groups. Second, once you adopt a new status, you find that you
must continually alter, adapt, and remake your roles to
fit changing circumstances. For example, a newly married couple must evolve new interpersonal skills because
much of the marital role is hidden by parents from their
children. Third, as we move through the life course, we
not only enter roles, but we disengage or exit from many
of them. Rituals such as graduation exercises, marriage,
retirement banquets, funerals, and other rites of passage
are socially established mechanisms for easing many
transitions.

Some role transitions require **resocialization**—the
learning of new patterns for behavior that run counter to
previously acquired patterns. Very likely your college

experiences have caused you to question and discard a number of your family's cherished values, beliefs, and customs and to replace them with others. Similarly, people who suddenly find themselves paralyzed or disabled have to relinquish earlier roles and identities and take on new expectations and self-definitions. And as we noted in Chapter 5, facilities such as prisons, monasteries, army boot camps, and mental hospitals are specifically designed to restructure people's lives. Erving Goffman (1961) has called these environments **total institutions**—places where people are isolated from the rest of society for an appreciable period of time and where their behavior is tightly regimented. Here "inmates" or "recruits" are exposed to resocialization experiences that systematically attempt to strip away old roles and identities and fashion new ones.

Agencies of Socialization

Since children are uninitiated in the ways of culture, the birth of new generations subjects society to a recurrent "barbarian invasion." Most infants are fairly malleable in the sense that within broad limits they are capable of becoming adults of quite different sorts. Through socialization, children become inducted into a society's cultural ways. As a related consequence, they may become more or less unfit for participation in many other societies. Anthropologist Edmund Carpenter (1965:55) recounts the difficulties he experienced when he lived for a period among the Aivilik, an Eskimo people:

> For months after I first arrived among the Aivilik, I felt empty, clumsy. I never knew what to do, even where to sit or stand. I was awkward in a busy world, as helpless as a child, yet a grown man. I felt like a mental defective.

Only as Carpenter learned the cultural patterns of the Aivilik and was accepted by them did he feel comfortable in the new setting.

In short, as an infant, you were born into a social environment; you could remain alive only in this environment; and from birth on you took your place in this environment. A number of *agencies of socialization* transformed you into a social being and equipped you for life in a social environment. Four agencies are especially important channels of cultural transmission: the family, the peer group, the school, and the mass media.

The family   In most cases, the family not only gets children first, it gets them during their most plastic phase and maintains an intensive and continuous relationship with them until they reach maturity. No other institution seriously rivals the family in its molding of the child. It is within the family that children acquire the chief facets of their personalities—those relatively enduring ways that people have for dealing with others in a wide variety of situations (for instance, friendliness, generosity, and aggressiveness). The family is the intermediary between the larger society and the child and is the chief culture-transmitting agency. Preparing children for membership within society is at best a long and tedious process. So the social fabrication of youngsters ideally should begin as soon as possible.

The family also plays a critical part in children's socialization because in many spheres of life other people locate the child in the social structure in terms of his or her family membership. As we noted in Chapter 4, a substantial number of ascribed statuses—social class, ethnic group, race, and religion—are assigned us on this basis. It is hardly surprising, then, that in some respects members of different social classes experience somewhat different conditions of life, come to see the world somewhat differently, develop different notions of social reality, and are prepared for somewhat different careers. Sociologist Melvin Kohn (1977) finds that white-collar parents stress the development of internal standards of conduct in their children. Consequently, they are more likely to discipline the child on the basis of their interpretation of the child's *intent*, or motive, for an act. Blue-collar parents, in contrast, place greater emphasis on conformity and tend to react to the *consequences* of the behavior. For instance, middle-class parents are more likely to punish children when they "lose their temper" than when they engage in "wild play"; working-class parents are equally likely to punish children in both situations because they are primarily concerned with the disruptive consequences of the behaviors. In recent years, however, the childrearing practices of American social classes have increasingly converged (Erlanger, 1974; Wright and Wright, 1976; Ellis, Lee, and Petersen, 1978).

Even so, parent-child relationships differ so much, both within the same family and among families, that in many respects each parent-child relation is unique. The Norman Rockwell portrait of the traditional family—the breadwinning husband greeted by the homemaker wife and kids—was prevalent in the early 1950s, when more than 60 percent of American families fitted that stereotype; today, less than 20 percent of all families look like that. Now there are many more single-parent families, stepfamilies, and two-income families (see Chapter 13). Other subtleties also operate. A child's position in the family (birth order) and the number and sex of siblings have major consequences for the child's development and socialization. For instance, an only child, an oldest child, a middle child, and a youngest child all seem to experience a somewhat different world because of the different social webs that encompass their lives. Reflecting these differences, first-borns are overrepresented in college populations, at the higher IQ levels, among National Merit and Rhodes scholars, in *Who's Who in America*, among American presidents (52 percent), and in the astronaut corps. However, later-borns seem to possess better social skills and are more popular among their classmates (Vander Zanden, 1985).

Peer groups   Across the life span we find ourselves immersed in countless relationships. Few are more important to us than those we have with our **peers**— individuals who are approximately the same age. Even at 10 to 12 months of age, youngsters will occasionally smile at one another, offer and accept toys, imitate each other, and struggle over or fuss about toys. By 2 years, children are capable of integrating their activities and engaging in social play (Eckerman, Whatley, and Kutz, 1975; Gottman, 1983). And children as young as 3 form friendships with other children that are surprisingly similar to those of adults (Rubin, 1980). Although young children may lack the insight that many adults bring to their relationships, they nevertheless often invest their friendships with an intense emotional quality. With increasing age, peer relationships are more likely to be formed and more likely to be successful (Brownell, 1986).

Peer groups serve a variety of functions. First, they provide an arena in which children can exercise independence from adult controls. And at adolescence, they furnish an impetus for young people to seek greater freedom. Second, peer groups give children experience with relationships in which they are on an equal footing with others. In the adult world, in contrast, children occupy the position of subordinates, with adults directing, guiding, and controlling their activities. But group living also calls for relationships characterized by sociability, self-assertion, competition, cooperation, and mutual understanding among equals—types of experiences offered by peer groups. Third, peer groups afford a social sphere in which the position of children is not marginal. In them, youngsters can acquire status and achieve an identity in which their own activities and concerns are paramount.

And fourth, peer groups are agencies for the transmission of informal knowledge, sexual information, deviant behaviors, superstitions, folklore, fads, jokes, riddles, and games. Peers are as necessary to children's development as adults are; the complexity of social life requires that children be involved in networks both of adults and peers.

The school   We commonly think of schools as agencies that provide formal, conscious, and systematic training. But schools teach more than the skills and information specified in the academic curriculum. Whether intentionally or unwittingly, they impart a whole complex of unarticulated values, attitudes, and behaviors—what is termed the **hidden curriculum.** Students learn not only from the official courses of study, but from the physical environment of the school, the attitudes teachers and pupils exhibit toward one another, the social climate, and the bureaucratic organization of the school.

The behaviors constituting the hidden curriculum are modeled by teachers and reinforced by them in their dealings with students. The characteristics preferred by teachers are those that embody middle-class values and morality—industry, responsibility, conscientiousness, reliability, thoroughness, self-control, efficiency, and emotional stability. These behaviors resemble those of the workplace and the marketplace, where the emphasis is on economically ambitious, materialistic, competitive, and conforming behavior.

Even first-graders learn the importance of "getting ahead." For instance, in working with reading series, 6-year-olds see that the main function of each task is to allow them to get to the next task—to finish the blue unit so they can get to the more advanced orange one, then to the purple one, and so on. And they become "social diagnosticians"—they throw out answers and guesses on the basis of the teacher's cues, smiles, nods, and body language, rather than focusing on the problem at hand (Radloff, 1975).

The mass media   Our capacity to learn from watching, as well as from doing, means that the mass media have important socialization consequences for us. The **mass media** consist of those organizations—television, radio, motion pictures, newspapers, and magazines—that convey information to a large segment of the public. All the mass media educate. The question is: What are they teaching? The good news from research is that prosocial (positive and helpful) models can have prosocial effects (Friedrich and Stein, 1975; Ball-Rokeach, Rokeach, and

Schools: Formal Agencies of Socialization
The members of a society may establish schools to train youths for roles they consider to be important. Here women are taught dancing skills at a school in Bali, Indonesia. *(Mary Ellen Mark/Archive)*

Grube, 1984). Children who view a prosocial television diet, including such programs as *Sesame Street* and *Mr. Roger's Neighborhood*, exhibit greater levels of helping behaviors, cooperation, sharing, and self-control than children who view a neutral or violent diet. Moreover, these programs have a positive effect on language development. The mass media have also contributed to anti-smoking campaigns by disseminating information on the relationship between smoking and lung cancer (McGuire, 1985; Roberts and Maccoby, 1985).

The bad news from television research is that there is a link between the mayhem and violence on children's programs and aggressive behavior in children. Although televised violence does not harm every child who watches it, many children imitate the violent attitudes and behaviors they see. Prime-time programs depict about 5 violent acts per hour, and Saturday-morning cartoons average 20 to 25 violent acts per hour (Coughlin, 1985). By the time most young people leave high school, they have spent more time before a television screen than in the classroom (see Figure 6.3). In the process they will have witnessed some 13,000 murders. Television not only provides opportunities for children and adults to learn new aggressive skills, it also weakens inhibitions against behaving in the same way. And television violence increases the toleration of aggression in real life—a "psychic numbing" effect—and reinforces the tendency to view the world as a dangerous place (Pearl, 1982; Singer, Singer, and Rapaczynski, 1984).

Complexity of socialization Although the family, the peer group, the school, and the mass media are major socializing agencies, all groups impart values, attitudes, beliefs, and norms to their members. Religious, work, business, youth, military, and recreational groups also influence people, although the various agencies may transmit different, and even conflicting, standards (see the box on corporate socialization on pages 160–161). Indeed, none of the agencies operate in a vacuum.

FIGURE 6.3 **Hours of Television Watched Weekly by Children Age 2 to 11**
Source: Why children's TV turns off so many parents. U.S. News & World Report, *February 18, 1985, p. 65.*

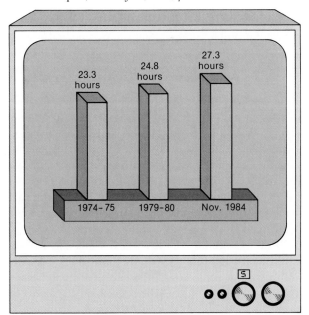

CULTIVATING A SOCIOLOGICAL CONSCIOUSNESS

Corporate Socialization

Corporations have cultures that foster a feeling of community among their members. Shared values, rules, beliefs, and legends supply employees with "horse sense"—what is "smart" and "approved" behavior. And they have invisible, matter-of-fact customs telling people how they are to relate to colleagues, subordinates, superiors, and outsiders. Some corporate cultures are strong; others are weak. In strong cultures, employees know the corporation's goals and how to attain them. Weak corporate cultures lack clear guidelines about how employees are to succeed (Deal and Kennedy, 1982). To illustrate, before its restructuring in 1984, AT&T had a solid tradition of service and quality built up over more than a hundred years. Employees knew the corporate legends of brave Bell System linemen fighting floods and blizzards to repair downed telephone wires. The breaking up of the Bell System had a pro-

Corporate Socialization
To function effectively in an organization, newcomers must come to know "how things are done around here." Much of corporate culture is subtle. For instance, one has to learn what are and are not appropriate topics for humor. *(John Coletti/The Picture Cube)*

found impact on its culture. Because AT&T no longer operates in a regulated environment, the company confronts fierce challenges from competitors. In the new environment, its leaders have had to downgrade earlier conservative traditions of caretaking to promote risk taking and competitive marketing.

Corporate socialization is the process by which organizational outsiders are transformed into organizational insiders. Newcomers are taught "the ropes" and fitted into corporate

Rather, the socialization process can best be described in terms of multiple, mutual interactions among the agencies and the person in question.

Any influence must be considered as only one among a good many contending forces. For example, heavy viewing of televised violence is followed by later aggression in daily life, but only under certain circumstances. More aggressive children identify more strongly than other children with aggressive television characters. And they are more likely to believe the shows they watch are an accurate reflection of life. Environmental factors are also closely linked to aggression: More aggressive children tend to do more poorly in school, are unpopular with peers, have aggressive mothers, and have parents with little education and low social status (Huesmann, Lagerspetz, and Eron, 1984). In sum, then, behavior results from the interaction of predispositions and experiences; no two children will respond to a potentially aggressive situation in precisely the same manner.

THINKING THROUGH THE ISSUES

Why is socialization always incomplete? Do you come into the world a social blank, devoid of biological needs or drives? Are the socializing influences of your class, ethnic, family, peer, religious, and occupational groups necessarily consistent or harmonious? When groups take pains to teach you certain rules, are they implicitly suggesting that it is possible to break the rules? If you were completely socialized, would you and the other members of society be capable of creative and innovative adaptations to the environment? In other words, can you be a *social* animal without being entirely a *socialized* animal?

life. A firm's culture comes to the forefront when novices violate assumptions, provoking responses from established employees. Through advice, ridicule, criticism, shunning, and corporate stories, the uninitiated are taught about "how things are done around here." In due course, most learn their roles, develop work skills, and accommodate themselves to the group's norms and values.

Socialization starts with the hiring or "getting in" process. In job interviews, recruits may be told that they will be supervised closely in their early assignments and that they will find some aspects of their work boring. Corporations often tell interviewees about themselves to ensure realistic expectations. Some firms grill applicants and tell them the bad as well as the good, hoping they will remove themselves from contention if they feel they will not fit in. Morgan Guaranty, a New York investment banking house, encourages applicants to discuss the demands of the job with spouses, girlfriends, or boyfriends because new recruits sometimes work 100 hours a week (Pascale, 1984).

Once employees begin to work, they must gain acceptance, develop competence in their work, have a clear understanding of their jobs, and concur with the system of performance evaluation. During this "breaking in" phase, some companies subject recruits to experiences designed to shake them up and make them susceptible to corporate values and norms. Many of the procedures resemble those of military boot camps (Goffman, 1961). Employees are pressured to assume the hair styles, clothing fashions, and standardized behaviors that establish an organizational identity. And they may be given more work than they can possibly accomplish. Such practices make people psychologically and emotionally receptive to the roles and identities demanded of them by the corporation.

As new employees settle in, they are evaluated and rewarded on the basis of their performance. At IBM, employees who violate a corporation norm—for example, handling subordinates inappropriately—find themselves assigned to what is called the "penalty box" (a fairly meaningless job at the same level at a less desirable location). The penalty box lets people know that they have erred, but that they will be given another chance in the future. All the while, the company supplies employees with role models—peers and superiors who are recognized as winners and who share the firm's exemplary traits. Protégés observe role models write memos, make presentations, and handle problems, and then attempt to duplicate the performance. By socializing employees in these ways, a corporation achieves order, continuity, and consistency (Pascale, 1984).

Chapter Highlights

1. Socialization is a lifetime process of social interaction by which people acquire those behaviors essential for effective participation in society. Were it not for socialization, renewal of culture could not occur from one generation to the next. And in the absence of socialization, society could not perpetuate itself beyond a single generation. Both the individual and society are mutually dependent on socialization.

2. You are a joint product of your nature—your inherited traits—and your nurture—your experiences. Some of your behaviors may be primarily a product of nature, some of nurture, but all are shaped by differing proportions of both. They interact in various ways to provide you with a distinct personality.

3. Learning occurs across the entire life span. It allows you to adapt your behavior to changing environmental conditions. Learning occurs in two principal ways: conditioning, and observing the behavior of others. In conditioning, you establish an association or linkage between two events. In observational learning, you learn new responses by observing other people without first having had the opportunity to make the responses yourself.

4. Developmental theorists stress the different processes that come into operation at various ages. Jean Piaget says that normal children pass through four stages of cognitive development: the sensorimotor, preoperational, concrete operational, and formal operational. What is learned in one stage differs from what was learned in the preceding stage. Lawrence Kohlberg has applied Piaget's stage approach to moral development.

5. Among your early childhood achievements was a growing self-awareness—the human sense of "I." By

naming yourself as others named you, you created the self. Charles Horton Cooley contended that consciousness arises in a social context. This notion is exemplified by his concept of the looking-glass self—a process by which we imaginatively assume the stance of other people and view ourselves as we believe they see us. It consists of three phases. First, we imagine how we appear to others. Second, we imagine how others judge our appearance. And third, we develop some sort of self-feeling such as pride or mortification on the basis of what we perceive others' judgments to be.

6. George Herbert Mead elaborated upon Cooley's ideas and contributed many insights of his own. He contended that we gain a sense of selfhood by acting toward ourself in much the same fashion that we act toward others. In so doing, we "take the role of the other toward ourself." We mentally assume a dual perspective: simultaneously we are the subject or "I" doing the viewing and the object or "me" being viewed. According to Mead, children typically pass through three stages in developing a full sense of selfhood: the imitation stage, the play stage, and the game stage.

7. Socialization continues across the entire life course. At first we master the information and skills essential for participating in the routines that compose daily life and evolve a self—primary socialization. Throughout life, we continually adopt new roles and shed old ones. Such role transitions commonly involve anticipatory socialization. Other role transitions require resocialization.

8. As an infant, we are born into a social environment; we remain alive only in this environment; and from birth on we take our place in this environment. A number of agencies of socialization transform us into social beings and equip us for life in a social environment. The four major channels of cultural transmission are the family, the peer group, the school, and the mass media.

The Sociologist's Vocabulary

anticipatory socialization People think about, experiment with, and try on the behaviors associated with a new role.

cognition Mental activity; the process of thinking whereby we receive raw sensory information that we in turn transform, elaborate, store, recover, and use.

conditioning The process of learning whereby we establish an association or link between two events.

egocentric bias The tendency to place yourself at the center of events.

generalized other The term George Herbert Mead applied to that social unit that gives to individuals their unity of self. The attitude of the generalized other is the attitude of the larger community.

hidden curriculum The whole complex of unarticulated values, attitudes, and behaviors that reflect the dominant views of the community, that are imparted by the school.

learning The more or less permanent modification of behavior that results from experiences in the environment.

looking-glass self The term Charles Horton Cooley applied to the process by which we imaginatively assume the stance of other people and view ourselves as we believe they see us.

mass media Those organizations—television, radio, motion pictures, newspapers, and magazines—that convey information to a large segment of the population.

nature Inherited traits; heredity.

nurture Experiences; environment.

observational learning By watching other people, we learn new responses without first having had the opportunity to make the responses ourselves.

operant conditioning Learning in which behavior is altered in strength by its consequences.

peers Individuals who are approximately the same age.

personality Unique and enduring behavior patterns of an individual.

primary socialization The process by which a person masters the information and skills essential for participating in the routines that compose daily life and evolves a self.

reinforcement The process whereby one event strengthens the probability of another event's occurring.

resocialization The learning of new patterns for behavior that run counter to previously acquired patterns.

role transition Continually adopting new roles and shedding old ones throughout life.

self The set of concepts we use in defining who we are.

self-concept An overriding view of yourself; a sense of self through time.

self-image A temporary mental conception or picture you have of yourself that changes as you move from one situation to another.

significant other The term sociologists apply to a social model, usually an important person in a person's life.

socialization A lifetime process of social interaction by which people acquire the knowledge, attitudes, values, and behaviors essential for effective participation in society.

stages Steplike levels into which human development is divided.

total institutions Places of residence where people are isolated from the rest of society for an appreciable period of time and where their behavior is tightly regimented.

7

Social Interaction

No man is an island, entire of itself.

—John Donne, *Devotions*, 1624

How might you respond if you were to spend six months completely alone in an inaccessible weather station at the South Pole? Admiral Richard Byrd volunteered for such an experiment in 1933. He had an adequate food supply, was well stocked with reading material, was in radio contact with people he knew, and had a demanding schedule of activities. Byrd looked forward to the experience and at first found great inner peace and exhilaration. But after twenty-four days of solitude, he began to write in his diary of a "brain-cracking loneliness":

> This morning I had to admit to myself that I was lonely. Try as I may, I find I can't take my loneliness casually, it is too big. But I must not dwell on it. Otherwise I am undone.
>
> At home I usually awaken instantly, in full possession of my faculties. But that's not the case here. It takes me some minutes to collect my wits; I seem to be groping in cold reaches of interstellar space, lost and bewildered. The room is a non-dimensional darkness, without shadow or substance; even after all these days I sometimes ask myself: Where am I? What am I doing here? I discover myself straining, as if trying to hear something in a place where no sound could possibly exist. [Byrd, 1938, pp. 95–96, 1958 edition]

Byrd tried to dispel the loneliness by imagining familiar scenes and people:

> Yet, I could, with a little imagination, make every walk seem different. One day I would imagine that my path was the Esplanade, on the water side of Beacon Hill in Boston, where, in my mind's eye, I often walked with my wife. I would meet people I knew along the bank, and drink in the perfection of a Boston spring. [p. 116]

After sixty-three days of being alone, Byrd became increasingly concerned with philosophical questions and the meaning of life:

The universe is not dead. Therefore, there is an intelligence there, and it is all pervading. At least one purpose, possibly the major purpose, of that intelligence is the achievement of universal harmony. Striving in the right direction for Peace (Harmony), therefore, as well as the achievement of it, is the result of accord with that intelligence. . . . The human race, then, is not alone in the universe. Though I am cut off from human beings, I am not alone. [p. 185]

Being alone for an extended period of time is a stressful experience for most of us. Although Byrd at first found the experience exhilarating, he soon became lonely and began to feel depressed and bored. And he had volunteered for the project and was in radio contact with others. For prisoners in solitary confinement, the circumstances are different; their orientation to the world about them is often profoundly altered.

One prisoner held in solitary confinement at the Massachusetts Correctional Institution at Walpole observes: "What really freaks me out is when a bee gets into the cell—such a small thing." Many inmates report difficulties with thinking, concentration, and memory. One prisoner reports: "I can't read. . . . Your mind's narcotized . . . sometimes I can't grasp words in my mind that I know." Some experience massive free-floating anxiety. One prisoner reports "shortness of breath a lot. My heart pumps real fast. I feel like I don't get enough oxygen. Get frantic." Another said, "I start to feel dizzy. I can't breathe." In some cases, those in solitary confinement impulsively mutilate themselves. "I cut my wrists—cut myself many times when in isolation. Now, it seems crazy. But every time I did it, I wasn't thinking—lost control—cut myself without knowing what I was doing" (Grassian, 1983:1452–1453).

These isolation experiences bring into stark relief the critical part relationships with others play in our lives. Indeed, you are the center of a good many social networks that link you to a rather large number of people. One network links you to your professor and classmates in your sociology course; other networks have strands that tie you to roommates, friends, parents, and perhaps coworkers. *Social interaction*, the topic of this chapter, is the essence of these relationships.

PLANNING AHEAD: TARGETED READING

1. What insights do each of the following perspectives provide regarding the nature of social interaction: symbolic interaction, dramaturgy, ethnomethodology, and social exchange?

2. How do we go about sizing up other people so that we know how to interact with them?

3. How do we transmit information, ideas, attitudes, and mental states to one another?

4. In what ways does physical space affect us as we interact with one another?

5. Why do we seek out other people and associate with them?

6. Under what circumstances are we likely to help others and expect no benefit to ourselves?

7. What does the prisoner's dilemma game tell us about people working with and against one another?

Perspectives on Social Interaction

Social life consists of the actions of people or, more precisely, social actions. **Social action** is behavior oriented to or influenced by other people. Whatever you do—wave to a friend, drive a car in traffic, ask your professor a question, cheer your team to victory, or call a relative on the telephone—you must immerse yourself in the world of others. What you say and do constitutes a flowing and developing process. You organize, bend, redirect, and forge your actions as you take other people into account. Indeed, the mere presence of another person influences your behavior (Guerin, 1986). For instance, while you are studying at the library, you may worry that the person at the next table will in some way evaluate you. Or you may have difficulty concentrating because you find the behavior of the other person distracting.

Very likely, while you are taking other people into account, they are simultaneously taking you into account. The result is **social interaction**—the mutual and reciprocal influencing by two or more people of each other's behavior. Put another way, social interaction consists of the interplay between your actions and those of other people. It is the building block that makes all other forms of social life possible. Without it, you could not acquire the knowledge and skills that permit you to become a functioning member of society. And without social interaction, organized society—family, political, economic, religious, and educational groups and institutions—would be impossible (see Chapter 4).

When we study social interaction, we examine behavior at the microsociological level. Microsociology involves the detailed study of what people say, do, and think moment by moment as they go about their daily lives. In contrast, macrosociology focuses on large-scale and long-term social processes. Microsociology is the province of **social psychology**—the scientific study of the nature and causes of social interaction and behavior. Many leading sociologists, including Charles Horton Cooley, George Herbert Mead, Emile Durkheim, Max Weber, and Georg Simmel, have dealt with social psychological matters as an integral part of their sociological studies. There are a number of sociological perspectives on social interaction, and each affords distinctive insights. The symbolic interactionist, dramaturgical, ethnomethodological, and social exchange perspectives all share a microsociological emphasis.

Symbolic Interaction: Fitting Actions Together

Symbolic interactionists say that we live our lives in both a symbolic and a physical environment. We mentally reflect on and interpret what goes on about us. We do not respond directly to the images, sounds, and sensations we receive from our sense organs; we first assign them meanings and then formulate actions based on these meanings. For example, a shirt is not merely a collection of visual, aural, and tactile stimuli. We give meaning to it by defining it as an "item of clothing" rather than a "cleaning cloth," "a bedspread," or a "flag." We may also infer from the design and quality of a shirt something about a person's social position and

Fitting Our Actions Together
Symbolic interactionists emphasize that people must continually fashion meanings and devise ways to link their actions in meaningful ways. Consequently, much of human behavior has a tentative and developing quality: People map, test, suspend, and revise their actions in response to the actions of others. *(Alan Mercer)*

rank. Indeed, we standardize some shirts as uniforms so that we can quickly discern a person's gender or occupation. At times we may even impute magical powers to a particular shirt as a "good luck" piece. In sum, we organize our behavior by the meanings we assign to our experiences. Without the assignment of meanings, our actions would become random and disorganized. Symbolic interactionists therefore say our definitions of the situation are critical to social interaction.

Definition of the situation   A **definition of the situation** is the interpretation we give to our immediate circumstances. We mentally represent our environment in symbolic terms so that we can size it up and make a preliminary assessment of the courses of action available to us. As viewed by symbolic interactionists, "facts" do not have an inherent or independent existence apart from the people who observe and assign meaning to them. "Real" facts are the ways in which people define various situations. A man mowing the lawn may be seen as beautifying his yard, avoiding his wife, getting exercise, supporting neighborhood property values, annoying a neighbor who is trying to sleep, or earning a living.

Although our definitions of the situation may differ, it is only as we arrive at common understandings that we are able to fit our action to the actions of other people. If you are to purchase toothpaste, rob a store, make love, cross a busy intersection, or sing in a church choir, you must attribute a similar meaning to the situation that others do. Only in this way can you achieve *joint* action with people. And once you arrive at a definition of the situation, you and others may carry it over to future occasions. Indeed, we can manage our lives as members of society because our definitions of most things roughly coincide. Viewed in this fashion, culture is the agreed-upon meanings—the shared definitions of situations—that we acquire as members of a society. Socialization is the process by which these shared definitions are transmitted from one generation to the next.

The Thomas theorem   Symbolic interactionists say that we *construct* reality by means of definitions. Sociologist William I. Thomas (1931:189) captured this insight in what has become known as the **Thomas theorem:** "If men [people] define situations as real, they are real in their consequences." The Thomas theorem draws our attention to the fact that we respond not only to the objective features of a situation, but also to the meaning the situation has for us. Once the meaning has been assigned, it serves to shape not only what we do or fail to

do, but also some of the consequences of our behavior. Suppose a rumor—a false definition—spreads that a certain bank is going bankrupt. A run starts on the bank as people try to withdraw their funds. Then, because no bank can immediately honor all claims upon it, the bank is forced to close. No conspiracy existed to make the false definition come true. Fulfillment occurred unintentionally when people acted *as if* it were true.

In race relations, the Thomas theorem contributes to minority disadvantage. If we think of blacks, whites, Chinese, or Jews as having certain characteristics, whether these beliefs are true or not, our definitions will influence our behavior. Throughout history, strongly negative ideas have periodically led to genocide and warfare. Generations of American whites, for example, held blacks to be racially inferior. Since whites controlled the centers of institutional power, they allocated blacks a lesser share of the privileges and opportunities of American society. By acting upon their racist definitions, whites fashioned institutional arrangements in which blacks are less well educated, hold more menial jobs, live in poorer housing, and enjoy poorer health than whites. So whites have *created* a social order characterized by institutional discrimination (see Chapter 10).

Negotiated action and order   As depicted by functionalists, social order seems to flow spontaneously from the fact that we obey rules, play our roles appropriately, and use culturally standardized procedures for dealing with everyday problems. If men are adequately socialized, they will know how and when to be fathers, breadwinners, or husbands, and their behavior will be integrated and coordinated with that of women as well as that of other men. Women will know the expectations for their behavior. Should men or women fail to play their roles appropriately, mechanisms of social control come into play (Hewitt, 1979).

Symbolic interactionists say that however elegant this vision may be, it scarcely does justice to what actually happens in everyday life. When we examine joint action, we see that the coordination of activities is produced by self-conscious effort. We achieve this coordinated activity and social order by bargaining, deliberating, reaching agreements, concluding temporary understandings, and deciding to suspend the rules. For example, the life of a middle-class American family can be described as a *negotiated order* among people who often have conflicting interests, competing demands on their time, and divided loyalties. The stuff of everyday family life consists of earning a living, maintaining peace among the children, finding time to do things around the house, reaching a compromise on the family vacation, and finding a balance between the husband's and wife's job (Hewitt, 1979).

In sum, symbolic interactionists see social action as something that develops in a tentative, groping, advancing, backtracking, and sounding out process. It is as if people "feel" their way along. They begin an act and fail to complete it. They disengage from a relationship or become further involved to the point of commitment (Cohen, 1965). Inherent in this vision is the idea that the essence of social interaction and order is negotiation. Indeed, social reality itself is negotiated in the course of social interaction. Things take on meaning through a process in which tentatively held definitions of the situation are repeatedly tested and reformulated on the basis of social experience (Stryker and Statham, 1985).

Dramaturgy: Staging Behavior

If situations do not define themselves but must be constructed through symbolic communication, then social life resembles a theater where reality is also constructed. Sociologist Erving Goffman (1959, 1983), in fact, portrays the social world as a natural theater, a perspective termed **dramaturgy**. For Goffman, we are both actors and members of the audience, and our parts are the roles we play in our daily lives. He takes great pains to show how the revelations and concealments that are the strengths of great drama are also the stuff of social interaction. In fact, theater is possible only because life is theatrical to begin with. Often we cannot draw a line between fiction and reality—between a stage, where the actors presumably know they are engaged in make-believe, and everyday life, where most of us believe that we are not (Wilshire, 1982; Perinbanayagam, 1982, 1985).

Impression management   One way life is like a theater is that we attempt to control the reality other people see. Goffman (1959) points out that only by influencing other people's ideas of us can we hope to predict or control what happens to us. We have a stake in presenting ourselves to others in ways that will lead them to view us in a favorable light, a process he labels **impression management**. We provide an audience with a definition of who and what we are in the hope that they will find us believable. And we seek to conceal behavior incompatible with the image we seek to project. For instance, we may attempt to hide errors we make and the steps we take

to correct them. Taxi drivers often attempt to cover up when they mistakenly take a passenger in the wrong direction. Or we may show only the end product and conceal the process involved. Young professors fresh out of graduate school frequently spend hours preparing and rehearsing a lecture because they want to appear "knowledgeable" to their students. You are probably aware of engaging in impression management when deciding what to wear for certain occasions, such as a party, a physician's appointment, a job interview, or a date. Indeed, as we note in the box on page 170, clothing is a key component of impression management.

Impression management also occurs in organizational life. Take the public lecture sponsored by a college or civic group. Goffman (1981) notes that the imparting of information is largely a pretext for an event that will allow the eminence of the speaker to confer prestige on the audience and the sponsoring organization. This fact helps explain the elaborate introductions, advertising, and publicity. Goffman contends that advertising is not done in anticipation of an informative talk by a prominent speaker. Rather, a prominent speaker is a device to present something that warrants wide advertising.

Front regions and back regions   Goffman (1959) carries his analogy between the stage and social interaction still further. In social interaction there is a **front region,** a place that parallels the stage seen by the audience. Both actors on stage and people in real life are interested in their appearance, wear costumes, and use props. There is also a **back region,** a place offstage where actors retire to prepare themselves for their performance. Here, away from an audience, we engage in behavior that contradicts the impressions we are attempting to convey and that we seek to screen from the audience's view. We "let down our hair," criticize outsiders, squabble with one another.

Goffman illustrates the distinction between front and back regions by describing the changes that occur in the behavior of waiters and waitresses as they move from the kitchen to the dining room. As the nature of the audience changes, so does their behavior. "Frontstage" in the dining room, they display a servile demeanor to the guests. "Backstage" in the kitchen, they openly ridicule the servility they must display "frontstage." Further, they seal off the dirty work of food preparation—the gristle, grease, and foul odors of spoiled food—from the appetizing and enticing "frontstage" atmosphere. Social bonds are typically strong among people who share com-

CULTIVATING A SOCIOLOGICAL CONSCIOUSNESS

Dressing for Effect

"Dress for success" is a persistent theme in American life. As early as 1772, a tract published in Philadelphia was entitled "Clothes Make Men." More than 200 years later, the piece still contains advice that is contemporary:

How can the world help it, that a great soul hides itself in a mean garment? This world is a stage, and on a stage we only take those for princes who appear in a princely dress. Not every one has patience enough to wait for the last scene, and the unraveling of the play. Let us change the clothes, and we shall find the world very equitable. [quoted by Lauer and Handel, 1983:168]

Clothing is a key source of information about people. Within seconds of encountering strangers, we confidently make assessments about their religious, political, and ethnic backgrounds and snap judgments about their social, professional, or sexual desirability. Clothes play a critical part in the conclusions we reach by providing clues to who people are, who they are not, and who they would like to be. They tell us a good deal about the wearer's background, personality, status, mood, and social outlook (Lauer and Lauer, 1981; Solomon, 1986).

Since clothes are such an important source of social information, we can use them to manipulate people's impression of us. Our appearance assumes particular significance in the initial phases of interaction and establishes the range of interaction that is likely to occur. An elderly middle-class man or woman may be alienated

Clothing: A Critical Source of Information
Based on their appearance, what do you conclude about each of these women? How does their clothing influence your perception of their roles, personality, and social ranking? If you were to strike up a conversation with each woman, how would your inferences affect your choice of topics and the levity of the encounter? *(left, Barbara Alper/Stock, Boston; middle, Christiana Dittmann/Rainbow; right, Bohdan Hrynewyc/Stock, Boston)*

by a young adult who looks like a punk, regardless of the person's education, background, or interests. In this sense, appearance defines the "universe" in which interaction is initiated and influences whether it starts off with friendliness, neutrality, or hostility (Lauer and Handel, 1983).

People tend to agree on what certain types of clothes mean. Adolescent girls can easily agree on the lifestyles of girls who wear certain outfits, including the number of boyfriends they likely have had and whether they smoke or drink. Newscasters are deemed more credible, honest, and competent when they are dressed conservatively. And college students who view themselves as taking an active role in their interpersonal relationships say they are concerned about the costumes they must wear to play these roles successfully. Moreover, many of us can relate instances in which the clothing we wore changed the way we felt about ourselves and how we acted. Perhaps you have used clothing to

gain confidence when you anticipated a stressful situation, such as a first date, a court appearance, or a job interview (Solomon, 1986).

In the workplace, men have long had well-defined precedents and role models for achieving success. It has been otherwise for women. A good many women in the business world are uncertain about the appropriate mixture of "masculine" and "feminine" attributes they should convey by their professional clothing. The array of clothing alternatives available to women has also been greater than that available for men. Male executives tend to appraise women more favorably for managerial positions when the women display less "feminine" grooming—shorter hair, moderate use of cosmetics, and plain tailored clothing. As one male executive confided, "A sexy-looking woman is definitely going to get a longer interview, but she won't get a job" (Solomon, 1986:28).

mon back regions, because they must trust one another to guard their secret strategies toward outsiders.

Although Goffman is commonly classed by sociologists with interactionists, his work departs in significant ways from traditional symbolic interactionist formulations (Gonos, 1977). Symbolic interactionists see each situation as freshly built up piece by piece out of the peculiar combinations of activities and meanings that operate in a particular setting. Goffman (1974) depicts social life as "frames"—structures—that have an invisible but real existence behind the visible social transactions of everyday life. These basic frameworks of understandings provide the stable rules people use in fashioning their behavior. Thus Goffman (1983) sees action as guided more by a mechanical adherence to rules—much as we follow the rules of syntax found in a language—than by an active, ongoing process of interpersonal negotiation.

Ethnomethodology: Uncovering the Rules

Symbolic interactionists suggest that social reality is what we believe it to be. If this is true, how do we go about constructing in our own minds and conversations a view of social life that is orderly and patterned? How do we analyze events so that they appear to be connected? What procedures do we use to investigate our activities and report them? How do we establish the factual character of our interpretations and accounts? These are the questions addressed by sociologist Harold Garfinkel (1964, 1967) and a number of his colleagues (Zimmerman and Wieder, 1970; Mehan and Wood, 1975). They have undertaken to describe the common, taken-for-granted activities that constitute our daily experience by an approach they call ethnomethodology. *Ethno*, borrowed from the Greek, means "people" or "folk," while *methodology* refers to the procedures by which something is done or analyzed. So in its most literal sense, **ethnomethodology** refers to the procedures—the rules and activities—that we use to make social life and society intelligible to ourselves and others (Garfinkel, 1974).

Ethnomethodologists build on the insights of the German social philosopher Alfred Schutz (1967). Schutz observes that in our daily experience, we assume that a real world exists "out there" independent of our experience of it. He contends that this view reflects a certain mind set; other mind sets suggest a world with quite different characteristics. These include such "realities" as dreams, hypnotic states, hallucinations, and the

theater. With different premises and types of logic, we create different worlds. Ethnomethodologists investigate how we go about creating and sustaining for one another the *presumption* that there is an external social reality and order. More particularly, they study the background understandings that supply the material out of which stable social interaction emerges.

One method that Garfinkel has used in his studies is the **demonstration experiment.** He introduces a nasty surprise into a situation in order to reveal its masked expectations. Garfinkel may fail to perform acts that others expect or perform acts that they have no reason to expect. For instance, he has his students get into a conversation and then ask for a clarification of meanings (Garfinkel, 1967:42–43):

> Subject: Hi, Ray. How is your girlfriend feeling?
> Experimenter: What do you mean, "How is she feeling?" Do you mean physical or mental?
> Subject: I mean how is she feeling? What's the matter with you? [He looked peeved.]
> Experimenter: Nothing. Just explain a little clearer what you mean.
> Subject: Skip it. How are your Med school applications coming?
> Experimenter: What do you mean, "How are they?"
> Subject: You know what I mean.
> Experimenter: I really don't.
> Subject: What's the matter with you? Are you sick?

Through such methods, Garfinkel seeks to reveal the subtle understandings that are taken for granted in conversations and incidents—the "you know what I mean" aspects that characterize everyday life. Demonstration experiments wrench us out of our selves and force us to take a different perspective. We are asked to transcend ourselves, and for a brief moment wonder who we are and what we are about.

Ethnomethodologists find that we act as if reality were solid, given, and unambiguous. But the social world we communicate about is actually fluid and not easily discoverable. We do not usually ask one another to clarify statements, even when they lack clarity. We give each other the benefit of the doubt; we assume there is a solid meaning in what others say and that in due course it will be made clear. Viewed this way, the social world is a flimsy thing. But we do not realize this; we act as if it were solid and assume that what is ordinarily done is proper and necessary. We accept our roles as docile customers, clients, employees. Garfinkel illustrates the

Ethnomethodology
What insights do events like the pre-Lenten Mardi Gras celebrations in New Orleans provide regarding the nature of external social reality and order? How do they reveal some of the subtle understandings that we take for granted in everyday life? What do they tell us about rules and social structure? *(Milton Potts/Photo Researchers)*

point by having his students go into a department store and offer a small fraction of the marked price for some item. At first the students feel uncomfortable because there is an implicit understanding in most American stores that an item must be purchased for its marked price. As the students overcome their initial discomfort and begin bargaining, the salespeople become flustered and ill at ease. At times the students sense that they actually stand a chance of having their offers accepted. Clearly, the rule that "The price you see is the price you pay" has force only because everyone *assumes* it will be followed; most of that force derives from the fact that the rule is never challenged.

The ethnomethodological perspective has potentially revolutionary implications. If rules and social structures exist only because we believe they exist, then we can successfully challenge them. The everyday fabric of interpersonal ceremony, deference, politeness, and authority exists because we take it for granted. The hippies of the 1960s led a cultural revolution against constraining formal definitions by their capacity to formulate counterdefinitions of everyday realities. Of course, as we will see in Chapter 16, not all invisible social structures are so easily challenged. Behind some stands the state—the police and the army. Yet the state and its agencies exist only because enough people agree to act as if rules and governmental agencies are real things. Revolutions take place when large numbers of people come to doubt the power of the state, much the same way that a bank is destroyed when there is a run on it (Collins and Makowsky, 1984).

THINKING THROUGH THE ISSUES

In one of his experiments, Garfinkel had his students act as if they were guests and not sons or daughters when they returned home to their families. They were to address their parents as "Mr." and "Mrs.," display gracious table manners, politely ask for permission to eat a snack, and so on. Garfinkel instructed the students to maintain this polite distance for fifteen minutes to an hour. Try this experiment or a variation of it (do not engage in behavior that provokes harm to yourself or others). What unspoken assumptions regarding social interaction do you uncover? Why is it difficult for you to maintain the role? What does this tell you about social interaction? Explain why it may pay you to go along with the tacit understandings that characterize daily life. By going along with these hidden expectations, how do you contribute to your own and other people's sense that social life has structure?

Social Exchange: Marketing Ourselves

When we interact with one another, an enormous number of things happen all at once. No theoretical perspective can possibly encompass all the dimensions of social interaction; nor can we comprehend them all at once. The aim of any perspective is to distinguish a few features and subject them to close scrutiny (Emerson, 1981). This is the task the **social exchange** perspective sets for itself. It depicts us as "social bookkeepers" who order relationships by maintaining a mental ledger of rewards, costs, and profits. *Rewards* are anything we will incur costs to obtain. *Costs* are whatever we attempt to avoid. And *profits* are rewards less costs. We exchange not only money and material things, but also social goods—affection, security, prestige, and information. In so doing we use a "minimax" strategy—we minimize costs and maximize rewards. Most of us do not keep track of the good and bad things about a relationship in an organized way. But we do focus on the overall outcome, a process reflected in such statements as "I'm really getting a lot out of this relationship," or "I don't think it's worth it anymore."

In this view, social interaction consists of an exchange of activity between at least two people that involves both rewards and costs. Assume, for instance, that you and I are co-workers. I am constantly asking you for advice, and you provide me with it. You and I are engaged in an exchange. I exchange my approval, recognition, and gratitude for your help. You exchange your help for my approval, recognition, and gratitude. Both you and I are rewarded. But we also face some costs. I suffer in self-esteem; you find that I disrupt your work schedule. So long as you and I find profit (reward minus cost) in the relationship, we are likely to continue it, much as in marketplace decisions. But we will end the relationship when the expected benefits are no longer forthcoming.

Sociologist Peter Blau (1967) contends that we end up with the friends, lovers, and marriage partners we "deserve." If we want to reap the benefits of associating with others, we must offer our partners enough to make it worth their while to remain in the relationship. The more people have to offer, the greater will be the demand for their company. Others will have to offer more if they hope to win the friendship of popular people. In this fashion, the principle of supply and demand ensures that we get only the partners we can socially "afford." Social exchange theory emphasizes that we make comparative judgments; we assess the profits we get from one person against the profits we get from another.

Social exchange underlies the **norm of reciprocity,** the social rule that we should help (and not harm) those who help us (Gouldner, 1960). It finds expression in maxims like "One good turn deserves another," and "You scratch my back and I'll scratch yours." More broadly, the norm of reciprocity embodies the expectation that we return good for good and evil for evil. In addition to its positive aspect, then, the norm of reciprocity has a negative component, one embodied in the ancient code of "An eye for an eye and a tooth for a tooth." The norm of reciprocity has implications at many levels of social life. It even affects international relations, as Kenneth and Mary Gergen (1971) found when they interviewed officials from more than a dozen nations. There was considerable hostility toward their benefactors among recipients of foreign aid. They preferred gifts that could be repaid by the fulfillment of definite obligations to those that could not be repaid or that required excessive reciprocation. This finding may help to explain the difficulty the United States has had in mustering support for its positions at the United Nations among nations receiving American aid (see Figure 7.1).

Relating to Others

The social exchange perspective draws our attention to the fact that social interaction has both positive and negative aspects. Over 300 years ago, the French writer Duc François La Rochefoucauld made much the same point when he observed, "People's natures are like most houses—many sided; some aspects are pleasant and some not." In brief, we relate to one another in many ways with many possible outcomes. It is hardly surprising, therefore, that we spend much of our time when alone thinking about our relationships with others. We try to figure out why someone did something that bothers us. We wonder why we like one person and dislike another. We examine out attitudes and think about how they compare to those of our professor or other students. We are not the only ones who ask these kinds of questions: Sociologists do too, only they use more systematic methods. Let us begin our discussion by looking at how we go about processing information about people.

Sizing Others Up

As we perceive, judge, and think about people, two basic social processes are at work. We form impressions of them, and we attribute causes to their behavior.

Forming impressions   When you come in contact with another person, what do you see? Very likely you notice physical characteristics—age, sex, skin color, height, clothing, and so on. But people are not merely observable objects like mountains, trees, and buildings. You also notice gestures, manner of speaking, tone of voice, firmness of handshake, and other traits. You use these cues to make inferences and generalizations; you try to construct coherent pictures of what you think these people are like. We need these pictures if we are to figure out

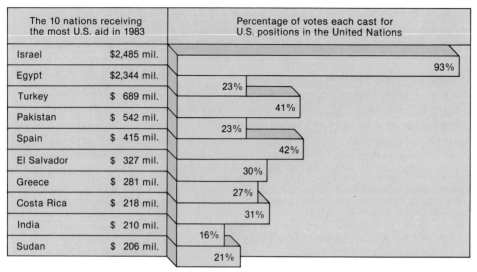

The 10 nations receiving the most U.S. aid in 1983		Percentage of votes each cast for U.S. positions in the United Nations
Israel	$2,485 mil.	93%
Egypt	$2,344 mil.	23%
Turkey	$ 689 mil.	41%
Pakistan	$ 542 mil.	23%
Spain	$ 415 mil.	42%
El Salvador	$ 327 mil.	30%
Greece	$ 281 mil.	27%
Costa Rica	$ 218 mil.	31%
India	$ 210 mil.	16%
Sudan	$ 206 mil.	21%

FIGURE 7.1 **United States Foreign Aid and Support for American Stands at the United Nations**
In a study of voting trends at the 1983 General Assembly, on 10 key issues the 10 major recipients of American military and economic aid supported the United States less than half the time. Despite receiving more than $1 billion, African states backed the United States in only 1 of every 5 votes. The most consistent support came from Western European nations, which get little aid. *Source: Agency for International Development, U.S. Department of State.*

how each person is likely to behave. And the picture we form of people influences how we act and feel toward them.

In sizing people up in this fashion, we usually fit them into readymade *categories*. For instance, we classify people in terms of statuses (nun, male, Hispanic, lawyer, mother) or personalities (surly, talkative, cheer-

Drawing by W. Miller; © 1986 The New Yorker Magazine, Inc.

ful, helpful, introverted). People are too complex for us to take into account every detail each time we meet someone. We like to solve problems quickly and easily, even to cut corners. Categories allow us to simplify and generalize large quantities of information about people—to sort individuals into meaningful and manageable classes and assign labels to these classes. And by pigeonholing people, we can relate current encounters with them to past experience. We view the person as the same despite a change in his or her mood and activities.

Categories that are mental structures for processing and organizing information are called **schemas**. You use person schemas as loose guides in perceiving, appraising, and thinking about people. **Stereotypes** are one type of person schema: They are the unscientific and unreliable generalizations that we make about people based on their group membership. With stereotypes, we commonly infer that a cluster of traits will apply to all the members of a social category (Lord, Lepper, and Mackie, 1984). For instance, you may have stereotypes of women who work, football players, fraternity members, and college professors. Indeed, knowing that a woman is pursuing a career and is a hard worker leads some men to assume that she is also competitive and unfeminine. So based on a few pieces of information about a person, we fill in the

Stereotypes: Fuzzy Guides to Action
What stereotype comes to mind as you size up the man in this photo? What pieces of information seem most significant to you? How do you attempt to "fill in" the gaps in your knowledge using the information supplied by your stereotype? How do stereotypes allow us to make snap judgments about people? Although stereotypes are convenient and efficient, are they necessarily accurate? *(Richard Hutchings/Photo Researchers)*

gaps in our knowledge with the "information" supplied by the schema.

Attributing causes to people's behavior Sizing people up goes beyond simply forming impressions of them. In order to make sense of people's behavior, you also try to uncover the reasons why they act as they do, a process termed **attribution**. Suppose you are walking across campus, and you encounter a friend. You greet her warmly, but she mutters "Hi" and continues on her way. You feel snubbed and wonder why she acted as she did. Did her behavior have something to do with the way she is—some trait such as moodiness or haughtiness? Or did it have something to do with the particular situation she is currently in—did she just fail a test or break up with her boyfriend? You will feel quite differently depending on which of these explanations is correct. There are two

kinds of attribution: *Dispositional*—you judge that people do something because of internal factors such as their personal traits and qualities; and *situational*—you judge that people do something because of external factors such as environmental circumstances.

Which way we explain people's behavior can have far-reaching implications. For instance, do children do poorly in school because they lack innate ability or motivation (dispositional factors), or because they are the victims of poor schools, inadequate teachers, racism, and poverty (situational factors)? Do people become criminals because of inner psychological pathologies, conflicts, and problems (dispositional factors) or because of their immersion in social settings where social pressures and learning experiences propel them into crime (situational factors)? Should we hold individuals accountable for their behavior (dispositional factors), rewarding conformity and punishing deviance? Or should we hold society responsible for human shortcomings (situational factors) and seek to remedy unhealthy social conditions through directed social change?

We usually tend to overestimate the extent to which the actions of *other* people derive from their underlying dispositions or personality—the **fundamental attribution error** (Ross, 1977). Consider what happens when a student who is doing poorly in school discusses the problem with a professor. The two are likely to see the matter somewhat differently:

> The student, in attempting to understand and explain his inadequate performance, is usually able to point to environmental obstacles such as a particularly onerous course load, to temporary emotional stress . . . , or to a transitory confusion about life goals that is now resolved. The faculty adviser may nod and may wish to believe, but in his heart of hearts he usually disagrees. The adviser is convinced that the poor performance is due neither to the student's environment nor to transient emotional states. He believes instead that the failure is due to enduring qualities of the student—to lack of ability, to irremediable laziness, to neurotic ineptitude. [Jones and Nisbett, 1971:1]

A primary bias in the attribution process is that we tend to attribute our own actions to situational factors and the behavior of others to internal or personal factors. We believe that we choose our actions to fit particular educational requirements, but we believe that others do what they do by virtue of their inherent dispositions and qualities.

Communicating with Others

Have you had the experience of being in a group of people who were speaking a foreign language? You could not determine what they were saying, nor could you tell what they were thinking or feeling. Without the ability to express your thoughts and to learn theirs, you very likely had a hard time figuring out how to relate to them. Such experiences highlight the important part communication plays in social interaction. Indeed, all social interaction involves communication (Grimshaw, 1980)

Communication refers to the process by which people transmit information, ideas, attitudes, and mental states to one another (see Figure 7.2). It includes all those verbal and nonverbal processes by which you send and receive messages. Without the ability to communicate, we would be locked within a highly private world. Communication allows us to establish commonness with one another so that we can become tuned together for a given message. Communication is an indispensable mechanism for attaining social goals. It permits us to coordinate complex group activities, and as such it is a foundation for institutional life.

Verbal communication   As we pointed out in Chapter 3, we use language to communicate information ("A car is approaching") and to influence actions ("Get off the road!"). Many other species also have communication systems. Dogs bark, bees dance, birds call, dolphins whistle, and bats shriek. But these signaling systems are simple and rigid. They are more like a knee-jerk reaction to a specific stimulus, something like the "Ouch!" that escapes our lips when we bump our knee against a table. Human language, by contrast, is incredibly complex and flexible.

Interaction is the essence of verbal communication. For example, conversations must be initiated with some sort of attention-getting device. Greetings, questions, or the ringing of a telephone function as summons. Yet conversations do not get under way unless the potential partners signal their availability. We often inform others that we are attending to them and willing to converse by establishing eye contact. We may also respond verbally to what they say. A common lead into conversation is a summons-answer sequence, and our response indicates our availability: "Kind of windy out today, isn't it?" "Sure is."

Once we gain another person's attention, we have to coordinate our speech (Clark, 1985). When two people wish to pass through a narrow doorway about the same time, they must determine who goes first. Like-

FIGURE 7.2   **A Simplified Model of the Communication Process**

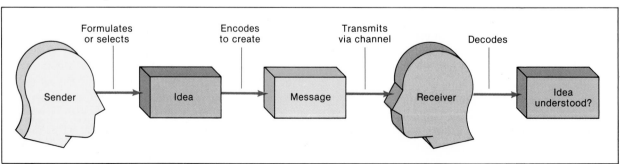

wise, in conversations we have to coordinate turn taking—who speaks when and for how long. Coordination is achieved by a system that allows or obligates us to talk at certain times, what sociologists call *turn-taking conventions*. One way we maintain the floor is to look away from the listener and only occasionally make eye contact. Or we may keep the floor by filling our pauses with something like "ah . . . um . . . you know . . ." We signal to others that it is their turn to speak by raising or lowering our voice as evidence of a terminal clause. Or we may speak the terminal clause in a slow, drawn-out manner. Recordings of conversations reveal that our utterances overlap only about 3 percent of the time because we are so skilled at using these types of mechanisms (Sacks et al., 1974). To carry on a conversation with a person requires that we continually assess how we are affecting our partner's interest and understanding. Based on these assessments, we shape and reshape our speech.

Nonverbal communication "Actions speak louder than words." Indeed, we are frequently more eloquent with our bodies than we realize. Verbal symbols are only the tip of the communication iceberg. Nonverbal messages abound, and we "read" a good deal into them without necessarily being aware of doing so. Based on his experiments, Albert Mehrabian (1968) concludes that the total impact of a message is 7 percent verbal, 38 percent vocal, and 55 percent facial. Another specialist, Raymond L. Birdwhistell (1970:197), suggests that "no more than 30 to 35 percent of the social meaning of a conversation or an interaction is carried by its words." "Video" information tends to be a lot more important than "audio" information (DePaulo et al., 1978).

Nonverbal communication affects our interaction in a good many ways. Consider the following illustration. As a white teacher asks a black student a question, the student shifts her eye gaze away from the teacher and down toward the floor. The teacher concludes that the student does not understand the question and rephrases it in simpler terms. The student responds with a cryptic "um-hum" and keeps her eyes averted. The teacher then assumes that the student does not understand the concept and turns to another student in frustration.

Although this situation appears to present a case in which a student fails to respond to a teacher's query, it may also represent a failure in cross-racial nonverbal communication. Black parents often teach their children that looking an adult in the eye is a sign of disrespect. In contrast, white children are socialized to do the opposite;

looking away from a speaker is seen as disrespectful. Further, black listeners sometimes indicate that they are listening to what the speaker is saying by looking away and uttering an "um-hum," "yeah," or a "mm-hmm" (what is termed a *back-channel behavior*). Hence, the black student who averted her eyes but accompanied the behavior with an "um-hum" is as likely to be attentive as the white student who gazes directly at the teacher (Feldman, 1985). As noted in the box, nonverbal communication also plays a central role in establishing dominance.

There are a good many nonverbal communication systems, including the following:

- *Body Language*: Slouching, hand motions, smiles, and grimaces are often more revealing than words. Physical movements and gestures function as signals (see Figure 7.3 on page 178). The "preening behavior" that accompanies courtship is a good illustration. Women frequently stroke their hair, check their makeup, rearrange their clothes, or push their hair away from the face. Men may straighten their hair, tug at their tie, readjust their clothes, or pull up their socks. These are signals that say, "I'm interested in you. Notice me. I'm an attractive person."

- *Paralanguage*: Nonverbal vocal cues surrounding speech—pitch, loudness, tempo, hesitations, and sighs—provide a rich source of information. Paralanguage has to do with *how* something is said rather than with *what* is said. For instance, sarcasm is indicated almost entirely by tone rather than words.

- *Proxemics*: The way we employ social and personal space also contains messages. For instance, if you are at a party and someone stands very close to you even though there is a good deal of room, you sense that the person is interested in you.

- *Touch*: Through physical contact—touching, stroking, hitting, holding, and greeting (handshakes)—we convey our feelings to one another. Among Americans, touch—especially nonreciprocal touch—is less a sign of affection than of status. For example, women are more likely to be touched by men than the reverse. The nonreciprocal touch symbolizes, albeit subtly, the greater status afforded men (Henley, 1973, 1977; Major, 1981). Likewise, bosses are permitted to pat employees on the back,

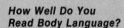

**How Well Do You
Read Body Language?**

Take this quick test to find out.
Circle the phrase that you
believe best communicates
what is being said in each
picture. You'll find the correct
answers below, printed
upside down.

1. a. "I can handle this easily."
   b. "Let me think about it for
      a while."
   c. "That will never work."

2. a. "Look, it's out of my
      league. Sorry."
   b. "I'll do anything I can to
      help."
   c. "You've got to be kidding!"

3. a. "This meeting is making
      me very tense."
   b. "Don't bore me with
      details—get to the
      point."
   c. "I'm frustrated that we
      can't agree."

4. a. "Can it wait until later?"
   b. "I'm ready to negotiate."
   c. "I'm much better at my
      job than you are."

5. a. "I've finally come to a
      conclusion."
   b. "That's worth considering."
   c. "I can't believe I just said
      that."

Answers: 1. a; 2. b; 3. a; 4. c; 5. c

Photos: Stacey Pleasant/Random House

FIGURE 7.3   How Well Do You Read Body Language?

but the same behavior is deemed inappropriate for
the subordinate.

- *Artifacts:* We commonly employ objects, including
  certain types of clothing, lipstick, hair pieces, eyeglasses, beauty aids, perfume, and jewelry, that tell
  other people our gender, rank, status, and up-to-
  dateness. For instance, at a singles bar clothing and
  hairstyle tell potential mates what we are and are
  not and say "see me" or "skip me."

"I know you didn't tell me to sell, Arthur, but when I said 'Maybe this is the time to sell' you paused."

Drawing by Saxon; © 1986 The New Yorker Magazine, Inc.

Gestures are especially susceptible to cultural influence (Ekman, Friesen, and Bear, 1984). The American "A-Okay" gesture made by joining the thumb and forefinger in a circle takes on quite different meanings in different cultures. An American tourist will find that what is a friendly sign in the United States has an insulting connotation in France and Belgium: "You're worth zero!" in southern Italy it means a jerk, and in Greece and Turkey it conveys an insulting or vulgar sexual invitation. Body language is also bilingual. When foreigners converse in English, their bodies seem to do likewise. For example, Arabs, South Americans, and Eastern Europeans favor close conversational encounters; Asians, Northern Europeans, and North Americans prefer to keep their distance. Should bilingual individuals of the former groups switch to English, they typically also adjust to the English-speaking distance norm. All this suggests that communicative competence is a total mul-

FIGURE 7.4 **Facial Expressions**
The data in this figure show that there is substantial agreement among the members of different cultures about the meaning of various facial expressions. Your facial action provides a window by which other people can gain access to your inner emotional life and by which you gain similar access to their inner life. *Source: After Paul Ekman, Ed. 1982. Emotion in the Human Face. 2nd ed. New York: Cambridge University Press.*

Photograph judged						
Judgment	Happiness	Disgust	Surprise	Sadness	Anger	Fear
Culture	Percent who agreed with judgment					
99 Americans	97	92	95	84	67	85
40 Brazilians	95	97	87	59	90	67
119 Chileans	95	92	93	88	94	68
168 Argentinians	98	92	95	78	90	54
29 Japanese	100	90	100	62	90	66

CULTIVATING A SOCIOLOGICAL CONSCIOUSNESS

Nonverbal Cues to Social Ranking

If you are verbally fluent, you are more likely to be listened to than are quiet types. Yet you can also be perceived as dominant and important without uttering a single word. Much depends on your nonverbal communication. How do you go about establishing the impression of high rank? For one thing, people who "outglance" their peers in first encounters typically become the most influential members of a group. Based on subtle cues obtained during the first few seconds of interaction, we rank one another in a dominance hierarchy (Rose and Mazur, 1979). Consider what happens when your eyes meet those of a stranger across the room. Let us say you decide to hold the stare. Chances are the eye contact has now become a dominance encounter. Your stare makes the stranger uncomfortable. The stranger may cut eye contact, relieving his or her discomfort and in

Submissive Behaviors among Wolves
A subordinate male wolf (left) pays his respects by nuzzling the mouth of a higher-ranking male. Note the flattened ears and pulled-back lip line on the subordinate wolf, both additional displays of a submissive posture. *(Scott Barry/ The Image Works)*

effect surrendering. Or the stranger may stare back, making you feel uncomfortable. In this case, who is going to "outstress" whom? The staredown continues until one of you succumbs by averting your eyes. The matter thus settled, the yielder usually avoids further eye contact although the winner may occasionally glance at the loser as if to verify the victory (Mazur, 1985;

tichannel cultural package (Sussman and Rosenfeld, 1982).

Social scientists find, however, that some facial expressions seem to have universal meanings. For instance, in situations of threat and intimidation, people often use glares that very closely resemble the stare-down behavior observed in monkeys and apes. To investigate these matters, Paul Ekman and his associates (1972, 1980) selected a group of photographs they thought depicted surprise, disgust, fear, anger, sadness, and happiness. Then they showed the photos to people from five different cultures and asked them to say what the person in each photo was feeling. The overwhelming majority of the subjects identified the emotions in the same way (see Figure 7.4). Even the Fore, a people in a remote part of New Guinea who have had little contact with Westerners, labeled the pictures in the same basic way. It appears, then, that the ways of displaying and interpreting certain feelings may be universal, which suggests a

strong biological component. Even so, each culture provides its own *display rules*, the norms that govern the public expression of emotions. These rules define the appropriateness of emotional expression and regulate the who, when, where, what kind, how strong, and how long of emotional displays.

THINKING THROUGH THE ISSUES

Look at Figure 7.5*a* and *b*. Assume you are interviewing this woman for a job. In each case, what is your first impression? In which photo does the woman seem more alert? In which photo does the woman seem more attentive? If you are like most people, you found the woman in photo *a* more alert and attentive. Why? Would another setting— for instance, a social encounter—make a difference? Might you then see the woman as shy and demure?

Ridgeway, Berger, and Smith, 1985).

You also create an impression of high rank when you convey a sense of certainty, self-control, and authority. Captains of industry have this talent. So do successful politicians and great generals. You do so by moving slowly, smoothly, and purposefully, while planting some strategic pauses along the way. Your movements are integrated, so that your neck and shoulders or hand, wrist, and arm move together as a unit. You use hand gestures carefully and appear charismatic. Your posture is erect (a modified West-Point cadet look is especially effective). You hold your head still while speaking. Your speech rate is even and measured; your sentences are complete. You command physical space by spreading out your arms and your legs (Schlenker, 1980). And before sitting in a chair, you move it one inch to establish territory while sliding into it from front to back.

You create an impression of low rank when you convey a sense of insecurity, of not being worthy of others' attention, and by a willingness to be submissive. You achieve this appearance when you fidget, fuss, move jerkily, touch your face and hair, shift your position frequently, hold onto objects in the room, stand with your feet pointed in, assume a restricted space, smile with your teeth covering your bottom lip, and speak breathlessly with periodic giggles or laughs.

Dominance contests may also occur in a conversation. If you interrupt another person, you are acting dominantly. If the other person pauses, he or she has deferred to you. If you both continue speaking, you are vying for dominance. The high-ranking person tends to set the pace and mood of the conversation, and the low-ranking person follows. The dominant person achieves this outcome with smiles, jokes, frowns, exclamations, loudness, and rapidity of speech. Similarly, the dominant person introduces and terminates major topics of conversation. In brief, the person of higher rank takes command of the conversation (Mazur, 1985).

Scientists find that a good many animal species also use gestures and actions that convey dominance and submission. These include physical threats or cowering, erect or stooped posture, direct stare or eye aversion, advancing or retreating, relaxed demeanor or nervousness, and a growl or a grin (Burgoon and Saine, 1978). Wolves provide a good illustration. Subordinates show submission toward dominants much in the manner that dogs do. They lower their heads and tails, flatten their ears, and, under extreme threat, roll over on their backs. Likewise, subordinate members display affection for the dominant wolf by nuzzling the pack leader's mouth, using the food-begging gesture of pups. The ceremony also occurs when wolves wake up, when group members return after a separation, and when the pack is ready to start on a hunt.

a   b

FIGURE 7.5 **A Job Interview**
Appraise these photos by answering the questions in the Thinking Through the Issues insert. (*Stacey Pleasant/Random House*)

Relating to Others in Physical Space

Talking, listening, and nonverbal displays take place in physical settings that color social relationships. You have around you an invisible social bubble of space that contracts and expands depending on your emotional state, the activity you are performing, and your cultural background (Hall and Hall, 1971). This bubble—**personal space**—is a kind of portable territory that others cannot intrude upon without making us feel uncomfortable and that we defend against intrusion (Hayduk, 1978). If someone stands too close to you, your first inclination is to back up. If this is not possible, you lean away, tense your muscles, and pull yourself in. If the intruder does not respond to these body signals, you may place an umbrella, briefcase, or raincoat between you. Pickpockets strategically violate your personal space—"pratt the mark"—to get you to position your body to make your wallet accessible (Goffman, 1971).

The Social Significance of Space
Strangers align themselves at about five-foot intervals, the distance at which conversation ceases to be comfortable. When possible, people observe this distance in seating themselves in public places. People may also defend territory against intrusion by placing a barrier such as books or articles of clothing between themselves and others. *(Peter Menzel/Stock, Boston)*

Most white middle-class Americans use four primary distances in their business and social relations: intimate, personal, social, and public (Hall, 1966). Each of these distances has a near and a far phase and is accompanied by changes in the loudness of the voice. *Intimate distance* varies from direct physical contact to a distance of 6 to 18 inches. It is used for private activities, such as caressing another person or making love. At this distance you are enveloped by sensory inputs from another person, including fragrances and the sounds of breathing. Even at the far phase you are easily within touching distance.

In the second zone—*personal distance*—the close phase occurs at 1.5 to 2.5 feet. Wives and husbands frequently find it threatening if another woman or man moves into this zone with their partner, since it may signal that the person has designs on their spouse. Conversations are carried on in soft voices indoors and at moderate volume outside. The far phase—2.5 to 4 feet—is the distance you use to "keep someone at arm's length" and to carry on an ordinary conversation.

The third zone—*social distance*—is used to transact impersonal business. In the close phase—4 to 7 feet—Americans tend to shift their gaze back and forth from eye to eye or from eyes to mouth. It is the distance maintained between customers and clerks in stores, or between householders and delivery personnel. The far phase—7 to 12 feet—is where you stand when someone says, "Stand back so I can look at you." In an executive office, the desk functions to keep people at this distance. Speaking is at full voice.

The fourth zone—*public distance*—is used by speakers at public gatherings and teachers in a classroom. At its farthest phase—25 feet and beyond—it is the distance given to important public figures such as the president of the United States. Panhandlers exploit the unwritten, unspoken conventions of space by beginning at this distance. Once having caught the eye of a "mark," panhandlers then lock on, not letting go until they move through the public zone, the social zone, the personal zone, and finally into the intimate sphere, where you are most vulnerable.

Affiliating with Others

A popular song says that those of us who need people are the luckiest people in the world. Indeed, most of us are acutely aware that our relationships play a critical part in our lives. When we are asked what it is that makes life most meaningful, we usually answer by mentioning friends, relatives, and lovers. We say it is important to have relationships and to feel "loved and wanted" (Berscheid and Peplau, 1983). Sociologists view a **relationship** as social interaction that continues long enough so that we become linked to another person by a relatively stable set of expectations.

Chances are that you spend a good deal of your average day in the company of other people. In one carefully controlled study of time use, researchers asked a sample of teenagers and adults to carry electronic pagers for a week. At random times during the day, the researchers activated the pager, sounding a beep that signaled participants to fill out a short questionnaire indicating what they were doing and whether they were alone or with other people. Adults spent 71 percent of their waking hours with someone else; for teenagers, the average was 74 percent (Czkiszentmihalyi and Larson, 1984) (see Figure 7.6 on page 184).

Why do we seek others out and want to associate with them? There is no single answer to this question. One reason seems to be that without other people, many of us feel unwanted. Sigmund Freud and countless psychologists have said that we like to know that we matter to someone else and are worth loving (Middlebrook, 1980). And some of us need to bestow love on others as much as we need to be loved ourselves. Moreover, life alone can get pretty boring. Although a book, a television program, or a hike alone can be fulfilling, they can never replace the stimulation of social interaction.

Still another reason we affiliate with other people is that we may find them comforting. Fear and anxiety are often reduced in the presence of other people (Berscheid, 1985). For example, if you are on a plane during a bumpy flight and your heart is racing and your hands are clammy, you may find it comforting to strike up a conversation with the calm-looking person sitting next to you. Likewise, there seems to be considerable truth in the adage that "misery loves company" (Schachter, 1959). Presumably the desire for affiliation arises in part from our experiences as infants, when we were dependent on our caretakers. Unless we were abused or neglected as children, we learn to look to others for security and a sense of well-being. And if something upsets us or we have a personal problem, we may turn to them for help.

We also need other people if we are to have a framework for fashioning our behavior. When we are in a state of uncertainty about impending events or what we should do, we can determine the "correctness" of a projected course of action by comparing our attitudes or beliefs with those of others. We find it especially helpful to compare ourselves with others who are relatively similar to us in opinion, ability, or ideals (Wetzel and Insko, 1982). For example, if you are a graduating senior in computer science trying to decide about a job opportunity, you do not typically seek out opinions of dance majors, registered nurses, or anthropologists. Rather, you are likely to compare your thinking with others like yourself, such as other computer science majors or your roommates—individuals of similar age, training, and academic level. Presumably, the more uncertain or unverifiable an opinion is, the greater your need for social evaluation and support (Festinger, 1954; Berscheid, 1985).

Helping Others

Admittedly a good deal of our social interaction is motivated by self-interest. You may offer to run an errand for a professor because you hope that he or she will take that help into account when awarding grades. Or you may offer to take care of the neighbors' dog while they are away on vacation because you want them to take care of your cat when you go on vacation. But if behavior that benefits others is *not* linked to personal gain, it is called **altruistic** or **prosocial behavior**. Many people go to considerable trouble to help a sick neighbor, take in a family left homeless by fire, or serve as hospital aides. Charitable contributions are often directed at strangers and made anonymously.

A good many factors influence whether or not we will engage in helping behavior. One of the most important is the situation. This line of investigation was inspired by a well-publicized incident in New York City some years ago. A young woman named Kitty Genovese was returning home from a night job when a male assailant attacked and stabbed her; she died of her wounds. In response to her screams, at least thirty-eight neighbors looked out their apartment windows and witnessed the attack. Although the assault went on for half an hour and many of the spectators watched the entire time, none of them went to the woman's assistance or called the police. Why? Experiments show that as the number of bystanders increases, the likelihood decreases that any one of them will help someone in trouble (Latané and Darley, 1970; Latané and Nida, 1981). Where others are present, both the obligation to assist and the potential blame for not acting are spread around. In the Genovese murder, each observer, seeing lights and people in nearby windows, knew that others were also watching. Contrary to popular belief, safety does not necessarily reside in numbers; a "surplus" of helpers diffuses responsibility, producing what is called the *bystander effect*.

Another key aspect of the situation is its ambiguity. Circumstances that make it harder for us to recognize a genuine emergency reduce the likelihood that we will help. A woman staggering about may be having a heart attack, experiencing the onset of a diabetic episode, or simply suffering from drunkenness. What appears to be smoke pouring from a building may be caused by fire or escaping steam. Consequently, much depends on how we define a situation.

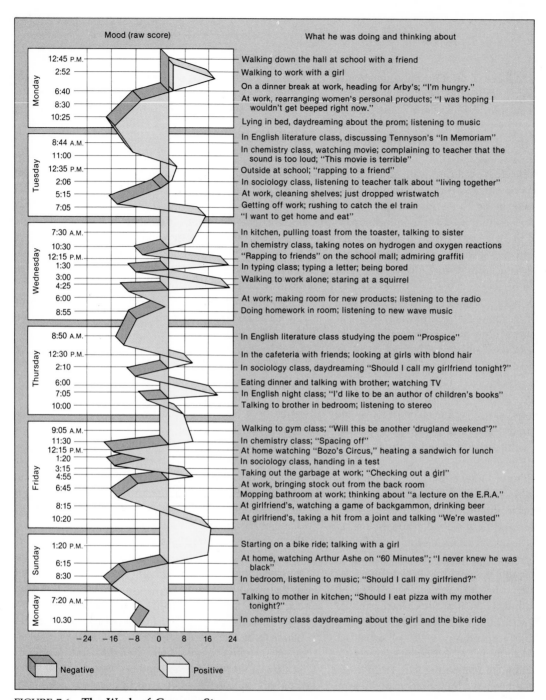

FIGURE 7.6 The Week of Gregory Stone
Researchers at the University of Chicago studied 75 teenagers in a Chicago suburb. The teenagers were equipped with small electronic pagers that were activated at random moments during the week, signaling the teenagers to record their thoughts, feelings, and activities at the time. *Source: Adapted from Mihaly Czkiszentmihalyi and Reed Larson.* Being Adolescent: Conflict and Growth in the Teen-Age Years. *New York: Basic Books, 1984.*

Other factors are also at work. Not all strangers are equally likely to be assisted. In a subway experiment, a young man with a cane was helped 95 percent of the time when he staggered forward and collapsed shortly after entering the train. When the young man carried a bottle and smelled of liquor, he was offered help only 50 percent of the time (Piliavin, Rodin, and Piliavin, 1969). Help is also less likely to be forthcoming as the costs of helping mount. For instance, it is significantly slower and less frequent if the sober victim with a cane is seen "bleeding" from the mouth because many people experience revulsion at the sight of blood (Piliavin and Piliavin, 1972). In real-life situations in which we expect negative outcomes—possible retaliation from the criminal or days spent in court testifying—we are also discouraged from helping by the prospect of incurring costs.

Working with and against Others

We may offer aid or assistance to others, even though we do not expect immediate or direct reward for our actions. Although one-way help occurs in a variety of settings, it is less common than working with or against others. One way social scientists have explored cooperation and competition is by the prisoner's dilemma game. It is based on a problem faced by two suspects at a police station. The district attorney thinks both are guilty of a crime, but he lacks adequate evidence to convict them at a trial. He places the prisoners in separate rooms and presents each with two alternatives—confess or not confess. The district attorney states that if neither confesses, they will be booked on a minor charge, such as petty larceny or illegal possession of a weapon, and they will both receive minor punishments. If both prisoners confess, the district attorney will prosecute them, but will recommend leniency. However, should one confess and the other not confess, the confessor will be released for helping the state, whereas the other suspect will get the maximum penalty.

The prisoner's dilemma provides a mixed-motive situation in which players must choose between cooperation and competition. Using Figure 7.7 as your point of reference, consider the situation in which the dilemma places you. If you both remain silent—stonewall—you and your co-conspirator will receive two years in prison. If only you confess, you will get off without a sentence and your partner will receive ten years. If your partner confesses and you hold out, you will receive the ten-year term. If both of you confess, each of you will spend seven years in jail.

What would you do? The "don't confess" choice is the cooperative one. You demonstrate that you trust your partner not to take advantage of the situation by turning state's evidence. But you run the risk that your partner will confess and you will pay dearly. The "confess" choice is the competitive one. You attempt to improve your circumstances by betraying your partner. But again you must run the risk that your partner will also confess,

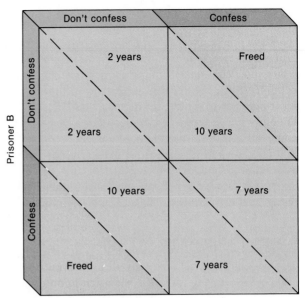

FIGURE 7.7 **The Prisoner's Dilemma Game**
The numbers in the matrix cells show the number of years each person would spend in jail.

ensuring that you both will receive ten years' imprisonment. In brief, what is the best choice for you individually results in a particularly punishing outcome if you both choose it.

Experimenters can adapt the game by altering the length of the prison terms or substituting chips, money, or course points for prison sentences. A series of games can be played. Researchers find that players are most likely to cooperate when they can communicate with one another, thereby establishing mutual trust and coordinating their strategies. What your opponent consistently does in early games also influences your own strategy. Where your opponent is consistently (and even foolishly) cooperative, you are more likely to respond in later games by a competitive strategy. Should your opponent reciprocate a cooperative move while remaining ready to compete if cooperation is not reciprocated, you become more inclined to cooperate. On the other hand, competition begets competition (Wichman, 1972).

Robert Axelrod (1984) finds that the simplest and most effective strategy for playing the prisoner's dilemma game is one he calls TIT FOR TAT. Your first move is one of cooperation. Then you do whatever your partner does on the previous move. The strategy appears to be successful because it combines four properties: It is nice, retaliatory, forgiving, and clear. It is *nice* because it avoids unnecessary conflict so long as the other side reciprocates. TIT FOR TAT is *retaliatory* because it responds to provocation. When the other player makes an unjustified competitive move, it results in immediate retaliation; delay in retaliation sends the signal that competition can pay. The strategy is *forgiving* in allowing the other player to back off following retaliation. So, should the other party resume cooperation after having made a competitive move, forgiveness results and cooperation again becomes possible. Finally, TIT FOR TAT is *clear* and predictable. Clarity is essential so that the other party can adapt his or her pattern of action, thereby fostering long-term cooperation.

Chapter Highlights

1. Symbolic interactionists say that we organize our behavior by the meanings we assign to our experiences. Accordingly, our definitions of the situation are critical to social interaction. It is only as we arrive at common understandings that we are able to fit our action to the actions of other people. We also construct reality by means of definitions. Social action develops in a tentative, groping, advancing, backtracking, and sounding out process. Inherent in this vision is the idea that the essence of social interaction and order is negotiation.

2. Sociologist Erving Goffman depicts the social world as a natural theater akin to the dramatic performances that take place on the stage, a perspective termed dramaturgy. One way life is like a theater is that we attempt to control the reality that other people see—a process called impression management. Another way life is like a theater is that in social interaction there is a front region and a back region.

3. Ethnomethodologists undertake to illuminate the commonplace, taken-for-granted aspects of everyday life. They investigate how we go about creating and sustaining for one another the presumption that there is an external social reality and order. More particularly, they study the background understandings that constitute the material out of which stable social interaction emerges.

4. The social exchange perspective portrays us as social bookkeepers who order our relationships by maintaining a mental ledger of rewards, costs, and profits. Rewards are anything we will incur costs to obtain. Costs are whatever we attempt to avoid. And profits are rewards less costs. Viewed in this man-

THINKING THROUGH THE ISSUES

How might the TIT FOR TAT strategy find application in marital relationships? In American-Soviet relations? How do real situations differ from the prisoner's game? In real life can the parties communicate with one another and attempt to bluff and deceive each other? Do the parties enjoy equal power; can one party bring greater resources to bear to gain a favorable outcome? Are the actual risks limited to those contained within the game, or do they encompass other spheres of one's life? What part do group norms and expectations play? Does the audience matter? Explain.

ner, social interaction consists of an exchange of activity between at least two people that involves both rewards and costs.

5. As we perceive, judge, and think about people, two basic social processes are at work. We form impressions of them, and we attribute causes to their behavior. In sizing them up, we fit them into standard categories. In order to make sense of people's behavior, we also try to uncover the reasons why they act as they do. A primary bias in the attribution process is that we tend to attribute our own actions to situational factors and the behavior of other people to internal or personal factors.

6. Communication allows us to transmit information, ideas, attitudes, and mental states to one another. It permits us to coordinate complex group activities, and as such it is a foundation of institutional life. Language is a central component of much communication. Yet verbal symbols are only the tip of the communication iceberg. Nonverbal meanings abound, and we "read" a good deal into them without necessarily being aware of doing so.

7. Physical space colors our social relationships. We have around us an invisible social bubble of space that contracts and expands depending on our emotional state, the activity we are performing, and our cultural background. White middle-class Americans use four primary distances in their business and social relationships: intimate, personal, social, and public.

8. We seek out and associate with other people for a good many reasons. One reason seems to be that without other people, many of us feel unwanted and

unloved. Moreover, life alone can get pretty boring. Additionally, we find other people comforting. And we need other people if we are to have a framework for fashioning our behavior.

9. At times we engage in behavior that benefits others but is not linked to personal gain—altruistic or prosocial behavior. We are less likely to help others when other people are present because both the obligation to assist and the potential blame for not act-

ing are spread around. Circumstances that make it harder for us to recognize a genuine emergency also reduce the likelihood that we will help.

10. The prisoner's dilemma game is used in the study of cooperation and competition. Researchers find that players are most likely to cooperate when they can communicate with one another, thereby establishing mutual trust and coordinating strategies. In contrast, competition tends to breed competition.

The Sociologist's Vocabulary

altruistic behavior (also *prosocial behavior*) Behavior that benefits others and is not linked to personal gain.

attribution A process by which we attempt to make sense of behavior by uncovering the reasons why people act as they do.

back region A place in social life offstage where actors retire to prepare themselves for their social performance.

body language Physical motions and gestures that provide social signals.

communication The process by which people transmit information, ideas, attitudes, and mental states to one another.

definition of the situation The interpretation we give to our immediate circumstances; we mentally represent our environment in symbolic terms so that we can size it up and gain a preliminary assessment of the courses of action available to us.

demonstration experiment A procedure that introduces a nasty surprise in a situation in order to reveal the underlying expectations of which we are normally unaware.

dramaturgy A sociological perspective in which the social world is portrayed as a natural theater akin to the dramatic performances on the stage.

ethnomethodology Procedures—the rules and activities—that people employ in making social life and society intelligible to themselves and others.

front region A place in social life that parallels the stage seen by the audience.

fundamental attribution error Overestimating the extent to which the actions of other people derive from their underlying dispositions or "personality."

impression management The term Erving Goffman applied to the process by which we present ourselves to others in ways that will lead them to view us in a favorable light.

norm of reciprocity The social rule that we should help and not harm those who help us.

paralanguage Nonverbal cues surrounding speech—pitch, loudness, tempo, hesitations, and sighs—that are a rich source of communicative information.

personal space A kind of portable territory that others cannot intrude upon without making us feel uncomfortable and that we defend against intrusion.

prosocial behavior (also *altruistic behavior*) Behavior that benefits others and is not linked to personal gain.

proxemics The way we employ social and personal space to transmit messages.

relationship Social interaction that continues long enough so that we become linked to another person by a relatively stable set of expectations.

schema A category that is a mental structure for processing and organizing information.

social action Behavior that is oriented to or influenced by other people.

social exchange A sociological perspective that depicts human beings as social bookkeepers who order their relationships by maintaining a mental ledger of rewards, costs, and profits.

social interaction The mutual and reciprocal influencing by two or more people of each other's behavior.

social psychology The scientific study of the nature and causes of social interaction and behavior.

stereotype An unscientific and hence unreliable generalization that we make about people based on our group membership.

Thomas theorem The notion that our definitions influence our construction of reality. It was stated by William I. Thomas: "If men [people] define situations as real, they are real in their consequences."

8

Social Control, Deviance, and Crime

The more laws, the more offenders.

—Thomas Fuller, M.D., *Gnomologia*, 1732

What is sanity, and what is insanity? How do you determine whether a behavior is sane or insane? We have all read accounts of murder trials in which eminent psychiatrists for the prosecution are contradicted by equally eminent psychiatrists for the defense on the issue of a defendant's sanity. Does a diagnosis of sanity or insanity reside in the people themselves? Or does the diagnosis depend on the context in which observers find them? For example, if you were to get a number of ordinary people without any history of mental disorder admitted to a psychiatric hospital, would the staff discover that they are sane? If so, how would this be done? On what basis would the decision be made?

To gain some insight into these questions, David L. Rosenhan (1973) and seven others, including several psychologists, a pediatrician, and a psychiatrist, pretended to hear voices that said "empty," "hollow," and "thud" to gain admission to twelve different psychiatric hospitals. On this basis they were diagnosed as schizophrenic, and admitted as patients. (Except for the voices, the researchers presented all the other events of their life histories as they actually had occurred.) Once the researchers had entered a hospital, they went back to their ordinary behavior. They dropped the claims of hearing voices, spoke to other patients and staff as they would to people outside the hospital, and told everyone they were feeling fine and no longer experiencing symptoms. In none of the hospitals did the staff become suspicious of these changes or entertain the idea that the "patients" were faking. The researchers took detailed notes of their experiences while in the hospital. Based on this and other aspects of their behavior, the real patients soon figured out that they were researchers or journalists—*not* real patients. The staff placed a quite different interpretation on the notetaking: They saw the behavior as a symptom of disturbance and pathology. One nurse wrote on the "patient's" chart that the writing behavior was indicative of a disordered, abnormal compulsion. On another occasion, a kindly nurse found a researcher pacing the hospital corridors. "Nervous, Mr. X?" she asked. "No, bored," he said.

Rosenhan concluded that once a person is assigned the label "mentally ill," the staff interprets that individual's actions in a way consistent with the label. Indeed, the label was so powerful that "normal" behaviors were overlooked or misinterpreted. When the researchers were finally released, they were described as "recovered schizophrenics" or "schizophrenics in remission," rather than as not mentally ill. In sum, the researchers were stuck with a label that took on a life of its own (Shoham-Salomon, 1985). Matters of this sort are the topics of this chapter, *deviance*.

PLANNING AHEAD: TARGETED READING

1. How do you determine whether or not behavior is deviant?

2. Why do most people conform to the rules most of the time?

3. What are the social effects of deviance?

4. Why do people violate social rules?

5. How effective is the criminal justice system?

6. Do crime-fighting programs, including imprisonment, work?

The Nature of Deviance

What some people say and do at times goes beyond the behavior permitted by their societies. Norms tell us only what we are supposed or not supposed to do; they do not tell us what people *actually* do. And what some of us actually do often runs counter to what other people judge to be acceptable behavior. Social life is characterized not only by conformity, but by nonconformity, or deviance. **Deviance** is behavior a considerable number of people view as reprehensible and beyond the limits of tolerance. We typically view behavior that is negatively valued and provokes hostile reactions as deviant.

THINKING THROUGH THE ISSUES

Are some acts inherently deviant? Is an act either deviant or not, regardless of who commits it, whether it is detected, why it is committed, or the circumstances under which it is carried out? For instance, "Thou shalt not kill" is a firm moral precept in the Judeo-Christian world. Western nations have complex sets of laws defining various degrees and forms of homicide and manslaughter. Are all acts of killing punishable offenses? Can a homeowner kill an intruder? Can police officers kill in the performance of their duties? Can killing win you the Congressional Medal of Honor? What do your answers tell you about deviance?

Social Properties of Deviance

As viewed by most sociologists, deviance is not a property *inherent* in certain forms of behavior (Erikson, 1962; Becker, 1963; Lemert, 1972). Instead, it is a property *conferred* upon behaviors by social definitions. This is not to say that the acts we label homicide, stealing, sexual perversion, mental disturbance, alcoholism, gambling, and child abuse would not occur in the absence of these definitions. Rather, a social audience decides whether or not some behavior is deviant. In this sense, deviance is what people say it is.

The relativity of deviance Definitions of which acts are deviant vary greatly from time to time, place to place, and group to group. For example, when ordinary people break into tombs, they are labeled looters. When archeologists break into tombs, they are hailed as scientists who are advancing the frontiers of knowledge. Yet in both cases burial sites are disturbed and items are carted away. Some Native Americans (Indians) are calling for

the immediate reburial of the thousands of Indian skeletons now in museums and university laboratories across the country. And they are seeking limits on the scientific study of newly discovered remains (Lewis, 1986). Or consider that Boris Pasternak, Aleksandr Solzhenitsyn, and countless other Soviet writers have been punished severely for doing what many people in Western nations hail as outstanding literary achievements.

Within recent years, many behaviors that Americans have traditionally judged to be deviant have undergone redefinition. Not too long ago we defined compulsive gambling, alcoholism, drug addiction, and even many forms of mental illness as evil and sinful. While such notions still persist, we now increasingly view these behaviors as "medical problems." They are "illnesses," like physical ailments such as ulcers, diabetes, and high blood pressure. Sufferers are placed in "hospitals" where they are termed "patients" and provided "treatment" by "physicians."

Making definitions stick   When people have differing definitions of what is and is not deviant behavior, the question becomes, who will prevail? In 1776 George Washington was labeled a traitor by British authorities. Twenty years later, he was the first president of the United States and beloved as "The Father of His Country." In the 1940s Menachem Begin was portrayed by British authorities in Palestine as a "Zionist terrorist" (he was the leader of the Irgun Zvai Leumi, the underground military organization so instrumental in forcing the British to leave Palestine). Thirty years later, he was the respected head of state of Israel. Had the Americans

and Jews lost their wars for independence, very likely both Washington and Begin would have been executed, or given long prison terms.

If deviance depends on social definitions and power relations, then notions of what is and is not deviant behavior can be changed. In recent years, some groups, including homosexuals, lesbians, the handicapped, and

"I don't know how you and I would be rated by the psychiatrists in the Soviet Union, but I'd say we're fairly sane by New York standards."

Drawing by Handelsman; © 1983 The New Yorker Magazine, Inc.

welfare mothers, have entered the political arena and successfully challenged official definitions that have portrayed them as "social problems." Indeed, people stigmatized and victimized by prevailing social definitions see their circumstances quite differently from those who enjoy power. Only a few hundred years ago, the political and religious "establishment" of Salem, Massachusetts, was preoccupied with hunting down "witches."

Stigmatized Minorities
Would Abraham Lincoln be ruled out as a presidential candidate today because of the stigma associated with mental illness? Throughout his life, Lincoln suffered recurrent periods of severe depression. When he was 29, Lincoln was plunged into a deep depression by the death of his first love, Ann Rutledge. He was often observed wandering along the river banks, distracted and filled with grief. Believing that he might be suicidal, friends deprived him of knives and razors. He experienced other depressive episodes at the time of the Lincoln-Douglas debates and later on the death of his son, Willie. The photo above, taken in 1857, shows the profoundly sad look characteristic of depression. In 1972, Thomas Eagleton's vice-presidential candidacy on the Democratic ticket with George McGovern was ended after disclosure that he had received electroshock therapy for mental depression. (*Alexander Hesler/The Bettmann Archive*)

Stigmatized minorities **Stigmatized minorities** are people who possess some attribute that leads other people to deny them full social acceptance (Goffman, 1963; Jones et al., 1984). They may be crippled, blind, deaf, or obese, or suffer from a feared disease such as AIDS. Or the stigma may have to do with the assumptions that other people make about their character. They may have a known record of mental illness, imprisonment, alcoholism, drug addiction, or homosexuality. Because they are stigmatized, other people do not see them as whole beings but as unusual people who are tainted and so discredited. The stigma intrudes itself in social interaction and interferes with it. These people are not given the respect and regard they would otherwise have. Indeed, even the families of stigmatized persons may be subjected to stares, embarrassed silences, rude comments, and disrespectful questions (Collins, 1986).

Stigmatized minorities often feel unsure of how others will react to them. Deaf, blind, or crippled people can never be certain whether they will be rejected or accepted by a new acquaintance. And they often feel they are "on stage," and are self-conscious and calculating about the impression they are making. By virtue of their problems, stigmatized minorities may take special measures when interacting with others. They may attempt to conceal the symbols that reveal their status, such as facial disfigurement. Others withdraw to groups of similar people. Still others assume a stance of hostile bravado. And some actively organize to combat their social discrimination. Clearly, not all people benefit from the social standards that a society devises. Why then are they expected to behave in accordance with the standards? This question brings us to a consideration of social control.

Social Control and Deviance

If the work of the world is to get done, people must follow rules. Social order dictates that people be kept in line—at least most people—and the line must be kept within allowable limits (Sagarin, 1975; Black, 1984a, 1984b). Without social order, we would have difficulty interacting with one another because we would not know what to expect. So societies seek to ensure that their members conform with basic norms by means of social control. **Social control** refers to the methods and strategies that regulate people's behavior within society. (Social control is not necessarily always a positive good, a matter discussed in the box on pages 194–195).

There are three main types of social control processes. First, there are the processes we call *socialization* (see Chapter 7). At first, conformity is primarily a product of external controls. However, as we grow older, an increasing proportion of our behaviors become governed by *internal* monitors. **Internalization** occurs—we incorporate within our personalities the standards of behavior prevalent in our society. For the most part, we accept these standards without thought or question; they become "second nature." As we immerse ourselves within the life of a group, we develop self-conceptions that regulate our conduct in accordance with the norms of the group. By doing what other group members do, we acquire our identities and a sense of well-being. The group is *our* group, and its norms are *our* norms. Social control thus becomes *self-control.*

Second, there are the processes that structure our social experiences. In large part we unconsciously build up our notions of reality by the way our society orders its social agendas and structures social alternatives. As long as we are locked within the social environment provided by our culture, we inhabit a somewhat restricted world. It usually does not occur to us that alternative standards exist. In this sense, we are "culture-bound." Very often nonconformist patterns do not come to our minds because the alternatives are not known to our society. For this reason, the most important thing we can often know about a people is what they take for granted.

Finally, we conform to the norms of our society because we realize that to do otherwise is to risk punishment, while conformity brings rewards. Those who break rules meet dislike, hostility, gossip, and ostracism—even imprisonment and death. The conformist wins praise, popularity, prestige, and other socially defined good things. It does not take us long to appreciate that there are disadvantages to nonconformity and advantages to conformity.

THINKING THROUGH THE ISSUES

Why are people who systematically violate societal norms nonetheless dependent on them (Goffman, 1983)? Do they violate all norms, or only certain norms? How do they exploit other people's conformity? For instance, how do terrorist assassins rely on and profit from understandings regarding normal appearances? How do Wall Street "insiders" who arrange mergers and buybacks that will push up stock prices once the deals become public depend on the orderly operation of the stock market in order to realize illegal trading profits? Why is organized crime dependent upon the criminalization of drugs, pornography, gambling, and loan-sharking?

Collective Retribution
The members of a community may act to punish the violation of norms they consider to represent a serious breach of morality. This French woman collaborated with the Germans during World War II. When Allied troops liberated the village in 1944, villagers punished her by shaving her head and driving her and her child from the community. (*Robert Capa/Magnum*)

ISSUES THAT SHAPE OUR LIVES

Totalitarian Conformity

Assume for the moment that the year is 1940 and you have been drafted into the German army. You are assigned to a post at a concentration camp in which your immediate superior is Adolf Eichmann. Eichmann orders you to send forty Jews to a gas chamber, where they will certainly meet their death. What would you do?

Imagine it is 1969 and you are an American draftee serving in Vietnam under the command of Lieutenant William Calley. Your helicopter lands near the village of My Lai, whose inhabitants are suspected of harboring Vietcong guerrillas. You and the other members of your unit move into the village and round up everyone—men, women, children, babies. Calley comes over to you and says: "You know what to do with them, don't you?" You say "Yes," assuming that your commanding officer wants you to guard them. Ten or fifteen minutes later, Calley returns and says: "How come you ain't killed them yet?" You say you thought he just wanted you to watch the civilians. Angered, Calley says: "No. I want them dead." What do you do? The Americans at My Lai backed away about fifteen feet and fired their automatics into the group, killing some 370 men, women, and children (*New York Times,* November 25, 1969, p. 16).

The Holocaust
The tragedy of the Holocaust reveals how many ordinary people, like the Germans during the Nazi era, could carry out a crusade of horror that resulted in the cruel and inhuman death of more than 12 million other ordinary people. This photo was taken at the Buchenwald concentration camp in 1945. (*The Bettmann Archive*)

You are a student at Yale University. You have responded to an advertisement and are now at the psychology department to participate in an experiment. Professor Stanley Milgram (1974) or one of his assistants informs you that Yale psychologists are studying the effect punishment has on learning. You and another "subject"—a mild-mannered 47- year-old accountant—draw slips out of a hat to determine which of you will be the "teacher" and which the "learner." You select the teacher slip. The other subject, the learner, is then led to an adjoining room. He is strapped into a chair, and an electrode is attached to his wrist. Before you is a Shock Generator with switches ranging in 15-volt increments

The Social Effects of Deviance

Most of us think of deviance as "bad"—as behavior that causes problems for society. This view is not surprising, given the negative or disruptive consequences of deviance, what sociologists term *dysfunctions*. But deviance also has positive consequences for social life, what sociologists term *functions* (see Chapter 2). Sociologists like Lewis A. Coser (1962), Albert K. Cohen (1965), and

Edward Sagarin (1975) have contributed much to our understanding of these matters.

Dysfunctions of deviance Apparently most societies can absorb a good deal of deviance without serious consequences. But persistant and widespread deviance can impair and even severely undermine organized social life. Social organization derives from the coordinated actions of numerous people. Should some people fail to

from 15 to 450 volts. The switches have labels going in order from "Slight Shock" to "Danger: Severe Shock," and finally to "XXX" (under the 435- and 450-volt switches). You are told to "move one level higher on the shock generator" and administer an electrical shock each time the learner provides an incorrect answer. When you flick the switch, lights flash and you hear a buzzing sound.

If you follow the experimenter's instructions, you hear the learner grunt at 75, 90, and 105 volts. When the time comes to activate 120 volts, the learner shouts out that he is in pain. At 150 volts he cries, "Experimenter, get me out of here! I won't be in the experiment anymore! I refuse to go on!" Perhaps you hesitate, but the experimenter prods you: "Please continue—the experiment requires that you continue." If you resist, he will inform you, "You have no other choice, you must go on." Should you obey, you hear the learner's protestations escalate to shrieks of agony as you administer a greater electrical charge with each succeeding error. Finally, at the 330-volt level, the learner falls silent. But the experimenter insists you continue, and eventually you are told to flick the XXX switch. How compliant do you think you would be with the experimenter's commands? (The learner was actually Milgram's confederate and received no shocks.)

Like most people, you probably believe that you would stop administering shocks about the time the learner said he was experiencing pain. But when Milgram actually undertook the experiment with forty men from a wide range of occupations, 65 percent obeyed and gave the highest shock voltage—450 volts. No subject stopped before administering 300 volts, at which point the learner began kicking the wall. When Milgram varied the experiment with other subjects so that the learner mentioned he had a "slight heart condition," 65 percent of the subjects still complied fully. Milgram pressed on and introduced other experimental variations, until almost a thousand subjects had taken part. The results remained basically the same. It seems that although many subjects were torn by the dilemma in which they found themselves, kindness took a back seat to obedience. Milgram concluded that obedience is not so much a product of our moral qualities or lack of them, but of the situation in which we are placed. This research has since been strongly criticized on moral grounds because people were deceived and led to engage in actions potentially harmful to their self-respect. It would no longer meet the ethical requirements set by universities and professional organizations for the conduct of social research.

THINKING THROUGH THE ISSUES

Based on the material in this box, what conclusions might you reach regarding the social pressures we experience for conformity? Under what circumstances would you think citizens might become *cheerful* robots and embrace their servitude? How is it possible to impose a totalitarian system of control on a society? In recent decades a number of writers—C. Wright Mills (1967), Erich Fromm (1968), and Aldous Huxley (1955, 1965)—have suggested that we are faced with the bureaucratic control of our lives by managers and their technical staffs. The resulting regimentation reduces curiosity, questioning, spontaneity, and dissent. Do you agree or disagree? What are your reasons?

perform their actions at the proper time in accordance with accepted expectations, institutional life may be threatened. For instance, when a parent deserts a family, it commonly complicates the tasks of child care and rearing. And when in the midst of battle a squad of soldiers fails to obey and runs away, an entire army may be overwhelmed and defeated.

Deviance also undermines our willingness to play our roles and contribute to the larger social enterprise. If some people get rewards, even disproportionate rewards, without playing by the rules—for instance, "idlers," "fakers," and "chiselers"—we develop resentment and bitterness. Our morale, self-discipline, and loyalty suffer. Consider what your reaction would be if you knew that a number of students in a particularly difficult course were getting the top grades by cheating on exams. Your motivation to struggle with the material and to study long hours would very likely be undermined.

Moreover, social life dictates that by and large we *trust* one another (Lewis and Weigert, 1985). We must have confidence that others will play by the rules. In committing ourselves to the collective enterprise, we allocate some resources, forgo some alternatives, and make some investment in the future. We do so because we assume that other people will do the same. But should others not reciprocate our trust—should they betray it—we feel that somehow our own efforts are pointless, wasted, and foolish. So we become less willing to play by the rules.

Functions of deviance   Although deviance may undermine social organization, it may simultaneously facilitate social functioning in a number of ways. First, it may promote social conformity. Sociologist Edward Sagarin (1975:14) observes:

> One of the most effective methods of keeping most people in line is to throw some people out of line. This leaves the remainder not only in better alignment but at the same time in fear of exclusion. . . . By reacting in a hostile manner to those who are not the good and the proper, a majority of the people or a powerful group may reinforce the idea of goodness and propriety and thus perpetuate a society of individuals who are more conforming, more obedient, and more loyal to their ideology and rules of behavior.

Second, many norms are not expressed as firm rules or in official codes (see Chapter 3). As Emile Durkheim (1893/1964) emphasized, each time people censure some act, they highlight and sharpen the contours of a norm. Their negative reactions clarify precisely what behavior the "collective conscience" will and will not allow. Indeed, societies at times "manufacture" deviance—the witchcraft hysterias of the Puritan colonists, McCarthyism in the 1950s, and the Cultural Revolution in China—to ensure that their moral boundaries and norms are reaffirmed (Erikson, 1966).

Third, by directing attention to the deviant, a group may strengthen itself. A shared enemy arouses common sentiments and cements feelings of solidarity. The emotions surrounding "ain't it awful" deeds quicken passions and solidify "our kind of people" ties. As we saw in Chapter 5, frictions and antagonisms between ingroups and outgroups highlight group boundaries and memberships. Campaigns against witches, traitors, perverts, and criminals reinforce social cohesion among "the good people." Sociologist Randall Collins (1982) says that the main object of our criminal trials is not the wrongdoer, but the larger society. The trial—a social ritual—reaffirms belief in laws and creates emotional bonds that tie us together. Even a society of saints would find things to make crimes of.

Fourth, deviance is a catalyst for change. Every time we violate a law, we contest it. The challenges serve as a warning that the social system is not functioning properly. For instance, high robbery rates are not likely to suggest to a political elite that robbery should be legalized and the wealth of the society redistributed. But they

Highlighting and Sharpening the Collective Conscience
Sociologist Kai T. Erikson (1962) notes that one of the interesting features of agencies of control is the amount of publicity they attract. In earlier times, the punishment of offenders took place in the public market in full view of the crowd. Today we achieve much the same result through heavy media coverage of criminal trials and executions. It is as if morality and immorality meet at the public scaffold, informing us which kinds of behavior belong within the group and which kinds belong outside it. *(Historical Pictures Services)*

"I hate to mention this, but one of our pearls on the Pearly Gate is missing. . . ."

From The Wall Street Journal; permission, Cartoon Features Syndicate

do proclaim that there are large numbers of disaffected people, that institutions for socializing youth are faltering, that power relations are being questioned, and that the moral structures of the society require reexamination. So deviance may be a vehicle for placing on a society's agenda the need for social change. By the same token, the deviant practice offers an alternative to existing practices (Sagarin, 1975). Martin Luther King, Jr., and his supporters called the nation's attention to the undemocratic nature of southern segregation laws by disobeying them en masse.

Sociological Perspectives on Deviance

Deviance may have both positive and negative consequences for the functioning and survival of groups and societies. But why do people violate social rules? Why are some acts defined as deviant, and not others? Why are some people labeled deviants when they engage in essentially the same behaviors as others who escape punishment and who may even enjoy acclaim? And why does the incidence of deviance vary from group to group and society to society? These are the types of questions that interest sociologists.

Other disciplines, particularly biology and psychology, are also concerned with deviance. But they typically ask somewhat different questions, and they make somewhat different contributions to our knowledge. Sociologists focus on factors that generate deviance; biologists and psychologists typically look at the deviant actors and ask what is "wrong"—or at least different—about them. They seek to explain rule breaking in terms of the individuals themselves and their unique characteristics.

Sociology, biology, and psychology, then, do not provide competing answers to the same question. Rather, they attempt to answer different questions about similar behavior. Controversies of the sort discussed in the box arise when differences among disciplines are ignored. Consequently, an understanding of the biological and psychological factors involved in a disorder like schizophrenia does not provide us with the full story; we need to take into account sociological factors as well.

Sources of Deviance
In the Middle Ages and the Renaissance, deviant behavior was taken as evidence of the devil's work, and the detection and treatment of the mentally disturbed was the responsibility of the religious establishment. This late-fifteenth-century painting portrays St. Catherine of Siena casting the devil out of a possessed woman. The devil is pictured as a tiny imp fleeing from the woman's head, apparently to escape the forces of prayer and goodness. *(The Bettmann Archive)*

ISSUES THAT SHAPE OUR LIVES

Controversy: The Roots of Criminal Behavior

Are criminals made or born? The arguments people use in this debate are usually closely related to their political ideology. Conservatives favor biological explanations, largely because no major social change is required if the problems are all inside the skin. Those on the other side—liberals, radicals, and social environmentalists—have favored social models that require better parenting and social change to increase social justice, reduce powerlessness, and lessen the stresses of a competitive society (Albee, 1985).

During the political upheavals of the 1960s, sociological explanations were in the ascendancy, and sociological findings had a considerable impact on federal policy toward crime and delinquency. After reading Richard A. Cloward and Lloyd E. Ohlin's *Delinquency and Opportunity: A Theory of Delinquent Gangs* (1960), Attorney General Robert Kennedy asked Ohlin to help develop a new federal policy on juvenile delinquency. The result

Crimes Rates Vary Widely Throughout the World
Sociologists look to social rather than biological factors for understanding variations in crime rates among peoples of the world. Biological explanations seem inadequate for explaining why someone is 208 times more likely to be robbed in the United States than in Japan. *(Peter Menzel)*

was the passage of the Juvenile Delinquency Prevention and Control Act of 1961. The law was based on a comprehensive action program the two sociologists had developed in connection with their book. The program included improving education, creating work opportunities, organizing

---

Consider the following example. A man living in the Ozarks has a vision in which God speaks to him. He begins preaching to his relatives and neighbors, and soon he has his entire community in a state of religious fervor. People say he has a "calling." His reputation as a prophet and healer spreads, and he attracts large audiences in rural communities of Arkansas and Missouri. However, when he ventures into St. Louis and attempts to hold a prayer meeting on a downtown thoroughfare during rush hour, he is arrested. When he tells the police officers about his conversations with God, they take him to a mental hospital. Attending psychiatrists say he is "schizophrenic" and hospitalize him for mental illness (Slotkin, 1955). Thus we return full circle to sociological concerns. Again we are reminded that deviance is not a

property inherent in behavior but is a property conferred upon it by social definitions. Let us turn, then, to a consideration of four sociological approaches to deviance: anomie, cultural transmission, conflict, and labeling perspectives.

The Structural-Strain Perspective

As we noted earlier in the chapter, Emile Durkheim (1893/1964, 1897/1951) contended that deviance is functional for a society. He said that deviance and its punishment reinforce the boundaries of acceptable behavior and serve as occasions on which people reaffirm their commitment to the society's moral order. Durkheim also made another contribution to our understand-

lower-class communities, and providing services to families and gangs. It was later expanded to include all lower-class people and became the foundation for the Johnson administration's War on Poverty (Vold and Bernard, 1986).

In the 1980s, as the nation moved in a conservative political direction, public policy toward crime and delinquency moved in a similar direction. The new point of view is reflected in a widely heralded book by a conservative political scientist, James Q. Wilson, and a controversial psychologist, Richard J. Herrnstein, entitled *Crime and Human Nature* (1985). Wilson and Herrnstein undertake to debunk notions that crime rates and unemployment are associated or that poverty causes crime. They say certain genetic traits predispose people to commit crimes. For instance, they find a clear and consistent link between criminality and low intelligence: The average offender differs from the average nonoffender by about 10 points in measured IQ. They do not know why this is important, but they speculate that people who have lower IQs do poorly in school,

get frustrated, and turn to crime. Likewise, individuals who have a rather athletic, muscular build that runs to fat have a greater tendency than individuals with other physiques to engage in crime. They think it is not the build that causes crime, but the aggressive temperament often associated with it. Criminals also tend to be young males with impulsive, "now"-oriented personalities that make postponing gratification or even thinking about the future difficult. Persistent offenders display disruptive behavior early in life; by third grade, they are often out of control.

Wilson and Herrnstein contend that criminality runs in families. Identical twins are more likely to have identical delinquency records than fraternal twins. Identical twins are genetically the same, while fraternal twins are no more alike genetically than ordinary brothers and sisters. They say adoption studies point in a similar direction. When the sons of criminals are adopted as infants by noncriminal parents, they are three times more likely to become criminals than the adopted sons of noncriminal biological parents. Wilson and Herrn-

stein conclude that even though no one is born a criminal, genes predispose people to criminality much as they do toward alcoholism or Alzheimer's disease. Criminality arises as individual predispositions interact with social circumstances.

Most sociologists do not find Wilson and Herrnstein's arguments particularly convincing. Sociologists point out that biology does not explain why someone is 208 times more likely to be robbed in the United States than in Japan. Nor does it explain why the murder rate in the United States is 5 times that in Australia, despite the fact that a significant fraction of the Australian population was descended from English convicts (Jencks, 1987). How can Americans have a monopoly on bad genes? Civil libertarians also warn that a biological emphasis could lead to wrongly classifying people as crime-prone. In sum, Wilson and Herrnstein fail to give adequate attention to the social forces that affect people, the ways people interpret social situations, and how they learn these interpretations (Cohen, 1987).

ing of deviance with his idea of **anomie**. He pointed out that during times of rapid social change people become unsure of what is expected of them, and they find it difficult to fashion their actions in terms of conventional norms. Old norms do not seem relevant to current conditions, and emerging norms are too ambiguous and poorly formulated to provide effective and meaningful guidelines for behavior. Under these circumstances, Durkheim believed, an upsurge in deviant behavior could be expected.

Robert K. Merton and structural strain Sociologist Robert K. Merton (1968) has built upon Durkheim's notions of anomie and social cohesion, linking them to American life in his structural-strain perspective. He says

that for large numbers of Americans, worldly success—especially as it finds expression in material wealth—has become a cultural *goal*. However, only certain cultural *means*—most commonly securing a good education and acquiring high-paying jobs—are approved for achieving success. There might not be a problem if all Americans had equal access to the approved means for realizing monetary success. But this is not the case. The poor and minorities often find themselves handicapped by little formal education and few economic resources.

For those Americans who internalize the goal of material success—and not all individuals do—strong strains push them toward nonconformity and the use of unorthodox practices. They cannot achieve the culturally approved goals by using the culturally approved means for attaining them. One answer to this dilemma is to obtain the prestige-laden ends by any means, including vice and crime. Contemporary professional criminals, members of organized crime, and drug dealers find much in common with Al Capone, the notorious bootlegger and mobster of the 1920s and early 1930s, who contended:

> I make my money by supplying a public demand. If I break the law, my customers . . . are as guilty as I am. The only difference between us is that I sell and they buy. Everybody calls me a racketeer. I call myself a businessman. [Klein, 1980:1]

Merton identifies five responses to the ends-means dilemma, four of them being deviant adaptations to conditions of anomie (see Figure 8.1):

- *Conformity.* Conformity exists when people accept both the cultural goal of material success and the culturally approved means to achieve the goal. Such behavior is the bedrock of a stable society.

- *Innovation.* In innovation, people hold fast to the culturally emphasized goal of success while abandoning the culturally approved ways of seeking it. People may engage in prostitution, peddle drugs, forge checks, swindle, embezzle, steal, burglarize, rob, or extort to secure money and purchase the symbols of success.

- *Ritualism.* Ritualism involves abandoning or scaling down lofty success goals, but all the while abiding compulsively by the approved means. For instance, the ends of the organization become irrelevant for many zealous bureaucrats. Instead, they cultivate the means for their own sake, and make a fetish of regulations and red tape (see Chapter 5).

- *Retreatism.* In retreatism people reject *both* the cultural goals and the approved means without substituting new norms. Skid Row alcoholics, drug addicts, vagabonds, and derelicts have dropped out of society; they "are in society but not of it."

- *Rebellion.* Rebels reject both the cultural goals and the approved means and substitute *new* norms for them. They transfer their loyalties from existing social arrangements to new groups with new ideologies. Radical social movements provide a good illustration of this type of adaptation.

Merton's modes of individual adaptation have to do with role behavior—not personality. The same person—depending on the situation—may at one time or another employ any one of the five responses.

Applying the structural-strain perspective A number of sociologists have applied the structural-strain perspective to the study of juvenile delinquency. Albert Cohen

People at a Speakeasy Bar during Prohibition

In 1920 the Prohibition amendment to the Constitution imposed severe restrictions on the manufacture and distribution of alcoholic products. People who had used alcoholic beverages were outraged and some began to make beer and wine at home. Others resented what they viewed as a violation of their personal liberty by government. It quickly became the fashionable thing to serve liquor. The tremendous profits made in the illicit manufacture and sale of alcoholic beverages built up a powerful underworld organization. Stress theorists say that Al Capone and other bootleggers of the period simply took advantage of the opportunities they were presented to pursue the American dream of worldly success by illicit means. *(Chronicle Pictures/Photo Researchers)*

Modes of adaptation	Cultural goals	Institutionalized means
I Conformity	+	+
II Innovation	+	−
III Ritualism	−	+
IV Retreatism	−	−
V Rebellion	±	±

+ = Acceptance
− = Rejection
± = Rejection of prevailing values and substitution of new values

FIGURE 8.1   Merton's Typology of Modes of Individual Adaptation to Anomie
Source: Robert K. Merton, Social Theory and Social Structure, rev. ed. New York: Free Press, 1957.

(1955) suggests that lower-class boys are attracted to gangs because they are constantly being judged by a middle-class measuring rod. They find themselves failing in middle-class school environments that reward verbal skills, neatness, and an ability to defer gratification. The boys respond by banding together in juvenile gangs where they evolve "macho" standards rewarding "toughness," "street smarts," and "troublemaking"—standards that allow them to succeed. Indeed, Delbert S. Elliott (1966) finds that delinquent boys who drop out of school have a lower rate of juvenile court referrals after dropping out of school than when in school. Leaving school presumably provides a temporary solution to the frustrations they experience in meeting middle-class expectations.

Evaluating the structural-strain perspective   The structural-strain perspective draws our attention to those processes by which society itself generates deviance. It is a very appealing approach because it takes an optimistic view of human nature: Criminals are driven to commit crimes by societal pressures, and they would be law-abiding citizens if only given a chance. Crime is seen as concentrated among the lower classes because its members lack the opportunity to succeed in legitimate ways. The solution to the crime problem, then, lies in reforming society so that it lives up to its ideals of democracy and egalitarianism. The perspective enjoyed wide acceptance during the 1960s and provided the ideological underpinning for President Lyndon Johnson's War on Poverty. But when the programs failed to achieve their goals, they were dismantled by later administrations (Vold and Bernard, 1986).

Critics have faulted the structural-strain perspective on a number of grounds. For one thing, if it is correct, delinquency should be greatest when aspirations are high and expectations are low. Yet most researchers find that delinquency is highest when both aspirations and expectations are low, and delinquency is lowest when both aspirations and expectations are high. Nor, as we will see later in the chapter, is delinquency necessarily concentrated in the lower classes. The relationship between class and many types of delinquency is slight (Agnew, 1985). Moreover, Merton provides an image of American society in which there is a consensus on values and goals. But critics say that American society is pluralistic, with a good many different subcultures (see Chapter 3). Numerous examples exist of "deviant" behavior that can be explained as a failure to accept the same norms that govern most of the population: violations of fish and game laws among Indians; common law marriage among some ethnic minorities; the producing of moonshine among some Appalachian groups; and marijuana use among many teenagers.

The Cultural Transmission Perspective

The structural-strain perspective provides us with insight on how society may contribute to deviance by the way it structures goals and opportunities. A number of other sociologists have emphasized the similarities between the way deviant behavior is acquired and the way in which other behavior is acquired. During the 1920s and 1930s, sociologists at the University of Chicago were struck by the concentration of high delinquency rates in some areas of Chicago (Thrasher, 1927; Shaw, 1930; Shaw and McKay, 1942). They undertook a series of investigations and found that in certain neighborhoods the delinquency rates were stable from one period to another, despite changes in ethnic composition. The sociologists concluded that delinquent and criminal behavior are culturally transmitted from one generation to the next. Viewed in this fashion, it is "natural" that youths living in high-crime areas should acquire delinquent life styles. Moreover, as new ethnic groups enter a neighborhood, their children learn the delinquent patterns from those already there. Hence, the Chicago sociologists contended that youths become delinquent because they associate and make friends with other juveniles who are already delinquent.

Edwin H. Sutherland and differential association
Edwin H. Sutherland (1939), a sociologist associated with the Chicago tradition of sociology, elaborated upon these conclusions in developing his ideas regarding **differential association.** Sutherland said that people become deviant to the extent to which they participate in settings where deviant ideas, motivations, and techniques are viewed favorably. For example, they may learn how to use and obtain illegal drugs, how to enjoy and go about making homosexual contacts, or how to steal and then sell stolen items. The earlier, the more frequently, the more intensely, and the longer the duration of the contacts people have in such settings, the greater the probability that they too will become deviant. But more is involved than simply imitation. Deviant behavior is not only learned; it is taught. Thus the perspective focuses on *what* is learned and *who* it is learned from. More recently, Ronald L. Akers (1977; Akers et al., 1979) has taken Sutherland's relatively loose formulation and applied the principles of conditioning to a variety of deviant behaviors (see Chapter 7). Akers focuses on how the rewards and punishments obtained in associations with others shape our behavior in deviant or nondeviant directions.

The differential association perspective provides a sophisticated version of the old saying that "good companions make good boys; bad companions make bad boys." When parents move to a new neighborhood to "get Mike away from his bad friends," they are applying the principle of differential association. So are parole officers who try to restrict the associations of the paroled

prisoners they supervise. The theory also suggests that imprisonment may be counterproductive when juveniles are incarcerated with experienced criminals.

Applying the cultural transmission perspective   In pluralistic societies with multiple subcultures, groups differ in some of their values and norms. Sociologist Walter B. Miller (1958, 1975) builds on this notion in his study of unlawful activity among lower-class juveniles. He sees their behavior not as deviance, but as conformity to cultural patterns prevalent in ghetto and inner-city settings. Lower-class culture, he says, attaches high value to a number of "focal concerns": *trouble*—welcoming "encounters" with police officers, school officials, welfare investigators, and other agents of the larger society; *toughness*—showing skills in physical combat and an ability to "take it"; *smartness*—being able to outwit, dupe, and outsmart others; *excitement*—seeking thrills, taking risks, and flirting with danger; *fate*—assuming that most of life's crucial events are beyond one's control and governed by chance and destiny; and *autonomy*—desiring to be free of external controls and coercive authority. Although these focuses are not necessarily delinquent, valuing them creates situations in which unlawful activity is likely to occur. For instance, an emphasis on toughness contributes to verbal insults and physical attack, and a craving for excitement promotes auto theft.

Evaluating the cultural transmission perspective   The cultural transmission perspective shows that socially dis-

Cultural Transmission
Behavior that society views as deviant is often acquired in the same way in which other behavior is acquired. Youths living in neighborhoods where gangs are prevalent grow up in social settings where gang membership is seen as attractive and even necessary for protection. *(Edward Lettau/Photo Researchers)*

approved behaviors can arise through the same processes of socialization as socially approved ones. As such it is a particularly useful tool for understanding why deviance varies from group to group and from society to society. However, the approach is not applicable to some forms of deviance, particularly those in which neither the techniques nor the appropriate definitions and attitudes are acquired from other deviants. Illustrations include criminal violators of financial trust; check forgers; occasional, incidental, and situational offenders; nonprofessional shoplifters; non-career criminals; and people who commit "crimes of passion." Further, deviants and nondeviants often grow up in the same environments—criminal patterns are presented to two persons, but only one of them becomes a criminal. Two people may be confronted with the same patterns but perceive them quite differently, producing different outcomes.

The Conflict Perspective

Cultural transmission theorists emphasize that people of different subcultures exhibit different behaviors because they are socialized in traditions that have unique values and norms. To this idea conflict theorists respond: "True, groups have differing values and norms. But the question is 'Which group will be able to translate its values into the rules of a society and make these rules stick?'" Consider, for instance, that during the Vietnam war, antiwar groups contended that the real criminals were those running the war. Consumer and ecology groups assert that the real criminals are corporate executives whose firms gouge the public and pollute the environment. Community organizers say that the real criminals in inner-city neighborhoods are absentee landlords and greedy store owners. Moreover, there are often clashing interests among major social groups—classes, sexes, racial and ethnic groups, business organizations, labor unions, and farm associations. Accordingly, conflict theorists say we also need to ask: "Who gets the lion's share of the benefits from particular social arrangements?" Or, put another way, "How is society structured so that some groups are advantaged while other groups are disadvantaged and even stigmatized as deviant?"

Although in recent decades the conflict perspective has taken many new directions, its early roots can be traced to the Marxist tradition (see Chapter 1). According to orthodox Marxism, a capitalist ruling class exploits and robs the masses, yet avoids punishment for its crimes. The victims of capitalist oppression, in their struggle to survive, are driven to commit acts that the ruling class brands as criminal (Bonger, 1936). Other types of deviance—alcoholism, drug abuse, family violence, sexual immorality, prostitution—are results of a social order founded on the unprincipled pursuit of profit and the subjugation of the poor, women, blacks, and other minorities. Mental and emotional problems are common because people become estranged from one another and from themselves. The estrangement ultimately comes from the separation of people from the means from which they derive their livelihood (see Chapter 15).

Richard Quinney: Class, state, and crime   The contemporary Marxist approach to deviance has been articulated by the sociologist Richard Quinney (1974, 1980). "Law," he says, "is the tool of the ruling class" (1974:8). The capitalist legal system makes illegal behavior that is offensive to the powerful and threatens their privileges and property. Even common behaviors—gambling, illicit sex, drinking, loitering, truancy—jeopardize powerful vested interests by challenging such basic capitalist values as sobriety, individual responsibility, deferred gratification, and industriousness (Hepburn, 1977).

In striving to maintain itself against the internal contradictions eating away at its foundations, Quinney (1980:57) says that capitalism commits *crimes of domination*: "One of the contradictions of capitalism is that some of its laws must be violated in order to secure the existing system." These crimes include those committed by corporations, which range from price fixing to pollution of the environment. But there are also *crimes of government* committed by the officials—for example, Watergate in the 1970s and the Iranian-Contra arms scandal in the 1980s. In contrast, much of the criminal behavior of ordinary people, or *predatory crime*—burglary, robbery, drug dealing, and hustling of various sorts—is "pursued out of the need to survive" in a capitalist social order. *Personal crime*—murder, assault, rape—is "pursued by those who are already brutalized by the conditions of capitalism." And then there are *crimes of resistance*, in which workers engage in sloppy work and clandestine acts of sabotage against their employers.

Applying the conflict perspective   The conflict perspective has led social scientists to investigate how the making and administering of law is controlled by powerful interests. Many sociologists have noted that crime is defined primarily in terms of offenses against property (burglary, robbery, auto theft, and vandalism), while **corporate crime**—crime committed by business firms—

Crime Committed by Government?
Some conflict theorists contend that government, acting as the agent of elites, has periodically acted to suppress political dissent contrary to American constitutional guarantees. In the late 1940s and early 1950s, the intensity of anti-Communist feeling reached hysterical proportions and was sometimes politically inspired. During this period, congressional committees investigated charges of subversive activities in the State Department and elsewhere in American life. Senator Joseph R. McCarthy (standing) was an important figure in the crusade against communism. *(UPI/Bettmann Newsphotos)*

is deemphasized (Sutherland, 1949; Coleman, 1985). Moreover, the penalty for crimes against property is imprisonment, while the most common form of penalty for business-related offenses is a monetary fine. Sociologist Amitai Etzioni (1985) found that between 1975 and 1984, 62 percent of the nation's 500 largest corporations were involved in one or more illegal practices; 42 percent, in two or more, and 15 percent, in five or more. The offenses included price fixing and overcharging, domestic and foreign bribes, fraud and deception, and patent infringements. Yet unlike robbers and muggers, corporations and their executives got off easy. For example, the Justice Department sought only misdemeanor charges against Smith Kline Beckman Corporation after the company failed to report to the Food and Drug Administration adverse reactions to Selacryn, a drug used to treat high blood pressure. Even though the drug was linked to 36 deaths and 500 injuries, the company was fined and three people were sentenced to perform community service work (Burnett, 1986). And while the Federal Bureau of Investigation keeps track of every murder, rape, assault, and auto theft reported in the United States, no agency keeps track of crimes committed by corporations. (We will have more to say about corporate crime in Chapters 16 and 19).

Evaluating the conflict perspective   There is a good deal of truth in the conflict perspective. It is obvious to most people that powerful individuals and groups make and administer the laws. In this sense, then, laws are not neutral, but favor some group's interests and some

group's values. Yet critics charge that intuitive insights like these hardly satisfy the canons of scientific inquiry (Hagan and Leon, 1977). Many conflict formulations need to be refined. It is not always clear which specific individuals or groups are covered by such terms as "ruling elites," "governing classes," and "powerful interests." And conflict hypotheses need to be tested. For instance, the notion that unemployment causes crime, when tested, yields contradictory findings (Cantor and Land, 1985; Wilson and Cook, 1985). Much depends on the type of crime involved and whether one focuses on the effects unemployment has on motivations to engage in crime or the opportunities to do so. Moreover, simply because corporations often seek to influence legislation and governmental policy, they do not necessarily win out over other interest groups (Hagan, 1980). Conflict propositions cannot be accepted as articles of faith, then; they require rigorous scientific investigation.

THINKING THROUGH THE ISSUES

Are economic motives the sole or even the supreme cause of crime? Do they explain, for example, the massive illegal mail interception programs by the CIA (Ermann and Lundman, 1978) or the U.S. army intentionally exposing soldiers to fallout from nuclear explosions (Stone, 1982)? Do all organizations, capitalist or socialist, experience pressure to resort to illegitimate means of

Corporate Crime

We typically think of crime as acts committed by individuals, not organizations. Conflict theorists draw our attention to unlawful activities undertaken by business firms. In 1986, an agency of the Labor Department assessed a 1.4 million-dollar fine against Union Carbide for health and safety violations at its plant in Institute, West Virginia (left). The inspection was prompted by the rupturing of a tank containing a toxic chemical, spewing a cloud of gas that forced the hospitalization of six workers and 135 nearby residents. On August 28, 1986, the United States said Lockheed had overcharged the government hundreds of millions of dollars in the production of the C-5B military transport plane (right). *(left, Tannenbaum/Sygma; right, Gamma–Liaison)*

goal attainment when legitimate means are unavailable to them (Los, 1982)? Consider the following statement: "Some organizations seek profits, others seek survival, still others seek to fulfill government-imposed quotas, others seek to service a body of professionals who run them, some seek to win wars, and some seek to serve a clientele. Whatever the goals might be, it is the emphasis on them that creates the trouble" (Gross, 1978:72).

The Labeling Perspective

Conflict theorists contend that people are often at odds with one another because interests diverge and values clash. Some people gain the power to translate their value preferences into the rules governing institutional life. They then successfully place negative labels on violators of these rules. A number of sociologists have taken this notion and expanded on it. They are interested in the process whereby some people come to be tagged as "deviants," begin to think of themselves as deviants, and

follow deviant careers. The approach is a version of symbolic interactionism.

Edwin Lemert, Howard S. Becker, and Kai Erikson: Societal reaction to deviance   Proponents of the labeling perspective—sociologists like Edwin M. Lemert (1951, 1972), Howard S. Becker (1963), and Kai Erikson (1962, 1966)—make a number of points. First, they contend that no act by itself is criminal or noncriminal. The "badness" of an act does not come from its content but from the way other people define and react to it. In this sense, then, deviance, like beauty, is in the eye of the beholder.

Second, labeling theorists point out that we all engage in deviant behavior by violating some norms. They reject the popular idea that human beings can be divided into those who are "normal" and those who are not. Some of us exceed the speed limit, experiment with cocaine, shoplift, cheat on a homework assignment, sample homosexual publications, underreport our income to tax authorities, swim in the nude, become intoxicated, commit vandalism in celebration of a football victory, trespass on private property, or ride in a friend's car without permission. Labeling theorists call these actions **pri-**

mary deviance—behavior that violates social norms but usually goes unnoticed by the agents of social control. Third, labeling theorists say that whether acts will be seen as deviant depends *both* on what they are *and* what other people do about it. In short, deviance depends on which rules society chooses to enforce, in which situations, and with respect to which people. Not everyone is arrested for speeding, shoplifting, underreporting income on tax returns, trespassing, or the like. Blacks may be censured for behaviors whites may display without comment; women, for what men may do; certain individuals, for what their friends are also doing. Some people may be labeled deviant simply because they are accused of something (for instance, they appear "effeminate" and are tagged as "gay"). What is critical is the social audience and how it *labels* the person.

Fourth, labeling people as deviant has consequences for them. It sets up conditions conducive to **secondary deviance**—deviance individuals adopt in response to the reactions of other individuals. In brief, labeling theorists contend that new deviance is *manufactured* by the hostile reaction of rule makers and rule abiders. A person is publicly identified, stereotyped, and denounced as a "delinquent," "mental fruitcake," "forger," "rapist," "drug addict," "bum," "pervert," "criminal." The label serves to lock the person into a master "outsider" status (Palamara, Cullen, and Gersten, 1986). Such a master status overrides other statuses in shaping a person's social experiences and results in a self-fulfilling prophecy. Rule breakers come to accept their status as a deviant and organize their lives around it.

Fifth, people labeled deviant typically find themselves rejected and isolated by "law-abiding" people. Friends and relatives may withdraw from them. In some cases, they may be institutionalized in prisons or mental hospitals. Rejection and isolation push stigmatized individuals toward other people who share a common fate. Participation in a deviant subculture becomes a way of coping with frustrating situations and finding emotional support and personal acceptance. In turn, joining a deviant group solidifies a deviant self-image, fosters a deviant life style, and weakens ties to the law-abiding community.

In sum, labeling theorists say that it is the societal response to an act and not the behavior itself that determines deviance. When behavior is seen as departing from prevailing norms, it "sets off a chain of social reactions." Others define, evaluate, and label the behavior. Norm violators then take into account these definitions as they plan further actions. In many cases, they evolve an identity consistent with the label and enter on a career of deviance.

Applying the labeling perspective   Sociologist William J. Chambliss (1973) used the labeling perspective to explain the differing perceptions and definitions community members had of the behavior of two teenage gangs. While at Hanibal High School, Chambliss observed the activities of the Saints, a gang of eight white upper-

The Labeling Perspective
Street people and bag ladies are a common sight today in most American cities. The line between acceptable and deviant behavior is a fine one and has much to do with the observer and the standard being used. What some people may see as merely different, others may consider as deviant. *(Robert V. Eckert, Jr./EKM–Nepenthe)*

middle-class boys, and the Roughnecks, a gang of six lower-class white boys. Although the Saints engaged in as many delinquent acts as the Roughnecks, it was the Roughnecks who were in "constant trouble" and called "delinquent."

The Saints had an image as "good students" headed for college. Yet they were often truant from school and spent their weekends drinking, driving recklessly at high speeds, deliberately running red lights, shouting obscenities at women, vandalizing empty houses, removing warning signs from road repair sites, and erecting stolen barricades on highways where unsuspecting motorists would crash into them. The Hanibal townspeople overlooked the Saints' high level of delinquency. They saw the Saints as law-abiding youths who simply went in for an occasional prank—"good boys sowing wild oats." After all, they were well dressed, displayed middle-class manners, and drove nice cars.

It was otherwise for the Roughnecks. Everyone agreed that "the not-so-well-dressed, not-so-well-mannered, not-so-rich boys were heading for trouble." Thier brawls and petty stealing were well known throughout the community. Moreover, a high level of mutual distrust and hostility existed between the Roughnecks and the police. Several of the Roughnecks were periodically arrested, and two of the boys were sentenced to six months in boys' schools. The community, the school, and the police treated the Saints as good, upstanding youths with bright futures, but they treated the Roughnecks as young criminals headed for trouble.

Chambliss (1973:30–31) concludes:

> The community responded to the Roughnecks as boys in trouble, and the boys agreed with that perception. Their pattern of deviancy was reinforced, and breaking away from it became increasingly unlikely. Once the boys acquired an image of themselves as deviants, they selected new friends who affirmed that self-image. As that self-conception became more firmly entrenched, they also became willing to try new and more extreme deviances. With their growing alienation came freer expression of disrespect and hostility for representatives of the legitimate society. This disrespect increased the community's negativism, perpetuating the entire process of commitment to deviance.

Evaluating the labeling perspective   Unlike the structural-strain and cultural transmission perspectives, the labeling perspective does not focus on why some people engage in deviant behavior. Rather, the labeling perspective seeks to explain why the same act may or may not be considered deviant, depending on the situation and the characteristics of the people involved. In recent years, a number of labeling theorists have incorporated insights from conflict theory. They have looked to societal inequalities to see how institutions are structured and how rules are made and enforced.

But the labeling perspective also has its critics. For one thing, while labeling may help us understand how individuals become career deviants, it tells us little about what initially contributed to their deviant behavior. Indeed, in many forms of deviance it is the behavior or condition of the people themselves that is primarily responsible for their being labeled in the first place. Take mental illness. It seems that the vast majority of hospitalized people suffer acute disturbance that is associated with *internal* psychological or neurological malfunctioning (Gove, 1970). Their inner turmoil and suffering cannot be explained solely in terms of the reactions of other people. In fact, if a family member develops symptoms of mental disorder, other family members typically resist labeling the person as "mentally ill." They invoke notions like job stress and long-standing personality quirks as explanations for the symptoms (Whitt and Meile, 1985). Deviance too cannot be understood without reference to norms. If behavior is not deviant unless it is labeled, how are we to classify secret and undetected deviance, such as the embezzlement of funds, failure to pay taxes, and clandestine sexual molestation of children?

None of the sociological perspectives we have examined provides a complete explanation of deviant behavior, although each one highlights an important source of deviance (see Table 8.1 on page 208). Deviant behavior has many forms, so we must approach each form in its own right to determine the specific factors involved. We turn next to a consideration of crime, a form of deviance that is particularly prevalent in modern industrialized societies.

Crime and the Criminal Justice System

Within modern societies, law is a crucial element in social control. Unlike informal norms such as folkways and mores, laws are rules that are enforced by the state. **Crime** is merely an act that is prohibited by law. Not all deviant acts are crime; for an act to be considered criminal, the state must make it illegal—or *criminalize* it. What distinguishes crimes is not that they are acts we

Table 8.1   Perspectives on Deviance

Perspective	Issue It Addresses	Premise	Source of Deviance	Best Explains
Structural-strain	Why do people violate social rules?	Society generates deviance through structural strains.	People cannot achieve cultural goals by culturally approved means.	Crime engaged in by lower-class people that provides monetary gain.
Cultural transmission	Why is deviance more prevalent among some groups than others?	Deviant behavior is learned in the same fashion as any other behavior.	People are immersed in different subcultures and countercultures. They learn the attitudes and practices associated with their peers.	Delinquent gangs and members of deviant subcultures.
Conflict	How is society structured so that some groups are advantaged while others are disadvantaged and stigmatized as deviant?	The institutional order generates clashing interests among major groups.	Social arrangements that breed social inequality and competition.	Economic and political crimes.
Labeling	How do behaviors and people come to be labeled as deviant?	No act or person is inherently deviant. Deviance is a matter of social definition.	People who are labeled as deviants enter careers as deviants.	Deviance among the powerless.

regard as immoral or wicked. For instance, a good many Americans consider it no more "evil" to cheat on their income taxes than their parents and grandparents did to purchase and consume illegal alcoholic beverages during Prohibition. The distinguishing property of crime is that people who violate the law are liable to be arrested, tried, pronounced guilty, and deprived of lives, liberty, or property. In brief, they are likely to become caught up in the elaborate social machinery of the **criminal justice system**—the reactive agencies of the state that include the police, the courts, and prisons. Let us briefly consider each of these.

The Criminal Justice System

Judged by what they see on television, the American public is enamored with crime. The scenario of most television series invariably runs along these lines: A serious crime is committed; the police or detective hero sifts through the clues and tracks down the culprits; the prosecutor throws the book at them; judge and jury do their duty; and the criminals are sent to prison. In real life, however, the picture is quite different. According to statistics from the Justice Department, of every 100 felonies

committed in the United States, only 33 are reported to the police. Of the 33 that are reported, only 6 are cleared by arrest. Of the 6 who are arrested, only 3 are prosecuted and convicted. Of these, only 1 is sent to prison; the other 2 are rejected or dismissed due to problems with the evidence or witnesses or diverted into treatment programs. Of those sent to prison, more than half receive a sentence of at least five years. However, the average inmate is released in about two years (see Figure 8.2). Even those sentenced to life imprisonment serve a median time of eight years and seven months.

The police   Within the United States, there are 490,000 police officers, plus 210,000 support employees. Of this number, 525,000 work for local governments, 100,000 for states, and 75,000 for the federal government. The police are a citizen's first link with the criminal justice system, and in many ways the most important one. When a crime occurs, the police are usually the first agents of the state to become involved.

Police officers are expected not only to catch lawbreakers, but also to perform a variety of community roles, from providers of emergency first aid to dog catching. Some police officers call themselves "do-everything

uncollected trash, and responding to medical emergency calls.

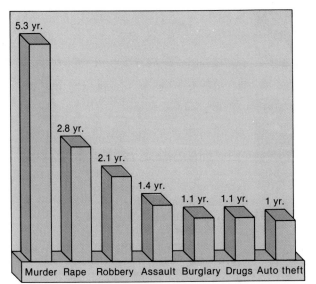

FIGURE 8.2 **Time behind Bars: Median Prison Terms Served by First Offenders**
Source: Justice Department. U.S. News & World Report, *April 15, 1985:43.*

guys" (despite affirmative action programs, 95 percent of police officers are male). In towns of 50,000 population or more, on average only 45 officers are actually on patrol out of every 100 who are on duty at any given time. Indeed, police officers spend only about 15 percent of their time dealing with crime. The rest is spent filling out reports, directing traffic, handling complaints about

THINKING THROUGH THE ISSUES

One suggestion for combatting crime is to "add more cops." But how much more crime is likely to be prevented by additional police resources? Or put another way, how many police are enough? Is there a simple answer to these questions? Look at Table 8.2. Detroit and Philadelphia have almost the same ratio of police to population, yet Detroit has more than twice as much reported crime. Detroit and San Diego have comparable crime rates, even though Detroit has twice the ratio of police to population.

The courts In the United States, the criminal justice system is an *adversary* system. The accused person—the *defendant*—is presumed to be innocent until proved guilty in a court of law by the representative of the state—the *prosecutor*. In other nations the questioning of witnesses is handled by judges, and guilt and innocence is decided by a judge or panel of judges. But the American system assumes that justice is best served by pitting opposing lawyers against one another before a neutral judge and jury.

In practice, the fate of most of those accused of crime is determined by prosecutors. Prosecutors typically

Table 8.2 Crime Rates and Police/Population Ratios, Ten Major Cities, 1978

City	Number of police officers	1978 Crimes per 10,000 Population	1978 Police per 10,000 Population
New York	29,443	762.3	39.3
Chicago	14,324	618.2	46.4
Los Angeles	9,649	837.7	34.6
Philadelphia	9,255	384.4	48.8
Houston	3,873	818.2	24.0
Detroit	6,371	839.5	48.4
Dallas	2,574	990.8	29.5
San Diego	1,557	847.6	19.7
Baltimore	3,912	839.4	47.3
San Antonio	1,386	687.3	18.1

Source: Adapted from Herbet Jacob and Robert L. Lineberry, Governmental Responses to Crime. Washington, D.C.: Government Printing Office, 1982.

Law Enforcement: The Guardian Angels
Frustrated by what they view as soaring crime rates, growing numbers of Americans are helping to patrol their neighborhoods, securing their homes like fortresses, or carrying guns. Here Guardian Angels keep an outlook for criminals on a New York subway. (*Eve Arnold/Magnum*)

reject or reduce the severity of 50 to 80 percent of the charges filed by police. The reasons that prosecutors cite range from case overload to police inefficiency in producing evidence. Of the some 2 million serious criminal cases filed each year in the United States, fewer than 1 in 5 go to trial, the others end in dismissals or guilty pleas.

When prosecutors decide to take a case to trial, judges must make a number of decisions. They must decide whether a defendant should be released on bail, how fast a case will come to trial, the legality of police and prosecution tactics, and when the defendant is found guilty, the penalty. Should a defendant be sent to prison, the sentence can vary substantially, depending on the judge. And once early releases granted by parole boards are factored in, disparities in time served can vary enormously. The average period spent in prison by convicted felons ranges from 13 months in South Dakota to 53 months in Massachusetts.

Prisons   American prisons vary from dingy, fortresslike state penitentiaries built in the 1800s to ultramodern lockups. And the convict population is increasing more rapidly than the capacity of prisons to hold them. In 1986, the nation's prison population reached a record 546,659 inmates (a 66 percent increase since 1980 and double the total of ten years earlier). Another 230,000 were in local jails awaiting trial or doing time for minor infractions. In all, 1 of every 382 adult males and 1 of every 5,422 adult females is behind bars (1 of every 35 adult men is on probation, under parole supervision, or imprisoned). The cost runs in excess of $10 billion a

year—$18,000 or more per inmate. On average, state prisons are estimated to be one-third over capacity, while federal facilities are 28 percent overfilled, leading to doubling up and even tripling up in cells designed for one person. We will have more to say later in the chapter about the impact of prisons on inmates. But first, let us take a closer look at crime.

Forms of Crime

Since crime is an act prohibited by law, it is the state that defines crime by the laws it promulgates, administers, and enforces. An infinite variety of acts can be crimes. In Eastern Europe and the Soviet Union, it is a crime to organize political parties in opposition to the regimes. In some nations like Iran, it is a crime to belong to religious groups barred by the dominant religious authorities. In the United States, interracial marriages were barred by many states prior to a 1967 Supreme Court decision prohibiting such statutes. And in many communities in the United States, "blue laws" make it a crime to sell various items on Sunday, particularly alcoholic beverages. Since we cannot then examine something we can call crime everywhere, we will consider a number of forms of crime within the United States.

White-collar crime   One type of crime that has been of particular interest to sociologists is **white-collar crime**—crime committed by persons of affluence, often in the course of their business activities (Sutherland, 1949).

Included in white-collar crime are corporate crime, fraud, embezzlement, corruption, bribery, tax fraud or evasion, stock manipulation, misrepresentation in advertising, restraint of trade, and infringements of patents. Fraud and theft in the retail industry increases the cost of many items by at least 15 percent. The cost of public construction is increased between 10 and 50 percent by bribery, kickbacks, and payoffs resulting in overcharges to taxpayers of more than $2 billion annually. Insurance frauds are common. In fact, the biggest theft in American history was not the robbery of a bank or an armored car, but the $1 billion Equity Funding fraud masterminded by executives of a Los Angeles–based insurance conglomerate in the late 1970s. And taxpayers who do not tell the Internal Revenue Service exactly how much they earn cost the government an estimated $100 billion in 1986 (Klott, 1986).

The American criminal justice system is not equipped to deal with white-collar crime. Unlike a robbery, a stock or insurance fraud is complex and difficult to unravel. Local law enforcement officials commonly lack the skills and resources necessary to tackle crimes outside the sphere of street crime. Federal agencies will handle only the more serious white-collar crimes. And the handful of white-collar criminals who are prosecuted and convicted are given a slap on the wrist. Street criminals who steal $100 may find their way to prison, while the dishonest executive who embezzles $1 million may receive a suspended sentence and a relatively small fine.

"*Warrington Trently, this court has found you guilty of price-fixing, bribing a government official, and conspiring to act in restraint of trade. I sentence you to six months in jail, suspended. You will now step forward for the ceremonial tapping of the wrist.*"

Drawing by Lorenz; © 1976 The New Yorker Magazine, Inc.

Federal statistics indicate that embezzlers at banks steal nine times more than bank robbers. Yet whereas only 17 percent of the embezzlers go to jail, 91 percent of bank robbers end up in jail.

Organized crime   **Organized crime** refers to large-scale organizations that provide illegal goods and services in public demand. The President's Commission on Organized Crime estimated that it reaped about $100 billion in the United States in 1986 (Shenon, 1986). Organized crime is likely to arise when the state criminalizes certain activities—prostitution, drugs, pornography, gambling, and loan sharking—that large numbers of citizens desire and are willing to pay for. Since Prohibition, organized crimes has largely been conducted by a syndicate variously termed the Mafia or the Cosa Nostra. So much has been written about this group that it is difficult to separate myth from fact. However, it seems to be a loose network or confederation of regional syndicates coordinated by a "commission" composed of the heads of the most powerful crime "families" (Cressey, 1969; Powell, 1986). The Mafia operates a vast system of political corruption and employs violence and intimidation against its victims, rivals, and "renegades." Having piled up enormous profits from drug dealing and gambling, the Mafia has diversified into entertainment, labor unions, construction, trucking, vending machines, garbage carting, toxic waste disposal, banking, stock fraud, and insurance.

The media often depict organized crime as an Italian monopoly. However, Irish and Jewish crime figures have long cooperated with the Mafia. In New York and Philadelphia, black groups and the Mafia run gambling and narcotics operations in concert. In San Francisco, Chinese gangs shake down merchants and are involved in gambling, robberies, and prostitution; the self-proclaimed Israeli Mafia extorts money in Los Angeles; and Colombian and Cuban drug rings have flooded Florida with their products (Raab, 1984; Powell, 1986; Kerr, 1987).

Violent crime   The Federal Bureau of Investigation (FBI) annually reports on eight types of crime in its *Uniform Crime Report*. These offenses are termed **index crimes** and consist of four categories of violent crimes against people—murder, rape, robbery, and assault—and four categories of crimes against property—burglary, theft, motor vehicle theft, and arson. It is these crimes that are emphasized by the news media, most feared by the public, and most denounced by public officials. In 1983, there were 30.9 violent crimes for every 1,000 people in the United States. Table 8.3 shows the odds of a person becoming a victim of robbery and assault based on Justice Department data.

Table 8.3   Odds of Becoming a Victim of Robbery or Assault (Rates per 100,000 Persons in 1981)

	Robbery	*Assault*
Sex		
Male	10	36
Female	5	18
Age		
12–15	12	46
16–19	12	53
20–24	12	54
25–34	8	35
35–49	5	17
50–64	5	8
65 or older	4	4
Race		
White	6	26
Black	17	31
Hispanic	12	25
Income		
$3,000 or less	16	47
$3,000–$7,499	12	31
$7,500–$9,999	9	32
$10,000–$14,999	8	31
$15,000–$24,999	6	25
$25,000 or more	5	23
Job Status		
Retired	6	4
Keeping house	4	11
Unable to work	6	18
Employed	7	29
In school	11	44
Unemployed	13	60
Residence		
Central city	15	35
Suburb	6	26
Rural	3	21

Source: U.S. Department of Justice.

Victimless crime   **Victimless crimes** are offenses in which the parties involved do not consider themselves to be "victims" (Schur, 1965; Box, 1984). They include gambling, the sale and use of illicit drugs, and prohibited sexual relationships between consenting adults (such as prostitution and homosexuality). Usually a crime has an identifiable victim who suffers as a result of the criminal behavior. But in victimless crime only the offenders themselves are likely to suffer. The behavior is criminalized because society, or powerful groups within society, define the behaviors as immoral.

In recent years there has been a movement to decriminalize many victimless crimes. Proponents argue that these crimes consume an inordinate amount of the time and resources of the criminal justice system and clog already congested courts and jails. Additionally, making illegal goods and services that many people desire and are willing to purchase almost invariably leads to the development of a black market supplied by organized crime. Victimless crimes are often related to the corruption of police officers and others in the criminal justice system who receive bribes and payoffs from illegal suppliers and practitioners. Finally, there are those who argue that victimless crime involves acts that are private matters, acts that are not rightfully the concern of government or other people. But others suggest that some acts are "inherently evil" and justify public action. So once again we find that deviance and crime are not matters upon which all people can agree and arrive at a universal standard. Instead, competing groups seek to gain the support of the state for their morality and values.

Measuring Crime

Statistics on crime are among the most unsatisfactory of all social data. Official crime records—such as the FBI's annual *Uniform Crime Reports* based on incidents filed with more than 15,000 law enforcement agencies—suffer from numerous limitations (see Figure 8.3). For one thing, a large proportion of the crimes that are committed go undetected; others are detected but not reported; and still others are reported but not officially recorded when police officers and politicians manipulate their reports to show low crime rates for political purposes. For another, perceptions of crime vary from community to community; what is viewed as a serious crime by a citizen of a small town may be shrugged off by a city resident as an unpleasant bit of everyday life.

When the *Uniform Crime Reports* are compared with victim-based measures of crime (based on survey

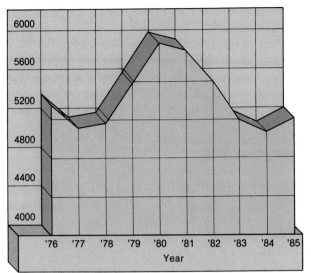

FIGURE 8.3 **Crimes Reported to Law Enforcement Officials per 100,000 Population**
The crimes include murder, rape, robbery, aggravated assault, burglary, larceny, and motor vehicle theft.
Source: Bureau of Justice Statistics, Federal Bureau of Investigation.

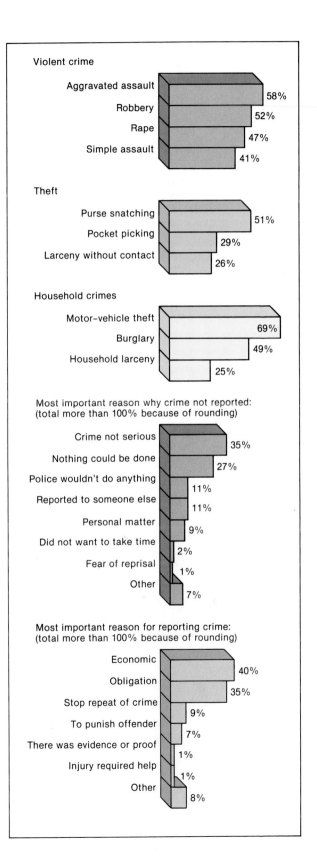

samples of American households in which individuals are asked if they or any member of their household had been victims of crime during the previous year), the rates of various crimes in the United States are substantially higher. A National Crime Survey based on 1983 data showed that only 35 percent of crimes were made known to the police (Katz, 1985). Among offenses against the person, reported crimes of violence ranged from a 41 percent rate for simple assault to a high of 58 percent for aggravated assault. Reporting rates for offenses against property ranged from 25 percent of the household larcenies to 69 percent of car thefts (see Figure 8.4).

Self-report-based measures of crime—anonymous questionnaires that ask people which offenses they have committed—also reveal much higher rates than those found in official crime statistics. For instance, studies of juvenile crime show that a good many youngsters of all social classes break some criminal laws, that the amount of unreported crime is enormous, and that convicted offenders are unrepresentative of persons violating the criminal law (Erickson and Empey, 1963; Hindelang,

FIGURE 8.4 **Crimes Reported and Reasons Why Crimes Were or Were Not Reported, 1983**
Source: Bureau of Justice Statistics.

Hirschi, and Weis, 1981; Thornberry and Farnworth, 1982). Youths who are arrested and placed in juvenile facilities are typically individuals with limited resources and/or those who commit serious offenses and do so frequently.

The *Uniform Crime Reports* focus on crimes that are most likely to be committed by young people and individuals of lower socioeconomic backgrounds. Consequently, many categories of crime, such as white-collar crime and organized crime, are not routinely reported on. Many crimes committed by those of upper socioeconomic status in the courses of their businesses are handled by quasi-judicial bodies, such as the Federal Trade Commission and the National Labor Relations Board, or by civil courts. As a result, businesspeople are generally able to avoid being stigmatized as criminals. Additionally, in the case of some criminal offenses, such as income tax evasion and fraud, the crimes are also unlikely to be reported in victimization studies.

The Purposes of Imprisonment

Many Americans take a rather gloomy view of crime-fighting programs. They question whether anything works. Experts themselves are unsure of the most effective methods for dealing with the prison population. Let us consider the four traditional purposes of imprisonment: punishment, rehabilitation, deterrence, and selective incapacitation.

Punishment   Prior to 1800 it was widely assumed that the punishment of deviants is required if the community is to feel morally satisfied. Toward the latter part of the eighteenth and the early part of the nineteenth centuries, the focus changed, and the idea that prisons might *rehabilitate* criminals came to the forefront. The word "penitentiary" was coined to describe a place where a criminal might repent and resolve to follow a law-abiding life. In recent years there has been a renewed interest in punishment—not to satisfy a desire for vengeance, but to restore a sense of moral order.

Rehabilitation   During the last century and a half, the concept of rehabilitation has dominated penal philosophy. It has drawn on a humanistic tradition that has pressed for the individualization of justice and demanded treatment for criminals. In this view, crime resembles "disease," something foreign and abnormal to most people. Inherent in the definition of a sick person is a presumption that individuals are not to blame for the disease, and that we should focus on curing them. Beginning in the 1960s, however, a number of criminologists began questioning the assumptions underlying rehabilitation strategies. Critics of rehabilitation contend

Convict Labor
At the turn of the century, the use of prison labor was widespread. Here convicts work in a quarry near a Georgia prison in 1919. The brutality of the system, the harshness of the working conditions, and the exploitation of the prisoners contributed to prison reform and the ending of prison labor in most states by 1940. Wider acceptance was won for the view that prisons and reform schools are primarily for reformation rather than punishment. *(The Bettmann Archive)*

that education and psychotherapy cannot overcome or reduce the powerful tendency for some individuals to continue a criminal career. They cite statistics on the high rate of *recidivism* (relapse into criminal behavior) to back up their arguments (Martinson, 1974; Lipton, Martinson, and Wilks, 1975).

Deterrence The notion of deterrence rests on assumptions about human nature that are difficult to prove. Even so, sociological studies seem to suggest that the *certainty* of apprehension and punishment does tend to lower crime rates (Wolfgang, Figlio, and Sellin, 1972; Waldo and Chiricos, 1972). Few studies, however, find an association between the *severity* of punishment and crime (Gibbs, 1975; Grasmick and Bryjak, 1980; Paternoster and Iovanni, 1986). While sociologists recognize that the prospect of punishment has some deterrent effect under some circumstances, they have been more concerned with specifying the *conditions* under which punishment influences behavior (Brown, 1978; Erickson and Gibbs, 1978). For instance, people often discount the chances that they will incur punishment (Piliavin et al., 1986). Moreover, allegiance to a group and its norms typically operates as a stronger force than the threat of societal punishment to bring about conformity (Anderson, Chiricos, and Waldo, 1977; Meier and Johnson, 1977). On the other hand, informal standards and pressures within delinquent subcultures may counteract the deterrent effects of legal penalties (Tittle, 1980).

Selective confinement There are those who argue, like Peter W. Greenwood (1982) of the Rand Corporation, that neither rehabilitation nor deterrence really works, so it is useless to send people to prison with these goals in mind. Imprisonment *can* be used to reduce crime rates by keeping "hard core" criminals off the streets. For example, Marvin E. Wolfgang and his colleagues (1972) tracked the criminal records of about 10,000 young men born in 1945 who lived in Philadephia. They found that about 6 percent of the men were responsible for more than half the crime committed by the entire group, including most of the serious offenses. A second study of 13,000 boys born in 1958 continued the pattern, with 7.5 percent becoming chronic delinquents and accounting for 60 percent of the offenses recorded by the police for the entire group (Schmeck, 1985). About 80 percent of chronic juvenile offenders later become chronic adult offenders.

Yet selective incarceration poses difficulties. For instance, people who engage in robbery and burglary typically retire from these careers fairly early in life; the "out years" in a long sentence might then be a waste of prison capacity. There is also the legal and constitutional difficulty in a democratic nation in sentencing individuals based on forecasts of their future behavior rather than on a verdict arising out of an actual crime. Further, comparable attempts by psychologists and psychiatrists to predict behavior on the basis of certain profile characteristics have been notoriously inaccurate. Indeed, any number of sociologists argue that some amount of crime is normal within modern societies. And they say that a large proportion of offenders is likewise normal, given the realities of contemporary social and economic life (Martinson, 1974). In sum, deviance is and is likely to remain an integral component of social life.

Chapter Highlights

1. In all societies, the behavior of some people at times goes beyond that which is permitted by the norms. Norms only tell us what we are supposed to do or what we are not supposed to do. They do not tell us what people actually do. And what some of us actually do very often runs counter to what other people judge to be acceptable behavior.

2. Implicit in a sociological definition of deviance is the notion that deviance is not something inherent in certain forms of behavior; it is a property conferred upon particular behaviors by social definitions. In this sense, deviance is what people say it is. Accordingly, definitions as to which acts are deviant vary greatly from time to time, place to place, and group to group.

3. Social order dictates that people have to be kept in line, at least most people, and the line must be followed within allowable limits. There are three main types of social control processes operating within social life: (1) those that lead us to internalize our society's normative expectations; (2) those that structure our world of social experience; and (3) those

that employ various formal and informal social sanctions.

4. It seems that most societies can absorb a good deal of deviance without serious consequences. But persistent and widespread deviance can be dysfunctional, impairing and even severely undermining organized social life. It weakens people's willingness to play their roles and to obey the rules of society. Deviance may also be functional: It may promote social solidarity, clarify norms, strengthen group allegiances, and provide a catalyst for change.

5. According to the anomie perspective, deviance derives from societal stresses. Robert K. Merton contends that American society sets goals of worldly success for the population at large, but withholds the means for realizing these goals from significant segments of the population. He identifies five responses to the ends-means dilemma: conformity, innovation, ritualism, retreatism, and rebellion. Critics, however, point out that delinquency is not necessarily concentrated in the lower class.

6. Edwin H. Sutherland developed an approach based on the notion of differential association. He said that individuals become deviant to the extent to which they participate in settings where deviant ideas, motivations, and techniques are viewed favorably. However, the perspective is not applicable to some forms of deviance, particularly those in which neither the techniques nor the appropriate definitions and attitudes are acquired from other deviants.

7. Conflict theorists examine a variety of questions with respect to deviance. They ask "Which group will be able to translate its values into the rules of a society and make these rules stick?" and "Who reaps the lion's share of benefits from particular social arrangements?" Critics charge that conflict formulations have given new directions to our understanding of deviance, but that the insights require scientific inquiry.

8. Labeling theorists study the processes whereby some individuals come to be tagged as deviants, begin to think of themselves as deviants, and enter on deviant careers. They say that it is the societal response to an act and not the behavior itself that determines deviance. Critics point out that the labeling perspective may help us understand how individuals become career deviants, but it tells us little about what contributed to the deviant behavior in the first place.

9. Crime is an act prohibited by law. The distinguishing property of crime is that people who violate the law are liable to be arrested, tried, pronounced guilty, and deprived of lives, liberty, or property. They become caught up in the elaborate social machinery of the criminal justice system—the reactive agencies of the state that include the police, the courts, and prisons.

10. Since crime is an act prohibited by law, it is the state that defines crime by the laws it promulgates, administers, and enforces. An infinite variety of acts can be crimes, including white-collar crime, organized crime, violent crime, and victimless crime.

11. Statistics on crime are among the most unsatisfactory of all social data. Official crime records suffer from numerous limitations. A large proportion of the crimes that are committed go undetected; others are detected but not reported; and still others are reported but not officially recorded. Official crime records are often supplemented by victim-based measures and self-report-based measures.

12. There have been four traditional purposes of imprisonment; punishment, rehabilitation, deterrence, and selective incapacitation. The rationale behind punishment is that it serves to restore a sense of moral order. Rehabilitation is based on the notion that crime resembles disease and needs to be cured. Deterrence is based on the notion that if the price of crime is too high, people will not engage in it. And selective confinement suggests that crime rates can be reduced by keeping hard core criminals off the streets.

The Sociologist's Vocabulary

anomie People are unsure of what is expected of them, and they find it difficult to fashion their actions in terms of conventional norms.

corporate crime Crime committed by business organizations.

crime An act prohibited by law.

criminal justice system The reactive agencies of the state that include the police, the courts, and prisons.

deviance Behavior a considerable number of people view as reprehensible and beyond the limits of tolerance.

differential association The notion that the earlier, the more frequently, the more intensely, and the longer the duration of the contacts people have in deviant settings, the greater the probability that they too will become deviant.

index crime Crimes reported by the Federal Bureau of Investigation in its *Uniform Crime Report*. These offenses consist of four categories of violent crimes against people—murder, rape, robbery, and assault—and four categories of crimes against property—burglary, theft, motor vehicle theft, and arson.

internalization Incorporating within one's personality the standards of behavior prevalent within the large society.

organized crime Large-scale bureaucratic organizations that provide illegal goods and services in public demand.

primary deviance Behavior that violates social norms but goes unnoticed by they agents of social control.

secondary deviance Deviance individuals adopt in response to the reactions of other individuals.

social control Those methods and strategies that regulate people's behavior within society.

stigmatized minorities People who possess some attribute that leads other people to deny them full social acceptance.

victimless crime Offenses in which the parties involved do not consider themselves to be victims.

white-collar crime Crimes committed by persons of affluence, often in the course of business activities.

PART FOUR

Social Differentiation and Inequality

9

Social
Stratification
and Social
Classes

There are but two families in the world—Have-much and Have-little.

—Cervantes, *Don Quixote*, 1615

Social inequality—slavery, serfdom, and poverty amid enormous wealth, splendor, and pomp—is a tale told countless times in human history. Throughout the world we find the high and the low, and in some societies, a big in-between. But why is this so? Why can't we pool resources, treat one another as equals, and live a caring, cooperative life? Such a dream led many young Jews in the ghettos of Eastern Europe to embark on a venture in utopia in what is now the state of Israel. Beginning in 1909, they founded some 280 rural settlements—*kibbutzim*—based on the values of social equality, collective production and education, and direct participatory democracy. Their guiding principle is a Marxist one: "From everyone according to ability, to everyone according to need."

Today, Israel's kibbutzim are home to 125,000 people, 3 percent of the country's population. They produce 10 percent of the nation's total output and supply more than 40 percent of its agricultural products (their sales now run more than $2 billion a year). Kibbutz enterprises are organized on communal principles of common ownership of the means of production and property. Consumption is also communal: All incomes are pooled, members use a communal dining hall, and children are cared for and educated in communal children's homes. All major decisions are taken at a general assembly of the members, which meets 35 to 40 times a year. A smaller secretariat, which meets weekly, includes managers in charge of labor, education, and finances.

The kibbutzim provided one answer to the historical crisis of the Jewish people, who have experienced anti-Semitism, dependence, alienation— and the challenge to their survival known as the Holocaust. Kibbutzniks played a major role in the establishment of the Jewish homeland. But the movement's idealistic pioneers had also dreamed of creating a whole society in which there would be no oppression or exploitation and where people would devote themselves to the common good. How well did they succeed?

Most kibbutzim have proved to be highly productive. Over 90 percent of kibbutz enterprises now include some form of light or heavy industry (Maital, 1982). They make pianos, plastics, cryogenic instruments, color TVs, microprocessors, and oscilloscopes. Many of these products compete favorably in world markets. And although industrialization has severely taxed the norm against hiring outside labor and experts, most have responded to industrial development by severely limiting managerial perquisites and periodically rotating managers back to the production line.

Despite their success in achieving equality in material rewards, inequality has not been eliminated from kibbutz life (Rosenfeld, 1951; Gerson, 1978). Differences in prestige and power remain. Since collective farms typically have suffered from a lack of specially talented men and women, their scarcity gains such people recognition and advantages. These individuals have opportunities to travel throughout Israel on kibbutz business and enjoy pleasures the rank-and-file do not. And they experience the ego-expanding gratification of being the representatives of a whole community in dealings with bankers, merchants, and government officials.

Time and new circumstances have also altered kibbutz arrangements. Many kibbutzim have sought a compromise between their original communal ideals and the values of family living (Ichilov and Bar, 1980; Shipler, 1984). Increasingly, the family has become the center of personal relationships, in sharp contrast to the antifamily attitudes that prevailed in the early days of the kibbutz movement. More and more children have moved out of dormitories and into their parents' apartments. Some families enjoy material advantages not enjoyed by others. With economic prosperity, the kibbutzim have deferred increasingly to private desires and needs. The experiences of the Israeli kibbutzim, then, testify to the difficulty of establishing equalitarian societies in the modern world. This is the topic of this chapter—*social stratification*, the issue of who gets what, and why.

PLANNING AHEAD: TARGETED READING

1. Is social stratification an inevitable feature of contemporary life?

2. Why is social stratification so widespread?

3. What are the components of a stratification system?

4. How do sociologists identify social classes?

5. What is the significance of social class for everyday life?

6. How are American class patterns changing?

7. What is happening among the poor within the United States?

8. What are the prospects that you will rise or fall in social ranking?

The Nature of Social Stratification

Group living confers a good many benefits on the members of a society. Together, they can accomplish a great many things that they could not otherwise achieve. But the advantages and disadvantages of the collective enterprise are not evenly shared. Most societies are organized so that their institutions systematically distribute benefits and burdens unequally among different categories of people. Social arrangements are not neutral, but serve and promote the goals and interests of some people more than they do those of other people. Sociologists term this structured ranking of people and groups **social stratification.**

Social Differentiation

Social stratification depends upon but is not the same thing as **social differentiation**—the process by which the members of a society divide up activities and become "different" by virtue of playing distinctive roles. Very early in their history, human beings discovered that a division of functions and labor contributed to greater social efficiency. In all societies, we find a separation of statuses and roles (see Chapter 4). This arrangement requires that people be distributed within the social structure so that the various statuses are filled and their accompanying roles performed. In other words, we must know what we are to do, when, by what means, for how

long, and in what relationships with others. Nature helps us accomplish this task by dictating that only women bear children. But nature does not go very much beyond this; the rest we have to figure out for ourselves.

Although the statuses within a social structure may be differentiated, they do not need to be *ranked* with respect to one another. Americans differentiate between the statuses of an infant and a child. However, we do not say the one is superior in rank to the other. They are merely different. Social differentiation sets the stage for social ranking. In other words, whenever we encounter social stratification, we find social differentiation—but not the other way around.

Dimensions of Stratification

The metaphor suggested by stratification is one in which human societies look like layers of a cake or the rungs on a ladder. The imagery contained in the formulations of Karl Marx has contributed to a view of stratification in which established groups are neatly separated from one another along a single dimension. Marx believed that the central feature of capitalist societies is the division between those who own and control the crucial means of production—the oppressing capitalist class or bourgeoisie—and those who have only their labor to sell—the oppressed working class or proletariat. But sociologist Max Weber (1946) contended that Marx had an overly simplistic image of stratification. Weber said that other divisions within society are at times independent of the class or economic aspect. He took a multidimensional

Social Stratification in Antiquity
The emergence of agrarian societies, like that of ancient Egypt, rested not only on new modes of production but on the evolution of more complex forms of social organization. The economic surplus generated by the agricultural revolution laid the foundations for a system of stratification in which privilege and power were concentrated in the hands of pharaohs, or hereditary monarchs. The scene in a pharaoh's tomb at left depicts the social cleavage between ruler and slaves. (*Robert Caputo/Stock, Boston*)

view of stratification, and identified three components: *class* (economic), *status* (prestige), and *party* (power). Each of these dimensions constitutes a distinct aspect of social ranking. Some statuses, such as that of physician, rank high in wealth, prestige, and power. Prostitutes and professional criminals enjoy economic privilege, although they possess little prestige or power. Members of university faculties and the clergy, while enjoying a good deal of prestige, typically rank comparatively low in wealth and power. And some public officials may wield considerable power, but receive low salaries and little prestige. For the most part, however, these three dimensions feed into and support one another (Wright, 1979, 1985). Let us examine each in turn.

Economic   The economic dimension of stratification consists of wealth and income. **Wealth** has to do with what people own. **Income** refers to the amount of money people receive. In other words, wealth is based on what people *have*, whereas income consists of what people *get*. For example, a person may have a good deal of wealth but receive little income from it, as someone who collects rare coins, precious gems, or works of art. Another person may receive a high salary, but spend it on the good life and have little wealth.

Based on data gathered in late 1984, the Census Bureau estimates that American families with incomes exceeding $48,000 a year—the top 12 percent—control 38 percent of household wealth and have a median net worth of $123,474. This group controlled 63 percent of all stocks and 53 percent of all bonds and money market funds. It was predominantly white, with its members employed in white-collar jobs or owners of their own businesses. Overall, the typical American family had a net worth of $32,667, with by far the biggest portion of this wealth, 41 percent, accounted for by equity in a home.

Prestige   **Prestige** refers to the social respect, admiration, and recognition we associate with a social status. It involves the feeling that we are admired and thought well of by others. Prestige is intangible, something that we carry about in our heads. However, in our daily lives we typically seek to give it a tangible existence through titles, deference rituals, honorary degrees, emblems, and conspicuous displays of leisure and consumption. These activities and objects serve as symbols of prestige to which we attribute social significance and meaning.

Much of our interaction with others consists of subtle negotiation over just how much deference, honor, respect, and awe we are to extend and receive. Even a simple conversation frequently involves a bargain that we will be attentive to what others say to us if they in turn will be attentive to what we say—a mutual exchange of "ego messages."

Some ninety years ago, Thorstein Veblen (1899) highlighted the part that *conspicuous leisure* and *conspicuous consumption* play in revealing social rank, what today we call "status seeking." Veblen observed that if we are to gain and hold prestige, it is not enough to possess wealth and power. We must put the wealth and power on public view by using money for nonessential goods and services. The ancient Egyptians revealed their station in life by how many things were put in their tombs. In England in the 1700s, castles were in vogue among the aristocracy. One way Americans currently display a luxurious style of life is through lavish expenditures on clothing. The requirement that we dress in the latest fashion, coupled with the fact that the fashion changes from season to season, adds greatly to the amount we must spend on a wardrobe and hence increases its symbolic significance (Solomon, 1986; Kleinfield, 1986). Automobiles serve a similar purpose. Rolls-Royces, Ferarris, and Maseratis look great in the driveway—and most important, cost more than $50,000.

The prestige of most Americans today rests primarily on income, occupation, and lifestyle (Coleman and Rainwater, 1978). Family background and wealth count for less than they did a generation or so ago. Simultaneously, individual "personality" and "gregariousness" have taken on greater importance. Although Americans still think money is the most important thing, the lifestyle people display and the values they hold now assume a critical part in determining prestige.

Power   As we will see in Chapter 16, power determines which people and groups will be able to translate their preferences into reality. **Power** refers to the ability of individuals and groups to realize their will in human affairs, even against the will of others. As such, it provides answers to the question of whose interests will be served and whose values will reign. Wherever we look, from families to juvenile gangs to nation-states, we find that some parties have their way much more than others. Even in such a matter as simple as a conversation, we note the operation of power. People high in power typically dominate a conversation by using a disproportionate amount of the time and by interrupting people low in

Conspicuous Consumption and Leisure
If people are to derive full social benefit and recognition from their wealth, others must be made aware of it. Accordingly, the wealthy place their money on public view by consuming it in lavish but nonessential ways. Expensive parties and automobiles serve this purpose admirably well. (*Abigail Heyman/Archive*)

power. The sociologist Amos Hawley (1963:422) observes: "Every social act is an exercise of power, every social relationship is a power equation, and every social group or system is an organization of power."

The bases of power fall into three categories. First, there are **constraints**, the resources that allow one party to add *new disadvantages* to a situation. People typically view constraints as punishment because they entail harming the body, psyche, or possessions of others. Second, there are **inducements**, the resources that allow one party to add *new advantages* to a situation. Individuals usually think of inducements as rewards because they involve the transfer of socially defined good things—such as material objects, services, or social positions—in exchange for compliance with the wishes of the power wielder. Third, there is **persuasion**, the resources that enable one person to change the minds of others *without* adding either advantages or disadvantages to a situation. Through persuasion—based on reputation, wisdom, personal attractiveness, or control of the media—individuals or groups are led to prefer the outcomes that the power wielder prefers.

Power affects our ability to make the world work on our behalf. To gain mastery of critical resources, then, is to gain mastery of people. To control key resources is to interpose oneself (or one's group) between people and the means whereby people meet their biological, psychological, and social needs. To the extent to which some groups command rewards, punishments, and persuasive communications, they are able to dictate the terms by which the game of life is played. They set the agendas, determine the issues that may be contested, and also decide the rules of the game.

THINKING THROUGH THE ISSUES

How are social agendas—conceptions of the things to be done and the matters to be acted upon—set within a society? To what extent are agendas taken for granted? Do people typically have realistic alternatives to those contained in their society's agenda? Does each socioeconomic system have a "built in" unique agenda? When are people likely to challenge an agenda? If there is to be social inequality, why must the underprivileged participate in their own disadvantage? Put another way, what processes of reality making sustain established social arrangements?

"*For your convenience, sir, the items starred are dishes associated with success, riches, power, and the like.*"

Drawing by Ed Fisher; © 1986 The New Yorker Magazine, Inc.

Open and Closed Systems

Stratification systems differ in the ease with which they permit people to move in or out of particular strata. As we will see later in the chapter when we discuss social mobility, people often move up or down in rank or horizontally to another status of roughly similar rank. Where people can change status with relative ease, we refer to the arrangement as an **open system.** Where people have great difficulty in changing status, we term the arrangement a **closed system.** A somewhat similar distinction is conveyed by the concepts *achieved status* and *ascribed status* we considered in Chapter 4. Achieved statuses are open to people on the basis of individual choice and competition, whereas ascribed statuses are assigned by the group or society.

Although there are no societies that are entirely open or entirely closed, the United States provides a good example of a relatively open system. It is based on a **class system** in which achieved statuses provide the principal basis for the unequal distribution of social resources. The American dream portrays a society in which all people can improve their lot. The American folk hero is Abe Lincoln, the "poor boy who made good," the "rail-splitter" who through hard work managed to move from log cabin to the White House. The United States is founded not on the idea that all people should enjoy equal status, nor on the notion of a classless society. Rather, the democratic creed holds that all people should have an equal opportunity to rise in the class system. In theory, the rewards of social life flow to people in accordance with their merit and competence and in proportion to their contribution to the larger social enterprise. In practice, the American system places some reliance on ascription, particularly in assigning status on the basis of race, age, and gender. (We will examine matters of race, age, and gender at greater length in the three chapters that follow.)

One example of a closed system is traditional Hindu society, particularly as it operated in India before World War II. It is based on a **caste system** in which ascribed statuses provide the principal basis for the unequal distribution of social resources. People inherit their social status at birth from their parents and cannot change it. Historically there have been thousands of castes in India, although all of them have fallen into four major castes. The Brahmin, or priestly caste, represent about 3 percent of the population. The Kshatriya, allegedly descendants of warriors, and the Vaisya, the traders, together account for about 7 percent of Indians. The Sudra, peasants and artisans, constitute about 70 percent of the population. The remaining 20 percent are the Harijans, or Untouchables, who traditionally served as sweepers, scavengers, leather workers, and swineherders.

Members of the lower castes were deemed inferior, scorned, snubbed, and oppressed by higher caste members regardless of their personal merit and behavior. Rigid rules of avoidance operated within the system because contact with lower caste members was believed to spiritually pollute and defile upper caste members. Even today, caste shapes behavior in some localities, especially in rural areas, setting the rules of courtship, diet, housing, and employment. The concept of *dharma,* the idea that enduring one's lot in life with grace is the only

Untouchables in India
Membership in the Hindu caste system is ascribed and unalterable. Untouchables are considered inherently inferior and occupy the least desirable social positions. Members of higher castes regard contact with untouchables as spiritually polluting, and rigid rules of avoidance bar certain types of contacts. In recent years discontent among untouchables and their political mobilization (as shown at left) have contributed to the emergence of more egalitarian practices. *(Marilyn Silverstone/Magnum)*

morally acceptable way to live, legitimates the system. But even at its zenith, the caste system never foreclosed mobility up and down the social ladder. Different birth and death rates among the castes, discontent among the disadvantaged and exploited, competition between members of different castes, the introduction of modern farming technologies, conversions to Buddhism and Islam, and other factors have operated against a completely closed system (Davis, 1949; Berreman, 1960; Critchfield, 1984). Today, powered by industrialization, a consumer boom, and a "green revolution" in the northern farm belt, a new generation of Indian leaders is redefining the old rules in politics, government, and the economy (Weisman, 1986).

Perspectives on Social Stratification

Why are all societies characterized by social inequality? This question has always intrigued us (Lenski, 1966). Early Hebrew prophets and classical Greek philosophers debated the issue, and today it provides a central focus for sociological study. Across history, two quite different answers have emerged. The first—the conservative thesis—has supported existing social arrangements. It says that an unequal distribution of social rewards is necessary to get the essential tasks of society done. The second view—the radical thesis—has been highly critical of the existing arrangements. It contends that social inequality arises out of a struggle for valued goods and services in short supply. Contemporary theories of inequality fall broadly into one or the other tradition. Those with roots in the conservative tradition are labeled *functionalist* theories; those stemming from the radical tradition are called *conflict* theories. Debates over the different perspectives are often academic substitutes for a real conflict over political orientations.

The Functionalist Perspective

The functionalist perspective holds that stratification exists because it is beneficial for society. In 1945, sociologists Kingsley Davis and Wilbert Moore set forth the classical statement of the theory, although it has since been modified and refined by other sociologists. Davis and Moore argued that social stratification is both universal and necessary, and hence no society is ever totally classless. In their view, all societies require stratification if they are to fill all the statuses comprising the social structure and motivate people to perform the duties associated with these positions.

Human motivation is important because the duties associated with the various statuses are not all equally pleasant, equally important to social survival, and equally in need of the same abilities and talents. Otherwise, it would make little difference who got which positions, and the problem of social placement would be greatly reduced. Moreover, the duties associated with a good many positions are viewed by their occupants as onerous. Without some motivation, many people would not carry out their roles. So a society must have rewards it can use as inducements for its members, and some way of distributing these rewards. Inequality provides the motivational incentive. And since the rewards are built into the system, social stratification is a structural feature of all societies.

Using the economists' model of supply and demand, Davis and Moore say the positions most highly rewarded are those (1) that are occupied by the most talented or qualified incumbents (supply) and (2) that are functionally most important (demand). For instance, to ensure sufficient physicians, a society needs to offer them high salaries and great prestige. If it did not offer them these rewards, Davis and Moore suggest that we could not expect people to undertake the "burdensome" and "expensive" process of medical education. People at the top must receive rewards; if they did not, the positions would remain unfilled and society would disintegrate.

The structure-function approach to stratification has been the subject of much criticism (Tumin, 1953, 1985; Collins, 1975). For one thing, critics charge that people are *born* into family positions of privilege and disadvantage (Anderson, 1971). As we will see later in our discussion of social mobility, where people end up in the stratification system depends a good deal on birth. Even in open class systems like that of the United States, the starting blocks in the competitive race are so widely staggered that the runners in the rear have only a remote chance of catching up with those ahead, while those starting ahead must virtually quit to lose ground. Indeed, conflict theorists contend society is structured so that individuals *maintain* a ranking that is determined by birth and that has nothing to do with their abilities (Bottomore, 1966).

Critics also point out that many of the positions of highest responsibility in the United States are not financially well rewarded. The officers of large corporations earn considerably more than does the president of the

United States, members of the cabinet, and Supreme Court justices. In 1986 the median pay of chairpersons of large corporations was $1.2 million (Rosenthal, 1986). Moreover, despite their lower pay and prestige, garbage collectors may be more important to the survival of the United States than athletes who receive million-dollar incomes. The idea that many low-paying positions are functionally less important to society than high-paying positions is difficult to support.

THINKING THROUGH THE ISSUES

Is it possible to get people with special talents to perform tasks without the promise of unequal rewards? What about family life? Do parents take on parenthood and discharge their responsibilities without regard for rewards other than those associated with the gratifications of family life? Can the conditions prevailing in family life be duplicated in large-scale, bureaucratic societies? Could duty, morality, obligation, and acceptance achieve the desired ends? Is a system of unequal rewards the most efficient method for discovering and recruiting the best talent? Is it primarily the promise of high rewards that attracts the most talented people to particular positions? Do those who get the greatest rewards necessarily perform their roles the best (Tumin, 1985)?

The Conflict Perspective

The conflict theory of social equality holds that stratification exists because it benefits individuals and groups who have the power to dominate and exploit others. Whereas functionalists stress the common interests members of society share, conflict theorists focus on the interests that divide people. Viewed from the conflict perspective, society is an arena in which people struggle for privilege, prestige, and power, and groups enforce their advantage through coercion.

The conflict theory draws heavily upon the ideas of Karl Marx. As we noted in Chapter 1, Marx believed that a historical perspective is essential for understanding any society. To grasp how a particular economic system works, he said we must keep in mind the predecessor from which it evolved and the process by which it grew. According to Marx, the current state of technology and the method of organizing production are the primary determinants of the evolutionary direction of a society.

At each stage of history, these factors determine the group that will dominate the society and the groups that will be subjugated. Under the feudal arrangement, medieval lords were in control of the economy and dominated the serfs. Under the capitalist system, the lord has been replaced by the modern capitalist and the serf by the "free" laborer—in reality a propertyless worker who "has nothing to sell but his hands."

Marx contended that the capitalist drive to realize surplus value is the foundation of modern class struggle—an irreconcilable clash of interests between workers and capitalists. *Surplus value* is the difference between the value workers create (as determined by the labor time embodied in a commodity they produce) and the value they receive (as determined by the subsistence level of their wages). Capitalists do not create surplus value; they appropriate it through exploitation of workers. As portrayed by Marx, capitalists are thieves who steal the fruits of labor. The accumulation of capital (wealth) derives from surplus value and is the key to—indeed, the incentive for—the development of contemporary capitalism. Marx believed that the class struggle will eventually be resolved when the working class overthrows the capitalist class and establishes a new social order.

Marx held that classes do not exist in isolation, independent of other classes to which they are opposed: "Individuals form a class only in so far as they are engaged in a common struggle with another class" (quoted by Dahrendorf, 1959:14). Under capitalism, workers at first are blinded by a *false consciousness*—an incorrect assessment of how the system works and of their subjugation and exploitation by capitalists. But through struggle with capitalists, the workers' "objective" class interests become translated into a "subjective" recognition of their true circumstances. They then formulate goals for organized action—in brief, they acquire *class consciousness*. Class consciousness is crucial for turning a "class in itself" into a "class for itself" (turning a mere category of people into a self-conscious, militant group). Hence, according to Marxists, if the working class is to fulfill its historic role of overturning capitalism, "it must become a class not only 'as against capital' but also 'for itself'; that is to say, the class struggle must be raised from the level of economic necessity to the level of conscious aim and effective consciousness" (Lukacs, 1968:76).

Much of the appeal of Marx lies in his seeming simplicity and directness. But the simplicity is deceiving; conflict is a pervasive feature of human life and is not restricted to economic relations. As Ralf Dahrendorf (1959:208) observes: "It appears that not only in social

Which Position Makes the Greater Social Contribution?
Migratory farm workers are paid notoriously low wages yet provide much of our nation's essential agricultural produce. In contrast, tennis star Jimmy Connors is awarded a check for $110,000 on winning the Suntory Cup Tennis Tournament in Tokyo. Functionalists say that a large supply of immigrant farm laborers has resulted in a surplus of people capable of filling a position that requires few skills whereas Jimmy Connors possesses an unusual talent and skill. Moreover, his successes are the "stuff" of which the American dream is made and serve to reinforce the public's allegiance to the free enterprise system. *(left, Fred McConnaughey/Photo Researchers; right, AP/Wide World Photos)*

life, but wherever there is life, there is conflict." Dahrendorf holds that group conflict is an inevitable aspect of any human society, and rejects Marx's view that the proletarian revolution will eliminate class conflict.

Even in the realm of property, Marx's dichotomy between the capitalist class and the working class hides or distorts other dynamic processes. Debtor and creditor have also stood against each other throughout history. A dominant feature of nineteenth-century American politics was the farmers' cry for cheap money (the Greenback and Free Silver movements). Consumers and sellers have also confronted one another, such as in the ghetto outbreaks of the 1960s (Dynes and Quarantilli, 1968). Divisions and hostility between racial and ethnic groups, skilled workers and unskilled laborers, and union organizations have been recurrent features of American life. These and other factors have blunted the sharp class polarization that Marx thought would lead to revolutionary class struggle and the end of capitalist society.

Ownership of property in the form of the means of production is only one source of power (Wright, 1985). The possession of the *means of administration* is an-

other. The Soviet Union and Eastern European nations are good illustrations of this. Even within the United

THINKING THROUGH THE ISSUES

Why do class interests, even when "seen," fail to translate automatically into class movements (Roy, 1984; Griffin, Wallace, and Rubin, 1986)? Why has the United States failed to develop a mass labor-based party such as the strong socialist parties of Europe? What part have racial and ethnic membership played in undermining class cohesion? May smaller conflicting groups fail to amalgamate into larger ones, so that conflict is not simplified into a classic two-sided battle? How has corporate paternalism, as embodied in company unions and "welfare capitalism," impaired collective action by labor? How did the civil rights movement of the 1960s and early 1970s differ from a class-based movement? Did the civil rights movement call into question the principles of a capitalist democracy?

The Means of Administration as a Source of Power
Milovan Djilas (1957), a Yugoslav Marxist and one-time Tito lieutenant, has vigorously condemned the rise of what he calls "the new class" in the Soviet Union and Eastern European nations. The new class is "made up of those who have special privileges and economic preference because of the administrative monopoly they hold" (39). The Communist party bureaucracy comprises the new elite who use, administer, and control nationalized and socialized property. *(Frederique Hibon/Sygma)*

States, one can go a long way nowadays without property. As we will see in Chapter 15, a good deal of power derives from office rather than ownership in large multinational corporations. Not only do executives hold comparatively little in the way of property, but their influence lasts only as long as they hold their positions. They are easily replaced. Much the same is true in government. Neither Harry Truman, Dwight Eisenhower, Lyndon Johnson, Richard Nixon, Gerald Ford, or Ronald Reagan launched their careers from a base of financial, industrial, or landed property, yet each reached the pinnacle of power in the United States—the presidency.

A Synthesis: Lenski's Evolutionary Perspective

Any number of sociologists have noted that both the functionalist and conflict perspectives contain useful insights, and so they have undertaken to integrate them (Sorokin, 1959; van den Berghe, 1963) (see Table 9.1). Harold R. Kerbo (1983) observes that a supply and demand relationship, such as that proposed by structure-function theorists, explains some aspects of the unequal distribution of rewards within the occupational structure. Yet, as pointed out by conflict theorists, he finds that economic conflicts are among the most important sources of division in capitalist societies. Ralf Dahrendorf (1959) contends that functionalist and conflict theorists simply study two aspects of the *same* reality.

In his evolutionary approach to stratification systems, sociologist Gerhard E. Lenski (1966) has sought a

workable synthesis that combines the two perspectives. He agrees with functionalists that the chief resources of society are allocated as rewards to people who occupy vital positions and that stratification fosters a rough match between scarce talent and rewards. *But* as a society advances in technology, it becomes capable of producing a surplus of goods and services. As the amount of economic surplus increases, conflicts arise over its distribution. Those individuals and groups with access to power then come to control social wealth.

Lenski finds that the most severe inequalities occur in societies where there is a sizable surplus *and* where power is concentrated in the hands of a few. Historically, agrarian empires have best fitted this description (see Chapter 3). In industrial societies, there is greater equality in the distribution of wealth to the extent to which the masses acquire political power. The foundation for this leverage is the emergence and expansion of the middle classes. Socialist societies contain the potential for an even greater reduction in economic inequality. Lenski says the inequalities that remain in socialist states result not from economic maldistribution, but from concentration of power in the hands of bureaucrats and party officials.

The American Class System

Sociologists may disagree about the sources of stratification, but they agree that inequality is a *structured* aspect of contemporary life. When sociologists say that social inequality is structured, they mean more than that individuals and groups differ in the privileges they enjoy, the

Table 9.1   Stratification Perspectives: A Comparative View

Functionalist Perspective	*Conflict Perspective*	*Lenski's Evolutionary Perspective*
1. Stratification is universal, necessary, and inevitable.	1. Stratification may be universal but it is neither necessary nor inevitable.	1. Stratification is prevalent, but some of it is not necessary or inevitable.
2. Societal requirements shape the stratification system.	2. Powerful groups shape the stratification system to benefit themselves.	2. The nature of a society's subsistence patterns shapes its stratification system.
3. Stratification arises from the need to fill all the statuses making up the social structure and to motivate individuals to perform the duties associated with these statuses.	3. Stratifications arises from group competition and conflict.	3. Stratification arises from the need to fill social statuses and from group competition and conflict.
4. Stratification reflects the commonly held values within a society.	4. Stratification reflects the values of the ruling classes.	4. Stratification reflects both commonly held societal values and the values of powerful groups.
5. Tasks and rewards are equitably allocated.	5. Tasks and rewards are unfairly allocated.	5. Although some tasks and rewards are fairly allocated, many are not.
6. Stratification facilitates the optimal functioning of society and its members.	6. Stratification impedes the optimal functioning of society and its members.	6. Stratification facilitates some aspects of societal functioning while impeding other aspects.

Source: Adapted from Arthur L. Stinchcombe. 1969. Some empirical consequences of the Davis-Moore theory of stratification. In Jack L. Roach, Llewellyn Gross, and Orville R. Gursslin. Eds. *Social Stratification in the United States.* Englewood Cliffs, NJ: Prentice-Hall, p. 55.

prestige they receive, and the power they hold. *Structured* means that inequality is hardened or institutionalized; there is a system of social relationships determining who gets what. Inequality follows recurrent, relatively consistent, and stable patterns. Further, inequalities are typically passed on from one generation to the next. Individuals and groups that are advantaged commonly find ways to ensure that their offspring will also be advantaged.

Sociologists have borrowed the term stratification from geology. However, it is more difficult to classify people within strata than it is to categorize rocks. Geologists usually find it rather easy to determine where one layer of rocks ends and another begins, but social strata often shade off into one another, so that their boundaries are dim and indistinct. Human societies, then, do not necessarily look like rock layers. As sociologist Randall Collins (1975:51) observes, what society looks like "is nothing more than people in houses, buildings, automobiles, streets—some of whom give orders, get deference, hold material property, talk about particular subjects, and so on." Even so, sociologists and lay people typically use the labels "upper class," "middle class," "working class," and "lower class" in discussing the American system, and we will follow this usage here.

Identifying Social Classes

Sociologists are of two minds regarding the nature of the American class system. One view contends that classes are real, bounded strata. Although this position has been a central element in Marxist formulations (Marx and Engels, 1848/1955; Anderson, 1971; Wright, 1979), it also emerges in the work of other sociologists who have identified a blue-collar–white-collar division in American life (Blau and Duncan, 1972; Vanneman and Pampel, 1977). The second view portrays American society as essentially classless, one in which class divisions are blurred. "Social classes" are culturally quite alike and merely reflect gradations in rank rather than hard-and-fast social groups (Rodman, 1968; Nisbet, 1970).

The differing conceptions derive in large measure from three different approaches to identifying social classes: (1) the objective method, (2) the self-placement method, and (3) the reputational method. Although all the approaches produce some overlap, there are real differences in the results (Kerbo, 1983). Moreover, each approach has advantages and disadvantages. Let us consider each of the methods more carefully.

The objective method   The **objective method** views social class as a statistical category. Categories are formed not by members, but by sociologists or statisticians. Usually people are assigned to social classes on the basis of income, occupation, or education (or some combination of these). The label "objective" can be misleading, for it does not mean that the approach is more "scientific" or "unbiased" than either of the others. Rather, it is objective in that numerically measurable criteria are employed for the placement of individuals. Table 9.2, for example, shows one way of depicting the distribution of Americans by median family income.

The objective method provides a rather clear-cut statistical measure for investigating various correlates of class, such as life expectancy, mental illness, divorce,

Table 9.2   Where You Rank Based on Median Income, 1984

If Your Family Income Is . . .	You Fall in This Bracket
More than $75,000	Top 5%
More than $50,000	Top 16%
More than $40,000	Top 27%
More than $30,000	Top 43%
More than $25,000	Top 53%
Less than $20,000	Bottom 36%
Less than $15,000	Bottom 25%
Less than $10,000	Bottom 14%
Less than $5,000	Bottom 5%

Source: U.S. Department of Commerce.

political attitudes, crime rates, and leisure activities. It is usually the simplest and cheapest approach, since detailed statistical data can be obtained from federal government agencies. But there is more to class than simply statistics. In the course of their daily lives people size one another up according to many standards. Morover, it is not only actual income, occupation, or education that matters, but the meanings and definitions others assign to these qualities.

The self-placement method   The **self-placement method** (also known as the *subjective method*) has people identify the social class to which they think they belong. Class is viewed as a social category, one in which people group themselves with other individuals they perceive as having certain attributes in common with them. These class lines may or may not conform to what social scientists think are logical lines of cleavage in the objective sense.

The major advantage of the self-placement approach is that it can be used for a large population, whereas the reputational approach is limited to small communities. Table 9.3 shows how Americans rank the prestige of various occupations when they are asked to do so. The self-placement method is also an especially useful tool for predicting political behavior, since who people *think* they are influences how they vote. However, the approach has its limitations. The class with which people identify may represent their aspirations rather than their current associations or the appraisals of other people. Further, when placing themselves in a national class structure, people commonly use fewer categories than they do when interacting with actual people and sizing them up in terms of subtle distinctions.

Knowledge as a Source of Power
We often overlook the power that derives from knowledge. Among Jews, mastery of the Talmud is an important source of authority and of inequality between mentor and student. Within contemporary American life, engineers and technicians derive organizational and social power by virtue of their expertise. *(Cary Wolinsky/Stock, Boston)*

The reputational method   In the self-placement method, people are asked to rank themselves; in the **reputational method,** they are asked how they classify *other* individuals. This approach views class as a social group, one in which people share a feeling of oneness and are bound together in relatively stable patterns of interaction. Class rests on knowledge of who associates with whom. The approach gained prominence in the 1930s when W. Lloyd Warner and his associates studied the class structure of three communities: "Yankee City" (Newburyport, Massachusetts), a New England town of some 17,000 people (Warner and Lunt, 1941, 1942); "Old City" (Natchez, Mississippi), a southern community of about 10,000 (Davis, Gardner, and Gardner, 1941); and "Jonesville" (Morris, Illinois), a midwestern town of about 6,000 (Warner, 1949). In Yankee City and Old City, Warner identified six classes: upper-upper, lower-upper, upper-middle, lower-middle, upper-lower, and lower-lower. In the more recently settled and smaller midwestern community of Jonesville he found five classes, since individuals made no distinction between the upper-upper and lower-upper classes (the former was an "old family" class representing "an aristocracy of birth and wealth" and the letter a class composed of the "new rich"; see Figure 9.1).

The reputational method is a valuable tool for investigating social distinctions in small groups and small communities. It is particularly useful for predicting associational patterns among people. But it is difficult to use in large samples where people have little or no knowledge of one another.

Combining approaches   Warner undertook most of his research before World War II. Recently the sociologists Richard D. Coleman and Lee Rainwater (1978) have updated our understanding of the class structure of urban America by combining the self-placement and reputational methods. In interviews of residents of Kansas and Boston, they asked them about their perception of the social levels of contemporary America. The urbanites ranked one another and themselves in the following way (Vander Zanden, 1983):

1. *People who have really made it.* At the very top of the American class structure is an elite class of wealthy individuals. Some of these are old rich (the Rockefellers); others are the celebrity rich (Paul Newman); still others are the anonymous rich (a millionaire shopping center developer); yet another group is made up of the run-of-the-mill rich (a well-heeled physician).

Table 9.3   Prestige Rankings of Occupations, 1972–1982

Occupation	Score
Physician	82
College teacher	78
Lawyer	76
Dentist	74
Bank officer	72
Airline pilot	70
Clergy	69
Sociologist	66
Secondary school teacher	63
Registered nurse	62
Pharmacist	61
Elementary school teacher	60
Accountant	56
Librarian	55
Actor	55
Funeral director	52
Athlete	51
Reporter	51
Bank teller	50
Electrician	49
Police officer	48
Insurance agent	47
Secretary	46
Mail carrier	42
Owner of a farm	41
Restaurant manager	39
Automobile mechanic	37
Baker	34
Salesclerk	29
Gas station attendant	22
Waiter and waitress	20
Garbage collector	17
Janitor	16
Shoeshiner	12

Note: Americans ranked a number of occupations in terms of prestige in national surveys conducted between 1972 and 1982. The highest possible score an occupation could receive was 90 and the lowest 10. The table shows the ranking of a number of the occupations.

Source: National Opinion Research Center, 1982:299–314.

2. *People who are doing very well.* Corporate executives and professional people make up this class. These individuals have large, comfortable homes, belong to relatively exclusive country clubs, occasionally vacation in Europe and places known for their elite clientele, and send their children to private colleges or reputable, large state universities.

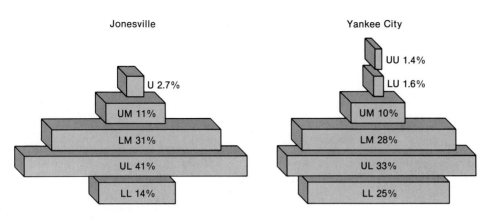

U = upper class   LM = lower-middle class
UU = upper-upper class   UL = upper-lower class
LU = lower-upper class   LL = lower-lower class
UM = upper-middle class

FIGURE 9.1 **Stratification in Jonesville and Yankee City**
In Jonesville, a midwestern community, W. Lloyd Warner and his associates found
five classes: one upper class, two middle classes, and two lower classes. In Yankee
City, a considerably older eastern seaboard community, they identified six classes,
the upper class being divided by an "old family"–"new family" chasm. Birth was
crucial for membership in the "old-family" (upper-upper) class. Its members could
trace their lineage and wealth through many generations. In terms of wealth, the
"new-family" (lower-upper) class could meet the means test, but its members failed
to meet the lineage test so essential for upper-upper class membership. *Source: Adapted
from W. Lloyd Warner. 1949.* Democracy in Jonesville. *New York: Harper & Row.*

3. *People who have achieved the middle-class dream.*
   These individuals enjoy the "good life" as defined
   in material terms, but they lack the luxuries of
   those in the higher classes. More often than not
   they are suburbanites who live in a three-bedroom
   home with a family-TV room.

4. *People who have a comfortable life.* While enjoying a "comfortable" life, the members of this class
   have less money at their disposal than the people
   above them, and they live in less fashionable suburbs.

5. *People who are just getting by.* Some Americans
   enjoy "respectable" jobs, but "the pay is not the
   greatest." The husband may be employed as a
   blue-collar worker and the wife as a waitress or
   store clerk. The couple may own or rent a small
   home, but they find that "getting by" puts a strain
   on their joint income.

6. *People who are having a difficult time.* Members
   of this group find "the going tough." Both the hus-

band and the wife work (although periodically
they may experience unemployment), but their
total income is low. Much leisure time is spent
watching television. They do, however, have one
consolation: "They are not on welfare."

7. *People who are poor.* At the bottom are "people
   who are down and out." Many of them receive
   government assistance and benefits.

   Still, the labels "upper class," "middle class,"
"working class," and "lower class" (poor people) continue to be widely used by both sociologists and lay people. Research suggests that these terms correspond reasonably well with objective class indicators such as
income, education, occupational-skill level, and manual versus nonmanual jobs (Kerbo, 1983). However, the
terms have the disadvantage of masking important divisions and interests among groups in American society.
And they do not necessarily correspond with self-placement identifications. So we need to exercise care when
using these class terms for sociological purposes.

The Significance of Social Classes

The American novelist F. Scott Fitzgerald once observed that the rich are different from the rest of us. Ernest Hemingway added that they have more money. No one will argue with the accuracy of the second half of the proposition, and sociological research supports the first. Few aspects of life affect the way people behave and think as much as social class.

Life chances Our social class largely determines our **life chances**—the likelihood that we will enjoy desired goods and services, fulfilling experiences, and opportunities for living long and healthy lives. Broadly considered, life chances have to do with our options and choices. For instance, the members of the upper social classes devote a smaller part of their resources to survival needs than do members of the lower classes. Sociologist Paul Blumberg (1980) finds that Americans in the highest tenth of the class hierarchy spend about 11 percent of their income for food, as compared to over 40 percent for those in the lowest tenth. And the members of the higher classes also benefit in nonmaterial ways. Their children are more likely to go farther in school and perform better than children whose parents occupy lower socioeconomic positions (DiMaggio, 1982).

During wars, it is the sons of the lower classes who are most likely to be the casualties. In Vietnam, a rainbow coalition of black, brown, and poor white youth were about twice as likely as their better-off peers to serve in the military, go to Southeast Asia, and see combat.

The sons of the higher classes often managed to escape military service through college deferments and a pandemic of asthma, bad backs, trick knees, flat feet, and skin rashes (Dunne, 1986). Also, the infants of parents of the higher classes are more likely to survive than are infants of parents of the lower classes (Wicks and Stockwell, 1984; Wise et al., 1985). The active life expectancy is also longer for the nonpoor than for the poor (Katz, 1983). And research consistently shows that lower social classes have higher rates of mental illness (Goodman et al., 1983; Link, Dohrenwend, and Skodol, 1986).

Style of life Social class also affects our **style of life**, the magnitude and manner of our consumption of goods and services. Convenience foods—TV dinners, potato chips, frozen pizza, and Hamburger Helper—are more frequently on the menus of lower-income than higher-income households. Lower-class families drink less vodka, scotch, bourbon, and imported wine, but consume more blended whiskey and beer. Families in the middle and upper classes tend to buy furniture one piece at a time from specialty stores; lower-class families are more likely to buy matched sets from discount department stores or regular furniture stores. And lower-income families spend more of their leisure time watching television than do higher-income families (Bridgwater, 1982).

Institutional patterns Social class is also associated with institutional patterns of behavior. For instance, there are differences in religious affiliation. Among

Differing Life Chances
Black and other minority youths are disproportionately overrepresented in the nation's military. Technological developments in industry and foreign competition have eliminated many unskilled and semi-skilled jobs that once provided avenues for upward social mobility in American life. Service in the armed forces is one of the few sources of employment available to inner-city youth. *(Liaison)*

Americans, income averages $16,300 for Lutherans, $17,000 for Methodists, $20,500 for Presbyterians, $21,700 for Episcopalians, $17,400 for Catholics, $23,000 for Jews, and $17,600 for people with no religious affiliation (Smith, 1984). Class also influences political participation. Voting increases with socioeconomic status in most Western nations (Verba, Nie, and Kim, 1978; Zipp, Landerman, and Luebke, 1982). And class is an important determinant of sexual behavior (Weinberg and Williams, 1980). For example, the lower classes are more likely to experience sexual intercourse and other sexual behaviors at earlier ages than are the higher classes.

One's social class leaves few areas of life untouched. And changes in the distribution of social classes can have major social consequences, a matter discussed in the boxed insert.

Poverty in the United States

Historians may well look back on the 1980s in the United States as a time of rising affluence and of rising poverty. The growth in affluence is attributable to an increase in professional and technical jobs, along with more two-career couples whose combined incomes provide a "comfortable living." Simultaneously, Census Bureau statistics reveal a 38 percent increase in poverty since 1978.

Defining poverty   The definition of poverty is a matter of debate. In 1795, a group of English magistrates decided that a minimum income should be "the cost of a gallon loaf of bread, multiplied by three, plus an allowance for each dependent" (Schorr, 1984). Today the Census Bureau defines the threshold of poverty in the United States as the minimum amount of money families need to purchase a nutritionally adequate diet, assuming they use one-third of their income for food. By this definition, roughly half the American population was poor in the aftermath of the Great Depression of the 1930s. By 1950, the proportion of poor had fallen to 30 percent and by 1964 to 20 percent. With the adoption of the Johnson administration's antipoverty programs, the poverty rate dropped to 12 percent in 1969. But since

---

ISSUES THAT SHAPE OUR LIVES

The American Middle Class: An Endangered Species?

Is the American middle class shrinking? Or is it alive and well? According to the first view, middle-class jobs are vanishing (Blackburn and Bloom, 1985; Greenhouse, 1986; Thurow, 1986). But others say that such conclusions are "Chicken Little" alarmism (Lawrence, 1985; Baldwin, 1986). Each side cites impressive statistical data in support of its view. Those who see the middle class shrinking point to data showing that families with annual earnings of between $11,000 and $46,800 (using the purchasing power of 1986 dollars as a basis) made up 44.3 percent of all families in 1986, down from 52.3 per-

cent in 1978 (Rose, 1986). Moreover, the richest one-fifth of American families received nearly 43 percent of the country's total money income in 1986—nine times as much as the poorest fifth, up from seven and a half times as much a decade earlier. These trends seem to suggest that the United States is becoming a nation of "haves" and "have nots," with fewer in the middle.

Those who claim the middle class is shrinking link the trend to industrial changes in the United States that are replacing high-paying jobs with low-paying ones. Smokestack industries, like machine tools, autos, and steel, with their high-wage, skilled blue-collar workers, have provided many middle-income jobs. Over the last decade, their share of total employment has fallen sharply. And when these industries shrink, the middle class shrinks with them. For

instance, while jobs in manufacturing fell over the past decade, nearly nine out of the ten new jobs that were created were in the service and trade sectors of the economy (over half of them in health, business services, finance, and eating and drinking places). According to the economists Barry Bluestone and Bennett Harrison (1982, 1987), it takes two department store jobs or three restaurant jobs to equal the earnings of one manufacturing job. Overall, service industries display a two-hump distribution in income—high and low. Reflecting these changes, average hourly earnings, adjusted for inflation, boomed in the 1950s and 1960s, but fell in the 1970s and displayed no real growth in the first half of the 1980s. As a result of these trends, many members of the baby boom generation, now in their thirties, are finding they cannot match their parents' middle-class

then it has stopped falling. In 1985 the Census Bureau classified 33.1 million, or 14 percent, of Americans as poor (see Figure 9.2 on page 238). However, liberals contend that this figure is too low because it fails to take into account changes in standard of living. Conservatives say it is too high because the poor receive in-kind income in the form of food stamps, housing subsidies, and health care (Nasar, 1986b).

Who are the poor? Over the past quarter century, poverty has become increasingly the fate of single-parent families headed by women. Although fatherless families today represent 15 percent of the nation's families, they are 48.6 percent of the households living in poverty. Children in particular are the victims: In 1985, one out of every four American children under 6 years of age and one of every five children under age 18 were poor (Pear, 1986). Nearly 50 percent of all black children, 40 percent of all Hispanic youngsters, and slightly more than 15 percent of all white children live in poverty.

Children under 16 years of age and elderly individuals over age 65 account, respectively, for 36 percent and 11 percent of the American poor. Farmers are also more likely to be poor than their city cousins. About 22 percent of white farmers and 49 percent of black farmers have incomes below the poverty line (Schreiner, 1983). Thousands of American farm workers are also poor; many of them lack toilets and clean water at their work sites and suffer kinds of illness rarely seen outside the Third World (Keller, 1984; Solis, 1985). And if individuals are handicapped, they are more than twice as likely as other workers to be poor (Census Bureau, 1984). About 23 percent of working-age people who receive food stamps and 37 percent of Medicaid recipients are disabled.

Theories of poverty Various theories have been advanced through the years to explain poverty. One approach uses the characteristics of the poor to explain their difficulties. According to this **culture of poverty** thesis, the poor in capitalist societies lack effective participation and integration opportunities within the larger society (Lewis, 1959, 1961, 1966). Clustered in large urban ghettos in places like New York, Mexico City, and

---

achievements of nice homes, financial security, and good education for their children. Working mothers are preserving family living standards in two-parent households that otherwise would have experienced a decline in income.

Whereas political liberals have tended to accept the notion of a shrinking middle class, conservative analysts take a more optimistic view. Fabian Linden (1984, 1986) blames the statistics showing a shrinking middle class primarily on the postwar baby boom. As young baby boomers have entered the workforce in recent years, they have swelled the ranks of low-income households. But as the baby boomers grow older, Linden says their incomes will rise. He also points out that the second-fastest-growing age group in the United States has been people 65 and over. All told, some three-fifths of all homes with incomes under $15,000 consist of individuals under 35 and over 65. Simultaneously, with the increase in separations and divorces, families headed by women grew from 12 percent of all households in 1970 to 16 percent today. Linden concludes that the demise of the middle class is a fiction based on a misreading of the effects of large changes in the age structure and living arrangements of adult Americans.

Those who see the emergence of a bipolar income distribution and the eclipse of the middle class express concern for American democracy. According to conventional sociological wisdom, a healthy middle class is essential for a healthy democracy. A society composed of rich and poor lacks a mediating group. This observation underlay Marx's prediction that revolution would follow as the economy generated a bipolar income distribution consisting of the rich and the poor. In part Marx was proved wrong because he did not foresee the rise of a middle class that had an interest in preserving capitalism and whose presence gave the poor hope that they could escape poverty. A shrinking middle class may now contribute to a Marxian polarization. Downward mobility for large numbers of a population can have many negative social effects. A. Gary Shilling, president of an economics consulting firm, says: "Most Americans seem to regard as their birthright their belief that they will live higher on the hog than their parents. They don't want to admit that what they thought was happening economically no longer is. When they are finally forced to bite the bullet, there could be a tough situation with potential social and political overtones" (quoted by Greenhouse, 1986:10F).

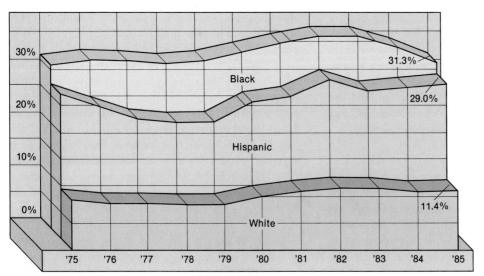

FIGURE 9.2 Poverty in the United States, 1985
The poverty level for a family of four was $10,980 in 1985. *Source: U.S. Bureau of the Census.*

San Juan, these people develop feelings of marginality, helplessness, dependence, and inferiority. Their circumstances breed a variety of survival mechanisms: a sense of passivity and resignation because of enduring poverty; a present-time orientation because of the survival pressures; feelings of fatalism and powerlessness deriving from lack of political resources; low aspirations because of lack of opportunity; feelings of inferiority because of the larger society's contempt; and the creation of female-headed families because of the inability of poor men to be adequate breadwinners. The patterns become self-perpetuating as the values associated with the culture of poverty are transmitted to successive generations.

Many sociologists argue that the culture of poverty thesis has serious shortcomings (Valentine, 1968; Critchfield, 1978). For instance, as we pointed out in Chapter 1, Elliot Liebow depicts the economically poor streetcorner men of Washington, DC, as very much immersed in American life. They too want what other American men want, but they are blocked from achieving their goals by a racist social order. Critics say that the so-called pathological consequences of poverty will disappear when the poor are provided with decent jobs and other social resources.

Another view is that poverty is largely *situational*. A study undertaken by the University of Michigan's Institute for Social Research (Duncan, 1984) portrays the poverty population as a kind of pool, with people flowing in and out. The findings are based on a survey of 5,000 American families chosen in 1968 and followed for a decade thereafter. The results cast doubt on the culture of poverty idea that being poor at one time means being poor always. During the ten-year period, only 2.6 percent of the sample could be classed as persistently poor, as failing to meet the government's income standard in eight or more of the ten years. The 25 percent of the families in the sample who had received welfare at some point in the decade often received it for very short periods. Many people who slip into poverty do so for a limited time after major adverse events, such as divorce or illness. For many families, welfare serves as a type of insurance protection, something they use for a brief period but dispose of as quickly as they can. The Michigan researchers conclude there is "little evidence that individual attitudes and behavior patterns affect individual economic progress." To a far greater extent, individuals "are the victims of their past, their environment, luck, and chance."

Even so, 70 percent of the women who are less than 25 years old when they first receive welfare remain on welfare for a least five years, and more than one-third stay on the rolls for at least a decade. For older and previously married women, welfare tends to be a benign source of help. Teenagers and women in their early twenties who have babies out of wedlock do not get married as often as their peers, do not remarry as quickly, and do not get into the paid labor force with the same degree of success. While the Michigan data show that the majority of people who have *ever* been on welfare have been on the rolls for less than five years, a majority of the people on the rolls *at any point in time* are in the midst of long spells of welfare dependence (Pear, 1986).

Still another view portrays poverty as a *structural* feature of capitalist societies. The cyclical movements of the economy—boom and bust—contribute to sharp fluctuations in employment. Marx contended that an *industrial reserve army* is essential for capitalist economies. This army consists of individuals at the bottom of the class structure who are laid off during times of economic stagnation, then rehired as needed during times of economic prosperity. It is composed mostly of minorities, who traditionally have been last hired and first fired. Proponents of the structural view charge that it is workers who bear the brunt of changes in industry, as seen in the persistent unemployment currently being experienced by many former workers in the American auto and steel industries (Kerbo, 1983).

An American underclass? The notion that a permanent *underclass* has emerged in American life, primarily black and isolated from mainstream America, has stirred controversy both inside and outside sociology. On one side are the proponents of the culture of poverty and structural positions; on the other, adherents of the situational position. The former see a "second nation" growing up within black America that is outside the economic mainstream, a permanent class of have-nots; the latter do not agree. There is also controversy over whether the term *underclass* is the right one to describe this category of poor people. Critics say it gives the impression that the problem cannot be solved (Auletta, 1983).

Simply being poor does not make a person a part of the underclass. For instance, poor blacks are not a solid, homogeneous group. Although a third of all blacks live in poverty, most of them—like most poor whites—hold jobs or use welfare only sometimes. The underclass, in contrast, is a core of poor inner-city blacks, people trapped in a cycle of joblessness and dependent on welfare or various forms of illicit earnings. Their communities are plagued by open lawlessness, drug abuse, violence, and poor schools. The underclass group is estimated to number about 2 to 3.5 million, or about one-third of all poor blacks (Whitman and Thornton, 1986).

Many women of the underclass are long-term welfare mothers who tend to be unwed and high-school dropouts. The vast majority were teenage mothers who found themselves sidetracked and without the resources or skills to escape a life of poverty (Ellwood and Bane, 1984). Many men of the underclass have borne the brunt of the decline in the manufacturing industries. They no longer find the opportunity blacks had in the 1940s, 1950s, and 1960s to move into higher-paying jobs in the industrial sector (young black men took only 1 out of every 1,000 new jobs created between 1970 and 1983). In 1985, with economic recovery in full swing, only 36 percent of black male youths aged 18 and 19 and 60 percent of those aged 20 to 24 were employed. Nearly half of black men between the ages of 16 and 24 had no work experience at all in 1984. Lacking skills and facing a shortage of jobs with career prospects, many young black men consider street life an attractive and rational alternative (Whitman and Thornton, 1986; Freeman, 1986).

Poverty in Contemporary America
A trash-barrel fire on a New York City street corner draws homeless people seeking a bit of warmth. *(Kevin Bubriski/Archive)*

Poverty programs "The poor you have always with you," says the Gospel of St. John. But the poor have not always been treated in the same way. Prior to the Civil War, most Americans saw poverty primarily as the product of personal misfortune, an individual problem that was not the fault of society. For much of Western history, assistance to the poor took the form of private almsgiving, augmented with public relief in times of crisis. Because of the merit in giving, charity served a dual purpose: It improved the spiritual state of the almsgiver and helped relieve want. Governments also intervened, although not necessarily in a charitable manner. For instance, the poor laws of eighteenth-century England provided workhouses for the able-bodied indigent to discourage people from joining the ranks of paupers. Much of the eighteenth- and nineteenth-century debate over the definitions of poverty and remedies for it is startlingly similar to that of today (Himmelfarb, 1984).

In this century in the United States, Lyndon Johnson's Great Society produced a flurry of social programs rivaling those of Franklin Roosevelt's New Deal. Now some are gone, and others have been severely cut or revamped by the Reagan administration. In 1980, federal transfers for the poor equaled 2.4 percent of the nation's Gross National Product (GNP), versus 2.2 percent of GNP in 1984 (Nasar, 1986b). The box examines

---

ISSUES THAT SHAPE OUR LIVES

Popular Myths about Poverty

Programs for dealing with poverty have become the source of a growing controversy. With the number of poor increasing 38 percent between 1978 and 1986, serious questions are being raised regarding the effectiveness of government programs. Indeed, critics of the antipoverty programs of the 1960s contend that they actually made the problem worse by promoting unstable families, encouraging out-of-wedlock births, and eroding the work ethic. This view is hardly new. Over a century and a half ago, the French writer Alexis de Tocqueville contended: "Any measure which establishes legal charity on a permanent basis and gives it an administrative form thereby creates an idle and lazy class, living at the expense of the industrial and working class" (quoted by Raspberry, 1986:13A). Others argue that the problem of rising poverty is caused by government *inaction*. They insist that without a massive effort, there is no real hope of eradicating poverty. Since our perceptions of the poor shape our views on public policy, let's see what

Seeking Work
In 1986 some 3,000 applicants converged on a Memphis meatpacking plant that had advertised some 250 openings. Here the applicants are pictured surging forward with outstretched hands to reach for job application forms. *(David Smart/ Picture Group)*

myths impair a realistic appraisal of the situation.

Myth: *The poor refuse to work and just live off welfare.*
Fact: Of 7.3 million families living in poverty in 1984, more than half had at least one worker, and more than 20 percent had two or more workers. An additional 1.4 million able-bodied poor sought work but were unable to find it. All the while, only one-third of poor families received public assistance, and only 43 percent received food stamps (O'Hare, 1986).

Myth: *Most poor people are black, are members of households headed*

some popular myths regarding poverty and America's antipoverty programs.

Two explanations have been proposed for the growth of welfare expenditures in contemporary Western nations. One holds that relief institutions are responsive to societal problems. As people's "needs" increase and the "capacity" of the economy grows, both consequences of industrialization and economic development, so do the responses of governmental relief-giving agencies. The state is a "neutral arbiter" serving the common good. The other view portrays the state as an agency of ruling elites. The state doles out welfare to keep the rebellious poor quiet and lessen popular opposition to ex-

isting social arrangements. The sociologists Larry Isaac and William R. Kelly (1981), using data from the black protest movement of the 1960s and early 1970s, found some support for both explanations—but more support for the latter. As one observer (Kerbo, 1983:326) notes: "Hungry people in need don't bring more welfare; an angry poor who take their anger to the streets do."

Allocating Social Resources: What Constitutes Justice?

The Declaration of Independence proclaims as a self-evident truth that "all men are created equal." Yet this

---

by women, and reside in inner-city ghettos.

Fact: In 1984 more than two-thirds of the 34 million poor were white, and fewer than 10 million were black. Indeed, between 1978 and 1984, the number of whites in poverty grew by 41 percent, compared to a growth of 25 percent for blacks. Only one-third of the poor live in female-headed families, and two-thirds of all poor families are found in rural or suburban areas. Less than one-fifth of the poor live in inner-city ghettos. In recent years, poverty has increased more rapidly among persons living in married-couple or male-headed households than among those in female-headed households (O'Hare, 1986; Nasar, 1986b).

Myth: Welfare payments are a major factor underlying the growing federal deficit.

Fact: The government's main cash-assistance program, Aid to Families with Dependent Children, cost $8 billion in fiscal 1984—only 5 percent of the amount spent on social security and less than 4 percent of defense expenditures. Since 1972, median benefits have declined 33 percent in purchasing power, while programs aiding

the middle class and the elderly have typically kept pace with inflation (O'Hare, 1986; Nasar, 1986b).

Myth: Welfare payments foster a "culture of dependency" and encourage teenagers to have children because the government will take care of them.

Fact: The Children's Defense Fund compared states' rates of teenage births with 1983 payment levels of Aid for Dependent Children (AFDC). Practically every state whose payments were more than 50 percent of the federal poverty level had teenage birth rates below the national average. In contrast, almost every state with low payments had teenage birth rates higher than the national average (Stein, 1986). Other researchers find that AFDC has virtually no effect on the fertility of unmarried black and white women (Ellwood and Bane, 1984). Higher benefits simply seem to encourage single mothers to establish separate households, whereas in low-benefit states they are more likely to live with relatives. Sociologist William Julius Wilson suggests that welfare is not a primary cause of female-headed households. He contends that the increase in female-headed families among whites has occurred primarily

in response to the rising earning power of white women. In contrast, the growth of female-headed households among blacks has stemmed from the worsening fortunes of black men in the labor market (the ratio of gainfully employed black men to all black women declined about 50 percent from 1960 to 1980) (Nasar, 1986b). Finally, at least 50 percent of the people who use AFDC leave the program within two years; most people do not seem to become trapped by welfare assistance (Ellwood and Summers, 1986).

Myth: Workfare programs—in which participants work for their welfare benefits—will solve the poverty problem.

Fact: Work programs do not guarantee jobs. Of the 10,000 welfare recipients in West Virginia who took workfare jobs in 1985, only 13 percent ended up with permanent employment. At the time, West Virginia's unemployment rate was 11.7 percent (Nasar, 1986a). The Job Corps, which provides remedial education and job training for the young, hard-core unemployed, is expensive ($15,000 a year for each participant) and has a high dropout rate.

Massive Poverty and Despair during the Great Depression of the 1930s
The stock-market collapse in 1929 heralded a business depression that was the most prolonged and devastating in American experience. Over 5,000 banks collapsed in the first three years of the Great Depression. By 1933, one-quarter of the labor force was unemployed and farm prices had fallen 63 percent. Thousands of people searched fruitlessly for work and suffered the effects of poverty and malnutrition. *(Dorothea Lange/Culver Pictures)*

pronouncement by the Founding Fathers is contradicted by widespread social inequality. In practice, the ideal has proved quite elusive: The American promise has primarily been one of equality of *opportunity*, not of *results*. It has been a vision in which individuals—freed from discrimination based on race, religion, family, gender, or community—find their places on the basis of merit and fair competition. The American dream, then, is not of a classless society; rather, it is of a class society in which all people have equal access to the top positions.

Americans have never been levelers; the vast majority agree that some income variation is both desirable and appropriate. Even the strong reform movements of

this century—the New Deal and the Great Society—were not advocating redistribution of wealth. On the other hand, the Reagan administration, although seeking to cut social programs substantially, promised to provide a safety net for the truly needy. Overall, Americans' general opposition to radical income redistribution and their support of some government protection for the truly disadvantaged have defined the outer limits of income inequality (Verba and Orren, 1985).

There are, of course, any number of ways that group resources can be allocated: (1) *equity*, in which rewards are distributed among members in proportion to their contributions; (2) *self-interest*, in which those with power maximize their own rewards, independent of their contributions; (3) *equality*, in which each person receives the same quantity of rewards as everyone else regardless of contribution; and (4) *need*, in which rewards are allocated in terms of each person's wants or requirements. Equity patterns typically appear when an allocator wishes to maximize the performance of group members. Self-interest—also termed "greed"—arises where rewards are lucrative and the allocator need not be concerned with the retaliatory power of others. Equality—based on the credo of "All for one and one for all—share and share alike"—most often occurs within families and closely bonded ingroups. Finally, distribution may rest

"There's no justice in the world, Kirkby, but I'm not convinced that this is an entirely bad thing."
Drawing by Handelsman; © 1986 The New Yorker Magazine, Inc.

upon notions of justice such as that contained in the Marxist slogan "From everyone according to ability, to everyone according to need" (Vander Zanden, 1987). Resources, then, can be awarded in terms of merit, power, equality, or need. Which criteria will be applied and under which circumstances has been a recurrent source of human conflict.

Opportunity and Social Mobility

America has long been called the "land of opportunity." Early in this century, the Horatio Alger rags-to-riches stories enjoyed wide appeal. They told of poor boys who made good by reason of personal virtue, pluck, diligence, and hard work. More recently, best seller lists have been filled with books describing how individuals can achieve success through investing in real estate, bonds, collectibles, or the stock market; dressing right; intimidating others; getting right with God; or psyching themselves up. Underlying these notions is the assumption that individuals or groups can move from one level (stratum) to another, a process termed **social mobility.** Social inequality has to do with differences in the distribution of benefits and burdens and social stratification with a structured system of inequality. Social mobility refers to the shift of individuals or groups from one social status to another.

Forms of Social Mobility

Social mobility may be vertical or horizontal. **Vertical mobility** involves movement from one social status to another of higher or lower rank. As Table 9.3 on page 233 shows, Americans differ in the prestige ratings of various occupations. If an auto mechanic (score 37) became a bank officer (score 72), this shift would be upward mobility. On the other hand, if the auto mechanic became a garbage collector (score 17), this change would involve downward mobility. If the auto mechanic left that position and took a job as a restaurant manager (score 39), this shift would represent horizontal mobility. **Horizontal mobility** is movement from one social status to another that is approximately equivalent in rank.

Sociologists also distinguish between intergenerational and intragenerational mobility. **Intergenerational mobility** involves a comparison of the social status of parents and their children at some point in their respec-

tive careers (for example, as assessed by the rankings of their occupations at roughly the same age). Research shows that a large minority, perhaps even a majority of the American population, moves up or down at least a little in the class hierarchy in every generation. **Intragenerational mobility** is a comparison of the social status of a person over an extended time period. Studies show that a large proportion of Americans have worked in different jobs and occupations in their lifetimes (Sorensen, 1975, Duncan, 1984). But there are limits to the variety of most people's mobility experience. Short-distance movements tend to be the rule, and long-distance movements the exception.

Social Mobility in the United States

When sociologists talk about social mobility, they usually have intergenerational occupational mobility in mind. Given the traditional operation of sexism in the labor market, which until recent decades relegated women to the home or to low-paying jobs, much more is known about the mobility of men than of women. Perhaps the most impressive studies of social mobility in the United States have been undertaken by Peter M. Blau and Otis Dudley Duncan (1972), and more recently by David Featherman and Robert Hauser (1978). The Blau and Duncan study used data collected by the Census Bureau in 1962 from a sample of over 20,000 men, while that of Featherman and Hauser consisted of a sample of over 30,000 employed men in 1973.

If we summarize the data from these and related studies, it seems that about 50 percent of American men are immobile; they remain in their father's stratum (Davis, 1982). About 25 percent are upwardly mobile, moving from farm or blue-collar jobs to white-collar jobs. Another 10 percent are downwardly mobile, moving from white-collar to blue-collar jobs. And 15 percent move from farm to blue-collar positions.

There are two primary explanations for the higher rate of upward intergenerational mobility in the United States. First, the *occupational structure* has been changing. As the nation advanced technologically, more jobs were created toward the top of the occupational structure than toward the bottom. Whether this pattern reversed in the 1980s is a matter of some controversy. There are those who say that over the past decade the American economy has been in a quiet depression in which real wages, real family incomes, and the proportion of better-paying positions have not grown (Levy and Michel, 1985; Longman, 1985). Others find that most young

Social Mobility among European Immigrants in the United States
Between 1901 and 1910, some 2 million Italians migrated to the United States (top left). By this time, the frontier and free lands had virtually vanished, and many Italians settled in Northeast and Atlantic seaboard communities. Some became pushcart vendors and small shopkeepers (top right). Others earned low wages in the sweatshops of New York City where unskilled workers, some of them children, were exploited. Many lived in crowded tenements in predominantly Italian neighborhoods. For the most part, however, the children of Italian immigrants were immersed into the mainstream of American life by the public school system. As adults, they entered the larger American political, economic, and social arena and became progressively Americanized. In the process many of them moved socially upward into the middle class. The appointment of Supreme Court Justice Antonin Scalia in 1986 signaled that Italian-Americans are now reaching top positions of power and authority in the United States (bottom). *(clockwise from top left: Lewis Hine photo, International Museum of Photography at George Eastman House; Culver Pictures; J. L. Atlan/Sygma)*

adults today believe that their living standards are equal to or more comfortable than those of their parents (Linden, 1986). Second, *fertility* plays a role; white-collar fathers have fewer sons than blue-collar fathers. With higher-occupation fathers producing fewer sons and the top of the occupational structure expanding, there is more room toward the top of the class hierarchy. Overall, more than twice as many men have moved into white-collar jobs as have moved out of them (Davis, 1982).

In Chapters 10 and 12 we will consider the special circumstances of blacks and women in the United States and how racism and sexism have affected their mobility opportunities. However, we need to point out here that the class system has proved to be much more rigid for blacks than for the general population (Blau and Duncan, 1972; Featherman and Hauser, 1978; Wright, 1978b). Moreover, historically black fathers who have attained white-collar jobs have had greater difficulty than white fathers in passing their advantage on to their sons. This pattern may now be changing for those blacks able to break into higher occupational positions (Clark, 1983). Research also shows that working women are less likely to be in an occupational status close to their father's than are men (Hauser and Featherman, 1977). Traditionally women have been concentrated in lower nonmanual and white-collar clerical jobs. Thus, regardless of whether their fathers are higher or lower in occupational rank, women are commonly pushed up to, or down to, lower white-collar positions.

THINKING THROUGH THE ISSUES

Sociologists say that the amount of mobility in a society is closely connected to other societal features. How do you think that it affects political freedom and democracy; social and political solidarity; racial and ethnic harmony; the rates for some kinds of crime; the amount of violence in social relations; the role of the schools; the quality of personal friendships and community patterns? What does the ratio of upward to downward mobility have to do with these issues? Does it matter from what positions the upwardly mobile people have risen and the downwardly mobile people have fallen? What sorts of positions are most susceptible to shifts in mobility patterns?

Social Mobility in Industrialized Societies

Sociologists' concern with social mobility reflects interest in the extent to which various societies have realized the ideal of equality of opportunity. Sociological evidence reveals that no contemporary society comes close to allowing all its members the same chances. In all industrial societies, a family's class position plays a large part in determining the status placement of offspring. On the other hand, no modern society denies its male members the opportunity to be upwardly mobile. In each nation for which data are available, a large proportion of men have moved up or down between generations (Lipset, 1982).

Overall there is little difference among various industrialized countries in rates of occupational mobility between blue-collar and white-collar classes. The basic processes affecting rates of social mobility, once people of rural origin are set aside, appear to be structural—linked to the pace of economic development, rather than to political or economic systems. Rates of mobility are in fact comparable in socialist and capitalist nations. A comparison of social mobility in six Communist countries (Bulgaria, Czechoslovakia, Hungary, Poland, Romania, and Yugoslavia) and seven non-Communist ones (Australia, France, Italy, Norway, Sweden, the United States, and West Germany) reveals that blue-collar non-farm sons (workers) are mobile into nonmanual jobs in 29.2 percent of the cases in the Communist average, and 28.2 percent in the non-Communist sample (Connor, 1979). Although upward mobility may be somewhat higher in the United States than in most other countries, the United States does not appear to be significantly more open than other industrialized nations (Tyree, Semyonov, and Hodge, 1979; Grusky and Hauser, 1984; Kerckhoff, Campbell, and Winfield-Laird, 1985).

Status Attainment Processes

In recent years considerable sociological research has dealt with the factors underlying status transmission and attainment. Blau and Duncan (1972) have developed a technique for studying the course of an individual's oc-

"Say, Pop, where do you stand in the pecking order?"
Drawing by Joe Mirachi; © 1986 The New Yorker Magazine, Inc.

cupational status over the life course. Termed the **socio-economic life cycle,** it involves a sequence of stages that begins with birth into a family with a specific social status and proceeds through childhood, socialization, schooling, job seeking, occupational achievement, marriage, and the formation and functioning of a new family unit. The outcomes of each stage are seen as affecting *subsequent* stages in the cycle. In order to capture the specific contributions of each stage, Blau and Duncan (1972:163) analyze their data by means of a statistical procedure called *path analysis:*

> We think of the individual's life cycle as a sequence in time that can be described, however partially and crudely, by a set of classificatory or quantitative measurements taken at successive stages. . . . Given this scheme, the questions we are continually raising in one form or another are: how and to what degree do the circumstances of birth condition [determine] subsequent status? And how does status attained . . . at one stage of the life cycle affect the prospects for a subsequent stage?

Blau and Duncan conclude that the social status of a man's parents typically has little *direct* impact on his occupational attainment. Instead, the primary influence of parental status is *indirect*, through its effect on level of schooling. (One of the virtues of path analysis is its ability to separate direct from indirect effects). Overall, education (years of schooling completed) is the factor that has the greatest influence on a man's occupational attainment, both early and late. Another factor that has a sizable effect is the level of the occupational status ladder at which a man starts his career. The lower he begins, the higher he has to rise, and the less likely he is to reach the top positions.

William Sewell and his associates have also investigated the status attainment process. They based their work on a survey of Wisconsin high school seniors conducted in 1957 and a follow-up study of one-third of them from 1964 through 1967. They conclude that educational and occupational attainment are the outcome of two related processes: those by which status aspirations are formed, and those by which the aspirations become translated into an actual position in the status hierarchy. The Wisconsin data reveal that practically the entire effect of a family's socioeconomic status on a child's educational and occupational attainments is the result of the personal influence it exerts on the child's status aspirations during adolescence. Other early factors that play a part are parental and teacher encouragement to attend college and the college plans of the adolescent's best friend. But once these factors are controlled (statistically taken into account and allowed for), the effects of parental social status become insignificant and have no other direct influence upon status attainment. Rather, as Blau and Duncan also conclude, it is level of schooling that has the primary influence on subsequent occupational attainment.

Status attainment research has its limitations. Critics contend that it has a functionalist bias (Coser, 1975; Horan, 1978). The approach assumes that the job market is fully open to all comers who acquire positions on the basis of competence (Knottnerus, 1987). In contrast, conflict theorists argue that people are channeled into class positions based on their family's ownership or lack of ownership of the means of production. In sum, critics say that the attainment process is quite unequal for the members of a capitalist society (Wright, 1978a, 1978b; Smith, 1981).

Chapter Highlights

1. Most societies are organized so that their institutions systematically distribute benefits and burdens unequally among different categories of people. Sociologists call the structured ranking of individuals and groups social stratification. Social stratification depends upon but is not the same thing as social differentiation—the process by which the members of a society become increasingly specialized over time.

2. Sociologists typically take a multidimensional view of stratification, and identify three components: economic (wealth and income), prestige, and power. The rankings of some statuses may be dissimilar. For the most part, however, these three dimensions feed into and support one another.

3. Stratification systems differ in the ease with which they permit people to move in or out of particular strata. Where people can change their status with relative ease, sociologists refer to the arrangement as an open system. Where people have great difficulty in changing their status, sociologists term the arrangement a closed system.

4. The functionalist theory of social inequality holds that stratification exists because it is beneficial for society. According to the sociologists Kingsley Davis and Wilbert Moore, society must concern itself with human motivation because the duties associated with the various statuses are not all equally pleasant, equally important to social survival, and equally in need of the same abilities and talents. Consequently, society must have, first, some kind of rewards that it can use as inducements for its members, and second, some way of distributing these rewards differentially among the various statuses.

5. The conflict theory of social inequality holds that stratification exists because it benefits individuals and groups who have the power to dominate and exploit others. The conflict perspective draws heavily on the ideas of Karl Marx. Marx contended that the capitalist drive to realize surplus value is the foundation of the modern class struggle—an irreconcilable clash of interests between workers and capitalists. Initially workers are blinded by false consciousness, but through struggle with capitalists, they evolve class consciousness.

6. Any number of sociologists have noted that both the functionalist and conflict theories have merit, but that each is better than the other in answering different questions. They have sought a synthesis of the two positions. The sociologist Gerhard E. Lenski has looked for ways of integrating the two perspectives.

7. Three primary methods are employed by sociologists for identifying social classes. The *objective method* views social class as a statistical category. People are assigned to classes on the basis of income, occupation, or education (or some combination of these characteristics). The *self-placement* method has people identify the social class to which they think they belong. Class is viewed as a social category, one in which people group themselves with other individuals they perceive as having certain attributes in common with them. The *reputational method* asks people how they classify other individuals. This approach views class as a social group.

8. Few aspects of social life affect the way people behave and think as strongly as social class. For one thing, it largely determines their life chances—the likelihood that individuals and groups will enjoy desired goods and services, fulfilling experiences, and opportunities for living healthy and long lives. Social class also affects people's style of life—the magnitude and manner of their consumption of goods and services.

9. The Census Bureau defines the threshold of poverty in the United States as the minimum amount of money families need to purchase a nutritionally adequate diet, assuming they use one-third of their income for food. Children and the elderly account for nearly half of Americans living in poverty. Three theories regarding poverty predominate: One explains the difficulties of the poor as stemming from a culture of poverty. Another view sees poverty as largely situational. Still another view portrays poverty as a structural feature of capitalist societies.

10. Social mobility takes a number of forms. It may be vertical or horizontal; it may be intergenerational or intragenerational. When sociologists talk about social mobility, they usually mean intergenerational occupational mobility. Although upward mobility may be somewhat greater in the United States than in most other countries, the United States does not appear to be significantly more open than other modern, industrialized nations.

11. Sociologists see education as a critical factor in the social mobility of individuals in the United States. It seems that education has the greatest influence on occupational attainment. William Sewell and his associates contend that educational and occupational attainment are the outcome of two related processes: those by which status aspirations are formed, and those by which the aspirations become translated into an actual position in the status hierarchy. Critics of status attainment research contend that it has a functionalist bias.

The Sociologist's Vocabulary

caste system A system in which ascribed statuses provide the principal basis for the unequal distribution of social resources.

class system A system in which achieved statuses provide the principal basis for the unequal distribution of social resources.

closed system A stratification system in which people have great difficulty changing status.

constraints Resources that allow one party to add new disadvantages to a situation.

culture of poverty The view that the poor have self-perpetuating lifeways characterized by weak ego structures, lack of impulse control, present-time orientation, and a sense of resignation and fatalism.

horizontal mobility Movement from one social status to another that is approximately equivalent in rank.

income The amount of money people receive.

inducements Resources that allow one party to add new advantages to a situation.

intergenerational mobility A comparison of the social status of parents and their children at some point in their respective careers.

intragenerational mobility A comparison of the social status of a person over an extended period of time.

life chances The likelihood that individuals and groups will enjoy desired goods and services, fulfilling experiences, and opportunities for living healthy and long lives.

objective method An approach to the identification of social classes that employs such yardsticks as income, occupation, and education.

open system A stratification system in which people can change status with relative ease.

persuasion Resources that enable one party to change the minds of other people without adding either advantages or disadvantages to the situation.

power The ability of individuals and groups to realize their will in human affairs, even if it involves overcoming the resistance of others.

prestige The social respect, admiration, and recognition associated with a particular social status.

reputational method An approach for identifying social classes that involves asking people how they classify others.

self-placement method An approach for identifying social classes that involves self-classification.

social differentiation The process by which the members of a society divide activities and become "different" by virtue of playing distinctive roles.

social mobility Individuals or groups move from one level (stratum) to another in the stratification system.

social stratification The structured ranking of individuals and groups; their grading into horizontal layers or strata.

socioeconomic life cycle A sequence of stages that begins with birth into a family with a specific social status and proceeds through childhood, socialization, schooling, job seeking, occupational achievement, marriage, and the formation and functioning of a new family unit.

style of life The magnitude and manner of people's consumption of goods and services.

vertical mobility The movement of individuals from one social status to another of higher or lower rank.

wealth What people own.

10

Racial and Ethnic Relations

I have a dream that my four little children will one day live in a nation where they will not be judged by the color of their skin but by the content of their character.

—Martin Luther King, Jr., Speech, June 15, 1963

The world seems convulsed by intergroup hatreds. South Africa is ablaze in racial antipathy and violence. Car bombs and terrorist acts are commonplace among Lebanon's warring factions. Northern Ireland's Catholics and Protestants remain consumed by age-old animosities. And headlines tell of separatist-inspired violence among the Tamil minority in Sri Lanka, the Sikhs in India's Punjab, and Palestinians in the Middle East. Not too many of us are willing to battle to the death over class-related ideologies of capitalism and Marxism. But a great many of us seem ready to kill each other over differences of color, height, facial configuration, religion, language, and dietary practices (Greeley, 1974). It would seem that conflict is an inevitable accompaniment of contact between different groups. Is this necessarily the case?

That humankind is capable of living together harmoniously and cooperatively is demonstrated by two peoples in northwestern Manchuria who were studied by anthropologist Ethel John Lindgren (1938). Racially the one group, the Reindeer Tungus, are a Mongoloid people with physical characteristics quite similar to those of the Chinese; the other, Russian Cossacks, are a burly Caucasoid people. The two people are also culturally dissimilar. The Tungus are an illiterate, nomadic people who live in tents and depend upon their domesticated reindeer, hunting, and trade with the Cossacks for subsistence. The Cossacks are a literate, sedentary people who dwell in village homes and rely for their subsistence upon agriculture, stock-raising, some squirrel hunting, and trading with the Tungus. Religiously the Tungus are Christians, yet their ancient religious beliefs persist; they place considerable reliance upon shamans, who are skilled in curing the sick, predicting the future, and communicating with spirits. For their part, the Cossacks are zealous Christians, although they are not without their superstitions and folk beliefs.

Despite their racial and cultural differences, Lindgren (1938:607), who lived among both peoples for a time during the 1930s, observes:

> I heard no Tungus or Cossack express fear, contempt, or hatred in relation to the other group as a whole or any individual composing it. A few traits of the opposite group are habitually criticized, and a few praised, on the basis of a comparison with the corresponding traits of the speaker's culture.

The Tungus criticize the Russians because thefts occur in their community, a crime unknown among the Tungus. For their part, the Cossacks praise the Tungus for their honesty, implying it is superior to their own. The Cossacks criticize the Tungus for the random violence they engage in when under the influence of alcohol, behavior the Tungus themselves deplore. Despite such criticisms, Lindgren notes, "Expressions of dislike and distrust with regard to individuals in the other group are of exactly the same type as those applied within the group itself, and admiration seems to predominate over criticism" (p. 607). Even though ethnocentric notions prevail, Lindgren was unable to discover any tradition or record that relations between the two groups had ever been other than amicable, although she looked for evidence and asked the elderly to search their memories.

The Tungus and Cossacks come into contact periodically during the year, so there is certainly enough opportunity for intergroup hostilities. Markets provide one occasion. Two or three times each winter, when the Tungus are busy hunting squirrels, Cossack traders travel up the frozen rivers with horse-drawn sledges and meet the Tungus at a forest rendezvous, where a market is held. Two or three times each summer, when the Cossacks are busy farming, the Tungus come to the Cossack settlements. The markets last from two to five days. The Tungus trade furs in exchange for needles, thread, axes, iron pots, copper kettles, gunpowder, lead, flour, and shirts, coats, and jackets made up, roughly to measure, by the traders' families. The trade is conducted between individuals who call each other *andak*, or "friend." A Tungus often boasts about the wealth and superior products of his Cossack *andak*, who in turn boasts of his Tungus hunter's achievements.

The Tungus and Cossacks also encounter one another in forested areas while hunting. Neither the Tungus or the Cossacks divide the hunting grounds within their own groups, nor do they come to a collective agreement with the other group. Nonetheless, the first to arrive in a valley, Tungus or Cossack, is left undisturbed. If members of either group discover fresh marks of the other, they will eagerly seek out the other's camp for the sake of company, and probably a little trade. Longer visits also occasionally occur.

How are we to explain the apparent lack of discord between the Tungus and Cossacks? Lindgren suggests a number of factors. First, the two groups have always been small in number and about equal in size. Consequently, personal relationships could develop among their members, and no group threatened to engulf the other. Second, the two groups were not in competition for land or resources. Third, outside pressures drew the two together. About 1908, the Chinese imposed a tax upon the fur trade, a development that both groups resented, and that strengthened the bonds between them. Fourth, the cultures of the two groups complemented one another. Both peoples benefited from their trading activities. The groups were also compatible religiously. The Tungus were nominally Christians, while the Cossacks took delight in praising the insight of the Tungus shamans and describing shaman prophecies that had come true. Friction arising from intermarriage did not occur, since the groups seldom intermarried, chiefly due to the fact that the opposite sexes of the two groups had little opportunity to meet. The Tungus and Cossacks provide a bright spot in a world of intergroup frictions and tensions.

PLANNING AHEAD: TARGETED READING

1. How do racial and ethnic systems of stratification differ from other systems of stratification?

2. What properties distinguish minority groups from other groups within a society?

3. What are the social implications of prejudice and discrimination for Americans?

4. How does institutional discrimination differ from individual discrimination?

5. What are some of the principal types of policies dominant groups pursue toward minority groups?

6. Why do systems of racial and ethnic stratification exist within a society?

7. How are America's major minority groups currently faring?

Intergroup Relations

Stratification contains the answer to the question of *who gets what, when, and how.* As a consequence, a society's "good things"—particularly income, wealth, prestige, and power—are distributed in an uneven manner. The burdens and unpleasant chores are also unequally allocated. So stratification represents institutionalized inequality in the distribution of social rewards and burdens. People find themselves in a social arena in which they differ sharply in their life chances and styles of living.

The class system is one type of stratification; race and ethnicity are another. Humankind contains peoples with quite different skin colors, languages, religions, and customs. These physical and cultural traits provide high social visibility and serve as identifying symbols of group membership. The distinctions are assigned social meanings that are translated into structured inequalities. For example, within the United States, blacks, Hispanics, Indians (Native Americans), Asian-Americans, and Jews have been the victims of prejudice and discrimination. They have historically been confined to subordinate statuses that are not justified by their individual abilities and talents. Figure 10.1 on page 255 reflects population trends in the United States for the nation's major racial and ethnic categories.

Although racial and ethnic stratification is similar to other systems of stratification in its essential features, there is one major difference. Racial and ethnic groups often have the *potential* for carving their own independent nation from an existing state. At times, political separatism offers a solution to disadvantaged racial and ethnic groups that is not possible for disadvantaged class and gender groups. Class and gender groups typically lack the possibility of becoming self-sufficient political states because they do not function as self-sufficient social or economic groups.

While separatist tendencies and their chances for success vary enormously, the underlying potential for such movements exists in most nations with diverse racial and ethnic groups. Unlike class stratification, the issue is not replacement of one elite by another, or even a revolutionary change in the political system. Instead, the question is one of whether the various racial and ethnic groups are willing to remain part of the existing nation-state (Lieberson, 1970). Class conflicts threaten

Racial Stratification: South Africa
A maid cleans the rug as a South African white carries on a telephone conversation. This black woman is viewed as a taken-for-granted fixture in a system in which social benefits and burdens are unequally distributed among the members of a racially stratified society. *(David Turnley/Detroit Free Press/Black Star)*

governments, but they rarely pose alternative definitions of the territorial boundaries of the nation (Geertz, 1963). Examples abound in the contemporary world of separatist movements, including the Palestinians in the Middle East, the Irish Catholics of Northern Ireland, the Ibo of Nigeria, the Katangese of Zaire, the various Muslim and Christian factions in Lebanon, and the French of Quebec, Canada. Nor have Communist societies escaped ethnic difficulties. Ethnic attachments remain a significant political fact in the Soviet Union, especially among residents of the Baltic region, Jews, and the Muslims along the southern border. According to the Soviet military paper *Red Star*, the bulk of the nation's armed forces are members of non-Russian ethnic groups, many of whom speak little or no Russian and who share a mutual antipathy toward ethnic Russians (Quinn-Judge, 1987). Given the intense loyalties ethnic affiliations generate, contemporary governments typically try to solidify the allegiance of their populations to a shared national standard rooted in a common territory (Yinger, 1985).

THINKING THROUGH THE ISSUES

How do ethnic attachments affect international relations? How did ethnic friction and tension in the Balkans spark World War I? What part has the treatment of Soviet Jews played in Soviet-American relationships? How have ethnic affiliations contributed to Middle Eastern turbulence? What have been the international consequences of white South Africa's apartheid policies? In the United States, how have various ethnic groups influenced American policies toward Cuba, Israel, the Arabic states, the USSR, Ireland, Vietnam, and South Africa?

Races

We all know—scientists and the public alike—that people in various parts of the world differ in certain hereditary features, including color of skin, texture of hair, facial features, stature, and shape of the head. It is equally true that the features humankind everywhere share are substantially larger and of considerably greater importance than their differences. Even so, differences do exist. We readily recognize that *groups* of Norwegians, Chinese, and Ugandans differ in their physical characteristics. Scientists call a population that differs from others in the incidence of certain hereditary traits a **race**.

Although we have little difficulty observing physical differences among people, scientists have considerable trouble identifying races and categorizing people in terms of them. People differ in a great many ways. Classifications based on one characteristic, such as skin color, do not necessarily yield the same results as those based on some other trait. For example, extremely kinky hair is found among the moderately pigmented San of South Africa, and straight or wavy hair among some otherwise dark-pigmented peoples of southern India

(Vander Zanden, 1983). Complicating matters, people interbreed, so that genetic lines become quite blurred. Populations grade into one another in skin color, hair form, stature, and head shape. Consequently, it is often next to impossible to tell where one population ends and another begins. Within the United States, 80 percent of black Americans have European ancestors; 50 percent or more of Mexican-Americans have both Indian and European ancestors; and some 20 percent of "white" Americans are estimated to have African or Indian ancestors (Stuckert, 1976).

Scientists today are far from agreement on dividing human populations into races. But what interests us here is the social significance we attach to various traits. By virtue of our social definitions, skin color or some other trait becomes a "sign" or "mark" of social status.

Ethnic Groups

Groups that we identify chiefly on cultural grounds—language, folk practices, dress, gestures, mannerisms, or religion—are termed **ethnic groups.** Within the United States, examples include Jewish-Americans, Italian-Americans, and Hispanics. Figure 10.2 on page 256 depicts the geographic distribution of major ethnic groups in the United States. Very often ethnic groups experience a sense of peoplehood. Their members entertain the belief that they share a common descent. This notion commonly results in a deep-seated feeling of "community" and entails a longing not to belong to any other group. Sociologist Pierre Van den Berghe (1981) views ethnic sentiments as extensions of kinship sentiments.

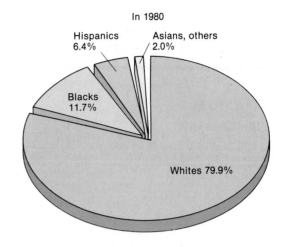

In 1980

Hispanics 6.4%
Asians, others 2.0%
Blacks 11.7%
Whites 79.9%

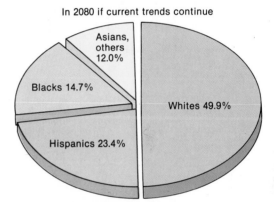

In 2080 if current trends continue

Asians, others 12.0%
Blacks 14.7%
Whites 49.9%
Hispanics 23.4%

FIGURE 10.1   **U.S. Population Trends: Major Racial and Ethnic Categories**
Source: Population Reference Bureau.

The Social Definition of Race
The people on "The Cosby Show" are actually white, or so figures Lucas DeLange, the manager of media relations for the South African Broadcasting Corp., which airs the program in the land of apartheid: "You call the Cosbys (the Huxtables) black, but here they'd be considered part of the white community, although of the colored persuasion." DeLange implied that a genetic mutation was possibly responsible for Dr. and Mrs. Huxtable's high social and economic status. Such success skews the usual rules of South African racial categorization (Wilson, 1986). *(R.M. Lewis, Jr./ NBC)*

ENGLISH*

Utah 61%, Kentucky 50%, Maine 48% Tennessee 45%, West Virginia 44%, Idaho 43%, Vermont 42%, North Carolina 41%, Virginia 41%

GERMAN

Wisconsin 56%, Iowa 53%, South Dakota 52%, Nebraska 52%, North Dakota 50%, Minnesota 48%, Kansas 43%, Indiana 42%, Ohio 41%

ITALIAN

Rhode Island 22%, Connecticut 20%, New Jersey 20%, New York 18%, Massachusetts 15%, Pennsylvania 12%, Delaware 9%

SCOTTISH

Maine 10%, Oregon 9%, North Carolina 9%, Washington 9%, Vermont 9%, New Hampshire 9%, Wyoming 8%, Montana 8%, South Carolina 8%

IRISH

Oklahoma 31%, Massachusetts 31%, Arkansas 29%, Missouri 29%, West Virginia 28%, Tennessee 26%, Kentucky 26%, Delaware 26%, Oregon 25%, Rhode Island 25%

AFRO-AMERICAN

Mississippi 38%, South Carolina 31%, Georgia 29%, Alabama 29%, Louisiana 28%, North Carolina 24%

FRENCH

Vermont 34%, New Hampshire 30%, Louisiana 29%, Maine 28%, Rhode Island 21%, Massachusetts 17%, Connecticut 12%

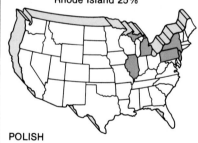

POLISH

Wisconsin 11%, Connecticut 10%, Michigan 10%, New Jersey 9%, Illinois 9%, Pennsylvania 8%, New York 8%, Massachusetts 7%

MEXICAN

Texas 22%, California 16%, Arizona 16%, New Mexico 14%, Colorado 6%, Illinois 4%, Wyoming 3%, Kansas 2%

AMERICAN INDIAN

Oklahoma 17%, New Mexico 11%, Arkansas 11%, Alaska 11%, Arizona 9%, South Dakota 7%, Missouri 6%, West Virginia 6%

 States in color are those with at least 500,000 persons of the indicated ethnic groups in the latest census—

*States with the highest concentration of the ethnic group. Percentages indicate percentages of total population.

FIGURE 10.2   **Distribution of Major Ethnic Groups**

Source: U.S. Bureau of the Census, U.S. News & World Report, July 7, 1986, 30–31.

We often confuse nationalism (a feeling of loyalty to a nation or an ethnic group) with a feeling of loyalty to the state (a political unit). Yet a nation and a state are not the same. Consider Europe. Virtually every territory of Europe has combined at some time or other with almost every one of its neighbors. In fact, the territories covered by European political states have never been, and could not possibly be, exactly the same as the territories inhabited by various ethnic groups. Very often ethnic groups occupy small pieces of territory or are dispersed by residence and place of occupation throughout a territory. So political self-determination for one ethnic nationality is often incompatible with political self-determination for another. Many European political states contain multiple nationality groups: Great Britain (English, Scotch, Welsh, Northern Irish), Belgium (Flemish and Walloons), Czechoslovakia (Czecks and Slovaks), and Switzerland (Germans, French, Italians). Consequently, many political states periodically experience ethnic strife and even violence that derives from the minority status of some groups. It is hardly surprising that any overly exuberant celebration of ethnicity is viewed with suspicion by political states that have multiple ethnic groups.

THINKING THROUGH THE ISSUES

How do intense ethnic allegiances, as contrasted with those rooted in class differences, influence the level and nature of conflict within a society? When societal strains are organized along ethnic lines, why are they typically less negotiable, more intractable, and more emotional than most other social divisions? How do ethnic identifications make it possible for an otherwise powerless population to mobilize resources that are out of reach when individuals act alone (Nielsen, 1985)? How may special interests be promoted by ethnically based movements? Who within an ethnic group profits in terms of wealth, prestige, and power by an emphasis on ethnic divisions? If ethnic movements are typically inspired and led by higher-status persons, why may they be the ones who have the most to gain (Yinger, 1985)?

Minority Groups

We hear a good deal nowadays about *minority groups*—or simply *minorities*. The choice of terms is unfortunate, because they have numerical connotations. Despite its literal meaning, a minority is *not* a statistical category.

For instance, within South Africa, blacks constitute a numerical majority but suffer disadvantage at the hands of a numerical minority of whites. And until relatively recently, small numbers of Europeans dominated "minority" peoples in colonial arrangements in Asia, Africa, and Latin America. In short, "minority" refers to a social status. A **minority group** is a racially and/or culturally self-conscious population, with hereditary membership and a high degree of ingroup marriage, that suffers disadvantage at the hands of a dominant segment of a nation-state (Williams, 1964).

Five properties typically characterize minority groups (Wagley and Harris, 1964; Vander Zanden, 1983):

1. A minority is a social group whose members experience discrimination, segregation, oppression, or persecution at the hands of another social group, termed the *dominant group*. By virtue of the power differences between the two groups, the members of a minority are disadvantaged. Equally important, they are the source of the dominant group's advantages, since the oppression of one people confers privilege and status on another.

2. A minority is characterized by physical and/or cultural traits that distinguish it from the dominant group. By virtue of these traits, its members are lumped together and placed in less desirable positions in the social structure.

3. A minority is a self-conscious social group characterized by a consciousness of oneness. Its members possess a social and psychological affinity with others like themselves, providing a sense of *peoplehood*. This consciousness of oneness is often accentuated by common suffering and burdens.

4. Membership in a minority group is generally not voluntary. Minority membership is an ascribed position, since an individual is typically born into the status—a person does not usually choose to be a black or a white.

5. The members of a minority, by choice or necessity, typically marry within their own group (endogamy) (Stevens and Swicegood, 1987). The dominant group discourages its members from marrying members of the minority group, and usually scorns those who do. The minority may encourage its members to marry among themselves to preserve their unique cultural heritage. It

Intergroup Marriage
The incidence of intergroup dating and marriage is a particularly sensitive measure of ethnic and racial attitudes in a society. Intergroup marriage represents an important means through which both assimilation and racial amalgamation are achieved. In the United States, intermarriage between people of different nationalities is a frequent occurrence; religious intermarriage is somewhat less common; while racial intermarriage is relatively infrequent. (*E. Roth/The Picture Cube*)

is hardly surprising, therefore, that many sociologists view intergroup marriage as a particularly sensitive barometer of ethnic and racial friction. The higher the rate of intergroup marriage, the less intense the prejudice and discrimination, the lower the rate of intergroup marriage, the more intense the prejudice and discrimination.

Prejudice

Prejudice is so prevalent in contemporary life that we often assume it is "part of human nature." Yet this view ignores the fact that individuals and societies vary enormously in their levels of prejudice. Even in Nazi Germany of the 1930s, some "Aryans" helped Jews flee the Holocaust. And whereas Asians have found acceptance in Hawaii and have prospered there, on the West Coast and in British Columbia they have a long history of persecution (Glick, 1980). Similarly, whites held a positive image of blacks in the ancient world, a situation sharply in contrast with recent history (Snowden, 1983).

Prejudice refers to attitudes of aversion and hostility toward the members of a group simply because they belong to it and so are presumed to have the objectionable qualities that are ascribed to it (Allport, 1954). Prejudice is a state of mind—a feeling, opinion, or disposition. Sociologist Herbert Blumer (1961) notes that four feelings typically characterize dominant group members: (1) a sense that they are superior to members of the minority group; (2) a feeling that minority members are by their nature different and alien; (3) a sense that domi-

nant-group members have a proprietary claim on privilege, power, and prestige; and (4) a fear and suspicion that members of the minority have designs on dominant-group benefits. In this respect, prejudice frequently reflects a sense of "group position."

Some sociologists say that a new form of antiblack prejudice has arisen over the past decade among affluent, suburban whites (McConahay and Hough, 1976; Kluegel and Smith, 1982; Kinder, 1986). They label it **symbolic racism.** Symbolic racism is not the racism of the Old South, with its doctrines of racial inferiority and legally instituted segregation. Instead, it is a new form of racism in which three elements converge. First, many whites feel that blacks have become too demanding, too pushy, and too angry, and that they are getting more than they deserve. Second, many whites believe that blacks do not play by "the rules of the game," typified by the traditional American values of hard work, self-reliance, individualism, and the delay of gratification. Third, many whites stereotype blacks in the imagery of black welfare, crime, and quota systems. Such attitudes lead whites to vote against black candidates, to oppose busing and affirmative action programs, and to consider racism to be "somebody else's" problem (Kinder and Sears, 1981; Sears and Kinder, 1985). In sum, whites reject racial injustice in principle without lowering resistance to social policies that would correct the injustice. When whites feel their jobs or neighborhoods are threatened by blacks, symbolic racism can become real—and nasty. Said one white ethnic in a Jewish and Italian neighborhood in Brooklyn: "A bigot hates without basis, but we have reasons to hate the [racial epithet]. . . . It's not blind unreason. I hate them with my eyes open" (Rieder, 1985:245).

Discrimination

Whereas prejudice is an attitude or a state of mind, **discrimination** involves the arbitrary denial of privilege, prestige, and power to members of a minority group whose qualifications are equal to those of members of the dominant group. Prejudice does not necessarily coincide with discrimination; a one-to-one relationship does not inevitably hold between attitudes and actions. Sociologist Robert K. Merton (1968) identifies four relationships between prejudice and discrimination and adds folk labels to the types of individuals he describes:

1. *The all-weather liberal*—the unprejudiced person who does not discriminate.

2. *The reluctant liberal*—the unprejudiced person who discriminates in response to social pressures.

3. *The timid bigot*—the prejudiced person who does not discriminate in response to social pressures.

4. *The all-weather bigot*—the prejudiced person who unhesitatingly acts on the beliefs he or she holds.

Merton points out that equal opportunity legislation has the greatest impact on the reluctant liberal and the timid bigot. The civil rights movement of the 1960s established new norms of nondiscrimination that such individuals are likely to follow when their behavior is under surveillance or they experience costs from discriminating.

In the years since World War II, whites have shifted from more blatant forms of discrimination to more subtle forms (Crosby, Bromley, and Saxe, 1980). Attitudes have also changed over the past forty years. While only 32 percent of whites in 1942 felt that white and black students should go to the same school, the number jumped to 64 percent in 1964, and 90 percent in 1982. In 1964, 35 percent of whites felt they should have the right to keep blacks out of their neighborhoods. In a recent poll, only 12 percent agreed. In 1944, 45 percent of whites favored equal job opportunities for blacks; by 1972, the figure had risen to 97 percent (Friedman, 1987). Much of the long-term change derives from people born after 1940, who are typically less prejudiced than those born earlier in the century (Taylor, Sheatsley, and Greeley, 1978; Opinion Roundup, 1982).

Discrimination has far-reaching consequences: look at how the older patterns of school segregation and the newer patterns of school desegregation have permeated and influenced other spheres of life. Traditionally, whites attending predominantly white schools have held a near-monopoly on critical information about higher educational and job opportunities. Desegregation has allowed minority youth to gain access to cross-racial networks and interpersonal channels leading to higher education and better-paying jobs (Blau and Schwartz, 1984). Additionally, segregation disadvantaged blacks because degrees, grades, and reference letters from predominantly white institutions have typically been accorded greater weight than equivalent records from predominantly black institutions. Finally, segregated schools reinforced patterns of adult racial separation whereas desegregated schooling allows white and black youngsters to polish the interpersonal skills necessary for successful interracial interaction (Pettigrew, 1985). Desegregation, then, allows the members of dominant and minority groups to move across traditional boundaries, to cement interpersonal ties, and to strengthen the bonds making for social solidarity.

Institutional Discrimination

It is not just individuals who practice discrimination. In their daily operation, the institutions of society also systematically discriminate against the members of some groups, what sociologists call **institutional discrimination**. Businesses, schools, hospitals, governments, and other key institutions need not be staffed by prejudiced people in order for discrimination to occur (Carmichael and Hamilton, 1967). Consider employment. Employers often specify the qualifications candidates must have in order to be considered for certain jobs. Usually the qualifications have to do with prior job-related experience and some measure of formal education. The standards appear nondiscriminatory because they apply to all individuals regardless of race, creed, or color. But when members of some racial and ethnic groups lack equal opportunities to gain on the job experience and to receive college and professional degrees, they enter the job market at disadvantage.

Blacks in particular have been subjected to institutional discrimination (Dreeben and Gamoran, 1986); for centuries they have been the victims of inequality and low status. As we will see later in the chapter, the handicaps associated with poverty, lack of skills, inadequate education, and low job seniority have been left largely untouched by civil rights legislation. Indeed, low status tends to be self-perpetuating. Twenty years ago, President Lyndon B. Johnson made this point in his June 1965 commencement address at Howard University. He asserted:

> You do not take a person who for years has been hobbled by chains and liberate him, bring him up to the starting line of a race and . . . say, you're free to compete with all the others, and still justly believe that you have been completely fair.

In brief, equality of opportunity, even if realized in American life, does not necessarily produce equality of outcome. On the contrary, to the extent that winners imply losers, equality of opportunity almost ensures inequality. Blacks and many other minorities have therefore concerned themselves not merely with removing the barriers to full opportunity, but with achieving the fact of *equality of outcome*—parity in family income, in housing, and in the other necessities for keeping families

strong and healthy. It has been this sentiment that has motivated proponents of affirmative action programs (see the box).

One mechanism by which institutional discrimination is maintained is **gatekeeping**, the decision-making process whereby people are admitted to offices and positions of privilege, prestige, and power within a society. Generally gatekeepers are professionals with experience and credentials in the fields they monitor—for example, people in personnel, school admission, and counseling offices. Although in theory they assess candidates on the basis of merit, skills, and talents (and not in terms of race, ethnicity, class, family, or religion), their decisions have been biased (Erickson, 1975). Merit, skills, and talent are relative matters. The issue of which group's *values* will be used for judging who is "capable," "bright," "conscientious," and "resourceful" comes to the forefront. Which community will supply the standards of excellence: the white? the black? the Puerto Rican? or the Chinese-American? And which group's members will determine who meets the qualifications? Historically, gatekeepers have been white and male, and they

---

ISSUES THAT SHAPE OUR LIVES

Affirmative Action versus Self-Help

Equality of opportunity holds that positions should be open to all people, regardless of race, gender, national origin, or religion. But a good many minorities have been excluded from "better" positions in American life by discrimination and institutional arrangements. Civil rights programs, such as those enacted in the 1960s, seek to end discrimination and achieve equality of opportunity. However, antidiscriminatory programs do not guarantee that minorities will be found in employment and other areas of social life in numbers equal to their proportion in the population. *Affirmative action programs* are designed to speed the process. They typically set "target" figures for blacks, Hispanics, women, and other groups that have

been victimized by discrimination. In practice, this emphasis has meant establishing priorities in the recruitment and hiring of minorities and the setting of timetables for reaching given employment goals. Blacks, Hispanics, and women are then hired as a matter of right, in proportion to their numbers. In some cases, the requirements of professional qualification or individual achievement may be relaxed.

Affirmative action is intended to right historic wrongs. Whereas discrimination denies a justly earned position to people based upon group membership, affirmative action requires that people be placed *because* of their membership in a particular group. The argument is made that since the members of a group were discriminated against in the past *because* they were members of the group, they should be hired to bring

them in to the system *because* they are members of the group. Proponents contend that affirmative action is needed to undo the consequences of institutional racism and sexism.

Critics claim that the programs entail "reverse discrimination" and victimize whites, particularly white males. They say that the programs lower standards and do an injustice to the more talented, whose only crime is that they do not belong to the right minority group (Etzioni-Halevy, 1981). And critics question whether affirmative action actually assists minorities with employment problems. They argue that jobs gained through quota systems very often have large attrition rates and result in those chosen becoming bitter and bruised by the experience. All members of minority groups frequently have to contend with the suspicion among co-

have selected candidates who have resembled themselves in family patterns, dress, hair style, personal behavior, and the ownership and use of property.

Dominant Group Policies

Dominant groups have pursued a variety of policies toward minorities. At times, these policies may parallel those of the minority; at other times, they run counter to minority group aims. Sociologists George E. Simpson and J. Milton Yinger (1972) identify six major types of policies: assimilation, pluralism, legal protection of minorities, population transfer, continued subjugation, and extermination. These policies are not mutually exclusive; many of them may be practiced simultaneously. Let us examine each of these more closely:

Assimilation   One way that dominant groups seek to "solve" a minority group "problem" is to eliminate the minority by absorbing it through assimilation. **Assimilation** refers to those processes whereby groups with distinctive identities become culturally and socially fused.

As a result of assimilation, a group's boundaries become more penetrable and permeable. In some cases, minorities may also prefer this approach; this has been true of European-origin groups in the United States. However, dominant groups and minority groups often approach assimilation differently. Within the United States, two views toward assimilation have dominated. One—the "melting pot" tradition—has seen assimilation as a process whereby peoples and cultures would fuse to produce a new people and a new civilization. The other—the "Americanization" tradition—has viewed American culture as an essentially finished product on the Anglo-Saxon pattern, and has insisted that immigrants give up their cultural traits for those of the dominant American group.

Pluralism   Another policy involves **pluralism**—diverse groups coexist and mutually accommodate themselves to their differences. The groups cooperate in areas where cooperation is essential to their mutual well-being—say, in political and economic matters. Pluralism may reflect dominant group restraints as well as minority group pref-

---

workers that they would not have been appointed or promoted on their own.

Until the past several years, the Urban League and many other black advocacy groups saw government programs as the way to bring poor blacks into the American mainstream (Perkins, 1986). But faced with evidence that the programs have done little to eliminate poverty—and in some cases have contributed to dependency among the poor—these groups have looked to blacks themselves to take greater responsibility for solving their problems. Toward this end, the Urban League has launched a number of programs meant to address such problems as teenage pregnancy, inner-city crime, and educational underachievement among blacks. Among its more publicized campaigns are those admonishing young black

males "Don't Make a Baby If You Can't Be a Father," and urging church members to fight crime through its "No Crime Sundays."

A growing number of black intellectuals—including sociologists like William Julius Wilson (1978, 1985) and political economist Glenn C. Loury (1985)—have expressed skepticism toward traditional programs promoted by the "civil rights establishment." They focus instead on the motivations of black Americans and emphasize the need to alter the social structure within black communities. The economist Thomas Sowell (1975, 1980) was one of the first black scholars to contend that racism has little to do with black inequalities in income and academic performance; he argues that social class and family stability rather than skin color are more important in determining success. While

applauding the civil rights movement for breaking down racial barriers and fostering the emergence of a black middle class, these black intellectuals believe it has not stopped the growth of a black underclass. Much of the Old Guard has criticized the new approach as misguided and dangerous. It contends that the new thinkers are catering to current prejudices. Even so, many traditional civil rights leaders are placing greater emphasis on self-help as a way of dealing with the problems of ghetto life. The debate is not unprecedented. At the turn of the century, Booker T. Washington contended that poor blacks should develop agricultural and industrial skills and not try to battle white prejudices. He was challenged by W. E. B. DuBois, who demanded the right to vote and higher education for blacks (Lamar, 1985; Williams, 1986).

Institutional Racism: Massacre of Native Americans
In the frigid Plains winter of 1890, an army unit armed with Hotchkiss machine guns killed nearly 300 Sioux men, women, and children at Wounded Knee, South Dakota. The photo depicts over 100 Sioux being buried in a mass grave. Although a treaty ratified by Congress in 1868 created the Great Sioux Reservation, covering nearly half of South Dakota (which was set aside for the "sole, absolute and undisturbed use and occupation" of the Sioux), the government promptly reneged on the treaty and required the Sioux to cede back much of the land. *(Courtesy Amon Carter Museum, Fort Worth, Texas)*

erences. Switzerland provides a good example: Historically, the Swiss nation arose from the desire of culturally distinctive communities to preserve their local independence, identities, and customs while simultaneously providing for a shared defense. There is no Swiss language. Instead, the Swiss speak German, French, or Italian, with all federal documents translated into the three "official" languages. The various cantons or provinces, in addition to language differences, also have somewhat different cultural patterns. And while the majority of Swiss are Protestant, there is a sizable Catholic population. Although religious and ethnic prejudices are by no means absent, the Swiss have learned to live harmoniously with their differences.

Legal protection of minorities   Closely related to pluralism is the legal protection of minorities through constitutional and diplomatic means. In some nations, significant segments of the population reject coexistence with minorities on equal terms. Under these circumstances, the government may make legal provision for the protection of the interests and rights of all individuals. The Thirteenth, Fourteenth, and Fifteenth amendments to the United States Constitution have attempted to protect the rights of minorities, especially those of blacks. Recent civil rights legislation has had a similar objective.

Population transfer   At times, dominant groups have resorted to population transfer to reduce the presence of the minority. This approach matches the secessionist aim of some minorities—both groups hope to reduce

intergroup difficulties through physical separation. At times, the migration can be forced. For instance, the separation of Pakistan from India after World War II was accompanied by the migration of more than 12 million Muslims and Hindus, a movement in part induced by terrorism and in part arranged under government auspices. During the nineteenth century, the United States relocated countless Native American tribes, with profound hardship and loss of life. People may also flee invaders. Recently Afghans have fled to Pakistan and Cambodians to Thailand in the face of the Russian and Vietnamese invasions of their respective homelands.

Continued subjugation   The policies just discussed attempt to incorporate minorities into a society or to drive them out. Often, however, the dominant group prefers to retain its minorities, although it seeks to keep them subservient and exploitable. This approach often finds expression in "internal colonialism." For example, South African whites have sought apartheid arrangements that allow for the political and economic subjugation of blacks and other non-Europeans (see Figure 10.3). Likewise, as we will see later in the chapter, it has been difficult to enforce laws restricting the migration of Mexicans into the United States because powerful business groups in the Southwest and elsewhere want an exploitable minority—cheap labor.

Extermination   Intergroup conflict may become so intense that the physical destruction of one group by the other becomes the overriding goal. History abounds with examples of **genocide**, the deliberate and systematic ex-

Where they live

A look at the primary population centers for the major ethnic groups within South Africa:

Venda
Transvaal
Pretoria
Johannesburg
Swaziland*
Bophuthatswana
Orange Free State
Lesotho
Natal
Durban
Cape Province
Transkei
Ciskei
Cape Town
Port Elizabeth

Blacks   Indians   Black homelands

Coloreds   Whites

Population shares

Coloreds 8.7%   Asians 2.7%

Whites 14.8%

Blacks 73.8%

Source: South African Institute of Race Relations Survey, 1984

BLACK

Population/Languages: 24.1 million; Zulu, Xhosa, Tswana and Sotho, also English and Afrikaans.
Work: Unskilled and semi-skilled, mostly farm and domestic laborers; few professionals.
Income: 1983 monthly average (excluding farm laborers and domestics) 310 rand ($150).
Political representation: None in national government.
History: Settled as early as the fifth century A.D., British white domination began in 1800s, was institutionalized beginning in 1910. In 1948, Afrikaner whites took power and instituted apartheid. Turning point in protest of apartheid came in 1960 when police killed 69 pass-law protesters at Sharpeville. African National Congress, formed in 1912 to work for better black conditions, subsequently banned and it abandoned peaceful protest strategy. Nelson Mandela and other ANC leaders captured in 1964 and jailed for life. Education and political protests continued with major violent confrontation in 1976-1977, after Soweto student demonstrations, and 1984 to present.

WHITE/AFRIKANER

Population/Language: About 3 million (60 percent of whites); Afrikaans (derived from Dutch with French and German influence), also English.
Jobs: Civil service, also heavily concentrated in farming, mining, light manufacturing and business.
Income: 1983 monthly average for all whites (no separate breakdown for Afrikaners), 1,210 rand ($605).
Political representation: Full. Two-thirds vote for National Party, in power since 1948. Control ruling white chamber in Parliament (colored, Indian chambers added in 1984).
History: Dutch who settled in Cape Town in 1652 mixed with German and French Huguenot settlers forming Afrikaners. When British seized Cape in 1806, Afrikaners (Boers) trekked north to found Transvaal and Orange Free State. Britain annexed both after discovery of diamonds (1867) and gold (1886); quelled Afrikaner rebellion in Anglo-Boer War, 1899-1902. In that conflict, the British interred Boer women and children in camps: 26,000, plus 13,000 black servants died from starvation and disease, a bitter legacy affecting Afrikaner thought and policy to this day. Afrikaners won political power in 1948, introduced apartheid. Pulled out of British Commonwealth in 1961.

WHITE/ENGLISH

Population/Language: 2 million (40 percent of whites); English, some Afrikaans.
Jobs: Concentrated in business and industry.
Income: 1983 monthly average, 1,210 rand ($605).
Political representation: Full, but denied vote if retain British passports. Most support Progressive Federal Party.
History: British seizure of Dutch Cape colony in 1806 recognized in 1815 settlement of Napoleonic Wars. British influx began in 1820, with second wave after discovery of diamonds (1867) and gold (1886). After quelling Afrikaner rebellion in Anglo-Boer War, 1899-1902, Britain united Cape, Natal, Orange-Free State and Transvaal provinces, forming Union of South Africa in 1910.

COLORED

Population/Language: 2.8 million; Afrikaans and English.
Income: Monthly average 417 rand ($206).
Jobs: Semi-skilled labor, fishermen, a few professionals.
Political representation: 1984 constitution gave vote for essentially powerless colored chamber in Parliament.
History: A mixture of black, white and Indian peoples. "Colored" classification disliked. "Black" is preferred.

INDIAN

Population: 890,292; Indian languages and English.
Income: Averages 584 rand ($292).
Jobs: Professionals, businessmen, shop owners, semi-skilled and skilled labor.
Political representation: 1984 constitution gave vote for essentially powerless Indian chamber in Parliament.
History: Indians arrived in Natal Province in the mid-1800s as indentured laborers to work on the sugar plantations.

*Lesotho and Swaziland are not part of South Africa; they are independent countries.

FIGURE 10.3   **Apartheid: Groups as Classified by South African Law**
Source: John Omicinski and Karen DeWitt. 1986. Apartheid. USA Today (April 11):6A.

Doctrines of Racial Superiority
Racism has had wide currency in the modern age. It
is the doctrine that one racial or ethnic group is condemned by nature to inferiority and another group is
destined to superiority. Racism was a cornerstone of
official government policy in Nazi Germany. An estimated 6 million Jews perished in the Nazi endeavor
to exterminate all Jews. *(The Bettmann Archive)*

termination of a racial or ethnic group. North American
whites destroyed more than two-thirds of the Indian population. Even as late as 1890, U. S. Army forces armed
with Hotchkiss machine guns mowed down nearly 300
Sioux at Wounded Knee, South Dakota. The Boers of
South Africa looked upon the Hottentots as scarcely
more than animals and hunted them ruthlessly. And
between 1933 and 1945, the Nazis murdered 6 million
Jews. In recent years, hundreds of thousands of Laotians
in Southeast Asia have lost their lives at the hands of Pol
Pot forces.

Perspectives on Intergroup Relations

Functionalist and conflict theorists offer different interpretations of racial and ethnic stratification. Yet as we
noted in earlier chapters, the perspectives complement
one another. Indeed, once more we see that society is
basically "Janus-headed," and that functionalists and
conflict theorists simply focus on different aspects of the
same reality. Each draws our attention to aspects of social life that the other tends to overlook.

The Functionalist Perspective

Functionalists compare society to a living organism in
which the various parts contribute to the survival of the
whole. They then examine the functions and dysfunctions associated with various social arrangements. Although at first sight racial and ethnic conflict would
seem to impair social solidarity and stability, functionalists contend that conflict may in fact be functional for a
society. First, conflict promotes group formation, and
groups are the foundation blocks of a society. It facilitates
a consciousness of kind—an awareness of shared or similar values. The distinction between "we," or the ingroup, and "they," or the outgroup, is established in and
through conflict (see Chapter 5). Groups in turn bind
people together within a set of social relationships. And
they define the statuses people occupy in the social structure, particularly those positions that are ascribed (Coser,
1956).

Second, not only is a group defined and its boundaries established through conflict, but conflict promotes
group cohesion. It makes groups members more conscious of their bonds and may increase their social participation. Some social scientists say that anti-Semitism
and anti-black sentiment may provide dominant-group
members who lack a sense of cohesion within the society
with an anchor—with a sense of group membership
(Ackerman and Jahoda, 1950; Bettelheim and Janowitz,
1950; Adorno et al., 1950). It highlights their racial and
ethnic membership, providing them with a means of
identification in an estranged world.

Third, ethnic and racial conflict may function as a
safety valve for the society as a whole. Prejudice provides
for the "safe" release of hostile and aggressive impulses
that are culturally taboo within other social contexts. By
channeling hostilities from within family, occupational,
and other crucial settings onto permissible targets, the
stability of existing social structures may be promoted.
This is the well-known *scapegoating* mechanism.

Fourth, functionalists point out that multiple conflicts between groups undergird a democratic order.
Each group strives, at the expense of the others, to enhance its interests. This compels individuals and groups
to enter into coalitions, creating social networks that
crisscross society. Individuals and groups who are allies

on one level (for instance, on the location of a new high school) often find themselves in competition on another level (for example, the location of a bus stop). Cooperation on one level and competition on another restrain and defuse the intensity of social conflict. Additionally, competing groups act as a check against one another. One individual's participation in numerous groups, rather than his or her absorption by one group, results in a kind of balancing mechanism and prevents deep cleavages along one axis (for instance, it prevents cleavage along rigid class lines that lead to class struggle). In totalitarian societies, in contrast, power is concentrated in one institution—the monolithic state (see Chapter 16).

The dysfunctions of racial and ethnic conflict are often more readily apparent than the functions. Conflict may reach a frequency and intensity that threatens the social system, as is the case in modern-day Lebanon. Energy and resources that might otherwise be used more productively and cooperatively are drained and dissipated by friction.

Additionally, fears and expectations of conflict may lead to an inefficient and ineffective employment of human resources and individual talents.

The Conflict Perspective

Whereas functionalists emphasize social stability and the mechanisms that promote or interfere with it, conflict theorists see the world as in continual struggle and contend that prejudice and discrimination can best be understood in terms of tension or conflict among competing groups. Various sociologists give a somewhat different twist to this fundamental notion.

Emergence of racism   According to one view, three ingredients commonly come into play in the emergence and initial stabilization of racism (Noel, 1972; Vander Zanden, 1983): ethnocentrism, competition, and unequal power. As we noted in Chapter 3, *ethnocentrism* is the tendency to judge the behavior of other groups by the standards of one's own. People assume that it is in the nature of things that all groups should be organized according to the same assumptions that characterize their own group. When people are strongly ethnocentric, they find it easy to perceive the outgroup as an object of loathing—as a symbol of evil, and even danger. Ethnocentrism provides a fertile soil in which stereotypes and prejudicial attitudes readily germinate (Pettigrew, 1979; McCann et al., 1985).

Competition intensifies ethnocentric sentiments and may lead to intergroup strife. Conflict theorists point out that people typically seek to improve their outcomes with regard to those things they define as good, worthwhile, and desirable—particularly privilege, prestige, and power. When they perceive their group outcomes as mutually exclusive and legitimate, so that each can realize its goals only at the expense of the other, intergroup tensions are likely to mount. For the most part, the attitudes people evolve toward outgroups reflect their perceptions of the relationships they have with its members. Consequently, where the relations between two groups are viewed as competitive, negative attitudes—prejudice—will be generated toward the outgroup. The boys' camp experiment undertaken by Muzafer Sherif and his associates (1961) and described in Chapter 5 documents this process.

Professional Boxing and Ethnic Status
The overrepresentation of racial and ethnic minorities in sports is frequently a response to disadvantaged circumstances and an effort to escape the bottom rungs of the social ladder. In the 1890s, Irish fighters predominated. In the photo at right, James Corbett dethroned John L. Sullivan in a 1892 world heavyweight championship match in New York's Madison Square Garden. In due course Jewish fighters became the nation's top professional boxers; they were succeeded by Italian and Eastern European boxers who in turn were displaced by black champions. Today Hispanics are coming to the foreground. *(The Bettmann Archive)*

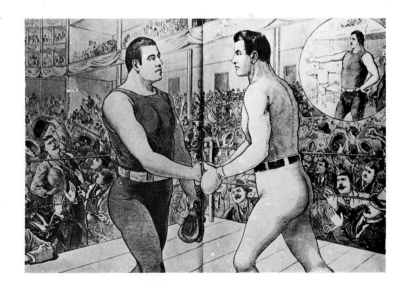

Whereas competition provides the motivation for systems of social inequality and ethnocentrism channels competition along racial and ethnic lines, *power* determines which group will subordinate the other (Noel, 1972). Without power, prejudices cannot be translated into discrimination and groups cannot turn their claims upon scarce resources into institutional discrimination. In brief, power is the mechanism by which domination and subjugation are achieved.

Marxist interpretations Marxists and neo-Marxists take the conflict thesis even further. They say that racial prejudice and exploitation arose in the Western world with the rise of capitalism (Cox, 1948; Szymanski, 1976, 1978; Geschwender, 1978). These theorists contend that racist notions serve the economic interests of the capitalist class in four ways. First, ideologies of racial superiority make colonialism and racist practices palatable and acceptable to the white masses. Second, racism is profitable, since capitalists can pay minority workers less and thus generate greater profits for themselves. Third, racist ideologies divide the working class by pitting white workers and minority workers against one another—a tactic of "divide and conquer." Fourth, capitalists require minority workers as an industrial reserve army who can be fired during times of economic stagnation and rehired when they are needed during times of prosperity (see Chapter 9).

The concept of a split labor market Whereas Marxists blame capitalists for generating racism, sociologist Edna Bonacich (1972, 1975; Cheng and Bonacich, 1984) says that economic competition within a **split labor market** is the source of tensions among ethnic groups. A split labor market is an economic arena in which large differences exist in the price of labor at the same occupational level. Bonacich notes that when a group sells its labor at rates substantially lower than the prevailing ones, higher-paid labor faces severe competition to maintain its advantage. When the cheaper labor is of a different racial or ethnic group, the resulting class antagonism takes the form of racism. That is, the antagonism focuses on racial or ethnic issues, although the source of the conflict is class.

Bonacich contends that the more expensive labor resists displacement through either exclusion or a caste system. The anti-Chinese movement, which flourished in California in the 1870s, illustrates an exclusion strategy. White workers sought to drive the Chinese from their communities through harassment and violence and to shut off the entry of new immigrants (Boswell, 1986). The caste system is the strategy that was employed in the post–Civil War period. White labor erected social and legal barriers—Jim Crow segregation arrangements—to avoid competition with black workers.

Racial and Ethnic Groups in the United States

We have considered the nature of minority groups, prejudice, discrimination, and institutional discrimination and discussed the functionalist and conflict perspectives. Let us now illustrate these concepts and patterns by examining the circumstances of a number of groups within

Nativistic Movements: The Ghost Dance Under conditions of dominance whereby one society holds another in subjugation, nativistic movements often arise. The Ghost Dance that spread among the Plains tribes in the 1890s was such a movement. It centered in the belief that a folk hero would one day appear and lead Native Americans to a terrestrial paradise. In anticipation of the millennium, believers were instructed to abandon white ways and return to their traditional tribal customs. Messengers went from tribe to tribe, bringing with them the new religion and teaching a dance in which some participants wore a "ghost shirt." *(Topham/The Image Works)*

Exclusion as a Response to a Split Labor Market
The engraving shows the massacre of Chinese immigrant workers at Rock Springs, Wyoming, in 1885. The anti-Chinese movement was a response by white workers to the economic threat they believed Chinese workers posed to their jobs. *(The Bettmann Archive)*

the United States: blacks, Hispanics, Native Americans (Indians), Asian-Americans, and white ethnics.

Blacks

Current black-white relations are more subtle, indirect, and ostensibly "nonracial" than they were a number of decades ago. Yet the American racist past—with its roots in slavery—remains an important ingredient of the contemporary scene. It seems that the first black came to the New World with Columbus. However, black settlement in the New World did not begin until 1619, when English colonists at Jamestown, Virginia, purchased twenty blacks from a Dutch man-of-war. At first, blacks were accorded the status of indentured servants. But in the 1660s legal recognition was given to the enslavement of blacks for life, and the first law was passed banning interracial sexual relations. During the colonial period, slaves were used primarily in commercial agriculture based on tobacco, rice, indigo, and naval stores. It was not until Eli Whitney invented the cotton gin in 1793 that cotton became the major crop of the South, increasing the demand for slaves by southern plantation owners.

Slavery in the new American nation The subjugation of blacks had become well established in the British colonies, and the tradition was carried on by the new American nation. By the time of the first federal census, taken in 1790, there were 757,208 blacks in the United States, 20 percent of the total population. At the Constitutional Convention of 1787, southerners succeeded in winning additional representation on the basis of slavery, securing

federal support for the capture and return of fugitive slaves, and preventing the closing of the African slave trade before 1808. In its early years, then, the United States operated as a Greek-style democracy, one in which democratic rights were extended only to the male, white population. The doctrine of black inferiority or "differences" was used to place blacks beyond the pale of the American democratic creed.

The Civil War and the postwar period Although American mythology says that the Civil War was fought to free the slaves, historians agree that the political struggle that unfolded between the North and the South was primarily a contest between a southern plantation elite and northern industrial, mercantile, and agrarian interests. It was political pressure and the necessities of war that led Lincoln to announce the Emancipation Proclamation in September 1862. But the proclamation did not in fact end slavery: it did not apply to areas under Union control—border slave states and Confederate areas occupied by northern armies. Critics pointed out the proclamation freed slaves only in those areas where they could not be reached. Even so, the proclamation served notice on the South that the war had become a social revolution; if the Confederacy were defeated, the slave-based society of the South would also fall.

When the war was over in 1865, the future of the former slaves was uncertain. The nation, still divided in spirit, plunged into a decade of political and social turmoil. In shaping their Reconstruction policies, the Radical Republicans were in part motivated by the abolitionist argument that a legalized caste system was not compatible with American institutions. But they were also concerned that the southern states not reenter the Union with the old planter elite still in control. It was the North's lack of commitment to black rights that ultimately doomed Reconstruction; in 1877, when the last occupation forces were withdrawn from the South, the region was on its own again. However, Jim Crow—legalized segregation—did not follow at once (Woodward, 1966). It was during the 1890s and early 1900s that lynching attained staggering proportions and that Jim Crow laws mandating segregation were passed throughout the South. Before this time, blacks still voted in substantial numbers and received equal treatment on common carriers, trains, and streetcars. But blacks and whites attended separate schools, and whites did not accept blacks as social equals.

Black migration from the South   In 1910 some 90 percent of the nation's black population was located in the South, and 77 percent were in rural communities. About this time, both "push" and "pull" factors began to encourage migration (see Chapter 20). Within the South, the "infiltration" of whites into types of work traditionally monopolized by blacks, the shift westward of cotton agriculture, the destruction of cotton crops by the boll weevil, and the droughts of 1916 and 1917 provided the impetus to black population movement. World War I accelerated the trend. The military draft took large numbers of young black men from their communities. Simultaneously, the military induction of white workers, the shutting down of European immigration, and conditions of wartime prosperity prompted northern industry to recruit southern blacks as workers.

The post–World War II period   With World War II came a new era of change in the South. Major assaults were directed against segregation from a good many quarters. The stage was set for even more drastic change when the Supreme Court ruled on May 17, 1954, in *Brown* v. *Board of Education*, that mandatory school segregation was unconstitutional. In the years that followed, the Supreme Court moved toward outlawing legalized segregation in all areas of American life. Simultaneously, the civil rights movement of the 1960s galvanized popular support for the enactment of the Civil Rights Acts of 1964, 1965, and 1968. The upsurge in black militancy during the 1960s and early 1970s was associated with a broad crisis of legitimacy within American life. Draft resisters, antiwar activists, student protesters, and liberated women challenged the traditional authority exercised by the military, college officials, and white males. Black unrest also found expression in episodes of property-oriented rioting that flared in most major Americans cities between 1964 and 1970.

As the United States entered the 1970s, resistance to welfare and affirmative action programs mounted among segments of the white community. By the 1980s, under the Reagan administration, the nation began moving down a road that involved the dismantling of the war on poverty and various federal measures for minorities and the poor.

The dynamics of class and race   One of the most important controversies centering on American race relations involves the relative importance of class and race. Are opportunities for black economic advancement affected by class position or by race? Sociologist William

Black Migration from the South
This painting by Jacob Lawrence, a black artist, depicts the migration northward of southern blacks. Census data reveal that the mounting inability of southern agriculture to absorb black tenants and workers induced a net migration of more than 700,000 blacks between 1920 and 1930. During the depression of the 1930s, net black migration fell to less than 350,000. During the decade of World War II, the demand for unskilled workers encouraged 1.2 million blacks to leave the South. Heavy migration continued in the 1950s and 1960s, but migration patterns began to reverse in the 1970s. *(The Phillips Collection, Washington, D.C.)*

Julius Wilson (1978; Wilson and Aponte, 1985) contends that class has superseded race as the most important factor explaining the life chances of black Americans. Once civil rights legislation and affirmative action programs removed the cap segregation had imposed on black social mobility, greater educational, income, and occupational differentiation occurred within the black community. Two countervailing trends resulted. Blacks with education and job skills experienced unprecedented opportunities for upward social mobility. Simultaneously, blacks lacking education and job skills experienced soaring unemployment rates, growing restriction to low-wage occupations, and increasing reliance on welfare. Structural factors—primarily the movement of industries out of central cities and the elimination of many jobs in agriculture and manufacturing once filled by blacks—have meant that only a small percentage of the total black population has been able to take advantage of the new opportunities. The black lower class, then, continues to be disadvantaged, but current discrimination is not the chief cause. Rather, past discrimination created a large black lower class that contemporary economic and structural factors perpetuate (see Chapters 15 and 22).

Other sociologists have challenged Wilson's thesis of "the declining significance of race" (Collins, 1983; Pomer, 1986). Charles V. Willie (1979) says that discrimination and racism still confront all blacks regardless of their social class, and that the problems associated with being a black in the United States are worsening. He interprets income, education, and housing data as showing that blacks and whites with similar qualifications are not treated alike in the marketplace—evidence of a "racial tax" levied on blacks for not being white. Sociologists Melvin E. Thomas and Michael Hughes (1986) find that considerable differences also exist in psychological well-being between blacks and whites regardless of social class, suggesting that the cost of being black is psychological as well.

Still other sociologists look at the same evidence and conclude that both class and race remain important factors shaping the black experience (Farley, 1984; Allen and Farley, 1986). In some domains, blacks have improved their status. The educational attainment, occupational status, and individual earnings of blacks have increased. As Table 10.1 shows, the gap, while still substantial, has progressively closed between black and white male wages. Even so, black family income has not improved relative to that of white families. Simultaneously, employment, poverty, and higher educational

Table 10.1 Closing the Gap: Black Male Wages as a Percent of White Male Wages

Years of Experience	1940	1950	1960	1970	1980
1–5	46.7%	61.8%	60.2%	75.1%	84.2%
6–10	47.5	61.0	59.1	70.1	76.6
11–15	44.4	58.3	59.4	66.2	73.5
16–20	44.4	56.6	58.4	62.8	71.2
21–25	42.3	54.1	57.6	62.7	67.8
26–30	41.7	53.2	56.2	60.6	66.9
31–35	40.2	50.3	53.8	60.0	66.5
36–40	39.8	46.9	55.9	60.3	68.5
All men	43.3	55.2	57.5	64.4	72.6

Source: Data from the Rand Corporation, February 1986. *The New York Times*, March 2, 1986, p. 8E.

data present a picture of worsening black plight. Overall, the gap between whites and blacks remains substantial. Class, then, is not replacing race as a significant factor in the black experience. Rather, class is interacting with race to produce the social cleavages that remain a continuing feature of American life (Colasanto and Williams, 1987).

Hispanics

Hispanics, America's Spanish-speaking ethnic groups, have been growing rapidly. As of 1985, there were 16.9 million Hispanics in the United States, up from the 9 million recorded in the 1970 census and the 14.8 million in the 1980 head count. California and Texas account for more than half the nation's Hispanics, who are primarily Mexican-Americans. Puerto Ricans predominate in New York, where about half of mainland Puerto Ricans reside; Cubans are the largest Hispanic group in Florida, where about 60 percent of Cuban-origin Hispanics live. Some 88 percent of all Hispanics live in metropolitan areas, compared with 75 percent of the general population.

Mexican-Americans have a long history in the United States; it stretches back to the period before New England was colonized. Many trace their ancestry to the merging of the native Indian population with Spanish settlers. In 1821 Mexico secured its independence from Spain, and shortly thereafter a substantial portion of the new Mexico nation became part of the United States (the result of the annexation of Texas, the conquest of north-

ISSUES THAT SHAPE OUR LIVES

A Disappearing Border?

It is often said that the United States is a nation of immigrants. Even so, beginning with the anti-Catholic Know-Nothing party in the 1850s, the United States has witnessed a succession of anti-immigrant movements. And in recent years, mounting sentiment has emerged to curb the tide of illegal aliens. Some media commentators assert that the United States "has lost control of its borders." Complicating matters, growing numbers of Americans are worried that both drugs and terrorists are streaming across the borders with the illegal immigrants. In Arizona, armed civilians—self-proclaimed vigilantes—patrol border areas. A 1986 New York Times/CBS poll found that half of the Americans surveyed favored lower immigration levels, against 33 percent in 1965. Paradoxically, 45 percent said that new immigrants work harder than native-born Americans, while 47 percent believed that most end up on welfare. And a third of the public thought that immigrants take jobs away from Americans, whereas slightly more than half said that immigrants generally take jobs Americans do not want (Pear, 1986).

The impact of illegal aliens on the economy is difficult to determine (Borjas and Tienda, 1987). Alien workers seldom displace American workers in agriculture, where the work is arduous and the wages low. Only about 15 percent of the illegal alien population picks crops, but in some cases they make up to 85 percent of migrant farm crews. Growers, espe-

Mexican Nationals Attempting to Cross Illegally into the United States
To curb the influx of illegal aliens, Congress enacted in 1986 the most sweeping immigration law revision in two decades. It permits millions of illegal immigrants to stay legally and imposes criminal sanctions on employers who hire undocumented foreign workers. (*Alon Reininger/Contact/Woodfin Camp & Associates*)

cially in the West, depend on migrant labor for harvesting. In many respects, noncitizen Hispanic workers are the backbone of the Southwest economy. In California's Silicon Valley, they make printed-circuit boards for IBM personal computers and assemble microchips for use in guided missiles. In Los Angeles, center of the $3-billion-a-year California apparel industry, two-thirds of the garment labor is estimated to consist of illegal aliens. In Houston, one-third of all construction workers (70 percent of the highway construction workforce) are "illegals" (Petzinger et al., 1985).

How much illegal immigrants compete with Americans for jobs is a matter of debate. Economist Donald Huddle calculates that in 1985, for every 100 illegal aliens, 70 United States citizens could not get jobs; in 1982, the figure was 65. However, not everyone buys this assessment. Says one California landscaper: "I couldn't be in business if there were no illegal immigrants. No one else will do this kind of back-bending labor" (Plattner, 1986:21). The safest conclusion is that the jury is still out on whether immigration reduces the national pool of job opportunities for low-wage workers (Slater, 1986). However, since illegal aliens tend to be unskilled workers, the immigrant labor force in the years ahead may find itself increasingly out of sync with the growing high-tech needs of employers (Briggs, 1985; Borjas and Tienda, 1987).

Some economists contend that immigration generates economic growth (Simon, 1986). One study sug-

ern Mexico, and the Gadsden Purchase). Like blacks and American Indians, people of Mexican ancestry did not originally become part of American society through voluntary immigration. With the exception of the American Indians, they are the only American minority to

enter the society through conquest of their homeland (Vander Zanden, 1983).

In recent decades the Spanish-speaking population of the United States has grown substantially through immigration. Persons of Hispanic origin now account

gests that Mexican immigrants, both legal and illegal, contribute more to the economy than they take out in the form of public assistance, the major exception being education. Less than 5 percent of all Mexican immigrants receive any cash public assistance. However, they contribute less than the roughly $2,900 it costs per year to educate a public school student. Most of those who come to the United States are young men, and not likely to need social services. In many cases immigrants have helped keep American manufacturing jobs from moving abroad because they work for comparatively low wages (Muller and Espenshade, 1985). And a Presidential Council of Economic Advisers' report concluded that alien workers have contributed to the nation's overall economic expansion. The benefits, it said, are "widely diffused" in the form of lower prices, new job opportunities, and higher profits for investors (Pear, 1986).

Over a hundred years ago, when the Statute of Liberty was dedicated, 90 percent of immigrants came from Europe. More than half still came from Europe in 1965, when Congress lowered immigration barriers that had been based on race. Today only 5 percent of legal immigrants come from Europe. Asians account for nearly half, and Latin Americans make up roughly 40 percent of legally admitted newcomers (see Figure A). Although public debate has focused on illegal immigration, the majority of immigrants arrive legally. And while public rhetoric talks of a "tidal wave" of migrants, immigration remains a comparative trickle as a proportion of the total population. Even including illegal entries, annual immigration amounts to about 0.3 percent of the population, as against 1.5 percent at the historic peak and a 0.6 percent average over the past two centuries (Reinhold, 1986).

The difficulty Congress has had in writing new immigration legislation reflects the split in national sentiment between our desire to offer a haven to hard-working, freedom-seeking new citizens and our fear of new competition for jobs, unfamilar lifestyles, and new tongues in our neighborhoods. Nonetheless, in 1986 Congress managed to pass the Immigration Reform and Control Act, a measure that seems to have made no one completely happy. The legislation prohibits the hiring of illegal aliens and offers legal status, or amnesty, to millions of illegals who have resided continuously in this country since December 31, 1981. The assumption is that keeping illegal immigrants out of the workforce is one way to deter impoverished foreigners from coming to the United States. But the ensuing controversy suggests that a tangle of rational and visceral concerns will continue to make American immigration policy a matter of debate in the years ahead.

FIGURE A   **Emigration from Mexico and China, 1820–1980**
Source: Jeffrey Albert and Marcy Eckroith-Mullins. 1986. The waves of immigration to the USA. USA Today (June 30):5E.

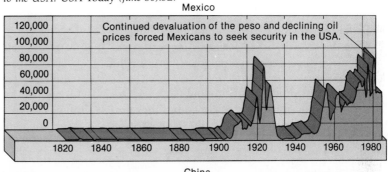

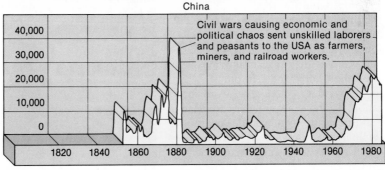

for about half the legal immigration to the United States, and vast numbers enter the United States illegally. An increasing number are Salvadorans and other Central Americans fleeing guerrilla war, political oppression, and economic deprivation. But the largest group continues to be Mexicans who see little chance of escaping poverty in their economically distressed nation. To enter the United States illegally, many must pay $350 to $700 each to smuggler-guides, called *coyotes*, who sometimes beat and rob them. If they elude the U.S Immigration and Naturalization Service (INS), the illegal aliens can usually find jobs paying less than the minimum wage as farm laborers, janitors, hospital orderlies, unskilled construction workers, chambermaids, or dishwashers. Estimates of the resident illegal population range from a low of about 3 million to a high of 15 million. The INS, which counts itself lucky to nab half the incoming illegal aliens, tabulated 1.8 million arrests during 1986, about double the figure for 1980. The overwhelming majority are from Central and Latin America, and at least 50 percent of those deported find their way back to the United States. (See the box for a discussion of the controversy surrounding this immigration.)

Hispanics are younger, less educated, and more likely to be living in poverty than Americans in general. In recent years only 50 percent of Hispanic 18- to 19-year-olds have graduated from high school, compared to 76 percent of whites and 59 percent of blacks. And only 12 percent of Mexican-American men in the labor force and 15 percent of Puerto Ricans, compared to 31 percent of all working men over 20, hold jobs in the highest-paid professional and administrative occupations (Population Reference Bureau, 1983). McAllen, Laredo, and Brownsville, Texas, communities along the Rio Grande Valley with large Mexican-American populations, rank as the poorest metropolitan areas in the United States.

Although Hispanics are commonly lumped together in the public mind as a single group, they embrace cultures as rich and varied as the United States itself. This fact is evident in the names used to describe them: Hispanic, Latino, Chicano, and Spanish-speaking. Some people of Spanish-speaking descent dislike the term Hispanic, preferring to identify themselves by their own ethnic group: Cuban, Nicaraguan, Guatemalan, Dominican, or Puerto Rican. Some Mexican-Americans like the name Chicano. Others groups of Spanish-speaking origin prefer Latino. While public opinion surveys reveal that 70 percent of Hispanics agree that the Spanish language creates a strong common bond among them, 30 percent perceive the existence of significant differences among the various Hispanic ethnic groups (Russell, 1983). In recent years there has been a blurring of differences among the Mexican, Puerto Rican, and Cuban communities, making Hispanic Americans more conscious of themselves as a homogeneous group (Rangel, 1984).

Native Americans (Indians)

The 1980 census counted 1.4 million Native Americans (Indians, Eskimos, and Aleuts) within the United States. They comprise the 173 tribes officially recognized by the U.S. government and the more than 300 tribes recognized by Native Americans themselves. The tribes or nations vary in size from those with fewer than 100 members (the Chumash of California and the Modocs of Oklahoma) to those with more than 160,000 members (the Navajos of the Southwest). An additional 50 or more tribes have vanished through massacre, disease,

Navajo-Hopi Land Conflict
Big Mountain Navajo are to be relocated because they live on the Hopi portion of the former Joint Use Area. Here Navajo women weep as they realize they must move off their homeland. "In our tongue," says one, "there is no word for relocation. To move away means to disappear and never be seen again." Powerful economic interests are seeking access to the water and other resources contained in the region. *(AP/Wide World Photos)*

destruction of their economic base, or absorption by other groups. Overall, Native American peoples vary substantially in their history, lifestyles, kin systems, language, political arrangements, religion, economy, current circumstances, and identities.

Estimates vary widely as to how many Native Americans were living north of the Rio Grande in 1492. Some anthropologists place the figure as low as 700,000, and others as high as 15 million. Contrary to popular mythology, most Native American societies were not composed of nomadic hunters, but of farming and fishing peoples with relatively sedentary communities. Initially the European powers treated the native groups as alien nations that could be enemies or allies against European adversaries. But as time passed, the tribal territories of the Native Americans were appropriated and their inhabitants either annihilated or driven inland.

After the Revolutionary War, the American government followed a policy of negotiating treaties of land cession with the Native Americans. When the Native Americans failed to agree, they were confronted with military force. The 1830 Removal Act provided for the relocation of all Eastern tribes to lands west of the Mississippi River. The process, called the Trail of Tears, is widely regarded as one of the most dishonorable chapters in American history. Of the at least 70,000 people removed, more than 20,000 died en route. Most were Creeks, Choctaws, Cherokees, Chickasaws, and Seminoles. West of the Mississippi, the tragedies of defeat and expropriation were repeated. The federal government merely extended to the western Indians the system of treaties and reservations it had used to dispossess the Indians of the East. When the Native Americans resisted, they were systematically slaughtered.

Until 1871, the United States treated the Native American tribes as sovereign yet dependent domestic nations with whom it entered into "treaties." In the 1870s it shifted its policies to one making Native Americans "wards" of the federal government. Forced assimilation, the core of the policy, had a devastating impact upon the Native American peoples and their cultures. It created massive poverty and terrible health problems. In 1929 the government reversed itself and encouraged Native Americans to retain their tribal identifications and cultures. But during the Eisenhower administration, the federal government reverted once more to an assimilationist course, prompting Native Americans to leave the reservations and settle in urban areas (Indians had been granted American citizenship in 1924). During the 1970s the goal of national policy was again reversed,

as the government sought to strengthen Native American control over their own affairs while maintaining federal support programs.

Lurking behind these policy shifts have been powerful interest groups with designs on Native American lands and resources. In recent decades, coal, gas, oil, uranium, and other minerals have been found in abundance on reservations, giving rise to intense pressure on the tribes to accelerate development of the resources (Cornell, 1984). This issue underlies the current Navajo-Hopi dispute over an arid chunk of Arizona (see Figure 10.4 on page 274). When the Hopi reservation was created in 1882, the federal government ignored the fact that Navajos lived inside the boundaries. Over the years, additional Navajos moved into these lands. In 1974, federal legislation divided the disputed lands between the Hopi and the Navajo and provided for the relocation of Navajos living on the Hopi side of the line. The struggle has involved traditional Hopis and Navajos and their white environmentalist allies on the one hand, and supporters of the tribal governments and coal leasing on the other. The resolution of the dispute will help determine whether the Los Angeles Department of Water and Power, Southern California Edison, and Arizona's Salt River Project will get more coal to generate electricity in adjacent power plants for the major cities of the Southwest (Gottlieb and Wiley, 1986).

Federal policies that vacillated between encouraging tribes to govern themselves on self-sufficient reservations and assimilating them into American society have caused severe problems. Native Americans have the lowest per capita income, lowest level of educational attainment, highest infant morality rate, and highest rate of illiteracy of any ethnic group in the nation. About 25 percent of Native Americans live on reservations, which cover 52.4 million acres in 27 states. The largest reservation, the Navajo in Arizona, New Mexico, and Utah, consists of 15 million acres. On the reservations, 41 percent live below the poverty line; 55 percent of the housing is substandard; 58 percent of children drop out of school before finishing eighth grade; and unemployment in some cases runs as high as 82 percent. Deaths caused by pneumonia, diabetes, tuberculosis, alcoholism, suicide, and homicide are two to eight times that of the entire population (Vander Zanden, 1983).

Native Americans have responded differently to their circumstances. Some have spun off into the larger community, becoming more or less assimilated. Others have chosen to stress their tribal identity and have undertaken the development of effective self-governing com-

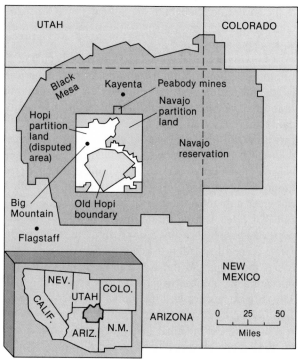

FIGURE 10.4 **Two Tribes, One Land: The Hopi-Navajo Dispute**

munities. Still others have found appeal in Pan-Indianism—a coming together of Native Americans regardless of tribal affiliation to achieve common ends and to develop an ethnic Indian community derived from a synthesis of diverse cultures.

Asian-Americans

The Census Bureau lumps together as Asians 3.5 million Americans, including 806,000 Chinese, 775,000 Filipinos, 701,000 Japanese, 362,000 Asian Indians, 355,000 Koreans, and 262,000 Vietnamese. Because 60 percent of Asian-Americans live in California, New York, or Hawaii, and 54 percent live in the top 25 metropolitan areas, many Americans know little about this country's Asian residents (Robey, 1985). But although they do not fit the image of the typical European immigrant arriving at Ellis Island, Asian-Americans have a long history in American life.

Chinese It was during the gold rush in California in the late 1840s that the first large-scale immigration of Chinese to the United States took place. The immigration of Chinese was encouraged as a source of cheap labor. Chinese were employed in building the transcontinental railroads—the Union Pacific, Northern Pacific, and Southern Pacific; in reclaiming swamplands; building levees and roads; in mining borax, quicksilver, and coal; and in making cigars, shoes, and garments in San Francisco factories. When the gold bubble burst, white miners and merchants were thrown into competition with Chinese workers. It was then that the cry "The Chinese must go" arose.

In the post–Civil War period, the Chinese were persecuted, victims of mob violence, pillage, and incendiarism. In 1882 Congress passed the Chinese Exclusion Act; it suspended all Chinese immigration, save for a small group of scholars, ministers, and merchants. California led the nation in the passage of anti-Chinese laws, many of which remained in effect until the 1950s (for instance, the California constitution provided that corporations could neither directly nor indirectly employ Chinese and empowered cities and towns to remove Chinese from within city limits). Although some Chinese responded by returning to China, most moved east. They took up residence in Chinatowns, ghettos made up of Chinese, in cities like New York.

By the end of World War II, few Chinatowns survived. However, in recent years the Chinatowns of New York City and San Francisco have been given a new lease on life as a result of sharp increases in new emigration from Hong Kong and Taiwan (made possible by legislation in 1965 that did away with the old quota system, under which only 105 Chinese were allowed entry each year). Above the gaudy storefronts of the nation's Chinatowns, Chinese families are jammed into tiny flats. In some cities, including San Francisco, more than a quarter of the residents of Chinatown live below the poverty level.

Japanese The Japanese in America have also been victims of intense prejudice and discrimination. On two occasions, the United States government undertook to exclude the Japanese from American life. In 1907 President Theodore Roosevelt reached an agreement with Japan to limit the immigration of its citizens to this country. Later, during the hysteria that followed the early months of World War II, military authorities placed some 120,000 Japanese (two-thirds of whom were American citizens) in ten concentration camps. The action was racial rather than political, since none of the nation's other so-called enemies-in-residence (Germans and Italians) were subjected to internment. Hawaii's Jap-

Japanese-Americans Registering at an Internment Camp in 1942
The Japanese attack on Pearl Harbor on December 7, 1941, intensified anti-Japanese sentiment on the West Coast. Rumors (later proved false) circulated of Japanese sabotage and "fifth-column" activities. Washington authorities, fearing that Japanese-Americans might be disloyal, herded them together in concentration camps, though some two-thirds of the victims were American-born citizens. This brutal precaution turned out to be unnecessary, for the loyalty and combat record of the Japanese-Americans proved exemplary. *(National Archives)*

anese population—one-third of the total and 3,000 miles closer to Japan—was, for the most part, allowed to go about its business.

The relocation caused Japanese-Americans great hardship. Merchants had to sell or liquidate their properties within a few weeks. Buyers, as a rule, were unwilling to pay reasonable prices. Farmers were in an even worse position, since evacuation came after planting and fertilizing but before harvesting (prior to World War II, Japanese-Americans raised about 42 percent of the produce crops in California, including berries, onions, asparagus, celery, lettuce, peppers, tomatoes, cucumbers, spinach, and cauliflower). Unable to harvest their crops, they had to make the best bargain possible. In December 1944, the military ban on the Japanese-Americans was lifted. Following the war, they found it difficult to reestablish earlier patterns of independent employment, and instead had to seek work from non-Japanese employers. The rapid upward social mobility of Japanese-Americans in the postwar years has led sociologists like William Petersen (1971) to observe that there have been few success stories in American history to parallel theirs.

Indochinese The collapse of the South Vietnamese government in 1975 and political upheavals in Cambodia and Laos have led to the admission of more than 500,000 Indochinese refugees to the United States over the past 15 years. Vietnamese have accounted for about 80 percent of these. Although many Vietnamese had middle-class positions in their homeland, in the United

States they have found that jobs open to them typically require little skill, pay low wages, and offer few opportunities for advancement. Even so, the Vietnamese have shown a remarkable ability to enter mainstream American economic life. Indochinese refugees are graduating from leading American universities and founding high-tech firms. They play a major role in the shrimp fishing industry in Texas's Galveston Bay and in small businesses in the nation's inner cities (Hume, 1985). They have also encountered a good deal of hostility. A 1975 Gallup Poll revealed that 54 percent of Americans felt that the Vietnamese should not be permitted to stay. And in some areas, like Manitowoc, Wisconsin, and the Houston-Galveston area of Texas, the Vietnamese have been subject to violence and harassment (Vander Zanden, 1983).

A "model minority"? In recent years, the nation's media have heralded Asian-Americans as "the model minority" (Kasindorf, 1982; McBee, 1984; McLeod, 1986). They now enjoy the highest median family income of the nation's ethnic groups ($22,075 in 1982). Through thrift, strong family ties, and sacrifice, many Asian-Americans have managed to achieve upward mobility. Recent immigrants have included a high proportion of doctors and engineers, and fully one-third of Asian adults have completed college (compared with 17.5 percent of whites). The National Center for Education Statistics finds that Asian-American students are more likely than other students to enroll in college preparatory programs (47 percent take the academic program compared with 37 percent of whites, 29 percent of blacks, and 23 percent of Hispanics). They also take more math and science courses and spend more time on homework than do other students (Zigli, 1984). But Asian-American leaders also point out that the "model minority" myth obscures such problems as crime, gang violence, high suicide rates, mental disorders, and disintegrating families among poor refugees and immigrants who have difficulty coping with a strange new society. Some Asian-Americans see prejudice as a major roadblock to advancement. Because Asian-Americans enjoy good reputations for technical competence, many companies are reluctant to see them as other than "high-tech coolies" (McLeod, 1986).

Sociologists who emphasize the emergent, flexible, and situational nature of ethnic memberships point to the beginning of Asian-American ethnic identities on some college campuses. In some cases students of Chinese, Japanese, Korean, Indian, Filipino, and Vietnamese backgrounds are coming together for a variety of purposes and in the process defining themselves as one ethnic group. This is quite different from seeing oneself as a Hakka from Fukien or a Kaoshan Chinese from Taiwan. In sum, the nature of ethnicity often changes, and drastically at that. In like manner, to think of oneself as an Oglala Sioux or Chippewa is quite different from thinking of oneself as a Native American in Chicago or St. Paul (Yinger, 1985).

White Ethnics

One notable change in recent years has been a renewed interest in ethnicity. Some observers have called it an "ethnic revival." Italian-Americans, Lithuanian-Americans, Slovakian-Americans, Polish-Americans, and many others have formed new ethnic organizations and revitalized old ones. Slogans printed on T-shirts and bumper stickers herald this ethnic awareness and pride. Prior to the 1960s it was considered poor taste to highlight ethnic membership, except on approved days like Columbus Day or St. Patrick's Day. But as black consciousness and militance grew, many other ethnic Americans saw no reason to continue hiding their own group memberships and pride.

Sociologists like Andrew M. Greeley (1974) have argued that the extent of assimilation in American life has been overestimated. He cites studies showing that ethnic cultures and organizations are still viable and functioning. Poles, Italians, Irish, and Jews are still set apart in behaviors and attitudes. Moreover, many ethnic groups continue to act and vote as political interest groups. Other sociologists like Herbert J. Gans (1979) say that ethnicity represents little more than a nostalgic search for an exotic tradition that can occasionally be savored in a museum or at an ethnic festival—a *symbolic ethnicity*. Viewed in this fashion, attendance at Polish picnics, membership in a Polish-American club, and a distaste for Polish jokes do not mean a strong ethnic

Ethnic Revival
Polish-American folk dancers celebrate their ethnic heritage in New York. For some people ethnicity represents a search for community in an impersonal urban world. It is one tool people use to shield themselves from the sharp edges of alienation. Ethnicity provides a basis for close, meaningful relationships that involve a high degree of personal intimacy, emotional depth, moral commitment, social acceptance, and continuity in time. During periods of confusion and crisis, such ties can be most reassuring. *(Guy Gillette/Photo Researchers)*

identity when the person does not speak Polish and adheres to few Polish traditions.

Still other social scientists find that assimilation is only a temporary process, and that ethnicity reemerges as third-generation nationalism (Hansen, 1952; Herberg, 1955). The second generation—the children of the immigrants—often feels keenly the discrimination directed against those who adhere to "foreign ways." Many seek to shed as quickly as possible the marks of ethnic identification. The third generation can afford to remember an ancestral culture. Equally significant, the third generation can no longer take its ethnic identity for granted. If its members wish to experience ethnicity, they must make it explicit and cultivate it. So the ethnic identity rejected by the second generation is often revived by the third. However, much depends on the group in question.

The Irish experience in the United States is illuminating. The Irish came to the United States in large numbers following the potato famine in Ireland in the 1840s. They experienced much hardship in America, and were victimized by prejudice and discrimination. But now, when they have made it—when for the first time it is legitimate for the Irish to act like Irish—many have forgotten how. In many respects they have become like "all other Americans." Some "Irish" compensate by attempting to regain their "roots." Yet parades on St. Patrick's Day are often merely an empty testimonial to a cultural tradition of which few participants are fully aware. In some circumstances, Irish ethnic solidarity has been heightened—as among those of South Boston—by the feeling that they are threatened by other ethnic and racial groups who are making inroads into "their" neighborhoods and who may jeopardize their newly won class positions. Just as ethnic groups have class reasons for tearing down ethnic barriers ahead of them, they often have class reasons for raising ethnic barriers behind them (Steinberg, 1981).

THINKING THROUGH THE ISSUES

The United States provides an unusual social laboratory for the study of race and ethnic relations. What social factors make it so (what has been the social significance of the nation's high degree of racial and cultural diversity, democratic political institutions, limited barriers to geographical mobility, and high levels of intergroup competition)? What social factors are likely to influence the rate of a group's assimilation within American society (consider such factors as the differences between the host and immigrant cultures; the ratio of the incoming group to the resident population; the length of the time period over which immigrants arrive; the geographical dispersion of the immigrant group; the educational and income levels of the host and incoming groups; the degree of economic competition between the host and immigrant people; and the geographical proximity of the immigrant group to its homeland)? Can you identify any ethnic groups in the United States whose members in time may find a separatist program (secession) appealing? What social and economic conditions are likely to increase the appeal of territorial separation from the dominant group?

Chapter Highlights

1. Race and ethnicity constitute one type of stratification system. Humankind contains peoples with quite different skin colors, languages, religions, and customs. These physical and cultural traits provide high social visibility and serve as identifying symbols of group membership. The distinctions are assigned social meanings that are translated into structured inequalities.

2. Although racial and ethnic stratification is similar to other systems of stratification in its essential features, there is one overriding difference. Racial and ethnic groups have the potential to carve their own independent nation from the existing state. Unlike class stratification, the issue is not replacement of one elite by another or even a revolutionary change in the political system. Instead, the question is one of whether the racial or ethnic segments of the society will be willing to participate within the existing nation-state.

3. Racial groups are populations who differ in the incidence of various hereditary traits. For the most part races are not characterized by fixed, clear-cut differences, but by fluid, continuous differences. It is often

next to impossible to tell where one population ends and another begins. Additionally, peoples differ in a great many ways, and these variations occur independently of one another.

4. Ethnic groups are identified on the basis of distinctive cultural backgrounds. Ethnic groups usually have a sense of peoplehood. Their members entertain the belief that they share a common descent.

5. Five properties characterize a minority: (1) Its members experience discrimination, segregation, oppression, or persecution at the hands of a dominant group. (2) It is characterized by physical or cultural traits that distinguish it from the dominant group. (3) It is a self-conscious social group. (4) Membership is generally involuntary. (5) The members of a minority, by choice or necessity, typically marry within their own group.

6. Prejudice is a state of mind—a feeling, opinion, or disposition. In contrast, discrimination is action, what people actually do in their daily activities. Discrimination is not practiced only by individuals; in their day-to-day operation, the institutions of society also systematically discriminate against the members of some group. Gatekeeping is one mechanism by which this institutional discrimination occurs.

7. Dominant groups have pursued a variety of policies toward minorities. At times these policies may parallel those of the minority; at other times they run counter to minority group aims. The chapter examined six types of dominant-group policies: assimilation, pluralism, legal protection of minorities, population transfer, continued subjugation, and extermination.

8. Functionalist and conflict theorists take differing views of racial and ethnic stratification. Functionalists look to the functions and dysfunctions it has for the survival of the social system and its parts. They note that conflict promotes group formation and solidarity. Simultaneously, conflict may imperil the larger social system. Conflict theorists contend that prejudice and discrimination can best be understood in terms of tension or conflict among competing groups. Often three ingredients come into play in the emergence and stabilization of racism: ethnocentrism, competition, and unequal power.

9. Within the United States blacks, Hispanics, Native Americans (Indians), and Asian-Americans have been victims of prejudice and discrimination. The subjugation of blacks extends to the period of exploration and colonization. Like blacks, people of Mexican heritage and Native Americans did not originally become part of American society voluntarily. Both Native Americans and Mexicans entered the society through conquest of their homeland. Asian-Americans have also encountered considerable difficulty in the United States, but in recent decades their circumstances have greatly improved.

The Sociologist's Vocabulary

affirmative action programs Government mandates that priorities be established in the recruitment and hiring of minorities and timetables be set for reaching employment goals; minorities are then hired as a matter of right in proportion to their numbers.

assimilation Processes whereby groups with distinctive identities become culturally and socially fused.

discrimination The arbitary denial of privilege, prestige, and power to members of a minority group whose qualifications are equal to those of members of the dominant group.

ethnic group A group that is identified chiefly on cultural grounds—language, folk practices, dress, gestures, mannerisms, religion.

gatekeeping The decision-making process whereby people are admitted to offices and positions of privilege, prestige, and power within a society.

genocide The deliberate and systematic extermination of a racial or ethnic group.

institutional discrimination The systematic discrimination against the members of some groups by the institutions of society.

minority group A racially or culturally self-conscious population, with hereditary membership and a high degree of ingroup marriage, which suffers at the hands of a dominant segment of a nation-state.

pluralism A situation where diverse groups coexist and accommodate themselves to their differences.

prejudice Attitudes of aversion and hostility toward the members of a group simply because they belong to it and hence are presumed to have the objectionable qualities ascribed to it.

race Populations who differ in the incidence of various hereditary traits.

split labor market An economic arena in which large differences exist in the price of labor at the same occupational level.

symbolic racism A form of racism in which whites feel that blacks are too aggressive, do not play by the rules, and have negative characteristics.

11

Age, Aging, and Ageism

Life is never a material, a substance to be molded. If you want to know, life is the principle of self-renewal; it is constantly renewing and remaking and changing and transfiguring itself.

—Boris Pasternak, *Doctor Zhivago*

The first cry of the normal newborn in Philadelphia or Conakry, in Moscow or Shanghai, has the same pitch and key. Each essentially says, "I am here! I am a member of your family and group." In all societies, babies arrive, suckle, and grow into restless and questioning youth. As adults they mate, toil, quarrel, seek, and hope (Sandburg, 1956). Ultimately, they too die. In sum, life is always an unfinished business, and death is its only cessation (Montagu, 1981).

Although you use chronological age as a convenient marker, the meaning of this dimension is a social one, with vast consequences for health, longevity, happiness, and well-being. This fact is highlighted by the inhabitants of Abkhasia, a small, mountainous Soviet republic wedged between the Black Sea and the High Caucasus. The Abkhasians are a tall, slender, narrow-faced, fair-skinned people. Older men develop bushy eyebrows which, together with their luxuriant mustaches, give them a dignified, stern demeanor. The women are a bit shorter than the men, graceful, with high foreheads and long, slender necks. A 1979 Soviet census found 548 Abkhasians, out of a population of 520,000, who claimed to be 100 years of age or older. When the cases were investigated, the number of centenarians was pared to 241—in proportion, a figure still five times higher than that of the United States (Sullivan, 1982).

Medical researchers are uniformly impressed by the alertness, excellent muscle tone, and mental and physical capabilities of Abkhasians of all ages. Consider Khfaf Lasuria, who at age 113 joined a troupe of thirty dancers, each of whom is 90 years of age or older. An able dancer, she was still performing happily before audiences when she was 131 years old. Not too far from her lived Akhutsa Kunach, age 114. While he was cutting timber in the woods, a tree fell on him and broke three of his ribs. Two months later, recovered, he had resumed forestry (Benet, 1974).

Social and cultural factors contribute to the long lives of the Abkhasians. Age is an honored and esteemed status, one that takes precedence over wealth and social position. Those of advanced age participate in the council of elders and are regularly sought out by the young. The elderly do not retire, but continue to work until they die, so at no stage of life does an Abkhasian become sedentary. Moreover, Abkhasian diets coincide with practices nutritionists define as ideal. And strong kinship ties pervade and regulate interpersonal relationships. The high degree of social integration and continuity that characterizes their personal lives allows the Abkhasians to adapt to changing circumstances at a comfortable pace. Although they have not discovered the fountain of youth, the people of Abkhasia seem to have developed the next best thing—an involved old age.

In this chapter, we consider the social transitions we undergo as we pass through infancy, childhood, adolescence, adulthood, and old age. In the course of our everyday lives, we use age as a critical dimension for differentiating among people. As we noted in Chapter 9, *social differentiation* is the process by which the members of a society split up activities and become "different" by virtue of playing distinctive roles. More often than not, age is among the taken for granted aspects of our social environment. But as we turn our sociological eye upon age, we see that it is an important foundation for social structure. In many cases, it becomes the basis for social ranking and the allocation of varying levels of wealth, power, and prestige among the members of a society. Like gender, which we consider in Chapter 12, it lays the framework within which our goals are fashioned and our socialization is carried out. For each of us personally, age contains much that is the core or essence of our social being.

PLANNING AHEAD: TARGETED READING

1. Why must all societies fashion social arrangements to deal with life course changes?

2. How are societies similar and dissimilar in the way they divide biological time into units of social time?

3. How do functionalist and conflict theorists differ in the way they view age strata?

4. How do our roles shift across the life course?

5. How does death pose a new social status for us by calling on us to redefine the self?

6. What evidence is there to support the notion that the elderly confront ageism in American life?

Social Age

The processes of sequential change that occur over the life course, beginning with conception and ending with death, are called **human development** (Featherman and Lerner, 1985). Throughout history people have woven varying social arrangements upon the rich tapestry supplied by the biological age grid. A 14-year-old girl may be expected to be a middle-school student in one culture and a mother of two in another. A 50-year-old man may be at the peak of a business career, still moving up in a political career, or retired from a career as a professional football player in our society, or dead and worshipped as an ancestor in some other (Datan, 1977). All cultures recognize **biological age**—the chronological time that elapses after birth and that is associated with changes in the organism. While birth, puberty, maturity, aging, and death are biological facts of life, it is society that

Elderly Abkhasians
Abkhasians of advanced age remain active and enjoy a prominent, prestigious, and authoritative role in their society. (both, Eve Arnold/Magnum)

gives each its distinctive meaning and assigns its social consequences (Neugarten and Hagestad, 1976; Riley, 1987). The life course, then, is punctuated by transition points—the relinquishing of familiar roles and the assuming of new ones. Biological time is translated into **social age**—the placement of people in the social structure based on phases of a socially defined life cycle.

Some cultures extend the stages of life to include the unborn and the deceased. The Australian aborigines think of the unborn as the spirits of departed ancestors. These spirits are believed to enter the womb of a passing woman and gain rebirth as a child (Murdock, 1935). Hindus regard the unborn as the spirits of persons or animals who lived in former incarnations (Davis, 1949). The dead may also be defined as continuing members of the community. For instance, when a Tanala of Madagascar dies, the person is seen as simply surrendering one set of rights and duties for another:

> Thus a Tanala clan has two sections which are equally real to its members, the living and the dead. In spite of rather half-hearted attempts by the living to explain to the dead that they are dead and to discourage their re-

turn, they remain an integral part of the clan. They must be informed of all important events, invited to all clan ceremonies, and remembered at every meal. In return they allow themselves to be consulted, take an active and helpful interest in the affairs of the community, and act as highly efficient guardians of the group's mores. [Linton, 1936:121–122]

Each society, then, shapes the processes of human development in its own image.

Social Structure and the Social Clock

Societal demands often define role-related tasks that are presented to us at certain phases of our lives. Most life course transitions are role transitions—entering school, completing school, getting a first job, marrying, having children, being promoted at work, seeing a youngest child married, becoming a grandparent, retiring, and so on. Age is a critical dimension by which we locate ourselves within society and in turn are located by others (Baltes and Nesselroade, 1984). It serves as a reference point that allows us to orient ourselves in terms of *what* and *where* we are within various social structures—family, school, church, workplace. In short, we use age as a key ingredient in answering the question, "Who am I?"

Age norms Like other social behaviors, rules—**age norms**—specify what constitutes appropriate and inappropriate behavior for people at various periods in the life span. In many cases an informal consensus provides the standards telling us how to "act your age." For instance, a child of 5 is thought "too young" to tend younger siblings in the absence of a parent. And a woman of 70 is thought "too old" to enter a bathing beauty contest. Laws also set floors and ceilings for some forms of behavior. There are laws restricting the marriage of minors without parental consent, entry into the workforce, and eligibility for Social Security and Medicare benefits. We even find apartment buildings limited to an age group, such as young singles, and cities designed for an age group, such as retirement communities.

A societal Big Ben A cultural timetable—a sort of societal Big Ben—defines the "best age" for a man or woman to finish school, settle on a career, marry, have children, hold a top job, become a grandparent, and retire (Kimmel, 1980). People tend to set their personal watches by this cultural Big Ben, which we call the **social clock**. They readily report whether they themselves are "early," "late," or "on time" with regard to major occupational and family events (Neugarten, 1968). However, variations do occur in the setting of one's social clock, so that the higher the social class, the later tends to be the pacing of age-linked events. Early adulthood typically lasts longer for a person in the middle class than for a member of the working class. And new generations may reset the social clock. For example, younger women currently prefer earlier ages for educational and occupational events and later ages for family events than did earlier generations (Ryff, 1985).

In recent years, the socially prescribed life course has become more fluid; many traditional norms and expectations are changing, and age is losing many of its customary meanings. As a result, we may be witnessing what sociologist Bernice L. Neugarten (1979) has called an "age-irrelevant society" in which there is no single appropriate age for taking on given roles. She notes that many Americans change careers in their forties and fifties, marry and remarry into their seventies and eighties, and go back to school at all ages. So it is no longer unusual to encounter the 28-year-old mayor, the 30-year-old college president, the 35-year-old grandmother, the 50-year-old retiree, the 65-year-old new father, and the 70-year-old student.

The Social Significance of Age Cohorts

People locate themselves across the life course not only in terms of social timetables, but also in terms of **life events**—turning points at which people change some direction in their lives (Hultsch and Plemmons, 1979; Brim, 1980). Some of these events are related to social clocks. But many are not, such as suffering severe injury in an accident, being raped, winning a lottery, undergoing a "born again" conversion, or living at the time of the antiwar protests of the early 1970s. Some life events are associated with internal growth or aging factors like puberty or old age. Others derive from happenings in the physical world, including storms, tidal waves, earthquakes, and avalanches. Still others have a strong inner or psychological component, such as a profound religious experience, the decision to leave a spouse, or the death of a parent. And some are the consequences of group life, including wars, national economic crises, and revolutions.

Societal influences on the aging process Although there is considerable cultural similarity among the members of a society, each **age cohort**—persons born in the same time interval—is unique because it is exposed to a unique segment of history (Mannheim, 1927; Ryder, 1965; Riley, 1987). Since society changes, the members of different cohorts age in different ways. Each new generation enters and leaves childhood, adolescence, adulthood, and old age at a similar point in time, and so its members experience certain decisive economic, social, political, and military events at similar junctures in life. As a consequence of the unique events of the era in which they live out their lives—for instance, the Great Depression of the 1930s, World War II, the Korean war, the prosperity of the 1950s, and the Vietnam war—each generation tends to fashion a somewhat unique style of thought and life. Not surprisingly, each cohort of American youth over the past sixty years has acquired a somewhat different popular image: the youth of the "roaring twenties," the "political radicals" of the 1930s, the "wild kids" of the war years, the "silent generation" of the 1950s, the "involved generation" of the 1960s, the "Me generation" of the 1970s, and the "materialistic generation" of the 1980s. Each new generation, then, confronts an environment different from that faced by earlier generations.

Cohort influences on social structure   Because people of different cohorts age in new ways, they contribute to changes in the social structure (Riley, 1987). As society moves through time, statuses and roles are altered. Older occupants of statuses are replaced by younger entrants from more recent cohorts, with more recent life experiences. The flow of new generations results in some loss to the cultural inventory, a reevaluation of some of its components, and the introduction of new elements. In sum, although parental generations play a crucial part in predisposing their offspring to particular values and behaviors, youth are not necessarily bound to replicate the views and perspectives of their elders (Kertzer, 1983; Demartini, 1985).

Imbalance between societal and cohort influences   Individuals age and societies change at different tempos. Within each cohort, people age according to a rhythm set by the biological properties of the human lifetime. In contrast, social change takes place unevenly, often in bursts and spurts (see Chapter 22). People who were young earlier in this century learned the age norms and patterns of behavior prevalent at that time. Most learned that they would need only a few years of schooling for most jobs. But now they are reaching their advanced years and are having to adjust to a world for which their early socialization left them unprepared. In similar fashion, you see the occupational ladder as it currently is. But twenty or thirty years from now, technological innovations will have altered the nation's job structure and opportunities. You will not be old in the same society in which you are now launching your career (Riley, 1987).

These difficulties are often accentuated when age cohorts are incorporated with age strata.

Perspectives on Age Strata

To one degree or another, all societies are divided into **age strata**—social layers based on time periods in the life cycle. Age strata are often the basis for structured social inequality. In our society, for instance, most young and old people do not have access to the most highly rewarded economic roles, and the middle-aged have more political power than the young. The treatment of infants and juveniles by adults has at times involved highly exploitative and physically and mentally punishing practices. Like class, racial, and gender hierarchies, the maltreatment and exploitation of children has often been rationalized by the superordinate group as occurring "for their own good." However, unlike movement up or down the class ladder, the mobility of people through the age strata is not dependent on motivation and recruitment. Mobility from one stratum to the next hinges primarily on biological considerations and is irreversible. The functionalist and conflict perspectives draw our attention to different aspects of this social ordering, each highlighting features that the other overlooks or tends to neglect.

The Functionalist Perspective

Functionalists point out that societies require ways for placing and motivating people in the social structure. If

Age Sets among the Masai of Eastern Africa
The Masai are a semi-nomadic people who tend their herds over a 45,000-square-mile area straddling Kenya and Tanzania. The men move from young warrior to junior elder to senior elder at prescribed periods. The passage from one age stratum to another is marked by a set of distinct rituals. Here senior elders gather around a ritual fire in preparation for a circumcision ceremony in which young warriors will move to the junior elder stratum. *(George Rodger/ Magnum)*

societies are to maintain and perpetuate themselves, they must somehow distribute their members in social positions and induce them to perform the duties associated with these positions. The evolution of age categories is one way of ordering biological aging and for ascribing statuses to people. Some societies accomplish these social ends by establishing **age sets,** groups of people of similar age and sex who move at prescribed intervals from one age stratum to another. Members of each age set are alike in life stage and have certain roles that are age-specific. For instance, all the boys of a certain age range may ceremonially enter "manhood" at the same time. Later in life, the same group may become "elders," and still later "retired elders." The Latuka of Sudan distinguish five age-sets: children, youths, rulers of the village, retired elders, and the very old. Such social arrangements permit the smooth passage of people across the life span. By culturally defining what is expected of people at various stages in the aging process, societies discourage the young, middle-aged, and elderly from competing for the same statuses and roles.

In the United States, we have few formalized rituals to mark the passage from one age stratum to another. High school and college graduation ceremonies are an exception, but not everyone graduates from high school or college. In some respects, age norms serve as a counterpart of the age set system in broadly defining what is appropriate for people to be and to do at various ages (Foner and Kertzer, 1978). Even so, Western societies allow "natural" forces considerable rein: Younger people assume adult roles when they are ready to do so, while older people give up roles when they are ready or when they become ill or die. This flexibility often contributes to tensions and conflicts. For instance, "middle age" is a sufficiently vague category that people approaching or leaving it often experience some measure of anxiety regarding their social placement and identity.

The Conflict Perspective

For conflict theorists, the tensions and conflicts associated with age divisions are the focus of scrutiny. Consider the matter of age sets. Greater rewards are bestowed on the members of some age sets than on others. Among the Kipsigis of Kenya, for example, there are three age grades: boyhood, warriorhood, and elderhood. The warriors enjoy the greatest prestige and personal freedom. Since social power and rewards are linked to one's age set, generation succession has widespread ramifications. And since the timing of transitions is a product of social

"I wish we could develop a better relationship, son, but the sad truth is that my generation doesn't trust anyone under 30."
Drawing by Harley L. Schwadron

deliberation rather than simple chronological determination, social discord is widespread. Age sets that stand to lose power and prestige through a transition often attempt to delay the ceremonies; those who stand to gain exert pressure to speed them up. It is not uncommon for current Kipsignis warriors to beat those who wish to replace them and for aspiring warriors to mobilize and attack the current warriors (Peristiany, 1939).

In our own society, conflict theorists note that all is not well among the age strata. The continuing debate over Social Security and health care funding and benefits reflects the tug between the young and the elderly. By the same token, young people wishing to enter the work force as full-time employees typically find that they need a high school diploma or a college degree, what is called *credentialism.* Very often, workers must have a degree for its own sake, not because it certifies they have skills needed for the performance of a job (see Chapter 17). Such requirements artificially extend the period of adolescence or preadulthood. One reaction of young American adults to their prolonged dependency has been collective action. The student movement of the 1960s claimed for young adults some of the rights and privileges of adulthood even before adult roles are assumed. College students no longer wait until they finish their schooling before they "live together" or get married.

Life Course Transitions

In all societies, people take notice of the changes that take place over the biological life course. These transi-

tions affect who and what we are. They also affect what we bring to others in the course of interacting with them. It is hardly surprising, then, that age should be a critical dimension in human affairs and that societies should have developed social forms for ordering relationships on the basis of major life course transitions.

Some social scientists depict life as a succession of *stages*—a sort of stairway made up of a series of steplike levels (see Chapter 6). Erik Erikson (1963) takes this approach, dividing psychosocial development into the eight major stages described in Table 11.1. Each stage is seen as posing a unique task that revolves about a crisis—a turning point of increased vulnerability and height-

ened potential. According to Erikson, the crisis posed by each stage must be successfully resolved if healthy development is to take place.

Daniel J. Levinson (1978, 1986) also takes a stage perspective in his approach to adulthood. He and his associates at Yale University have studied forty men and forty-five women. They designate nine periods, ranging from the late teens to the mid-sixties (see Figure 11.1). In Levinson's view, the overriding task confronting people throughout adulthood is the creation of a structure for their lives—the answer to the question "What is my life like now?" The primary components of a life structure are relationships with other people and the institu-

Table 11.1   Erikson's Eight Stages of Development

Development Stage	Psychosocial Crisis	Predominant Social Setting	Favorable Outcome
1. Infancy	Basic trust vs. mistrust	Family	The child develops trust in itself, its parents, and the world.
2. Early childhood	Autonomy vs. shame, doubt	Family	The child develops a sense of self-control without loss of self-esteem.
3. Fourth to fifth year	Initiative vs. guilt	Family	The child learns to acquire direction and purpose in activities.
4. Sixth year to onset of puberty	Industry vs. inferiority	Neighborhood; school	The child acquires a sense of mastery and competence.
5. Adolescence	Identity vs. role confusion	Peer groups and outgroups	The individual develops an *ego identity*—a coherent sense of self.
6. Young adulthood	Intimacy vs. isolation	Partners in friendship and sex	The individual develops the capacity to work toward a specific career and to involve himself or herself in an extended intimate relationship.
7. Adulthood	Generativity vs. stagnation	New family; work	The individual becomes concerned with others beyond the immediate family, with future generations, and with society.
8. Old age	Integrity vs. despair	Retirement and impending death	The individual acquires a sense of satisfaction in looking back upon his or her life.

Source: Erik Erikson. 1953. *Childhood and Society.* New York: Norton.

Autonomy versus Shame and Doubt
Erik Erikson suggests that as children begin to walk and climb, they gain a sense of independence and competence. When children are not permitted the freedom to explore, they become inhibited and develop a sense of shame and doubt.
(Diane M. Lowe/Stock, Boston)

tional context in which they are embedded. But the structure does not become established once and for all time; it must be continually modified and reappraised. Transition periods tend to loom within two or three years of, and on either side of, the symbolically significant birthdays—20, 30, 40, 50, and 60. By interacting with the environment, each person formulates goals, works out means to achieve them, and modifies assumptions.

Many sociologists contend that stage theories overlook the vast differences that characterize the social experience. They say that adult life is not the same thing for men and for women, for the rich and the poor, and even for people in different phases of the life course (see Figure 11.2). And, as we noted in the discussion of age cohorts, the social and historical era in which a person is born makes a difference. Moreover, these sociologists contend that people are prepared for the major transitions of life by age norms and social clocks. They tend to take the transitions in stride and do not experience them as crises or unusually stressful events. Let us take a closer look at some of the transitions that center on life course roles.

Childhood

The concept of childhood as we know it was unheard of in the Middle Ages. Then, children were regarded simply as small adults (Aries, 1962; Plumb, 1972). The arts and documents of the medieval world portray adults and children mingling, wearing the same clothes, and engaging in many of the same activities. The world we think

proper for children—fairy tales, games, toys, and books—is of comparatively recent origin. Only around 1600 did a new concept of childhood begin to emerge. Similarly, the notion that children should be attending school rather than working in factories, mines, and fields is of relatively recent origin. The first industrial workers in the United States were nine children hired in 1791 as employees of a Rhode Island textile mill. In the 1820s, half of the cotton mill workers in New England were children who worked 12- to 15-hour days. Even as late as 1924, the National Child Labor Committee estimated that 2 million American children under 15 were at work, the majority as farm laborers. In recent years, our view of children has changed dramatically. We no longer see childhood as an inconvenient "waiting" period, but as a special time for exploring, learning about, and mastering the world. Various laws and programs are designed to protect children from the excesses of the adult world, including child labor laws, special systems of juvenile justice, and government economic aid programs.

Whatever definitions they hold of children, societies begin socializing them as soon as possible. Most infants are fairly flexible in that within broad limits they are capable of becoming adults of quite different sorts. Even so, youngsters not only acquire the social standards of their social environment, they also become a part of this environment. In entering the family, they influence and alter it. They affect their parents' marital relations, modify the bonds between parents and grandparents, transform the domestic division of labor, and alter existing operating rules (Furstenberg, 1985). Children are

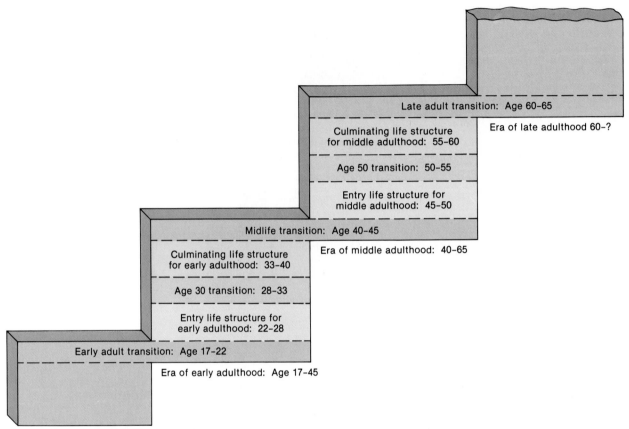

FIGURE 11.1 **Levinson's Periods in Early and Middle Adulthood**
Levinson conceives of development in adulthood as characterized by a succession of stages. Each stage requires the restructuring of critical aspects of a person's self-assumptions and the world. *Source: Daniel J. Levinson. 1986. A conception of adult development.* American Psychologist, *41:3–13.*

hardly passive beings, blank tablets on which the finger of experience writes. They are active agents in the socialization process: They are not only influenced by, but themselves influence their caretakers.

Children display people-oriented responses at very early ages. Even before their first birthdays, children are already contributors to social life (Rheingold, Hay, and West, 1976; Leung and Rheingold, 1981). For instance, they will point toward objects—a window display, an airplane, an automobile, a picture of a cereal box—to call other people's attention to them. By age 2, toddlers are already beginning to master and sharpen their role-playing capabilities. Three-year-olds can make a doll

	By age			
	18–29 years	30–44 years	45–59 years	60 years and over
Childhood	22%	22%	17%	14%
Teen-age years	29%	21%	16%	14%
The twenties	42%	28%	24%	19%
The thirties	9%	31%	22%	20%
The forties	4%	13%	20%	16%
The fifties	1%	4%	13%	11%
Retirement years	3%	5%	8%	31%

FIGURE 11.2 **The Best Years of Our Lives**
Source: Survey by the Roper Organization (Roper Report 84-4), March 17–24, 1984. Public Opinion, *8 (February/March, 1985):33.*

Children as Miniature Adults
Notice the way children are pictured in this seventeenth-century painting by
Diego Velázquez. They are dressed much like adults; their body proportions
resemble those of adults; and they are in the company of adults. *(Museo del Prado, Madrid)*

carry out several role-related activities (for instance, pretend to be a doctor and examine a doll). Four-year-olds can typically act out a role, meshing the behavior with that of a reciprocal role (for example, pretend that a patient doll is sick and a doctor examines it, in the course of which both dolls make appropriate responses). During the late preschool years, children become capable of combining roles in more complicated ways (for instance, being a doctor and a father simultaneously) (Lewis and

Brooks-Gunn, 1979; Lewis, Brooks-Gunn, and Jaskir, 1985). The number of dimensions along which children conceive of other people increases throughout childhood (Selman, 1980; Damon and Hart, 1982). The greatest surge occurs between 7 and 8 years of age. Indeed, the differences between children who are 7 years old and those who are 8 are frequently greater than the differences between 8-year-olds and 15-year-olds (Livesley and Bromley, 1973).

Child Labor

Children were widely employed in the textile mills and coal mines of the United States in the nineteenth century. In the intervening years our notions of childhood have changed so that we now see children as in need of protection from the dictates of the adult world. *(left, AFL-CIO Photo Library/Photo Researchers; right, Historical Pictures Service)*

Adolescence

During adolescence, young people undergo revolutionary changes in growth and development. They suddenly catch up with adults in physical size and strength. Accompanying these changes is the rapid development of the reproductive organs that signals sexual maturity. Yet in much of the world adolescence is not a socially distinct period in the human life course. Although young people everywhere undergo the physiological changes associated with puberty, children frequently assume adult responsibilities by age 13 and even younger. In the United States, adolescence appears to be an "invention" of the past hundred years (Demos and Demos, 1969; Kett, 1977; Lapsley, Enright, and Serlin, 1985). During this time, youth were displaced from the workforce and systematically excluded from adult roles. Countless teenagers lost their places as technological innovation made many jobs obsolete. For example, the spread of the telephone in the first decade of the twentieth century put large numbers of youths who found employment delivering telegrams out of work (Troen, 1985). Moreover, as the nation moved from a rural to an urban society, chil-

dren no longer had a significant economic function in the family. In time, mandatory school attendance, child labor laws, and special legal procedures for "juveniles" established adolescence as a well-defined social reality.

According to Erik Erikson (1963, 1968), adolescence is a time when youths, like trapeze artists, must release their hold on childhood in midair and reach for a firm grasp on adulthood. In the process of building a stable identity, Erikson says, many young people experience role confusion and a blurred self-image. These difficulties and uncertainties lead them to seek a social and emotional anchorage in intense commitments to cliques, allegiances, loves, and social causes. Adolescence, then, is a period of "storm and stress." However, a growing body of research disputes this view (Adelson, 1979; Blyth and Traeger, 1983). Although the self-images and self-conceptions of young people change, the changes are not invariably turbulent (Offer and Offer, 1975; Dusek and Flaherty, 1981). The self-esteem of most youths actually *increases* across the adolescent years (O'Malley and Bachman, 1983; Savin-Williams and Demo, 1984). There are exceptions: Changes in the social environment, like the transitions to middle or junior

Puberty Rites

Some societies induct youth into adult status by means of initiation ceremonies. Boys may be terrorized, ceremonially painted, and circumcised; girls may be secluded at menarche. But the tasks and tests are clear-cut, and young people know that if they accomplish the goals set for them, they will acquire adult status. Here boys in Eastern New Guinea undergo an ordeal in a puberty rite. In the photo to the left, a boy is having his head shaved in preparation for the final event. In the photo to the right, the boys are standing behind their spears, clutching spear throwers in both hands; they are expected to remain in the position without moving for 60 hours. The ceremonies also include beating the boys with sticks in a series of 12 daily fights to teach them to withstand pain without whimpering. *(both, Jen and Des Bartlett/Photo Researchers)*

high school, can in some cases have a disturbing effect, especially for girls (Simmons and Rosenberg, 1973; Simmons et al., 1979).

The media make a good deal out of generational differences between adolescents and their parents. According to much popular belief, teenage peer groups specialize in negative conformity: using drugs, drinking, vandalizing, stealing, driving fast, and flouting adult rules. While it is true that adolescents often rebel in small and large ways, the notion of a generation gap vastly oversimplifies matters. For most teenagers, both the family and the peer group are important anchors in their lives. The relative influence of the two groups varies with the issue involved. The peer group has the greater influence when the issues have to do with musical tastes, personal adornment, and entertainment idols, and in some cases with marijuana use and drinking. But

the family has the greater influence when the issues have to do with future life goals, fundamental behavior codes, and core values (Davies and Kandel, 1981; Krosnick and Judd, 1982; Sebald, 1986).

Some sociologists have suggested that Western nations make the transition from childhood to adulthood a particularly difficult one (Elkind, 1979; Magnusson, Stattin, and Allen, 1985; Lerner, 1985). At adolescence, boys and girls are expected to stop being children, yet they are not expected to be men and women. The definitions given them by society are inconsistent. Many non-Western societies make the shift in status more definitive by providing **puberty rites**—initiation ceremonies that symbolize the transition from childhood to adulthood. Adolescents may be subjected to thoroughly distasteful, painful, and humiliating experiences during such rituals, but they are then pronounced grown up (Herdt,

1982). Mild versions of puberty rites in Western societies include the Jewish Bar Mitzvah and Bat Mitzvah, the Catholic confirmation, securing a driver's license, and graduation from high school and college.

Young Adulthood

Recent developments in the Western world—the growth of service industries, the prolongation of education, and the enormously high educational demands of a postindustrial society—have lengthened the transition to adulthood. In some respects, our society appears to be evolving a new status between adolescence and adulthood: youth—men and women of college and graduate school age (Keniston, 1970). In leaving home, youths in their late teens or early twenties may choose a transitional institution, such as the military or college, to start them on their way. Or young people may work (provided they can find a job) while continuing to live at home. During this time, a roughly equal balance persists between "being in" the family and "moving out." Individuals become less financially dependent, enter new roles and living arrangements, and achieve greater autonomy and responsibility. With the passage of time, the center of gravity in young people's lives gradually shifts away from the family of origin (Levinson, 1978, 1986; Gould, 1978).

The developmental tasks confronting individuals from 18 to 30 years of age typically center on the two core tasks that Sigmund Freud (1938) termed *love* and *work*. Through adult friendships, sexual relationships, and work experiences, they arrive at initial definitions of themselves as adults. Ideally they develop the capacity to experience a trusting, supportive, and tender relationship with another person (Erikson, 1963; Kahn et al., 1985; White et al., 1986). They may cohabit with a sexual partner or marry and begin a family. And they may lay the groundwork for a career, develop one career and then discard it, or drift aimlessly, often precipitating a crisis at about age 30.

Middle Adulthood

Middle adulthood lacks the concreteness of "infancy," "childhood," and "adolescence." It is a catchall category that is rather nebulous. Sometimes middle adulthood is used to refer to "people over 30," a time in life when men and women presumably have "settled down" with families and careers. But it is also employed to denote "middle-aged" people—those roughly between 45 and 64 years of age. Whichever meaning is attached to middle adulthood, the core tasks remain much the same as they did for men and women in young adulthood and revolve about love and work. We will consider the love dimension at length in Chapter 13 and work in Chapter 15.

Levinson (1978, 1986) finds that in their late twenties and early thirties, people tend to establish their niche in the world, dig in, build a nest, and make and pursue long-range plans and goals. They usually have some "dream" or vision of the future. In their mid- to late thirties, they attempt to realize their aspirations. From about 40 to 45, they enter a major transitional period. People begin assessing where they stand in relation to the goals they earlier set for themselves. They may sense a gap between "what I've got now" and "what it is I really want." There may be an interval of soul-searching. In some respects, Levinson's periods reflect the social clock patterns that prevail among different generational cohorts. So the mid-life transition is in part a social artifact associated with the way our society organizes work and defines an ideal career (Dannefer, 1984).

Although some social scientists talk about "adult development," the life courses of men and women differ in important ways (Baruch and Brooks-Gunn, 1984). For one thing, until relatively recently, work and family were not separate spheres of life for most women. For another, women may leave the paid labor force to have and care for children, complicating their career opportunities. And every marriage tends to be two marriages—his and hers (White et al., 1986). We will have more to say on these matters in Chapter 12, when we examine gender roles in American life.

Later Adulthood

Like other periods of the life span, the time at which later adulthood begins is a matter of social definition. In preindustrial societies, life expectancy is typically short, and old age comes early. Literary evidence reveals that during the European Renaissance, men were already considered old in their forties (Gilbert, 1967). Currently, as Neugarten (1977) suggests, a new division is emerging in many Western nations between the "young-old" and the "old-old." The young-old are early retirees who enjoy physical vigor, new leisure time, and new opportunities for community service and self-fulfillment; the old-old include those who are of advanced age and suffer various infirmities.

Societies differ in the prestige and dignity they accord the aged. In many rural societies, including that of imperial China, elders enjoyed a prominent, esteemed, and honored position (Lang, 1946). Among the agricultural Palaung of North Burma, long life was deemed a privilege that befell those who had lived virtuously in a previous incarnation. People showed their respect to older people by being careful not to step on their shadow. And young women cultivated an older appearance because women acquired honor and privilege in proportion to their years (Milne, 1924). In contrast to these cultural patterns, youth is the favored age in the United States.

Old age entails exiting from some social roles. One of the most important of these is retirement from a job. On the whole, Americans are now retiring at earlier ages then they did in previous generations. The proportion of men aged 65 and over who were gainfully employed dropped from 68 percent in 1890, to 48 percent in 1947, to only 17 percent today. About 8 percent of women over 65 hold jobs or are seeking work, down from 9.5 percent in 1971. Of equal social significance, the proportion of men retiring between ages 55 and 64 is steadily rising. The growing availability of pensions and early retirement programs have contributed to these trends (Collins, 1986).

A decade or so ago, sociologists depicted retirement as having negative consequences for the elderly because occupational status is a master status—an anchoring point for adult identity (Blau, 1973). Much of postretirement life was portrayed as aimless, and giving structure to the long, shapeless day was believed to be the retired person's most urgent challenge (Rosow, 1974). Recent research has challenged this negative image (George and Maddox, 1977; Beck, 1982; Palmore et al., 1985). One survey of 5,000 elderly men found that when people are healthy and their incomes adequate, they express satisfaction with retirement (Parnes, 1981).

Many elderly individuals experience an additional role loss, that of being married. Although three out of four American men 65 and over are married and living with their wives, the same holds true for only one out of three women. This results from the fact that women typically outlive men by seven to eight years and from the tradition that women marry men older than themselves. Sociologists find that when negative long-term consequences are associated with widowhood, they typically derive more from socioeconomic deprivation than from widowhood itself (Balkwell, 1981; Hyman, 1983).

Aging, then, is not an immutable or biologically fixed process. It varies with social structure and social

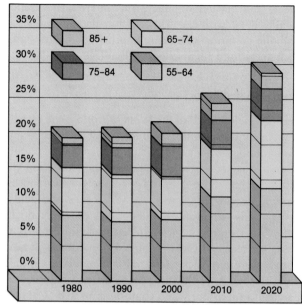

FIGURE 11.3 **The Aging of America**
By 2020, almost one-third of the U.S. population is expected to be at least age 55. *Source: U.S. Bureau of the Census.*

change. Being old is not like suddenly falling off a cliff; people do not stop being themselves and all at once turn into "old people." Aging does not destroy the continuity of what we have been, what we are, and what we will be. By counterposing youth and age we lose sight of the fact that our lives are a seamless whole.

THINKING THROUGH THE ISSUES

More and more Americans are living into their eighties and nineties. What are some of the social consequences of this development? For example, it is estimated that if all the people who died prematurely from heart attacks in 1978 had lived out their full lives, it would have cost the federal government an extra $15 billion in benefits for the elderly. What are likely to be the social and institutional consequences of the "aging of America" (see Figure 11.3)? What are the implications for retirement (retirement, which scarcely existed early in the century, now accounts for over one-fourth of the adult life course [Torrey, 1982])? How does longevity alter the social structure by increasing structural complexity and the options open to people as they age (for changing jobs, careers, marriages, educational plans)? How does longevity alter the aging process by prolonging the opportunity for accumulating social, psychological, and biological experiences (Riley, 1985)? How does longevity contribute to more role transitions for men? for women?

Death

A diagnosis of impending death requires that a person adjust to a new definition of self. To be defined as dying implies more than biochemical processes (DeVries, 1981). It entails the assumption of a social status, one in which social structuring not only attends but shapes the dying experience. Consider, for instance, the different social definitions we typically impute to a 20-year-old who has been given a five-year life expectancy and those we attribute to a healthy 80-year-old. Hospital personnel

---

Bereavement Ceremonies
Societies throughout the world have evolved funerals and other rituals that assist their members in coming to terms with the death of a loved one. The events highlight the finality of death. Here mourners in Ghana express their grief in a funeral ceremony.
(Hector R. Acebes/Photo Researchers)

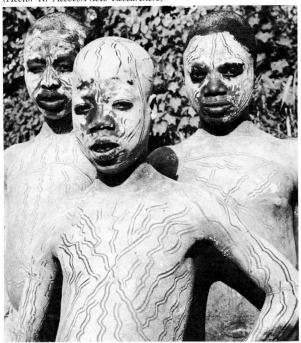

also give different care to patients based on their perceived social worth. In a study of a hospital emergency room, sociologist David Sudnow (1967) found that different social evaluations led the staff to work frantically to revive a young child, but to acquiesce in the death of an elderly woman. Finally, although death is a biological event, it is made a social reality through such culturally fashioned events as wakes and funerals.

Often there is an interval of "living-dying" that follows the crisis precipitated by learning of one's impending death (Pattison, 1977). People take stock of their lives and reflect and reminisce about them—a process termed **life review** (Butler, 1963, 1971). Often the review proceeds silently and provides a positive force in personality reorganization. As a part of the process, people engage in "the legitimation of their biography" (Marshall, 1980). The life review process is an important element in the overall adjustment to death, a continuation of human development right to the very end of life. On the whole, only a relatively small proportion of the elderly express profound fear of death. The uncertainty of the experience may be a source of concern to them, but on the whole they show less fear of death than younger people do. When people do fear death, it is largely because death deprives them of the opportunity for achieving important goals (Riley, 1983).

Elisabeth Kübler-Ross (1969, 1981) has contributed a good deal to the movement to restore dignity and humanity to death. She contends that when medical personnel and the family know that a patient is dying and attempt to hide the fact, they construct a barrier that prevents all the parties from preparing for death. Moreover, the dying person typically sees through the make-believe. Kübler-Ross has found that it is better if everyone is allowed to express his or her genuine emotions and if these feelings are respected. Surveys show that four out of five persons would want to be told if they had an incurable illness.

Although there are different styles for dying—just as there are different styles for living—Kübler-Ross (1969) finds that dying people typically pass through five stages in accommodating themselves to impending death: *denial* that they will die, *anger* that life will shortly end, *bargaining* with God or fate to arrange a temporary truce, *depression* or "preparatory grief," and *acceptance*. Not everyone passes through all of the stages, and individuals slip back and forth between them. A great many other factors also influence the dying experience, including differences in gender, ethnic membership, personality, the death environment, and the nature of the disease itself. Death cannot be understood except in the total context of a person's previous life and current circumstances. In sum, over the past decade or so, public and professional awareness of the dying person's experience has increased dramatically and has given impetus to a more humane approach to death (see the box).

THINKING THROUGH THE ISSUES

Are the meanings of death undergoing transformation in American life (Riley, 1983)? Will dying people demand and achieve an even greater sense of autonomy? Will passive euthanasia ("mercy killing") achieve greater moral acceptance, or will the issue enter the political arena, as abortion has, and contribute to intense social division? Will suicide become a more acceptable "final alternative"? As people are living longer and death is increasingly postponed, will new patterns of bereavement emerge? Will new caring environments for the terminally ill be institutionalized? What new lay-care arrangements (social, mental, and spiritual) may arise? Will the concept of a "good" death gain growing acceptance? What will be the impact of new medical technologies for dying people?

ISSUES THAT SHAPE OUR LIVES

Death with Dignity?

Changes in medical technology and social conditions have made death a different experience from that of earlier times. Dying in the modern world is often drawn out and enmeshed in formal bureaucratic processes (Lofland, 1978). Only a few generations ago, most people died at home and the family assumed responsibility for preparing the body and the funeral. In recent times, death has been surrounded by taboos that in large measure have kept the subject out of sight and out of mind. Today the nursing home or hospital cares for the terminally ill and manages the dying experience. A mortuary—euphemistically called a "home"—prepares the body and makes the funeral arrangements or undertakes the cremation of the remains. As a result, the average American's exposure to death is minimized. The dying and the dead are segregated from others and placed with specialists for whom contact with death has become a routine and impersonal matter (Strauss and Glasser, 1970; Arias, 1981).

The control of dying by organizations has reduced individual autonomy. Personal needs and desires are often subordinated to organizational needs. The very meaning of life—consciousness, self-control, and decision making—is all too frequently taken away from the dying person. Indeed, much criticism has been leveled at the way modern organizations and technology structure the care of the terminally ill. Public opinion surveys reveal that 73 percent of Americans believe that patients with terminal illnesses should be allowed to halt treatment even if it means certain death; 65 percent believe that physicians should be allowed to stop treating an unconscious, terminally ill patient if asked by the patient's family (Kenny, 1984). And 44 percent of Americans approve of suicide for a person with an incurable disease, suggesting that suicide may not be as taboo a subject as we often think (Hale, 1986).

For the most part, Americans favor a quick transition between life and death. But the belief that "the less dying, the better" has come up against an altered biomedical technology, in which people are increasingly approaching death through a "lingering trajectory." Many of us have a profound fear of being held captive in a state between life and death—as "vegetables" sustained entirely by life-support equipment. Consequently, growing numbers of Americans are coming to the view that too much is done for too long a period at too high a cost, all at the expense of basic human considerations and sensitivities. It may be that a new medical-moral battle, possibly as divisive as the conflict over abortion, is about to explode into the political arena (Otten, 1986).

Over the past decade, the hospice movement has arisen to provide a more humane approach for the care of the terminally ill. A *hospice* is a program or mode of care that attempts to make the dying experience less painful and emotionally traumatic for patients and their families. Advocates of the hospice approach say that it is difficult for physicians and nurses in hospital settings to accept the inevitability of death. Hospitals are geared to curing illness and prolonging life, and consequently incurable illness and death are sources of embarrassment to them. Proponents of hospice care insist that other institutional arrangements are required.

Whenever possible, hospice treatment is administered in the patient's home. Visiting physicians, nurses, social workers, and volunteers provide emotional and spiritual help in addition to medical care. A num-

Institutional Ageism

Along with institutional racism and sexism, critics charge our society with **institutional ageism**—the systematic negative stereotyping of and discrimination against people because they are old. We have restricted the roles open to the elderly and accord them little prestige. Indeed, the older the elderly become, especially as they reach quite advanced ages, the more likely they are to be unfavorably stereotyped (Lachman and McArthur, 1986). At times they are depicted as "cute", and thus assumed to be like clever children. At other times they are portrayed as "funny" creatures who behave inappropriately and chatter endlessly about the past. And at still other times they are seen as troublesome, cranky, touchy, sickly beings. Yet *most* elderly Americans do not fit popular stereotypes and mythology.

Myth and Reality

The facts of aging are befogged by a great many myths that have little to do with the actual process of growing old:

- *Myth:* Most elderly Americans live in hospitals, nursing homes, homes for the aged, and other such institutions.

ber of hospitals and nursing homes have also established care units. The emphasis of hospice approaches falls on "comfort care" rather than on attempts to prolong life. Patients receive painkilling medication on a regularly scheduled basis, and they are also provided with antidepressive and anti-anxiety drugs should they be required. Most hospice programs also offer follow-up bereavement care for family members.

A presidential commission has proposed that decisions on whether to continue life-sustaining medical treatment be left to mentally competent patients. Family members would be permitted to make similar decisions for mentally incompetent patients. But the commission said that the ending of a patient's life intentionally could not be sanctioned on moral grounds. Even so, doctors would be allowed to administer a pain-relieving drug that hastens death, provided that the sole reason for giving the drug is to relieve the pain (Schmeck, 1983). A growing number of states, now numbering more than fifteen, have enacted "living will" laws that afford protection against dehumanized dying and confer immunity upon physicians and hospital personnel who comply with a patient's wishes.

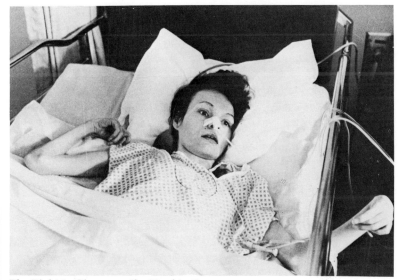

The Right to Die versus the Need to Care
Normally the law allows competent adults to decide whether or not to accept medical treatment. But there are a good many gray areas. In 1984 the case of Elizabeth Bouvia drew national attention to the question, "Under what circumstances does a person have the right to die with dignity by refusing medical treatment?" Bouvia, a 26-year-old quadriplegic almost totally paralyzed by cerebral palsy and suffering from severe arthritis, asked for a court injunction to block the hospital that was caring for her from force-feeding her. Not terminally ill but incapable of feeding herself and weary of fighting her handicap, she wanted to be allowed to starve herself to death, asserting, "I want control over my own body and destiny." But a California court denied her request. The judge held that the claim of a constitutional right to privacy was outweighed by the rights of society. Some doctors and nurses had feared that had the case been decided in Bouvia's favor, they would have been made accomplices to a suicide. *(AP/Wide World Photos)*

Stereotypes of the Elderly
Americans are increasingly being pulled between conflicting stereotypes of the elderly. On the one hand elderly people are portrayed as lonely and socially isolated. On the other, they are depicted as enjoying a life of leisure and affluence at the expense of hardworking younger generations. *(left, Elliott Erwitt/Magnum; right, Paul Fusco/Magnum)*

Fact: Only 12 people out of 1,000 in the 65 to 74 age group live in nursing homes. The figure rises to 59 for those 75 to 84, and to 237 for those over 85. Overall, only one American in five who is over 65 will ever be relegated to a nursing home (Rosenwaike and Logue, 1985).

- *Myth:* Many of the elderly are incapacitated and spend much of their time in bed because of illness.
  Fact: About 3 percent of the elderly who live at home are bedridden, 5 percent are seriously incapacitated, and another 11 to 16 percent are restricted in mobility. On the other hand, from one-half to three-fifths of the elderly function without any limitation (and 37 percent of those 85 and over report no incapacitating limitation on their activity) (Shanas, 1982).

- *Myth:* Most people over 65 find themselves in serious financial straits.
  Fact: Elderly people do not constitute a homogeneous mass. When people turn 65, nobody waves a magic wand that makes them all alike. Some are economically well off; others are not so well off; and still others fare poorly. Conventional wisdom depicts the elderly as living on fixed incomes in drab apartments and struggling for the necessities of life. Although 25 years ago the elderly were a disadvantaged group, much has changed. In 1967 some 30 percent of aged Americans lived in poverty—twice the rate of the general population. In 1985,

the poverty rate for the elderly was 12.6 percent, lower than the 14 percent for Americans overall. Today, 92 percent of Americans over 65 receive social security benefits (compared with 60 percent in 1965). Nearly three-quarters of elderly householders own their own homes, half of them without a mortgage (older Americans have substantial equity in their homes, averaging over $65,000, more than twice the equity of homeowners younger than age 35). On the whole, elderly Americans see themselves as faring better financially than do younger Americans.

- *Myth:* Most elderly people are "prisoners of fear" who are "under house arrest" by virtue of their fear of crime.
  Fact: Although 74 percent of the public view fear of crime as a major concern of people over 65, only 25 percent of the elderly agree (Harris, 1981). Meanwhile, crimes against the person, such as rape, robbery, and assault, occur at a rate of 30 per 1,000 to the elderly, less than the rate of 130 per 1,000 to the population as a whole. And the burglary rate for elderly households is 50 per 1,000, compared with 89 per 1,000 for all households (Russell, 1980).

- *Myth:* Most elderly people are lonely and isolated from their families and other meaningful social ties.
  Fact: A Harris poll (1981) found that although 65

percent of the public assume that most of the elderly are frequently lonely, only 13 percent of people 65 and over view loneliness as a serious problem. Moreover, about four of every five of the elderly have living children. Of this group, reputable surveys show that 85 percent live within an hour's travel of at least one child, 55 percent see their children every day or so, and another 26 percent see them about every week (Cupito, 1986; *Public Opinion*, December–January, 1986:36).

Dangers in stereotyping   By and large there is a considerable gap between the actual experiences of most older Americans and the circumstances attributed to them by others. Most of the elderly are resilient and very much alive, not a hopeless, inert mass teetering on the edge of senility and death. Generalizations that depict the elderly as an economically and socially deprived group may actually do them a disservice by tagging them with unfavorable social definitions and reflected appraisals. Such stereotypes allow younger people to separate themselves comfortably from older ones and to relegate the elderly to inferior status.

New stereotypes   The changing economic fortunes of the elderly are overhauling how Americans view them. The elderly are increasingly seen as "haves" while the young are the "have nots." Indeed, organizations of the retired worry lest old stereotypes are being replaced by new ones in which the elderly are portrayed as carefree, buoyant, and selfish consumers, sallying forth from Florida condominiums each morning to frolic on the golf course. Should the new images gain wide acceptance, they could be used to reduce social security retirement payments and Medicare health insurance benefits, the very programs that enabled many of the elderly to escape poverty. Altogether, the proportion of the federal budget aimed at the elderly rose from 16 percent in 1965 to 28 percent in 1986. Besides endangering existing benefits for the elderly, changed perceptions could also set generation against generation on other issues. Although it long has been accepted that there is no politics of age in the United States, uneasiness that age divisiveness may appear is increasing (see the box on page 300).

The elderly poor   Not all elderly Americans are faring well, and worst off are blacks and single or widowed women. The poverty rate for black women over 65 is 41.7 percent. Half of all women past 65 have incomes below or within $800 a year of the official poverty level.

Women live longer than men, and so they are more likely to exhaust savings and other resources. Their income disadvantage is also built into the system of retirement benefits. Retired men are more likely than women to receive maximum benefits and to be eligible for private pensions. So long as the husband lives, a couple can maintain a comfortable standard of living. But upon the husband's death, income from private pensions is typically terminated and social security benefits are reduced. For most widowed older women, their deceased husbands' social security check is their primary source of income. Additionally, their longer life expectancy means that older women are more likely than men to experience the debilitation of chronic illness in an era of high medical costs (Hess, 1985; Warlick, 1985). Overall, financial hardship among the aged is less a matter of growing old than a result of the factors that lead to low incomes at any age, primarily a person's work history and education. In large measure, postretirement benefits are pegged to preretirement earning levels. So in many cases, today's old-poor were yesterday's young-poor.

The Aging of the Aged

A steadily increasing percentage of Americans is living past 65, the long-accepted benchmark for entry into old age—what is commonly termed "the graying of America" (see Table 11.2). What is dramatically new is the second phase of the gerontological explosion: the aging of the aged. As science has learned to stave off heart disease, strokes, cancer, and other killers, more and more Americans are living into their eighties and nineties. In 1940, only 365,000 Americans were 85 or over, a mere 0.3 percent of the population. But now the number has zoomed to 2.5 million, 1.1 percent of all Americans. By the end of this century, the number will top 5.1 million, almost 2 percent of the population. Addition-

Table 11.2   The Graying of the United States

Year	Population 65 or older	Percentage of total population
1985	28.6 million	12.0%
1990	31.1 million	12.7%
2000	35.0 million	13.0%
2015	44.8 million	15.4%
2030	64.6 million	21.2%

Source: U.S. Bureau of the Census.

How Should Resources Be Allocated among Generations?

The issue of generational equity is wending its way into political discourse. The debate has to do with whether the generation currently in power is passing the bill for its gratifications to its successors. Indeed, many Americans are becoming increasingly concerned that as a nation we are mortgaging our children's and our children's children's futures. The national debt doubled in the first five years of the Reagan administration. Since 1973, yearly earnings for workers younger than 35 have declined 15 percent, adjusting for inflation. Younger families are finding it increasingly difficult to purchase their own homes. And the percentage of children who live below the poverty line has increased 50 percent since 1980 (Greenhouse, 1986).

Retirement programs are one area of controversy. Consider the social security system. It is a "pay-as-you-go" arrangement that depends on the continuing collection of taxes from the working to support the retired and disabled. In 1986 the system paid out more than $182 billion in benefits. If income to the system had stopped for any reason, benefits could have continued for only three months. As long as government can take money from one group of citizens and pass it along to another, no one needs to worry about receiving benefits. But a problem looms in the years ahead: About one-third of Americans are baby boomers. Most have now entered the workforce, and their taxes will swell the coffers of social security over the next thirty years. The baby boom generation is much larger than the generation following it. Currently there are about 3.4 working Americans to support each elderly retiree. But population projections show that there will be fewer than 2 by 2035. All the while, medical advances since 1960 have added five years to the average American's life expectancy and retirement. By the year 2008, based on current trends, the system is projected to pay out more than it takes in. Not surprisingly, many Americans have lost confidence in the social security system. A 1985 ABC/*Washington Post* poll (January 16, 1985) revealed that 64 percent of Americans aged 45 to 60 were confident that they would receive social security benefits. However, only 33 percent of those aged 18 to 30 were equally confident about their prospects.

It is often argued that social security, as currently constructed, is a mechanism for redistributing income from the younger to the older generation. The elderly who retired in the early years of social security had to pay the program's taxes for only a few years before retiring, and the initial taxes were low. The maximum annual social security tax, including both employer and employee shares, was $189 in 1958 and still only $348 in 1965. However, today's young workers must pay taxes of several thousand dollars a year for their entire working careers (Ferrar, 1984). Stanford University economist Michael J. Boskin (1986) estimates that, adjusted for inflation and investment potential, payroll taxes paid by a middle-income 25-year-old will exceed benefits by nearly $40,000. In contrast, today's 70-year-old retiree who had the same inflation-adjusted salary at age 25 would receive $20,000 more in benefits than he or she had paid in taxes.

One answer to the problems of the social security system has been later retirement. Legislation already passed raises the age for drawing full benefits to 66 beginning in 2009 and to 67 in 2027. Another is to raise payroll taxes. Some estimates project that in order to pay all the benefits promised to today's younger workers, social security payroll tax rates would have to be raised to at least 33 percent (perhaps even 40 percent), compared with 14 percent today. Given this state of affairs, some contend that the system should be financed from a national trust fund made up of government revenues and based on a percentage of the gross national product (Hess, 1985).

Many people do not realize that

ally, as reflected in Figure 11.4 on page 302, more than 100,000 Americans will be 100 or over, three times the present number.

Medical authorities say that, roughly speaking, 85 tends to be a turning point in life. After that, problems usually come faster. Although today's population 85 and older is healthier and more active than its predecessors, they nonetheless become increasingly likely to suffer from chronic illnesses and other disabilities that require care for longer and longer periods. From the population of the very old come most of the million or more Americans who are so disabled that they require round-the-clock care in nursing homes (whereas only 6.4 percent of 75- to 84-year-olds are in nursing homes, the figure rises to 23.7 percent for those 85 and over). There are another 2 million equally disabled who are not in institutions, and some 6 million others who need less intensive services. Among the most incapacitating chronic condi-

social security was never intended to provide for all their needs when they retire or are disabled. Pension planners typically view social security as one leg of a three-legged stool, with private pensions and savings providing the other two kinds of support. Critics of the system contend that most people could do much better if they were able to put their social security contributions into a private pension plan. But this argument fails to consider the disability and survivor's benefits that workers or their families may begin drawing at an early age. Moreover, economists say that it is not feasible to make social security voluntary. Some people would get out because they could get better investment returns and benefits elsewhere. The high-cost people would stay in, and the system would collapse. Overall, the nation is confronting the problem of how to allocate its resources among generations. But politicians have been reluctant to address issues associated with generational equity for fear of offending elderly voters.

THINKING THROUGH THE ISSUES

There is "the potential for real generational warfare in the next century," say Senator David Durenberger (R., Minn.), who heads Americans for Generational Equity, or AGE. AGE campaigns to reduce the federal budget deficit, overhaul social security, and spur savings and investment. Generations United is a coalition of groups (the National Council on the Aging and the Child Welfare League of America) promoting what it sees as the common interests of children, youths, families, and the elderly. Groups like Generations United believe generational warfare will not occur, and cite the following arguments (Otten, 1987):

- Polls consistently show that social security, Medicare, and Medicaid enjoy strong support in every age group.

- Young people appreciate the "debt" they owe older generations. Not only have older generations cared for them and educated them as youngsters, but many parents and grandparents are providing the down payments on homes and helping divorced daughters and sons who have young children to support.

- Young people realize that the elderly receiving government benefits are their own parents and grandparents, and that if the benefits are unavailable, the children might have to provide help directly.

- When the baby boom generation starts to retire, employers will face a shrinking workforce and will respond by offering flexible work hours and other inducements to keep many of their elderly workers.

How do you appraise each of these arguments? What do you make of the argument that, in the final analysis, the amount of intergenerational conflict will be determined primarily by the overall rate of economic growth?

tions are Alzheimer's disease and other forms of mental impairment. Other chronic problems that strike with increasing frequency and severity as people become very old include arthritis, heart conditions and hypertension, osteoporosis (brittleness of the bones), incontinence, depression, and problems with hearing and vision (Otten, 1984).

Despite the popular image of families dumping aged parents into nursing homes, surveys show that most infirm and disabled elderly are cared for by a spouse, child, or other relative. Generally, most families turn to a nursing home placement only as a last resort. Adult children usually find the decision excruciating, and they commonly experience high levels of ambivalence, shame, and guilt. Some nursing homes afford high-quality care, but they are often costly. And there are also those that are little more than warehouses for the elderly and dying—catacombs for the not-quite-living. Overall,

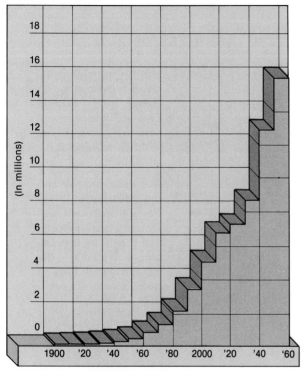

FIGURE 11.4   Population 85 Years and Over, 1900–2050
Source: U.S. Bureau of the Census.

staffing is a major problem in most nursing homes. Patients too often are overmedicated on the premise that "a quiet patient is a good patient." Complicating matters, government regulations have cast nursing homes in the role of miniature hospitals. The quality of life they provide is largely determined by bureaucratic requirements associated with Medicare and Medicaid and by state regulations mandating standards for licensing. The resulting organization emphasizes meeting medical needs but frequently at the expense of fostering psychological and economic dependency among the elderly. The hospital model has imposed a medical solution on a variety of *social* problems: Residents are defined as "patients," and their day-to-day activities are controlled by the staff.

Many of the difficulties confronting the nursing-home elderly are more social than medical. Some residents could be maintained independently in the community if our societal bias toward institutionalizing the old did not exist. They could be more economically cared for in their homes—with the help of visiting nurses and "meals-on-wheels" services. Another alternative is sheltered housing—a type of protected community arranged in apartment complexes or detached cottages—that provide supportive services such as meals, recreation, and health care. And for those living with relatives, day care centers could afford harried family members a chance to work or catch up on tasks (Vander Zanden, 1985).

Because aging is subject to social and medical interventions, it can be modified by changes in social and health care arrangements. This is not to say that human beings can expect to enjoy perpetual youth. But a mounting body of evidence demonstrates that the process of aging can be slowed, and functioning improved, by altering the social expectations and supports available to the elderly. Although life expectancy has increased to 70 years for men and 78 years for women, our societal role structures and opportunities have lagged (Haug, Ford, and Shaefor, 1985).

The Very Old

Our image of growing old may be worse than the reality. Researchers find that younger people worry far more than older people about aging and death. An international study of 13 countries, including the United States, found that people over 60 were far more content than young people. (Gundersen, 1987). *(James H. Karales/Peter Arnold)*

Chapter Highlights

1. All societies must deal with the life cycle that begins with conception and continues through old age and ultimately death. Upon the rich tapestry supplied by the biological age grid, people throughout history have woven varying social arrangements. Each society shapes the processes of human development in its own image, defining the phases and roles it recognizes as significant.

2. Societal demands often represent role-related tasks that are presented for us at particular phases of our lives. Age norms specify what constitutes appropriate and inappropriate behavior at various periods in the life span. A cultural timetable—a sort of societal Big Ben—defines the "best age" for a man or woman to finish school, settle on a career, marry, have children, hold a top job, become a grandparent, and retire. People also locate themselves across the life span in terms of life events.

3. Since society changes, the members of different cohorts age in different ways. And because people of different cohorts age in new ways, they contribute to changes in the social structure. Matters are complicated because individuals age and societies change at different tempos.

4. To one degree or another, all societies are divided into age strata. They are frequently the basis for structured social inequality. Functionalists point out that societies require ways for placing and motivating people in the social structure and that age strata serve this purpose. Conflict theorists see age strata as a vehicle to benefit some age groups at the expense of others.

5. A number of social scientists have undertaken a search for the critical periods and transitions in the life cycle. For instance, Erik Erikson depicts life as a succession of stages that resembles a sort of stairway made up of a series of discrete steplike levels. But some sociologists contend that stage theories overlook the vast differences that characterize the human experience.

6. Along with institutional racism and sexism, critics charge our society with institutional ageism. However, elderly people do not constitute a homogeneous mass. Although many older Americans fare quite well, this is not the case for many blacks and single or widowed women. Likewise, the circumstances of those over 85 are frequently difficult.

The Sociologist's Vocabulary

age cohort Persons born in the same time interval.

age norms Rules that specify what constitutes appropriate and inappropriate behavior for people at various periods of the life span.

age sets Groups of people of similar age and sex who move at prescribed intervals from one age grade to another.

age strata Social layers based on time periods in life; they serve as a basis for allocating roles and for drawing social divisions.

biological age The chronological time that elapses after birth and is associated with changes in the organism.

hospice A program or mode of care that attempts to make the dying experience less painful and emotionally traumatic for patients and their families.

human development The processes of sequential change that takes place over the life span, beginning with conception and ending with death.

institutional ageism The systematic negative stereotyping of and discrimination against people because they are old.

life events Turning points at which people change some direction in the course of their lives.

life review The taking stock of one's life that often occurs when people learn of their impending death.

puberty rites Initiation ceremonies that symbolize the transition from childhood to adulthood.

social age The placement of people in the social structure based upon socially differentiated phases of the life cycle.

social clock A set of internalized concepts that regulates our progression through the age-related milestones of the adult years.

12

Gender and Sexuality

What are little boys made of? What are little boys made of?
Frogs and snails and puppy dogs' tails,
that's what little boys are made of.
What are little girls made of? What are little girls made of?
Sugar and spice and all that is nice,
and that's what little girls are made of.

—J. O. Halliwell, *Nursery Rhymes of England*, 1844

As you go about your daily activities, you assume that every person you encounter is either a male or a female. When you come across someone whose gender identity is not obvious—perhaps someone wearing unisex clothes—you are puzzled. You scrutinize the person for gender cues that will "tell" you what the person "really" is. But what cues do you and others use? If you ask people how they tell men from women, you will find that most of them answer in terms of a person's sexual characteristics. Yet in most of our day-to-day dealings with others, we rarely see the genitals of those we "know" to be male or female.

That there are two sexes—male and female—seems to be a "fact" of life. Indeed, most Americans accept the following "facts" about gender (Garfinkel, 1967:122–128):

1. There are two, and only two, genders [female or male].

2. One's gender is invariant. [If you are female/male, you always *were* female/male and you always *will be* female/male.]

3. Genitals are the essential sign of gender. [A female is a person with a vagina; a male is a person with a penis.]

4. Any exceptions to two genders are not to be taken seriously. [They must be jokes.]

5. There are no transfers from one gender to another except ceremonial ones [masquerades].

6. Everyone must be classified as a member of one gender or another. [There are no cases where gender is not imputed to a person.]

7. The male/female dichotomy is a "natural" one. [Males and females exist independently of scientists', or anyone else's, criteria for being male or female.]

8. Membership in one or the other gender is "natural." [Being female or male is not dependent on someone's deciding that you are male or female.]

Yet these "facts" do not necessarily hold (Kessler and McKenna, 1978). Transsexuals provide one type of disconfirming evidence and give us insight as to how we go about *constructing* a world of gender in our everyday interactions. **Transsexuals** are people who have normal sexual organs but who psychologically feel like members of the opposite sex. The writer James Morris, who became Jan Morris (1974) after a sex-change operation, put it in these terms: "I was born with the wrong body, being feminine by gender but male by sex, and I could achieve completeness only when the one was adjusted to the other." Transsexuals do not just want to dress like the opposite sex. Male transsexuals reject their penises; women transsexuals loathe their breasts. Like homosexuals, transsexuals have a sexual preference for individuals of the same sex as themselves. But *unlike* homosexuals, they redefine themselves as members of the opposite sex. So having sex with a man is not seen by a transsexual as "homosexuality" because he is, in his self-view, a woman.

Although transsexuals take their own gender for granted, they cannot assume that other people will do likewise. They must "manage" themselves as "males" or "females" so that others will attribute the "correct" gender to them. Transsexuals make obvious what nontranssexuals do "naturally." For instance, in order to carry off their masquerade—to "pass" in everyday activities, use the women's restroom, work undetected as a woman, and take a male lover—requires countless stratagems. So transsexuals have to learn gender-specific speech skills—to talk like a "man" or a "woman" and use a "masculine" or "feminine" vocabulary. They must affect masculine or feminine mannerisms that go beyond merely dressing as a male or female (for example, wearing padding, a scarf, and gloves to camouflage broad shoulders, an Adam's apple, and large hands). Those who have not had surgery must manage so that others do not see them undressed (genital surgery is often sufficiently successful that most people are unlikely to question the authenticity of transsexuals' genitals). Finally, transsexuals must create the impression that they have always had the gender to which they lay claim.

Research with transsexuals highlights for us how we use various "gender markers" in making day-to-day gender attributions. People need not have the physical anatomy of a male or female for us to treat them as a man or a woman. Clothes and other devices can conceal irregularities. To be a "man" or a "woman" requires only that a person be competent in the use of interpretive skills and in presenting himself or herself convincingly to others. If this conclusion applies to fundamental, anatomically based characteristics, such as one's sex, think how much easier it is to pass oneself off as the occupant of an even more ambiguous status!

In the previous chapters we saw how skin color and age frequently become the focus for social differentiation and inequality. So does gender (Walker and Fennell, 1986). The social experience is different for men and for women. Social relations across the life course are structured along gender lines. For example, kin relations are not simply relationships involving parents, grandparents, children, siblings, and other relatives. The relationships are typically gender-specific, having to do with mothers, fathers, sons, daughters, sisters, brothers, nieces, nephews, grandsons, granddaughters. And the gender roles defined by a society have profound consequences for us: They provide master statuses that carry primary weight in our interactions and relationships with others.

Gender roles place us in the social structure, establishing where and what we are in social terms. They lay the framework within which we gain our identities, formulate our goals, and carry out our training. Additionally, gender roles are a major source of social inequality. Just as our society structures inequalities based on race, ethnicity, and age, so it institutionalizes inequalities based on **gender**—the social creation of girls, boys, women, and men (Berg, 1987).

PLANNING AHEAD: TARGETED READING

1. In what ways is gender a socially constructed reality?

2. Sociologically speaking, do women meet the criteria of a minority group?

3. What gender inequalities do women encounter in American life?

4. How is rape linked to the social system?

5. What have been the contributions of the women's movement to the equality of the sexes?

6. How is sexual behavior filtered through a social screen that defines its meaning and significance?

Gender Roles

It seems that all societies have used the anatomical differences between men and women to assign **gender roles**—sets of cultural expectations that define the ways in which the members of each sex should behave. Gender roles represent the earliest division of labor among human beings. We all are born into societies with well-established cultural guidelines for the behavior of men and of women.

Gender Roles and Culture

Cross-cultural evidence reveals that men and women are capable of great behavioral variety. As reflected in Table 12.1 on page 308, a survey of 244 societies reveals the sharp differences in the allocation of duties by gender (Murdock, 1935). For generations, American communities have had laws restricting the weights that a working woman is permitted to lift. Women have been excluded from many jobs because the men who control the jobs define women as "stupid," "delicate," and "emotional." Yet among the Arapesh of New Guinea, it was the women who were assigned the task of carrying heavy loads because their heads were believed to be harder and stronger than those of men. Among the Tasmanians of the South Pacific, the most dangerous type of hunting—swimming out to remote rocks in the sea to stalk and club sea otters—was assigned to women. Women formed the bodyguard of Dahomeyan kings because they were thought to be particularly fierce fighters. And although most peoples believe that it is the men who should take the initiative in sexual matters, among the Maoris and the Trobriand Islanders, this responsibility falls to women (Ford and Beach, 1951).

Cultural variation in the gender roles of men and women points to a social foundation for most of these differences. So do the changes observed from one time to another in sex-linked behavior patterns within the same society. Not too long ago in Western history, the dashing cavalier wore long curls and perfume; he had a rapier and a stallion; and he also wore powder and lace and soft leather boots that revealed a well-turned calf. In the 1950s, men who wore long hair were labeled "sissies" and "queers." By the 1970s, long hair came into style. Today, more intermediate hair styles are in vogue. All

Table 12.1   The Division of Labor by Sex in 244 Societies

Activity	Number of Societies and Sex of Person by Whom Activity Is Performed				
	Men Always	Men Usually	Either Sex	Women Usually	Women Always
Hunting	166	13	0	0	0
Trapping small animals	128	13	4	1	2
Herding	38	8	4	0	5
Fishing	98	34	19	3	4
Clearing agricultural land	73	22	17	5	13
Dairy operations	17	4	3	1	13
Preparing and planting soil	31	23	33	20	37
Erecting and dismantling shelter	14	2	5	6	22
Tending and harvesting crops	10	15	35	39	44
Bearing burdens	12	6	35	20	57
Cooking	5	1	9	28	158
Metalworking	78	0	0	0	0
Boat building	91	4	4	0	1
Working in stone	68	3	2	0	2
Basket making	25	3	10	6	82
Weaving	19	2	2	6	67
Manufacturing and repairing of clothing	12	3	8	9	95

Source: Adapted from George P. Murdock, "Comparative Data on the Division of Labor by Sex," *Social Forces* (1935), 15:551–553.

this suggests that gender roles are largely a matter of social definition and socially constructed meanings.

Not surprisingly, when given only a person's gender label, we attribute a good many gender-related characteristics to the person (Deaux and Lewis, 1984; McCann et al., 1985). Americans have traditionally stereotyped men and women as polar opposites: Men are dominant, independent, competitive, self-confident, aggressive, and logical; women are submissive, dependent, emotional, conforming, affectionate, and nurturant. These stereotypes have proved remarkably resilent across the past several decades (Skrypnek and Snyder, 1982). They

Cultural Norms Dictate Masculine and Feminine Patterns
The dominant American culture defines the masculine and feminine way for carrying books: Men carry books at the side, the arm extended downward; women carry books against the chest or against the side with the arm bent at a right angle. *(Dan McCoy/Rainbow)*

Cultural Variations in Gender Roles
Americans typically accept the notion that men are "naturally" stronger than women and so are the ones who should do the hard physical work. But definitions of what constitutes "men's" and "women's" work differ from culture to culture. In many societies, women are the ones who are assigned the task of carrying heavy burdens, including Fulani women of Mali (top left), lower caste Hindu women in India (top right), and Haitian women (right). *(clockwise from top left: Richard Wood/The Picture Cube; Kent Reno/Jeroboam; Burt Clinn/Magnum)*

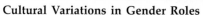

reflect the division of labor and social structure in our society. They mirror social patterns in which men garner the more prestigious, higher-paying, and responsible positions and women bear primary responsibility for child care and domestic chores (Eagly and Steffen, 1984).

It is often easier for society to allow women to occupy new roles than to allow them a new style in performing these roles. A woman can become a college professor, a corporate executive, a surgeon, or a tennis player, but "she should still act like a woman" (Spradley and Mann, 1975). When men and women use stereotyped beliefs as guides for relating to one another, they restrict each other's behavioral options in ways that gen-

erate traditional gender behaviors. For example, women dress more traditionally for job interviews when they expect to be interviewed by a male holding traditional views of women than they do when they believe the interviewer does not hold such views (von Baeyer, Sherk, and Zanna, 1981; Skrypnek and Snyder, 1982). Gender, then, is a social fact constraining our behavior.

Gender Roles and Biology

Until about 35 years ago, scientists did not use the term *gender;* they spoke of *sex.* The underlying assumption was that our gonads determine our *true sex* and identity. It is of course indisputable that men and women differ physically: Women have the capacity to menstruate, carry a fetus until delivery, and provide it with milk after birth; men have the ability to produce and transmit sperm. But beyond these matters, the role biology plays in producing identity and behavioral differences between men and women is shrouded in controversy. Consider the matter of **hermaphrodites,** individuals whose reproductive structures are sufficiently ambiguous that it is difficult to define them exclusively as male or female. This condition arises when the developmental process goes awry in the embryo (Money and Tucker, 1975; Ehrhardt and Meyer-Bahlberg, 1981; Ehrhardt, 1985).

Researchers at the Johns Hopkins Medical Center find that social definitions play a crucial part in influencing the gender identities of hermaphrodites. **Gender identities** are the conceptions we have of ourselves as being male or female. Consider that at birth a child will be classed as a boy or girl, and a whole series of environmental forces then come into play (Money and Tucker, 1975:86–89):

> The label "boy" or "girl" . . . has tremendous force as a self-fulfilling prophecy, for it throws the full weight of society to one side or other as the newborn heads for the gender fork [in the road], and the most decisive sex turning point of all. . . . [At birth you were limited to] something that was ready to become your gender identity. You were wired but not programmed for gender in the same sense that you were wired but not programmed for language.

Some researchers suggest that the human embryo has a bisexual potential: It seems that biological factors do not themselves produce differences in male or female behavior, but affect the threshold for eliciting such behavior. Hormonal differences may "ready" a person for one kind of gender behavior or another. Even so, hormones do not dictate that the behavior be learned. Rather, hormones make it easier for a person to learn certain gender-related behaviors. And these behaviors are constantly being shaped and modified by the environment (Money and Tucker, 1975; Scarf, 1976; Imperato-McGinley et al., 1981).

Intense debate currently surrounds questions regarding the "essential" or "basic" nature of men and women. Aggression—physical or verbal behavior that is intended to hurt someone—is a case in point. In her well-publicized review of research, psychologist Eleanor E. Maccoby (1980:216) concluded: "The tendency of males to be more aggressive than females is perhaps the most firmly established sex difference and is a characteristic that transcends culture." But psychologist Todd Tieger (1980), on the basis of his independent survey of the literature, says that such differences become observable in children's spontaneous behavior only at around 5 years of age. During these early years, adults encourage boys to display aggression, whereas girls are pressured to inhibit it. Commenting on Tieger's review, Maccoby acknowledges that aggressiveness is less a trait of individuals than it is behavior that characterizes people in certain situations (Maccoby and Jacklin, 1980). Moreover, when differences are found between men and women in aggression, they usually are not large (Hyde, 1984). So women, like men, can be expected to be aggressive when the norms support aggression, and inhibit it in domains when it is barred by the norms (Perry, Perry, and Rasmussen, 1986). Overall, the variations within each sex far exceed the differences between the sexes. It is little wonder that when asked whether man or woman is more intelligent, the English scholar and poet Samuel Johnson replied: "Which man? Which woman?"

Even in many demanding physical tasks, the overlap between men and women is considerable. Tiffany Cohen's winning time in the 1984 women's Olympic 400-meter freestyle swim was 5 seconds faster than the 1964 men's winner. And the winner of the 1932 men's Olympic marathon held in Los Angeles would have finished tenth in the 1984 women's Olympic marathon in the same city. It seems that there is little that is inherently either male or female, although our cultural definitions often make it appear so. What nature initiates, culture accentuates.

THINKING THROUGH THE ISSUES

Does the idea that biological factors may contribute to gender differences threaten the ideal that men and women should enjoy social equality? The subjugation and oppression of women has long been supported by notions that men and women are naturally different. However, does social equality require biological sameness? If there are to be equal educational and job opportunities in a society, must all the citizens be alike? What implications does your answer have for such social positions as priest, minister, and rabbi? Are biological differences necessarily deficits or deficiencies? Identify some ways in which men differ from one another, such as in height, weight, and muscular build. Have these differ-

Aggression: A Gender Behavior?
Although scientists continue to debate whether or not aggression is a sex difference that transcends culture, sociologists find considerable evidence that our society encourages boys to display aggression and girls to inhibit it. *(Barbara Laing/Picture Group)*

ences been institutionalized so that large categories of men are systematically barred (regardless of their other talents) from a great many job and educational opportunities? How may minor biological differences trigger major social differences? In what ways has this happened in the realm of gender differences? What part do our social definitions have in elevating biological differences to social significance?

Acquiring Gender Identities

Although we come into the world with the biological equipment of a male or female, our physical organs do not assure us of a sense of "maleness" or "femaleness." Our gender identities are invisible, something that cannot be established by appearance. For most people, there is a good fit between anatomy and gender identity. Boys generally come to behave in ways that their culture labels "masculine," and girls learn to be "feminine." Learning plays a key part in the acquisition of our gender identities. However, the exact nature of this learning has been the subject of considerable debate.

Identification theory   According to Sigmund Freud and his followers, the adoption of gender identities and sex-typed behaviors are the result of an *Oedipus conflict* that emerges between the ages of 3 and 6. During this period, children discover the genital differences between the sexes. According to Freudians, this discovery prompts children to see themselves as rivals of their same-sex parent for the affection of the parent of the opposite sex. Such desires and feelings give rise to considerable anxiety. This anxiety is resolved through complicated psychological maneuvers in which children come to identify with the same-sex parent. By virtue of this identification, boys acquire masculine self-conceptions and girls learn feminine self-conceptions. However, research that has tried to test Freud's theory has been either inconclusive or at odds with it. Additionally, cross-cultural research suggests that the Oedipus conflict does not occur among all peoples, including the Trobriand Islanders of the South Pacific (Malinowski, 1929).

Cultural transmission theory   Unlike Freud and his followers, *cultural transmission* theorists contend that the acquisition of gender identities and behaviors is not the product of an Oedipus conflict, but rather is a gradual process of learning (Bandura, 1971, 1973; Bussey and Bandura, 1984). They suggest that parents, teachers, and other adults shape a child's behavior by reinforcing responses that are deemed appropriate to the child's gender role and discouraging inappropriate ones (see Chapter 6). Moreover, children are motivated to attend to, learn from, and imitate same-sex models because they think of same-sex models as more like themselves (Mischel, 1970). Children are cued to gender roles in a great variety of ways. Parents often furnish boys' and girls' rooms differently, decorating those of boys with animal motifs and those of girls with floral motifs, lace, fringe, and ruffles (Rheingold and Cook, 1975). The toys found in the rooms also differ. Boys are provided with more vehicles, military toys, sports equipment, toy animals, and mechanical toys; girls, more dolls, doll houses, and domestic toys. Moreover, fathers are rougher with their infant sons and play more active, physical games with them than they do with their daughters. And they encourage their daughters but not their sons to ask for "help" (Huston, 1983).

Labeling and self-socialization theory   Cultural transmission theory draws our attention to the part that socialization plays in fashioning the sex-typed behavior of children. However, the image we gain from the theory is one of essentially passive individuals who are programmed for behavior by adult bearers of culture. *Labeling theory* (also called cognitive-developmental theory) provides a corrective by calling our attention to the fact that children actively seek to acquire gender identities and roles (see Chapter 5).

Acquiring a Gender Identity

Apparently children construct an image of maleness and femaleness and then cultivate the behavior appropriate to their gender. Fathers tend to be more concerned than mothers over their children's development of culturally appropriate gender roles. They treat their sons differently from their daughters. For instance, whereas fathers give trucks and dolls with equal frequency to their daughters, most fathers withhold dolls from their sons (Vander Zanden, 1985).

(James Holland/Stock, Boston)

According to Lawrence Kohlberg (1966, 1969; Kohlberg and Ullian, 1973), children come to label themselves as "boys" or "girls" when they are between 18 months and 3 years of age. Once they have identified themselves as males or females, they then want to adopt the behaviors consistent with their newly discovered status. This process is termed *self-socialization*. According to Kohlberg, children form a stereotyped conception of maleness and femaleness—an oversimplified, exaggerated, cartoonlike image revolving about such highly visible traits as hair style, dress, stature, and occupation. Just as children growing up in a bilingual environment are presented with two languages, so children are presented with two gender scripts or schemes (Money and Ehrhardt, 1972). They then use their stereotyped images of maleness and femaleness in organizing their behavior and cultivating the attitudes and actions associated with being a boy or a girl. For example, once girls of about $2\frac{1}{2}$ years of age become aware that boys and girls belong to different categories, they begin to modify their behavior to conform to feminine gender expectations. They become less aggressive, while boys of comparable age are more likely to become more aggressive (Fagot, Leinbach, and Hagan, 1986).

Both the cultural transmission and labeling theories of gender-role learning have received research support (Maccoby and Jacklin, 1974). Children may construct a gender scheme for maleness and femaleness, much in the manner suggested by labeling theorists. The content—the attitudes and behaviors deemed appropriate for males and females—is then provided by cultural transmission. So over time, children gain a conception of what it means to be male or female, compare themselves to their gender scheme, and adjust their behavior accordingly (Bem, 1985).

THINKING THROUGH THE ISSUES

Is masculine behavior the cultural ideal in American society? In attempting to move toward a society where gender roles assume less importance, are men encouraged to "act like women," or are women encouraged to "act like men"? For example, insofar as clothing symbolizes relationships between the sexes, have men accepted female clothing to the same extent as women have accepted male clothing? Why is it often necessary that working women wear a dark tailored suit, along with a silk bow or colorful scarf that says

"I'm feminine underneath"? Girls are increasingly being treated like boys and given the same opportunities for participation in athletic events, Little League activities, and the like. But are boys socialized in the ways girls traditionally have been socialized? Are boys encouraged to develop socially positive qualities such as tenderness, sensitivity to feelings, nurturance, cooperativeness, and esthetic appreciation? What do you think might be the consequences for the level of violence in American society if males were socialized to subscribe to the same standards of behavior as those traditionally encouraged for women (Eron, 1980)?

Institutional Sexism

Throughout human history men and women have differed in their access to privilege, prestige, and power. The distribution problem of who gets what, when, and how has traditionally been answered in favor of males, giving rise to gender stratification. Even today, despite the breakdown of many discriminatory barriers in American life, old patterns persist. Although women have gained some positions of power, these tend to be the exception, as evidenced by newspaper accounts that note "she is the only female" or "she is the first woman." The term **institutional sexism** is applied to those social arrangements and enduring patterns by which members of one gender group realize more benefits and fewer burdens than members of the other gender group. Noting that sexist practices pervade America's social fabric, sociologist Jessie Bernard observes:

> [Sexism is] the unconscious, taken-for-granted, assumed, unquestioned, unexamined, unchallenged acceptance of the belief that the world as it looks to men is the only world, that the way of dealing with it which men have created is the only way, that the values which men have evolved are the only ones, that the way sex looks to men is the only way it can look to anyone, that what men think about what women are like is the only way to think about what women are like. [Quoted in Gornick and Moran, 1971:xxv]

Until relatively recently, most Americans did not recognize women as being a subordinate group. For the most part, women have not resided in ghettos, although this is increasingly becoming the fate of black women who are single parents. And even though prestigious Ivy League institutions and medical, engineering, law, and business schools traditionally catered to male students, women have not been segregated in inferior schools. Moreover, they freely interact with—even live with—men, the presumed dominant group. How then can they be viewed as a minority? Let us return to the five properties of a minority group we considered in Chapter 10:

1. Historically, women have encountered *prejudice and discrimination*.

2. Women possess *physical and cultural traits* that distinguish them from men, the dominant group.

3. Through the efforts of the women's liberation movement and consciousness-raising groups, women have increasingly become a *self-conscious social group* characterized by an awareness of oneness.

4. *Membership is involuntary*, since gender is an ascribed status assigned to a person at birth.

5. Only the fifth characteristic does not apply to women, since *endogamy* (in-group marriage) is not the rule.

It is clear that women and racial and ethnic minorities have many characteristics in common.

Perspectives on Gender Stratification

The functionalist and conflict perspectives offer interpretations of gender stratification that resemble and parallel their positions on class, racial/ethnic, and age stratification. Each line of thought has drawn our attention to important aspects of gender behavior, and allowed sociologists to acquire increasingly sophisticated insights.

The functionalist perspective Functionalists suggest that a division of labor originally arose between men and women because of the woman's role in reproduction. By virtue of the fact that women were often pregnant or nursing, preindustrial societies assigned domestic and childrearing tasks to them. In contrast, by virtue of their larger size and greater muscular strength, men were assigned hunting and defense tasks. Functionalists contend that a gender division of labor promoted the survival of the species and hence has been retained.

Sociologists Talcott Parsons and Robert Bales (1955) have built upon principles of small group research

The Door Ceremony

Many Americans say that acts of chivalry, such as holding open a door for a woman or pulling out a chair for her, are acts of respect. But sociologist Laurel Walum Richardson suggests a different explanation based on her field experiments in which teams of students violated the rules of the "door ceremony." The researchers found that men have considerable difficulty entering a door in front of a woman. Richardson says the hand that holds the doorknob controls the situation; it is a sign of power and authority. So men feel threatened when they are deprived of their "possession" of the door, a symbolic expression of social dominance. *(Stacey Pleasant/Random House)*

in refining the functionalist position. They argue that two types of leaders are essential if a small group is to function effectively (see Chapter 5). *Instrumental leaders* (task specialists) devote their attention to appraising the problem at hand and organizing people's activity in dealing with it. *Expressive leaders* (social-emotional specialists) focus on overcoming interpersonal problems in the group, defusing tensions, and promoting solidarity. Parsons and Bales suggest that families are also organized along instrumental-expressive lines. Men specialize in instrumental tasks (particularly roles that are associated with deriving a livelihood) and women in expressive tasks (nurturing and comforting roles that allegedly are an extension of their reproductive and nursing functions).

The conflict perspective   Conflict theorists reject functionalist arguments as offering a rationale for male dominance. They contend that a sexual division of labor is a social vehicle devised by men to assure themselves of privilege, prestige, and power in their relationships with women. By relegating women to the home, men have been able to deny women the resources they need to succeed in the larger world. More particularly, conflict theorists have advanced a number of explanations for gender stratification (Collins, 1975; Vogel, 1983). Some argue that the motivation for gender stratification derives from the economic exploitation of women's labor. Others say it derives from men's desire for sexual gratification; men appropriate and guard rights of sexual access in the same way as advantaged social classes do rights to use economic property (Engels, 1884). Still others emphasize that the appropriation of women is not for sexual gratification but for procreation, especially to produce males heirs and daughters who can be used as exchanges in cementing political and economic alliances with other families.

A number of social scientists find a relationship between the social power and freedom women enjoy and the extent to which they contribute to economic production *and* control economic resources. Among hunters-and-gatherers and horticulturalists, women typically have greater power where they *both* contribute to subsistence and have opportunities to distribute and exchange valued goods and services (Friedl, 1984; Chafetz, 1984; Warner, Lee, and Lee, 1986). For instance, among the horticultural Bemba of Zambia, women play a vital role in raising crops and collecting and distributing the food. Power, privilege, and opportunities for autonomy and self-esteem are relatively balanced between Bemba men and women. But it is otherwise among the Inuit peoples (Eskimos) of Alaska, where women contribute negligible amounts to the food supply and depend on men for the basic resources (Friedl, 1984).

It also seems that where kin groups and marital residence are organized around women, women have somewhat higher status. For example, among the Iroquois Indians, women held considerable authority within and beyond the household. Related women lived together in longhouses with husbands who belonged to other kin groups. In the longhouse, women could insist that objectionable men leave, and they controlled the allocation of the food they produced. However, when we survey the world, we find such variability in economic patterns that it is difficult to establish any definite association between the contribution women make to subsistence and their overall status (Whyte, 1978; Leacock and Safa, 1986).

Gender Inequalities

As Table 12.2 shows, sociologists David B. Sugarman and Murray A. Straus have recently ranked the states in terms of gender equality. They indexed 29 categories, including the proportion of women in professional and managerial posts and in political and judicial offices, and state legislation protecting women's rights. With a score of 100 reflecting full equality, Oregon ranked highest with a score of 59.9 and Mississippi lowest with a score of 19.2.

Table 12.2   Rating the States: Women's Equality with Men

Top 10 States		Bottom 10 States	
Oregon	59.9	North Dakota	34.1
Michigan	56.1	Wyoming	33.5
Alaska	55.5	Oklahoma	32.7
Maine	54.7	Louisiana	31.2
Maryland	53.9	Texas	30.5
Minnesota	52.5	Vermont	29.7
California	51.8	Arkansas	27.6
Connecticut	51.6	South Carolina	24.0
Hawaii	51.3	Alabama	20.1
Massachusetts	50.6	Mississippi	19.2

Note: Full equality = 100.

Source: Newsweek, October 6, 1986, p. 4.

The domestic sphere   Historically, patterns of sexual inequality have been sustained by assigning the economic-provider role to men and the child-rearing role to women. The division between the public and domestic spheres has been a compelling one. Labor in the public sphere has been rewarded by money, prestige, and power; labor in the domestic sphere has been typically isolated and undervalued. Surveys of occupational ratings show considerable complexities in evaluations of the domestic role. Overall, the public ranks homemaking on a par with skilled clerical work; only women with jobs in the professions, the arts, and management are assigned higher prestige (Nilson, 1978).

The gender division of labor has operated to bind women to their reproductive function. Until the past decade or so, motherhood has been central to American definitions of the female role. Each woman has been expected to raise one man's children in an individual household viewed as private property and private space. A man typically thought he "owned" a woman's sexuality. A woman was viewed as exchanging sexual and domestic services for financial support. Within this arrangement, a sexual double standard prevailed which permitted men considerable sexual freedom and adventure not permitted to women. Until the twentieth century, English and American common law viewed women as committing "civil death" upon marriage. Wives lost their legal identity and, in the eyes of the law, became "incorporated and consolidated" with their husbands. A wife could not own property in her own right or sign a contract. A husband could require his wife to submit to sexual intercourse against her will and to live wherever he chose.

Although American men, particularly younger men, are shifting their views on doing housework, the burden still falls primarily upon women (Juster, 1985). There is a striking gap between men's intentions and actions when it comes to housework and caring for children. One study finds that husbands of women with full-time jobs spend 57 minutes doing housework each weekday. This is not much more than the 48 minutes of housework done by the husbands of women who work part-time, and the 43 minutes of housework done each day by the husbands of full-time homemakers (Michelson, 1985). Overall, men today are not doing appreciably more in the home; rather, women are doing less. If a married woman is employed outside the home, she spends 7 to 21 fewer hours a week doing housework than a married woman who is not (Jordan, 1985). With fewer "diligent cleaners" today and more women prepared to cut corners and purchase TV dinners, the total time women spend on housework decreases, and their husbands' proportional share goes up (Russell, 1985; Pleck, 1985). Still, as women are taking jobs outside the home, they are setting in motion changes in the household division of labor. In turn, these changes undermine the traditional norms and values that have historically governed the behavior of men (Ross, 1987).

The workplace   At the turn of the century, less than 20 percent of women worked outside the home (Silk, 1987). Over the past several decades, the employment picture has changed appreciably. In 1960, some 35 percent of American women were working outside the home. Today the figure is 55 percent (the percentage of men is 76 percent). Women hold 44 percent of all available jobs, and since 1980, they have taken 80 percent of the new jobs created in the economy (Hacker, 1986). Less than 11 percent of women today are the stereotyped "housewife"—a married woman, not in the labor force, with children at home. Indeed, most women prefer to work. A 1986 Gallup Poll found that 71 percent of the at-home mothers said they would like to work. And some 75 percent of working mothers said they would work even if they did not need the money (Kantrowitz, 1986).

Despite these changes, many of the current figures on the employment of women bear a striking resemblance to those of previous decades. Overall, there has been little substantial change in the gender segregation of occupations since 1900 (Scott, 1982; Reskin and Hartmann, 1986). Between 1970 and 1985, some 290,000 more women found employment in the fields of law, medicine, journalism, and higher education. An additional 220,000 women became police officers, bartenders, typesetters, and telephone installers. Yet against the gain of 510,000 women in fields hitherto the domain of men, 3.3 million women joined the workforce as secretaries, nurses, bookkeepers, and cashiers, augmenting the occupations in which women have predominated (Hacker, 1986). As Table 12.3 shows, women fill more than 90 percent of all secretarial, bookkeeping, and receptionist positions. And although women constitute 71 percent of the nation's classroom teachers, they account for less than 2 percent of school district superintendents.

Women also earn less than men. In 1985 a woman working full time earned 65 cents for each dollar earned by her male counterpart. Earnings in traditional "female" jobs and professions are substantially lower than those in comparable male-dominated occupations. A decade ago, sociologists David L. Featherman and Rob-

ert M. Hauser (1978) calculated that discrimination in one form or another accounts for 84 percent of the earnings gap between men and women. More recently, economist Barbara R. Bergmann (1987) has calculated that discrimination accounts for about half of the wage gap; differences in experience, training, and related factors account for the other half. Significantly, the earnings of a woman with four years of college are only 65 percent of those of a man with equal education. As Figure 12.1 shows, the earnings of contemporary women

---

Changing Gender Patterns?
Many Americans point to the admission of women to traditional male jobs as evidence that gender is now of little significance in the world of work. Yet despite recent changes, many of the current figures on the employment of women in American industry are quite similar to those of previous decades. Although the proportion of women in the labor force has greatly increased, there has been little substantial change in the sex labeling or sex segregation of occupations since 1900. Even so, we should not overlook the social significance of the breakdown in traditional occupational patterns that has taken place in recent years. *(Theodore Vogel/Rapho/Photo Researchers)*

Table 12.3   Sexism in the Labor Force, 1982

Occupation	Percent Women	Median Income*	Occupation	Percent Men	Median Income*
Secretaries	99.2%	$12,636	RR switch operators	100%	$22,828
Receptionists	97.5	$10,764	Firefighters	99.5	$20,438
Typists	96.6	$11,804	Plumbers, pipefitters	99.2	$21,944
Registered nurses	95.6	$18,980	Auto mechanics	99.1	$15,964
Sewers, stitchers	95.5	$8,632	Carpet installers	98.8	$15,392
Keypunch operators	94.5	$12,480	Surveyors	98.5	$17,472
Bank tellers	92.0	$10,348	Truckdrivers	97.9	$17,160
Telephone operators	91.9	$13,988	Garbage collectors	97.3	$12,116

*For full-time workers.

Source: U.S. Bureau of Labor Statistics, 1984.

still seem to be determined by the Old Testament rule, as stated in Leviticus 27:3–4: "A male between 20 and 60 years old shall be valued at 50 silver shekels. . . . If it is a female, she shall be valued at 30 shekels."

Overall, the career patterns of women are quite different from those of men. More than one humorist has observed, "It's all right for both husband and wife to work, but only until one or the other gets pregnant." The median annual earnings for full-time, year-round workers who are female and married are 60 percent of those of married men. When we compare single women with single men, however, the ratio rises to 90 percent—a much smaller difference in earnings. Similarly, single men working full-time earn 62 percent as much as married men. It may be that family responsibilities make a man all the more eager to maximize his earning potential. But by the same token, a man with a wife to bear the greater share of their child care and domestic responsibilities has more time to devote to his job, and the flexibility to adopt uncertain schedules and change job loca-

FIGURE 12.1   **Men and Women: Same Job; Different Pay, 1985**
Source: U.S. Bureau of Labor Statistics.

Profession	Average weekly pay		Percentage of mens' salary paid to women for performing same job
	Men	Women	
Managers	$670	$421	62.8%
Accountants/auditors	$507	$356	70.2%
Engineers	$628	$554	88.2%
Reg. nurses	$445	$408	89.7%
Teachers	$456	$372	81.6%
Lawyers	$753	$504	67.0%
Real estate	$506	$307	60.7%
Cashiers	$203	$167	82.3%
Secretaries	$356	$258	72.5%
Police	$408	$355	87%
Food service	$213	$155	72.8%
Machine operators	$331	$208	62.8%

tions, thus increasing his earning power (Gwartney, 1987).

Given our contemporary family and work arrangements, the economic advancement of women is complicated by the social organization of child care (Van Velsor and O'Rand, 1984). A number of economists point out that women who have children encounter a substantial career disadvantage (Thurow, 1981; Hewlett, 1986a, 1986b; Fuchs, 1986). The years between 25 and 35 are especially critical in the development of a career. During this period of life, lawyers and accountants become partners in the top firms; business managers make it onto the fast track; college professors secure tenure at good universities; and blue-collar workers find positions that generate high earnings and seniority. Yet it is these years when women are most likely to leave the labor force to have children. When they do, they suffer in their ability to acquire critical skills and to achieve promotions. Even when new mothers return to work within a few months, men typically conclude that they are no longer free to take on time-consuming tasks, and the women are passed over for promotion (Fraker, 1984). Not surprisingly, when economist David E. Bloom (1986) compared women managers with similar educational backgrounds, he found that those with children made about 20 percent less than those who remained childless. Additionally, responsibility for children often affects the choice of a job; women accept lower wages in exchange for shorter or more flexible hours, a location near home, and limited travel.

Only 2 percent of the nation's 1,362 top executives are women, and just one woman, Katharine Graham of the Washington Post Company, heads a Fortune 500 company (Graham acknowledges that she got the job because her family owns a controlling share of the corporation). A *Wall Street Journal* supplement on corporate women cited the biggest obstacle to their advancement: "Men at the top feel uncomfortable with women beside them" (Hymowitz and Schellhardt, 1986:1). Much of the discrimination is subtle. Forming friendships and exchanging valuable business advice take place informally in all-male preserves, especially golf courses, squash courts, and private male clubs. Male nuances and humor draw on athletic allusions that are heavily tinged with sexual and military overtones. Women entering such circles sense that men view them as outsiders, if not intruders. Yet recent research by the American Management Association shows that women bosses do not manage any differently from men, and that women are more committed to their careers than men are

Women in War Production
During World Wars I and II, mobilization of the nation's labor resources resulted in women being drawn into war work, where "Rosie the Riveter" won laurels for herself. The old saying took a new twist: "A Woman's Place Is in the War." But when men returned home, women were expected to relinquish their jobs and resume a domestic existence of baking, cleaning, sewing, and caring for children. (*Historical Pictures Service*)

(Hymowitz and Schellhardt, 1986).

For most men, work and family have traditionally been separate spheres of living. But for most women, they have not. Even today, single mothers or married women tend to work primarily in the interest of the family and only after all the other needs of its members have been addressed. Additionally, the more successful a man is, the more likely it is that he will marry and have a family. But for women it is the other way around. Whereas 51 percent of women executives at top corporations are single, only 4 percent of their male counterparts are single. Moreover, whereas 61 percent of the women are childless, only 3 percent of the men have no children (Fraker, 1984). Clearly, the choice is more immediate and the cost more apparent for women (Gerson, 1986). While more and more women have gained what men have at work, many of them have had to sacrifice what men have at home—children and a familial refuge. (The box on page 320 examines some of the personal costs of sexism.)

Academia and science   Historically, academic institutions and science have not been work environments that have welcomed women (Kahn and Robbins, 1985). In 1972, federal legislation (Title IX of the Educational Amendments of 1972) was enacted that prohibited discrimination on the basis of sex in educational programs or activities that receive federal assistance. Even so, sexism still prevails. After nearly two decades of affirmative action, the number and distribution of women in American colleges and universities have changed little. Women still constitute less than 15 percent of the chief academic officers at universities, and most of these women are employed either at small liberal arts and community colleges or in the lower ranks of prestigious research universities.

Women in academia are found in the lower, untenured ranks, where they remain for longer periods than do equally qualified men. As of 1985, women were only 4.2 percent of the full professors at Harvard; 3.2 percent at Princeton; 3.9 percent at Yale; and 2.6 percent at Stanford. Among all academically employed doctoral scientists and engineers in 1985, 63 percent of men but only 38 percent of women were tenured. Women and men who start out with similar credentials, including the same graduate department and subfield, have very different career outcomes. Women are less likely to receive tenure, do so at later ages, and have substantially lower average salaries than men of comparable rank and experience. The pattern holds regardless of whether they are married or whether they have children (Pfafflin, 1984; Robbins and Kahn, 1985; Vetter, 1986).

Women make up only about 13 percent of the science and engineering workforce. They are most underrepresented in engineering and the physical sciences, more numerous in the biological sciences, and best represented in the behavioral and social sciences (National Science Foundation, 1984). Although women have been moving into science in larger numbers, by 1985 women constituted only 17 percent of all employed Ph.D.s in science, while 35 percent of women with science doctorates were involuntarily unemployed. Regardless of field, they are less likely than men to be employed in industry or by the federal government. But women are more likely than men to work in hospitals and clinics, nonprofit organizations, state and local governments, and academic institutions (Vetter, 1986).

Politics and government   In 1984, for the first time in American history, a woman was named to the presidential ticket of a major political party. Geraldine Ferraro became the Democratic party's vice-presidential candidate. Her nomination reflected other gains, especially at the state and local levels. Between 1969 and 1986, the number of women elected to state legislatures rose from 301, or 4 percent, to 1,100, or nearly 15 percent. By 1986, two women were state governors; some forty women held other statewide posts such as attorney general, treasurer, and lieutenant governor; and 2 were United States senators and 23 were members of the House of Representatives. Locally, 7 percent of mayors, 10 percent of city council members, and 36 percent of school board members were women. And Justice Sandra Day O'Connor of the United States Supreme Court headed a list of 72 women on federal benches (of 27,845 judges presiding in the United States, 4,762 were women).

Although women have shown increasing strength in the political arena, their numbers as officeholders still do not reflect the fact that 53 percent of the voting-age population are women and that more women vote than men. And even though in 1972 both houses of Congress approved the Equal Rights Amendment, the proposal died in June 1982, still 3 states short of the 38 state legislatures needed for ratification.

THINKING THROUGH THE ISSUES

In their book, *The Longest War,* Carol Tavris and Carole Offir (1977) find that the vast majority of societies are male dominated. They also reach another conclusion. See if you can determine what it is from the following information:

Among the Toda of India, men do the domestic chores: such work is too sacred for a mere female. If the women of a tribe grow sweet potatoes and men grow yams, yams will be the tribe's prestige food, the food distributed at feasts. . . . And if women take over a formerly all-male occupation, it loses status, as happened to the professions of typing and teaching in the United States, medicine in the Soviet Union, and cultivating cassavas in Nigeria. [p. 16]

The rule, say Tavris and Offir, is this: Men's work, no matter what it is, is accorded greater

ISSUES THAT SHAPE OUR LIVES

What Are the Personal Costs of Sexism?

The women's movement has highlighted the consequences of sexism for the identities of women. In a sexist world, a woman gains a reflection of herself not as a person with individual worth, talents, and dignity, but as a commodity (Landy and Sigall, 1974). Within American culture we continue to rely heavily on physical appearance and attractiveness to make inferences about other aspects of a person (Webster and Driskell, 1983; Deaux and Lewis, 1984). But even more for women than for men, the ultimate test of their value has traditionally been their beauty. Historically, Western society has compelled a woman to barter her looks for love and a man. Repeatedly women get the message: "If you are unlovely, you are unloved" (Berscheid and Walster, 1974).

In turn, a man has traditionally been judged by the beauty of "his woman"—her looks are viewed as a tangible measure of his manhood and sexual prowess (Zetterberg, 1966). Nearly a century ago the social critic Thorstein Veblen (1899) pointed out

that women serve as status symbols for men. High-heeled shoes, long fingernails and hair, and awkward skirts hamper women at every turn and attempt to convey the impression (more often than not a fiction) that the wearers do not habitually engage in useful work. The late Grace Kelly, movie star and princess of Monaco, said when she turned 40 that although 40 is a marvelous age for a man, it is torture for a woman because it means "the end." And Brigitte Bardot, viewed as a "sex siren" in the 1960s, attempted suicide on her forty-ninth birthday, observing: "It's really tough to age. . . . It's half a century. Welcome to the senior citizens' club" (Columbus Dispatch, September 20, 1984, p. 3).

Much is made of the benefits men derive from institutional sexism. But men also pay a price for their dominance; they are trapped within the same system as women (Spence and Helmreich, 1978). Although the male prison may be much bigger and more luxurious, it is still a prison (Gitlin, 1971; Komarovsky, 1976). Men are expected to live up to male stereotypes (Cicone and Ruble, 1978). These stereotypes tell men that they

"should be" active and achievement-oriented, adventurous, ambitious, independent, courageous, competitive, and active. They "should be" dominant, and exhibit such qualities as aggressiveness, power, and assertiveness. And they "should" control their emotions, and display a cool level-headedness. But these stereotypes have consequences for almost every aspect of men's lives. The dictate that men project a tough, impersonal front and maintain a competitive stance frequently makes friendships between men shallow and superficial. Tenderness, warmth, and sensitivity are defined as weakness, even when men relate to women and their own children. And by making women sex objects, men become sex machines (Fasteau, 1974). It is little wonder that these traditional expectations have weakened over the past two decades, and that many men, particularly younger ones, no longer subscribe to them.

Shirley Sloan Fader (1987) points out that today's men have much to lose if they were to go back to the full-time pressures of being the sole breadwinner. It is wives' financial contribu-

prestige. Within the United States, as women enter a field, earnings tend to drop—not only for themselves but for the men who remain. Each time women gain a percentage point in an occupation, the field as a whole falls $42 in median annual earnings (Reskin and Hartmann, 1986).

Rape

Rape—sexual relations obtained through physical force, threats, or intimidation—has a long and disturbing history. However, societal attention to the problems that surround rape is a recent phenomenon. It seems that behavior in which some people are victimized is ac-

corded public concern only when the victims have enough power to demand attention. The current focus on rape has paralleled the emergence of the women's movement (Cann et al., 1981). Like other behaviors, rape is linked to the social system (Schwendinger and Schwendinger, 1983). It varies across cultures, with some societies, such as the Gusii of southwestern Kenya, being "rape prone," and other societies, such as the Tuareg of the Sahara, being relatively "rape free" (Sanday, 1981).

In part, the incidence of rape in Western societies reflects a legal system that has defined women as the property of men and that even today often operates on such an assumption. Indeed, as of 1986, only 23 states had laws allowing prosecution of husbands for raping

tions that are boosting modest-income families into the middle and affluent brackets. When a family reaches $40,000–$50,000 annually, 70 percent have working wives. Should a wife give up her job, living standards drop for her *and* for her husband. Fader identifies other benefits men have realized as their wives have entered the paid workforce:

- Twenty years ago men who tried a midlife career change were almost universally condemned for "jeopardizing the family's welfare." Today husbands have approval for a career change largely because they have working wives. The woman's ability to tide the family over economically during his career change increases the man's options.

- Should a husband lose his job, many of the torments of unemployment are lessened by his wife's earnings. And he has the luxury of search time to locate the best job opportunity.

- Contemporary men whose wives have jobs feel less pressure to devote themselves singlemindedly to work. Men can say no to overtime, heavy travel assignments, and unpleasant work conditions. The opportunity to have a better life is purchased by a second income, that of the wife.

- Men—no longer simply income machines—seem to be discovering the joys of fatherhood. In earlier generations, fathers were so busy earning a living they had little chance to know their children.

Redefining traditional gender roles has not been easy. But by pursuing a more equitable sharing of economic and domestic responsibilities, many couples are finding that both husband and wife come out winners. New standards of behavior are emerging that allow men and women to express the full range of human emotions and role options without regard to gender stereotypes. The expanded range of social possibilities is called *androgyny* (from "andro," male, and "gyne," female).

Male Gains: Expanded Role Options In the traditional division of labor, women took care of the children and men earned a livelihood in jobs outside the home. These patterns served to isolate men from their families. With the erosion of old stereotypes and expectations, men are able to realize many of the rewards of parenthood. *(Joel Gordon)*

their wives. Moreover, in rape trials, a woman typically finds that she is the one who is actually on trial. Jurors admit to being influenced by a woman's character, appearance, reputation, and lifestyle. They treat more seriously the rape of a woman who seems chaste and conventional; they are more likely to exonerate men charged with raping women who reputedly are sexually active outside marriage or women who knew the assailant (Brozan, 1985).

Rape myths abound in American life. Psychologist Martha R. Burt (1980) found that over half of her representative sample of Minnesota residents agreed with such statements as "In the majority of rapes, the victim was promiscuous or had a bad reputation," and "A woman who goes to the home or apartment of a man on a first date implies she is willing to have sex." Of equal interest, a 1981 study of 432 teens by social scientists at UCLA indicated that 54 percent of the boys and 42 percent of the girls believed forced sexual intercourse was permissible under some circumstances (Seligmann, 1984). And studies of college males reveal that from 35 to 44 percent say they would personally rape a women if they could be assured of not being caught and punished (Malamuth, 1981, 1983; Check and Malamuth, 1983). Such attitudes form part of a larger and interrelated ideology that includes acceptance of traditional sex-role stereotyping, interpersonal violence (particularly when directed against women), the sexual harassment on the job of women by male bosses and co-workers, and the view that sexual relationships are adversary relationships.

The threat of rape affects women whether or not they are its actual victims. It limits women's freedom, keeps them off the streets at night, and at times imprisons them in their homes. Women who carry the highest burden of fear are those with the fewest resources—the elderly, ethnic minorities, and those with low incomes. Women who live in high-crime neighborhoods typically seek to avoid rape by staying away from areas known to be dangerous and through "street savvy." Even so, victims often are assaulted in their homes and know their attacker (Riger and Gordon, 1981; Bart and O'Brien, 1985; Warr, 1985).

Date rape is also a serious social problem. A recent three-year study of 6,200 male and female students on 32 campuses found that 15 percent of all women reported experiences that met legal definitions of forcible rape. More than half of the incidents were date rapes. Some 73 percent of the women forced into sex avoided using the term rape to describe their experiences, and only 5 percent reported the incident to authorities. Since acquaintance rape is such a paralyzing event, so outside the realm of normal events, women are left without a way of understanding it. Instead, they feel shame and guilt, and attempt to bury the experience. Many campuses and rape crisis centers sponsor programs directed at preventing date rape. But as Bernice Sandler of the Association of American Colleges points out: "Many schools are still unsure about whether date rape is rape or not. Schools just don't know what to do about it" (Leo, 1987). Clearly, the issue of date rape forces a society to confront its most basic assumptions about women and sexuality. By this measure, American society still has much work to do.

The Women's Movement

Over the past twenty years, no social movement has had a more substantial impact on the way Americans think and act than the women's movement. Its vision has been of a just society where women share equally in responsibilities and rewards. Such movements have arisen throughout human history, particularly within the context of social revolutions and movements for national independence. Initially women get caught up in the same broad currents that engulf a nation. But then they begin to extend the ideology of social justice and equality to their circumstances. The suffragist movement of the 1830s developed out of the abolitionist movement when women discovered strong parallels between their conditions and that of slaves. In the 1960s the women's move-

ment gained impetus from the civil rights movement (Freeman, 1973). Cross-national research reveals that women's movements gain impetus from industrialization and urbanization, but take on feminist directions only as women increase their participation in the labor force (Chafetz and Dworkin, 1986).

The revival of feminist activity in the 1960s was spearheaded by a variety of groups. Some, like the National Organization for Women (NOW), were organized at the national level by well-known women. Others were grassroots groups that engaged in campaigns for abortion reform or welfare rights, consciousness-raising rap sessions, or the promotion of the interests of professional or

The Women's Suffrage Movement
It was the refusal of the World's Antislavery Convention meeting in London in 1840 to seat eight American women delegates that led two of them, Lucretia Mott and Elizabeth Cady Stanton, eight years later to call together the first Women's Rights Convention at Seneca Falls, New York. Here a "Declaration of Sentiments" was drawn up, declaring that "all men and women were created equal" and launching a seventy years' battle for suffrage. The movement gained momentum in the pre-World War I period as women entered the work force in growing numbers. Female breadwinners rose from 2.5 million in 1880 to 4.5 million in 1890 and to over 5.3 million by 1900. A campaign to secure an amendment to the Constitution resulted in 1920 in the passage and ratification of the Nineteenth Amendment, giving women full political rights. The photo shows suffragettes parading in 1912 in Columbus, Ohio. *(Culver Pictures)*

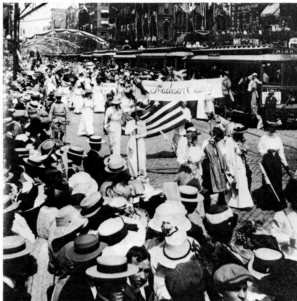

gay women. After nearly two decades of feminist activism, a Gallup Poll found that 71 percent of the respondents said the women's movement had improved their lives. Overall, the women's movement raised the nation's consciousness about the worth and dignity of women (Salholz, 1986). Said Betty Friedan, one of the founders of NOW, on the twentieth anniversary of the organization's formation: "NOW went beyond our wildest dreams. Our daughters take it for granted that they will play in the Little League, that they can be astronauts, and that they can run for President. It broke the barriers of explicit sex discrimination" (Brozan, 1986:22).

The Equal Rights Amendment (ERA) and abortion rights have been central issues for the women's movement. In the 1980s the concept of *comparable worth*—the idea that different jobs can be compared in a way that "equal pay for equal work" can become "equal pay for comparable work"—was added to the agenda of many women's groups. Pay equity calls for employers to assess the intrinsic value of different jobs by measuring the knowledge, skills, and effort required by employees, their responsibilities, and their work conditions. Employers, for instance, would compare what a secretary does with what a truckdriver does. If the two jobs end up at about the same place on a numerical scale, proponents of comparable worth contend that they should command the same pay.

Movements commonly beget countermovements, and this has happened with the women's movement. Antifeminism—particularly anti-abortion and anti-ERA sentiment—has found a strong constituency among people with conservative religious backgrounds and interpersonal networks who favor traditional family values and women's roles (Himmelstein, 1986). After a decade or so of gains, the movement now finds itself on the defensive in many arenas. An equal rights amendment to the Constitution seems dead for the present. Anti-abortion activists have put on strong campaigns. The Reagan administration appointed conservative judges who are reluctant to grant new legal protections of any kind. And in business, executives who have made their peace with affirmative action programs oppose comparable worth as an obstacle to free enterprise. For a discussion of some of these matters, see the box on pages 324–325.

Persistence and Change

Women have come a long way over the past two decades. Adult women are no longer "girls," and newspaper

Changing Gender Patterns
Traditional gender roles are changing throughout the world. Yet practices ingrained over many generations persist. Here contemporary Chinese children engage in new forms of role play while simultaneously wearing gender-typed clothing. It is often easier for society to allow women to occupy new roles than to allow them a new style in performing these roles. (*Mary Ellen Mark/Archive*)

want ads are no longer segregated by gender. Women are police officers, pipefitters, sheet-metal workers, coal miners, firefighters, and carpenters. They are receiving a larger share of college degrees and are being elected to lead cities and states. There is less gender-role stereotyping (see Figure 12.2 on page 326). So when viewed from the perspective of more than a century, much has changed. In 1848, when the Women's Rights Convention was held in Seneca Falls, New York, women lacked property rights. In 1872, Susan B. Anthony was arrested for voting, and women did not obtain the right to vote until 1920. As late as the 1930s, Maryland law permitted a man to divorce his wife for being unchaste before marriage. And the Oklahoma and Arizona state constitutions barred women from holding high public office.

New Directions in Feminism

A quarter-century ago, Betty Friedan (1963) articulated "the problem" that lay buried, unspoken, and with no name. She contended that middle-class American women were prisoners in gilded cages, unfulfilled by their roles as wives and mothers. Friedan gave "the problem" a name—"the feminine mystique"—and the book

Double Responsibilities: Mother and Worker

If gender equality is to be achieved in American life, feminists say that new social arrangements are required that will allow both men and women to earn a living and raise a family. Compared with many other industrial nations, the United States lacks a system of infant day care that is affordable and adequate. (*Steven McCurry/ Magnum*)

that described it provided the ideological foundations for the converging currents that gave rise to the contemporary women's movement. But as women entered the paid labor force, a sense of new unease emerged, a nagging suspicion that fulfillment was not at hand—in brief, a new problem with no name. The rigors of building careers, cultivating intimate relationships, and raising children have proved more difficult than had been anticipated in the heady days of feminism (Salholz, 1986).

Feminists of the 1960s and 1970s focused their energies on a struggle for formal equality with men. Psychologist Matina Horner (1984) says that women were looking at how they could get into law firms, medicine, and corporate management. But now a "postfeminist" generation of women in their twenties and thirties—women who have been the beneficiaries of the women's movement—are attempting to address the less tangible issues of the working environment:

> One of the things we did in the beginning was to turn our backs on some of our interpersonal needs in order to try for a job or career that had been denied us. . . . There was considerable emphasis on autonomy: The best way to relate to others was to be strong and happy and secure in your achievements. Now we're trying to reintegrate our lives, to grapple with personal aspirations as well as achievement in the outside world. . . . Also,

> some people who in the early part of this decade decided that they wouldn't have children, later decided they wanted to. [p. 44]

American feminists have long demanded a national child care policy. But for the most part, family issues took a back seat to the Equal Rights Amendment, legal abortion, and job opportunity. In their defense, many feminists argue that political and economic equality are central to women's personal lives—that changes in the social order are absolutely necessary for gender-based equality. Yet in some ways this early emphasis did not address many of the private problems women experience, and accordingly has made children a major item in feminism's new "personal agenda." "Second-wave" feminists are demanding a social framework in which *both* men and women are able to earn a living *and* have a family. In brief, neither men or women would be trapped by impossible choices that stress the virtues of independence and economic achievement in men and connection and nurturing in women.

In a book entitled *A Lesser Life: The Myth of Women's Liberation in America* (1986a), economist Sylvia Ann Hewlett says that feminism's traditional bias against protective legislation for women has done more harm than good. Calling herself a member of the loyal opposition, Hewlett insists that women are equal—but separate. Hewlett contends that as women struggled for equal rights in the 1960s and 1970s, they tried to clone the male competitive model, with their

Yet for all the current trends toward greater equality, women still fall behind men. As we saw in our survey of gender inequalities, sexism remains a potent force in American life. Men and women continue to cluster along traditional employment lines. Moreover, fewer than 2 percent of women workers have salaries over $35,000, compared with 15 percent of men. And although 1,150,000 men receive more than $75,000, only 60,000 women have reached this level (Hacker, 1986).

A recent Roper Organization poll (1985) found that

business suits and briefcases. Women were "trying to be men." She believes that the movement not only oversold the joys and benefits of careers, but underestimated the importance to women of other experiences. What feminists like Betty Friedan and Gloria Steinem "forgot" was that "90 percent of women do choose to become mothers and that family life is still the most passionate attachment." Hewlett (1986b:9A) would "like to move away from an exclusive emphasis on the ERA and abortion rights and widen the agenda to put family support center stage." She insists that equal access to jobs and education has to be supplemented by family support systems if women are to improve their economic position. (Eleanor Smeal, president of NOW, disputes Hewlett's portrayal of the women's movement [Brozan, 1986:22]: "We have always been involved in the full range of child care and family issues, in pregnancy leave issues, in employment issues for lower-income women. To say that we have not always done so distorts the truth: child care was in fact a part of our 1967 bill of rights.")

Hewlett points out that 60 percent of American working women are not guaranteed their old jobs back after they give birth—a basic right in 117 other nations. Working mothers without maternity leave confront the choice of losing their jobs or placing their infants in day care situations that frequently are inadequate—little more than "kennels" for children. She notes that no other society forces these choices on working women (see Figure A). In Europe, the average

maternity leave is five months at full pay. In France, 90 percent of 3-year-olds spend their days in government-sponsored preschools. In Sweden, parents can opt for a six-hour workday until a child is 8 years old. And in Italy, women receive two years' credit toward seniority every time they give birth to a child.

Hewlett argues that until our society helps women resolve their double burden as mothers and workers, they are bound to remain second-class citizens. And by too often ignoring working mothers and their children,

the women's movement has allowed the ultra-right to take over the family. She would like to see prenatal care, maternity benefits, job-protected parental leave (for men as well as women), and high-quality child care more vigorously promoted by feminists. Overall, it seems that the goals for feminism's second wave are coming to center on the quality of life for women, their children, and their families. Women are increasingly engaged in a major struggle to reconcile the demands of childbirth and childrearing with those of earning a living.

FIGURE A **Parental Leave Policies Set by Governments in Other Countries**
Source: U.S. News & World Report, *March 10, 1986, p. 52.*

		Maximum leave	Pay while on leave	Parent on leave
Sweden		52 wk.	90%/ 38 wk.	either
Finland		39 wk.	80%/ 39 wk.	either
Canada		37 wk.	60%/ 15 wk.	mother
Italy		24 wk.	80%/ 24 wk.	mother
Austria		20 wk.	100%/ 20 wk.	mother
Chile		18 wk.	100%/ 18 wk.	either
West Germany		14 wk.	100%/ 14 wk.	mother

fewer than 10 percent of Americans believe it is better to be a woman than a man, and about 4 in 10 think one's sex makes no difference in the drive for success. Majorities of men and women say it is easier for men to get top jobs in business, as well as mortgages and substantial

loans. Some 77 percent of American women agree that a woman generally must be much better at what she does than a man if she is to get ahead. Whereas in 1974 half of the women and 48 percent of the men said the most satisfying lifestyle was a traditional marriage where the

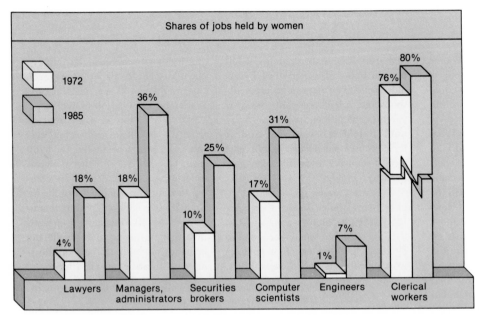

FIGURE 12.2   **New Opportunities for Women**
Source: U.S. Department of Labor.

husband worked and the wife stayed home and took care of the house and children, only 37 percent of women and 43 percent of men thought this the most satisfying arrangement in 1985. Overall, only about 10 percent of Americans believe that women will return to more traditional roles. And 69 percent of men and 67 percent of women say that women's roles should continue to change. Both persistence and change, then, characterize the status of women in American life.

Sexuality

One aspect that we typically associate with gender is our sexuality. Indeed, we are very sexy animals. We engage in a good deal more sex than other primates do. Our love of sex is one reason why our species has not only survived, but has peopled the globe. Not surprisingly, then, sexuality is an integral component of the human experience across the life course. Observations of male and female infants suggest that some of them may be capable of sexual arousal and orgasm. And at very early ages youngsters show interest in exploring their own bodies. Even at 4 months of age, babies respond to genital stimulation in a way that suggests that they are experiencing

erotic pleasure. When children reach 2 and 3 years of age, they will investigate their playmates' genitals and, if permitted, those of adults as well. But by this time, strong social prohibitions come into effect, and children are socialized to constrain these behaviors (Rosen and Hall, 1984). Nor does erotic interest and activity necessarily disappear as people age (Jasso, 1985). The research of William H. Masters and Virginia E. Johnson (1966) shows that many healthy men and women function sexually into their eighties. Although time takes its toll, it need not eliminate sexual desire or bar its fulfillment.

The Social Nature of Sexuality

Most of us think of sexual arousal and orgasm as purely physiological experiences. Although sexual behavior undeniably has a biological component, we approach it, as we do other activities, in terms of social symbols and meanings. Teenagers often report feelings of anxiety, nausea, and even fear for what they later categorize (or disregard, should the feelings persist) as sexual arousal. Preadolescent boys typically regard kissing as "sissy stuff"; girls consider it asexual. But as adolescents begin "hanging out" together, they come to see kissing as erotically exciting. The act has not changed, only the meaning attached to it. Or consider that when the Thonga of Africa first saw Europeans kissing, they laughed and commented: "Look at them; they eat each other's saliva and dirt." In contrast, the Kwakiutl of British Columbia and the Trobriand Islanders of the South Pacific "kiss" by sucking the lips and tongue of their partner, allowing the exchange of saliva (Hyde, 1979). Even nudity is not intrinsically erotic. Although in some societies people wear little clothing, they typically do not attach erotic meanings to their exposure (Victor, 1980). The same holds true among members of nudist camps in the United States (Weinberg, 1965). In sum, we filter physiological events through a social screen that defines for us their meaning and significance.

Many of the same physical acts that occur in sexual encounters between men and women also occur in other situations—a gynecological or penal examination, the palpation of the breast for cancer, the insertion of a tampon, and mouth-to-mouth resuscitation. Yet we usually do not define these activities as sexual. For behavior to be seen as sexual, we typically require that "certain" words and gestures be introduced into a situation—saying the "right things," wearing "seductive" clothing, establishing "sexy" eye contact, "deftly" removing clothing, and petting in the "proper" ritualistic sequence. Additionally, we must define the other person as an "appropriate" sexual partner in terms of gender, age, physical attractiveness, and social status. Genitals, copulation, and orgasms do not have "sexual meaning" in their own right. We must *bestow* meanings upon them, meanings we acquire in the course of social interaction (Plummer, 1975; Gagnon, 1977).

By the same token, much sexual behavior also has "nonsexual" motivations. Health faddists may engage in sex at prescribed intervals in the same way they eat health foods and for the same purpose. A married couple may have sexual relations because each believes the other expects it, even though neither actually wants it. A prostitute or stripper uses sex as a means for earning a living. A man may seek a great many sexual partners in the hope of sustaining his public image of masculinity and virility. And a student may masturbate while studying for a test as a mechanism to reduce boredom or anxiety (Plummer, 1975).

Heterosexual Behavior

Heterosexuality entails a sexual preference for a person of the opposite sex as a partner. Within Western societies, heterosexual interests and activities are thought to begin with puberty. Indeed, the notion has long been prevalent in American life that childhood is ideally a period of "innocence"—one in which children are ignorant of sexuality and excluded from sexual concerns (Winn, 1983). Yet ours is a highly sexualized society, and much interaction is flavored by our obsession with sex. Moreover, television, movies, and magazines bombard young and old alike with sexual stimuli on an unprecedented scale. So in practice, children are hardly shielded from sexual matters. Although Sigmund Freud depicted the elementary school years as a kind of developmental plateau in which sexual impulses are repressed (a period he termed *latency*), research casts doubts on his formulation. One sample of Pennsylvania school children between 10 and 12 years of age demonstrated the developing roots of adult heterosexual interests and activities. Some 84 percent of the girls and 62 percent of the boys said that they expected to get married; 71 percent of the girls indicated that they had a boyfriend and 56 percent of the boys that they had a girlfriend; and 51 percent of the girls and 47 percent of the boys admitted to having been in love (Broderick and Rowe, 1968). And sexual play among young children is common (Rosen and Hall, 1984).

This century has witnessed *two* periods of very rapid change regarding sexual attitudes and behavior. The first period occurred around the time of World War I; the second, during the Vietnam war years. Before 1915, approximately 75 percent of all middle-class first-time brides were virgins. By 1920, the figure had dropped to around 50 percent as more women had premarital relations with their future husbands. During the same period, the proportion of middle-class men who were virgins at marriage declined from about 51 percent to around 33 percent. The incidence of premarital sexual experience was higher among members of the working and lower classes (Reiss, 1976).

Between 1920 and 1965, little overall change occurred in the actual premarital sexual *behavior* of Americans. However, in the post–World War II period, *attitudes* did become more permissive. Dramatic changes in sexual behavior showed up again after 1965. Growing proportions of teenagers became sexually active and began their sexual activity at earlier ages. National surveys revealed that by 1980, only a third of adolescent females had not had intercourse by age 19. And three out of ten teenage girls who have premarital sexual experience become pregnant (teenage sex results in about one million pregnancies a year). Among never-married women, 80 percent of all pregnancies and 72 percent of births are unwanted (Stewart, 1985). Much of the change in the sexual behavior of young people has resulted from the growing power of the young to run their

Emerging Cross-Gender Friendships
Among American first-grade children, both boys and girls can be observed playing together on school playgrounds during recess. By the third grade, however, children have divided themselves into two gender camps. This separation tends to reach its peak around the fifth grade. Even though same-gender friendships predominate among 10- and 11-year-old children, most children show a steady and progressive development of cross-sex interests as they advance toward puberty. *(Jeffry W. Myers/Stock, Boston)*

own lives without interference by parents, schools, churches, and the law (Reiss, 1976, 1986).

In the 1980s the United States entered a new phase characterized by more conservative attitudes toward sexuality than those of the 1960s and 1970s. The proportion of white teenage women who engaged in premarital intercourse leveled off, while it declined among blacks. And the number of people who said that extramarital sex is wrong increased. Moreover, the number of Americans who favor sex education in the schools dropped, while larger numbers now oppose pornography on grounds that it leads to a breakdown in morals (Goleman, 1985). Casual sex has also declined dramatically as fear of sexually transmitted disease and AIDS has increased (Hellmich, 1986; Nordheimer, 1986).

Homosexual Behavior

Few people within the history of Western society have been more scorned, feared, and stigmatized than homosexuals. **Homosexuality** is a sexual preference for a person of the *same* sex. A person's gender identity and *sexual preference* are distinct. Most gay men and lesbian women have no confusion about their gender identity; they simply prefer sexual partners of the same sex. People show varying degrees of sexual preference, including *bisexuality*, in which both opposite- and same-sex partners are about equally preferred. Some homosexual behavior is also situational. Prisoners, for example, often enter into homosexual relationships, but return to heterosexual relationships when they are released. Although

there is no shortage of theories or research on the matter, the current state of scientific knowledge does not allow us to arrive at firm conclusions regarding the determinants of a person's sexual orientation.

The Alfred C. Kinsey Institute for Sex Research estimates that 5 to 6 percent of the adult population is predominantly homosexual. However, since there are so many gradations in sexual behavior and preferences, many sociologists take the view that there are heterosexual or homosexual practices, but not heterosexual or homosexual individuals (Bell, Weinberg, and Hammersmith, 1981). It is estimated that some 25 percent of American men and 15 percent of American women have had some homosexual experience (Hyde, 1986). Further, gays are a varied group (Bell and Weinberg, 1978). They are found in all occupational fields, political persuasions, religious faiths, and racial and ethnic groups. Some are married, have children, and lead lives that in most respects are indistinguishable from those of the larger population. Others enter homosexual unions that are relatively durable. Still others engage in casual sex with a good many partners. In 1973, the American Psychiatric Association officially removed homosexuality from its list of mental disorders, thus endorsing the view that the choice of a sexual partner of the same sex is no more indicative of mental illness than is the choice of a sexual partner of the opposite sex. Its action also reveals how our definitions of "abnormal sexual behavior" can alter with time.

Although American society has stigmatized homosexuality, in 64 percent of the tribal societies for which information is available, homosexual activities of one sort or another are accepted or approved of under some circumstances (Ford and Beach, 1951). The Siwans of North Africa expected all males to engage in homosexual relations. Fathers arranged for their unmarried sons to enter a relationship with an older man. Later, between age 16 and 20, the young men married women (Allah, 1917). Among the ancient Greeks, erotic relationships between younger and older men were common. However, little is known about female homosexuality, probably because most of the early Greek writers were men. In some parts of the world, including the New Guinea Highlands, homosexual behavior is seen as a path to heterosexuality and is widely supported. Preadolescent boys involve themselves with older men and ingest their sperm so that they will become capable of producing their own sperm in adulthood and thereby impregnate their wives (Herdt, 1982, 1984). And in the United States, sexual experimentation between members of the same sex is relatively common during adolescence, especially among boys, although participants typically do not regard it as "homosexual" (Rosen and Hall, 1984).

As among heterosexuals, casual sex has decreased markedly in recent years among homosexuals. Part of the reason can be traced to new fear of such diseases as acquired immune deficiency syndrome (AIDS) and herpes. But, as noted above, it also reflects a trend toward greater conservatism after the sexual revolution of the 1960s and 1970s. The AIDS epidemic has created a high degree of anxiety within gay communities throughout the United States because many victims of this fatal disease have been male homosexuals (lesbians have a low incidence of any kind of venereal disease and are not among the high-risk groups for AIDS). The AIDS organism is a virus that is spread by bodily secretions, particularly semen and blood. It results in the collapse of the body's immune system, rendering the victim susceptible to cancers and various fatal infections.

Because of the hostility of the larger community, homosexuals and lesbians have often had to live double lives, "gay" at home and "straight" on the job. However, shifts in public attitudes and gay rights laws have prompted many to live openly. This has been most noticeable in large cities like San Francisco, Los Angeles, and New York. Further, gay and lesbian organizations and political caucuses have vigorously championed gay rights measures. But in recent years the tendency of many Americans to equate gays with AIDS has resulted in a setback to the movement. Gay bashing—physical assaults on homosexual men and lesbian women—has

markedly increased in recent years (Wilson, 1987). The 1986 Supreme Court ruling that there is no constitutionally protected right to engage in homosexual conduct has also made it more difficult for homosexual advocates to gain their objectives.

In conclusion, human sexual behavior is highly variable. The Judeo-Christian religious tradition maintains that only sexual behavior that can lead to conception within marriage is moral. Other sexual acts are seen as immoral. Yet what is considered moral in one culture may be immoral or at least disapproved, in another. In some societies, premarital intercourse is considered both moral and necessary—in fact, no man will take a bride who has not already demonstrated her fertility by producing a child (Rosen and Hall, 1984). The sociological perspective, then, rather than defining what behavior is moral or immoral, offers us insight regarding the varied sexual behavior of men and women.

Acceptance of Homosexual Relationships in Ancient Greece

Among the ancient Greeks, sexual pleasure was defined as a valuable goal, and the naked male body symbolized the ideal of both physical and emotional love. Homosexual relationships were common among Greek men of all ages. It seems that the Greeks regarded homosexual feelings as "natural" and made no attempt to explain why one man was sexually attracted to another (Rosen and Hall, 1984). *(North Wind Picture Archives)*

Chapter Highlights

1. Gender roles represent the earliest division of labor among human beings. Cross-cultural evidence reveals that while it is obvious that men and women differ biologically, both sexes are capable of great behavioral variety. This variation points to a social foundation for most gender differences. So do the changes observed from one time to another in sex-linked behavior patterns within the same society.

2. Three major theories have been advanced to explain the process whereby we acquire our gender identities. According to Freudian theory, the key involves complicated psychological maneuvers in which children come to identify with the parent of the same sex as themselves. Cultural transmission theory looks to a gradual process of learning that begins in infancy and shapes a child's gender responses. And labeling theory draws our attention to the fact that children actively seek to acquire gender identities and roles.

3. Throughout human history men and women have differed in their access to privilege, prestige, and power. The distribution problem of who gets what, when, and how has traditionally been answered in favor of males, giving rise to gender stratification. Women exhibit four of the five properties usually associated with a minority group. Just as our society structures inequalities based on race, ethnic group, and age, so it institutionalizes inequalities based on gender.

4. Functionalists suggest that a division of labor originally arose between men and women because of the woman's role in reproduction. In contrast, conflict theorists contend that a sexual division of labor is a social vehicle devised by men to assure themselves of privilege, prestige, and power in their relationships with women.

5. Rape has a long and disturbing history. It seems that behavior in which some people are victimized is accorded public concern only when the victims have enough power to demand attention. Like other behaviors, rape is linked to the social system and varies across cultures.

6. Over the past 20 years no social movement has had a more substantial impact on the way Americans think and act than the women's movement. Its vision has been a just society where women share equally the responsibilities and rewards of men. Such movements have arisen throughout human history, particularly within the context of social revolutions and movements for national independence. However, movement commonly begets counter-movement and so has the women's movement.

7. Women have come a long way over the past two decades. Yet for all the current trends toward greater equality, women still fall behind men. So both old and new patterns characterize the status of women in American life.

8. Most of us think of sexual arousal and orgasm as purely physiological experiences. Although sexual behavior undeniably has a biological component, like any other activity we approach it in terms of social symbols and meanings.

9. Heterosexuality entails a sexual preference for a person of the opposite sex as a partner. In contrast, homosexuality involves a sexual preference for a person of the same sex as a partner. A person's gender identity and sexual preference are distinct. Among both heterosexuals and homosexuals, a marked decrease has taken place in recent years in casual or promiscuous sex. Fear of AIDS is reshaping sexual life.

The Sociologist's Vocabulary

androgyny A standard that allows individuals to express the full range of human emotions and role possibilities without regard to gender stereotypes.

gender The social creation of girls, boys, women, and men.

gender identities The conceptions we have of ourselves as being male or female.

gender roles Sets of cultural expectations that define the ways in which the members of each sex should behave.

hermaphrodites Individuals whose reproductive structures are sufficiently ambiguous that it is difficult to define them exclusively as male or female.

heterosexuality A sexual preference for a person of the opposite sex as a partner.

homosexuality A sexual preference for a person of the same sex as a partner.

institutional sexism Those social arrangements and enduring patterns by which members of one gender group realize more benefits and fewer burdens than members of the other gender group.

transsexuals Individuals who have normal sexual organs but who psychologically feel like members of the opposite sex.

PART FIVE

Social
Institutions

13

Marriage, Family, and Alternative Lifestyles

The happiest moments of my life have been the few which I have passed at home in the bosom of my family.

—Thomas Jefferson, Letter to Francis Willis, 1790

Much is made of "the American Dream." It is the label we apply to our unique national inspiration—a term laden with a sense of promise and possibility. Yet which promises the dream contains and whether the nation is keeping its word is a matter of public debate. One of these issues has to do with marriage. Public opinion polls overwhelmingly show that the vast majority of Americans want the closeness and intimacy of a happily married life. So it came as somewhat of a shock when a study by sociologists Neil Bennett and Patricia Craig and economist David Bloom concluded that college-educated white women who have not married by the age of 25 have only a 50 percent chance of marrying. Perhaps even more ominously, it said that 95 percent of those not married by age 35 would never wed. College-educated black women face even more unfavorable odds (Greer, 1986; Salholz, 1986).

The study, based on 1982 Census Bureau data, received major media attention and resulted in some misunderstandings. For one thing, 8 out of 10 female college graduates *will* marry. The predictions also represent statistical averages, not individual odds. And a woman's chances of marrying rise considerably if one removes from the statistical calculations women who choose to remain single and those who favor a live-in relationship or sequential relationships (Brooks, 1986).

More recently, Jeanne Moorman of the Census Bureau has taken a new look at the matter and has come up with a different forecast: If a woman is single, college-educated, and 30, she stands a 58 to 66 percent chance of marrying someday; at 35, her odds are between 32 and 41 percent; and at 40 there is still a 17 to 23 percent chance that she will wed (Norton and Moorman, 1987; Heller, 1987).

We will have to wait twenty or more years to find out who is right. Some sociologists think both may be off the mark, viewing the methods and assump-

tions used by Bennett as overly complicated and those of Moorman as overly simplistic (Mitchell, 1987). Regardless of which conclusions we find most convincing, it would be well to remember that people who remain single are not doomed to misery or unhappy lives. Moreover, the controversy does draw our attention to the substantial changes that are under way in American life. Growing numbers of women are pursuing careers, postponing marriage, and reducing their childbearing. Yet, as we noted in the previous chapter, while men say they respect women's career aspirations, in practice they retain rather traditional gender expectations when it comes to domestic chores and child care. So men and women are having to struggle in search of new accommodations.

Women who postpone marriage to secure a higher education and pursue careers are often among the brightest and most gifted. Indeed, some find it relatively easy to conclude, as does sociologist Nancy Chodorow, "When you look at the men who don't marry, you're looking at the bottom of the barrel. When you look at the women who don't marry, you're looking at the cream of the crop" (quoted by Salholz, 1986:56). Of course, not all women—much less all men—wish to get married. They find a good life and satisfying relationships in a different lifestyle. Some women, as well as men, have come to terms with remaining single, preferring it to lowering their standards or settling for the wrong person. Still other women are not waiting around for a husband and are having children on their own.

Many women who have singlemindedly pursued their careers had assumed that when they were ready to marry, they could simply pencil in a husband. But now, in their thirties and finding biology's clock for having children ticking away, they discover that marriage has eluded them. One difficulty has been the "marriage squeeze." Between 1946 and 1956, each year's new crop of births was larger than the previous one. Since men typically marry women several years younger than themselves, many millions of women are left out. The problem is not so much a shortage of men in the marriage market as the practice that men have of marrying (and when divorced, remarrying) younger women—usually to impress others. Perhaps you have noted that college men of all ages compete for freshman women. Realistically, older women do not enjoy a similar option (complicating matters, undergraduate women now outnumber undergraduate men in the United States). And with demographics and biology on their side, men come to exercise "ultimate power." Once more we see the operation of social structure. It plays a critical part in shaping our aspirations and in influencing our ability to realize them.

PLANNING AHEAD: TARGETED READING

1. What makes the family a unique social institution?

2. What are some of the cultural and subcultural variations in the family and marriage?

3. What theoretical perspectives are available to sociologists in interpreting the family?

4. What are some of the major changes occurring in American family life?

5. What are some of the social implications of these changes?

6. What are some of the alternative lifestyles open to Americans?

Structure of the Family

What is the family? Although we all use the term and doubtless have a notion of what we mean by it, the "family" is exceedingly difficult to define. When we set about separating families from nonfamilies, we encounter all sorts of problems (Stephens, 1963). Many of us think of the family as a social unit consisting of a married couple and their children—Mom, Dad, and the kids. But as we will see in the course of the chapter, this definition is too limited. In many societies it is the kin group, and not a married couple and their children, that is the basic family unit. Sociologists have traditionally viewed the **family** as a social group whose members are related by ancestry, marriage, or adoption and who live together, cooperate economically, and care for the young (Murdock, 1949). But those who are unhappy with this definition argue that psychological bonds are what families are all about. Defined in this fashion, long-term relationships, heterosexual or homosexual, should be considered families. Clearly, defining the family is not simply an academic exercise: How we define it determines the kinds of intimate groups we consider normal and the kinds we consider deviant, and what rights and obligations we recognize as legally and socially binding (Skolnick, 1981).

Forms of the Family

The family is a unique institution. In no sphere of social life are the differences in human societies more evident and striking than in kin and marriage patterns. Throughout the world there are many arrangements for regulating mating and reproduction, caring for and bringing up children, and meeting personal needs. Let us begin our discussion by considering a number of these differences.

Composition   Every society has a family system, although not every society has organized and relatively independent religious, economic, political, educational, and medical institutions. Social relationships between adult males and females can be organized within families by emphasizing either spouse or kin relationships. In the **nuclear family** arrangement, spouses and their offspring constitute the core relationship; blood relatives are functionally marginal. In contrast, in the **extended family** arrangement, *kin*—individuals related by common ancestry—provide the core relationship; spouses are functionally marginal. The nuclear family pattern is the preferred arrangement for most Americans. In the course of their lives, Americans typically are members of two

nuclear families. First, a person belongs to a nuclear family that consists of oneself and one's father, mother, and siblings, what sociologists call the **family of orientation.** Second, since over 90 percent of Americans marry at least once, the vast majority of people are members of a nuclear family that consists of themselves and a spouse and children, what sociologists call the **family of procreation.**

Extended families are found throughout the world. In one case, that of the Nayar—a warrior caste group in pre-British southwestern India—spouse ties were virtually absent (Gough, 1959, 1965; Dumont, 1970; Fuller, 1976). About the time of puberty, a Nayar woman took a ritual husband chosen for her by a neighborhood assembly. The union was recognized in a ceremony during which the husband tied a gold ornament around the neck of his bride. In the marriage ritual, the man acted as a representative of all the men of his group, an act that accorded them sexual rights with the woman. Without this ritual, no offspring could be considered legitimate. After three days, the woman was ritually separated from her "husband" and was then free to take on a series of "visiting husbands" or "lovers." Although a woman's lovers gave her regular gifts on prescribed occasions, they did not provide her with support. When a woman had a child, one of the men—not necessarily the biological father—paid a fee to the midwife. However, the man assumed no economic, social, legal, or ritual rights or obligations toward the child: It was the *mother's* blood relatives who took responsibility for the child.

For some time, sociologists assumed that industrialization undercut extended family patterns while fostering nuclear family arrangements (Goode, 1963). For one thing, industrialism requires that people move about in search of new job and professional opportunities, weakening kin obligations that depend on frequent and intimate interaction. For another, industrialism substitutes nonkin agencies for kin groups in handling such common problems as police protection, education, military defense, and money lending. Now sociologists have taken a new look and have found that industrialization and extended family arrangements are not necessarily incompatible (Laslett, 1974, 1976; Quadagno, 1982; Cherlin, 1983). Although industrializing peoples make new demands on kin, industrialization also makes it possible to respond to family claims with new resources. For instance, when the Tonga of Malawi went off to work in the mines of Zimbabwe and South Africa, they did not take their wives and children with them. The men relied on their kin to look after their wives and children, while

The Family: A Universal Social Institution
All societies have a family institution. However, they display considerable variation in the structural and cultural forms that the institution assumes. The photos show families in Papua, New Guinea (top left), Oman, Arabia (top right), and China (right). *(clockwise from top left: David Austen/Stock, Boston; Robert Azzi/Woodfin Camp & Associates; Stan Ries/The Picture Cube)*

they sent home as much of their wages as they could. The men continued to exert their claims to status and land in the village and took part in village politics (Goldthorpe, 1984). Similarly, when Tamara K. Hareven (1982) examined family life in a textile community of New Hampshire in the nineteenth century, she discovered that industrialism had promoted kin ties. Not only did different generations often reside in the same household, they provided a good deal of assistance to one another.

Descent Societies trace descent and pass property on from one generation to the next in one of three ways. Under a **patrilineal** arrangement, a people reckon descent and transmit property through the line of the father. Under the **matrilineal** arrangement, descent and

inheritance takes place through the mother's side of the family. The Nayar, for example, were a matrilineal people. A child owed allegiance to the mother's brother, and not the father. Property and position passed from maternal uncle to nephew. Under the **bilineal** arrangement, both sides of an individual's family are equally important. Americans are typically bilineal, reckoning descent through both father and mother (however, the surname is transmitted in a patrilineal manner).

Kin, then, are people who act like kin—who relate to us in certain ways and expect to be treated in certain ways—as well as people who are biologically related to us. For instance, we typically use the terms "aunt" and "uncle" for people who are married to the sisters and brothers of our mother and father, even though such relationships lack a biological reference. We call them

Aunt Bee or Uncle Ed because of social definitions. And we behave toward them, and they toward us, much as if they were biologically our aunts and uncles (Cole, 1982).

Residence   Societies differ in the location where a couple takes up residence after marriage. In the case of **patrilocal** residence, the bride and groom live in the household or community of the husband's family. The opposite pattern prevails in **matrilocal** residence. For example, among the Hopi, a Southwest Pueblo people, upon marriage the husband moves into the dwelling of his wife's family, and it is here that he eats and sleeps. In the mainstream American culture, newlyweds tend to follow **neolocal** patterns in which they set up a new place of residence independent of parents or other relatives.

Authority   Although the authority men and women exercise in family decision making is influenced by their personalities, societies nonetheless dictate who is expected to be the dominant figure. Under **patriarchal** arrangements, it is usually the eldest male or the husband who fills this role. The ancient Hebrews, Greeks, and Romans and the nineteenth-century Chinese and Japanese provide examples. Logically, the construction of a **matriarchal** family type is very simple and would involve the vesting of power in women. Yet true matriarchies are rare, and considerable controversy exists as to whether the balance of power actually rests with the wife in any known society (Stephens, 1963). Although matriarchies may not be the preferred arrangement in most societies, they often arise through default upon the death or desertion of the husband. Moreover, in some societies cultural norms provide that husband and wife each has spheres of authority. In a third type of family, the **equalitarian** arrangement, power and authority is equally distributed between the husband and wife. This pattern has been on the increase in recent years in the United States, where marriage is changing from a one-vote system in which men make the decisions to a system in which the couple sort out choices jointly.

Forms of Marriage

The fact that the parties to a marriage must be members of two different kin groups has crucial implications for the structure of the family. Indeed, the continuity, and therefore the long-term welfare, of any kin group depends on obtaining spouses for the unmarried members of the group from other groups. A kin group also has a stake in retaining some measure of control over at least a portion of its members after they marry (Lee, 1977). Accordingly, we need to take a closer look at mating arrangements, particularly **marriage**, a socially approved sexual union between two or more individuals that is undertaken with some idea of permanence.

Exogamy and endogamy   All societies regulate the pool of eligibles from which individuals are expected to select a mate. A child's kin generally have more in mind than simply getting a child married. They want the child married to the *right* spouse, especially where marriage has consequences for the kin group. Two types of marital regulations define the "right" spouse: endogamy and exogamy. **Endogamy** is the requirement that marriage occur within a group. People must marry within their

The Navaho: Matrilineal Descent
The Navaho of the American Southwest trace descent through the mother's side of the family. The women and children shown here belong to the same matrilocal extended family. *(Shostak/Anthro-Photo)*

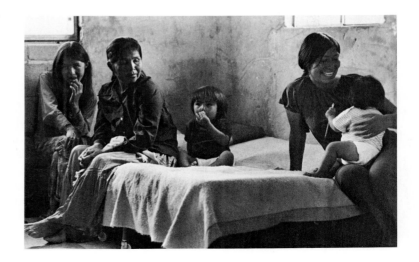

class, caste, race, ethnic group, or religion. **Exogamy** is the requirement that marriage occur outside a group. People must marry outside their kin group, be it their immediate nuclear family, clan, or tribe.

Regulations relating to exogamy are based primarily on kinship and usually entail **incest taboos,** rules that prohibit sexual intercourse with close blood relatives. But who constitutes a "close blood relative" is a matter of social definition. Consider the case of two young lovers in Seoul, South Korea, whose family names both happen to be Soh. At first the couple gave little thought to the matter, since Koreans have only 249 surnames (for instance, people named Kim account for 20 percent of the 41 million South Koreans). When the Sohs wanted to get married, an inspection of their family registers revealed they had a common ancestor. Both traced their lineage to a Soh who had lived, 30 generations ago, in the town of Talsong. Under Korean family law, the lovers might as well have been brother and sister. Men and women who share the same name and ancestral village may not marry, since the relationship is considered incestuous. Despite the prohibition, the Sohs married in a civil ceremony. The couple could not legally register their marriage, so the two children born to them were considered illegitimate and ran the risk of being barred from public school. Because of their difficulties, the Sohs recently migrated to the United States (Haberman, 1987).

Incest taboos were once singled out by social scientists as the only universal norm in a world of diverse moral codes. But the sociologist Russell Middleton (1962) found that brother-sister marriage was not only permitted, but frequently practiced, by the ancient Egyptians (Cleopatra was married to two of her younger brothers at different times). He speculates that brother-sister marriages served to maintain the power and property of a family and prevented the splintering of an estate through inheritance. A similar arrangement apparently also occurred among the royal families of Hawaii, the Inca rulers of Peru, and the Dahomey of West Africa. Additionally, the degree of kinship covered by incest varies from society to society. For example, in colonial New England it was incestuous if a man married his deceased wife's sister. But among the ancient Hebrews, the custom of the levirate required that a man marry his brother's widow under some circumstances.

Incestuous relationships are not just prohibited by a society; most people react to them with aversion and disgust. The intensity of such feelings and the worldwide prevalance of incest taboos have led scholars to search for explanations. The psychoanalyst Sigmund Freud (1917) alleged that incest taboos are a psychological reaction against unconscious incestuous desires. The anthropologist Claude Levi-Strauss (1956) suggested that incest taboos promote alliances between families and reinforce their social interdependence. The anthropologist Bronislaw Malinowski (1927) said that incest taboos prevent destructive sexual jealousies and rivalries within the family. The sociologist Kingsley Davis (1960) contends that incestuous relationships would hopelessly confuse family statuses (for example, the incestuous male offspring of a father-daughter union would be the son of his own sister, a stepson of his own grandmother, and a grandson of his own father). And some anthropologists and sociobiologists, noting that children brought up together avoid sexual relationships and marriage among themselves (such as children raised on Israeli kibbutzim), argue that the behavior is set by genes (Wilson, 1975; Lumsden and Wilson, 1981). These issues remain unresolved, and social scientists continue to find themselves perplexed about the real causes of incest taboos (Dinnage, 1986).

Types of marriage   The relationship between a husband and wife may be structured in one of four ways: **monogamy,** one husband and one wife; **polygyny,** one husband and two or more wives; **polyandry,** two or more husbands and one wife; and **group marriage,** two or more husbands and two or more wives. Monogamy appears in all societies, although other forms may not only be permitted, but preferred. Monogamy was the preferred or ideal type of marriage in less than 20 percent of the 862 societies included in one cross-cultural sample (Murdock, 1967). Not too long ago, members of Western societies believed that monogamy was one of the hallmarks of civilization and that other forms of marriage were signs of barbarism.

Polygyny has enjoyed a wide distribution throughout the world, with 83 percent of the 862 societies permitting husbands to take plural wives. The Old Testament, for example, records polygynous practices among the Hebrews. Gideon's many wives bore him seventy sons; King David had several wives; King Solomon reportedly had seven hundred wives and three hundred concubines; King Solomon's son Rehoboam had eighteen wives and sixty concubines; and Rehoboam's sons also had many wives. As among the ancient Hebrews, it is usually only the economically advantaged males who can afford to have more than one wife. The arrangement is closely tied with economic production and status con-

Fraternal Polyandry
Ethnic Tibetans along the Tibet-Nepal border practice polyandry. A number of brothers jointly take a wife. Although the eldest brother is usually the dominant figure in the household, all the brothers share the work and participate as sexual partners with the wife. Here a 12-year-old bride stands with three of her five husbands-to-be. The grooms, ages 19, 17, and 7, are brothers. Two other brothers, ages 14 and 21, are off on a trading trip. The cultural ideal calls on the wife to show all the brothers equal affection and sexual favor, but deviations from the ideal occur, particularly when there are considerable age differences. *(Thomas L. Kelly)*

siderations. Polygyny tends to be favored where large families are advantageous and women make substantial contributions to subsistence (Oliver, 1955; Heath, 1958).

Whereas polygyny has a wide distribution, polyandry is exceedingly rare. Polyandry usually does not represent freedom of sexual choice for women. It often involves the right or the opportunity of younger brothers to have sexual access to the wife of an older brother. Where a family cannot afford wives or marriages for each of its sons, it may find a wife for the eldest son only. The anthropologist W. H. R. Rivers (1906:515) studied polyandrous practices among the Todas, a non-Hindu people in India, and observed:

> The Todas have a completely organized and definite system of polyandry. When a woman marries a man, it is understood that she becomes the wife of his brothers at the same time. When a boy is married to a girl, not only are his brothers usually regarded as also the husbands of the girl, but any brother born later will similarly be regarded as sharing his older brother's rights. . . . The brothers live together, and my informants seemed to regard it as a ridiculous idea that there should even be disputes or jealousies of the kind that might be expected in such a household. . . . Instead of adultery being regarded as immoral . . . according to the Toda idea, immorality attaches rather to the man who grudges his wife to another.

Social scientists are far from agreement on whether group marriage has ever existed as a cultural norm. There is some evidence that it did occur among the

Kaingang of the jungles of Brazil, the Marquesans of the South Pacific, the Chukchee of Siberia, and the Todas of India. At times, as among the Todas, polyandry appears to slip into group marriage when a number of brothers share more than one wife (Stephens, 1963).

Some societies also recognize marriages between individuals of the same sex. The Cheyenne Indians permitted married men to take on *berdaches*, or male transvestites, as second wives (Hoebel, 1960). And the Azande of the African Sudan allowed warriors who could not afford wives to marry "boy-wives" to satisfy their sexual needs. The boy-wives not only had sexual relations with their husbands, but performed many of the chores Azande wives performed for their husbands. Additionally, the husband could sue a lover of his boy-wife in court for adultery (Evans-Pritchard, 1970). Female-female marriages are also found in some African societies, although a sexual relationship is not involved (O'Brien, 1977; Oboler, 1980).

THINKING THROUGH THE ISSUES

Our discussion has highlighted the vast variation that occurs in marriage and family patterns throughout the world. How would you go about finding explanations for a particular social arrangement? Why is an explanation implying a structure is "natural," "functional," or "decreed by culture" really not an explanation? To get a grip on variations in the family system, why would it make sense to find arrangements that are

Perspectives on the Family

Since the family institution is found in all known societies and plays such a critical role in human affairs, it is hardly surprising that proponents of each of the major sociological schools should undertake to examine it. Functionalists focus on the structural properties and functions of family systems. Conflict theorists portray the family as a system of perpetual "give and take" and conflict regulation (Dahrendorf, 1965). And symbolic interactionists see the family as a dynamic entity through which people continually fashion ongoing relationships and construct a group existence. Each perspective yields insights, and each offers a complementary lens through which to view families.

The Functionalist Perspective

As we have noted in other chapters, functionalist theorists stress that if a society is to survive and operate with some measure of effectiveness, it must guarantee that certain essential tasks are performed. The performance of these tasks—termed *functions*—cannot be left to chance (see Chapter 2). To do so would run the risk that some activities would not be carried out, and the society would disintegrate. Although acknowledging that families show a good deal of variation throughout the world, functionalists seek to identify a number of recurrent functions families typically perform.

Reproduction   If a society is to perpetuate itself, new members have to be created. Sexual drives do not necessarily take care of the matter, because many people are aware that they can satisfy their sexual needs in the absence of procreation. For instance, the "pill," coitus interruptus, intrauterine devices (IUDs), condoms, abortion, infanticide, the rhythm method, and countless other techniques allow couples to separate sexual enjoyment from reproduction. Consequently, societies commonly motivate people to have children. Among peasant peoples, children are often defined as an economic asset. Religious considerations may operate. In pre-Communist China, where ancestor worship provided the foundation for religious life, one's comfort in the hereafter could only be assured by having numerous sons. And in the United States, many Americans still define marriage and children as affording the "good life"; in fact, the absence of children is often viewed as a misfortune (in a Gallup survey, 45 percent of the respondents said that childless people are more likely to be unfulfilled, and 64 percent felt that the childless are lonely) (Pebley and Bloom, 1982).

Socialization   At birth, children are not initiated into the ways of their culture, and thus each new generation subjects society to "barbarian invasion" (see Chapter 6). Most infants are fairly malleable, in that within broad limits they are capable of becoming adults of quite different sorts. It is urgent, therefore, that they become the "right" kind of adults. Through the process of socialization, children become inducted into their society's ways. It is the family that usually serves as the chief culture-transmitting agency. The family functions as an intermediary between the larger community and the individual.

"*Fred Homerson! How are you? How's the wife? The kids? The traditional family values?*"

Drawing by Dana Fradon; © 1986 The New Yorker Magazine, Inc.

Care, protection, and emotional support   Whereas the offspring of lower animals can survive independently of their parents within a matter of days or weeks, this is not true of human children. Their prolonged dependency dictates that they be fed, clothed, and provided with shelter well into puberty. Throughout the world, the family has been assigned the responsibility for shielding, protecting, sustaining, and otherwise maintaining children, the infirm, and other dependent members of the community. Moreover, since people are social beings, they have a variety of emotional and interpersonal needs that can be met only through interaction with other human beings. The family provides an important setting for intimate, face-to-face contact with others. Healthy family relationships afford companionship, love, security, a sense of worth, and a general feeling of well-being.

Assignment of status   Societies constantly confront a continual stream of raw material in the form of new infants who must be placed within the social structure. This function can be accomplished by assigning some statuses to an individual on the basis of family membership, what sociologists term *ascribed statuses* (see Chapter 4). The family confers statuses that (1) orient a person to a variety of interpersonal relationships, including those involving parents (parent-child), siblings (brothers and sisters), and kin (aunts, uncles, cousins, and grandparents); and that (2) orient a person to basic group memberships, including racial, ethnic, religious, class, national, and community relationships.

Regulation of sexual behavior   As we noted earlier in the chapter, a society's norms regulate sexual behavior by specifying who may engage in sexual behavior with whom and under what circumstances. In no known society are people given total freedom for sexual expression. Although some 70 percent of the world's societies permit some form of sexual license, even these societies typically do not approve of childbirth out of wedlock—the **norm of legitimacy** (like other norms, this one is occasionally violated, and those who violate it are usually punished). Legitimacy has to do with the placement of a child in a kinship network that defines the rights the newborn has to care, inheritance, and instruction (Goode, 1960; Malinowski, 1964). A great many complications result when the norm is violated. Consider the matter of the small but growing number of unmarried women who are becoming pregnant through artificial insemination by a male donor. The artificially conceived child is born into a legal limbo.

In sum, the functionalist perspective draws our attention to the requirements of group life and to the structural arrangements whereby these requirements are fulfilled. But critics point out that these tasks can be performed in other ways. Indeed, by virtue of social change, many of the economic, child care, and educational functions once performed by the family have been taken over by other institutions. Even so, the family tends to be that social unit most commonly responsible for reproduction, socialization, and the other functions considered here.

THINKING THROUGH THE ISSUES

On April 13, 1986, a baby girl was born who had been conceived under rather unusual circumstances (Goodman, 1986). The egg and sperm were from a New York couple and were brought together in a glass dish in a Cleveland laboratory. From this union there came an embryo that was implanted in the womb of a woman from Detroit. The second woman was paid a fee of $10,000 for fetus care, and at birth the baby was turned over to the couple from New York. The girl was the product of one woman's genes and another woman's womb. Who was the "mother" of the child? Should the surrogate mother have decided to keep the child after she was born, would the woman have been entitled to custody? If tests had shown after her birth that the infant girl was the offspring of the second woman and a lover, who would have been the "father" and "mother" of the child? Had the embryo been created from a sperm donor, who would have been the "father"? If the embryo had been created from a sperm donor and an egg donor, implanted into a second woman, and adopted by a third couple, who would have been the child's "father" and "mother"? Did the surrogate mother, who was paid to gestate an unborn child, sell her baby? Had the child been born handicapped and none of the parties wanted her, who would be responsible for her? Do donors have the right to know "their" children and do children have a right to know their donor parents?

The Conflict Perspective

Functionalists spotlight the tasks that serve the interests of society as a whole. In contrast, many conflict theorists

Surrogate Motherhood: Controversy and Anguish
Surrogate motherhood occurs when a woman, usually for pay, agrees to be inseminated by a man whose wife is infertile, to carry the embryo to birth, and then to turn the child over to the couple to rear as its own. The practice has given rise to disputes, such as the case of Baby M in which the surrogate mother, Mary Beth Whitehead changed her mind after she gave birth to the child. Whitehead was artificially inseminated with sperm from William Stern, whose wife, Elizabeth, contended she could not bear a child without significant risk to her health. In 1987, New Jersey Superior Court Judge Harvey Sorkow awarded custody of Baby M to Stern. *(Ricki Rosen/Picture Group)*

have seen the family as a social arrangement benefiting some people more than others. Friedrich Engels (1884/ 1902), Karl Marx's associate, viewed the family as a class society in miniature, with one class (men) oppressing another class (women). He contended that marriage was the first form of class antagonism in which the well-being of one group derived from the misery and repression of another group. The motivation for sexual domination was the economic exploitation of a woman's labor.

Sociologist Randall Collins (1975) says that historically men have been the "sexual aggressors" and women the "sexual prizes for men." He traces male dominance to the greater strength, size, and aggressiveness of men. Women, he says, have been victimized by smaller size and their vulnerability as childbearers. Across an entire spectrum of societies women have been seen as sexual property, taken as booty in war, used by their fathers in economic bargaining, and considered the property of their husbands. Collins (1975:232) says: "Men have appropriated women primarily for their beds rather than their kitchens and fields, although they could certainly be pressed into service in the daytime too."

According to Collins, men have ordered society so that women are their sexual property. They claim exclusive sexual rights to a woman much in the manner that they determine access to economic property like buildings and land. Marriage becomes a socially enforced contract of sexual property. Hence, within Western tradition, a marriage was not legal until sexually consummated; sexual assault within marriage was not legally rape; and the principal ground for divorce was sexual infidelity. A woman's virginity was the property of her father, and her sexuality the property of her husband. Rape has often been seen less as a crime perpetuated by a man against a woman than as a crime perpetuated by one man against another man.

In recent years, however, economic and political changes have improved women's bargaining position. When they were no longer under the control of their fathers, they became potentially free to negotiate their own sexual relationships. But women often found that within the free marriage market they had to trade their sexuality for the economic and status resources of men. Collins suggests that in an economic world dominated by men, the most favorable female strategy became one in which a woman maximized her bargaining power by appearing both as sexually alluring and as inaccessible as possible. She had to hold her sexuality in reserve as a sort of grand prize that she exchanged for male wealth and status stabilized by a marriage contract. Under such an arrangement, femininity and female virginity came to be idealized, and women were placed on a pedestal so that an element of sexual repression was built into courtship. But as women have bettered their economic opportunities, freeing themselves from economic dependence on men, they have gained the resources to challenge the double standard. The sexual bargains they strike can focus less upon marriage and more upon immediate entertainment, companionship, and sexual gratification.

Women as Property: A Wife Auction, England, 1832
Historically in the West, male dominance involved the notion that a father "owned" his daughter and a husband his wife. Until the twentieth century, English and American common law viewed a woman as civilly dead when she married. She lost her legal and social identity for she had to forsake her own name for that of her husband, she became "incorporated and consolidated" with her husband. A wife could not own property in her own right or sign a contract; her husband had claim to all her property, inherited or earned. *(North Wind Picture Archives)*

Although conflict theory reverberates with the seminal ideas of Friedrich Engels and Karl Marx, other social scientists have approached the issues somewhat differently. At the turn of the century, the psychoanalyst Sigmund Freud (1930/1961) and the sociologist Georg Simmel (1908/1955, 1908/1959) also advanced a conflict approach to the family. They contended that intimate relationships inevitably involve antagonism as well as love. More recently, sociologists like Jetse Sprey (1979) have suggested that conflict is a part of all systems and interactions, including family systems and marital interactions. They see family members as confronting two conflicting demands: to compete with one another for autonomy, authority, and privilege, and simultaneously to share one another's fate in order to survive and even flourish. Viewed in this fashion, the family is a social arrangement that structures close interpersonal relationships through ongoing processes of negotiation, problem solving, and conflict management. This view is quite compatible with the interactionist perspective.

The Interactionist Perspective

As we saw in Chapters 2 and 7, symbolic interactionists emphasize that human beings create, use, and communicate with symbols. They interact through role taking, a process of reading the symbols used by others and attributing meaning to them. Interactionists portray humans as a unique species because they have a mind and self. The mind and self arise out of interaction and provide the foundation for enduring social relationships and group life. When they enter interactive situations, people define the situation by identifying the expectations that it will hold for themselves and others. They then organize their own behavior in terms of these understandings.

As viewed by symbolic interactionists, marriage involves the fashioning of new definitions so that two people with separate and distinct biographies can come together and construct a "couple subworld." The marriage partners restructure their definitions of themselves, their daily lives, their past experiences, and their futures. Relationships with relatives, friends, and co-workers are redefined in ways that accommodate the marriage partner. New conceptions of reality emerge as each partner shapes his or her actions in conjunction with the other. As a result, the couple construct a joint biography with a mutually coordinated common memory. These patterns enable them to align their sentiments and actions on an ongoing basis, so their interaction can proceed smoothly (Berger and Kellner, 1964).

The symbolic interactionist perspective is a useful tool for examining the complexities of a relationship (Stryker and Statham, 1985). Thus, for example, should the roles of one family member change, invariably there are consequences for other family members as well. Later in the chapter we will see that parenthood alters the husband-wife relationship by creating new roles and increasing the complexity of the family unit. Likewise, family life is somewhat different in homes where a mother is in the paid labor force or where an economic provider is unemployed. And the loss of critical family roles, such as occurs through divorce, has vast implications for personal and family functioning. The symbolic interactionist perspective draws our attention to the complex interconnections that bind people within relationships. Through it, we encounter individuals as active beings who evolve, negotiate, and rework the social fabric that constitutes the mosaic of family life.

Marriage and the Family in the United States

The issues that divide sociological theorists are also found among the American public. Indeed, the family has become such a debated topic that sociologists Brigitte Berger and Peter L. Berger (1983) titled their recent book *The War Over the Family*. To its critics on the political left and among some feminists, the nuclear family is the source of many modern woes. To political conservatives, the family is the last bastion of morality in a world that is becoming increasingly decadent. And to the army of helping professionals, the family is an institution in grave difficulty. Let us see what we can make of these matters by taking a closer look at marriage and the family in American life.

Romantic Love

Americans look favorably upon love as a foundation for courtship and marriage. Although love has many meanings, we usually think of the strong physical and emotional attraction between a man and a woman as **romantic love**. Americans have capitalized on these feelings and elevated them to an exalted position. Many other peoples have viewed romantic love quite differently. Consider these words of the elders of an African tribe who, in discussing the problems of "runaway" marriages and illegitimacy, complained to the 1883 Commission on Native Law and Custom: "It is all this thing called love. We do not understand it at all" (quoted by Gluckman, 1955:76). The elders saw romantic love as a disruptive force. Given their cultural traditions, marriage did not mean a romantic attraction toward the spouse-to-be, marriage was not the free choice of children, and considerations other than love determined the selection of a mate.

The sociologist William J. Goode (1959) finds that romantic love is given more emphasis in some societies than in others. At one extreme, societies view marriage without love as mildly shameful; at the other, they define strong romantic attachment as a laughable or tragic aberration. The American middle class falls toward the pole of positive approval; the nineteenth-century Chinese

Romantic Love

Romantic love involves intense absorption in, acute longing for and dependency on, and strong bodily sensations in response to a loved one. It is a love that is quite fragile and dwindles after long interaction. Marriage partners find that the abrasions of ordinary living dull the idealization of the partner, and regular sexual gratification and growing predictability of the partner undermine high levels of arousal. (*Love Letters by Jean Honoré Fragonard*, © *The Frick Collection, New York*)

toward the pole of disapproval; and the Greeks after Alexander and the Romans of the Empire took a middle course. Goode offers a functional explanation for these differences. The extended kinship system of China, linked with a patriarchal household economy, contrasts with a middle-class American nuclear family that carries out few functions other than childrearing and recreation. Goode concludes that love is frowned upon in China because it is dysfunctional for the system. In the United States it is favored because there are few bonds except emotion to hold the family unit together.

Factors in Mate Selection

Given a field of eligible mates, why do we fall in love with and marry one person and not another? A variety of factors seem to be at work. One is **homogamy**, the tendency of "like to marry like." People of similar ages, races, religions, nationalities, education, intelligence, health, stature, attitudes, and countless other traits tend to marry one another to a degree greater than would be found by chance. Although homogamy seems to operate with respect to social characteristics, the evidence is less clear for such psychological factors as personality and temperament.

Physical attractiveness also plays a part in mate selection. On the whole, Americans share similar standards for evaluating physical attractiveness (Udry, 1965). Moreover, we prefer the companionship and friendship of attractive people to that of unattractive people (Reis, Nezlek, and Wheeler, 1980; Marks, Miller, and Maruyama, 1981). And we believe that attractive people are more likely to find good jobs, to marry well, and to lead happy and fulfilling lives—in brief, we think that "what is beautiful is good" (Dion, 1972; Dion, Berscheid, and Walster, 1972). When talking on the telephone to a man whom they believe to be physically attractive, women are more poised, more sociable, and more vivacious than when they talk to a man they believe to be physically unattractive (Brody, 1981). However, since the supply of unusually beautiful or handsome partners is limited, in real life we tend to select partners who have a degree of physical attractiveness similar to ours (Murstein, 1972, 1976; White, 1980). According to the **matching hypothesis**, we typically experience the greatest payoff and the least cost when we follow this course, since individuals of equal attractiveness are the ones most likely to reciprocate our advances.

Still another factor operates in choosing a mate. We feel most comfortable with people who have certain personality traits, while those with other traits "rub us the wrong way." Sociologist Robert F. Winch (1958) has taken this everyday observation and formulated a theory of **complementary needs** based on it. This concept refers to two different personality traits that are the counterparts of each other and that provide a sense of completeness when they are joined. For instance, dominant people find a complementary relationship with passive people, and talkative people find themselves attracted to good listeners. Roles also complement one another (Murstein, 1976). By way of illustration, a bedroom athlete is likely to be attracted to a lusty, passionate partner. Thus interpersonal attraction also depends on how well each partner fulfills the role expectations of the other and how mutually gratifying they find their "role fit."

Social exchange theory provides a unifying link among these three factors. It is based on the notion that we like those who reward us and dislike those who punish us (Blau, 1964; Sabatelli and Cecil-Pigo, 1985; England and Farkas, 1985). Many of our acts derive from confidence that from them will flow some benefit—perhaps a desired expression of love, gratitude, recognition, security, or material reward. In the course of interacting with one another, we reinforce the relationship by rewarding each other. Thus people with similar social traits, attitudes, and values are mutually rewarded by validating one another's lifestyle and supporting it at very

The Tendency of Like to Marry Like
A good deal of research reveals that we tend to like others who are similar to us. Indeed, the greater the proportion of similar attitudes that two people share, the greater is the likelihood that they will be attracted to one another (Gonzales et al., 1983). This is one factor that contributes to ingroup ethnic marriages. (*Abigail Heyman/Archive*)

low cost. In selecting partners of comparable physical attractiveness, we minimize the risk of rejection while maximizing the profit from such a conquest. And the parties in complementary relationships offer each other high rewards at low cost to themselves. In sum, social exchange theory proposes that people involved in a mutually satisfying relationship will exchange behaviors that have low cost and high reward.

In support of social exchange formulations, social psychologists find that partners who believe they are getting far more in exchange than they give feel insecure and guilty, while those who believe give more than they get feel angry (Golesman, 1986). Indeed, the best single predictor of satisfaction in loving relationships is how closely your perceptions of what the other person feels about you compare with what you want the partner to feel. Relationships tend to go bad when there is a mismatch between what you want from the other person and what you think you are getting (Trotter, 1986).

Married Couples

Most adult Americans hope to establish a close and meaningful relationship with another person and make the relationship work. This finding underlies a recent study of American couples undertaken by sociologists Philip Blumstein and Pepper Schwartz (1983). They investigated the experiences of four types of couples: married, cohabiting, homosexual male, and lesbian. The study centered on New York City, Seattle, and San Francisco, where the researchers secured 12,000 completed questionnaires. From these, Blumstein and Schwartz selected 300 couples for in-depth interviews. Eighteen months later they sent half the couples a follow-up questionnaire to determine if they were still living together. As with most volunteer samples, the survey was not wholly representative, since it was overweighted with white, affluent, well-educated Americans. The researchers believe that any bias is toward the liberal side, and that the nation is probably even more conservative in its family patterns than the results reveal.

Blumstein and Schwartz had expected American couples to be less conventional than they were. Consider work. Although 60 percent of the wives were employed outside the home, only 30 percent of the men and 39 percent of the women believed that both spouses should work. Even when the wives had full-time jobs, they did the greater part of the housework. Whereas 59 percent of the women contributed eleven or more hours a week to household chores, only 22 percent of the men contributed this amount of time. Indeed, husbands so objected

to doing housework that the more they did of it, the more unhappy they were, the more they argued with their wives, and the greater were the chances the couple would divorce. In contrast, if a man did not contribute what a women felt to be his fair share of the housework, the relationship was not usually jeopardized.

American men seem preoccupied with dominance and power. In fact, they could take pleasure in their partner's success only if it was not superior to their own. In contrast, women were found to be happier and relationships were more stable when the male partners were ambitious and successful. Most married couples pooled their money. However, regardless of how much the wife earned, they measured their financial success by the husband's income.

Early in the marriage men were more likely than women to feel encroached upon by the relationship and to complain that they needed more "private time." But in longstanding marriages it was the wives who more often complained that they did not have enough time by themselves. Further, women were more likely than men to say they were the emotional caretakers of the family, although 39 percent of the men indicated that they fo-

Successful Marriages

Sociologists Jeanette Lauer and Robert Lauer (1985) surveyed 300 happily married couples, asking them why their marriages survived. The most frequently cited reason was having a positive attitude toward one's spouse. The partners commonly said that "my spouse is my best friend" and "I like my spouse as a person." A second key to a lasting marriage was a belief that marriage is a long-term commitment and a sacred institution. *(Comstock)*

cused more on their marriage than they did on their work. In about a quarter of the marriages, both partners claimed they were relationship-centered.

Like Blumstein and Schwartz, Theodore Caplow and his colleagues (1982) expected to find the American nuclear family in trouble when they undertook a restudy of Middletown, a pseudonym for Muncie, Indiana. Robert S. and Helen Merrill Lynd (1929, 1937) had made Middletown into a "sociological laboratory" in their celebrated 1920s study. Sociologists generally agree that the Lynds' research represents one of the best large-scale uses of anthropological methods in the study of an American community. The Lynds portrayed Middletown as a small city whose residents were straining to enter the twentieth century, but nevertheless clung to a nineteenth-century faith in the value of work, church, family, and country.

On the surface, much seems to have changed in Middletown in the intervening fifty years. High school students wear blue jeans and T-shirts to classes; mothers leave their children at day care centers and take jobs; there is bloodshed on television and graphic sex in the movies; and junior high school girls line up at the Planned Parenthood center to get their birth control pills. But Caplow and his associates conclude that doom-sayers are wrong and the family has not lost its attractiveness. They observe (1982:323).

> Tracing the changes from the 1920s to the 1970s, we discovered increased family solidarity, a smaller generation gap, closer marital communication, more religion, and less mobility. With respect to the major features of family life, the trend of the past two generations has run in the opposite direction from the trend nearly everyone perceives and talks about.

They say their findings were as surprising to them "as they may be to our readers."

Although divorce rates have soared, the research described above and other studies reveal that Americans have not given up on marriage. Public opinion surveys confirm that Americans depend on marriage for their psychological well-being (Glenn and Weaver, 1981). As Figure 13.1 shows, marriage is the most prevalent American lifestyle, and the Census Bureau projects that it will remain so. However, increasing numbers of Americans no longer view marriage as a permanent institution, but rather as something that can be ended and reentered. These matters are examined more closely in the box on pages 350–351.

FIGURE 13.1.   **Household Composition Now and Census Bureau Projections**
The Census Bureau expects nonfamily households (singles and unmarried or unrelated couples living together) to grow to almost one-third of the total by the year 2000. Fairly high divorce rates are cited as one factor. In addition, young adults continue to put off marriage. And an increasingly elderly population, with more women outliving husbands, is also contributing to the growth in single households. *Source: U.S. Bureau of the Census.*

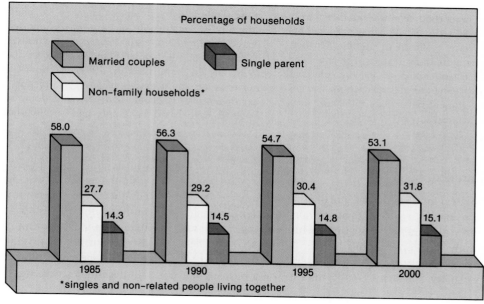

Is the Family Endangered or Merely Changing?

Some 90 percent of American men and women still think that marriage is the best way to live (Walsh, 1986). Given this sentiment, it is hardly surprising that a good many Americans have been concerned about the directions in which family life has been moving in recent decades. But they tend to be of two minds. There are those who say that the family is timeless, rooted in our social and animal nature. But since the institutional structure of society is always changing, the family must change to reflect this fact. Accordingly, although a durable feature of the human experience, the family is said to be a resilient institution (Bane, 1976). The other view holds that the family is in crisis, with decay and disintegration stalking it at every turn. This latter view is currently the most fashionable. The evidence in support of it seems dramatic and, on the surface, incontrovertible (see Table A). Divorce rates have soared; birth rates have fallen; the proportion of unwed mothers has increased; single-parent households have proliferated; mothers of young children have entered the labor force in large numbers; and the elderly are placing growing reliance on the government rather than the family for financial support (Fuchs, 1983).

Table A SYNOPSIS OF THE CHANGING AMERICAN FAMILY

	1965	1980	1985
Working women (percentage of all women 16 and over)	36.7	51.1	54.7
Fertility rate (number of children the average woman will have at the end of her childbearing years)*	2.9	1.8	1.8
Marriage rate (number of marriages per 1,000 population)†	9.3	10.6	10.2
Median age at first marriage			
Men	22.8	24.7	25.5
Women	20.6	22.0	23.3
Divorce rate (number of couples divorcing per 1,000 population)	2.5	5.2	5.0
Single-parent families (percentage of all families with children under 18)	10.1	19.5	26.3
Premarital births (percentage of all births)	7.7	18.4	21.5
Living alone (percentage of all households occupied by single person)	15.0	22.6	23.7

*A 2.1 rate is needed for the natural replacement of the population.
†Remarriages account for about one-third of the recent totals.

Sources: U.S. Census Bureau; National Center for Health Statistics; U.S. Department of Labor.

Laments about the current decline of the family imply that at an earlier time in history the family was more stable and harmonious than it currently is. Yet, despite massive research, historians have not located a golden age of the family (Flandrin, 1979; Degler, 1980; Cherlin, 1983). For instance, the marriages of seventeenth-century England and New England were based on family and property needs, not on affection. Loveless marriages, the tyranny of husbands, and the beating and abuse of children give us a grim picture (Shorter, 1975). And families were riddled by desertion and death. Indeed, because of fewer deaths, disruptions of marriage up through the completion of childrearing have been *declining* in the United States since 1900 (Uhlenberg, 1980).

Parenthood

Nuclear families that are not disrupted by divorce, desertion, or death typically pass through a series of changes and realignments across time, what sociologists call the **family life cycle** (Hill, 1964; Nock, 1979). These changes and realignments are related to the altered expectations and requirements imposed on a husband and wife as children are born and grow up. The family begins with the husband-wife pair and becomes increasingly complex as members are added, creating new roles and multiplying the number of relationships. The family then stabilizes for a time, after which it begins shrinking as each of the adult children is launched. Finally, it returns once more to the husband-wife pair, and eventually terminates with the death of a spouse.

The notion that the family should consist of a breadwinner husband, a homemaker wife, and their dependent children is of recent origin. The rural, preindustrial family was a relatively self-sufficient unit that produced most of what it consumed. Husbands, wives, children, and lodgers were all engaged in gainful work. With the onset of industrialization, more and more family members sought work for wages in factories and workshops. This trend led Karl Marx and Friedrich Engels to deplore the capitalists' use of cheap female and child labor to run factory machines. They termed it "shameless" and "unconscionable" that able-bodied men, their strength and skills no longer needed, should find themselves dismissed or compelled to accept "children's work at children's wages." Throughout the Western world, the nascent labor movement pressed for the establishment of a "living wage," an income sufficient for a male breadwinner to support a wife and children in modest comfort.

It was during the nineteenth century that Americans culturally sorted jobs into male and female categories. Women's jobs were deemed to be either of short duration until they married, or a lifetime commitment of secular celibacy as nurses and schoolteachers. Women's special place became defined as the "domestic sphere." The restriction of large numbers of married women to domestic activities took place only after industrialization was well established (Cherlin, 1983; Carlson, 1986).

Prior to the 1950s, family life tended to be relatively disorderly. Young adults were expected to postpone leaving home or put off marriage to help the family face an unexpected economic crisis or a death in the family. At the turn of the century, young adults married relatively late because they were often obligated to help support parents and siblings. But with the economic prosperity that followed World War II, the average age at marriage dropped sharply. Today's young adults seem to have reversed the trend, and are marrying at later ages (Cherlin, 1983). The emphasis on emotional satisfactions and the associated transformation of the family into a private institution did not become widespread beyond the middle class until this century. In the early 1900s, such trends as the decline in the boarding and lodging of nonfamily members, the growing tendency for unmarried adults to leave home, and the fall in fertility created the conditions for increasingly private and affectionate bonds within the small nuclear family (Laslett, 1973).

All in all, reports of the death of the American family are greatly exaggerated. Public-opinion polls show that the vast majority of Americans—97 percent—believe that when families are happy and healthy, the world is a better place. And nearly 9 out of 10 Americans regard their family as one of the most important facets of their lives. However, Americans now want a different kind of marriage. In 1974, half of women and 48 percent of men said that the most satisfying lifestyle was one where the husband worked and the wife stayed home and took care of the home and children. By 1985, only 37 percent of women and 43 percent of men thought this arrangement the best. Fifty-seven percent of women and 50 percent of men picked a marriage where the husband and wife share work, housekeeping, and child care. Seven in ten Americans also agree "strongly" that it is important for fathers to spend as much time with their children as mothers do, and an additional 20 percent agree "to some extent" (*Public Opinion*, 1986; Schwartz, 1987).

Concerns about the family have a long history (Greer, 1979; Demos, 1987). Educators of the European medieval and Enlightenment periods worried about the strength and character of the family. In colonial and frontier times, people expressed anxiety about the disruption of family life. And in the nineteenth and early twentieth centuries worry about the family was cloaked in recurrent public hysteria regarding the "peril" posed to the nation's Anglo-American institutions by the arrival of immigrant groups with "alien cultures." So the "family question" is not new. Although we may think that the grindstones of social change are pulverizing family organization, the family remains a vital, adaptive, resilient human institution.

Each modification in the role content of one family member has implications for all the other members. The arrival of the first child compels the reorganization of the couple's life, since living as a trio is more complicated than living as a pair. Parents have to juggle work roles, alter their time schedules, change their communication patterns, and relinquish some measure of privacy. And parenthood competes with the husband-wife role. Couples report that the "romantic" qualities of their relationship lessen, and they share fewer leisure activities. On the whole, marital quality ratings fall after the birth of a first child, although more substantially for women than for men and for nontraditional than for gender-typed women (Belsky, Lang, and Rovine, 1985; Belsky, Lang, and Huston, 1986).

Even so, having a first baby seems to have a stabilizing effect on marriages over the short run. By the time their children are 2 years of age, parents have a divorce rate under 8 percent, compared to more than 20 percent for childless couples (Waite, Haggstrom, and Kanouse, 1985). However, it may simply be that people who decide to have children are happier together than those who decide against having them. Couples commonly report that having a baby increases their sense of partnership. Overall, while their initial encounter with parenthood may be stressful, most couples do not find it sufficiently stressful to warrant calling the experience a crisis (Lamb, 1978; McLaughlin and Micklin, 1983). Contemporary parents seem to have a less romantic and more realistic view of the probable effects of children on their lives than did earlier generations. And despite the changes a child brings to their lives, most couples report enormous satisfaction with parenthood (Elias, 1986).

Clinical psychologists and psychiatrists have stressed the problem parents face when their children leave home. It is most common among couples who use their children to disguise the emptiness of their own relationship. But most couples do not experience difficulty with the "empty-nest" period of their life. The majority view this stage "as a time of new freedoms." Indeed, national surveys show that middle-aged women whose children have left home experience greater general happiness and enjoyment of life, in addition to greater marital happiness, than middle-aged women with children still living at home (Vander Zanden, 1985).

New Patterns and Pressure Points

American family life has undergone a good many changes in recent decades. For this reason, the family-life-cycle approach is unrepresentative of more and more American families. The traditional concept of the family—in which the husband is the only breadwinner, the wife is a homemaker who is not part of the paid labor force, and there are minor children—may be useful for some purposes, but it does not represent the typical American family today. In fact, less than 7 out of 100 American families currently fit this description. The family-life-cycle approach barely touches on the father's family contribution, and then only at the time of retirement. It makes no reference at all to the mother's work. Indeed, it fosters the notion that there are two categories of women: those who are married and those with careers.

Yet increasing numbers of women are spending a larger amount of time in roles that lie outside the traditional family. So the career woman and the mother may be one and the same person. A good place to begin our consideration of changing family patterns and pressure points, then, is with employed mothers.

Employed Mothers

As we pointed out in Chapter 12, sexual inequality has been sustained historically by assigning the economic provider role to men and the childrearing role to women. However, over the past several decades increasing numbers of mothers with children have found employment outside the home. As reflected in the data in Figure 13.2, in 1986 some 63 percent of children under age 18 had working mothers, comprising some 32 million children and 20.8 million working mothers (72 percent of the mothers work full-time). Nearly 51 percent of all mothers with preschool children were employed outside the home (some 66 percent of the mothers work full-time), as were 48.4 percent of mothers with children under age 1.

FIGURE 13.2   Mothers in the Labor Force by the Age of Children
Source: U.S. Department of Labor.

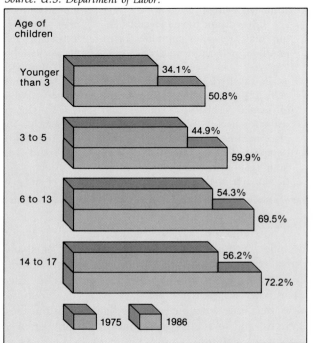

Corporate Day Care Centers
In contrast to their counterparts in most other industrialized nations, American parents are pretty much on their own in finding and providing day care for their youngsters while they work. However, a number of firms have pioneered programs that provide care for the children of their employees on corporate premises, such as the child care center at Wang Laboratories. But many companies have decided to leave the child care issue alone. *(Rich Friedman/Black Star)*

Serious concern is frequently voiced about the future of the nation's children as more and more mothers enter the workforce (Ricks, 1987). A good many working mothers also experience guilt for not staying home with their children (Berg, 1986). Many people fear that the working mother represents a loss to children in terms of supervision, love, and cognitive enrichment. Yet overall, an accumulating body of research suggests that there is little difference in the development of children whose mothers work and children whose mothers remain at home (Stith and Davis, 1984; Cochran and Gunnarsson, 1985; Meredith, 1986). In fact, many psychologists and sociologists are no longer asking whether it is good or bad that mothers work. Instead, they are finding that a more important issue is whether the mother, regardless of employment, is satisfied with her situation (Stuckey, McGhee, and Bell, 1982; Ainslie, 1984). The working mother who obtains personal satisfaction from employment, who does not feel excessive guilt, and who has adequate household arrangements is likely to perform as well as or better than the nonworking mother. Women who are not working and would like to, and working mothers whose lives are beset by harassment and strain, are the ones whose children are mostly likely to display maladjustment and behavior problems.

With the entry of women into the labor force, arrangements for child care are shifting from care in the home to care outside the home. But even so, between 1977 and 1984 the use of group care rose only from 13 to 15 percent, with most children being cared for at home or in another person's home. In 1986 some 5 million American children under the age of 10 had no one to look after them when they came home from school in the afternoon. An additional 500,000 preschoolers were in the same predicament. For significant portions of the day or night, many working parents are unable to care personally for their children, and they lack relatives or friends to whom they can turn for reliable babysitting. One answer to this problem is day care. But the quality of the day care currently available and affordable leaves many people dissatisfied. Ralph Nader, the consumer activist, describes some centers as "children's warehouses." And sex-abuse scandals at centers from California to New York have terrified a good many parents. Additionally, low-quality facilities function as networks for spreading a variety of diseases, especially colds, diarrhea, and dysentery (Ricks, 1984; Brody, 1986).

The United States is one of the few industrialized nations that does not have a comprehensive day care program. European nations—particularly Sweden—have established nationally subsidized support systems. In contrast, a 1985 study by the Conference Board, a business research group, found that American parents pay about $3,000 per child a year for out-of-home child care services (Noble, 1986). Some 2,500 American companies offer help with day care, up from 110 in 1978, but such programs are still in their infancy. Schools are also under pressure to offer services to 3- and 4-year-olds and to provide a safe haven beyond the normal school day for older children (Seligson, 1986). Child care advocates warn that the failure to develop a national policy will result in "a generation of neglected children" (Palmer, 1984).

There is, however, one encouraging note. Most child psychologists agree that *high-quality* day care and nursery schools afford acceptable child care arrangements (Clarke-Stewart and Gruber, 1984; Meredith, 1986). Such programs are characterized by small group size, high staff-child ratios, well-trained staffs, good equipment, and attractive and nurturing environments. Most children show remarkable resilience. Throughout the world, children are raised under a great variety of conditions, and the day care arrangement is just one of them. What is crucial is that children have consistent and warm relationships with their caregivers. Moreover, working mothers provide a somewhat different role model for their children, imparting less traditional gender-role concepts and a higher evaluation of female competence (Shreve, 1984; Stephan and Corder, 1985).

Two-Income Couples

Some 27.7 million American households—67 percent of all married couples—have two breadwinners. Even so, as we saw in Chapter 12, women still continue to shoulder the primary responsibility for household tasks and child care. The result is that overwhelming numbers of working women report they do not have enough time to meet their responsibilities (General Mills, 1981). When women are expected to contribute more than men to the household division of labor, role strains may be created, especially when husbands view their wives as failing to live up to traditional gender expectations as wives and mothers (Chassin et al., 1985). And women may be less effective on the job than they otherwise could be and fail to realize their true career potential. Alternatively, women may fall victim to the super-woman syndrome and attempt to excel both on the job and at home.

In two-income families, the man typically has a larger voice in major household decisions than the woman does. Junior-senior relationships commonly operate, with the wife usually secondary (O'Barr, 1979; Gappa, O'Barr, and St. John-Parsons, 1980; Cooper et al., 1986). For instance, should a husband be offered a better position elsewhere in the nation, the wife typically makes the move regardless of the effect the transfer has on her career. Moreover, some wives fear that should they take responsibility for their own finances, their husbands will feel that their masculinity is threatened. However, should they relinquish control of their income to the husband, they often experience resentment and bitterness. Consequently, many couples maintain separate accounts or pool a portion of their incomes.

Scheduling time together is a frequent source of tension for dual-career couples (Moore, 1984). But the conflict often masks problems of commitment, lack of intimacy, and divergent goals. Arguments over work schedules usually have more to do with "how much does he/she care" than with the amount of time the couple actually spends together. Another source of tension derives from income differences. On average, wives earn only 60 percent as much as their husbands do as full-time, year-round workers. However, in nearly one-fifth of dual-earner couples, the wife brings home more money than the husband (Census Bureau, 1986). Men often feel their self-esteem threatened under this arrangement, and the couples run a higher risk of psychological and physical abuse, marital conflict, and sexual problems (Kessler and McRae, 1981; Rubenstein, 1982). Yet the difficulties are not insurmountable, provided

---

Two-Earner Couples
Dual-earner couples now substantially outnumber single-earner couples in the United States. The work time of dual-earner couples reduces the time they have with one another in domestic life, including time together for eating meals, watching TV, and enjoying shared leisure. It is through face-to-face conversations and common activities, however, that marriage partners construct a mutual sense of oneness and place in the social world. Consequently, dual-earner couples may have to pay closer attention to cultivating the companionable aspects of their marriage (Kingston and Nock, 1987). *(Cathey Cheney/EKM-Nepenthe)*

couples can come to terms with old expectations and new realities and learn what works best for them. Women are growing more confident of their knowledge and abilities, while increasing numbers of men are learning to share family responsibility and power. The dynamics of family decision making are currently in transition as many dual-income couples evolve new patterns and traditions (Huber and Spitze, 1983; Bird, Bird, and Scruggs, 1984; Cooper et al., 1986).

The separation of work and family life finds its most extreme expression in *commuter marriages*—relationships in which the spouses maintain separate residences in order to meet the requirements of their work and yet are married and expect to remain so. The separation commonly comes about as a result of the husband and wife pursuing careers that require different geographic locations. Some estimates place the number of commuter marriages at about 700,000 couples. Increasingly, university faculty members confront this type of relationship. They are finding that getting a university teaching job is hard enough, and getting two jobs in the same place is nearly impossible. The chief motivation for commuting tends to be the personal satisfaction and fulfillment provided by career involvement. Women in commuter marriages typically report that they spend less time at traditional household chores and more time developing their careers than would otherwise be the case. But unlike co-resident dual-career couples, when the husband and wife do get together, they do not allow work to encroach on their time. Commuter marriages demonstrate that co-residence and a shared economic fate can no longer be taken for granted as defining conditions for the family (Gerstel and Gross, 1984). They also highlight some of the pressures that come to bear on contemporary families, at times producing family breakup and divorce.

Divorce

Although divorce rates have been on the upswing in recent decades, they seem to have stabilized in the 1980s. Even so, should current rates persist, Census Bureau experts predict that six out of ten American women now in their thirties will go through at least one divorce. For the 70 percent who remarry, 52 percent will experience a second divorce. The projection for women in their forties is an eventual 46 percent divorce rate; for those in their fifties, a 24 percent rate; and for those now in their twenties, a 50 percent rate (Census Bureau projections refer only to women because women's responses to cen-

sus surveys have been found to be more accurate than men's). It seems that women currently in their thirties are a somewhat unique group. They were the ones who led the way through the turbulent Vietnam war era. They had been brought up on traditions that were already on the way out. Parents had taught them to go out and find a man, settle down, and raise a family. Yet they were the trendsetters who entered the workforce in extraordinary numbers and created new social standards. This generation confronted an era of change and uncertainty that included new ideas about husband-wife relationships.

Those now in their twenties are heirs to the new traditions and so may escape some of the stresses experienced by the baby-boom generation. If younger adults divorce less frequently than their older baby-boom counterparts, the overall rate of divorce should be slowed (Clancy, 1986; Norton and Moorman, 1987). Whereas a decade ago Americans seemed more willing to take a chance on divorce, they have become more conservative and more realistic in their marital expectations. In brief, more and more couples are finding it better to make up than break up (Kantrowitz, 1987). These trends are not untypical, since there have been noteworthy fluctuations in the divorce rate over the past century. A low point of 1.3 divorces per 1,000 population occurred in 1933 at the depth of the Great Depression; the rate rose sharply after World War II to a peak of 4.3 in 1946. Thereafter, the rate declined slowly, reaching a low of 2.1 in 1958. It then moved upward, peaking at 5.3 in 1979 and again in 1981 (Glick and Lin, 1986).

Statistics on divorce present people minus the tears. Although more common today than among earlier generations, divorce is hardly a routine experience. In many cases, divorce exacts a greater emotional and physical toll than almost any other type of stress, including widowhood (Brody et al., 1983; Masterson, 1984). Separated and divorced people are overrepresented in mental institutions, more likely to die from cardiovascular disease, cancer, pneumonia, and cirrhosis of the liver, and more prone to die from accidents, homicides, and suicides. Women in middle and late life are especially devastated by divorce. These women—termed *displaced homemakers*—often dedicated themselves to managing a home and raising children, and then find themselves jettisoned after years of marriage. Divorced mothers with young children frequently feel overwhelmed: They commonly find themselves in tight financial straits; they may be working and simultaneously attempting to go back to school; they may also be trying to revive their own social

ISSUES THAT SHAPE OUR LIVES

Do We Need New Divorce Laws?

Social intervention in society—no matter how beneficent its purposes—often has unexpected outcomes. A good example is the dramatic transformation of the marriage contract since the advent of no-fault divorce laws in 1970. In *The Divorce Revolution* (1985), sociologist Lenore Weitzman explores the economic and social consequences of the new divorce laws for women and children in the United States. She had begun her research assuming that no-fault divorce was a real improvement for women and families, but she found otherwise. The laws, designed to treat women and men equally, have in practice created hardship for divorced women and their children. In the first year after the divorce, the standard of living of the typical divorced woman with young children plummets 73 percent, while that of her divorced husband goes up 42 percent.

Weitzman analyzed some 2,500 divorce decrees issued both before and since California's no-fault reforms became law in 1970. Additionally, she interviewed family court judges and prominent divorce lawyers and more than 100 recently divorced couples in the Los Angeles area. Weitzman wanted to find out why divorce has become "a financial catastrophe for most women." She found that most courts do not require husbands to contribute more than one-third of their income to the support of their ex-wives and children. Moreover, judges frequently order the family home to be sold, with half the proceeds going to the wife, resulting in the woman having to find a much smaller house with less room for herself and her children. Further, valuable but often intangible assets acquired during the marriage—credit, pensions, insurance, entitlements, professional credentials, and future earning power—usually go with the husband. Finally, a divorced woman is likely to enter a competitive labor market without skills, seniority, or opportunity for training. Weitzman says that the new laws give a clear message to young women in planning their futures. Divorce may send you into poverty if you invest in your family ahead of your career.

Weitzman identifies three categories of women who are particularly vulnerable but who rarely get assistance: mothers with custody of young children, women requiring transitional support, and older homemakers. The plight of the last is especially difficult, says Weitzman, because both their husbands and society had promised the women that marriage is a lifetime commitment and homemaking an honorable occupation. Instead, no-fault divorce changed the rules in the middle of the game—after the women had fulfilled their share of the bargain. Now the women find that they are unable to make up for the 25 or so years they spent out of the labor force. Weitzman urges judges and legislators to rethink current notions about alimony and to recognize it as an acceptable way to compensate long-married women for their contributions.

Weitzman also targets the nonsupport of children by divorced fathers, a record of inadequate awards, rampant default, and insufficient enforcement. She does not favor a return to the earlier system, with its rancorous charges of cruelty and adultery and legal wrangling over the assignment of guilt. Most of her recommendations consist primarily of adjustments in the interpretation, enforcement, and administration of current laws: the inclusion of "career assets"—pensions and retirement benefits, education and training, enhanced earning capacity, medical and health insurance, and other entitlements—along with material goods when marital assets are divided; effective child support enforcement measures such as withholding wages, property liens, and the threat of jail; and assurance of an equal share of the marital property to long-married, older homemakers. In sum, Weitzman places the problems that divorced women and their children face in the context of society, and traces the structural forces that generate poverty and hardship. Although no-fault laws in many states differ from those in California, which may bias her research, this does not seem to invalidate her findings.

lives; and all the while they have the primary responsibility for rearing and caring for their dependent children. The box dealing with American divorce laws examines these matters more closely. But even though divorce is a disruptive experience—often frightening, frustrating, and depressing—it can simultaneously be an exciting and potentially liberating one (Spanier and Thompson, 1984). Young divorced people, especially women, often experience a greater sense of personal competence and independence once they have adjusted to their divorce (Yarrow, 1987).

More than half of the couples who divorce have children. Researchers find that the households of divorced mothers and fathers are substantially more disor-

Divorce: Although More Common, Hardly a Routine Experience
When a couple who are in their forties or fifties divorce, the woman usually anticipates the breakup much sooner than the man does. Wives typically recognize that their marriage is not working 10 years or more before the actual divorce. In contrast, men usually come to realize that their marriage is crumbling fewer than 3 years before the divorce. It thus seems that women monitor their marriages more closely than men do. Consequently, more women than men report that the worst part of the divorce is the period before the divorce decree (Hagestad and Smyer, 1983). *(Joel Gordon)*

ganized than are those of intact families (Hetherington, Cox, and Cox, 1982; Guidubaldi and Perry, 1985). The first two years after divorce are especially difficult: Divorced parents do not communicate as well with their children, are less affectionate, and are more inconsistent discipliners than parents in intact families (Wallerstein and Kelly, 1980; Fine, Moreland, and Schwebel, 1983). Divorced mothers with teenage sons find their situation particularly stressful. And financial problems complicate the difficulties of many women. Less than half of divorced mothers receive any money from their children's fathers; those who do seldom receive much.

Overall, the negative effects of divorce seem less severe if a child lives with the same-sex parent or maintains a good relationship with at least one parent and is able to return to a consistent, reliable family routine (Peterson and Zill, 1986). Of course, not all the difficulties children experience can be attributed to the divorce of their parents. Many problem behaviors commonly viewed as a consequence of divorce result from family tensions that were present prior to the parental splitup (Block, Block, and Gjerde, 1986). The adjustment of many children, especially those of educated, well-off parents, improves by the third year following a divorce. And in many cases, children are less depressed and do better academically than before the divorce (Elias, 1987).

THINKING THROUGH THE ISSUES

How does divorce provide an opportunity for society to articulate what it expects of husbands and wives? If a court fails to award alimony to a 50-year-old woman who has been a homemaker and mother for 25 years, what does it say about her contributions? If it expects her to secure a job and support herself, what message does it give younger women? Does marital property consist of intangible property—pensions and retirement benefits, licenses to practice a profession, medical insurance, and government benefits—as well as tangible assets—homes, cars, and TV sets? Consider the kinds of inheritance we currently give our children. Does it consist of the family farm or business? Or do middle-class parents attempt to give their children an education so that they can make their way in the world? These new forms of property are usually worth more than the tangible assets of a marriage. If one career asset—earning capacity—is left with the husband, is "property" being divided equally at divorce (Weitzman, 1986)? How might ex-husbands and their new wives or companions define the situation? How would you go about restructuring American divorce laws in dealing with the disposition of assets in divorce proceedings?

Stepfamilies

Most divorced people remarry. Because 60 percent of remarried persons are parents, their new partners become stepparents. One in six American families is a stepfamily; 35 million Americans live in one. Some 35 percent of children born today will live in a stepfamily before they are 18 (Johnson, 1986). Clearly, biological and sociological parenthood are not necessarily one and the same. Nor is being a sibling. Almost one in five children share the home with half-siblings, and many more have step-siblings (Bumpass, 1984).

Most stepparents attempt to re-create a traditional family because it is the only model they have. But a stepfamily functions differently from the traditional nuclear family (Mills, 1984). For one thing, the stepparent role does not necessarily approximate that of a biological parent, particularly in authority, legitimacy, and respect. For another, stepparents and stepchildren lack a mutual history and a previous opportunity to bond. Further complicating matters, society lacks a clear picture of how members should relate to one another. For instance, how should a son relate to his stepparent and vice versa, and how should the custodial stepparent relate to the former spouse? Overall, the family tree of a stepfamily can be complex and convoluted, populated not only by children of both spouses, but by six sets of grandparents, relatives of former spouses, relatives of new spouses, and the people former spouses marry. The more complex the social system of the remarriage, the greater the ambiguity about roles within the family and the greater the likelihood of difficulties (Clingempeel, 1981). Because stepfamilies lack a clear definition of the expectations and roles for each family member, sociologist Andrew Cherlin (1978) terms them "an incomplete institution."

Stepfamilies often start on an idealistic note. Each spouse typically expects the other to be a new and improved version of the old one. As the months go by, family members gain a more realistic view. Misunderstandings in stepfamilies take many forms. Often, they are caused by conflicting family traditions, unfulfilled expectations, financial pressures, loyalty conflicts, unresolved power struggles, and ill-defined behavior standards for the children. Discipline is a frequent problem, because children often see the stepparent as an intruder. Accordingly, it is hardly surprising that stepparents report significantly less satisfaction with their family life than do married couples with biological children. Recent research shows that 17 percent of remarriages which involve stepchildren on both sides wind up in divorce within three years, compared with 6 percent of first-time marriages and 10 percent of remarriages without stepchildren (White and Booth, 1985).

Most stepparents are stepfathers. Although growing numbers of fathers are winning child custody cases, the vast majority of children still live primarily with their mothers. Stepfathers usually underrate their parenting skills and their contributions to the lives of their stepchildren. Indeed, their stepchildren and spouses give them higher marks than they give themselves (Bohannan and Erickson, 1978). Children living with stepfathers apparently do just as well, or just as poorly, in school and in their social life as children living with natural fathers. And children with stepfathers on the whole do better than children from father-absent homes (Robinson, 1984; Ganong and Coleman, 1984).

The stepfamily must adjust to many types of challenges not encountered by most natural families. In order to succeed, the stepfamily must loosen the bound-

A Stepfamily Wedding
The number of stepfamilies is growing rapidly in the United States. On the basis of the research currently available, it seems fair to conclude that children may turn out well or poorly in either a stepfamily or a natural family. Clearly, the stepfamily is required to adjust to many types of challenges not encountered by most natural families. Yet the opportunities for personal growth and satisfaction are considerable. (Ulrike Welsch)

aries that encapsulated the two previous biological families and structure a new social unit (Paernow, 1984). As old arrangements "unfreeze," members must create enough mutual empathy to support a shared awareness so that the family can mobilize and act to meet its members' needs. Most workable solutions leave some of the "old" ways of doing things intact while fashioning new rituals, expectations, and rules that define differences between the stepfamily and the previous family. When the restructuring is successful, the members need no longer give constant attention to relationships and can interact spontaneously and comfortably. Although certain strains are associated with stepfamilies, so is a good deal of positive adaptation (Furstenberg and Spanier, 1984).

Family Violence, Child Abuse, and Incest

In recent years problems of family violence, child abuse, and incest have become the focus of public attention. The expression "coming out of the closet" is an apt one when applied to battered women and victims of child abuse and sexual molestation. They have been as reluctant to reveal their plight as gay persons have been to reveal their sexual preferences. Traditionally they have attempted to keep the indignities they have experienced inside the family home. But there has been a growing recognition in recent years that family violence is rooted in the social system. Since physical force is the ultimate tool for keeping subordinate groups in their place, women and children have often been the victims of physical assault by men (Straus and Gelles, 1986). Since the family is a private institution, the violence that occurs within it often is unknown to outsiders, and so men can get away with it.

Estimates of family violence vary widely. It is difficult to obtain valid information about family behavior, especially when the behavior is socially unacceptable. The best estimates suggest that some 1.6 million wives are beaten each year. At least one in ten married women has experienced marital rape. Some 1.1 million of the nation's elderly may be abuse victims. And some 1.5 million children are victims of abuse (Gelles and Cornell, 1985; Straus and Gelles, 1986). Although both men and women engage in violence, men typically do more damage than their female partners. Some men find it easier to control the weaker members of the family by force, because it does not require negotiation or interpersonal skills. Women put up with battering for a variety of reasons (Strube and Barbour, 1983; Gelles, 1985). For

one thing, the fewer the resources a wife has in the way of education or job skills, the more vulnerable she is in the marriage. For another, American society places the burden of family harmony on women, with the implication that they have failed if the marriage disintegrates. And finally, the more a wife was abused by her parents and witnessed violence in her childhood home, the more likely she is to remain with an abusive husband.

Children also suffer abuse and neglect. You need spend only an hour or so in a shopping mall or supermarket to observe instances of children being verbally abused or hit. And the public behavior is but the tip of the iceberg. Neglect of children—the absence of adequate social, emotional, and physical care—is a closely related problem. In many cases of abuse and neglect, the parent is an unwed teenage woman living in poverty, without a great deal of support for her parental duties (Pagelow, 1984). Overall, researchers find that social stress, including the loss of a job or divorce, is associated with the maltreatment of children (Wolfe, 1985). Moreover, families that are socially isolated and outside neighborhood support networks are more at risk for child abuse than are families with rich social ties (Garbarino and Sherman, 1980). Additionally, abusive parents are themselves likely to have been abused when they were children (Kalmuss, 1984; Gelles, 1985).

Although incest has been called the last taboo, its status as a taboo has not kept it from taking place, but only from being talked about. Indeed, most people find the idea that parents may be sexually attracted to their children so offensive that they prefer not to think about it. There are about 10 female victims of incest for every male victim (Hinds, 1981). The perpetrator is commonly the father, stepfather, or other male authority figure in the household. In cases of father-daughter incest, the fathers are typically "family tyrants" who use physical force and fear to control their families. The mothers in such families are frequently passive, have a poor self-image, and are overly dependent on their husbands, much the same traits found among battered wives. Often an illness or disability causes the mother to be absent from the home or restricts her ability to meet the requirements of her role (Finkelhor, 1979, 1984; Swanson and Biaggio, 1985). The victims of molestation are usually shamed or terrified into treating the experience as a dirty secret (Gordon and O'Keefe, 1984). Not uncommonly, childhood incest leads to serious emotional and psychological problems, low self-esteem, guilt, isolation, mistrust of men, difficulties in establishing intimate relationships, sexual precociousness, drug and alcohol abuse, and even suicide. Victimized women tend to show lifetime patterns of psychological shame and stigmatization (Stark, 1984; Herman, 1986).

Although the problems of family violence, child abuse, and incest have emerged as major issues, considerable ambivalence still exists on these subjects, and much needs to be done to assist the victims. Social service agencies need to be restructured so that battered family members can find help ("shelters" and "safe havens" have mostly been a private endeavor of the women's movement). Remedial laws need to be enacted, and existing laws need to be enforced. Researchers find that arrest of offenders is the most effective means for preventing new incidents of wife battery (Berk and Newton, 1985). Perhaps even more important, a cultural revolution of attitudes and values is required to eradicate the abuse of women and children (Vander Zanden, 1985).

Care of the Elderly

One pressure point for many Americans is often overlooked in discussions of contemporary family life. Grown children still bear the primary responsibility for their aged parents. The sense of obligation is strong even when the emotional ties between the parent and child are weak (Cicirelli, 1981, 1983; Baruch and Barnett, 1983; Fischer, 1986). In 80 percent of the cases, any care an elderly person requires is provided by the family. This assistance supplements what the elderly receive from savings, pensions, Social Security, Medicare, and Medicaid. But although at some point the elderly may need help, they often do more for their children than is done for them. Until they reach age 75 or older, the majority of elders are resources for the family. They frequently provide financial help and assist with babysitting (Gelman, 1985).

Some 40 percent of Americans between the ages of 55 and 59 and 20 percent of those 60 to 64 have at least one living parent (Brody et al., 1983). Social scientists call middle-aged adults the *sandwich generation* because they find themselves with responsibilities for their own teenage and college-age children on the one side and for their elderly parents on the other. Care for the elderly falls most often on daughters and daughters-in-law. These women have historically functioned as our society's "kin-keepers." Despite the changing roles of women, when it comes to the elderly, the old maxim still applies: "A son's a son till he takes a wife, but a daughter's a daughter for the rest of her life." Yet 61 percent of the women also work. While being employed

substantially reduces the hours of assistance that sons provide their elderly parents, it does not have an appreciable effect on that provided by daughters (Stoller, 1983; Brozan, 1986).

Not surprisingly, women of the sandwich generation are often subjected to role-overload stresses that are compounded by their own age-related problems, including lower energy levels, the onset of chronic ailments, and family losses (Brody et al., 1983). Often they are confronted with parent care at the very time they are struggling to make changes in their own work status or trying to return to work after raising children. And large numbers of these middle-aged women will end up caring for their husbands in the years ahead because women generally marry older men (Day, 1986). Increasingly the disproportionate burden that falls on women is coming to be seen as a "women's issue" on a par with job discrimination, pay inequity, and child care (Brozan, 1986).

The motivations, expectations, and aspirations of the middle-aged and the elderly at times differ because of their different positions in the life course. Intergenerational strain is usually less where financial independence allows each generation to maintain separate residences. Both the elderly and their adult offspring seem to prefer intimacy "at a distance" and opt for independent households as long as possible. Elderly parents who call upon their children for assistance are more likely to be frail, severely disabled, gravely ill, or failing mentally. When middle-aged adults fail to take responsibility for an ailing parent, it may reflect not "hardheartedness," but a realization that the situation is more stressful than they can cope with. To do so, however, commonly produces strong feelings of guilt (Hess and Waring, 1978). Indeed, most children would rather make sacrifices to care for their parents than put them in a nursing home (Hull, 1985).

Alternative Lifestyles

Despite popular perceptions that the American family is a dying institution, the evidence we have reviewed in this chapter suggests that the family tree is as deeply rooted as ever in the nation's social landscape. It is, however, sprouting a variety of branches. Family relationships are becoming more tangled as a result of people living longer and occasionally changing mates to suit the seasons of their lives. Increasing numbers of children are growing up with several sets of parents and an assortment of half- and step-brothers and -sisters. Simultaneously, by virtue of the rapid expansion in lifestyle options, Americans now enjoy more alternatives in tailoring their relationships to individual choice. A **lifestyle** is the overall pattern of living people evolve to meet their biological, social, and emotional needs. Let us examine a number of options.

Singlehood

Despite our couples-oriented society, single-person households are outpacing the growth of most other household types. Between 1970 and 1985, the share of married couples among the nation's 86.8 million households fell from 70.5 to 58 percent. Simultaneously, there has been a marked increase in single people living alone. Some 20.6 million Americans now live by themselves, a 90 percent jump in one-person households over 15 years (see Figure 13.3). Overall, the singles population is hardly a monolithic group, with the divorced (11.5 million), widowed (12.7 million), and never-married (45.7 million) comprising distinct groups of those aged 15 and older. The high incidence of divorce, the ability of the elderly to maintain their own homes alone, and the deferral of marriage among young adults have contributed to the high rate of increase in the number of nonfamily households. Singlehood is also a reclaimable status. A person may be single, then choose to cohabit or marry, and perhaps decide later to divorce and become single again.

In 1986 almost 14.2 percent of women and 22.2 percent of men aged 30 to 34 had never married. These figures were more than double the proportion of never-married singles in 1970, when 6.2 percent of women and 9.4 percent of men had never married. A similar trend is evident among people in their mid to late twenties. Overall, the median age at first marriage has been trending upward (see Figure 13.4 on page 362). While many men and women have simply postponed marriage, the changes suggest that a growing proportion of Americans will elect never to marry at all. Even so, the population remaining single today is smaller than it was at the turn of the century, when fully 42 percent of all American adult men and 33 percent of adult women never married (Kain, 1984).

In recent years the notion that people must marry if they are to achieve happiness and well-being has been questioned (Cargan and Melko, 1982; Peterson and Lee, 1985). A good many Americans no longer think of singlehood as a residual category for the unchosen and lonely. The single have found that as their numbers have

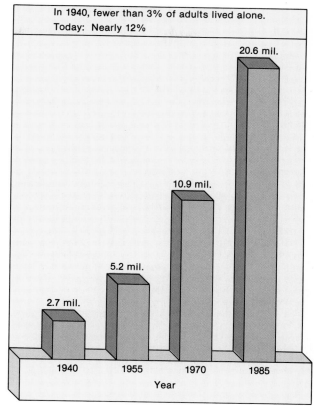

FIGURE 13.3   **The Singles Population, 1985**
Source: U.S. Department of Commerce.

grown, a singles subculture is available to them in most metropolitan areas. They can move into a singles apartment, go to a singles bar, take a singles vacation, join a singles consciousness-raising group, and so on. And if they wish, they can lead an active sex life without acquiring an unwanted mate, child, or reputation. However, there has been a marked decrease in casual sex in the United States in recent years, in part a response to fears surrounding such diseases as acquired immune deficiency syndrome (AIDS) and genital herpes.

Unmarried Cohabitation

The number of adults who share living quarters with an unrelated adult of the opposite sex has risen in recent decades to 2.2 million in 1986, 4 percent of all couples. About half of all people living together have been married previously, and three in ten unmarried couples have one or more children present in the household. Cohabi-

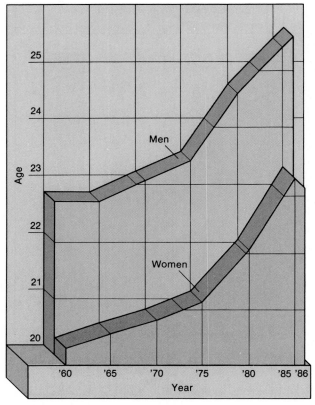

FIGURE 13.4   **Median Age at First Marriage**
Source: U.S. Bureau of the Census.

tation is especially attractive to young adults. One-fourth of the men and nearly two-fifths of the women are under 25 years of age; two-thirds of the men and three-fourths of the women are under 35 (Spanier, 1983). The dramatic increase in the numbers and proportion of unmarried couples is related to the growing acceptance of the arrangement. Indeed, a study of a representative Oregon county found that premarital cohabitation increased between 1970 and 1980 from 13 to 53 percent for couples seeking marriage licenses. The high proportion of married couples who live together prior to marriage suggests that premarital cohabitation may become institutionalized as a new step between dating and marriage (Gwartney-Gibbs, 1986).

Although the media often label cohabiters "unmarried marrieds" and their relationships "trial marriages," couples do not necessarily see themselves this way. College students commonly define cohabitation as part of the courtship process rather than as a long-term alterna-

tive to marriage. One study of students in the Boston area found cohabiting couples to be no less likely to marry, and no more likely to break up, than noncohabiting students who were "going together" (Risman et al., 1981). Nor does cohabitation hold any particular advantage in assuring compatibility in marriage. This contradicts the popularly held belief that one of the potential benefits of cohabitation is improved mate selection (Newcomb, 1979; Brothers, 1986).

Although about a fourth to a third of students at major universities had cohabiting experiences in the mid-1970s (Macklin, 1974, 1978), the pattern has reversed itself in the 1980s. Many college students look upon cohabitation as a restricting and demanding lifestyle. At the same time, there has been a shift toward more conservative values and stronger religious conviction among students (Pentella, 1983).

Couples living together but not married are far less liberated about money, sex, and housework than their nontraditional living arrangement might suggest. As with married men, cohabiting men are more likely to be the ones who initiate sexual activity, make most of the spending decisions, and do far less of the housework than their working women partners (Blumstein and Schwartz, 1983). Cohabiting couples experience many of the same sorts of problems as do married couples (Gross, 1977). However, unmarried couples see themselves as less securely anchored than married couples, and accordingly they feel more tentative about their ability to endure difficult periods. Perhaps these insecurities contribute to the higher incidence of interpersonal violence among cohabiting than among married couples (Yllo and Straus, 1981). Still, the number of unmarried couples is growing, as is the number of childless couples.

Childless Marriages

Historically the adage has held, "First comes love, then comes marriage, then comes the baby in the baby carriage." But in recent decades married couples have begun to break with this rule. Whereas in 1960 some 13 percent of married women between 25 and 29 were childless, 29 percent did not have a child in 1985. Moreover, today 1 out of 4 ever-married women between the ages of 25 and 34 has not had a child, compared with 1 out of 10 in 1960. It is still possible that some will go on and have children. Medical advances have made it easier for women to have healthy babies into their late thirties or early forties. Yet there are not enough women over 35 having children to make up for all the younger ones who

Catering to Single Lifestyles
With the growth in the young adult population, new institutional arrangements have evolved in response to their needs and preferences. Singles bars are a good illustration of this. However, the impersonal nature of singles bars has led them to be labeled "meat racks," "body works," and other nicknames that signify a sexual marketplace. *(Howard Dratch/The Image Works)*

are deciding to remain childless (Kantrowitz, 1986; Bloom and Bennett, 1986).

Increasing numbers of couples have come to view childbearing not as an inevitable part of their lives, but as a choice to be made after a rational weighing of pros and cons (in addition, some couples are involuntarily childless due to infertility). Couples cite a variety of reasons for not wanting to have children. Some feel that they are unsuited to parenthood. Others desire a lifestyle that allows for greater freedom, spontaneity, privacy, and leisure than that permitted by children. And still others say that a career is the primary focus of their lives. Indeed, as women draw closer to men in social and economic status, childbirth becomes more disruptive to their careers.

As couples enter their thirties, some of them change their minds and decide that they want to undertake parenthood. As a result, the birth rate among women in their early thirties is beginning to rise (Langer, 1985). The delay in childbearing has occurred primarily among urban professional women. Many of these women undertook to complete their education and establish their careers before beginning a family. They repeatedly deferred having children and then came to see that a deadline was approaching. Further, during the 1980s a renewed family traditionalism set in. And many couples find that the thirties are a more comfortable time to have children, because they have already faced and gone through a good many of their own crises. In some cases, the desire to nurture and undertake parenthood is strong enough to inspire deliberate unwed motherhood (McKaughan, 1987).

Single Parenthood

If current trends continue, about 60 percent of all children born in the 1980s will live in a single parent household for at least a portion of their childhood. Of 33.4 million families with children in 1985, 8.8 million—26.3 percent—were headed by a single parent (compared with 12.9 percent in 1970). The overwhelming majority of single-parent families are headed by women. About 70 percent of these families originate through divorce or separation. Another 10 percent result from the death of a spouse, and still another 20 percent through the birth of a child to an unmarried woman. In about half of the households, the parent marries or remarries within five years, creating a parent-stepparent arrangement.

As we pointed out in Chapter 9, female-headed households are likely to be low-income households (Norton and Glick, 1986). Nearly half of families headed by single-parent mothers live below the poverty level, and many are dependent on government agencies for assistance. There is a critical difference between the married poor with children and the single-parent poor: On average the married poor move out of poverty; the single-parent poor do not (Weiss, 1984). Moreover, women heading a single-parent family typically experience greater stress than do women in two-parent families (McLanahan, 1983; Sanik and Mauldin, 1986). For one thing, their lower incomes are sources of chronic strain. For another, the responsibilities for the family fall entirely on one adult rather than two. Female heads report much lower self-esteem, a lower sense of effectiveness,

Single-Parent Fathers
What was portrayed in the hit movie *Kramer vs. Kramer* is becoming a way of life for increasing numbers of American men: rearing children alone. Not too long ago parenting was equated with "mothering." A father was awarded custody of his children only if he could demonstrate in court that the mother was "unfit" for motherhood. But now more men are awarded custody of children in divorce proceedings. *(Jim Harrison/Stock, Boston)*

and less optimism about the future than do their counterparts in two-parent settings. Many single-parent mothers complain of a lack of free time, spiraling child care costs, loneliness, and unrelenting pressures associated with the dual demands of home and job.

Single-parent fathers comprise about 11 percent of single-parent families. They encounter many of the same problems as single-parent mothers. Juggling work and child care poses a good deal of difficulty, especially for fathers with preschool youngsters. On the whole, the care provided by custodial fathers and mothers is rather similar. They provide about the same amount of hugs, well-balanced meals, and piano lessons. Very often, however, fathers have more money and greater job flexibility, allowing them somewhat greater leeway in adjusting to their children's daily needs (Meredith, 1985). Many single fathers report that their greatest difficulty in making the transition to single parenthood is losing their wife's help and companionship; they say that it is more difficult for them to become single than to become a single parent (Smith and Smith, 1981). Overall, the single father is neither the extraordinary human being nor bumbling "Mr. Mom" depicted in many popular stereotypes (Greif, 1985; Risman, 1986).

Many families headed by single parents survive their hardships with few ill effects. Some even blossom as a result of the spirit of cooperation engendered by their difficulties. However, a disturbing number of children and their parents are saddled with problems. Some studies show that juvenile delinquency is twice as likely to occur in a single-parent home as in a two-parent home. Lack of parental supervision and persistent social and psychological strains are usually complicated by problems of poverty (Mann, 1983). Moreover, children living in single-parent families are much more likely to be enrolled below the grade that is modal for their age and to be experiencing school difficulties than are children living with both parents (Bianchi, 1984; Milne et al., 1986). Single parents are in need of a variety of services not currently available in most communities: day care facilities that are affordable and convenient to home or work, various forms of counseling, child care enrichment, after-school programs, and parent education (Turner and Smith, 1983; Campbell, Breitmayer, and Ramey, 1986).

Gay Couples

As we pointed out in Chapter 12, homosexuality involves a sexual preference for a person of the same sex. Researchers at the Kinsey Institute for Sex Research at Indiana University have examined the social and psychological adjustment of a sample of nearly 1,000 homosexual men and women living in the San Francisco Bay area (Bell and Weinberg, 1978; Bell, Weinberg, and Hammersmith, 1981). They find that, on the whole, homosexual adults resemble heterosexual adults in their reports about their physical health and their feelings of happiness or unhappiness. The Kinsey Institute researchers (Bell and Weinberg, 1978:216) have concluded that "homosexual adults who have come to terms with their homosexuality, who do not regret their sexual orientation, and who can function effectively sexually and socially, are no more distressed psychologically than are heterosexual men and women."

Lesbians tend to form more lasting ties than do male homosexuals. However, whereas lesbian and heterosexual couples place considerable emphasis upon fidelity, male homosexual couples tolerate outside sexual relations quite well (Blumstein and Schwartz, 1983). About 90 percent of homosexual men with established partners engage in sexual relations with other men. On the whole the men define fidelity not in terms of sexual behavior, but in terms of each individual's commitment to the other. Homosexual men are more likely to break up over money issues and other incompatibilities than over matters of sexual faithfulness. They tend to sort household duties out according to each person's skills and preferences and only rarely on the basis of stereotyped roles of "husband" and wife."

Communes

Communes are groups or communities that people intentionally form in order to establish family-like relationships among unrelated individuals. The idea of communal living dates back far into antiquity. And communes have had a long history in American life, including such groups as the Shakers, Fourierists, Zoarites, Spiritualists, the Hutterites, the Amana Community, and the Oneida Community. Communal living underwent a revival in the late 1960s and early 1970s when some two to three thousand communes were formed in the United States. Not uncommonly, communes spring up during periods when people feel that traditional institutions are disintegrating and they long for a meaningful new order (Zablocki, 1980).

Communes vary greatly. There are those that assume an anarchistic form and stress warmth, intimacy, and involvement, have few or no formal rules, demand no long-term commitment, provide a vague philosophical foundation, are open to all comers, and have a weak financial base. At the opposite extreme, there are those that are rigorously structured and set stringent entrance requirements, enforce a strict normative code, demand a firm philosophical commitment, and foster economic survival through communal financial enterprises. Some communes, such as the nineteenth-century Shakers, have insisted on celibacy; others have practiced monogamy; and still others have encouraged unrestricted sexual promiscuity. Although historically most communes were founded in rural settings, many modern communes have taken the form of collective households in urban areas where the members have renovated old townhouses (Cornfield, 1983).

Chapter Highlights

1. The family is an institution. As we look about the world, and even in our own society, we encounter a good many differences in the ways in which families are organized. Families vary in their composition and in their descent, residence, and authority patterns.

2. Social relationships between adult males and females can be organized within families by emphasizing either spouse or kin relationships. In the nuclear family arrangement, spouses and their offspring constitute the core relationship; blood relatives are functionally marginal and peripheral. In contrast, in the extended family arrangement, kin provide the core relationship; spouses are functionally peripheral.

3. The fact that the parties to a marriage must be members of two different kin groups has crucial implications for the structure of the family. All societies regulate the pool of eligibles from which individuals are expected to select a mate. And they also structure the relationship between a husband and wife in one of four ways: monogamy, polygyny, polyandry, and group marriage.

4. Functionalist theorists stress that if a society is to survive and operate with some measure of effectiveness, it must guarantee that essential tasks are performed. The performance of these tasks—termed functions—cannot be left to chance. Although acknowledging that families show a good deal of variation throughout the world, functionalists identify a

number of functions that families typically perform: reproduction; socialization; care, protection, and emotional support; assignment of status; and regulation of sexual behavior.

5. Functionalists spotlight the tasks carried out by the family that serve the interests of society as a whole. In contrast, many conflict theorists have seen the family as a social arrangement benefiting some people more than others. Randall Collins sees the family as an instrument for maintaining male claims to women as sexual property. Other conflict sociologists say that intimate relationships inevitably involve antagonism as well as love.

6. Societies regulate the process whereby young people choose a marriage partner. Societies "control" love in different ways, including child marriage, social isolation of young people, close supervision of couples, and peer and parental pressures. A variety of factors operate in the selection of a mate: homogamy, physical attractiveness, and complementary needs. Social exchange theory provides a unifying link among these factors. It proposes that people involved in a mutually satisfying relationship will exchange behaviors that have low cost and high reward.

7. Most adult Americans hope to establish a close and meaningful relationship with another person and make the relationship work. Despite the considerable change in family patterns in recent years, American couples remain rather conventional in their marital relationships. Although divorce rates have soared, Americans have not given up on marriage. Yet increasing numbers of Americans no longer view marriage as a permanent institution, but rather as something that can be ended and reentered.

8. Nuclear families that are not disrupted by divorce, desertion, or death typically pass through a series of changes and realignments across time—the family life cycle. These changes and realignments are related to the altered expectations and requirements imposed on a couple as children are born and grow up. Each modification in the role content of one family member has implications for all the other members.

9. Increasing numbers of mothers are working. Many social scientists are no longer asking whether it is good or bad that mothers work. Instead, they are finding that a more important issue is whether the mother, regardless of employment, is satisfied in her situation. Two-income couples are also on the increase. Even so, women continue to shoulder the primary responsibility for household tasks and child care.

10. Divorce is on the upswing in American life. But although it may be more common, it is hardly a routine experience. Most divorced people remarry. Remarriage frequently results in stepfamilies. Despite the significant changes that have occurred in family roles in recent decades, it is grown children who still bear the primary responsibility for their aged parents.

11. By virtue of the rapid expansion of lifestyle options, Americans now enjoy more alternatives in tailoring their relationships to individual choice. A lifestyle is the overall pattern of living people evolve to meet their biological, social, and emotional needs. Among the varying lifestyle options open to Americans are singlehood, unmarried cohabitation, childless marriage, single parenthood, gay relationships, and communes.

The Sociologist's Vocabulary

bilineal Reckoning descent and transmitting property through both the father's and mother's sides of the family.

commune A group or community people intentionally form in order to establish family-like relationships among unrelated individuals.

complementary needs Two different personality traits that are the counterparts of each other and provide a sense of completeness when they are joined.

endogamy The requirement that marriage occur within a group.

equalitarian An arrangement in which power is equally distributed between husband and wife.

exogamy The requirement that marriage occur outside a group.

extended family A family arrangement in which kin—individuals related by common ancestry—provide the core relationship; spouses are functionally marginal.

family A social group whose members are related by ancestry, marriage, or adoption and who live together, cooperate economically, and care for the young.

family life cycle Changes and realignments related to the altered expectations and requirements imposed on a husband and wife as children are born and grow up.

family of orientation A nuclear family that consists of oneself and one's father, mother, and siblings.

family of procreation A nuclear family that consists of oneself and one's spouse and children.

group marriage The marriage of two or more husbands and two or more wives.

homogamy The tendency of like to marry like.

incest taboos Rules that prohibit sexual intercourse with close blood relatives.

lifestyle The overall pattern of living people evolve to meet their biological, social, and emotional needs.

marriage A socially approved sexual union between two or more individuals that is undertaken with some idea of permanence.

matching hypothesis The notion that we typically experience the greatest payoff and the least cost when we select partners who have a degree of physical attractiveness similar to our own.

matriarchy Reckoning descent and inheritance through the mother's side of the family.

matrilineal Reckoning descent and inheritance through the mother's side of the family.

matrilocal Bride and groom living in the household or community of the wife's family.

monogamy The marriage of one husband and one wife.

neolocal Newlyweds set up a new place of residence independent of either their parents or other relatives.

norm of legitimacy The rule that children not be born out of wedlock.

nuclear family A family arrangement in which the spouses and their offspring constitute the core relationship; blood relatives are functionally marginal.

patriarchy The vesting of power in the family in men.

patrilineal Reckoning descent and inheritance through the father's side of the family.

patrilocal A bride and groom living in the household or community of the husband's family.

polyandry The marriage of two or more husbands and one wife.

polygyny The marriage of one husband and two or more wives.

romantic love The strong physical and emotional attraction between a man and a woman.

social exchange theory The view which proposes that people involved in a mutually satisfying relationship will exchange behaviors that have low cost and high reward.

14

Religion

The propitiation or conciliation of powers superior to man which are believed to control the course of nature or of human life.

—James G. Frazer, *The Golden Bough*, 1, 1890

Father Rolando Nueva, 31 years old, a slight, curly-haired man, is the Roman Catholic parish priest in Candoni, a small rural hamlet in the Philippines. There is no doctor within 50 miles of the town, no public high school, no telephone system, and, except in the town itself, no electricity. Candoni is Father Nueva's first parish assignment. He says his seminary training did not prepare him for his work. The people are poor and come to him with financial, medical, and political problems. He had thought his role would be one of "saving souls," but he soon found himself having to assume responsibility for running a school, a feeding program, and an agricultural cooperative. Father Nueva says:

As a churchman, I am here to bring Christ to the people. But as a practical matter, you also have to organize the people. The concepts of the church must be brought to the level of everyday life through, let's say, a better price for their produce. Otherwise, these philosophical concepts are just floating in the air. [quoted by Mydans, 1986:144]

As Father Nueva was drawn into the life of his parishioners, he became increasingly concerned with his nation's social system. One afternoon he was very worried about the health of a parishioner; this started him thinking:

. . . why are other people able to afford surgeons and specialists? And the answer was: it's the system. The injustice is in the system, and that's evil. I think sin produces this injustice, and the sin is personal, because social structures are made by man. [quoted by Mydans, 1986:144]

As a result, Father Nueva has immersed himself in the Basic Christian Communities movement. Local priests and small groups of laypeople not only explore religion together, but enter cooperative ventures in health care, feeding programs for the poor, legal aid, and agricultural marketing.

Father's Nueva's superior, Bishop Antonio Y. Fortich, likewise has been drawn into social activism. Communist insurgents asked him to enter into discussions to assist in finding a peaceful resolution to the nation's many problems. His own residence was destroyed in a fire that he believes the military set to destroy documents he had collected on human rights abuses. And he was recently called upon to quiet a crowd of 7,000 who were protesting the appointment of an unpopular official by Manila authorities (Mydans, 1986).

The Catholic Archbishop of the Philippines, Jaime Cardinal Sin, has also assumed an increasingly temporal role. The Roman Catholic Church holds the allegiance of some 84 percent of the nation's 54 million people and historically has been a powerful institution in Philippine life. Cardinal Sin led the church-backed National Movement for Free Elections in 1986 that played a critical role in the ouster of the Ferdinand Marcos government. Before the election, he issued a pastoral letter suggesting that Marcos renounce "the office he has obtained by fraud." And the Church's nationwide infrastructure—its networks and pulpits—became, in effect, the political infrastructure for the Corazon Aquino campaign. When the military staged a revolt against Marcos in February 1986, the Catholic prelate called on the faithful to gather in the streets and block the President's tanks, a decisive factor in the events that led to Marcos's capitulation. After the peaceful revolution in which Aquino was brought to power, Sin was called to Rome and criticized privately by Pope John Paul II for his actions.

Despite Vatican opposition, Catholic clergy in Latin America have also entered the political arena. Liberation theology, developed by priests working with the poor, holds that the teachings of Jesus require the Church to take responsibility for changing social, economic, and political conditions that deprive people of dignity. And in Poland, the Roman Catholic Church has periodically placed itself in opposition to the Communist government and backed the outlawed Solidarity trade union movement.

But the Catholic Church is not the only religious organization playing a critical role in politics. In Iran, the Islamic fundamentalist movement led by the Ayatollah Khomeini toppled the government of the Shah. And in the United States, under the leadership of the Reverend Martin Luther King, Jr., a religious-based civil rights movement successfully overturned the nation's racist institutions.

Clearly, religion is not a staid institution limited to otherworldly concerns and thisworldly churches and temples. In this chapter, we examine the powerful social forces that are contained within and generated by religion. Sociologists do not deal with the philosophical issue of whether religious beliefs are true or false; rather, they explore the part religion plays in human behavior. Indeed, if religious beliefs and practices are found in every known society, as seems to be the case, then no study of society that neglected religion would be complete.

PLANNING AHEAD: TARGETED READING

1. What forms and kinds of organization characterize religious life?

2. How can people's sense of the sacred contribute to social solidarity and moral authority?

3. How can religion hold in check the explosive social tensions that are produced by inequality and injustice?

4. What are some of the ways religion can be employed in the clash between traditional and modern social arrangements?

5. What are some of the major trends characterizing religious life in the United States?

6. What part does religion play in American politics?

The Nature of Religion

Religion refers to those socially shared ways of thinking, feeling, and acting that have to do with the supernatural or "beyond." As sociologist Emile Durkheim (1912/1965) suggests, religious beliefs and practices relate to *sacred* as opposed to *profane* things. The **sacred** is anything that is extraordinary, mysterious, awe-inspiring, and even potentially dangerous—something that "sticks out" from normal, routine life (Berger, 1967). As such, the sacred is set apart, or forbidden. The **profane**, in contrast, has to do with those aspects of life that are everyday and commonplace. Whether something is profane or sacred depends on how people define it. A wafer made of flour when seen as bread is a profane object. However, it becomes sacred to Catholics as the body of Christ when it is consecrated in Communion. Because the sacred is caught up with strong feelings of reverence and awe, it can usually be approached only through **rituals**—formal procedures that dictate how people should comport themselves in the presence of the sacred.

In their religious behavior, then, people fashion a social world of rules and meanings that governs their experiences much in the manner they do in other realms of life. Once more we encounter a vital link between a society's institutional arrangements and the private experiences of its members. Something social in origin becomes lodged in the individual consciousness. Here it is embedded in the personality and influences a person's strategies for coping with life.

Varieties of Religious Behavior

Because religious behavior finds expression in so many aspects of everyday life, we find it difficult to disentangle religion from other institutional spheres. In fact, classifying behavior as religious or political or economic is a relatively recent custom. For instance, although the ancient Greeks had notions regarding various gods, they did not have a word for religion (Ember and Ember, 1985). But precisely because religious behavior is so varied, we have difficulty thinking about it unless we find

The Sacred: Extraordinary, Mysterious, and Awe-Inspiring
In recent decades, hundreds of churches and countless individuals have reported seeing moisture coming from the eyes of a Madonna figure or blood coming from the hands of a Christ figure. Religious authorities do not agree on the meaning of the events, but theories on the subject abound. In some cases, the events are found to be hoaxes. Others remain a mystery. Some clerics say that reports of miracles place them in an awkward position. They are tempted to uncover hoaxes, when they exist, but investigating the events makes believers angry. Here visitors pass before a weeping Madonna in a Chicago church. *(Keinstein/Gamma-Liaison)*

some way to sort it into relevant categories. Although no categories do justice to the diversity and richness of the human religious experience, sociologist Reece McGee (1975) has provided a scheme that is both intelligent and manageable: simple supernaturalism, animism, theism, and a system of abstract ideals.

Simple supernaturalism prevails in preindustrial societies. Believers attribute a diffuse, impersonal, supernatural quality to nature, what some South Pacific peoples call **mana.** No spirits or gods are involved, but rather a "force" that influences events for better or worse. People *compel* the superhuman power to behave as they wish by mechanically manipulating it. For instance, a four-leaf clover has mana; a three-leaf clover does not. Carrying the four-leaf clover in your wallet is thought to bring good luck. You need not talk to the four-leaf clover or offer it gifts—only carry it. Similarly, the act of uttering the words "open Sesame" serves to manipulate impersonal supernatural power: you say it, and the door swings open on Aladdin's cave. Many athletes use lucky charms, elaborate routines, and superstitious rituals to ward off injury and bad luck in activities based on uncertainty (Zimmer, 1984). Mana is usually employed to reach practical, immediate goals—control of the weather, assurance of a good crop, the cure of an illness, good performance on a test, success in love, or victory in battle. It functions much like an old-fashioned book of recipes or a home medical manual.

A belief in spirits or otherworldly beings is called **animism.** People have imputed spirits to animals, plants, rocks, stars, rivers, and, at times, other people. Spirits are commonly thought to have the same emotions and motives that activate ordinary mortals. So humans deal with them by techniques they find useful in their own social relationships. Love, punishment, reverence, and gifts—even cajolery, bribery, and false pretenses—have been used in dealing with spirits. Occasionally, as with mana, supernatural power is harnessed through rituals that compel a spirit to act in a desired way—what we call spells.

In **theism** religion is centered in a belief in gods who are thought to be powerful, to have an interest in human affairs, and to merit worship. Judaism, Christianity, and Islam are forms of **monotheism,** or belief in one god. They all have established religious organizations, religious leaders or priests, traditional rituals, and sacred writings. Ancient Greek religion and Hinduism (practiced primarily in India) are forms of **polytheism,** or belief in many gods with equal or relatively similar power. Gods of the Hindus are often tribal, village, or caste deities associated with a particular place—a building, field, or mountain—or a certain object—animal or tree.

Finally, some religions focus on a set of abstract ideals. Rather than centering on the worship of a god, they are dedicated to achieving moral and spiritual excellence. Many of the religions of Asia are of this type, including Taoism and Buddhism. Buddhism is directed toward reaching an elevated state of consciousness, a method of purification that provides a release from suffering, ignorance, selfishness, and the cycle of birth and rebirth. In the Western world, humanism is a religion

The Antiquity of Religion
The hunter-gatherers of the upper Paleolithic period painted and engraved on the walls of caves and rock shelters. Lascaux, the most famous cave in France (pictured at right), dates to about 15,000 B.C. The paintings feature wild bulls prancing with horses, deer, and other animals. Archaeologists speculate that the Ice Age paintings had a religious or ceremonial purpose. Additionally, many burial sites include special items such as elaborate stone tools and remains of animals that are interpreted as offerings for use in the afterlife. *(Topham/The Image Works)*

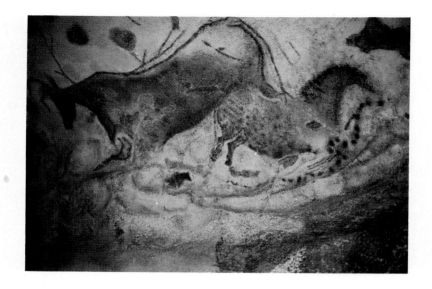

Religious Healing

The treatment of illness is often the responsibility of faith healers and shamans, individuals who work with supernatural power. Modern medicine is taking a closer and more sympathetic look at folk healers such as the !Kung shaman in South Africa who puts his arms around a patient in a healing trance (left). Although folk medicine has generated much skepticism, people who believe they are victims of a malevolent spirit not only think they are sick but are sick. Not surprisingly, then, they often respond to the supernatural entreaties of traditional healers. Faith healing is not uncommon in the United States (above). (Levine, 1987). *(left, Irven DeVore/Anthro-Photo; above, James R. Rolland/Stock, Boston)*

The cult   The **cult** accepts the legimitacy of other religious groups but often finds fault with the dominant society. Like the denomination, the cult does not lay claim to *the* truth, but unlike the denomination it tends to be critical of society. The cult lacks many of the features of a traditional religion; sees the source of unhappiness and injustice as incorporated within each person; holds the promise of finding truth and contentment by following its tenets; believes it possesses the means for people to unlock a hidden or potential strength within themselves without necessarily withdrawing from the world; and holds a relatively individualized, universalized, and secularized view of the Divine (Wallis, 1984, 1986).

The cult does not require its members to pass strict doctrinal tests, but instead invites all to join its ranks. It usually lacks the tight discipline of sects whose rank-and-file members hold one another "up to the mark." And unlike a sect, it usually lacks prior ties with an established religion: it is instead a new and independent religious tradition (Stark and Bainbridge, 1979). The cult

frequently focuses on the problems of its members, especially loneliness, fear, inferiority, tension, and kindred troubles. Some cults are built about a single function, such as spiritual healing or spiritualism. Others, like various "New Thought" and "New Age" cults, seek to combine elements of conventional religion with ideas and practices that are essentially nonreligious. Still others direct their attention toward the pursuit of "self-awareness," "self-realization," wisdom, or insight, such as Vedanta, Soto Zen, the Human Potential Movement, and Transcendental Meditation.

Perspectives on Religion

What part does religion play in social life? Why it is such a pervasive component in the social experience? Why should people come to believe that the world about them is filled with invisible forces, spirits, and gods? From functionalists following in the tradition of Durkheim we learn of social rituals that create social solidarity. And we discern that we are infused with ideas that place a moral sanction against undertaking actions that run counter to established practices. From conflict theorists we learn that ideas are weapons and that ideas serve the interests of privileged groups. In few other areas of sociology do we find the positions of the functionalist and conflict schools so clearly articulated.

The Functionalist Perspective

Functionalist theorists look to the contributions religion makes to societal survival. They reason that if every known society seems to have something called religion, its presence cannot be dismissed as a social accident (Davis, 1951). If religion were not adaptive, societies would long since have evolved without it. So they ask what functions are performed by religion in social life.

Durkheim: Religion as a societal glue   In *The Elementary Forms of Religious Life* (1912/1965), the last of his major works, Emile Durkheim brought his concern with group forces to an analysis of the functions of religion. He selected for his study the Arunta, an Australian hunting-and-gathering people. The Arunta practice **totemism,** a religious system in which a clan (a kin group) takes the name of, claims descent from, and attributes sacred properties to a plant or animal. Durkheim says that the totem plant or animal is not the source of totemism but a *stand-in* for the real source, society itself. He contends that the supernatural—the totem ancestor, God, or some other spiritual force—is *a symbol of society.* By means of religious rituals the group, in effect, worships itself. Society harnesses the awesome force inherent in people's perception of the sacred for animating a sense of oneness and moral authority. The primary functions of religion are the creation, reinforcement, and maintenance of social solidarity and social control.

But how is a societal sense of oneness and moral authority achieved? Durkheim observes that if we are left to ourselves, our individual consciousness—our inner mental states—are closed to one another. Our separate minds cannot come in contact and communicate except by "coming out of themselves." Consequently, social life dictates that the internal be made external—the intangible, tangible. Our inner consciousness is transformed into a *collective consciousness* through the symbolic device of religious rituals. By uttering the same cry, pronouncing the same word, or performing the same gesture, we inform other people that we are united with

Religious Taboos
Cattle are considered sacred among the Hindu population of India. Religious taboo forbids the eating of cattle even as an alternative to starvation. This religious practice may be dysfunctional in times of perilous hunger, but functionalists point out that it assures the survival of cattle and their continued availability for milk and milk-related products. *(Paolo Koch/Photo Researchers)*

them in a shared state of mind. Simultaneously, we mentally fuse ourselves within a social whole. We generate a sort of electricity or collective euphoria that lifts us to an intense state of exaltation which overrides our individual beings. Religious rituals thus operate in two ways: First, they provide vehicles by which we *reveal* to one another that we have a common mental state; second, they *create* among us a shared consciousness that contributes to social bonding and moral authority.

Durkheim stresses that our attitudes toward God parallel our attitudes toward society. Society inspires the sensation of divinity in the minds of its members because of its life and death power over them. Moreover, society, like God, possesses moral authority and can inspire self-sacrifice and devotion. Finally, religion is capable of endowing individuals with exceptional powers and motivation—as, for example, in times of war. Accordingly,

Durkheim says that the religious person is not the victim of an illusion. Behind the symbol—religion—there is a real force and reality: *society*. Like God, society is simultaneously both outside us and inside the core of our consciousness. Durkheim says society is in jeopardy when religion is imperiled and not replaced by a satisfying substitute; people then pursue their private interests without regard for the dictates of the larger social enterprise. In sum, for functionalists, human society achieves its unity primarily through the common possession by its members of ultimate values and ends.

THINKING THROUGH THE ISSUES

If Durkheim is correct and God is a symbolic stand-in for society, does it follow that different types of society should have different types of gods? Among horticultural peoples in which women make a major contribution to the economy, why might you expect the religion to have a heavily female emphasis, with fertility rites that symbolically equate sexual intercourse and child-bearing with planting and harvesting crops? Among rigidly class-stratified societies with a centralized political organization, why might you expect to find a high god presiding over all the others, like the Greeks' Zeus presiding over Mt. Olympus? With the rise of literate, cosmopolitan civilizations—like the Roman Empire and comparable periods in India and China—why might you expect that a single God or mystical condition would emerge that would take on the properties of "world religions" like Christianity, Buddhism, Hindu mysticism, and Islam (Collins, 1982)? What social mechanisms do you think might foster compatibility between secular and religious institutions?

Social control   Durkheim draws our attention to how religion functions as a "societal glue." But he points out that it does even more. When a society links its morality to religion, social control may be heightened. The enforcement of the norms is greatly enhanced if recourse can be had to priests, the unknown, the divine, idealism, and supernatural agents. Religion, then, becomes a moral force beyond any individual, a collective force that makes demands and punishes transgressions. Viewed in this fashion, Heaven and Hell become realities that are embedded within the group. Heaven sym-

bolizes the secure sense of being a member in good standing in society; Hell, the banishment of the sinner from society. By equating thisworldly with otherworldly morality, the members of society come to internalize societal standards so that social control becomes self-control (Collins, 1982). As the box shows, witchcraft can be an especially effective mechanism of social control.

Dealing with life's "breaking points"   Religion also helps people in dealing with life's "breaking points" (Pargament and Hahn, 1986). Much of the human experience is uncertain and insecure. Humankind is recurrently confronted with crises and haunting perplexities: floods, epidemics, droughts, famines, wars, accidents, sickness, social disorder, personal defeat, humiliation, injustice, the meaning of life, the mystery of death, and the enigma of the hereafter. Religion deals with these ultimate problems of life, provides "answers," and often offers the prospect of hope through magical control or spiritual intercession. It is a "social bandage" that protects an inner being made bloody by adversity. Religion, then, provides a sense of personal integration, meaning, and a unified self-identity (Habermas, 1979; Wuthnow, 1986). Moreover, it assists people in the transitions of life. Most religions celebrate and explain the major events of the life cycle—birth, puberty, marriage, and death—through *rites of passage* (ceremonies marking the transition from one status to another).

An impetus to social change   Religion may also be an impetus to social change. For instance, black religion has historically made a significant contribution to the mobilization of protest, as was evident in the civil rights movement of the 1950s and 1960s. The black ministers of Montgomery, Alabama, organized a bus boycott in 1955 and 1956 that was instrumental in bringing about the desegregation of the city's buses after Mrs. Rosa Parks was arrested for violating a local bus segregation ordinance. And the Southern Christian Leadership Conference (SCLC), led by the Reverend Martin Luther King, Jr., and other black ministers, was at the forefront of the black protest movement of the 1960s.

Functional equivalents   We frequently overlook the religious overtones in behavior that is otherwise thought to be nonreligious and even antireligious. The search for a doctrine that reveals the meaning of existence and answers fundamental questions may lead one person to God and another to "the party," nationalism, science, or sport. It is a mistake to disregard the differences these

Witchcraft: A Mechanism for Social Control?

For believers and victims alike, witchcraft can be a terrifying reality (Erikson, 1966). Supernatural powers are imputed to beings who use it for evil purposes. Even more frightening, its practitioners can seldom be detected. Complicating matters, that a person does not practice witchcraft is no safeguard against accusations that one may be a witch. We may well ask, "Do not human beings live in a fearful enough world without compounding it by invoking spirits who work harm against people?" Sociologists answer that humankind gives birth to witchcraft precisely because it is such a formidable power.

Consider how beliefs in witchcraft may function as a means of social control. How can you protect yourself against false accusations that you may be a witch? You can conduct yourself in a friendly and generous manner, avoid quarrels, and act in ways that do not alienate you from kin or community members (Dole, 1966). Evidence suggests that witchcraft is more im-portant in societies lacking judicial officials than in societies possessing them (Whiting, 1950; Swanson, 1969). Without authorities who might otherwise deter antisocial behavior, witchcraft becomes an exceedingly effective mechanism of social control. If you misbehave or cause offense, you may either be called a witch or become the victim of a witch.

Nor has witchcraft been limited to non-Western societies. The witch craze in Europe during the sixteenth and seventeenth centuries and the witch trials of 1692 in Salem, Massachusetts, remind us that the Western world has also been susceptible to witch hunts. Sociologist Guy E. Swanson (1969) suggests that political turmoil contributed to the European witchcraft epidemic. At the time, small and regional political units were being incorporated into larger nation-states, and political allegiances were changing. The erosion of feudalism was giving birth to new social classes that were amenable to Protestantism and other heresies from Roman Catholicism. In Massachusetts of 1692, the colony was left without a governor and judicial practices broke down. Swanson speculates that the undermining of legitimate political procedures made the colonists susceptible to fears that generated a concern with witches.

Studies of African societies suggest that witchcraft accusations also serve to perpetuate the status quo by identifying the witch as a person who does not fulfill social expectations and thereby arouses community frustration and wrath (Nadel, 1952). By the same token, the established order can rid itself of the deviant or the person who questions existing values and behavior patterns. In the 1950s of our own society, under the leadership of Senator Joseph McCarthy, the evils of American society were to be purged through "witch hunts" of Communists and "fellow travelers." Congressional committees investigated "Communist influence" in a host of professions, while the Truman administration ordered a sweeping loyalty program for federal employees. All the while, state and local governments chipped in with loyalty oaths and lesser remedies. Birmingham, Ala-

choices indicate, but it is equally a mistake to overlook the similar functions they often perform.

Communist movements share a variety of elements with many Christian groups (Stark and Bainbridge, 1985). Communism provides a philosophical world view; a promise of a Messianic era in Communist utopia; an explicit program for personal conduct; a priesthood of Party theologians and officials; saints and martyrs of the "cause"; annual rites of renewal such as May Day parades; party missionaries; revered texts such as the *Communist Manifesto* and *Das Kapital*; heresies; inquisitions; sacred shrines like Lenin's tomb in Moscow's Red Square; and iconic statues of Marx, Lenin, Mao, and other "prophets." The novelist Arthur Koestler (1949:23) describes his "conversion" to communism (which he later recanted) in terms reminiscent of converts to religious sects:

> By the time I had finished with *Feuerbach* and *State and Revolution* [books by Marx and Lenin], something had clicked in my brain which shook me like a mental explosion. To say that one had "seen the light" is a poor description of the mental rapture which only the convert knows (regardless of what faith he has been converted to). The new light seems to pour from all directions across the skull; the whole universe falls into pattern like the stray pieces of a jigsaw puzzle assembled by magic at one stroke. There is now an answer to every question, doubts and conflicts are a matter of the tortured past—a past already remote, when one had lived in dismal ignorance in the tasteless, colorless world of those who *don't know.*

bama, ordered Communists to leave town, and Ohio declared them ineligible for unemployment benefits.

Colleges and universities were among the targets of the anti-Communist purgers. Testimony provided by "expert" witnesses like J. B. Matthews, a former missionary and anti-Communist crusader, claimed, among other things, that Dwight D. Eisenhower, then president of Columbia University, was coddling Communists there. The fact that there were few Communists on the campuses did not really matter to those who were determined to preserve the status quo. What did seem to matter was that many witch hunt victims had criticized the American Legion, or stayed away from church, or supported unpopular causes like civil rights. In brief, the target was often "radical" professors who did not come from the surrounding area, who did not fit into the local culture, and who seemed to mock the community's traditional beliefs (Schrecker, 1986).

The Salem Witch Trials of 1692
Many colonial inhabitants of New England believed in witches, actively hunted them down, and put them on trial. And some 200,000 to 500,000 witches, 85 percent of whom were women, were executed in Europe between the fourteenth and seventeenth centuries. Because people attribute terrifying qualities to witchcraft, it can be used as a mechanism to deter deviant behavior. (*Culver Pictures*)

Nationalism has also taken on many religious qualities. Political scientist Frederick Schuman (1933:287–288) observes:

> The cult of nationalism has its high priests, its rituals, and its theology no less than other cults. . . . The patriot has learned reverence for the land of his ancestors—for merrie England, America the beautiful, *la Patrie*, or *das Vaterland*. This involves both ancestor worship and territorial fetishism. . . . Living political leaders are judged by the degree to which they appear to come up to or fall short of the traditional standards set by the departed figures of national myths and legend. Similarly, the patriot worships the land of his nation—the hallowed soil, watered by the blood of heroes. . . . The national flag is everywhere a peculiarly sacred symbol, always to be respected and never to be defiled.

In sum, nationalism has assumed properties of a political religion.

For some, science has come to be the source of meaning in life, serving for them as a sort of secular religion. Similarly, sport in America, for a good many athletes and spectators, is like a religion (Vance, 1984; Lipsyte, 1986). Some runners, wrestlers, and other athletes describe their sport experiences as a profound communion and oneness with nature that propels them out of ordinary space and time. Athletes and sportswriters often employ words in talking and writing about sport that are traditionally associated with religion, including "faith," "dedication," "sacrifice," "ritual," "commitment," "spirit," and "peace." And each sport has its system of elevation to "sainthood" temporarily as all-stars

Marxist-Leninism: A Secular Religion?
Functionalists note that Marxist-Leninism bears a number of resemblances to more traditional religion, including its statuary and shrines deifying leaders like Mao Tse-tung (pictured above), Karl Marx, and Vladimir llyich Lenin. *(Ira Kirschenbaum/Stock, Boston)*

and permanently as members of a Hall of Fame. But although communism, nationalism, science, and sport function somewhat like religions, they are not religions in the sense that Christianity or Judaism are religions.

The Conflict Perspective

From the writings of functionalist theorists we gain a view of religion as a vital source for social integration and solidarity. We derive a quite different image from conflict theorists. Some of them depict religion as a weapon in the service of ruling elites who use it to hold in check the explosive tensions produced by social inequality and injustice. Others see religion as a source of social conflict and point to the religious wars of the Middle Ages and to present-day religious strife in the Middle East, India, and Ireland. And still others see religion as a source of social change.

Marx: Religion as the opium of the people   The stimulus for many of the contributions made by conflict theorists comes from the work of Karl Marx. Marx (1844/1963:43–44) portrayed religion as a painkiller for the frustration, deprivation, and subjugation experienced by oppressed peoples. He said it soothes their distress, but any relief it may provide is illusory, because religion is a social narcotic:

> Religious suffering is at the same time an expression of real suffering and a protest against real suffering. Religion is the sigh of the oppressed creature, the sentiment of a heartless world, and the soul of soulless conditions. It is the opium of the people.

Marx saw religion as producing an otherworldly focus that diverts the oppressed from seeking thisworldly social change. It leads people to project their needs and desires into the realm of "make-believe" and obscures the real sources of social misery and class conflict. More particularly, religion engenders a false consciousness among the working class that interferes with its attainment of true class consciousness. For instance, the members of fundamentalist sects in Appalachia are well aware that fancy clothes, material luxuries, and opulent lifestyles exist. But they are also well aware that they have little chance of gaining access to them. So they define these things as sinful and accept the compensatory belief that by accepting privation in this world, they will triumph in the next, where "the first shall be last, and the last, first." Interestingly, the Russian revolutionary Leon Trotsky was so aware of the similarity of revolutionary Marxism to religious sectarianism that in the late 1890s he successfully recruited the first working-class members of the South Russian Workers' Union among adherents to religious sects.

Marx viewed religion as an expression of human alienation. People shape social institutions with the expectation that they will serve their needs, but find instead that they themselves become the servants of the institutions they have created. Social institutions, rather than providing for the wants of the entire community and enriching lives, are taken over by the ruling class and used to oppress and victimize people. Thus people fashion gods, lose their knowledge that they have done so, and then find themselves having to live their lives at the behest of these same gods. As with economic, family, and legal institutions, people no longer see themselves as the authors of their own products, but as part of an encompassing natural order that dominates and directs them. Hence, in much the manner that they are alienated from their labor (see Chapter 15), the members of the working class are alienated from the larger social environment: "the more powerful becomes the world of

Black Religion: Opiate or Inspiration?

Karl Marx contended that religion is a tool by which a ruling class keeps the oppressed in check by offering them salvation in the next world in return for subservience in this world. Although many blacks turned to religion as a solace for their worldly tribulations, black preachers like Denmark Vesey and Nat Turner (leaders of slave revolts) and the religiously inspired abolitionists actively fought slavery. More recently, black religion has made significant contributions to the mobilization of the civil rights movement. It seems that religion has contributed both to black quietism and activism. This lithograph depicts a southern black camp meeting in 1872. *(North Wind Picture Archives)*

objects which they create . . . the poorer they become in their inner lives, and the less they belong to themselves. It is just the same as in religion. The more of themselves humankind attributes to God the less they have in themselves" (Marx, 1844/1963:122).

Any number of sociologists have agreed with Marx that there often is an inherently conservative aspect to religion (Yinger, 1957; Glock, Ringer, and Babbie, 1967). The sense of the sacred links a person's present experience with meanings derived from the group's traditional past. Religious beliefs and practices provide taken-for-granted truths that constitute powerful forces against new ways of thinking and behaving. Practices handed down from previous generations, including institutional inequalities and inequities, become defined as God-approved ways and highly resistant to change. For instance, American slavery was justified as part of God's "natural order." Thus in 1863, the Presbyterian church, South, met in General Synod and passed a resolution declaring slavery to be a divine institution, ordained by God. More recently segregation was justified on similar grounds. Said Louisiana State Senator W. M. Rainach in defending segregation in 1954: "Segregation is a natural order—created by God, in His wisdom, who made black men black and white men white" (*Southern School News*, 1954:3). Likewise, Hindu religion threatens believers who fail to obey caste rules with reincarnation at a lower caste level or as an animal.

Religion may also legitimate changes favoring powerful and wealthy groups. Imperialism has often been supported by religious or quasi-religious motivations and

beliefs. President William McKinley explained his decision to wage the expansionist war against Spain and seize Cuba and the Philippines as follows (quoted by McGuire, 1981:188):

> I am not ashamed to tell you, gentlemen, that I went down on my knees and prayed to Almighty God for light and guidance more than one night. And one night late it came to me this way. . . . There was nothing left for us to do but to take them all and to educate the Filipinos and uplift and civilize and Christianize them and by God's grace do the very best we could by them, as our fellow men for whom Christ also died.

Religion, then, can be a potent force in the service of the established order. Additionally, religious organizations themselves are frequently motivated to legitimate the status quo because they also have vested interests to protect, including power, land, and wealth (Collins, 1981).

A force for social change   A number of conflict theorists have recently taken a new look at the relationship between religion and social change (McGuire, 1981). They see religion not as a passive response to the social relations of production, but as an active force shaping the contours of social life. It can play a critical part in the birth and consolidation of new social structures and arrangements. While acknowledging that some aspects of religion inhibit change, they point out that other aspects challenge existing social arrangements and encourage change. Under some circumstances religion can be a profoundly revolutionary force that holds out a vision to people of how things might or ought to be. So religion is not invariably a functional or conservative factor in society, but often one of the chief, and at times the only, channel for bringing about a social revolution.

Throughout history, religion has provided an unusually effective vehicle for change because of its ability to link what people say and do with what they think. American history has been no exception: The religious movements associated with the Great Awakening in the late eighteenth and early nineteenth centuries were an important impetus to the abolitionist movement and later to the temperance and prohibition movements. And they had an impact on the democratization of the American political system, for they promoted popular participation in what was largely an oligarchy of the economically privileged. The civil rights and peace movements of recent decades drew strength from religious motivations and the resources of religious organizations. As we noted earlier in the chapter, functionalists concur with conflict theorists that religion can be an impetus to social change, a matter that deserves closer inspection.

Religion and Social Change

Sociologist Peter L. Berger (1979) suggests that in the clash between traditional and modern social arrangements, religious sentiments and organizations can be employed in three contrasting ways. First, religion can be mobilized in opposition to modernization and to the reaffirmation of traditional authority. This is the route taken by the Ayatollah Khomeini and his Islamic Shiite followers in present-day Iran. Second, religion can adapt to the secular world and harness religious motivations for secular purposes. This was the road taken by John Calvin and his Protestant followers in Reformation Europe. And third, religion can retain its fundamental roots while applying them to contemporary concerns. This is the path reflected in the religious revival that took place in the United States during the 1980s. Let us examine each alternative in turn.

Reaffirming Tradition: The Iranian Islamic Revolution

In February 1979, the Ayatollah Khomeini returned to Iran from exile in Paris and led a revolution that toppled Shah Mohammed Riza Pahlevi. The Iranian monarchy was replaced by a theocratic regime rooted in Islamic traditions and anti-Western fervor. Nine months later, a

The Iranian Islamic Revolution
The religious fundamentalist movement led by Ayatollah Khomeini represents an organized effort to restore traditional Islamic values and practices to Iranian society. Islam is a communal faith with a comprehensive way of life that knows no distinction between public and private, sacred and secular, belief and behavior. In the Koran and the Hadith (the sayings and life of the Prophet), devout Muslims believe they can discover all they need to know about creating a society worthy of God. Islamic fundamentalists see many of their ills as deriving from Western influences. (Chauvel/Sygma)

militant crowd seized control of the United States Embassy in Teheran and launched 444 days of tension that appreciably affected the 1980 American presidential election. In the intervening years, the new Islamic state has weathered a power struggle and the purging of many of the revolution's prominent figures, a campaign of bombings and assassinations by internal enemies, severe economic difficulties, and a costly war with neighboring Iraq (Mottahedeh, 1985; Hiro, 1985). The Khomeini-inspired revolution is now ranked by some scholars as the second most important revolution of the twentieth century—second only to the 1917 Russian Revolution in terms of ideologies shaping the world political arena (Wright, 1987). The Islamic Republic has challenged the concept of a bipolar world divided into capitalist and Communist blocs.

A number of forces converged to produce this revolution (Akhavi, 1980; Fischer, 1980; Abrahamian, 1986). For one thing, Shiite Muslims do not make a distinction between the public and private—the secular and sacred—spheres of life. The Western concept of separation of church and state is an alien one. Many Shiites insist that solutions to social and economic difficulties can best be found through religious leaders and by interpreting the guidelines of traditional Islam. In the shah's drive to modernize and secularize the nation, the Islamic clergy, or mullahs, found their authority and wealth eroded. The threat to their position tightened the cohesiveness of the clergy and transformed the mullahs into a revolutionary force. The clergy used the network provided by the mosques as a power base to attack the shah's regime and ultimately to bring the state apparatus under clerical domination.

The rural migrants who were flooding into Iranian cities—the "disinherited" as they were called by anti-shah activists—steadfastedly supported the Islamic clergy. From them, the mullahs recruited and organized the Revolutionary Guards, the paramilitary force that served as the footsoldiers of the revolution. The clergy rallied the Iranian masses against the decadence and degradation they saw in Iranian life, against Western practices and fashions, and against rampant materialism and modernization. Religion became an idiom for political and nationalistic expression.

In the face of intense foreign pressures and destabilizing internal conditions and tensions, the beleaguered masses increasingly took refugee in religion. Resentment against persistent Western dominance and the imposition of Western ways fed revolutionary fervor. Young people rediscovered their grandparents' traditions as they sought a religious source for their social and cultural identities. And the new power that oil conferred and the West's insatiable dependence on it made defiance seem feasible. Additionally, the oil boom had enriched a privileged class, brought accusations that the money had not been spent for the good of the people, and upset traditional economic and social patterns. Complicating matters, the brutality of the shah's secret police alienated Westernized intellectuals, students, civil servants, technical experts, and traditionalist merchants of the bazaar (Green, 1986).

Since the revolution, the mullahs have secured political dominance by filling nearly all the seats in Parliament through their Islamic Republican party. The local mosques have served as the building blocks of power, functioning as an amalgam of political clubhouse, government office, police station, and educational center. A system of Islamic law and justice has superseded secular law and a formal judiciary. A systematic campaign has been undertaken to purge Western ways, alcohol, gambling, prostitution, and pornography from Iranian life. Women must wear head scarves, and those who neglect to do so may be sent to a "reeducation center." The Islamic state employs surveillance and intimidation to impose strict conformity to rules of dress, social conduct, and religious observance. Iranian authorities admit to some 2,000 to 3,000 executions of dissidents, although opposition leaders say the figure is closer to 30,000. Homosexuals, drug dealers, and unfaithful wives have also been targets for firing squads.

On the international scene, the Iranian regime sees as its religious duty the export of revolution until an Islamic empire once again stretches from the Persian Gulf to the Mediterranean and beyond, as it did in ancient times. Since Khomeini's triumph in 1979, the Shiite movement has been catapulted into prominence in war-ravaged Lebanon. And Muslim leaders who are seen as compromising the integrity of Islam by embracing Western ideas of democracy and secularization—such as those in Iraq, Egypt, and Tunisia—have become objects of wrath (Woodward, 1985; Kifner, 1987).

Promoting Secular Change: The Protestant Ethic

Orientations to gods and the supernatural can inhibit secular change and modernization. But religious beliefs and practices can also promote socioeconomic change. The sociologist Max Weber (1904, 1916, 1917) studied several world religions in order to discern how a religious **ethic,** the perspective and values engendered by a religious way of thinking, can affect behavior. He suggests that there are periods in historical development when circumstances push a society toward a reaffirmation of old ways or toward new ways. At such critical junctures, religion—by supplying sources of individual motivation and defining people's relationship to their society—can be a source of historical breakthrough. While a religious ethic does not mechanically determine social action, it can give social action impetus by shaping people's perceptions and definitions of their interests.

The Protestant Ethic

Grant Wood's painting, *American Gothic* (1930), reflects the ethic of hard work, sobriety, and frugal living that has long been a theme in American culture. Max Weber said these values were nurtured by Calvinism and gave impetus to capitalist economic activity. He thought that religion is a powerful vehicle for social change. *(© 1987 The Art Institute of Chicago. All rights reserved.)*

In *The Protestant Ethic and the Spirit of Capitalism* (1904), Weber turned his sociological eye to one historical breakthrough—the development of capitalism. He sought a link between the rise of the Protestant view of life and the emergence of capitalist social arrangements in Western society. He maintained that the development of capitalism depended upon the creation of a pool of individuals who had the attitudes and values necessary to function as entrepreneurs. Once capitalism is established, it is self-perpetuating. The critical problem, Weber said, is to uncover the origin of the motivating spirit of capitalism in precapitalist society. He believed that Protestantism, particularly Calvinism, was one crucial factor in the rise of this spirit. Calvinism, based on the teachings of the French theologian and reformer John Calvin (1509–1564), has found expression in a variety of religious movements, including Puritanism,

Pietism, and Anabaptism. Central to the doctrine is the **Protestant ethic,** an "attitude which seeks profit rationally and systematically" (Weber, 1904/1958:64). Weber thought that Benjamin Franklin's writings expressed this spirit in "classical purity" (see Table 14.3).

Weber noted that Protestantism and modern capitalism appeared on the historical scene at roughly the same time. There were other linkages as well. First, capitalism initially attained its highest development in Protestant countries, particularly the United States and England, whereas Catholic nations like Spain and Italy lagged behind. Second, in nations with both Protestant and Catholic regions, such as Germany, it seemed to be the Protestant—not the Catholic—regions that pioneered in capitalist development. Third, Weber marshaled evidence which suggested it was by and large the Protestants, not the Catholics, who became the early capitalist entrepreneurs.

The Calvinist ethos also had other elements that fed capitalist motivation, particularly its **doctrine of predestination.** Calvin rejected the idea prevalent in the Catholicism of the Middle Ages that a person's status in the afterlife is determined by the way one behaves here on earth. Instead, Calvin taught that at birth every soul is already predestined for Heaven or Hell. This notion was especially disquieting, since people did not know whether they were among the saved or the damned. According to Weber, Calvin's followers, in their search for reassurance, came to accept certain earthly signs of **asceticism** as proof of salvation and genuine faith: hard work, sobriety, thrift, restraint, and the avoidance of earthly pleasures. As people are wont to do, the Calvinists, preoccupied with their fate, began to cultivate these very behaviors. More important, self-discipline and a willingness to deter gratification are qualities that lead people to amass capital and achieve economic success. Capitalist entrepreneurs could ruthlessly pursue profit and feel that they were fulfilling their Christian obligation. So the Calvinist ethos took the spirit of capitalism out of the realm of individual ambition and translated it into an ethical duty.

A good many scholars since Weber have raised serious questions regarding this hypothesis (Tawney, 1926; Robertson, 1933; Samuelsson, 1961; Cohen, 1980). They have looked to other factors in explaining the origins of capitalism, including a surge in commerce during the fifteenth and sixteenth centuries, technological innovations, the influx of resources from New World colonies, unrestrained markets, and the availability of a free labor force. Further, sociologist Randall G. Stokes

Table 14.3 The Sayings of Benjamin Franklin: The Protestant Ethic

Early to bed and early to rise makes a man healthy, wealthy and wise.

Time is money.

Be ashamed to catch yourself idle.

The way to wealth . . . depends on two words, industry and frugality; waste neither time nor money, but make the best use of both.

God helps them who helps themselves.

Little strokes fell great oaks.

Women and wine, game and deceit, make the wealth small and the wants great.

If you would know the value of money, go and try to borrow some.

Beware of little expenses; a small leak will sink a great ship.

A sleeping fox catches no poultry.

For age and want, save while you may; no morning sun lasts a whole day.

But dost thou love life? Then do not squander time, for that's the stuff life is made of.

Remember that money is of a prolific, generating nature. Man can beget money, and its offspring can beget more, and so on.

Sloth makes all things difficult, but industry all things easy.

From *Advice to a Young Tradesman* (1748) and *Poor Richard's Almanac* (1757).

(1975) has shown that the beliefs comprising the Protestant ethic do not necessarily lead people to engage in entrepreneurial activities. Calvinism did not produce capitalist outcomes when it was transplanted by Dutch and French Huguenot settlers (Afrikaners) to South Africa. Although Afrikaner Calvinism was theologically identical to European Calvinism, it had a conservative rather than an innovative economic impact.

It is worth noting that *The Protestant Ethic and the Spirit of Capitalism* was one of Weber's earlier works. In lectures given shortly before his death, Weber incorporated many new elements into his analysis of the origins of large-scale capitalism (Collins, 1980). Even so, his early work remains a sociological landmark in demonstrating the impact religion can have on human affairs, producing outcomes that are not necessarily intended or foreseen by its adherents.

Adapting Tradition: The Revival of Religious Interest

We have seen that religion may be a conservative force, impeding modernization and reaffirming traditional authority, as in contemporary Iran. It may also be a powerful agent for social change, creating a perception of the world that gives an impetus to innovation and rationalized economic activity, as in the case of Calvinism. Religion may also draw upon a people's spiritual yearnings and adapt them to modern life. The revival of religious interest in the United States during the 1980s represents an attempt to capture the roots of religious inspiration and shape them to the contemporary world.

Perhaps the most appropriate words to describe the religious character of the United States over the past fifty years are "continuity" and "stability" (Caplow, Bahr, and Chadwick, 1983; Gallup, 1985; Hadden, 1987). Basic religious beliefs, and even religious practice, differ remarkably little from the levels recorded a half-century ago. Indeed, the nation has remained rather orthodox in its beliefs. For instance, nearly half of all Americans currently accept "creationism"—the notion that God created humankind during the last 10,000 years—and a consistent one-third of the population believes the Bible to be literally true, word for word. Even so, there have been notable swings in the religious life of the nation. Following World War II, interest in religion rose, associated with increased church membership and attendance, a growth in Bible reading, increased giving to churches, and extensive building. Religious leaders like Billy Graham, Norman Vincent Peale, and Bishop Fulton Sheen had substantial followings. The surge lasted until the early 1960s. Religious interest and involvement declined during the 1960s and 1970s, but "bottomed out" in the 1980s, and in some cases reversed (Gallup, 1985).

Despite a renewed search for spiritual moorings, polls show church memberships still hovering around 70 percent of the nation's population in the 1980s, unchanged since the early 1970s. Attendance has also been static—about 40 percent of the American public attends religious services weekly (Gallup, 1985). It appears that many people feel more comfortable expressing their newfound fervor outside organized religion. Informal, quiet gatherings and discussion groups are a particularly popular mode of expression. Unlike the more impassioned swing to Eastern religions in the late 1960s and to "born again" Christianity in the late 1970s, the 1980s revival has been a more sober affair, with tradition back on the agenda as a positive force. The "born again" movement was marked by outward revivalism and a dramatic conversion, whereas the newer movement has emphasized the inward nurture of the soul and a deepening of faith. Many Americans seem to be searching for a religious rootedness, as opposed to the extreme emphasis on individualism and self that was the focus of the 1970s. Simultaneously, the desire for a direct relationship with God has been coupled in some measure with a rejection of the authority of churches.

The campus religious revival   Religion has also enjoyed a rebirth on college campuses. The Gallup Organization finds that the number of Americans between the ages of 18 and 29 taking part in religious education more than doubled to 35 percent between 1980 and 1984. And the proportion of college students who say religion is important to them grew from 39 to 50 percent (Mann, 1984). A majority of college freshmen believe in life after death, a God who intervenes in people's lives, and prayer. Almost half of freshmen students say that the Bible is "literally true and we should believe everything it says," although only 37 percent of seniors retain this belief (Greene, 1986).

Students of all major religious faiths—various Protestant denominations, Catholics, and Jews—displayed a renewed interest in spiritual matters during the 1980s, with enrollment in theology courses, involvement in volunteer work, and attendance at campus worship services increasing over that of the previous decade. Religious workers found students more concerned with basic values and religious essentials than students of the 1960s and 1970s. Students, like their elders, appear to be looking for a quiet, secure religious life that is both humane and compassionate. Many of them have lost confidence in social engineering and are searching for something worth living for. Overall, the 1980s have witnessed a revived interest in traditional religion and the questions it raises and seeks to answer. Many of the older baby boomers—those now 31 to 42 years of age—are returning to churches and synagogues. Some 43 percent report attending worship services three or more times a month. Polls taken among people representing the same group in the early 1970s found that only 34 percent reported attending church that frequently (Berger, 1986).

The electronic church   Television has become a major vehicle for religious expression in American life. Slightly more than a third of the American public say they watch religious programs on television. Viewers are disproportionately older, female, southern, small-town, and less well educated than people who do not watch religious programs (Clymer, 1987; Lord, 1987). To a considerable extent, the audience uses television as a supplement, rather than as a substitute, for attendance at religious services. Although complicated theological issues are rarely debated, political issues are discussed on more than half the programs. Over the past decade a flurry of new religious-oriented talk shows, soap operas, documentaries, gospel music, and magazine-format programs has been added to the fare of television programming. In

"*A fantastic evangelist was on TV, and I sent him everything.*"

Drawing by W. Miller; © 1987 The New Yorker Magazine, Inc.

addition, about 1,000 of the 9,642 radio stations in the United States have a religious format.

The vast majority of religious programming is fundamentalist or evangelical in tone. *Fundamentalism* is a conservative Protestant movement that seeks to conserve the principles underlying the Christian system; it views the Bible as the literal and unerring word of God. *Evangelism* is a "good news" or "glad tidings" movement whose members profess a personal relationship with Jesus Christ. Adherents believe that Scripture provides the only authoritative basis for faith, stress the importance of personal conversion rather than ritualistic practices for salvation, and emphasize the importance of intense zeal for Christian living. Over half of the nation's evangelicals live outside the South, over a third have family incomes of $30,000 or more, and the number who have attended college has risen to over 20 percent (Gergen, 1987).

The practitioners of televangelism have pressed hard to restore "morality" and traditional family values to American life. They see "secular humanism" as the root of contemporary ills—liberal policies that seek to deal with social life "independently of God." They say that non-Fundamentalist efforts are empty, futile, or apostate, because there cannot be a rationale for life apart from God. Televangelists equate abortion with murder, define homosexuality as an ungodly perversion, vigorously denounce pornography and smut (including sex education in the public schools), and promote prayer in the nation's classrooms. Running throughout their messages is the notion that God has a message and a plan ("Believe in Him; trust in Him") and that enormous benefit can be derived from taking a positive approach to life. Television allows viewers to "privatize" religious worship, to gain a feeling of immediate and personal help in coping with their "troubles," and to enjoy the illusion of a face-to-face relationship with a dynamic religious leader (Hadden and Swann, 1981; Korpi and Kim, 1986).

The Christian Right In 1965, priests, nuns, rabbis, and ministers marched in Selma, Alabama, in an effort to secure a national voting rights act. In the decade that followed, many mainstream Protestant denominations, including the Methodists, Episcopalians, Congregationalists, and Presbyterians, made active efforts on behalf of civil rights, peace, and other social issues, usually on the side embraced by political liberals. Many of these religious groups were characterized by a "modern theology," the attempt to make traditional religious teachings

plausible and understandable in the modern world. These developments raised the ire of fundamentalists. As the nation moved in a more politically conservative direction, fundamentalists began to organize in the late 1970s around issues that were of interest to them. Among these groups were the Moral Majority (later renamed The Liberty Foundation) associated with the Reverend Jerry Falwell, Christian Voice, and the Religious Roundtable (Guth, 1983).

The nation's major television networks and popular magazines "discovered" the Christian Right during the 1980 election and for the most part viewed it with alarm. During the next two years the media sought to ascertain the movement's "true" strength and resources. When poll results showed unfavorable attitudes among Americans outweighing favorable views by about a 2-to-1 ratio, there followed a period of debunking and dismissal. Since then, the movement has been depicted as a minor actor, unworthy of either alarm or major attention. Yet with its access to the evangelical media, money, and organization, it may be premature to dismiss the Christian Right (Bromley and Shupe, 1984; Gailey, 1986). In close local and congressional races—elections decided by a few thousand votes—Fundamentalists can tip the scales in favor of one or another candidate. Moreover, followers of Pat Robertson have successfully mobilized evangelical Christians to take over local Republican party offices in some communities and run for political office in others (Hume, 1986).

Fundamentalists have insisted that discussing public policy and politics without reference to moral and biblical principles is wrong. They are skeptical of modern science and technology, and place their faith in the search for spiritual answers rather than purely technical solutions to modern problems. Among the issues that galvanized the Fundamentalists for political action have been freedom for Christian schools, prayer and Bible reading in the public schools, a constitutional ban on abortions, tighter restrictions on pornography and homosexuality, free enterprise, anticommunism, and a stronger military (Ostling, 1985; Clendinen, 1986). They became deeply involved in partisan support of Ronald Reagan in the 1980 and 1984 elections. The Christian Right has relied on up-to-date methods of computerized direct mail solicitation, fundraising, mass media publicity, political organization, and targeted lobbying. Whether fundamentalist political organizations will fade as did the civil rights movement's Southern Christian Leadership Conference and the Student Nonviolent Coordinating Committee (SNCC) or whether they will continue as an important force on the national political scene remains to be determined.

Religion in the United States

If religious denominations were basically the same, then it would matter little that Americans are divided among more than a thousand religious groups (see Table 14.4). However, surveys find substantial differences in attitudes and practices among Americans of different denominations (T. Smith, 1984). Nearly 90 percent of Protestant Fundamentalists believe in an afterlife, but among more moderate and liberal Protestant groups the figure slips to 80 percent. About 75 percent of Catholics believe in an afterlife, compared with 46 percent of those with no religious affiliation and 25 percent of Jews. While only 20 percent of Protestant Fundamentalists are willing to allow an atheist to make a speech, teach in college, or have a book in a public library, about 40 percent of all Catholics, 54 percent of Episcopalians, 61 percent of Jews, and 72 percent of those with no religious affiliation support all three civil rights for atheists. Similar patterns hold in other spheres as well, with Fundamentalists taking the strictest view of sin and biblical teachings, and being the least likely to smoke, drink, go to bars, or favor the legalization of marijuana. Overall, Catholics tend to resemble the Protestant center with respect to traditional values, while Jews fall toward the liberal pole.

Protestants

Protestants comprise about 64 percent of the adult population of the United States. American Protestant groups can be ranked along a continuum in terms of religious traditionalism (T. Smith, 1984; Gallup, 1985). At the conservative end are the Fundamentalists, including the Southern Baptists, Pentecostals, and Jehovah's Witnesses. Near the middle fall the moderate religious groups, including Lutherans and Methodists. At the liberal end of the continuum come the Unitarians, Congregationalists, Presbyterians, and Episcopalians. Religious attachment is strongest among Fundamentalist groups, with 51 percent reporting that they attend church weekly and 58 percent rating their faith as strong. Among Lutherans and Methodists, weekly attendance is about 23 percent, and the proportion with strong religious faith ranges between 33 and 40 percent. In contrast, about 18 percent of Episcopalians attend church weekly, and 31 percent rate their faith as strong.

Table 14.4 Largest American Christian Denominations, 1982

	Total Members	Share of U.S. Population (%)
Roman Catholic	52,088,774	22.5%
Southern Baptist	13,991,709	6.0
United Methodist	9,457,012*	4.1
Lutheran Church in America	2,925,655	1.3
Mormon	2,864,000	1.2
Episcopal	2,794,139	1.2
Lutheran, Missouri Synod	2,630,823	1.1
American Lutheran	2,346,710	1.0
United Presbyterian	2,342,441	1.0
United Church of Christ	1,716,723	0.9

*Latest Methodist figure is for 1981.
Source: National Council of Churches, 1984.

Over the past two decades mainline Protestant denominations (Methodist, Lutheran, Presbyterian, Disciples of Christ, and Episcopal groups) have seen their memberships shrink. During the same period, conservative and Fundamentalist groups have grown. A variety of factors have contributed to the mainliners' decline: First, many of the denominations lack a clear sense of institutional identity and suffer from diffuseness and a lack of cohesion (Woodward, 1986). Second, the trend toward greater individualism, personal freedom, and tolerance of diversity that took place during the sixties and seventies, especially among baby boomers, turned many younger people away from the religious patterns of their parents and fostered a "pick-and-choose" type of Christianity (Chittister and Marty, 1983; Gallup, 1985). Third, mainliners frequently marry outside their own denomination and relinquish their church memberships in the process. And finally, the mainline denominations have run against a swelling tide of religious and political conservatism. In order to meet these challenges, some groups like the Methodists have cut back on "left" political issues and placed greater emphasis on building a strong spiritual base (Briggs, 1984a, 1984b; Woodward, 1986).

Roman Catholics

Roman Catholics constitute the nation's largest religious denomination, representing nearly a quarter of the adult population. About 42 percent of Catholics attend mass

Levels of Religious Involvement
According to the Princeton Religion Research Center, only 4 percent of American adults can be described as "totally nonreligious." These are people who are not members of a church, rarely if ever attend church, and say religion is not important to them. Most are men and younger persons. At the other end of the scale are the "superchurched." Thirty-one percent fall into this category and tend to be women, older persons, and residents of the Midwest and South. These are people who state a religious preference, are members of a church, attend church regularly, and say religion is very important to them. (Roswell Angier/Archive)

each week, and some 41 percent say their faith is strong (Smith, 1984). Catholics have seen their church undergo an astounding array of changes since the Second Vatican Council in 1962–1965: Mass is said in English rather than Latin; the laity can receive communion wafers into their own hands or take wine from the chalice; power is less rigorously centralized; the role of lay members has been expanded; secrecy in Church affairs has been diminished; and non-Catholics are no longer defined as heretics.

Yet on the issues of birth control, divorce, abortion, women's inclusion in the priesthood, and mandatory celibacy for priests, large numbers of American Catholics seem to be turning a deaf ear to the Pope's firm insistence on traditional beliefs and practices. Only 29 percent approve all the things that Pope John Paul II has done. On questions of sexual morality the differences are most marked, with 83 percent of young Catholic adults approving of artificial birth control and 80 percent approving of remarriage after divorce (positions at odds with official Church teaching). Nearly half of American Catholics do not consider premarital sex wrong, 36 percent favor legal abortion, and 32 percent say that sexual activity between members of the same sex is not categorically wrong. Of the estimated 1.5 million American women who have an abortion in a given year, about one-quarter are Catholic (Sciolino, 1984; Berger, 1985).

These shifts in sentiment have resulted in a growing tension between the Vatican and segments of the American Church—a "contested accommodation" (Seidler, 1986; Suro, 1986). Underlying the changes have been

the success and power Catholics have achieved in the United States. In a few generations, large numbers of Catholics have made their way from immigrant status—many of them poor and crowded into industrial cities of the Northeast and Middle West—into the mainstream of American life as well-educated, affluent suburbanites (Greeley, 1982).

The growing independence of conscience is accepted—or at least tolerated—by many parish priests and nuns, who define their chief pastoral mission as one of meeting the everyday needs of the faithful (Sciolino, 1984). But turbulence in the American Church has contributed to about a fifth of the priests and a higher proportion of nuns withdrawing from the active ministry. The result has been a growing shortage. Two decades ago, the American Church had 48,000 seminarians; currently there are fewer than 11,000, of whom only 60 percent are likely to take their final vows. Fewer Catholic families regard the priesthood as a higher calling than marriage, and more and more young men are hesitating to make a permanent commitment to a life of celibacy and service to others. Complicating matters, 20 percent of younger priests quit within the first ten years; an additional 17 percent quit by fifteen years; by their twenty-fifth anniversary, 50 percent have left the priesthood (Briggs, 1984; Canerdy, 1986). At the same time, the ranks of nuns are dwindling, dropping 35 percent since reaching a peak of 181,421 in 1966 (half of all nuns in the United States are now 60 years of age or older). Increasing numbers of nuns are rebelling against their second-class ecclesiastical status. Following the Second

Vatican Council, many jettisoned their cumbersome habits, relaxed rigid convent rules, and made social justice central to their mission. Although 10 percent of the nuns still choose cloistered lives in a traditional convent setting, another 10 percent have pursued secular careers as lawyers, academics, administrators, social activists, and government officials (Woodward, 1984).

The priorities of the American Church have changed in recent years, with the issues of peace and the lot of the poor moving to the forefront of the concerns of The National Conference of Catholic Bishops. The bishops have supported a freeze on nuclear weapons production, called the level of poverty and unemployment in the United States a "social and moral scandal," and endorsed economic sanctions against South Africa. And although Catholics who go the church every week or almost every week are evenly split over a constitutional amendment banning abortions, many bishops have militantly opposed abortion. The result has been an increasingly bitter debate within the Church on the activist direction taken by the nation's bishops.

Jews

Jews constitute about 2 to 3 percent of the nation's adult population. Like their Protestant and Catholic counterparts, the nation's Jews have experienced a good deal of change over the past two decades. A particularly significant statistic has been the rapid increase in intergroup marriages, with indications that the rate of Jewish-Gentile intermarriage may be approaching 50 percent. However, this does not necessarily represent a loss to the Jewish community, since the non-Jewish partner often converts to Judaism. Overall, Jewish leaders have been concerned with the passive erosion of religious practice among their members. While many Jews continue to identify themselves with their faith, they often do not take an active part in religious pursuits. Only 8 percent of the nation's Jewish population reports attending religious services each week, although 42 percent rate their faith as strong (T. Smith, 1984). A commitment to the survival of Israel has also given psychological unity to the Jewish community (Sanoff, 1983).

The American Jewish Committee places the world's Jewish population at about 14.3 million. The United States, with about 5.8 million Jews, has the largest group, outstripping Israel, which counts a Jewish population of 3.1 million, and the Soviet Union, with 2.7 million. A threefold division is found among American Jews that resembles Christian denominationalism in shades of belief and practice (Harrison and Lazerwitz, 1982; Goldman, 1986). Orthodox Jews display the greatest degree of traditionalism, followed by Conservative Jews, who are intermediate in rank, and Reform Jews, who are the least traditional. The split has widened in recent years over each group's standards for marriage, divorce, and conversion. One matter at issue is the 1983 decision of Reform rabbis to accept as Jews children of intermarriages where either the father or the mother is Jewish. Until then, all branches of Judaism held to the standard that Jewish identity derived from the mother (Berger, 1986a).

In a manner paralleling the Protestant and Catholic communities, many Jews have turned to a more personal type of religion for solace and sustenance. Some are returning to a number of the old ways, while remaining contemporary in outlook. Many Reform Jews are again wearing skullcaps and prayer shawls during services. Attendance at all-day Jewish schools has doubled in the past two decades, despite a decline in birth rates. Large numbers of Jews have also turned to *havurah*, a movement designed to make the Jewish religious experience more meaningful. A *havurah* usually consists of about ten families who meet together on a regular basis to pursue Jewish interests. The members may study together, worship and celebrate holidays with one another, and render service to the Jewish community. Simultaneously, more Jews are turning to makeshift synagogues tucked away in small buildings and family houses—*shtiblekh*—to gain a greater sense of intimacy and identity (Berger, 1986b). Given developments such as these, Jewish leaders tend to be optimistic regarding the continued vitality of Judaism in the United States in the years ahead.

Mormons

Mormons, the Church of Jesus Christ of Latter-Day Saints, are the largest and wealthiest religion originating in the United States. They are 5.8 million strong, with 30,000 young missionaries in the field from Tahiti to Tonga to Topeka. A basic tenet of the Mormons is that in 1823 an angel named Moroni directed Joseph Smith to a secret cache of gold tablets. Smith translated them into the Book of Mormon, an addition and correction to the Bible. Many Mormon doctrines, as they evolved under Smith, were and remain unorthodox by mainstream religious standards: God lives on a planet and looks very human; Mormons themselves may aspire one day to become Godlike and preside over their own planets; Adam

ISSUES THAT SHAPE OUR LIVES

Does Religion Make a Difference?

It is sometimes said that the United States is at once the most religious and the most secular of nations— enthusiastically churchgoing, yet showing little evidence of actually living its several faiths. Indeed, there seems to be a rather profound gulf between America's avowed ethical standards and the observable realities of everyday life. All this raises the question of whether or not religion makes a difference in people's personal lives. Sociologist Theodore Caplow and his associates (1983), in their recent followup study of religion in Muncie, Indiana, conclude that differences in behavior between the religiously active and inactive are minimal and hardly dramatic. Like other researchers, they also find that religious involvement is correlated with countless attitudes and behaviors, including political conservatism and conventionality (for instance, being happily married rather than divorced). But, as we pointed out in Chapter 2, correlations do not inform us about cause-and-effect relationships. We do not know whether religious involvement fosters political conservatism and conventionality, whether political conservatism and

conventionality promote religious involvement, or whether some third variable is responsible for the correlation.

Whatever the case may be, Americans *believe* their religious beliefs do make a difference. Some 8 in 10 report that their religious beliefs help them to respect and assist other people. And a like number say their religious beliefs and values help them to respect themselves. Moreover, 63 percent state that their beliefs "keep me from doing things I know I shouldn't do." Currently, one-third claim they give money to or work with charities associated with a church or synagogue. The figure rises to 47 percent among college graduates, and 51 percent among those from households with annual incomes of more than $50,000. Some 70 percent of the nation's adults believe there have been times in their lives when important prayers were answered. And nearly 4 in 10 claim to have had an important religious experience or revelation that reinforced their faith (Princeton Religion Research Center, 1986).

Counterbalancing these statistics are others that suggest religion is not a particularly influential force in the day-to-day lives of Americans. Only one-tenth of Christians fall into the category of "highly spiritually com-

mitted." And there is ample evidence of a self-centered kind of faith. The effect of reading the Bible, prayer and meditation, and religion programs is much more often stated in terms of "it makes me feel good" than in terms of making people repentant or willing to do God's will regardless of the cost (Gallup, 1985).

In sum, it seems we can answer the question of whether religion makes a difference either affirmatively or negatively. As with most other behaviors, much undoubtedly has to do with the situation in which people find themselves, so that a clear overriding answer is hard to come by. In some circumstances, religion can be a powerful social force. Protestant, Catholic, and Jewish groups have spearheaded protests against South Africa's racial policies and ties with that nation. More than 280 houses of worship have declared themselves sanctuaries for people fleeing from Central America, and some parishioners have risked imprisonment to shelter illegal immigrants. Liberal church groups have also been involved with various disarmament and peace issues. And on the political Right, church activists have spearheaded the anti-abortion and anti-ERA movements (Hertel and Hughes, 1987).

teenth Amendment. It has provided the foundation for the principle of "the separation of church and state" in which organized religion and government have remained substantially independent of each other. Compared with many other nations, the United States has maintained a remarkably hands-off attitude toward religion. In a number of cases, however, laws have been enacted and upheld by the Supreme Court that have impinged upon religious practices, including those against polygamy among Mormons and against snake handling by charismatic Christians.

The separation of church and state has not denied a religious dimension to the American political scene. Although most Americans think an individual's religious beliefs and practices are a strictly private matter, there are nonetheless certain common elements of religious orientation that most Americans share. These religious dimensions are expressed in a set of beliefs, symbols, and rituals that sociologist Robert Bellah (1970; Bellah and Hammond, 1980) calls **civil religion**. Its basic tenet is that the American nation is not an ultimate end in itself, but a nation under God with a divine mission. Although

THANKSGIVING-DAY, NOVEMBER 26, 1863.

Civil Religion

According to sociologist Robert Bellah, a recurrent theme running throughout American history has been the notion that the United States is a nation under God with a divine mission. Many of our national holidays have religious overtones. Cartoonist Thomas Nast reflected this theme in his 1863 Thanksgiving Day lithograph. *(North Wind Picture Archives)*

religious pluralism prevents any one denomination from supplying all Americans with a single source of meaning, civil religion compensates by providing an overarching sacred canopy. President Reagan captured this sentiment when he observed at a Dallas prayer breakfast in August, 1984: "I believe that faith and religion play a critical role in the political life of our nation, and always have, and that the church—and by that I mean all churches, all denominations—has had a strong influence on the state, and this has worked to our benefit as a

nation." Like Durkheim, Bellah recognizes that much of the traditional importance of religion lay in its capacity to instill an integrative sense of community. He thinks civil religion continues to fulfull this function.

Civil religion finds expression in the statements and documents of the Founding Fathers, presidential inaugural addresses, national holidays, historic shrines, mottos, and patriotic expressions in times of crisis. There are four references to God in the Declaration of Independence. Every president has mentioned God in his inaugural address (except George Washington in his second inauguration). Thanksgiving is a national holiday celebrated as a day of public thanksgiving and prayer. And the government engages in many religious practices, from placing the phrase "In God We Trust" on its currency to the prayers said in Congress. Thus a set of religious values and sentiments pervades the American political system.

Throughout American history, the influence of religion on secular politics and government has remained strong. Religion has historically played a major role in a good many American social movements. Today groups armed with moral agendas are also seeking to gain public support for their programs. For instance, liberal religious organizations and the nation's Catholic bishops are pushing a set of issues that includes disarmament and improved social services for the disadvantaged. The Christian Right has also come to the fore with an appeal to recover the Christian roots, heritage, and values of an older America. The result has been a reopening of the debate over the role religion should play in public policy. At issue is not the right of religious activists to enter the political arena and lobby for laws consistent with their beliefs, but defining the place of a religiously defined morality in a pluralistic society. The main controversies have been in those areas in which private morality and public policy overlap. Abortion is a good illustration. There are those who insist that abortion is a private moral choice and that the state has no right to make the practice illegal. Others, particularly pro-life groups, contend that abortion is no more a matter of private moral choice than slavery was and that the state has an obligation to stop it. Other equally emotional issues have related to prayer in public schools, pornography, and the rights of homosexuals.

The current debates suggest that religion remains a powerful force in American life. In some respects, Americans are no closer to resolving how to relate people's religious lives to their civil lives than was the case in the days of Thomas Jefferson and James Madison.

Clearly the issue is not one to be decided once and for all ages. Each generation of Americans must tackle its own version of the church–state question. The strength of the nation's pluralistic system has historically resided in a built-in check in which a backlash or countermovement sets in when any one group pushes too hard for its religious values.

THINKING THROUGH THE ISSUES

How has the "tension" between religious groups and the state contributed to the flourishing of America's democratic institutions? How has a panorama of religious groups contributed to a social climate conducive to pluralistic attitudes? How do you account for the differences between the United States and contemporary Lebanon, where groups are killing one another over religion? Also consider this matter: Historian R. Laurence Moore (1985) shows that women, deprived of power in the secular realm as well as in the religious one, were particularly drawn to Mary Baker Eddy's Christian Science movement. By providing avenues for Americans to adjust to their difficulties, how have "religious outsiders" contributed to making America work?

Chapter Highlights

1. Religion is centered in beliefs and practices that are related to sacred as opposed to profane things. The sacred is extraordinary, mysterious, awe-inspiring, and even potentially dangerous. Because the sacred is caught up with strong feelings of reverence and awe, it can usually be approached only through rituals.

2. One approach to religious behavior distinguishes between simple supernaturalism, animism, theism, and a system of abstract ideals. Simple supernaturalism entails the notion of mana—a diffuse, impersonal, supernatural force that exists in nature for good or evil. Animism involves a belief in spirits or otherworldly beings. Theism is a religion centered in a belief in gods who are thought to be powerful, to have an interest in human affairs, and to merit worship. Some religions focus on a set of abstract ideals that are oriented to achieving moral and spiritual excellence.

3. Sociologists distinguish among four ideal types of religious organization: churches, denominations, sects, and cults. Whereas churches and denominations accommodate themselves to the larger society, sects and cults do not. Cults differ from sects in that cults are viewed by their members as being pluralistically legitimate, providing one among many alternative paths to truth or salvation. In this respect, cults resemble denominations. In contrast, the sect, like the church, believes it is uniquely legitimate and possesses exclusive access to truth or salvation.

4. Functionalist theorists look to the contributions religion makes to societal survival. According to Emile Durkheim, religion—the totem ancestor, God, or some other supernatural force—is a symbol for society. By means of religious rituals the group, in effect, worships itself. Viewed in this manner, the primary functions of religion are the creation, reinforcement, and maintenance of social solidarity and social control. In addition, religion helps people in dealing with life's "breaking points." And it may be an impetus to social change.

5. Some conflict theorists depict religion as a weapon in the service of ruling elites, who use it to hold in check the explosive tensions produced by social inequality and injustice. Karl Marx portrayed religion as a painkiller for the frustration, deprivation, and subjugation experienced by oppressed peoples. Other conflict theorists see religion not as a passive response to the social relations of production, but as an active force shaping the contours of social life.

6. The sociologist Peter L. Berger suggests that religion can be employed in three contrasting ways. First, it can be mobilized in opposition to modernization and to the reaffirmation of traditional authority. This is the route taken by the Ayatollah Khomeini and his Islamic Shiite followers in Iran. Second, religion can adapt to the secular world and harness religious motivations for secular purposes. According to Max Weber, this is the path taken by John Calvin and his

Protestant followers. Third, religion can retain its fundamental roots while applying them to contemporary concerns. This is the road reflected in the religious revival that took place in the United States during the 1980s.

7. If religious denominations were basically the same, it would matter little that Americans are divided among more than a thousand religious groups. However, surveys find substantial differences in attitudes and practices among Americans of different denominations. All religious denominations have confronted major pressures for change in recent decades. Perhaps this has been most notable in the Roman Catholic Church. And many Americans seem to be turning to a more personal type of religion for solace and sustenance.

8. Compared with many other nations, the United States has maintained a remarkably hands-off attitude toward religion. However, the separation of church and state has not denied a religious dimension to the American political scene, which finds expression in civil religion.

The Sociologist's Vocabulary

animism A belief in spirits or otherworldly beings.

asceticism A way of life characterized by hard work, sobriety, thrift, restraint, and the avoidance of earthly pleasures.

church A religious organization that asserts its lone legitimacy and seeks a positive relationship with the dominant institutions of society.

civil religion Elements of nationalism and patriotism that take on the properties of a religion.

cult A religious organization that accepts the legitimacy of other groups but often finds fault with the dominant society.

denomination A religious organization that accepts the legitimacy claims of other religions and enjoys a positive relationship with the dominant society.

doctrine of predestination The idea taught by John Calvin that a person's status in the afterlife is predetermined and not affected by how one behaves on earth.

ethic The perspective and values engendered by a religious way of thinking.

mana The notion that there is in nature a diffuse, impersonal, supernatural force operating for good or evil.

monotheism The belief in one god.

polytheism The belief in many gods with equal or relatively similar power.

privatization The transformation of religion from a public to a personal matter, anchored in individual consciousness.

profane Those aspects of social reality that are everyday and commonplace.

Protestant ethic The Calvinist ethos that embodied the spirit of capitalism; an attitude that seeks profit rationally and systematically.

religion Those socially shared ways of thinking, feeling, and acting that have do with the supernatural or "beyond."

rituals Formal procedures that dictate how people should comport themselves in the presence of the sacred.

sacred Anything that is extraordinary, mysterious, awe-inspiring, and even potentially dangerous; those aspects of reality that are set apart and forbidden.

sect A religious organization that asserts its lone legitimacy and rejects the lifeways and values of the dominant society.

secularization thesis The notion that profane (nonreligious) considerations gain ascendancy over sacred (religious) considerations in the course of social evolution.

theism A religion centered in a belief in gods who are thought to be powerful, to have an interest in human affairs, and to merit worship.

totemism A religious system in which a clan (a kin group) takes the name of, claims descent from, and attributes sacred properties to a plant or animal.

15

The Economy, Work, and Leisure

Work keeps at bay three great evils: boredom, vice, and need.

—Voltaire, *Candide*, XXX, 1759

For decades the American auto and steel industries symbolized American capitalism. During World War II they were called "the arsenals of democracy," and in the postwar years they fueled several decades of economic growth. In recent years, these industries have fallen on hard times. Small, cheaper foreign imports have undercut American-made cars and now capture a third of the domestic auto market. Steel production has fallen by nearly half from its 1973 levels.

The problems of the auto and steel industries are symptomatic of the troubles and uncertainties that have engulfed much of American manufacturing in the past decade. The nation is coping with one of the most wrenching economic transitions since the turn of the century. Idle smokestack industries and their crippled communities blot many corners of the American landscape and bring hardship to countless workers and their families. Since the economic institution is closely bound up with other institutions, the effects of the closed plants have reverberated throughout the social structure. Merchants have lost customers; banks have lost depositors; churches have lost congregations; governments have lost taxpayers; and schools have lost pupils. Many industrial scholars, labor leaders, and politicians worry lest the process they call "deindustrialization" may undercut American welfare and security through the loss of capacities that kept the nation strong for decades. Fear of deindustrialization has kindled a crescendo of national and congressional sentiment in favor of protectionist trade measures aimed at sheltering American industries from foreign competition.

Yet throughout our history, change has been a central feature of American life. The decline of the great canal networks and the rise of railways, the demise of rail travel with the invention and popularization of the automobile, and the idling of long-distance truck carriers by modern aviation have heralded the passages from one economic era to another. And the changes have always been unsettling: They have involved disruptions in livelihoods, relocation, and social stress.

Although the number of blue-collar jobs has been slipping since the 1960s, those in service industries—retail trade, fast-food, repair, finance, insurance, real estate, technology, and government—have steadily increased. The U.S. Department of Labor projects that 90 percent of the new jobs that will be added by the year 2000 will be in services. Further, manufacturing jobs are shifting away from the large-scale older concerns to smaller, more efficient enterprises. In the steel business, minimills that make steel by reprocessing scrap and by continuous casting have flourished. In Detroit, hundreds of small machine-tool companies are appearing even as the older firms that formerly supplied the auto industry disappear. In brief, as in the past, there are economic winners and economic losers.

Once more, we see that social arrangements which initially seem somewhat remote nonetheless structure our experiences and place constraints on our behavior. Major changes in the economic realm always have consequences for our personal lives. Take Bill Gorol, Jr., a 27-year-old former steelworker who has embarked on a new career selling cars. He grew up near the sprawling Homestead steel plant in the Monongahela Valley of Pennsylvania. After graduation from Steel Valley High, he found employment in the local mill—known to high school graduates as "13th Grade" or "Riverside Academy"—just as his father had in 1944, his grandfather in 1913, and his great-grandfather in the 1890s. Bill worked at the mill for five years before being laid off in 1982.

The move into the white-collar world was not easy for Bill. For more than a year, he bounced about from job to job—car mechanic, service station attendant, shoe clerk—before answering an ad for a car salesperson. He was ill-prepared for the competitive world of selling cars. At first, more aggressive co-workers interrupted his sales pitches and stole his customers. But in due course Bill mastered the wide smile and outstretched hand essential for success.

Even though he experiences frequent headaches now, he prefers the pressure of sales to mill work. Bill's father, himself laid off, cannot understand his son's thinking. Bill says: "My father can't accept what I'm doing. He thinks it's stupid." The lifestyles of father and son have also diverged. Bill's mother quit her job when she and her husband began having children. But Bill, in talking about beginning a family, says he has offered to quit his own job so that his wife can keep working. He has not mentioned this possibility to his father, who he says "would disown me" (Burrough and Hymowitz, 1986).

Given the important part that the economic order and its changing character plays in our lives, we need to examine it closely. We will concentrate here on the social basis and implications of economic activity and leave consideration of the actual mechanics of the economy to economists.

PLANNING AHEAD: TARGETED READING

1. How do capitalist market economies differ from socialist command economies?

2. What part do corporations play in American life; who controls the decisions made by corporations?

3. What are the consequences for a nation as its domestic economy is drawn increasingly into a global economy?

4. What has been the impact of recent social and economic change on work and the workplace?

5. What insights do sociologists provide regarding satisfaction and alienation in work?

6. In what respects are leisure and sport a microcosm of the larger society?

The Economic System

The **economic system** is the social institution responsible for the production and distribution of goods and services. It supplies answers to three basic problems all societies confront. *What* goods and services should they produce, and in what quantities? *How* should they employ their limited resources—land, water, minerals, fuel, and labor—to produce the desired goods and services? And *for whom* should they produce the goods and services? The manner in which societies answer these questions has profound consequences for their culture and social structure. For instance, if they decide to produce guns and weapons in large quantities, their citizens' standard of living will be lower than if they emphasize the satisfaction of consumer needs. How they go about producing the desired goods and services shapes the world of work, how it is organized, the satisfactions it provides, and the status it accords. And decisions regarding the "for whom" question influence the distribution of wealth, income, and prestige—the stratification system.

As we pointed out in Chapter 4, people have responded somewhat differently across history to the problems posed by economic survival. Hunting and gathering economies are the earliest form of organized social life. Horticultural, agrarian, and industrial modes of production followed. And some social analysts say that advanced nations are currently moving in the direction of postindustrial social organization (see Chapter 22). Changes in the way people produce, distribute, and consume goods and services have usually been accompanied by changes in the family, religious, and political institutions as well.

Contemporary Economic Systems

In the contemporary world, two different types of economic systems are competing for people's allegiance. One is characterized by a capitalist market economy and the other by a socialist command economy. The two systems differ from one another in two important respects. First, they provide a different answer to the question, "How is economic activity organized—by the market or by the plan?" Second, they provide a different answer to the question, "Who owns the means of production—individuals or the state?"

These questions do not demand an "either/or" answer. Each question allows for a range of choice, with a great many gradations in between. No contemporary nation falls totally at one or the other pole, although the United States and the Soviet Union typically supply opposite answers to both questions. In practice, we usually merge the two features and talk about contrasting economic systems. We think of **capitalist economies** as relying heavily on free markets and privately held property and **socialist economies** as relying primarily on state planning and publicly held property. In truth, however, the answers to the two questions do not necessarily go together. Nazi Germany had a government controlled and planned economy, although ownership remained mainly in private hands. And in contemporary Yugoslavia the means of production are socially owned, although the economy is largely organized by markets.

Capitalist and socialist economies have a somewhat different image of the role the state should play in economic life. And each takes a quite different approach to property. We will have a good deal more to say about the state in Chapter 16. But let us examine the social notion of property here, because property ownership is a major source of difference between proponents of the two approaches.

The social notion of property We typically think of property as having to do with tangible, material things. In point of fact, however, **property** is a social reality consisting of a set of rights that indicates what one party can do and what another party cannot do. It is an *enforceable claim* with respect to some scarce object (Collins, 1975). The notion of property seems to be a cultural universal—all societies have rules governing the possession, handling, and disposition of property. Societies differ, however, in the emphasis they place on the "private

Trade and Markets

The evolution of exchange relationships can be traced to prehistoric times. Hunters and gatherers often desired salt, obsidian, red ochre, flint, reeds, and honey that they themselves did not produce or control. So trade relations evolved and in due course led to trading partnerships like those found today among inhabitants of the Niger in Africa (top left), markets like those of the Indian population of contemporary Bolivia (top right), and bazaars like those still prominent among merchants of Morocco (bottom left). Balanced reciprocity and barter are traditionally relied on as methods for distributing goods and services. However, such arrangements work only so long as people are assured of finding someone who has an excess of what they want to obtain and a shortage of what they want to give away. This difficulty encourages the use of money as a medium of exchange. *(clockwise from top left: Philip Jon Bailey/Stock, Boston; Christiana Dittmann/Rainbow; Burt Glinn/Magnum)*

property" rights of some individuals as opposed to the "public ownership" of property by the state or the "communal ownership" of property by families, clans, or the community.

No society carries individual ownership to the point where no one but the party concerned has jurisdiction over the objects. Societies impose social limitations on property, including building codes, taxation, licensing, and maintenance requirements. No society, no matter how collectivist, lacks individual ownership of some objects—clothing and various "personal" possessions, for example. Even in communes that stress ideals of equality and sharing, people commonly have a sense of ownership about a room, bed, chair, or table—one that is "theirs" by virtue of consistent use. In monasteries and convents, monks and nuns can come to feel possessive about "their" individual cells.

Comparing market and command economies

Capitalist market and socialist command economies supply different solutions to the three problems we noted at the beginning of the chapter. Consider the question of what goods and services should be produced, and in what quantities. In a market economy, consumers determine the answer by their dollar votes. What they buy or fail to buy acts as a signal to profit-making individuals and firms. This mechanism is called *consumer sovereignty*. Underlying this approach is the notion that if each economic unit is allowed to make free choices in pursuit of its own best interests, the interests of all will be best served. Critics fault the arrangement because people's best interests are not necessarily well served when consumer tastes are manipulated to pursue profits. Children, for instance, may end up eating high-sugar, low-nutrient cereals for breakfast. In contrast, in command economies the state or central planning authority determines the items that will be produced and their quantities. The problem with this arrangement is highlighted by the situation in the Soviet Union, where there are fewer automobiles and more copies of Lenin's books than consumers want.

Free market and command economies also differ in how they deal with the problem of allocating scarce resources among productive activities. In free market economies, competition among suppliers of goods and labor services is thought to ensure the most efficient and productive use of resources. If we try to grow oranges in South Dakota and wheat in Florida, we are unlikely to have as much success as if we reverse the patterns. Command economies, in contrast, are based on the assumption that rational decision making gives better results than the haphazard operation of market forces.

Finally, market and command economies differ in how they handle the "for whom" question of income distribution. Market economies rely on the same price system that determines wages, interest rates, and profits for determining the distribution of income among people. The major beneficiaries are capitalists—the private owners of capital. Critics condemn the arrangement because of the social inequality and injustice they believe results from it. Their solution is to have the state own the primary instruments of production and direct their use in "the public good."

Capitalist economies   The capitalist market economy began somewhat tentatively in the Middle Ages. Between 1500 and 1750 or so, traders evolved such essential capitalist arrangements as private property rights, banks, insurance, commercial law, and accounting procedures. After 1750, other innovations—especially the introduction of steam power, factories, and ferrous metals—fundamentally altered production. Beginning about 1850, industry embraced science and began to use it as a system of innovation. In this century, most capitalist enterprises have adopted a corporate form that facilitates the accumulation of capital while permitting diversity in size and technology (Rosenberg and Birdzell, 1986).

Sociologist Peter L. Berger (1986) has sought a deeper understanding of capitalism by taking a look at the underlying culture and social structures that promote it. He asks two questions: What kinds of societies are associated with this type of economic system? What type

Capitalism: Singapore
Bustling, robust growth has come to characterize the economies of the Pacific Rim nations such as Singapore, a small island republic in the South China Sea. Like Hong Kong, Japan, Taiwan, and South Korea, Singapore is on the periphery of the huge Asian land mass, strategically located for carrying on global commerce and for attracting migrants willing to work in its burgeoning industries. Stressing hard work, education, and social harmony, state and business sectors have cooperated to produce the exports that fuel development. *(Brian Brake/Photo Researchers)*

of people does it produce? Max Weber had addressed somewhat similar issues in *The Protestant Ethic and the Spirit of Capitalism* (1904)(see Chapter 14). Until the great postwar economic booms in East Asia—Singapore, Hong Kong, Japan, South Korea, and Taiwan—it seemed reasonable to believe that capitalism thrived only in environments sympathetic to individual autonomy and independent action. But the East Asian experience has shown this idea to be wrong. It has enabled sociologists to distinguish between those social ingredients favorable to capitalist institutions and those rooted in specifically European traditions.

East Asian cultures emphasize group solidarity and respect for tradition, rather than individual achievement. Indeed, Berger concludes that the East Asian evidence shows that a high degree of state intervention in an economy is quite compatible with successful capitalist development. In Singapore, Hong Kong, Japan, South Korea, and Taiwan, government has intervened massively in economic life and fostered a "government-business symbiosis" quite different from the situation in Europe and North America. In brief, laissez-faire capitalism—"let the state leave business alone"—is only one version of capitalism. Communal capitalism—the East Asian version—is another.

Berger finds that capitalism, whatever its form, creates strong pressures for political and personal freedom. Indeed, he concludes that capitalism is a necessary but not sufficient condition of democracy. Berger cannot find a democracy without a capitalist economy, although he finds cases, like Taiwan, of vigorous capitalism without much democracy. Moreover, based on his survey of cross-national studies, Berger concludes that capitalist development is more likely than socialist development to improve the material standard of life in Third World nations.

Socialist economies   Berger fails to consider that capitalism has defects as well as virtues. One of its main defects is its instability—its proneness to what in the nineteenth century were called "financial panics" and in this century "recessions" or "depressions." The most powerful critic of capitalism was, of course, Karl Marx (see Chapter 1). As the Industrial Revolution gathered force in the early nineteenth century, it had produced considerable social hardship. Capitalists treated their workers as harshly as machines, and even young children were pressed into factory service for 14-hour days under wretched and often dangerous conditions. Surveying the capitalist system of his day, Marx predicted it would be overthrown and replaced by a socialist state, where workers rather than profit-seeking capitalists would run the economy. He believed that socialism would evolve into communism, a utopian society in which class distinctions and the state would no longer exist. The Marxist vision inspired social movements that led to the establishment of the Soviet system and to the less rigidly dogmatic, welfare-oriented Democratic Socialist parties of Western Europe.

The Great Depression of the 1930s and World War II set the stage for the advance of socialist and welfare notions. People sought reforms to curb the abuses of capitalism and to lessen the severity of its boom and bust cycles. In the United States, the New Deal created a

Soviet-style Economies: Difficulty Satisfying Consumer Needs
The centrally planned economies of the Soviet Union and Eastern European nations have had problems meeting the wants of the countries' citizens. Chronic shortages and low-quality goods are commonplace. Here Poles wait in a line at a foodstore in Gdansk. Mikhail Gorbachev has sought to loosen the state's grip on Soviet industry and agriculture. But translating the program into an economic revival has pitted Gorbachev against the inertia of Stalinist central control. Soviet managers are inexperienced in decentralized, market-oriented planning. *(Paula Allen/Archive)*

variety of programs, including public works projects and the social security system. In postwar Europe, governments went even further. They enacted social legislation creating programs such as free medical care, and they nationalized a number of major industries (the British nationalized the steel industry and the French their largest automaker, Renault). Third World nations turned to socialism, in part as a response to the ending of colonial rule. In sum, following World War II, much of the world favored state planning over a market system and public over private enterprise.

By the 1980s, however, it had become increasingly difficult to deny the poor performance of most existing socialist societies with respect to economic growth, individual freedom, and even social equality. More and more European and Third World governments sought to reduce the public spheres and to expand the market sectors of their economies. Many of their welfare programs had become increasingly difficult to pay for (for example, by the mid-1980s, one-third of West Germany's total economic output went for old age pensions, medical insurance, and other welfare programs) (O'Boyle and Gumbel, 1987). Moreover, conservatives charged that generous social benefits had had a serious impact on individual initiative and worker incentive. In North America and Western Europe, voters brought into office conservative governments such as that of Ronald Reagan in the United States, Margaret Thatcher in Great Britain, and Helmut Kohl in West Germany. The shift was not so much a call for the dismantling of social service programs as support for policies that promised to encourage national economic growth. It seems that while capital-

ism may have difficulty coexisting with the welfare state, it also has difficulty existing without social programs that manage the hardships produced by the unbridled operation of market processes (Mishra, 1984; Offe, 1984).

The Soviet experience is also enlightening. The centrally planned economy is capable of doing some things reasonably well, particularly adding to the nation's military arsenal. Yet the Soviet system remains remarkably inflexible. Shortages, corruption, pessimism, economic drift, and low worker discipline have characterized the Soviet economy in recent years. The requirements of growth and technology clash with the determination of the Soviet political elite to retain the status quo and preserve their immense power. By wielding strong control over the economy, the Soviet leadership has left little room for innovation, experimentation, or individual enterprise (Bialer, 1986). Under the leadership of Mikhail Gorbachev, the Soviet Union has permitted a touch of free enterprise, but has retained its ban on hired labor (Taubman, 1986). On its western border, the Soviet-style economy of Poland collapsed in the late 1970s, leading to the rise and suppression of the independent trade union Solidarity in 1980–1981.

China's current Communist leaders have also allowed the introduction of free market principles in selected spheres of economic life. Large privately owned companies are still banned, and nowhere do the changes seem so radical as to threaten the Party's monopoly on political power. In 1986, the output of private manufacturing enterprises in China grew by 60 percent, though it accounted for less than 1 percent of total industrial output. Although the Chinese are experimenting with and

Free Markets: People's Republic of China
In recent years free-market principles have been introduced in selected areas of the Chinese economy. Free markets can be found in major cities, like that in Shanghai pictured at right. Bureaucrats who stand to lose authority and diehard Maoists in the party and armed forces are uneasy about the new direction. Although the spirit of free enterprise has gained momentum, the explosive growth of entrepreneurship is not without problems. Opponents warn that it threatens social polarization of the sort that fueled the Chinese revolution more than 50 years ago. *(J.P. Laffont/Sygma)*

redefining socialism, they do not plan to set up a capitalist market system (Baum, 1987). And a question remains whether Deng Xiaopeng's "opening" will be shut down by traditionalists.

Mixed economies   Our discussion suggests that as we look about the contemporary world, we are hard pressed to find a pure form of either a capitalist market economy or a socialist command economy. To one degree or another, most nations are characterized by mixed economies. Consider the United States (see the box dealing with the issue of whether government should save failing businesses). The nation's tax laws influence investment decisions by providing incentives and shelters for investors in real estate and mineral exploration. Regulatory agencies impose pollution controls, standards for work conditions, rates for electric utility companies, and licensing of prescription drugs. Additionally, some enterprises, such as the Tennessee Valley Authority (TVA), the Postal Service, and Amtrak operate as publicly owned agencies. For its part, the Soviet Union allows a small "capitalist" sector in which peasants are permitted to sell what they grow on small private plots of land.

Western European nations are even more mixed. In Great Britain, for instance, most industries are privately owned, except for those deemed "basic" to the economy (coal, steel, and railroads). Scandinavian capitalism— sometimes mistakenly taken for socialism—is a form of "welfare statism." For example, in Sweden some 90 percent of the nation's enterprises are privately owned, although income taxes on profits run as high as 80 percent. The revenues secured in this fashion are used for an extensive system of social benefits that provide cradle-to-grave care for everyone. Japan has also evolved a unique system whereby industry and government work closely together. Some large firms, particularly those engaged in exporting, receive substantial government preferences.

Corporate Capitalism

The government is an important participant in the American economy, but the primary productive role is played by private business. In 1987 there were some 17 million businesses in the United States. Most were small, owned by an individual or family, and concentrated in services, construction, and retail and wholesale trade. Although most American businesses are small, large corporations have the greatest impact on the economy. The 275 largest industrial corporations own two-thirds of the assets of manufacturing firms and realize nearly three-fourths of the profits (*Statistical Abstract of the United States*, 1984). The largest American industrial corporation, General Motors, netted a profit of nearly $4 billion in 1985. IBM made the most profit— $6.6 billion.

The power and influence of national corporations   When you drive a car, work on a computer terminal, replace a lightbulb, purchase gasoline, or eat a breakfast cereal, you are using products manufactured by an oligopoly. An **oligopoly** is a market dominated by a few firms. When we look at such giants of American business as General Motors, IBM, and General Electric, we find oligopolies. General Motors must compete with Ford, Chrysler, Toyota, and Honda; IBM with Apple, Control Data, and Hewlett-Packard; and General Electric with Westinghouse (in the electrical generator market) and with Pratt and Whitney (in the jet engine market).

Such gigantic firms exercise enormous power. Decisions made by their officials have implications and ramifications that reach throughout the nation. Take the automobile industry. Until recently, the car business pumped $40 billion a year into 30,000 suppliers, made products equivalent to 8 percent of the nation's gross national product (GNP) and 26 percent of total retail sales, and employed a large fraction of the workforce (Abernathy, Clark, and Kantrow, 1983; Halberstam, 1986). But as the big auto firms matured, their managements failed to adapt in ways that would sustain both efficiency and innovation. Meanwhile, Japanese car makers learned to make subcompacts for about $2,000 less than their American counterparts (in 1985, the Japanese needed only 80 to 100 hours to make a car, whereas American auto companies required 150 to 160 hours to do the same job) (Holusha, 1986; Karmin, 1987). And because of the superior quality image of Japanese cars, Americans wanted more of them. Consequently, American auto companies lost a substantial market share to foreign manufacturers, found themselves with outdated plants and equipment, and underwent plant closings and massive layoffs. They sought and won voluntary agreements between the United States and Japan limiting Japanese auto imports. The import limits result in high price tags that cost American consumers an extra $5 billion a year for cars (Crandall, 1986). Whereas in 1972 it took the average consumer 30 weeks to earn enough to afford the average automobile, in 1984 it took 40 weeks (Anderson, 1984).

ISSUES THAT SHAPE OUR LIVES

Should Government Bail Out Big Corporations?

President Calvin Coolidge summarized the matter well when he observed in 1925 that "The business of America is business." So did Charles Wilson, the president of General Motors, who in his 1953 Senate confirmation hearings as secretary of defense commented: "What's good for the country is good for General Motors and vice versa." Asked to elaborate on his statement, Wilson said that the interests of General Motors and the nation went hand in hand.

Few of us would deny that government and business are closely intertwined in American life. Government affects business in countless ways, particularly by spending, taxation, and regulatory policies. And as we will observe later in the chapter, the decisions made by business leaders have a profound impact on the nation. Given the many bonds binding government and business, there are those who express concern lest the ties become so close that they imperil the interests of the many for the advantage of the few. One matter that has generated considerable debate is whether or not the government should intervene in a free-market system to save ailing corporations.

The issue is not a new one. Although in theory large corporations operate in the private sector, their impact on national life and the nation's welfare is so enormous that governments have often intervened to bail them out when they are threatened with bankruptcy. Italy under Mussolini was a pioneer. A huge sector of troubled Italian industry and banking was brought into government hands. After the war, in Britain, France, Germany, and Spain, older industries—coal mining, steel and steel fabricating, shipbuilding, and chemicals—were likewise rescued by government (Galbraith, 1985).

In 1970, the United States Congress for the first time underwrote an ailing private enterprise, the Penn Central Transportation Co., with a multibillion-dollar loan guarantee. Later the federal government rescued Chrysler and Lockheed. And in 1984 it saved the Continental Illinois National Bank & Trust Co. of Chicago. The Comptroller of the Currency, Todd Conover, told Congress that the federal government could not allow any of the nation's eleven largest banks to fail. Recounting a discussion with the heads of the Federal Reserve Board, the Federal Deposit Insurance Corporation, and the Treasury Department, Conover said: "We recognized that we could very well have seen a national, if not an international, financial crisis" if the government did not rescue Continental. He estimated that more than 100 banks with deposits in the troubled Chicago bank would have failed, and that dozens of the bank's corporate customers could also have collapsed had the government not intervened with its $4.5 billion rescue (Carrington, 1984). The bailout of Continental Illinois ultimately cost the government about $1 billion (Nash, 1986). The federal government and the Federal Reserve have also reassured the nation's banks that they will not be permitted to fail if Argentina, Brazil, and Mexico are unable to repay their loans (Norton, 1986).

Although the government may have taken the sting out of capitalism for large corporations with political and economic muscle, it has not done so for countless small business firms and hundreds of thousands of farmers who have confronted bankruptcy. Likewise, Wheeling-Pittsburgh Steel was allowed to go under, but it was only the seventh largest in the industry. It is quite likely that in the years ahead there will be more rescues for firms that are defined as "vital" to the national well-being. Karl Marx had thought that the workers would be the ones who would force the pace to socialism. Yet in our time, it is large industrial and banking interests that seem to be leading the march when they find capitalist enterprise in difficulty (Galbraith, 1985).

The American steel industry affords another illustration of the impact large corporations have on American life. Steel was once the backbone of the nation's economy, but miscalculations by the steel corporations have devastated the industry. Between 1979 and 1986, industry employment plummeted from 450,000 to 200,000 (Greenhouse, 1986). For the three decades following 1940, the major steel companies—unchallenged by either foreign or domestic competitors—could charge what the market would bear, so they had little incentive for innovation. In 1982, less than a third of American crude steel was produced with more efficient continuous-casting methods, contrasted with 90 percent in Japan and 66 percent in Europe. According to a report by the Congressional Budget Office, steel companies spent an average of $2.2 billion annually on capital projects between 1980 and 1984, $3.3 billion less than required if they were to remain competitive (Williams,

Has the American Job Machine Broken Down?
Although the American ability to create jobs has long
been the envy of the rest of the world, there are
growing concerns that the United States is undergoing "deindustrialization." Many factories have closed
in the midwestern "rust belt." Workers are losing
their jobs because they do not have the skills currently required and because companies are leaving
aging cities for suburbs. But some analysts are more
upbeat about the changes in the nation's employment
profile. They see the United States as undergoing a
rapid transition from an industrial-based, goods-
producing society to an information-based, service-
producing society. *(Bill Campbell/Picture Group)*

1984). What money they did invest was often diverted to
nonsteel areas. For example, United States Steel (since
renamed USX) purchased Marathon Oil for $6 billion in
1982 and Texas Oil & Gas for $3 billion in stock in
1985. Clearly, auto and steel executives have made decisions with enormous consequences not only for their
companies and employees, but for the nation and economy as a whole. Their decisions have had a substantial

impact on employment opportunities, economic conditions (depression and inflation), consumer choices, and
political authority. This raises the question of who controls corporations—who are the decision makers?

The control of corporations   In 1932 Adoph Berle, Jr.,
and Gardiner C. Means sought to answer the question of
corporate control in their book, *The Modern Corporation
and Private Property.* They said that corporate power re-
sides with chief executives who themselves have little
financial stake in the firms they manage. The logic of
their argument rested on the assertion that the stock of
most large corporations is widely dispersed. Consequently, no shareholder or group of shareholders possess
a sufficient block of stock to impose policy on the managers who make the day-to-day decisions. The separation
of ownership and effective control was labeled "the managerial revolution" (Burnham, 1941). This portrait of
management dominated the social sciences for some
thirty years.

The view that a company's top officers enjoy considerable discretion in making decisions has been challenged in recent years. Sociologists are finding strong
constraints on managers in discharging their responsibilities (Mintz and Schwartz, 1981a; Glasberg and
Schwartz, 1983). For one thing, suppliers of raw materials and customers for finished products place limits on
executive maneuverability. Even greater constraints are
imposed by large banks (eight major New York City
commercial banks are responsible for over 50 percent of
all industrial bank loans in the United States). Through
their control of capital resources, major corporate lend-
ers can decide which projects will be pursued and which
will remain unfunded. Other constraints also operate.
Large institutional investors—mutual, trust, and pension funds—now control at least 70 percent of all stock
traded (Glasberg and Schwartz, 1983). The buying and
selling of large blocks of stock by institutional investors
has enormous consequences for corporate affairs. For
instance, when they sell in tandem, they can squelch
financing and expansion plans and undermine a firm's
morale. Similarly, **corporate interlocks**—networks of
individuals who serve on the boards of directors of multiple corporations—place constraints on what the managers of one firm can undertake without reference to the
needs and requirements of other firms (Mintz and
Schwartz, 1981b; Burt, 1983; Palmer, Friedland, and
Singh, 1986). Figure 15.1 on page 412 shows the corporate interlocks of the individuals who sit on the board of
directors of General Motors.

Some large investors and speculators—called corporate raiders—have found that a good deal of money can be made by buying and selling companies. They commonly see a corporation as a salable bundle of assets, rather than as a producer of goods and services. One example of this trend has been corporate mergers that have given rise to **conglomerates,** companies whose components operate in completely different markets and produce largely unrelated products. For example, in the early 1980s Beatrice Foods pursued an aggressive acquisitions strategy that steadily transformed the Chicago concern into a $10-billion-a-year conglomerate with 50 companies selling everything from cosmetics to luggage to orange juice. However, in late 1985 and early 1986, very focused companies—those having a limited range of diversification—became the stock-market favorites. This provided a climate in which Beatrice Foods was taken over by a new group of investors who promptly sought to recoup their investment and make a profit by selling off the nonfood subsidiaries (McCormick, 1986).

By virtue of these trends, managers often run their businesses like stock portfolios, with companies bought and sold because they provide a good return on investment at the moment. Held accountable by owners who focus on immediate earnings, managers lack the independence and power to set a course that will reap sound payoffs in future years. For example, fearing a dip in today's profits, executives skimp on research and technology, the investment critical to competitiveness tomorrow. The auto and steel industries provide good illustrations. Moreover, takeovers and divestitures have far-reaching ramifications that call into question existing social arrangement such as plant and headquarters locations; product lines; union contracts; pension and retirement benefits; and ties with local suppliers, banks, and community organizations (Hirsch, 1986).

In sum, professional managers do not typically enjoy the wide range of latitude in decision making that Berle and Means credited them as having. Executive officers are governed by the requirement that they optimize profits. That corporate managers own little or none of a corporation's stock does not mean corporations have been freed to pursue goals and policies that consistently run counter to profit maximization. The vision of a "soulful corporation" has not been realized. Rather, an arrangement characterized by a "constrained management" has evolved. Although in many cases the separation of ownership from control has given managers greater range of autonomy, it has also rendered them subservient to the constraints of a highly institutionalized system of rational profit-seeking (Herman, 1981). The dictates of the drive for profits limit managerial discretion by tying managerial compensation and promotion to investors' rate of return. Hence, corporations remain fundamentally capitalist in goal and in practice.

Restructuring American industry   Between 1980 and 1987, well over half of the 1,000 largest U. S. corporations underwent some form of significant reorganization, variously known as downsizing, rationalizing, streamlining and, most commonly, restructuring. IBM closed three domestic plants, cut back on employee overtime, and reduced its workforce 7 percent. Eastman Kodak undertook a revitalization program by forming small entrepreneurial business units and slashing its workforce of 128,950 by 10 percent. And Gulf & Western sold some 65 diverse subsidiaries worth more than $4 billion. Re-

"*Then it's agreed. We'll close our plants in Raleigh, Scranton, Kansas City, Toledo, Newark, Sacramento, Wheeling, and Houston. Thank you, gentlemen. It was a very productive meeting.*"

Drawing by C. Barsotti; © 1986 The New Yorker Magazine, Inc.

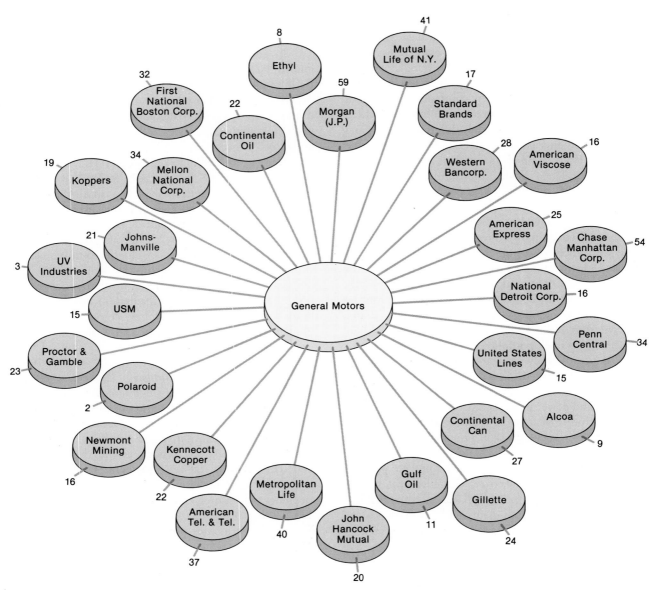

FIGURE 15.1   The Interlocking Directorate of General Motors and Other Firms
Individuals who sit on the board of directors of General Motors also sit on the boards of directors of 29 other firms. In turn, the members of each of the 29 firms sit on the boards of directors of still other firms. For instance, the people who sit on the board of J. P. Morgan are also linked to the boards of 59 other firms. Through such ties, General Motors is embedded in a network of 728 corporations. *Source: Beth Mintz and Michael Schwartz, Interlocking directorates and interest group formation,* American Sociological Review, *46 (December 1981), figure 3, p. 857.*

structuring has entailed cutting back on costs to make dramatic and durable improvements in long-term profitability and growth. It has also involved retrenchment, as corporations cut back on marginal operations, strip away

unnecessary layers of management and staff, and refocus attention on proven money-making areas. The new leanness has had its human costs. Between 1983 and 1987, some 600,000 to 1.2 million middle- and upper-level executives with annual salaries of $40,000 or more lost their jobs (Ansberry, 1987; Russell, 1987).

Chief among the forces prompting restructuring has been foreign competition. In addition to traditional rivals in Europe and Japan, United States companies face an expanding roster of formidable competitors in South Korea and Brazil. By 1987, imports to the United States amounted to 14.5 percent of the Gross National Product, up from 10.6 percent in 1982. Another force behind restructuring has been the sharp rise in corporate mergers and acquisitions. More than 4,000 mergers worth $190 billion took place in 1986. Following the buyouts, most merged companies eliminate staff duplications and unprofitable divisions. Between 1981 and 1987, for instance, General Electric spent $11.1 billion to buy 338 companies, including RCA (a $6.3 billion acquisition). During the same period, GE sold 232 businesses worth $5.9 billion and closed 73 plants and offices. Overall, "competitiveness"—defined as the ability of the United States to remain the world's premier economy—is a buzzword that has pushed to center stage in business and government (Russell, 1987; Karmin, 1987).

THINKING THROUGH THE ISSUES

Peter F. Drucker (1986), a leading authority on business management, contends that American capitalism is in crisis. He notes that pension funds now own 50 percent or more of the equity in the nation's biggest companies. Pension funds typically turn the management of their monies over to companies that specialize in making investment decisions that will generate the greatest financial returns. Drucker finds that managers of investment companies focus on short-term results. Should their investment decisions prove less profitable than those made by rivals who manage the monies of other pension funds, they will be replaced. Because they must show immediate gains, investment managers demand the companies whose stock they have purchased for a pension fund make quick profits. Corporate executives, then, be they with General Motors, Hewlett-Packard, Allied Supermarkets, or Sonoco Products, are compelled to subordinate long-range considerations—their firm's technological requirements and market standing—to short-term profits. Drucker says that no American company currently produces VCRs because the recorders would have required a few years of investment and would not have yielded immediate gains. If Drucker is correct in his assessment of American management practice, what are the long-term consequences for the nation's major corporations? How are they likely to fare in competition with foreign firms? What ripple effects are likely to be produced in the economy as a whole and in other institutional sectors? How might some of the difficulties corporate managers experience be remedied?

The Global Economy and Multinational Corporations

Domestic economies are increasingly being drawn into a global economy. The world's markets are now linked by modern telecommunications, so that trading goes on around the clock. If terrorists knock out an oil pipeline in the Middle East or American auto sales prove stronger than expected, within minutes the prices of world oil contracts, and U.S. Treasury bonds, South African gold, American stock market prices, and commodity futures—an entire spectrum of financial instruments—respond by moving up or down. Each day billions of dollars flow across national boundaries in countless transactions. Major corporations and governments no longer care whether they raise money in New York, London, Tokyo, or Hong Kong. General Motors packages car loans as securities and sells them in Japan and Europe. Japanese banks and brokerage firms routinely underwrite bond issues in Europe for General Electric, Exxon, and IBM and occasionally buy 60 percent of a new U.S. Treasury bond offering. The West German Deutsche Bank Capital Corporation arranges for an American company to issue bonds in European currencies and switch the proceeds into dollars with American, Japanese, French, and West German banks and companies.

Round-the-clock trading sets new values for the dollar, the Japanese yen, the German mark, the Swiss franc, and more than 100 other currencies. By 1986, the foreign exchange market had grown into a $150-billion-a-day industry. The stability of governments can rest on the outcome of these transactions. Exchange rates—such as the amount of marks or yen a dollar will fetch—influence which products people buy, which factories hum and which close, who loses jobs, and whose savings are depleted by inflation. The magnitude and speed of the capital flows has eroded the ability of presidents and prime ministers to manage their domestic economies. Further, if companies do not like the political or economic climate in one nation, they can switch their investments to another country. For example, the amount of money Americans invested in French businesses *grew* by an annual rate of 11 percent between 1965 and 1981. But with the victory of François Mitterrand's Socialist party in the 1981 French elections, American investment *fell* at an average rate of 9 percent a year over the following five years. In contrast, the economic policies of Ronald Reagan gave a powerful boost to the flow of Western European and Japanese capital to the United States (Bowles and Gintis, 1986). Complicating matters even more, decisions reached by such giant international cartels as OPEC, by regulating the price of critical commodities like oil, send economic shock waves around the globe.

Multinational corporations   The internationalization of the world economy and the rise of multinational corporations have given a new dimension to economic power (Bornschier, Chase-Dunn, and Rubinson, 1978; Szymanski, 1981; Fennema, 1982). **Multinational corporations** are firms that have their central office in one country and subsidiaries in other countries. Since World War II, multinational corporations have played a growing role in the structuring of the division of labor within the world economy. Table 15.1 lists the world's 30 largest public corporations. The annual income from sales of the largest corporations exceeds the gross national products of most countries in which they do business. In

fact, about half of the largest economic units in the world are not nations but multinational corporations.

But multinational firms do not only rival nations in wealth; together, such companies form a distinct "supranational" economy that operates beyond public regulation or the usual international rules. They pursue their own global strategic interests in search of profit, oblivious to the domestic goals of individual nations (Wachtel, 1986). In some instances, multinational corporations have posed a threat to the sovereignty of the nations in which they operate. For instance, International Telephone and Telegraph (ITT) flagrantly intervened in Chile's domestic political life in the early 1970s by aiding the opponents of Marxist Salvador Allende. When Allende was elected president, ITT worked with the CIA to overthrow his legally constituted government with a coup that assassinated Allende and installed a military dictatorship. Nor have developed nations been spared. In an attempt to secure foreign military contracts, Lockheed made payments to politically influential people in a number of countries. Among those touched by the scandal were a former Japanese prime minister and a member of the Dutch royal family. Since their operations extend across a great many national boundaries, any one government has difficulty holding multinational firms accountable. And governments find it more difficult to deal with a multinational corporation than with a domestic firm, because the multinational corporation will simply take its business and leave.

More and more multinational companies are taking on a transnational character (Drucker, 1986). Consider the oil and petrochemical business. The major oil com-

Multinational Corporations Operating in the United States
Billions of dollars from Britain, the Netherlands, West Germany, Japan, and other lands have poured into the United States in recent years, creating jobs, filling the federal government's borrowing needs, and reviving some industrial areas. Japanese firms have had a particularly strong impact on the American automobile industry. It has spawned Japanese industrial centers such as "Auto Alley," stretching into the mid-South. Here American workers in Marysville, Ohio, assemble Honda Civics and Accords. *(Andy Snow/Picture Group)*

Table 15.1   The World's 30 Largest Public Companies
(By market value on June 30, 1986, converted into U.S. dollars at exchange rate for that date)

	Company Name	Headquarters	Market Value (In millions of U.S. dollars)	Earnings, 1985 (In millions of home currency)	Sales, 1985 (In millions of home currency)	Worldwide Employment (In thousands)	Percent Employed Outside Home Country
1	IBM	Armonk, N.Y.	$87,697	6,560	50,100	405	40%
2	Exxon	New York	44,015	4,870	92,000	146	54
3	General Electric	Fairfield, Conn.	36,820	2,340	28,300	300	20
4	Tokyo Electric	Tokyo	32,421	113,000	3,915,000	39	*
5	AT&T	New York	27,138	1,560	34,900	350	2
6	Sumitomo Bank	Osaka, Japan	25,962	77,200	31,034	17	21
7	Toyota Motor	Toyota City, Japan	25,197	406,000	6,770,000	80	20
8	General Motors	Detroit	24,751	4,000	96,400	890	40
9	Dai-Ichi Kangyo Bank	Tokyo	23,729	N.A.	35,863	20	4
10	Nomura Securities	Tokyo	23,151	111,000	2,178	10	2
11	Royal Dutch Petroleum	The Hague, Netherlands	21,592	3,030	73,100	141	60
12	Mitsubishi Bank	Tokyo	21,461	62,100	26,772	16	5
13	Fuji Bank	Tokyo	21,460	60,700	30,653	15	2
14	Daimler-Benz	Stuttgart, W.Germany	20,874	1,630	52,409	311	19
15	British Telecom	London	20,430	904	7,653	234	1
16	Du Pont	Wilmington, Del.	20,093	1,120	29,500	140	21
17	BellSouth	Atlanta	19,246	1,418	10,664	96	*
18	Industrial Bank of Japan	Tokyo	19,092	44,800	21,447	5	N.A.
19	Sanwa Bank	Osaka, Japan	18,346	58,700	27,384	20	25
20	Philip Morris	New York	17,813	1,260	16,000	114	38
21	Sears Roebuck	Chicago	17,659	1,300	40,700	466	12
22	British Petroleum	London	16,651	1,600	41,000	129	77
23	Matsushita Electric Industrial	Osaka, Japan	16,210	247,000	5,053,000	150	3
24	Coca-Cola	Atlanta	16,147	678	7,904	39	56
25	Amoco	Chicago	15,588	1,950	28,900	50	19
26	Mitsubishi Estate	Tokyo	15,112	20,500	192,000	2	1
27	Hitachi	Tokyo	14,923	210,000	5,013,000	165	18
28	Merck	Rahway, N.J.	14,666	540	3,547	31	53
29	Wal-Mart Stores	Bentonville, Ark.	14,579	271	6,401	120	*
30	Ford Motor	Dearborn, Mich.	14,313	2,520	52,800	369	53

Source: A special report: Global finances & investing. *Wall Street Journal* (September 29, 1986), p. 16d.

panies secure their crude oil from the Middle East, Nigeria, Venezuela, Mexico, Alaska, Indonesia, and the North Sea. They coordinate their purchases with markets, refining operations, and chemical plants in the United States, Japan, Europe, and elsewhere. The companies optimize refinery capacity on an international rather than a national basis and set a global price for their products. Their survival and strategic advantage are not located in any individual nation, but in their ability to coordinate and link resources and activities internationally. Earnings from one unit are shifted from nation to nation so that income realized in the United States, Japan, or Germany may be invested in Brazil, or vice versa.

Although American-based multinational corporations have long held assets in other countries, in recent years foreign-based multinational corporations have increased their investments in the United States. As of 1987, some 2.5 million to 3 million American jobs are with companies owned by foreign nationals (the total U.S. labor force is 118 million). Much concern about foreign investment has focused on the Japanese. Yet only 2 to 3 percent of U.S. industry is foreign-owned, and no more than 20 percent of that amount is in the hands of any one nation (Great Britain). Holland is second, and only recently has Japan moved ahead of Canada into third place. For the most part, Americans do not worry about British, Dutch, or Canadian ownership. So why are Americans so bothered by the Japanese? Sociologists and economists suspect racism (Yemma, 1987).

Core and periphery regions   Although the pace at which local economies are being internationalized is accelerating, the development is hardly a new one. The economic integration of less developed nations into the structures of a world economy can be traced to European exploration and colonization beginning in the fifteenth century. The arrangement has been characterized by the differentiation of core and periphery regions (Wallerstein, 1974, 1980). **Core regions** consist of geographical areas that dominate the world economy and exploit the rest of the system; **periphery regions** consist of those areas that provide raw materials to the core and are exploited by it. At first the peripheral areas exported spices, coffee, tea, and tobacco to Europe. Later they became suppliers of agricultural and mineral raw materials, while their advantaged classes provided markets for industrial goods from Europe (Bornschier and Hoby, 1981).

There is considerable controversy regarding the impact that multinational corporations have upon less developed or peripheral nations in the Third World. One view, associated with mainstream Marxism, asserts that international capitalism has transformed the economies of precapitalist countries, made them capitalist, and established the foundation for worker-led socialist revolutions. Sociologist Albert Szymanski (1981) contends that prior to the 1960s, Western colonialism posed obstacles to Third World industrialization. But he says that in recent decades imperialist obstacles have been removed, and capital has flowed to low-wage areas. The contrasting view argues that Third World nations have been capitalist for centuries, have de-developed in the face of the onslaught from advanced capitalist nations, and continue to be exploited (Baran and Sweezy, 1966; Wallerstein, 1974, 1980). Thus sociologist Volker Bornschier and his associates (1978, 1981) claim that foreign investment in a country creates dependencies that have a long-term negative effect on the nation's rate of economic growth. Moreover, they find that the penetration of multinational corporations weakens the power of labor and middle-class groups and strengthens the hand of traditional powerholders (Rubinson, 1976).

It is difficult to arrive at overall generalizations regarding the economic impact of multinational corporations on Third World nations because the impact often differs from one time to another and from country to country (Newman, 1979, 1983; Evans, 1981). Nations like South Korea, Taiwan, Hong Kong, and Singapore

"It doesn't look good. Some of our nationals are at war with some of our other nationals."

Drawing by S. Harris; © 1983 The New Yorker Magazine, Inc.

have used multinational firms as organizational vehicles to begin taking their populations out of poverty. But in many other cases, trade and investment by multinational firms have made jobs disappear. For example, the introduction of machinery has often led to a loss of agricultural jobs. Moreover, the economies of Third World nations frequently become tied to a single industry, increasing the dependency on foreign investors, distorting patterns of national economic development, and rendering these nations especially vulnerable to bust and boom cycles. We will return to these matters in Chapter 22 when we consider modernization and world system analysis.

Work

Few aspects of the social experience touch us more closely and intimately than work. It typically provides us with our income, influences our class position, and shapes key components of our identity. It is hardly surprising, then, that upon meeting someone for the first time, we usually try to ascertain how that person earns a living. Once again we see the powerful links that bind our individual experiences with larger social forces. The world of work is in large measure shaped by the social structures in which we are immersed. They determine whether or not work will be available, how work will be organized, and the manner in which work will be remunerated. Since work is so central to the social experience, sociologists have sought a better understanding of its social significance.

The Significance of Work

Why do people work? Undoubtedly you have periodically asked yourself the same question, perhaps focused on why *you* have to work. "Self-interest" in its broadest sense, including the interests of family and friends, is a basic motivation for work in all societies. But self-interest can involve more than providing for subsistence or accumulating wealth. For instance, among the Maori, a Polynesian people of the South Pacific, a desire for approval, a sense of duty, a wish to conform to custom and tradition, a feeling of emulation, and a pleasure in craftsmanship are additional reasons for working (Hsu, 1943). Even within the United States, we cannot understand work as simply a response to economic necessity. Studies show that the vast majority of Americans would continue to work even if they inherited enough money to live

Why Do People Work?
Work cannot be understood as simply a response to economic necessity. People work because they are members of a human group that institutionally structures economic activity. People work out of a sense of duty, to gain approval from others, to escape boredom, to derive a sense of accomplishment, and to realize the benefits of group fellowship. Here Chinese farmers harvest vegetables. *(Brian Brake/Photo Researchers)*

comfortably (Morse and Weiss, 1955; Kaplan and Tausky, 1972; Opinion Roundup, 1980). Indeed, only one in four million-dollar lottery winners quits working after hitting the jackpot. So for a great many Americans, work is more than merely a means to food, shelter, and physical warmth.

When people work, they gain a contributing place in society. The fact that they receive pay for their work indicates that what they do is needed by other people, and that they are a necessary part of the social fabric. Work is also a major social mechanism for placing people in the larger social structure and for providing them with identities. Much of who individuals are, to themselves and others, is interwoven with how they earn their livelihood. In the United States, it is a blunt and ruthlessly public fact that to do nothing is to be nothing and to do little is to be little. Work is commonly seen as the measure of an individual (Levinson, 1964).

Sociologist Melvin L. Kohn and his associates (1983) have shown some of the ways work affects our lives. Consider those who have a college education. They are more likely to acquire jobs that require independent judgment and lead to higher rankings in the stratification system. By virtue of the intellectual demands of their work, the college-educated evolve an intellectual prowess that carries over to their nonoccupational lives. They even seek out intellectually demanding activities in their leisure pursuits. Generally, people who engage in self-directed work come to value self-direction more highly, to be more open to new ideas, and to be less authoritarian in their relationships with others (Miller, Slomczynski, and Kohn, 1985). Moreover, they develop self-conceptions consistent with these values, and as parents they pass these characteristics on to their children. Our work, then, is an important socializing experience that influences who and what we are (Lorence and Mortimer, 1985; Schwalbe, 1985).

Satisfaction and Alienation in Work

Sociologists find that people in occupations that combine high economic, occupational, and educational prestige typically show the greatest satisfaction with their work and the strongest job attachment (Blauner, 1969; Kohn and Schooler, 1973, 1982). However, the prestige factor partly subsumes a number of other elements, including the amount of control and responsibility that goes with an occupation. The opportunity to exercise discretion, accept challenges, and make decisions has an important bearing on how people feel about their work (Gruenberg, 1980; Mottaz, 1985; Schwalbe, 1985). The most potent factors in job satisfaction are those that relate to workers' self-respect, their chance to perform well, their opportunities for achievement and growth, and the chance to contribute something personal and quite unique. Public opinion polls show that on the whole, the vast majority of Americans (at least 85 percent) are satisfied with the work they are doing (Opinion Roundup, 1980). Even so, only about 40 percent would keep their present jobs if they had the opportunity to choose some other job.

When people fail to find their work fulfilling and satisfying, they may experience alienation (Erikson, 1986). **Alienation** refers to a pervasive sense of powerlessness, meaninglessness, normlessness, social isolation, and self-estrangement (Seeman, 1959). One expression of alienation is *job burnout*—people no longer find their work fulfilling and satisfying and instead may experience boredom, apathy, fatigue, frustration, and despondency. In burnout, people complain that they feel drained and used up, and that they have nothing more to give to their work. They become cynical, callous, and insensitive toward the people they encounter in the work setting. Frequently, victims of burnout are highly efficient, competent, talented, and energetic individuals with high ideals and expectations. Nurses, teachers, and police officers seem to be particularly prone to burnout (Farber, 1983).

Marx and alienation   Two somewhat different perspectives on alienation are provided by Karl Marx and Emile Durkheim (Lukes, 1977). Marx saw alienation as rooted in capitalist social arrangements. For Marx, work is our most important activity as human beings. Through work, we create our world and ourselves. The products of our labor reflect our nature and form the basis for our self-evaluations. The things we produce become an extension of ourselves, a part of us, because we breathe life into them—shape a bowl, work a piece of leather, or stitch a garment. Further, through work we experience ourselves as beings who actively shape the world. In the course of working, then, we come to know ourselves; we see ourselves reflected in the world that we have constructed. But according to Marx (1844/1960:500), people in capitalist societies lose control of their labor and become commodities, objects used by others:

> Labor . . . is external to the worker, i.e., it does not belong to his essential being; . . . in his work, therefore, he does not affirm himself but denies himself. . . . His labor is . . . merely a *means* to satisfy needs external to it. . . . It belongs to another; it is the loss of self.

Marx portrayed workers under capitalism as alienated from productive activity, the products of their labor, their co-workers, and their own human potential. Rather than being a process that is inherently satisfying, work becomes an unfulfilling activity that simply produces a subsistence wage. By virtue of the private ownership of factories, mines, and land, the means by which workers produce objects and the objects they produce no longer belong to them but to capitalists. When the things that workers produce are taken away from them—stored in someone else's warehouse or sold on someone else's terms—their makers are reduced in stature and diminished in spirit. Moreover, human labor itself becomes a commodity like all other commodities. Workers sell their labor to capitalists, who use the workers in any manner they see fit. As a result, human beings are reduced to animal status, becoming little more than beasts of burden or inanimate machines. Work ceases to be a creative, fulfilling act when workers are dominated by the machinery with which they work. Under capitalism, then, work violates people and deadens the human spirit.

Durkheim and anomie   Marx saw alienation as the outcome of social forces that inhere in capitalist arrangements and separate human beings from meaningful, creative, and self-realizing work. In contrast, Durkheim depicted alienation as arising from the breakdown of the cohesive ties that bind individuals to society. For Durkheim, the central question was whether or not people are immersed in a structure of group experiences and memberships that provide a meaningful and valued context for their behavior.

As we noted in Chapter 1, Durkheim contended that traditional societies are held together by *mechanical solidarity*. People gain a sense of oneness from the fact that they experience much the same social world. The division of labor is relatively simple, and so all members of the society engage in relatively similar tasks and activities. They share beliefs and sentiments that serve as a social glue binding them as one within a collective whole. By contrast, modern societies are characterized by complex social arrangements and a sophisticated division of labor, with many different occupations. People experience quite different life circumstances and they have little in common. Durkheim thought that modern societies endure because they are held together by *organic solidarity*—their members are motivated to cooperate to realize goals that individually they cannot achieve. But as societies come increasingly to rely upon organic solidarity, common loyalties, allegiances, beliefs, and sentiments are weakened. Moreover, people no longer know what is expected of them, and they find it difficult to fashion their actions in terms of traditional guidelines—they experience *anomie* (see Chapter 8). In sum, whereas Marx emphasized freedom from social constraint as the source of human happiness, Durkheim stressed that human happiness depends on a society that provides people with rules. Rules, said Durkheim, integrate individuals into cohesive social groups and give direction and meaning to their activity.

Both Marx and Durkheim identify forces that can result in alienation. Since much of life is spent at work, people's work experiences profoundly affect how they come to think about themselves and their satisfactions. Yet people show considerable differences in reactions to work and group experiences. What one person finds a challenge, another may view as an unendurable pressure. Even assessments of monotony vary widely. In fact, almost any job will seem boring to some people (Stagner, 1975). And we need hardly be reminded that people differ enormously in what they view as adequate or inadequate contact with other people and in their requirements for formal rules and direction (Lowenthal, 1964).

THINKING THROUGH THE ISSUES

Management often asks, "Why aren't our workers more productive? We pay good wages and provide good working conditions. Yet people do not seem to put forth more than their normal effort." How does this statement accord with your work experiences? What were the rewards provided you by management? Did these rewards satisfy your needs when you were on the job *or* only when you left the job? Is pay the principal incentive that moved you to perform your responsibilities? Have you had a job where you did not involve yourself in the tasks because you found them unfulfilling? If you answer this question affirmatively, could the job have been made fulfilling? Would job rotation—shifting from one work station to another periodically during the day—have made you a more productive worker? Would job enlargement—providing you with a greater variety of tasks—have increased your motivation? Would job enrichment—providing you with more tasks that involved variety plus complexity and discretion—have increased your productivity? Would "pay based on performance" serve as a job motivator for you? Would you find opportunities for advancement a work incentive? Do your answers to these questions depend on the job—for instance, whether it was blue-collar or white-collar, part-time or full-time, temporary or relatively permanent work? Explain.

Changes in Work and the Workforce

Work is also influenced by the types of industry that predominate in a society. In preindustrial societies, the

Cottage Industry
Prior to the Industrial Revolution, the spinning of wool and the weaving of cloth took place in the home. Merchants in turn marketed the textiles in cities and foreign lands. In nonindustrial societies the workplace was not physically segregated from the home and working time was not temporally separated in the daily cycle from leisure time. *(North Wind Picture Archives)*

vast majority of the labor force is found in **primary production**, the extraction of undeveloped natural resources from nature through hunting, gathering, forestry, fishing, farming, herding, and mining. Hunting-and-gathering, horticultural, and agrarian societies are characterized by primary production (see Chapter 3). Industrialization brings a shift to **secondary production**, the processing or converting of raw materials in a fashion that enhances their final consumption value (for instance, iron ore is converted into steel that in turn is used in making bridges and automobiles). The productivity of industrial economies frees increasing numbers of people for tasks less immediately associated with meeting survival needs, especially for the production of services— **tertiary production**. These changes are accompanied by rapid advances in knowledge and technology, giving rise to what is sometimes called *postindustrial society* (see Chapters 3 and 22). Let us examine some of these changes more closely.

Social structure The work experience of Americans has undergone a significant change over the past 150 years. Although more than 70 percent of the labor force worked on the farm in 1820, by 1910 only 31 percent of Americans were engaged in agriculture. Today employment in the service industries—transportation and pub-

lic utilities, wholesale and retail trade, finance, insurance, real estate, and government—is approaching the same 70 percent that were involved in farming a century and a half ago (see Table 15.2). Indeed, since 1850, more American jobs have originated in service-producing industries than in goods production. The trend has become more pronounced in recent years. Of the 23.3 million people added to nonagricultural payrolls from 1970 to 1984, 94 percent were in the service sector. But even though the proportion of jobs captured by goods-producing industries has been declining, goods output accounts for nearly the same proportion of real gross national product (46.6 percent in 1950 and 42.6 percent in 1985). Since World War II, new technology has been responsible for roughly half of all productivity gains, far more than those due to capital, education, resource allocation, or economies of scale (Couch, 1986; Bloch, 1986). These changes have had wide-ranging social consequences.

Table 15.2 Percentage of the Labor Force in Various Sectors of the U.S. Economy, 1910–1980

Year	Agriculture	Blue Collar/ Manufacturing	White Collar/ Service Workers
1910	31%	38%	31%
1920	27	40	33
1930	21	40	39
1940	17	40	43
1950	12	41	47
1960	6	41	54
1970	3	37	60
1980	3	30	67
1995*	2	26	71

*Projected.

Source: Data from U.S. Bureau of the Census and U.S. Bureau of Labor Statistics.

Changes in the workforce have been accompanied by a shift from a nonindustrial to an industrial society. In nonindustrial societies, the family overshadows and dominates other institutional spheres. Work (earning a living) is not readily distinguishable from other social activities. The situation is quite different in industrial societies (Dubin, 1976). First, the workplace is physically segregated from the home. Second, "working time" is temporally separated in the daily cycle from "leisure time." Third, specialized organizational structures— complex authority hierarchies—take over the management of work activities (Stinchcombe, 1983). And finally, the economic institution becomes increasingly the focus of other institutions, with the family, government, religion, and education accommodating to its needs.

Segmentation of the labor market The economies of advanced capitalist nations like the United States have tended to segment into a **dual labor market.** The primary sector offers jobs that provide high pay, security, and ample promotion possibilities. The secondary sector consists of jobs that provide low pay, undesirable working conditions, high turnover, and little room for promotion. The segmented markets are characterized by different skill and job requirements. Recruitment to the two sectors varies, with blacks and women found more often in the secondary sector (Beck, Horan, and Tolbert, 1978, 1980; Kalleberg, Wallace, and Althauser, 1981). Within this latter sector, control is based on more open and arbitrary power. In contrast, control in the primary sector rests primarily on corporate career ladders and the proliferation of administrative job titles, all of which encourage workers to exercise self-discipline in the expectation that they will receive "promotions" (Baron, Davis-Blake, and Bielby, 1986).

Professions The growing productivity of contemporary economic systems, rapid advances in technology, and the creation of unprecedented wealth have contributed to the emergence of the professions. A **profession** is an occupation based on systematic and formal knowledge. By virtue of this property, the occupations are usually well-paid and prestigious, as in the case of law and medicine. Professions have a number of distinguishing properties. First, professionals must undergo a period of formal training that is based on a body of theoretical knowledge and applied toward the solution of problems. Second, their members exercise a good deal of control over their work. The people they serve are thought to lack the competence necessary to arrive at judgments concerning the problems with which the profession deals, such as handling an estate or treating a serious illness. Third, the members of a profession control entry and enjoy a legal monopoly in establishing procedures for recruiting and policing members. Commonly, a person must acquire the proper credentials—pass an examination, receive a license, and be accorded a title—to practice a profession. You do not become a university professor or a surgeon simply by asserting that you are one. And fourth, a code of ethics governs the behavior of the members of a profession, and members who breach that code may be expelled.

An occupation is unlikely to be granted professional status if its knowledge is either common sense or so thoroughly codified as to be easily split into routine procedures. If the technical base of an occupation consists of knowledge and a vocabulary most people can readily learn, it has difficulty laying claim to a monopoly on skill and exclusive jurisdiction. When tasks are so varied that the best way to do them cannot be routinized, workers are likely to enjoy considerable autonomy in what they do and how they do it. The "art" of medicine is a good example of this. Semi-professions such as teaching, nursing, librarianship, and social work have failed to achieve full professional stature because they do not rest on theoretical knowledge that goes substantially beyond what the public knows (or thinks it knows). Moreover, the body of theoretical knowledge to which they lay claim is often already monopolized by some other profession; for instance, medicine in the case of nursing and psychiatric social work. People have difficulty controlling their services if someone else can redefine what they do and when they do it (Simpson, 1985).

Part-time jobs One of the most significant trends over the past decade has been the growing reliance of employers on part-time workers. By 1986, some 19 million people, nearly a fifth of the nation's employed workers, were employed part-time. Many homemakers and parents with small children welcome the opportunities afforded by part-time work. But part-time workers who want full-time work find themselves frustrated and dissatisfied. Although part-time jobs have traditionally been most prevalent in office work and retail selling, they are rapidly spreading into janitorial services, health care, private security, legal services, and computer and data processing (Serrin, 1986).

Employers frequently turn to part-time workers to save on costs. Wages are generally lower than they are with full-time work. Part-time employees usually do not receive sick pay, vacations, and health, hospital, or life insurance—benefits employers find now represent an increasing part of their costs. Employers also gain flexibility in scheduling. For example, fast-food chains use part-time workers, primarily students and women who are homemakers, during peak business hours. Another benefit accruing to employers is that a temporary, transient labor force is difficult for unions to organize.

Labor unions In confronting employers, individual workers have little power. To balance the scales and give themselves leverage in the workplace, workers have formed labor unions. **Labor unions** are organizations formed by workers to bargain collectively with employers for higher wages, improved working conditions, job security, fringe benefits, and grievance procedures. Workers have often used unions to reduce the uncertainties they encounter in the labor market. For example, high unemployment may lead employers to replace their workers by new and cheaper employees. So workers have favored seniority and other guarantees as criteria for determining the order of temporary layoffs as well as promotions. These efforts have contributed to an increase in a firm's formal operating and administrative procedures—what sociologists call *bureaucracy* (see Chapter 5). For instance, in the American auto and steel industries, the relationships between management and labor are contractually governed by narrow job classifications arranged on hierarchical ladders and regulated by a system of formal procedures (Stark, 1986).

In the 1930s, during the formative years of the Congress of Industrial Organizations (CIO), the American labor movement was plagued by countless court battles and widespread and bloody strikes. In the intervening fifty years, the major labor federations (the AFL and CIO) have merged, labor organizations have enjoyed considerable popular support, and the labor movement has been at the cutting edge of many social reforms. But in recent years organized labor has undergone a dramatic and accelerating reversal of its fortunes (Bloom and Bloom, 1985).

Union membership as a percent of the workforce has fallen from 33 percent in 1960 to less than 18 percent in 1986. Public faith in trade union leaders has also fallen. In a 1985 Gallup survey about ethical standards, labor leaders placed next to the bottom of twenty-five occupations (only used-car salespersons ranked lower). In the same year, a Harris poll found that 73 percent of employed Americans believe that unions improve wages and working conditions, but a sizable majority, 58 percent, also thought that "most employees today don't need unions to get fair treatment from employers" (Lipset, 1986).

Behind the eroding power of the labor unions have been changes in the American workforce, the growing technological sophistication of the workplace, and the increasing competition American industries are facing from foreign producers. Young, educated, and female workers have historically been less likely to join unions than have other workers; yet these workers have been the most rapidly growing segments of the labor force for the past two decades. The "second industrial revolution"—the widespread introduction of computers and the automation of production—and the shift of work toward the service sector has altered the settings in which people do their work. And international competition has led to the contraction of such key industries as auto and steel, traditional strongholds of organized labor (Bloom and Bloom, 1985). As we noted in the opening to the chapter, these trends have resulted in unemployment for many workers.

Unemployment

People typically find unemployment a painful experience. It may result from the inability to find a first job,

Union Victories Were Not Achieved Easily
In the 1930s, employers used company unions, propaganda, and force ("service" units) against union organizers. Here strikers advance toward the South Chicago plant of the Republic Steel Corporation on May 30, 1937. When the workers refused to disperse on police orders, clouds of tear gas were released. Bricks were thrown and pistols were fired. When the smoke cleared, four strikers were dead and nearly a hundred were injured. (*UPI/Bettmann Newsphotos*)

layoffs, dismissal because of poor job performance, or even quitting a job voluntarily. Sociologists find that unemployment has adverse effects on physical and mental health (Kessler, House, and Turner, 1987). M. Harvey Brenner (1973, 1976) has calculated that a rise of one percentage point in the national rate of unemployment, when sustained over a number of years, is associated with 4.1 percent increase in suicide and a 4.3 percent increase in first-time male admissions to state mental institutions.

Many people pass through several stages in reacting to their unemployment (Kaufman, 1982). At first they undergo a sequence of shock, relief, and relaxation. In many cases they had anticipated that they were about to lose their jobs, so when the dismissal comes, they may feel a sense of relief that at last the suspense is over. On the whole they remain confident and hopeful that they will find a new job when they are ready. During this time, they maintain normal relationships with their family and friends. The first stage lasts for about a month or two. The second stage centers on a concerted effort to find a new job. If workers have been upset or angry about losing their jobs, the feeling tends to evaporate as they marshal their resources and concentrate on finding a new job. This stage may last for up to four months. But if another job is not found during this time, people move into the third stage, which lasts about six weeks. Their self-esteem begins to crumble, and they experience high levels of self-doubt and anxiety.

The fourth stage finds unemployed workers drifting into a state of resignation and withdrawal. They become exceedingly discouraged and convinced that they are not going to find work. They either stop looking for work or search for it only halfheartedly and intermittently. Some come through the stage and look back on it as a "cleansing" experience. They may make a conscious decision to change careers or to settle for some other line of work. And they may look for other sources of self-esteem, including family, friends, and hobbies.

However, people who undergo long-term unemployment often find that their family life deteriorates. Unemployment benefits end, and most Americans lose their health insurance when they lose their jobs. Financial pressures mount. People are unable to keep up their mortgage payments, or they fall behind in the rent. They see cars and furniture repossessed. It is little wonder that they feel they are losing control of their lives. Child abuse, violence, family quarreling, alcoholism, and other evidences of maladjustment mount. The divorce rate soars among the long-term unemployed. Many men feel emasculated when confronted by an involuntary change of roles in the family, and they lash out with destructive reactions.

As pointed out in Chapter 1, some categories of Americans are more vulnerable to unemployment than others. As reflected in Figure 15.2, groups that have historically borne the brunt of discrimination are disproportionately without jobs, especially blacks and Hispanics. A heritage associated with poverty, inadequate education, limited technical skills, and low job seniority has impaired their ability to find jobs (see Chapter 10). The difficulties of minority peoples have been compounded by the shift of the economy away from manufacturing, traditional employment entry points for immigrant groups, and toward the service sectors. The severe and persistent problems that have plagued the American economy in recent years allow little optimism that these disparities will be corrected in the foreseeable future (Baily, 1986). Nor should we conclude that simply because unemployment typically results in a good deal of "free time," most people experience it as "leisure time."

Leisure

Mark Twain observed that work consists of whatever we are obligated to do, while play consists of whatever we are not obliged to do. Work, then, is a means to an end, whereas play is an end in itself. Like play, **leisure** is an activity we choose for its own sake. As we noted above, leisure is not simply "free time"—the portion of the day left over after we fulfill our work, family, household, and other obligations. It is the quality rather than the form of the activity that makes it leisure—the element of choice

FIGURE 15.2 Unemployment Rates, 1986
Source: U.S. Bureau of Labor Statistics.

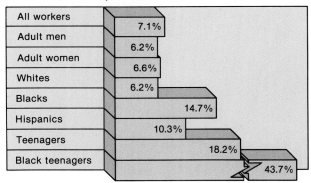

and the meaning the experience has for us. Virtually any activity can be leisure or not, depending on how we define it (Kelly, 1981).

Leisure in American Life

Colonial America and the new United States viewed leisure with suspicion. In keeping with the Puritan heritage, work was regarded as part of God's plan and necessary for salvation—fostering the notion that "Idle hands are the devil's workshop." Time came to be seen as a commodity to be rationally "used." But life was not devoid of free time and leisure. There were holidays, turkey shoots, and fairs, but these generally were the by-product of work. Over time, the popular view of leisure changed. As the factory system became established, demands arose for the shortening of the work day. However, it was not until 1840 that President Van Buren issued an executive order establishing a 10-hour day in government work. Through the years, the work day has been progressively shortened, and the work week, once six or seven days, has been steadily reduced. However, simultaneously, second jobs—"moonlighting"—have been increasing.

In earlier times, the working time of laborers and clerks typically exceeded that of their "superiors." But in contemporary America, a paradoxical situation has developed. Blue-collar workers generally work shorter hours than professionals, engineers, managers, and the self-employed. Although the affluent society may foster a preference for leisure, the nation's opportunity structure is increasingly dictating that a growing minority work very long hours while millions, especially the unemployed, are reluctant victims of too much free time.

When Americans do get away from work, their leisure activities often have the characteristics of work. The notion is widespread that playtime should be used "productively." About 7 out of 10 Americans say that hardly any of their free time is "wasted." And about 6 out of 10 say leisure time is best spent focused on certain goals (Brozan, 1982). This sentiment finds expression in the recent concern with fitness. The health-conscious chart their weekly progress in jogging or on muscle-building machines much as they monitor sales and profits at the office. The travel industry also packages bite-size, three-day getaways for those who cannot take a week off from work, yet want to cram as much as they can into a vacation trip. And racketball, golf, tennis, and aerobics are viewed as opportunities to make contacts and secure new clients. For its part, the leisure industry exploits the drive to perform by marketing everyday activities like walking as trendy sports requiring the right equipment. Such regimens hardly promote the sense of "pure enjoyment" that many sociologists deem to be the basis of genuine leisure (Solomon, 1986; Robinson, 1987).

Changes in the economy have had consequences for leisure activity and have affected spending patterns, national sports, and vacation patterns. More than half of all adult women now are employed full time outside the home. Most return home from work to assume domestic

Must Leisure Time Be Used Productively? If leisure is an activity people choose for its own sake, can the physical fitness preoccupation of many Americans be defined as "leisure"? (*Ethan Hoffman/Archive*)

chores and care of children. Conflicting schedules make it increasingly difficult for families to participate in leisure activities together. Simultaneously, spending for leisure products—from skateboards to compact disk players—is growing each year, and more than doubled between 1975 and 1985 to $181.1 billion. However, the size of leisure business is almost anybody's guess, partly because it is embedded in many industries that are considered utilitarian (see Table 15.3). For example, the big shift in the multibillion-dollar clothing industry has been toward "casual" clothes, reflecting the growth of leisure activities.

Sport

Sport, commonly viewed as leisure activity, also permeates many levels of contemporary society and is deeply embedded in the nation's business life, status systems, patterns of gender and race relations, automotive design, ethical values, and language. Indeed, in many respects sport is a microcosm of the larger society. Let us view **sport** as competitive physical activity based upon a set of rules. Sport, then, is an institutional structure—a form of organized social behavior—with norms, values, symbols, statuses, and roles.

Table 15.3 Leisure Spending
(In millions of dollars)

	1975	1980	1985
Food bought in restaurant/carry out	$45,318	$83,674	$121,412
Alcohol bought in restaurant/bar	10,458	16,551	20,662
Toys and sports supplies	8,954	14,633	20,621
Magazines and newspapers	6,356	10,438	13,375
Hotels and motels	3,351	7,469	11,084
Cable TV	783	2,489	8,610
Boats	2,117	3,784	5,999
Flowers, seeds, potted plants	2,659	4,047	5,542
Live theater and entertainment	787	1,786	2,977
Spectator sports	1,333	2,033	2,840
Parimutuel net receipts	1,662	2,095	2,605
Pleasure aircraft	308	530	838

Source: U.S. Department of Commerce, 1986.

A big business   Within the United States, sport is also a big business (see Figure 15.3). Spectator sports garner nearly $3 billion each year. Billions more are spent betting, legally or illegally, on sporting events. Top athletes are awarded multimillion-dollar contracts, more than the incomes of the nation's most successful scientists, physicians, and public officials. NBC paid $17 million to the National Football League for the right to telecast the 1986 Super Bowl game; in turn, it charged $550,000 for a 30-second commercial, producing $32 million for about 6 hours of programming. Baseball teams like the Los Angeles Dodgers and New York Yankees are reportedly worth between $91 and $100 million, and football teams like the New York Giants and Dallas Cowboys between $76 and $90 million (*Fortune*, August 4, 1986:167).

Instilling values   Sport is often touted as a builder of physical and emotional health. And it is seen as instilling teamwork, esprit de corps, and character. Viewed from a functionalist perspective, sport is one vehicle by which a society transmits important values and norms to its members. For instance, in the United States sport supports such values as competition, achievement, and teamwork. And it teaches obedience to authority in the pursuit of collective goals. These values find expression in such maxims as "There is no I in TEAM," "Who passed you the ball when you scored," "When the going gets tough, the tough get going," and "A quitter never

FIGURE 15.3 Who Goes to the Game?
Number of Americans who attended a sporting event in 1985. *Source: Adapted from Marc Yergin. 1986. Who goes to the game?* American Demographics, 8 (July):42–43.

Major-league baseball — 21 million
Pro football — 9.5 million
College football — 9.3 million
College basketball — 7.6 million
Pro basketball — 6.4 million
Ice hockey — 3.9 million
Boxing — 3.6 million
Wrestling — 3.6 million
Golf — 3.2 million
Tennis — 2.5 million

"The Assassin": Oakland Raider Safety Jack Tatum
During his playing days with the Oakland Raiders, Jack Tatum's bruising tackles made him one of football's most feared defensive players. His tackle of New England Patriots receiver Darryl Stingley in a 1978 game left Stingley paralyzed from the neck down. In his book, *They Call Me Assassin*, Tatum prides himself on his "mean and nasty" play. *(Mario Ruiz/Picture Group)*

scribe to the cliché." But whether or not sport builds character is a debatable matter. There are those who contend that sport selects from a pool of youth those individuals who are already predisposed to be competitive, industrious, and disciplined. Youths who lack these traits are likely to avoid sport, drop out, or be cut from a team. Moreover, critics of sport ask, "How do you define 'character'?" Does character include empathy, honesty, and integrity? If so, what becomes of Vince Lombardi's dictum, "Winning isn't everything; it's the only thing"? Are unrestrained aggression, violence, and cheating— even the use of health-endangering steroids—acceptable in the pursuit of victory? Is sport necessarily an ennobling experience? For example, heavyweight champion Larry Holmes reveals that a key to his success was to say to himself before entering the ring: "I have to change, I have to leave the goodness out and bring all the bad in, like Dr. Jekyll and Mr. Hyde" (Bredemeier and Shields, 1985:23). Additionally, sporting events are often occasions for drinking and rowdy behavior. In Chapter 17, we will examine some of the negative consequences that "big-time" sports programs have had for many colleges and universities.

A people–place bond   A sports team may also function as a powerful unifying source for a community—a people–place bond. For many emerging and rebuilding cities, professional sports franchises are seen as a potent symbol of urban progres Partly for this reason, Indianapolis risked $77.5 million on a new stadium *before* any team was signed to play in it, and Baltimore spent $500,000 on a losing legal battle to get its team (the Colts) back. Significantly, Boston, a city that produced Paul Revere, John Adams, and John F. Kennedy, has deified only one man by erecting a statue to him in his lifetime—Arnold Auerbach (whose leadership of the Celtics produced 16 championships in 30 years). The inscription on the bronze monument to Auerbach reads simply: "He has made winning synonymous with Boston." Says Edward L. Martin, a Boston investment portfolio manager: "The Celtics mean everything to Boston. They are part of the working class, the professional class, the whole city" (Butterfield, 1986). In sum, winning teams make people feel good about themselves and their city. They feel expanded, and gain a sense of triumph, mastery, and completeness.

wins; a winner never quits" (Snyder, 1972). Viewed in this manner, athletes are significant social figures because they are symbolic stand-ins for important societal values like courage, integrity, and poise (Birrell, 1981).

Does sport build character?   The notion that sport is good for both the athlete and society is a popular one in American life. Former President Gerald Ford, himself a football player while at the University of Michigan, summarized this belief when he observed: "Few things are more important to a country's growth and well-being than competitive athletics. If it is a cliché to say that athletics builds character as well as muscle, then I sub-

A focus for patriotic sentiment   A team may likewise become a symbolic stand-in for a nation—a rallying

point for patriotic fervor—in the course of international competition. In 1980, while American hostages were held in Iran and Americans suffered severe economic times, the Olympic hockey team sparked strong nationalistic sentiment with its gold medal performance in defeating the Russians at Lake Placid, New York. At times national loyalties reach such a feverish pitch during world soccer games that riots ensue and people lose their lives. In ancient times, victories in the Greek or Roman games redounded to the credit of the city and the ruler they represented. It is little wonder that boycotts and the exclusion of nations for political reasons have been an integral part of the Olympics since their revival in 1896. Russia, under the czars and the Soviets, refused to compete until 1952. Germany and Japan were barred from the 1948 games because they lost World War II. Spain, Switzerland, and the Netherlands boycotted the 1956 games to protest the invasion of Hungary by the Soviet Union. The United States boycotted the 1980 games in Moscow in response to the Soviet invasion of Afghanistan, and the Soviets boycotted the 1984 games in the United States.

Social opiate and cloak for profit?

Some conflict theorists debunk sport for being a social sedative—a "fix" or opiate—that distracts people from the more critical issues of life. And perhaps somewhat cynically, they point out that tangible financial benefit underlies much "civic pride." Indianapolis estimated that the Colts would add $21 million a year to business. Oakland figures the Raiders' defection to Los Angeles took $30 million annually from its economy. Referring to the Celtics and other Boston-area teams, Jonathan Hyde of the Massachusetts Division of Tourism says: "But winning is an important thing. There's a psychology in travel that relates to success. People like to go to places that appear successful. . . . To have an image out there of Massachusetts as a winning state is certainly very helpful to us" (Terry, 1986). Conflict theorists also contend that sport buttresses a stratification system that disadvantages women and minorities, a matter that deserves closer examination.

Sport and sexism

Sport is perhaps our society's most prominent masculinity rite. Men have participated in sport to affirm their manliness. The point eludes few men who grow up actively engaging in competitive athletics. Sport is a setting where men can test their masculinity against other men—where "the men are separated from the boys" and where a losing effort is applauded because "he stood there and took it like a man."

Through Little League baseball and Pop Warner football and interscholastic sports, boys are encouraged to develop the skills and assertive traits prized in business (Leonard, 1980).

By the same token, the division of labor in sports has been tied to traditional values and beliefs, with women historically relegated to secondary roles as spectators, sexual prizes, and cheerleaders (even today, spurred by the Dallas Cowboy cheerleaders, many NFL teams feature cheerleading squads made up of women wearing revealing halter tops and skimpy shorts). Women were thought to have no active place in sport. For example, Katherine Switzer ran in the Boston Marathon eight times—the first in 1967. That year she participated as an uninvited, unwelcome guest because women were barred from the event. When women ran their first Olympic marathon in 1984, Switzer noted:

Sport: American Society's Most Prominent Masculinity Rite?
One way American males are taught to affirm their manliness is through sport. Little League baseball and Pop Warner football teams are thought to encourage the development of those competitive skills and qualities of teamwork deemed essential by the business community. *(Therese Frare/The Picture Cube)*

When I was first running marathons, we were sailing on a flat earth. We were afraid we'd get big legs, grow mustaches, not get boyfriends, not be able to have babies. Women thought that something would happen to them, that they'd break down or turn into men, something shadowy, when they were only limited by their own and society's sense of limitations. [Gross, 1982:23]

And Sheila Young, an Olympic champion speed skater and world champion cyclist, says that when she was growing up she would tell people she was visiting friends rather than competing when she went out of town on weekends. She did not want to be labeled a woman who wore "ugly black skates and unattractive costumes" rather than the more traditionally feminine garb of the figure skater. In sum, whereas men who competed and won proved their masculinity, women who did the same thing still had to prove their femininity.

Much has changed in recent years. The increased participation of female athletes at the high school and college level has been aided by the passage of the Title IX clause in the Education Act of 1972 forbidding discrimination on the basis of sex in schools receiving federal funds. When the act was passed, 7 percent of the interscholastic athletes and 2 percent of the intercollegiate athletes in the United States were women, compared with 35 percent of the high school athletes and 30 percent of the college athletes ten years later. And whereas men have been taking seconds off their performance records, by virtue of the improvement in their coaching methods and training, women have been taking minutes off their records. Ideals of feminine beauty have also altered to favor a taut, fit body.

Yet even though times have changed, remnants of past traditions still live on. Despite the progress since the enactment of the Title IX legislation, the law has not always been zealously enforced and there have been conflicting court interpretations as to the law's intent. And spectator sport is still primarily male sport. Professional women's leagues in baseball, basketball, and football have not succeeded (tennis is an exception—Martina Navratilova earned an estimated $21.8 million between 1974 and 1987). Likewise, women who are sportscasters have had considerable difficulty breaking the network TV barrier as studio hosts, play-by-play announcers, and field reporters. These gender patterns mirror life in modern industrial societies.

Sport and racism On April 15, 1947, Jackie Robinson, the Brooklyn Dodgers' rookie first baseman, made his debut at Ebbets Field in a game against the Boston Braves. In so doing, he became the first black in modern times to break the color line that dominated professional baseball. Professional football had excluded blacks from 1933 until the Los Angeles Rams signed Kenny Washington for the 1946 season. And in 1950 Chuck Cooper and Nat (Sweetwater) Clinton became the first black players in the National Basketball Association when they were signed, respectively, by the Boston Celtics and New York Knicks. It took even longer for blacks to gain positions on southern college teams. At the University of Alabama in 1971, Wilbur Jackson, a running back, became the first black to play for Paul (Bear) Bryant. At the University of Arkansas, Frank Broyles did not have a black player on his football squad until 1972 when Jon Richardson became a wide receiver for the Razorbacks.

Sport has done much to bring blacks high visibility in a white-dominated society. Blacks have also had a substantial impact upon sport. According to Hank Aaron, baseball's all-time home run champion, it was the black athlete who helped "open up" baseball from its earlier "one base, one run, and wait-for-the-big-hit" type of game. In football, running back Jim Brown says that the development of "option blocking" and the "flare pass"—now basic football—were instituted to take advantage of his quickness and strength. And in basketball, Bill Russell, an intimidating shot-blocker, rebounder, and shooter, was the creator of the vaunted Boston Celtic fast break (Johnson, 1982).

Despite black gains in sport, black athletes have had difficulty coming to be accepted by the white public as human beings in their own right. Says sociologist Harry Edwards, "The dynamics involved in channeling the black athlete into sports meant simply that he was needed. But when it comes to discerning between being needed and being desired, one is walking a very fine line" (Johnson, 1982:26). Moreover, the percentage of American blacks in the major baseball leagues has fallen since the early 1970s. In part, this trend reflects the fact that teams are now signing more of their young prospects from the colleges rather than from high schools and the sandlots.

Vestiges of discrimination still remain in organized sport. Black athletes have had little success in transferring their gains to positions as coaches, managers, and "front office" personnel (in 1987, blacks held only 1.9 percent of major-league baseball's 879 top administrative positions). Blacks are also more likely to play peripheral positions in football that are away from the decision of play, including wide receiver, running back, and defen-

A Wrenching Transition: Retirement from Professional Sports

Professional baseball, basketball, football, and hockey players are symbols of adoration and envy among large segments of the American public. But after 20 or so years as elite athletes, they must crawl out of the protective cocoon of a team and drop from hero to zero overnight. They experience a kind of "social death." Many discover they are not equipped to deal with the realities of life as ordinary citizens. Willie Davis, a Football Hall of Fame player on Vince Lombardi's Green Bay Packer teams of the 1960s, has made a successful transition as a West Coast beer and wine distributor. Davis (pictured at right) says that most athletes fail to carry out of the locker room the discipline and hard work ethic that made their sports careers possible. *(Jim Caccavo/Picture Group)*

sive back. Few blacks play quarterback, center, or middle linebacker. Similarly, in basketball white players are more apt to fill the guard position, the leadership position on the court. And in baseball, blacks are more likely to be fielders than they are to be catchers or pitchers. In brief, institutional arrangements structure the opportunities available to blacks and contribute to the perpetuation of social inequalities.

THINKING THROUGH THE ISSUES

What social and cultural factors account for the disproportionate representation of blacks on American professional baseball, basketball, and football teams? What are the opportunity structures open to black youth? What role models do the media present for black youth? How do you account for the fact that at many colleges and universities, black students are vastly underrepresented in the student body and in programs leading to the most prestigious and remunerative professions and occupations, yet constitute a significant proportion of the football and basketball players (for instance, although blacks comprise about 10 percent of the population of Ohio, they represent 4.8 percent of undergraduates, 4.9 percent of graduate students, 3.8 percent of students in the professional colleges, and more than 50 percent of the varsity basketball and football players at Ohio State University–Columbus)? Why are black youths less likely than suburban white youths to excel at golf, tennis, skiing, and swimming? What training facilities, equipment, coaching, and travel opportunities are available to black youths? Does sport offer blacks a fast lane out of the ghetto? Consider professional football. There are fewer than 1,600 full-time players in the National Football League. Of this number, about 40 percent or so are black. If you were urged to aspire to a career in which there were some 650 jobs—and on average you would hold the job for only three or four years—would the idea appeal to you? What career opportunities are likely to be open to you once your career as a professional black athlete is over?

Chapter Highlights

1. The economic institution supplies answers to three basic problems all societies confront. What goods and services should they produce and in what quantities? How should they employ their limited resources to produce the desired goods and services? And for whom should they produce the goods and services?

2. Capitalist economies rely heavily on free markets and privately held property. Socialist economies rely primarily on state planning and publicly held property. To one degree or another, most nations are characterized by mixed economies.

3. Large corporations exercise enormous power in American life. The decisions made by their officials have implications and ramifications that reach throughout the nation. The separation of ownership from the control of corporations has not meant that managers enjoy a wide range of latitude in corporate decision making. Executive officers are still governed by the requirement that they optimize profits.

4. Domestic economies are increasingly being drawn into a global economy. Multinational corporations rival nations not only in wealth, but in power. The economic integration of less developed nations into the structures of a world economy can be traced to European exploration and colonization beginning in the fifteenth century. It contributed to the differentiation of core and periphery regions.

5. Self-interest is a basic motivation for working in all societies. But work also has a good many social meanings, including a sense of self-worth. When people fail to find their work fulfilling and satisfying, they may experience alienation. Karl Marx saw alienation as rooted in capitalist social arrangements that turned labor into a commodity. In contrast, Emile Durkheim saw alienation as associated with the shift from mechanical solidarity to organic solidarity, producing conditions of anomie (circumstances in which people find it difficult to guide their behavior by norms that they experience as weak, unclear, or conflicting).

6. The work experience of Americans has undergone a significant change over the past 150 years. Today employment in the service industries outpaces that in other sectors of the economy. These changes have been accompanied by structural changes in other institutional spheres.

7. Leisure consists of activity that people choose for its own sake. When Americans do get away from work, their leisure activities often have the characteristics of work. Changes in the economy have had consequences for leisure time and have affected spending patterns, national sports, and vacation patterns.

8. In many respects, sport is a microcosm of the larger society. Within the United States it is also a big business. Viewed from a functionalist perspective, sport is one vehicle by which a society transmits important values and norms to its members while simultaneously reinforcing them. Conflict theorists view sport as a bulwark of a stratification system that disadvantages women and minorities.

The Sociologist's Vocabulary

alienation A pervasive sense of powerlessness, meaninglessness, normlessness, social isolation, and self-estrangement.

capitalist economies Economic systems that rely heavily on free markets and privately held property.

conglomerates Companies whose components operate in completely different markets and produce largely unrelated products.

core regions Geographical areas that dominate the economy of the world and exploit the rest of the system.

corporate interlocks Networks of individuals who serve on the boards of directors of multiple corporations.

dual labor market An economy characterized by two sectors. The primary sector offers "good jobs" and the secondary sector offers "bad jobs."

economic system The social institution responsible for the production and distribution of goods and services.

labor unions Organizations formed by workers to bargain collectively with employers for higher wages, improved working conditions, job security, fringe benefits, and grievance procedures.

leisure An activity we choose for its own sake.

multinational corporations Firms that have their central office in one country and subsidiaries in other countries.

oligopoly A market dominated by a few firms.

periphery regions Geographical areas that provide raw materials to core regions and are exploited by it.

primary production The extraction of undeveloped natural resources from nature through hunting, gathering, forestry, fishing, farming, herding, and mining.

profession An occupation based on systematic and formal knowledge.

property A set of rights that indicates what one party can do and what another party cannot do.

secondary production The processing or converting of raw materials in a fashion that enhances their final consumption value.

socialist economies Economic systems that rely primarily on state planning and publicly held property.

sport Competitive physical activity based upon a set of rules.

tertiary production Service activities of one sort or another.

16

The Political System

The great question which, in all ages, has disturbed mankind, and brought on them the greatest part of those mischiefs which have ruined cities, depopulated countries, and disordered the peace of the world, has been, not whether there be power in the world, not whence it came, but who should have it.

—John Locke, *Treatises on Government,* 1690

When Ronald Reagan assumed the presidency in 1981, he selected a 34-year-old member of Congress, David Stockman, to be director of the Office of Management and Budget. The position was a critical one if the Reagan Revolution were to succeed. The administration's agenda called for an economic revolution that would drastically reduce the role of the government as taxer, spender, borrower, and regulator. But it was an agenda that also emphasized a drastic increase in military spending. After five years as one of the chief architects of American domestic policy, Stockman resigned. In his memoirs, *The Triumph of Politics: Why the Reagan Revolution Failed* (1986), Stockman traces his disenchantment with the White House staff, political gamesmanship, turf battles, and even the chaos that characterized Reagan's first term. Disillusioned, Stockman accepted more than 2 million dollars from Harper & Row to write the book and took a job as a managing director of the Salomon Brothers investment banking firm.

Stockman had joined the Reagan team with ideological fervor and unflagging enthusiasm. But even before the 1980 election, he sensed that the Reagan game plan would not work. The proposed tax cuts and defense increases were inconsistent with Reagan's promises to achieve a balanced budget by 1983. As a result, the nation's debt nearly doubled in Reagan's first four years in office. Stockman says Congress showed little interest in cutting expenditures while giving lip service to the need for reining in the mounting deficit. Cabinet secretaries were as determined as their predecessors to expand their own budgets. And the public wanted its taxes cut, yet insisted upon keeping its benefits and subsidies.

Stockman concludes that the Reagan Revolution failed because "it defied all of the overwhelming forces, interests, and impulses of American democracy." He says he learned the welfare state is here to stay, the United States is a heartbreaker for revolutionaries, and politics is ruled by power, not ideas: "The abortive Reagan Revolution proved that the American electorate wants a moderate social democracy to shield it from capitalism's rougher edges" (394). Indeed, public opinion polls reveal that 85 percent of Americans believe there must be substantial government involvement to handle the problem of poverty, and a similar proportion agree that the federal government should help finance long-term care of the elderly (Opinion Roundup, *Public Opinion*, 1987).

Stockman gives us a glimpse of what went on backstage during Reagan's first term. We learn of the roles played by such key figures as Donald Regan, Edwin Meese 3d, James A. Baker, Michael K. Deaver, and Caspar W. Weinberger in shaping policy, and we witness power at work. Yet we are also reminded that there is much more to government than merely personalities who come and go from one administration to the next. Over a quarter century ago, James Reston (1963) of the *New York Times* made a similar point at the time of the assassination of President John F. Kennedy, when the nation was collectively shocked, grieved, and even dazed. Reston wrote:

> This is not a bad time to remember that the Government of the United States has a life of its own. It is a permenant institution. It cannot be assassinated by anything less than the destruction of the nation.

Eleven years later, at the time of President Richard M. Nixon's resignation in the face of his impending impeachment, Reston's colleague, Clifton Daniel (1974), also observed:

> Watergate has now joined Teapot Dome, Credit Mobilier and the Whisky Ring in the lexicon of political infamy. Yet, in millions of minds it also symbolized the finest hour of American democracy. A President has been deposed, but the Republic endures. Its institutions have survived, and some are saying they have been strengthened as well.

And in the mid-1980s, the United States government survived the Iran-Contra scandal. These observations lead us to a closer look at a remarkable and resilient institution—*the political system*.

PLANNING AHEAD: TARGETED READING

1. Why does power play such a critical role in social life?

2. What factors are responsible for the emergence of the state?

3. How does democratic government differ from its totalitarian counterpart?

4. What insights do we gain from the functionalist and conflict perspectives into the social forces that underlie the state arrangement?

5. What structures provide the foundations for the American political system?

6. What is the nature and basis for power in the United States?

7. What social forces make for war and peace?

Power, Authority, and the State

The **political institution** is the social structure concerned with the use and distribution of power within a society. Because group life makes us mutually dependent on one another, we can achieve many of our goals only by influencing other people's behavior. Power gives direction to human affairs; it channels people's actions along one course rather than another so that collective goals can be achieved. Of course, some expressions of power are more critical than others. The power that makes a real difference in the way society operates is institutionalized power. Such power is embedded in social arrangements and is the bedrock of social organization (Bierstedt, 1950).

As we noted in Chapter 9, *power* refers to the ability of individuals and groups to realize their will in human affairs even if it involves the resistance of others. Power brings about change in people—in attitude, behavior, motivation, or direction—that would not have occurred in its absence. It entails the ability not only to get things done, but to get them done in the way that one party prefers. Those individuals and groups who control critical social resources—rewards, punishments, and persuasive communications—are able to influence, even dictate, the way social life is ordered. In sum, power affects the ability of people to make the world work on their behalf. To command key organizations and institutions, particularly the state, is to command people.

Social Foundations of the State

The **state** is a social organization that exercises within a given territory an effective monopoly in the use of physical coercion. In the final analysis the state rests on **force,** power whose basis is the threat or application of punishment. The ability to inflict suffering and take life gives a crucial advantage in human affairs. In effect, force constitutes a final court of appeals; there is usually no appeal from force except the exercise of superior force. For this reason, sovereign nations restrict, and even prohibit, the independent exercise of force by their subjects. If it were otherwise, governments could not suppress forceful challenges to their authority (Lenski, 1966). But even though force is ultimately the basis of the state, it is only in unusual situations that societal power actually takes this form.

David Stockman: Former Reagan Warrior on Wall Street
In the early days of the Reagan administration, David Stockman held the critical post of director of the Office of Management and Budget (below). Disillusioned when the promised Reagan economic revolution sputtered, Stockman went to work for Salomon Brothers, a Wall Street financial firm (right). Sociologists like C. Wright Mills have noted the frequency with which elite personnel flow back and forth between top positions in government and business. *(below, Halstead/Gamma-Liaison; right, Nancy Moran/Outline Press)*

One of the peculiarities of state power is that it may be exercised without corresponding to the letter of the law. Having delegated the right to act for the society as a whole, the citizenry finds it difficult to maintain control over its rulers who, by virtue of their power, can bear down upon them (see the discussion of Michels's iron law of oligarchy in Chapter 5). Moreover, any group that can secure sufficient power may overthrow the legally constituted government and establish itself as the ruling group. This has been the recurrent pattern in many Latin American nations, where periodic coups and "palace revolutions" displace one ruling elite with another.

Evolution of the state   As we pointed out in our discussion of the types of society in Chapter 3, the state is a relatively recent institution. It arose with changes in subsistence patterns and the production of a social surplus. But states have emerged not just as a response to internal factors. They have arisen as a *system* of states called *nation-states*. States are part of a larger social arrangement—a sort of culture—that legitimates sovereignty, state purposes, and territorial jurisdication. A set of rules defines permissible spheres of military action, the alloca-

tion of sea and air space, allowable weaponry, diplomatic etiquette, the provision of embassies, and treaty obligations. Widespread military competition also puts a premium on large-scale and strongly organized governments (Thomas and Meyer, 1984; Giddens, 1985). In medieval times Europe was characterized by a decentralized system of relatively minute, independent domains ruled by feudal lords. But military dictates prompted a process of territorial and governmental centralization in which these domains were progressively incorporated into larger and considerably more effective political entities.

As smaller domains were integrated into an encompassing nation-state, their many languages were incorporated into, or replaced by, one national language. This language then became the carrier of an emerging national culture, and both together became the hallmarks of the nation. In turn, the nation became the focus of intense identification and loyalty. By the sixteenth century, several European nation-states had came into existence. England, Spain, and France were among the earliest. Others were added throughout the following centuries with the unification of smaller ones (including

Using the State for Private Advantage: The Marcos Regime
During the 20 years of his rule in the Philippines, Ferdinand Marcos, his wife, Imelda, family members, and friends amassed a fortune estimated to be worth between 5 and 10 billion dollars through fraud, corporate kickbacks, and alleged embezzlement of U.S. aid. Jovito Salonga, the lawyer who headed the Philippine commission charged with recovering Marcos's wealth, said, "There was no distinction between private funds and public wealth." An American official observed: "The robber barons took over the government and declared martial law." *(both photos, Andy Hernandez/Sygma)*

Germany and Italy during the nineteenth century) and the dismantling of the Austro-Hungarian Empire following World War I (Etzioni-Halevy, 1981). After World War II, the Western nation-state model was exported to Africa and Asia with the breakup of the former British, French, Spanish, and Portuguese colonial empires.

Expansion of the state's jurisdiction

Within the Western world, the jurisdiction of the state has expanded across time. More and more aspects of social life have been incorporated within its "general welfare" function. Courts and taxing structures were early components. A whole arena of public finance evolved to control credit, currency, and national debt. And education, medicine, the family, religion, working conditions, and technology have been increasingly drawn within its sphere (Skocpol and Amenta, 1986). All the while, the size of government has grown dramatically. In 1986, as shown in Figure 16.1, nearly 17 million Americans were employed in federal, state, and local government, and 8 million more owed their jobs to the direct federal procurement of

goods and services (Newitt, 1986). Altogether the $1.7 trillion spent by American government in 1986 represented 35 percent of the gross national product (up from 21 percent in 1950)—$7,017 for each man, woman, and child in the nation.

Rationalization of state structures

As the state has grown and assumed more activities, its role has become increasingly *rationalized* through the introduction of explicit rules and procedures based on a division of function and authority that Max Weber called a *bureaucracy* (see Chapter 5). Bureaucratic administration standardizes and routinizes operations in ways that permit the performance of tasks on a regular and orderly basis and the planning and coordination of activities in an efficient manner. Clearly, bureaucratic structure has become a powerful tool of the modern nation-state. In fact, some observers believe modern bureaucracy has turned from an instrument of power to a master of power in its own right. American presidents, secretaries of state, and other officials have repeatedly decried their inability to translate political programs into day-to-day policies because of entrenched bureaucracies that operate in terms of their own agendas (see Table 16.1 on page 438).

Types of Authority

Although force may be an effective means for seizing power and serves as the foundation of the state, it is not the most effective means for political rule (Lenski, 1966). As the officials of the Soviet-imposed regime in modern-day Poland are discovering, force is both inefficient and costly. Moreover, honor, normally a prized possession, is denied to those who rule by force alone. Finally, if leaders are inspired by revolutionary visions for building a new social order, those ideals remain unfulfilled unless the masses come to embrace the new order as their own. The English leader and orator Edmund Burke (1729–1797) captured the essence of these matters when he noted that the use of force alone is temporary: "It may subdue for a moment; but it does not remove the necessity of subduing again; and a nation is not governed, which is perpetually to be conquered."

All this highlights the importance of the distinction sociologists make between power that people view as legitimate and power they define as illegitimate. Legitimate power is **authority**. In contrast, **coercion** is illegitimate power. When individuals possess authority, they have a recognized and established *right* to determine policies, pronounce judgments, and settle controversies—

FIGURE 16.1 **Expansion of Government**
State and local governments are growing at a rate faster than that of the federal government. Myth has it that the federal government is a swollen, ever-growing bureaucracy, gorging itself at the public trough, while state and local governments practice ascetic restraint, contentedly munching on the same old lean fare. *Source: U.S. Bureau of Labor Statistics.*

Table 16.1   Reshaping Bureaucracy: An Old Problem

Andrew Jackson (1837)
I am accused of usurping power, when my whole life has been one continual battle against the tendency of bureaucracy or aristocracy—the concentration of power in the hands of the few.

Woodrow Wilson (1914)
Very few governments are organized, I venture to say, as wise and experienced businessmen would organize them if they had a clean sheet of paper to write on.

Herbert Hoover (1928)
Bureaucracy is ever desirous of spreading its influence and its power.

Harry Truman (1955)
There was too much duplication of functions, too much "passing the buck," and too much confusion and waste . . . Reorganization should be an unending process.

Lyndon Johnson (1965)
I am busy currently reviewing the structure of the executive branch of this Government. I hope to reshape it and reorganize it to meet more effectively the tasks of the twentieth century.

Richard Nixon (1971)
It is important that we move boldly to consolidate the major activities of the Government.

Jimmy Carter (1976)
We must give top priority to a drastic and thorough revision and reorganization of the federal bureaucracy.

Ronald Reagan (1986)
We must get Government off the back of the American people.

---

to act as leaders. Max Weber (1921/1968) suggested that *legitimacy*, the social justification of power, finds expression in three types of authority: legal-rational, traditional, and charismatic.

Traditional authority   In **traditional authority**, power is legitimated by the sanctity of age-old customs. People obey their rulers because "this is the way things have always been done." Additionally, they may view a ruler's power as eternal, inviolable, and sacred. Many Roman Catholics invest the pope with infallibility deriving from divine guidance when he acts in matters pertaining to the Church. Similarly, medieval kings and queens ruled in the name of "a divine right" ordained by God. It was this type of authority that Emperor Hirohito of Japan enjoyed until the American occupation imposed a legal-rational system on the country following World War II. A good deal of moral force stands behind traditional authority. Often the claim to such authority rests on birthright, royal blood being thought superior to the blood of commoners.

Legal-rational authority   In **legal-rational authority**, power is legitimated by explicit rules and rational procedures that define the rights and duties of the occupants of given positions. It is this type of authority that Weber depicted in his ideal-type bureaucracy, discussed in Chapter 5. Under this arrangement, officials claim obedience on grounds that their commands fall within the impersonal, formally defined scope of their office. Obedience is owed not to the person, but to a set of impersonal, rationally devised principles. For instance, in the United States the authority of government leaders is for the most part accepted because Americans accept the premise that the law is supreme and that policies and orders are formulated in accordance with rules to which they subscribe. They accept the authority of a newly elected president even when the election campaign was waged in bitterness and anger. The system would crumble were large numbers to reject these as "the rules of the game." In fact, this occurred in 1861, when southern states rejected the election of Abraham Lincoln and federal authority. And it was the perception among Americans that President Nixon had failed to abide by the rules in the Watergate case that led to his downfall. A similar perception surrounding the Iran-Contra scandal led to a sharp drop in President Reagan's popularity during his second term. Ideally, then, legal-rational authority is "a government of laws, not of people."

Charismatic authority   In **charismatic authority**, power is legitimated by the extraordinary superhuman or supernatural attributes that people impute to a leader. Founders of world religions, prophets, military victors, and political heroes commonly derive their authority from charisma (meaning literally "gift of grace"). Miracles, revelations, exceptional feats, and baffling successes are their trademarks. They are the Christs, Napoleons, Caesars, Castros, Joan of Arcs, Gandhis, and Ayatollah Khomeinis that dot the pages of history. At times such leaders have a sense of being "called" to spread the word. They communicate a sense that the past is decadent and that a new day awaits people who follow them, as symbolized in Christ's injunction, "It is written . . . but I say unto you . . . "

Charismatic Authority: Martin Luther King, Jr.
During the 1960s, the Reverend Martin Luther King, Jr., enjoyed a preeminent position among black leaders. Here he is shown speaking at the time of the 1963 "March on Washington" when 200,000 civil rights marchers demonstrated "for jobs and freedom."
(The Bettmann Archive)

Weber viewed each of these three bases of authority as ideal types. As we noted in Chapter 1, ideal types are concepts sociologists construct to portray the principal characteristics of something. In practice, any specific form of authority may involve various combinations of all three. For example, Franklin Delano Roosevelt gained the presidency through legal-rational principles. By the time he was elected president for the fourth time, his leadership had a good many traditional elements to it. And many Americans viewed him as a charismatic leader.

Authority in new nations   A basic problem faced by all new nations and postrevolutionary societies is a crisis of

The "Cult" of George Washington
In monarchies the king symbolizes the nation; in republics a great hero may play a comparable role. George Washington was the national hero of the new American nation. The European traveler Paul Svinin observed in 1815: "Every American considers it his sacred duty to have a likeness of Washington in his home, just as we have the image of God's saints." *(North Wind Picture Archives)*

legitimacy. An old order is abolished and with it the set of beliefs that justified its system of authority. Since traditional authority is absent, legitimacy can be developed only through reliance on legal-rational or charismatic authority. But legal-rational authority is usually weak, since the law is identified with the previous regime. Charismatic authority, in contrast, is suited to the needs of newly developing nations. A charismatic leader serves as a symbol of the nation—a hero who embodies national values and aspirations. Not surprisingly, the early American Republic, like many contemporary new nations in Africa and Asia, was initially legitimized by charisma. It is easy to forget that, in his time, George Washington was idolized as much as many of the contemporary leaders of new nation-states. In the words of the Virginian Henry Lee, Washington was "first in war, first in peace and first in the hearts of his countrymen" (Lipset, 1963).

Comparative Political Systems

Clearly, power can be exercised in a good many ways, both legitimately and illegitimately. There are also multiple sources of power. Historically, Marxist theorists have highlighted the power that is realized by those who control a society's means of production (see Chapters 9 and 15). The possession of the means of administration is, as Max Weber contended, an alternative basis of social power. Consider the case of the Soviet Union and Eastern European nations, in which there is no ownership of the means of production and the state controls the economy. Additionally, Western nations contain a rather large array of fairly distinct arenas of power, including those found in religion, science, the arts, medicine, education, and the media. Sociologist Suzanne Keller (1963) suggests that each of these spheres often has its own set of powerful individuals and groups—what she terms *strategic elites*. These elites—people with significant power—operate primarily in their own rather specialized domains.

Although there may be many arenas of power within modern societies, the study of power—especially power that make a real difference—invariably brings us to a consideration of government. Let us view **government** as those individuals and groups who control the state apparatus and direct state power. These individuals and groups formulate the rules and policies that are authoritative, binding, and pervasive throughout a society. The decisions they make profoundly affect the everyday lives of a nation's citizenry, and very often the citizenry

of other nations as well. Policies relating to the economy, military expenditures, issues of war and peace, drug trafficking, education, health care, social welfare, and environmental issues leave no individual untouched by their consequences and ramifications. In dealing with these matters, two quite different types of government have competed in recent generations for people's allegiance: democracy and totalitarianism. Each can be considered an ideal type, for in practice many nations have regimes with mixtures of democratic and totalitarian elements. Indeed, more often than not, the most significant difference between various regimes is not *type* of government, but *degree* of government.

Democracy **Democracy** is a political system in which the powers of government derive from the consent of the governed, and in which regular constitutional avenues exist for changing officials. The populace has a voice in decision making by virtue of its right to choose among contenders for political office. Quite clearly, democratic governments do not differ from totalitarian regimes by the absence of powerful officials (indeed, it is questionable whether on the critical issues that affect the survival of humankind, the president of the United States has less power than his or her Soviet counterpart). And for the most part democracy is not characterized by the rule of the people themselves. Only in relatively rare instances, such as the New England town meeting of colonial times, do we find *direct democracy*, face-to-face participation and decision making among the citizenry. Rather, most democratic nations are characterized by *representative democracy*—officials are held accountable to the public through periodic elections that either confirm them in power or replace them with new officials.

Sociologists have undertaken a search for those social conditions that favor a stable democracy (Kornhauser, 1959; Gusfield, 1962; Nisbet, 1962; Lipset, 1963). One factor is *political pluralism*, a social arrangement characterized by a competitive struggle for positions of power, challenges to incumbents, and shifts in the parties holding office. Many well-organized but countervailing interest groups serve as a check against one another. Each group is limited in influence because, in the process of governing, officials must also take into account the interests of other groups as well. Simultaneously, interest groups provide independent power bases from which citizens can interact with the government. Many mediating structures and intermediary levels of human association—voluntary organizations, churches, and labor unions—bridge the abyss separating individual and state. Consequently, citizens have the protection of many groups and institutions against the encroachment of any one of them. No group or institution can attain a monopoly of power. This arrangement contrasts sharply with totalitarian societies, where isolated and vulnerable individuals confront an omnipotent state.

Multiple loyalties likewise prevent the rigid polarization of society into hostile camps (Blau and Schwartz, 1984). Each person is a member of multiple groups, with membership in one group cutting across membership in others. For instance, American Catholics are found in both the working and upper classes, and the same holds for Protestants. Consequently, in terms of religious affiliation, Catholics and Protestants are counterposed to one another. At the same time, working-class Catholics and Protestants are united on many economic issues by their class membership and set apart from upper-class Catholics and Protestants. In sum, people's loyalties cleave along plural axes, a crisscrossing of ties that does not allow for clear-cut political divisions. In contrast, deep-seated religious divisions in Northern Ireland and Lebanon and racial divisions in South Africa divide people into militant camps that make compromise difficult.

Relatively stable economic and social conditions also seem to favor a democratic order. Significant institutional failure confronts people with stressful circumstances that can make them vulnerable to extremist social movements (see Chapter 21). For example, Germany underwent a ruinous inflation and economic dislocation in the 1920s that made the middle classes susceptible to Nazism. In this economic and social environment, the middle classes felt their status eroding and their financial fortunes collapsing before the onslaught of large-scale capitalist enterprise and a powerful labor movement. They turned to Nazism as a road to salvation. The result was the death knell of Germany's fragile democratic institutions. In somewhat like fashion, the chaos and social breakdown accompanying their defeat in war made the Russian people susceptible to revolutionary slogans in 1917.

Finally, a stable democracy benefits from an underlying consensus among the populace that a democratic government is desirable and valid. Democracy is more than a set of organizational structures; it is a spirit, a kind of secular religion, that holds the rights of the individual sacred. In turn, people give legitimacy to the political institution. They believe they can realize their goals within the existing organizational framework because they enjoy "fair play" access to the seats of power. Voting is a key mechanism for achieving this consensus. Consider that although Americans wage their election campaigns with great fury and fervor, once the election returns are in, the candidates and the parties accede to the results. The losers recognize the legitimacy of the process and do not resort to extralegal and violent remedies. Rather, they criticize the incumbent officials and prepare to "throw the rascals out" at the *next* election.

Totalitarianism   It is exceedingly difficult for most of us to maintain value neutrality in considering totalitarianism, since this type of government runs counter to many of our fundamental values. **Totalitarianism** is a "total state," one in which the government undertakes to extend control over all parts of the society and all aspects of social life (Olsen, 1978). Those individuals and groups who dominate the state apparatus—elites—seek to control all subordinate units, all institutions (including the economy, education, religion, medicine, the arts, science, and communciation), all associations (labor unions, churches, occupational and professional organizations, special interest associations, and youth groups), and even individual families and cliques. All forms of social organization become an extension of the state and are expected to act as its agent. The hallmark of totalitarianism is its power structure, not its economic order. The two major prototypes of twentieth-century totalitarianism—Nazi Germany under Hitler and Communist Russia under Stalin—remind us that this form of government can incorporate either a capitalistic or a socialistic economy.

A totalitarian society typically has three characteristics: a monolithic political party, a compelling ideology, and pervasive social control. First, totalitarianism permits one political party that brooks no opposition. Only a small proportion of the population are party members, although party membership is a requisite for all important positions. Intermediate structures standing between the individual and the state are eradicated. Second, totalitarian ideology is utopian in nature, encompasses all areas and aspects of life, and establishes universal goals. It sets grandiose schemes for social reconstruction and societal betterment that provide the moral basis for the extension of state power to all parts of social life. Third, to maximize its power and propagate its ideology, a totalitarian regime centralizes control. It regiments education and the media while simultaneously using police terror to compel compliance.

The Soviet leader Nikita Khrushchev vividly depicted his nation's experience with terror in his 1956

Khrushchev: Stalin Had More Communists Killed Than Did "Capitalist Enemies"!
In his famous "secret" speech to the 20th Party Congress in 1956, Soviet leader Nikita Khrushchev detailed the crimes of the Stalin era. Among Stalin's "errors" were the purging of the top officers of the Red army in the 1930s, severely crippling the Russians' ability to defend their nation against the German invasion of June 22, 1941. Khrushchev also amended the Leninist doctrine of the inevitability of war; in the nuclear age, he said, the conflict between capitalism and communism would be decided by peaceful competition between social systems. *(Sovfoto)*

"secret" speech to the 20th Communist Party Congress. Stalin, Khrushchev said, "practiced brutal violence, not only toward everything that opposed him, but also toward that which seemed, to his capricious and despotic character, contrary to his concepts . . . Mass arrests and deportations of many thousands of people, executed without trial and without normal investigation created conditions of insecurity, fear and even desperation." Since Stalin's death in 1953, repression has become more selective and the range of permissible discussion and debate within the Soviet Union has broadened. And since assuming power on March 11, 1985, Mikhail Gorbachev has made it clear that he plans a degree of structural change unprecedented in Soviet history. His decisions and proposals seem crafted to galvanize his nation's lethargic economy, ease the grip of the state, and improve his country's international image (Quinn-Judge, 1987; Manning, 1987). A question remains, however, whether Gorbachev and *glasnost* (meaning "opening") will last, or whether—like Khrushchev—he will be removed by the same bureaucracies that brought him to power. Some scholars see the loosening of repression in the Soviet system as a means for furthering its stability, while others see the changes as signs that the regime is losing its vigor (Cohen, 1985; Heller and Nekrich, 1986; Bialer, 1986).

Since disagreement and competition are permitted in the Soviet Union, it may be more appropriate to characterize its political structure as authoritarian rather than totalitarian. **Authoritarianism** is a political system in which the government tolerates little or no opposition to its rule, but permits nongovernmental centers of influence and allows debate on some issues of public policy. Many African and Latin American countries ruled by military regimes are also authoritarian. Since issues of liberty and equality invariably arise in discussions of these topics, let us turn to a consideration of them.

Liberty and Equality

In his first term, President Reagan labeled the Soviet Union "an evil Empire," in part because of its violation of human rights. For its part, the Soviet Union has long criticized the considerable income inequalities and the treatment of minority groups in the United States. And while Americans think their nation is a uniquely democratic society and its Soviet-style counterparts undemocratic, many of the latter nations call themselves "People's Democracies." Indeed, whether they be identified with the Western or Eastern blocs, most contemporary nations lay claim to being "free" societies.

Part of the problem arises from what people mean by "freedom." When Americans talk about freedom, they talk about freedom "of"—freedom of speech, freedom of the press, freedom of religion, freedom of assembly, and freedom of property. In Soviet-style societies, the emphasis falls on freedom "from"—freedom from want, freedom from unemployment, freedom from huge medical bills, and freedom from exploitation by the propertied. Americans have defined freedom as meaning "liberty," whereas the citizenry of Communist nations have viewed it as meaning "equality."

In important respects, liberty and equality are at odds with one another. Americans have chosen to stress the equality of rights. Our version of democracy is individual, willingly accepting the inequalities that result from competition, so long as the competition is fair. In competition, there are invariably winners and losers. If there are to be the wealthy and advantaged, there must also be the poor and disadvantaged. So if a society accords each member the right to pursue his or her individual fortune, the society virtually ensures that inequality will be the outcome. The Soviet Union and Eastern European nations have instead emphasized equality, but they too have had to pay a price. The price has been the infringement of individual liberty. Some nations have sought a middle road, one of "democratic socialism"—an approach taken by Sweden and to one degree or another by many Western European nations. Regardless of the course nations take, visions of liberty and equality provide powerful counterforces in the shaping of national life. They have also influenced the sociological perspectives that have evolved for analyzing and understanding the state, particularly as they have found expression in functionalist and conflict formulations.

Perspectives on the State

Functionalists find the state to be a necessary social institution that evolved as societies moved from more traditional to modern ways of life. This notion predates modern sociological theory. It found particularly cogent expression in the thinking of the conservative English philosopher Thomas Hobbes (1588–1679). Hobbes contended that by nature, human beings are a perverse and destructive lot. He conjectured that rampant brutality, violence, and chaos haunted humankind before the establishment of law and government. In order to improve their lot, Hobbes thought that early humans voluntarily entered into a social contract, an agreement that provided for a central authority and a collective defense. But not all philosophers have agreed. Jean Rousseau (1712–

1778) took a contrary view, arguing that in their original "state of nature," human beings were "noble savages"—spontaneous, outgoing, loving, kind, and peaceful. They lived in harmony with their environment. However, the advent of private property ended this idyllic state, brought corruption and oppression, and substituted obedience to a privileged class for obedience to the "common will." Rousseau's thinking foreshadowed the contemporary conflict perspective on the state.

The Functionalist Perspective

Functionalists contend that there is a good reason why the state arose, and why today it has assumed a dominant position in contemporary life. They say that society must maintain order and provide for the common good. Emile Durkheim viewed the state as above all a moral agency that concentrates within itself the values of the broader social community—a coordinating mechanism for the social organism (Giddens, 1978). More particularly, functionalists point to four primary functions performed by the state.

Enforcement of norms It is easy to take the state for granted. Yet the eminent anthropologist George Peter Murdock (1950:716) tells us:

> . . . for 99 percent of the approximately one million years that man has inhabited this earth, he lived, thrived, and developed without any true government whatsoever, and . . . as late as 100 years ago half the peoples of the world—not half the population but half the tribes or nations—still ordered their lives exclusively through informal controls without benefit of political institutions.

As we pointed out in Chapter 3, where people lack a formal political institution, they enforce their folkways and mores through the spontaneous and collective action of community members. Thus the Iban of Borneo subjected violators of their mores to scathing ridicule. But in modern, complex societies characterized by a preponderance of secondary relationships, these arrangements are no longer adequate. A special body or organization is required to assure law and order—the state.

Planning and direction Rapid social change dictates that people can no longer rely upon the gradual, more-or-less spontaneous evolution of folkways and mores to provide the guidelines for their daily lives. New norms become indispensable. Such norms, *laws*, result from

A Preindustrial Political System
Dogun village elders in Mali assemble to settle a dispute. Functionalists see the political institution arising to arbitrate conflicting interests, enforce norms, and deal with outsiders. But conflict theorists say it arose in the desire of elites to give permanence to institutional inequality. *(Arthur Tress/Magnum)*

conscious thought, deliberate planning, and formal declaration (see Chapter 3). Additionally, laws have the added advantage that they can be changed more readily than folkways and mores. For example, the folkways that regulated traffic in horse and buggy days are no longer adequate for the congested conditions of the nation's highways. Nor are laws governing automobiles suitable for handling air traffic.

In addition, the complexity and scope of many activities generate and require a specialized mechanism of coordination and integration. Under contemporary urban conditions, people find that personal and informal arrangements no longer suffice to provide highways, fire and police protection, public sanitation, safeguards to public health, assistance to the poor and infirm, and fiduciary money. These and many other activities dictate central direction. Similarly, in times of war, financial panic, or natural disaster, people often cannot cope with the magnitude of the crisis through independent and individual actions. The efficient and effective coordination and channeling of the human endeavor requires planning and direction. This task can be performed by only one or at most a few individuals. And these individuals must have the power and authority to implement their plans (Davis, 1949).

Arbitration of conflicting interests   Because such resources as privilege, prestige, and power are scarce and divisible, people find themselves in conflict over them. If no bonds other than the pursuit of immediate self-interest were to unite people, there would be chaos. The entire social fabric would be imperiled if conflict among

different social strata, races, religions, and special interest groups were to become deep and intense. Some agency must be capable of containing conflict within tolerable limits, and that agency is the state (Goode, 1972).

Protection against other societies   Throughout human history, societies have felt it necessary to protect their members and interests against outside groups, and to advance their fortunes through aggression against other groups. Two primary means for achieving these ends have been war and diplomacy. If a society is to maximize its position against adversaries through war and diplomacy, it needs the state to centralize control and mobilize the population.

The Conflict Perspective

Functionalists see the state as a rather benign institution. Conflict theorists contend that the state is a vehicle by which one or more groups imposes its values and structured inequality upon other groups. As they see the matter, the state has its origin in the desire of ruling elites to give permanence to social arrangements that benefit themselves. More fundamentally, they depict the state as an instrument of violence and oppression. Randall Collins (1975:351–352) asserts:

> What we mean by the state is the way in which violence is organized. The state consists of those people who have the guns or the other weapons and are prepared to use them; in the version of political organization found in the modern world, they claim monopoly on their use.

The State: An Instrument of Capitalist Oppression?

Here police attempt to disperse demonstrators in New York City in 1972 who were protesting the Vietnam war. Marxists portray the state as an agency that serves the interests of a ruling class. They say that the true nature of the state is revealed in times of social unrest and political crisis when the army and police engage in violence against those who challenge the authority of established elites. *(Charles Harbutt/Archive)*

The state *is*, above all, the army and the police, and if these groups did not have weapons we would not have a state in the classical sense. This is a type of definition much disputed by those who like to believe that the state is a kind of grade-school assembly in which people get together to operate for their common good. . . . [However, the basic question is] who will fight or threaten whom and who will win what?

Conflict theorists see the state arising in history with the production of goods and services over and above what is necessary for human survival. In hunting and gathering societies, land is communally owned and the members of the community share the food derived from it. People have more to gain by sharing than by hoarding because they earn the right to be repaid in the future when they are unsuccessful in the search for food or are disabled. Agricultural societies are more highly stratified than hunting and gathering groups (see Chapter 3). Intensive agriculture produces food surpluses, and hence it is no longer essential that every human hand be employed in subsistence activities. Some people can then apply their talents and abilities to new occupations, such as pottery, masonry, and weaving. Of equal significance, some members of society, elites who become the beneficiaries of privilege, can live off the surplus produced by others (Lenski, 1966).

The rise of the state had other social consequences. It gave rise to subject peoples (dominant-minority group relationships):

Only with the development of the state did human societies become equipped with a form of social organization which could bind masses of culturally and physically heterogeneous "strangers" in a single social entity. Whereas primitive peoples derive their cohesion largely from a common culture and from kinship and other kinds of personal ties, state societies are held together largely by the existence of a central political authority which claims a monopoly of coercive power over all persons within a given territory. Theoretically, with a sufficiently strong development of the apparatus of government, a state society can extend law and order over limitless subgroups of strangers who neither speak the same language, worship the same gods, not strive for the same values. [Wagley and Harris, 1964:24]

There is a difference of opinion among conflict theorists regarding the nature of the state. Some Marxists (*instrumental Marxists*) have taken literally the *Communist Manifesto*'s dictum that "the executive of the modern state is but a committee for managing the common affairs of the whole bourgeoisie." Seen in this manner, the state is an instrument that is manipulated, virtually at will, by the capitalist class (Beirne, 1979). As we will see later in the chapter, several studies seek to show that economic power inheres in the ownership or control of the means of production (factories, banks, and large farms) and is typically transformed into political influence (Kolko, 1962; Miliband, 1969; Domhoff, 1970, 1983). Capitalists, it is alleged, accomplish this transformation through lobbying, campaign financing, intermarriage within the capitalist class, and the corruption by business of the judiciary and federal and state legislatures.

Other Marxists (*structural Marxists*) contend that the state apparatus exercises "relative autonomy" in its relationship with the capitalist class. State structures are said to have independent histories that are not simply the products of dominant class interests or class struggles (Quadagno, 1984; Carnoy, 1984; Evans, Rueschemeyer, and Skocpol, 1985). According to this view, relentless class war between capitalists and workers, boom and bust economic cycles, and intercorporate conflict place constraints on the ability of the capitalist class to manipulate political institutions at will. Although the state may promote a climate favorable to capitalist enterprise, it must also legitimate the sanctity of the social order and maintain internal peace (O'Connor, 1973; McNall, 1984). By virtue of this latter requirement, the state routinely pursues policies that are at variance with the interests of *some* capitalists. For instance, it enacts welfare legislation that supports unemployed and nonproductive workers; places restrictions on rent that inhibit the ability of landlords to receive open market rentals; passes and enforces antitrust legislation; and imposes taxes on corporations (Beirne, 1979). The state apparatus, then, is seen as standing above individual economic units, even though it promotes a social environment conducive to capitalist arrangements. In this way the unity of the capitalist class is maintained and capitalist arrangements persist (Poulantzas, 1973; Mollenkopf, 1975; Block, 1977; Jessop, 1985). Even though Marxists may differ in their views on some matters, they nonetheless tend to agree that the state is the servant of capitalist interests.

THINKING THROUGH THE ISSUES

Most sociologists agree with Marx that the state is not a socially neutral organization. It supports the interests of a society's dominant classes. But is this the only function that the state performs? Are there functions performed by the state that are not related to class conflict and to the maintenance of existing stratification systems? Marx and Engels predicted that under conditions of communism—a classless society—the state would "wither away." In the absence of classes in modern societies, would the state still be necessary? Why? Can you integrate the functionalist and conflict approaches to provide a better understanding of social reality?

American Political Structure

Totalitarian, authoritarian, and democratic governments are marked by competition for positions of power. What distinguishes democracies is that the contest is usually regarded as legitimate. Norms define political competition as expected and opposition as appropriate. Free and competitive elections, the right to form opposition parties, freedom to criticize those in power, freedom to seek public office, and popular participation are among the commonly accepted hallmarks of democratic procedures. In practice, these processes have often proven difficult to achieve. Central to their implementation are political parties, popular electoral participation, interest group lobbying, and the mass media.

Political Parties

A **political party** is a durable organization formed to gain control of the government by putting its people in public office. It is not the same thing as an interest group—an organization that undertakes to affect policy without assuming the responsibilities of running the government. Members of an interest group seek control over government decisions as a means to an end. But a political party pursues the control of government as an end in itself. Accordingly, mass-based political parties tend to abandon or modify positions that interfere with gaining or maintaining political office.

Within American life, the major political parties function as brokers or intermediaries between people and government. Because of this and the structural dictates of a two-party system, parties steer a relatively pragmatic course. To win control of the government, each party must shape itself in ways that provide the greatest electoral appeal. This requirement exerts a centrist pull away from the political fringes. In close elections, both the Republican and Democratic parties strive for the support of the same uncommitted, often middle-of-the-road, voters. Not surprisingly, they often end up championing programs that seem to be Tweedledum and Tweedledee versions of one another. Occasionally a more doctrinaire faction gains control of the presidential nominating machinery. But then the party typically suffers electoral disaster, the fate of the Goldwater Republican Right in 1964 and the McGovern Democratic Left in 1972. Critics of the American system say that centrist forces and pressures result in the voters not getting a real choice. But proponents point out that what is really happening is that the parties are performing one of their chief func-

A Tilt Too Far to the Political Left?
Senator George McGovern won the 1972 Democratic presidential nomination. But McGovern's campaign was soon thrown badly off stride when Senator Thomas Eagleton, McGovern's running mate, retired from the ticket after disclosing he had a history of psychiatric treatment. In addition, McGovern's proposal of a guaranteed minimum income won him a reputation for radicalism. Republicans denounced him as the champion of "acid [hard drugs], abortion, and amnesty [for draft evaders]." Given the centrist forces that traditionally have operated in American politics, McGovern received the lowest margin of votes in the Electoral College (520 to 17) since 1936. *(Lee Goff/Magnum)*

tions: compromising different and conflicting points of view prior to the election (Olson and Meyer, 1975).

Electoral Participation and Voting Patterns

Citizens participate in the American political system through periodic elections. The principle that each person has one vote is seen as a basic mechanism for offsetting class, gender, and racial inequalities. Yet many Americans do not vote. Over the past 50 years, between 52 and 64 percent of the electorate has voted in presidential elections. Nonvoters are apt to be younger, less educated, and poorer than those who do vote. In the 1984 presidential elections, 69 percent of those aged 45 to 64 voted, compared with 40 percent of those aged 18 to 24; 79 percent of college graduates went to the polls, compared with only 44 percent of those whose schooling stopped before they received their high school diploma; and 74 percent of those with family incomes of $35,000 or more voted, compared with 46 percent of those with family incomes under $10,000. And whites (61 percent) were more likely to vote than blacks (56 percent) or Hispanics (33 percent).

The turnout rate in presidential elections is typically 25 to 30 percent lower in the United States than in major elections in most Western European nations. At least 9 percentage points of the difference is attributable to American registration statutes (Glass, Squire, and Wolfinger, 1984). The United States is the only nation where the entire burden of registration falls on the individual rather than the government. In Western Europe, Canada, Australia, and New Zealand, the state has the

responsibility for compiling and maintaining the electoral registers. Additionally, many nonvoters view their success or lack of success in life as a matter of "luck." So they do not see their fate as something that can be influenced by political participation (Hadley, 1978). Generally speaking, higher-status people discern a relationship between politics and their own lives. But many lower-status people do not see the political system as offering them anything, or anything they can relate to effectively.

As reflected in Table 16.2 on page 448, there are also important differences in how various segments of the population vote. As a general rule, better-off voters tend to favor Republican candidates and the poor favor Democratic candidates. Even so, Democrats still receive a significant proportion of their support from higher-income groups, while the Republican Ronald Reagan got many blue-collar votes. Prior to the 1930s, black voters tended to support the party of Abraham Lincoln and black emancipation, but since Franklin D. Roosevelt and the New Deal, they have voted overwhelming Democratic. Although the voting patterns of men and women have not traditionally differed, in recent years women have been more apt to support the Democratic party. Overall, there is a persistence of voter identification with particular parties. Changes do occur, although not as quickly and sharply as is often imagined.

Interest Group Lobbying

People who have common concerns or points of view are called **interests,** and the groups that organize them are called **interest groups.** Special interest groups differ from

Table 16.2   Portrait of the Electorate: The Vote for House of Representatives

Percent of 1986 Total		1982		1984		1986	
		Democrat	Republican	Democrat	Republican	Democrat	Republican
—	Total	57%	43%	51%	49%	52%	48%
48	Men	55	45	48	52	51	49
52	Women	58	42	54	46	54	46
87	Whites	54	46	46	54	49	51
8	Blacks	89	11	92	8	86	14
3	Hispanics	75	25	69	31	75	25
16	18–29 years old	59	41	51	49	51	49
32	30–44 years old	54	46	54	46	52	48
24	45–59 years old	56	44	50	50	54	46
28	60 and older	58	42	48	52	52	48
8	Not a high school graduate	—	—	60	40	57	43
32	High school graduate	—	—	51	49	55	45
29	Some college	—	—	49	51	50	50
31	College graduate	—	—	50	50	51	49
26	From the East	65	35	54	46	52	48
37	From the Midwest	49	51	50	50	53	47
12	From the South	59	41	52	48	56	44
25	From the West	53	47	48	52	51	49
46	White Protestant	43	57	38	62	43	57
32	Catholic	63	37	58	42	55	45
4	Jewish	82	18	70	30	70	30
—	White born-again Christian	46	54	35	65	—	—
8	White Fundamentalist or Evangelical Christian	—	—	—	—	31	69
15	Under $12,500 in income	73	27	63	37	56	44
26	$12,500–$24,999	60	40	54	46	53	47
21	$25,000–$34,999	56	44	50	50	52	48
21	$35,000–$50,000	49	51	47	53	53	47
17	Over $50,000	37	63	39	61	47	53
16	Liberal	80	20	76	24	71	29
46	Moderate	60	40	57	43	58	42
34	Conservative	35	65	31	69	35	65
—	Professional or white collar	48	52	—	—	—	—
29	Professional or manager	—	—	48	52	50	50
14	Other white collar worker	—	—	53	47	54	46
14	Blue collar worker	64	36	58	42	55	45
2	Agricultural worker	55	45	26	74	56	44
13	Homemaker	—	—	48	52	50	50
2	Full-time student	—	—	59	41	57	43
11	Government employee	—	—	58	42	62	38
2	Unemployed	71	29	70	30	63	37
19	Retired	61	39	48	52	52	48
27	Union household	68	32	64	36	63	37

Source: *The New York Times*, November 6, 1986, p. 15.

public interest groups. **Special interest groups** are interest groups that primarily seek benefits from which their members would derive more gains than the society as a whole. Examples include chambers of commerce, trade associations, labor unions, and farm organizations. **Public interest groups** are interest groups which pursue policies that presumably would be of no greater benefit to their members than to the larger society. Consumer protection organizations are good illustrations of public interest groups.

One type of special interest group that has attracted considerable controversy are **political action committees (PACs)**, interest groups set up to elect or defeat candidates independently of regular party organizations. PACs were specifically authorized by the 1971 Federal Election Campaign Act, although they had operated well before then. In 1986, political action committees established by unions, corporations, and special interests numbered more than 4,092. Money is important in an era of multimillion-dollar campaigns, especially for purchasing media advertising. In the 1986 elections, winning a seat in the House of Representatives cost on average about $400,000 (Shribman, 1987). A Senate seat cost five times this amount. Even before elections are in full swing, PACs are in action. For instance, Common Cause, the public interest lobby, estimates that in 1985—a year with no national elections—the 27 incumbent United States senators who were running for reelection spent $15.9 million on their campaigns, with 62 percent of the money coming from PACs. The 399 House incumbents running for reelection spent $25.9 million, 73 percent from PACs (Edmondson, 1986). Many political action committees cover their bets by contributing to both candidates in a campaign, assuring that they later will have access to the winner.

Drawing by Dana Fradon; © 1986 The New Yorker Magazine, Inc.

The Mass Media

The **mass media** consist of those organizations—newspapers, magazines, television, radio, and motion pictures—that undertake to communicate with a large segment of the public. For effective political participation, the public must have access to information on what is going on in government. Whereas earlier generations of Americans depended primarily upon newspapers for their political information, recent generations have depended chiefly upon television. Studies show that two-thirds of Americans get most of their news from television, and over half get *all* of their news in this manner (Shea, 1984). The public secures information about candidates from television through news broadcasts and paid advertising. Although there is little credible evidence that the television networks knowingly favor particular presidential candidates, they do influence public attitudes by their selection of news events. They slant their programs toward the exciting, the provocative, the timely, and the unusual, which encourages candidates to make "news" and provide good "visuals."

For example, Jimmy Carter and his advisers correctly judged that the winner of the Iowa caucuses, the first real event of the 1976 campaign season, would emerge as the "front runner." Accordingly, beginning in 1974 and for two years thereafter, the Carter campaign concentrated on Iowa. Even though Carter did not really win Iowa (he finished second to "uncommitted"), the media portrayed him as the winner and he quickly became the center of media attention. One month earlier, only 3 percent of the American public knew who Jimmy Carter was (a former governor of Georgia). The rest is history.

> **THINKING THROUGH THE ISSUES**
>
> How may the proliferation of interest groups contribute to the proliferation of government agencies? Do new interest groups mean new problems for government? How is government going to mediate the conflicts born of the frictions generated by new interest groups? If government intervenes to control the relations among groups and to fashion public policy in new areas, does it stimulate the formation of still more new groups that feel threatened by the growth of government? Does organization beget organization in an ongoing chain of interaction (Key, 1958)?

Jimmy Who?
Jimmy Carter was virtually unknown to
the American public before the nation's
media depicted him as the winner of the
Iowa primary in the 1976 Democratic presidential nomination race. The former governor of Georgia went on to win his
party's nomination, and he defeated the
Republican Gerald Ford in the general
election. The American public saw Carter
as "Mr. Clean" and as a "Washington outsider" who would restore honesty and
dignity to the presidential office after it
had been severely tainted by the political
turmoil of the Vietnam war years and the
Watergate scandals. *(Alex Webb/Magnum)*

In a television age, campaigns are based on partisan
posturing and polemics, skills that contrast sharply with
the skills of quiet compromise demanded for effective
governing. In conducting their campaigns, more and
more candidates are turning to high-powered professionals who advise them on every detail, ranging from which
issues they should tackle to the images they should project in media appearances. Physical appearance and
"good looks" are surfacing as paramount matters in an
era when packaging candidates for the media is so critical. Moreover, TV advertising, for which candidates
spend nearly half their campaign funds, means giving
greater emphasis to style and personality over substance.

Professionals cite evidence showing that a colorful event
in which a candidate utters a few catchy one-liners wins
more votes than an earnest discussion of the issues.
Computer technology is also being employed to target
specific voter groups, and then bombard them with TV
advertising and direct-mail appeals specifically tailored
to them. Campaign managers are employing public
opinion polls not only to find out how voters perceive
their candidates, but to determine what voters want to
hear their candidates say (Walsh, 1984; Morrow, 1986).

In the American political system, incumbents have
a decided advantage. For one thing, they set the agenda
by being primary sources of news. Clearly, newsworthiness is not something that inheres in most events. Journalists and television anchors must select the happenings
that they will portray and translate them into public
events for a mass constituency (Lester, 1980). By virtue
of their official positions, incumbents can upstage others
through news conferences, press briefings, public
speeches, and television interviews, as well as indirectly
through news leaks, trial balloons, and off-the-record
confidences. These matters raise the question, "How
does the political system actually operate and who makes
it run?" Different answers have been proposed to this
question.

Models of Power in the United States

One of the longest running debates in sociology has to do
with nature of power in the United States. Is power con-

*"No, no. When I say this new secret weapon can slip past their defenses
undetected, I'm not referring to the Russians, I'm referring to Congress."*

Drawing by Stevenson; © 1986 The New Yorker Magazine, Inc.

centrated in the hands of the few, or distributed somewhat among various groups within American life? What is the basis of power? Is the exercise of power in the United States unrestricted, or is it limited by the competing interests of numerous groups? Sociologists have supplied quite different answers to these questions, represented by three theoretical models: the Marxist (or ruling class), the elitist, and the pluralist.

Marxist Models

Marxist theory has had a profound impact upon sociological thinking on power and social organization. Not only has it influenced the work of conflict sociologists, but it has provided a backdrop—even a target—in terms of which non-Marxist sociologists have formulated their rival interpretations. Sociologists following in the Marxist tradition, like J. Allen Whitt (1979, 1982), hold that political processes must be understood in terms of a society's institutional structure as it is shaped by underlying class interests and conflict. Whitt contends that the ways in which the major social institutions (especially the economic institution) are organized have critical implications for how power is exercised. Rather than focusing primarily upon the individuals who control the seats of power (as do power elite theorists), Whitt looks to the *biases* inherent in social institutions as shaping political outcomes. He portrays society as structured in ways that place constraints on decision makers and render their formulation of policy largely a foregone conclusion. When General Motors believes its profits can be improved by closing countless plants and laying off thousands of workers, the system dictates that it do so, with little regard for the broader social consequences of its actions. Indeed, given the capitalist logic of institutions in Western nations, the ruling class usually need not take direct action to fashion outcomes favorable to its interests. The political outcomes are built within the capitalist ordering of affairs by the way agendas are set and alternatives are defined.

A number of contemporary Marxist theorists like Nicos Poulantzas (1973, 1975) distinguish between ruling and governing. Ruling has to do with the possession of decisive power, the kind of power that constrains political processes and serves underlying capitalist interests. Governing, in contrast, has to do with day-to-day administration and decision making that allows the political system to run smoothly. It matters little who *governs* the capitalist societies; it is the capitalist class, the bourgeoisie, that *rules*. Poulantzas suggests that the state best

serves the interests of the capitalist ruling class when the latter distances itself from the routine of everyday, and often controversial, decision making.

Elitist Models

The elitist perspective found early expression in the ideas of such late nineteenth- and early twentieth-century European sociologists as Vilfredo Pareto, Gaetano Mosca, and Robert Michels. They undertook to show that the concentration of power in a small group of elites is inevitable within modern societies. These sociologists rejected Marx's idealistic vision that social change would bring about a classless and stateless society. Instead, they depicted all societies beyond the bare subsistence level— be they totalitarian, monarchical, or democratic—as dominated by the few who rule and the many who are ruled. The masses, they held, cannot and do not govern themselves. Even so, change occurs across time through the gradual circulation of elites: one elite comes to replace another. Viewed in this fashion, democracy gives the masses the ability to choose between competing elites, but not necessarily the ability to influence policies once an elite is in power.

Within the United States, elitist theory has taken a somewhat unique twist, particularly in the hands of sociologist C. Wright Mills (1956). Mills contends that the major decisions affecting Americans and others, especially those having to do with issues of war and peace, are made by a very small number of individuals and groups whom he calls "the Power Elite." The real rulers of the United States, says Mills, come from three interlocking groups: corporation executives, the military, and high-ranking political office holders. They are the ones who make such fateful decisions as those surrounding the Bay of Pigs invasion of Cuba, the bombing of North Vietnam, the supplying of military assistance to pro-American elements in Central America, and the procurement of major weapon systems. Elite personnel flow back and forth among the three realms: Corporate officials take top positions in the president's cabinet and then return to business; generals and admirals retire from the military to assume leading posts in the business community; and former senators and members of Congress become special interest lobbyists. All the while, large segments of the population such as the disadvantaged and minorities have become increasingly powerless, politically impotent, and therefore apathetic (Mills, 1959) (see the box on page 452).

Elitist models typically depict elites as unified in purpose and outlook because of similar social back-

A Military–Industrial Complex?

In a farewell address to the nation on January 17, 1961, four days before he turned over his office to John F. Kennedy, President Dwight D. Eisenhower warned Americans of the "conjunction of an immense military establishment and a large arms industry"—what he labeled the "military-industrial complex." He said the total influence of it ". . . is felt in every city, every state house, every office of the federal Government," and that "only an alert and knowledgeable citizenry" can so manage this complex that "security and liberty may prosper together."

What has happened in the years intervening since the late General-President issued his warning? There are those like *New York Times* columnist Anthony Lewis (1985:23) who contend that "the influence of that complex has grown beyond his worst nightmares." Lewis notes that on the day the 1985 summit meeting began in Geneva between President Ronald Reagan and Soviet leader Mikhail Gorbachev, *The Washington Post* published a story under the headline: "Defense Contractors Are Worried Arms-Control Plan Could Cost Them: Lucrative Contracts Might Be Affected by Superpower Talks." The story said defense contractors viewed the proposals for 50 percent cuts in nuclear weapons as "ominous." On the same day, the *New York Times* also carried an article listing the contracts already awarded in the Strategic Defense Initiative or Star Wars pro-

gram. "The most lucrative missiles contracts," the article said, "have gone to many of the same companies . . . that also build Minuteman missiles, the MX missile and military satellites." A defense analyst for the First Boston Corporation, Wolfgang H. Demisch, said the aerospace companies were looking to Star Wars because "the traditional defense budget clearly isn't going to grow much in the near future. Every company is on notice that, if they want to be a long-term player, they can't let S.D.I. get away."

In contrast, others, like Bruce Weinrod of the conservative Heritage Foundation, say that Eisenhower's phrase has become "an old chestnut" that liberals pull out to oppose Pentagon budgets (*Columbus Dispatch*, January 17, 1986:7A). According to this view, defense spending actually plays a smaller proportional role in the economy than in Eisenhower's time. In 1960, defense spending accounted for 49 percent of the federal budget, compared with about 28 percent today. However, Eisenhower's budgets did not include Social Security benefit payments or expenditures for the Great Society programs inaugurated in the mid-1960s by the Johnson administration. Looked at another way, in 1960 defense spending accounted for 9.5 percent of the gross national product, the value of all goods and services produced by the economy, compared with 6.5 percent in 1985.

People trying to figure out whether the United States is spending the right amount on defense, or spending in the right ways, quickly

learn that many critical details are known only to a few specialists, and that wide gaps exist in their knowledge as well (Stubbing, 1986). In 1984, a high-ranking Pentagon official, A. Ernest Fitzgerald, charged that reports about the military's paying $500 for a hammer and $7,000 for a coffee brewer barely scratch the surface. Defense companies, he said, charge similarly excessive prices for all items—wasting $30 billion to $50 billion a year (*Columbus Dispatch*, October 11, 1984:F7). The publicly reported profits of defense companies (affording a 25.6 percent return on shareholder equity) run substantially higher than the profits of companies in other segments of the economy (the 1,000 largest companies show an average 15.1 percent return on shareholder equity). Additionally, as revealed in Figure A, considerable controversy surrounds the performance capabilities of the equipment provided by defense contractors.

A Commission on Defense Management appointed by President Reagan reported that as of May 1985, 45 of the nation's top 100 military contractors were the targets of 131 separate investigations, involving such issues as pricing, kickbacks, product substitution, and false claims. A chronic problem has been scandals in military procurement, such as Lockheed Corporation's overbilling by hundreds of millions of dollars for the C-5B military transport (Cushman, 1986). Congress is often part of the problem. Members of Congress want to be seen cutting budgets, but they oppose closing bases or factories in their states and districts.

FIGURE A   **Controversy Surrounds How the Pentagon Spends Its Billions**
The Pentagon budget for 1987 was in excess of 300 billion dollars. Spending on weapons procurement had doubled since 1980, and spending on weapons research had risen 80 percent. *Source: The Defense Budget Project and congressional testimony.*

DIVAD Antiaircraft Gun Self-propelled

Authorized cost per unit* (1978): $5.2 million
Actual cost: $6.7 million
Increase: 29.7 percent

The DIVAD air-defense gun was authorized in 1978 at a cost of $5.2 million per unit. The equipment did not operate properly and the program was eventually cancelled at a loss of $1.8 billion. (Department of the Army)

*Rounded cost figures in 1984 dollars.

M-1 Abrams Tank

Authorized cost per unit (1972): $2 million
Actual cost: $2.8 million
Increase: 42.4 percent

The M-1 Abrams tank was authorized in 1972 at a cost of $2 million per unit. The design of the tank was affected by the Ford Administration's desire to help out Chrysler, then a major tank producer. The design finally adopted was based on a Chrysler-Avco proposal featuring a "hybrid turret" that increased the vulnerability of the tank to enemy fire. (Larry Downing/Woodfin Camp & Associates)

Bradley Infantry Fighting Vehicle

Authorized cost per unit (1979): $686,000
Actual cost: $1.5 million
Increase: 113.5 percent

The Bradley Infantry Fighting Vehicle was authorized in 1979. Well after the Bradley had gone into production, it was disclosed that the Army had never fully tested it to see how it would fare under combat conditions. When Army officials finally agreed to its test, some officers charged that the procedures were rigged so they would not reveal the vehicle's inherent flaws. It seems the Bradley is too lightly armored to protect soldiers in combat and too heavy and unwieldly to safely ford streams. (Larry Downing/Woodfin Camp & Associates)

F-18 Fighter-Bomber

Authorized cost per unit (1975): $19.3 million
Actual cost: $29 million
Increase: 50 percent

The F-18 fighter was authorized in 1975. Its range is less than the A-7 attack aircraft it is replacing and so it increases the vulnerability of carrier forces. From the beginning, the program was influenced by pressures from powerful members of Congress concerned with jobs created in their districts by the F-18 program. (George Hall/Woodfin Camp & Associates)

grounds, dominant and overlapping positions in key social institutions, and the convergence of their economic interests (Domhoff, 1970, 1983; Orum and Feagin, 1987). For instance, sociologist Michael Unseem (1983) contends that an "inner circle" of interconnected corporate officers and directors assumes the stewardship of American political and social affairs. He finds that inner group members are more likely to belong to an exclusive social club, have upper-class parents, participate in major business associations, serve on government advisory boards, belong to the upper levels of nonprofit and charitable organizations, gain media coverage for themselves, maintain informal contacts with government leaders, and prefer one another's company. According to elitist theorists, elites invariably get their way whenever important public decisions are at stake. They manage conflicts in the larger society in such a way as to keep the distribution of power in their hands and to produce outcomes favorable to themselves. Their power is pervasive and leaves few areas of social life untouched.

THINKING THROUGH THE ISSUES

Both Marxist and elitist sociologists emphasize the pervasiveness of political manipulation by the "ruling class" or "elites" in modern societies. **Can you identify a number of mechanisms of political manipulation? What role does** cooptation **play—when a political structure is threatened by particular groups (for instance, labor unions or civil rights groups), the leaders of these groups are incorporated into positions of power within the existing structure? What part does** gerrymandering **play—the mapping of electoral boundaries so that a party gains a majority in a number of electorates rather than simply a minority in a good many (see Figure 16.2)? How do political elites undertake to manufacture consent through the release or withholding of vital information? How do political elites undertake to "create" events and fashion their portrayal in ways that conform with their needs and interests (Lester, 1980)? How is support for American foreign policy mobilized through instilling in Americans a sense of mission against international communism?**

Pluralist Models

The pluralist perspective contrasts sharply with both the Marxist and power elite models. Rather than seeing

FIGURE 16.2   **Gerrymandering: Drawing the Lines in Indianapolis**
Source: Republican National Committee.

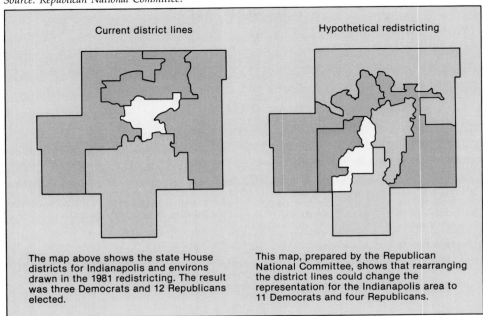

Current district lines	Hypothetical redistricting
The map above shows the state House districts for Indianapolis and environs drawn in the 1981 redistricting. The result was three Democrats and 12 Republicans elected.	This map, prepared by the Republican National Committee, shows that rearranging the district lines could change the representation for the Indianapolis area to 11 Democrats and four Republicans.

power as centralized in the hands of an elite or ruling class, pluralist theorists portray it as politically fragmented and diffused. These sociologists start with interest groups as the basic feature of organized political life. They say that no one group really runs the government, although many groups have the power to veto policies that run counter to their interests (Riesman, 1953; Dahl, 1961). Important decisions are made by different groups, depending on the institutional arena—business organizations, labor unions, farm blocs, racial and ethnic associations, and religious groups. When their interests diverge, the various groups compete for allies among the more or less unorganized public. But the same group or coalition of groups does not set policies across the board. Instead, their power varies with the issue.

Most groups remain inactive on most issues and mobilize their resources only when their interests are immediately at stake. Viewed in this fashion, the resulting distribution of power tends to be unstable because interests and alliances are typically short-lived, and new groups and coalitions are always being organized as old ones disintegrate. Moreover, government achieves substantial autonomy by operating as a broker or balancing agent among competing interest groups.

Some pluralists say that so many interest groups have sprung up in the United States in recent years, each demanding special attention to its own concern, that government has become paralyzed. All too often it is unable to respond effectively and efficiently in dealing with major problems (Shea, 1984). Stalemate results when there are powerful and nearly equal opposing interests on an issue. Additionally, policymakers become preoccupied with certain highly focused and emotional issues, and ignore the less dramatic but vital ones. Whether it is abortion, gun control, antipollution, nuclear power, or tax deductions for business lunches, increasing numbers of groups are singlemindedly pursuing their narrow interests. Single-issue politics, then, come to dominate the political process.

Conclusions

What conclusions can we draw from these contending models of power? At the outset, it should be stressed that elitist theorists like Mills and even Marxian-oriented theorists do not argue that a power elite or governing class totally dominates American society. Given the many interest groups in the United States, no one group can achieve dominance. Even so, when important decisions on such critical issues as war and peace and on matters

fundamentally affecting the economy are made, some corporate and political power centers clearly have greater input than other groups. While conceding that the people in modern Western democracies may not really govern themselves, sociologists point out that they nonetheless can stir up a deafening commotion when they dislike the way their leaders are governing them.

Yet given the divisions within the highest echelons of American government on the B-1 bomber, the MX missile, levels of defense spending, military intervention in Central America, the American position in arms talks with the Soviet Union, and tax policies, it is exceedingly difficult to make a convincing case for a unified power elite. At the same time, it is hard to deny that major corporate, military, and political interests have a common stake in preserving the essential components of existing institutional arrangements. And it is also true, as structural Marxists remind us, that the political and economic institutions seem to gain an existence separate from the specific individuals who have ownership or positions of authority within them. So the question is not only one of "Who runs America?" but also one of "What runs America?" In sum, each model contains a kernel of truth, and a synthesis of the formulations seems at present to provide the most satisfactory approach.

War and Peace

As we noted earlier in the chapter, a state exists as part of a system of nation-states. What occurs in the international arena—especially with respect to issues of war and peace—has profound consequences for a nation's internal life. Since World War II, the centralizing of power in two superpower states—the United States and the Soviet Union—has meant that in large measure history-making has been a product of the decisions and defaults of American and Soviet leaders. Over thirty years ago, C. Wright Mills observed:

> But what was Caesar's power at its peak compared with the power of the changing inner circle of Soviet Russia or of America's temporary administrations? The men of either circle can cause great cities to be wiped out in a single night, and in a few weeks turn continents into thermonuclear wastelands. That the facilities of power are enormously enlarged and decisively centralized means that the decisions of small groups are now more consequential. [1956:23]

The dropping of atomic bombs on Nagasaki and Hiroshima in the final days of World War II ushered in

"*Essentially, it's a disagreement over turf.*"

Drawing by Ed Fisher; © 1986 The New Yorker Magazine, Inc.

the atomic age. Because the survival of humankind is at stake, the nuclear threat is perhaps the foremost social issue of our time, especially as nuclear arsenals are spreading to more and more nations (see Figure 16.3). Two competing views promptly surfaced in the nuclear debate. One has held that nuclear weapons have made national sovereignty obsolete and that the safety of humankind can be secured only by establishing a global political order—"world state or world doom." The opposing view has found expression in policies of deterrence (the box evaluates the effectiveness of deterrence as a strategy for avoiding nuclear war). This latter approach was articulated in the mid-1940s by General Leslie R. Groves, military chief of the Manhattan Project that had developed the atomic bomb: "If there are to be atomic weapons in the world, we must have the best, the biggest, and the most." On whole, the view typified by General Groves has prevailed. Even today, as expressed in the Star Wars program, the conviction has persisted among many American military leaders that somewhere down an endlessly receding road there exists the defini-

tive technological solution that will make the United States safe and secure in a nuclear world (Boyer, 1985).

The nuclear threat differs from other social problems that sociologists usually study in that the unwanted behavior is created by governments, and all the world's most powerful governments are directly implicated. With government as the source of the problem, the usual approaches to problem solving do not apply (Caplow, 1986). Partly for this reason—as well as the unimaginable horror of large-scale nuclear war— sociologists have been slow to study nuclear issues. But in the past several years this has been changing, and the matter of war and peace is a topic gaining sociological scrutiny (Kramer and Marullo, 1985).

Warfare

War is a socially organized form of aggression that involves violent, armed conflict between political contestants. War has been common throughout human history. Sociologist Pitrim Sorokin (1937) recorded all the major European wars from 500 B.C. to A.D. 1925. Included among the combatants were ancient Rome, Austria, England, France, Germany, Greece, Italy, Lithuania, the Netherlands, Russia, and Spain. All told he registered 967 wars, an average of one war every 2 to 3 years. Spain had the highest record, at 67 percent of the years studied; Germany, the lowest at 28 percent. Russia was at war 46 percent of the time, so that it had experienced only one peaceful quarter-century during the thousand-year period. Indeed, before A.D. 1500, there is little point in trying to tote up statistics on European wars, because war was endemic to the continent.

In recent times, war has grown steadily less common. Even so, in 1986—the year the United Nations had hopefully designated the International Year of Peace—at least 43 countries were at war. Among them, Iraq and Iran were locked in a six-year-old border war; Afghanistan was the focus of stepped-up Soviet and Afghan government action against anti-Communist rebels; in Cambodia, 15,000 Communist and non-Communist guerrillas were fighting a Vietnamese-sponsored Cambodian government backed by 150,000 Vietnamese troops; in El Salvador, the U.S.-equipped Salvadoran army had put the 4,000 guerrilla forces on the defensive; and in Nicaragua, the Sandinista government was girding for an escalation in fighting as new United States aid was arriving for the Contras. During the International Year of Peace, only one major arms control agreement was reached between the superpowers. It provides for notification of military maneuvers in Europe as a way of lessening the chances of surprise attack.

Sources of Warfare

Why do people resort to war? In the early years of sociology, Social Darwinists like Herbert Spencer and William Graham Sumner contended that war is the "natural way" for human beings gathered in societies to compete, and competition is a "fixed law of nature." Sumner (1911:5–6) wrote: "War arises from the competition of life . . . a fundamental condition of human existence. . . . It is the competition of life, therefore, which makes war, and that is why war always has existed and always will." The explanations of the Social Darwinists, however, have not stood the test of scientific scrutiny. Not all societies chose to deal with one another by war. The Arunta of Australia, the Andaman Islanders of the Bay of Bengal, the Eskimo peoples of the Arctic have cultural

FIGURE 16.3   **The Spread of Nuclear Weapons**
While the United States and the Soviet Union are negotiating possible cuts in nuclear weapons, some nations are expanding their nuclear arsenals, and others are joining the ranks. In the 1960s, the United States, the Soviet Union, and Great Britain completed a treaty on nonproliferation in an effort to curb the spread of nuclear weapons beyond the nations already possessing them. The treaty has been joined by more than 120 non-nuclear-weapon countries that have pledged not to divert nuclear materials to arms. The treaty was not signed by France and China, declared nuclear weapon countries. And some nations who have signed the treaty have not acted in strict accordance with its provisions. *Source: Nuclear Control Institute.*

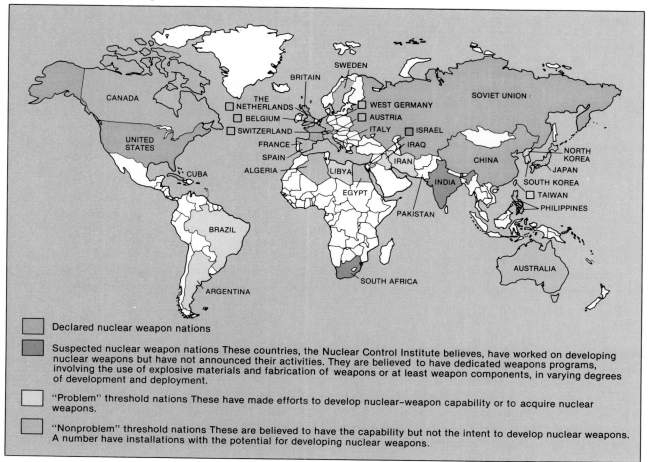

Declared nuclear weapon nations

Suspected nuclear weapon nations These countries, the Nuclear Control Institute believes, have worked on developing nuclear weapons but have not announced their activities. They are believed to have dedicated weapons programs, involving the use of explosive materials and fabrication of weapons or at least weapon components, in varying degrees of development and deployment.

"Problem" threshold nations These have made efforts to develop nuclear–weapon capability or to acquire nuclear weapons.

"Nonproblem" threshold nations These are believed to have the capability but not the intent to develop nuclear weapons. A number have installations with the potential for developing nuclear weapons.

ISSUES THAT SHAPE OUR LIVES

Does Deterrence Work?

Two competing images have dominated the thinking of American leaders over the past thirty years in formulating our nation's nuclear policy toward the Soviet Union (Tetlock, 1983; Marullo, 1985). The one is the "hard line" or deterrence image of the international environment; the other, the "soft line" or conflict-spiral image.

The deterrence approach holds that serious dangers to world peace arise whenever an aggressor state (as the Soviet Union is presumed to be) doubts either the capability or resolve of a status quo power (as the United States is presumed to be) to resist encroachments on its sovereignty and strategic interests. Therefore, the United States must convince the Soviet Union that it possesses sufficient nuclear forces to inflict "unacceptably large" losses upon the Soviet Union—even to the point of annihilation—in the event the Soviets launch a "first-strike" attack on American forces or those of its allies. On the other hand, policies that suggest the United States lacks either the capacity or determination to maintain a viable nuclear deterrent destablize the international system by inviting Soviet aggression and expansionism.

The deterrence image rests on the notion that the objectives of the United States and the Soviet Union are fundamentally incompatible and

"And I say one bomb is worth a thousand words."
Drawing by Dana Fradon; © 1986 The New Yorker Magazine, Inc.

that only mutual fear stays the hands of warmakers. The spiral-conflict image challenges this assumption. Its proponents contend that mutual fear frequently destabilizes rather than stabilizes the international system. The superpowers readily misinterpret each other's "defensive" preparations as offensive, laying the basis for an escalation of military competition and mutual hostility. For instance, whereas President Reagan portrayed his Strategic Defense Initiative—Star Wars—as a "defensive" umbrella to shield American cities from Soviet ballistic missiles, Soviet leaders viewed it as a program that would allow the United States to carry out a first-strike attack without fear of Soviet retaliation. Each side sees its own nuclear preparations as defensive precautions against attack, whereas it views the preparations of its adversary as evidence of an intention to attack. Consequently, a continuing spiral of escalation traps both parties.

The conflict-spiral approach also has policy implications. It says that a

patterns for dealing with quarrels and aggression, but they do not include organized battles in which one group is pitted against another. Apparently these societies even lack a word for war (Lesser, 1968). Nor are human beings necessarily aggressive and warlike. In fact, Zbigniew Brzezinski (1986), the former National Security Adviser in the Carter administration, contends that "pacifism"—"the willingness to disarm unilaterally in the proclaimed belief 'better Red than dead'"—is a primary danger confronting the Western World in its contest with the Soviet Union. Moreover, contemporary governments typically find it necessary to mobilize mass support for a war effort through propaganda, and then must assure support through legal and social constraints. Although a population may display collective enthusiasm and determination at the outbreak of war, maintaining public support

nation engaged in intense rivalry with another nation must convince the other side that it does not seek to destroy it. For example, the United States might make a conciliatory gesture to the Soviet Union that entails some small risk but does not jeopardize its own security. Consider the Berlin crisis of the early 1960s. American and Soviet tanks confronted one another barrel-to-barrel. The crisis was defused when the Americans pulled back their tanks step by step and the Soviets reciprocated each step (Rubin, 1981). Such a policy seeks to unwind conflict spirals by initiating a gradually expanding cycle of confidence-building and trust-enhancing actions. While recognizing that real conflicts of interest divide the two superpowers, proponents of these policies would accentuate bases for cooperation.

Both the deterrence and conflict-spiral approaches are concerned about the danger of international misunderstanding. But the deterrers worry that aggressors will underestimate their resolve, while spiral theorists worry that each side will overestimate the hostility of the other (Jervis, 1976). Who is right? Neither model totally fits the historical evidence. Judged by the wars since 1815, it seems that military buildups in and of themselves have little direct effect on the likelihood that rival nations will or will not go to war. Other factors are also at work.

Among them are high defense burdens, a conflict over a site bordering one of the nation-states, and the presence of a series of disputes between the rival nations (Diehl, 1985).

Even so, one can find cases that support each model. Consider deterrence theory. Appeasement did not stop Hitler, who gradually escalated his territorial demands in Europe—from the Rhineland (1936), to Austria (1938), to the Sudetenland (1938), to all of Czechoslovakia (1939), and then to Poland (1939). Other cases fit the spiral approach quite well. An upward spiral in the naval race between Britain and Germany and French-German competition in troops and armor were largely responsible for the outbreak of World War I in 1914.

Some social scientists point out that the nuclear age has radically tilted the balance of cost and benefit by which leaders calculate the decision to go to war. In the "good old days" of conventional forces, they could visualize circumstances in which their nation might emerge from a war in better shape. Or, more often, they could conceive of circumstances when if they did *not* go to war, they would be in even worse shape than if they did. For instance, Britain went to war with Germany in 1939 not because it had greater affection for the Poles than it had for the Czechs, for whom it had not fought in 1938, but because its leadership believed that if

the Germans were not stopped then, it would be impossible to stop them later. But in the nuclear age, rational calculations as to whether the prospective gains of war outweigh the likely costs no longer make sense. Viewed in this manner, world peace may be promoted by fearful restraint—the doctrine of mutual assured destruction (MAD) (Howard, 1984).

Critics of deterrence reject this conclusion. They say that in practice political leaders rarely make "rational" calculations. Their information is typically ambiguous; they lack the time to survey all their options thoroughly; and they find the trade-offs among options often impossible to weigh. For instance, misperceptions plagued both Argentina and Great Britain in the 1982 Falklands war. Despite abundant intelligence, the British failed to comprehend that Argentina was preparing to attack the islands. For their part, the Argentinians were so confident Britain would not fight that they gave little or no thought to what they would do if their assumption was wrong. And emotional pressures also operate on decision makers in crisis situations. Backed into a corner, leaders are even more prone to miscalculation. In fact, threats may actually increase the chances of an aggressive response, whereas creditable reassurances may defuse the situation (Jervis, Lebow, and Stein, 1986).

becomes increasingly difficult when fighting is prolonged and the sacrifices great (Shibutani, 1986).

Mounting evidence supports the contention that cooperation, not aggression, is the hallmark of humankind. Even warfare requires cooperation, since efficient coordination maximizes the chances of victory. One of the most intense and complex forms of cooperation is the fielding of a modern army (Leakey, 1982). War is, in fact, a social institution. The procedures of warfare have been established in custom and at times formalized into law. For instance, the Geneva Convention of 1929 set forth the legal rights of prisoners of war, and most combatants abide by restrictions on the use of outlawed weapons such as poison gas and germ warfare. Leaders of nation-states typically define guerrilla and terrorist groups as "deviant" precisely because they do not follow basic military rules. Guerrillas and terrorists fight and disappear and so fail to follow the conventions for surrender; it is unclear whether they have been defeated or have just retired to fight again on another day (Shibutani, 1986).

In searching for a more sophisticated explanation of warfare than that provided by Social Darwinists, sociologist Nicholas S. Timasheff (1965) has identified three conditions that typically pave the way for military action. First, a state has a cultural tradition that makes war a viable alternative. When it finds itself enveloped in rivalry with another nation, it already possesses a set of expectations and values that encourages the resolution of conflict by warfare. Second, two or more states confront a situation in which they all are pursuing the same, mutually exclusive objectives. Each can realize what it defines as a rightful outcome—be it in territory, resources, or international influence—only at the expense of another. And third, combat is resorted to when an antagonistic situation is "fueled" by one or more factors: an attempt to settle "old scores" and right "old wrongs"; to impose one's will upon a weaker state; to protect or enhance national "honor"; to court offense with another nation in order to overcome domestic dissension by uniting rival factions against an external threat; to enhance the position of the military and its leaders; to satisfy the national aspirations of an ethnic group by uniting "our people" within one nation-state; or to convert others to cherished religious or ideological beliefs.

Immanuel Wallerstein (1974, 1980) extends our sociological understanding with a geopolitical perspective on military expansion and contraction. He looks to the larger world system, seeking to discover some of the laws by which it operates (see Chapters 15 and 22). Wallerstein contends that war is not fueled by the actions of one nation. Rather, a shift in the balance of power occurs over time in the long-term world economic cycle. At critical historical junctures, "turning point" wars take place that give political expression to the new economic alignments. He views World Wars I and II as expressions of a realignment that took place between 1914 and 1945. Other periods of large-scale world convulsion were the 30 years of war between the French Revolution of 1789 and the downfall of Napoleon in 1815, and the decline of Spanish power in Europe in the Counterreformation wars of 1618–1648. Based on this logic, Wallerstein predicts that our globe's smaller wars are not structurally due to escalate into another encompassing world war until the twenty-first century. Others disagree: They say that the advent of nuclear weapons has shifted the balance of cost and benefit in undertaking war, especially if there is the slightest prospect that the weapons could be used against oneself (Howard, 1984).

The Social Effects of Military Spending

Weapons do not have to be used in order for them to have an effect on contemporary social life. For over 40 years, a competitive arms race has dominated not only relations between the United States and the Soviet Union, but a generation of world affairs as well. The building and maintenance of weapon systems have had substantial social and economic costs. The decision of the Reagan administration to accelerate the American arms program pushed military spending to new levels. Unwilling to raise taxes or cut other expenditures, the United States has run up massive fiscal deficits. In the Soviet Union, the arms race has exacted a heavy toll on living standards and has diverted resources from sorely needed modernization. With an economic output only half that of the United States, the Soviet Union devotes twice as much of its national product to the military effort, putting its economy in deep trouble. Together the two superpowers, with less than 11 percent of the world's population, account for 23 percent of the world's armed forces, 60 percent of the military expenditures, more than 80 percent of the weapons research, and 97 percent of all nuclear warheads and bombs. Overall, the estimated $980 billion spent worldwide by all countries in 1986 was more than the combined income of the poorest half of the world's nations.

A long held and popular view has been that military spending contributes to the health of a nation's economy by maintaining employment and providing economic stability. Supporters of the defense buildup argue, for example, that defense spending can be an effective jobs-creating counterweight to recession, as happened in the United States in 1981 and 1982. But critics say that huge military expenditures are undermining our nation's broad industrial base. They contend that military spending lowers our standard of living, because dollars spent on military hardware cannot be used to produce consumer goods. And large military outlays make for large federal deficits that periodically contribute to strong inflationary pressures (Adams, 1983; Melman, 1983).

It is also claimed that military expenditures, especially for research, spur growth in the economy as a whole. But this image of military spending has come into question in recent years. Nearly 75 percent of the 1987 federal research and development budget was tic-

Table 16.3   Military Spending and Industrial Performance

Country	Military Research and Development as Percent of G. D. P.		Civil Research and Development as Percent of G. D. P.		Competitiveness Indicator*	
	1979	1982	1979	1982	1979	1982
Britain	0.68%	0.68%	1.6%	1.6%	99.0	94.3
United States	0.58	0.72	1.8	2.0	100.3	99.7
France	0.50	0.38	1.4	1.6	103.5	100.2
Sweden	0.22	0.24	1.7	1.7	102.9	117.2
West Germany	0.13	0.11	2.2	2.5	111.3	128.9
Japan	0.01	0.01	2.3	2.5	110.3	138.3

*Competitiveness indicator represents excess of output over domestic absorption.
Source: *The New York Times*, Nov. 11, 1986, p. 25.

keted for defense items, meaning that basic research in universities was shortchanged while high-tech programs like Star Wars got funded. Complicating matters, modern weaponry is becoming so sophisticated that the technologies it requires are becoming increasingly removed from civilian needs. Significantly, as shown in Table 16.3, the United States and Britain—nations that consistently spend more than other Western countries on military research—tend to score low on a gauge of economic competitiveness based on a nation's trade surplus (the excess of output over domestic absorption). In contrast, Japan and West Germany, which spend little on military research, have highly efficient industries (Lewis, 1986). Indeed, Japan and Germany, two of the most militaristic states of previous times, were forced by the victorious World War II powers to redirect their formidable energies into industry and trade. Japan, by keeping its armed forces to a minimum, has become so successful that it is overtaking the Soviet Union in terms of gross national product (Rosecrance, 1985).

There are other costs as well to the international arms race. An extreme emphasis on secrecy and national security has in the past led the FBI, the CIA, and other governmental agencies to violate the civil liberties of Americans. And it has led to "disinformation campaigns"—the spreading of false information for political ends—such as that undertaken by the CIA in 1986 aimed at undermining Libyan leader Muammar Kaddafi by generating false reports that the United States and Libya were again on a collision course. Moreover, given

their own vested interests, military-industrial structures in the United States and military-bureaucratic structures in the Soviet Union exert inexorable pressure to build more and more weapon systems (Kramer and Marullo, 1985).

Arms Control

Despite those forces feeding military buildups, arms control has come to occupy a central place in world politics. Because the rivalry between the United States and the Soviet Union is so dangerous and the cost of a conflict between them potentially so high, there is considerable pressure for the two superpowers to reach agreements on limiting nuclear weaponry. Although deep-seated hostility and profound distrust have blocked significant progress on issues of human rights and regional competition, the superpowers have been able to negotiate on the composition of their nuclear arsenals and have reached periodic understandings.

Given the intensity of their political rivalry, it is conceivable the United States and the Soviet Union would have gone to war at one time or another following World War II had it not been for the existence of nuclear weapons. Rather than using these weapons to wage war, the two nations have used them to maneuver for political advantage while at the same time seeking to diminish the danger of military conflict. Over 150 years ago the Prussian military strategist and theoretician Karl von Clausewitz (1780–1831) wrote: "War is nothing but the continuation of politics by other means." In some respects the two superpowers have inverted this famous maxim, so that politics has become the conduct of war by other means. Indeed, this is the core of arms control: a joint effort to achieve military peace while simultaneously pursuing the political contest.

During the 1970s, arms control became a firmly established aspect of Soviet-American relations. Bureaucracies have evolved in both nations that have institutionalized the monitoring of prior agreements and the negotiation of new agreements. In many respects, arms control has become the centerpiece of the two nations' relations. It has survived opposition from powerful military interests in both countries, disruptive events in other arenas of competition, and persistent attempts to "link" specific proposals with non-arms issues. We cannot predict whether or not a specific round of negotiations will end in specific agreements. But it does seem a safe conclusion that agreements in the foreseeable future will not abolish significant weapons, as Ronald Reagan and Mikhail Gorbachev proposed to do at the Reykjavik summit meeting in 1986. As with previous accords, any arms control agreements are likely to be modest in scope. So long as the United States and the Soviet Union remain bitter rivals, the world will confront the continuing threat of nuclear destruction, and arms control will remain a lively issue (Mandelbaum and Talbott, 1987).

Chapter Highlights

1. Power pervades all aspects of social life. It gives direction to human affairs so that collective goals can be achieved. And it determines which individuals and groups will be able to translate their preferences into the reality of day-to-day social organization. The state is a social organization whose power is based on the threat or application of punishment.

2. Although force may be an effective means for seizing power, and though it remains the ultimate foundation of the state, it is not the most effective means for political rule. Sociologists distinguish between power that is legitimate and power that is illegitimate. Legitimate power is authority. The sociologist Max Weber suggests that power may be legitimated by traditional, legal-rational, or charismatic means.

3. Functionalists contend that there is a good reason why the state arose, and why today it has assumed a dominant position in contemporary society. They point to four primary functions performed by the state: the enforcement of norms, overall social planning and direction, the arbitration of conflicting interests, and the protection of a society's members and interests against outside groups.

4. Conflict theorists contend that the state is a vehicle by which one or more groups impose their values and stratification system upon other groups. As they view the matter, the state has its origin in the desire of ruling elites to give permanence to social arrangements that benefit themselves. More fundamentally, they depict the state as an instrument of violence and oppression.

5. A number of factors promote a social climate favorable to a stable democracy: countervailing interest groups, multiple loyalties, stable economic and social conditions, and an underlying political consensus. A totalitarian society typically has three characteristics: a monolithic political party, a compelling ideology, and pervasive social control.

6. A constitutional system of government defines and prescribes the boundaries within which political power is pursued in the United States. Central to American political processes are political parties, popular electoral participation, interest group lobbying, and the mass media.

7. One of the longest running debates in the social sciences has to do with the nature of power in the United States. Marxist theory holds that political processes must be understood in terms of the institutional structure of society as it is shaped by underlying class interests and conflict. The elitist model depicts major decisions as being made by a power elite who constitute the real rulers of the United States. The pluralistic perspective contends that no one group really runs the government because interest groups constitute countervailing and balancing political forces. Each model contains a kernel of truth, and a

synthesis of the formulations seems at present to afford the most satisfactory approach.

8. A state exists as part of a system of nation-states. What occurs in the international arena—especially with respect to issues of war and peace—has profound consequences for all people. Nations go to war for both internal and external reasons. But whether used for military purposes or not, weapon systems have vast social and economic costs.

The Sociologist's Vocabulary

authoritarianism A political system in which the government tolerates little or no opposition to its rules, but permits nongovernmental centers of influence and allows debate on issues of public policy.

authority Legitimate power.

charismatic authority Power that is legitimated by the extraordinary superhuman or supernatural attributes people impute to a leader.

coercion Illegitimate power.

democracy A political system in which the powers of government derive from the consent of the governed, and in which regular constitutional avenues exist for changing government officials.

force Power whose basis is the threat or application of punishment.

government Those individuals and groups who control the state apparatus and direct state power.

interest People who share common concern or points of view.

interest groups Organizations of people who have common concerns or points of view.

legal-rational authority Power that is legitimated by explicit rules and rational procedures which define the rights and duties of the occupants of given positions.

mass media Those organizations—newspapers, magazines, television, radio, and motion pictures—that undertake to communicate with a large segment of the public.

political action committees Interest groups set up to elect or defeat candidates independently of regular party organizations.

political institution The social structure concerned with the use and distribution of power within a society.

political party A durable organization formed to gain control of the government by putting its people in public office.

public interest groups Interest groups that pursue policies which presumably would be of no greater benefit to their members than to the larger society.

special interest groups Interest groups that primarily seek benefits from which their members would derive more gains than the society as a whole.

state A social organization that exercises within a given territory an effective monopoly on the use of physical coercion.

totalitarianism A "total state"—one in which the government undertakes to extend control over all parts of the society and all aspects of social life.

traditional authority Power that is legitimated by the sanctity of age-old customs.

war A socially organized form of aggression that involves violent, armed conflict between political contestants.

Perspectives on Education
  The Functionalist Perspective
  The Conflict Perspective

Education and Social Inequality
  Class, Race, and Education
  Effects of School Desegregation
  Availability of Higher Education

The American School System
  The Formal Structure of Schools
  The Effectiveness of the Schools
  Revamping the Ivory Tower

17

Education

The children at a Philadelphia preschool were puzzled: They had been promised chicken for lunch, but got liver instead. The mixup occurred because Mable Crisp, the school's cook, could not read. Distressed by difficulties like these, she enrolled in a literacy program. "I feel like a little bud that's blossomed into a flower," says Ms. Crisp, who recently read her first book at age 45. Previously, the school's director would read her the week's menu each Monday and she would try to memorize it. Occasionally she would forget and have to make do with whatever was available. Similar mistakes, sometimes with far more serious consequences, occur because millions of Americans are illiterate (Gruson, 1986).

Imagine how illiteracy would affect you! What would you do if you were unable to read street signs, menus, letters, simple instructions, want ads, grocery labels, ballots, telephone bills, and bank statements? What would you do if you were unable to use calendars, note pads, date books, bus schedules, telephone directories, and street maps? How could you function as an active participant in American society without reading skills?

In 1982 the Census Bureau tested the basic reading ability of a sample of adult Americans; Table 17.1 on page 467 reproduces several of the questions. The researchers found that 13 percent of the sample was illiterate in English (9 percent of those whose native language is English and 48 percent of those whose native language is not English). Of the native English speakers who were unable to answer at least 20 of 26 simple questions, 70 percent had not completed high school and 42 percent had earned no money in the year before they were tested (Werner, 1986).

The ability of the United States to compete in the world economy is damaged by the illiteracy or limited literacy of many of its citizens. Nor are college students exempt. A 1986 study commissioned by the U.S. Department of Education found that one in three young adults with a college degree from a two- or four-year school failed to answer this question correctly: "If one purchases a sandwich for $1.95 and a bowl of soup for 60 cents, and gives the cashier $3, how much change should he receive?" The answer is 45 cents (Kiresch and Jungeblut, 1986). Although Americans live in a high-tech world, a National Science Foundation poll of 1,992 adults revealed that only 19 percent of us know that a phone converts sound into electric energy; only 24 percent know how computer software operates, and only 31 percent can explain radiation accurately (Rothschild, 1986). As the United States moves increasingly toward a service economy, in which people have to be able to read and assimilate information, it becomes imperative that its people acquire basic competencies and skills. The educational institution is usually assigned this responsibility.

PLANNING AHEAD: TARGETED READING

1. What functions does the educational institution play in modern societies?

2. How does the educational institution benefit some people at the expense of others?

3. How is the educational system linked to the stratification system?

4. What have been the effects of school desegregation on American youth?

5. How available is higher education to all Americans?

6. What makes for effective schools?

7. In what ways is the American undergraduate college a "troubled institution"?

Perspectives on Education

Most of us have a substantial stake in the educational enterprise. The reason is not difficult to come by: Learning is a fundamental mechanism for adapting to our environment. As we saw in Chapter 6, *learning* involves a more or less permanent modification in behavior that results from experience. Since learning is critical to social life, societies do not leave it to chance. Many societies transmit certain attitudes, knowledge, and skills to their members through formal, systematic training—the institution we call **education.** Some people assume the status of teacher and others the status of student, and both carry out their associated roles. Education is one aspect of the many-sided process of socialization by which people acquire those behaviors essential for effective participation in a society. Both the functionalist and conflict perspectives are in agreement on the importance of education, but they differ in their conception of the part it plays in modern life.

The Functionalist Perspective

Schools came into existence several thousand years ago in advanced horticultural and agricultural societies to prepare a select few for leadership and professional positions (see Chapter 3). Until the last century or so, no society could afford more than a handful of educated people. With the emergence of large-scale industrial and bureaucratic organizations, however, came a need for an abundant supply of literate and educated people. The school system became the primary vehicle by which a nation's citizens were taught the three Rs, and higher education became the custodian of a nation's intellectual capital. Education today is a crucial investment in the economy, and a major economic resource. It has also become a major military resource; today it is the classrooms of higher education that give a nation its advantage in the struggle for military preeminence. Throughout the world, schools are increasingly being viewed as a branch of the state and as serving state purposes (Carnoy and Levin, 1985; Ramirez and Boli, 1987). Functionalists elaborate on this portrayal of the schools, depicting education as an essential modern-day institution.

Completing socialization Many preliterate and peasant societies lack schools. They socialize their youngsters in the same "natural" way that parents teach their children to walk or talk. Anthropologist Farley Mowat (1952) describes the process among the Ihalmiut, an Eskimo

**Table 17.1   13 Percent of Adult Americans Failed This Test:
Sample Questions Given to 3,400 Adults in 1982 by the Census Bureau**

Directions: Choose the answer that means the same as the word or phrase with a line under it.

We cannot see you today. <u>When can you return</u>?
  a. When was the last time you came?
  b. Who should you call when you come?
  c. On what date can you come again?
  d. Are those the papers you can return?

<u>Enter</u> your Social Security number here.
  a. Find
  b. Check
  c. Show
  d. Write

Directions: Choose the best answer to the question.

You should ask a friend or relative to help you fill out the forms if you cannot read or understand the application.

What should you do if you do not understand the questions on the application form?
  a. Answer all the questions by writing "None."
  b. Return the application unsigned.
  c. Write to the notary public.
  d. Ask a friend or relative to help you.

Directions: Read all of the paragraph first. Draw a line under the best word or phrase to complete each sentence.

Soon, you'll receive a new medical services program identification card. It will replace all other medical _____.
  a. bills
  b. cards
  c. types
  d. checks
Before using the card you must sign _____ on the back. Don't allow your
  a. the
  b. it
  c. on
  d. a
medical identification card to _____ by
  a. be used
  b. have destroy
  c. go lose
  d. get expired
any other person.

people. If an Ihalmiut boy indicates he wishes to become a hunter, a great hunter, all at once, his parents do not make him feel foolish; nor do they condescend to his childish fancy. Instead, his father sets to work to make a small bow that is an efficient weapon on a reduced scale. The father then presents the boy with the bow and the boy

. . . sets out for his hunting grounds—a ridge, perhaps, a hundred yards away, with the time-honored words of good luck ringing in his ears. These are the same words which are spoken by the People to their mightiest hunter when he starts on a two-month trip for musk ox. . . . There is no distinction, and this lack of distinction is not a pretense; it is perfectly real. The boy wants to be a

The Absence of a Formal Educational Institution
Here Indian youngsters of the Venezuelan Amazon learn to make blow guns by observing their fathers and experimenting with the bamboo. They acquire the content of culture mostly in an informal, unconscious manner in the course of daily living. In societies characterized by rapid change, the transmission of critical knowledge and skills can no longer take place simply in this way. Adults cannot afford to shape their children in their own image, because the adults often find themselves with obsolete skills. (*Jacques Jangoux/ Peter Arnold*)

hunter? Very well, he shall be a hunter—not a boy with toy bow! . . . When he returns at last with hunger gnawing at his stomach, he is greeted gravely as if he were his father. The whole camp wishes to hear about his hunt. He can expect the same ridicule at failure, or the same praise if he managed to kill a little bird, which would come to a full-grown man. [Mowat, 1952:156–157]

The content of culture among the Ihalmiut is quite similar for everyone, and people acquire it mostly through daily living. Unlike the Ihalmiut, adults in modern societies cannot afford to shape their children in their own image. Too often parents find themselves with obsolete skills, trained for jobs that are no longer needed. The knowledge and skills required by contemporary living cannot be satisfied in a more or less automatic and "natural" way. Instead, a specialized educational agency is needed to transmit to the young the ways of thinking, feeling, and acting required by a rapidly changing urban and technologically based society.

Social integration   Functionalists say that the educational system functions to instill the dominant values of a society and shape a common national mind. Within the United States, students learn what it means to be an American, become literate in the English language, gain a common heritage, and acquire mainstream standards and rules. Youngsters from diverse ethnic, religious, and racial backgrounds are immersed within the same Anglo-American culture and prepared for "responsible" citizen-

ship. Historically, the nation's schools have played a prominent part in Americanizing the children of immigrants, helping to stamp out "alien" ways and assimilate the youngsters within American life. Likewise, the schools are geared to integrating the poor and disadvantaged within the fabric of dominant, mainstream institutions. How well the educational institution performs these functions is a debatable matter.

Screening and selecting   As we noted in Chapter 4, all societies ascribe some statuses to people independent of their unique qualities or abilities. Other statuses are achieved through choice and competition. No society ignores individual differences or overlooks individual accomplishment and failure. Modern societies in partic-

"It may be society's report card, but it has your name on it."

Cartoon by Randy Glasbergen

ular must select certain youths for positions that require special talents. The educational institution commonly performs this function, serving as an agency for screening and selecting individuals for different types of jobs. By conferring degrees, diplomas, and credentials that are prerequisites for many technical, managerial, and professional positions, it determines which young people will have access to scarce positions and offices of power, privilege, and status. For many Americans, the schools function as "mobility escalators," allowing gifted people to ascend the social ladder.

Research and development   For the most part, schools are designed to produce people who fit into society, not people who set out to change it. However, schools, particularly universities, may not only transmit culture; they may add to the cultural heritage. Contemporary American society places a good deal of emphasis on the development of new knowledge, especially in the physical and biological sciences, medicine, and engineering. In recent decades, the nation's leading universities have increasingly become research centers. Indeed, by virtue of their research roles, some 88 colleges and universities are among the top 500 contractors for the U.S. Department of Defense (in 1985, the Massachusetts Institute of Technology was the fourteenth leading contractor, with contracts of $360 million, and Johns Hopkins University, with $304 million, was ranked eighteenth). Nearly two-thirds of the $9.6 billion spent on research done on college campuses in 1985 came from the federal government (see Table 17.2 on page 470).

An emphasis on research has led universities to judge professors not primarily in terms of their competence as teachers, but as researchers. Promotions, salary increases, and other benefits are usually dependent on research and publication, with "publish or perish" and "publish and prosper" the governing tenets of university life. Critics contend that academic success is most likely to come to those who have learned to "neglect" their teaching duties to pursue research activities. Defenders say that even when students are not themselves involved in research projects, they benefit from the intellectual stimulation that a research orientation brings to university life.

Latent functions   Schools perform a good many latent functions, consequences that may not be recognized or intended (see Chapter 2). Within American life, the educational institution performs a number of these functions. First, it provides a custodial or babysitting service,

keeping youngsters from under the feet of adults and the wheels of automobiles (as the number of households in which both parents work increases, pressure has mounted to start public schooling at age 4 and to have the schools provide supervised settings for latchkey youngsters before and after school). Second, schools serve as a marriage market, providing young people with opportunities to select mates of similar class and social background. Third, schools provide settings in which students develop a variety of interpersonal skills needed for entering into friendships, participating in community affairs, and relating to others in the workplace. Fourth, the age segregation of students in school environments encourages the formation of youth subcultures. Finally, formal compulsory education keeps children and adolescents out of the labor market and so out of competition with adults for jobs.

The Conflict Perspective

Conflict theorists say the educational institution reproduces and legitimates the current social order. By doing so, it serves some people at the expense of others (Collins, 1977, 1979).

Reproducing the social relations of production   As portrayed by some conflict theorists, American schools promote capitalist arrangements by popularizing the idea that private ownership and profit are just and benefit the entire society (Apple, 1982; Apple and Weis, 1983; Carnoy and Levin, 1985). But the schools do even more for the privileged. In *Schooling and Capitalist America* (1976), Samuel Bowles and Herbert Gintis contend the social relations of work find expression in the social relations of the school—what they call the **correspondence principle.** They say schools mirror the workplace and on a day-to-day basis prepare children for adult roles in the job market. The authoritarian structure of the school reproduces the bureaucratic hierarchy of the corporation by rewarding diligence, submissiveness, and compliance; and the system of grades employed to motivate students parallels the wage system for motivating workers. The schools, then, socialize a compliant labor force for the capitalist economy. And like their counterparts in industry, students experience alienation (see Chapter 15). Robert B. Everhart (1983) found that junior high students suffer boredom from having their labor controlled by others, yet are collectively unaware of the source of their discontent.

Table 17.2   The Top Research Colleges and Universities
Fiscal 1985 research and development spending, in millions of dollars

Institution	Total Spending	Percent U.S. Govt.	Percent State and Local Govts.	Percent Industry	Percent Institutional	Percent Other
1 Johns Hopkins	$ 388.6	94%	*	0%	1%	4%
2 MIT	243.0	78	*	13	*	8
3 Univ. of Wisconsin (Madison)	208.4	60	18%	3	13	6
4 Cornell	203.2	59	14	6	11	10
5 Stanford	199.2	87	*	4	4	5
6 Univ. of Minnesota	173.3	51	11	5	22	11
7 Univ. of Washington	164.0	83	1	5	3	8
8 Univ. of Michigan	163.7	65	1	7	22	5
9 Univ. of Calif., Berkeley	149.9	65	1	0	26	8
10 Univ. of Calif., Los Angeles	149.7	73	*	0	13	13
11 Texas A & M	146.4	49	36	8	2	5
12 Univ. of Calif., San Diego	145.6	79	*	0	10	10
13 Univ. of Illinois (Urbana)	139.6	58	13	5	21	3
14 Harvard	137.7†	75	*	4	6	14
15 Columbia (main division)	136.6	88	*	3	1	7
16 Univ. of Calif., San Francisco	131.3	73	2	0	12	13
17 Univ. of Pennsylvania	130.4	71	*	3	11	15
18 Univ. of Texas (Austin)	123.3	51	4	2	33	10
19 Univ. of Calif., Davis	114.9	41	3	0	46	10
20 Penn State	113.2	62	4	14	20	*
21 Yale	107.2	83	3	2	11	2
22 Univ. of Arizona	105.8	49	1	9	36	5
23 Ohio State	103.4	51	12	7	17	13
24 USC	97.3	79	*	6	14	*
25 Univ. of Maryland (College Park)	96.5	41	28	9	22	0
Total (all institutions)	$9,503.7	63%	7%	6%	17%	7%

*Less than 1%   †Estimated

Source: National Science Foundation, 1986.

The hidden curriculum   In the eyes of conflict theorists, the *hidden curriculum* of the schools also serves the interests of economic elites. As we noted in Chapter 6, the hidden curriculum consists of a set of unarticulated values, attitudes, and behaviors that subtly mold children in the image of the dominant institutions. Teachers model and reinforce traits that embody middle-class standards—industry, responsibility, conscientiousness, reliability, thoroughness, self-control, and efficiency. Children learn to be quiet, to be punctual, to line up, to wait their turn, to please their teachers, and to conform to group pressures. In short, schools bridge the intimate and accepting structure found in many families and the demanding, impersonal structure of the larger society.

Control devices   Conflict theorists agree with functionalist theorists that schools are agencies for drawing minorities and the disadvantaged into the dominant culture. But they do not see the function in benign terms. Sociologist Randall Collins (1976) contends that the educational system serves the interests of the dominant group by defusing the threat posed by minority ethnic groups. In large, conflict-ridden, multi-ethnic societies like the United States and the Soviet Union, schools

Are Schools Mirrors of the Workplace? Paternalistic control was firmly in place in American high schools by 1940. The fortress-like architecture of the buildings and the hall passes required of students reminded teachers and students alike that submissiveness and propriety were the order of the day. Conflict theorists contend that this atmosphere sought to develop a compliant labor force for the capitalist economy. *(Betsy Cole/The Picture Cube)*

become instruments to "Americanize" or "Sovietize" minority peoples. Compulsory education erodes ethnic differences and loyalties and transmits to minorities and those at the bottom of the social hierarchy the values and lifeways of the dominant group. Schools, then, are viewed as control devices.

Productive capital Conflict theorists see the research and development function of the universities quite differently than do functionalist theorists. For instance, Michael W. Apple (1982) gives a Marxist twist to the functionalist argument by contending that the educational institution produces the technical and administrative knowledge necessary for running a capitalist order. Viewed in this manner, education is part of the system of production. It not only reproduces existing social arrangements, but develops the knowhow needed by capitalists to fuel the economy and gain a competitive advantage in world markets. Although some colleges have always had ties to business, according to a recent National Academy of Sciences report, there has been "a virtual explosion over the past several years in the number and variety of university-industry alliances." Universities are entering research agreements with companies, setting up research parks, and encouraging the founding of new high-tech businesses on campus (Main, 1987; Kenney, 1987). Moreover, universities serve as research centers for the defense establishment. Recently, universities have been pressured to participate in the Strategic Defense Initiative (SDI), despite a consensus within the scientific community that the Star Wars enterprise is technically flawed and incapable of providing a perfect space shield against enemy missiles (Piel, 1986).

A Hidden Curriculum? Children do not only learn the formal subject matter provided by their teachers. From their teachers' comments, children learn that they should be punctual, write legibly, not waste paper, and be quiet when authority figures are speaking. In group games, they learn that they should take turns and play fairly. From the total setting, they gain considerable experience in social control: Teachers restrict their behavior, subject them to supervision, put them through various drills, and require that they fit themselves into a regimen that they do not control. *(Charles Gupton/Southern Light)*

Credentialism   Collins (1979) also downplays the functionalist contention that schools serve as mobility escalators. He cites evidence showing that students acquire little technical knowledge in school and learn technical skills on the job. Although employers demand more and more schooling from job applicants, Collins says that this trend is not explained by the changing technical requirements of work. The level of skill required by typists, receptionists, salesclerks, teachers, assembly-line workers, and many others differs little from that of a generation or so ago. Collins calls these tendencies **credentialism**—the requirement that a worker have a degree attesting to skills not dictated by the job. By virtue of credentialism, education functions more as a certification of class membership than of technical skills, and so it becomes a means of class inheritance.

Whereas at one time a college degree brought an elite occupational status with elite pay, today it brings a middle-class status with middle-class pay. There has been a progressive reduction in the occupational and income return for each year of education (Featherman and Hauser, 1978; Jencks et al., 1979). Conflict theorists portray junior and community colleges as an extension of the public school tracking system, keeping minority and working-class youngsters at the same class level as their parents (Karabel, 1977). These youths are led to believe that a junior college or community college education will increase their chances for upward mobility. Yet their schooling does not typically bring opportunities for corporate or professional careers. For instance, fewer than 10 percent of the students who enroll at one of California's 106 two-year community colleges (with 1.1 million students in 1985) complete a two-year program and move on to a four-year college (Lindsey, 1985). In short, as the population gains more education, the relative position of different groups in the stratification system remains basically the same.

> **THINKING THROUGH THE ISSUES**
>
> College instructors often complain about the passiveness of their students and the difficulty they have stimulating them intellectually. A favorite student question is, "Do we need to know this for the exam?" Why are students so concerned with tests? Does the lecture format encourage discussion or intellectual curiosity? Notice how the classroom is laid out. Students are placed in rows of undifferentiated seats, often bolted to the floor. What message does this give students? How does this seating arrangement discourage egalitarian exchanges in a classroom? A solid table or lectern typically sets the instructor apart from the students. What does this tell students? In sum, how do teaching practice and the structure of the American classroom encourage student passivity?

Education and Social Inequality

Education is simultaneously linked forward and backward to the stratification system (see Chapter 9). It is linked forward through the effects schooling has on the occupational placement of upcoming generations. It is linked backward in time to a preexisting system of stratification through the ways in which social class, gender, and race affect school achievement. Often, these links join over time to form a circle of low social rank leading to unfavorable educational opportunities and then on to low rank, or of high social rank leading to favorable educational opportunities and then on to high rank. At other times, education breaks the circle and fosters social mobility. The issue, then, is one of weighting: To what extend does education serve as a vehicle of social inheritance (stabilizing social rankings across generations) compared to its role as a mechanism of social mobility (placing children in different statuses from those of their parents)?

Class, Race, and Education

It certainly is no secret that occupational success is related to educational achievement. As Table 17.3 shows, those with college educations generally get the best jobs,

Table 17.3   How Education Raises Income, 1986

Education, Head of Household	Median Household Income
Less than high school	$13,900
High school graduate	24,300
1–3 years of college	28,800
4 years of college	37,500
5 or more years of college	45,900

Source: U.S. Bureau of the Census.

as reflected in wealth, power, and prestige. A cross-section study of 20,000 American men found that the proportion of those who experience intergenerational upward mobility increases steadily with education—from 12 percent of those who have little schooling, to 76 percent of those who go on to graduate or professional school (Blau and Duncan, 1972). Education's forward link to adult placement, then, is strong. So is its backward link to family position. As we pointed out in Chapter 9, a family's socioeconomic position affects how far youths will go in schooling and how well they will perform in school. Families influence the careers of their children by socializing them to high educational and occupational aspirations and by providing them with the support necessary for achieving these aspirations (Sewell, 1981). Early schooling experiences are especially important. Although early academic success does not assure later success, early academic failure strongly predicts later academic failure (Temple and Polk, 1986).

On average, the higher the social class of children's families, the greater will be the number of formal grades the children complete. This pattern holds even for youngsters of above-average ability. According to data from the Census Bureau, in 1980 the college-going rate for *medium*-ability but wealthy youths was 89 percent;

high-ability but low-wealth high school graduates attended college at a 70 percent rate. Wealthy youths of *low* ability went to college at a rate of 54 percent (Hodgkinson, 1986). Other measures also show that the higher the socioeconomic status of students' families, the more academic honors and awards the children are likely to receive, the more elective offices they are likely to hold, and the greater the children's participation in extracurricular activities is likely to be. In sum, success depends heavily on the socioeconomic position of one's family of origin (Kerckoff, 1985). Sociologists have offered a number of explanations for these patterns, including a middle-class bias in schools, subcultural differences among students, and educational self-fulfilling prophecies.

Middle-class bias   Most American teachers, regardless of social origin, fit into middle-class life and share its outlook on such matters as ambition, cleanliness, punctuality, respect for property and established authority, sexual morality, and neatness. It is little wonder, then, that schools succeed reasonably well with middle- and upper-class youngsters. In contrast, middle-class teachers, without necessarily being aware of their prejudice,

Equality of Opportunity?
Americans have traditionally viewed education as the road to opportunity and upward mobility. Functionalists have portrayed the schools as "mobility" escalators. But conflict theorists say schools guarantee that the sons and daughters of the elite—having attended the "best" schools and having acquired the "proper" credentials—secure the best positions. *(left, Bohdan Hrynewyck/Stock, Boston; right, Kit Hedman/Jeroboam)*

often see children from other backgrounds as unacceptable—different and even depressing. Their students frequently respond by taking the attitude "If you don't like me, I won't cooperate with you." And so many youngsters fail to acquire basic reading, writing, and math skills.

Subcultural differences   Subcultural differences also play a part. Middle- and upper-class parents usually make it clear to their children that they are *expected* to apply themselves to school tasks. Their children typically enter school already possessing a variety of skills that children from other backgrounds lack, including conceptions regarding books, crayons, pencils, drawing paper, numbers, and the alphabet. Perhaps even more important, middle-class children are much more likely than lower-class youngsters to have the conviction that they can affect their environments and their futures (Friend and Neale, 1972; Stephens and Delys, 1973). Children who speak Spanish or black English find themselves doubly handicapped in schools where standard English is used (Seitz, 1975; Gay and Tweney, 1975).

Educational self-fulfilling prophecies   Finally, lower-class and minority children are often the victims of **educational self-fulfilling prophecies** or *teacher-expectation effects*. They frequently fail to learn because those who are charged with teaching them do not believe that they will learn, do not expect that they can learn, and do not act toward them in ways that help them to learn (Clark, 1965; Crano and Mellon, 1978; Dusek, 1985). Researchers find that teachers' assessments of students are affected by the stereotypes the teachers hold of racial groups and social classes. In general, white teachers rate white students higher than either their black or their Hispanic counterparts (Jensen and Rosenfeld, 1974). Nor are schools or districts equal in the learning opportunities they provide, particularly in facilities, equipment, and teacher quality. Black and Hispanic students are disadvantaged by schools in very much the same ways that their communities are disadvantaged in their interactions with major societal institutions (Cummins, 1986; Dreeben and Gamoran, 1986). Minority and lower-class students often respond by dropping out. Hispanics have the highest high school dropout rate—19.1 percent—compared to 17.2 percent for blacks and 13.0 percent for whites. Overall, youths from low-income families are three times as likely to drop out of high school as are youths from high-income families (Riche, 1986). These patterns highlight the social context in which schooling occurs and raise questions regarding the effectiveness of schools, how they are effective, for whom, and for how many.

THINKING THROUGH THE ISSUES

Consider that 3.6 million 4-year-olds are now moving toward becoming a freshman class of higher education in the early twenty-first century. About a fourth of them live below the poverty line. One-third are nonwhite. Eighteen percent are born out of wedlock, and more than 45 percent will be raised by a single parent before they reach 18 years of age. A higher percentage of 4-year-olds today than in the past do not speak English. Twenty percent of the girls among the 4-year-olds will become pregnant during their teen years. Armed with this information, what can the public schools and higher education do to equip the nation's youth with the skills and knowledge necessary to function effectively in a college environment? Examine your own background and attempt to identify the factors that handicapped or advantaged you.

Effects of School Desegregation

In 1954 the United States Supreme Court ruled in *Brown* v. *Board of Education* that mandatory school segregation is unconstitutional. It said that separate schools for black and white children are inherently unequal. Today, three decades later, a fifth of the nation's black students attend schools that are almost all black in enrollment and more than half still attend schools in which the majority of students are black. The greatest difficulty in achieving desegregation is that black children typically outnumber white children in big cities and that each race is concentrated in different neighborhoods. Let us examine some of the effects of school desegregation.

Academic achievement   During the 1950s, a rather naive optimism pervaded the scientific community. It assumed that school desegregation would almost automatically improve the education of black youth. The voluminous Coleman Report, which appeared in 1966, seemed to support this conclusion. The study, funded by Congress, involved tests and surveys of 645,000 pupils and 60,000 teachers in 4,000 schools. The data from the work of sociologist James S. Coleman and his associates suggested that the academic achievement of blacks rose as the proportion of white students in a school increased. Many social scientists concluded that this was due to the higher levels of educational motivation present in predominantly white student bodies—*the lateral transmission of values thesis* (Maruyama, Miller, and Holtz, 1986). Accordingly to this view, black students acquire the achievement-oriented values held by whites when immersed within predominantly white schools. Black critics immediately challenged this interpretation. They contended that it is not the presence of white children by itself that leads to a higher achievement for black children; it is the quality of the education that white community leaders provide *because* white children are in these schools that makes the difference. A growing body of findings supports this contention (Patchen, 1982; Dreeben and Gamoran, 1986).

Studies investigating the impact of desegregation on student achievement turn up more positive than negative effects in the performance of minority students and, in general, no effect on that of white students (Longshore and Prager, 1985). Black achievement seems most enhanced when desegregation occurs at the earliest grades (Crain and Mahard, 1983). Even so, the effects of desegregation on black children's achievement are not uniform. This is because other factors, such as socioeconomic status, family background, degree of racial tension in the community, and interracial acceptance in the schools, also play a part (Schofield, 1982; Miller and Brewer, 1984). There is much more to effective integration than simply mixing children from different racial backgrounds (Epstein, 1985; Damico and Sparks, 1986).

Schools do not teach just academic skills; they also socialize youngsters for membership in the larger society. One of the long-term consequences of racial segregation is its tendency to become self-perpetuating. School segregation leads blacks and whites to mistrust and avoid one another, attitudes and patterns that in adulthood solidify racial separation. The reverse situation also holds: School desegregation contributes to desegregation in later life. Blacks who attend racially mixed schools are more likely than those who attend predominantly black schools to graduate from high school, attend predominantly white colleges, complete more years of college, have more frequent social contact with whites outside school, and live in desegregated neighborhoods as adults (Braddock, Crain, and McPartland, 1984; Braddock, 1985).

White flight   Popular belief holds that school desegregation has contributed to "white flight" from big cities and is fostering resegregation of urban school districts. Yet the evidence in support of this view is mixed. For one thing, white migration from central cities is a long-term trend that predated school desegregation (see Chapter 20). For another, in many cities the same level of white outmigration can be observed whether or not the cities have implemented desegregation plans (Willie, 1984). Much depends on the conditions under which desegregation occurs. It seems that school desegregation accelerates the long-term decline in white public school enrollment in the year of implementation if a school district is above 30 to 35 percent black or if it involves the reassignment of whites to formerly black schools. Even

How Is School Desegregation to Be Achieved?

More than 30 years after the Supreme Court ruled mandatory school segregation unconstitutional, most of the nation's black youths still attend predominantly black schools. Courts have redrawn school-district boundaries, altered school locations, scrutinized transfer policies, reassigned students, and ordered busing as remedies to correct racial imbalances in the schools. But the considerable chasm between minorities in central cities and whites in suburbs has frustrated efforts to achieve integration. Schools mirror the racial patterns of the larger society. (*Susan Lapides/Design Conceptions*)

so, metropolitan plans (involving a central city and its suburbs) result in less "white flight" than city-only plans (Hawley, 1979; Longshore and Prager, 1985; Wilson, 1985).

Conclusions   The failure to bring about many of the hoped-for benefits of desegregation is not surprising, because schools mirror the patterns of the larger society. Moreover, it is unreasonable to expect the schools to undo what the larger society continually reestablishes in its daily operation. An intriguing current runs below the surface in virtually all school desegregation research. There are indications that desegregation works if people really want it to work, and there are disturbing signs of ulterior motives for not really wanting it to work. We need to abandon the simplistic question "Does desegregation work?" and study the *conditions* for effective desegregation. We need to find out a good deal more about how students learn in interracial settings.

Availability of Higher Education

The average tuition charges for public and private four-year colleges have more than doubled since 1977 (since 1980, the costs of a college education have surged ahead at twice the rate of inflation)(Solorzano, 1987). There are many reasons for this. For one thing, education is a labor-intensive industry, with about three-quarters of a college's budget going for faculty and staff salaries. Yet compared with other professionals, college professors do not seem overpaid. In 1987, full professors earned an average of $45,530 a year; assistant professors made $27,920, less than most executive secretaries (Heller, 1987). Indeed, college faculty members make 19 percent *less* than they did in 1971, adjusting for inflation. Other costs have also mounted. Utility bills, for example, have doubled over the past decade. And years of deferred maintenance have meant growing costs to keep buildings open and facilities working (Williams, 1985).

As reflected in Table 17.4, some 47 percent of male students and 51 percent of female students now work full-time. Additionally, by 1986 more than 3.4 million college students were receiving financial help from federally sponsored programs, primarily in the form of loans. In 1987, on average, students at public four-year colleges graduated with $6,685 in loans; those at private four-year colleges with $8,950 (Evangelauf, 1987). Student debt was substantially higher for those graduating from professional schools: about $30,000 for new doctors

Table 17.4   Percentage of Full- and Part-time Students in the Labor Force, 1985

Fall Survey	Men		Women	
	Full-time	*Part-time*	*Full-time*	*Part-time*
1960	32%	97%	20%	75%
1965	35%	96%	23%	73%
1970	41%	97%	38%	75%
1975	45%	94%	41%	82%
1980	46%	96%	45%	85%
1985	47%	92%	51%	91%

Note: The figures in the table probably understate the proportion of students who work, because in recent years the Department of Labor has limited its survey to students aged 16 to 24, instead of those 16 to 34.

Source: U.S. Department of Labor.

and dentists, $25,000 for lawyers, $15,000 for MBAs, and $10,000 for new Ph.D.s (Fiske, 1986).

The cutback in federal subsidies during the Reagan administration has complicated the financial crunch for many students. Youths from middle-income, working-class, and minority families have been especially affected. According to the American Association of State Colleges and Universities, financial obstacles were taking a growing toll in the college enrollment of minority and disadvantaged students even prior to the cutback in federal funds (Ordovensky, 1985). Although more blacks and Hispanics have graduated from high school in recent years than in 1975, smaller percentages are attending college. Whereas 29 percent more blacks graduated from high school in 1982 than in 1975, black college enrollment fell 11 percent. During the same time period, the Hispanic high school graduation rate was up 38 percent, but enrollment in college was down 16 percent. In contrast, white high school graduates were up 7 percent, and white college enrollment was down less than 1 percent. The prevalence of such educational inequalities calls our attention to the structure of the American school system.

The American School System

Americans have a tremendous faith in the worth of education. For many, it is a magic carpet. Do we have social problems—crime, marital breakdown, drug addiction, teenage pregnancies, racial discrimination, poverty,

How Well Are They Doing?
A 1986 "report card" on the writing skills of students by the Educational Testing Service of Princeton, New Jersey, found:

Fewer than one-fourth of 11th graders perform adequately on writing tasks involving skills required for success in academic studies, business, or the professions.

Fewer than one-fourth of 11th graders can write a letter to their principals offering adequate reasons for changing a school rule.

Three-fourths of students say an ability to write is not necessary to get a job.
(Joel Gordon)

war? Then let us educate people! This appeal to "education" as a cure-all for social problems is deeply rooted in the ideology of American life. Many Americans stand in awe of education and of those individuals who enjoy its trappings. The rawest Ph.D. can often command a deference in the community at large that would be inconceivable on a college campus. Expenditures for education are also impressive, with schools consuming a large share of local tax expenditures. Attendance at elementary and secondary schools is compulsory. And comparatively speaking, our colleges and universities are richly endowed. Foreign travelers comment that in American towns the local school or college dominates the scene much as the cathedral dominates the towns of Latin America and Western Europe.

Along with a strong faith in education has also gone a considerable distrust—a sort of Dr. Jekyll and Mr. Hyde image. Americans often attack education as "too impractical," as too expensive, as corrosive of established beliefs and values, and as preoccupied with fads and frills. Education in general receives much acclaim; education in particular is the object of widespread criticism and low esteem. Teacher salaries tend to be low, and the public school teacher has a social rank that does not correspond with his or her years of education. The image of educators, especially those in higher education, is that of impractical visionaries who could not meet the competition of the less protected world of practical affairs. Even so, educators continue to be called on to serve in critical government positions, a fact that reflects the

ambivalence underlying American attitudes toward education and educators (Williams, 1960).

The Formal Structure of Schools

Until a few generations ago, schooling in the United States usually took place in a one-room schoolhouse. One teacher taught all eight grades, with the more advanced and older students helping the less capable and younger students with their lessons. So long as the schools remained relatively small, they could operate on the basis of face-to-face interaction. But like hospitals, factories, and businesses, schools grew larger and more complex. In order to attain their goals, they had to standardize and routinize many of their operations and establish formal operating and administrative procedures. So school officials turned increasingly to the bureaucratic arrangement, a social structure made up of a hierarchy of statuses and roles defined by explicit rules and procedures and based on a division of function and authority.

Like other complex organizations, schools do not exist in a vacuum, but are tightly connected to other institutions. At the very top of this organizational arrangement is the federal government, which through a variety of agencies, including the Department of Education and the federal court system, profoundly influences educational life. Consider, for instance, court rulings in desegregation cases and recent policies mandating practices relating to the education of handicapped children. State educational authorities also provide standards and regulations, like those setting the number of days in a school year, and they allocate state monies for specified programs.

The formal organization of American schools and colleges typically consists of four levels: (1) the board of education or trustees, (2) administrators, (3) teachers or professors, and (4) students. The control of most schools and colleges is vested in an elected or appointed board of laypeople. It generally appoints and assigns administrators and teachers, decides on the nature of curricular programs, determines building construction, and approves operational budgets. The administrators—superintendents, principals, presidents, chancellors, and deans—are responsible for executing the policies of the board. Although in theory the board determines policy, in actual practice many policy questions are settled by administrators. Teachers are the immediate day-to-day link between the larger system and individual students. The latter occupy the lowest position in the school bureaucracy. The school system, then, is characterized by a chain of command, a network of positions functionally interrelated for the purpose of accomplishing educational objectives.

School environments are remarkably standardized in physical and social characteristics. Physical objects, social relations, and major activities remain much the same from day to day, week to week, and even year to year. These patterns are most apparent at the elementary- and secondary-school levels. For instance, time is highly formalized. The pledge of allegiance is followed by math at 8:35, which is followed by reading at 9:10, which is followed by recess, and so on over the course of the day. There is almost a holy aura about the "daily grind." Additionally, individual behavior is rigidly governed by sets of rules—no loud talking during seat work, raise your hand to talk during discussions, keep your eyes on your paper during tests, and no running in the halls. The physical layout of the school and the omnipresent symbols of adult authority emphasize and reinforce the subordinate status of the pupils. Cloakrooms and lunchrooms have a special space reserved for the teachers. The system encourages student passivity and makes the school a relatively uninteresting place, resembling in many ways what sociologist Erving Goffman (1961) has termed a *total institution* (see Chapter 5).

Although there is much about the American school system that resembles the bureaucratic model, its structure is far from being rock-solid. For one thing, teachers enjoy considerable autonomy in what they do in the classroom. Teachers and their organizations have ad-

"No Arnold, you do not have the right to remain silent!"
From The Wall Street Journal; permission, Cartoon Features Syndicate

vanced and promoted a professional model that emphasizes the need for teachers to exercise discretion in planning, organizing, and conducting their work. Professionals stress the importance of developing strong personal relationships with their clients and doing the job that *they* feel is necessary (see Chapter 15). Countervailing forces are also at work. Students, parents, and community leaders make many facets of schooling precarious undertakings in which negotiated rules and informal understandings—not programmed routines—are the stuff of everyday social encounters. In many respects, the school is a "loosely coupled" system in which the components often take on an independent existence (Tyler, 1985).

The Effectiveness of the Schools

In recent years an outpouring of reports have decried the state of the American educational system. In 1983 *A Nation at Risk*, a product of a National Commission on Excellence in Education, set an alarmist tone that pointed to a "rising tide of mediocrity" in the schools. Others reports, criticisms, and recommendations followed. The National Task Force on Education for Economic Growth (1983) said "a real emergency is upon us"; a 1986 report by the secretary of education said that while elementary schools around the nation are in "pretty good shape" for the first three grades, large numbers of them are failing to do an adequate job in teaching the more complicated subject matter that begins around the fourth grade (Bennett, 1986); and the Carnegie Forum on Education and the Economy (1986) charged that, as currently structured, American schools are poorly equipped to provide workers for an increasingly technological society.

The reports mention many of the same indicators, including poor achievement test scores, a long-term fall in college entrance test scores (see Table 17.5), declines in both enrollments and achievement in science and mathematics, low levels of communication, writing, and critical-thinking skills, the poor performance of American students on international tests (see Table 17.6), the high cost incurred by business and the military for remedial and training programs, and the substantial levels of functional illiteracy among American adults and children.

Table 17.6   Twelfth-Grade Math Skills (Average percentage of correctly answered questions)

	U.S.	World*
Sets and relations	59%	62%
Number systems	45	50
Algebra	48	57
Geometry	37	42
Elementary functions/ calculus	36	44
Probability and statistics	45	50
Finite mathematics	36	44†

* In addition to the United States, the countries covered in the survey were Australia, Belgium, Canada, Chile, England, Finland, France, Hong Kong, Hungary, Ireland, Israel, Ivory Coast, Japan, Luxembourg, Netherlands, New Zealand, Nigeria, Scotland, Swaziland, Sweden, and Thailand.
† Estimated average score.
Source: Second International Mathematics Study, 1984.

Table 17.5   Average Scores on National College Entrance Examinations

Testing Year	ACT*	SAT†
1970	19.9	948
1971	19.2	943
1972	19.1	937
1973	19.2	926
1974	18.9	924
1975	18.6	906
1976	18.3	903
1977	18.4	899
1978	18.5	897
1979	18.6	894
1980	18.5	890
1981	18.5	890
1982	18.4	893
1983	18.3	893
1984	18.5	897
1985	18.6	906
1986	18.8	906

* The ACT (American College Testing Program Assessment) is scored on a scale of 1 to 36. The ACT test is used primarily by schools in Midwest, South, Southwest, Mountain, and Plains states.
† SAT's (Scholastic Aptitude Test) total possible score is 1,600. It is used primarily by elite colleges and universities on the East and West coasts.
Source: American College Testing Program and College Board.

A University of Michigan study shows that American schoolchildren lag behind children in Japan and Taiwan from the day they enter school (see Table 17.7 on page 480). The poorer performance of the American youngsters seems to be related to the way American schools manage instruction. For one thing, the average school year is shorter in the United States—180 days versus 240 in Japan and Taiwan—and the school day is a half hour to two hours shorter. Also, American children spend less than half as much time as the Taiwanese and less than two-thirds as much as the Japanese on academic activities. Cultural differences also appear to affect performance. Japanese and Taiwanese parents place greater emphasis than their American counterparts on the importance of children working hard at school and on homework. Despite the lower achievement levels of American children, parents in the United States are more satisfied with their children's schools than are parents in Japan and Taiwan (Stevenson, Lee, and Stigler, 1986). (See the box on page 482 dealing with the academic success of Asian-Americans in the United States.)

Social scientists have also examined what makes a school effective. Michael Rutter (1979) led a University of London team in a three-year study of students entering twelve London intercity secondary schools. The researchers found that schools only a scant distance apart and with students of similar social backgrounds and intellectual abilities had quite different educational results. The critical element distinguishing the schools was their

Table 17.7   Academic Achievement in the United States, Japan, and Taiwan

	Mean Number of Questions Answered Correctly		Percent of Class Time Spent on Reading	Percent of Class Time Spent on Math	Percent of the Time Students Paid Attention in Class
	Math	Reading Comprehension			
First Grade					
United States	17.1	21.3	50.6%	13.8%	45.3%
Japan	20.1	22.8	36.2	24.5	66.2
Taiwan	21.2	25.6	44.7	16.5	65.0
Fifth Grade					
United States	44.4	82.6	41.6	17.2	46.5
Japan	53.8	82.5	24.0	23.4	64.6
Taiwan	50.8	84.6	27.6	28.2	77.7

Source: Harold W. Stevenson, University of Michigan, 1984.

"ethos" or "climate." The successful schools fostered expectations that order would prevail in the classrooms; they did not leave matters of student discipline to be worked out by individual teachers. As a result, it was easier to be a good teacher in some schools than in others. Additionally, the effective schools emphasized academic concerns—care by teachers in lesson planning, group instruction, high achievement expectations for students, a high proportion of time spent on instruction and learning activities, the assignment and checking of homework, and student use of the library. The researchers also found that schools which fostered respect for students as responsible people and held high expectations for appropriate behavior achieved better academic results.

Other research confirms the conclusion successful schools foster expectations that order will prevail and that learning is a serious matter (Clark, Lotto, and McCarthy, 1980; Winn, 1981). Much of the success enjoyed by private and Catholic schools has derived from their ability to provide students with an ordered environment and strong academic demands (Coleman et al., 1982a; Jensen, 1986). Academic achievement is just as high in the public sector when the policies and resulting behavior are like those in the private sector (Coleman et al., 1982b). In sum, successful schools possess "coherence";

A Tokyo Public Primary School
The Japanese have produced educational results in basic competencies that place their average 18-year-old on a par with the average American college graduate. On achievement tests, the 50 percentile Japanese high-school student would score in the 98 percentile on an American examination. Japanese schools provide a more orderly, focused, and faster-paced education than do their American counterparts. However, American colleges and universities seem to do a better job than do those in Japan. *(J.P. Laffont/Sygma)*

things work together and have predictable relationships with one another.

Revamping the Ivory Tower

With the founding of Harvard University in 1636, American higher education came into being. In the intervening 350 or so years, higher education has evolved into a huge $100 billion a year enterprise. The 3,340 American colleges and universities with almost 700,000 faculty turn out 1.4 million graduates a year (Fiske, 1986). Like its public school counterparts, higher education has been the subject of reports warning that the quality of education is declining (Bloom, 1987). A recent study by the Carnegie Foundation for the Advancement of Teaching concludes that the American undergraduate college is a "troubled institution," as much in need of reform as public schools (Boyer, 1987).

The Carnegie report identifies eight "points of tension" that sap the vitality of the undergraduate experience:

A discontinuity between schools and higher education: Students find the transition to college haphazard and confusing. Many young people who go to college lack basic skills in reading, writing, and computation—essential prerequisites for academic success.

Confusion over goals: In a scramble for students and driven by marketplace demands, colleges have lost their sense of mission; a narrow vocationalism has come to dominate campus communities.

Divided loyalties among faculty members: Promotion and tenure hang on research and publication, but undergraduate education calls for a commitment to students and effective teaching.

Tensions between conformity and creativity in the classroom: An absence of vigorous intellectual exchange characterizes most classrooms. Faculty members complain about the passivity of students whose interest is stirred only when they are reminded that the material will be covered on a test.

Gulf between spheres of campus life: A great separation divides academic and social life, especially in resident hall living.

Disagreement over how the college should be governed: College administrators are caught in the crossfire of conflicting pressures and groups; faculty feel greater loyalty to their discipline than to the institutions where they teach; and students only sporadically involve themselves in campus governance.

Debate over how a successful college education should be measured. Increasingly, educators, lawmakers, parents, and students are wondering just how much is being learned in the nation's colleges.

A disturbing gap between the college and the larger world: An intellectual and social isolation dominates higher education, reducing the effectiveness of faculty and limiting the vision of students.

The Carnegie Foundation report says that many colleges have tried to be "all things to all people" (see the box on big-time college sports). In doing so, they have increasingly catered to a parochial careerism while failing to cultivate a global vision among their students. The current crisis, it contends, does not derive from a legitimate desire to put learning to productive ends. The problem is that in too many academic fields, the work has no context; skills, rather than being means, have become ends. Students are offered a smorgasbord of options and allowed to pick their way to a degree. In short, driven by careerism, "the nation's colleges and universities are more successful in credentialing than in providing a quality education for their students." The report concludes that the special challenge confronting the undergraduate college is one of shaping an "integrated core" of common learning. Such a core would introduce students "to essential knowledge, to connections across the disciplines, and in the end, to application of knowledge to life beyond the campus."

Although the key to a good college is a high-quality faculty, the Carnegie study found that most colleges do very little to encourage good teaching. In fact, they do much to undermine it. As one professor observed: "Teaching is important, we are told, and yet faculty know that research and publication matter most." Not surprisingly, over the last twenty years colleges and universities have failed to graduate half of their four-year degree candidates (all the while, high schools are severely criticized for graduating only three-fourths of their students). Faculty members who dedicate themselves to teaching soon discover that they will not be granted tenure, promotions, or substantial salary increases. Yet 70 percent of all faculty say their interests lie more in teaching than in research. Additionally, a frequent complaint among young scholars is that "There is pressure to publish, although there is virtually no interest among ad-

ISSUES THAT SHAPE OUR LIVES

What Can We Learn from the Academic Success of Asian-Americans?

"Thank God for the Asians," exclaims a middle-aged Eastern suburbanite. "They're bringing back standards to our schools. And they're so successful in small businesses. It all happened overnight. How do you explain it?"

Does Good Parenting Make a Difference?
Sociologists and psychologists find that the quality of the parent-infant relationship plays a key part in children's early cognitive and language competence.
(Adam Stoltman/Duomo)

(Oxnam, 1986; 72). Sociologists have asked the same question. Although a scant 2.1 percent of the United States population is Asian, they account for 12 percent of the 1986 freshman class at Harvard, 19 percent at the Massachussets Institute of Technology, and 20 percent at the University of California at Berkeley. In 1986, the Westinghouse Science Talent Search, probably the nation's most prestigious high school science contest, awarded all five of its top scholarships to Asians.

One explanation for the success of Asian-Americans lies in the Confucian ethic that still infuses China, Korea, Japan, and Vietnam. The Confucian legacy—an ethical code rather than a religion—centers on tightly knit families, discipline, and a high respect for all forms of learning. Children have the strong support and encouragement of their families throughout their schooling. In turn, children work hard to bring honor to their families. Educational commitment often takes on the properties of an obsession. "When I was second-highest on a test," recalls Agnes Lin, now a professor of educational psychology, "my father scolded me for not trying hard enough. When I was first, he said the test was too easy" (Oxnam, 1986:88).

In some respects, Asian-Americans are similar to the Jewish immigrants of the 1930s and 1940s, who also emphasized family values, education, and advancement in American life. A survey in the San Francisco area found that male Asian-Americans spend an average of 11.7 hours a week doing homework, compared with 8 hours for whites and 6.3 hours for blacks. Among females, the figures are 12.3 hours a week for Asian-Americans, 8.6 for whites, and 9.2 for blacks. Asian-Americans are more likely than other ethnic groups to enroll in college-preparatory courses, earn more total high school credits, and take more courses in science, math, and foreign languages. Not surprisingly, San Francisco's Asian-Americans get consistently better grades than other students regardless of their parents' level of education or their families' social and economic status. However, the highest level of academic performance typically comes in the first and second generation. By the third generation, more socialized in American ways, many Asian-American youths seem less interested in school (Butterfield, 1986).

Another explanation for Asian-American success is that the children are the offspring of a unique group of immigrants, drawn largely from the intellectual and professional elites of their native lands. The first of these groups were students from China who remained in the United States after the Communist triumph there in 1949. Later, many middle-class and well-educated Vietnamese fled to the United States on the Communist takeover of South Vietnam. All the while there has also been a brain-drain of engineers, physicians, and scientists

ministrators or colleagues in the content of the publications" (Hechinger, 1986).

Between 1960 and 1983, undergraduate enrollments trebled, growing from 3,227,000 to 9,707,000. Less than half this increase came from the baby boom; most of it came from the increase in the proportion of youths attending college, from 34 percent to 58 percent. The greatest growth occurred in state schools of the second tier and in two-year colleges (Hacker, 1986). Almost all the student diversity in higher education—by race, cultural background, and age—is handled by junior and community colleges. Indeed, they are often viewed as

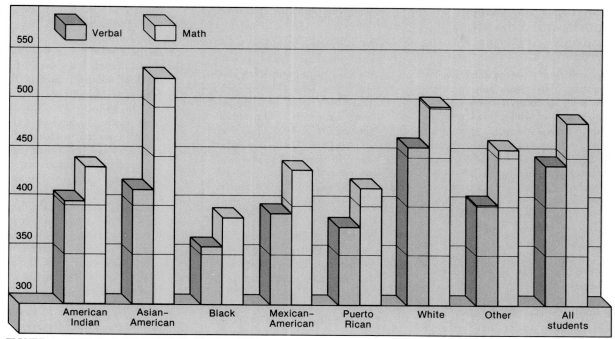

FIGURE A   SAT Averages by Ethnic Groups, 1985
Range of scores in 200 to 800. *Source: College Board.*

from Taiwan, South Korea, and other Asian nations. Significantly, earlier generations of youngsters from the nation's older Chinatowns did not perform nearly as well as have recent arrivals.

Although many Asian-American youths enjoy remarkable academic success, some Asian-American leaders say their young people are encountering increasing discrimination when they apply to the nation's most prestigious universities (Lindsey, 1987).

At Harvard, 12.5 percent of Asian-American applications were accepted in 1985, as against 15.9 percent of all applicants. At Brown, another Ivy League school, 18 percent of the Asian-Americans were accepted, compared with 21 percent of the whites. The Asian-American students who were admitted averaged 1 point higher on the verbal portion of the SAT than successful white applicants and 18 points higher on the math portion (see Figure A). Moreover, instructors at a

number of colleges report that some white students withdraw from courses with a large number of Asian-Americans because they fear their standings on the grading curve will suffer (Butterfield, 1986; Biemiller, 1986). Stereotypes do a disservice to people, whether the images equate blacks and athletics or Asians and academics. For instance, some white managers, defining Asian-Americans as technicians, fail to promote them to executive positions.

"second rate" *because* they have taken the issue of student diversity seriously and have stressed teaching (Hodgkinson, 1986).

One of the bright spots in higher education is that American colleges are opening up to "nontraditional" students, those over 25 who for one reason or another

have put off getting a degree. Over the last decade, the number of people 25 and over enrolled in colleges and universities grew by over 70 percent. Part-timers now account for over 45 percent of all college students, and the College Board estimates that by 1990 these "nontraditional" students will be the majority. The older stu-

Can Big-Time College Sports and Education Coexist?

Big-time sports pose a dilemma for educators. The games provide entertainment, spectacle, excitement, and festival—all of which bond together administrators, faculty, staff, students, and alumni. As Alabama's Bear Bryant once noted, "It's kind of hard to rally round a math class." Simultaneously, big-time sports have severely compromised many of the nation's colleges and universities. The quest for big money and fame has superseded the pursuit of educational goals (Eitzen, 1986). College sports now generate more than $1 billion a year. The pressure to keep the money rolling in is what contributes to abuse and corruption (Ivey, 1986). Since winning programs produce huge revenues from gate receipts, television, bowl games, tournament appearances, and state legislative funding, many athletic departments are governed by a winning-at-any-cost philosophy. Consider these examples:

- A federal jury ruled in 1986 that a University of Georgia instructor, Jan Kemp, had been dismissed illegally in retaliation for opposing favored treatment for athletes. She said university officials changed the failing grades of nine football players so they could remain eligible for the 1982 Sugar Bowl, in which Georgia lost to Pitt, 24–20. The president of the University of Georgia, Fred C. Davison, testified at the Kemp trial that most athletes at Georgia do not graduate, saying the athletes have a "utilitarian value" to the university because of their revenue-producing potential (Goodwin, 1986).

- Many college coaches report that they are under growing pressure to bring in more revenue. Says Dale Brown, men's basketball coach at Louisiana State University: "The bottom line used to be W's [wins]. Now it is dollars. There is a lot of greed because college presidents see a way to enhance their budgets by putting their teams on TV" (Farrell, 1986).

- By virtue of recruiting infractions, Southern Methodist University in Dallas had its football program placed on probation by the National Collegiate Athletic Association (NCAA) for two years in 1974, for another year in 1976, for two years in 1981, and for three more years in 1985. In 1986 it was revealed that a former football player, David Stanley, was paid $25,000 in 1983 to sign a national letter of intent with Southern Methodist and was being paid $750 a month through December 1985, four months after the school was placed on probation for previous violations (Applebome, 1986). Citing a "record of violations [that is] nothing short of abysmal," the NCAA canceled Mustang football for 1987 and cut the team's schedule from 11 to 7 games in 1988; it also limited the number of athletic scholarships the school could grant and the size of its coaching staff.

- When hired at the University of Nebraska, a coach joked, "I don't expect to win enough games to be put on N.C.A.A. probation. I just want to win

enough to warrant an investigation" (Will, 1986).

- At the close of the 1986 football season, Ted Tollner was fired as the head football coach at the University of Southern California. In Tollner's four years as head coach, the Trojans had a 26–19–1 record, with one Pacific Ten Conference championship and three appearances in postseason bowl games, including the 1985 Rose Bowl. Fred Akers was also fired. The University of Texas football coach had won 75 percent of his games and led his team to nine bowl games in as many years. But influential boosters would not tolerate "mediocre" seasons.

- Pennsylvania State University likes to claim that 90 percent of its varsity football players graduate. But the figure is valid only if you count players who reach their senior years. The Pittsburgh *Post-Gazette* calculates the rate is 67 percent if dropouts are included. The National Football League Players Association says that 61 percent of the Penn State products in the NFL are degree-holders (Klein, 1984). Overall, barely one-third of the players in the National Football League hold college degrees, and some estimates for the National Basketball Association are even lower. At Memphis State University, only 6 of 58 basketball players graduated in ten years (Bowen, 1985; Sanoff, 1986).

Perhaps most troubling to educators is what happens to college athletes. Many football and basketball programs prosper by taking advantage of the belief of poor and minority youth that sports are a broad, paved road to riches. Big-time college sports have become little more than farm systems for professional basketball and football teams. Sociologists Peter Adler and Patricia A. Adler (1985) conducted a participant-observation study of a major college basketball program over a four-year period. They found that most athletes enter college feeling idealistic about their impending academic experience and optimistic about their prospects for graduating. But soon sport comes to occupy a central role in their lives. *Professionalization* ensues. The media, fans, coaches, classmates, and professors relate to them as athletes, not as students. Time spent in athletically related activities interferes and conflicts with academic time. All the while, they are socially isolated, housed in a special dorm, and cut off from other students by the demands of practices, games, study halls, and booster functions. When classmates relate to them, it is in terms of athletics and not with respect to academic, cultural, political, or intellectual pursuits.

Over time, the relentless pressures they experience lead athletes to distance themselves from their studies. As freshmen they expect that their professors will accord them sympathetic understanding, special privileges, and greater tolerance. When professors hold them to the same standards as other students, or stereotype them as "dumb jocks," they become disillusioned. Their difficulties are often compounded by inadequate academic backgrounds, poor study habits, tight schedules, and peer distractions. The positive feedback they expected from academics is replaced by low grades and failed courses. They

grow increasingly cynical and gradually resign themselves to inferior academic performance. The peer subculture of athletes widens the gulf by devaluing academic involvement and neutralizing academic failure.

The Adlers identify the structural forces within big-time university athletic programs that undermine the professed goals of the educational system. They also make a number of policy suggestions derived from their research. First, athletes should be sheltered from the enticing whirlwind of celebrity status by making freshmen ineligible for varsity sports. Second, athletic dorms should be abolished and athletes integrated within the larger college culture. And third, athletes should be provided with academic role models and advisers—not athletic personnel masquerading as models and advisers—who can assist them in pursuing academic goals. In sum, academic institutions need to make a commitment to their athletes as students (Eitzen, 1986).

Scandal of College Athletic Programs
Critics charge that the worst scandal of college sports programs does not involve cash or cars. It involves slipping academically unqualified youths in the back doors of academic institutions, wringing them dry of their athletic-commercial usefulness, then slinging them out the back door (Will, 1986). Pictured above is Sammy Drummer, who averaged 22 points a game while at Georgia Tech. He quit college to go pro, was cut early, and now works as a maintenance supervisor. *(left,* Atlanta Journal and Constitution; *right,* John Starkey for *USN&WR)*

"The school gets $800,000 if we make it to the Final Four, boys, but paying you to get there is a no-no."

Cartoon by Cochran; © 1986, USA TODAY. Reprinted with permission.

They have a sense that "the whole world has opened up before me." Because of their eagerness to learn, many professors find that they feel more exhilarated teaching "nontrads" in evening continuing education classes than they do their younger counterparts during the day (Rowe, 1986; Boyer, 1987).

THINKING THROUGH THE ISSUES

What obstacles block a fundamental reform of American higher education? How do you think faculty members would respond to an "integrated curriculum" that did away with the "unruly cafeteria line of course offerings"? How do you think students would feel about a return to a curriculum grounded in the traditional liberal arts? Note that a recent study of nearly 6 million freshmen revealed that 80 percent rated "being well-off financially" as important (up from 43.8 percent in 1966) and 43 percent rated "developing a meaningful philosophy of life" as an important goal (down from 80 percent in 1967) (Hellmich, 1986). What might employers find attractive and unattractive about a liberal arts curriculum? How does higher education mirror the values of the larger society? If financial achievement is a major national goal, is it realistic to expect higher education to focus on other objectives?

---

dents are more likely to come from working-class backgrounds, and strive for the kind of education that people from more affluent backgrounds take for granted. Although their high school grades are often lower than those of younger students, "nontrads' " college grades tend to be higher.

Many of the older students report that although they may have gone back to school for career reasons, they find their overall college experiences enriching.

Is Anybody Learning Here?
The verdict is a mixed one for large lecture classes. Yet they have become an established part of higher education, even though many professors find them harder to teach and many students report that they are harder to learn in than smaller classes. They are popular with university officials because they are cheaper. At Ohio State University, an average-size class of 60 students costs 37 dollars per student hour; a megaclass of 400 or so students costs 7 dollars. *(Laimute E. Druskis/Jeroboam)*

Chapter Highlights

1. Education is one aspect of the many-sided process of socialization by which people acquire those behaviors essential for effective participation in society. It entails an explicit process in which some people assume the status of teacher and others the status of student and carry out their associated roles.

2. Viewed from the functionalist perspective, the schools make a number of vital contributions to the survival and perpetuation of modern societies. A specialized educational agency is needed to transmit to young people the ways of thinking, feeling, and acting mandated by a rapidly changing urban and technologically based society. The educational system serves to inculcate the dominant values of a society and shape a common national mind. It functions as an agency for screening and selecting individuals for different types of jobs. And schools, particularly universities, may add to the cultural heritage through research and development.

3. Conflict theorists see the schools as agencies that reproduce and legitimate the current social order through the functions they perform. By reproducing and legitimating the existing social order, the educational institution is seen as benefitting some individuals and groups at the expense of others. Some conflict theorists depict American schools as reflecting the needs of capitalist production and as social instruments for convincing the population that private ownership and profit are just and in the best interests of the entire society.

4. Education has simultaneous forward and backward links to the stratification system. It links forward through the effects schooling has on the occupational placement of upcoming generations. It links backward in time to a preexisting system of stratification through the ways in which social class, gender, and race affect school achievement.

5. School desegregation works if people really want it to work, and there are disturbing signs of ulterior motives for not really wanting it to work. Schools mirror the racial patterns of the larger society. It is unreasonable to expect the schools to undo what the larger society continually reestablishes in its daily operation.

6. So long as the schools remained relatively small, they could operate on the basis of face-to-face interaction. But like hospitals, factories, and businesses, schools grew larger and more complex. In order to attain their goals, they had to standardize and routinize many of their operations and establish formal operating and administrative procedures. Like other complex organizations, schools do not exist in a social vacuum, but are connected to other institutions. The formal organization of American schools and colleges typically consist of four levels: (1) the board of education or trustees, (2) administrators, (3) teachers or professors, and (4) students.

7. Social scientists have examined what makes a school effective. Successful schools foster expectations that order will prevail and that learning is a serious matter. Much of the success enjoyed by private and Catholic schools has derived from their ability to provide students with an ordered environment and strong academic demands.

8. Like its public schools counterparts, higher education has been the subject of reports warning that the quality of education is declining. One major criticism is that colleges have increasingly catered to a parochial careerism while failing to cultivate a global vision among their students. Moreover, most colleges do very little to encourage good teaching.

The Sociologist's Vocabulary

correspondence principle The notion set forth by Samuel Bowles and Herbert Gintis that the social relations of work find expression in the social relations of the school.

credentialism The requirement that a worker have a degree attesting to skills not needed for the performance of a job.

education The transmission of certain attitudes, knowledge, and skills to the members of a society through formal, systematic training.

educational self-fulfilling prophecies (also called *teacher-expectation effects*) The fact that many children fail to learn, espcially lower-class and minority children, because those who are charged with teaching them do not believe that they will learn, do not expect that they can learn, and do not act toward them in ways that help them to learn.

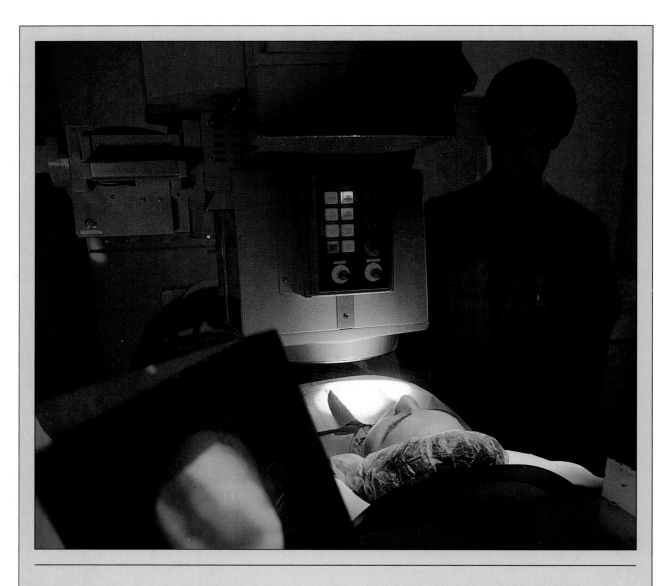

18

Medicine and Health

How well I should be if it were not for all these people shouting that I am ill!

—André Gide, *Pretexts*

An epidemic of yellow fever—a virus infection transmitted by mosquitoes—struck Philadelphia in the summer of 1793. Its victims experienced severe headache and stomach pain, jaundice, high fever, and delirium. Many people died—not only in isolated cases here and there, but in clusters. Since Philadelphians did not know the cause of the illness, a plague mentality soon came to haunt the citizenry. Friends and acquaintances recoiled when they encountered one another on the street. Even the air seemed diseased. People would seek to pass each other on the windward side of the street in case the disease was airborne. Husbands were known to abandon stricken wives, and some parents deserted their ailing children. Corpses were carted off without benefit of funerals and buried in mass graves. By the time the cold weather arrived, killing off the mosquitoes, about 10 percent of Philadelphia's population had died (Morrow, 1985).

A plague mentality has been likened to the sense of terror that befalls a city under siege, except that in a siege, the enemy waits outside, whereas in an epidemic it stalks within. Death seems to travel in mysterious ways, drifting in when one least expects it. Everything and everyone becomes suspect: the doorknob, the toilet seat, rain, bugs, saliva, blood, a kiss, the stranger. Society polarizes, divided between the world of the healthy and that of the afflicted. Terror and fear breed fanaticism (Morrow, 1985). During the terrible Black Death that swept Europe in the fourteenth century, thousands of Jews were massacred in countless communities because they were blamed for the disease.

Elements of a plague mentality have also begun to appear among segments of the American public with regard to AIDS. AIDS victims are stigmatized. Parents have withdrawn their youngsters from school upon learning that a classmate has AIDS. The public identification of AIDS with homosexual men has led to a marked rise in gay bashing in recent years (Wilson, 1987). Those afflicted with AIDS have been denied jobs, housing, schooling, dental care, and insurance; those with jobs are often harassed and threatened by co-workers (Siwolop,

1987). Nor does a clean bill of health place one beyond suspicion: An insurance company refused a policy to a Colorado man who voluntarily provided the results of an AIDS test that came out negative; the company said the fact that he got tested at all made him too great a risk (Silverman, 1987). Overall, a 1987 Roper Organization poll found that 77 percent of adult Americans approved of AIDS tests for couples planning to be married; 74 percent, for immigrants; 51 percent, for foreigners visiting the United States; 37 percent, for job applicants; and 33 percent, for children entering school (Comarow, 1987).

Although AIDS has been likened to the plagues that struck Europe in the Middle Ages, it is much harder to catch. Adults can usually control their exposure to the disease. Moreover, in one year, 1348, the Black Death is estimated to have killed one-fourth of the population of Europe. AIDS would have to kill 60 million Americans in a single year to have the same impact. Since it is a disease transmitted in the course of sexual encounters, fear of contracting AIDS has had the social effect of compelling a good many Americans to alter their sexual practices (Leishman, 1987; Russell, 1987). The AIDS epidemic has also led countless private citizens, researchers, and governments to search for effective ways for preventing and curing the disease. In sum, issues of health and illness play an important part in what we do and fail to do, how we relate to others, and how they relate to us. These considerations lead us to the subject matter of this chapter, **medicine**—the social institution responsible for problems of health and illness (Bloom, 1986).

PLANNING AHEAD: TARGETED READING

1. **What part do social and cultural factors play in causing disease and in its effective treatment and management?**

2. **How do stress and social support affect our ability to stay well?**

3. **What unique insights do the functionalist, conflict, and interactionist perspectives provide for health and illness?**

4. **How is the American health care system organized?**

5. **What fundamental changes are taking place in how doctors practice medicine and in how hospitals care for the sick?**

Sociocultural Aspects of Health and Illness

As you go about your daily activities, you are asked countless times, "How are you?" And you invariably reply with a standardized response like, "Fine. How about you?" It is little wonder we inquire about one another's health: How we feel plays a pivotal part in our sense of well-being. Indeed, health is more than the absence of illness. The World Health Organization defines **health** as "a state of complete physical, mental, and social well-being and not merely the absence of disease or

infirmity." We usually assess people's health by how well they are able to function in their daily lives and adapt to a changing environment. Health, then, has a somewhat different meaning for a nun or monk, a professional athlete, an unemployed worker, an airline pilot, a coal miner, a presidential candidate, a nursing home resident, and a homemaker.

Most of us think of disease as a serious, prolonged condition. The word **disease** literally means "dis-eased"—not feeling at ease. It is a condition in which an organism does not function properly due to biological causes. The problems may result from microbial infection, dietary deficiency, heredity, or a harmful environmental agent. The notion of disease, as opposed to explanations rooted in beliefs regarding malevolent spirits or ill humors, is a relatively recent one in Western culture. **Illness** is the sense we have that we are afflicted by a disease. **Sickness**, is contrast, refers to a social status in which other people define us as having a disease and alter their behavior toward us. So we may define ourselves as "ill," be diagnosed as having a "disease" by a medical practitioner, or come to be seen as "sick" by parents, friends, teachers, and co-workers (Clark, 1983).

Our American belief system sees disease and illness as the result of foreign organisms attacking the body or as some malfunction of the body itself. This orientation has contributed to a "person-centered" as opposed to a societally, environmentally, or supernaturally centered view of health problems. So our search for the sources, treatment, and cure of disease has focused on the individual.

The considerable success of *germ theory* in controlling microbial infections has contributed to this thrust in Western medicine. Yet germ theory is not particularly helpful for understanding many forms of degenerative, chronic, and mental illnesses (Twaddle and Hessler, 1977; Clark, 1983). Despite our reliance on the traditional biological model of disease, we have become increasingly aware in recent years that any health problem is also a consequence of social and cultural factors (Strauss, 1975; Arney and Bergen, 1984; Krantz, Grunberg, and Baum, 1985). Let us consider the part that social and cultural factors play in causing disease and in its effective treatment and management.

Health Behaviors and Practices

Patterns of health and illness vary from society to society and from group to group within a society. **Epidemiol-**

Mass Hysteria: Response to the Medieval Plague
A dancing mania swept Europe during the fourteenth century as the bubonic plague, or "Black Death," ravaged hundreds of communities. Congested towns were hardest hit by the plague, but the countryside was not spared. Economic life was adversely affected not only by the Black Death itself but by the shortage of labor that followed in its wake. Penitents (depicted here) believed dancing and pray would ward off the evil forces responsible for the disease. *(The Bettmann Archive)*

ogy, the study of the distribution of diseases among and within populations, reveals that these differences can be substantial. For instance, cancer is more prevalent among some people than among others. Breast cancer is quite common among northern Europeans and relatively rare among Asians. But this finding does not necessarily mean that there is a genetically inherited predisposition to cancer. Many things run in ethnic groups besides genes, including diet and other lifestyle factors. Japanese-American women are more susceptible to breast cancer the longer they have lived in the United States and the more they have adopted American culture. The probability of developing some cancers also changes with socioeconomic class. White women are more likely than black women to develop breast cancer, but among black women who have moved up the socioeconomic ladder, the rate of breast cancer is the same as for white women at the same class level (Taylor, 1986).

Social habits and styles of life   Social habits and styles of life affect our health in many ways. As Figure 18.1 shows, large numbers of Americans have poor health habits. For example, cigarette smoking is the single most important source of preventable death in the United States today. The annual death toll of 350,000 Americans from diseases attributed to smoking is seven times the fatality rate of motor vehicle crashes and more than the total number of Americans killed in World War I, Korea, and Vietnam combined (Fielding, 1985). Diets high in cholesterol, excessive consumption of alcohol, lack of exercise, and poor hygienic practices have also been linked to illnesses, including coronary heart disease (Pell and Fayerweather, 1985; Stamler, 1985). Many of these practices are rooted in American cultural patterns that define what constitutes a "hearty meal" and that say we should use alochol as a "social lubricant." Most of the behaviors are socially acquired—for instance, smoking to obtain the approval of peers. Research similarly documents the part that social and cultural factors play in increasing our susceptibility to cancer. Consider skin cancer: An estimated 400,000 new cases are detected each year in the United States, and the vast majority are attributable to overexposure to the sun (Fitzpatrick and Sober, 1985).

Clearly, each of us can do more for our own health than can most hospitals, doctors, medical treatments, or drugs. A program at Johnson & Johnson encouraging employees to quit smoking and to eat and exercise properly has slashed absenteeism by 20 percent and hospitalization by 35 percent. And the corporation recaptured three times the cost of its effort (Califano, 1986).

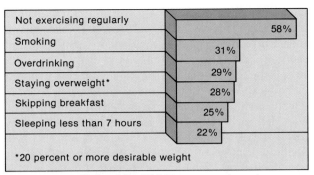

Not exercising regularly	58%
Smoking	31%
Overdrinking	29%
Staying overweight*	28%
Skipping breakfast	25%
Sleeping less than 7 hours	22%

*20 percent or more desirable weight

FIGURE 18.1   Unhealthy Habits among Americans, 1986
Although we have become more health conscious, we still practice what many medical practitioners consider bad health habits. *Source: U.S. Department of Health and Human Services.*

Seeking medical treatment   Social and cultural factors influence whether or not we seek formal treatment and how we respond to it. Our society says that for certain illnesses like a flu virus we should stay in bed, even "call the doctor." For others—a pulled muscle, a broken finger, or poison ivy—we should continue our daily activities because our society does not label them as sicknesses. People living in insular ethnic communities often share folk beliefs that do not correspond to those of physicians and that keep them from seeking medical treatment. And they differ in how they describe a symptom to a medical practitioner. For instance, as Table 18.1 shows, Irish patients often impassively report a very specific complaint to the doctor ("I have an upset stomach"), whereas Italian patients are likely to voice concern about more general complaints ("I just feel achy all over") (Zola, 1966). Since people from different ethnic backgrounds react to different aspects of their complaints, they are reassured by different types of information. Italian patients commonly react to the pain sensations they are experiencing and are comforted by medication that makes the pain go away; Jewish patients typically react to the significance of the pain and are comforted when they are given an adequate explanation for it (Zborowski, 1952).

Class factors   Sociologists also find that the higher our social class, the more likely we are to enjoy good health, receive good medical care, and live a long life (see Chapter 9). Overall, poor people experience more disability and lower levels of health than do affluent people. Even though access to health care among the poor has improved in recent years, when level of disability is taken into account, the poor receive less care for their illnesses than the nonpoor (Dutton, 1978, 1982a). Life expectancy is also longer for the nonpoor than for the poor: The difference in favor of the nonpoor ranges from 2.4 additional years for those aged 65 to 69, to less than 1 additional year for those aged 75 or over (Katz, 1983).

Many factors account for these patterns. As we will see later in the chapter, cost operates as one constraint on the ability of the poor to afford the services they need; their incomes are low and they often lack adequate health insurance. The American health care system also reflects the needs of the affluent more than those of the poor. Physicians tend to be scarce in poor areas and travel difficulties are often complicated by inadequate public transportation. In practice, a dual system of medical care operates in which the poor utilize public sources (hospital outpatient departments, emergency rooms, and

Table 18.1 Ethnic Group and Symptoms

Each set of responses was given by a patient of Italian or Irish background who was of similar age and sex with a disorder of approximately the same duration and with the same diagnosis. In the first two cases, the Irish-American patient focused on a specific malfunctioning as the main concern, whereas the Italian-American patient did not mention this aspect of the problem but went on to mention more diffuse qualities of the condition. The last four responses contrast the Irish-American and Italian-American response to questions about pain and interpersonal relations.

Diagnosis	Question of Interviewer	Irish Patient	Italian Patient
1. Presbyopia and hyperopia (farsightedness)	What seems to be the trouble?	I can't see to thread a needle or read a paper.	I have a constant headache and my eyes seem to get all red and burny.
	Anything else?	No, I can't recall any.	No, just that it lasts all day long and I even wake up with it sometimes.
2. Myopia (nearsightedness)	What seems to be the trouble?	I can't see across the street.	My eyes seem very burny, especially the right eye . . . Two or three months ago I woke up with my eye swollen. I bathed it and it did go away but there was still the burny sensation.
	Anything else?	I had been experiencing headaches, but it may be that I'm in early menopause.	Yes, there always seems to be a red spot beneath this eye . . .
	Anything else?	No.	Well, my eyes feel very heavy . . . at night they bother me most.
3. Otitis externa A.D. (inflammation of the external ear)	Is there any pain?	There's a congestion . . . but it's a pressure not really a pain.	Yes . . . if I rub it, it disappears . . . I had a pain from my shoulder up to my neck and thought it might be a cold.
4. Pharyngitis (inflammation of the throat)	Is there any pain?	No, maybe a slight headache but nothing that lasts.	Yes, I have had a headache a few days. Oh, yes, every time I swallow it's annoying.
5. Presbyopia and hyperopia (farsightedness)	Do you think the symptoms affected how you got along with your family? your friends?	No, I have had loads of trouble. I can't imagine this bothering me.	Yes, when I have a headache, I'm very irritable, very tense, very short-tempered.
6. Deafness, hearing loss	Did you become more irritable?	No, not me . . . maybe everybody else but not me.	Oh, yes . . . the least little thing aggravates me . . . and I take it out on the children.

Source: Irving Kenneth Zola. 1966. Culture and symptoms—An analysis of patients' presenting complaints. *American Sociological Review*, 31:625.

public clinics) while middle- and upper-income Americans use private sources (physicians in private or group practice). Patients using public sources must often maneuver between multiple clinics to obtain their services, and the services are usually disease-oriented rather than preventive (Wan and Gray, 1978). In addition, the atmosphere in these institutions is often dehumanizing (Dutton, 1978b). Since blacks, Hispanics, and Native Americans (Indians) are more likely to be poor than are whites, these groups also experience higher rates of disease and shorter life expectancies (see Chapter 10).

Stigmatized illnesses   As we pointed out in the chapter opening, social and cultural factors influence how we regard various diseases and their victims. (The box takes a closer look at the AIDS epidemic.) Cancer patients have long suffered from a host of socially created problems associated with their illness. One survey found that 85 percent of cancer patients encountered problems interacting with friends and relatives because these friends and relatives felt uncomfortable about cancer; 70 percent reported they experienced tension in talking with their spouses about their illness; 91 percent said that their sex lives were adversely affected; and 72 percent admitted having difficulties telling physicians and nurses about their feelings, symptoms, and concerns (Bridgwater, 1985). Indeed, medical anthropologist Horacio Fabrega (1974) concludes from his research that, in all known societies, designating a person as sick inevitably entails an element of discreditation. Even though people may not be blamed for their health problems and may receive the sympathy of others, they are not viewed as being as worthy, as creditable, as reliable, or as adequate as are the healthy.

Stress and Social Support

Social and cultural factors similarly affect our ability to stay well. Stress and social support are especially important. As we noted in Chapter 15, sociologists find that unemployment has adverse effects on physical and mental health (Kessler, House, and Turner, 1987). In fact, a stressful job or financial difficulties nearly double the odds that we will become ill or injured (Catalano and Dooley, 1983). Traumatic life events are also correlated with disease onset. Rape victims show a significant increase in health-related problems in the year following the rape (Kilpatrick, Resick, and Veronen, 1981; King and Webb, 1981). Many studies investigating the social effects of wartime destruction, military combat, nuclear accidents, and natural disasters reveal similar patterns. For instance, in the seven months following the Mount Saint Helens eruption and ashfall on the nearby town of Othello, Washington, emergency room visits rose 21 percent, deaths rose 19 percent, and stress-related illness complaints at the local mental health clinic doubled, compared with a comparable period during the previous year (Adams and Adams, 1984).

Social support plays a crucial role in our physical and mental health through its health-sustaining and stress-buffering functions. People with social ties live longer and have better health than those without such

A Young Victim of AIDS
Although Americans typically think of AIDS as a disease of adults, growing numbers of youngsters are AIDS victims. Some have acquired the virus from blood transfusions. Others have been born to women who have been exposed to the AIDS virus. Fighting the spread of the disease has proved especially difficult because most infants with AIDS are born to mothers with no outward signs of disease.
(Abraham Menashe/Science Source/Photo Researchers)

ties (Berkman and Breslow, 1983). Studies over a range of illnesses, from depression to arthritis to heart disease, reveal that the presence of social support helps people fend off illness, and the absence of such support make poor health more likely (Wallston et al., 1984; Reis et al., 1985). The incidence of death from all causes is greater among people with relatively low levels of group and community supports (Blazer, 1982; House, Robbins, and Metzner, 1982). Large social networks provide us with positive social experiences and a set of stable, socially rewarding roles in the community.

Perspectives in Medical Sociology

Health and health care can be usefully examined from the functionalist, conflict, and interactionist perspectives. Our conception of the part that health, illness, and sickness play in social life varies, depending on the perspective we adopt.

The Functionalist Perspective

Functionalists point out that health is essential to the preservation of the human species and organized social life. If societies are to function smoothly and effectively, there must be a reasonable supply of productive members to carry out vital tasks. Should large numbers of people be ill or physically unfit, as in some Third World

nations where malaria is widespread, low vitality, low productivity, and poverty are the result. Moreover, community personnel, resources, facilities, and funds must be withdrawn from other essential activities to care for the nonproductive sick (Hertzler, 1961).

Given these considerations, functionalists reason, it should not surprise us that many societies have evolved a medical institution. More specifically, they see the medical institution performing a number of key functions in modern societies. First, it treats and seeks to cure disease. Second, the medical institution attempts to prevent disease through health maintenance programs, including vaccination, education, periodic checkups, and public health and safety standards. Third, it undertakes research in the prevention, treatment, and cure of health problems. And fourth, it serves as an agency of social control by defining some behaviors as "normal" and "healthy" and others as "deviant" and "unhealthy."

Talcott Parsons (1951) expands on the functionalist position in his analysis of the **sick role**, a set of cultural expectations that define what is appropriate and inappropriate behavior for people with a disease or health problem. Like other functionalists, Parsons assumes illness must be socially controlled lest it impair societal functioning. He says one way societies contain the negative effects of health problems is through institutionalizing illness in a special role, one having the following characteristics:

- Sick people are exempt from their usual social roles and responsibilities. They need not attend school

Spiritual Healing

Spiritism offers an alternative to traditional health care and services. A spiritist healing most frequently takes place in a group setting. Mediums receive spirit messages or become possessed by either good or evil spirits in order to diagnose, counsel, prescribe ritual and herbal remedies, and predict the future. Researchers find that among both traditional therapists and spiritist healers positive patient expectations tend to be associated with positive outcomes. Patients often report that they "feel better," due in part to a restructuring of their definitions regarding their condition (Koss, 1987). *(Peter Simon/Stock, Boston)*

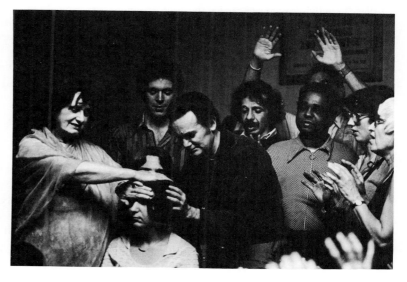

ISSUES THAT SHAPE OUR LIVES

AIDS: The Dawn of an Age of Fear?

The Nobel laureate David Baltimore, a biochemist, puts it bluntly: "AIDS is a problem for everyone—gay and straight, urban and rural. We are at a critical point in the progress of the epidemic [and] we are quite honestly frightened by the future prospects" (Morganthau, 1986:20). By 1987, Otis R. Bowen, secretary of health and human services in the Reagan administration, was speaking in alarmist terms. He said the worldwide AIDS epidemic would become so serious it would dwarf such earlier medical disasters as the Black Plague, smallpox, and typhoid: "You haven't heard or read anything yet" (Columbus, Ohio, *Dispatch*, January 30, 1987:6A). As the incidence of AIDS has risen, so have public fears. A plague mentality is beginning to surface in American life.

According to conservative estimates, by 1991, 270,000 Americans will have been stricken with AIDS and 179,000 will have died (killing more Americans than the Korean and Vietnam wars combined). In 1987, the Centers for Disease Control estimated that 1.5 million Americans carried the virus but displayed no symptoms. We still do not know what proportion of those infected with the AIDS virus will eventually develop symptoms. In

Ugandan Mother and Child: Both Victims of AIDS
In central Africa AIDS has reached epidemic dimensions. By 1987, the World Health Organization estimated that 50,000 people had died of the disease in 11 nations stretching from the Congo to Tanzania. But leading AIDS researchers privately said that the death toll was in excess of several hundred thousand. The same scientists estimated that some 5 million Africans were carriers of the virus (Morganthau, 1986; Quinn et al., 1986). *(Neveu/Gamma-Liaison)*

1987, most AIDS cases fell into three categories: homosexual men, intravenous drug users, and hemophiliacs. In the same year, blood tests on heterosexual Americans indicated that fewer than 1 percent had been exposed to the virus (Morganthau, 1986; Cupito, 1987; McAuliffe, 1987).

A 1986 panel of 28 scientists assembled by the prestigious Institute of Medicine of the National Academy of Sciences concluded that the United States no longer can entirely avert catastrophe. It said the choice the nation confronts is between a lesser catastrophe and a much larger one. Even at present levels, AIDS cases

threaten to swamp the nation's health care system with immense costs and a sizable caseload of slowly dying patients (Church, 1986). On an international scale, AIDS is undermining nations, especially in Africa. In Zaire, for example, an estimated 10 percent of the population is infected with the AIDS virus (Cupito, 1987). In neighboring Uganda, health authorities project that by the year 2000, one in every two sexually active adults will be infected. The Geneva-based World Health Organization estimates that 2 to 5 million Africans are now carriers of the virus. The African experience reveals how widespread AIDS can

or go to work, and other people will not censure them for doing so.

- Sick people are not thought to be at fault for their condition. Being sick is a physical matter, not a moral one.

- Sick people have the duty to get well and "not enjoy themselves too much." Because being sick is an undesirable state, sick people are obligated to seek competent help from medical practitioners.

- Sick people should cooperate with medical practitioners and follow their instructions.

The sick role shares many characteristics with the deviant role. We are excused from our usual responsibilities, but only so long as we dedicate ourselves to getting well. If other people conclude we are sick through our own fault or we are not attempting to get well, they are likely to redefine us as deviant—as "bad" rather than "sick." The reverse process also may hold: A generation

become and how difficult it can be to convince people to alter their sexual behaviors, even in the face of death (Serrill, 1987).

Hysteria surrounding AIDS has fed xenophobia (fear of foreigners). When several African students who were studying in India were found carrying the AIDS virus—although they had no symptoms—officials promptly forced them to leave. Belgium has ordered that AIDS tests be administered to foreign scholarship students, most of them Africans from its former colony of Zaire. In Cuba, Bulgaria, and Romania, African students are routinely tested for the AIDS virus—and expelled if they have it (Norland, 1987).

Within the United States, AIDS is having a substantially different impact on society than traditional killers like cancer and heart disease. Not only is the disease usually lethal and its victims the young and middle-aged, but it is also transmitted sexually. Given the nation's historic ambivalence toward sex, it is hardly surprising that AIDS has charged public emotions. As in earlier times, calls for quarantines—social exile—have been heard from a variety of quarters. Among them have been the religious Right, who see AIDS as divine punishment for the "sin of homosexuality."

While health authorities inside and outside government describe the situation as potentially catastrophic, government and public health officials have been slow to mount an assault on the disease. Part of the reason is that AIDS so far has struck chiefly groups outside the mainstream. Official projections assume that the disease will spread slowly among heterosexuals and continue to be centered mostly among male homosexuals. However, in New York City an almost equal ratio of male and female military applicants are showing signs of infection. Critics charge that health officials, well-intentioned as they may be in wishing to avoid public alarm, are lulling people into a false complacency (McAuliffe, 1987).

The panel of the Institute of Medicine said that checking the spread of AIDS will require "perhaps the most wide-ranging and intensive efforts ever made against an infectious disease" and will necessitate research and education programs costing $2 billion a year by 1991 (Church, 1986). Scientists have learned a good deal about how AIDS infects cells. But efforts to devise a vaccine or a treatment have been complicated by the fact that AIDS is caused by two, perhaps three, similar viruses, and that the virus mutates frequently. At present, education is the nation's lone "vaccine." Consequently, the Institute of Medicine scientists have recommended a massive national educational campaign centering on two precepts: First, random sex of any sort is dangerous (when people have sex, they're not just having it with that partner; they're having it with everybody that partner had it with for the past 10 years). Second, all sex outside monogamous relationships with well-known partners should be accompanied by the use of a condom.

Significantly, the panel of distinguished scientists rejected ideas for a massive national quarantine program or mandatory blood testing to detect the AIDS virus. The panel argued that those in high-risk groups were not likely to comply with quarantine or mandatory screening programs and that it would be neither ethical nor in keeping with American civil liberties to compel them to do so. Moreover, AIDS is not likely to become another Black Death—the plague that killed a quarter to half of Europe's population in a three-year spasm from 1347 to 1350. Unlike the plagues of old, AIDS does not spread through casual contact: It cannot be contracted from doorknobs, drinking glasses, toilet seats, or social kissing. The AIDS epidemic reminds us that—as in many other social realms—the domains of individual private troubles and public policy cannot be segregated; they constantly merge and remerge in complex configurations (Berg, 1986).

or so ago Americans viewed alcoholism as resulting from a moral shortcoming. Today, we have increasingly come to see it as a disease associated with chemical dependency.

The Conflict Perspective

Implicit to the functionalist image of the sick role is the assumption that health care services are available to all members of a society, regardless of class, race, age, gender, or creed. This image is challenged by conflict theorists (Waitzkin, 1983). They say that people of all societies prefer health to illness. Yet some people achieve better health than others because they have access to those resources that contribute to good health and to recovery should they become ill. These inequities are embedded in the stratification system (see Chapter 9).

Conflict theorists charge that many of the primary providers of American medical care and services—physicians, health maintenance organizations, hospitals, nursing homes, pharmaceutical firms, and insurance companies—have their behaviors shaped by incentive systems that are anatgonistic to good health care. A system dominated by profit means that considerations of private gain prevail. The result, critics say, is that medical practitioners become more sensitive to profits than to their patients' best interests and more responsive to the affluent than to the poor (Iglehart, 1986; Anderson, 1987). Some 28 million Americans—12 percent of the population—have problems that hinder their access to the health care system. And some 40 million Americans live in federally designated areas with a shortage of primary medical care, a disproportionate percentage of whom are poor and members of minority groups (Strelnick et al., 1986). Currently, the United States is the only industrialized nation, except for South Africa, that does not cover as a right of citizenship the medical expenses of all those who become seriously ill (Light, 1986; Gray, 1986).

In 1986, investor-owned hospitals like Humana, Hospital Corporation of America, and American Medical International accounted for 15 percent of the 6,100 hospitals in the United States. By 1995, according to a projection by the American College of Hospital Administrators, their market share will rise to 60 percent (Kennedy, 1985). A major study by the National Academy of Sciences found that nonprofit and investor-owned hospitals offer health care of similar quality, but the for-profit hospitals charge higher prices and provide less charity care. It costs these hospitals from 3 percent to 10 percent more than nonprofit centers to deliver the same care, and their bills to insurance companies and government agencies run between 8 and 24 percent higher.

The report warns that the most insidious danger in the trend toward profit-oriented health care is doctors themselves. With pressure building on nursing homes, hospitals, group practices, and health maintenance organizations to attract a greater share of the market for health services, doctors are succumbing to the temptation to put their economic well-being ahead of the welfare of patients. Two developments are particularly troubling. First, many hospitals and corporate concerns that provide physician care are giving doctors cash incentive bonuses if they refrain from using certain types of expensive services. Second, growing numbers of doctors hold hidden ownership in for-profit diagnostic laboratories, radiology clinics, home care corporations, and weight-loss and drug-abuse clinics to which they refer patients (Gray, 1986; Watt et al., 1986).

Perhaps the sharpest criticisms of the for-profit health chains is that they are inattentive to the needs of those who cannot afford to pay hospital bills on their

Unequal Care: Treating Those with Money and Those without
Parkland (left) is the only public hospital in Dallas, Texas. It gets nearly 60 percent of its 147-million-dollar budget from taxpayers because most of its patients lack health insurance and 72 percent of its bills cannot be collected. Across town at Humana Medical City (right), about 11 percent of its budget goes to charity and another 25 percent to Medicare. "We have the world's greatest health-care system if you have the money," says Humana's spokesperson Ira Corman. *(Mark Perlstein/USN&WR)*

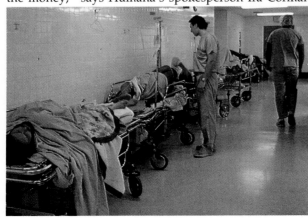

own, who lack medical insurance, and who are ineligible for government assistance. For-profit hospitals have acquired and built hospitals in areas that have relatively few patients who are uninsured or who are covered by the lower reimbursement Medicaid program. Moreover, private hospitals often engage in cream skimming. They provide only profitable services to paying patients and leave costly services and medically indigent patients to public hospitals. Transfers of indigent patients from private hospitals to Cook County Hospital—a public hospital in Chicago—rose from about 70 per month in 1983 to 500 per month in 1985 (Eisenberg, 1986; Schiff et al., 1986).

Critics also charge that for-profit hospitals neglect teaching and research. University teaching hospitals are 33 percent more costly than nonteaching hospitals. Yet they educate the next generation of health professionals and develop new knowledge essential to the improvement of health care. There are exceptions, the best known being Humana's corporate investment in the artificial heart. Yet the case is instructive. It involves a procedure of dubious value (associated with disabling strokes), but one that generates enormous publicity for the sponsor. From Humana's viewpoint, it represented what its officials have termed "a wise investment" because Humana's name has become "a household word" (Eisenberg, 1986).

THINKING THROUGH THE ISSUES

Not too long ago it was possible to joke that the value of the human body, based on its chemical components, was about $1.98. Now, by virtue of new technological developments that allow the transplanting of kidneys, hearts, and corneas, its value exceeds $200,000. In 1984, in response to a concern that human organs not be merchandised, Congress passed the National Organ Transplantation Act prohibiting sales of organs for transplantation. However, in 1985 a series of articles in *The Pittsburgh Press* reported that, while 10,000 Americans were awaiting transplants, some hospitals were allowing foreigners to move ahead of the line and receive 30 percent of the kidney replacements. Significantly, the surgeons' fees were often four times and hospital charges almost twice as high for foreigners as for Americans. The Department of Health and Human Services confirmed that a high percentage of American kidneys were being transplanted into foreigners who are charged fees several times those charged Americans. In brief, while some people are donating their organs upon their death for transplant purposes, other individuals and groups are profiting from their generosity. All this raises a number of questions. Should the families of organ donors be paid for the organs? Or should Congress enact a nationwide organ procurement system, finance transplants for the poor, and perhaps limit transplants to foreigners to a specified ratio (Thorne and Langner, 1986)?

The Interactionist Perspective

Symbolic interactionists contend that "sicknesses" are culturally created meanings we attach to certain conditions. To use an analogy, the blight that attacks corn or potatoes is a human invention, for if we wish to cultivate parasites, rather than corn or potatoes, there would be no "blight." By the same token, the invasion of a person's body by cholera germs no more carries with it the stamp of "sickness" than does the souring of milk by other forms of bacteria. In order for a condition to be seen or interpreted as a sickness, the members of society must define it as such. Frequently, the definition is a negotiated one (Clark, 1983). You usually attempt to "validate" your interpretation of your symptoms by checking with others: "Mom, do you think this rash is poison ivy?" or "Doctor, do I have a sore throat?" Your mother may reply, "It looks to me more like a couple of mosquito bites," and your doctor may say, "Your throat doesn't *look* too bad to me, but how does it *feel*? Does it hurt when you swallow?"

Some conditions are so prevalent among a population that they are not considered "symptomatic" or unusual. Among many Hispanics in the Southwest, diarrhea, sweating, and coughing are everyday experiences, while among certain groups of Greeks trachoma—an eye disorder—is virtually universal. Lower back pain is a common condition among lower-class American women, who typically see it not as a product of any disease or disorder, but part of their expected everyday existence. And although the incidence of hernia is no higher among American men of Southern European background (Italy or Greece) than among those of Eastern European background (Austria, Czechoslovakia, Russia, and Poland), they are more likely to seek medical assistance for the condition. It seems that the Southern Europeans are more concerned with groin problems and so readily seek aid, whereas Eastern Europeans are threatened or ashamed by genital-area symptoms and keep them to themselves (Graham, 1956; Zola, 1966).

In some cases, the medical profession comes to view certain conditions as diseases even though there is little evidence that they have biological causes, and no effective medical treatment exists (Conrad and Schneider, 1980). For instance, prior to 1973 the American Psychiatric Association included homosexuality in its manual of mental illnesses. A major lobbying effort by various homosexual organizations led psychiatrists to reevaluate their position. Similarly, some early American physicians viewed "Negritude" (the state of being a black person) as a disease and used drugs, poultices, and other procedures to try to change blacks into whites (Szasz, 1970).

In other cases, a medical treatment is discovered *before* the condition is seen as a medical one. The discovery that the amphetamine Ritalin has a calming effect on certain children led to the conclusion that their disruptive behavior, short attention span, impulsiveness, and fidgeting is a disease—hyperkinesis or attention deficit disorder. Previously, the children were defined as "bad" and dealt with by their parents and teachers as such (Conrad, 1975). Today, more and more behaviors earlier generations considered immoral or sinful are coming to be regarded as forms of sickness, a process sociologists call the **medicalization of deviance.** Increasingly, alcoholism, drug abuse, child abuse, and emotional difficulties are defined as "medical" problems requiring treatment by physicians, particularly psychiatrists. As yet, however, it remains a controversial and unsettled issue whether incest, murder, and rape should be viewed as "crimes" that are best handled by jailers or as "sicknesses" best treated by medical practitioners. Whether we define them as deviance or sickness, interactionists point out that imprisonment, fines, gossip, stares, hospitalization, and the prescription of antibiotics have one thing in common: They are all behaviors or social arrangements that encourage people to conform to social norms—to think, to act, and to look in ways that are within the culture's acceptable limits (Clark, 1983; Schneider, 1985).

Alcoholism: Moral Flaw or Medical Problem?

Not too long ago alcoholism was seen as a moral failing, and inebriated members of the community, particularly the poor, were imprisoned. Here they often suffered the torment of withdrawal symptoms, which were thought to be divine retribution for their shortcomings (left). But in recent years, alcoholism has increasingly come to be defined as a medical problem requiring professional treatment (right). *(left, The Bettmann Archive; right, Kit Hedman/Jeroboam)*

The American Health Care Delivery System

Rather than trusting solely to the motivation and abilities of afflicted people to get better, all societies have evolved one or more "specialist" positions to deal with sickness (Hughes, 1968). Curers, shamans, physicians, nurses, and other practitioners are relied upon to explain illness and to offer means for eliminating or controlling it. Drugs, poultices, surgery, bone setting, confinement, acupuncture, electric shock, leeching, talking, ritual, magic, and appeal to the supernatural are all techniques used by medical practitioners. Additionally, medical practitioners serve as gatekeepers who legitimately channel people into the sick role. And in modern societies, physicians certify that people have been born, have died, are fit to work, are eligible for disability benefits, are entitled to accident claims, and are a danger to themselves or society.

From a virtual cottage industry dominated by individual physicians and not-for-profit hospitals, health care is evolving into a network of corporations running everything from hospitals and home health care services to retirement homes and health spas. In 1985, American health care spending totaled $424 billion, or an average of $1,721 for every person in the United States. These expenditures accounted for 10.7 percent of the nation's gross national product (the total output of goods and services), up from 5.9 percent in 1965 (Pear, 1986). (Figure 18.2 shows where American health dollars came from and where they went.) The health care industry employed some 6.5 million people, 5.9 percent of civilian jobs. The number is expected to rise to 9 million, or 7 percent of civilian jobs, in the 1990s (Prokesch, 1986). So formidable has the medical care industry become that critics have labeled it "the medical-industrial complex" (Relman, 1980). Let us take a closer look.

Hospitals

Separate facilities for the sick came into existence among the ancient Greeks, but it was not until the Middle Ages in Western Europe that the hospital movement began in earnest. By 1450, there were some 600 hospitals in England alone. Most hospitals were run by Catholic religious orders because healing and health care were the province of religion. The hospitals also cared for the poor, the disabled, and the itinerant. The linking of the medical and social functions had grave health consequences. Travelers housed with sick people in one hospital would then carry the germs to the next hospital, readily infecting those whose resistance to disease was already low. Toward the end of the 1600s and 1700s, financial abuses and the mismanagement of funds by some religious orders led local governments to take on greater responsibility for the management of hospitals. About the same time, care of the indigent was physically segregated in separate facilities (Rosen, 1963).

By the late 1800s, hospitals were improving. Advances in medical research, especially bacteriology, provided a stronger scientific basis for treatment and the control of infection. New diagnostic tools, such as the X ray, and advances in surgical procedures made many diseases, injuries, and deformities more amenable to medical techniques. By the turn of the century, the trustees of charity hospitals began to woo doctors who cared for well-to-do patients at home. More and more

FIGURE 18.2 **American Health Dollars, 1985** In 1985, Americans spent $425 billion on health care. The figure shows where the money came from and where it went. *Source: U.S. Department of Health and Human Services.*

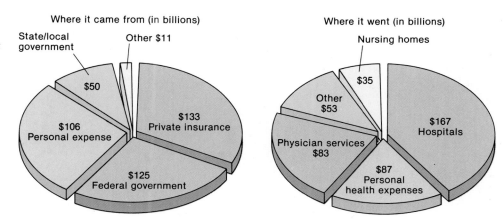

Where it came from (in billions)

State/local government — $50
Other $11
$133 Private insurance
$106 Personal expense
$125 Federal government

Where it went (in billions)

Nursing homes — $35
Other $53
Physician services $83
$167 Hospitals
$87 Personal health expenses

charity hospitals refurbished their rooms and advertised their amenities. In the process, the hospitals ceded considerable control to private physicians, who were more concerned with making the hospital a workshop for the treatment of paying patients than a center for administering charitable care. Hospitals became businesses governed by commercial incentives. As insurance developed first for hospital bills and later for physicians' bills, the hospital industry and the medical profession flourished. By 1965, Congress established Medicare to pay some of the health care costs of the elderly and Medicaid for those of the "deserving" poor. By the mid-1960s, hospitals, physicians, private insurers, and the government had devised a system for financing health care that was ripe for big business and the emergence of for-profit hospital chains (Light, 1986).

In recent years controversy has mounted as to whether an excessive use of hospitals has contributed to unnecessarily high hospital costs. Studies conducted over the past 25 years suggest that a substantial fraction of hospital use is inappropriate. One recent study found that 40 percent of hospital stays were unnecessary be-

cause patients could get the same treatment much more cheaply at outpatient facilities: 23 percent involved services available at less cost in a doctor's office or clinical lab, and 17 percent were for surgery that could be done on an outpatient basis (Siu et al., 1986). Other research suggests that hospital payments by Medicare could be reduced by at least 40 percent if the comparatively low costs of care in Madison, Wisconsin, Iowa City, New Haven, and Rochester, New York, were the national norm (Davidson, 1986). As Figure 18.3 shows, growing pressures to curb health costs have contributed to a drop in both hospital admissions and average patient stay.

Physicians

Sociologist Paul Starr (1982) has traced the transformation of health care from a household service to a market commodity and the rise of the private medical practice. He shows that well into the nineteenth century, most American doctors eked out scant incomes. However, following the Civil War, a contracting household economy, a growing urban population, and more efficient

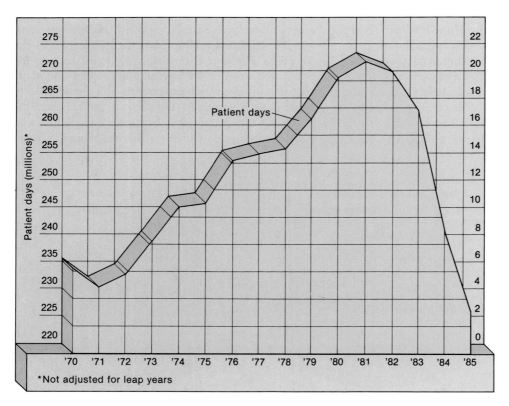

FIGURE 18.3 **Decline in Hospital Use**
The figure reflects the drop in hospital admissions and the average length of hospital stay. For instance, the average hospital stay fell from 6.6 days in 1984 to 6.4 days in 1985. However, the average cost per stay rose 7.5 percent, from $3,571 to $3,840. *Source: American Hospital Association.*

transportation and communication expanded the market for medical services. By the turn of the twentieth century, doctors were well on the road to endowing their profession with a "cultural authority" sufficient to justify claims to self-regulation, state protection, client deference, and control of the means of work. Doctors capitalized on these gains to develop medical specialties and mutual networks that decreased competition and increased their economic and political power. By the 1930s, private practitioners had acquired sufficient influence and prestige to establish themselves as virtually the sole arbiters of medicine in the United States. They dominated hospitals, medical technology, and other health practitioners, including nurses and pharmacists. Additionally, doctors institutionalized their authority through a system of medical education and standardized educational licensing.

Although the private practitioner still remains the primary figure in health care, medicine is increasingly becoming a corporate undertaking. Many physicians have set up professional corporations to achieve the benefits of group practice and to take advantage of special tax-shelter provisions. Walk-in clinics—quick treatment centers that do not require an appointment—are being established in countless communities, usually in busy shopping malls (detractors refer to them as "Docs-in-a-Box" and "7-Eleven Medicine"). Private corporations like Humana hire physicians for their health care clinics. And health maintenance organizations (HMOs) are winning growing numbers of patients, compelling doctors to practice their profession in unaccustomed surroundings (the box on page 504 provides additional information on HMOs). In short, health care is being reshaped into centralized and well-structured organizations designed for a competitive market.

Many young doctors are also finding private practice less attractive than did earlier generations (an American Medical Association survey in 1983 found that 39 percent of doctors younger than 36 years old were employees rather than owners of their practices, while only 23 percent of those between 36 and 45 were employees). A good many factors have contributed to the trend. Some are financial. For one thing, the typical 1985 medical student owed $30,000 upon graduation, a burden that made financing a new practice difficult. For another, malpractice premiums are climbing, and private practitioners do not have an employer to pick up the bill. At the same time, competition for patients from HMOs and other corporate providers has been growing.

Personal factors are also at work. Many young doctors are more interested in freedom *from* the job, allowing them time to be with family and friends. And pressure from government and employers to cut health care costs is eliminating some of the independence that private practitioners once enjoyed, while adding to their paperwork (Starr, 1982; Wessel, 1986). In sum, there are mounting signs that the institutional system built up around the domination of private physicians is breaking

Quick–Service Health Clinics
Borrowing a page from McDonald's and Burger King, entrepreneurs and doctors are undertaking to provide patients with more convenient and less costly health care at walk-in medical clinics. The quick-service centers are springing up in shopping malls and along major highways. They offer an alternative to hospital emergency rooms and doctors' offices. Also gaining popularity in an age of "fast-food medicine" are independent one-day surgical units where physicians perform minor operations (such as hernia repairs and knee arthroscopies) and patients go home the same day. (*Paul N. Bryan/Southern Light*)

ISSUES THAT SHAPE OUR LIVES

Is the Quality of American Medical Care in Jeopardy?

Fundamental changes are taking place in how doctors practice medicine and hospitals care for the sick. With health costs soaring, some of the traditional incentives in financing health care have been reversed. Perhaps the most substantial change has occurred in the way the federal government funds the care of some 30 million elderly and disabled Americans who are covered by Medicare. Rather than reimbursing hospitals for the actual costs of treating Medicare patients, the government now pays a set fee according to 467 "diagnostic related groups," or DRGs. As of 1988, all hospitals from Maine to California receive the same rate. So if a hospital spends more on a patient than the fixed amount for that category of illness, it must absorb the loss. If it spends less, it makes money.

In the past, doctors and hospitals were encouraged to do more in treating a patient. Neither the medical community nor the patient was particularly worried about the costs because insurance companies or Medicare picked up most of the tab. But fee-for-service payment encouraged unnecessary tests, procedures, and surgery—a gravy train for unscrupulous doctors and a major drain on corporate and public coffers. Some estimates placed medical costs resulting from waste, duplication, fraud, and abuse at 30 percent of the nation's annual medical bill. Medicare was

headed for bankruptcy. And corporations found that their ability to compete with foreign firms was undermined by the high costs of employee benefit programs. For instance, one-tenth of Chrysler's costs in making the K-car was accounted for by health expenditures (Trafford and Dworkin, 1986).

To cope with rising medical expenses, various cost-cutting alternatives have emerged. Many of them reward doctors and hospitals for keeping costs down by doing less for patients and getting them in and out as quickly as possible. The current drive by corporations to contain health care costs is based on a variety of managed-care programs, primarily health maintenance organizations and preferred provider organizations (by some estimates, three-fourths of the American population will be enrolled in these delivery systems by the mid-1990s):

- *Health-maintenance organizations (HMOs)* offer prepaid health plans. For a fixed sum of money each year, the HMO (a physician, a group of physicians, a hospital, or other organization) provides its members with comprehensive health care. If total costs go higher than the sum of the prepayments, the HMO loses money; if they stay below the estimate, the HMO gets to keep the difference. The provider benefits financially from delivering less care rather than more. On average, HMOs use 30 percent fewer hospital days than the traditional fee-for-service

provider (Schwartz, 1984). By 1987, HMOs claimed to provide care for more than 25 million Americans.

- The *preferred-provider organization (PPO)* is an arrangement whereby an insurer or employer contracts with a group of physicians to provide its members or employees with care. PPOs commonly pay each doctor, in advance, a set amount per patient. The doctor, in return, must cover the costs for all services to that patient. The same doctor may have fee-for-service as well as prepaid patients.

The essence of all managed care is to restrict medical practice thought to be overly elaborate and too expensive. But new arrangements for containing costs may be placing the *quality* of health services in jeopardy. Critics charge that patients are being discharged "quicker and sicker," without post-hospital support. Moreover, HMOs have an economic incentive to weed out doctors who provide the most lab tests and specialist referrals and to replace them with more "manageable" practitioners. It is also financially beneficial to an HMO if those patients who use its services the most (particularly elderly patients) become sufficiently annoyed by a lack of care that they drop out of the plan. In sum, critics worry that incentives are skewed toward the *pretense* of care delivery, and that there is a disincentive to provide actual care (Brannigan, 1986; Anderson, 1987).

down. The control of health care by doctors is shifting to large corporations and the government because those who ultimately pay the bills can determine the way the money is spent.

The Nursing Profession

The nursing profession grew out of the religious and charitable activities of early hospitals. Religious orders of

Unacceptable Realism?
Thomas Eakins, an American artist, portrayed Dr. Samuel D. Gross performing an operation and lecturing to students at the Jefferson Medical College of Philadelphia in 1875. The uncompromising truth of a few square inches of blood was repellent to the times, and Eakins had difficulty exhibiting the painting. *(Jefferson Medical College of Thomas Jefferson University, Philadelphia)*

nuns took on the care of the sick and the poor. Because nursing is so closely associated with its religious origins, the term "sister" is still used to mean "nurse" in many European nations. By the latter half of the 1800s, however, increasing numbers of nonreligious personnel were employed to perform various custodial functions in hospitals. Since the jobs required no formal training and were deemed to be menial labor, many poor and uneducated women entered the field. This heritage has contributed to the undeservedly low prestige the profession of nursing has long endured (Mauksch, 1972).

The professionalization of nursing—the emergence of professional standards, education, and nursing organizations—received impetus from the activities of Florence Nightingale and her organization of nurses during the Crimean War (an 1853–1856 war with Great Britain, France, and Turkey on one side and Russia on the other). Nightingale sought to strengthen cooperative ties between physicians and nurses in the care of patients. Although her efforts carved out a special niche in patient care for nurses, it had the side effect of establishing nursing as a profession under the jurisdiction of physicians. By World War I, most nurses were educated in two- or three-year nursing programs with a hospital apprentice-

ship. Today, most nurses earn a bachelor of science degree in nursing in a four-year college degree program, and many go on to secure master's degrees in specialized areas.

Through the years nursing has remained almost exclusively female (97 percent of America's 1.5 million nurses are women). Even though nurses have traditionally spent more time with hospitalized patients than doctors, physicians have rarely acknowledged their significance and have seldom approached them as colleagues. However, the old pattern of dominance based on doctors being men and nurses being women is changing as more and more women are becoming physicians. Increasing numbers of nurses are also going into private practice as nurse-midwives, nurse-practitioners, nurse-anesthetists, and critical-care nurses. But as many communities are experiencing an oversupply of doctors, physicians have intensified their efforts to bar nurses from performing midwife services (Easterbrook, 1987). Historically, physicians ignored midwives as long as they served rural and poor patients; they even endorsed midwife programs for urban ghettos and poor rural areas in the South (De-Vries, 1985).

About 60 percent of all registered nurses work in hospitals, where they serve simultaneously as managers of hospital wards and assistants to physicians. These dual functions often place nurses in situations of role conflict because they are responsible to both administrative and medical authorities. And in an era of high technology and intensive-care units, nurses have had to assume more responsibilities, leading many to experience role overload. Compounding the problems of nurses on hospital wards, bureaucratic dictates are filling their time with mounting paperwork. These requirements have made it increasingly difficult for nurses to listen to patients and provide them with emotional support—critical tasks historically performed by the nursing profession (Taylor, 1986).

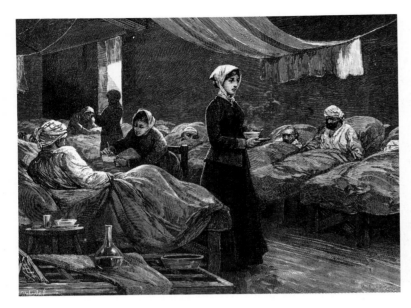

Florence Nightingale in the Hospital at Scutari
The care that Florence Nightingale and other nurses afforded wounded and sick soldiers during the Crimean War received considerable popular acclaim and helped to establish nursing as a distinct profession. Gross military inefficiency characterized both sides in the war, with sickness causing more deaths than bullets. *(Mary Evans Picture Library/Photo Researchers)*

Wages in nursing, as in other fields with a large concentration of women, remain low (see Chapter 12). Starting nurses average about $18,000 a year. From a career standpoint, nurses achieve peak earnings (about $25,000) and responsibility in their late twenties, with few if any opportunities for later advancement. These factors—coupled with an ambiguous image of nursing in the media, widespread dissatisfaction with working conditions, and women's increased access to other professions—have contributed to a critical shortage of nurses. Enrollments in nursing schools have been dropping in recent years. Meanwhile, the number of registered nurses needed over the next decade is expected to increase by 33 percent (Echenique, 1986; Wright, 1986; Easterbrook, 1987).

Patients

Some 9 out of 10 Americans say they are in excellent or pretty good health, although 1 in 4 suffers from a serious chronic disease. Moreover, 87 percent are satisfied with the health care they receive, but 39 percent have switched doctors or stopped going to a doctor because they were dissatisfied. The most frequent reasons patients cite for leaving doctors is that the doctor did not spend enough time with them; the doctor did not have a friendly personality; the doctor did not answer their questions honestly or completely; and the treatment did not work. About 26 percent of Americans have been told they have high blood pressure or a heart condition; 18

percent have arthritis; 9 percent suffer from anxiety or depression; 10 percent have ulcers; and 5 percent have diabetes (Findlay, 1985).

A person's relationship with the health care system is far more complex than in the past. The rapidly changing social environment and the speed of scientific and technological advances have all made for change. The simple one-to-one relationship that existed between patient and doctor is often replaced by a "patient-care team" made up of physicians, nurses, and paramedical staff. Typically, stable, face-to-face, long-term relationships evolved between patients and their doctors. But the growth in medical specialization and general population mobility have eroded many of these earlier ties.

Interaction between a physician and patient was traditionally governed by inequality. Like other professionals, doctors derived their power from their command of an esoteric body of knowledge, acquired through academic training and leavened by a service orientation toward the client (see Chapter 15). The "competence gap" justified both the physician's assumption of authority and the client's trust, confidence, and compliance. However, over the past decade or so, a new type of relationship has emerged between many physicians and their patients that is based on consumerism. It focuses on the purchaser's (the patient's) rights and the seller's (the physician's) obligations. In a consumer relationship, the seller lacks authority because the buyer can make the decision to buy or not to buy. With many patients coming to view doctors as self-interested vendors of their ser-

A Legendary Figure: The Family Physician?
Toward the end of the nineteenth century and in the early decades of the twentieth century, the American doctor was depicted as a trusted, kindly, and gentle healer. The state of medical technology was limited and often the physician could offer patients and their families little more than solace. Consequently, the human dimension was at the forefront of medicine. But as medical technology has become increasingly sophisticated, the one-to-one relationship between doctor and patient has eroded, replaced by a patient-care team. The new climate is fostering consumer-driven attitudes that are incompatible with earlier notions and practices. (*The Bettmann Archive*)

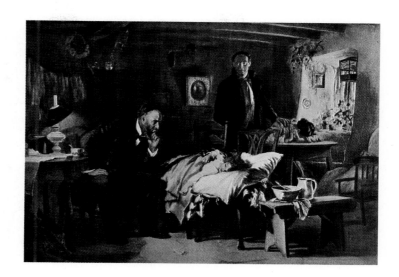

vices, the practice of medicine is becoming customer-driven.

On the basis of the knowledge they have acquired through experience, education, or the media, many younger and better-educated patients now make their own assessments of their health. One indicator of the new trend is the spate of do-it-yourself health books. Underlying these developments is the notion that self-care is appropriate, and that physicians are not essential. These new attitudes are incompatible with the sick-role model of the dependent patient and the doctor authority figure. Additionally, patients are becoming more distrustful of doctors, while simultaneously holding the medical profession to higher standards of accountability. As a result, physician and patient often do not know what to expect of one another (Betz and O'Connell, 1983; Haug and Lavin, 1983; Arney and Bergen, 1984). Moreover, growing numbers of physicians are reporting more aggravation than satisfaction in practicing medicine these days (Steptoe, 1987).

Financing Health Care

The United States seems to be moving toward a three-tiered system for the financing of health care. The first tier is a set of government programs that provides a minimal level of care for the elderly and disabled (Medicare) and the poor (Medicaid). The government pays care providers a fixed fee for various categories of treatment and care. The second tier involves the financing of health

care by private corporations and depends on the level of care employers are prepared to provide for their employees. A corporation typically enters a fixed-price contract with health providers—a health maintenance organization (HMO) or a preferred provider organization (PPO)—to cover its workers for some fixed period (see the box entitled, "Is the Quality of American Medical Care in Jeopardy?"). The third tier consists of a free-market, individual health care system. In this market people can buy health care in excess of that provided by the government or their employers. The only limit on treatment is the amount of money individuals are willing to spend on themselves or their family (Thurow, 1985). Soaring health costs have been a major factor in the evolution of these arrangements.

Soaring health costs As Figure 18.4 on page 508 shows, the nation's health expenditures have increased steadily in recent decades. Between 1980 and 1986, hospital costs rose nearly 70 percent. A variety of forces have operated to push costs up:

1. *Incentive systems.* The classical rules that govern marketplace exchanges have not been applied to the health industry. The sellers, doctors and hospitals, have traditionally determined the price and product options; the buyers, the patients, rather than shopping around, have bought what the sellers have ordered. And since doctors and hospitals have been paid for what they do, regardless of

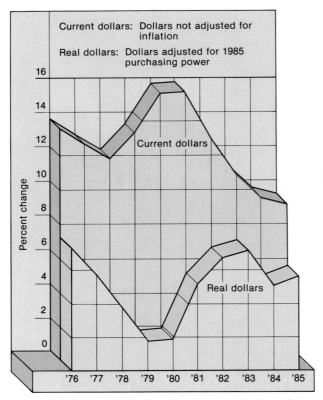

FIGURE 18.4 Annual Percentage Growth in American Health Expenditures

If one measures national health expenditures in current (nonadjusted) dollars, it appears that the expenditures have been rising at ever-falling annual rates since 1981. In terms of constant purchasing power (inflation-adjusted dollars), the picture is quite different. The Medical Care Price Index is still rising about three times as fast as the Consumer Price Index for all goods and services. *Source: Uwe E. Reinhardt. 1986. Battle over medical costs isn't over.* Wall Street Journal *(October 22):28.*

whether the care actually benefits the patient, they have had few incentives not to use every service and technique available. Each year corporate and government health programs are estimated to pay $60 billion for medical procedures that are not needed by patients. For example, Americans who go to fee-for-service doctors are twice as likely to have coronary bypass surgery as those who belong to health maintenance organizations and four times more likely than their European and Canadian counterparts (Califano, 1986). As reflected in

Table 18.2, there are also erratic geographic variations in medical practice. Boston residents are half as likely to have their tonsils removed as people in Springfield, Massachusetts, just 95 miles away. The chance of being admitted to a hospital because of gastroenteritis, a digestive system disorder, is nearly twice as great in Stockton, California, as in Pal Alto, only 75 miles away (Davidson, 1986).

2. *Mounting labor, administrative, and insurance costs.* Labor costs have risen sharply (since 1950 the number of hospital workers per bed has more than tripled). Simultaneously, administrative costs—personnel for such activities as billing, accounting, and institutional planning—have grown three times faster since 1970 than costs for health care personnel (administrative costs accounted for 22 percent, or $77.7 billion, of American medical bills in 1983) (Himmelstein and Woolhandler, 1986). Liability insurance costs have also increased dramatically as more and more patients have brought lawsuits against doctors they believe have provided them with negligent health care. Currently, malpractice insurance premiums average about 5 percent of physicians' revenues (however, obstetricians often pay premiums that average 25 percent of their in-

"With the cost of real estate and my son's tuition, how can they say these are unnecessary operations?"

From The Wall Street Journal; permission, Cartoon Features Syndicate

Table 18.2 Frequency of Hospitalization or Operations (per 10,000 population)

	Gastroenteritis	Major Cardio-vascular	Hysterectomy	Tonsillectomy
Stockton, Calif.	35.2	19.6	31.8	15.6
Sacramento, Calif.	28.3	16.9	24.3	7.3
Palo Alto, Calif.	19.1	13.8	17.8	7.7
North San Diego, Calif.	24.8	23.0	27.7	11.9
Springfield, Mass.	45.4	13.0	20.6	11.8
Boston, Mass.	33.3	11.2	12.1	6.2
Des Moines, Iowa	83.6	NA	26.7	NA
Iowa City, Iowa	40.8	NA	14.1	NA

NA = Not available.

Source: Joe Davidson. 1986. Research mystery: Use of surgery, hospitals varies greatly by region. *Wall Street Journal* (March 5):33.

come) and 2 percent of hospital costs. Moreover, to protect themselves against litigation, doctors often practice defensive medicine, ordering countless but unnecessary tests (Freudenheim, 1986).

3. *More costly technologies.* The continual upgrading in the scope and intensity of medical services is costly. Technological advances include such accepted practices as hip-replacement and coronary-bypass surgery (now costing more than $4 billion a year), new therapies such as liver and heart transplant, and new diagnostic techniques such as computerized axial tomography (CAT) and magnetic resonance imaging (MRI) devices (often costing $2 million apiece) (Schwartz, 1984).

4. *Aging population.* Our population is getting larger and older, and this fact alone contributes about one percentage point a year to the increase in real costs. More and more Americans are living beyond age 85. It is this age group in which the chronic diseases and disorders of aging take their main toll. The risk of developing Alzheimer's disease is only 1 in 20 at the age of 65, but this figure rises to 1 in 4 among those who live past their 85th birthday. While Americans 85 years of age and older currently constitute less than 1 percent of the population, they fill more than 20 percent of the beds in nursing homes.

5. *High expectations.* Americans have come to expect a high level of medical care, and they show

no signs of accepting less when it is their turn to go to the hospital. Surveys show that Americans want a system that provides first-class care with a human face, that is accessible to everyone, including the poor and the old, and that is affordable. Quality, accessibility, and cost, then, are the major criteria (Taylor, 1985).

Containing costs As exploding costs have led the two major payers of the nation's health bill, government and employers, to reduce their health care outlays, new arrangements for financing health care have appeared. The new arrangements have developed piecemeal over the past fifteen years. Their theme is "competition"— the notion that physicians, hospitals, and other health providers should compete for patients in a price-sensitive market, not unlike the markets for other goods and services (Relman, 1986). The air of competition is changing the ways Americans use and pay doctors and hospitals. It is also reshaping the financial incentives that have encouraged unnecessary care (Califano, 1986).

Another approach to holding down costs is to keep people out of hospitals. Increasingly, hospitals and independent medical companies are setting up satellite outpatient surgical centers, mobile diagnostic laboratories, hospices, and walk-in clinics for routine care. Even so, little is being done about the estimated 30 or 40 million Americans who lack adequate medical care. Indeed, since 1975, as a result of changes in Medicaid eligibility requirements, the proportion of low-income Americans

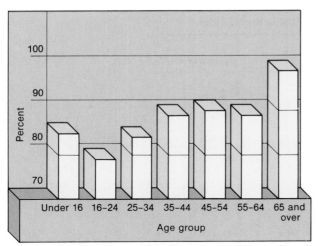

FIGURE 18.5   **Percentage of Americans with Health Insurance, by Age, 1985**
Source: U.S. Bureau of the Census.

insured by Medicaid has fallen from 63 to 46 percent (Blendon et al., 1986). Although about 87 percent of Americans have private or government health insurance, at least 13 percent lack health coverage (see Figure 18.5). These inadequacies have led some critics to contend that the United States should provide all citizens, as an entitlement, with the essentials of adequate health care, regardless of ability to pay (Relman, 1986). The British system illustrates this approach.

The British health care system   Following World War II, the British created a system of "socialized medicine" in which health care is approached in much the way that Americans handle the public school education of their children (Mechanic, 1971; Fox, 1986). The British National Health Service finances access to high-quality health care for all citizens through taxation. The state, not the individual, assumes payments for visits to a physician and hospital care. Doctors receive from the government a basic salary and a small annual fee for each patient on their registers. They may also accept private, fee-paying patients if they wish. Each person is free to select a physician of his or her own choosing. The primary complaint against the system is that patients often have a long waiting time in a doctor's office, and there are long waiting lists for the treatment of medical problems considered nonessential, like hernia and hip replacement surgery.

The central government limits expenditure on medical care by rigid budgetary control. In no year has the global sum exceeded 6.2 percent of the gross national product. Many physicians and other health care workers believe the British National Health Service is underfinanced. Even so, life expectancy and infant mortality are almost identical in Britain and the United States. Since the British austerity budget allows about half the level of expenditures of the United States, some beneficial services and procedures have had to be rationed. The British, for instance, use less X-ray film, provide little treatment for cancerous solid tumors, and generally

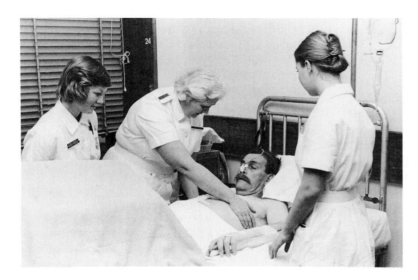

The British Health Care System
The British provide health care services to the public under an arrangement that resembles the way Americans provide for public school education. The state assumes payment of medical bills which it finances through taxation. *(Charles Kennard/Stock, Boston)*

do not offer kidney dialysis to the elderly (Daniels, 1986; Lister, 1986).

THINKING THROUGH THE ISSUES

As a growing number of Americans live to age 85 and beyond, will healthy Americans below age 65 support massive health care expenditures to keep alive the extremely ill or the very old? Or will there be some attempt to ration expensive life-saving technologies? For instance, more than 30 percent of Medicare's money goes to patients with less than a year to live. And in 1984, a mere 3.4 percent of Chrysler's insured employees accounted for 43.5 percent of the company's health care payments. These high-cost cases often involved chronic or terminal illness (Califano, 1986). The idea of rationing care is alien to most Americans. The British, however, have been living for a long time with a system that requires hard choices. For instance, up to the age of 45 or 50, the rate of kidney dialysis and transplant in Great Britain is nearly the same as in the United States. But only a small number of patients over age 55 are placed on dialysis. There is no official age cutoff; instead, British doctors typically do not refer elderly people who are ill with other diseases such as diabetes or heart trouble to dialysis centers. Since funds for medical care are not infinite, will Americans be confronted in the near future with a similar kind of moral dilemma? Consider this situation raised by William Schwartz (1984), a physician and professor of medicine: If we know that keeping someone alive for another few months at a cost of $100,000 will mean that this money is not available for the care of several people with hip or heart disease, should we use the limited resource for maintaining a life of poor quality for a few months and deny care to others?

Chapter Highlights

1. Patterns of health and illness vary from society to society and from group to group within a society. In part, these differences reflect differences in social habits and styles of life. Social and cultural factors also influence whether or not people seek formal treatment and how they respond to it.

2. Stress and social support affect our ability to stay well. A stressful job or financial difficulties nearly double the odds that we will become ill or injured. Social support plays a crucial role in our physical and mental health through its health-sustaining and stress-buffering functions.

3. Functionalists point out that a society's well-being depends upon a healthy labor force for carrying out vital tasks. Consequently, disease and illness must be socially controlled lest it impair societal functioning. Conflict theorists emphasize that some members of modern societies achieve better health than others because they are socially advantaged. And symbolic interactionists focus on the culturally created meanings we attach to certain conditions and come to view as illness and sickness.

4. Rather than trusting solely to the motivation and abilities of afflicted people to get better, all societies have evolved one or more "specialist" positions to deal with sickness. Curers, shamans, physicians, nurses, and other practitioners are relied upon to explain illness and to offer means for eliminating or controlling it. From a virtual cottage industry dominated by individual physicians and not-for-profit hospitals, health care in the United States is evolving into a network of corporations running everything from hospitals and home services to retirement homes and health spas.

5. Fundamental changes are taking place in how doctors practice medicine and hospitals care for the sick. With health costs soaring, some of the traditional incentives in financing health care have been reversed. Various cost-cutting alternatives have emerged. Many of them reward doctors and hospitals for keeping costs down by doing less for patients and getting them in and out as quickly as possible.

6. Although the private practitioner continues to be the norm in medicine, the practice of medicine is increasingly becoming a corporate undertaking. Tech-

nological trends, social policy, lifestyle changes, government- and employer-paid health insurance plans, a scarcity of capital, and an increasing number of physicians and health care facilities are factors combining to reshape health care into centralized and well-structured organizations designed for a competitive market.

7. Ninety-seven percent of America's 1.5 million nurses are women. Wages in nursing, as in other fields with a large concentration of women, remain low. This factor, and widespread dissatisfaction with working conditions and the ambiguous public image of the profession, have contributed to a critical shortage of nurses.

8. The United States is moving toward a three-tier system for the financing of health care. The first tier is a set of government programs that provides a minimal level of care for the elderly and disabled and the poor. The second tier involves the financing of health care by private corporations and depends on the level of care employers are prepared to provide for their employees. The third tier consists of a free-market, individual health care system.

The Sociologist's Vocabulary

disease A condition in which an organism does not function properly due to presumed biological causes.

epidemiology The study of the distribution of diseases among and within populations.

health A state of complete physical, mental, and social well-being, and not merely the absence of disease or infirmity.

health-maintenance organizations (HMOs) A physician, a group of physicians, a hospital, or other organization providing members with comprehensive health care for a fixed sum of money each year.

illness The sense we have that we are afflicted by a disease.

medicalization of deviance More and more behaviors earlier generations considered immoral or sinful coming to be regarded as forms of sickness.

medicine The social institution responsible for problems of health and illness.

preferred provider organization (PPO) An arrangement whereby an insurer or employer contracts with a group of physicians to provide its members or employees with health care.

sickness A social status in which other people define us as having a disease and accordingly alter their behavior toward us.

sick role A role in which people are exempted from their usual social roles and responsibilities.

PART SIX

Changing Society

19

Population and Ecology

Man can improve the quality of his life, not by imposing himself on nature as a conqueror, but by participating in the continuous act of creation in which all living things are engaged. Otherwise, he may be doomed to survive as something less than human.

—René Dubos, as quoted in *Life*, July 28, 1970

Earth is not simply an inanimate rock that happens to support life. Our planet has been likened to a space vehicle in a deadly vacuum, with a life support system as precious as the astronaut's backpack. Like the spacecraft, Earth is an integrated system in which all the parts—including the living part—interact and contribute to the survival of the whole. Because people have become such an important force in nature, in terms of both numbers and activity, sociologists and other scientists are taking a closer look at what we are doing to our planet (Cowen, 1987).

The magnitude of our species's impact on the earth is enormous. We are eroding soil, destroying forests, contaminating water sources, extinguishing plant and animal species, and creating deserts. We are making and releasing chemicals, including spray-can propellants and refrigerator coolants, that threaten the outer ozone shield. We are polluting the air with carbon dioxide and other heat-trapping gases to a degree that is changing the world's climate. One of the most dramatic consequences of atmospheric pollution—the greenhouse effect—would be the melting of the polar ice sheets. If this should happen, the oceans would rise 15 to 25 feet and change coastlines. Cities like Charleston and Galveston would be completely flooded; Miami, Baltimore, Boston, New York, and San Francisco would lose significant chunks of real estate. Members of Congress would arrive by boat at Capitol Hill, which would be the waterfront on a swollen Potomac River. Humankind, then, is joining wind, rain, snow, volcanoes, sun spots, and the ponderous drift of continents as a major force for global change (Begley, 1986; Maranto, 1986; Cowen, 1987).

The pressures of population growth are also taxing the earth's natural system. Although overall agricultural production has been growing, it has been declining in many countries, especially in Africa, because of soil erosion and the spread of deserts. Even in the United States, a sixth of the grain harvest comes from eroding lands or draws on diminishing sources of groundwater for irrigation, and cannot be sustained over the long run. Explosive population growth is having detrimental social consequences in many Third World countries. Not untypical are some Central American nations, where high population growth, deforestation, soil erosion, and high energy costs have contributed to political instability and social disintegration. In many parts of the world, efforts to improve living standards are themselves endangering the health of the global economy. Many of these changes threaten to make the Earth a less habitable planet for future generations (Shabecoff, 1987).

PLANNING AHEAD: TARGETED READING

1. What factors underlie population change?

2. What have been the long-term trends in world population change?

3. What policies are available for discouraging or encouraging population growth?

4. How is humankind linked within a complex web of interdependencies with other organisms and nature?

5. Need we be concerned about the depletion of critical resources and a deteriorating natural environment?

Demography

It is difficult to consider the social experience very long without turning rather quickly to a discussion of population. A **population** is a group of organisms who are members of the same species and occupy a certain territory. Each human population has a set of unique characteristics that are rooted in group forces and that cannot be explained solely in terms of the biological or mental characteristics of its individual members. For instance, although individuals are born and die, they do not have birth rates and death rates. These are characteristics of a population. **Demography** is the science dealing with the size, distribution, and composition of, and changes in, population.

The Social Significance of Demography

It would be easy to dismiss demographic research as the collection of statistics, if the statistics meant little. But demographic data in fact are vital for a society. Consider the United States. The periodic rise and fall in births has created waves of people who pass through the life course, alternately building up and eroding major institutional

arrangements and changing the social landscape. Usually demographic changes do not have overnight effects; they often sneak up on us slowly and modestly.

Many of the population effects the United States is now confronting result from a large "bulge" of those born between 1946 and the early 1960s. This cohort is currently making its way through the life course (see Chapter 11). Sandwiched between two much smaller generations—the children born during the Great Depression of the 1930s and the "baby bust" group of the 1970s—the baby boom generation has strained American institutions at every stage. Demographers liken this generation's progress across the decades to that of a watermelon swallowed by a python. The bumper crop of 64 million infants born between 1946 and 1961 are now nearly 30 to 45 years old and comprise about a third of the American population.

In the 1950s the baby boomers made the United States a child-oriented society of new schools, suburbs, and station wagons. The baby boomers born before 1955 provided the nation with Davy Crockett and rock 'n' roll, went to Woodstock and Vietnam, and fueled the student, civil rights, and peace movements of the 1960s and early 1970s. Younger boomers have been somewhat

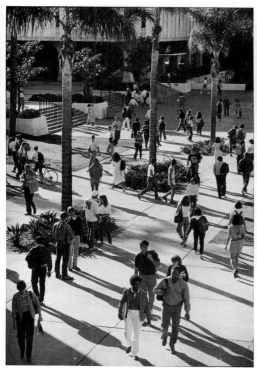

Major Institutions Are Affected by Population Changes
As the traditional college age population of youths between the ages of 18 and 24 declines (left), universities are increasingly turning to adult education and evening classes to fill their classrooms with older adults. The military (above) is also having growing difficulty recruiting young people, so proposals to revive the draft are beginning to be heard. *(left, Frank D. Smith/Jeroboam; above, Jane Scherr/Jeroboam)*

more conservative. They find that their older brothers and sisters have already taken the better positions, in many cases blocking career ladders. A 1986 Gallup poll found that 61 percent of Americans ages 22 to 40 said it was harder for them to afford a home "that fits their expectations" than it was for people of comparable age in the 1940s and 1950s. Even so, 57 percent felt better able to find a good-paying job (although 51 percent thought they were less able to find a job with long-term security), and 48 percent said they were better able to lead a fulfilling life than was true in their parents' generation (Hellmich, 1986).

Many of the schools built to accommodate the large number of baby boomers in the 1960s are now closed or half empty, and colleges are already scrambling to keep enrollments up. The college-age population (individuals aged 18 to 24) peaked in 1981 at 30 million people. By 1995, only 24 million people will be 18 to 24 years old, a 22 percent decline from 1981. College presidents are turning to adult education in hope of maintaining enrollments. The armed forces will also be hard hit as the young adult population declines. If they are to maintain current annual requirements, the military will have to recruit 55 percent of all qualified and available 18-year-

old men in 1995. They now recruit about 42 percent. So the once-unthinkable notion of reviving the draft is gaining ground in Congress (Carrington, 1986). Along with colleges and the armed forces, businesses that rely on young, low-wage workers, such as the food service, tourism, and hospitality industries, will feel the impact of the "baby bust" years. Already fast-food chains are recruiting older Americans to staff the grills and cash registers (DeMott, 1987).

The imbalance in the size of the nation's generations is likely to cause additional problems when the baby boom children reach old age. By the year 2030, one out of every five Americans will be 65 or older; they will be dependent on a social security and Medicare system that will have to be supported by the smaller generations behind them. The social security dependency ratio (the number of workers relative to the number of recipients) was 5 to 1 twenty years ago; it will drop to 2 to 1 by 2035.

So population changes have major social consequences. Educational, governmental, and business leaders would do well to undertake serious, long-term analysis and planning to prepare for swings in the sizes of generations. Population changes also touch our lives in less vital ways. Look at the influence they have on a college's football fortunes. As the population grows in southern, southwestern, and West Coast states, more high schools are built in these areas. And there are more talented and well-coached prep gridders available for southeastern, southwestern, and Pacific Coast teams. So the fortunes of the college teams in these regions improve. Those of the Northeast and Midwest (including the Big Ten) seem to deteriorate, especially in intersectional contests.

Components in Population Change

Overall, a human population grows because people in it have more children, or because people die less quickly, or because new members are added to it when they move from one place to another. In short, all population change within a society can be reduced to three factors: the birth rate, the death rate, and migration into or out of the society.

Birth rate   The **birth rate** is the number of live births per 1,000 members of a population in a given year. In 1986 the birth rate for Americans was 15.3 per thousand, down substantially from the nation's highest postwar rate of 26.5 per thousand in 1947. The American rate is also substantially lower than that of nations like Kenya in eastern Africa, which has a birth rate of 53.8 per thousand. Demographers are also interested in a society's **fertility**, the number of babies born to the average woman of childbearing age. Fertility differs from **fecundity**, the potential number of children that could be born if every woman of childbearing age bore all the children she possibly could. Fertility does not equal fecundity because health, cultural, and social factors intervene to curb prolific reproduction.

As Figure 19.1 shows, the number of children born in recent years is rising. In thinking about this pattern, we need to keep in mind that the momentum of population growth takes a number of generations to build or wind down. The primary reason for the increase in births is a national "baby boomlet," the echo effect of the baby boom: Women having babies now are the baby boomers of the 1950s. But the average number of children born to today's mothers is only about half the number born to women three decades ago. Overall, the birth rate among American women has continued its decline in the 1980s, with one exception: Childbearing is up among women in their early thirties who postponed having babies until their schooling was completed and their careers begun.

Young American women say they want so few children that, if they do as they say they will, their generation will not replace itself. From a postwar high of 3.8 births per woman at the peak of the baby boom the figure has tumbled to 1.8, where it has remained unchanged for a decade. It takes an average of 2.1 children per woman for a modern population to replace itself without immigration, the figure of **zero population growth** (ZPG). Some 12 percent of all American women aged 18 to 34 indicate that they do not plan to have children. These trends reflect the dramatically changing roles of women in American life and in the workforce. Were it not for the continued infusion of immigrants, the United States population would begin to decline before the middle of the next century (Westoff, 1986).

Death rate   The **death rate** is the number of deaths per 1,000 members of a population in a given year. In 1986 the death rate for Americans was 8.7 per thousand, substantially lower than that of a nation like Chad in central Africa, which has a death rate of 44.1 per thousand. The **infant mortality rate** is the number of deaths among infants under 1 year of age per 1,000 live births. In 1985 the infant mortality rate in the United States was 10.6 per 1,000. Eighteen nations report infant mortality rates lower than that, the lowest being Finland, Japan, and Sweden, with rates of 6.0, 6.6, and 6.8, respectively. In

FIGURE 19.1   Increase in U.S. Births, 1947 to 1985
Source: National Center for Health Statistics.

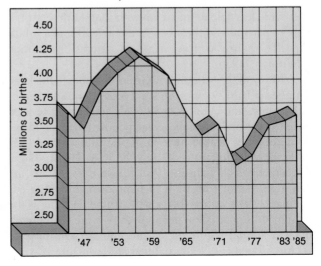

contrast, the infant mortality rate of the Soviet Union is 31 and that of Ethiopia, 229.

Life expectancy is the number of years of life remaining to an average person of a certain age. A 50-year-old man living in northern Europe in 1500 had only one chance in four of living to be 70. The odds increased to 45 percent by 1700 but remained at roughly this level until the beginning of the twentieth century. By 1983, even the average American newborn could expect to live 74.7 years. White female newborns could expect to live 78.8 years, and black female newborns, 73.8 years. In contrast, white males born in 1983 had a life expectancy of 71.6 years, and black males a life expectancy of 65.2 years. As a result of the greater longevity of women, there are currently in the United States three women for every two men over the age of 65; in the over-85 bracket, the margin is better than two to one. Genetic differences may play a part in these sex differences (Epstein, 1983). Women appear to be more durable because of an inherent sex-linked resistance to some types of life-threatening disease. For instance, the female hormone estrogen is a protective factor against cardiovascular disease. Lifestyle differences also seem to play a part. One factor has been the higher incidence of smoking among men (Holden, 1983). But with the increase of smoking among teenage girls, women may lose some of their statistical advantage in the years ahead.

Migration   **Migration** refers to the movement of people from one geographic area to another in order to establish a new residence. Migration is the product of two factors. *Push* factors encourage people to leave a habitat they already occupy; *pull* factors attract people to a new habitat. Before people actually migrate, they usually compare the relative opportunities offered by the present and the anticipated habitat. If the balance is on the side of the anticipated habitat, they typically migrate unless prevented from doing so by a Berlin Wall, immigration quotas, lack of financial resources, or some other compelling reason. In the 1840s the "push" of the potato famine in Ireland and the "pull" of employment opportunities in the United States made this country appear attractive to many Irish people. The "push" resulting from the failure of the 1848 Revolution and the "pull" of American political freedom also led many Germans to seek their fortunes in this country. At the present time, both "push" and "pull" factors are contributing to the entry into the United States of large numbers of illegal aliens from Mexico. Low agricultural productivity and commodity prices in Mexican agriculture have served as a "push" factor and high American wages have served as a "pull" factor (see Chapter 10). The movement of people from one nation to another is called **international migration.**

People also move about within a nation—**internal migration.** Within the United States, the South and the West have been the fastest growing regions. Consider the South. From 1910 to 1955, millions of people left the region. Most were poor whites and blacks heading North, away from the South's ailing farms and struggling

Anti-Immigrant Sentiment Has Been Mounting in Western Europe
In recent years, tightening job opportunities, mounting economic woes, and ethnic mistrust has fed an anti-immigrant backlash in many Western European nations. Most major cities have large communities of foreign-born workers whose cultures remain non-European, such as these Moslems kneeling in prayer in Marseilles, France. Nationalistic reactions and sentiments are increasingly closing Europe's doors to the foreign born (Zanker, 1986). (J. Pavlovsky/Sygma)

Haitian Refugees Arriving in Florida
Political oppression and diminishing economic opportunities in Haiti are "push" factors and political freedom and economic opportunities are "pull" factors that have encouraged Haitians to leave their Caribbean island homeland for the United States. The refugees often incur incredible risk in making their way to the United States, including setting sail in vessels that are marginally seaworthy. (*Randy Taylor/ Sygma*)

local economies. But then the tide shifted, so that between 1960 and 1985 the South gained over 17 million jobs, compared to a gain of just under 11 million in the West and 13 million in the Midwest and Northeast combined. During this period, the South became increasingly attractive to business. Additionally, more and more retired people sought the South's warmer climate; racial attitudes liberalized; a more cosmopolitan atmosphere pervaded southern cities, exemplified by Atlanta; and lower living and amenity costs than those of the Midwest and East attracted many younger people (Kasarda, Irwin, and Hughes, 1986).

Growth rate   The **growth rate** of a society is the difference between births and deaths, plus the difference between immigrants and emigrants per 1,000 population. In 1986, the United States had a growth rate of 0.9 percent. The highest annual population growth rate is 11.3 percent in the United Arab Emirates. The growth rate of the Soviet Union is roughly comparable to that of the United States. However, a number of nations, including East Germany, West Germany, and Hungary, have negative annual growth rates, which means that without immigration they will lose population. If we consider merely the difference between the birth and death rates (the rate of natural increase), it takes a population with an annual rate of increase of 1 percent 69 years to double its population; a 4 percent annual rate of increase leads to a doubling in 17 years. A nation's growth rate has many implications. For instance, assuming unchanged rates of investment and technological

progress, income in a population growing at 3 percent a year would be 13 percent lower than in one growing at 1 percent (Holden, 1986). We will have more to say about this issue later in the chapter.

Population Composition

Births, death, and migration affect population *size*. Sociologists are also interested in the *composition* or characteristics of a population. Among these characteristics are sex, age, rural or urban residence, race, religion, national origin, marital status, income, education, and occupation.

Sex composition   The sex composition of a population is of particular significance. It is measured by the *sex ratio*, the number of males per 100 females. About 124 males are conceived for every 100 females, but by virtue of their higher rate of miscarriage, the rate drops to approximately 105 for full-term births. Then, beginning about age 21, women begin to outnumber men, and the rate accelerates as people grow older. Typically, frontier, mining, cattle-raising, and lumbering areas attract a disproportionate number of men. Women are found in greatest numbers in areas concentrating on commercial and clerical activities (for instance, Long Island and Hartford, Connecticut) (Elias, 1986).

Age composition   Another important population characteristic is its age composition. A population heavily concentrated in the 20- to 65-year range has a large labor force relative to its nonproductive population. Dependency burdens tend to be light. In contrast, a population concentrated at either extreme of the age distribution—either under 20, over 65, or both—has a heavy dependency ratio (a large number of nonproductive individuals relative to productive population). We can gain an appreciation of the social significance of these facts by examining population pyramids.

Population pyramids　Figure 19.2 shows how the age and sex composition of a population can be portrayed by a **population pyramid,** often called the "tree of ages,"

based on absolute numbers or proportions. Age groupings are placed in order on a vertical scale, with the youngest age group located at the bottom and the oldest at the top. On the horizontal axis are plotted the numbers or proportions that each specified age group represents of the total, with the sum or portion corresponding to the male segment placed to the left of the central dividing line and that comprising the female segment placed to the right of it. The pyramid itself represents the entire population.

　　The population pyramid for 1900 shown in Figure 19.2 has the shape of a true pyramid, typical of a popula-

FIGURE 19.2 **Population Pyramids, United States**
Source: U.S. Bureau of the Census.

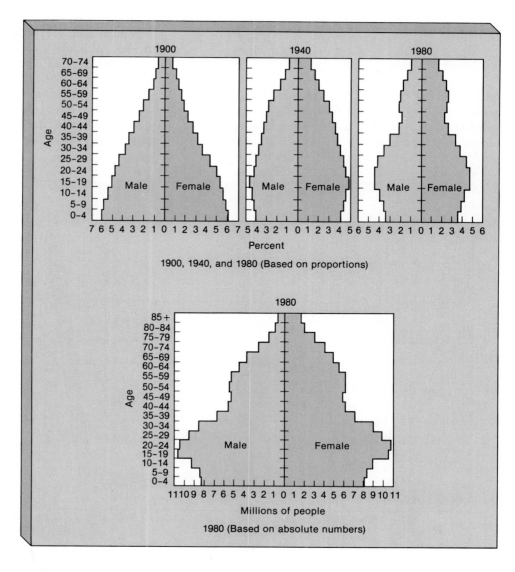

tion that is increasing by virtue of a high birth rate and a declining death rate. The 1940 and 1980 pyramids reveal a different picture. They are the product of a decline in both the birth rate and the death rate. Notice that the bases of the 1940 and 1980 pyramids are contracted, reflecting the decline in the birth rate in 1930 and 1970. Next notice the short bars in the 40 to 50 age group in the 1980 pyramid; those individuals occupying the base bars in the 1940 pyramid have now moved slightly above the middle-aged range. Pyramids based on absolute numbers, like that shown in Figure 19.2, are of particular value to public officials, educators, investors, and planners. From this type of pyramid it is possible to project the age structure of the population at various time intervals in the future.

World Population

As depicted in Figure 19.3, demographic data show that world population growth is at once both awesome and sobering. The earth gains 150 new human beings each minute, 9,100 each hour, 218,000 each day, and some 80 million each year. World population is growing so rapidly that every three years the new additions equal the total population of the United States. As we go back in time, population statistics become increasingly fragmentary and unreliable, so that the earliest figures are at best informed guesses (Wilford, 1981). It is estimated that some 40,000 years ago, the world population stood at about 3 million. At 8000 B.C., the dawn of agriculture, it was 5 million. At the time of Christ, it was 200 million. By 1650, it had climbed to 500 million, and by 1830, to 1 billion. Around 1985 or 1986, it passed the 5 billion mark.

Population Growth: A Ticking Bomb?

World population is expected to top 10.4 billion by the year 2100. Although growth rates are declining, the annual absolute increase continues. As Figure 19.4 shows, much of the large future increase will occur in less developed nations, including some of the poorest. But this growth is a concern to all inhabitants of the globe. For developing countries, it is a question of whether they will evolve into an underclass at the bottom of a two-tiered

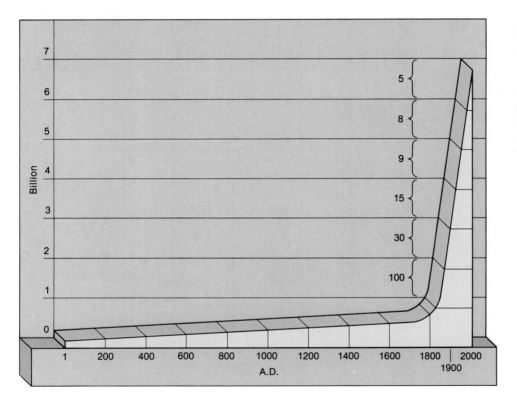

FIGURE 19.3 **World Population Growth** The bold numbers inside the graph indicate the rapidly decreasing number of years required to increase the world's population by 1 billion.
Source: Population Reference Bureau.

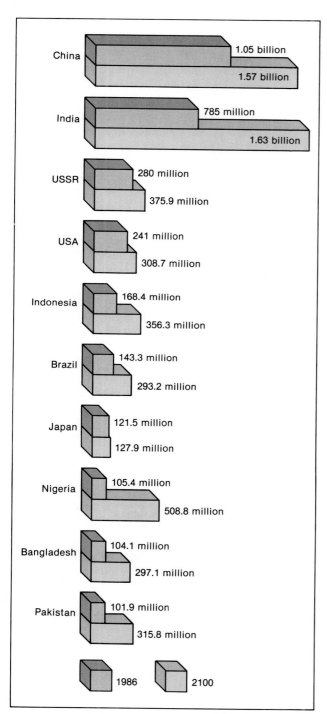

China — 1.05 billion / 1.57 billion

India — 785 million / 1.63 billion

USSR — 280 million / 375.9 million

USA — 241 million / 308.7 million

Indonesia — 168.4 million / 356.3 million

Brazil — 143.3 million / 293.2 million

Japan — 121.5 million / 127.9 million

Nigeria — 105.4 million / 508.8 million

Bangladesh — 104.1 million / 297.1 million

Pakistan — 101.9 million / 315.8 million

1986   2100

FIGURE 19.4 Projected World Population Growth
Source: Population Reference Bureau.

world economy. For more developed nations now approaching population stabilization, it may be difficult to continue as islands of prosperity in a sea of world poverty. The separation will be more difficult to maintain should the imbalance generate waves of immigration and international tensions (Merrick, 1986). We should remind ourselves, however, that projections are not predictions. They merely follow from the assumptions experts make regarding how they think people will plan family size in the future. Epidemics, famines, or major wars may alter the actual course of events. Conversely, population projections may turn out to be wrong if family size does not decrease as rapidly as demographers assume.

There is also an encouraging note. During the 1980s, world population was growing more slowly than in the 1960s and 1970s. The annual growth rate peaked at more than 2 percent in 1965 (2 percent of the population was added each year to the existing population, which itself consisted of the previous year's population enlarged by 2 percent). It fell to 1.6 percent in 1987, and is expected to decline to 1.5 percent by the year 2000. Rates have dropped in all regions except sub-Saharan Africa. Various reasons have been advanced for the slowdown. Population experts observe that the use of contraception and levels of education and literacy have been rising in many nations at the same time as population growth rates have been declining (Census Bureau, 1986).

Malthus and Marx

The relationship between population growth and welfare has long been of interest to social reformers. The English historian and political scientist Thomas Robert Malthus (1766–1834) articulated this concern in his 1798 *Essay on the Principle of Population*. Many of the issues he raised are still being debated today. Malthus took a pessimistic view and asserted that human populations tend to increase at a more rapid rate than the food supply needed to sustain them. Human beings, Malthus said, confront two unchangeable and antagonistic natural laws: (1) the "need for food," and (2) the "passion between the sexes." He contended that, whereas agricultural production tends to increase in arithmetic fashion (1-2-3-4-5-6-7-8), population has a tendency to increase in geometric fashion (1-2-4-8-16-32-64-128).

Based on this formulation, Malthus took a dim view of the future, for if populations always increase to the ultimate point of subsistence, progress can have no lasting effect. The population will invariably catch up and literally "eat" away the higher levels of living. He considered famine, war, and pestilence to be the chief deterrents to excessive growth. But Malthus also recognized that preventive checks might reduce the birth rate—what he called "moral restraint." However, Malthus did not foresee the possibility of new birth control methods or their application within a value system favoring small families. Since he was an ordained minister, it either did not occur to him that people might use birth control, or he viewed birth control as a sin.

Contrary to Malthusian contentions, there is no clear evidence that food always and everywhere can increase only in an arithmetic ratio. Indeed, recent scientific and technical advances in agriculture have resulted in harvests outpacing population growth. Food production in developing nations is now increasing by 4.4 percent annually, more than twice the rate of population growth. According to the Food and Agricultural Organization, between 1972 and 1982 per capita food output rose 16 percent in South America and by 10 percent in Asia. Much of the credit goes to the Green Revolution launched in the 1960s, when farmers began to achieve impressive improvements in grain and livestock production through crossbreeding and hybridizing. Today, biotechnology holds the promise of endowing plants and animals with new traits, such as disease resistance and larger size, by manipulating their genetic codes. Of course, even with these gains, hunger still remains a worldwide problem.

Karl Marx (1906) took issue with much of what Malthus had to say. Marx argued that excess population, especially among the working class, is actually a matter of limited employment opportunities, not a fixed supply of food. Marx believed that a deepening crisis of the capitalist system was forcing more and more workers into the ranks of the unemployed, leading capitalists and alarmist scholars to conclude that society is overpopulated. Population growth, then, was merely the excuse used for the failure of the capitalist system. Marx sought cures for the problems bred by capitalism in a fundamental restructuring of the social and economic order.

Whereas Malthus looked primarily to the individual to restrain population growth through self-control, Marx looked to collective action to refashion institutional life. Many of the issues raised by Malthus and Marx continue to be debated today (see the box on the effects of long-term economic growth).

Demographic Transition

A number of social scientists have employed the idea of **demographic transition** to map out the population growth that characterizes the modern era (Davis, 1945; Notestein, 1945). Viewed as history, the notion seeks to

The Green Revolution
By virtue of new and improved hybridized plants, the world's grain harvests more than doubled from 1960 to 1986, even though the amount of land on which grain was planted grew by less than 11 percent (Schneider, 1986). New corn varieties are now available that can double yields in Central America and West Africa (Avery, 1985). Expected breakthroughs in biotechnology will be even more powerful than those of the Green Revolution. Scientists predict that some varieties of self-fertilizing crops (nitrogen-producing plants) will become a reality by the late 1990s (Watts, 1986). *(J.P. Laffont/Sygma)*

ISSUES THAT SHAPE OUR LIVES

What Are the Effects of Long-Term Economic Growth?

Many scientists worry about the future of Earth. Some, like sociologist William R. Catton (1980; Catton, Lenski, and Buttel, 1986), say that capitalist and socialist nations have committed themselves to policies of economic growth that disregard the pollution of the biosphere and the rapid consumption of nonrenewable resources. Catton contends we have *already* exceeded the planet's carrying capacity. Complicating world problems, three-quarters of the earth's population uses about 25 percent of the resources; the other 75 percent is consumed by the affluent, industrialized quarter. Catton fears that large populations in an environment with too few resources will give rise to deep social divisions, including racism, social inequalities, popular unrest, and war.

Sobering conclusions are also contained in *The Global 2000 Report to the President* issued in 1980 by the Council on Environmental Quality. It contends we soon will run out of key natural resources. The report's main conclusion is this: "The world in 2000 will be more crowded, more polluted, less stable ecologically, and more vul-

nerable to disruption than the world we live in now." The council says nations must act decisively to alter current trends and calls for centralized government planning, controls on the allocation of scarce resources, and internationalism.

Not all scientists agree with these pessimistic projections. The economist Julian L. Simon and the late futurist Herman Kahn (1984) explicitly contradict the wording in *Global 2000,* saying: "If present trends continue, the world in 2000 will be less crowded (though more populated), less polluted, more stable ecologically, and less vulnerable to resource-supply disruption than the world we live in now." Citing historical trends, they predict declining scarcity, falling prices for raw materials, and increased wealth. Given time to adjust to shortages and innovations, Simon and Kahn say, people will create additional resources. For instance, plastics began as a substitute for elephant ivory in billiard balls after tusks began to grow scarce. An actual or perceived shortage eventually leaves us better off than if the shortage had never arisen, thanks to resulting new techniques.

Simon rejects the warnings of those who talk about "nonrenewable resources" in a "finite world," noting that our "spaceship Earth" is a body

of 260 billion cubic miles of material. Nor does he accept the specter of environmental ruin. He argues that pollution was far worse in nineteenth-century cities, with coal dust, horse manure, and human excrement posing serious health hazards. Simon seeks proof of environmental improvement in data showing lower age-specific death rates and increased life expectancies. According to Simon, people who engage in work and create knowledge are "the ultimate resource." More people means more minds at work to solve problems. He says government interference with market forces is more often the cause of, rather than a solution to, world problems.

A recent report by the National Research Council (Holden, 1986) offers a middle ground between these scenarios. It concludes that global population growth is unlikely to outrun world resources. Increased scarcity then stimulates technological advance and the search for economizing strategies. Yet beyond a certain point, the council recognizes that population growth by itself is insufficient to generate technological innovation. It seems to say that both pessimists and optimists overstate the case, although each position contains a kernel of truth.

describe what took place in European nations over the last two hundred years. As theory, it has been used to predict what will happen in developing nations in the future. Demographic transition theory holds that the process of modernization is associated with the three stages of population change (see Figure 19.5 on page 526).

Stage 1: High Potential Growth. Societies untouched by industrialization and urbanization are characterized by a high birth rate and a high death rate, and the population remains relatively stable. The stage is de-

scribed as being "coiled" or having "high potential growth" because, once the societies gain control over their death rates, growth is likely to be rapid.

Stage 2: Transitional Growth. Modernization has its initial impact on mortality levels. Improved housing, better levels of nutrition, and improvements in health and sanitary measures bring a steady decline in death rates. Since a decisive reduction in the death rate has traditionally been associated with a marked drop in the infant mortality rate, a larger proportion of the huge yearly crop of babies survives and in time becomes par-

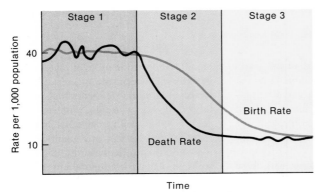

FIGURE 19.5 **Trends in Birth and Death Rates According to the Theory of Demographic Transition**

ents. So a drop in the death rate, while the birth rate remains unchanged, results in a marked increase in the rate of population growth. As time passes, couples begin to realize that with lower infant mortality rates, fewer births are required to produce the same number of surviving children, and they adjust their fertility accordingly. Moreover, the costs and benefits associated with children alter as modernization progresses, making smaller families economically advantageous. The second stage ends when the birth rate sinks to meet the death rate.

Stage 3: Population Stability. Modernization allows couples to gain control of their fertility through effective birth-control techniques while simultaneously undermining religious proscriptions against their use. The result, according to demographic transition theorists, is that modern societies come to be characterized by low mortality and low fertility, a situation approximating zero population growth.

Social scientists have debated whether modernization produces these stages in a reliable, regular way (Tilly, 1978; Eberstadt, 1981; Organski et al., 1984). For one thing, they are not sure that the stages represent an accurate portrayal of European demographic history. Demographer William Petersen (1960) finds that the Netherlands followed a quite different demographic course than that suggested by the theory. In the modern era, the Netherlands underwent a more or less continuous growth in population, although its death rate did not decline until the twentieth century. In the period between 1750 and 1850, the death rate actually rose. Petersen says the Dutch population grew because fertility

went up following the breakdown of traditional social barriers against procreation.

The transition process in many other European nations also did not follow the scenario outlined by proponents of the theory. Indeed, the Soviet Union is currently experiencing an increase in infant mortality and a decline in life expectancy. Between 1964 and 1984, the crude death rate in the Soviet Union increased 54 percent (Feshbach, 1986). Nor does demographic transition theory apply directly to the poor countries of today's world. In some nations, such as Jamaica, fertility has actually gone up in recent decades as an initial response to economic advances (Tilly, 1978). Apparently, a great many variables come to bear in quite different interrelationships to produce widely different demographic outcomes (Entwisle and Mason, 1985).

Population Policies

Few sociological topics reveal the human paradox more sharply than the matter of population growth. Humankind has shown remarkable success in coping with the unique environment posed by planet Earth. We have progressively multiplied until our very numbers threaten to overtax the Earth's natural systems. In recent decades, concern for the future has led to a growing chorus of voices calling for measures to curb our own expansion before it is curbed for us by come catastrophe. A variety of policies have been proposed to limit population growth. All the while, a new source of concern has come to the forefront in nations confronting low birth rates and population decline. In these nations we also hear a growing chorus of voices, but they are calling for measures to encourage citizens to have more children. In order to gain a better perspective on these matters, let us examine each of the issues in turn.

A "Population Bomb": Fertility-Reduction Policies

Over the past several decades some forecasters have ominously predicted that in the years ahead there will be "standing room only" on the earth. In 1960 a leading American demographer, Philip M. Hauser (1960:7), warned: "Projection of the post-World War II rate of increase gives a population of one person per square foot of the land surface of the earth in less than 800 years." Hauser believed fertility reduction was essential if hu-

Chinese Fertility Reduction Policies
Over the past decade China has undertaken policies designed to curb the nation's birth rate, including punishing couples who have two or more children and fining women who are pregnant with a second child 20 percent of their pay if they refuse to have an abortion. As a result of these policies, there were 74 abortions for 100 live births in Beijing in 1982, and 84 abortions for 100 live births in Shunyi County outside Beijing (Wren, 1984). However, the one-child policy now seems to be easing. *(Owen Franken)*

mankind were to defuse the "population bomb." Through the years, three quite different strategies have been proposed for reducing human fertility: the family planning, the developmental, and the societal (Grunstaff, 1981).

The family planning strategy The *family planning* strategy rests on the assumption that if contraceptives are made readily available, and information regarding the value and need for birth planning is disseminated

widely, people will reduce their fertility. In practice, however, the strategy often falls victim to the "technological fallacy." Blind faith is accorded the gadgetry of contraception while the *social* changes that may first be required if the technology is to be adopted are neglected. Even the best technique will not be used unless people want to use it. The simple truth is that people in many parts of the world do *not* want to limit their number of children. Kenya has had a family planning program since 1969, yet it is burdened with one of the world's highest growth rates—about 4 percent a year (Cordes, 1985). For many people, children are the chief protection against misfortune; they provide care when parents are unemployed, sick, or elderly. Children are a kind of old age insurance in societies without bank accounts and pensions (Cain, 1985). Birth rates come down when people are motivated to lower their fertility, whether or not they have modern contraceptives available. Throughout human history, people have shown considerable imagination in separating sexual enjoyment from procreation.

The developmental strategy According to proponents of the *developmental* strategy, fertility is closely tied to level of modernization. Whereas the economic incentives of an agricultural economy are thought to favor large families, those of an industrial society discourage them. Agriculturalists see children as an investment in the future; career-oriented men and women in industrial and postindustrial societies see them as an extra expense. At the 147-nation World Population Conference in Mexico City in 1984, the United States delegation placed itself in the developmental camp, saying there is no global population problem. It contended that governmental intervention in the economy hinders people's efforts to improve themselves and that free enterprise, by encouraging economic development, in time lessens population pressures (Lieberson, 1986).

The societal strategy While acknowledging that a decline in fertility often goes hand in hand with modernization, proponents of the *societal* strategy say the link is hardly firm enough to justify making it the foundation of a "do-nothing" population policy (Silk, 1986). They call on government to fashion policies that will change demographic behavior. Sociologist Kingsley Davis (1971:403) suggests a number of social reforms that would reduce fertility by rewarding low fertility and penalizing high fertility:

. . . the most effective social changes would be those that offer opportunities and goals that compete with family roles. For instance, giving advantages in housing, taxes, scholarships, and recreation to single as compared to married people, would discourage early marriage. Giving special educational and employment opportunities to women would foster career interests and therefore lessen motherhood as a woman's sole commitment. . . . Discontinuing the custom of family names, giving more complete control over children to nursery and elementary schools while holding parents responsible for the costs. . . . As for methods of birth control, including abortion, these could be provided free of charge.

A number of nations have employed coercion to reduce fertility. For a period in the 1970s, India inaugurated a program of forced sterilization that resulted in nearly one million vasectomies being performed each month (Kaufman, 1979). And in recent years China has instituted harsh methods to curb population growth, including punishing couples who have two or more children and fining a woman pregnant with a second child 20 percent of her pay if she refuses to have an abortion (Wren, 1984). Such programs have aroused considerable indignation among many citizens in Western nations. There is evidence, however, that China may be easing its one-child policy (Scheuer, 1987). Clearly, programs for reducing fertility remain quite controversial, in terms of both effectiveness and morality.

A "Population Collapse": Pronatalist Policies

Concern about population *growth* is now giving way to a new worry in many Western nations, population *loss* (Kelley, 1986; Wattenberg and Zinsmeister, 1986). Some governments are becoming increasingly nervous about the low level of births in their nations. Given present trends, the population of many European nations will start falling in the 1990s. In West Germany and Denmark, the birth rate has fallen to 1.3 per woman. British fertility has declined by a third since the mid-1970s. The French government, with a rate of 1.8 children per woman, has sought to stimulate births by paying mothers having a third or subsequent child a "temporary maternal salary" that can run to $280 a month for three years.

Eastern European nations have also seen their birth rates fall. Poland has been the exception, with average family size inching upward since 1981 (Kaufman, 1986). Most Eastern European nations are manipulating their

housing and employment systems to encourage childbearing. In 1976, the East German government introduced a set of profamily incentives, including extra vacation time and six months of maternity leave. The birth rate moved upward for several years as young couples cashed in, but by 1980 the boom had petered out. Attempts by other Eastern European nations to spur childbearing have likewise had no lasting results (Sullivan, 1986). Outlawing abortion, as was done in Rumania in 1966, had a temporary, though substantial, effect. Moreover, the Rumanian government imposes a tax on single adults and childless couples.

Soviet leaders have encouraged women, especially ethnic Russians, to have more children (Dunn, 1986). The government bestows the "Mother Heroine Award" on women who have 10 or more children. In 1986, it increased paid maternity leave from 12 to 18 months. Officially, the policies are aimed at increasing the labor force. But Western demographers believe they are also intended to increase the Russian population, which is not growing as rapidly as other ethnic minorities. The rate of growth among Central Asians of Islamic heritage is two to three times higher than that of ethnic Russians. Yet overall it may be easier ultimately to bring down fertility in developing countries than it is to raise it in developed ones (Westoff, 1986).

THINKING THROUGH THE ISSUES

Over the past two decades popular thinking in the Western world has apparently gone from a concern that there will be standing room only to a concern that there will not be enough of us left to stand. Some pro-natalists like Ben J. Wattenberg and Karl Zinsmeister (1986) paint a picture of a "starkly changing" demographic balance in the world, with the survival of Western cultural values and political democracy at stake. In the 1930s, the specter of a withered France, a vanishing Europe, and a doomed Western civilization also grabbed media headlines as European birth rates plummeted. The theme went into remission during the baby boom of the 1950s and 1960s. So, based on past history, reports of the "death of the West" may be premature (Teitelbaum and Winter, 1985). For the moment, however, assume that fertility in Western nations remains below replacement level. Among the questions demographers are asking, but having difficulty answering, are the following: Will economic prosperity be un-

A Kazakh Hunter from a Collective Farm in Soviet Kazakhstan
There are more than 100 nationalities in the Soviet Union that many Westerners often casually refer to as "Russia." Ethnic Russians make up about 52 percent of the Soviet population, but demographers forecast that before the end of the century the Russians will be in a numerical minority. The highest birth rates are in the Moslem belt of Kazakhstan and Central Asia. In late 1986, when Moscow replaced a long-time Kazakh party chief with an ethnic Russian, students took to the streets and burned cars in Alma-Ata, the Kazakh Republic's capital. *(TASS/Sovfoto)*

dermined? Will the character of society change from a vigorous, productive, creative one, to one that is conservative and risk-averse? Will opportunities for social advancement be limited? Will the pace of technological innovation slow? How will a relatively smaller workforce pay for the social security and health care benefits required by an elderly population? Will the United States be outnumbered by a more rapidly growing Soviet population, and thus find itself gravely threatened by Soviet power in the twenty-first century? How will NATO nations secure military recruits? If free nations coerce people to have more children, will they continue to be free nations? Will immigration provide an answer to Western population declines (AEI Symposium, 1986; Cherlin, 1987)?

Ecology

Population growth has enormous consequences. Like other organisms, we are a part of nature and depend on it for our welfare and existence (Hawley, 1950, 1984; Agnew, 1981; Micklin and Choldin, 1984). **Ecology** is the scientific study of the relationship between living organisms and their environment. Human beings confront the physical environment not so much as lone individuals as units in cooperation with one another—the "humanmade cocoon" we call society (Catton, Lenski, and Buttel, 1986). Among the chief adaptive mechanisms of this cocoon are social organization and technology. As we saw in Chapter 3, the subsistence strategy a population employs—hunting and gathering, horticulture, agriculture, or industrialism—has critical implications for its culture and social structure.

The Ecosystem

One way of viewing the environment is as an **ecosystem,** a relatively stable community of organisms that have established interlocking relationships and exchanges with one another in their natural habitat. The perspective is nicely captured by the notion of Spaceship Earth—the idea that our planet is a vessel in the void of the universe, a closed system with finite resources that, if destroyed or depleted, cannot be replaced. Life exists only in the biosphere, a thin skin of air, soil, and water on the surface of the planet. The earth's biosphere has served us well: We have multiplied to over 5 billion people and expanded to all corners of the globe. In large part our remarkable success has derived from our ability to alter the environment and take from it the resources we need. But ecologists stress that survival depends on our ability to

*"I think we agree, gentlemen, that one can respect
Mother Nature without coddling her."*

Drawing by Lorenz; © 1986 The New Yorker Magazine, Inc.

maintain a precarious balance among the living and nonliving components of the biosphere. They fear that pollution of the environment and depletion of the earth's natural resources are jeopardizing the very environment that is the basis for human life.

A graphic example of the reciprocal ties binding human beings and their physical environment is provided by the sub-Saharan region of Africa. Television has captured the human tragedy: pale deserts haunted by starving people, infant bellies swollen by want, and dead cattle. An estimated 35 million people in Africa live on the interfaces of deserts and arable land and are threatened by hunger. The overworking of marginal lands for crops, grazing, and firewood has resulted in "desert creep." Much of this "desertification" is not attributable to basic climate change. Rather, the introduction of Western techniques, such as irrigation, deep plowing, and chemical fertilizers, have served to compound the region's problems (Cowell, 1984a). Irrigated land becomes waterlogged, accumulates too much salt, and ends up useless. And wells dug in arid regions lead people and cattle to congregate in their vicinity, resulting in overgrazing and trampling of the earth by cattle. A vicious circle comes into being whereby people intensify their exploitation of the land to compensate for desert creep, only to complicate their problems as the misuse in turn feeds new desert expansion. In a dry or drought year, such as 1984, the desert of Chad advanced 125 miles, rather than the usual rate of 6 to 12 miles a year (Kamm, 1985). Ecologists emphasize that human beings must become more sensitive to the manifest and

latent consequences of their actions in order to avoid this type of damage to the ecosystem. Each species is seen as playing a role essential to the harmony and well-being of the entire community of living organisms (May and Seger, 1986). Viewed in this manner, all peoples and nations are part of a global network, deftly enmeshed in one shared ecosystem.

Conflict theorists think that some ecologists have overemphasized the harmony and balance to be found in nature: They see competition as "the principal game in town." Conflict theorists look at the same circumstances in Africa, but come to quite different conclusions. They point out, using World Bank figures, that sub-Saharan Africa's foreign debt increased almost tenfold between 1970 and 1982, from $5.7 to $51.3 billion (Cowell, 1984a). This growing indebtedness exerted pressure on African governments to promote cash crops for export rather than food crops for their people. Simultaneously, commodity prices have fallen on the world market. The African nations cannot repay their debt, nor can they afford to purchase food from other nations. Complicating matters, the money provided by Western aid agencies during the 1970s was diverted to highly visible projects, such as roads, port facilities, airports, and office buildings. In short, the aid money was recycled to Western corporations, while small African farmers were neglected. Moreover, when Western nations have provided food to African governments, they have found an outlet for surplus food and benefited their own farmers. Finally, assistance is often rendered to African governments that are favorable to the donor nations, in the process stabilizing pro-Western regimes (Cowell, 1984b).

For conflict theorists, environmental problems derive not so much from a limited supply of finite resources as from an unequal distribution of the world's resources. The question, then, is not "How much is available?" but "Which individuals and groups will secure a disproportionate share of what is available?" The critical decisions that affect the environment are made not in the interests of present and future generations, but in the self-interest of powerful groups.

The POET Complex

One way of viewing the human ecological complex is to explore interdependencies among four critical factors: population (P), organization (O), environment (E), and technology (T). An acronym for the complex—**POET**—is often used and easy to remember (Duncan,

1959, 1961). The intricate relationships among the POET factors is highlighted by the air pollution problems of Los Angeles. The city's residents experience periodic bouts of a bluish-gray haze in the atmosphere that reduces visibility and irritates the eyes and the respiratory tract (E → P). The smog also damages plants (E → E) and erodes a variety of metals (E → T). Over the past three decades, Los Angeles residents have organized civic movements that have sponsored and achieved adoption of regulatory measures (E → O). Among other things, industrial plants have been required to install abatement devices (O → T).

Meanwhile, chemists have confirmed the "factory in the sky" theory of smog formation. Combustion and related processes release unburned hydrocarbons and oxides of nitrogen into the atmosphere which, when subjected to strong sunlight, form smog (T → E). Temperature inversion in the Los Angeles area keeps polluted air from rising very high above ground level (E → E). Population growth has intensified the problem; residents have spread out over a wide territory (P → E), heightening dependence on the automobile as the principal means of transportation (T → O). Sociologist Otis Dudley Duncan (1961:146) notes the following paradox: "Where could one find a more poignant instance of the principle of circular causation . . . than that of the Los Angelenos speeding down their freeways in a rush to escape the smog produced by emissions from the very vehicles conveying them?"

The four factors of the POET complex have been in continuous interaction throughout human history. But among hunting and gathering peoples, the environment assumes the dominant role. In the course of sociocultural evolution, the other factors have become increasingly important (see Chapter 3). Responding to survival pressures, some of our ancestors set out in new directions and evolved new patterns of social organization and technology. In turn, our economies now support more and more people. But as our ruthless exploitation of the earth's ecosystem has increased, using up natural resources and spewing out toxic chemicals, sewage, and heaps of rubbish, environmental considerations are compelling us to introduce new forms of social organization and technological innovations and lessen population pressures. Let us take a closer look at the depletion of critical resources and the deteriorating environment.

Depletion of Resources

It seems that humankind has abused the earth from earliest times. Environmental myth has portrayed early humans as "noble savages" who lived in harmony with nature. But an accumulating body of archeological evidence is providing glaring examples of environmental abuse across human history. Paleolithic hunters eradicated the mammoth, the mastodon, the Pleistocene camel and horse, and numerous smaller mammals; New Zealand's Maori population contributed to the extinction of the moa (a large flightless bird); and early Polynesian settlers brought about the extinction of various Hawaiian birds. Early agriculturalists frequently contributed to their own demise by abusing the lands on which they lived (Catton, Lenski, and Buttel, 1986). These tendencies have changed little over the centuries.

Air Pollution: Downtown Los Angeles
In a normal pattern of air flow, warm air close to the ground rises, carrying with it most atmosphere pollutants. But in a thermal inversion, which frequently affects Los Angeles, a lid of warm air prevents the circulation of air from below. The result is that pollutants become trapped under the inversion layer. *(Georg Gerster/ Photo Researchers)*

It seems that today's human beings are neither more nor less destructive of the land than were their forebears. It is simply that the technology of destruction is vastly more efficient than it was in earlier times (Browne, 1987).

In few areas of life is the depletion of critical resources more evident than in shrinking water supplies. Since the beginning of this century, the population of the United States has increased about 200 percent, while per capita water use has shot up 500 to 800 percent. By 1980, water use in the nation came to some 2,000 gallons per day for each man, woman, and child. Americans use three times as much water per capita as do the Japanese (Sheets, 1983). Complicating matters, the nation's reserves of water are being stretched thin as more rivers, lakes, and aquifers become polluted and undrinkable. Forty-seven percent of the nation's major sewage treatment plants are still violating pollution standards (Tyson, 1986). And pristine waters like Yellowstone Lake in Yellowstone National Park are being damaged by the dumping of raw sewage (Anderson, 1987).

Another area of concern is the quiet apocalypse that seems to be occurring on a global scale. Life on earth has been punctuated by mass extinctions of a wide variety of plants and animals, possibly the result of the impact of giant meteors or comets. Currently a mass extinction of another sort is taking place at the hands of humankind. Each year, an estimated 17,500 species of plants and animals are lost, especially in tropical rain forests. Rain forests, such as those in the Amazon Basin, Indonesia, and Central Africa, are the world's most biologically diverse habitats. Although they occupy only 7 percent of the planet's land area, they contain half of all living species. In the past several hundred years, the globe's rain forests have decreased by 44 percent. If nothing is done to slow the rampant clearing of these lands, all tropical forests will disappear in 50 to 75 years. The loss will involve many species that almost certainly could have provided new drugs, new food sources, and many new opportunities for economic growth. Moreover, once the trees are gone, torrential rains erode the soil, and the

FIGURE 19.6 **Toxic Waste Dump Sites in the United States**

Source: Environmental Protection Agency.

EPA's 'dirty dozen' top cleanup priority list

1. Lipari Landfill Pitman, N.J.
2. Tybouts Corner Landfill New Castle County, Del.
3. Bruin Lagoon Bruin Borough, Pa.
4. Helen Kramer Landfill Mantua Township, N.J.
5. Industri–Plex Woburn, Mass.
6. Price Landfill Pleasantville, N.J.
7. Pollution Abatement Services Oswego, N.Y.
8. LaBounty Site Charles City, Iowa
9. Army Creek Landfill New Castle County, Del.
10. CPS/Madison Industries Old Bridge Township, N.J.
11. Nyanza Chemical Waste Dump Ashland, Mass.
12. GEMS Landfill Gloucester Township, N.J.

land quickly becomes like a moonscape where nothing grows. The destruction of Haiti's forests is a principal cause of that island's poverty, which in turn is one reason for the flood of Haitian immigrants to the United States (Lee, 1986; Murphy, 1986).

Pollution

Pollution involves the contamination of the environment by wastes or other substances that have a damaging effect upon public health and ecosystems. Within the United States, more than 71 billion gallons of waste chemicals from ammonia to zinc are generated by industry each year. According to the Environmental Protection Agency, up to 90 percent of this chemical debris is improperly disposed of in open pits and ponds or leaky barrels (Work and Taylor, 1984) (see Figure 19.6). A report of the Office of Technology Assessment says that more than 10,000 disposal sites for hazardous waste require cleanup on a priority basis to protect the public. It estimates that the total cost of cleaning up these sites could approach $100 billion (Shabecoff, 1985). Hazardous sites contain toxic chemicals, metals, and other substances that contaminate water sources and pose health hazards. For example, some 800 families had to leave Niagara's Love Canal area in 1979 after health experts linked unusually high rates of illness and death there to chemicals leaking from an old industrial dump.

Air pollution is also a serious problem. It periodically reduces the sunlight reaching Chicago by about 40 percent and New York City by 25 percent. Sources of pollution range from the smokestacks of power plants to the exhaust pipes of cars. Forests throughout the eastern United States and central Europe are in decline because of acid rain. As Figure 19.7 on page 534 shows, when coal, oil, and other fossil-based fuels are burned, the emissions are converted in the upper atmosphere into particles that return to earth in the form of highly acidic rain, snow, or fog (Taylor, 1984).

Chemical pesticides are another source of environmental pollution. They are used by everyone from farmers to public health authorities to suburban homeowners. Some, such as dieldrin and DDT, are resistant to environmental degradation, posing a threat to terrestrial and aquatic ecosystems. The process of exterminating harmful organisms also eradicates other forms of life. And as predators develop immunity to the pesticides, resistant flies, mosquitoes, and rodents require more powerful agents to kill them (at least 447 species of insects are resistant to some pesticides, compared with

seven prior to World War II; 20 of the worst are immune to all existing pesticides). Among alternatives to pesticides are the use of natural enemies, insect hormones, sex attractants, and the release of sterile males (Begley, 1986). Chemical pesticides also imperil human health (Shabecoff, 1984).

A comparatively modern form of pollution has resulted from radioactive pollutants. The buildup in nuclear weapons and power plants is particularly ominous (see Figure 19.8 on page 535). The danger was highlighted by the 1986 catastrophic meltdown and explosion of a Soviet nuclear reactor at Chernobyl that sent a radioactive plume across Europe. Experts project that from 24,000 to 75,000 Russians and Europeans will die prematurely from cancer due to radiation exposure from the Chernobyl accident (Diamond, 1986). In the United States, the biggest nuclear mishap occurred at Three Mile Island, near Harrisburg, Pennsylvania, on March 28, 1979. The loss of coolant caused the radioactive fuel in one of two reactors to overheat, leading to a partial meltdown and the escape of some radioactive material. Although no one is known to have died as a result of the accident, the hazard posed to local residents is still a matter of debate. Overall, then, advances in technology have accelerated the global impact of humankind on the environment.

THINKING THROUGH THE ISSUES

In June 1985, the Davis-Besse nuclear power plant at Oak Harbor, Ohio, suffered a series of operator errors and equipment malfunctions that produced, in the words of Jesse Ebersole, a senior federal atomic safety adviser, "40 minutes of chaos and fast-approaching disaster" before the reactor was brought under control. Five months later, an atomic plant in southern California flirted with a serious overheating of the reactor's nuclear fuel core that had gone undetected by plant personnel for twelve months. In December 1985, a nuclear reactor near Sacramento, California, went through a severe temperature gyration and dumped hundreds of gallons of radioactive cooling water outside the plant (Rose and Emshwiller, 1986). Between 1971 and 1986, nuclear plants in 14 countries have recorded 151 "significant" incidents, according to a report by the U.S. General Accounting Office. Scientists

Midwestern smokestacks spewing out pollutants that result in acid rain.

Acid rain from Midwestern smokestacks kills forest on North Carolina's Mount Mitchell.

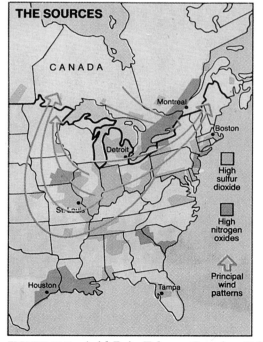

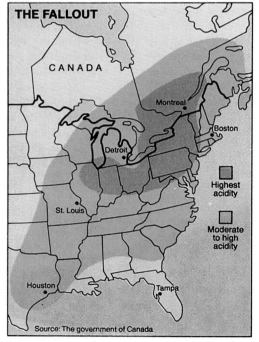

FIGURE 19.7 **Acid Rain Takes a Growing Toll, Killing Lakes and Destroying Timberland**
Acid precipitation—the product of industrial emissions—is severe in the Midwest and Northeast, but the South and parts of the West are also affected. U.S.-generated acid rain has long been a sore point in our nation's relationship with Canada. *Source: Maps: Formula for a Manmade Plague.* Newsweek *(April 25, 1983)37. Photos: left, Stuart Rosner/Stock, Boston; right, Katherine S. Thomas/ Taurus.*

Country	Operating Reactors	Percent of Electricity Supplied
Argentina	2	23
Belgium	8	60
Brazil	1	1
Britain	33	19
Bulgaria	4	32
Canada	16	12
Czechoslovakia	5	15
East Germany	5	12
Finland	4	38
France	40	65
Hungary	2	5
India	6	2
Italy	3	4
Japan	33	27
Netherlands	2	6
Pakistan	1	2
South Africa	4	18
South Korea	4	18
Spain	8	24
Sweden	12	42
Switzerland	5	34
Taiwan	6	59
U.S.S.R.	50	11
United States	101	17
West Germany	18	30
Yugoslavia	1	5

Living dangerously? The Rancho Seco nuclear reactor is 23 miles southeast of heavily populated Sacramento, California. In December 1985, a sudden cooldown nearly cracked the water vessel, which would have set off a nuclear accident. (*Tony O'Brien/Picture Group*)

FIGURE 19.8   **A Global Grid of Nuclear Power Plants** As of April 28, 1986, there were 374 commercial nuclear power plants in operation worldwide, turning out 15 percent of global electric power; 157 more had been ordered. In the United States there were 101 operating nuclear power plants; 27 percent more were under construction. *Source: International Atomic Energy Agency.*

say there is a limit to how much safety technology can guarantee. Warns Harvard University physicist Richard Wilson: "With 300 big reactors in place around the world, we'll average a meltdown every 30 years" (Trafford and Wellborn, 1986:21). Is there a realistic alternative to nuclear plants? Is it morally justifiable to continue to use nuclear energy after Chernobyl? Will governments agree to put safety above all other considerations—and can safety-first policies be enforced? Are American safety standards adequate? The Soviets established an evacuation zone of 18 miles around the stricken Chernobyl plant. This distance is 80 percent more than the American emergency planning zone. The nuclear industry insists that 10 miles is too large (Diamond, 1986). What would be the likely consequences if there were a serious Chernobyl-type accident in a nuclear power reactor in the New York City area (see Figure 19.9 on page 536)?

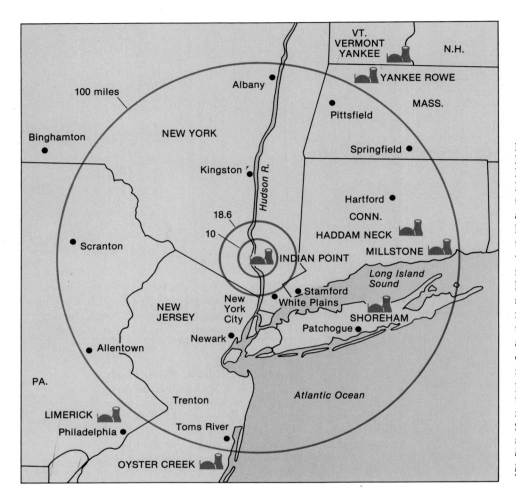

FIGURE 19.9 **Nuclear Power Reactors in the New York City Area** Nuclear experts agree that meltdowns like that at Chernobyl are likely to happen again. With reactors throughout the world continuing to suffer from control problems, fears mount for the safety of populations near the plants. Evacuation and significant radioactive contamination occurred up to 100 miles from the Chernobyl plant—a distance ten times the emergency zone in the United States. *Source: Stuart Diamond, 1986. Chernobyl causing big revisions in global nuclear power policies. New York Times (October 27):8.*

Chapter Highlights

1. The periodic rise and fall in U.S. births has created waves of people who move through the life course, alternately building up and eroding major institutional arrangements and changing the social landscape. Demographic changes do not have overnight effects; they sneak up on us slowly and modestly.

2. All population change within a society can be reduced to three factors: the birth rate, the death rate, and the migration rate into or out of the society. The number of children born in recent years in the United States has risen. The reason the number of births has risen is that the number of women of childbearing age has increased as the large generation born during the baby boom of the 1950s has reached adulthood. The life expectancy of Americans has now reached a high of 74.7 years. Migration is the product of two factors. Push factors encourage people to leave a habitat that they already occupy; pull factors attract people to a new habitat.

3. Births, death, and migration affect population size. Sociologists are also interested in the composition or characteristics of a population. They are particularly interested in the sex ratio (the number of males per 100 females) and age composition. A population pyramid is a useful tool for analyzing population change and discerning population trends.

4. Thomas Robert Malthus held that, whereas agricultural production tends to increase in arithmetic fashion, population has a tendency to increase in geomet-

ric fashion. Based on this formulation, Malthus took a dim view of the future, for if populations always increase to the ultimate point of subsistence, then progress can have no lasting effect. Karl Marx took issue with Malthus, insisting that an excess of population is relative to the availability of employment opportunities, not to a fixed supply of food.

5. A number of social scientists have employed the idea of demographic transition to map out the population growth characteristic of the modern era. Demographic transition theory holds that the process of modernization is associated with three stages in population change: Stage 1: high potential growth; Stage 2, transitional growth; and Stage 3, population stability. However, social scientists have debated whether modernization produces these stages in a reliable, regular way.

6. There are three basic schools of thought relating to fertility-reduction policies. The first approach involves family planning. Its proponents contend that if contraceptives are made readily available, and information regarding the value of and need for birth planning is disseminated throughout a society, people will reduce their fertility. A second approach entails a developmentalist strategy. It holds that modernization automatically decreases fertility. A third approach involves a societalist perspective. The government fashions policies designed to produce changes in people's demographic behavior.

7. Concern about population growth is now giving way to a new worry in many Western nations—population loss. Some governments are becoming increasingly nervous about the lack of births in their nations and are undertaking programs to encourage women to have more children.

8. Like other organisms, we are a part of the larger world of nature and depend on it for our welfare and existence. One way of viewing the environment is as an ecosystem—a complex web of interlocking relationships and exchanges among organisms, communities of organisms, and the natural habitat. Sociologists find its useful to study the interdependences among four critical factors: population (P), organization (O), environment (E), and technology (T). An acronym for the complex is POET.

9. Experts are in disagreement regarding the long-term effects of economic growth and development. Many authorities express grave concern about the prospects for our planet. They say that capitalist and socialist nations alike have committed themselves to policies of economic growth that disregard the pollution of the biosphere and the rapid consumption of nonrenewable resources. Other authorities take a more optimistic view: They look to technology to save us.

The Sociologist's Vocabulary

birth rate The number of live births per 1,000 members of a population in a given year.

death rate The number of deaths per 1,000 members of a population in a given year.

demographic transition A view of population change which holds that the process of modernization passes through three stages: high potential growth, transitional growth, and population stability.

demography The science dealing with the size, distribution, and composition of, and changes in, population.

ecology The scientific study of the relationship between living organisms and their environment.

ecosystem A relatively stable community of organisms that have established interlocking relationships and exchanges with one another in their natural habitat.

fecundity The potential number of children that could be born if every woman of childbearing age bore all the children she possibly could.

fertility The number of babies born to the average woman of childbearing age.

growth rate The difference between births and deaths, plus the difference between immigrants and emigrants per 1,000 population.

infant mortality rate The number of deaths among infants under 1 year of age per 1,000 live births.

internal migration Population movement within a nation.

international migration Population movement among nations.

life expectancy The number of years of life remaining to an average person of a certain age.

migration The movement of people from one geographic area to another in order to establish a new residence.

POET complex The interdependencies among four ecological factors: population (P), organization (O), environment (E), and technology (T).

pollution The contamination of the environment by wastes or other substances that have a damaging effect on public health and the ecosystem.

population A group of organisms who are members of the same species and occupy a certain territory.

population pyramid The age and sex composition of a population as portrayed in the tree of ages.

zero population growth A stable population: an average of 2.1 children per woman so that a population replaces itself without immigration.

20

Communities and Urban Life

We will neglect our cities to our peril, for in neglecting them we neglect the nation.

—John F. Kennedy, message to Congress, January 30, 1962

When you think of a city, what comes to mind? Noise, traffic-choked streets, crime, towering skyscrapers, sprawling slums, affluent suburbs, crowded shopping malls, aging factories, museums, smog? If you were to draw a map of your hometown or college town, what features would you include? Do you think your map would be similar to that made by the mayor, or a bill collector, or a drug dealer, or a county health official, or a police officer, or a banker?

Sociologists find that there is not one city, but many cities—as many as there are people to experience them. You are more familiar with some sections of the city than others, so your images of these areas are more complete and fine-grained. And if you live in a city like Boston, with many historic sites and well-defined ethnic neighborhoods, you are likely to have more detailed notions of the community than if you live in cities with fewer distinctive features like Los Angeles or Jersey City. Your age also makes a difference. Young children's maps are highly personal, with "scary" zones of empty stores, funeral parlors, "big boys' play areas," and "gas tanks that might blow up." Older children's maps more closely approximate geographical reality and are organized around key landmarks like schools or shopping centers. Adults' maps are typically more complex, showing major travel routes like rail lines or streets, city districts, and landmarks. Past experience also colors your images of a city. University of Michigan students from small towns view Ann Arbor as less safe and more cosmopolitan than do students from larger cities. And your notions of neighborhoods are likely to be biased by how you experienced them a decade or so ago (Goleman, 1985).

Your images of a city are as important to your behavior as the actual concrete and asphalt features, regardless of the accuracy of your ideas. For instance, middle-class Americans commonly view city slums as grim islands of pathology. From the perspective of many suburbanites, morality in the slums seems to be upside-down. Slum people appear to be drowning in a swamp of "urban ills":

high delinquency and crime rates, unwed teenage mothers, high unemployment, filthy streets and decaying buildings, juvenile gangs. Viewed from the inside, sociologists find that slum neighborhoods are often rich, orderly, disciplined, and composed mostly of conventional people (Gans, 1962; Suttles, 1968, 1972, 1984; Anderson, 1978). Ethnic membership provides an important foundation for social organization in many slum neighborhoods (Figure 20.1 shows the major ethnic neighborhoods of Chicago). Indeed, some behavior that the larger community labels "juvenile delinquency" is condoned by residents who see the illegal activities of their young as a means for protecting their life and property from the "dangerous" residents of adjacent neighborhoods (Heitgerd and Bursik, 1987).

None of us can escape the territorial dimension of our existence. The ebb and flow of social life in all societies occurs in the context of place. Most of us live in settlements of some sort: an open campsite, a village, a town, a city, or a metropolis. Sociologists term such settlements a **community,** and define it as a relatively self-contained social unit whose members share a sense of belonging together and a common territorial base. The concept of community has proved useful to sociologists, because it serves as a kind of prototype of society, or minisociety, in which we can observe aspects of social structure and social processes that would be difficult to study in society as a whole. To be sure, a community's boundaries are becoming increasingly difficult to ascertain in modern, large-scale societies. Yet the territorial imperative remains: to give meaning to space and to define the places of our lives in social terms (Spradley and Mann, 1975).

PLANNING AHEAD: TARGETED READING

1. Why have cities arisen and developed as they have?

2. How do the ways in which the members of society arrange and distribute themselves in space influence other aspects of their lives?

3. How is your hometown tied to a world system of cities?

4. Is the city best portrayed as a lonely crowd, an urban village, or an arena of conflict?

5. What major trends are shaping contemporary American cities?

The Origin and Growth of Cities

The emergence and growth of cities has been one of the most significant developments in human history. A **city** is a relatively dense and permanent concentration of people who secure their livelihood chiefly through nonagricultural activities. The influence of the urban mode of life extends far beyond a city's boundaries. Many of the characteristics of modern societies, including their problems, derive from an urban existence. Yet **urbanization**—the growth in the proportion of a population living in cities—is a comparatively recent development.

Preindustrial Cities

It was not until the Neolithic period (beginning about 10,000 B.C.) that conditions became ripe for the emergence of large settlements of people. The substitution of stockraising and farming for hunting and gathering set in motion a vast array of forces. Within a few thousand years, social life had changed more drastically than it had in the preceding 2 or 3 million years of cultural evolution. Human beings now became capable of "producing" food, and of creating a *social surplus*, goods and services over and above those necessary for human survival (see Chapter 3). This capability permitted the emergence of cities and more complex forms of culture

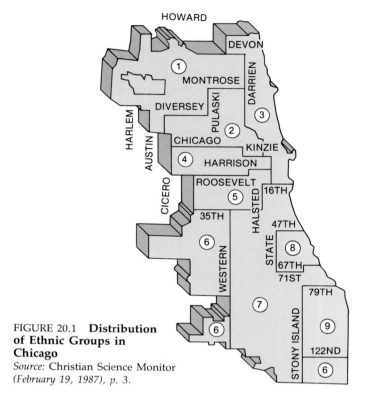

FIGURE 20.1 Distribution of Ethnic Groups in Chicago

Source: Christian Science Monitor *(February 19, 1987), p. 3.*

Ethnic Chicago

1. Northwest Side: mainly white ethnic
2. Near Northwest Side: predominantly Puerto Rican with some whites and blacks
3. North Lakefront: some Hispanics but overwhelmingly white
4. West Side: black, generally poorer than South Side blacks
5. Near Southwest: predominantly Mexican, but includes some blacks and whites
6. Southwest and South Side: mainly white ethnic, includes Hegewisch on the Southeast Side
7. South Side: black, includes middle class, but also includes housing projects
8. Hyde Park-Kenwood: black and white
9. Southeast Side: mainly white ethnic on East Side, rest of area black with some Mexicans and whites

and social structure (Childe, 1936, 1942, 1956; Redman, 1979; Wilson, 1984).

Early Neolithic communities were more a matter of small villages than of cities. A number of innovations had to be added to the Neolithic complex before towns evolved. Between 6000 and 4000 B.C., the invention of the ox-drawn plow, the wheeled cart, the sailboat, metallurgy, irrigation, and the addition of new plants, taken together, afforded a more intensive and productive use of Neolithic innovations. When this enriched technology came to be applied in locales where climate, soil, water, and topography were most favorable, the result was an economy that permitted the concentration in one place of people who did not grow their own food. These conditions were found in broad river valleys with alluvial soil that was not exhausted by successive use, a dry climate that minimized the leaching of soil, ample days of sunshine, and a nearby river that afforded a supply of water for irrigation. Among the early centers of urban development were Mesopotamia, the Nile Valley of Egypt, the Indus Valley of India, and the Yellow River basin of China (Davis, 1955, 1967).

The earliest cities took many forms, from the compact, walled settlements of Mesopotamia to the Central

American ceremonial center with a core population in close proximity and a rural population scattered in outlying villages. The cities of the Harappan civilization of the Indus were carefully planned and laid out with streets and assigned living quarters. And the palaces of early Crete and Greece served as economic and trading centers for nearby villagers (Feagan, 1986). Clearly, by itself a productive economy was not sufficient to allow for the growth of these complex urban arrangements. Rather than providing food for a surplus of city dwellers, cultivators could, at least in theory, have multiplied on the land until they ended up producing just enough to sustain themselves. New forms of social organization were obviously required. Bureaucratic structures and stratification systems arose that enabled government officials, religious personnel, merchants, and artisans to appropriate for themselves part of the produce grown by cultivators (see Chapters 5 and 9).

Yet preindustrial cities typically did not exceed 10 percent of the population of an area. Cities of 100,000 or more were rare, although under favorable social and economic conditions some cities surpassed this size. Rome in the second century A.D., Constantinople as the political successor to Rome, Baghdad before

A.D. 1000, the cities of Sung China between A.D. 1100 and 1300, and Tokyo, Kyoto, and Osaka in seventeenth- and eighteenth-century Japan all had populations well above 100,000, and in some cases, possibly even a million (Sjoberg, 1960).

A number of factors restricted the size of preindustrial cities. First, the roads and vehicles of the time could not accommodate the transportation of bulky materials for long distances. And the preservation of perishable commodities, including foodstuffs, was difficult. Second, early cities had trouble securing the hinterlands. Their inhabitants were constantly threatened and often conquered by neighboring cities and nonurban peoples. Indeed, even mighty Rome ultimately succumbed to foreign invaders. Third, the absence of modern medicine and sanitation meant that urban living was often fatal. The water supply was frequently polluted by sewage, and as commercial centers, cities attracted transients who served as carriers of contagious diseases (see Chapter 18). Finally, serf, slave, and caste arrangements bound the peasantry to the land and impaired rural-urban migration. These factors made early cities relatively small affairs (Davis, 1955).

Industrial–Urban Centers

Urbanization has proceeded quite rapidly during the past 180 years. In 1800 there were fewer than 50 cities in the world with 100,000 or more population. By 1950, there were 906 cities and by 1980, 2,202 cities with over 100,000 inhabitants. By size, there are currently 26 cities with over 5 million people, 71 cities with between 2 and 5 million inhabitants, and 128 cities with between 1 and 2 million people. Most early urban communities were city-states, and many modern nations have evolved from them. Even in cases in which the nation became large in both population and land area, the city has remained the focus for political and economic activities, and the core and magnet for much of social life. To people of other nations, the city often represents the nation. This tradition survives in the modern use of a city, such as Washington, London, and Moscow, as a synonym for a nation.

Both social factors and technological innovations speeded the processes of urbanization. Organizational changes permitted greater complexity in the division of labor (see Chapter 5). Simultaneously, the events labeled the Industrial Revolution allowed human beings to use steam as a source of energy, reinforcing the forces promoting the widespread use of machines. Power-driven machines accelerated social trends that were drawing manufacturing out of the home and placing it in a factory. As the factory system expanded, more and more workers were needed. People flocked to the factories, drawn not only by the novelty of urban life, but by the opportunity to gain its economic benefits. Throughout Europe, urban growth received impetus from the demise of the feudal system and the emergence of nation-states (see Chapter 16). Nationalism fostered the consolidation of local and regional economies, enlarging internal markets, integrating transportation systems, providing for common coinage and weights, and abolishing internal duties on goods.

Metropolitan Cities

Industrial-urban centers have typically been geographically scattered, and although dominating their hinterlands, have had only tenuous economic and social relations with them. More recently, metropolitan cities have emerged. This phase in urban development does not represent a sharp break with the industrial-urban tradition, but rather a widening and deepening of urban influences in every sphere of social life. The technological base for the metropolitan phase of urbanism is found in the tremendous increase in the application of science to industry, the widespread use of electric power (freeing industry from the limitations associated with steam and belt-and-pulley modes of power), and the advent of modern forms of transportation (the automobile and rapid transit systems have released cities from the limitations associated with foot and hoof travel, which had more or less restricted growth to a radius of 3 miles from the center).

By the late nineteenth century, a converging set of forces gained momentum, bucking earlier centripetal pressures. The growing availability of electric power, the telephone, rapid transit, and the automobile, coupled with a growing disenchantment with inner city life, encouraged thousands to migrate to outlying areas. Rising city taxes, increased land values, traffic and transportation problems, and decaying and obsolescent inner zones speeded the process. Satellite and suburban communities sprang up in growing numbers—broad, ballooning urban bands linked by beltways. In population, jobs, investment, construction, and shopping facilities, they rival the old inner cities. The communities are the sites of industrial plants, corporate offices and office towers, fine stores, independent newspapers, theaters, restaurants, superhotels, and big league sports stadiums.

The conventional distinction between cities and rural areas is eroding in many Western societies as the world is becoming, in Marshall McLuhan's oft-quoted phrase, a "global village." In many cases, the rural interstices between metropolitan centers have filled with urban development, making a "strip city" or **megalopolis.** The Northeastern seaboard is a good illustration of this process. A gigantic megalopolis lies along a 600-mile axis from southern New Hampshire to northern Virginia, encompassing 10 states, 117 counties, 32 cities larger than 500,000 people, and embracing nearly a fifth of U.S. population. As shown in Figure 20.2 on page 547, urban projections suggest that by the year 2050, if not sooner, another urbanized strip will extend from

Hamburg, Germany: 1663
Until relatively recent times, cities had a rural quality to them. This is hardly surprising, since many of the residents of cities were migrants from the countryside. And the cities had close social, economic, and political links with their rural hinterlands. *(Topham/The Image Works)*

OLD CHELTEM   10ᴹᴵ
CHELTEM   15ᴹᴵ
NEW CHELTEM   18ᴹᴵ
NEW, IMPROVED CHELTEM 25ᴹᴵ

Drawing by Levin; © 1986 The New Yorker Magazine, Inc.

New York State through Pennsylvania, Ohio, northern Indiana, and Illinois to Green Bay, Wisconsin, and Minneapolis-St. Paul.

Urban Ecology

Earlier in the text we noted that the members of a society differentiate among themselves in terms of such social characteristics as class, race, religion, nationality, age, and gender (see Chapters 9 through 12). They split up activities and become "different" by virtue of playing distinctive roles. In addition, every aspect of social organization has a spatial component; people differentiate among themselves and their activities territorially. The "where" may be an area as large as a continent or as small as a city block. Between these extremes are world regions, nations, national regions, states, cities, and rural areas.

The ways in which the members of a society arrange and distribute themselves in space has ramifications for all phases of social life. Your health, quality of education, access to employment, and exposure to crime depend in part on where you live (Massey and Denton, 1985). Moreover, space is not only a physical location, but "a piece of real estate" in a web of stratified relationships (Micklin and Choldin, 1984; Gottdiener, 1985). Consider, for instance, the affluent and white character of the suburbs and the poor and nonwhite character of inner cities. Not surprisingly, sociologists are interested in understanding how people order their relationships and conduct their activities within a spatial context.

Patterns of Urban Growth

Human ecology is the term sociologists have coined to describe the interrelationships that operate among people and their physical environment (Park and Burgess, 1921). Indeed, as ecologists observe, "Everything is connected to everything else." During the 1920s and 1930s, sociologists at the University of Chicago undertook to build on this insight and studied communities as a special case of adaptation to an ever-changing environment. More specifically, they sought to explain the patterns by which people and institutions come to be distributed in the physical space of a modern city. Their approach is known as **urban ecology.** As seen by the early Chicago sociologists, all cities have a center, be it a place of worship, a marketplace, a collection of office buildings, or a capitol. Around the center, a city spreads out like a patchwork quilt, "a mosaic of little worlds that touch but do not interpenetrate" (Park et al., 1925:40). Each area is characterized by a particular land use pattern, certain kinds of people, and distinctive lifestyles (Shibutani, 1986). Since the 1930s, other sociologists have also examined the processes of urban growth and have proposed new or modified models. This work has expanded our understanding of urban settlement patterns (these models are summarized in Figure 20.3 on page 548).

Concentric circle model The University of Chicago sociologists were struck by the fact that a city like Chicago is not a helter-skelter meshing of random elements. You rarely encounter a pretentious mansion in the midst of slum dwellings or the city's tallest office building next door to an electric generating plant. In scrutinizing the patterning of Chicago neighborhoods, the sociologists discerned a circular arrangement, what has been called the **concentric circle model** (Park, Burgess, and McKenzie, 1925) (review Figure 20.3). At the center of the city— *the central business district*—are retail stores, financial institutions, hotels, theaters, and businesses that cater to the needs of downtown shoppers. Surrounding the central business district is an area of residential deterioration caused by the encroachment of business and industry— *the zone in transition.* In earlier days these neighborhoods had contained the homes of wealthy and prominent citizens. In later years they became slum areas and havens for marginal business establishments (pawnshops, secondhand stores, pool halls, brothels, cheap hotels, and modest taverns and restaurants). Now the area is a mixed usage commercial and residential zone (Hunter, 1987). The zone in transition shades into the *zone of*

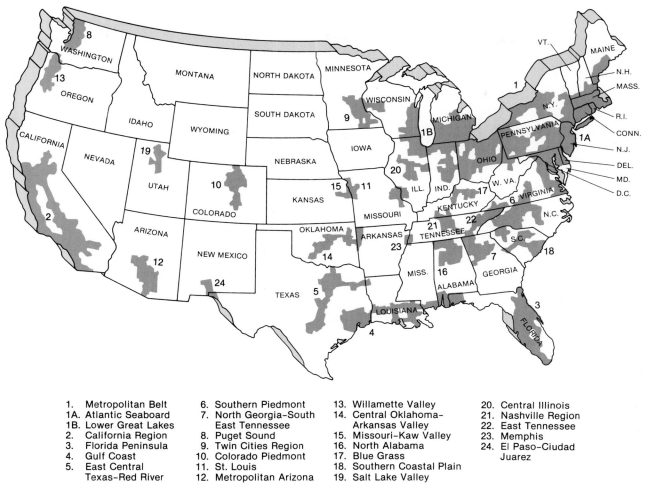

FIGURE 20.2 **Megalopolises in the Year 2000**
Projections suggest that the heavily urban shaded areas on the map will characterize
many sections of the United States by the year 2000. The megalopolitan areas shown
here are numbered in order of population size. *Source: Adapted from* Population Growth
and American Future. *Washington, D.C.: U.S. Government Printing Office.*

1. Metropolitan Belt
1A. Atlantic Seaboard
1B. Lower Great Lakes
2. California Region
3. Florida Peninsula
4. Gulf Coast
5. East Central
    Texas–Red River

6. Southern Piedmont
7. North Georgia–South
    East Tennessee
8. Puget Sound
9. Twin Cities Region
10. Colorado Piedmont
11. St. Louis
12. Metropolitan Arizona

13. Willamette Valley
14. Central Oklahoma–
    Arkansas Valley
15. Missouri–Kaw Valley
16. North Alabama
17. Blue Grass
18. Southern Coastal Plain
19. Salt Lake Valley

20. Central Illinois
21. Nashville Region
22. East Tennessee
23. Memphis
24. El Paso–Ciudad
    Juarez

working class homes. It contains flats, old single dwellings, and inexpensive apartments inhabited largely by
blue-collar workers and lower-paid white-collar workers.
Beyond the zone occupied by the working class are *residential zones* where primarily small business proprietors,
professional people, and managerial personnel live. Finally, out beyond the areas containing the more affluent
neighborhoods, there is a ring of encircling small cities,
towns, and hamlets, *the commuters' zone.*

The Chicago group viewed these zones as ideal
types, since in practice no city conforms entirely to the

scheme. For instance, as shown in Figure 20.4 on page
549, Chicago borders on Lake Michigan so it has a concentric semicircular rather than a circular arrangement.
Moreover, the hypothesis applies only to a growing community in a capitalist economy, one marked by little or
no citywide planning of housing, substantial distinctions
in social rank, and the leeway to live wherever one can
afford to (Shibutani, 1986). Consequently, the approach
is less descriptive of today's cities than cities at the turn of
the twentieth century. And even then, some cities never
took on a circular pattern (Davie, 1937). Likewise, cities

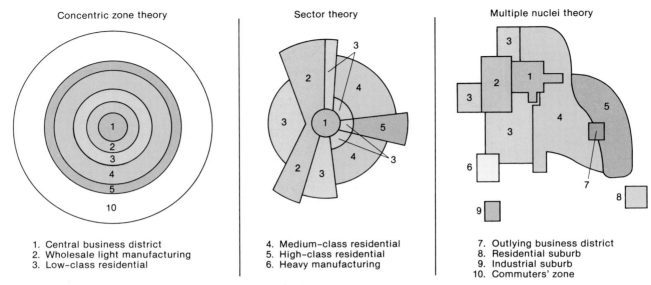

FIGURE 20.3 **Theoretical Patterns of Urban Structure**
Source: Chauncey D. Harris and Edward L. Ullman. 1945. The nature of cities. The Annals of The American Academy of Political and Social Science, 242.

in the Third World nations of Latin America, Asia, and Africa reveal less specialization in land use than do North American cities.

The sector model   Homer Hoyt (1939) portrays large cities as made up of a number of sectors rather than concentric circles—the **sector model** (review Figure 20.3). Low-rent districts often assume a wedge shape and extend from the center of the city to its periphery. In contrast, as a city grows, high-rent areas move outward, although remaining in the same sector. Districts within a sector that are abandoned by upper-income groups become obsolete and deteriorate. Rather than forming a concentric zone around the periphery of the city, Hoyt says, high-rent areas typically locate on the outer edge of a few sectors. Furthermore, industrial areas evolve along river valleys, water courses, and railroad lines, rather than forming a ring around the central business district. But like the concentric circle model, the sector model does not fit many urban communities, including Boston (Firey, 1947).

The multiple nuclei model   Another pattern—the **multiple nuclei model**—depicts the city as having not one center, but several (Harris and Ullman, 1945). Each center specializes in some activity and gives its distinctive cast to the surrounding area. For example, the down-

town business district has as its focus commercial and financial activities. Other centers include the "bright lights" (theater and recreation) area, "automobile row," a government center, a wholesaling center, a heavy manufacturing district, and a medical complex. Multiple centers evolve for a number of reasons. First, certain activities require specialized facilities—for instance, the retail district needs to be accessible to all parts of the city; the port district requires a suitable waterfront; and a manufacturing district dictates that a large block of land be available near water, rail, or highway connections. Second, similar activities often benefit from being clustered together—for instance, a retail district profits by drawing customers for a variety of shops. Third, dissimilar activities are often antagonistic to one another—for example, affluent residential development tends to be incompatible with industrial development. And finally, some activities cannot afford high-rent areas and hence locate in low-rent districts—for instance, bulk wholesaling and storage. The multiple nuclei model is less helpful in discovering universal spatial patterns in all cities than in describing the patterns peculiar to particular communities.

Social area analysis   The concentric circle, sector, and multiple nuclei models attempt to identify the spatial patterns that govern the ecological structure of urban

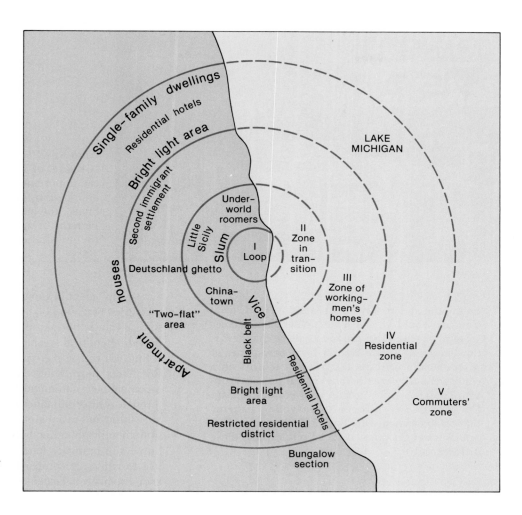

FIGURE 20.4 **Urban Areas in Chicago as Depicted by The University of Chicago Sociologists**
Source: Robert E. Park, Ernest W. Burgess, and R. D. McKenzie. The City. Chicago: University of Chicago Press, 1925.

centers. Eshref Shevky and Marilyn Williams (1949) provide a different approach—**social area analysis**—that focuses on the social characteristics of an urban population. They compile indexes of the social, family, and ethnic properties of a community to discern linkages between changing dimensions of social life and use of space. For example, people who reside in inner city neighborhoods tend to be unmarried and of lower socioeconomic rank. Those living in the suburbs are more likely to be married and of higher socioeconomic rank. By measuring these and related indexes at various points in time, sociologists can identify major trends and currents in urban living. It should be stressed, however, that all these models of urban growth rest primarily on studies of North American cities and are not necessarily applicable to cities in other parts of the world.

THINKING THROUGH THE ISSUES

Secure a map or make your own hand-drawn map of a city with which you are familiar, perhaps your college town or hometown. Identify the distinctive characteristics of various locales, particularly the dominant land use, social class, and ethnic group patterns. Which model or combination of models of city growth seems best fitted to the community? Can you provide a sociological explanation for the patterning you discern? Did unique historical factors play a part—for instance, the city's location at the intersection of two highways, along a river or lake that facilitated the transport of raw materials and manufactured products, or near a major governmental, religious, or university hub? If you were to make

Auto Row: Toyota City, Japan
A thicket of Toyota dealers' signs reflects the important role that the automobile has assumed in Japanese life. As in the United States, the automobile has influenced the patterns of urban growth and the use of the physical environment. *(Toshi Matsumoto/Sygma)*

a similar map ten or twenty years from now, what changes would you observe? What social forces seem to be at work in producing these changes? If time permits, secure from a local newspaper or from election officials the precinct returns on a controversial referendum or critical political contest. Locate the precincts on your ecological map. Do you observe differences in voting patterns that are associated with locale? Do the social characteristics of the population help to explain these differences?

Ecological Processes

The structural patterning of cities derives from a number of underlying ecological processes. As we have seen, people relate to one another and undertake their activities in ways that result in geographic areas taking the form of **natural areas** with distinctive characteristics. The Chicago sociologists of the 1920s suggested that natural areas are initially not the product of deliberate design, but of competition and natural selection.

One way natural areas emerge is through **segregation,** a process of clustering wherein individuals and groups are sifted and sorted out in space based on sharing certain traits or activities. This clustering takes place voluntarily when people find that close spatial proximity is advantageous. For instance, the multiple nuclei model of city growth suggests that certain similar activities profit from the cohesion provided by a segregated district. Likewise, some nationality and cultural groups prefer to live close to one another. Such an arrangement facilitates communication, understanding, and rapport, and fosters

"we-group" identifications and loyalties. Additionally, a segregated neighborhood protects against the intrusion of strange values, norms, and beliefs, while simultaneously providing political leverage with City Hall through bloc voting. Of course segregation may also be involuntary. Residential neighborhoods frequently attempt to exclude incompatible commercial and industrial activities through zoning ordinances. And as we noted in Chapter 10, ethnic and racial groups may systematically exclude from their neighborhoods other ethnic and racial groups. Surveys of mortgage lending practices reveal that, relative to whites of comparable income, black applicants are more likely to be denied mortgages (a practice termed *redlining*) and to pay higher interest rates when they do get mortgages. In brief, blacks compete with whites in a dual housing market in which realtors and financial institutions "contain" blacks in neighborhoods that whites no longer find desirable (Stearns and Logan, 1986).

Invasion and succession are also important ecological processes (Park, 1952; Schwirian, 1983). **Invasion** takes place when a new type of people, institution, or activity encroaches on an area occupied by a different type. Should the invasion continue until the encroaching type displaces the other, **succession** is said to have occurred. Although a neighborhood's ecological function may remain unchanged (for instance, residential), it typically becomes a less desirable place to live or work. Yet the reverse process, reinvasion, also takes place (Marullo, 1985). Georgetown, in Washington, D.C., was a terrible slum in the 1920s. More recently, private individuals have restored many of the pre–Civil War mansions, providing expensive and attractive housing in which government, business, and professional leaders now reside.

Urban Gentrification
In major cities throughout the United States, upwardly mobile whites are displacing the poor and minorities in some neighborhoods. In the process, older buildings go through renewal or removal. Pictured at right is the conversion of brownstone buildings to cooperative apartments in the Park Slope area of Brooklyn, a neighborhood undergoing gentrification. *(Hazel Hankin)*

One expression of reinvasion is **urban gentrification**—the return of the middle class, usually young, white professionals (sometimes called *Yuppies*), to older neighborhoods. Urban gentrification is happening in large cities throughout the United States (Haight-Ashbury in San Francisco, Queen Village in Philadelphia, Mount Adams in Cincinnati, New Town in Chicago, and German Village in Columbus, Ohio). The process typically culminates in the displacement of the poor and minorities from these neighborhoods by upwardly mobile whites with financial resources and clout. Many older cities are counting on urban gentrification to offset eroding population and tax bases. However, even though the "back-to-the-city" movement has transformed some neighborhoods, it has hardly been a panacea for urban ills. Indeed, it may compound the ills when the poor are displaced and pushed into adjoining neighborhoods (Schill and Nathan, 1983; Gale, 1984; Chall, 1984). Frequently, urban gentrification occurs as a process of change in which a neighborhood moves through a series of invasion-succession cycles—a sort of life cycle involving development, transition, downgrading, thinning out, and renewal (Schwirian, 1983).

Cities in a World System

According to ecological theory, communities are not self-contained forms of social organization, but rather parts of a larger division of labor and social whole. They are differentiated according to their primary sustenance activities, which allows them to exchange their surplus goods and services with other communities. Since cities are interdependent, their respective specializations reflect an adaptation to the specializations of other cities. Consequently, cities come in many forms and sizes. Some are highly specialized, like capital cities, college communities, auto municipalities, steel towns, research centers, and military bases. Others are more diversified, like Columbus, Ohio; Indianapolis; Minneapolis; Atlanta; and Austin. Interconnections among cities are promoted and sustained by large corporations and government units (Wilson, 1984; Meyer, 1986; Ross, 1987).

Cities mediate many of the relations a local population has with the physical environment and the larger social world. Indeed, most contemporary cities are caught up in a world system. Consider the importance of the global economy in shaping Detroit's decline following the surge in foreign auto imports and Houston's difficulties following the sharp drop in world oil prices (Hill, 1984; Feagin, 1985). Nor is it surprising, given an unequal world, that cities should be unequal. London, Amsterdam, Paris, Madrid, and Vienna evolved and prospered on the basis of foreign empires. Today metropolises are also ordered in a world hierarchy; those with the greatest power, cities like New York, London, and Paris, dominate the activities of cities of lesser power, both within their own nations and in the international arena. The world system of cities reaches across national and regional boundaries (Walton, 1976; Gilbert, 1982; Meyer, 1986).

The extent and influence of the linkages among cities are highlighted by the urban patterns found in Third World cities. European colonization altered the character of the urbanization process in Asia, Africa, and South America; it changed the structure of existing cities and built new ones to facilitate the extraction and export of natural resources. In many cases the process retarded and distorted the growth and development of these cities in ways that subverted the interests and needs of native populations. In recent decades, the penetration of developing nations by multinational corporations and the diffusion of Western lifestyles and technologies have reinforced earlier patterns of outside domination (Wilson, 1984; London, 1987).

Unequal relationships between developed and developing nations have hindered socioeconomic development in Third World countries in a variety of ways. They have fostered an imbalance in living standards between rural and urban areas, contributing to substantial rural-urban migration flows. One enormous metropolis, such as Mexico City or Sao Paolo, comes to dominate and intermediate sized cities never develop. The metropolis functions as a "core" city, with the remainder of the nation constituting the "periphery" (see Chapters 15 and 22). Urban growth typically occurs more rapidly in core cities than do employment opportunities, producing unemployment, underemployment, and misemployment. All the while demands for housing, education, transportation, water, and sanitation strain the budgets of developing countries. Consider, for instance, that between 1947 and 1981 the population of Cairo increased from 3.6 million to more than 10 million and is expected to reach 13 million by the year 2000. And as Table 20.1 shows, Mexico City, already the world's most populous metropolitan area, is expected to grow from nearly 19 million in 1985 to more than 26 million by the turn of the century. Even though urbanization may serve as a catalyst for socioeconomic development, the speed and extent of the growth can at times overwhelm the capacity of a nation to manage the process. In some cases the disproportionate growth of core cities seems to pull their nations toward political or environmental disaster (Wilson, 1984; Vining, 1985). We will have more to say on these matters in Chapter 22.

Table 20.1   Top 35 Cities in 2000

Metropolitan Area	2000 Pop. (in millions)
Mexico City	26.3
São Paulo, Brazil	24.0
Tokyo/Yokohama	17.1
Calcutta, India	16.6
Bombay, India	16.0
New York–northeastern New Jersey	15.5
Seoul, South Korea	13.5
Shanghai, China	13.5
Rio de Janeiro, Brazil	13.3
New Delhi, India	13.3
Buenos Aires, Argentina	13.2
Cairo, Egypt	13.2
Jakarta, Indonesia	12.8
Baghdad, Iraq	12.8
Tehran, Iran	12.7
Karachi, Pakistan	12.2
Istanbul, Turkey	11.9
Los Angeles–Long Beach	11.2
Dacca, Bangladesh	11.2
Manila, Philippines	11.1
Peking	10.8
Moscow	10.1
Bangkok, Thailand	9.5
Tianjin, China	9.2
Paris	9.2
Lima, Peru	9.1
London	9.1
Kinshasa, Zaire	8.9
Rhine-Ruhr, West Germany	8.6
Lagos, Nigeria	8.3
Madras, India	8.2
Bangalore, India	8.0
Osaka, Japan	7.7
Milan, Italy	7.5
Chicago	7.2

Source: United Nations.

THINKING THROUGH THE ISSUES

Consider your college town or hometown. How many ties or connections can you identify linking it to cities outside the United States? Imagine that intense protectionist sentiment led to a cutting off of foreign exports and imports. How would your community be affected? Which activities and industries would benefit? Which would suffer? How does the rise and fall in the price of world oil directly and indirectly affect the community?

In what ways does the import of foreign automobiles, computer chips, textiles, steel, and electronic equipment affect employment opportunities in your community? How dependent is the community on foreign students and on the export to foreign nations of American goods and services?

Urban Social Strains: Bombay, India
In Third World nations, cities have served as magnets attracting migrants from interior regions. But the urban populations grow more rapidly than do jobs and city services, overtaxing the capacity of cities to absorb and assimilate the new arrivals.
(Peter Menzel)

Perspectives on Urban Life

The emergence of urban settlements has conspicuously changed our planet's surface and profoundly altered our social relationships. Even after nearly 10,000 years of urban experience, many of us are uncertain whether our creation is a benefit or a curse. To the philosophers of the Enlightenment the city represented virtue and hope, but to later generations in the midst of the Industrial Revolution it seemed a tarnished nest of corruption and despair. Today Americans are also divided on the relative merits of city life. There are those who point out that life expectancy is higher for people in urban areas and infant mortality rates are lower. It seems that the potentially unhealthy aspects of urban living, including pollution, crime, and stress, are more than offset by better medical care, better water supplies, and better sewage systems. On the other side are those Americans who see cities as hotbeds of dehumanizing confrontations, grit and grime, high noise levels, tight spaces, and crime-ridden streets (Creekmore, 1985). This same ambivalence toward the city emerges in the perspectives sociologists have fashioned for describing and explaining the consequences of urban life.

The City as a Lonely Crowd

Many nineteenth-century sociologists distrusted cities. They maintained a commitment to rural life because they thought humans are best served by intimate associations of family, neighborhood, and community. These early sociologists saw large cities, with their complex divisions of labor, bureaucracies, and countless masses, as

imperiling the social fabric through distant and aloof relationships. This sentiment is captured by the terms *Gemeinschaft* and *Gesellschaft*, introduced by the German sociologist Ferdinand Toennies (1855–1936). The concepts have many of the same connotations as those asso-

"We love the view. It helps to remind us that we're part of a larger community."

Drawing by Weber; © 1986 The New Yorker Magazine, Inc.

ISSUES THAT SHAPE OUR LIVES

Do You Really Want to Live in a Small Town?

Given your choice of where to live, would you prefer a small town? Would you like "to return to nature"— to experience pleasant breezes, pure water and air, and ready access to wooded terrain, trickling brooks, and bountiful meadows? And how about the folksy, rustic charm of the small hamlet, its homespun values, and its unassuming, warm, and neighborly inhabitants? If you respond affirmatively to these questions, you are not alone. In recent decades surveys have consistently shown that almost half of all Americans say they would like to live in small town and rural settings. And across the United States, especially in the 1970s, significant numbers of Americans did opt for "simplicity of life and rural atmosphere" (Herbers, 1986).

The 1970s migrants were primarily the young and the elderly. The

Stereotyped Utopia: Rural America?
Stereotypes of the city have had their corollary in notions of rural life as a haven of natural purity, wholesome values, and a spirit of self-reliance. (*Hank Morgan/Rainbow*)

younger migrants were better educated than long-time residents, earned more money, and were more liberal in their attitudes and politics. Many of them experienced "culture shock" after their move, dismayed that small-town and rural life so little resembled

their stereotyped utopia. So they turned to "improving" the communities, pushing for water and sewer lines, better schools and libraries, public transportation, and community health programs. They sought to raise local taxes to pay for the amenities.

ciated with primary groups and secondary groups (see Chapter 5). **Gemeinschaft** describes binding, personal relationships rooted in customary roles, long-standing obligations, and mutual trust; **Gesellschaft** describes relationships dominated by self-interest and competition, with people's interests protected formally by contract and law—a social world where "everybody is by himself and isolated" (Toennies, 1887/1963:74). In practice, many sociologists have equated Gemeinschaft and Gesellschaft with rural-urban differences, attributing dissimilar ways of life to people in the two settings (Christenson, 1984; Gold, 1985). The rural environment is depicted as a personal world of friends, relatives, and neighbors, whereas the city is portrayed as an impersonal world of strangers (many Americans share this view, a matter discussed in the box).

This theme was elaborated by sociologist Louis Wirth (1938) in his classic essay, "Urbanism as a Way of Life." He thought that the city profoundly affects our attitudes by virtue of its *size, density,* and *heterogeneity.* A large population, Wirth said, makes the city a place

where impersonal, superficial, transitory, and segmental relationships prevail, so that urban dwellers are "largely anonymous" beings. Dense land use compels people and organizations to develop elaborate specializations, generating occupational, religious, ethnic, and social variation and their segregation in space. And heterogeneity— a mosaic of differing lifestyles—breeds weak social ties and fluid, unpredictable, and insecure relationships. Wirth believed these elements made urban residents more liberal, tolerant, and aloof than their rural counterparts. Moreover, the moral order, undergirded by strong person-to-person bonds in traditional villages, requires formal social controls in cities to mediate the competition, aggrandizement, and mutual exploitation that arise among strangers.

The City as an Urban Village

Not too many decades ago it seemed "obvious" both to the general public and to sociologists that modern society has disrupted people's natural relations, loosened their

And they thought it might be a good idea to foster local industry and manufacturing to provide a larger tax base and to expand employment opportunities. But elderly migrants disagreed. They did not like the idea of raising taxes. And they thought the local economy should be stimulated not by manufacturing and industry, but by increasing the population and developing recreational facilities. However, whether young or elderly, most smalltown newcomers have shown little interest in farming. Those with homes next to farms complain about the smell of fertilizer, the noise made by tractors, and their dusting by chemical carcinogens when farmer Bob sprays his crops (Mueller, 1987).

Since the 1970s, the growth in small towns has been slowing and the nation's metropolitan areas have reestablished themselves as magnets for people on the move (Peterson, 1986). Disillusion with village life has spread across the nation. Life in small towns and rural areas looks quite appealing

from a distance. Close-up experience reveals its shortcomings. In 1985, the Farmers Home Administration studied 520 randomly selected communities in the United States, all with populations of under 2,500. The survey revealed that many small communities endure poor facilities. For example, 60 percent of the towns in the Midwest lack public water. Well water is of questionable purity; many small towns inadequately monitor surrounding water supplies for coliform bacteria and other organic contaminants. Waste and sewage disposal systems are in disarray, with families making do as best they can with septic tanks and open landfills. Roads are often poor, and inhabitants have limited access to hospitals. People living in smalltown America may not have to lock their doors at night, but they may die of a heart attack because they cannot be reached in time (Mueller, 1987).

Nor have small towns provided a robust business climate for local mer-

chants. In recent years, the slump in the farm economy has hurt sales. People like to have certain services close at hand, like grocery stores, auto repair shops, lawyers, insurance companies, and hair stylists. But when they want freezers, cars, ranges, dryers, furniture, clothes, and shoes, they are willing to go farther from home. Airline and telephone deregulation have compounded smalltown problems, since these services become less frequent and more expensive outside transportation and business hubs like Denver and Salt Lake City. Despite ailing economies and a high rate of business failure, each year new entrepreneurs try their hand at making a living in craft and antique shops in small towns across the United States. But for most people, smalltown life does not provide the life they long for. What they really seem to be looking for is a frontier stocked with urban amenities (Herbers, 1986; Mueller, 1987).

commitments to kin and neighbors, and substituted in their place shallow encounters with passing acquaintances. However, in recent years a growing body of research has revealed that the "obvious" is not true (Lewis, 1952; Gans, 1962; Fischer, 1982). It seems that if you are a city resident, you typically know a smaller proportion of your neighbors than you do if you are a resident of a smaller community. But, for the most part, this fact has few significant consequences. It does not necessarily follow that if you know few of your neighbors you will know no one else.

Even in very large cities, people sustain intimate social ties within small, private social worlds. Indeed, the number and quality of meaningful relationships do not differ between more and less urban people. Smalltown residents are involved more with kin than are bigcity residents. Yet city dwellers compensate by developing friendships with people who share similar interests and activities, such as those found among a group of bowlers or poker players, friends at the office or shop, and hockey or opera goers. Urbanism may produce a

different *style* of life, but the *quality* of life does not differ between town and city. Nor are residents of large communities any likelier to display psychological symptoms of pathology, stress, or alienation than are residents of smaller communities. However, city dwellers do worry more about crime, and this leads them to a distrust of strangers (Fischer, 1981, 1982).

These findings do not imply that urbanism makes little or no difference. If neighbors are strangers to one another, they are less likely to alternate babysitting duties, shovel the sidewalk of an elderly couple living next door, or keep an eye out for youthful mischief and deviance (Freudenburg, 1986). Moreover, as Wirth suggested, there may be a link between a community's population size and its social heterogeneity. For instance, sociologists have found much evidence that the size of a community is associated with "moral deviance," including gambling, narcotics, prostitution, topless nightclubs, and liberal attitudes toward premarital and extramarital sex. Large-city urbanites are also more likely than their smalltown counterparts to have a cosmopolitan outlook,

An Ethnic Neighborhood in New York City: 1900
Flourishing street markets like the one depicted above
on the Lower East Side of Manhattan were commonplace in neighborhoods with large immigrant populations. Many of the residents had come from rural villages of Europe and sought to replicate the ways of
the small community in the anonymous urban environment of New York City. In their ethnic neighborhoods the immigrants evolved a social cohesion
rooted in their common experiences and shared culture. *(The Bettmann Archive)*

to display less commitment to traditional kinship roles,
to vote for leftist political candidates, and to be tolerant
of winos, bag ladies, nontraditional religious cults, unpopular political groups, and so-called undesirables (Stephan and McMullin, 1982; Wilson, 1985). Everything
considered, heterogeneity and unconventionality seem
to be outcomes of large population size (Wilson, 1986).

Sociologist Claude Fischer (1982, 1984) offers one
explanation for the link between population size and heterogeneity. He says that large populations increase social
heterogeneity by increasing the variety of *subcultures* to
be found among them (see Chapter 3). His argument
runs as follows. First, the more people there are in a
community, the greater the likelihood that an untypical
or unconventional person will be able to find others who
share similar traits and needs. Second, the larger the
population, the greater the probability that a group of
people will be numerous enough to attain "critical mass"
and so be able to support distinctive subcultural institutions. Third, to the extent that subcultural institutions
emerge and flourish, the distinctive features of the subculture receive support and are intensified. And finally,
the more numerous the subcultures, the more likely it is
that new blends and hybrids of subcultures will arise.

The City as an Arena of Conflict

In still another view of urban life, conflict is the central
feature of cities. The city is seen as an arena of struggle.
"Who gets what?" is the critical question. Urban life and
place depend on a crucial dimension of social structure:
power and class hierarchy. Land, the basic stuff of place,
is a market commodity that provides wealth and power.
Those at the top of the power structure set the priorities
within which decisions affecting land use, the public
budget, and urban social life are formulated. The winners are always the powerful and monied; the losers, always the poor and minority groups. In sum, a city's physical layout and social characteristics are an expression
and consequence of conflict (Molotch, 1976; Whitt,
1982).

Sociologist Harvey Molotch (1973, 1976) observes
that we have a stake or interest in our parcels of land.
Should the land's value be enhanced, our wealth is increased. Each component of a community strives, at the
expense of others, to maximize its land-use potential.
Shopkeepers at each end of a block contend with one
another to determine whether the bus stop will be in
front of the one or the other building. Hotel owners on
the south side of a city compete with those on the north
side for a convention center nearby. Areas fight over
highway routes, traffic intersections, one-way street des-
ignations, park development, airport location, campus
expansion, and defense contracts. The city, then, is a
mosaic of interest groups.

In the Marxist version of conflict theory, the control
of economic production, and of the surplus it generates,
has powered the evolution of the city through the stages
of mercantile, industrial, and corporate capitalism (Gordon, 1978; Mollenkopf, 1981; Jaret, 1983). The profit
requirements of merchant capitalism in the 1600s and
1700s created colonial port cities along the Atlantic and
Gulf coasts. These cities were tied to the waterfront
wharves that linked them in trade with foreign cities. All
social classes lived in close proximity along zigzag
streets. With the coming of industrial capitalism in the

Mercantile Capitalism: Shaping Colonial Port Cities?

As portrayed by Marxists, colonial cities along the Atlantic and Gulf coasts reflected the profit motivations of seventeenth- and eighteenth-century mercantile capitalists. The focus of urban life was the waterfront that linked the cities in trade with world commerce. Members of all social classes lived in close proximity along zigzag streets. Depicted here is the harbor of Charles Town (Charleston), South Carolina. *(The I.N. Phelps Stokes Collection of American Historical Prints, Prints Division, The New York Public Library)*

1800s, profits were sought primarily through manufacturing. A sifting and winnowing process set in whereby people were segregated by class within different neighborhoods; simultaneously, tight urban centralization facilitated industrial production and the control of labor. Under corporate capitalism, the third stage beginning in the 1890s, the dictates of huge corporations brought about the decentralization of industry and residential areas. Business leaders believed they would have fewer labor problems, lower taxes, and greater control over production outside the cities. Marxists say that profit-seeking motives are the source of current urban ills: A capitalist enterprise remains in an area until it exhausts its profit-making potential, and then moves on to new domains (Smith, 1984).

As seen by Marxists, the capitalist mode of production creates the type of city in which we live, and our cities have changed as the requirements of capitalism have changed (Harvey, 1985a, 1985b). Unfortunately, the theory fails to explain why cities in contemporary socialist nations resemble so closely those of contemporary capitalist nations (Castells, 1977; Szelyni, 1978). And it gives little hint as to how the city will evolve. Strangely, the Marxist dynamo of history seems to give a last turn, stopping forever with the triumph of socialism (Lynch, 1984).

THINKING THROUGH THE ISSUES

In recent decades, the issue of urban exploitation has aroused concern. Critics—typically city officials and planners—charge that the suburbs are "exploiting" central cities. They argue that suburbanites who work in, visit, and play in the city make demands on the municipal budget for facilities and services, but avoid their costs by virtue of living elsewhere (Slovak, 1985). How many services can you identify that central cities provide and that suburbanites use on a "free-ride" basis (for instance, street maintenance, rapid transit, and police protection)? How have cities attempted to remedy this situation (for example, placing earning taxes on commuters, creating special metropolitan taxing districts, and providing fees for services)? What arguments do you think suburban officials use in fighting these measures (for instance, "our commuting workers and shoppers subsidize central city shops, theaters, and services")? Taking the matter of exploitation a step further, there are those who say that central cities function as reservations for the poor, the deviant, the unwanted, and people who make a business or career of managing them (keeping them "safe") for the rest of society. What do you make of this position? What sorts of social programs do you think its adherents advocate?

American Cities in Flux

Looking out over Chicago from the 94th-floor observatory of the John Hancock building, one sees a city that resembles an old Oriental rug: bright and vital in some places and worn and bare in others. Chicago's development has become a tale of two cities. The gleaming new office towers in the downtown—the "Loop," State

Street, and Michigan Avenue—mask the boarded-up storefronts, abandoned houses, and idle factories in adjoining neighborhoods (Klein, 1980; Helyar and Johnson, 1986). The bare spots on the face of Chicago and other older American cities began to appear in the mid-1950s, and by the 1970s the exodus of residents and corporations had become a serious problem. St. Louis, Cleveland, Pittsburgh, and Detroit suffered population declines of 13 percent or more in the early 1970s, a rate that, had it continued, would have resulted in their being virtually uninhabited by the year 2000. Large numbers of people from northeastern and east-central states moved to southwestern and western states. People tend to follow jobs and migrate to areas where they believe there are better employment opportunities. However, the tightening of the job market in the Southwest in the 1980s has slowed the big-city population drain. Indeed, between 1980 and 1983, New York, Los Angeles, Chicago, Philadelphia, and San Francisco gained

1.2 million people, compared to a gain of 1.6 million in the entire 1970s (Engels and Forstall, 1985; Fuguitt, 1985). (Figure 20.5 shows cities that may offer you the best job prospects in the 1990s.)

The "donut" analogy is a useful description of the course of post–World War II metropolitan development. The hole in the donut is the decaying central city, and the ring is a prosperous and growing suburban and satellite-city region. In some cases, such as Chicago's Loop district and portions of Manhattan, the hole is a core area that is being revitalized and the ring is a surrounding part of the city that is becoming progressively blighted. A number of trends have contributed to the doughnut phenomenon. Since World War II, the suburbs of most American cities have grown more rapidly than have central cities, so that by 1984, nearly a half of the nation's population lived in suburbs (105,247,000 people compared to 83.5 million in 1970). Recent changes in the workplace and society have accelerated

FIGURE 20.5 Looking for a Job? Locations that Are Good and Poor Bets
Fortune magazine, based on its expectations for the nation's economy in the 1990s, believes the areas where job growth is likely to be the highest are those "with a big concentration of brains plus an array of amenities that attract creative people." The most promising spots are near prestigious, research-oriented universities, such as Massachusetts Institute of Technology, Stanford, Cal Tech, Carnegie-Mellon, Georgia Tech, and the Universities of Washington and Michigan. Whereas most low-growth areas are in the Midwest, the high-growth prospects cluster near the nation's coasts.
Source: Gurney Breckenfeld. 1987. Where to live—and prosper. Fortune *(February 2), p. 54.*

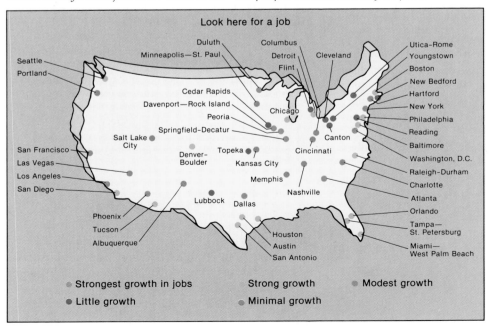

"Now that we're away from it all—let's go back."

From The Wall Street Journal; permission, Cartoon Features Syndicate

the movement of many corporations to outlying areas. Computer and communications technology and the growth of service industries have allowed companies to shift many routine office and other operations to the suburbs. Rents there are often one-third to one-half those of downtown locations. Additionally, by moving to the suburbs, many companies have been able to tap an educated, largely female work force that business firms secure at comparatively low salaries. By the same token, two-income households need a variety of employment opportunities, and the suburbs now offer this variety— upstaging the central city (Dentzer, 1986; Lueck, 1986; Hughes and Sternlieb, 1986; Frey, 1987). Let us take a closer look at what is happening to the nation's cities.

Suburbs: No Longer *Sub*

"Our property seems to me the most beautiful in the world. We enjoy all the advantages of the city, and yet when we come home we are away from all the noise and dust." This testimonial to suburban life was not written this year or even in the twentieth century. It is an excerpt from a letter written on a clay tablet in cuneiform script. The city? Babylon. The year? 539 B.C. The recipient? The king of Persia. If this Babylonian summation rings true today, it is because the suburb is not the modern invention we often imagine it to be: The history of the

suburb is the flip side of the history of cities. Growing and prospering cities invariably spawn outlying communities (Binford, 1985; Kimmel, 1986).

Following World War II, when the trickle of people out of central cities became a tide, the stereotype of suburbia arose. Despite their diversity, the suburbs became framed in the American mind as the land of green velvet lawns, two-car garages, swimming pools, the bridge club set, picture windows, and Republicanism. Yet the stereotype is unreal and for the most part, always has been. Although Americans still speak of suburbs, they are no longer *sub*. Many of them are broad, ballooning bands, linked by beltways, that constitute cities in their own right. In population, jobs, investment, construction, and stores, they rival older inner cities (Logan and Golden, 1986).

King of Prussia, Pennsylvania, a suburban "minicity" 20 miles from the center of Philadelphia, is the home of a shopping mall with 6 department stores and 200 smaller shops, a half-dozen factories and warehouses, and office parks occupied by more than 30 small- to medium-size companies. The Metro subway and rail system in the Washington area has turned Bethesda, Maryland, from a comfortable residential suburb to a booming "outer city" with tall hotels and even taller office buildings. And Southfield, Michigan, now boasts more office space than downtown Detroit, a 20-minute drive away. The community has 75,000 residents, 4,000 businesses, and a workforce of 300,000. Nor is Southfield an exception. In 1980, 57 percent of all office space in the United States was in traditional downtown areas and 43 percent elsewhere; by 1987, the figures had reversed (Barron, 1986).

The old image of the metropolis as a radial city, one in which residents go downtown to work in the morning and return home at night, is clearly wrong. One-time "bedroom hamlets" have been transformed into places where residents both sleep and work. Increasingly, more and more people who live in suburbs also work there. For instance, none of the New York counties surrounding New York City's five boroughs now sends even half of its workers to jobs in the city. Of interest, many suburbs are becoming net importers of labor, especially blue-collar and service workers. The central cities, with their vast supply of apartments and aging single-family houses, are becoming dormitories for those who work beyond the city limits.

Whereas a few decades ago a central city was relatively compact, in suburbia everything is spread over a much larger crescent of development. The broad multi-

Sprawling Office Development in a Washington, D.C., "Suburb"
Tyson's Corner, Virginia, 10 miles from the White House, is no longer "crabgrass frontier" but a booming community in its own right. But a major shortcoming of congested areas like Tyson's Corner is that development occurs with little overall thought or planning. Strong county government headquartered elsewhere has a half dozen other megacenters scattered about and does not think of any of them as "downtown." *(John Troha/Black Star)*

your parents: a better life for their children. But the effort to escape mounting congestion simply creates more congestion; it is self-defeating. Families want ranch houses on half-acre plots; retailers want one-floor supermarkets and acres for parking; manufacturers want one-floor factories and parklike grounds; and motorists want eight-lane superhighways and cloverleaf turns. Americans fashion more and more subdivisions named after the kinds of trees that are then cut down to make room for them. As each new area fills up, the quest for space takes the suburbs farther out. In time, the home that once was "in the country" or in "a pleasant suburb" becomes a dot in a continuous sea of housing developments and shopping centers. In the process, inner-ring suburbs age and begin to experience many of the ills that have long plagued big cities (Fitzpatrick and Logan, 1985; Lublin, 1985).

Central Cities in Crisis

According to many urban experts, U.S. industrial cities are institutions of a bygone era, and they "must simply accept a less exalted place in American political and social life than they once enjoyed" (Peterson, 1985). Technological and demographic change have relentlessly undermined the position of smokestack cities. Technological change is transforming them from centers that primarily produce and distribute goods to centers that administer and that produce and distribute information and services (see Chapters 15 and 22). On the population front, large cities are continuing to lose middle-class residents and becoming the repository of a dependent, minority underclass. The urban minorities confront a triple handicap of shrinking job opportunities, limited education, and low-quality neighborhoods (see Chapters 9 and 10). Some cities seem capable of retaining or luring back higher-income urban residents, but they tend to be single professionals, empty-nesters, childless dual-income couples, and people leading unconventional lifestyles.

Urban decline is both descriptive and functional. *Descriptive decline* has to do with the loss of population or jobs. It occurs as people who have the resources to leave the city do, while those who are poor have little choice but to remain. The proportion of poor residents increases as their number is swelled by recent migrants who are also poor. In turn, urban ills are aggravated and require an increasing share of a city's resources. Life in the city then becomes less agreeable and more costly for middle- and upper-income residents, who move out. This reinforcing pattern hurts the city and complicates

lane beltways and expressways that ring most large cities have in their own way become the new main streets of the outer cities. The sleek highways, designed in the 1950s to route interstate traffic around cities, make an interlinked metropolis possible. In many cases, the residents use the suburbs collectively as a city, a centerless city. They may live in one suburb, work in another, shop in still another, and go to a doctor in yet another.

As the population of large metropolitan centers has grown, the space consumed by urban development has progressively expanded. Many of your parents sought to escape the mounting congestion of the central cities by moving to suburban areas. Today's young Americans are leaving the cities for many of the same reasons as did

Cities in Trouble
Communities like the South Bronx in New York City confront a decline in population, jobs, services, and social amenities. Urban ills are aggravated by growing fiscal woes. Critics say that central cities make the suburbs possible by serving as "reservations" for the poor, the deviant, and the unwanted. *(C. Vergara/Photo Researchers)*

its ability to be responsive to the needs of its citizenry. All this means that American cities are less able to fulfill one of their historical functions, helping society assimilate and integrate the poor and immigrants (Bradbury, Downs, and Small, 1982).

Functional decline refers to a deterioration in city services and the social amenities of urban life. It is reflected in the decay in older industrial cities of the urban infrastructure—the network of roads, bridges, sewers, rails, and mass transit systems. Currently half of all American communities cannot expand because their water-treatment systems are at or near capacity. Many roads and bridges are bearing far greater burdens than they were designed to accommodate. For instance, Boston's six-lane Southeast Expressway, built in 1959 for 75,000 autos a day, now carries 150,000 cars daily. Forty-five percent of the nation's 248,500 bridges are structurally deficient or obsolete. Work needed by the year 2000 will cost $1 trillion, according to the Joint Economic Committee of Congress ($720 billion for highways and bridges, $178 billion for mass transit, $96 billion for water supply, and $163 billion for sewage systems). Yet in response to city fiscal crises of recent years, many local officials have balanced budgets by canceling preventive maintenance and deferring necessary public works projects. One major obstacle to infrastructure maintenance is the diversity and multiplicity of responsibility, falling upon more than 100 federal agencies, not to mention 50 states, more than 3,000 counties, and thousands of local agencies.

American cities, already besieged by lagging local economies and population shifts, have seen their financial difficulties compounded by a sharp curtailing of federal urban aid programs. In part, the cutbacks have reflected government deficit cutting and austerity policies. But they have also been an expression of a decline in the political muscle of central cities (of the 435 districts of the House of Representatives, the *Congressional Quarterly* counts only 79, or 18 percent, as urban in the 1980s, versus 148 districts, or 34 percent, in 1970). The tightening economic crunch is compelling municipal officials to seek new remedies. The remedies have included tax increases and charging for an increasing number of city services. For example, officials in St. Paul, Minnesota, charge residents and businesses when police respond to burglar alarms (Powell, 1986). Yet many of the policies designed to save central cities have been counterproductive, and have accelerated their decline. In the case of a city like Chicago, city taxes are already four or five times higher than those in the suburbs and construction costs run 20 to 25 percent higher. So middle-class residents and businesses find it economically advantageous to flee to the suburbs, widening the gap between the haves and the have-nots (Herbers, 1986). Today's hard choices, then, will determine the shape of urban life for decades to come.

Chapter Highlights

1. It was not until the Neolithic period that conditions became ripe for the emergence of large settlements of people. Preindustrial cities were usually rather small affairs. Only in the past 180 years or so has the pace of urbanization accelerated, giving rise to industrial-urban centers. More recently, metropolitan cities have emerged. This phase in urban development does not represent a sharp break with the industrial-urban tradition, but rather a widening and deepening of urban influences in every area of social life. In many cases, the rural interstices between metropolitan centers have filled with urban development, making for a "strip city" or megalopolis.

2. Every aspect of social organization has a spatial component. Sociologists seek to understand how people order their relationships and conduct their activities in space. They provide a number of models that attempt to capture the ecological patterns and structures of city growth: the concentric circle model, the sector model, the multiple nuclei model, and social area analysis.

3. The structural patterning of cities derives from a number of underlying ecological processes. People relate to one another and undertake their activities in ways that result in geographic areas taking the form of natural areas with distinctive characteristics. One process by which natural areas are formed is segregation. Invasion and succession are also critical ecological processes.

4. Communities are not self-contained forms of social organization, but rather parts of a larger division of labor and social whole. They are differentiated according to their primary sustenance activities, allowing them to exchange their surplus goods and services with other communities. Most contemporary cities are caught up in a world system of cities.

5. Three perspectives have dominated sociological thinking regarding the city. The first sees the city as a world of impersonal strangers. The second challenges this image, portraying the city as little different from small-town communities in the number and quality of meaningful relationships. And the third sees conflict as the central feature of city making.

6. The "donut" analogy is a useful description of the course of post–World War II metropolitan development. The hole in the donut is the decaying central city and the ring is a prosperous and growing suburban and satellite-city region. Since World War II, suburbs have grown more rapidly than have central cities. Today suburbs are rivaling central cities in population, jobs, investment, construction, and stores.

7. Urban decline in many American cities has been both descriptive and functional. Descriptive decline has to do with the loss of population or jobs. Functional decline refers to a deterioration in city services and the social amenities of urban life. Descriptive decline occurs as people who have the resources to leave the city do, while those who are poor have little choice but to remain. Functional decline is reflected in the decay in older industrial cities of the urban infrastructure—the network of roads, bridges, sewers, rails, and mass transit systems.

The Sociologist's Vocabulary

city A relatively dense and permanent concentration of people who secure their livelihood chiefly through nonagricultural activities.

community A relatively self-contained social unit whose members share a sense of belonging together and a common territorial base.

concentric circle model The approach to city growth that says that the modern city assumes a pattern of concentric circles, each with distinctive characteristics.

Gemeinschaft A concept introduced by Ferdinand Toennies that describes binding, personal relationships rooted in customary roles, long-standing obligations, and mutual trust.

Gesellschaft A concept introduced by Ferdinand Toennies that describes relationships dominated by self-interest and competition, with people's interests protected formally by contract and law.

human ecology The interrelationships that operate among people and their physical environment.

invasion A new type of people, institution, or activity encroaching on an area occupied by a different type.

megalopolis A strip city formed when the rural interstices between metropolitan centers fill with urban development.

multiple nuclei model The approach to city growth that assumes a city has several centers, each of which specializes in some activity and gives its distinctive cast to the surrounding area.

natural areas Geographic areas with distinctive characteristics.

sector model The approach to city growth which assumes that large cities are made up of sectors—wedge-shaped areas—rather than concentric circles.

segregation A process of clustering wherein individuals and groups are sifted and sorted out in space based on sharing certain traits or activities.

social area analysis An approach to examining urban patterns that focuses on the social characteristics of the population by areas.

succession An invasion continuing until the encroaching type of people, institution, or activity displaces the previous type.

urban ecology An approach to the study of communities that seeks to explain the patterns by which people and institutions come to be distributed in space as an expression of humankind's adaptation to an ever-changing environment.

urban gentrification The return of the middle class—usually young, white, childless professionals—to older urban neighborhoods.

urbanization Growth in the proportion of a population living in cities.

21

Collective Behavior and Social Movements

A *universal feeling, whether well or ill founded, cannot be safely disregarded.*

—Abraham Lincoln, speech, Peoria, Illinois, October 16, 1854

Students attending Atlantic Coast Conference colleges take their basketball games quite seriously. Consider some of the antics of Duke fans in recent years:

- When former Maryland coach Charles "Lefty" Driesell clumped onto the Cameron Indoor Stadium court wearing a cast to protect an injured foot, a half-dozen Duke students followed him in single file wearing fake foot casts. When the bald-headed coach sat down, he was surrounded by Duke students with bald-headed masks.

- When Detlef Schrempf, the German-born star of the University of Washington team, would go to the free-throw line, Duke fans would shout "*Fehlwurf!*"—the German-language equivalent of "airball."

- When television broadcaster Billy Packer went on the air at Duke, students chanted, "We want McGuire," McGuire being Al, another television broadcaster.

The displays earned Duke students some bad press, so the university's president appealed to them to spruce up their act. For the next home game, against North Carolina, some students showed up wearing halos and presented a bouquet of flowers to UNC coach Dean Smith (Klein, 1986)

About the same time that Duke basketball enthusiasts were engaged in their antics, students at colleges across the nation were erecting shanties on campuses as part of the anti-apartheid movement. From coast to coast—from Dartmouth

College to the University of California at Berkeley—students protested university investments in companies doing business in South Africa and racism in the United States. The shanties symbolized the living conditions of blacks under Apartheid. University officials invariably had the shanties removed on grounds that they violated campus regulations and state fire and safety laws.

Such episodes are not uncommon. Yet as you survey your life, you find that it is rather patterned and repetitive, much of it caught up in routine. You carry out your roles as student, worker, friend, spouse, parent, and so on. You guide your behavior by norms that define what you are supposed to do in various situations. Yet it is easy to overemphasize the structured nature of society: Some forms of social life are not organized in terms of established norms and institutionalized arrangements. This is most apparent in **collective behavior**—ways of thinking, feeling, and acting that develop among a large number of people and that are relatively novel and not well defined. Human history is full of episodes labeled by contemporaries as "collective seizures," "group outbursts," "mass delusions," "crazes," and "group pathologies." Indeed, from earliest recorded times, people have thrown themselves into a great many types of mass behavior, including social unrest, riots, manias, fads, panics, mass flights, lynchings, religious revivals, and rebellions.

Collective behavior occurs most often during times of rapid social change. In turn, it provides an impetus to social change. The same is true of a **social movement,** a more or less persistent and organized effort on the part of a relatively fairly large number of people to bring about or resist change. Both collective behavior and social movements occur outside the institutional framework of everyday life, and they break through the familiar web of ordered expectations. But even though social movements and collective behavior resemble one another, they differ in an important respect (Traugott, 1978; Hannigan, 1985). Whereas collective behavior is characterized by spontaneity and a lack of internal structure, social movements possess a considerable measure of internal order and purposeful action. It is this organizational potential that allows social movements to challenge established institutions. In this chapter we examine both collective behavior and social movements.

PLANNING AHEAD: TARGETED READING

1. How do rumors, fashions and fads, crowds, and other forms of collective behavior affect your lives?

2. Given the organized nature of much of social life, why do people engage in collective behavior?

3. If you wish to institute or oppose a social change, how might you go about it?

4. Under what conditions would you expect a social revolution to occur?

5. Does terrorism pay?

6. Do people participate in a social movement primarily as a result of deprivation, or in response to a rational decision-making process?

Collective Behavior

When you find yourself in a situation that falls outside the routine—and somehow you feel impelled to do

something about it—you become susceptible to collective behavior. It may be that a fire breaks out in your workplace, you learn that a world leader has been assassinated, you witness a horrible traffic accident, the stock market takes a sudden plunge, your team wins a championship, you are marching in a protest when the police begin arresting demonstrators, you hear a rumor that a brand of food you use is contaminated, or you undergo a conversion experience at a religious revival. In these situations, the usual responses do not seem appropriate.

Dispersed Collective Behavior

Modern societies are usually quite large. You cannot know or have face-to-face contact with millions upon millions of Americans, yet they influence your behavior and you influence their behavior. Sociologists apply the term **mass** to people who—although physically dispersed—respond to the same event in much the same way. Anything that simultaneously catches the attention of large numbers of people can become involved in mass behavior—for instance, all the people who watch the same television program, rush to buy the same corporate stock, follow the same murder trial in the press, switch to the same style of clothing, sing the same song, or are absorbed by the same national event. Sometimes objects catch the popular eye by chance. For instance, at the height of his popularity in 1931, Rudy Vallee introduced the song "As Time Goes By." It had only moderate success and soon dropped from sight. In 1943 it was revived in the hit movie *Casablanca*, and to the surprise of people in the music industry, gained an enduring place among the nation's favorite songs (Shibutani, 1986).

Mass communication is the critical vehicle that allows dispersed people to establish "commonness" and become "tuned" for some message. It is the process by which the media, particularly the press, television, and radio, transmit information, ideas, and attitudes among a large population. Another mechanism is an *interaction chain* in which communication proceeds from person to person and from small group to small group.

Rumors   Rumors are both a form of collective behavior and an important element in other types of collective behavior. A **rumor** is a difficult-to-verify piece of information that people transmit to one another in relatively rapid fashion. Although many rumors are false, some are accurate, or contain a measure of truth (for instance, a local plant will close or a product will be discontinued). Rumors typically arise in times of tension and sagging economic conditions in which we lack information or distrust official sources of information. They are a substitute for hard news (Shibutani, 1966; Rosnow and Fine, 1976). Rumors regarding alleged contamination and conspiracy are quite common (Rosnow and Kimmel,

1979; Koenig, 1982, 1985). Unfounded rumors have hurt the sales of some of the nation's largest corporations. For instance, McDonald's and Wendy's have had to fight rumors that they put earthworms in hamburgers (perhaps suggested by the fact that raw hamburger resembles red worms). Some people have seen a Communist connection in the bent-elbow, clenched fist symbol of Arm And Hammer, the baking soda. And Procter & Gamble removed its 135-year-old moon-and-stars trademark from its products when it was unable to dispel the rumor that the symbol is a sign of devil worship (Solomon, 1984; Salmans, 1985).

Rumors evolve and take on new details as we talk and interact. People who are eager to listen to or pass on a rumor typically wish to attract attention; they are people who often are on the edge of the group or of relatively low status. For a brief instant—when they are circulating a sensational story—rumor tellers become minor celebrities. People also listen to and pass on hearsay because it verifies their shared beliefs, heightens group solidarity by identifying a conspiratorial enemy, and cuts the successful down to size (Koenig, 1982, 1985).

Fashions and fads   We typically think of folkways and mores as having considerable durability, as being relatively fixed and slow to change. Yet we often yearn for something new, for variety and novelty. At first it may seem impossible that this desire could be satisfied through norms, since norms emphasize conformity (see Chapter 3). Yet curiously, we manage to be conformists even when we seek change. We achieve this strange outcome by a set of norms that demand some measure of conformity while they endure, but that last only a short time (Davis, 1948). These norms are termed *fashions* and *fads*.

A **fashion** is a folkway that lasts for a short time and enjoys widespread acceptance within society. Fashion finds expression in such things as styles of clothing, auto design, and home architecture. By virtue of fashion, the suit that was in vogue five years ago often seems out of place today. The automobile of three years past that appeared so beautiful and appropriate looks outdated and even somewhat odd now. And "gingerbread" and brownstone houses no longer suit most of our tastes.

A **fad** is a folkway that lasts for a short time and enjoys acceptance among only a segment of the population. Indeed, the behavior is often scorned by most members of society. Fads appear in amusements, new games, popular tunes, dance steps, health practices, movie idols, and slang. Adolescents seem to be particularly fascinated by fads. Since clothing and gestures can

Fads of an Earlier Generation of College Students
During a period in the 1950s, college students
throughout the United States undertook to see how
many persons they could get in a phone booth. Such
fads are highly transitory and often involve somewhat
bizarre behavior. Other widely publicized student fads
of the 1950s included the swallowing of goldfish, sitting on flagpoles, and shaving the top of one's head.
Fads provide an opportunity for quick recognition and
momentary notoriety. *(Joe Munroe/Photo Researchers)*

arbitrarily serve as signs of ingroup or outgroup status,
fads provide young people with a sense of identity and
belonging (Erikson, 1968).

Fashions and fads are found in all spheres and walks
of life. They appear in medicine, especially when the
effectiveness of new drugs or of novel treatments is still
uncertain (Coleman, Katz, and Menzel, 1959). Intellectuals who often scorn the "sheeplike" behavior of the
masses themselves follow the latest plays, books, esoteric
foods, and scholarly theories currently in vogue in their
social worlds (Shibutani, 1986).

Crazes   For the most part, fads usually play only an
incidental part in the lives of those who adopt them.

Some fads, however, come to preoccupy individuals,
and become all-consuming passions. Such fads are
termed **crazes.** Financial speculations at times assume
craze proportions. In the famous Holland tulip mania in
the seventeenth century, the value of tulip bulbs came to
exceed their weight in gold; the bulbs were not planted,
but bought and sold among speculators. In the Florida
land boom of the 1920s, parcels were sold and resold at
skyrocketing prices without the purchasers ever even seeing their purchases.

Mass hysteria   **Mass hysteria** involves the rapid spreading of frenzied fears and activity among large numbers of
people who feel threatened by a mysterious force. The
people become obsessed with some object of attention—
a psychotic rapist on the loose, hidden enemies inside
government, a demonic religious cult, a contagious illness, or a fanatic enemy. For instance, medieval
witchhunts rested on the belief that many social ills were
caused by witches, the Red Scare of the 1950s resulted in
the hounding and persecution of people believed to be
part of an "international Communist conspiracy," and
the contemporary fear of AIDS has led to excited agita-
tion against AIDS victims and homosexuals (see Chapter 18).

Some "epidemics" of assembly-line illness—
termed *mass psychogenic illness*—derive from hysterical
contagion. In recent years they have occurred among
workers in American plants packing frozen fish, punch-
ing computer cards, assembling electrical switches, sewing shoes, making dresses, and manufacturing lawn furniture. In most cases, the workers complain of
headaches, nausea, dizziness, weakness, and breathing
difficulty. However, health authorities, including physicians, industrial hygienists, and toxicologists, find no
bacteria, virus, toxic material, or other pathogenic agent
to explain the symptoms. The episodes are prevalent
among poorly paid women workers who perform the
same repetitive task over and over. Mass psychogenic
illness is usually a collective response to severe stress
caused by job dissatisfaction, monotony, overwork,
noise, crowding, or poor management. An event such as
a speedup or required overtime typically triggers the outbreak (Colligan, Pennebaker, and Murphy, 1982).

Panic   **Panic** involves the uncoordinated flight of people from some perceived danger. It occurs only if we
believe that we have some avenue of escape and that this
avenue is closing. On the other hand, should we conclude there is no way out and that disaster is imminent,

we may experience terror but remain in place (Smelser, 1963). An Ohio State University student describes a panic episode (Vander Zanden, 1979:221):

> In our dorm we had a fire drill at 2:30 this morning. Being awakened in the middle of the night is bad enough but to a fire alarm is really scary. My roommates started screaming and running to the window to look outside and see if anything was happening. Someone down the hall started yelling "Fire" and ran for the stairs. Naturally everyone dropped the idea of it being only a false alarm (which it really was) and thought the dorm really was on fire. We all jammed up at the stairway door and could not get through. We were all pushing and shoving. It was just horrible. It seemed forever before we managed to get outside.

In a panic, people experience collective fear. The threat seems so overwhelming and imminent that it temporarily alters and constricts people's perspective. So they become susceptible to desperate measures. Observers invariably comment that panic behavior seems exceedingly irrational, foolish, and self-defeating. People jam their only escape route, jump from a high-story window, precipitously flee their homes, or stampede to withdraw their funds from an otherwise solvent bank. To the participants, their actions seem the most appropriate and reasonable thing to do. The atmosphere of impending calamity is augmented by the screams, cries, and frenzied gestures that contribute to mutual reinforcement and selective communication.

Publics and public opinion   A **public** consists of a collection of people who share an interest in some issue and seek to influence the actions of decision makers. It is not an established group, nor does it have a fixed membership. Some of the interaction of a public involves direct face-to-face discussion, as in arguments with acquaintances, friends, and family members. However, most of the interaction is carried on indirectly through the mass media. Publics arise in societies having institutions that permit argument and discussion as methods for settling controversial issues. In such societies, there is not just one public but many publics, one for every controversy that arises and attracts the attention of a sizable number of people. In the United States today, for example, abortion, gun control, mandatory drug testing, affirmative action programs, and arms control policies have all attracted publics. When Congress is in session, there is a public for every controversial bill that receives attention. Clearly, publics overlap in membership, yet each public is a separate and distinct unit.

"A Ms. Ramona Bissell, of West Allison, Vermont, writes, 'What the hell is going on?' We here at WVCN think that question deserves an answer."

Drawing by Leo Cullum; © 1987 The New Yorker Magazine, Inc.

Public opinion is the behavior of a public. It emerges out of the give-and-take among people divided on an issue. The existence of active concern and discussion on an issue transforms individual private opinions into some sort of public opinion. When the points of view on an issue coalesce so that most members of the public agree, the matter passes from the realm of public opinion and enters that of consensus. At times, however, people simply tire of a controversy, and it fades from view. Despite romantic renditions that portray democracy as a system in which each citizen is attentive and informed about the persons and problems of public life, public knowledge thins out rapidly beyond the biggest and most captivating events. It seems that the trials and tribulations of daily life are compelling in ways that politics can never be for the ordinary citizen (Kinder and Sears, 1985).

Converging Collective Behavior: The Crowd

The **crowd** is one of the most familiar and at times spectacular forms of collective behavior. It is a temporary, relatively unorganized gathering of people who are in close physical proximity. Since a wide range of behavior is encompassed by the concept, sociologist Herbert Blumer (1946) distinguishes among four basic types of crowd behavior. The first, a **casual crowd** is a collection of people who have little in common except that they may be participating in a common event, such as looking through a department-store window. The second, a **conventional crowd,** entails a number of people who

Expressive Crowd: Argentine Soccer Enthusiasts
Although baseball, football, and basketball are the leading spectator sports in the United States, soccer holds center stage in Latin America and Europe. Rioting and loss of life have occasionally followed an intensely contested game between teams from differing nations. *(Yoram Lehmann/Peter Arnold)*

have assembled for some specific purpose and who typically act in accordance with established norms, such as people attending a baseball game or concert. The third, an **expressive crowd**, is an aggregation of people who have gotten together for self-stimulation and personal gratification, such as at a religious revival or a rock festival. And fourth, an **acting crowd** is an excited, volatile collection of people who are engaged in rioting, looting, or other forms of aggressive behavior in which established norms carry little weight.

Although crowds differ in many ways, they also share a number of characteristics:

1. *Suggestibility.* When we are in a crowd, we are usually more suggestible than we are in established social settings. Conventional norms do not guide our behavior in a straightforward manner. But even though we may be more susceptible to images, directions, and ideas coming from others, our behavior need not take antisocial directions. In some instances, sentiment shifts to caution, and the crowd simply melts away (Johnson and Feinberg, 1977).

2. *Deindividualization.* In a crowd we may temporarily lose our sense of personal identity and responsibility, which can lead us to do things we would usually not do when we are alone—a process called **deindividualization** (Zimbardo, 1969). Anonymity, a sense that we are among strangers and "lost in the crowd," contributes to deindividualization. Under these circumstances, we no longer feel as inhibited in committing disap-

proved acts as we would among close associates (Mann, Newton, and Innes, 1982). Deindividualization helps explain the brutal inhumanity of the lynch mob and the savage cruelty of the baiting crowd in taunting and urging a victim to jump in episodes of threatened suicide (Mann, 1981; Mullen, 1986).

3. *Invulnerability.* In crowd settings we often acquire a sense that we are more powerful and invincible than we are in routine, everyday settings. Under these conditions, we may be more willing to engage in behavior not normally approved by society, such as aggression, risk-taking, self-enhancement, stealing, vandalism, and the uttering of obscenities (Dipboye, 1977; Mann, Newton, and Innes, 1982).

The convergence of people who are similarly aroused amplifies each crowd member's feelings. The closed circuit context affords positive feedback, since each person's emotions are intensified in exchanges with other crowd members. At times the buildup of acute tension is necessary to accomplish some difficult goal, such as a suicidal infantry charge or the rescue of a drowning person by bystanders (Shibutani, 1986). We will return to a consideration of crowds shortly. But first, let us look at a number of preconditions that underlie collective behavior.

Preconditions for Collective Behavior

Sociologist Neil J. Smelser (1963) provides a framework for examining collective behavior that is based on the value-added model popular among economists. **Value-added** is the idea that each step in the production process—from raw materials to the finished product—increases the economic value of manufactured goods. Consider, for instance, the stages by which iron ore is converted into finished automobiles. As raw ore, the iron can be fashioned into an auto fender, a kitchen range, a steel girder, or the muzzle of a cannon. Once it is converted into thin sheets of steel, however, its possible uses are narrowed. Although it can still be fashioned into an auto fender or a kitchen range, it can no longer be employed for making a steel girder or the muzzle of a cannon. After the steel sheet is cut and molded in the shape of a fender, its use is further limited; it is no longer suitable for making a kitchen range. Each step in the process adds a specific "value" to the iron ore while simultaneously subtracting from previous possibilities.

As viewed by Smelser, episodes of collective behavior are like automobiles in that they are produced in a sequence of steps. In order of occurrence, these are (1) structural conduciveness, (2) structural strain, (3) growth and spread of a generalized belief, (4) precipitating factors, (5) mobilization of participants for action, and (6) the operation of social control. Each determinant is shaped by those that precede it and in turn shapes the ones that follow. Moreover, as in the case of automobiles, as each successive determinant is introduced in the value-added sequence, the range of potential final outcomes becomes progressively narrowed. Smelser contends that each of the six factors in the scheme is a *necessary* condition for the production of collective behavior, while all six are believed to make collective behavior virtually inevitable. Let us take a closer look at each of the determinants in Smelser's model.

Structural conduciveness Structural conduciveness refers to social conditions that *permit* a particular variety of collective behavior to occur. For instance, before a financial panic is possible, such as the stock market crash of 1929, there must be a money market where assets can be exchanged freely and rapidly. This basic arrangement does not exist in societies where property can be transferred only to the firstborn son on the father's death, because the holders of property lack sufficient maneuverability to dispose of their assets on short notice. In like manner a race riot—a battle between two racial groups—dictates that two racial populations be in close physical proximity.

Structural strain Structural strain is said to occur when important aspects of a social system are "out of joint" with each other. Wars, economic crises, natural disasters, and technological change disrupt the traditional rhythm of life and interfere with the way we normally carry out our activities. As stress accumulates, Smelser says, we become increasingly susceptible to courses of action not defined by existing institutional arrangements. We experience *social malaise*, a feeling of underlying and pervasive discontent. As we noted earlier in the chapter, mass psychogenic illness is one response to job strain when workers are under pressure to increase production. What the workers seem to be saying when they become ill is, "This place makes me sick."

Acting Crowd: The Draft Riots of 1863
In 1863, when volunteering for the Union Army slackened off, Congress enacted legislation establishing a military draft. The provisions were grossly unfair to the poor since a man could escape service by paying 300 dollars or hiring a substitute. The draft was especially detested in Democratic party strongholds of the North. A four-day uprising in New York City left over a thousand people killed or wounded. Many of the rioters were anti-black and anti-abolitionist and hostile to the Lincoln administration. Here rioters destroy The Coloured Orphan Asylum in New York City. *(Historical Pictures Service)*

Structural Conduciveness: The 1929 Stock Market Crash
The dramatic collapse of the prices of corporate stocks in October 1929 set the stage for the Great Depression. When foreign investors and wary domestic speculators began to unload their stocks, an orgy of desperate selling followed. Financial panics occur in capitalist economies, which rely on free markets and privately held property. These structural ingredients are lacking in socialist economies, which rely on state planning and publicly held property. Here crowds mill about New York's Wall Street on October 24, 1929, as stock prices tumbled. (*The Bettmann Archive*)

The growth of a generalized belief Structural strain and a sense of social malaise by themselves are not enough to produce collective behavior. Smelser says we must define a situation as a problem in need of a solution. In the course of social interaction, we evolve a shared view of reality and common ideas as to how we should respond to it. We require a generalized belief that provides us with "answers." For instance, in panic behavior, we evolve a belief that empowers some element in the environment with a generalized capacity to threaten or destroy us.

Precipitating factors Still another ingredient is required: Some sort of event is needed to "touch off" mass action. A precipitating event creates, sharpens, or exaggerates conditions of conduciveness and strain. Additionally, the event affords explicit evidence of the workings of evil forces and a promise of success in combating them. Revolutions may be triggered in this manner: General Gage's 1775 march from Boston to Concord and Lexington; the seizure of the royal prison fortress by an angry French crowd in 1789; and the March 11, 1917, tsarist decrees against Petrograd (Leningrad) strikers. Likewise, in panic behavior it is usually a specific event that sets the flight in motion. A dramatic event—a cry of "Fire," an explosion, a governmental collapse, or a bank failure—provides the stimulus for the frenzied behavior.

The mobilization of participants for action Once these determinants are in place, the only necessary condition that remains is to bring the participants into action. This point marks the outbreak of crowd hostilities, the onset of panic, or the beginning of a revolution. It seems that collective action depends on a *critical mass*. For physicists, the term "critical mass" refers to the amount of radioactive material that is needed for a nuclear fission explosion to take place. Sociologists apply the concept to the threshold or number of participants that must be reached before collective behavior "erupts" or "explodes" (Oliver, Marwell, and Teixeira, 1985).

Conversion is often central to the process. For instance, Pentecostal converts usually explain their conversion by saying, "I was saved because God spoke to me!" However, closer scrutiny reveals that some person they already knew—someone they trusted and felt rapport with—took them to a revival meeting or otherwise influenced their behavior. Recruitment typically follows lines of preexisting social relationships, through relatives, work associates, friends, and neighbors (Snow and Machalek, 1984; Lofland, 1985). In other cases, people actively search for "meaningful encounters," "identity change," and "creative-transformation experiences." Those who join UFO cults, the Divine Light Mission, and the Unification Church frequently describe themselves as "seekers" before joining (Balch, 1979; Downton, 1979; Barker, 1984).

Operation of social control The sixth factor in Smelser's scheme is the operation of social control. It is not like the other determinants of collective behavior. Social control is basically a counterdeterminant that prevents, interrupts, deflects, or inhibits the accumulation of the others. Social control typically takes two forms. First,

Social Control: Whose Interests Are Served?
The wave of demonstrations organized by civil rights activists in the 1960s were instrumental in bringing about the enactment of the Civil Rights Acts of 1964 and 1965. Southern segregationist officials sought to repress the movement and on occasion unleashed violence against black protestors. Here one of several hundred black activists is dragged to a paddy wagon in a 1965 demonstration in Tuscaloosa, Alabama. *(AP/Wide World Photos)*

there are controls designed to *prevent* the occurrence of an episode of collective behavior by lessening conductiveness and strain (for example, welfare programs that seek to pacify the underclasses). Second, there are controls that attempt to *repress* an episode of collective behavior *after* it has begun (for example, repressive police measures and curfews).

In some instances, however, the activities of the agents of social control precipitate collective behavior and even violence. A good illustration of this occurred in the spring of 1963 when the Reverend Martin Luther King, Jr., took the civil rights fight to Birmingham, Alabama, alleged to be the most segregated large city in the South. He and his followers organized a "siege of demonstrations" against Birmingham's segregation ordinances.

More than 3,000 Birmingham blacks were arrested, while newspapers, magazines, and television stations beamed to the nation pictures of blacks facing snarling police dogs and being bowled over by high-pressure fire hoses.

Although the demonstrations did not immediately succeed in overturning Birmingham's racist laws, the civil rights issue quickly became the number-one topic not only in the South, but throughout the United States and then the world. The brutality against Birmingham blacks gave impetus to some 1,122 demonstrations in the following four months in cities throughout the nation. These demonstrations culminated on August 28, 1963, in the March on Washington, in which some 200,000 civil rights marchers demonstrated "for jobs and freedom." The wave of demonstrations spurred the Kennedy administration to sponsor new civil rights legislation, which was passed by Congress the following year.

Assessing the value-added model Smelser's value-added model provides a useful tool for grasping the complexity of collective behavior. We see that collective behavior requires more than discontent and effective leaders (Marx and Woods, 1975). But the approach does have serious limitations. In some cases of collective action, all six stages do not necessarily occur, or they do not take place in the sequence Smelser specifies (Milgram, 1977). And some forms of crowd behavior are better explained by other perspectives. Let us consider a number of these approaches.

Explanations of Crowd Behavior

One of the characteristics of crowd behavior is the substitution of new forms and patterns of behavior for those that normally prevail in everyday life. Although crowd members differ in a great many ways, their behavior seems to derive from a common impulse and to be dominated by a single spirit. But is this indeed the case? What happens in the course of crowd behavior? And what processes fashion behavior under crowd conditions? Sociologists have supplied three somewhat differing answers to these questions.

Contagion theory Contagion theory emphasizes the part that rapidly communicated and uncritically accepted feelings, attitudes, and actions play in crowd settings. Its proponents assume that unanimity prevails within a crowd, since crowd members often seem to act in identical ways and to be dominated by a similar impulse. A crowd is often spoken of in the singular, as if it were a real being—"the crowd roars" and "the angry mob surges forward." This view of the crowd is embodied in the work of the nineteenth-century French writer Gustave Le Bon (1896:23–24), who set forth the "law of the mental unity of crowds":

> Under certain given circumstances . . . an agglomeration of men [people] presents new characteristics very different from those of the individuals composing it. The sentiments and ideas of all the persons in the gathering take one and the same direction, and their conscious personality vanishes.

Le Bon believed that individuals undergo a radical transformation in a crowd. They can become cruel, savage, and irrational—Jekylls turned into Hydes. In the crowd people become capable of violent, destructive actions that would horrify them if they engaged in the actions when alone.

Le Bon's contagion theory depicts the crowd as characterized by a "mob mind" that overpowers and submerges the individual. A uniform mood and imagery evolve contagiously through three mechanisms: *imitation*—the tendency for one person to do the same thing that others are doing; *suggestibility*—a state in which individuals become susceptible to images, directions, and propositions emanating from others; and *circular reaction*—a process in which the emotions of others elicit the same emotions in oneself, in turn intensifying the emotions of others in a reciprocal manner (you see your friend becoming excited and in response you also become excited, intensifying the excitement of your friend, leading you to become all the more excited, and so on).

Le Bon's concept of the crowd mind as some sort of supra-individual entity—one that is endowed with thinking processes and a capacity for feeling and believing—is rejected by most social scientists (Milgram and Toch, 1969). Indeed, sociologists like Richard A. Berk (1974a, 1974b) find a good deal of rationality in what crowd members do (McPhail and Wohlstein, 1986). Berk sees the crowd as a case of collective problem solving in which people try to make the most of a situation by maximizing their outcomes, constrained only by the need to gain the support of others.

Convergence theory The spread of an infectious disease is a good analogy for the contagion theory. In contrast, the heart surgery ward of a hospital provides the best analogy for **convergence theory.** The patients on the

ward share a common problem, but not because they have transmitted the infection to one another. Rather, they select themselves out from the public because they have a common complaint and assemble on the ward with a common purpose. Likewise, some social scientists say that crowds select out a special class or category of people who are "crowd-prone." Whereas contagion theorists see "normal, decent people" being *transformed* under crowd influence, convergence theorists propose that a crowd consists of a highly unrepresentative body of people who assemble *because* they share the same predispositions. For instance, the social psychologist Hadley Cantril (1941), in his study of a lynching in Leeville, Texas, contends that the active members came chiefly from the lowest economic bracket, and several had previous police records. As a class, poor whites were most likely to compete for jobs with blacks and were most likely to find their own status threatened by the presence of successful blacks. These individuals provided a reservoir of people who were ready for a lynching with a minimum of provocation.

Emergent-norm theory The **emergent-norm theory** challenges the image of the crowd contained in both contagion and convergence theories. It stresses the *lack* of unanimity in many crowd situations and the *differences* in motives, attitudes, and actions that characterize crowd members: the presence of impulsives; suggestibles; opportunistic yielders; passive supporters; cautious activists; passersby; and so on. The approach denies that people find themselves spontaneously infected with the emotions of others to the extent that they want to behave as others do (Turner, 1964; Turner and Killian, 1972).

Emergent-norm theory draws upon the work of Muzafer Sherif (1936) and Solomon Asch (1952), which deals with social conformity in ambiguous situations (see Chapter 5). According to sociologists like Ralph H. Turner and Lewis M. Killian (1972), collective behavior occurs when people seek to find meaning in an uncertain social setting. They search for cues to appropriate and acceptable behavior. And like the subjects in Sherif's experiments, who developed group norms that were different from the standards they developed when they were alone, crowd members collectively evolve new standards for behavior. For example, they may develop a norm that one should loot, burn, or harass police. Crowd members then proceed to enforce the norm: They reward behavior consistent with it, inhibit behavior contrary to it, justify proselytizing, and institute actions that restrain dissenters. Since the new behavior differs from that in noncrowd situations, the norm must be specific to the situation—hence, an *emergent* norm.

Seen in this way, agitators, although often said to be the "cause" of a disturbance, are simply those who are more deeply involved and feel more strongly about an event than the others. Agitators, then, are pacesetters; they contribute disproportionately to the developing mood. However, only those who do and say things consistent with the mood of a crowd are heard. Leaders are chosen by the led; they simply express more appropriately and eloquently what the listeners already feel. The secret of the leader's power is the crowd itself. As the collective excitement intensifies, the self-selection of personnel continues. Those who disagree find it difficult to be heard; they may even be taunted and assaulted. In this manner, dissidents are silenced and excluded (Shibutani, 1986).

Assessing the perspectives   The three perspectives provide differing views of crowd behavior. Even so, they are not mutually exclusive. Consider what happens at a homecoming football game. Contagion contributes to the excitement through a process of circular reaction. Convergence operates, since loyal alumni and football enthusiasts are selected out from the larger population and come together in the stadium. Finally, an emergent norm defines what constitutes an appropriate response to a particular event and suppresses incompatible behavior.

Social Movements

Earlier in the chapter we defined a social movement as a more or less persistent and organized effort on the part of a relatively large number of people to bring about or resist change. Central to the concept is the idea that people intervene in the process of social change. Rather than responding passively to the flow of life or to its troubling aspects, they seek to alter the course of history. Of equal significance, they undertake joint activity. People consciously act together with a sense of engaging in a common enterprise. So, social movements are vehicles whereby people collectively seek to influence the course of human events through formal organization (see Chapter 5). It is little wonder, then, that social movements are the stuff of which history books are written: accounts of great leaders, the rise and fall of political movements, and the social dislocations and changes brought about by revolutions. Christianity, the Crusades, the Reforma-

tion, the American Revolution, the antislavery movement, the suffragist movement, Zionism, and fascism, like other social movements, have profoundly affected the societies that they have touched.

Types of Social Movements

Historian Crane Brinton (1938), in his classic study *The Anatomy of Revolution*, writes: "No ideas, no revolution." He might equally well have noted, "No ideas, no social movement." An **ideology,** a set of beliefs and myths, is critical to a social movement. An ideology provides people with conceptions of the movement's purposes, its rationale for existence, its indictment of existing social arrangements, and its design for action. An ideology functions as a kind of glue that joins people together in a fellowship of belief, thereby cementing solidarity. But an ideology does even more. It not only binds together otherwise isolated and separated individuals; it unites them with a *cause.* In doing so, it prepares them for self-sacrifice on behalf of the movement—even to laying down their lives for the "True God," "the New Nation," or "the Revolution."

Social movements can be distinguished on the basis of their ideologies, or more particularly, by the goals their ideologies set. Some movements pursue objectives that aim to change society through challenging fundamental values or by seeking modifications within the framework of the existing value scheme. The former, **revolutionary movements,** advocate the *replacement* of the existing value scheme; the latter, **reform movements,** pursue changes that will *implement* the existing value scheme more adequately. The civil rights movement identified with the leadership of the Reverend Martin Luther King, Jr., had a reform emphasis. It sought to extend values that were already acknowledged to inhere in political democracy to the black population of the United States. In contrast, a number of black nationalist groups that arose in the late 1960s had a revolutionary emphasis. They sought to institute basic changes in the American form of government, to rearrange the American class structure, and to inaugurate a system of greater black autonomy.

Movements arise not only for the purpose of instituting change, but also to block change or to eliminate a previously instituted change. These are **resistance movements.** Indeed, movement begets countermovement. The southern movement for civil rights unleashed a white counterattack beginning in the 1950s that found expression in the organization of White Citizens Coun-

Reform Movement: The 1965 Selma-to-Montgomery Civil Rights March
The civil rights movement led by the Reverend Martin Luther King, Jr., was a reform movement that sought to extend the nation's accepted democratic values to blacks. In order to secure congressional enactment of legislation to protect black voting rights, King took his campaign in 1965 to Selma, Alabama. In response to the brutality, thousands of sympathizers descended on Selma. Here the Reverend King gives an "On to the state capitol" signal, officially starting the last leg of the march on March 25. With King are his wife, Coretta, Dr. Ralph Bunche, and the Reverend Ralph Abernathy. *(UPI/Bettmann Newsphotos)*

cils and Ku Klux Klan groups. Historian Arthur Schlesinger, Jr. (1986), argues that from its earliest days the United States has been dominated by alternating political currents that run in cycles of roughly thirty years: the conservative (Tory or Hamiltonian) philosophy and the liberal (Whig or Jeffersonian) philosophy. Liberal periods witness an emphasis on "public purpose"—popular rights, programs of reform, and efforts to share power with the unrepresented. The emphasis during conservative periods falls on "private interest"—property rights, safety of the propertied classes, and efforts to perpetuate the power of the status quo. Liberal gains typically remain on the statute books even after the conservatives recover power. The conservatives acquiesce in the new social arrangements. However, they attempt to sabotage the reform measures by halfhearted enforcement and reduced appropriations.

Other types of movements, called **expressive movements,** are less concerned with institutional change than with a renovating or renewing of people from *within* (frequently with the promise of some future redemption). Pentecostal and holiness religious sects illustrate this kind of movement. Although they arise primarily among the underprivileged, the sects do not seek comprehensive social change; they do not aim to save the world, but to save individuals out of a world that is becoming progressively degenerate. They often believe that the second coming of the Messiah is at hand and that there is no hope for the unsaved except through conversion and regeneration.

Social Revolution

A **social revolution** involves the overthrow of a society's state and class structures and the fashioning of new social arrangements. Revolutions are most likely to occur under the following conditions (Skocpol, 1979; Taylor, 1984; Goldstone, 1986a):

- First, a good deal of political power is concentrated in the state so that there is a centralized governing apparatus (for example, the monarchy in pre-1789 France, the tsarist order in pre-1917 Russia, and the Kuomintang regime in pre-1949 China). Consequently, the state can become the focus for collective anger and attack.

- Second, the military's allegiance to the established regime is weakened so that the army is no longer a reliable tool for suppressing domestic disorder. Where army officers are drawn from elites in conflict with the central government, or where troops sympathize with their civilian counterparts, the unreliability of the army increases the vulnerability of the state (for instance, the defection of the Philippine military sealed the fate of the Ferdinand Marcos regime in 1986).

- Third, a severe political crisis weakens the existing regime and contributes to the collapse of the state apparatus. The crisis is often associated with long-term international conflicts that result in military defeat (for instance, French defeats by the British in the 1700s, Russian defeats in the Russo-Japanese War of 1905 and World War I, and the Chinese defeat by the Japanese in World War II).

- Fourth, a substantial segment of the population must mobilize in uprisings that bring a new elite to power. Peasant revolts usually stem from landlords taking over peasant lands, a substantial increase in taxation or rents, or famines. Urban uprisings are commonly precipitated by sharp jumps in food prices and unusually high levels of unemployment (Markoff, 1985; Goldstone, 1986a; Tilly, 1986).

A number of historians and sociologists have surveyed important revolutions in the West in search of common stages and patterns in their development (Edwards, 1927; Brinton, 1938; Goldstone, 1986a; Shibutani, 1986). Among the revolutions they have examined are the English Revolution of 1640, the American Revolution of 1776, the French Revolution of 1789, and the Russian Revolution of 1917. From this work has stemmed a number of observations regarding the typical sequence of events in the course of major social revolutions, an approach termed the **natural history of revolutions.**

Prior to the revolution, intellectuals—journalists, poets, playwrights, essayists, lawyers, and others—withdraw support from the existing regime and demand major reforms. Under increasing attack, the state attempts to meet the criticisms by instituting a number of reforms (for example, the reforms of Louis XVI in France, the Stolypin reforms in Russia, and the Boxer reforms in China). The onset of the revolution is heralded by the weakening or paralysis of the state, usually brought on by the government's inability to deal with a major military, economic, or political problem. The collapse of the old regime brings to the forefront divisions among conservatives who attempt to minimize change, radicals who seek fundamental change, and moderates who try to steer a middle course. Coups or civil war often ensue. The first group to gain the reins of power is usually the moderate reformers (for instance, in Iran, Bazargan, the moderate critic, first took power after the Shah's government was forced out).

The moderates seek to reconstruct governmental authority on the basis of limited reform, often employing organizational structures left over from the old regime. Simultaneously, radical centers of mass mobilization spring up with new organizations (in France, the moderate Girondin assembly confronted the radical Jacobin clubs; in America, the moderate Continental Congress was outpaced by the radical Patriots Societies; and in contemporary Iran the moderates led by Bazargan, Bani-Sader, and Gotzbadeh were supplanted by the radical Islamic clerics). The moderates find themselves heirs to the same problems and liabilities that brought down the old regime, and in turn they are replaced by the radicals.

Storming the Bastille
In the winter of 1788–1789, France was in the throes of a severe depression and near famine. All the while, nationalistic and libertarian sentiment mounted, leading to a series of political crises as King Louis XVI vacillated. When rumors spread in early July that the monarch was concentrating troops to intimidate the National Assembly, three days of disorder erupted in Paris. Shops were looted and on the third day rioters attacked the royal prison-fortress of the Bastille. The scanty garrison was overwhelmed and slaughtered. The fall of the Bastille was interpreted as a defeat for the king, and revolutionary violence spread to the provinces. The French Revolution was under way. (*North Wind Picture Archives*)

The disorder that follows the revolution and the seizure of power by the radicals results in coercive rule. This is the stage of Terror that characterized the guillotine days of the French Revolution, Stalin's *gulag*, and Mao's Cultural Revolution. Turmoil persists and allows military leaders to move into ascendancy (for instance, Washington, Cromwell, Napoleon, Attaturk, Mao, Tito, Boumedienne, and Mugabe). Finally, radicalism gives way to a phase of pragmatism and the consolidation of a new status quo. The "excesses" of the revolution are condemned, and the emphasis falls on the fashioning of stable institutions. In France, this phase was marked by the fall of Robespierre; in the Soviet Union, by Khrushchev's repudiation of Stalin; and in China, by the fall of Mao's allies (the Gang of Four). Although not all revolutions pass through the identical sequence of stages, the natural history of revolution approach does draw our attention to recurrent patterns.

What can we conclude regarding the outcomes of revolution? First, revolutions do not create a "clean slate." The conditions and cultural traditions that held under the old regime bias the outcome. For instance, the Bolsheviks carried over patterns of authoritarian rule that dominated Russian life under the tsarist state in establishing their new order. Second, the outcomes reveal zigs and zags in state policies and their effects, so that the new social world is never quite what the revolution's leaders and supporters had anticipated. Although in the short run revolutions may reduce inequality, in the long run it is likely to reemerge. Even the American Revolution, though more successful than most in promoting equality, liberty, and political freedoms, perpetuated slavery in the United States long after it had been abolished in England. In sum, revolutions are human creations, and as such share the flaws of their creators (Kelley and Klein, 1980; Goldstone, 1986b).

THINKING THROUGH THE ISSUES

What image do you have of revolution? Is your view colored by a handful of successful revolutions—the American colonies in 1776, France in 1789, Russia in 1917, and China in 1949? Do you regard revolutions as popular uprisings in which the oppressed overthrow their oppressors, where decadent rulers are toppled and a new society comes into being in which security, justice, and freedom reign? How do your images correspond with those of sociological formulations? In re-flecting on these matters, also think about these questions: Was the overthrow of the Ferdinand Marcos regime in the Philippines in 1986 a revolution? Was the secession of the Confederacy in the 1860s a revolution? Was the Nazi movement in Germany a revolution? Is a coup by disgruntled military officers in a Latin American nation a revolution?

Terrorism

Terrorism may be viewed as the use of force or violence against persons or property to intimidate or coerce a government, a formal organization, or a civilian population in furtherance of political, religious, or social objectives. Since terrorists commonly use violence against civilian targets, their actions are widely condemned as morally unacceptable. In practice, as with a great many other behaviors, what constitutes terrorism is a matter of social definition. When nations resort to violence to further their interests, the results are construed as being legal warfare. In many respects, terrorism is an extension of that approach by people who lack the armies of a state (Cordes, 1986).

It is also difficult in practice to distinguish "your terrorist" from "our freedom-fighter" or to differentiate aid to "terrorists" from "covert support of friendly forces" like the Nicaraguan Contras, or counterrevolutionary fighters (in 1984, an 89-page booklet was prepared under the auspices of the Central Intelligence Agency that advocated blackmailing, kidnapping, and assassinating Nicaraguan government officials). In like fashion, the Federal Bureau of Investigation labeled a "terrorist" the antinuclear activist who in 1982 drove up to the Washington Monument in a truck that he pretended was loaded with explosives, whereas the agency has failed to apply a similar label to those responsible for firebombing countless abortion clinics.

For many years the public, government officials, and scholars treated terrorism primarily as a "nuisance." The powerful images of World War II led us to think of aggression as panzer divisions racing across an international frontier. More recently, we have come to see terrorism as a new mode of warfare with far-reaching implications. Terrorism serves as an avenue of political expression for some militants, whether they are motivated by ideology, ethnicity, or religion. However, what distinguishes much contemporary terrorism is not so much its motivation or purpose, but rather the extent of

The 1985 Scuttling of the *Rainbow Warrior* by French Agents
Greenpeace's flagship, the *Rainbow Warrior*, was sunk in a New Zealand port by French agents with two bomb blasts and the loss of one life. Subsequent investigation revealed the French government was attempting to terrorize those who would challenge its practice of testing nuclear devices in the South Pacific. *(C. Animals/ Sygma)*

state involvement in carrying out well-planned and highly destructive acts against adversary nations. Trials of terrorists in a number of nations have established that Syria, Iran, and Libya have actively sponsored terrorist activities. But these nations have merely been the most visible participants. In 1985, French agents clamped two bombs to the hull of the *Rainbow Warrior* in a New Zealand port, sinking the vessel and killing one crew member (the ship belonged to the environmentalist group Greenpeace that was challenging the French government's testing of nuclear devices in the South Pacific). Moreover, aiding your neighbors' enemies is a common practice throughout the world, as Figure 21.1 on page 580 shows (also see the box on page 582).

Another feature of contemporary terrorism has been the extent to which it has become a media event. Terrorism is usually aimed at a media audience, not the actual victims. Although the terrorists write the script and perform the drama, the "theater of terror" becomes possible only when the media afford the stage and access to a worldwide audience. So terrorists undertake spectacular, attention-grabbing events to ensure that television, radio, and the press will tell their story, escalating the violence as necessary to hold public attention. The personal involvement of the president of the United States, the pope, and other world leaders contributes to the drama. Measured in terms of the worldwide attention terrorism garners, and not in terms of the number of lives lost, the method can be quite effective in the amount of interest it generates at relatively low cost to the perpetrators (Rubin and Friedland, 1986; Shipler, 1987).

The act of media coverage also enhances the importance of "the problem" that allegedly led to the terrorist activities. Newspaper readers and television viewers see "the problem" as of substantially greater importance and as justifying national or international action. Terrorism forcibly introduces its sponsor's interest into the foreign policy decisions of countless nations. For instance, the 1983 bombing of the Beirut Marine barracks led many Americans, including members of Congress, to oppose American involvement in Lebanon. The media portrayed grotesque scenes of young Marines being pulled out of the rubble and the death of 241 others, making the American public desirous of avoiding further entanglement in Lebanon's affairs.

According to some social scientists, terrorists see themselves as victims, as members of a mistreated and despised group. Fanaticism breeds in deep-rooted social upheavals that derive from defeat in war or rapid social change. People feel dislocated, as though they and their worlds are falling apart. They become susceptible to extreme ideologies, to a view of the world as split into the forces of good and evil. This vision is found in groups as diverse as the Baader-Meinhof Gang in West Germany, Pol Pot's Khmer Rouge in Cambodia, and the Ayatollah Khomeini's Party of God in Iran.

Terrorists are often teenagers and young adults who experience a strong sense of political powerlessness and helplessness that boils into burning rage. When they engage in brutality in the service of a cause, they see themselves as acting to save the world and destroy evil (Cordes, 1986; Goleman, 1986). Somewhat similar patterns find expression in issue-oriented terrorism (in

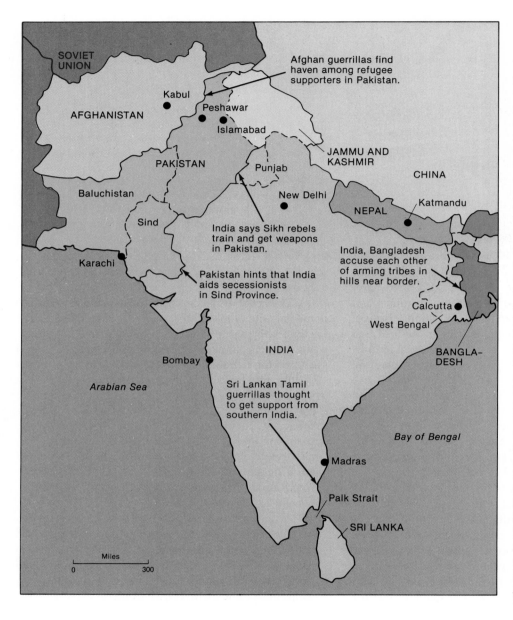

FIGURE 21.1 **Patterns of Regional Interference in South Asia**
Long-standing rivalries in South Asia have led nations to assist their neighbors' enemies. One explanation for regional interference is that it is easier to engage in subversion by proxy than in open warfare. Terrorism permits governments to engage in aggression while evading responsibility or retaliation. Internal pressures also operate. For instance, in the early 1980s, leaders of the 50 million Tamils in south India pressured the Indian government to back the insurgency in Sri Lanka. Cross-border interference has been cited as one reason for Moscow's wariness about the prospect of an unfriendly government coming to power in Afghanistan. A number of Afghan guerrilla leaders have vowed not only to take back their nation from Soviet occupiers, but also to "liberate" the Muslim Soviet republics on Afghanistan's northern border. *Source: Steven R. Weisman. 1987. Aiding your neighbors' enemies. New York Times (February 1):E3.*

France, the Committee for the Liquidation of Computers has bombed computer centers; in the United Kingdom, the Animal Rights Militia has set off bombs and incendiary devices at laboratories conducting animal experiments; in Canada, the Wimmins Fire Brigade has made arson attacks on video shops selling pornography; and in Iceland environmentalists sank two whaling vessels in Reykjavik harbor).

Nor has the United States been exempt from terrorism. Over the past decade or so, a variety of terrorist groups have surfaced, such as the Symbionese Liberation Army, the Weather Underground, the Armed Resistance Group, United Freedom Front, the Black Liberation Army, and the World Liberation Front. A number of groups have had nationalistic aims, including anti-Turkish Armenians, nationalist Puerto Ricans, Croatian separatists, and anti-Castro Cubans. Some groups have advanced programs of racial and religious hatred, including such right-wing extremist organizations as the Order, the Silent Brotherhood, the Covenant, the Ku

Political Assassination: 44 B.C.
Julius Caesar's military successes, his conquest of France (Gaul), and the vanquishing of his rival Pompey enabled the Roman general and consul to assume dictatorial power. The assassins who struck him down regarded themselves as patriots removing a tyrant. Caesar's death plunged Rome into civil war which lasted until 31 B.C. (*Historical Pictures Service*)

Klux Klan, and the Aryan Nations. Many of the same factors that underlie social movements also feed terrorist activities.

Causes of Social Movements

Clearly the concept of social movement covers a good many different kinds of behavior. But why should a social movement form? What factors lead people to undertake joint action on behalf of some cause? Sociologists have been of two minds on these matters. There are those who seek the roots of social movements in social misery, and more particularly, in social and economic deprivation. Others do not find this argument particularly convincing. They note that most societies contain a considerable reservoir of social discontent and that oppression and misery have been widespread throughout history. Yet social movements are relatively rare. These sociologists look to the resources and organizations that aggrieved persons can muster as providing the key to an understanding of social movements. Let us examine each of these approaches at greater length.

Strain approaches   As noted in earlier chapters, Karl Marx held that capitalist exploitation leads to the progressive impoverishment of the working class. He expected that over time conditions would become so disagreeable that workers would be compelled to recognize the social roots of their misery and overthrow their oppressors. Yet Marx also saw that abject misery and exploitation do not necessarily result in revolutionary fer-

vor. He pointed out that the suffering of the underclasses (what he labeled the *lumpenproletariat*) can be so intense and their resulting alienation so massive that all social and revolutionary consciousness is deadened. Although the "progressive misery," or *absolute deprivation*, argument is found in Marx's more political writings, he also recognized a type of *relative deprivation*. He foresaw that the working class could become better off as capitalism advanced, but that the gap between owners and workers would widen, causing workers to feel their comparative disadvantage intensely (Giddens, 1973; Anderson, 1974; Harrington, 1976).

Some sociologists have suggested that a major factor in the evolution of the black protest movement in the 1960s was the emergence among blacks of a growing sense of **relative deprivation**—a gap between what people actually have and what they have come to expect and feel to be their due (Geschwender, 1964; Gurr, 1970; Vander Zanden, 1983). The prosperity of the 1950s and 1960s gave many blacks a taste of the affluent society. They gained enough to hope realistically for more. Hence, grievances revolved about squalid housing, limited job opportunities, persistent unemployment, low pay, and police brutality. The civil rights movement arose not so much as a protest fed by despair as one fed by *rising* expectations.

Sociologist James Davies (1962, 1969, 1974) finds that relative deprivation may also be fostered under another condition depicted by his "rise-and-drop," or "J-curve," hypothesis (see Figure 21.2 on page 584). He contends that revolutions most likely occur when a prolonged period of social and economic betterment is fol-

Does Terrorism Pay?

Next week an airplane will be hijacked with American passengers on it or Americans will be taken hostage somewhere in the world. If not next week, it will happen the following week or next month or the following month. But it will happen. And one reason it will happen is that terrorists find that terrorism often pays dividends. Terrorists have discovered that they can gain far more by selecting victims from the nationals of foreign countries than by focusing on their specific enemies. They gain world attention and blackmail power by the horror that results from an airplane hijacking or kidnappings (Rosenthal, 1987).

Governments have acted against terrorists or have launched attacks in retaliation for terror: the July 3, 1976, Israeli raid at Entebbe Airport in Uganda; the ill-fated 1980 Carter administration attempt to free the Iranian hostages in Operation Blue Light; the 1980 British storming of the Iranian embassy in London; the 1982 rescue of American General James L. Dozier from the hands of Red Brigades by Italian antiterrorist forces; the 1985 storming of the Palace of Justice in Bogota by Colombian troops; and the 1986 American raid on Libya. Even so, victim nations, despite protests to the contrary, have demonstrated that they do cave in and make concessions when hostages are taken:

- The United States delivered blackmail arms to Iran in the hope of winning freedom for Americans held by Lebanese pro-Iranian groups, even though Iran was believed to be the nation that sponsored the 1983 Beiruit attack that killed 241 American Marines.

- Israel turned over 1,150 Arab and Palestinian prisoners for three Israeli captives.

- Italy allowed the terrorist Abul Abbas to escape to Yugoslavia, even though he had been implicated in the 1985 hijacking of the *Achille Lauro,* an Italian cruise ship.

- The French, for nearly a generation, have had a policy of dealing with terrorists, or at the very least looking the other way, with the expectation of buying immunity from attacks on French soil. Although French leaders have publicly spoken out against terrorism, they have shown a willingness to strike deals in private (Lief, 1986).

All this raises the question, "Does terrorism pay?" The answer is both yes and no. Immediate terrorist demands—the release of terrorist colleagues, ransoms, or political concessions—have almost uniformly been rejected. Yet long-term advantages do frequently result to movements or governments that sponsor terrorist actions. First, well-publicized terrorism bestows instant political visibility on groups that might otherwise be ignored. The Palestinian movement was little known or heeded until it began terrorist operations after the 1967 Arab-Israeli war. Second, insurgents are strengthened by their capacity to intimidate civilians into cooperating with them, practices of the Viet Cong, Khmer Rouge, Afghan *mujahideen,* and Nicaraguan Contras. Third, policy goals are occasionally achieved, such as the reduction of the American presence in Lebanon. And in the 1940s, terrorism by the Israeli Irgun Zvai Leumi and the LEHI (or Stern gang) helped drive the British out of Palestine and that by the Front de Liberation Nationale compelled the French to leave Algeria. Fourth, while governments typically do not pay outright ransom, private companies usually have no such scruples in securing the release of business executives. And fifth, violence provokes reactions in its target areas that create a climate for intensified strife (Waterman, 1986).

Faced with the problem of terrorist extortion, and acknowledging the principle that rewarding an act encourages its repetition, Western leaders continually endorse the notion that there must be no negotiations for hostages. Yet when hostages are taken, they have shown themselves willing to negotiate. There are those who insist that any policy involving negotiations and concessions is fundamentally flawed. Benjamin Netanyahu (1986),

lowed by a period of sharp reversal. People fear that the gains they achieved with great effort will be lost, and their mood becomes revolutionary. Davies illustrates this hypothesis by events as varied as Dorr's Rebellion in Rhode Island in 1842, the Pullman Strike of 1894, the Russian Revolution of 1917, and the Egyptian Revolution of 1953. The breakdown and disintegration of prison conditions has also been implicated in prisoner discontent and the outbreak of riots (Useem, 1985).

Resource mobilization approaches Deprivation approaches seek to find out why people in general are moti-

an Israel official, insists that the United States and Western nations must apply pressure on those regimes that sponsor terrorism and make them pay for what they are doing. He sees terrorism as a method of warfare sustained and supported by Marxist and radical Islamic states and not a sporadic phenomenon born of social misery and frustration. Netanyahu says that going after terrorists is not enough. He applauds the 1986 American raid on Libya and the shutting down of embassies of nations implicated in terrorism. Viewed in this manner, human lives may have to be sacrificed during a crisis to deter future incidents and thus protect more lives.

Others reject this reasoning. They say that the hard-line stance reflects an overly rational image of terrorists' behavior. It assumes that terrorists will be deterred if they know they will be captured and punished. But terrorists have varied and complex motives, and estimating the odds of getting caught is only one of many calculations (Cordes, 1986). For some, death in a suicidal mission may represent ultimate fulfillment (Tagliabue, 1986). Viewed in this fashion, governments should determine on a case-by-case basis whether negotiation is wise and whether or not concessions should be made.

Terrorism is unlikely to go away. In fact, experts warn that in the years ahead terrorist attacks may include the use of nuclear weapons, or instruments of biological or chemical war-

fare. In the international sphere, conventional combat, classic guerrilla war, and terrorism are increasingly coexisting side by side. To some extent, terrorism is becoming institutionalized. Some governments not only provide logistical backing and sanctuary, but fashion a bureaucracy to oversee relations with terrorists. And the security measures taken against terrorism are acquiring a permanent place in the social landscape (Gelman, 1986).

In studying terrorism, we should keep in mind that terrorist groups also need to be examined on their own terms, and not merely as "security threats." They are social movements of real people, acting in concrete social and political contexts, with intense hopes and fears (Paul, 1986). Political conflict often involves a good deal of what we would otherwise call criminal behavior. Rebellions and revolutions are almost always accompanied by murder, sabotage, the seizure of private property, and many other offenses against the criminal code. And, as we noted in Chapter 8, successful revolutions make criminals out of the government officials in old regimes, and unsuccessful revolutions make its leaders into outlaws and traitors (Vold and Bernard, 1986).

Gunmen Hold a Hijacked TWA Jetliner, Beirut Airport, 1985
Terrorists seek ways of exercising influence beyond their actual numbers or means. In order to be believable, they engage in the wizardry of the stage to capture the attention of an international audience. An airliner with civilian men, women, and children is a far more dramatic target than a military aircraft. (Gamma/Liaison)

vated to join social movements. Resource mobilization approaches take a different tack. They ask, "Why does one person get involved, while another remains inactive?" According to the resource mobilization school, social discontent is more or less constant and thus always present within modern societies (Tilly, 1978; Zald and McCarthy, 1979; Jenkins, 1983, 1985). Even the Russian revolutionary Leon Trotsky (1932/1959:249) came to a somewhat similar conclusion, noting that if privations were enough to cause a revolution, the masses would always be in revolt. So resource mobilization proponents deem it unnecessary to explain the forces that

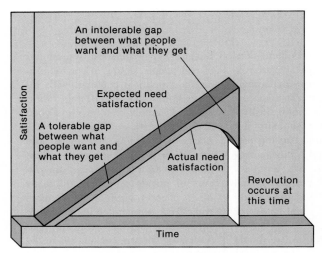

FIGURE 21.2   **Davies's J-curve Theory of Revolution**
The figure illustrates Davies's theory that revolutions are often fostered when a period of social and economic betterment is succeeded by sharp reversals, fueling concern that the gains will be lost. *Source: James C. Davies. 1962. Toward a theory of revolution. American Sociological Review, 27 (February): Fig. 1, p. 6.*

Resource Mobilization Approaches
According to resource mobilization theory, collective action is seldom a viable option for deprived groups because they lack the resources to challenge elites. When deprived groups do mobilize, sociologists who advocate this approach say it is usually due to the infusion of outside help and the garnering of assistance from established groups and institutions. They credit the success of Cesar Chavez's National Farm Workers Association (NFWA) pictured here to the support of a liberal-labor coalition during the 1960s and early 1970s. *(Paul Fusco/Magnum)*

energize and activate a social movement. Instead, they emphasize the importance of structural factors, such as the availability of resources for pursuing particular goals and the network of interpersonal relationships that serve as the focus for recruitment. People become involved in a social movement not as the result of deprivation, but as a response to a rational decision-making process whereby they weigh the costs and benefits of participation.

In many cases, resources and organizations outside the protest group are crucial in determining the scope and outcomes of collective action. External support is especially critical for movements of the poor. Sociologist J. Craig Jenkins (1985) illustrates the point with historical materials dealing with farm worker insurgencies within the United States. He contrasts the unsuccessful attempt to organize farm workers by the National Farm Labor Union from 1946 to 1952 with the successful organization of Mexican farm workers by the United Farm Workers from 1965 to 1972. Both groups pursued similar ends (union contracts), employed similar tactics (mass agricultural strikes and boycotts supported by organized labor), and encountered comparable obstacles. Yet the United Farm Workers prevailed where the National Farm Labor Union failed. Jenkins contends that the United Farm Workers succeeded because internal divi-

sions in government neutralized opposition elites, while the support of the liberal-labor coalition during the reform years of the 1960s and early 1970s turned the tide in favor of the farm workers. The grievances of the farm workers did not change in the post–World War II period, nor did the basic conflicts of interest that were embedded in the nation's institutional life. What changed were the resources and opportunities for collective action available to the farm workers, particularly the availability of powerful allies.

Assessing the approaches   At times, proponents of both the deprivation and resource mobilization approaches overstate their respective cases. Relative deprivation theory neglects the part that resources and organization play in social movements, and instead focuses primarily on people's grievances and psychological frustrations (Downey, 1986; Snow et al., 1986). On the other hand, it may be true, as resource mobilization theorists say, that social unrest is always present within society. Yet there are instances where suddenly grievances do generate organized protest. For example, organized action groups sprang up rapidly in the communities surrounding the Three Mile Island area following the 1979 nuclear accident there (Walsh, 1981). Much the same holds for countermovements—resistance or "anti" movements—that arise in response to the social change pursued by other movements (Mottl, 1980). The antisegregation movement in the South (Vander Zanden, 1965) and the antifeminist and anti-ERA movements (Marshall, 1985; Himmelstein, 1986) provide examples of movements that gain support among people who believe themselves threatened by impending change.

Resource mobilization approaches, however, have the advantage of drawing social movement analysis within the larger arena of social and political conflict. We gain an image of social movements as formal organizations clashing over the direction of public policy and

the use of political power. Indeed, we come to view social movements as instruments or vehicles of power. A study of collective action allows us to study social movements and political events "from the bottom up," since it is through collective action that common people make their own history (Tilly, 1978, 1986).

THINKING THROUGH THE ISSUES

Identify one or two grievances you and your classmates share regarding some aspect of campus life. What, if any, action have you undertaken to remedy the problems? Or have you simply reconciled yourself to the problems? How do you account for your action or inaction? If you wanted to take action on a campus grievance, do you think it would be more effective to form an entirely new organization or to gain the support of an existing campus organization like student government, a religious group, or a fraternity or sorority? Explain your answer. What insights does your examination of these matters provide regarding the relative merits of the deprivation and resource mobilization approaches?

Chapter Highlights

1. Some forms of group behavior are not organized in terms of established norms and institutionalized lines of action. This is particularly true of collective behavior. When people find themselves in a situation that falls outside the routine, and somehow they feel impelled to do something about it, they become susceptible to collective behavior.

2. Anything that simultaneously catches the attention of large numbers of people can become involved in mass behavior. Mass communication is a critical vehicle allowing people to establish "commonness" and become "tuned" for some message. Another mechanism is an interaction chain in which communication proceeds from individual to individual and from small group to small group. Dispersed collective behavior comes in a great many forms, including rumors, fashions, fads, crazes, mass hysteria, panic, and publics.

3. A crowd is one of the most spectacular forms of collective behavior. Sociologists distinguish among casual, conventional, expressive, and acting crowds. Although crowds differ from one another in many ways, they also share a number of characteristics: suggestibility, deindividualization, and a sense of invulnerability.

4. Sociologist Neil J. Smelser provides a framework for examining collective behavior that is based on the value-added model popular among economists. As viewed by Smelser, episodes of collective behavior are produced in a sequence of steps that constitute six determinants of collective behavior. In order of occurrence, they are (1) structural conduciveness, (2) structural strain, (3) growth and spread of a generalized belief, (4) precipitating factors, (5) mobilization of participants for action, and (6) the operation of

social control. Each determinant is shaped by those that precede it and in turn shapes the ones that follow.

5. Sociologists offer three somewhat different approaches to crowd behavior. According to contagion theory, rapidly communicated and uncritically accepted feelings, attitudes, and actions play a critical part in crowd settings through processes of imitation, suggestibility, and circular reaction. Convergence theory suggests that a crowd consists of a highly unrepresentative body of people who assemble because they share the same predispositions. The emergent-norm theory challenges the image of the crowd contained in both contagion and convergence theory. According to this view, crowd members evolve new standards for behavior which they then enforce in normative ways.

6. Central to the concept of social movement is the idea that people intervene in the process of social change. Of equal significance, they undertake joint activity. Social movements are vehicles whereby people collectively seek to influence the course of human events through formal organizations. Common forms of social movement include revolutionary, reform, resistance, and expressive movements.

7. Social revolutions are most likely to occur under certain conditions. First, a good deal of political power is concentrated in the state so that there is a centralized governing apparatus. Second, the military's allegiance to the established regime is weakened so that the army is no longer a reliable tool for suppressing domestic disorders. Third, political crises weaken the existing regime and contribute to the collapse of the state apparatus. And fourth, a substantial segment of the population must mobilize in uprisings that bring a new elite to power. A number of historians and sociologists have surveyed important revolutions of the West in search of common stages and patterns in their development, giving rise to the natural history of revolutions approach.

8. As with a great many other behaviors, what constitutes terrorism is a matter of social definition. When nations resort to violence to further their interests, the results are construed as being legal warfare. In many respects, terrorism is an extension of that approach by people who lack the armies of a state.

9. Sociologists are of two minds regarding the causes of social movements. There are those who seek the roots of social movement in social misery, and more particularly, in social and economic deprivation. Other sociologists do not find this argument particularly convincing. They note that most societies contain a considerable reservoir of social discontent and that oppression and misery have been widespread throughout history. These sociologists look to the resources and organizations that aggrieved persons can muster as providing the key to an understanding of social movements.

The Sociologist's Vocabulary

acting crowd An excited, volatile collection of people who are engaged in rioting, looting, or other forms of aggressive behavior in which established norms carry little weight.

casual crowd A collection of people who have little in common except that they may be participating in a common event, such as looking through a department-store window.

collective behavior Ways of thinking, feeling, and acting that develop among a large number of people and that are relatively novel and not well defined.

contagion theory An approach to crowd behavior that emphasizes the part rapidly communicated and uncritically accepted feelings, attitudes, and actions play in crowd settings.

conventional crowd A number of people who have assembled for some specific purpose and who typically act in accordance with established norms, such as people attending a baseball game or concert.

convergence theory An approach to crowd behavior that says a crowd consists of a highly unrepresentative body of people who assemble because they share the same predispositions.

crazes Fads that become virtually all-consuming passions.

crowd A temporary, relatively unorganized gathering of people who are in close physical proximity.

deindividualization People temporarily losing their sense of personal identity and responsibility, which can lead them to do things they would usually not do when alone.

emergent-norm theory An approach to crowd behavior that says crowd members evolve new standards for behavior in a crowd setting and then enforce the expectations in the manner of norms.

expressive crowd An aggregation of people who have gotten together for self-stimulation and personal gratification, such as at a religious revival or a rock festival.

expressive movement Movements that are less concerned with institutional change than with a renovating or renewing of people from within.

fad A folkway that lasts for a short time and enjoys acceptance among only a segment of the population.

fashion A folkway that lasts for a short time and enjoys widespread acceptance within society.

ideology A set of beliefs and myths; the ideas that provide individuals with conceptions of the purposes of a social movement, a rationale for the movement's existence, an indictment of existing conditions, and a design for action.

mass People who, even though physically dispersed, respond to the same event in much the same way.

mass hysteria The rapid spreading of frenzied fears and activity among large numbers of people who feel threatened by a mysterious force.

natural history of revolutions The view that social revolutions past through a set of common stages and patterns in the course of development.

panic The uncoordinated flight of people from some perceived danger.

public A collection of people who share an interest in some issue and seek to influence the actions of decision makers.

public opinion The behavior of a public.

reform movement A social movement that pursues changes which will implement the existing value scheme of a society more adequately.

relative deprivation A gap between what people actually have and what they have come to expect and feel to be their just due.

resistance movement A social movement that arises to block change or eliminate a previously instituted change.

revolutionary movement A social movement that advocates the replacement of a society's existing value scheme.

rumor A difficult-to-verify piece of information that is transmitted from person to person in relatively rapid fashion.

social movement A more or less persistent and organized effort on the part of a relatively large number of people to bring about or resist change.

social revolution The overthrow of a society's state and class structures and the fashioning of new social arrangements.

structural conduciveness Social conditions that permit a particular variety of collective behavior to occur.

structural strain A condition in which important aspects of a social system are "out of joint" with each other.

terrorism The use of force or violence against persons or property to intimidate or coerce a government, a formal organization, or a civilian population in furtherance of political, religious, or social objectives.

value-added The idea that each step in the production process—from raw materials to the finished product—increases the economic value of manufactured goods. Smelser has applied the notion to collective behavior.

22

Social Change, Technology, and Modernization

The actual world is a process. . . .
The flux of things is one ultimate generalization.

—Alfred North Whitehead, *Process and Reality*, 1929

There are designer shirts, skirts, and jeans, and now there's a designer sport: wallyball. Wallyball is a version of volleyball played on a racquetball court. It is hardly an old folk recreation that modern-day enthusiasts revived. Rather, Joe Garcia designed the sport when the racquetball boom peaked about 1980. The game is suitable for teams of two to four persons. Says Garcia: "Wallyball is a better way than racquetball for guys to meet girls, and vice versa. In a team sport, you get more people to choose from." Owners of racquetball clubs and their adjoining watering holes appreciate this quality. Instead of two people drinking beer after an hour on a racquetball court, wallyball provides up to eight.

But let us backtrack a moment. In the beginning, there was handball. People played it in firehouses and drafty YMCA gyms. The problem with handball is that it is played with a hard little rubber ball that stings the hands, and it requires that people use both hands equally well, which few people do. Then someone discovered that a hollow rubber ball and a short, strung racket could be used on hardball courts, and racquetball became fashionable. But alas, the masses soon tired of the game. While racquetball is easy to play poorly, the game is difficult to master and play well. When the masses took to jogging and aerobics, owners of racquetball clubs found they could no longer make a living on racquetball alone. Enter Joe Garcia and wallyball (Klein, 1986).

Wallyball seems a relatively trivial innovation. But its origins call our attention to the ever-changing, dynamic quality of life. We are led by a commonsense orientation to regard the world as stable. For practical purposes, most objects and events seem sufficiently durable to allow us to treat them as if they are unchanging. Indeed, we often think of permanence as being the natural state of affairs and change as something requiring special explanation (Shibutani, 1986). In reality, however, social life is an ongoing process, constantly renewing, remaking, and transforming itself. Events in the world compel people to change. As people change, they influence events in the social world of which they are a part. People like Joe Garcia, then, bring about change as they confront and deal with social life.

PLANNING AHEAD: TARGETED READING

1. How does social change affect your life?

2. Why does society change?

3. Are there any patterns or recurrent themes in social change?

4. What implications does the computer revolution have for your life and career?

5. Do new technologies result in a loss of jobs?

6. How are we to understand the torrents of social change now convulsing many Third World nations?

7. What is the future likely to hold for us?

The World of Change

Sociologists refer to the fundamental alterations that occur over time in patterns of culture, structure, and social behavior as **social change**. It is a process by which society becomes something different while remaining in some respects the same. Society is in constant flux. Most changes take place in small increments over long periods of time and pass unnoticed. We begin to appreciate this quality of life when the elderly tell us things were different in the "good old days" (Strasser and Randall, 1981; Shibutani, 1986). Of course, social change can also occur in response to a natural disaster, war, acts of terrorism, collective behavior, or social revolution (see Chapter 21).

The impact of social change is strikingly apparent when we reflect on events that influenced the national mood only a few years ago. Now they have faded in importance as millions of Americans who are too young to have experienced them have entered adulthood. If we assume that by age 10 we are capable of forming lasting memories of events, then of today's Americans (*U.S. News & World Report*, January 23, 1984):

- 98 percent do not remember a United States without a federal income tax (1913)

- 94 percent are too young to remember the first time women voted (1920)

- 89 percent cannot recollect Charles Lindbergh's solo flight to Paris (1927)

- 87 percent do not remember the stock market crash that marked the onset of the Great Depression (1929)

- 76 percent do not recall Pearl Harbor and the entry of the United States in World War II (1941)

- 69 percent are too young to recall life without television (1948)

- 49 percent have no recollection of the assassination of President John F. Kennedy (1963)

- 30 percent cannot recall the end of the Vietnam war or the Arab oil embargo (1973)

- 25 percent do not remember the nation's Bicentennial (1976)

Given the impact that social change has on our lives, let us begin our discussion by examining some of its sources.

Sources of Social Change

Social change confronts us with new situations and compels us to fashion new forms of action. Consequently, societies develop in a succession of collective adaptations to troublesome events (Malinowski, 1945). Many factors interact to generate changes in our behavior and in the culture and structure of our society. Sociologists have identified a number of particularly critical factors, the impact of which differs with time and place.

The physical environment   As we saw in Chapter 19, humans are physical beings who are located in space in some sort of habitat. If we are to survive, we must achieve a working relationship with our environment. Among the chief adaptive mechanisms available to us are social organization and technology. But the social organization and technology that is adaptive to one environment is not necessarily adaptive to another. Hunting-and-gathering, horticulture, agricultural, industrial, and postindustrial societies all require different types of adaptations. Should the environment change for any reason, populations who have evolved a given type of adaptation must respond by making appropriate adjustments and by fashioning new forms of social organization and new technologies. Droughts, floods, epidemics, earthquakes, and other natural disasters are among the realities that compel people to alter their lifeways. Additionally, as we noted in Chapter 19, human beings also have an impact on their physical environment. Hazardous-waste dumps, acid rain, pollution of the water and the air, overtaxing water resources, erosion of topsoil, and desertification result from human damage to the ecosystem. So human beings are tied to their environment in complex interchanges.

Population   Changes in size, composition, and distribution of a population also affect culture and social structure. In Chapter 19 we noted the impact that the baby boom generation is having on American life as the large bulge of persons born after World War II makes its way through the age structure. Already they have left their mark on musical tastes and the political climate.

And what some have called the "narcissism of the '70s" appears to be on the wane as maturing members of the generation look for close relationships and commitments. The graying of the American population is also having vast social ramifications. It is a principal factor in the nation's soaring social security, Medicare, and health care costs. And the graying of the society is posing thorny dilemmas in the workplace as large numbers of middle-aged workers jockey for advancement. Increasing numbers of people are lining up for promotions, but there are fewer slots opening up than there are people willing to fill them. This situation can lead to frustration and an increase in midlife career changes, although some people respond by pouring more of their energies into hobbies or family and community pursuits.

Clashes over resources and values   As we have repeatedly noted in this text, conflict is a form of interaction in which people are involved in a struggle over resources or values. Individuals and groups find themselves at odds; they feel separated by incompatible objectives. Not surprisingly, conflict is a basic source of social change. Members of a group must marshal resources for competition. For instance, during wartime they must alter their customary ways of ordering their daily lives, and they may invest greater authority in military leaders. Of course, conflict often involves negotiation, compromise, or accommodation. The swirling currents produced by these dynamic processes result in new institutional arrangements. Yet history demonstrates that the outcomes are rarely the total fulfillment of the goal or goals of the parties involved (see Chapter 21). Most commonly the

War as an Impetus to Social Change
In the battle of Marston Moor (1644) depicted here, the royal army of King Charles I was crushed by the English parliamentary forces. By 1649 the authority of the monarchy had been so weakened that a "high court of justice" had Charles I beheaded. Oliver Cromwell, leader of the parliamentary army, assumed dictatorial powers. Under his strict enforcement of order, commerce thrived. His conduct of foreign affairs was so skillful that it increased English patriotism and brought profit to many English purses. However, within two years of Cromwell's death in 1658, the monarchy was restored. Even so, the English monarchy was never the same again. (*North Wind Picture Archives*)

result is not a simple quantitative mixing of aspects of the opposing programs, but a completely new qualitative entity. Who could have blueprinted in 1870 the South that eventually emerged from the contest between the Reconstructionists and their opponents? In 1918, the Europe and Russia that arose following a war "to end all wars" and "to make the world safe for democracy"? In 1933, the economic and social America that developed from the struggle between Roosevelt supporters and anti–New Dealers? In 1965, the nation that would emerge twenty years later after a decade of social turbulence? Old social orders continually erode and new ones arise.

Supporting values and norms   A society's values and norms act as watchdogs or censors permitting or inhibiting certain innovations. They may also serve as stimulants. It is interesting to compare our readiness to accept technological innovations with our resistance to changes in economic theory, religion, or the family. The semantics of our use of the word "inventor" reflects this cultural bias. The inventor is one who innovates in material things, whereas the inventor of intangible ideas is often called a "revolutionary" or "radical," words with odious connotations. Among Samoans, considerable allowance is made for innovation in decorative arts, yet this freedom is negated by the culture's failure to give the innovator much recognition. Contrast this outlook with the Israelites of the eighth and seventh centuries B.C. who felt a strong need for spiritual interpretation and so gave honor to prophets who could find ways of interpreting the will of God in the interests of the society (Herskovits, 1945).

Innovation   A **discovery** represents an addition to knowledge, whereas an **invention** uses existing knowledge in some new form. A discovery involves the perception of a relationship or fact that had not previously been recognized or understood. Einstein's theory of relativity and Mendel's theory of genes were discoveries. In contrast, an invention involves a new combination of old elements. The automobile was composed of six old elements in a new combination: a liquid gas engine, a liquid gas receptacle, a running-gear mechanism, an intermediate clutch, a driving shaft, and a carriage body.

Innovations—both discoveries and inventions—are not a single act but a cumulative series of transmitted increments plus a series of new elements. Consequently, the greater the number of cultural elements on which innovators may draw, the greater the frequency of discovery and invention. And just as a prolific couple gives birth to descendants who may multiply geometrically, so a pregnant invention may bring forth a geometrically increasing number of progeny. For example, glass gave birth to lenses, costume jewelry, drinking goblets, windowpanes, test tubes, X-ray tubes, lightbulbs, radio and television tubes, mirrors, and many other products. Lenses in turn gave birth to eyeglasses, magnifying glasses, telescopes, cameras, searchlights, and so on. Such developments reflect the *exponential principle*—as the cultural base increases, its possible uses tend to grow in geometric ratio. Table 22.1 lists some of the goods and services that in the opinion of the editors of *Consumer Reports* magazine most revolutionized our lives during the past fifty years.

Diffusion   **Diffusion** is the process by which cultural

The Cotton Gin: The Social Impact of a Significant Invention

After the American Revolution, agriculture faced hard times in the South. Southern planters could not easily slash costs, and many of them complained that their slaves had become an economic burden. Eli Whitney's invention of the cotton gin in 1793 changed all this. The cotton gin efficiently solved the technological problem of separating seeds from the lint of cotton. The spread of cotton cultivation was rapid and gave a powerful impetus to the southern plantation system and slavery. This is an early engraving of the gin and its impact on southern life as seen by the white plantation elite. *(The Bettmann Archive)*

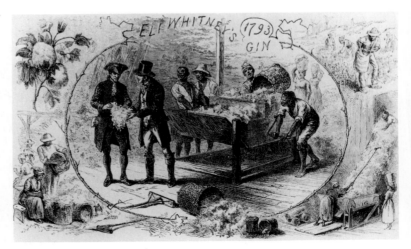

Table 22.1   The Goods and Services that Most Revolutionized Our Lives during the Past Half-Century

Air conditioners	Pensions and Social
Air travel	Security
Antibiotics	Personal computers
Austin/Morris Mini, '59	Plymouth Voyager, '84
Automatic	Polio vaccine
transmissions	Power mowers
Birth control pill	Refrigerators/freezers
Black-and-white TV	Running shoes
Color TV	Safety belts
Compact discs	Shopping malls
Credit cards	Smoke detectors
Detergents	Dr. Spock's *Baby and*
Disposable diapers	*Child Care*
Enriched bread	Fast food
Fluoridation	Suburbia
Ford Mustang, '65	Supermarkets
Frozen foods	Synthetic fabrics
GI Bill of Rights	Tampons
Health insurance	Toyato Corona, '65
Hi-fis	Transistors
Jeep, '42	Transparent tape
Latex paint	VA and FHA
LP records	mortgages
Magnetic tape	VCRs
Nash 600, '41	Volkswagen
Olds/Cadillac V-8	Beetle, '51
Olds Toronado, '66	Washers and dryers
Paperbacks	

Source: Copyright 1986 by Consumers Union of United States, Inc., Mount Vernon, NY 10553. Reprinted by permission from *Consumer Report Books.*

traits spread from one social unit to another. As we pointed out in Chapter 3, each culture contains a minimum of traits and patterns unique to or actually invented by it. Americans take considerable pride in the impact our nation has had on other societies. A quick swing around the globe leaves a traveler dazed by the prevalence of Americanisms. McDonald's, Kentucky Fried Chicken, and Pizza Hut dot urban landscapes. In Bangkok, Thailand, a teenager walks by in an orange Snoopy T-shirt and another in a yellow sweatshirt with the message, "HOW ARE YOU?" American films dominate the market in Tokyo, Paris, London, Stockholm, Copenhagen, Helsinki, and Oslo. And in Romania, leading professionals dress from head to toe in blue denim (Grenier, 1986).

We commonly overlook the fact that diffusion is a two-way street. For example, did you begin the morning by putting in contact lenses, switching on the television set, or brewing coffee on the gas range? Did you ride to school by subway or go to work in a plant making machine tools, automobile parts, or military rocket casings? Do you end your day by popping open a can of beer? If you have done any of these things, you have benefited from Soviet bloc technology purchased by American companies. In 1986, the Soviet Union and Eastern European countries held some 5,300 United States patents for their inventions, and Soviet bloc nations earned about $80 million in licensing fees and royalties from American firms. The Soviet Union has done an especially brisk business in technologies related to electric welding and metallurgical processes. Soviet scientists have also pioneered methods for applying thin coatings of diamond film to make radiation-resistant computer chips, superhard tools, and other useful products (Browne, 1986). A great number of social forces are at work in a continual process of social change (see the box on foreign development programs.)

THINKING THROUGH THE ISSUES

How would you go about selling a new invention like a lightbulb that, for all practical purposes, never burns out? Kevin Keating, the co-inventor of such a bulb, figured he had a sure thing. When he set out to break into the lightbulb market, he thought his only problem would be technological—all he had to do was come up with a better lightbulb. But when he sought someone to produce it, domestic and foreign manufacturers told him: "No way. We are in the bulb-replacement business!" Wholesalers and distributors were not interested either. They reasoned that every eternal bulb they sold was equivalent to 80 GE bulbs they would not sell. Additionally, not many people wanted to spend $5.99 for a light bulb. Had you been Keating, how would you have dealt with this situation? See the answer in the caption to Keating's photo on page 596.

Perspectives on Social Change

Many of sociology's roots lie in an endeavor to unravel the "meaning" of history and to establish laws of social change and development. The founders of sociology,

ISSUES THAT SHAPE OUR LIVES

Why Do Development Programs Often Fail?

During the Kennedy years, the United States launched the Peace Corps to assist citizens of Third World countries in the execution of agricultural, educational, and public health programs. And in recent years we have witnessed concerts and other activities designed to raise funds to aid the starving in Africa. Although these and other programs have been undertaken with high hopes, all too often they have failed to achieve their goals. In many cases the difficulties can be traced to the resistance of the intended beneficiaries. For instance, many U.S. foreign-aid programs display on trucks, equipment, and walls the symbol of a pair of hands clasped in friendship. But the symbol is often given different interpretations in other cultures. In some parts of the world, the two hands coming from opposite directions are considered proof that Americans go to other countries to pull their peoples into slavery. And to local Thai villagers, the symbol connotes the spirit world because no bodies are attached to the hands (Foster, 1969).

Cultural barriers can impede the acceptance of an innovation even when it is designed to save lives. Consider the experience of the British in Nigeria. Prior to World War II, British medical teams established that sleeping sickness had reached epidemic proportions among the Hausa population. The disease is transmitted by the tsetse fly, an insect that can survive only in a relatively cool environment, such as the bushes along shaded banks of streams. Tests revealed that the flies would die if the brush were chopped down. So British officials, ruling "indirectly" through local emirs, ordered the job to be undertaken. Then, the emirs issued commands to their subordinates, and the trouble began.

The British overlooked certain features of Hausa culture. The peasants believed that evil spirits inhabited certain patches of brush; sacred spirits, others. Nor did the Hausa share British definitions of sleeping sickness. The peasants identified the illness solely with its most severe symptom—total somnolence—and not with its more common symptoms: sporadic fever, headache, swelling of the face and limbs, and persistent weakness. The peasants thought that

evil spirits were responsible for the disease. And since the Hausa isolated and shunned disease victims, people were loath to admit they were sick.

Because the British did not take the Hausa beliefs into account, their efforts initally failed. The Hausa refused to cut the sacred brush. So the British imported non-Hausa natives from the French Sudan to cut it. In due course, the British succeeded in bringing the disease under control. Yet forty years later, the Hausa still had not changed their attitudes. They would cut down the flies' cover, but only under orders from the emirs. The peasants readily admitted that were it not for the coercion exercised by the emirs, they would not clear the banks (Miner, 1960).

Clearly, when the aim of a project is to inaugurate new practices, it is not sufficient simply to acquaint local residents with their benefits, even when those benefits seem readily apparent. For instance, agricultural extension agents succeeded in introducing an improved breed of hybrid corn among Spanish-American farmers in Arizona. But after a few years, the farmers returned to the old variety. Government officials found that the

particularly Auguste Comte and Herbert Spencer, looked to the grand sweep of history for an understanding of how and why societies change. Many contemporary sociologists continue to be intrigued by these "big questions." The major sociological perspectives dealing with social change fall within four broad categories: evolutionary, cyclical, functionalist, and conflict.

Evolutionary perspectives Much sociological thinking during the nineteenth century was dominated by the doctrine of social progress and a search for underlying evolutionary laws. According to Social Darwinists like Spencer, social evolution resembles biological evolution and results in the world growing progressively better. In

his theory of *unilinear evolution*, Spencer contended that change has persistently moved society from homogeneous and simple units toward progressively heterogeneous and interdependent units. He viewed the "struggle for existence" and "the survival of the fittest" as basic natural laws. Spencer equated this struggle with "free competition," insisting that "men ignore it to their sorrow." If unimpeded by outside intervention, particularly government, those individuals and social institutions that are "fit" will survive and proliferate while those that are "unfit" will in time die out.

As we pointed out in Chapter 1, Spencer's Social Darwinism mirrored the orientation of laissez-faire capitalism. Governmental regulation and welfare legislation

project had failed because the farmer's wives felt the new corn was too difficult to grind, and they preferred the taste of the older variety in their tortillas (Arensberg and Niehoff, 1964).

At times the introduction of Western measures have unintended and harmful consequences. For example, Western experts sponsored a program of crop irrigation in the Gezira region of the Sudan to increase the crop yield. The program succeeded in its intended purpose. But the irrigated canals offered lush breeding opportunities for a snail that carries *bilharziasis,* a parasitic disease which is seldom fatal but greatly weakens its victims. In due course, some 80 percent of local children contracted the disease. Only by halting the irrigation program could bilharziasis be brought under control (Foster, 1969).

Again and again, those concerned with bringing innovations to Third World nations encounter situations similar to these. Planners often ignore the human factor. They fail to comprehend the interrelated set of beliefs, traditions, rituals, taboos, fables, and physical realities that govern the people of other cultures (Creekmore, 1986).

The Peace Corps
The Peace Corps, launched during the Kennedy administration, seeks to channel the idealism of individual Americans into face-to-face cooperation with Third World peoples. Its purpose is to promote world peace and friendship by sending skilled American volunteers to Asian, African, and Latin American nations to help with health, poverty, agricultural, and related problems. Here a Peace Corps worker provides medical care for a child in Senegal. (*Olivier Rebbot/Woodfin Camp & Associates*)

were depicted as fostering social degeneration by "artificially preserving" the unfit and restricting the fit in their inheritance of the earth. Social Darwinism was a doctrine suited to expansionist imperialism and provided a justification for Western colonialism. The white race and its cultures were extolled as the highest forms of "humanity" and "civilization." Other peoples and cultures were "lower" in evolutionary development, and so it was only proper the Europeans, being "fitter," should triumph. However, such blatant ethnocentrism did not stand the test of scientific research. As the notion of unilinear evolution came under scientific scrutiny, it was found wanting. Anthropologists demonstrated that non-Western societies—and many European nations as well—did not pass through the same sequence of stages. There is not one scenario but many scenarios of social change.

Although evolutionary theory fell into disrepute for some fifty years, it has undergone a revival in recent decades (Steward, 1955; White, 1959; Lenski, 1966; Service, 1971). Contemporary approaches take a *multilinear* view of evolution. Their proponents recognize that "change" does not necessarily imply "progress," that change occurs in different ways, and that change proceeds in different directions. Indeed, interest in evolutionary theory has moved so centrally into mainstream sociology that even such a leading structural-functionalist sociologist as the late Talcott Parsons (1966, 1977) came to fashion a theory of "evolutionary change." While disclaiming that societal evolution is either a continuous or a simple linear process, Parsons suggests that societies tend to become increasingly *differentiated* in their structures and functions. But differentiation is not sufficient, since the new structural arrangements must be more functionally adaptive than the previous ones, which leads to *adaptive upgrading.*

Sociologist Gerhard Lenski (1966; Lenski and Lenski, 1982) likewise takes an evolutionary perspective that does not regard changes in social organization as necessarily leading to greater human happiness or satisfaction. He holds that evolution depends largely on

Kevin Keating and His Eternal Bulb

Big corporations and retail outlets had little interest in a lightbulb that almost never burned out. So Keating and his associates promoted the bulb as "one *hell* of a gimmick." And they depicted Keating as a David going up against Goliath (entrenched big electrical corporations). The Cable News Network, *USA Today, Newsweek,* and other publications picked up the human interest story. Keating and his bulb gained the kind of credibility that advertising could not buy. Orders poured in and distributors called wanting to market the bulb. Keating even secured an unexpected customer: The General Electric Supply Co., a division of GE, bought the bulbs to resell to Radio Shack (Richman, 1986). *(Peter Yates/NYT Pictures)*

changes in a society's level of technology and its mode of economic production. These changes in turn have consequences for other aspects of social life, including stratification systems, the organization of power, and family structures. According to Lenski, there is an underlying continuum in terms of which all societies can be ranked: hunting and gathering societies, simple horticultural societies, advanced horticultural societies, agrarian societies, and industrial societies. More specialized evolutionary bypaths include herding societies and "hybrid societies" such as fishing and maritime societies (see Chapter 3).

Cyclical perspectives Evolutionary theories, particularly those with a unilinear focus, depict history as divided into steplike levels of sequential stages. Cyclical theorists take a different approach and look to the rise and fall of civilizations. Their objective is not to predict the long-term direction of human history, but rather to predict the course of a civilization or society. Nor do cyclical theorists seek to place societies on some sort of lineal or historical scale. Instead, they compare societies in search for generalizations regarding their stages of growth and decline. Evolutionists tend to be relatively jolly people who see humankind as striving to reach new heights in a challenging future, whereas cyclical theorists tend to be relatively pessimistic people who forecast the demise of every civilization.

The nineteenth century was a time of faith in evolution and human progress. But the catastrophe of World War I and the recurrent economic crises that have plagued industrial nations led some scholars to express doubt regarding the course of human history. One of these was the German scholar Oswald Spengler (1880–1936), whose *The Decline of the West* (1918) became a best seller. He contended that culture passes through the same stages of growth and decline as individuals: a period of development, followed by maturity, eventual decline, and death. Based on his examination of eight cultures, Spengler says that each culture possesses a life span of approximately a thousand years. Western culture, he held, emerged about A.D. 900, and therefore its end is near (hence the title of his book and the interest it provoked).

English historian Arnold J. Toynbee (1934/1954) also sought to depict uniformities in the growth and decline of civilizations and to identify the principles that underlie this development. Like Spengler, he believed that the course of most civilizations is uniform, although he did not ascribe a time interval to their rise and de-

Cyclical Theories: The Rise and Fall of Rome
Although once dominating Western Europe and the lands adjoining the Mediterranean Sea, the greatness and strength of the Roman Empire progressively eroded. By the third and fourth centuries, internal chaos and pressure from foreign invaders had taken a serious toll. In 455 A.D. the Vandals sacked Rome (depicted above). *(North Wind Picture Archives)*

cline. Toynbee said that civilizations arise in response to some challenge. A challenge may derive from natural forces, such as a severe climate, or from human factors, such as warlike neighbors. A civilization grows and flourishes when the challenge is not too severe and when a creative minority (an intelligent elite) finds an adequate response to it. When the creative minority fails to respond adequately to a challenge, the civilization breaks down and disintegrates. In the course of disintegrating, the minority, no longer creative, transforms itself into a ruling elite and imposes its will by force. This develop-

ment hastens decline, because it intensifies internal strife. However, careful examination of Toynbee's work shows it relies primarily on Hellenic and Western experiences and neglects Arabic, Egyptian, and Chinese histories, which have somewhat different patterns. It seems he arbitrarily imposed his theory on the history of non-Western civilizations rather than inductively deriving his theory from a study of them.

Functionalist perspectives   As we saw in Chapter 2, the concept of system is central to the structure-function model of society. A system is a combination of things or parts that form a larger whole. One feature of a system is its tendency toward *equilibrium*—a society responds to uncertainties and disturbances with adaptive measures that restore it to a steady course. While time can be introduced as a factor within the model, American functionalists have typically stressed the static properties of social life—a cross-sectional view of social structure at a particular point in time. This approach allows sociologists to control the fluid quality of social organization so they may grasp, describe, and analyze it, and make it understandable and intelligible. Such a portrait, however, does not imply that things are static in the sense of being dead. Functionalists recognize that things happen all the time; children are born, people die, and institutional structures regularly perform essential tasks (Dahrendorf, 1968).

As we pointed out earlier in the chapter, functionalists like Parsons (1966, 1977) have added evolutionary elements to the perspective. In so doing, they have attempted to broaden the notion of equilibrium to include *developing* properties in addition to those that are *self-maintaining*. Following the organic analogy, they portray the social group as living in a state of dynamic or moving equilibrium. Upsetting forces intrude, functioning as innovative stimuli. The social system adjusts to these disturbances by establishing a new level of equilibruim. Hence, even though society changes, it remains stable by achieving new forms of social integration.

Sociologist William F. Ogburn (1922) drew upon evolutionary models to fashion a functionalist approach to social change. He distinguishes between *material* and *nonmaterial culture* and locates the source of change in material invention—tools, weapons, and technical processes. Nonmaterial culture refers to social values, norms, beliefs, and social arrangements, including law, religion, and the family (see Chapter 3). Ogburn saw the impetus for social change coming from material culture.

Nonmaterial culture must adapt or respond to changes in material culture. Since nonmaterial culture must constantly "catch up" with material culture, an adjustment gap develops between the two. Ogburn called this gap **cultural lag.**

Social life abounds with examples in which uneven rates of change result in social dislocation. Consider the social consequences of the automobile. It spawned secondary industries like oil refineries, tire and glass conglomerates, and the giant accident insurance industry. It induced massive investments in single-family homes and interstate highway systems. But in doing so, the automobile has contributed to a dispoiling of the natural environment and to an exodus of the central city's affluent population. Ogburn says these sorts of problems arise when social institutions lag behind changing technology, what some sociologists have called "social disorganization." Although Ogburn's notion of cultural lag contains a valuable insight, it vastly oversimplifies matters. No single factor explains social change, since in real life a great many forces converge to give society its dynamic qualities.

Conflict perspectives   Conflict theorists hold that tensions among competing groups are the basic source of social change. Nowhere do we find a clearer exposition of the conflict perspective than in the writings of Karl Marx, particularly those espousing *dialectical materialism.* As we saw in Chapter 1, dialectical materialism depicts the world in dynamic terms—terms of *becoming* rather than *being.* Marx said that every economic order grows to a state of maximum efficiency while it develops internal contradictions or weaknesses that result in it decay. Class conflict is the driving force of social change—the key to human history. As we noted in Chapter 9, class conflict derives from the struggle between those who own the means of producing wealth and those who do not.

For Marx, all change is the product of a constant conflict between opposites. It arises from the contradictions inherent to all things and processes. All development—be it social, economic, or human—has to do with producing and resolving contradictions. Contradictions are not decided through compromise, through an averaging out of differences. Rather, they give birth to something entirely new. By means of struggle, a working through of opposing forces, people and societies change. All facets of social life, therefore, are dynamic and ever-changing. As Marx (1906) observed: "By acting on the external world and changing it, he [the individual] at the same time changes his own nature."

We have dealt with conflict theories at some length in several chapters. We have noted that many conflict theorists say Marx's view that "all history is the history of class conflict" is much too simple (Coser, 1956, 1957; Dahrendorf, 1958). They contend that other types of conflict are equally and in some instances more important, including conflict among nations, ethnic groups, religions, and economic interest groups. Sociologist Ralf Dahrendorf (1958:174–175) exemplifies the thinking of many contemporary conflict theorists in his capsule summary of the perspective.

Cultural Lag

As viewed by cultural lag theorists, the various parts of culture do not change at the same rate. Some parts, especially those associated with new technologies, change more rapidly than others. Since there is an interdependence among cultural parts, a rapid change in one part requires readjustments through change in other parts. In this fashion material culture gives impetus to change in nonmaterial culture. The uneven rate of change may be accompanied by some degree of social disorder or chaos. Depicted below are Kayapo Indians of Brazil with a radio recorder. What would you expect to be the likely social consequences of the introduction of this new technology? *(Rio Branco/Magnum)*

1. Every society is subjected at every moment to change: social change is ubiquitous.

2. Every society experiences at every moment social conflict: social conflict is ubiquitous.

3. Every element in a society contributes to its change.

4. Every society rests on constraint of some of its members by others.

Dahrendorf sees these components as complementing the functionalist model, providing an integrated image of social life as an encompassing whole or configuration.

Technology and Social Change

To live in the United States today is to gain an appreciation for Dahrendorf's assertion that social change is ubiquitous (meaning "being everywhere"). Technology, the application of knowledge for practical ends, is a major source of social change (see Chapter 3). Thousands of years ago, in the process of evolving a human form, our ancestors learned how to fashion tools—stone axes, bone fish hooks, wooden spearheads, and countless other instruments and utensils. Each innovation gave them a little more power over nature and provided a cultural base for additional innovations.

In recent centuries, humankind has succeeded in creating all kinds of new technologies of increasing sophistication. Today, technology is advancing at what seems to be a breakneck speed. Indeed, in some laboratory somewhere in the United States today, amid a clutter of vacuum chambers, thermoses of liquid chemicals, and computer screens, scientists are engaged in research that will win Nobel Prizes in the next century. Technology now promises greater power than we have ever experienced before.

Yet we would do well to remind ourselves that technology is a human creation; it does not exist naturally. A spear or a robot is as much a cultural as a physical object. Until humans use a spear to hunt game or a robot to produce machine bolts, neither is much more than a solid mass of matter. For a butterfly or sparrow looking for an object on which to alight, a spear or robot serves the purpose equally well. The chemical catastrophe at Bhopal, India, the explosion of the Challenger space shuttle, and the Russian nuclear accident at Chernobyl drive home the human quality of technology; they provide cases in which well-planned systems suddenly went haywire and there was no ready hand to set them right. Since technology is a human creation, we are responsible for what is done with it. Pessimists worry that we will use our technology eventually to blow our world and ourselves to pieces. But they have been saying this for decades, and so far we have managed to survive and even prosper. Whether we will continue to do so in the years ahead remains uncertain. Clearly, the impact of technology on our lives warrants a closer examination.

The Computer Revolution

Few technological developments have had a greater impact on our lives than the computer revolution. Scientists and engineers have designed specialized machines that can do tasks that once only people could do. There are those who contend that the switch to an information-

The Dawn of the Railroad Age
During the early 1830s, many short stretches of railroad track were laid and initial runs were made, including that of the *De Witt Clinton* in 1831 between Albany and Schenectady (right). The railroads stimulated the flow of goods between east and west and had important political and economic significance in binding the Middle West to the East during the critical years of Southern secession. In the long run, American railroads would supply the cheap transportation essential to large-scale specialized agriculture and mass production industry. *(The Bettmann Archive)*

based economy is in the same camp as other great historical milestones, particularly the Industrial Revolution. Yet when we ask why the Industrial Revolution was a revolution, we find that it was not the machines. Certainly the steam engine, the cotton gin, the locomotive and rails, and the power loom were extraordinary inventions. But the primary reason they were revolutionary is that they were agents for great social change. They took people out of the fields and brought them into factories. They gave rise to mass production and, through mass production, to a society in which wealth was not confined to the few (Diebold, 1983).

In somewhat similar fashion, computers promise to revolutionize the structure of American life, particularly as they free the human mind and open new vistas in knowledge and communication (Feigenbaum and McCorduck, 1983). These advances are making it possible for machines to perform many chores more cheaply than people. The Industrial Revolution supplemented and replaced the *muscles* of humans and animals by mechanical methods. The computer extends this development to supplement and replace some aspects of the *mind* of human beings by electronic methods. It is the capacity of the computer for solving problems and making decisions that represents its greatest potential and that poses the greatest difficulties in predicting its impact on society.

Expanding human options　　As computers are becoming smaller, faster, and cheaper, they are becoming accessible to increasing numbers of people. In 1986, 6.6 million personal computers were sold in the United States, of which 2.4 million were purchased for the home. Within twenty to thirty years, it is projected that desktop computers will have 10,000 times the capability of current personal computers, which means that machines on a desk will be able to do what expensive mainframe computers do today. In the early days of the computer revolution, a commonly voiced fear was that computers would force people into a common mold and regiment their lives. Yet the new technology seems to be encouraging individuality. For instance, Chevrolet has developed an experimental promotion that consists of a disk allowing users of personal computers to assemble, on their screen, the truck they want from a vast list of options—and then determine its performance standards, calculate its cost, and test drive it around a simulated track. Shoppers in the future may be able to use computers to assemble preprogrammed options in a way that is best for them. In so doing, computers afford new opportunities for individual choice and diversity.

Smaller, cheaper, and faster computers also help equalize small and big business. In the past, the capacity to handle large amounts of information set large businesses apart from smaller ones. But new computer technologies are lowering this threshold. Similarly, education is benefiting from the proliferation of personal computers. Consider, for instance, that many textbooks are accompanied by computer disks providing databases and models that help students study the subject matter. Computer simulation is being applied in many areas of education, including the training of pilots. And advances in artificial intelligence hold promise of allowing computers to develop their own expert decision-making

The Computer Revolution
Computers are having enormous consequences for the ways people carry out their work and live their lives. They are opening vast new vistas in knowledge and communication and supplementing and replacing some aspects of the human mind by electronic technology. But the computer revolution, while expanding human options, also poses threats to civil liberties. And it alters some of the ways people relate to one another and has implications for the exercise of social power in corporations, schools, and government. *(Tom Hollyman/Photo Researchers)*

systems, and even permit them to learn from their mistakes (Kidder, 1987).

Affording a source of social power   The expansion of computer technology is giving new dimensions to social power. Consider the experience of New Hampshire. There is an old adage among the state's politicians: "He who has the information rules. He who has the information has the power." So when the New Hampshire legislature passed a bill giving itself access to the information stored in the state's computer, the governor insisted on veto power over who can look at the data. The information the governor sought to protect is not the personal information of the kind held by welfare and mental health agencies, but the basic financial information on which key government decisions are based. The governor and legislative leaders agreed that the outcome of the conflict would very likely determine the balance of power between the two branches of state government in the years ahead (Clendinen, 1985).

The issue confronting New Hampshire officialdom is one that is emerging in countless forms throughout American life: Will access to information be widespread, or will it be concentrated in the hands of the few? The centralized accumulation of data permits the concentration of considerable power in those who have access to the computer. A power gap tends to develop between those who are trained to use and understand computers and those who are not.

The computer revolution is also posing an agonizing dilemma for the leaders of the Soviet Union and Eastern European nations. Their regimes are secretive and highly centralized. The leaders maintain political power, in part, by controlling information. In the past the Kremlin has treated most computers the way it has treated copiers: as dangerous weapons that must be kept under lock and key. Current Soviet and East European leaders want to modernize their economies, but they cannot do so unless they adopt new technologies that weaken their monopoly on information and loosen their grip on political power. It remains to be seen whether they will be successful in selectively adopting Western technology, while minimizing features that may cause internal dissent (Nagorski and Watson, 1986).

Affecting people's relationships   Computers alter the way people relate to one another. On a telephone, we hear the other person's voice. In face-to-face contact we see people smile, frown, and nod. But there is no such feedback in computer exchanges. When people employ

a computer to send electronic mail, they lack access to nonverbal cues. As a result, computer exchanges become less predictable. For one thing, people are less likely to hold back strong feelings when communicating by computers; they show a greater tendency to swear, insult others, and communicate abruptly. For another, in face-to-face meetings, one person is likely to talk considerably more than another. But on a computer, people talk about the same amount because they are less self-conscious and are protected by a feeling of anonymity. Moreover, computer technology changes people's awareness of themselves, of one another, and of their relationship with the world. Machines that give the appearance of "thinking" challenge our notions not only of time and distance, but of mind (Turkle, 1984).

The introduction of computer technology has compelled organizations to change as well. Like thousands of companies in the 1980s, the Shenandoah Life Insurance Company moved eagerly into the age of high technology. It installed a $2 million system to computerize processing and claims operations at its Virginia headquarters. Even so, it still took 27 working days—and handling by 32 clerks in three departments—to process an application for a policy conversion. Shenandoah's problems stemmed from its bureaucratic maze, not from defects in its equipment. Only when it radically reorganized its work structure was Shenandoah able to reap the benefits of the new technology. It now groups clerks in teams of 5 to 7 members. Each team performs all the functions that

"Sir, I'm leaving my high-paying job in the manufacturing industry for a low-paying job in a service industry, because that's what's happening."

Drawing by Dana Fradon; © 1985 The New Yorker Magazine, Inc.

previously were spread over 3 departments. In the process, case-handling time has dropped to 2 days and the firm is processing 50 percent more applications with 10 percent fewer employees (Hoerr, 1986).

Endangering civil liberties   Computers also have implications for our privacy and the confidentiality of our communications and personal data. The use of computers to collect data and store information provides the technical capability for integrating several information files into networks of computerized data banks. With such networks, personal data that we provide for one purpose (the Internal Revenue Service, the Social Security Administration, Motor Vehicle departments, courts, credit bureaus, banks, hospitals, and insurance companies) can potentially be accessed for other purposes. As people handle more and more of their activities through electronic instruments—mail, banking, shopping, entertainment, and travel plans—it becomes technically feasible for government and private concerns to monitor these activities with unprecedented ease. To its critics, computer technology represents the ultimate intrusion of Big Brother into our lives. According to the Office of Technology Assessment, a congressional agency, the federal government has built a vast capacity for computerized surveillance of Americans, while failing to devise adequate safeguards against abuses (Davis, 1986).

Technology and Jobs

Visionaries look to technology to make human lives richer and freer. They say that the new electronics allow people to have access to vast stores of information, expanded human resources, and opportunities for working and relating with one another on a more flexible, cheaper, and convenient basis (Hiltz and Turoff, 1978). More specifically, they see a variety of benefits deriving from technological advances. For one thing, tasks that are boring, repetitive, and narrowly defined can be performed by machines. As automation removes low-level work, opportunities grow for greater free time in which people can be more creative and productive. For another, new technologies dictate that workers understand how the entire production process fits together, and no longer see themselves as working with only a small piece of it. And as routine tasks are taken over by computers and robots, the ability and willingness of workers to solve unexpected problems and to meet shifting requirements assumes greater significance (Eckholm, 1984). Further, some experts see computer systems as offering opportuni-

ties to disadvantaged groups to acquire the skills and social ties they require to become fully functioning members of society.

Do new technologies eliminate jobs?   Although optimists see technology as affording opportunities for improving the human condition, there are those who express considerable concern about the economic impact of technology on jobs. Across the decades the automating of industrial processes has aroused fear that machines will replace human beings and create mass unemployment. Indeed, at the dawn of the Industrial Revolution (1811–1816), English textile workers called Luddites destroyed the machinery they thought would put them out of work. Strictly speaking, all technological change within industry has meant "automation" in that low-level skills are taken over by the automatic operation of machines. The ballad of John Henry tells how a legendary steel driver of the 1870s sought to combat the steam drill. John Henry wielded a 20-pound hammer in each hand to drill two 7-foot holes in rock faster than the machine. "A man ain't nothing but a man," John Henry told his foreman, "but before I let that steam drill beat me in the ground, I'll die with a hammer in my hand." John Henry succeeded but died in the process.

We hear growing expressions of fear nowadays that as computers and robots take over many office and factory duties, the only work that will remain will be primarily for janitors, hospital orderlies, cashiers, truck drivers, sales personnel, and fast-food helpers (Bluestone and Harrison, 1987; Kuttner, 1987). According to this view, technology has the double impact of job creation and job displacement, eliminating semiskilled and unskilled jobs while increasing the demand for technically trained workers. Many blue-collar workers and even some managers from the industrial sector have difficulty crossing over the line to fill new service jobs. So despite persistently high unemployment, large numbers of service jobs go unfilled (Supple, 1986; Brookes, 1987). In other industrial nations as well, the growth of the service industries is occurring at the expense of manufacturing and farming (see Figure 22.1).

A few years ago, experts were predicting that millions of dangerous and repetitive jobs would be taken over by an army of robots, the vanguard in a new industrial revolution. But the wave of robots seems to be creeping, rather than sweeping, across the nation's industrial landscape (by 1987, some 14,000 robots had been installed in American factories) (Karmin, 1987). Even by 1995, robots are expected to perform fewer than

Technology: A Threat to Jobs?
The acres of machinery at a number of Chrysler plants move in a carefully choreographed fashion. Robots shower sparks, weld car bodies, and spray paint the autos' sheet-metal skin. But what about the workers who once performed these operations? Many auto workers believe that they have been replaced by robots in a frantic effort by American firms to compete with cheaper foreign imports. Yet robots have not fulfilled many early expectations regarding their feasibility, cost, and productivity, all factors slowing their introduction within American industry. *(George Haling/Science Source/Photo Researchers)*

5 percent of factory jobs (Stricharchuk and Winter, 1985). Automation also has consequences for many white-collar workers. Engineers are finding that CAE/CAD (computer-aided engineering/design) is making inroads on many of their traditional responsibilities. You can think of CAE/CAD as replacing the pencil and paper in an engineer's hand with computers that reduce, by 50 percent or more, the time and cost of creating products (Hillkirk, 1986).

FIGURE 22.1   The Growth in Service Industries
Service jobs include finance, insurance, restaurant, hotel, education, legal, and social services. *Source: The Conference Board, 1987.*

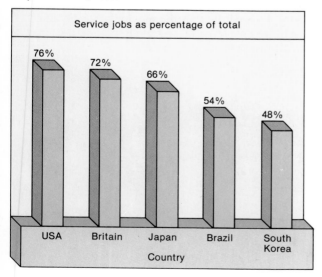

One leading economist—Wassily Leontief, recipient of the Nobel Prize in economics in 1973—has long argued that the application of new technologies results in the loss of jobs. But recently, in a new study he undertook with Faye Duchin (1986), Leontief concludes that while robots will wipe out about 400,000 semiskilled jobs by 1990 and nearly 2 million by the year 2000, roughly the same number of jobs will be needed to make the machines and use the new technology. However, his analysis seeks to determine total employment levels by occupation and does not deal with the question of whether the available workforce will fit the occupational demands. All this raises the question of what is happening to the American economy.

Is technology atomizing the American economy?
Economist David L. Birch (1987) draws our attention to a significant trend in the American economy: It is breaking into pieces—"atomizing." More and smaller businesses are now doing what fewer and larger ones did before. In 1985, 700,000 new companies were formed, compared with 90,000 startups in 1950 and 200,000 in 1965. In addition, there were some 400,000 new partnerships and 300,000 newly self-employed people—about 1.4 million new enterprises created in one year. New enterprises mean the creation of new jobs. Small service businesses generate about 40 percent of the U.S. gross national product and 62 percent of U.S. jobs (Cook, 1986). While small businesses are becoming more numerous, the nation's 500 largest corporations have been under growing competitive pressure to become leaner and more flexible. As a result, they employed 2.2 million fewer people at the end of 1985 than

they did at the beginning of 1980. Nearly 10 percent of the blue-collar workers displaced by these trends have returned to work operating their own businesses (Richards, 1986).

How are these changes likely to affect your careers? Birch says that if you work for someone else, you are bound to feel it. The days when an employee worked for one company and received a gold watch at retirement are virtually gone. One of five American workers changes jobs each year. To stay alive economically, Birch says, you must be prepared to switch careers and employers often. Rapid technological change means you will enjoy less job security and will confront a constant need to stay current in what you do. (See the box dealing with multiple careers.)

How does the new technology affect the work environment? In Charlie Chaplin's now classic film *Modern Times*, a factory boss keeps speeding up an assembly line while Chaplin, wrench in hand, works faster and faster in a futile—and hilarious—effort to keep up. The scene captures a persistent concern: the dehumanization of the workplace. Now critics are contending that the new technology is dehumanizing the lot of office workers.

Indeed, some labor leaders contend that office automation has created the electronic equivalent of the moving assembly line, with the computer system programmed to monitor workers' performance. A study by the U.S Public Health Service offers some support for the criticism. Clerical workers who use video-display terminals report substantially greater physical and mental stress than do their counterparts who do not use terminals. They have to follow rigid work procedures that allow them little control over their work. Contemporary "electronic factories" are mostly a creation of banks, insurance companies, credit-card concerns, and firms with large data-processing requirements (Andrew, 1983).

The new technologies often result in a two-tier workforce, with a small group of creative people performing spirit-enhancing and mind-challenging tasks at the top and a large workforce of people with low job skills who are paid correspondingly low wages at the bottom. What appear to be missing from the service industries are the high-wage blue-collar jobs, such as those traditionally found in the auto and steel industries. Indeed, in recent years it has become fashionable to deplore the decline of the industrial sector of the American economy—popularly dubbed "deindustrialization"—

The Dehumanization of the Workplace?
Charlie Chaplin's classic film *Modern Times* depicts a factory worker of the 1920s who is caught in the grip of a mechanized age and dehumanized as an appendage of the machine (left). He must work faster and faster in a futile attempt to keep pace with an assembly line that is continually being speeded up. There are those who contend that something of a similar sort is occurring among office workers in today's "electronic factories" (below). They say video-display terminals are the equivalent of the moving assembly line and the source of severe physical and mental stress. *(left, Columbia Pictures Industries; below, Tom Hollyman/Photo Researchers)*

ISSUES THAT SHAPE OUR LIVES

Will You Have More Than One Career?

Are you having difficulty choosing a career? If you answer "yes," you are among the vast majority of college students. Selecting a career is far more difficult today than ever before. New ones spring up every day, and old ones are caught up in currents of continual change. Complicating matters, you are likely to live longer than your parents or grandparents. It is hardly surprising, then, that many students have difficulty deciding on a career.

A new ingredient has also entered the picture. The notion that you should make a lifelong commitment to a single career is going out of style. Not too long ago, students would choose a career and expect to stick with it. Even today, professionals—physicians, lawyers, accountants, engineers, and college professors—start out on the assumption that they will spend their lives in one line of work. In late adolescence and early adulthood these people dedicate themselves to the acquisition of special skills and credentials. Family, friends, and associates also assume that they will spend their remaining years successfully pursuing a career that will remain a lifetime commitment. A career is expected to provide a sense of achievement and fulfillment. Moreover, professionals typically anticipate that their careers will unfold in an orderly progression of steps from an entry position to eventual retirement. Each step—for example, assistant professor, associate professor, and professor for academics, and staff, senior, manager, and partner for accountants—is assumed to bring new levels of satisfaction and well-being.

Yet many people find these goals unattainable. Seymour B. Sarason (1977) tracked the careers of some 2,300 individuals listed in *Who's Who*. Roughly 40 percent of them had experienced a career shift. And nearly 10 percent of the shifts represented a substantial movement from one area to another, such as from medicine to business or vice versa. Men and women switch careers for a variety of reasons. Some find that their career has not provided the fulfillment they had expected, or it has lost its challenge. One 57-year-old former physician told the author:

I was born with a good head on my shoulders and people seem to like me. I went into medicine not so much because I was interested in being a doctor but because I was interested in making money. I get a big kick out of finding new financial ventures. When I was 34, I interested five other doctors in joining with me in setting up a centralized billing service for physicians. At the time it was a pretty novel idea. Even when I was in medical school I played the stock market. Throughout my adult years my favorite pastime has always been reading financial publications. I like playing around with measures and models of stock market action. And since I follow a disciplined and systematic approach, I have made considerably more money than I have lost. I never really found medicine all that interesting. By the time I was 45, I was burned out and resented the intrusions that patients were making in my life. I did not have any financial worries, so I decided to give up medicine and do what I really enjoyed—manage investment portfolios. It was a natural extension of my billing corporation. I specialize in putting together portfolios for professionals.

Others leave one career for another because they became bored, because they would like to give a new direction to their lives, or because they are having difficulty with their employer. As people move through life, it is not uncommon for them to take stock of themselves periodically and reassess what they are doing with their lives and where they are going (see Chapter 11). Some return to college to secure new skills. Others build on contacts, interests, skills, or hobbies they have developed. You too may reach a point in your life in which you experience a sense of disenchantment and decide you want something different. Rather than remain alienated in a one-career trap, you will want to strike out in new directions. Switching is easier if you have a working spouse whose income makes it less essential to work at a distasteful job simply to earn a livelihood.

For these reasons, it may be shortsighted to look upon your college experiences as simply enhancing your chances to secure a good job on graduation. The far greater payoff may be the analytical and problem-solving skills that you acquire and that enable you to cope with challenges. Seen in this way, a college education should not merely provide you with a fund of current knowledge; it should increase your capacity to acquire knowledge and to function rationally and effectively in the years ahead. As a result, you should be better able to capitalize on your strengths, compensate for your weaknesses, and modify your environment so that it will better fit your skills.

and to lament the "McDonaldization of America."

However, many people mistakenly assume that the number of employees an industry loses is proportional to the decline of its output. A more accurate measure of the health of the manufacturing sector is the percentage of gross national product (GNP) it produces, and this percentage has remained relatively stable. In 1950, the production of goods accounted for 46.6 percent of the real GNP; in 1960, 43.6 percent; in 1970, 42.6 percent; in 1980, 42.1 percent; and in 1985, 42.9 percent. The share of *employment* in manufacturing is declining steadily because *productivity* has increased more rapidly in manufacturing than in services. In the years ahead, the balance of employment is likely to continue its shift toward services. This fact does not mean that the United States will cease to be a manufacturing nation It simply means that manufacturers are not going to need as many people to produce goods as they did in the past (Couch, 1986; Heskett, 1987). Figure 22.2 shows the job projections of the Bureau of Labor Statistics.

Does society have a responsibility for those who are the losers? Although considerable controversy surrounds the impact technology has on the workplace, it is clear that some people do come out the losers. The human consequences of new technologies are frequently so massive and pervasive that a single company, industry, or state cannot cope with them. Under these circumstances, a national response is essential with programs for shifting workers to industries and regions with jobs and for retraining workers for new jobs.

The United States has only begun to explore extensive retraining programs to insulate its workers from unemployment. For instance, from 1977 to 1984, 1.2 million workers received "basic trade readjustment benefits"—payments to workers in industries the government determined to be in distress. Only 70,000 of these

workers began retraining. Of the 28,000 who completed the courses, fewer than 4,500 found jobs that used their new skills (Barron, 1986). The problem of retraining America's workers is expected to intensify in the years ahead. By the year 2000, according to the American Society for Training and Development (1986), 75 percent of all workers currently employed will need retraining. A related problem is the increasing obsolescence of the nation's school system. As we pointed out in Chapter 17, the schools simulate factory life, a pattern of work that is becoming increasingly irrelevant as Americans move into the twenty-first century. Clearly, a modern society ignores at its peril a situation where a growing proportion of its population cannot find gainful employment.

Social Change in Third World Nations

It is difficult today to read a newspaper or view a television newscast without gaining a feeling for the powerful currents of change that are at work in the world. Iran, the Middle East, Central America, South Africa, and countless other global centers conjure images of boiling cauldrons of social transition and transformation. Sociologists have approached social change in Third World nations from two somewhat different perspectives: modernization and world systems. Sociologists use the term "Third World nations" more or less interchangeably with "developing countries" and "poor countries" (Goldthorpe, 1984).

Modernization

Modernization describes the process by which a society moves from traditional or preindustrial social and eco-

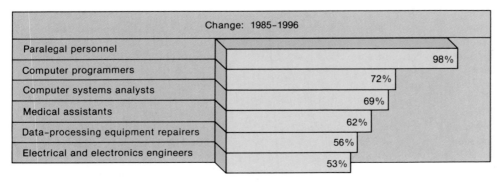

FIGURE 22.2   **Where the Jobs Are**
These occupations are projected by the Bureau of Labor Statistics to have the fastest rate of growth in the next decade. *Source: U.S. Bureau of Labor Statistics.*

New Overseas Empire Building: The Late Nineteenth Century
From 1815 to 1880, there was a slackening in the colonial activities of the great powers. It was and is still clear that most colonies do not "pay" in the ordinary sense of bringing in more money than they cost. Even so, by 1880, the new imperialism was gathering strength. The British Empire was by far the largest. The richest and most populous unit of the Empire was India. The British enlisted Indian military units in the pursuit of British imperial objectives elsewhere in the world. Pictured at left is the 9th Bengal Cavalry. *(North Wind Picture Archives)*

nomic arrangements to those characteristic of industrial societies. It rests on the assumption that there is basically one underlying path of development, that followed by advanced Western nations and Japan. Traditional societies are portrayed as relatively static, rooted in subsistence economies using "biblical" methods: hand sowing and planting, the ox-drawn wooden plow, and "cottage industries" employing little or no mechanical power. Religious institutions are powerful and dogmatic, engendering fatalism and political submissiveness. Kin ties predominate, and fertility rates are high.

By contrast, modern societies are depicted as dynamically changing, rooted in economies fostering development, innovation, and technological advance. Re-

ligious dogma and traditional political authority are weak, replaced by modern-minded attitudes. Members of industrial societies display independence in making important decisions, including the number of children they will have. Viewed in this manner, modernization involves a pattern of *convergence* as societies become increasingly urban, industry comes to overshadow agriculture, the size and density of the population increases, the division of labor becomes more specialized, and the knowledge base grows larger and more complex (Lerner, 1958; Parsons, 1966; Goldthorpe, 1984).

The momentum for modernization is said to derive from *internal* forces and processes. The chances that a Third World country will evolve in the direction of lib-

Social Change in the Third World
As portrayed by modernization theorists, Third World nations must follow the same path of social and economic development as that taken by advanced Western nations and Japan. In contrast, world-system theorists say that Third World nations experience difficulty in growing and developing because they are dominated and exploited by developed capitalist nations. They argue that an international economic system limits Third World enterprise to the extraction of natural resources like petroleum. What do you make of these conflicting arguments as they apply to Middle Eastern oil-producing nations? *(Minosa-Scorpio/Sygma)*

eral Western democracies is enhanced when a nation provides for literacy and education, encourages free media, creates a pluralistic rather than a centrally dominated social order, and prevents extreme inequalities among the various social strata (Dahl, 1971). The crowning achievement of modern society is the informed participation of its citizens in public life through a democratic order affording choices of leaders and policies. To be "modern" means to see life as alternatives and preferences (Apter, 1965). Clearly, the picture we gain from modernization theorists is an optimistic and rosy one—although far too optimistic and too rosy. Nations do not just take off after the appropriate infusion of technology and then keep flying. Some take off and then crash, like contemporary Poland.

World Systems

Explanations of the poverty of Third World nations in terms of their alleged backwardness have not been appreciated by the citizens of these nations (Frank, 1969, 1978; Goldthorpe, 1984). They have looked more favorably on **world system** (or *dependency*) explanations in which development is seen within the context of an international, geographic division of labor. World system theorists reject the idea of traditional and modern societies and assert that there is only one world economy. Third World nations are poor not because they are *unde*veloped or backward, but because they have been exploited and actively *under*developed by rich nations.

World system theorists start with the proposition that a huge gulf has opened up in productivity and living standards between the advanced capitalist countries and the rest of the world. Sociologist Immanuel Wallerstein (1974, 1979, 1980) says capitalism and a world economy are merely two sides of the same coin. He sees the capitalist world system as divided into three tiers of nations: the core, the periphery, and the semiperiphery (see Chapter 15). In general, the core nations dominate the world economy and exploit other social and economic units. The *periphery* consists of those regions that supply raw materials to the core and are exploited by it. The *semiperiphery* are those areas that fall somewhere between the exploiting and exploited segments of the world economy.

According to world system analysis, the major capitalist nations are not permitting Third World nations to develop and grow. An unequal exchange operates between core and periphery nations, with development at the former end of the chain coming at the cost of underdevelopment at the other end (Delacroix and Ragin, 1981). The waves of debt restructurings, defaults, and near-defaults that have occupied the international monetary stage in recent years have had as their counterpart a deepening of human misery in Mexico and other Latin American nations (Walsh and Witcher, 1986). Specialization in the production and export of raw materials is also said to be detrimental to the long-term growth prospects of developing nations. Specialization makes these nations' economies responsive to the demands of the world market, rather than to their own internal developmental needs. This distortion becomes most apparent in the multibillion-dollar cocaine industry that is causing untold problems for Bolivia, Peru, and Colombia (Ricks,

Andean Economies: Addicted to the Drug Traffic?
All along the high slopes of the Andes, Indians have for centuries chewed the coca leaf as a hunger and fatigue suppressant. But in recent years, coca has become a major cash crop (right). In many ways, coca is an ideal crop because it matures in six months, and its leaves can be harvested three times a year. In Bolivia, the drug trade accounts for about 25 percent of the gross national product. Some Bolivian leaders fear that drug barons will gain control over the nation's government and economy. A major drawback of the drug trade is that it is stifling the much-needed development of Bolivia's manufacturing base. (Ryser, 1986). *(Peter MacFarren/Sygma)*

1986). So the momentum and course of development in Third World nations is shaped primarily by *external* forces and processes (Wolf, 1982). Further, class formation in the dependent nations results in a small elite whose economic interests are linked to foreign investors in the core countries (Rubinson, 1976).

During the 1970s, it seemed as if modernization and world system theorists were simply two mutually incompatible ways of looking at change in the Third World. It would be wrong to call it a debate, because there was little or no dialogue; the two schools of thought merely talked past each other. But in recent years, other sociologists have looked at the same matters and have offered a "third force" perspective that draws on both approaches. These sociologists are aware that backwash effects (for instance, attracting capital and educated people from depressed world regions) can impoverish poorer nations while accelerating development in richer ones. They attach considerable importance to the distorted economic growth imposed on Third World nations by their colonial pasts. And they give much weight to the international economic system with which Third World nations must cope (Goldthorpe, 1984; McCord and McCord, 1986; Hall, 1986). Moreover, they have suggested a number of new ideas. For instance, Gunnar Myrdal (1979) has shown that economic growth in Third World nations is often hampered by "soft state" arrangements; the effectiveness of the political institution is impaired by deficiencies in law enforcement, momentous corruption, and widespread tax evasion. Many forces, then, converge in hindering development.

THINKING THROUGH THE ISSUES

Industrial nations make lavish use of energy. Ever since the steam engine was invented, heat engines burning fossil fuels have placed enormous power at the elbows of the inhabitants of affluent countries. Now that the citizens of the world are confronting high social and environmental costs associated with the pollution of the land, sea, and atmosphere, Americans are demanding that industries engage in pollution abatement. Would the United States be justified in demanding that developing Third World nations transfer a significant fraction of their limited industrial resources from development to the abatement of pollution? Now that "we have ours," are we entitled to request a change in the rules of the game (under the old rules the cost of industrialization was underwritten in part by environmental pollution)? What happens to ecological balances if 1 billion Chinese and 800 million Indians "modernize" to the point where they pollute at the rate of 235 million Americans (Gamst, 1974)?

Looking to the Future

We look to the past for the roots of the present and to both the past and the present for what the future may hold. In fact, we undertake many of our daily activities in anticipation of the future. We carry out our job responsibilities in the expectation that we will be remunerated at the end of the week or the month. We make arrangements for future events, including football games, parties, spring break, final examinations, and graduation exercises. We invest our money, energy, and time in an education based on the assumption that there will be a job payoff down the road. We may involve ourselves in environmental and antinuclear movements in order to have a voice in the fashioning of tomorrow's world. Because the future is so important to us, we look to experts from a wide range of disciplines to give us some idea of what we can expect in the weeks, years, and decades ahead. Some scholars, known as **futurists,** specialize in the study of the future.

Ways of Anticipating the Future

Futurists are not in the business of *predicting* the future, they know that the future is not predictable. Obviously, we cannot *know* what will happen tomorrow. But we can attempt to anticipate what is likely to happen. In doing so, we can devise strategies that we hope will alter undesirable trends or cushion their impact. Consider the case of the emperor of Japan. Toward the conclusion of World War II, Allied leaders had to decide what to do about the Japanese emperor. American public opinion would have overwhelmingly favored his being tried and executed for war crimes. But social scientists familiar with Japanese culture said that the Japanese were intensely loyal to their emperor. His execution might lead to massive unrest and could cost countless lives. On the other hand, he could be a vital asset in rallying the Japanese to support the occupation forces. The emperor's life was spared and, at his urging, American troops secured the full cooperation of his people in the postwar era. Clearly, futurists could not have known in advance whether or not the plan would succeed; the emperor might have abdicated or been assassinated. But, although thinking ahead does not guarantee success, it can certainly contribute to success (World Future Society, 1986).

What methods are available to us for anticipating the future?

- *Trend projection:* We can take data regarding past and present events, depict the data on a chart or graph, and with lines or rays extend the trend into the future. The Census Bureau uses this procedure in making many of its projections. For instance, it projects that the proportion of the labor force from 16 to 24 years old will shrink from 30 percent in 1985 to 16 percent in the year 2000. Higher education, business, and the military will be competing for this segment of the population for students, employees, and recruits.

- *Models:* We can imitate events that occur in the real world in ways that help us to understand them better. Architects use this approach when they fashion a miniature model of a skyscraper to gain an idea of how the finished product will look. Sociologists do much the same thing when they use maps—two-dimensional models—to anticipate how the American population is likely to be distributed in the year 2000.

- *Simulations:* A model is a static representation of something. Its dynamic twin is the simulation. Generals and admirals simulate battles when they engage in war games that involve real troops and weapons. If you have played Monopoly, you have simulated the real estate market. Sociologists simulate group behavior when they undertake jury research in which they vary social status, education, age, gender, marital status, ethnic origin, religion, and personality traits of the members.

- *Computer simulations:* Complex systems, such as the United States economy, can be modeled by means of mathematical equations that researchers can then feed into a computer. Economists follow this procedure when they ask "What if" questions, such as "What if we increase the income tax rate by 15 percent?" Such a policy change is likely to have

far-reaching ramifications, many of which the economists would not have anticipated, due to the complex interaction of many variables. Sociologists engage in computer simulations when they seek to track the impact of family background and educational variables in status attainment processes (see Chapter 9).

- *Consulting experts:* Since "two heads are often better than one," we can ask experts for their opinions about the future. For example, Louis Harris and Associates, a polling organization, interviewed 227 biomedical specialists (including 6 who had won the Nobel Prize) to gain some idea regarding medical priorities and promising areas of research as the next century dawns. The survey found that 34 percent of the scientists said cardiovascular diseases would be the leading health problem in industrialized countries in the year 2000, while 27 percent specified age-related problems. Seven percent chose AIDS, and the remainder selected other illnesses (Schmeck, 1987).

Again, let us remind ourselves of this point: When social scientists use these techniques, they are not predicting the future. Many popular writers on social change confuse predictions with projections and descriptions with prescriptions by claiming to do the former when actually indulging in the latter (Nimbark, 1986).

Coping with a Different Future

The complexity of society makes it exceedingly difficult to predict the distant future with accuracy, and even the not too distant future is often hard to anticipate. Even so, one thing seems certain: We will not live all of our lives in the world into which we were born, nor will we die in the world in which we worked in our maturity. Futurists have identified two changes that seem to be central to contemporary social life. First, the United States is being restructured from an industrial to an information society. Second, modern societies are increasingly shifting from a national to a global economy. Futurists have applied to a good many metaphors to these changes, including Daniel Bell's "postindustrial society," Alvin Toffler's (1980) "the third wave," and John Naisbitt's (1982) "megatrends." Common to these metaphors is the notion that American society is shifting from the production of goods to the production of services and from a society based on the coordination of people and ma-

Human Settlement of Other Planets?
What do you think would be the social implications of the settlement of other planets for the people on planet Earth? What changes would be required in our social structures? What problems would confront the colonists on other planets? What institutional arrangements would they have to evolve? *(David A. Hardy/Science Photo Library/Photo Researchers)*

chines to a society organized around knowledge. These changes, it is contended, will afford a myriad of choices. The world will increasingly be one of many flavors, not just vanilla or chocolate.

Many observers of contemporary American life believe that we are witnessing a historical change and the first major impact of the shift from an energy economy to an information economy (Drucker, 1985). For three hundred years technology has been cast in a mechanical model, one based on the combustion processes that go on inside a star like the sun. The steam engine opened the mechanical age, and it reached its apex with the discovery of nuclear fission and nuclear fusion, which replicated the energy-producing processes of a star. We now seem to be moving toward a biological model based on information and involving the intensive use of materials. Although biological processes need physical energy and materials, they tend to substitute information for both. Biological processes "miniaturize" size, energy, and materials by "exploding" information. The human

brain is some ten times the size and weight of the brain of a lemur (a lower primate), but it handles a billion times more information. The miniaturization is on the order of 10 to the ninth power, and it is far ahead of what the microchip has achieved. As a result, high-tech industries are information-intensive rather than energy- or materials-intensive. Sociologists have played and will continue to play an important role in assessing and interpreting these developments and other aspects of change.

THINKING THROUGH THE ISSUES

The Census Bureau has made a number of projections regarding the nation's population. What national policies do you think the following projections call for?

1. The proportion of the labor force from 16 to 24 years old will shrink from 30 percent in 1985 to 16 percent in the year 2000.

2. An estimated 29 percent of the net growth in the workforce during the next 15 years will be in minority groups. Yet high school dropout rates, which run nearly 30 percent nationally, are 40 to 50 percent higher in inner-city areas with large minority populations.

3. Women will account for about 63 percent of the new entrants into the labor force between 1985 and 2000 and will increase their demand for child care.

4. Between 2 and 3 percent of the nation's labor force—which is projected to reach about 135 million by the year 2000—will need to be retrained each year.

5. In the next decade, about 6 million more jobs are projected in the most skilled occupations—executive, professional, and technical—compared to only about a million new jobs in the less-skilled and laborer categories.

6. About 13 percent of U.S. adults are illiterate in English. This statistic means that between 17 and 21 million Americans will have difficulty reading a job notice, filling out an employment application, or understanding an instruction manual.

Chapter Highlights

1. Society is in constant flux. Most changes take place in small increments over long periods of time and pass unnoticed. Of course, social change can also occur precipitously in response to a natural disaster, war, acts of terrorism, collective behavior, or social revolution.

2. Social change confronts people with new situations and compels them to fashion new forms of action. A great many factors interact to generate changes in behavior and in the culture and structure of a society. Sociologists identify a number of particularly critical factors, including the physical environment, population, clashes over resources and values, supporting values and norms, innovation, and diffusion.

3. Many of sociology's roots lie in the effort to unravel the "meaning" of history and to establish laws of social change and development. The major sociological perspectives on social change fall within four broad categories: evolutionary perspectives, cyclical perspectives, functionalist perspectives, and conflict perspectives. Evolutionary theorists, particularly those with a unilinear focus, depict history as divided into steplike levels that constitute sequential stages and that are characterized by an underlying trend. Cyclical theorists look to the course of a civilization or society, searching for generalizations regarding their stages of growth and decline. Functionalist theorists see society as a system that tends toward equilibrium. And conflict theorists hold that tensions between competing groups are the basic source of social change.

4. The computer revolution is having a broad impact on people's lives. Computers promise to automate some workplace activities that are now performed by people. They have consequences for the use and manipulation of social power. Computers alter the manner in which people relate to one another. And they have implications for individual privacy and the confidentiality of communications and personal data.

5. Visionaries look to technology to make human lives richer and freer. But not all experts are optimistic about the economic impact of technology on our lives. They worry that machines will replace human beings and create mass unemployment. And they express concern that technology will dehumanize the workplace. It seems that technology has the double impact of job creation and job displacement, eliminating semiskilled and unskilled jobs while increasing the demand for technically trained workers.

6. Sociologists have approached social change in Third World nations from two somewhat differing perspectives. The modernization approach sees development as entailing a pattern of convergence as societies become increasingly urban, industry comes to overshadow agriculture, the size and density of the population increases, the division of labor becomes more specialized, and the knowledge base grows larger and more complex. The world system or dependency approach views development within the context of an international, geographic division of labor. According to world system analysis, an unequal exchange takes place between core and periphery nations, with development at the former end of the chain coming at the cost of underdevelopment at the other end.

7. Because the future is so important to us, we look to experts from a wide range of disciplines to give us some idea of what we can expect in the weeks, years, and decades ahead. However, futurists are not in the business of predicting the future. The future is not predictable; we can only attempt to anticipate what is likely to happen. In anticipating the future, futurists use a variety of methods: trend projection, models, simulations, computer simulations, and consulting experts.

The Sociologist's Vocabulary

cultural lag The view that nonmaterial culture must constantly "catch up" with material culture, resulting in an adjustment gap between the two forms of culture.

diffusion The process by which cultural traits spread from one social unit to another.

discovery An addition to knowledge.

futurists Scholars specializing in the study of the future who seek to understand, anticipate, and plan the future of society.

invention The use of existing knowledge in a new form.

modernization The process by which a society moves from traditional or preindustrial social and economic arrangements to those characteristic of industrial societies.

social change Fundamental alterations in the patterns of culture, structure, and social behavior over time.

world system An approach that views development as involving an unequal exchange between core and periphery nations, with development at the former end of the chain coming at the cost of underdevelopment at the other end.

achieved status A status people secure on the basis of choice and competition.

acting crowd An excited, volatile collection of people who are engaged in rioting, looting, or other forms of aggressive behavior in which established norms carry little weight.

affirmative action programs Government mandates that priorities be established in the recruitment and hiring of minorities and timetables be set for reaching employment goals; minorities are then hired as a matter of right in proportion to their numbers.

age cohort Persons born in the same time interval.

age norms Rules that specify what constitutes appropriate and inappropriate behavior for people at various periods of the life span.

age sets Groups of people of similar age and sex who move at prescribed intervals from one age grade to another.

age strata Social layers based on time periods in life; they serve as a basis for allocating roles and for drawing social divisions.

aggregate A collection of anonymous people who are in one place at the same time.

agrarian societies Peasant societies based on plow agriculture that allow for the emergence of complex forms of social organization and stratification.

alienation A pervasive sense of powerlessness, meaninglessness, normlessness, social isolation, and self-estrangement.

altruistic behavior (also *prosocial behavior*) Behavior that benefits others and is not linked to personal gain.

androgyny A standard that allows individuals to express the full range of human emotions and role possibilities without regard to gender stereotypes.

animism A belief in spirits or otherworldly beings.

anomie People are unsure of what is expected of them, and they find it difficult to fashion their actions in terms of conventional norms.

anticipatory socialization People think about, experiment with, and try on the behaviors associated with a new role.

archival research The use of existing records that have been produced or maintained by persons or organizations other than the researcher.

asceticism A way of life characterized by hard work, sobriety, thrift, restraint, and the avoidance of earthly pleasures.

ascribed status A position arbitrarily assigned to an individual by a group or society.

assimilation Processes whereby groups with distinctive identities become culturally and socially fused.

attribution A process by which we attempt to make sense of behavior by uncovering the reasons why people act as they do.

authoritarianism A political system in which the government tolerates little or no opposition to its rules, but permits nongovernmental centers of influence and allows debate on issues of public policy.

authority Legitimate power.

back region A place in social life offstage where actors retire to prepare themselves for their social performance.

bilineal Reckoning descent and transmitting property through both the father's and mother's sides of the family.

biological age The chronological time that elapses after birth and is associated with changes in the organism.

birth rate The number of live births per 1,000 members of a population in a given year.

body language Physical motions and gestures that provide social signals.

bureaucracy A social structure made up of a hierarchy of statuses and roles that is prescribed by explicit rules and procedures and based on a division of function and authority.

capitalist economies Economic systems that rely heavily on free markets and privately held property.

caste system A system in which ascribed statuses provide the principal basis for the unequal distribution of social resources.

casual crowd A collection of people who have little in common except that they may be participating in a common event, such as looking through a department-store window.

category A collection of people who share a characteristic that is deemed to be of social significance.

charismatic authority Power that is legitimated by the extraordinary superhuman or supernatural attributes people impute to a leader.

church A religious organization that asserts its lone legitimacy and seeks a positive relationship with the dominant institutions of society.

city A relatively dense and permanent concentration of people who secure their livelihood chiefly through nonagricultural activities.

civil religion Elements of nationalism and patriotism that take on the properties of a religion.

class conflict The notion advanced by Karl Marx that all history is composed of struggles between classes.

class system A system in which achieved statuses provide the principal basis for the unequal distribution of social resources.

closed system A stratification system in which people have great difficulty changing status.

coercion Illegitimate power.

coercive organization A formal organization that people become members of against their will.

cognition Mental activity; the process of thinking whereby we receive raw sensory information that we in turn transform, elaborate, store, recover, and use.

collective behavior Ways of thinking, feeling, and acting that develop among a large number of people and that are relatively novel and not well defined.

commune A group or community people intentionally form in order to establish family-like relationships among unrelated individuals.

communication The process by which people transmit information, ideas, attitudes, and mental states to one another.

community A relatively self-contained social unit whose members share a sense of belonging together and a common territorial base.

complementary needs Two different personality traits that are the counterparts of each other and provide a sense of completeness when they are joined.

concentric circle model The approach to city growth that says that the modern city assumes a pattern of concentric circles, each with distinctive characteristics.

conditioning The process of learning whereby we establish an association or link between two events.

conglomerates Companies whose components operate in completely different markets and produce largely unrelated products.

constraints Resources that allow one party to add new disadvantages to a situation.

constructed reality Meaning is not something that inheres in things; it is a property that derives from, or arises out of, the interaction that takes place among people in the course of their daily lives.

contagion theory An approach to crowd behavior that emphasizes the part rapidly communicated and un-

critically accepted feelings, attitudes, and actions play in crowd settings.

control group In scientific research, the group that provides a neutral standard against which the changes in an experimental group can be measured.

conventional crowd A number of people who have assembled for some specific purpose and who typically act in accordance with established norms, such as people attending a baseball game or concert.

convergence theory An approach to crowd behavior that says a crowd consists of a highly unrepresentative body of people who assemble because they share the same predispositions.

core regions Geographical areas that dominate the economy of the world and exploit the rest of the system.

corporate crime Crime committed by business organizations.

corporate interlocks Networks of individuals who serve on the boards of directors of multiple corporations.

correlation The term—or measurement—employed in scientific research referring to change in one variable that is associated with change in another variable.

correspondence principle The notion set forth by Samuel Bowles and Herbert Gintis that the social relations of work find expression in the social relations of the school.

counterculture A subculture—norms, values, traditions, and a lifestyle—that is at odds with the ways of the larger society.

crazes Fads that become virtually all-consuming passions.

credentialism The requirement that a worker have a degree attesting to skills not needed for the performance of a job.

crime An act prohibited by law.

criminal justice system The reactive agencies of the state that include the police, the courts, and prisons.

crowd A temporary, relatively unorganized gathering of people who are in close physical proximity.

cult A religious organization that accepts the legitimacy of other groups but often finds fault with the dominant society.

cultural lag The view that nonmaterial culture must constantly "catch up" with material culture, resulting in an adjustment gap between the two forms of culture.

cultural relativism A value-free or neutral approach that views the behavior of a people from the perspective of their own culture.

cultural universals Patterned and recurrent aspects of social life that appear in all known societies.

culture The social heritage of a people; learned patterns for thinking, feeling, and acting that characterize a population or society, including the expression of these patterns in material and nonmaterial ways.

culture of poverty The view that the poor have self-perpetuating lifeways characterized by weak ego structures, lack of impulse control, present-time orientation, and a sense of resignation and fatalism.

death rate The number of deaths per 1,000 members of a population in a given year.

definition of the situation The interpretation we give to our immediate circumstances; we mentally represent our environment in symbolic terms so that we can size it up and gain a preliminary assessment of the courses of action available to us.

deindividualization People temporarily losing their sense of personal identity and responsibility, which can lead them to do things they would usually not do when alone.

democracy A political system in which the powers of government derive from the consent of the governed, and in which regular constitutional avenues exist for changing government officials.

demographic transition A view of population change which holds that the process of modernization passes through three stages: high potential growth, transitional growth, and population stability.

demography The science dealing with the size, distribution, and composition of, and changes in, population.

demonstration experiment A procedure that introduces a nasty surprise in a situation in order to reveal the underlying expectations of which we are normally unaware.

denomination A religious organization that accepts the legitimacy claims of other religions and enjoys a positive relationship with the dominant society.

dependent variable The variable that is affected in a scientific study; it is preceded in time by the independent variable.

deviance Behavior a considerable number of people view as reprehensible and beyond the limits of tolerance.

dialectical materialism The notion contained in the works of Karl Marx that development depends on the clash of contradictions and the creation of new, more advanced structures out of these clashes.

differential association The notion that the earlier, the more frequently, the more intensely, and the longer the duration of the contacts people have in deviant settings, the greater the probability that they too will become deviant.

diffusion The process by which cultural traits spread from one social unit to another.

discovery An addition to knowledge.

discrimination The arbitrary denial of privilege, prestige, and power to members of a minority group whose qualifications are equal to those of members of the dominant group.

disease A condition in which an organism does not function properly due to presumed biological causes.

doctrine of predestination The idea taught by John Calvin that a person's status in the afterlife is predetermined and not affected by how one behaves on earth.

dramaturgy A sociological perspective in which the social world is portrayed as a natural theater akin to the dramatic performances on the stage.

dual labor market An economy characterized by two sectors. The primary sector offers "good jobs" and the secondary sector offers "bad jobs."

duties Actions others can legitimately insist that we perform.

dyad A two-member group.

dysfunctions Those consequences that lessen the adaptation or adjustment of a system.

ecology The scientific study of the relationship between living organisms and their environment.

economic system The social institution responsible for the production and distribution of goods and services.

ecosystem A relatively stable community of organisms that have established interlocking relationships and exchanges with one another in their natural habitat.

education The transmission of certain attitudes, knowledge, and skills to the members of a society through formal, systematic training.

educational self-fulfilling prophecies (also called *teacher-expectation effects*) The fact that many children fail to learn, especially lower-class and minority children, because those who are charged with teaching them do not believe that they will learn, do not expect that they can learn, and do not act toward them in ways that help them to learn.

egocentric bias The tendency to place yourself at the center of events.

emergent-norm theory An approach to crowd behavior that says crowd members evolve new standards for behavior in a crowd setting and then enforce the expectations in the manner of norms.

endogamy The requirement that marriage occur within a group.

epidemiology The study of the distribution of diseases among and within populations.

equalitarian An arrangement in which power is equally distributed between husband and wife.

equilibrium A self-maintaining order; the tendency for a system to achieve some sort of balance among contending forces.

ethic The perspective and values engendered by a religious way of thinking.

ethnic group A group that is identified chiefly on cultural grounds—language, folk practices, dress, gestures, mannerisms, religion.

ethnocentrism Judging the behavior of other groups by the standards of our own culture.

ethnomethodology Procedures—the rules and activities—that people employ in making social life and society intelligible to themselves and others.

exogamy The requirement that marriage occur outside a group.

experiment Researchers work with two groups that are identical in all relevant respects. They introduce a change in one group, but not in the other group. The procedure permits researchers to test the effects of an independent variable on a dependent variable.

experimental group The group in which researchers introduce a change in an experiment.

expressive crowd An aggregation of people who have gotten together for self-stimulation and personal gratification, such as at a religious revival or a rock festival.

expressive movement Movements that are less concerned with institutional change than with a renovating or renewing of people from within.

extended family A family arrangement in which kin—individuals related by common ancestry—provide the core relationship; spouses are functionally marginal.

facts Agreed-upon statements about what we observe.

fad A folkway that lasts for a short time and enjoys acceptance among only a segment of the population.

family A social group whose members are related by ancestry, marriage, or adoption and who live together, cooperate economically, and care for the young.

family life cycle Changes and realignments related to the altered expectations and requirements imposed on a husband and wife as children are born and grow up.

family of orientation A nuclear family that consists of oneself and one's father, mother, and siblings.

family of procreation A nuclear family that consists of oneself and one's spouse and children.

fashion A folkway that lasts for a short time and enjoys widespread acceptance within society.

fecundity The potential number of children that could be born if every woman of childbearing age bore all the children she possibly could.

fertility The number of babies born to the average woman of childbearing age.

folkways Norms people do not deem to be of great importance and to which they exact less stringent conformity.

force Power whose basis is the threat or application of punishment.

formal organization A social group that is deliberately created for the achievement of specific objectives.

free-rider mechanism Left to our own rational self-interest, we often are tempted to take unfair advantage of contributions others make to the community as a whole.

front region A place in social life that parallels the stage seen by the audience.

functions Those consequences that permit the adaptation or adjustment of a system.

fundamental attribution error Overestimating the extent to which the actions of other people derive from their underlying dispositions or "personality."

futurists Scholars specializing in the study of the future who seek to understand, anticipate, and plan the future of society.

gatekeeping The decision-making process whereby people are admitted to offices and positions of privilege, prestige, and power within a society.

Gemeinschaft A concept introduced by Ferdinand Toennies that describes binding, personal relationships rooted in customary roles, long-standing obligations, and mutual trust.

gender The social creation of girls, boys, women, and men.

gender identities The conceptions we have of ourselves as being male or female.

gender roles Sets of cultural expectations that define the ways in which the members of each sex should behave.

generalized other The term George Herbert Mead applied to that social unit that gives to individuals their unity of self. The attitude of the generalized other is the attitude of the larger community.

genocide The deliberate and systematic extermination of a racial or ethnic group.

Gesellschaft A concept introduced by Ferdinand Toennies that describes relationships dominated by self-interest and competition, with people's interests protected formally by contract and law.

government Those individuals and groups who control the state apparatus and direct state power.

group marriage The marriage of two or more husbands and two or more wives.

groupthink A decision-making process found in highly cohesive groups in which the members become so preoccupied with maintaining group consensus that their critical faculties become impaired.

growth rate The difference between births and deaths, plus the difference between immigrants and emigrants per 1,000 population.

health A state of complete physical, mental, and social well-being, and not merely the absence of disease or infirmity.

health-maintenance organizations (HMOs) A physician, a group of physicians, a hospital, or other organization providing members with comprehensive health care for a fixed sum of money each year.

hermaphrodites Individuals whose reproductive structures are sufficiently ambiguous that it is difficult to define them exclusively as male or female.

heterosexuality A sexual preference for a person of the opposite sex as a partner.

hidden curriculum The whole complex of unarticulated values, attitudes, and behaviors that reflect the dominant views of the community, that are imparted by the school.

homogamy The tendency of like to marry like.

homosexuality A sexual preference for a person of the same sex as a partner.

horizontal mobility Movement from one social status to another that is approximately equivalent in rank.

horticultural societies Societies in which members clear the land by means of slash and burn technology, raise crops with the digging stick or hoe, and move on to new plots as the soil becomes exhausted.

hospice A program or mode of care that attempts to make the dying experience less painful and emotionally traumatic for patients and their families.

human development The processes of sequential change that take place over the life span, beginning with conception and ending with death.

human ecology The interrelationships that operate among people and their physical environment.

hunting and gathering societies Societies in which individuals survive by foraging for edible foods, fishing, collecting shellfish, and hunting animals.

hypothesis A trial idea; a testable statement that an expected outcome will result from particular conditions.

ideal type A concept constructed by a sociologist to portray the principal characteristics of a phenomenon.

ideology A set of beliefs and myths; the ideas that provide individuals with conceptions of the purposes of a social movement, a rationale for the movement's existence, an indictment of existing conditions, and a design for action.

illness The sense we have that we are afflicted by a disease.

impression management The term Erving Goffman applied to the process by which we present ourselves to others in ways that will lead them to view us in a favorable light.

incest taboos Rules that prohibit sexual intercourse with close blood relatives.

income The amount of money people receive.

independent variable The variable that causes an effect in a scientific study; it precedes in time the phenomenon it causes, the dependent variable.

index crime Crimes reported by the Federal Bureau of Investigation in its *Uniform Crime Report*. These offenses consist of four categories of violent crimes against people—murder, rape, robbery, and assault—and four categories of crimes against property—burglary, theft, motor vehicle theft, and arson.

inducements Resources that allow one party to add new advantages to a situation.

industrial societies Societies based on machine technologies in which the energy needed for work activities comes from hydroelectric plants, petroleum, and natural gas, rather than from people or animals.

infant mortality rate The number of deaths among infants under 1 year of age per 1,000 live births.

informal organization Interpersonal networks and ties that arise in a formal organization but that are not defined or prescribed by it.

ingroup A group with which we identify and to which we belong.

institution An enduring set of cultural patterns and social relationships organized to accomplish basic social tasks.

institutional ageism The systematic negative stereotyping of and discrimination against people because they are old.

institutional discrimination The systematic discrimination against the members of some groups by the institutions of society.

institutional sexism Those social arrangements and enduring patterns by which members of one gender group realize more benefits and fewer burdens than members of the other gender group.

interest People who share common concerns or points of view.

interest groups Organizations of people who have common concerns or points of view.

intergenerational mobility A comparison of the social status of parents and their children at some point in their respective careers.

internal migration Population movement within a nation.

internalization Incorporating within one's personality the standards of behavior prevalent within the large society.

international migration Population movement among nations.

intragenerational mobility A comparison of the social status of a person over an extended period of time.

invasion A new type of people, institution, or activity encroaching on an area occupied by a different type.

invention The use of existing knowledge in a new form.

the iron law of oligarchy The principle set forth by Robert Michels that leaders seldom reflect the democratic aspirations espoused by their organizations. Instead, they use their offices to advance their own fortunes and self-interests.

kin selection Evolution favoring genes that improve the chances of the group's survival.

labor unions Organizations formed by workers to bargain collectively with employers for higher wages, improved working conditions, job security, fringe benefits, and grievance procedures.

language A socially structured system of sound patterns (words and sentences) with specific and arbitrary meanings.

latent functions Those consequences that are unintended and often not recognized by the participants in a system.

laws Rules that are enforced by a political body (the state) composed of people who enjoy the right to employ force.

learning The more or less permanent modification of behavior that results from experiences in the environment.

legal-rational authority Power that is legitimated by explicit rules and rational procedures which define the rights and duties of the occupants of given positions.

leisure An activity we choose for its own sake.

life chances The likelihood that individuals and groups will enjoy desired goods and services, fulfilling experiences, and opportunities for living healthy and long lives.

life events Turning points at which people change some direction in the course of their lives.

life expectancy The number of years of life remaining to an average person of a certain age.

life review The taking stock of one's life that often occurs when people learn of their impending death.

lifestyle The overall pattern of living people evolve to meet their biological, social, and emotional needs.

linguistic relativity hypothesis The view that each language "slices up" the world differently; the limits of our language become the limits of our world.

looking-glass self The term Charles Horton Cooley applied to the process by which we imaginatively assume the stance of other people and view ourselves as we believe they see us.

macrosociology The study of large-scale and long-term social processes.

mana The notion that there is in nature a diffuse, impersonal, supernatural force operating for good or evil.

manifest functions Those consequences that are intended and usually recognized by the participants in a system.

marriage A socially approved sexual union between two or more individuals that is undertaken with some idea of permanence.

mass People who, even though physically dispersed, respond to the same event in much the same way.

mass hysteria The rapid spreading of frenzied fears and activity among large numbers of people who feel threatened by a mysterious force.

mass media Those organizations—television, radio, motion pictures, newspapers, and magazines—that convey information to a large segment of the population.

master status A key or core status that carries primary weight in a person's interactions and relationships with others.

matching hypothesis The notion that we typically experience the greatest payoff and the least cost when we select partners who have a degree of physical attractiveness similar to our own.

material culture Physical artifacts or objects that are made by humans.

matriarchy Reckoning descent and inheritance through the mother's side of the family.

matrilineal Reckoning descent and inheritance through the mother's side of the family.

matrilocal Bride and groom living in the household or community of the wife's family.

mechanical solidarity A form of social integration that characterized early societies in which a sense of oneness was derived from the fact that all the members of the society engaged in essentially similar tasks.

medicalization of deviance More and more behaviors earlier generations considered immoral or sinful coming to be regarded as forms of sickness.

medicine The social institution responsible for problems of health and illness.

megalopolis A strip city formed when the rural interstices between metropolitan centers fill with urban development.

microsociology The detailed study of what individuals say, do, and think as they go about their daily lives.

migration The movement of people from one geographic area to another in order to establish a new residence.

minority group A racially or culturally self-conscious population, with hereditary membership and a high degree of ingroup marriage, which suffers at the hands of a dominant segment of a nation-state.

modernization The process by which a society moves from traditional or preindustrial social and economic arrangements to those characteristic of industrial societies.

monogamy The marriage of one husband and one wife.

monotheism The belief in one god.

mores Norms to which people attach a good deal of importance and exact strict conformity.

mortification Rituals employed by coercive organizations that render individuals vulnerable to institutional control, discipline, and resocialization.

multinational corporations Firms that have their central office in one country and subsidiaries in other countries.

multiple nuclei model The approach to city growth that assumes a city has several centers, each of which specializes in some activity and gives its distinctive cast to the surrounding area.

natural areas Geographic areas with distinctive characteristics.

natural history of revolutions The view that social revolutions past through a set of common stages and patterns in the course of development.

natural selection A notion central to evolutionary theory that those organisms best adapted survive and pass on their genetic characteristics to their offspring. Consequently, later generations resemble their better-adapted ancestors.

nature Inherited traits; heredity.

negotiated order The fluid, ongoing understandings and agreements that people reach with one another as they go about their daily activities.

neolocal Newlyweds set up a new place of residence independent of either their parents or other relatives.

nonmaterial culture Abstract creations like values, beliefs, symbols, norms, customs, and institutional arrangements formed by the members of a society.

norm of legitimacy The rule that children not be born out of wedlock.

norm of reciprocity The social rule that we should help and not harm those who help us.

norms Social rules or guidelines that specify the behavior that is and is not appropriate in given situations.

nuclear family A family arrangement in which the spouses and their offspring constitute the core relationship; blood relatives are functionally marginal.

nurture Experiences; environment.

objective method An approach to the identification of social classes that employs such yardsticks as income, occupation, and education.

observational learning By watching other people, we learn new responses without first having had the opportunity to make the responses ourselves.

oligarchy The concentration of power in the hands of a few individuals who use their offices to advance their own fortunes and self-interests.

oligopoly A market dominated by a few firms.

open system A stratification system in which people can change status with relative ease.

operant conditioning Learning in which behavior is altered in strength by its consequences.

operational definition Taking an abstract concept and putting it in a form that permits its measurement.

organic solidarity A form of social integration that characterizes modern societies. A society is held together by the interdependence fostered by the differences among people.

organized crime Large-scale bureaucratic organizations that provide illegal goods and services in public demand.

outgroups Groups with which we do not identify and to which we do not belong.

panic The uncoordinated flight of people from some perceived danger.

paradigm A fundamental image or vision regarding the nature of the world.

paralanguage Nonverbal cues surrounding speech—pitch, loudness, tempo, hesitations, and sighs—that are a rich source of communicative information.

Parkinson's law Work expands so as to fill the time available for its completion.

participant observation A research technique in which investigators engage in activities with the people that they are observing.

pastoral societies Societies that depend primarily on domesticated herds of animals for their livelihood.

patriarchy The vesting of power in the family in men.

patrilineal Reckoning descent and inheritance through the father's side of the family.

patrilocal A bride and groom living in the household or community of the husband's family.

peers Individuals who are approximately the same age.

periphery regions Geographical areas that provide raw materials to core regions and are exploited by it.

personal space A kind of portable territory that others cannot intrude upon without making us feel uncomfortable and that we defend against intrusion.

personality Unique and enduring behavior patterns of an individual.

persuasion Resources that enable one party to change the minds of other people without adding either advantages or disadvantages to the situation.

pluralism A situation where diverse groups coexist and accommodate themselves to their differences.

POET complex The interdependencies among four ecological factors: population (P), organization (O), environment (E), and technology (T).

political action committees Interest groups set up to elect or defeat candidates independently of regular party organizations.

political institution The social structure concerned with the use and distribution of power within a society.

political party A durable organization formed to gain control of the government by putting its people in public office.

pollution The contamination of the environment by wastes or other substances that have a damaging effect on public health and the ecosystem.

polyandry The marriage of two or more husbands and one wife.

polygyny The marriage of one husband and two or more wives.

polytheism The belief in many gods with equal or relatively similar power.

population A group of organisms who are members of the same species and occupy a certain territory.

population pyramid The age and sex composition of a population as portrayed in the tree of ages.

postindustrial societies Societies that center on the provision of services rather than the extracting of raw materials and the manufacturing of goods and that permit the automation of many processes in the workplace.

power The ability of individuals and groups to realize their will in human affairs, even if it involves overcoming the resistance of others.

preferred provider organization (PPO) An arrangement whereby an insurer or employer contracts with a group of physicians to provide its members or employees with health care.

prejudice Attitudes of aversion and hostility toward the members of a group simply because they belong to it and hence are presumed to have the objectionable qualities ascribed to it.

prestige The social respect, admiration, and recognition associated with a particular social status.

primary deviance Behavior that violates social norms but goes unnoticed by the agents of social control.

primary group Two or more people who enjoy a direct, intimate, cohesive relationship with one another.

primary production The extraction of undeveloped natural resources from nature through hunting, gathering, forestry, fishing, farming, herding, and mining.

primary socialization The process by which a person masters the information and skills essential for participating in the routines that compose daily life and evolves a self.

principle of determinism The notion that relations in the world are organized in terms of cause and effect.

privatization The transformation of religion from a public to a personal matter, anchored in individual consciousness.

profane Those aspects of social reality that are everyday and commonplace.

profession An occupation based on systematic and formal knowledge.

property A set of rights that indicates what one party can do and what another party cannot do.

prosocial behavior (also *altruistic behavior*) Behavior that benefits others and is not linked to personal gain.

Protestant ethic The Calvinist ethos that embodied the spirit of capitalism; an attitude that seeks profit rationally and systematically.

proxemics The way we employ social and personal space to transmit messages.

puberty rites Initiation ceremonies that symbolize the transition from childhood to adulthood.

public A collection of people who share an interest in some issue and seek to influence the actions of decision makers.

public interest groups Interest groups that pursue policies which presumably would be of no greater benefit to their members than to the larger society.

public opinion The behavior of a public.

qualitative methodology An approach that seeks to understand behavior without undertaking a precise measurement of it.

quantitative methodology An approach that seeks to understand behavior by counting instances of it.

race Populations who differ in the incidence of various hereditary traits.

random sample Researchers select subjects on the basis of chance so that every individual in the population has the same opportunity to be chosen.

reference group A social unit we use for appraising and shaping our attitudes, feelings, and actions.

reform movement A social movement that pursues changes which will implement the existing value scheme of a society more adequately.

reinforcement The process whereby one event strengthens the probability of another event's occurring.

relationship Social interaction that continues long enough so that we become linked to another person by a relatively stable set of expectations.

relative deprivation A gap between what people actually have and what they have come to expect and feel to be their just due.

religion Those socially shared ways of thinking, feeling, and acting that have do with the supernatural or "beyond."

reputational method An approach for identifying social classes that involves asking people how they classify others.

resistance movement A social movement that arises to block change or eliminate a previously instituted change.

resocialization The learning of new patterns for behavior that run counter to previously acquired patterns.

revolutionary movement A social movement that advocates the replacement of a society's existing value scheme.

rights The actions we can legitimately insist that others perform.

rituals Formal procedures that dictate how people should comport themselves in the presence of the sacred.

role Expectations (rights and duties) that define the behavior people view as appropriate and inappropriate for the occupant of a status.

role conflict A situation in which individuals are confronted with incompatible role requirements.

role making The process of improvising and innovating new features of a role; creating, shaping, and modifying a role as we go about interacting with others.

role performance The actual behavior of the person who occupies a status.

role set The multiple roles associated with a single status.

role strain The stress individuals experience when they encounter difficulties in meeting the requirements of a role.

role taking The process by which we devise our performance based on the feedback other people provide regarding their expectations of us and their assessments of our behavior.

role transition Continually adopting new roles and shedding old ones throughout life.

romantic love The strong physical and emotional attraction between a man and a woman.

rumor A difficult-to-verify piece of information that is transmitted from person to person in relatively rapid fashion.

sacred Anything that is extraordinary, mysterious, awe-inspiring, and even potentially dangerous; those aspects of reality that are set apart and forbidden.

sample Researchers select subjects for study in such a way that they are representative of the larger group or population.

schema A category that is a mental structure for processing and organizing information.

secondary deviance Deviance individuals adopt in response to the reactions of other individuals.

secondary group Two or more people who are involved in an impersonal way and have come together for a specific, practical purpose.

secondary production The processing or converting of raw materials in a fashion that enhances their final consumption value.

sect A religious organization that asserts its lone legitimacy and rejects the lifeways and values of the dominant society.

sector model The approach to city growth which assumes that large cities are made up of sectors—wedge-shaped areas—rather than concentric circles.

secularization thesis The notion that profane (nonreligious) considerations gain ascendancy over sacred (religious) considerations in the course of social evolution.

segregation A process of clustering wherein individuals and groups are sifted and sorted out in space based on sharing certain traits or activities.

self The set of concepts we use in defining who we are.

self-concept An overriding view of yourself; a sense of self through time.

self-image A temporary mental conception or picture you have of yourself that changes as you move from one situation to another.

self-placement method An approach for identifying social classes that involves self-classification.

sick role A role in which people are exempted from their usual social roles and responsibilities.

sickness A social status in which other people define us as having a disease and accordingly alter their behavior toward us.

significant other The term sociologists apply to a social model, usually an important person in a person's life.

social action Behavior that is oriented to or influenced by other people.

social age The placement of people in the social structure based upon socially differentiated phases of the life cycle.

social area analysis An approach to examining urban patterns that focuses on the social characteristics of the population by areas.

social change Fundamental alterations in the patterns of culture, structure, and social behavior over time.

social clock A set of internalized concepts that regulates our progression through the age-related milestones of the adult years.

social control Those methods and strategies that regulate people's behavior within society.

social Darwinism The application of evolutionary notions and the concept of the survival of the fittest to the social world.

social differentiation The process by which the members of a society divide activities and become "different" by virtue of playing distinctive roles.

social dilemma A situation in which members of a group are faced with a conflict between maximizing their personal interests and maximizing the collective welfare.

social dynamics Those aspects of social life that have to do with social change and that pattern institutional development.

social-emotional specialist A leadership role that focuses on overcoming interpersonal problems in a group, defusing tensions, and promoting solidarity.

social exchange A sociological perspective that depicts human beings as social bookkeepers who order their relationships by maintaining a mental ledger of rewards, costs, and profits.

social exchange theory The view which proposes that people involved in a mutually satisfying relationship will exchange behaviors that have low cost and high reward.

social facts Those aspects of social life that cannot be explained in terms of the biological or mental characteristics of the individual. People experience the social fact as external to themselves in the sense that it has an independent reality and forms a part of their objective environment.

social group Two or more people who share a feeling of unity and who are bound together in relatively stable patterns of social interaction.

social interaction The mutual and reciprocal influencing by two or more people of each other's behavior.

social loafing When individuals work in groups, they work less hard than they do when working individually.

social mobility Individuals or groups move from one level (stratum) to another in the stratification system.

social movement A more or less persistent and organized effort on the part of a relatively large number of people to bring about or resist change.

social psychology The scientific study of the nature and causes of social interaction and behavior.

social revolution The overthrow of a society's state and class structures and the fashioning of new social arrangements.

social statics Those aspects of social life that have to do with order and stability and that allow societies to hold together and endure.

social stratification The structured ranking of individuals and groups; their grading into horizontal layers or strata.

social structure The recurrent and patterned relationships that exist among the components of a social system.

social surplus Goods and services over and above those necessary for a society's survival.

socialist economies Economic systems that rely primarily on state planning and publicly held property.

socialization A lifetime process of social interaction by which people acquire the knowledge, attitudes, values, and behaviors essential for effective participation in society.

society A relatively independent, self-perpetuating group of people who occupy the same territory and participate in a common culture.

sociobiology A new and controversial discipline that focuses on the biological foundations for social behavior in species ranging from amoeba colonies to human societies.

sociocultural evolution The long-run trend for societies to change by becoming increasingly complex.

socioeconomic life cycle A sequence of stages that begins with birth into a family with a specific social status and proceeds through childhood, socialization, schooling, job seeking, occupational achievement, marriage, and the formation and functioning of a new family unit.

the sociological imagination The ability to see our lives, concerns, problems, and hopes entwined within the larger social and historical context in which we live.

sociology The scientific study of society, particularly the study of human organization.

special interest groups Interest groups that primarily seek benefits from which their members would derive more gains than the society as a whole.

split labor market An economic arena in which large differences exist in the price of labor at the same occupational level.

sport Competitive physical activity based upon a set of rules.

stages Steplike levels into which human development is divided.

state A social organization that exercises within a given territory an effective monopoly on the use of physical coercion.

status A position in a social structure.

stereotype An unscientific and hence unreliable generalization that we make about people based on our group membership.

stigmatized minorities People who possess some attribute that leads other people to deny them full social acceptance.

strategic elites Powerful individuals and groups who exercise significant power in their own rather specialized domains.

stratified random sample Researchers divide a population into relevant categories and draw a random sample from each of the categories.

structural conduciveness Social conditions that permit a particular variety of collective behavior to occur.

structural strain A condition in which important aspects of a social system are "out of joint" with each other.

style of life The magnitude and manner of people's consumption of goods and services.

subculture A group whose members participate in the mainstream culture of society while simultaneously sharing unique values, norms, traditions, and lifestyles.

succession An invasion continuing until the encroaching type of people, institution, or activity displaces the previous type.

superstructure The notion of Karl Marx that political ideologies, religion, family organization, law, education, and government constitute a level of social life that is shaped primarily by the economic institution.

survey The gathering of information by asking people a number of questions.

symbol Anything that socially has come to stand for something else; an arbitrary sign.

symbolic racism A form of racism in which whites feel that blacks are too aggressive, do not play by the rules, and have negative characteristics.

system A combination of things or parts that form a larger whole.

taboo Prohibition against violating certain mores.

task specialist A leadership role that focuses on appraising the problem at hand and organizing people's activity in dealing with it.

terrorism The use of force or violence against persons or property to intimidate or coerce a government, a formal organization, or a civilian population in furtherance of political, religious, or social objectives.

tertiary production Service activities of one sort or another.

theism A religion centered in a belief in gods who are thought to be powerful, to have an interest in human affairs, and to merit worship.

theoretical perspective A way of looking at various features of the world; an orientation that provides methods for studying various aspects of the social experience and finding explanations for them.

theory A set of interrelated statements that provides an explanation for a class of events.

Thomas theorem The notion that our definitions influence our construction of reality. It was stated by William I. Thomas: "If men [people] define situations as real, they are real in their consequences."

total institutions Places of residence where people are isolated from the rest of society for an appreciable period of time and where their behavior is tightly regimented.

totalitarianism A "total state"—one in which the government undertakes to extend control over all parts of the society and all aspects of social life.

totemism A religious system in which a clan (a kin group) takes the name of, claims descent from, and attributes sacred properties to a plant or animal.

traditional authority Power that is legitimated by the sanctity of age-old customs.

trained incapacity The term Thorstein Veblen applies to the tendency within bureaucracies for members to rely upon established rules and regulations and to apply them in an unimaginative and mechanical fashion.

transsexuals Individuals who have normal sexual organs but who psychologically feel like members of the opposite sex.

triad A three-member group.

unobtrusive observation A research technique in which investigators observe the activities of people without intruding or participating in the activities.

urban ecology An approach to the study of communities that seeks to explain the patterns by which people and institutions come to be distributed in space as an expression of humankind's adaptation to an ever-changing environment.

urban gentrification The return of the middle class—usually young, white, childless professionals—to older urban neighborhoods.

urbanization Growth in the proportion of a population living in cities.

utilitarian organization A formal organization formed to achieve practical ends.

value-added The idea that each step in the production process—from raw materials to the finished product—increases the economic value of manufactured goods. Smelser has applied the notion to collective behavior.

value-free sociology The view of Max Weber that sociologists must not allow their personal biases to affect the conduct of their scientific research.

values Abstract ideas of the desirable, correct, and good that most members of a society share. Values are general and encompassing and do not explicitly specify which behaviors are and are not acceptable.

variable A trait or characteristic that changes under different conditions.

Verstehen An approach to the study of social life developed by Max Weber in which sociologists mentally attempt to place themselves in the shoes of other people and identify what they think and how they feel.

vertical mobility The movement of individuals from one social status to another of higher or lower rank.

victimless crime Offenses in which the parties involved do not consider themselves to be victims.

voluntary organization A formal organization that people enter and leave freely.

war A socially organized form of aggression that involves violent, armed conflict between political contestants.

wealth What people own.

white-collar crime Crimes committed by persons of affluence, often in the course of business activities.

world system An approach that views development as involving an unequal exchange between core and periphery nations, with development at the former end of the chain coming at the cost of underdevelopment at the other end.

zero population growth A stable population: an average of 2.1 children per woman so that a population replaces itself without immigration.

References

Numbers in italic indicate page references in *The Social Experience*.

ABERNATHY, WILLIAM J., KIM B. CLARK, and ALAN M. KANTROW. 1983. *Industrial Renaissance*. New York: Basic Books. *408*

ABRAHAMIAN, ERVAND. 1986. Structural causes of the Iranian revolution. In J. A. Goldstone, Ed., *Revolutions: Theoretical, Comparative, and Historical Studies*. San Diego: Harcourt Brace Jovanovich. *385*

ABRAHAMSON, MARK. 1978. *Functionalism*. Englewood Cliffs, NJ: Prentice-Hall. *31*

ACKERMAN, NATHAN W., and MARIE JAHODA. 1950. *Anti-Semitism and Emotional Disorder*. New York: Harper & Row. *264*

ADAMS, PAUL R., and GERALD R. ADAMS. 1984. Mount Saint Helens' ashfall: Evidence for a disaster stress reaction. *American Psychologist*, 39: 252–260. *494*

ADAMS, ROBERT M. 1982. *Behavioral and Social Science Research: A National Resource*. Washington, DC: National Academy Press. *10*

ADAMS, GORDON. 1983. The 'iron triangle' and the American economy. In Ronald V. Dellums, Ed., *Defense Sense: The Search for a Rational Military Policy*. Cambridge, MA: Ballinger. *460*

ADELSON, JOSEPH. 1979. Adolescence and the generation gap. *Psychology Today*, 12 (February):33–37. *291*

ADLER, PETER, and PATRICIA A. ADLER. 1985. From idealism to pragmatic detachment: The academic performance of college athletes. *Sociology of Education*, 58:241–250. *485*

ADORNO, T. W., ELSE FRENKEL-BRUNSWIK, DANIEL J. LEVINSON, and R. NEVITT SANFORD. 1950. *The Authoritarian Personality*. New York: Harper & Row. *264*

AEI SYMPOSIUM. 1986. The birth dearth. *Public Opinion*, 8 (December/January):18–20. *529*

AGNEW, ROBERT. 1981. The individual and values in human ecology: An examination of the adaptive processes. *The Sociological Quarterly*, 22:105–117. *529*

AGNEW, ROBERT. 1985. A revised strain theory of delinquency. *Social Forces*, 64:151–167. *201*

AINSLIE, RICARDO C., Ed. 1984. *The Child and the Day Care Setting: Qualitative Variations and Development*. New York: Praeger. *353*

AKERS, RONALD L. 1977. *Deviant Behavior*. Belmont, CA: Wadsworth. *202*

AKERS, RONALD L., MARVIN D. KROHN, LONN LANZA-KADUCE, and MARCIA RADOSEVICH. 1979. Social learning and deviant behavior. *American Sociological Review*, 44:636–655. *202*

AKHAVI, SHAHROUGH. 1980. *Religion and Politics in Contemporary Iran: Clergy-State Relations in the Pahlavi Period*. Albany: State University of New York Press. *385*

ALBEE, GEORGE W. 1985. The answer is prevention. *Psychology Today*, 19 (February):60–64. *198*

ALEXANDER, JEFFREY C. 1984. *Theoretical Logic in Sociology, Vol. 4: The Modern Reconstruction of Classical Thought: Talcott Parsons*. Berkeley: University of California Press. *29*

ALEXEYEV, VLADIMIR. 1986. Soviets safeguard basic human rights. *USA Today* (February 13):8A. *66*

'ABD ALLAH, MAHMUD M. 1917. Siwan customs. *Harvard African Studies*, 1:7,20. *329*

ALLEN, WALTER R., and REYNOLDS FARLEY. 1986. The shifting social and economic tides of black America, 1950–1980. *Annual Review of Sociology*, 12:277–306. *269*

ALLPORT, GORDON W. 1954. *The Nature of Prejudice*. Cambridge, MA: Addison-Wesley. *258*

AMERICAN SOCIETY FOR TRAINING AND DEVELOPMENT. 1986. *Serving the New Corporation*. Alexandria, VA: American Society for Training and Development. *606*

AMERICAN SOCIOLOGICAL ASSOCIATION. 1980. Revised ASA code of ethics. *ASA Footnotes* (August):12–13. *52*

ANDERSON, CHARLES H. 1971. *Toward a New Sociology*. Homewood, IL: Dorsey Press. *227,231*

ANDERSON, CHARLES H. 1974. *The Polit-*ical Economy of Social Class*. Englewood Cliffs, NJ: Prentice-Hall. *581*

ANDERSON, ELIJAH. 1978. *A Place On the Corner*. Chicago: University of Chicago Press. *542*

ANDERSON, HARRY. 1984. Carving up the car buyer. *Newsweek* (March 5):72–73. *408*

ANDERSON, TERRY L. 1987. Camped out in another era. *Wall Street Journal* (January 14):16. *532*

ANDERSON, WILLIAM H. 1987. HMOs' incentives: A prescription for failure. *Wall Street Journal* (January 2):12. *494,504*

ANDREW, JOHN. 1983. As computers change the nature of work, some jobs lose savor. *Wall Street Journal* (May 6):1, 16. *604*

ANSBERRY, CLARE. 1987. Eastman Kodak Co. has arduous struggle to regain lost edge. *Wall Street Journal* (April 2):1, 12. *413*

APPLE, MICHAEL W. 1982. *Education and Power*. London: Routledge & Kegan Paul. *469,471*

APPLE, MICHAEL W., and LOIS WEIS. 1983. *Ideology and Practice in Schooling*. Philadelphia: Temple University Press. *469*

APPLEBOME, PETER. 1986. S.M.U. president, citing health, resigns amid sports dispute. *New York Times* (November 22):8. *484*

APTER, DAVID. 1965. *The Politics of Modernization*. Chicago: University of Chicago Press. *608*

ARENSBERG, CONRAD M., and ARTHUR NIEHOFF. 1964. *Introducing Social Change: A Manual for Americans Overseas*. Chicago: Aldine. *595*

ANDERSON, L. S., THEODORE G. CHIRICOS, and GORDON P. WALDO. 1977. Formal and informal sanctions: A comparison of deterrent effects. *Social Problems*: 25:103–114. *215*

ARIES, PHILIPPE. 1962. *Centuries of Childhood*. Trans. R. Baldick. New York: Random House. *288*

ARIES, PHILIPPE. 1981. *The Hour of Our Death*. New York: Knopf. *296*

ARNEY, WILLIAM R., and BERNARD J. BERGEN. 1984. *Medicine and the*

Management of Living: Taming the Last Great Beast. Chicago: University of Chicago. *491,507*

ARONSON, ELLIOT, MARILYNN BREWER, and J. MERRILL CARLSMITH. 1985. Experimentation in social psychology. In G. Lindzey and E. Aronson, Eds., *Handbook of Social Psychology*, 3rd ed. Vol. 2. New York: Random House. *42*

ARONSON, ELLIOT, and J. MERRILL CARLSMITH. 1962. Performance expectancy as a determinant of actual performance. *Journal of Abnormal and Social Psychology*, 65:178–182. *151*

ASCH, SOLOMON. 1952. *Social Psychology.* Englewood Cliffs, NJ: Prentice-Hall. *120,574*

ASIMOV, ISAAC. 1972. *Asimov's Guide to Science.* New York: Basic Books. *62*

AULETTA, KEN. 1983. *The Underclass.* New York: Vintage Books. *239*

AVERY, DENNIS. 1985. U.S. farm dilemma: The global bad news is wrong. *Science*, 230:408–412. *524*

AXELROD, ROBERT. 1984. *The Evolution of Cooperation.* New York: Basic Books. *185*

BAILY, MARTIN NEIL. 1986. What has happened to productivity growth? *Science*, 234:443–451. *423*

BALCH, ROBERT W. 1979. Two models of conversion and commitment in a UFO cult. Paper presented at the annual meeting of the Pacific Sociological Association, Anaheim, California. *572*

BALDWIN, WILLIAM. 1986. Chicken Little's income statistics. *Forbes* (March 24):68–69. *236*

BALES, ROBERT F. 1970. *Personality and Interpersonal Behavior.* New York: Holt, Rinehart, and Winston. *114*

BALES, ROBERT F., and EDGAR F. BORGATTA. 1955. Size of group as a factor in the interaction profile. In A. P. Hare, E. F. Borgatta, and R. F. Bales, Eds., *Small Groups: Studies in Social Interaction.* New York: Knopf. *114*

BALKWELL, CAROLYN. 1981. Transition to widowhood: A review of the literature. *Family Relations*, 30:117–127. *294*

BALL-ROKEACH, SANDRA J., MILTON ROKEACH, and JOEL W. GRUBE. 1984. *The Great American Values Test: Influencing Behavior and Belief through*

Television. New York: Free Press. *158*

BALTES, PAUL B., and JOHN R. NESSELROADE. 1984. Paradigm lost and paradigm regained: Critique of Dannefer's portrayal of life-span developmental psychology. *American Sociological Review*, 49:841–847. *283*

BANDURA, ALBERT. 1971. *Psychological Modeling: Conflicting Theories.* Chicago: Aldine-Atherton. *311*

BANDURA, ALBERT. 1973. *Aggression: A Social Learning Analysis.* Englewood Cliffs, NJ: Prentice-Hall. *311*

BANE, MARY JO. 1976. *Here to Stay: American Families in the Twentieth Century.* New York: Basic Books. *350*

BAPTIST, BOB. 1984. Football makes it all happen. *Columbus Ohio Dispatch* (March 5):C–1. *108*

BARAN, PAUL, and PAUL M. SWEEZY. 1966. *Monopoly Capital: An Essay on the American Economic and Social Order.* New York: Monthly Review Press. *416*

BARCLAY, A. M. and R. N. HABER. 1965. The relation of aggression to sexual motivation. *Journal of Personality*, 33:462–475. *44*

BARKER, EILEEN. 1984. *The Making of a Moonie.* New York: Basil Blackwell. *572*

BARKER, EILEEN. 1986. Religious movements: Cult and anticult since Jonestown. *Annual Review of Sociology*, 12:329–346. *374*

BARRON, JAMES. 1986. Boom in high-rise offices turning suburbs into satellite 'downtowns.' *New York Times* (August 22):11. *559*

BARRON, JAMES. 1986. Gaps in retraining are seen in era of industrial change. *New York Times* (August 10):1,14. *606*

BART, PAULINE B., and PATRICIA H. O'BRIEN. 1985. *Stopping Rape: Successful Survival Strategies.* New York: Pergamon. *322*

BARTH, FREDRIK. 1960. Nomadism in the mountain and plateau areas of South West Asia. In *The Problems of the Arid Zone.* Paris: UNESCO. *79*

BARTH, FREDRIK. 1968. *Nomads of South Persia.* Boston: Little, Brown. *79*

BARUCH, GRACE, and ROSALIND C. BARNETT. 1983. Adult daughters' relationships with their mothers. *Journal of Marriage and the Family*, 45:601–606. *360*

BARUCH, GRACE, and JAMES BROOKS-GUNN, EDS. 1984. *Women in Midlife:*

Women in Context, Development and Stresses. New York: Plenum Press. *293*

BASS, BERNARD M. 1960. *Leadership, Psychology, and Organizational Behavior.* New York: Harper & Row. *115*

BAUM, JULIAN. 1987. Working on the edge. *Christian Science Monitor* (February 27):16–17. *408*

BAUMEISTER, ROY F. 1984. Choking under pressure: Self-consciousness and paradoxical effects of incentives on skillful performance. *Journal of Personality and Social Psychology*, 46:610–620. *152*

BAUMEISTER, ROY F., and ANDREW STEINHILBER. 1984. Paradoxical effects of supportive audiences on performance under pressure: The home field disadvantage in sports championships. *Journal of Personality and Social Psychology*, 47:85–93. *153*

BECK, E. M., PATRICK HORAN, and CHARLES TOLBERT. 1978. Stratification in a dual economy: A structural model of earnings determination. *American Sociological Review*, 43:704–720. *421*

BECK, E. M., PATRICK HORAN, and CHARLES TOLBERT. 1980. Social stratification in industrial society: Further evidence for a structural alternative. *American Sociological Review*, 45:712–719. *421*

BECK, SCOTT H. 1982. Adjustment to and satisfaction with retirement. *Journal of Gerontology*, 37:616–624. *294*

BECKER, HOWARD S. 1963. *Outsiders: Studies in the Sociology of Deviance.* New York: Free Press. *190,205*

BECKMAN, LINDA J. 1981. Effects of social interaction and children's relative inputs on older women's psychological well-being. *Journal of Personality and Social Psychology*, 41:1075–1086.

BEGLEY, SHARON. 1986. The silent summer. *Newsweek* (June 23):64–65. *515,533*

BEGLEY, SHARON. 1986. Silent spring revisited? *Newsweek* (July 14):72–73. *515,532*

BEIRNE, PIERS. 1979. Empiricism and the critique of Marxism on law and crime. *Social Problems*, 26:373–385. *445*

BELL, ALAN P., and MARTIN S. WEINBERG. 1978. *Homosexualities: A Study of Diversity among Men and Women.*

New York: Simon & Schuster. 328,364

BELL, ALAN P., MARTIN S. WEINBERG, and SUE K. HAMMERSMITH. 1981. *Sexual Preference: Its Development in Men and Women*. Bloomington, IN: Indiana University Press. 328,364

BELL, DANIEL. 1973. *The Coming of the Post-Industrial Society*. New York: Basic Books. 81,610

BELLAH, ROBERT N. 1970. *Beyond Belief*. New York: Harper & Row. 373,394, 395

BELLAH, ROBERT N. 1976. New religious consciousness and the crisis of modernity. In C. Y. Glock and R. N. Bellah, Eds., *The New Religious Consciousness*. Berkeley: University of California Press. 373,394

BELLAH, ROBERT N., and PHILLIP E. HAMMOND. 1980. *Varieties of Civil Religions*. New York: Harper & Row. 395

BELLAH, ROBERT N., RICHARD MADSEN, ANNE SWIDLER, WILLIAM M. SULLIVAN, and STEVEN M. TIPTON. 1985. *Habits of the Heart: Individualism and Commitment in American Life*. Berkeley: University of California Press. 66

BELSKY, JAY, MARY LANG, and TED L. HUSTON. 1986. Sex typing and division of labor as determinants of marital change across the transition to parenthood. *Journal of Personality and Social Psychology*, 50:517–522. 351

BELSKY, JAY, MARY E. LANG, and MICHAEL ROVINE. 1985. Stability and change in marriage across the transition to parenthood: A second study. *Journal of Marriage and the Family*, 47:855–865. 351

BEM, SANDRA L. 1985. Androgeny and gender schema theory: A conceptual and empirical integration. *Nebraska Symposium on Motivation*, 32:179–226. 312

BENDIX, REINHARD. 1977. Bureaucracy. *International Encyclopedia of the Social Sciences*. New York: Free Press. 124

BENET, SULA. 1974. *Abkhasians: The Long-Living People of the Caucasus*. New York: Holt, Rinehart, and Winston. 281

BENNETT, WILLIAM J. 1986. *First Lessons: A Report on Elementary Education in America*. Washington, DC: Government Printing Office. 479

BENSON, J. KENNETH. 1977. Organiza-tions: A dialectical view. *Administrative Science Quarterly*, 22:1–21. 129

BERG, BARBARA. 1986. *The Crisis of the Working Mother*. New York: Summit Books. 353

BERG, ELLEN. 1986. Sociological perspectives on AIDS. *Footnotes* (December):8–9. 497

BERG, ELLEN. 1987. Feminist theory: Moving sociology from the "malestream." *Footnotes* (March):5, 11. 307

BERGER, BRIGITTE, and PETER L. BERGER. 1983. *The War Over the Family: Capturing the Middle Ground*. New York: Anchor Press. 346

BERGER, JOSEPH. 1985. Catholic dissent on church rules found. *New York Times* (November 25):7. 391

BERGER, JOSEPH. 1986a. Split widens on a basic issue: What is a Jew? *New York Times* (February 28):1,18. 392

BERGER, JOSEPH. 1986b. More Jews turning to small congregations for a sense of community. *New York Times* (August 5):11. 392

BERGER, JOSEPH. 1986. Religious surge found among 'baby boomers.' *New York Times* (November 19):9. 388

BERGER, PETER. 1961. *The Noise of Solemn Assemblies*. Garden City, NY: Doubleday. 384,393

BERGER, PETER L. 1963. *Invitation to Sociology*. Garden City, NY: Anchor Books. 5,17,99,100

BERGER, PETER L. 1967. *The Sacred Canopy: Elements of a Sociological Theory of Religion*. Garden City, NY: Doubleday. 371

BERGER, PETER L. 1986. *The Capitalist Revolution*. New York: Basic Books. 405–406

BERGER, PETER L., and HANSFRIED KELLNER. 1964. Marriage and the construction of reality. *Diogenes*, 45:1–25. 345

BERGMANN, BARBARA R. 1987. *The Economic Emergence of Women*. New York: Basic Books. 316

BERK, RICHARD A. 1974a. A gaming approach to crowd behavior. *American Sociological Review*, 39:355–373. 574

BERK, RICHARD A. 1974b. *Collective Behavior*. Dubuque, IA: William C. Brown. 574

BERK, RICHARD A., and PHYLLIS J. NEWTON. 1985. Does arrest really deter wife battery? An effort to replicate the findings of the Minneapolis spouse abuse experiment. *American Sociological Review*, 50:253–262. 360

BERKMAN, L. F., and L. BRESLOW. 1983. *Health and Ways of Living: The Alameda County Study*. New York: Oxford University Press. 495

BERLE, ADOLPH, JR., and GARDINER C. MEANS. 1932. *The Modern Corporation and Private Property*. New York: Harcourt, Brace, and World. 410

BERREMAN, GERALD. 1960. Caste in India and the United States. *American Journal of Sociology*, 66:120–127. 227

BERSCHEID, ELLEN. 1985. Interpersonal attraction. In G. Lindzey and E. Aronson, Eds., *Handbook of Social Psychology*, 3rd ed. Vol. 2. New York: Random House. 183

BERSCHEID, ELLEN, and LETITIA ANNE PEPLAU. 1983. The emerging science of relationships. In H. H. Kelley, Ed., *Close Relationships*. New York: W. H. Freeman. 182

BERSCHEID, ELLEN, and ELAINE WALSTER. 1974. Physical attractiveness. In L. Berkowitz, Ed., *Advances in Experimental Social Psychology*, Vol. 7. New York: Academic Press. 320

BETTELHEIM, BRUNO, and MORRIS JANOWITZ. 1950. *Dynamics of Prejudice*. New York: Harper & Row. 264

BETZ, MICHAEL, and LENAHAN O'CONNELL. 1983. Changing doctor-patient relationships and the rise in concern for accountability. *Social Problems*, 31:84–95. 507

BIALER SEWERYN. 1986. *The Soviet Paradox: External Expansion, Internal Decline*. New York: Knopf. 407,442

BIANCHI, SUZANNE M. 1984. Wives who earn more than their husbands. *American Demographics*, 6 (July): 19–23+. 364

BIEMILLER, LAWRENCE. 1986. Asian students fear top colleges use quota systems. *Chronicle of Higher Education* (November 19):1,34. 483

BIERSTEDT, ROBERT. 1950. An analysis of social power. *American Sociological Review*, 15:730–738. 435

BINFORD, HENRY C. 1985. *The First Suburbs: Residential Communities on the Boston Periphery, 1815–1860*. Chicago: University of Chicago Press. 559

BIRCH, DAVID L. 1987. The atomization of America. *INC* (March):21–22. 603

BIRD, GLORIA W., GERALD A. BIRD, and MARGUERITE SCRUGGS. 1984. Determinants of family task sharing: A study of husbands and wives. *Journal of Marriage and the Family,* 46:345–355. *355*

BIRDWHISTELL, RAYMOND L. 1970. *Kinesics and Context.* Philadelphia: University of Pennsylvania Press. *177*

BIRRELL, SUSAN. 1981. Sport as ritual: Interpretations from Durkheim to Goffman. *Social Forces,* 60:354–376. *426*

BLACK, DONALD. 1984a. *Toward a General Theory of Social Control. Vol. 1: Fundamentals.* Orlando, Fl: Academic Press. *192*

BLACK, DONALD. 1984b. *Toward a General Theory of Social Control. Vol. 2: Selected Problems.* Orlando, Fl: Academic Press. *192*

BLACKBURN, MCKINLEY L., and DAVID E. BLOOM. 1985. What is happening to the middle class? *American Demographics,* 7 (January):19–25. *236*

BLAKE, ROBERT, and JANE MOUTON. 1979. Intergroup problem solving in organizations: From theory to practice. In W. G. Austin and S. Worchel, Eds., *The Social Psychology of Intergroup Relations.* Monterey, CA: Brooks/Cole. *112*

BLAU, PETER M. 1964. *Exchange and Power in Social Life.* New York: Wiley. *173,347*

BLAU, PETER M., and OTIS DUDLEY DUNCAN. 1972. *The American Occupational Structure,* 2nd ed. New York: Wiley. *231,243,245,246,473*

BLAU, PETER M., and RICHARD A. SCHOENHERR. 1971. *The Structure of Organization.* New York: Basic Books. *129*

BLAU, PETER, M., and JOSEPH E. SCHWARTZ. 1984. *Crosscutting Social Circles: Testing a Macrostructural Theory of Intergroup Relations.* Orlando, Fl: Academic Press. *86,259, 441*

BLAU, PETER and RICHARD SCOTT. 1962. *Formal Organizations.* San Francisco: Chandler. *125*

BLAU, ZENA SMITH. 1973. *Old Age in a Changing Society.* New York: New Viewpoints. *294*

BLAUNER, ROBERT. 1969. Work satisfaction and industrial trends. In A. Etzioni, Ed., *A Sociological Reader on Complex Organizations.* New York: Holt, Rinehart and Winston. *418*

BLAZER, D. G. 1982. Social support and mortality in an elderly community

population. *American Journal of Epidemiology,* 115:684–694. *495*

BLENDON, ROBERT J., LINDA H. AIKEN, HOWARD E. FREEMAN, BRADFORD L. KIRKMAN-LIFF, and JOHN W. MURPHY. 1986. Uncompensated care by hospitals or public insurance for the poor. *New England Journal of Medicine,* 314:1160–1163. *510*

BLOCH, ERICH. 1986. Basic research and economic health: The coming challenge. *Science,* 232:595–599. *420*

BLOCK, FRED. 1977. The ruling class does not rule: Notes on the Marxist theory of the state. *Socialist Revolution,* 7:6–28. *446*

BLOCK, JACK. 1981. Some enduring and consequential structures of personality. In A. I. Rubin, Ed., *Further Explorations in Personality.* New York: Wiley. *151*

BLOCK, JEANNE H., JACK BLOCK, and PER F. GJERDE. 1986. The personality of children prior to divorce: A prospective study. *Child Development,* 57:827–840. *357*

BLOOM, ALLAN. 1987. *The Closing of the American Mind: How Higher Education Has Failed Democracy and Impoverished the Souls of Today's Students.* New York: Simon and Schuster. *481*

BLOOM, DAVID E. 1986. Women and work. *American Demographics,* 8 (September):25–30. *318*

BLOOM, DAVID E., and NEIL G. BENNETT. 1986. Childless couples. *American Demographics,* 8 (August):23–25 +. *363*

BLOOM, SAMUEL W. 1986. Institutional trends in medical sociology. *Journal of Health and Social Behavior,* 27:265–276. *490*

BLOOM, STEVEN M., and DAVID E. BLOOM. 1985. American labor at the crossroads. *American Demographics,* 7 (September):31–33 +. *422*

BLUESTONE, BARRY, and BENNETT HARRISON. 1982. *The Deindustrialization of America.* New York: Basic Books. *236*

BLUESTONE, BARRY, and BENNETT HARRISON. 1987. The grim truth about the job 'miracle.' *New York Times* (February 1):F–3. *236,602*

BLUMBERG, PAUL. 1980. *Inequality in the Age of Decline.* New York: Oxford University Press. *235*

BLUMER, HERBERT. 1946. Collective behavior. In A. M. Lee, Ed., *New*

Outline of the Principles of Sociology. New York: Barnes & Noble. *569*

BLUMER, HERBERT. 1961. Race prejudice as a sense of group position. In J. Masuoka and P. Valien, Eds., *Race Relations.* Chapel Hill, NC: University of North Carolina Press. *258*

BLUMER, HERBERT. 1969. *Symbolic Interaction: Perspective and Method.* Englewood Cliffs, NJ: Prentice-Hall. *34,35,39,88,130*

BLUMSTEIN, PHILIP, and PEPPER SCHWARTZ. 1983. *American Couples.* New York: William Morrow. *348,362,365*

BLYTH, DALE A., and CAROL M. TRAEGER. 1983. The self-concept and self-esteem of early adolescents. *Theory into Practice,* 22:91–97. *291*

BOHANNON, PAUL, and ROSEMARY ERICKSON. 1978. Stepping in. *Psychology Today,* 11 (January):53–59. *358*

BONACICH, EDNA. 1972. A theory of ethnic antagonism: A split-labor market. *American Sociological Review,* 37:547–559. *266*

BONACICH, EDNA. 1975. Abolition, the extension of slavery, and the position of free blacks: A study of split-labor markets in the United States, 1830–1863. *American Journal of Sociology,* 81:601–628. *266*

BONGER, WILLIAM A. 1936. *An Introduction to Criminology.* London: Methuen. *203*

BORJAS, GEORGE J., and MARTA TIENDA. 1987. The economic consequences of immigration. *Science,* 235:645–651. *270*

BORNSCHIER, VOLKER, CHRISTOPHER CHASE-DUNN, and RICHARD RUBINSON. 1978. Cross-national evidence of the effects of foreign investment and aid on economic growth and inequality. *American Journal of Sociology,* 84:651–683. *414,416*

BORNSCHIER, VOLKER, and JEAN-PIERRE HOBY. 1981. Economic policy and multinational corporations in development. *Social Problems,* 28:363–377. *416*

BOSKIN, MICHAEL J. 1986. *Too Many Promises: The Uncertain Future of Social Security.* New York: Dow Jones-Irwin. *300*

BOSWELL, TERRY E. 1986. A split labor market analysis of discrimination against Chinese immigrants, 1850–1882. *American Sociological Review,*

51:352–371. 266

BOTTOMORE, THOMAS B. 1966. *Classes in Modern Society*. New York: Pantheon Books. 227

BOTTOMORE, TOM. 1981. A Marxist consideration of Durkheim. *Social Forces*, 59:902–917. 17

BOWEN, EZRA. 1986. Losing the war of letters. *Time* (May 5):68. 484

BOWLES, SAMUEL, and HERBERT GINTIS. 1976. *Schooling and Capitalist America*. New York: Basic Books. 469

BOWLES, SAMUEL, and HERBERT GINTIS. 1986. When investment capital goes on strike. *New York Times* (June 29): F–3. 414

BOX, STEVEN. 1984. Power, Crime, and Mystification. London: Tavistock. 212

BOYER, ERNEST L. 1986. A narrowing of vision. *New York Times* (December 7): 7E. 486

BOYER, ERNEST L. 1987. *College—The Undergraduate Experience in America*. New York: Harper & Row. 481,486

BRADBURY, KATHARINE L., ANTHONY DOWNS, and KENNETH A. SMALL. 1982. *Urban Decline and the Future of American Cities*. Washington, DC: Brookings Institution. 561

BRADDOCK II, JOMILLS H. 1985. School desegregation and black assimilation. *Journal of Social Issues*, 41:9–22. 475

BRADDOCK II, JOMILLS H., ROBERT L. CRAIN, and JAMES M. MCPARTLAND. 1984. A long-term view of school desegregation: Some recent studies of graduates as adults. *Phi Delta Kappan*, 66:259–264. 475

BRADY, ERIK. 1983. Our colleges give a cheer for mascots. *USA Today* (December 1):D–1. 107

BRANNIGAN, MARTHA. 1986. A fast-growing HMO shows its's tough to make a profit caring for the elderly. *Wall Street Journal* (August 27):17. 504

BREDEMEIER, BRENDA JO, and DAVID L. SHIELDS. 1985. Values and violence in sports today. *Psychology Today*, 19 (October):23–28 +. 426

BRENNER, M. HARVEY. 1973. *Mental Illness and the Economy*. Cambridge: Harvard University Press. 423

BRENNER, M. HARVEY. 1975. Trends in alcohol consumption and associated illnesses: Some effects of economic changes. *American Journal of Public Health*, 65:1279–1292. 423

BRENNER, M. HARVEY. 1976. Estimating the social costs of national economic policy: Implications for mental and physical health and criminal aggression. Paper No. 5., *Report to the Congressional Research Service of the Library of Congress and Joint Committee of Congress*. Washington, DC: Government Printing Office. 423

BREWER, MARILYNN B., and RODERICK M. KRAMER. 1986. Choice behavior in social dilemmas: Effects of social identity, group size, and decision framing. *Journal of Personality and Social Psychology*, 50:543–549. 117,119

BRIDGEWATER, CAROL AUSTIN. 1982. Consumer psychology. *Psychology Today*, 16 (May):16–20. 235

BRIDGEWATER, CAROL AUSTIN. 1985. Cancer: The psychosocial effects. *Psychology Today*, 19 (April):13. 494

BRIGGS, KENNETH A. 1984a. Methodist church foresees renewal. New York Times (May 7):1,15. 390

BRIGGS, KENNETH A. 1984b. Methodists' conference: Some signs of a rebirth. *New York Times* (May 14):8. 390

BRIGGS, KENNETH A. 1984c. Catholics aren't collaring enough priests. *New York Times* (February 26):18E. 391

BRIGGS, VERNON, JR. 1985. *Immigration Policy and the American Labor Force*. Baltimore: The Johns Hopkins University Press. 270

BRIM, ORVILLE G., JR. 1966. Socialization through the life cycle. In O. G. Brim and S. Wheeler, Eds., *Socialization after Childhood*. New York: Wiley. 156

BRIM, ORVILLE G., JR. 1980. Types of life events. *Journal of Social Issues*, 36:148–157. 284

BRINT, STEVEN. 1984. "New-class" and cumulative trend explanations of the liberal political attitudes of professionals. *American Journal of Sociology*, 90:30–71. 82

BRINTON, CRANE. 1938. *The Anatomy of Revolution*. New York: Vintage Books. 575,577

BRODERICK, CARLFRED B., and GEORGE P. ROWE. 1968. A scale of preadolescent heterosexual development. *Journal of Marriage and the Family*, 30:97–101. 327

BRODY, ELAINE M., PAULINE T. JOHNSEN, MARK C. FULCOMER, and ABIGAIL M. LANG. 1983. Women's changing roles and help to elderly parents. *Journal of Gerontology*, 38:597–607. 355,360

BRODY, JANE E. 1986. Assessing illnesses related to day care. *New York Times* (September 10):25. 353

BROMLEY, DAVID G., and ANSON SHUPE, Eds. 1984. *New Christian Politics*. Macon: Mercer University Press. 389

BRONFENBRENNER, MARTIN, WERNER SICHEL, and WAYLAND GARDNER. 1984. *Economics*. Boston: Houghton Mifflin. 17

BROOKES, WARREN T. 1987. Low-pay jobs: The big lie. *Wall Street Journal* (March 25):26. 602

BROOKS, ANDREE. 1986. When studies mislead. *New York Times* (December 29):17. 492

BROTHERS, JOYCE. 1986. When unmarried couples live together. *Readers Digest* (March):11–16. 362

BROWN, DON W. 1978. Arrest rates and crime rates: When does a tipping effect occur? *Social Forces*, 57:671–682. 215

BROWNE, MALCOLM W. 1986. Technology from Russia finds a niche in U. S. life. *New York Times* (December 16):17,18. 593

BROWNE, MALCOLM W. 1987. New findings reveal ancient abuse of lands. *New York Times* (January 13):13,15. 532

BROWNELL, CELIA A. 1986. Convergent developments: Cognitive-developmental correlates of growth in infant/toddler peer skills. *Child Development*, 57:275–286. 158

BROZAN, NADINE. 1982. Family is focus of leisure time, study finds. *New York Times* (December 15):19. 424

BROZAN, NADINE. 1985. Jurors in rape trials studied. *New York Times* (June 17):20. 321

BROZAN, NADINE. 1986. Care of infirm relatives: A new potent issue for women. *New York Times* (November 13):17. 360

BROZAN, NADINE. 1986. NOW at 20: Reassessment in a new era. *New York Times* (December 1):22. 323,325

BRZEZINSKI, ZBIGNIEW. 1986. *Game Plan*. New York: Altantic Monthly Press. 458

BULMER, MARTIN. 1985. *The Chicago School of Sociology*. Chicago: University of Chicago Press. 21

BUMPASS, LARRY. 1984. Some characteristics of children's second families. *American Journal of Sociology*,

90:608–623. *358*

BURAWOY, MICHAEL. 1979. *Manufacturing Consent*. Chicago: University of Chicago Press. *128*

BURAWOY, MICHAEL. 1983. Factory regimes under advanced capitalism. *American Sociological Review*, 48:587–605. *128,129*

BURGOON, JUDEE, and THOMAS SAINE. 1978. *The Unspoken Dialogue*. Boston: Houghton Mifflin. *181*

BURNETT, R. CHRIS. 1986. Senator: U. S. lax on corporate crime. *Columbus Ohio Dispatch* (February 28):6A. *204*

BURROUGH, BRYAN, and CAROL HYMOWITZ. 1986. As steel jobs dwindle, blue-collar families face vexing changes. *Wall Street Journal* (August 8):1,7. *402*

BURNHAM, JAMES. 1941. *The Managerial Revolution*. New York: John Day Co. *410*

BURT, MARTHA R. 1980. Cultural myths and supports for rape. *Journal of Personality and Social Psychology*, 38:217–230. *321*

BURT, RONALD S. 1983. *Corporate Profits and Cooptation*. New York: Academic Press. *410*

BUSSEY, KAY, and ALBERT BANDURA. 1984. Influence of gender constancy and social power on sex-linked modeling. *Journal of Personality and Social Psychology*, 47:1292–1302. *311*

BUTLER, ROBERT N. 1963. The life review. An interpretation of reminiscence in the aged. *Psychiatry*, 26:65–76. *295*

BUTLER, ROBERT N. The life review. *Psychology Today*, 5 (December):49–51+. *295*

BUTTERFIELD, FOX. 1986. What has red, green and joy all over? *New York Times* (June 11):1,10. *426*

BUTTERFIELD, FOX. 1986. Why Asians are going to the head of the class. *New York Times* (August 3):18–23 EDUC. *482*

BYRD, RICHARD. 1938. *Alone*. London: Neville Spearman. *165–166*

CAIN, MEAD. 1985. Fertility as an adjustment to risk. In A. S. Rossi, Ed., *Gender and the Life Course*. New York: Aldine. *527*

CALIFANO, JOSEPH A., Jr. 1986. A revolution looms in American health. *New York Times* (March 25):25. *492,508,511*

CAMPBELL, FRANCES A., BONNIE BREITMAYER, and CRAIG T. RAMEY. 1986. Disadvantaged single teenage mothers and their children: Consequences of free educational day care. *Family Relations*, 35:63–68. *364*

CANERDY, BEVERLY. 1986. Catholic orders losing numbers. *USA Today* (May 28):3A. *391*

CANN, ARNIE, LAWRENCE G. CALHOUN, JAMES W. SELBY, and H. ELIZABETH KING. 1981. Rape: A contemporary overview and analysis. *Journal of Social Issues*, 37:1–4. *320*

CANTOR, DAVID and KENNETH C. LAND. 1985. Unemployment and crime rates in the post-World War II United States: A theoretical and empirical analysis. *American Sociological Review*, 50:317–332. *204*

CANTRIL, HADLEY. 1941. *The Psychology of Social Movements*. New York: Wiley. *574*

CAPLOW, THEODORE. 1986. Sociology and the nuclear debate. In J. E. Short, Jr., Ed., *The Social Fabric*. Beverly Hills, CA: Sage. *456*

CAPLOW, THEODORE, HOWARD M. BAHR, and BRUCE A. CHADWICK. 1983. *All Faithful People: Change and Continuity in Middletown's Religion*. Minneapolis: University of Minnesota Press. *387,395*

CAPLOW, THEODORE, HOWARD M. BAHR, BRUCE A. CHADWICK, REUBEN HILL, and MARGARET H. WILLIAMSON. 1982. *Middletown Families: Fifty Years of Change and Continuity*. Minneapolis: University of Minnesota Press. *349*

CARGAN, LEONARD, and MATTHEW MELKO. 1982. *Singles: Myths and Realities*. Beverly Hills, CA: Sage. *361*

CARLSON, ALLAN C. 1986. What happened to the "family wage"? *The Public Interest*, 83:3–17. *351*

CARMICHAEL, STOKELY, and CHARLES HAMILTON. 1967. *Black Power*. New York: Random House. *259*

Carnegie Foundation for the Advancement of Teaching. 1986. Report. *Change: The Magazine of Higher Learning* (May–June). *479*

Carnegie Forum on Education and the Economy. 1986. *A Nation Prepared: Teachers for the 21st Century*. New York: Carnegie Corporation. *479*

CARNOY, MARTIN. 1984. *The State and Political Theory*. Princeton, NJ: Princeton University Press. *446*

CARNOY, MARTIN, and HENRY M. LEVIN. 1985. *Schooling and Work in the Democratic State*. Stanford: Stanford University Press. *466,469*

CARPENTER, EDMUND. 1965. *Comments*. Current Anthropology, 6:55. *157*

CARPENTER, ELIZABETH. 1985. Conditioning: It's the thought that counts. *Psychology Today*, 19 (May):8–10. *146*

CARRINGTON, TIM. 1984. U.S. won't let 11 biggest banks in nation fail. *Wall Street Journal* (September 20):2. *409*

CARRINGTON, TIM. 1986. Some Democrats weigh reviving draft to bolster armed services and make their mark on defense. *Wall Street Journal* (November 17):66. *517*

CARVER, CHARLES, S. and CHARLENE HUMPHRIES. 1981. Havana daydreaming: A study of self-consciousness and the negative reference group among Cuban Americans. *Journal of Personality and Social Psychology*, 40:545–552. *113*

CASTEEL, RICHARD W. 1975. The relationship between population size and carrying capacity in a sample of North American hunter-gatherers. In D. Browman, W. Irving, and W. Powers, Eds., *Prehistoric Cultural Adaptations in Western North America*. The Hague: Mouton. *73*

CASTELLS, MANUEL. 1977. *The Urban Question*. London: Edward Arnold. *557*

CATALANO, RALPH, and DAVID DOOLEY. 1983. Health effects of economic instability: A test of economic stress hypothesis. *Journal of Health and Social Behavior*. 24:46–60. *494*

CATTON, WILLIAM R., JR. 1980. *Overshoot: The Ecological Basis of Revolutionary Change*. Urbana: University of Illinois Press. *525*

CATTON, WILLIAM R., JR., GERHARD LENSKI, and FREDERICK H. BUTTEL. 1986. To what degree is a social system dependent on its resource base? In J. E. Short, Jr., Ed., *The Social Fabric: Dimensions and Issues*. Beverly Hills, CA: Sage. *525,529,531*

Census Bureau. 1986. Earnings in 1983 of Married-Couple Families, by Characteristics of Husbands and Wives. *Current Population Reports*, Series P–60, No. 153. Washington, DC: U.S. Bureau of the Census. *354*

Census Bureau. 1986. *World Population Profile: 1985*. Washington, DC: Government Printing Office. *523*

CHAFETZ, JANET SALTZMAN. 1984. *Sex and Advantage: A Comparative, Macro-Structural Theory of Sex Stratification*. Totowa, NJ: Rowman & Allanheld. *314*

CHAFETZ, JANET SALTZMAN, and ANTHONY GARY DWORKIN. 1986. *Female Revolt: Women's Movements in World and Historical Perspective*. Totowa, NJ: Rowman & Allanheld. *322*

CHAGNON, NAPOLEON A., 1983. *Yanomano*. New York: Holt, Rinehart and Winston. *68–69,75*

CHALL, DANIEL E. 1984. Neighborhood changes in New York City. *American Demographics*, 6 (October):19–23+. *551*

CHAMBLISS, WILLIAM J. 1973. The Saints and the Roughnecks. *Society*, 2 (November)24–31. *206–207*

CHASSIN, LAURIE, ANTONETTE ZEISS, KRISTINA COOPER, and JUDITH REAVEN. 1985. Role perceptions, self-role congruence and marital satisfaction in dual-worker couples with preschool children. *Social Psychology Quarterly*. 48:301–311. *354*

CHECK, JAMES V. P., and NEIL M. MALAMUTH. 1983. Sex role stereotyping and reactions to depictions of stranger versus acquaintance rape. *Journal of Personality and Social Psychology*, 45:344–356. *321*

CHENG, LUCIE, and EDNA BONACICH. 1984. *Labor Immigration Under Capitalism*. Berkeley: University of California Press. *266*

CHERLIN, ANDREW. 1978. Remarriage as an incomplete institution. *American Journal of Sociology*, 86:636–650. *358*

CHERLIN, ANDREW. 1983. Changing family and household: Contemporary lessons from historical research. *Annual Review of Sociology*, 9:51–66. *337,350,353*

CHERLIN, ANDREW. 1987. Don't fear the 'depopulation bomb.' *Christian Science Monitor* (January 5):16. *529*

CHILDE, V. GORDON. 1936. *Man Makes Himself*. London: Watts. *80,543*

CHILDE, V. GORDON. 1941. *Man Makes Himself*. London: Watts & Co., Ltd. *80,543*

CHILDE, V. GORDON. 1942. *What Happened in History*. London: Routledge and Kegan Paul. *543*

CHILDE, V. GORDON. 1952. *New Light on the Most Ancient East*. London: Routledge and Kegan Paul. *543*

CHILDE, V. GORDON. 1956. *Piecing Together the Past*. London: Routledge and Kegan Paul. *543*

CHITTISTER, JOAN D., and MARTIN E. MARTY. 1983. *Faith & Ferment*. Minneapolis: Augsburg Publishing House. *390*

CHRISTENSON, JAMES A. 1984. Gemeinschaft and Gesellschaft: Testing the spatial and communal hypotheses. *Social Forces*, 63:160–168. *554*

CHURCH, GEORGE J. 1986. Call to battle. *Time* (November 10):18–20. *496*

CICIRELLI, VICTOR G. 1981. *Helping Elderly Parents: The Role of Adult Children*. Boston: Auburn House. *360*

CICIRELLI, VICTOR G. 1983. Adult children's attachment and helping behavior to elderly parents: A path model. *Journal of Marriage and the Family*, 45:815–825. *360*

CICONE, MICHAEL V., and DIANE N. RUBLE. 1978. Beliefs about males. *Journal of Social Issues*, 34:5–16. *320*

CLANCY, PAUL. 1986. For women in 30s, 6 of 10 marriages fail. *USA Today* (April 4):1, 2. *355*

CLARK, CANDACE. 1983. Sickness and social control. In H. Robboy and C. Clark, Eds., *Social Interaction: Readings in Sociology*. New York: St. Martin's Press. *491,499*

CLARK, DAVID L., LINDA S. LOTTO, and MARTHA M. MCCARTHY. 1980. Factors associated with success in urban elementary schools. *Phi Delta Kappan*, 61:467–470. *480*

CLARK, KENNETH B. 1965. *Dark Ghetto*. New York: Harper & Row. *474*

CLARK, R. A. 1952. The projective measurement of experimentally induced levels of sexual motivation. *Journal of Experimental Psychology*, 44:391–399. *44*

CLARK, REGINALD M. 1983. *Family Life and School Achievement: Why Poor Black Children Succeed or Fail*. Chicago: University of Chicago Press. *245*

CLARKE-STEWART, ALISON, and CHRISTIAN GRUBER. 1984. Day care forms and features. In R. C. Ainslie, Ed., *The Child and the Day Care Setting: Qualitative Variation and Development*. New York: Praeger. *354*

CLENDINEN, DUDLEY. 1985. New computer splits New Hampshire officials. *New York Times* (May 6):11. *601*

CLENDINEN, DUDLEY. 1986. Conservative Christians again take issue of religion in schools to courts. *New York Times* (February 28):11. *389*

CLINGEMPEEL, W. GLEN. 1981. Quasi-kin relationships and marital quality in stepfather families. *Journal of Personality and Social Psychology*, 41:890–901. *358*

CLOWARD, RICHARD A., and LLOYD E. OHLIN. 1960. *Delinquency and Opportunity: A Theory of Delinquent Gangs*. New York: Free Press. *198*

CLYMER, ADAM. 1987. Survey finds many skeptics among evangelists' viewers. *New York Times* (March 31):1, 14. *388*

COCHRAN, MONCRIEFF M., and LARS GUNNARSSON. 1985. A follow-up study of group day care and family-based childrearing patterns. *Journal of Marriage and the Family*, 47:297–309. *353*

COHEN, ALBERT K. 1955. *Delinquent Boys*. New York: Free Press. *200–201*

COHEN, ALBERT K. 1965. The sociology of the deviant act: Anomie theory and beyond. *American Sociological Review*, 30:5–13. *169,194*

COHEN, ALBERT K. 1966. *Deviance and Control*. Englewood Cliffs, NJ: Prentice-Hall. *64,150*

COHEN, JERE. 1980. Rational capitalism in Renaissance Italy. *American Journal of Sociology*, 85:1340–1355. *386*

COHEN, LAWRENCE E. 1987. Throwing down the gauntlet: A challenge to the relevance of sociology for the etiology of criminal behavior. *Contemporary Sociology*, 16:202–205. *199*

COHEN, STEPHEN F. 1985. *Rethinking the Soviet Experience: Politics and History Since 1917*. New York: Oxford University Press. *442*

COLASANTO, DIANE, and LINDA WILLIAMS. 1987. The changing dynamics of race and class. *Public Opinion*, 9 (January/February):50–53. *269*

COLE, JOHNNETTA B. 1982. *Anthropology for the Eighties*. New York: Free Press. *339*

COLE, STEPHEN. 1972. *The Sociological Method*. Chicago: Markham. *42*

COLEMAN, JAMES S. 1966. *Equality of Educational Opportunity*. Washington, DC: Government Printing Office. *474–475*

COLEMAN, JAMES S. 1985. Schools and the communities they serve. *Phi Delta Kappan*, 66 (April):527–532. *480*

COLEMAN, JAMES W. 1985. *The Criminal Elite: The Sociology of White-Collar Crime*. New York: St. Martin's Press. 204

COLEMAN, JAMES S., THOMAS HOFFER, and SALLY KILGORE. 1982a, 1982b. High School Achievement: Public, Catholic and Other Private Schools Compared. New York: Basic Books. 480

COLEMAN, JAMES S. and LEE RAIN-WATER. 1978. *Social Standing in America*. New York: Basic Books. 224,233

COLGAN, PATRICK. 1983. *Comparative Social Recognition*. New York: Wiley. 63

COLLIGAN, MICHAEL J., JAMES W. PENNEBAKER, and LAWRENCE R. MURPHY, Eds., 1982. *Mass Psychogenic Illness: A Social Psychological Analysis*. Hillsdale, NJ: Erlbaum. 568

COLLINS, GLENN. 1986. More women work longer. *New York Times* (April 3):17,19. 294

COLLINS, GLENN. 1986. Insensitivity to the disabled. *New York Times* (August 11):18. 192

COLLINS, RANDALL. 1975. *Conflict Sociology*. New York: Academic Press. 32,65,227,231,314,344,403,444

COLLINS, RANDALL. 1976. Review of "Schooling in Capitalist America." *Harvard Educational Review*, 46:246–251. 470

COLLINS, RANDALL. 1977. Some comparative principles of educational stratification. *Harvard Educational Review*, 47:1–27. 469

COLLINS, RANDALL. 1979. *Credential Society*. New York: Academic Press. 469,472

COLLINS, RANDALL. 1980. Weber's last theory of capitalism: A systematization. *American Sociological Review*, 45:925–942. 387

COLLINS, RANDALL. 1981. *Sociology since Midcentury: Essays in Theory Cumulation*. New York: Academic Press. 383

COLLINS, RANDALL. 1981. On the microfoundations of macrosociology. *American Journal of Sociology*, 86:984–1014. 88

COLLINS, RANDALL. 1982. *Sociological Insight*. New York: Oxford University Press. 8,32,119,125,126,196,342,379

COLLINS, RANDALL. and MICHAEL MAKOWSKY. 1984. *The Discovery of Society*. 3rd ed. New York: Random House. 172

COLLINS, SHARON. 1983. The making of the black middle class. *Social Problems*, 30:340–377. 269

COMAROW, AVERY. 1987. AIDS: A time of testing. *U.S. News & World Report* (April 20):56–59. 490

CONNOR, WALTER D. 1979. *Socialism, Politics, and Equality*. New York: Columbia University Press. 245

CONRAD, PETER. 1975. The discovery of hyperkinesis: Notes on the medicalization of deviant behavior. *Social Problems*, 23:12–21. 500

CONRAD, PETER, and JOSEPH SCHNEIDER. 1980. *Deviance and Medicalization: From Badness to Sickness*. St. Louis: Mosby. 500

COOK, JAMES. 1986. The knack. . .and how to get it. *Forbes* (March 24):56–66. 603

COOK, STUART W. 1984. The 1954 social science statement and school desegregation. *American Psychologist*, 39:819–832. 9

COOKSON, PETER W., Jr. and CAROLINE HODGES PERSELL. 1986. The price of privilege. *Psychology Today*, 20 (March):31–35. 123–124

COOLEY, CHARLES HORTON. 1902. *Human Nature and the Social Order*. New York: Scribner's. 35,150

COOLEY, CHARLES HORTON. 1909. *Social Organization*. New York: Charles Scribner's Sons. 109

COOPER, KRISTINA, LAURIE CHASSIN, SANFORD BRAVER, ANTONETTE ZEISS, and KATHERINE AKHTAR KHAVARI. 1986. Correlates of mood and marital satisfaction among dual-worker and single-worker couples. *Social Psychology Quarterly*, 49:322–329. 354,355

COOPERSMITH, STANLEY. 1967. *Antecedents of Self-Esteem*. San Francisco: Freeman. 151

CORDES, COLLEEN. 1984. Behavior therapists examine how emotion, cognition relate. *Monitor* (February):18. 111

CORDES, COLLEEN. 1985. Officials overlook roles of culture, self-motivation in family planning. *APA Monitor* (May):14–16. 527

CORDES, COLLEEN. 1986. Responding to terrorism. *APA Monitor* (May):36–37. 578

CORNELL, STEPHEN. 1984. Crisis and response in Indian-white relations: 1960–1984. *Social Problems*, 32:44–59. 273

CORNFIELD, NOREEN. 1983. The success of urban communes. *Journal of Marriage and the Family*, 45:115–126. 365

COSER, LEWIS A. 1956. *The Functions of Social Conflict*. New York: Free Press. 32,264,598

COSER, LEWIS A. 1957. Social conflict and the theory of social change. *British Journal of Sociology*, 8:170–183. 598

COSER, LEWIS A. 1962. Some functions of deviant behavior and normative flexibility. *American Journal of Sociology*, 68:172–181. 194

COSER, LEWIS A. 1975. Presidential address: Two methods in search of a substance. *American Sociological Review*, 40:691–700. 246

COSTA, PAUL T., Jr., and ROBERT R. McCRAE. 1980. Still stable after all those years: Personality as a key to some issues in adulthood and old age. In P. B. Baltes and O. G. Brim, Jr., Eds., *Life Span Development and Behavior.*, Vol. 3. New York: Academic Press. 151

COUCH, KENNETH A. 1986. How edonomic change shapes new dreams. *Public Opinion*, 9 (September/October): 9–10. 420,606

COUGHLIN, ELLEN K. 1985. Is violence on TV harmful to our health? *The Chronicle of Higher Education* (March 13):5, 8. 159

Council On Environmental Quality. 1980. *The Global 2000 Report to the President*. Washington, DC: Government Printing Office. 525

COWELL, ALAN. 1984. African famine battle: Aid has been a villain. *New York Times* (November 29):1, 6. 530

COWELL, ALAN. 1984b. South of Sahara, the intrusive politics of hunger. *New York Times* (December 3):1, 4. 530

COWEN, ROBERT C. 1987. Spaceship earth: Mankind as a force of nature. *Christian Science Monitor* (March 31): 16–17. 515

COX, OLIVER C. 1948. *Caste, Class, and Race*. New York: Doubleday & Co. 266

CRAIN, ROBERT L., and RITA E. MAHARD. 1983. The effect of research methodology on desegregation-achievement studies. *American Journal of Sociology*, 88:839–854. 475

CRANDALL, ROBERT W. 1986. Detroit rode quotas to prosperity. *Wall Street*

Journal (January 29):26. *408*

Crano, William D., and Phyllis M. Mellon. 1978. Causal influence of teachers' expectancies on children's academic performance: A cross-lagged panel analysis. *Journal of Educational Psychology*, 70:39–49. *474*

Creekmore, C. R. 1985. Cities won't drive you crazy. *Psychology Today*, 19 (January):46–53. *553*

Creekmore, Charoles. 1986. Misunderstanding Africa. *Psychology Today*, 20 (December):38–45. *595*

Cressey, Donald R. 1969. *Theft of the Nation: The Structure and Operations of Organized Crime in America*. New York: Harper & Row. *211*

Critchfield, R. 1978. The culture of poverty. *Human Behavior*, 7 (January):65–69. *238*

Critchfield, Richard. 1984. Modern farming sows turmoil among India's Sikhs. *Wall Street Journal* (July 16):15. *227*

Crosby, Faye, Stephanie Bromley, and Leonard Saxe. 1980. Recent unobtrusive studies of black and white discrimination and prejudice: A literature review. *Psychological Bulletin*, 87:546–563. *259*

Crossette, Barbara. 1987. Boat people: Fresh faces, new horrors. *New York Times* (February 14):1, 5. *69*

Cskiszentmihalyi, Mihaly, and Reed Larson. 1984. *Being Adolescent: Conflict and Growth in the Teen-age Years*. New York: Basic Books. *183,184*

Cummins, Jim. 1986. Empowering minority students: A framework for intervention. *Harvard Educational Review*, 56:18–36. *474*

Cupito, Mary Carmen. 1986. Children do help elderly. Columbus, Ohio, *Dispatch* (October 23):C1. *299*

Cupito, Mary Carmen. 1987. No rampant AIDS seen for U.S. heterosexuals. Columbus, Ohio, *Dispatch* (January 27):1E. *496*

Cushman, John H., Jr. 1986. U.S. says Lockheed overcharged by hundreds of millions on plane. *New York Times* (August 29):1, 26. *452*

Dahl, Robert. 1961. *Who Governs? Democracy and Power in an American City*. New Haven: Yale University Press. *455*

Dahl, Robert A. 1971. *Polyarchy: Participation and Opposition*. New

Haven: Yale University Press. *608*

Dahrendorf, Ralf. 1958. Toward a theory of social conflict. *Journal of Conflict Resolution*, 2:170–183. *598*

Dahrendorf, Ralf. 1959. *Class and Class Conflict in Industrial Society*. Stanford, CA: Stanford University Press. *31,33,228,230*

Dahrendorf, Ralf. 1965. *Gesellshaft und Demokratie in Deutschland*. München: Piper Verlag. *342*

Dahrendorf, Ralf. 1968. *Essays in the Theory of Society*. Stanford, CA: Stanford University Press. *597*

Damico, Sandra Bowman, and Christopher Sparks. 1986. Cross-group contact opportunities: Impact on interpersonal relationships in desegregated middle schools. *Sociology of Education*. 59:113–123. *475*

Damon, William, and Daniel Hart. 1982. The development of self-understanding from infancy through adolescence. *Child Development*, 53:841–864. *290*

Daniel, Clifton. 1974. Gains of Watergate. *New York Times* (August 10):17. *434*

Daniels, Norman. 1986. Why saying no to patients in the United States is so hard. *New England Journal of Medicine*, 314:1380–1383. *511*

Dannefer, Dale. 1984. Adult development and social theory. *American Sociological Review*, 49:100–116. *293*

Datan, Nancy. 1977. After the apple: Post-Newtonian metatheory for jaded psychologists. In N. Datan and H. W. Reese, Eds., *Life-Span Developmental Psychology: Dialectical Perspectives on Experimental Research*. New York: Academic Press. *282*

Davidson, Joe. 1986. Research mystery: Use of surgery, hospitals varies greatly by region. *Wall Street Journal* (March 5):33. *502,508*

Davie, Maurice R. 1937. The patterns of urban growth. In George P. Murdock, Ed., *Studies in the Science of Society*. New Haven: Yale University Press. *547*

Davies, James. 1962. Toward a theory of revolution. *American Sociological Review*, 27:5–19. *581*

Davies, James. 1969. The J-curve of rising and declining satisfactions as a cause of some great revolutions and a contained revolution. In H. D. Graham and T. R. Gurr, Eds., *The History of Violence in America*. New

York: Bantam. *581*

Davies, James. 1974. The J-curve and power struggle theories of collective violence. *American Sociological Review*, 39:607–610. *581*

Davies, Mark, and Denise B. Kandel. 1981. Parental and peer influences on adolescents' educational plans: Some further evidence. *American Journal of Sociology*, 87:363–387. *292*

Davis, Allison, B. B. Gardner, and M. R. Gardner. 1941. *Deep South*. Chicago: University of Chicago Press. *233*

Davis, Bob. 1986. Report says U.S. computer surveillance lacks means to protect privacy rights. *Wall Street Journal* (July 1):11. *602*

Davis, James. 1982. Up and down opportunity's ladder. *Public Opinion*, 5 (June/July):11–15+. *243,244*

Davis, Kingsley. 1945. The world demographic transition. *Annals of the American Academy of Political and Social Science*, 237:1–11. *524*

Davis, Kingsley. 1949. *Human Society*. New York: Macmillan. *65,227,283, 444,567*

Davis, Kingsley. 1951. Introduction. In William J. Goode, *Religion among the Primitives*. New York: Free Press. *378*

Davis, Kingsley. 1955. The origin and growth of urbanization in the world. *American Journal of Sociology*, 60:429–437. *543,544*

Davis, Kingsley. 1960. Legitimacy and the incest taboo. In Norman W. Bell and Ezra F. Vogel, Eds., *A Modern Introduction to the Family*. New York: The Free Press. *340*

Davis, Kingsley. 1967. The urbanization of the human population. In *Cities*. New York: Knopf. *543*

Davis, Kingsley. 1971. The world's population crisis. In Robert K. Merton and Robert A. Nisbet, Eds., *Contemporary Social Problems*, 3rd ed. New York: Harcourt Brace Jovanovich. *527*

Davis, Kingsley, and Wilbert Moore. 1945. Some principles of stratification. *American Sociological Review*, 10:242–249. *227*

Dawes, Robyn M., Jeanne McTavish, and Harriet Shaklee. 1977. Behavior, communication, and assumptions about other people's behavior in a common dilemma situation. *Journal of Personality and Social Psychol-*

ogy, 35:1–11. *119*

DAY, ALICE T. 1986. *Who Cares? Demographic Trends Challenge Family Care for the Elderly.* Washington, DC: Population Reference Bureau. *360*

DEAL, TERRENCE E., and ALLEN A. KENNEDY. 1982. *Corporate Cultures: The Rites and Rituals of Corporate Life.* Reading, MA: Addison-Wesley. *160*

DEAUX, KAY, and LAURIE L. LEWIS. 1984. Structure of gender stereotypes: Interrelationships among components and gender labels. *Journal of Personality and Social Psychology,* 46:991–1004. *308,320*

DEGLER, CARL. 1980. *At Odds: Women and the Family in America from the Revolution to the Present.* New York: Oxford University Press. *350*

DELACROIX, JACQUES, and CHARLES C. RAGIN. 1981. Structural blockage: A cross-national study of economic dependency, state efficacy, and underdevelopment. *American Journal of Sociology,* 86:1311–1347. *608*

DE LUCE, JUDITH, and HUGH T. WILDER. 1983. *Language in Primates.* New York: Springer-Verlag. *63*

DEMARTINI, JOSEPH R. 1985. Change agents and generational relationships: A reevaluation of Mannheim's problems of generations. *Social Forces,* 64:1–16. *285*

DEMOS, JOHN. and V. DEMOS. 1969. Adolescence in historical perspective. *Journal of Marriage and the Family,* 31:632–638. *291*

DEMOS, JOHN. 1987. *Past, Present, and Personal: The Family and the Life Course in American History.* New York: Oxford University Press. *351*

DEMOTT, JOHN S. 1987. Welcome, America, to the baby bust. *Time* (February 23):28–29. *517*

DENTZER, SUSAN. 1986. Back to the suburbs. *Newsweek* (April 21):60–62. *559*

DEPAULO, BELLA M., ROBERT ROSENTHAL, RUSSELL A. EISENSTAT, PETER L. ROGERS, AND SUSAN FINKELSTEIN. 1978. Decoding discrepant nonverbal cues. *Journal of Personality and Social Psychology,* 36:313–323. *177*

DE VRIES, RAYMOND G. 1981. Birth and death: Social construction of the poles of existance. *Social Forces,* 59:1074–1093. *295*

DE VRIES, RAYMOND G. 1985. *Regulat-*

ing Birth: Midwives, Medicine, and the Law. Philadelphia: Temple University Press. *505*

DIAMOND, STUART. 1986. Chernobyl rouses bad memories, new fears. *New York Times* (May 4):3E. *533*

DIEBOLD, JOHN. 1983. Innovation and new institutional structures. In Howard F. Didsbury, Jr., Ed., *The World of Work.* Bethesda, MD: World Future Society. *600*

DIEHL, PAUL F. 1985. Arms races to war: Testing some empirical linkages. *Sociological Quarterly,* 26:331–349. *459*

DIENSTBIER, R. A. 1978. Attribution, socialization, and moral decisionmaking. In J. Harvey, W. Ickes, and R. F. Kidd, Eds., New Directions in Attribution Research. Hillsdale, NJ: Erlbaum. *45*

DIMAGGIO, PAUL. 1982. Cultural capital and school success: The impact of status culture participation on the grades of U.S. high school students. *American Sociological Review,* 47:189–201. *235*

DINNAGE, ROSEMARY. 1986. All in the family. *New York Review of Books* (December 4):39–40. *340*

DION, KAREN. 1972. Physical attractiveness and evaluations of children's transgressions. *Journal of Personality and Social Psychology,* 24:207–213. *347*

DION, KAREN, ELLEN BERSCHEID, and ELAINE WALSTER. 1972. What is beautiful is good. *Journal of Personality and Social Psychology,* 24:285–290. *347*

DIONNE, E. J., JR. 1985. Vatican criticizes Brazilian backer of new theology. *New York Times* (March 21):1,6. *375*

DIONNE, E. J., JR. 1986. Vatican backs struggle by poor to end injustice. *New York Times* (April 6):1,11. *375*

DIPBOYE, ROBERT L. 1977. Alternative approaches to deindividualization. *Psychological Bulletin,* 84:1057–1075. *570*

DJILAS, MILOVAN. 1957. *The New Class.* New York: Praeger. *130,230*

DOAN, MICHAEL. 1984. The "electronic church" spreads the word. *U.S. News & World Report* (April 23):68–69.

DOMHOFF, G. WILLIAM. 1970. *The Higher Circles.* New York: Random House. *445,454*

DOMHOFF, G. WILLIAM. 1983. *Who Rules America Now? A View for the*

'80's. Englewood Cliffs, NJ: Prentice-Hall. *445*

DOWNEY, GARY L. 1986. Ideology and the clamshell identity: Organizational dilemmas in the anti-nuclear power movement. *Social Problems,* 33:357–373. *585*

DOWNTON, JAMES V. 1979. *Sacred Journeys.* New York: Columbia University Press. *572*

DREEBEN, ROBERT, and ADAM GAMORAN. 1986. Race, instruction, and learning. *American Sociological Review,* 51:660–669. *259,474,475*

DRUCKER, PETER F. 1985. Depression cycle. *Wall Street Journal* (January 9):24. *611*

DRUCKER, PETER F. 1986. A crisis of capitalism. *Wall Street Journal* (September 30):32. *413*

DRUCKER, PETER F. 1986. The changing multinational, *Wall Street Journal* (January 15):18. *414*

DUBIN, ROBERT. 1976. Work in modern society. In Robert Dubin, Ed., *Handbook of Work, Organization, and Society.* Chicago: Rand McNally. *420*

DUMONT, L. 1970. *Homo Hierarchicus. The Caste System and Its Implications.* London: Weidenfeld and Nicolson. *337*

DUNCAN, GREG. 1984. *Years of Poverty, Years of Plenty.* Ann Arbor, MI: Institute for Social Research, University of Michigan. *238,243*

DUNCAN, OTIS DUDLEY. 1959. Human ecology and population studies. In Philip Hauser and Otis D. Duncan, Eds., *The Study of Population.* Chicago: The University of Chicago Press. *530–531*

DUNCAN, OTIS DUDLEY. 1961. From social system to ecosystem. *Sociological Inquiry,* 31:140–149. *530–531*

DUNN, WILLIAM. 1986. Europe: Children encourged. *USA Today* (December 22):8A. *528*

DUNNE, JOHN G. 1986. The war that won't go away. *New York Review of Books* (September 25):25–29. *235*

DURKHEIM, EMILE. 1893/1964. *The Division of Labor in Society.* New York: Free Press. *18,196,198*

DURKHEIM, EMILE. 1897/1951. *Suicide.* New York: Free Press. *19,198*

DURKHEIM, EMILE. 1912/1965. *The Elementary Forms of Religious Life.* New York: Free Press. *371,378–379*

DUSEK, JEROME B., Ed. 1985. *Teacher Expectancies.* Hillsdale, NJ: Erlbaum. *474*

DUSEK, JEROME B. and JOHN F. FLAHERTY. 1981. The development of the self-concept during the adolescent years. *Monographs of the Society for Research in Child Development* 46 (No. 191). *291*

DUTTON, DIANA B. 1978. Explaining the low use of health services by the poor: Costs, attitudes, or delivery systems? *American Sociological Review*, 43:348–368. *493*

DUTTON, DIANA B. 1982a. Re-blaming the victim. *American Sociological Review*, 47:557–560. *493*

DUTTON, DIANA B. 1982b. Children's health care: The myth of equal access. *Better Health for Our Children: A National Strategy*. Washington, DC: Government Printing Office. *494*

DUTTON, DONALD G., and ARTHUR P. ARON. 1974. Some evidence for heightened sexual attraction under conditions of high anxiety. *Journal of Personality and Social Psychology*, 30:510–517. *43–45*

DYNES, RUSSELL, and ENRICO QUARANTELLI. 1968. Looting in American cities: A new explanation. *Trans-action* (May):14. *229*

EAGLY, ALICE H. and VALERIE J. STEFFEN. 1984. Gender stereotypes stem from the distribution of women and men into social roles. *Journal of Personality and Social Psychology*, 46:735–754. *309*

EASTERBROOK, GREGG. 1987. The revolution in medicine. *Newsweek* (January 26):40–74. *505,506*

EATON, G. GRAY. 1976. The social order of Japanese macaques. *Scientific American*, 235 (October):96–106. *61*

EBERSTADT, NICK, Ed. 1981. *Fertility Decline in the Less Developed Countries*. New York: Praeger. *526*

ECHENIQUE, JEANNIE. 1986. Nursing shortage getting critical. *USA Today* (December 29):D1. *506*

ECKERMAN, CAROL O., JUDITH L. WHATLEY, and STUART L. KUTZ. 1975. Growth of social play with peers during the second year of life. *Developmental Psychology*, 11:42–49. *158*

ECKHOLM, ERIK. 1984. Computers on job may improve life. *New York Times* (September 30):31. *602*

ECKHOLM, ERIK. 1985a. Pygmy chimp readily learns language skills. *New York Times* (June 24):1, 14. *63*

ECKHOLM, ERIK. 1985b. Kanzi the chimp: A life in science. *New York Times* (June 25):19, 20. *63*

ECKHOLM, ERIK. 1986. What is the meaning of cannibalism? *New York Times* (December 9):19, 22. *69*

EDMONDSON, BRAD. 1986. The political sell. *American Demographics*, 8 (November):27–28+. *449*

EDWARDS, L. P. 1927. *The Natural History of Revolution*. Chicago: University of Chicago Press. *577*

EDWARDS, RICHARD. 1978. The social relations of production at the point of production. *The Insurgent Sociologist*, 8:109–125. *130*

EDWARDS, RICHARD. 1979. *Contested Terrain*. New York: Basic Books. *129*

EHRHARDT, ANKE A. 1985. The psychology of gender. In A. S. Rossi, Ed., *Gender and the Life Course*. New York: Aldine. *310*

EHRHARDT, ANKE A., and H. F. L. MEYER-BAHLBURG. 1981. Effects of prenatal sex hormones on gender-related behavior. *Science*, 176:123–128. *310*

EHRLICH, PAUL. 1968. *The Population Bomb*. New York: Ballatine Books. *550*

EISENBERG, LEON. 1986. Health care: For patients or for profits? *American Journal of Psychiatry*, 143:1015–1019. *499*

EITZEN, D. STANLEY. 1986. How we can clean up big-time college sports. *Chronicle of Higher Education* (February 12):96. *484*

EKMAN, PAUL. 1980. *The Face of Man: Expressions of Universal Emotions in a New Guinea Village*. New York: Garland STPM Press. *180*

EKMAN, PAUL, WALLACE V. FRIESEN, and JOHN BEAR. 1984. The international language of gestures. *Psychology Today*, 18 (May):64–67. *179*

EKMAN, PAUL, WALLACE V. FRIESEN, and P. ELLSWORTH. 1972. *Emotion in the Human Face: Guidelines for Research and an Integration of Findings*. New York: Pergamon Press. *180*

ELIAS, MARILYN. 1986. Kids a handful—but make us happier. *USA Today* (September 9):1A. *352*

ELIAS, MARILYN. 1987. Divorce is easier on well-off kids. *USA Today* (March 16):D–1. *357*

ELIAS, THOMAS D. 1986. Single women on lookout for love should look West. *Columbus, Ohio, Dispatch* (April

8):3B. *520*

ELKIND, DAVID. 1979. Growing up faster. *Psychology Today*, 12 (February):38–45. *292*

ELLIOTT, DELBERT S. 1966. Delinquency, school attendance and dropout. *Social Problems*, 13:307–314. *201*

ELLIS, GODFREY J., GARY R. LEE, and LARRY R. PETERSEN. 1978. Supervision and conformity: A cross-cultural analysis of parental socialization values. *American Journal of Sociology*, 84:386–403. *157*

ELLWOOD, DAVID T., and MARY JO BANE. 1984. *The impact of AFDC on family structure and living arrangements*. Washington, DC: Department of Health and Human Services (Grant No. 92A–82). *239,241*

ELLWOOD, DAVID T., and LAWRENCE H. SUMMERS. 1986. Is welfare really the problem? *The Public Interest*, 83:57–78. *241*

EMBER, CAROL R., and MELVIN EMBER. 1985. *Cultural Anthropology*, 4th ed. Englewood Cliffs, NJ: Prentice-Hall. *51,371*

EMERSON, RICHARD M. 1981. Social exchange theory. In M. Rosenberg and R. H. Turner, Eds., *Social Psychology: Sociological Perspectives*. New York: Basic Books. *172*

ENGELS, FRIEDRICH. 1884/1902. *The Origin of the Family, Private Property, and the State*. Chicago: Kerr. *314,344*

ENGELS, RICHARD A. and RICHARD L. FORSTALL. 1985. Metropolitan areas dominate growth again. *American Demographics*, 7 (April):22–25+. *558*

ENGLAND, PAULA, and GEORGE FARKAS. 1985. *Households, Employment and Gender*. New York: Aldine. *347*

ENTWISLE, BARBARA, and WILLIAM M. MASON. 1985. Multilevel effects of socioeconomic development and family planning programs on children ever born. *American Journal of Sociology*, 91:616–649. *526*

EPSTEIN, JOYCE L. 1985. After the bus arrives: Resegregation in desegregated schools. *Journal of Social Issues*, 41:23–44. *475*

EPSTEIN, SUE HOOVER. 1983. Why do women live longer than men? *Science 83*, 4 (October):30–31. *519*

ERICKSON, FREDERICK. 1975. Gatekeeping and the melting pot. *Harvard Educational Review*, 45:44–70. *260*

ERICKSON, MAYNARD L., and LAMAR T. EMPEY. 1963. Court records, undetected delinquency and decision-making. *Journal of Criminal Law, Criminology and Police Science*, 54:456–469. *213*

ERICKSON, MAYNARD L., and JACK P. GIBBS. 1978. Objective and perceptual properties of legal punishment and the deterrence doctrine. *Social Problems*, 25:253–264. *215*

ERIKSON, ERIK. 1963. *Childhood and Society*. New York: Norton. *287,291*

ERIKSON, ERIK. 1968. *Identity: Youth and Crisis*. New York: Norton. *291,568*

ERIKSON, KAI T. 1962. Notes on the Sociology of Deviance. *Social Problems*, 9:307–314. *190,196,205*

ERIKSON, KAI T. 1966. *Wayward Puritans: A Study in the Sociology of Deviance*. New York: Wiley. *196, 205,380*

EIRKSON, KAI. 1986. On work and alienation. *American Sociological Review*, 51:1–8. *418*

EIRKSON, KAI. 1986. War and peace in Oceania. In J. F. Short, Jr., Ed., *The Social Fabric*. Beverly Hills, CA: Sage. *112*

ERLANGER, HOWARD S. 1974. Social class and corporal punishment in childrearing: A reassessment. *American Sociological Review*, 39:68–85. *157*

ERMANN, M. DAVID, and RICHARD J. LUNDMAN. 1978. Deviant acts by complex organizations: Deviance and social control at the organizational level of analysis. *Sociological Quarterly*, 19:55–67. *204*

ERON, LEONARD. 1980. Prescription for reduction of aggression. *American Psychologist*, 35:244–252. *313*

ETZIONI, AMITAI. 1964. *Modern Organizations*. Englewood Cliffs, NJ: Prentice-Hall. *121*

ETZIONI, AMITAI. 1975. *A Comparative Analysis of Complex Organizations*. New York: Free Press. *121*

ETZIONI, AMITAI. 1985. Shady corporate practices. *New York Times* (November 15):27. *204*

ETZIONI-HALEVY, EVA. 1981. *Social Change: The Advent and Maturation of Modern Society*. London: Routledge & Kegan Paul. *260,437*

EVANGELAUF, JEAN. 1987. Students' borrowing quintuples in decade, raising the specter of a 'debtor generation.' *Chronicle of Higher Education* (January 7):1, 18. *476*

EVANS, PETER B. 1981. Recent research on multinational corporations. *Annual Review of Sociology*, 7: 199–223. *416*

EVANS, PETER B., DIETRICH RUESCHEMEYER, and THEDA SKOCPOL, Eds. 1985. *Bringing the State Back In*. Cambridge: Cambridge University Press. *446*

EVANS-PRITCHARD. E. E. 1970. Sexual inversion among the Azande. *American Anthropologist*, 72:1428–1438. *341*

EVERHART, ROBERT B. 1983. *Reading, Writing and Resistance: Adolescence and Labor in a Junior High School*. Boston: Routledge & Kegan Paul. *469*

EXTER, THOMAS. 1986. Looking for brand loyalty. *American Demographics*, 8 (April):32–33+. *49*

EZEKIEL, RAPHAEL S. 1984. *Voices from the Corner: Poverty and Racism in the Inner City*. Philadelphia, PA: Temple University Press. *6,10*

FABREGA, HORACIO, Jr. 1974. *Disease and Social Behavior*. Cambridge, MA: MIT Press. *494*

FADER, SHIRLEY SLOAN. 1987. Men lose freedom if women lose ground. *Wall Street Journal* (February 2):14. *320–321*

FAGOT, BEVERLY I., MARY D. LEINBACH, and RICHARD HAGAN. 1986. Gender labeling and the adoption of sex-typed behaviors. *Developmental Psychology*, 22:440–443. *312*

FARBER, B. A. 1983. *Stress and Burnout in the Human Service Professions*. Elmsford, NY: Pergamon Press. *418*

FARLEY, REYNOLDS. 1984. *Blacks and Whites: Narrowing the Gap?* Cambridge, MA: Harvard University Press. *269*

FARRELL, CHARLES S. 1986. Stress and the changing nature of the job could force many college coaches to quit. *Chronicle of Higher Education* (March 19):37. *484*

FEAGIN, JOE R. 1985. The global context of metropolitan growth: Houston and the oil industry. *American Journal of Sociology*, 90:1204–1230. *551*

FEATHERMAN, DAVID L., and ROBERT M. HAUSER. 1978. Sexual inequalities and socioeconomic achievement in the U.S., 1962–1973. *American Sociological Review*, 41:462–483. *243,245,316*

FEATHERMAN, DAVID, and ROBERT HAUSER. 1978. *Opportunity and Change*. New York: Academic Press. *243,245,472*

FEATHERMAN, DAVID, and RICHARD M. LERNER. 1985. Ontogenesis and sociogenesis: Problematics for theory and research about development and socialization across the lifespan. *American Sociological Review*, 50:659–676. *282*

FEIGENBAUM, EDWARD A., and PAMELA McCORDUCK. 1983. *The Fifth Generation*. Reading, MA: Addison-Wesley. *600*

FELDMAN, ROBERT S. 1985. Nonverbal behavior, race, and the classroom teacher. *Teacher into Practice*, 24:45–49. *177*

FELSON, RICHARD B. and MARK D. REED. 1986. Reference groups and self-appraisals of academic ability and performance. *Social Psychology Quarterly*, 49:103–109. *113*

FENIGSTEIN, ALAN. 1984. Self-consciousness and the overperception of self as a target. *Journal of Personality and Social Psychology*, 47:860–870. *153*

FENNEMA, MEINHERT. 1982. *International Networks of Banks and Industry*. Boston: Martinus Nijhoff. *414*

FERRAR, PETER J. 1984. Expand IRAs to Social Security. *Wall Street Journal* (December 7):24. *300*

FESHBACH, MURRAY. 1986. The birth dearth: An AEI symposium. *Public Opinion*, 8 (December/January):18–19. *526*

FESTINGER, LEON. 1954. A theory of social comparison processes. *Human Relations*, 7:117–140. *183*

FEYERABEND, PAUL K. 1975. *Against Method*. London: New Left Books. *41*

FIEDLER, FRED E. 1981. Leadership effectiveness. *American Behavioral Scientist*, 24 (5):619–632. *114*

FIELDING, JONATHAN E. 1985. Smoking: Health effects and control. *New England Journal of Medicine*, 313:491–498. *492*

FIEVE, RONALD R. 1975. *Moodswing*. New York: William Morrow. *170*

FINDLAY, STEVEN. 1985. We feel healthy, even with aches, pains. *USA Today* (January 31):1D. *506*

FINE, GARY A. 1984. Negotiated orders and organizational cultures. *Annual Review of Sociology*, 10:239–262. *130*

FINE, MARK A., JOHN R. MORELAND, and ANDREW I. SCHWEBEL. 1983. Long-term effects of divorce on parent-child relationships. *Developmental Psychology*, 19:703–713. 357

FINKELHOR, DAVID. 1979. *Sexually Victimized Children*. New York: Free Press. 359

FINKELHOR, DAVID. 1984. *Child Sexual Abuse: New Theory and Research*. New York: Free Press. 359

FIREY, WALTER. 1947. *Land Use in Central Boston*. Cambridge: Harvard University Press. 548

FISCHER, CLAUDE S. 1981. The public and private worlds of city life. *American Sociological Review*, 46:306–316. 555

FISCHER, CLAUDE S. 1982. *To Dwell among Friends: Personal Networks in Town and City*. Chicago: University of Chicago Press. 555

FISCHER, CLAUDE S. 1984. *The Urban Experience*, 2nd ed. New York: Harcourt, Brace and Jovanovich. 555

FISCHER, LUCY ROSE. 1986. *Linked Lives: Adult Daughters and Their Mothers*. New York: Harper & Row. 360

FISCHER, MICHAEL M. J. 1980. *Iran: From Religious Dispute to Revolution*. Cambridge: Harvard University Press. 385

FISHER, ANNE B. 1985. Coke's brand-loyalty lesson. *Fortune* (August 5):44–46. 49

FISKE, EDWARD B. 1986. Student debt reshaping colleges and careers. *New York Times* (August 3):34–41. 476

FITZPATRICK, KEVIN M., and JOHN R. LOGAN. 1985. The aging of the suburbs, 1960–1980. *American Sociological Review*, 50:106–117. 560

FITZPATRICK, THOMAS B., and ARTHUR J. SOBER. 1985. Sunlight and skin cancer. *New England Journal of Medicine*, 313:818–819. 492

FLANDRIN, J. F. 1979. *Families in Former Times: Kinship, Household, and Sexuality*. New York: Cambridge University Press. 350

FONER, ANNE, and DAVID KERTZER. 1978. Transitions over the life course: Lessons from age-set societies. *American Journal of Sociology*, 83:1081–1104. 286

FORD, CHELLAN S., and FRANK A. BEACH. 1951. *Patterns of Sexual Behavior*. New York: Harper & Row. 307,329

FORD, MAUREEN R., and CAROL R. LOWERY. 1986. Gender differences in moral reasoning: A comparison of the use of justice and care orientations. *Journal of Personality and Social Psychology*, 50:777–783. 149

FOSTER, GEORGE M. 1969. *Applied Anthropology*. Boston: Little, Brown. 595

FOSTER, THOMAS W. 1980. Amish simply prosper. Columbus (Ohio) *Dispatch* (December 3):B–3. 70

FOX, DANIEL M. 1986. *Health Policies, Health Politics: The British and American Experience, 1911–1965*. Princeton, NJ: Princeton University Press. 510

FRAKER, SUSAN. 1984. Why women aren't getting to the top. *Fortune* (April 16):40–45. 318

FRANK, ANDRE GUNDER. 1969. *Capitalism and Underdevelopment in Latin America*, Rev. ed. New York: Modern Reader Paperbacks. 608

FRANK, ANDRE GUNDER. 1978. *Dependent Accumulation and Underdevelopment*. London: Macmillan. 608

FREEMAN, JO. 1973. The origins of the women's liberation movement. *American Journal of Sociology*, 78:792–811. 322

FREEMAN, RICHARD B. 1986. Create jobs that pay as well as crime. *New York Times* (July 20):2F. 239

FREUD, SIGMUND. 1917/1943. *A General Introduction to Psychoanalysis*. Garden City, NY: Garden City Publishing Co. 340

FREUD, SIGMUND. 1938. *The Basic Writings of Sigmund Freud*, Trans. A. A. Brill. New York: Modern Library. 345

FREUDENBURG, WILLIAM R. 1986. The density of acquaintanceship: An overlooked variable in community research. *American Journal of Sociology*, 92:27–63. 555

FREY, WILLIAM H. 1987. Migration and depopulation of the metropolis: Regional restructuring or rural renaissance? *American Sociological Review*, 52:240–257. 559

FRIEDAN, BETTY. 1963. *The Feminine Mystique*. New York: Norton. 324

FRIEDL, ERNESTINE. 1984. *Women and Men*. Prospect Heights, IL: Waveland Press, Inc. 314

FRIEDMAN, ANDREW. 1977. *Industry and Labor, Class Struggle at Work and Monopoly Capitalism*. New York: Macmillan. 130

FRIEDMAN, MURRAY. 1987. America is not a racist society. *Wall Street Journal* (February 20):16. 259

FRIEDRICH, LYNETTE K., and ALETHA H. STEIN. 1975. Prosocial television and young children. *Child Development*, 46:27–38. 158

FRIEND, R. M. and J. M. NEALE. 1972. Children's perceptions of success and failure. *Developmental Psychology*, 7:124–128. 474

FROMM, ERICH. 1968. *The Revolution of Hope*. New York: Harper & Row. 195

FUCHS, VICTOR R. 1983. *How We Live: An Economic Perspective on Americans from Birth to Death*. Cambridge: Harvard University Press. 350

FUCHS, VICTOR R. 1986. Sex differences in economic well-being. *Science*, 232:459–464. 318

FULLER, C. J. 1976. *The Nayars Today*. Cambridge: Cambridge University Press. 337

FURSTENBERG, FRANK F., JR., and GRAHAM B. SPANIER. 1984. *Recycling the Family: Remarriage after Divorce*. Beverly Hills: Sage. 359

GAGNON, JOHN H. 1977. *Human Sexualities*. Glenview, IL: Scott, Foresman. 327

GALBRAITH, JOHN KENNETH. 1985. Taking the sting out of capitalism. *New York Times* (May 26):1, 27. 409

GAILEY, PHIL. 1986. Religious right challenging the G.O.P. *New York Times* (June 2):16. 389

GALE, DENNIS E. 1984. *Neighborhood Revitalization and the Postindustrial City*. Lexington, MA: Lexington Books. 551

GALLOWAY, JOSEPH. 1983. Mormon church faces a fresh challenge. *U.S. News & World Report* (November 21): 61–62. 393

GALLUP, GEORGE, JR. 1985. *Religion in America*. Princeton, NJ: The Gallup Report. 387,390,394

GAMST, FREDERICK C. 1974. *Peasants in Complex Society*. New York: Holt, Rinehart and Winston. 80,609

GANONG, LAWRENCE H., and MARILYN COLEMAN. 1984. The effects of remarriage on children: A review of the empirical literature. *Family Relations*, 33:389–406. 358

GANS, HERBERT J. 1962. *The Urban Villagers*. New York: Free Press. 542,555

GANS, HERBERT J. 1972. The positive

functions of poverty. *American Journal of Sociology*, 78:275–289. 6,30

GANS, HERBERT J. 1979. Symbolic ethnicity: The future of ethnic groups and cultures in America. *Ethnic and Racial Studies*, 2:1–20. 276

GAPPA, JUDITH M., JEAN F. O'BARR, and DONALD ST. JOHN-PARSONS. 1980. The dual-career couple and academe: Can both prosper? *Anthropology Newsletter*, 21 (April):12–16. 354

GARFINKEL, HAROLD. 1964. Studies of the routine grounds of everyday activities. *Social Problems*, 11:225–250. 171

GARFINKEL, HAROLD. 1967. *Studies in Ethnomethodology*. Englewood Cliffs, NJ: Prentice-Hall. 86,171,305

GARFINKEL, HAROLD. 1967. *Studies in Ethnomethodology*. Englewood Cliffs, NJ: Prentice-Hall. 171

GARFINKEL, HAROLD. 1974. The origins of the term "ethnomethodology." In R. Turner, Ed., *Ethnomethodology*. Middlesex, England: Penguin Books. 171

GAY, JUDY, and RYAN D. TWENEY. 1975. Comprehension and production of standard and black English by lower-class black children. *Developmental Psychology*, 12:262–268. 474

GECAS, VIKTOR, and MICHAEL L. SCHWALBE. 1986. Parental behavior and adolescent self-esteem. *Journal of Marriage and the Family*, 48:37–46. 151

GEERTZ, CLIFFORD. 1963. *Old Societies and New States*. New York: Free Press. 254

GELLES, RICHARD J. 1985. Family violence. *Annual Review of Sociology*, 11:347–367. 359

GELLES, RICHARD J. and CLAIRE P. CORNELL. 1985. *Intimate Violence in Families*. Beverly Hills: Sage. 359

GELMAN, DAVID. 1986. Banality and terror. *Newsweek* (January 6):60. 583

GENERAL MILLS. 1981. *The General Mills American Family Report, 1980–1981: Families: Strengths and Strains at Work*. Minneapolis: General Mills. 354

GEORGE, LINDA K. and GEORGE L. MADDOX. 1977. Subjective adaptation to loss of the work role: A longitudinal study. *Journal of Gerontology*, 32:456–462. 294

GERGEN, DAVID R. 1987. On Christian understanding. *U.S. News & World Report* (April 6):72. 389

GERGEN, KENNETH J., and MARY GERGEN. 1971. International assistance in psychological perspective. *Yearbook of World Affairs*, 25:87–103. 173

GERSON, KATHLEEN. 1986. *Hard Choices: How Women Decide about Work, Career, and Motherhood*. Berkeley: University of California Press. 318

GERSON, MENACHEM. 1978. *Family, Women, and Socialization in the Kibbutz*. Lexington, MA: D.C. Heath. 222

GERSTEL, NAOMI, and HARRIET GROSS. 1984. *Commuter Marriage: A Study of Work and Family*. New York: Guilford Press. 355

GESCHWENDER, JAMES A. 1964. Social structure and the Negro revolt: An examination of some hypotheses. *Social Forces*, 43:248–256. 581

GESCHWENDER, JAMES A. 1978. *Racial Stratification in America*. Dubuque, IA: William C. Brown. 266

GIBBS, JACK P. 1975. *Crime, Punishment, and Deterrence*. New York: Elsevier. 215

GIBBS, JOHN C., KEVIN D. ARNOLD, and JENNIFER E. BURKHART. 1984. Sex differences in the expression of moral development. *Child Development*, 55:1040–1043. 149

GIBBS, JOHN C. and STEVEN V. SCHNELL. 1985. Moral development "versus" socialization. *American Psychologist*, 40:1071–1080. 149

GIDDENS, ANTHONY. 1971. *Capitalism and Modern Social Theory*. London: Cambridge University Press. 15

GIDDENS, ANTHONY. 1973. *The Class Structure of the Advanced Societies*. New York: Harper & Row. 581

GIDDENS, ANTHONY. 1978. *Emile Durkheim*. New York: Penguin Books. 443

GIDDENS, ANTHONY. 1985. *The Nation-State and Violence: Vol. 2 of a Contemporary Critique of Historical Materialism*. Berkeley: University of California Press. 436

GILBERT, ALAN. 1982. Urban development in a world system. In A. Gilbert and J. Gugler, Eds., *Cities, Poverty, and Development: Urbanization in the Third World*. New York: Oxford University Press. 551

GILBERT, C. 1967. When did a man in the Renaissance grow old? *Studies in the Renaissance*, 14:7–32. 293

GILLIGAN, CAROL. 1982. *In a Different Voice: Psychological Theory and Women's Development*. Cambridge, MA: Harvard University Press. 149

GITLIN, T. 1971. The price men pay for supremacy. *New York Times* (December 11):31. 320

GLASBERG, DAVITA S., and MICHAEL SCHWARTZ. 1983. Ownership and control of corporations. *Annual Review of Sociology*, 9:311–332. 410

GLASS, DAVID, PEVERILL SQUIRE, and RAYMOND WOLFINGER. 1984. Voter turnout: An international comparison. *Public Opinion*, 6 (January):49–55. 447

GLENN, NORVAL, and C. N. WEAVER. 1981. The contribution of marital happiness to global happiness. *Journal of Marriage and the Family*, 43:161–168. 349

GLICK, CLARENCE. 1980. *Sojourners and Settlers: Chinese Migrants in Hawaii*. Honolulu: University of Hawaii Press. 258

GLICK, PAUL C., and SUNG-LING LIN. 1986. Recent changes in divorce and remarriage. *Journal of Marriage and the Family*, 48:737–747. 355

GLOCK, CHARLES Y., BENJAMIN B. RINGER, and EARL R. BABBIE. 1967. *To Comfort and Challenge: A Dilemma of the Contemporary Church*. Berkeley, CA: University of California Press. 383

GLUCKMAN, MAX. 1955. *Custom and Conflict in Africa*. Oxford: Blackwell. 346

GOFFMAN, ERVING. 1959. *The Presentation of Self in Everyday Life*. Garden City, NY: Doubleday. 169

GOFFMAN, ERVING. 1961. *Asylums: Essays on the Social Situation of Mental Patients and Other Inmates*. Chicago: Aldine. 122,157,161,478

GOFFMAN, ERVING. 1961. *Encounters*. Indianapolis: Bobbs-Merrill. 92

GOFFMAN, ERVING. 1963. *Behavior in Public Places*. New York: Free Press. 3

GOFFMAN, ERVING. 1963. *Stigma: Notes on the Management of Spoiled Identity*. Englewood Cliffs, NJ: Prentice-Hall. 192

GOFFMAN, ERVING. 1971. *Relations in Public*. New York: Basic Books. 101

GOFFMAN, ERVING. 1974. *Frame Analysis: An Essay on the Organization of Experience*. Cambridge, MA: Harvard University Press. 171

GOFFMAN, ERVING. 1981. *Forms of Talk*. Philadelphia: University of Pennsylvania Press. *169*

GOFFMAN, ERVING. 1983. The interaction order. *American Sociological Review*, 48:1–17. *169,171,193*

GOLD, RAYMOND L. 1985. *Ranching, Mining, and the Human Impact of Natural Resource Development*. New Brunswick, NJ: Rutgers University Press. *554*

GOLDSTONE, JACK A. 1986. The comparative and historical study of revolutions. In J. A. Goldstone, Ed., *Revolutions*. San Diego: Harcourt Brace Jovanovich. *576,577*

GOLDSTONE, JACK A. 1986b. Revolutions in world history. In J. A. Goldstone, Ed., *Revolution*. San Diego: Harcourt Brace Jovanovich. *578*

GOLDTHORPE, J. E. 1984. *The Sociology of the Third World*. 2nd Ed. New York: Cambridge University Press. *338,606,607,608*

GOLEMAN, DANIEL. 1984. A bias puts self at center of events. *New York Times* (June 12):18, 23. *153*

GOLEMAN, DANIEL. 1985. Scientists find city is a series of varying perceptions. *New York Times* (December 31):11, 14. *541–542*

GOLEMAN, DANIEL. 1986. Psychologists pursue the irrational aspects of love. *New York Times* (July 22):17, 20. *348*

GOLEMAN, DANIEL. 1986. The roots of terrorism are found in brutality of shattered childhood. *New York Times* (September 2):19, 23. *579*

GONOS, GEORGE. 1977. "Situation" versus "frame": The "interactionist" and the "structuralist" analyses of everyday life. *American Sociological Review*, 42:854–867. *171*

GOODE, WILLIAM J. 1959. The theoretical importance of love. *American Sociological Review*, 24:38–47. *346*

GOODE, WILLIAM J. 1960. Illegitimacy in Caribbean social structure. *American Sociological Review*, 25:21–31. *343*

GOODE, WILLIAM J. 1963. *World Revolution and Family Patterns*. New York: Basic Books. *337*

GOODE, WILLIAM J. 1972. The place of force in human society. *American Sociological Review*, 37:507–519. *444*

GOODE, WILLIAM J. 1986. Individual choice and the social order. In J.E. Short, Jr., Ed., *The Social Fabric*. Beverly Hills, CA: Sage. *11*

GOODMAN, ANN B., CAROLE SIEGEL, THOMAS J. CRAIG, and SHANG P. LIN. 1983. The relationship between socioeconomic class and prevalence of schizophrenia, alcoholism, and affective disorders treated by inpatient care in a suburban area. *American Journal of Psychiatry*, 140:166–170. *235*

GOODMAN, ELLEN. 1986. We need a law to define motherhood. *Columbus, Ohio, Dispatch* (April 25):7A. *343*

GORDON, DAVID M. 1978. Capitalist development and the history of American cities. In W. Tabb and L. Sawers, Eds., *Marxism and the Metropolis*. New York: Oxford University Press. *556*

GORDON, LINDA, and PAUL O'KEEFE. 1984. Incest as a form of family violence: Evidence from historical case records. *Journal of Marriage and the Family*, 46:27–34. *359*

GORNICK, V. and B. K. MORAN. 1971. *Women in Sexist Society*. New York: New American Library. *313*

GOTTDIENER, MARK. 1985. *The Social Production of Urban Space*. Austin: University of Texas Press. *546*

GOTTLIEB, BOB, and PETER WILEY. 1986. Hopis, Navajos and King Coal. *Wall Street Journal* (July 11):16. *273*

GOTTMAN, JOHN M. 1983. How children become friends. *Monographs of the Society for Research in Child Development*, 48 (201). *158*

GOUGH, E. KATHLEEN. 1959. The Nayars and the definition of marriage. *Journal of the Royal Anthropological Institute*, 89:23–24. *100,337*

GOULD, CAROL GRANT. 1983. Out of the mouths of beasts. *Science 83*, 4 (April):69–72. *63*

GOULDNER, ALVIN. 1960. The norm of reciprocity: A preliminary statement. *American Sociological Review*, 39:86–100. *173*

GOULDNER, ALVIN W. 1970. *The Coming Crisis of Western Sociology*. New York: Basic Books. *21,31*

GOVE, WALTER R. 1970. Societal reaction as an explanation of mental illness: An evaluation. *American Sociological Review*, 35:873–884. *207*

GOWLETT, JOHN. 1984. *Ascent to Civilization*. New York: Knopf. *73*

GRAHAM, SAXON. 1956. Ethnic background and illness in a Pennsylvania County. *Social Problems*, 4:76–81. *500*

GRASMICK, HAROLD G., and GEORGE J. BRYJAK. 1980. The deterrent effect of perceived severity of punishment. *Social Forces*, 59:471–491. *215*

GRASSIAN, STUART. 1983. Psychopathological effects of solitary confinement. *American Journal of Psychiatry*, 140:1450–1454. *166*

GRAY, BRADFORD H., Ed. 1986. *For-Profit Enterprise in Health Care*. Washington, DC: Institute of Medicine, National Academy Press. *498*

GREELEY, ANDREW M. 1974. *Ethnicity in the United States*. New York: Wiley. *251,276*

GREELEY, ANDREW M. 1982. American Catholics: Going their own way. *The New York Times Magazine* (October 10):28+. *391*

GREEN, JERROLD D. 1986. Countermobilization in the Iranian revolution. In J. A. Goldstone, Ed., *Revolutions: Theoretical, Comparative, and Historical Studies*. San Diego: Harcourt Brace Jovanovich. *385*

GREENE, ELIZABETH. 1986. Today's college students found embracing traditional values. *Chronicle of Higher Education* (April 30):31. *388*

GREENHOUSE, STEVEN. 1986. The average guy takes it on the chin. *New York Times* (July 13):F1+. *236,237*

GREENHOUSE, STEVEN. 1986. Passing the buck from one generation to the next. *New York Times* (August 17):5E. *300*

GREENHOUSE, STEVEN. 1986. LTV failure stirs questions on survival of steel industry. *New York Times* (July 28):1, 26. *409*

GREENWALD, ANTHONY G. 1980. The totalitarian ego: Fabrication and revision of personal history. *American Psychologist*, 35:608–616. *153*

GREENWALD, ANTHONY G., and A. R. PRATKANKS. 1984. The self. In R. S. Wyer and T. K. Srull, Eds., *Handbook of Social Cognition*. Hillsdale, NJ: Erlbaum. *153*

GREENWALD, JOHN. 1985. Coca-Cola's big fizzle. *Time* (July 22):48–52. *49*

GREENWOOD, PETER W. 1982. *Selective Incapacitation*. Santa Monica, CA: Rand. *215*

GREER, COLIN. 1979. Once again, the 'family question.' *New York Times* (October 14):19E. *351*

GREER, WILLIAM R. 1986. The changing women's marriage market. *New York Times* (February 22):16. *335*

GREIF, GEOFFREY L. 1985. *Single Fathers*. Lexington, MA: Lexington Books. *364*

GRENIER, RICHARD. 1986. Around the world in American ways. *Public*

Opinion, 9 (February/March):3–5+. *593*

GRIFFIN, LARRY J., MICHAEL E. WALLACE, and BETH A. RUBIN. 1986. Capitalist resistance to the organization of labor before the New Deal: Why? How? Success. *American Sociological Review,* 51:147–167. *229*

GRIMSHAW, ALLEN D. 1980. Social interactional and sociolinguistic rules. *Social Forces,* 58:789–810. *176*

GROSS, A. 1977. Marriage counseling for unwed couples. *New York Times Magazine* (April 24):52+. *362*

GROSS, E. 1978. Organizational crime: A theoretical perspective. In N. Denzin, Ed., *Studies in Symbolic Interaction.* Greenwich, CT: JAI. *205*

GROSS, JANE. 1982. Old images are fading rapidly. *New York Times* (October 29):23, 24. *428*

GRUENBERG, BARRY. 1980. The happy worker: An analysis of educational and occupational differences in determining job satisfaction. *American Journal of Sociology,* 86:247–271. *418*

GRUNDSTAFF, CARL F. 1981. *Population and Society: A Sociological Perspective.* West Hanover, MA: The Christopher Publishing House. *527*

GRUSKY, DAVID, and ROBERT M. HAUSER. 1984. Comparative social mobility revisited: Models of convergence and divergence in 16 countries. *American Sociological Review,* 49:19–38. *345*

GRUSON, LINDSEY. 1986. Widespread illiteracy burdens the nation. *New York Times* (July 22):17, 20. *465*

GUERIN, BERNARD. 1986. Mere presence effects in humans: A review. *Journal of Experimental Social Psychology,* 23:38–77. *167*

GUIDUBALDI, JOHN, and JOSEPH D. PERRY. 1985. Divorce and mental health sequelae for children: A two-year follow-up of a nationwide sample. *Journal of the American Academy of Child Psychiatry,* 24:531–537. *357*

GUNDERSEN, EDNA. 1987. Fear and facts often don't match. *USA Today* (May 19):6D. *302*

GURNEY, PATRICK J. 1981. Historical origins of ideological denial: The case of Marx in American sociology. *The American Sociologist,* 16:196–201. *15*

GURR, TED R. 1970. *Why Men Rebel.* Princeton: Princeton University Press. *581*

GUSFIELD, JOSEPH. 1962. Mass society

and extremist politics. *American Sociological Review,* 27:19–30. *440*

GUTH, JAMES L. 1983. The new Christian right. In Robert C. Liebman and Robert Wuthnow, Eds., *The New Christian Right.* New York: Aldine. *389*

GWARTNEY, JAMES D. 1987. Reasons behind the male-female pay gap. *Wall Street Journal* (March 20):10. *318*

GWARTNEY-GIBBS, PATRICIA A. 1986. The institutionalization of premarital cohabitation: Estimates from marriage license applications, 1970 and 1980. *Journal of Marriage and the Family,* 48:423–434. *362*

HABERMAN, CLYDE. 1987. Defining kith and kin in the land of Kim and Lee. *New York Times* (February 23):4. *340*

HABERMAS, JURGEN. 1979. *Communication and the Evolution of Society.* Boston: Beacon. *379*

HABERMAS, JURGEN. 1981. Talcott Parsons: Problems of theory construction. *Sociological Inquiry,* 51:173–196. *29*

HACKER, ANDREW. 1986. The decline of higher learning. *The New York Review of Books* (February 13):35–42. *482*

HACKER, ANDREW. 1986. Women at work. *The New York Review* (August 14):26–32. *316,324*

HADDEN, JEFFREY K. 1987. Toward desacralizing secularization theory. *Social Forces,* 65:587–611. *387,394*

HADDEN, JEFFREY K., and CHARLES E. SWANN. 1981. *Prime Time Preachers: The Rising Power of Televangelism.* Reading, MA: Addison-Wesley. *389*

HADLEY, ARTHUR T. 1978. *The Empty Polling Booth.* Englewood Cliffs, NJ: Prentice-Hall. *447*

HAGAN, JOHN. 1980. The legislation of crime and delinquency: A review of theory, method, and research. *Law and Society Review,* 14:603–628. *204*

HAGAN, JOHN, and JEFFREY LEON. 1977. Rediscovering delinquency: Social history, political ideology, and the sociology of law. *American Sociological Review,* 42:587–598. *204*

HAGESTAD, G., and M. SMYER. 1983. Divorce at middle-age. In Weissman, S., Cohen, R., and Cohler, B., Eds., *Dissolving Personal Relationships.* New York: Academic Press. *357*

HALE, ELLEN. 1984. Menopause: Few feel ill effects. *USA Today* (June 20):D–1. *296*

HALL, EDWARD T. 1966. *The Hidden Dimension.* Garden City: Doubleday. *182*

HALL, EDWARD T., and MILDRED R. HALL. 1971. The sounds of silence. *Playboy* (June):139–140, 204, 206. *181*

HALL, THOMAS D. 1986. Incorporation in the world-system: Toward a critique. *American Sociological Review,* 51:390–402. *609*

HANNIGAN, JOHN A. 1985. Alain Touraine, Manuel Castells and social movement theory: A critical appraisal. *Sociological Quarterly,* 26:435–454. *566*

HANSEN, MARCUS. 1952. The third generation in America. *Commentary,* 14:492–500. *277*

HARDIN, GARRETT J. 1968. The tragedy of the commons. *Science,* 162:1243–1248. *117,118*

HARE, A. PAUL. 1976. *Handbook of Small Group Research,* 2nd ed. New York: Free Press. *114*

HAREVEN, TAMARA K. 1982. *Family Time and Industrial Time.* New York: Cambridge University Press. *338*

HARRINGTON, MICHAEL. 1976. *The Twilight of Capitalism.* New York: Simon and Schuster. *581*

HARRIS, CHAUNCEY D., and EDWARD L. ULLMAN. 1945. The Nature of Cities. *The Annals of the American Academy of Political and Social Science,* 242:7–17.

HARRIS, LOUIS. 1981. *Aging in the Eighties: America in Transition.* Washington, DC: National Council on Aging. *298*

HARSANYI, ZSOLT, and RICHARD HUTTON. 1979. Those genes that tell the future. *New York Times Magazine* (November 18):194–205. *142*

HARVEY, DAVID. 1985a. *Consciousness and the Urban Experience.* Baltimore: Johns Hopkins University Press. *557*

HARVEY, DAVID. 1985b. *The Urbanization of Capital.* Baltimore: Johns Hopkins University Press. *557*

HAUG, MARIE, AMASA FORD, and MARIAN SHAEFOR, Eds. 1985. *The Physical and Mental Health of Aged Women.* New York: Springer. *302*

HAUG, MARIE R., and BEBE LAVIN. 1983. Practitioner or patient—who's in charge. *Journal of Health and Social Behavior,* 22:212–229. *507*

HAUG, MARIE, and BEBE LAVIN. 1983. *Consumerism in Medicine: Challeng-*

ing Physician Authority. Beverly Hills, CA: Sage. 507

HAUSER, PHILIP M. 1960. Population Pressures. New Brunswick, NJ: Rutgers University Press. 526

HAUSER, ROBERT, and DAVID FEATHERMAN. 1977. The Process of Stratification. New York: Academic Press. 245

HAWLEY, AMOS. 1950. Human Ecology: A Theory of Community Structure. New York: Ronald Press. 529

HAWLEY, AMOS. 1963. Community power and urban-renewal success. American Journal of Sociology, 68:422–431. 225

HAWLEY, W. D. 1979. Getting the facts straight about the effects of school desegregation. Educational Leadership, 36:314–321. 476

HAYDUK, LESLIE ALEC. 1978. Personal space: An evaluation and orienting overview. Psychological Bulletin, 85:117–134. 181

HAYS, CHARLOTTE. 1984. The evolution of Ann Landers: From prim to progressive. Public Opinion, 6 (January):11–13. 66

HEARST, PATRICIA CAMPBELL. 1981. Every Secret Thing. New York: Doubleday. 121

HEATH, DWIGHT B. 1958. Sexual division of labor and cross-cultural research. Social Forces, 37:77–79. 341

HECHINGER, FRED. 1986. Humanities' peer review is faulted. New York Times (September 30):19, 22. 482

HEINERMAN, JOHN, and ANSON SHUPE. 1986. The Mormon Corporate Empire. Boston: Beacon Press. 393

HEITGERD, JANET L., and ROBERT J. BURSIK, JR. 1987. Extracommunity dynamics and the ecology of delinquency. American Journal of Sociology, 92:775–787. 542

HELLER, MIKHAIL, and ALEKANDR NEKRICH. 1986. Utopia in Power: The History of the Soviet Union From 1917 to the Present. New York: Summit Books. 442

HELLER, SCOTT. 1987. Scholars spar over marriage-prospects study. Chronicle of Higher Education (January 28):12. 335

HELLER, SCOTT. 1987. Faculty pay up 5.9 pct. The Chronicle of Higher Education (April 8):1, 16. 476

HELLMICH, NANCI. 1986. Casual sex: Hot '60s, chilly '80s. USA Today (February 19):1D. 328

HELLMICH, NANCI. 1986. Boomers: We're happier than our folks. USA Today (October 10):D1. 517

HELLMICH, NANCI. 1986. Freshmen want cash, not ideals. USA Today (October 31):A1. 486

HELYAR, JOHN, and ROBERT JOHNSON. 1986. Chicago's busy center masks a loss of jobs in its outlying areas. Wall Street Journal (April 16):1, 23. 558

HENLEY, NANCY M. 1973. Status and sex: Some touching observations. Bulletin of the Psychonomic Society, 2:91–93. 177

HENLEY, NANCY M. 1977. Body Politics: Sex, Power, and Nonverbal Communication. Englewood Cliffs, NJ: Prentice-Hall. 177

HEPBURN, JOHN R. 1977. Social control and the legal order: Legitimated repression in a capitalist state. Contemporary Crises, 1:77–90. 203

HERBERG, WILL. 1955. Protestant-Catholic-Jew. Garden City, NY: Doubleday. 277,393

HERBERS, JOHN. 1986. The New Heartland: America's Flight Beyond the Suburbs and How It Is Changing Our Future. New York: Times Books. 554

HERBERS, JOHN. 1986. Experts see need for new approach to urban aid. New York Times (June 22):13. 561

HERDT, GILBERT. 1982. Rituals of Manhood: Male Initiation in Papua New Guinea. Berkeley: University of California Press. 292–293,329

HERDT, GILBERT, Ed. 1984. Ritualized Homosexuality in Melanesia. Berkeley: University of California Press. 329

HERMAN, EDWARD S. 1981. Corporate Control, Corporate Power. New York: Cambridge University Press. 411

HERMAN, JUDITH. 1986. How serious is incest? Harvard Medical School Mental Health Letter, 2 (May):8. 360

HERSKOVITS, MELVILLE J. 1945. The processes of cultural change. In Ralph Linton, Ed., The Science of Man in the World Crisis. New York: Columbia University Press. 592

HERTEL, BRADLEY R., and MICHAEL HUGHES. 1987. Religious affiliation, attendance, and support for "profamily" issues in the United States. Social Forces, 65:858–882. 395

HERTZLER, J. O. 1961. American Social Institutions. Boston: Allyn and Bacon. 495

HESKETT, JAMES L. 1987. Thank heaven for the service sector. Business Week (January 26):22. 606

HESS, BETH B. 1985. Aging policies and old women: The hidden agenda. In A. S. Rossi, Ed., Gender and the Life Course. New York: Aldine. 299,300

HESS, BETH B., and JUAN M. WARING. 1978. Parent and child in later life: Rethinking the relationship. In R. M. Lerner and G. B. Spanier, Eds., Child Influences on Marital and Family Interaction. New York: Academic Press. 360

HETHERINGTON, E. MAVIS. 1979. Divorce. American Psychologist, 34:851–858. 357

HETHERINGTON, E. MAVIS, MARTHA COX, and ROGER COX. 1982. Effects of divorce on parents and children. In M. E. Lamb, Ed., Nontraditional Families: Parenting and Child Development. Hillsdale, NJ: Erlbaum. 357

HEWITT, JOHN P. 1979. Self and Society: A Symbolic Interactionist Social Psychology, 2nd ed. Boston: Allyn and Bacon. 9,34,35,168,169

HEWLETT, SYLVIA ANN. 1986a. A Lesser Life: The Myth of Women's Liberation in America. New York: William Morrow & Company. 318,324–325

HEWLETT, SYLVIA ANN. 1986b. Family isn't getting the support it deserves. USA Today (May 2):9A. 318

HILL, REUBEN. 1964. Methodological issues in family development research. Family Process, 3:186–206. 350

HILL, RICHARD C. 1984. Urban political economy. In M. P. Smith, Ed., Cities in Transformation. Beverly Hills, CA: Sage. 551

HILLKIRK, JOHN. 1986. Computer-aided design looks for faster growth. USA Today (April 14):3B. 603

HILLKIRK, JOHN. 1987. Classic Coke is it; No. 1 in '86. USA Today (January 26):B–1. 49

HILTZ, STARR ROXANNE, and MURRAY TUROFF. 1978. The Network Nation. Reading, MA: Addison-Wesley. 602

HIMMELFARB, GERTRUDE. 1984. The Idea of Poverty: England in the Early Industrial Age. New York: Knopf. 240

HIMMELSTEIN, DAVID U., and STEFFIE WOOLHANDLER. 1986. Administrative waste in U.S. health care. New England Journal of Medicine, 314:441–445. 508

HIMMELSTEIN, JEROME L. 1986. The social basis of antifeminism: Religious networks and culture. *Journal for the Scientific Study of Religion*, 25: 1–15. 323,585

HINDELANG, MICHAEL J., TRAVIS HIRSCHI, and JOSEPH WEIS. 1981. *Measuring Delinquency*. Beverly Hills: Sage. 214

HINDS, MICHAEL. 1981. The child victim of incest. *New York Times* (June 15):22. 359

HINKLE, ROSCOE. 1980. *Founding Theory of American Sociology: 1881–1915*. London: Routledge and Kegan Paul. 20

HIRO, DILIP. 1985. *Iran Under the Ayatollahs*. London: Routledge & Kegan Paul. 384

HIRSCH, PAUL M. 1986. From ambushes to golden parachutes: Corporate takeovers as an instance of cultural framing and institutional integration. *American Journal of Sociology*, 91:800–837. 411

HODGKINSON, HAROLD L. 1986. Reform? Higher education? Don't be absurd! *Phi Delta Kappan*, 68 (December): 271–274. 473

HOEBEL, E. ADAMSON. 1958. *Man in the Primitive World*, 2nd ed. New York: McGraw-Hill. 65

HOEBEL, E. ADAMSON. 1960. *The Cheyennes: Indians of the Great Plains*. New York: Holt, Rinehart & Winston. 341

HOERR, JOHN. 1986. Management discovers the human side of automation. *Business Week* (September 29):70–75. 602

HOLDEN, CONSTANCE. 1983. Can smoking explain ultimate gender gap. *Science*, 221:1034. 519

HOLDEN, CONSTANCE. 1986. A revisionist look at population growth. *Science*, 231:1493–1494. 520,525

HOLUSHA, JOHN. 1986. Saturn's uncertain future. *New York Times* (April 7):21, 42. 408

HORAN, PATRICK. 1978. Is status attainment research atheoretical? *American Sociological Review*, 43:534–541. 246

HORNER, MATINA. 1984. My side. *Working Woman* (January): 44–46. 324

HORNING, DONALD. 1970. Blue collar theft: Conceptions of property, attitudes toward pilfering, and work group norms in a modern industrial plant. In Erwin O. Smigel and H. Laurence Ross, Eds., *Crimes Against Bureaucracy*. New York: Van

Nostrand Reinhold. 128

HOSTETLER, JOHN A. 1980. *Amish Society*. Baltimore: Johns Hopkins University Press. 70

HOUSE, J. S., C. ROBBINS, and H. L. METZNER. 1982. The association of social relationships and activities with mortality: Prospective evidence from the Tecumseh Community Health Study. *American Journal of Epidemiology*, 116:123–140. 495

HOWARD, MICHAEL. 1984. Nuclear arms make chance of war "far more remote." *U.S. News & World Report* (April 9): 37–38. 459,460

HOYT, HOMER. 1939. *The Structure and Growth of Residential Neighborhoods in American Cities*. Washington, DC: Federal Housing Administration. 548

HSU, FRANCIS L. K. 1943. Incentives to work in primitive communities. *American Sociological Review*, 8:638–642. 417

HUBER, JOAN, and GLENNA SPITZE. 1983. *Sex Stratification: Children, Housework, and Jobs*. New York: Academic Press. 355

HUESMANN, L. POWELL, KIRSTI LAGERSPETZ, and LEONARD D. ERON. 1984. Intervening variables in the TV violence-aggression relation: Evidence from two countries. *Developmental Psychology*, 20:746–775. 160

HUGHES, CHARLES C. 1968. Medical care: Ethnomedicine. In D. Sills, Ed., *International Encyclopedia of Social Sciences*, Vol. 10. New York: Macmillan. 501

HUGHES, JAMES W. and GEORGE STERNLIEB. 1986. The suburban growth corridor. *American Demographics*, 8 (April):34–37. 559

HULL, JENNIFER BINGHAM. 1985. Women find parents need them just when careers are resuming. *Wall Street Journal* (September):21. 360

HULTSCH, DAVID F., and J. K. PLEMMONS. 1979. Life events and life span development. In Paul B. Baltes and Orville G. Brim, Jr., Eds., *Life-Span Development and Behavior*, Vol. 2. New York: Academic Press. 284

HUME, ELLEN. 1985. Indochinese refugees adapt quickly in U.S., using survival skills. *Wall Street Journal* (March 21):1, 12. 275

HUME, ELLEN. 1986. Pat Robertson hopes to turn evangelical fervor into political constituency for a presiden-

tial bid. *Wall Street Journal* (July 18):36. 389

HUNTER, ALBERT. 1987. The sixth circle of "Dis must be the place." *Sociological Footnotes* (April):3. 546

HUNTLEY, STEVE. 1983. America's Indians: "Beggars in our own land." *U.S. News & World Report* (May 23):70–72. 273

HUSTON, ALETHA. 1983. Sex-typing. In P. H. Mussen, Ed., *Handbook of Child Psychology*, 4th ed. E. M. Hetherington, Ed., *Socialization, Personality, and Social Development*. New York: Wiley. 312

HUXLEY, ALDOUS. 1955. *Brave New World*. New York: Bantam Books. 195

HUXLEY, ALDOUS. 1965. *Brave New World Revisited*. New York: Harper & Row. 195

HYDE, JANET SHIBLEY. 1979. *Understanding Human Sexuality*. New York: McGraw-Hill. 327

HYDE, JANET SHIBLEY. 1984. How large are gender differences in aggression? A developmental meta-analysis. *Developmental Psychology*, 20:722–736. 310

HYMAN, HERBERT. 1983. *Of Time and Widowhood: Nationwide Studies of Enduring Effects*. Durham, NC: Duke University Press. 294

HYMAN, HERBERT H., and ELEANOR SINGER. 1968. Introduction. In H. H. Hyman and E. Singer, Eds., *Readings in Reference Group Theory and Research*. New York: Free Press. 113

HYMOWITZ, CAROL, and TIMOTHY D. SCHELLHARDT. 1986. The glass ceiling. *Wall Street Journal* (March 24):1, 4. 318

ICHILOV, ORIT, and SHMUEL BAR. 1980. Extended family ties and the allocation of social rewards in veteran kibbutzim in Israel. *Journal of Marriage and the Family*, 42:421–426. 222

IGLEHART, JOHN K. 1986. Canada's health care system. *New England Journal of Medicine*, 315:1623–1628. 498

IMPERATO-MCGINLEY, J., R. E. PETERSON, E. GAUTIER, and N. STURLA. 1979. Androgens and the evolution of male-gender identity among male pseudohermaphrodites with 5a-reductase deficiency. *New England Journal of Medicine*, 300:1233–1237. 310

IM THURN, E. F. 1883. *Among the Indians of Guiana*. London: Kegan Paul, Trench & Trubner. *364*

INGHAM, ALAN G. 1974. The Ringelmann effect: Studies of group size and group performance. *Journal of Experimental Social Psychology*, 10:371–384. *116*

INKELES, ALEX. 1964. *What Is Society?* Englewood Cliffs, NJ: Prentice-Hall. *102*

ISAAC, LARRY, and WILLIAM R. KELLY. 1981. Racial insurgency, the state, and welfare expansion: Local and national level evidence from the postwar United States. *American Journal of Sociology*, 86:1348–1386. *241*

ITANI, JUNICHIRO. 1961. The society of Japanese monkeys. *Japan Quarterly*, 8:421–430. *61*

IVEY, MARK. 1986. How educators are fighting big-money madness in athletics. *Business Week* (October 27):136–140). *484*

JACKSON, JEFFREY M., and STEPHEN G. HARKINS. 1985. Equity in effort: An explanation of the social loafing effect. *Journal of Personality and Social Psychology*, 49:1199–1206. *116*

JACKSON, JEFFREY M., and KIPLING D. WILLIAMS. 1985. Social loafing on difficult tasks: Working collectively can improve performance. *Journal of Personality and Social Psychology*, 49:937–942. *116*

JAMES, JOHN. 1951. A preliminary study of the size determinant in small group interaction. *American Sociological Review*, 16:474–477. *114*

JANIS, IRVING L. 1982. *Groupthink: Psychological Studies of Policy Decisions and Fiascoes*. Boston: Houghton Mifflin. *117,120*

JARET, CHARLES. 1983. Recent neo-Marxist urban analysis. *Annual Review of Sociology*, 9:499–525. *556*

JENCKS, CHRISTOPHER. 1987. Genes & crime. *New York Review of Books* (February 12):33–41. *199*

JENCKS, CHRISTOPHER, et al. 1979. *Who Gets Ahead? The Determinants of Economic Success in America*. New York: Basic Books. *472*

JENKINS, J. CRAIG. 1983. Resource mobilization theory and the study of social movements. *Annual Review of Sociology*, 9:527–553. *583*

JENKINS, J. CRAIG. 1985. *The Politics of Insurgency: The Farm Worker Movement in the 1960s*. New York: Columbia University Press. *583,584*

JENSEN, ARTHUR R., and L. B. ROSENFELD. 1974. Influence of mode presentation, ethnicity, and social class on teachers' evaluations of students. *Journal of Educational Psychology*, 66:540–547. *474*

JENSEN, GARY F. 1986. Explaining differences in academic behavior between public-school and Catholic-school students: A quantitative case study. *Sociology of Education*, 59:32–41. *480*

JERVIS, ROBERT. 1976. *Perception and Misperception in International Politics*. Princeton: Princeton University Press. *459*

JERVIS, ROBERT, RICHARD N. LEBOW, and JANICE G. STEIN. 1986. *Psychology and Deterrence*. Baltimore: Johns Hopkins Press. *459*

JESSOP, BOB. 1985. *Nicos Poulantzas: Marxist Theory and Political Strategy*. New York: St. Martin's Press. *446*

JOHNSON, JANIS. 1986. '90s home: Make room for stepfamilies. *USA Today* (March 6):1–A. *358*

JOHNSON, NORRIS R., and WILLIAM E. FEINBERG. 1977. A computer simulation of the emergence of consensus in crowds. *American Sociological Review*, 42:505–521. *570*

JOHNSON, ROY S. 1982. Jackie Robinson to now: A growing dominance. *New York Times* (October 28):25, 26. *428*

JOHNSTONE, RONALD L. 1975. *Religion and Society in Interaction: The Sociology of Religion*. Englewood Cliffs, NJ: Prentice-Hall. *373*

JONES, EDWARD E., AMERIGO FARINA, ALBERT H. HASTORF, HAZEL MARKUS, DALE T. MILLER, and ROBERT A. SCOTT. 1984. *Social Stigma: The Psychology of Marked Relationships*. New York: Freeman. *192*

JONES, EDWARD E., and RICHARD E. NISBETT. 1971. *The Actor and the Observer: Divergent Perceptions of the Causes of Behavior*. Morristown, NJ: General Learning. *175*

JORDAN, NICK. 1985. Labors neither loved nor lost. *Psychology Today*, 19 (October):70–72. *315*

JUSTER, F. THOMAS. 1985. *Time, Goods and Well-Being*. Ann Arbor: University of Michigan Press. *315*

KAHN, ETHEL D., and LILLIAN ROBBINS. 1985. Social-psychological issues in sex discrimination. *Journal of Social Issues*, 41:135–154. *319*

KAIN, EDWARD L. 1984. Surprising singles. *American Demographics*, 6 (August):16–19+. *361*

KALLEBERG, ARNE L., MICHAEL WALLACE, and ROBERT P. ALTHAUSER. 1981. Economic segmentation, worker power, and income inequality. *American Journal of Sociology*, 87:651–683. *421*

KALMUSS, DEBRA. 1984. The intergenerational transmission of marital aggression. *Journal of Marriage and the Family*, 46:11–19. *359*

KAMM, HENRY. 1985. In one year, Sahara engulfs much of Chad. *New York Times* (January 2):1, 4. *530*

KANTROWITZ, BARBARA. 1986. A mother's choice. *Newsweek* (March 31):46–51. *316*

KANTROWITZ, BARBARA. 1987. Portrait of divorce in America. *Newsweek* (February 2):78. *355*

KANTROWITZ, BARBARA. 1986. Three's a crowd. *Newsweek* (September 1):68–76. *363*

KAPLAN, H. ROY, and CURT TAUSKY. 1972. Work and the welfare Cadillac: The function of and commitment to work among the hard-core unemployed. *Social Problems*, 19:469–483. *417*

KARABEL, JEROME. 1977. Community colleges and social stratification: Submerged class conflict in American higher education. In Jerome Karabel and A. H. Halsey, Eds., *Power and Ideology in Education*. New York: Oxford University Press. *472*

KARMIN, MONROE W. 1987. Will the U.S. stay number one? *U.S. News & World Report* (February 2):18–22. *408,413,602*

KASARDA, JOHN D., MICHAEL D. IRWIN, and HOLLY L. HUGHES. 1986. The South is still rising. *American Demographics*, 8 (June):32–39+. *520*

KASINDORF, MARTIN. 1982. Asian-Americans: A "Model Minority." *Newsweek* (December 6):39–51. *275*

KATZ, GREGORY. 1985. It's a crime: Only 1 of 3 are reported. *USA Today* (December 2):1A. *213*

KATZ, SIDNEY. Active life expectancy. *The New England Journal of Medicine*, 309:1218–1224. *235,493*

KAUFMAN, HAROLD G. 1982. *Professionals in Search of Work: Coping with the*

Stress of Job Loss and Underemployment. New York: Wiley. 423

KAUFMAN, MICHAEL T. 1979. Abandoned effort after the Gandhi era. *New York Times* (November 11): E–7. 528

KAUFMAN, MICHAEL T. 1986. Polish birth rate: It's No. 1 in Europe. *New York Times* (October 16):6. 528

KAYE, HOWARD L. 1986. *The Social Meaning of Modern Biology: From Social Darwinism to Sociobiology*. New Haven: Yale University Press. 103

KELLER, BILL. 1984. Experts describe 'Third World' health conditions of farm workers in U.S. *New York Times* (May 24):15. 237

KELLER, SUZANNE. 1963. *Beyond the Ruling Class*. New York: Random House. 440

KELLEY, ALLEN. 1986. The birth dearth: The economic consequences. *Public Opinion*, 8 (December/January):14–17+. 528

KELLEY, HAROLD H. 1952. Two functions of reference groups. In G. E. Swanson, T. M. Newcomb and E. L. Maccoby, Eds., *Readings in Social Psychology*. New York: Henry Holt. 113

KELLEY, HAROLD H., and J. L. MICHELA. 1980. Attribution theory and research. *Annual Research of Psychology*, 31:457–501. 45

KELLEY, JONATHAN, and HERBERT S. KLEIN. 1980. *Revolution and the Rebirth of Inequality: Stratification in Post-Revolutionary Bolivia*. Berkeley, CA: University of California Press. 578

KELLY, JOHN R. 1981. Leisure interaction and the social dialectic. *Social Forces*, 60:304–322. 424

KENISTON, KENNETH. 1970. Youth: A "new" stage in life. *American Scholar* (Autumn):586–595. 293

KENNEDY, L. 1985. The proprietarization of voluntary hospitals. *Bulletin of the New York Academy of Medicine*, 61:81–89. 498

KENNEY, MARTIN. 1987. *Biotechnology: The University-Industrial Complex*. New Haven: Yale University Press. 471

KENNY, TIMONY. 1984. 73% polled back right to die. *USA Today* (January 3):3A. 296

KENTAN, ROBERT K. 1968. *The Semai: A Nonviolent People of Malaya*. New York: Holt, Rinehart & Winston. 67

KERBO, HAROLD R. 1983. *Social Stratification and Inequality*. New York: McGraw-Hill. 230,232,234,239,241

KERCKOFF, ALAN. 1985. Social class, ability, and school attainments. In John G. Richardson, Ed., *Handbook of Theory and Research in the Sociology of Education*. Westport, CT: Greenwood. 473

KERCKHOFF, ALAN C., RICHARD T. CAMPBELL, and IDEE WINFIELD-LAIRD. 1985. Social mobility in Great Britain and the United States. *American Journal of Sociology*, 91:281–308. 245

KERR, NORBERT L., and ROBERT J. MacCOUN. 1985. Role expectations in social dilemmas: Sex roles and task motivation in groups. *Journal of Personality and Social Psychology*, 49:1547–1556. 118–119

KERR, PETER. 1987. New breed of ethnic gangs smuggling heroin. *New York Times* (March 21):1, 11. 211

KERTZER, DAVID I. 1983. Generation as a sociological problem. *Annual Review of Sociology*, 9:125–149. 285

KESSLER, RONALD C., and JAMES A. McRAE, JR. 1981. Trends in sex and psychological distress. *American Sociological Review*, 46:443–452. 354

KESSLER, RONALD C., JAMES S. HOUSE, and J. BLAKE TURNER. 1987. Unemployment and health in a community sample. *Journal of Health and Social Behavior*, 28:51–59. 423,494

KESSLER, S. J., and W. McKENNA. 1978. *Gender: An Ethnomethodological Approach*. New York: Wiley. 306

KETT, J. F. 1977. *Rites of Passage: Adolescence in America, 1870 to the Present*. New York: Basic Books. 291

KEY, V. O. JR. 1958. *Politics, Parties and Pressure Groups*. New York: Crowell. 449

KIDDER, RUSHWORTH M. 1987. Theodore Gordon. *Christian Science Monitor* (April 22):16–17. 601

KIFNER, JOHN. 1987. Shiite radicals: Rising wrath jars the Mideast. *New York Times* (March 22):1, 8. 385

KILBORN, PETER T. 1986. U.S. whites 10 times wealthier than blacks, census study finds. *New York Times* (July 19):1, 26.

KILMAN, SCOTT, and TIMOTHY K. SMITH. 1986. New Coke gets its own ad campaign—and one more chance to find a market. *Wall Street Journal* (February 14):19. 48

KILPATRICK, DEAN G., PATRICIA RESICK,

and LOIS VERNONEN. 1981. Effects of rape experience: A longitudinal study. *Journal of Social Issues*, 37:105–122. 494

KIMMEL, D. C. 1980. *Adulthood and Aging*. New York: Wiley. 284

KIMMEL, MICHAEL S. 1986. Little boxes: Life in the 'burbs. *Psychology Today*, 20 (July):74–75. 559

KINDER, DONALD R. 1986. The continuing American dilemma. *Social Issues*, 42:151–171. 258

KINDER, DONALD B. and DAVID O. SEARS. 1981. Prejudice and politics: Symbolic racism versus racial threats to the good life. *Journal of Personality and Social Psychology*, 40:414–431. 258

KINDER, DONALD R., and DAVID O. SEARS. 1985. Public opinion and political action. In G. Lindzey and E. Aronson, Ed., *Handbook of Social Psychology*, 3rd ed. Vol. II. New York: Random House. 569

KING, H. ELIZABETH, and CAROL WEBB. 1981. Rape crisis centers. *Journal of Social Issues*, 37:93–104. 494

KINGSTON, PAUL W. and STEVEN L. NOCK. 1987. Time together among dual-earner couples. *American Sociological Review*, 52:391–400. 354

KIRESCH, IRWIN S. and ANN JUNGEBLUT. 1986. *Literacy: Profiles of America's young adults*. Washington, DC: Government Printing Office. 466

KLEIN, FREDERICK C. 1980. Big old cities of East, Midwest are reviving after years of decline. *Wall Street Journal* (May 19):1, 20. 558

KLEIN, FREDERICK C. 1980. The pot trade. *Wall Street Journal* (August 8):1, 7. 200

KLEIN, FREDERICK C. 1984. Do college jocks graduate? *Wall Street Journal* (November 9):26. 484

KLEIN, FREDERICK C. 1986. Creative harassment. *Wall Street Journal* (January 17):13. 565

KLEIN, FREDERICK C. 1986. A designer sport is born. *Wall Street Journal* (February 14):15. 589–590

KLEINFIELD, N. R. 1986. The art of selling to the very rich. *New York Times* (June 15):F1. 224

KLEINFIELD, N. R. 1986. An eternal light in every socket. *New York Times* (March 16): F11. 596

KLOTT, GARY. 1986. The IRS loses its muscles. *New York Times* (April 6):1F. 211

KLUCKHOHN, CLYDE. 1960. *Mirror for*

Man. Greenwich, CT: Fawcett. 59–60,67

KLUEGEL, JAMES R., and ELIOT R. SMITH. 1982. Whites' beliefs about blacks' opportunity. *American Sociological Review*, 47:518–532. 258

KOENIG, FREDERICK. 1985. *Rumor in the Marketplace: The Social Psychology of Commercial Hearsay*. Dover, MA: Auburn House. 567

KOENIG, FREDERICK. 1982. Today's conditions make U.S. "ripe for the rumor mill." *U.S. News & World Report* (December 6):40. 567

KOESTLER, ARTHUR. 1949. The God that failed. In R. Crossman, Ed., *The God That Failed*. New York: Harper & Row. 380

KOHLBERG, LAWRENCE. 1966. A cognitive-developmental analysis of children's sex-role concepts and attitudes. In Eleanor E. Maccoby, Ed., *The Development of Sex Differences*. Stanford, CA: Stanford University Press. 312

KOHLBERG, LAWRENCE. 1969. Stage and sequence: The cognitive-developmental approach to socialization. In D. A. Goslin, Ed., *Handbook of Socialization Theory and Research*. Chicago: Rand McNally. 312

KOHLBERG, LAWRENCE. 1981. *Essays on Moral Development*, Vol. 1. *The Philosophy of Moral Development*. San Francisco: Harper & Row. 148

KOHLBERG, LAWRENCE, and D. Z. ULLIAN. 1974. Stages in the development of psychosexual concepts and attitudes. In R. C. Friedman, R. N. Richart, and R. L. Vande Wiele, Eds., *Sex Differences in Behavior*. New York: Wiley. 312

KOHN, MELVIN. 1977. *Social Competence, Symptions and Underachievement in Childhood: A Longitudinal Perspective*. Washington, DC: Winston. 157

KOHN, MELVIN L., and CARMI SCHOOLER. 1973. Occupational experience and psychological functioning: An assessment of reciprocal effects. *American Sociological Review*, 38:97–118. 418

KOHN, MELVIN L., and CARMI SCHOOLER. 1982. Job conditions and personality: A longitudinal assessment of their reciprocal effects. *American Journal of Sociology*, 87:1257–1286. 418

KOHN, MELVIN L., and CARMI

SCHOOLER. 1983. *Work and Personality: An Inquiry into the Impact of Social Stratification*. Norwood, NJ: Ablex Publishing Company. 418

KOLKO, GABRIEL. 1962. *Wealth and Power in America*. New York: Praeger. 445

KOMAROVSKY, MIRRA. 1976. *Dilemmas of Masculinity: A Study of College Youth*. New York: Norton. 320

KOMORITA, SAMUEL S., and JOAN M. BARTH. 1985. Components of reward in social dilemmas. *Journal of Personality and Social Psychology*, 48:364–373. 117,119

KOMORITA, SAMUEL S., and C. WILLIAM LAPWORTH. 1982. Cooperative choice among individuals versus groups in an N-person dilemma situation. *Journal of Personality and Social Psychology*, 42:487–496. 119

KORNHAUSER, WILLIAM. 1959. *The Politics of Mass Society*. New York: Free Press. 440

KORPI, MICHAEL F., and KYONG LIONG KIM. 1986. The uses and effects of televangelism: A factorial model of support and contribution. *Journal of the Scientific Study of Religion*, 25:410–423. 389

KOTEN, JOHN, and SCOTT KILMAN. 1985. How Coke's decision to offer 2 Colas undid 4½ years of planning. *Wall Street Journal* (July 15):1, 13. 48

KNOTTNERUS, J. DAVID. 1987. Status attainment research and its image of society. *American Sociological Review*, 52:113–121. 246

KOTLOWITZ, ALEX. 1985. Failed farmers find more hardships as they trek to city for work. *Wall Street Journal* (December 3):1, 23. 93

KRAMER, RODERICK M., and MARILYNN B. BREWER. 1984. Effects of group identity on resource use in a simulated commons dilemma. *Journal of Personality and Social Psychology*, 46:1044–1057. 119

KRAMER, RONALD C., and SAM MARULLO. 1985. Toward a sociology of nuclear weapons. *Sociological Quarterly*, 26:277–292. 456,461

KRANTZ, DAVID S., NEIL E. GRUNBERG, and ANDREW BAUM. 1985. Health psychology. *Annual Review of Psychology*, 36:349–384. 93,491

KROSNICK, JON A., and CHARLES M. JUDD. 1982. Traditions in social influence at adolescence: Who induces cigarette smoking? *Developmental*

Psychology, 18:359–368. 292

KÜBLER-ROSS, ELISABETH. 1969. *On Death and Dying*. New York: Macmillan. 295

KÜBLER-ROSS, ELISABETH. 1981. *Living with Death and Dying*. New York: Macmillan. 295

KUHN, MANFORD. 1964. Major trends in symbolic interaction theory in the past twenty-five years. *The Sociological Quarterly*, 5:61–84. 34

KUHN, MANFORD, and THOMAS S. MCPARTLAND. 1954. An empirical investigation of self attitudes. *American Sociological Review*, 19:68–76. 151

KUHN, THOMAS. 1962. *The Structure of Scientific Revolutions*. Chicago: University of Chicago Press. 40–41

KUHN, THOMAS. 1977. *The Essential Tensions: Selected Studies in Scientific Tradition and Change*. Chicago: University of Chicago Press. 41

KUHN, THOMAS. 1986. What are scientific revolutions? In R. Daston, M. Heidelberger, and L. Kruger, Eds., *The Probabilistic Revolution. Vol. 1: Ideas in History*. New York: Bradford Books. 41

KURTZ, LESTER R. 1984. *Evaluating Chicago Sociology*. Chicago: University of Chicago Press. 21

KUTTNER, ROBERT. 1987. The debate over new jobs is turning into mudslinging. *Business Week* (April 13):22. 602

LAMB, MICHAEL E. 1978. Influence of the child on marital quality and family interaction during the prenatal, perinatal, and infancy periods. In Richard M. Lerner and Graham B. Spanier, Eds., *Child Influences on Marital and Family Interaction: A life-span perspective*. New York: Academic Press. 352

LANDY, DAVID, and HAROLD SIGALL. 1974. Beauty is talent: Task evaluation as a function of the performer's physical attractiveness. *Journal of Personality and Social Psychology*, 29: 299–304. 320

LANG, O. 1946. *Chinese Family and Society*. New Haven: Yale University Press. 294

LANGER, JUDITH. 1985. The new mature mothers. *American Demographics*, 7 (July):29–31+. 363

LANTZ, HERMAN R. 1984. Continuities and discontinuities in American sociology. *The Sociological Quarterly*, 25:581–596. *20,21*

LAPSLEY, DANIEL K., ROBERT D. ENRIGHT, and RONALD C. SERLIN. 1985. Toward a theoretical perspective on the legislation of adolescence. *Journal of Early Adolescence*, 5:441–466. *291*

LAQUEUR, WALTER. 1986. *A World of Secrets: The Uses and Limits of Intelligence.* New York: Basic Books. *30*

LARSON, ERIK, and CARRIE DOLAN. 1983. Large computer firms sprout little divisions for good, fast, work. *Wall Street Journal* (August 19): 1, 12. *132*

LASLETT, BARBARA. 1973. The family as a public and private institution: An historical perspective. *Journal of Marriage and the Family*, 35:480–492. *351*

LASLETT, PETER. 1974. *Household and Family in Past Time.* New York: Cambridge University Press. *337*

LASLETT, PETER. 1976. Societal development and aging. In R. Binstock and E. Shanas, Eds., *Handbook of Aging and the Social Sciences.* New York: Van Nostrand Reinhold. *337*

LATANE, BIBB, and JOHN M. DARLEY. 1970. *The Unresponsive Bystander.* New York: Appleton-Century-Crofts. *10,183*

LATANE, BIBB, and STEVE NIDA. 1981. Ten years of research on group size and helping. *Psychological Bulletin*, 89: 308–324. *10,183*

LATANE, BIBB, KIPLING WILLIAMS, and STEPHEN HARKINS. 1979. Many hands make light the work: The causes and consequences of social loafing. *Journal of Personality and Social Psychology*, 37:822–832. *116*

LAUER, JEANETTE C., and ROBERT H. LAUER. 1985. Marriages made to last. *Psychology Today*, 19 (June):22–26. *348*

LAUER, ROBERT H., and WARREN H. HANDEL. 1983. *Social Psychology*, 2nd ed. Englewood Cliffs, NJ: Prentice-Hall. *131,170*

LAUER, ROBERT H., and JEANETTE C. LAUER. 1981. *Fashion Power: The Meaning of Fashion in American Society.* Englewood Cliffs, NJ: Prentice-Hall. *170*

LAWRENCE, ROBERT Z. 1985. The middle class is alive and well. *New York Times* (June 23):F–3. *236*

LAZAR, IRVING, and RICHARD DARLING-TON. 1982. Lasting Effects of Early Education: A Report from the Consortium for Longitudinal Studies. *Monographs of the Society for Research in Child Development.*

LEACOCK, ELEANOR, and HELEN I. SAFA, Eds. 1986. *Women's Work.* South Hadley, MA: Bergin & Garvey. *315*

LEAKEY, RICHARD. 1982. Discarding the concept of man as "killer ape." *U.S. News & World Report* (January 18):62. *459*

LEAKEY, RICHARD E. and ROGER LEWIN. 1977. *Origins.* New York: Dutton. *73*

LE BON, GUSTAV. 1986. *The Crowd: A Study of the Popular Mind.* London: Ernest Benn, Ltd. *574*

LEE, GARY R. 1977. *Family Structure and Interactions: A Comparative Analysis.* New York: J. B. Lippincott. *339*

LEE, JOHN. 1986. Ravage in the rain forests. *U.S. News & World Report* (March 31):61–62. *533*

LEE, RICHARD. 1968. What hunters do for a living, or how to make out on scarce resources. In R. Lee and I. DeVore, Eds., *Man the Hunter.* Chicago: Aldine. *73*

LEE, RICHARD. 1969. !Kung Busman subsistence: An input-output analysis. In A. Vayda, Ed., *Environment and Cultural Behavior.* Garden City: NY: Natural History Press. *73*

LEE, RICHARD. 1984. *The Dobe !Kung.* New York: Holt, Rinehart, and Winston. *76,77,78*

LEE, RICHARD B., and IRVEN DEVORE. 1968. Problems in the study of hunters and gatherers. In R. B. Lee and I. DeVore, Eds., *Man the Hunter.* Chicago: Aldine. *73*

LEE, SUSAN H., and DANIEL G. BATES. 1974. The origins of specialized nomadic pastoralism: A systemic model. *American Antiquity*, 39:187–193. *79*

LEISHMAN, KATIE. 1987. Heterosexuals and AIDS. *Atlantic Monthly* (February):39–58. *490*

LEMERT, EDWIN M. 1951. *Social Pathology: A Systematic Approach to the Theory of Sociopathic Behavior.* New York: McGraw-Hill. *205*

LEMERT, EDWIN M. 1972. *Human Deviance, Social Problems and Social Control*, 2nd ed. Englewood Cliffs, NJ: Prentice-Hall. *190,205*

LENSKI, GERHARD. 1961. *The Religious Factor.* Garden City, NY: Doubleday. *393*

LENSKI, GERHARD E. 1966. *Power and Privilege.* New York: McGraw-Hill. *31,33,73,75,80,81,227,230,435,437, 445,595,596*

LENSKI, GERHARD, and JEAN LENSKI. 1982. *Human Societies: An Introduction to Macrosociology*, 4th ed. New York: McGraw-Hill. *79,80,596*

LENSKI, GERHARD, and PATRICK D. NOLAN. 1984. Trajectories of development: A test of ecological-evolutionary theory. *Social Forces*, 63:1–23. *71,76,78*

LENSKI, GERHARD, and PATRICK D. NOLAN. 1986. Trajectories of development: A further test. *Social Forces*, 64:794–795. *71,76*

LEO, JOHN. 1987. When the date turns into rape. *Time* (March 23):77. *322*

LEONARD, WILBERT MARCELLUS II. 1980. *A Sociological Perspective of Sport.* Minneapolis: Burgess Publishing Company. *427*

LEONTIEF, WASSILY, and FAYE DUCHIN. 1986. *The Future Impact of Automation on Workers.* New York: Oxford University Press. *603*

LERNER, DANIEL. 1958. *The Passing of Traditional Society.* New York: Free Press. *607*

LERNER, RICHARD M. 1985. Adolescent maturational changes and psychosocial development: A dynamic interactional perspective. *Journal of Youth and Adolescence*, 14:355–372. *292*

LESSER, ALEXANDER. 1968. War and the state. In *War: The Anthropology of Armed Conflict and Aggression.* Garden City, NY: Natural History. *458*

LESTER, MARILYN. 1980. Generating newsworthiness: The interpretive construction of public events. *American Sociological Review*, 45:984–994. *450,454*

LEUNG, ELEANOR H. L. and HARRIET L. RHEINGOLD. 1981. Development of pointing as a social gesture. *Developmental Psychology*, 17:215–220. *289*

LEVINSON, DANIEL J. 1978. *The Seasons of a Man's Life.* New York: Knopf. *287,293*

LEVINSON, DANIEL J. 1986. A conception of adult development. *American Psychologist*, 41:3–13. *287,293*

LEVINSON, HARRY. 1964. Money aside, why spend life working. *National Observer* (March 9):20. *418*

LEVI-STRAUSS, CLAUDE. 1956. The family. In Harry L. Shapiro, Ed., *Man, Culture and Society.* New York: Oxford University Press. *340*

LEVY, FRANK and RICHARD C. MICHEL. 1985. Are baby boomers selfish. *American Demography*, 7 (April):38–41. *243*

LEWIN, KURT, RONALD LIPPITT, and RALPH K. WHITE. 1939. Patterns of aggressive behavior in experimentally created "social climates." *Journal of Social Psychology*, 10:271–299. *114–115*

LEWIS, ANTHONY. 1985. The military-industrial complex. *New York Times* (November 21):23. *452*

LEWIS, PAUL. 1986. Military spending questioned. *New York Times* (November 11):25. *191*

LEWIS, J. DAVID, and ANDREW J. WEIGERT. 1985. Social atomism, holism, and trust. *Sociological Quarterly*, 26:455–471. *196*

LEWIS, MICHAEL and JEANNE BROOKS-GUNN. 1979. Toward a theory of social cognition: The development of the self. *New Directions for Child Development*, 4:1–20. *290*

LEWIS, MICHAEL, JEANNE BROOKS-GUNN, and JOHN JASKIR. 1985. Individual differences in visual self-recognition as a function of mother-infant attachment relationship. *Developmental Psychology*, 21:1181–1187. *290*

LEWIS, OSCAR. 1952. Urbanization without breakdown: A case study. *Scientific Monthly*, 75:31–41. *555*

LEWIS, OSCAR. 1959. *Five Families: Mexican Case Studies in the Culture of Poverty*. New York: Basic Books. *237*

LEWIS, OSCAR. 1961. *The Children of Sanchez*. New York: Random House. *237*

LEWIS, OSCAR. 1966. *La Vida: A Puerto Rican Family in the Culture of Poverty: San Juan and New York*. New York: Random House. *237*

LEWIS, PETER H. 1986. Indian bones: Balancing research goals and tribes' rights. *New York Times* (May 20):20. *191*

LEWONTIN, R. C., STEVEN ROSE, and LEON J. KAMIN. 1984. *Not in Our Genes*. New York: Pantheon. *15,103*

LIEBERMAN, JONATHAN. 1986. Too many people? *The New York Review* (June 26):36–42. *527*

LIEBERSON, STANLEY. 1970. Stratification and ethnic groups. *Sociological Inquiry*, 40:172–181. *253*

LIEBOW, ELLIOT. 1967. *Tally's Corner*. Boston: Little, Brown. *5–6,7*

LIEF, LOUISE. 1986. France sends mixed signals on terrorism and Mideast policy. *Christian Science Monitor* (November 3):11. *582*

LIGHT, DONALD W. 1986. Corporate medicine for profit. *Scientific American*, 255 (December):38–45. *498,502*

LIMBER, JOHN. 1977. Language in child and chimp? *American Psychologist*, 32:280–295. *63*

LINDEN, FABIAN. 1984. Myth of the disappearing middle class. *Wall Street Journal* (January 23):18. *237*

LINDEN, FABIAN. 1986. The dream is alive. *American Demographics*, 8 (June):4–6. *237*

LINDGREN, ETHEL JOHN. 1938. An example of culture contact without conflict: Reindeer Tungus and Cossacks of Northwestern Manchuria. *American Anthropologist*, 40:605–621. *251,252*

LINDSEY, ROBERT. 1985. Lack of students and money besets California 2-year colleges. *New York Times* (April 29):8. *472*

LINDSEY, ROBERT. 1986. The Mormons: Growth, prosperity and controversy. *New York Times Magazine* (January 12):19–23+. *393*

LINDSEY, ROBERT. 1987. Colleges accused of bias to stem Asians' gain. *New York Times* (January 19):8. *483*

LINK, BRUCE G., BRUCE P. DOHREN-WEND, and ANDREW E. SKODOL. 1986. Socio-economic status and schizophrenia. *American Sociological Review*, 51:242–258. *235*

LINTON, RALPH. 1936. *The Study of Man*. New York: Appleton-Century-Crofts. *89,90,283*

LINTON, RALPH. 1937. One hundred per cent American. *American Mercury*, 40 (April):427–429. *68*

LINTON, RALPH. 1945. *The Cultural Background of Personality*. New York: Appleton-Century-Crofts. *58–59*

LIPSET, SEYMOUR MARTIN. 1959. *Religion in America: What religious revival*. New York: Columbia University Forum. *394*

LIPSET, SEYMOUR MARTIN. 1963. *The First New Nation*. New York: Basic Books. *440*

LIPSET, SEYMOUR MARTIN. 1963. *Political Man*. Garden City, NY: Doubleday. *440*

LIPSET, SEYMOUR MARTIN. 1982. Social mobility in industrial societies. *Public Opinion*, 5 (June/July):41–44. *245*

LIPSET, SEYMOUR MARTIN. 1986. Unions in decline. *Public Opinion*, 9 (September/October):52–54. *422*

LIPSYTE, ROBERT. 1985. Time to stop exploiting "gladiators." *Columbus, Ohio, Dispatch* (September 22): C1. *381*

LIPTON, DOUGLAS, ROBERT MARTINSON, and JUDITH WILKS. 1975. *The Effectiveness of Correctional Treatment: A Survey of Treatment Evaluation Studies*. New York: Praeger. *215*

LISTER, JOHN. 1986. Shattuck lecture—The politics of medicine in Britain and the United States. *New England Journal of Medicine*, 315:168–174. *511*

LIVESLEY, W. J. and D. B. BROMLEY. 1973. *Person Perception in Childhood and Adolescence*. New York: Wiley. *290*

LOFLAND, LYN. 1978. *The Craft of Dying*. Beverly Hills: Sage. *296*

LOGAN, JOHN R., and REID M. GOLDEN. 1986. Suburbs and satellites: Two decades of change. *American Sociological Review*, 51:430–437. *559*

LONDON, BRUCE. 1987. Structural determinants of third world urban change: An ecological and political economic analysis. *American Sociological Review*, 52:28–43. *552*

LONGMAN, PHILLIP. 1985. The downwardly mobile baby boomers. *Wall Street Journal* (April 12):26. *243*

LONGSHORE, DOUGLAS, and JEFFREY PRAGER. 1985. The impact of school desegregation: A situational analysis. *Annual Review of Sociology*, 11:75–91. *475,476*

LOONEY, DOUGLAS S. 1979. Sis-boom-grrrr. *Sports Illustrated* (September 10):43–44. *107*

LORD, CHARLES G., MARK R. LEPPER, and DIANE MACHIE. 1984. Attitude prototypes as determinants of attitude-behavior consistency. *Journal of Personality and Social Psychology*, 46:1254–1266. *174*

LORD, LEWIS J. 1987. An unholy war in the TV pulpits. *U. S. News & World Report* (April 6):58–65. *388*

LORENCE, JON, and JEYLAN T. MORTIMER. 1985. Job involvement through the life course: A panel study of three age groups. *American Sociological Review*, 50:618–638. *418*

LOS, M. 1982. Crime and economy in the Communist countries. In P.

Wickman and T. Dailey, Eds., *White-Collar and Economic Crime*. Lexington, MA: Lexington. *205*

LOURY, GLENN C. 1985. The moral quandary of the black community. *The Public Interest*, 79:9–22. *261*

LOWENTHAL, MARJORIE F. 1964. Social isolation and mental illness in old age. *American Sociological Review*, 29:20–30. *419*

LUBLIN, JOANN S. 1985. Increasing numbers of suburbs face problems once confined to cities. *Wall Street Journal* (February 27):33. *560*

LUCKMANN, THOMAS. 1967. *The Invisible Religion*. New York: Macmillan. *394*

LUECK, THOMAS J. 1986. Baby-boomers: Reality vs. dream. *New York Times* (March 6):19, 20. *7*

LUECK, THOMAS J. 1986. New York suburbs offer jobs but a daunting cost of living. *New York Times* (September 1): 1, 5. *559*

LUHMANN, NIKLAS. 1982. *The Differentiation of Society*. New York: Columbia University Press. *394*

LUKACS, GEORGE. 1922/1968. *History and Class Consciousness*. Cambridge, MA: MIT Press. *228*

LUKES, STEVEN. 1977. Alienation and anomie. In *Essays in Social Theory*. New York: Columbia University Press. *418*

LUMSDEN, CHARLES J., and EDWARD O. WILSON. 1981. *Genes, Mind, and Culture*. Cambridge, MA: Harvard University Press. *340*

LYNCH, KEVIN. 1984. *Good City Form*. Cambridge, MA: MIT Press. *557*

LYND, ROBERT S., and HELEN MERRILL LYND. 1929. *Middletown: A Study in American Culture*. New York: Harcourt, Brace & World. *349*

LYND, ROBERT S., and HELEN MERRILL LYND. 1937. *Middletown in Transition: A Study in Cultural Conflicts*. New York: Harcourt, Brace & World. *349*

LYNN, MICHAEL, and ANDREW OLDENQUIST. 1986. Egoistic and nonegoistic motives in social dilemmas. *American Psychologist*, 41:529–534. *119*

MACCOBY, ELEANOR E., and CAROL N. JACKLIN. 1974. *The Psychology of Sex Differences*. Stanford, CA: Stanford University Press. *312*

MACCOBY, ELEANOR E., and CAROL N. JACKLIN. 1980. Sex differences in aggression: A rejoinder and reprise.

Child Development, 51:964–980. *310*

MACKLIN, ELEANOR D. 1974. Going very steady. *Psychology Today*, 8 (November):53–59. *362*

MACKLIN, ELEANOR D. 1978. Nonmarital heterosexual cohabitation. *Marriage and the Family Review*, 1:2–10. *362*

MAEROFF, GENE I. 1986. Exeter, at 205, expands on the basics. *New York Times* (February 16):14. *123*

MAGNUSSON, DAVID, HAKAN STATTIN, and VERNON L. ALLEN. 1985. Biological maturation and social development. *Journal of Youth and Adolescence*, 14:267–283. *292*

MAIN, JEREMY. 1984. The trouble with managing Japanese-style. *Fortune* (April 2):50–56. *132*

MAIN, JEREMY. 1987. Business goes to college for a brain gain. *Fortune* (March 16):80–86. *471*

MAITAL, SHLOMO. 1982. Kumquats to computers. *Barron's* (July 19):24–26. *222*

MAJOR, B. 1981. Gender patterns in touching behavior. In C. Mayo and N. Henley, Eds., *Gender and Nonverbal Behavior*. New York: Springer-Verlag. *177*

MALAMUTH, NEIL M. 1981. Rape proclivity among males. *Journal of Social Issues*, 37:138–157. *321*

MALAMUTH, NEIL M. 1983. Factors associated with rape predictors of laboratory aggression against women. *Journal of Personality and Social Psychology*, 45:432–442. *321*

MALCOLM, ANDREW H. 1987. What five families did after losing the farm. *New York Times* (February 4):1, 9. *92*

MALINOWSKI, BRONISLAW. 1922. *Argonauts of the Western Pacific*. New York: E. P. Dutton. *99*

MALINOWSKI, BRONISLAW. 1927. *Sex and Repression in Savage Society*. London: Routledge & Kegan Paul. *340*

MALINOWSKI, BRONISLAW. 1929. *The Sexual Life of Savages in Northwestern Melanesia*. New York: Eugenics Press. *99, 311*

MALINOWSKI, BRONISLAW. 1945. *The Dynamics of Culture Change*. New Haven: Yale University Press. *590*

MALINOWSKI, BRONISLAW. 1964. Parenthood—The basis of social structure. In Rose Coser, Ed., *The Family: Its Structure and Functions*. New York: St. Martin's Press. *343*

MANDELBAUM, MICHAEL, and STROBE

TALBOTT. 1987. What arms control is all about. *New York Times* (January 30):23. *462*

MANN, JAMES. 1983. One-parent family: The troubles and the joys. *Newsweek* (November 28):57–62. *364*

MANN, JAMES. 1984. A revival of religion on campus. *U.S. News & World Report* (January 9):44. *388*

MANN, LEON. 1981. The baiting crowd in episodes of threatened suicide. *Journal of Personality and Social Psychology*, 41:703–709. *570*

MANN, LEON, JAMES W. NEWTON, and J. M. INNES. 1982. A test between deindividuation and emergent norm theories of crowd aggression. *Journal of Personality and Social Psychology*, 42:260–272. *570*

MANNHEIM, KARL. 1927. The problems of generations. In K. Mannheim, *Essays on the Sociology of Knowledge*. London: Routledge & Kegan Paul. *284*

MANNING, ROBERT A. 1987. Gorbachev: Faster, faster. *U.S. News & World Report* (February 23):25–26. *442*

MARANTO, GINA. 1986. Are we close to the road's end? *Discover* (January):28–50. *515*

MARECEK, JEANNE, and DAVID R. METTEE. 1972. Avoidance of continued success as a function of self-esteem, level of esteem certainty, and responsibility for success. *Journal of Personality and Social Psychology*, 22:98–107. *151*

MARGLIN, STEPHEN. 1974. What the bosses do: The origins and functions of hierarchy in capitalist production. *Review of Radical Political Economics*, 6:60–112. *130*

MARKOFF, JOHN. 1985. The social geography of rural revolt at the beginning of the French Revolution. *American Sociological Review*, 50:761–781. *577*

MARKS, GARY, NORMAN MILLER, and GEOFFREY MARUYAMA. 1981. Effect of targets' physical attractiveness on assumptions of similarity. *Journal of Personality and Social Psychology*, 41:198–206. *347*

MARKS, MITCHELL L., PHILIP H. MIRVIS, EDWARD J. HACKETT, and JAMES F. GRADY, JR. 1986. Employee participation in a quality circle program: Impact on quality of work life, productivity, and absenteeism. *Journal of Applied Psychology*, 71:61–69. *132*

MARS, GERALD. 1974. Dock pilferage: A

case study in occupational theft. In *Deviance and Social Control*. London: Tavistock. 129

MARSHALL, SUSAN E. 1985. Ladies against women: Mobilization dilemmas of antifeminist movements. *Social Problems*, 32:348–362. 585

MARSHALL, THOMAS H. 1964. *Class, Citizenship and Social Development*. Garden City, NY: Doubleday. 81

MARSHALL, VICTOR. 1980. *Last Chapters: A Sociology of Aging and Dying*. Belmont, CA: Wadsworth. 295

MARTIN, HARRY J., and THEODORE N. GREENSTEIN. 1983. Individual differences in status generalization. *Journal of Personality and Social Psychology*, 45:641–662. 90

MARTINSON, ROBERT. 1974. What works?—Questions and answers about prison reform. *The Public Interest*, 35:22–54. 215

MARTY, MARTIN E. 1987. What people seek—and find—in belief. *U.S. News & World Report* (January 7):43. 394

MARULLO, SAM. 1985. The ideological nature of nuclear deterrence: Some causes and consequences. *Sociological Quarterly*, 26:311–330. 458

MARULLO, SAM. 1985. Targets for racial invasion and reinvasion: Housing units where racial turnovers occurred, 1974–1977. *Social Forces*, 63:748–774. 550

MARUYAMA, GEOFFREY, NORMAN MILLER, and ROLF HOLTZ. 1986. The relation between popularity and achievement: A longitudinal test of the lateral transmission of value hypothesis. *Journal of Personality and Social Psychology* 51:730–741. 475

MARX, GARY. 1969. *Protest and Prejudice*. New York: Harper & Row. 10

MARX, GARY T., and JAMES L. WOODS. 1975. Strands of theory and research in collective behavior. *Annual Review of Sociology*, 1:363–428. 573

MARX, KARL. 1844/1964. *Critique of the Hegelian Philosophy of the Right*. Reprinted in Tom B. Bottomore, *Karl Marx*. New York: McGraw-Hill. 382

MARX, KARL. 1844/1963. Estranged labour—Economic and philosophic manuscripts of 1844. In C. W. Mills, Ed., *Images of Man*. New York: George Braziller. 382,418

MARX, KARL. 1906. *Capital*, Vol. 1. New York: Modern Library. 129, 524,598

MARX, KARL. 1966. *The Civil War in France*. Peking: Foreign Languages Press. 130

MARX, KARL. 1970. *Critique of Hegel's "Philosophy of Right."* Trans. A. O'Malley and J. O'Malley. London: Cambridge University Press. 129

MARX, KARL, and FRIEDRICH ENGELS. 1848/1955. *The Communist Manifesto*. S. H. Beer, Ed., New York: Appleton-Century-Crofts. 15,231

MASSEY, DOUGLAS S., and NANCY A. DENTON. 1985. Spatial assimilation as a socioeconomic outcome. *American Sociological Review*, 50:94–106. 546

MASTERS, WILLIAM H., and VIRGINIA E. JOHNSON. 1966., *Human Sexual Response*. Boston: Little, Brown. 326

MASTERSON, JOHN. 1984. Divorce as health hazard. *Psychology Today*, 18 (October):24. 355

MAUKSCH, HANS O. 1972. Ideology, interaction, and patient care in hospitals. *Social Science and Medicine*, 7:817–830. 505

MAY, ROBERT M. and JOH SEGER. 1986. Ideas in ecology. *American Scientist*, 74:256–267. 530

MAZUR, ALLAN. 1985. A biosocial model of status in face-to-face primate groups. *Social Forces*, 64:377–402. 4,180,181

MCAULIFFE, KATHLEEN. 1987. AIDS: At the dawn of fear. *U.S. News & World Report* (January 12):60–69. 496,497

MCBEE, SUSANNA. 1984. Asian-Americans: Are they making the grade? *U.S. News & World Report* (April 2): 41–47. 275

MCCANN, C. DOUBLAS, THOMAS M. OSTROM, LINDA K. TYNER, and MARK L. MITCHELL. 1985. Person perception in heterogeneous groups. *Journal of Personality and Social Psychology*, 49:1449–1459. 265,309

MCCONAHAY, JOHN B., and JOSEPH C. HOUGH, JR. 1976. Symbolic racism. *Journal of Social Issues*, 32:23–45. 258

MCCORD, WILLIAM, and ARLINE MCCORD. 1986. *Paths to Progress*. New York: W. W. Norton. 609

MCCORMICK, JAY. 1986. Consumer goods giant trims the fat. *USA Today* (June 17):B1. 411

MCGEE, REECE. 1975. *Points of Departure*. Hinsdale, IL: Dryden. 372

MCGUIRE, MEREDITH B. 1981. *Religion: The Social Context*. Belmont, CA:

Wadsworth. 383

MCKAUGHAN, MOLLY. 1987. *The Biological Clock: Is Yours Ticking?* Garden City, NY: Doubleday. 363

MCLANAHAN, SARA S. 1983. Family structure and stress: A longitudinal comparison of two-parent and female-headed families. *Journal of Marriage and Family Living*, 45:347–357. 363

MCLAUGHLIN, STEVEN D., and MICHAEL MICKLIN. 1983. The timing of the first birth and changes in personal efficacy. *Journal of Marriage and the Family*, 45:47–55. 352

MCLEOD, BEVERLY. 1986. The Oriental express. *Psychology Today*, 20 (July): 48–52. 275, 276

MCPHAIL, CLARK, and ROBERT T. WOHLSTEIN. 1986. Collective locomotion as collective behavior. *American Sociological Review*, 51:447–463. 574

MEAD, GEORGE HERBERT. 1934. *Mind, Self, and Society*. Chicago: University of Chicago Press. 34,153

MEAD, MARGARET. 1935. *Sex and Temperament in Three Primitive Societies*. New York: William Morrow & Co. 89

MECHANIC, DAVID. 1971. The English National Health Service: Some comparisons with the United States. *Journal of Health and Social Behavior*, 12:18–29. 510

MEHAN, HUGH, and HOUSTON WOOD. 1975. *The Reality of Ethnomethodology*. New York: Wiley. 171

MEHRABIAN, ALBERT. 1968. Communication without words. *Psychology Today*, 2 (September):53–55. 177

MEIER, ROBERT F., and WELDON J. JOHNSON. 1977. Deterrence as social control: The legal and extralegal production of conformity. *American Sociological Review*, 42:292–304. 215

MELMAN, SEYMOUR. 1983. Military spending and domestic bankruptcy. In Ronald V. Dellums, Ed., *Defense Sense: The Search for a Rational Military Policy*. Cambridge, MA: Ballinger. 460

MELTZER, BERNARD, JAMES PETRAS, and LARRY REYNOLDS. 1975. *Symbolic Interactionism: Genesis, Varieties, and Criticisms*. London: Routledge and Kegan Paul. 35

MEREDITH, DENNIS. 1985. Dad and the kids. *Psychology Today*, 19 (June):62–67. 364

MEREDITH, DENNIS. 1986. Day-care: The nine-to-five dilemma. *Psychology Today*, 20 (February):36–44. 353,354

MERRICK, THOMAS W. 1986. *World Population in Transition.* Washington, DC: Population Research Bureau. 523

MERTON, ROBERT K. 1968. *Social Theory and Social Structure,* Rev. ed. New York: Free Press. 29,30,199,259

MERTON, ROBERT K. 1973. *The Sociology of Science.* Chicago: University of Chicago Press. 40

MESSICK, DAVID M., HENK WILKE, MARILYNN B. BREWER, RODERICK M. KRAMER, PATRICIA ENGLISH ZEMKE, and LAYTON LUI. 1983. Individual adaptations and structural change as solutions to social dilemmas. *Journal of Personality and Social Psychology,* 44:294–309. 118

MEYER, DAVID R. 1986. The world system of cities. *Social Forces,* 64:553–581. 551

MICHELS, ROBERT. 1911/1966. *Political Parties.* New York: Free Press. 127

MICHELSON, WILLIAM. 1985. *From Sun to Sun—Daily Obligations and Community Structure in the Lives of Employed Women and Their Families.* Totowa, NJ: Rowman & Allanheld. 315

MICKLIN, MICHAEL, and HARVEY M. CHOLDIN. 1984. *Sociological Human Ecology: Contemporary Issues and Applications.* Boulder, CO: Westview. 529,546

MIDDLEBROOK, PATRICIA NILES. 1980. *Social Psychology and Modern Life.* 2nd ed. New York: Knopf. 183

MIDDLETON, RUSSELL. 1962. A deviant case: Brother-sister and father-daughter marriage in ancient Egypt. *American Sociological Review,* 27:603–611. 340

MILGRAM, STANLEY. 1974. *Obedience to Authority.* New York: Harper & Row. 194–195

MILGRAM, STANLEY. 1977. *The Individual in a Social World.* Reading, MA: Addison-Wesley. 573

MILGRAM, STANLEY, and HANS TOCH. 1969. Collective behavior: Crowds and social movements. In G. Lindzey and E. Aronson, Eds., *The Handbook of Social Psychology,* 2nd ed. Vol. 4. Reading, MA: Addison-Wesley. 574

MILIBAND, RALPH. 1969. *The State in Capitalist Society.* New York: Basic Books. 445

MILLER, JOANNE, KAZIMIERZ M. SLOMCZYNSKI, and MELVIN L. KOHN. 1985. Continuity of learning-generalization: The effect of job on men's intellective process in the United States and Poland. *American Journal of Sociology,* 91:593–615. 418

MILLER, NORMAN, and MARILYNN B. BREWER, Eds. 1984. *Groups in Contact: The Psychology of Desegregation.* Orlando, FL: Academic Press. 475

MILLER, WALTER B. 1958. Lower-class culture as a generating milieu of gang delinquency. *Journal of Social Issues,* 14:5–19. 202

MILLER, WALTER B. 1975. *Violence by Youth Gangs and Youth Groups as a Crime Problem in Major American Cities.* Washington, DC: Government Printing Office. 202

MILLS, C. WRIGHT. 1956. *The Power Elite.* New York: Oxford University Press. 455

MILLS, C. WRIGHT. 1959. *The Sociological Imagination.* New York: Oxford University Press. 7–8,31,451

MILLS, C. WRIGHT. 1960. *The Causes of World War Three.* New York: Ballantine Books. 451

MILLS, C. WRIGHT. 1962. *The Marxists.* New York: Dell. 15

MILLS, C. WRIGHT. 1967. *Power, Politics and People.* New York: Oxford University Press. 195

MILLS, DAVID M. 1984. A model for stepfamily development. *Family Relations,* 33:365–372. 358

MILNE, ANN M., DAVID E. MYERS, ALVIN S. ROSENTHAL, and ALAN GINSBURG. 1986. Single parents, working mothers, and the educational achievement of school children. *Sociology of Education,* 59:125–139. 364

MILNE, L. 1924. *The Home of an Eastern Clan.* Oxford: Clarendon Press. 294

MINER, HORACE. 1956. Body ritual among the Nacirema. *American Anthropologist,* 58:503–507. 57–58

MINER, HORACE. 1960. Culture change under pressure: A Hausa case. *Human Organization,* 19:164–167. 594–595

MINTZ, BETH, and MICHAEL SCHWARTZ. 1981a. The structure of intercorporate unity in American business. *Social Problems,* 29:87–103. 410

MINTZ, BETH, and MICHAEL SCHWARTZ. 1981b. Interlocking directorates and interest group formation. *American Sociological Review,* 46:851–869. 410

MISCHEL, WALTER, 1970. Sex-typing and socialization. In P. H. Mussen, Ed., *Carmichael's Manual of Child Psychology,* 3rd ed. Vol. 2. New York: Wiley. 311

MISHRA, RAMESH. 1984. *The Welfare State in Crisis: Social Thought and Social Change.* New York: St. Martin's Press. 407

MITCHELL, CONSTANCE. 1987. Marriage rates: Which study do you believe? *Wall Street Journal* (January 15):21. 336

MIYALDI, D. 1967. Differences in social behavior among Japanese macaque troops. In D. Starch, R. Schneider, and J. Kuhn, Eds., *Progress in Primatology.* Stuttgart: Gustav Fischer. 61

MOLLENKOPF, JOHN. 1975. Theories of the state and power structure research. *Insurgent Sociologist,* 5:245–264. 446

MOLLENKOPF, JOHN. 1981. Neighborhood political development and the politics of urban growth: Boston and San Francisco 1958–1978. *International Journal of Urban and Regional Research,* 5:15–39. 556

MOLOTCH, HARVEY. 1973. *Managed Integration Dilemmas of Doing Good in the City.* Berkeley: University of California Press. 556

MOLOTCH, HARVEY. 1976. The city as a growth machine: Toward a political economy of place. *American Journal of Sociology,* 82:309–332. 556

MONEY, JOHN, and ANKE A. EHRHARDT. 1972. *Man & Woman, Boy & Girl.* Baltimore: Johns Hopkins University Press. 312

MONEY, JOHN, and P. TUCKER. 1975. *Sexual Signatures: On Being a Man or a Woman.* Boston: Little, Brown. 310

MONTAGU, ASHLEY. 1981. *Growing Young.* New York: McGraw-Hill. 281

MOORE, DIDI. 1984. It's either me or your job! *Working Woman* (April): 108–111. 354

MOORE, R. LAURENCE. 1985. *Religious Outsiders and the Making of Americans.* New York: Oxford University Press. 397

MORGANTHAU, TOM. 1986. AIDS: Grim prospects. *Newsweek* (November 10): 20–21. 496

MORGANTHAU, TOM. 1986. Future shock. *Newsweek* (November 24):30–39 496

MORLEY, JOHN VISCOUNT. 1901. *On Compromise.* London: Macmillan. 8

MORRIS, JAN. 1974. *Conundrum.* New York: Harcourt Brace Jovanovich. 306

MORROW, LANCE. 1985. The start of a plague mentality. *Time* (September

23):92. *489,490*

MORROW, LANCE. 1986. Yankee Doodle magic. *Time* (July 7):12–16. *450*

MORSE, NANCY C., and ROBERT S. WEISS. 1955. The function and meaning of work and the job. *American Sociological Review*, 20:191–198. *417*

MORTIMER, JEYLAN T., and ROBERTA G. SIMMONS. 1978. Adult socialization. *Annual Review of Sociology*, 4:421–454. *156*

MOTTAHEDEH, ROY. 1985. *The Mantle of the Prophet: Religion and Politics in Iran*. New York: Simon and Schuster. *384*

MOTTAZ, CLIFFORD J. 1985. The relative importance of intrinsic and extrinsic rewards as determinants of work satisfaction. *The Sociological Quarterly*, 26:365–385. *418*

MOTTL, TAHI L. 1980. The analysis of countermovements. *Social Problems*, 27:620–635. *585*

MOWAT, FARLEY. 1952. *People of the Deer*. Boston: Little, Brown & Co. *466*

MUELLER, WILLIAM. 1987. Do Americans really want to live in small towns? *American Demographics*, 9 (January):34–37+. *555*

MULLER, THOMAS, and THOMAS J. ESPENSHADE. 1985. *The Fourth Wave: California's Newest Immigrants*. Washington, DC: Urban Institute Press. *271*

MURDOCK, GEORGE PETER. 1934. *Our Primitive Contemporaries*. New York: Macmillan. *283*

MURDOCK, GEORGE P. 1935. Comparative data on the division of labor by sex. *Social Forces*, 15:551–553. *307*

MURDOCK, GEORGE P. 1949. *Social Structure*. New York: Macmillan. *337*

MURDOCK, GEORGE PETER. 1950. Feasibility and implementation of comparative community research. *American Sociological Review*, 15:713–720. *67,443*

MURDOCK, GEORGE P. 1950. *Outline of Cultural Materials*, 3rd ed. New Haven: Yale University Press. *67*

MURDOCK, GEORGE PETER. 1967. *Ethnographic Atlas*. Pittsburgh: University of Pittsburgh Press. *340*

MURPHY, JAMIE. 1986. The quiet apocalypse. *Time* (October 13):80. *533*

MURSTEIN, BERNARD I. 1972. Physical attractiveness and marital choice. *Journal of Personality and Social Psychology*, 22:8–12. *347*

MURSTEIN, BERNARD I. 1976. *Who Will Marry Whom?* New York: Springer. *347*

MYDANS, SETH. 1986. Dilemma of a priest in the Phillipines. *New York Times Magazine* (September 14):68–70+. *369–370*

MYERS, DAVID G. 1983. *Social Psychology*. New York: McGraw-Hill. *10,119*

MYRDAL, ALVA. 1976. *The Game of Disarmament*. New York: Pantheon. *22*

MYRDAL, GUNNAR. 1944. *An American Dilemma*. New York: Harper & Row. *9,23*

MYRDAL, GUNNAR. 1979. Underdevelopment and the evolutionary imperative. *Third World Quarterly*, 1:24–42. *609*

NADEL, SIEGFRIED F. 1952. Witchcraft in four African societies. *American Anthropologist*, 54:18–29. *380*

NAGORSKI, ANDREW, and RUSSELL WATSON. 1986. Moscow faces the new age. *Newsweek* (August 18):20–22. *601*

NAISBITT, JOHN. 1982. *Megatrends*. New York: Warner Books. *82,610*

NASAR, SYLVIA. 1986a. What should government do for the poor? *Fortune* (May 26):82–85. *241*

NASAR, SYLVIA. 1986b. America's poor: How big a problem. *Fortune* (May 26):74–80. *237,240,241*

NASH, NATHANIEL C. 1986. Continental Illinois stock sale. *New York Times* (October 17):29, 41. *409*

The National Commission on Excellence in Education. 1983. *A Nation at Risk: The Imperative for Educational Reform*. Washington, DC: U.S. Department of Education. *478*

National Science Foundation. 1984. *Women and Minorities in Science and Engineering*. Washington, DC: National Science Foundation. *319*

National Task Force on Education for Economic Growth. 1983. *Action for Excellence: A Comprehensive Plan to Improve our Nation's Schools*. Denver: Education Commission of the States. *478*

NEIDERT, LISA J., and REYNOLDS FARLEY. 1985. Assimilation in the United States: An analysis of ethnic and generation differences in status and achievement. *American Sociological Review*, 50:840–850. *242*

NETANYAHU, BENJAMIN. 1986. Terrorism. *USA Today* (September 29):13A. *582–583*

NEUGARTEN, BERNICE L. 1977. Personality and aging. In J. E. Birren and K. W. Schaie, Eds., *Handbook of Aging and the Social Sciences*. New York: Van Nostrand. *293*

NEUGARTEN, BERNICE L. 1979. Time, age, and the life cycle. *American Journal of Psychiatry*, 136: 887–894. *284*

NEUGARTEN, BERNICE L., and G. O. HAGESTAD. 1976. Age and the life course. In R. H. Binstock and E. Shanas, Eds., *Handbook of Aging and the Social Sciences*. New York: Van Nostrand. *283*

NEWCOMB, PAUL R. 1979. Cohabitation in America: An assessment of consequences. *Journal of Marriage and the Family*, 41:597–603. *362*

NEWCOMB, THEODORE M. 1950. *Social Psychology*. New York: Holt, Rinehart & Winston. *88*

NEWITT, JANE. 1986. In search of the bloated bureaucracy. *American Demographics*, 8 (March):26–29+. *437*

NEWMAN, BARRY. 1979. *Bounty* descendants in mutiny again—against Australia. *Wall Street Journal* (November 19):1, 26. *416*

NEWMAN, BARRY. 1979. Do multinationals really create jobs in the Third World? *Wall Street Journal* (September 25):1, 16. *416*

NIEBUHR, H. RICHARD. 1929. *The Social Sources of Denominationalism*. New York: Holt, Rinehart & Winston. *373*

NIELSEN, FRANCOIS. 1985. Toward a theory of ethnic solidarity in modern societies. *American Sociological Review*, 50:133–149.

NILSON, L. B. 1978. The social standing of a housewife. *Journal of Marriage and the Family*, 40:541–548. *315*

NIMBARK, ASHAKANT. 1986. Social change: Macro-, micro-, and medium. *Contemporary Sociology*, 15:515–519. *610*

NISBET, ROBERT. 1962. *Community and Power*. New York: Oxford University Press. *440*

NISBET, ROBERT A. 1970. *The Social Bond*, New York: Knopf. *231*

NOBLE, KENNETH B. 1986. Study finds 60 percent of 11 million who lost jobs got new ones. *New York Times* (February 7):1, 11. *7*

NOBLE, KENNETH B. 1986. 48% of mothers of infants are found to hold jobs. *New York Times* (March 16):14. *353*

NOCK, STEVEN L. 1979. The family life cycle: Empirical or conceptual tool? *Journal of Marriage and the Family*, 41:15–26. *350*

NOEL, DONALD M. 1972. *The Origins of American Slavery and Racism*. Columbus, OH: Charles E. Merrill. *265*

NORDHEIMER, JON. 1986. With AIDS about, heterosexuals are rethinking promiscuity. *New York Times* (March 22):7. *328*

NORLAND, ROD. 1987. AIDS: Fear of foreigners. *Newsweek* (April 6):36. *497*

NORTON, ARTHUR J., and PAUL C. GLICK. 1986. One parent families: A social and economic profile. *Family Relations*, 35:9–17. *363*

NORTON, ARTHUR J., and JEANNE E. MOORMAN. 1987. Current trends in marriage and divorce among American women. *Journal of Marriage and the Family*, 49:3–14. *335*

NORTON, ROBERT E. 1986. Banks are safer than you think. *Fortune* (August 18):53–56. *409*

NOTESTEIN, FRANK W. 1945. Population—the long view. In Theodore W. Schultz, Ed., *Food for the World*. Chicago: University of Chicago Press. *524*

O'BARR, JEAN F. 1979. *Conflict of Interest: A Growing Challenge for Working Couples*. Durham, NC: Duke University's Office of Continuing Education. *354*

OBOLER, REGINA SMITH. 1980. Is the female husband a man? Woman/woman marriage among the Nadi of Kenya. *Ethnology*, 19:69–88. *341*

O'BOYLE, THOMAS F., and PETER GUMBEL. 1987. Bonn now faces task of finding a solution for its welfare crisis. *Wall Street Journal* (January 28):1, 119. *407*

O'BRIEN, DENISE. 1977. Female husbands in Southern Bantu societies. In A. Schlegel, Ed., *Sexual Stratification: A Cross-Cultural View*. New York: Columbia University Press. *341*

O'CONNOR, JAMES. 1973. *The Fiscal Crisis of the State*. New York: St. Martin's Press. *446*

O'DELL, JERRY W. 1968. Group size and emotional interaction. *Journal of Personality and Social Psychology*, 8:75–78. *114*

OFFE, CLAUS. 1984. *Contradictions of the Welfare State*. Cambridge, MA: MIT Press. *407*

OFFER, DANIEL, and JUDITH B. OFFER. 1975. *From Teenage to Young Manhood*. New York: Basic Books. *291*

OGBURN, WILLIAM F. 1922. *Social Change*. New York: B. W. Huebsch. *597–598*

O'HARE, WILLIAM. 1986. The eight myths of poverty. *American Demographics*, 8 (May):22–25. *10,240,241*

OLIVER, DOUGLAS. 1955. *A Solomon Island Society*. Cambridge, MA: Harvard University Press. *341*

OLIVER, PAMELA, GERALD MARWELL, and RUY TEIXEIRA. 1985. A theory of the critical mass. I. Interdependence, group heterogeneity, and the production of collective action. *American Journal of Sociology*, 91:522–556. *572*

OLIVER, THOMAS. 1986. *The Real Coke, The Real Story*. New York: Random House. *48*

OLSEN, MARVIN E. 1978. *The Process of Social Organization*. 2nd ed. New York: Holt, Rinehart and Winston. *88*

OLSON, DAVID J., and PHILIP MEYER. 1975. *To Keep The Republic*. New York: McGraw-Hill. *447*

O'MALLEY, PATRICK M., and HERALD G. BACHMAN. 1983. Self-esteem: Change and stability between ages 13 and 23. *Developmental Psychology*, 19:257–268. *291*

Opinion Roundup. 1980. Work in the 70's. *Public Opinion*, 3 (December/January):36. *417*

Opinion Roundup. 1982. Race: A decade of progress. *Public Opinion*, 5 (October):34. *259*

Opinion Roundup. 1987. The role of government. *Public Opinion*, 9 (March/April):21. *434*

ORDOVENSKY, PAT. 1985. Lack of aid shuts door on minority grads. *USA Today* (March 21):1A. *476*

ORGANSKI, A. F. K., JACEK KUGLER, J. TIMOTHY JOHNSON, and YOUSSEF COHEN. 1984. *Births, Deaths, and Taxes: The Demographic and Political Transitions*. Chicago: University of Chicago Press.

ORUM, ANTHONY, and JOE FEAGIN. 1987. In defense of Domhoff. *American Journal of Sociology*, 92:975–977. *454*

OSTLING, RICHARD N. 1985. Jerry Falwell's crusade. *Newsweek* (September 2):48–57. *389*

OTTEN, ALAN L. 1986. Issue of force-feeding to keep patients alive enters political arena. *Wall Street Journal* (June 9):1, 12. *296*

OTTEN, ALAN L. 1987. Warning of generational fighting draws critics—led by the elderly. *Wall Street Journal* (January 13):35. *301*

OXNAM, ROBERT B. 1986. Why Asians succeed here. *New York Times Magazine* (November 30):71–74+. *482*

PAERNOW, PATRICIA L. 1984. The stepfamily cycle: An experiential model of stepfamily development. *Family Relations*, 33:355–363. *359*

PAGELOW, MILDRED DALEY. 1984. *Family Violence*. New York: Praeger. *359*

PALMER, BARBARA. 1984. Putting more care into child care. *USA Today* (April 19):1. *353*

PALMER, DONALD, ROGER FRIEDLAND, and JITENDRA V. SINGH. 1986. The ties that bind: Organizational and class bases of stability in a corporate interlock network. *American Sociological Review*, 51:781–796. *410*

PALMORE, ERDMAN B., BRUCE M. BURCHETT, GERDA G. FILLENBAUM, LINDA K. GEORGE, and LAWRENCE M. WALLMAN. 1985. *Retirement: Causes and Consequences*. New York: Springer. *294*

PARGAMENT, KENNETH I., and JUNE HAHN. 1986. God and the just world: Causal and coping attributions to God in health situations. *Journal for the Scientific Study of Religion*, 25:193–207. *379*

PARK, ROBERT E. 1952. *Human Communities*. Glencoe, IL: Free Press. *550*

PARK, ROBERT E., and ERNEST W. BURGESS. 1921. *Introduction to the Science of Sociology*. Chicago: University of Chicago Press. *546*

PARK, ROBERT E., ERNEST W. BURGESS, and RODERICK D. MCKENZIE. 1925. *The City*. Chicago: The University of Chicago Press. *546*

PARKINSON, C. NORTHCOTE. 1962. *Parkinson's Law*. Boston: Houghton Mifflin. *126–127*

PARNES, H. S. 1981. *Work and Retirement—A Longitudinal Study of Men*. Cambridge, MA: MIT Press. *294*

PARSONS, TALCOTT. 1949. *The Structure of Social Action*, 2nd ed. New York: McGraw-Hill. *495*

PARSONS, TALCOTT. 1951. *The Social*

System. New York: Free Press. *495*

PARSONS, TALCOTT. 1951. *Toward a General Theory of Action*. New York: Harper & Row. *495*

PARSONS, TALCOTT. 1966. *Societies: Evolutionary and Comparative Perspectives*. Englewood Cliffs, NJ: Prentice-Hall. *71,595,607*

PARSONS, TALCOTT. 1971. *The System of Modern Societies*. Englewood Cliffs, NJ: Prentice-Hall. *71*

PARSONS, TALCOTT. 1977. On building social system theory: A personal history. In Talcott Parsons, Ed., *Social Systems and the Evolution of Action Theory*. New York: Free Press. *595*

PARSONS, TALCOTT, and ROBERT F. BALES. 1955. *Family Socialization and Interaction Process*. New York: Free Press. *313–314*

PASCALE, RICHARD. 1984. Fitting new employees into the company culture. *Fortune* (May 28):28–38. *161*

PATCHEN, MARTIN. 1982. *Black-White Contact in Schools: Its Social and Academic Effects*. West Lafayette, IN: Purdue University Press. *475*

PATERNOSTER, RAYMOND, and LEEANN IOVANNI. 1986. The deterrent effect of perceived severity: A reexamination. *Social Forces*, 64:751–777. *215*

PATTISON, MANSELL. 1977. *The Experience of Dying*. Englewood Cliffs, NJ: Prentice-Hall. *295*

PAUL, ANGUS. 1986. Rise in terrorism around the world fuels scholars' attempts to fathom it. *Chronicle of Higher Education* (June 18):6–7+. *583*

PAULY, DAVID. 1986. Too much for defense? *Newsweek* (March 24):52–53. *452*

PEAR, ROBERT. 1986. Poverty rate shows slight drop for '85 census bureau says. *New York Times* (August 27):1, 9. *237*

PEAR, ROBERT. 1986. Reagan's advisers say bill on aliens can hurt economy. *New York Times* (January 23):1, 12. *270,271*

PEAR, ROBERT. 1986. Rising public support for limits on immigration is found in poll. *New York Times* (July 1):1, 14. *270,271*

PEAR, ROBERT. 1986. Spending for health care rose in '85 at lowest rate in 2 decades. *New York Times* (July 30):7. *501*

PEAR, ROBERT. 1986. Study examines profit role in hospitals. *New York Times* (June 5):8. *492,501*

PEAR, ROBERT. 1986. Young mothers stay on welfare for longer periods, study says. *New York Times* (September 10):15. *239*

PEARL, DAVID. 1982. *Television and Behavior: 10 Years of Scientific Research*. Washington, DC: Government Printing Office. *159*

PEBLEY, ANNE R., and DAVID E. BLOOM. 1982. Childless Americans. *American Demography*, 4 (January):18–21. *342*

PELL, SIDNEY, and WILLIAM E. FAYERWEATHER. 1985. Trends in the incidence of myocardial infarction and in associated mortality and morbidity in a large employed population, 1957–1983. *New England Journal of Medicine*, 312:1005–1011. *492*

PENTELLA, CHERYL. 1983. More students say good night at the front door. *On Campus* (January):16. *362*

PERINBANAYAGAM, R. S. 1982. *The Karmic Theater: Self, Society, and Astrology in Jaffna*. Amherst: University of Massachusetts Press. *169*

PERINBANAYAGAM, R. S. 1985. *Signifying Acts: Structure and Meaning in Everyday Life*. Carbondale: Southern Illinois University Press. *169*

PERISTIANY, J. G. 1939. *The Social Institutions of the Kipsigis*. London: Routledge & Sons. *286*

PERKINS, JOSEPH. 1986. Urban League heeds conservative call for self-help. *Wall Street Journal* (August 6):16. *261*

PERROW, CHARLES. 1979. *Complex Organizations*, rev. ed. Glenview, IL: Scott, Foresman and Company. *125*

PERROW, CHARLES. 1982. Disintegrating social sciences. *Phi Delta Kappan*, 63:684–688. *131*

PERRY, DAVID G., LOUISE C. PERRY, and PAUL RASMUSSEN. 1986. Cognitive social learning mediators of aggression. *Child Development*, 57:700–711. *310*

PETERSEN, WILLIAM. 1960. The demographic transition in the Netherlands. *American Sociological Review*, 25:334–347. *526*

PETERSEN, WILLIAM. 1971. *Japanese Americans*. New York: Random House. *275*

PETERSON, JAMES L., and NICHOLAS ZILL. 1986. Marital disruption, parent-child relationships, and behavior problems in children. *Journal of Marriage and the Family*, 48:295–307. *357*

PETERSON, IVAN. 1986. People moving back to cities, U.S. study says. *New York Times* (April 13):1, 12. *555*

PETERSON, KAREN S., and FELICIA LEE. 1985. Most find the single life isn't lonely. *USA Today* (April 5):1D. *361*

PETERSON, PAUL E., Ed. 1985. *The New Urban Reality*. Washington: Brookings Institution. *560*

PETTIGREW, THOMAS F. 1979. The ultimate attribution error: Extending Allport's cognitive analysis of prejudice. *Personality and Social Psychology Bulletin*, 5:461–476. *265*

PETTIGREW, THOMAS F. 1985. New black-white patterns. *Annual Review of Sociology*, 11:329–346. *259*

PETZINGER, THOMAS, JR., MARK ZIEMAN, BRYAN BURROUGH, and DIANNA SOLIS. 1985. Illegal immigrants are backbone of economy in states of Southwest. *Wall Street Journal* (May 7):1, 4. *270*

PFAFFLIN, SHEILA M. 1984. Women, science, and technology. *American Psychologist*, 39:1183–1186. *319*

PIEL, GERALD. 1986. Natural philosophy in the constitution. *Science*, 233:1056–1060. *471*

PILIAVIN, IRVING M., and JANE ALLYN PILIAVIN. 1972. Effects of blood on reactions to a victim. *Journal of Personality and Social Psychology*, 23:353–361. *184,185*

PILIAVIN, IRVING M., JUDITH RODIN, and JANE ALLYN PILIAVIN. 1969. Good Samaritanism: An underground phenomenon? *Journal of Personality and Social Psychology*, 13:289–299. *184*

PILIAVIN, IRVING, CRAIG THORNTON, ROSEMARY GARTNER, and ROSS L. MATSUEDA. 1986. Crime, deterrence, and rational choice. *American Sociological Review*, 51:101–119. *215*

PLATTNER, ANDY. 1986. Immigration reform: Weighing cost of failure. *U.S. News & World Report* (August 11):20–22. *270*

PLECK, JOSEPH H. 1985. *Working Wives/Working Husbands*. Beverly Hills: Sage. *316*

PLUMB, J. H. 1972. *Children*. London: Penguin. *288*

PLUMMER, KENNETH. 1975. *Sexual Stigma: An Interactionist Account*. London: Routledge & Kegal Paul. *327*

POMER, MARSHALL I. 1986. Labor market structure, intragenerational mobility, and discrimination: Black male advancement out of low-paying occupations, 1962–1973. *American Sociological Review*, 51:650–659. *269*

POWELL, STEWART. 1986. Busting the mob. *U.S. News & World Report* (February 3):24–31. *211*

POWELL, STEWART. 1986. One more blow for America's cities. *U.S. News & World Report* (September 29):31–32. *561*

PRESTHUS, ROBERT. 1978. *The Organizational Society*, rev. ed. New York: St. Martin's Press. *121*

Princeton Religion Research Center. 1986. Survey explores impact of religion on views toward self, other people. *PRRC Emerging Trends*, 8 (May):5. *395*

PROKESCH, STEVEN. 1986. Cleveland counts on a clinic. *New York Times* (December 29):23, 34. *501*

Public Opinion. 1986. Opinion roundup. *Public Opinion*, 8 (January):25–34. *299,351*

QUADAGNO, JILL S. 1982. *Aging in Early Industrial Society*. New York: Academic Press. *337*

QUADAGNO, JILL S. 1984. Welfare capitalism and the Social Security Act of 1935. *American Sociological Review*, 49:632–647. *446*

QUINN, THOMAS C., JONATHAN M. MANN, JAMES W. CURRAN, and PETER PIOT. 1986. AIDS in Africa: An epidemiologic paradigm. *Science*, 234:955–963. *496*

QUINN-JUDGE, PAUL. 1987. Gorbachev pushes for radical change. *Christian Science Monitor* (March 10):1. *442*

QUINN-JUDGE, PAUL. 1987. Soviet soldiers are tongue-tied. *Christian Science Monitor* (March 13):9. *254*

QUINNEY, RICHARD. 1974. *Criminal Justice in America*. Boston: Little, Brown. *203*

QUINNEY, RICHARD. 1980. *Class, State, & Crime*. New York: Longman. *203*

RAAB, SELWYN. 1984. Asia crime groups spreading in U.S., Smith tells panel. *New York Times* (October 24):1, 16. *211*

RADLOFF, B. 1975. The tot in the gray flannel suit. *New York Times* (May 4):8E. *158*

RAMIREZ, FRANCISCO O., and JOHN BOLI. 1987. The political construction of mass schooling: European origins and worldwide institutionalization. *Sociology of Education*, 60:2–17. *466*

RANGEL, JESUS. 1984. Survey finds Hispanic groups are more unified. *New York Times* (September 8):5. *272*

RASPBERRY, WILLIAM. 1986. Tocqueville predicted welfare woes. *Columbus, Ohio, Dispatch* (June 19):13A. *240*

REDMAN, CHARLES L. 1979. *The Rise of Civilization*. San Francisco: Freeman. *543*

REINHOLD, ROBERT. 1986. Flow of 3d world immigrants alters weave of U.S. society. *New York Times* (June 30):1, 11. *271*

REIS, HARRY T., JOHN NEZLEK, and LADD WHEELER. 1980. Physical attractiveness in social interaction. *Journal of Personality and Social Psychology*, 38:604–617. *347*

REIS, HARRY T., LADD WHEELER, MICHAEL H. KERNIS, NANCY SPIEGEL, and JOHN NEZLEK. 1985. On specificity in the impact of social participation on physical and psychological health. *Journal of Personality and Social Psychology*, 48:45⌐ -471. *495*

REISS, IRA L. 1976. *Family Systems in America*, 2nd ed. Hinsdale, IL: Dryden Press. *327,328*

REISS, IRA L. 1986. *Journey into Sexuality: An Exploratory Voyage*. New York: Prentice-Hall. *328*

RELMAN, ARNOLD S. 1980. The new medical-industrial complex. *New England Journal of Medicine*, 303:963–970. *501*

RELMAN, ARNOLD S. 1986. The United States and Canada: Different approaches to health care. *New England Journal of Medicine*, 315:1608–1610. *510*

RESCORLA, ROBERT A., and P. C. HOLLAND. 1982. Behavioral studies of associative learning in animals. *Annual Review of Psychology*, 33:265–308. *146*

RESKIN, BARBARA F., and HEIDI I. HARTMANN, Eds. 1986. *Women's Work, Men's Work: Sex Segregation on the Job*. Washington, DC: National Academy Press. *316*

RESTON, JAMES. 1963. Nobody can assassinate a government. *New York Times* (November 27):16. *434*

RHEINGOLD, HARRIET L., and K. V. COOK. 1975. The contents of boys' and girls' rooms as an index of parents' behavior. *Child Development*, 46:459–463. *311*

RHEINGOLD, HARRIET L., DALE F. HAY, and MEREDITH J. WEST. 1976. Sharing in the second year of life. *Child Development*, 47:1148–1158. *289*

RICHE, MARTHA F. 1986. The forking path. *American Demographics*, 8 (February):42–44. *474*

RICHMAN, TOM. 1986. How do you sell a light bulb that never burns out? *INC.* (March):90–94. *596*

RICKS, THOMAS E. 1984. Researchers say day-care centers are implicated in spread of disease. *Wall Street Journal* (September 5):15. *353*

RICKS, THOMAS E. 1986. The cocaine business: Big risks and profits, high labor turnover. *Wall Street Journal* (June 30):1, 14. *609*

RICKS, THOMAS E. 1987. Day care for infants is challenged by research on psychological risks. *Wall Street Journal* (March 3):37. *353*

RIDGEWAY, CECILIA L., JOSEPH BERGER, and LEROY SMITH. 1985. Nonverbal cues and status: An expectation states approach. *American Journal of Sociology*, 90:955–978. *181*

RIDGEWAY, C. L. 1983. *The Dynamics of Small Groups*. New York: St. Martin's Press. *115*

RIDING, ALAN. 1986. Vatican lifting 'silence' order on Brazil friar. *New York Times* (April 1):1, 8. *375*

RIEDER, JONATHAN. 1985. *Canarsie: The Jews and Italians of Brooklyn against Liberalism*. Cambridge, MA: Harvard University Press. *259*

RIESMAN, DAVID. 1953. *The Lonely Crowd*. Garden City, NY: Doubleday. *455*

RIGER, STEPHANIE, and MARGARET T. GORDON. 1981. The fear of rape: A study in social control. *Journal of Social Issues*, 37:71–92. *322*

RILEY, MATILDA WHITE. 1985. Women, men, and the lengthening life course. In A. S. Rossi, Ed., *Gender and the Life Course*. New York: Aldine. *295*

RILEY, MATILDA WHITE. 1987. On the significance of age in sociology. *American Sociological Review*, 52:1–14. *283,284,285*

RILEY, JOHN W., JR. 1983. Dying and the meanings of death: Sociological inquiries. *Annual Review of Sociology*, 9:191–216. *295*

RISMAN, BARBARA J. 1986. Can men "mother"? Life as a single father. *Family Relations*, 35:95–102. *364*

RISMAN, BARBARA J., CHARLES T. HILL,

ZICK RUBIN, and LETITIA ANNE PEPLAU. 1981. Living together in college: Implications for courtship. *Journal of Marriage and the Family*, 43:77–83. 362

RITZER, GEORGE. 1983. *Sociological Theory*. New York: Knopf. 12,15,20,41,125

RIVERS, W. H. R. 1906. *The Toda*. New York: Macmillan. 99,341

ROBBINS, LILLIAN, and ETHEL D. KAHN. 1985. Sex discrimination and sex equity for faculty women in the 1980s. *Journal of Social Issues*, 41:1–16. 319

ROBBINS, WILLIAM. 1986. Rising suicides in farm belt reflect surge in hardship and despondency. *New York Times* (January 14):9. 93

ROBERTS, DONALD F., and NATHAN MACCOBY. 1985. Effects of mass communication. In G. Lindzey and E. Aronson, Eds., *Handbook of Social Psychology*, 3rd ed. Vol. 2. New York: Random House. 159

ROBERTSON, HECTOR M. 1933. *Aspects of the Rise of Economic Individualism*. London: Cambridge University Press. 386

ROBEY, BRYANT. 1985. America's Asians. *Demography*, 7 (May):22–29. 274

ROBINSON, BRYAN E. 1984. The contemporary American stepfather. *Family Relations*, 33:381–388. 358

ROBINSON, JOHN P. 1987. Where's the boom. *American Demographics*, 9 (March):34–37, 56. 424

RODMAN, HYMAN. 1968. Class culture. In D. L. Sills, Ed., *International Encyclopedia of the Social Sciences*, Vol. 15. New York: Macmillan. 231

ROETHLISBERGER, FRITZ J., and WILLIAM J. DICKSON. 1939. *Management and the Worker*. Cambridge, MA: Harvard University Press. 128

ROONEY, JAMES F. 1980. Organizational success through program failure: Skid row rescue missions. *Social Forces*, 58:904–924. 122

Roper Organization. 1985. *Virginia Slims Poll*. New York: Richard Weiner, Inc. 324

ROSE, EUGENE, and ALLAN MAZUR. 1979. Incipient status in groups. *Social Forces*, 58:18–37. 180

ROSE, FREDERICK, and JOHN EMSHWILLER. 1986. U.S. nuclear industry also has safety perils, three accidents show. *Wall Street Journal* (May 5):1, 10. 533

ROSE, STEPHEN J. 1986. *The American Profile Poster*. New York: Pantheon Books. 236

ROSECRANCE, RICHARD. 1985. *The Rise of the Trading State: Commerce and Conquest in the Modern World*. New York: Basic Books. 461

ROSEN, COREY, KATHERINE J. KLEIN, and KAREN M. YOUNG. 1986. When employees share the profits. *Psychology Today*, 20 (January):30–36. 133

ROSEN, GEORGE. 1963. The hospital: Historical sociology of a community institution. In E. Freidson, Ed., *The Hospital in Modern Society*. New York: Free Press. 501

ROSEN, RAYMOND, and ELIZABETH HALL. 1984. *Sexuality*. New York: Random House. 326,327,329

ROSENBAUM, RON. 1987. Crack murder. *New York Times Magazine* (February 15):24–33+. 27,28

ROSENBERG, NATHAN, and L. E. BIRDZELL, JR. 1986. *How the West Grew Rich: The Economic Transformation of the Industrial World*. New York: Basic Books. 405

ROSENFELD, EVA. 1951. Social stratification in a "classless society." *American Sociological Review*, 16:766–774. 222

ROSENHAN, DAVID L. 1973. On being sane in insane places. *Science*, 179:250–258. 189

ROSENTHAL, A. M. 1987. The next hijacking. *New York Times* (January 27):23. 582

ROSENTHAL, MARC. 1986. Executive pay. *Business Week* (May 5):48–80. 228

ROSENWAIKE, I., and B. LOGUE. 1985. *The Extreme Aged in America*. Westport, CT: Greenwood Press. 298

ROSNOW, RALPH, and GARY ALAN FINE. 1976. *Rumor and Gossip: The Social Psychology of Hearsay*. New York: Elsevier. 567

ROSNOW, RALPH, and ALLAN J. KIMMEL. 1979. Lives of a rumor. *Psychology Today*, 13 (June):88–92. 567

ROSOW, IRVING. 1974. *Socialization to Old Age*. Berkeley: University of California Press. 294

ROSS, CATHERINE E. 1987. The division of labor at home. *Social Forces*, 65:816–833. 316

ROSS, CHRISTOPHER O. 1987. Organizational dimensions of metropolitan dominance: Prominence in the network of corporate control, 1955–1975. *American Sociological Review*, 52:258–267. 551

ROSS, LEE. 1977. The intuitive psychologist and his shortcomings: Distortions in the attribution process. In L. Berkowitz, Ed., *Advances in Experimental Social Psychology*, Vol. 10. New York: Academic Press. 175

ROSSI, PETER H., and JAMES D. WRIGHT. 1984. Evaluation research: An assessment. *Annual Review of Sociology*, 10:331–352. 9

ROTHSCHILD, BARBARA S. 1986. Our high-tech IQ is fairly low. *USA Today* (February 14):D1. 466

ROTTON, JAMES, and I. W. KELLY. 1985. Much ado about the full moon: A meta-analysis of lunar-lunacy research. *Psychological Bulletin*, 97:286–306. 10

ROWE, JONATHAN. 1986. Continuing ed sheds its second-class image. *Christian Science Monitor* (October 24):B1, B8. 486

ROY, WILLIAM G. 1984. Class conflict and social change in historical perspective. *Annual Review of Sociology*, 10:483–506. 229

RUBIN, JEFFREY Z., Ed. 1981. *Third Party Intervention in Conflict: Kissinger in the Middle East*. New York: Praeger. 459

RUBIN, JEFFREY Z., and NEHEMIA FRIEDLAND. 1986. Theater of terror. *Psychology Today*, 20 (March):18–28. 579

RUBIN, ZICK. 1980. *Children's Friendships*. Cambridge, MA: Harvard University Press. 158

RUBINSON, RICHARD. 1976. The world-economy and the distribution of income within states: A cross-national study. *American Sociological Review*, 41:638–659. 609

RUBENSTEIN, CARIN. 1982. Real men don't earn less than their wives. *Psychology Today*, 16 (November):36–41. 354

RUSSELL, CHERYL. 1980. The elderly: Myths and facts. *American Demographics*, 2:30–31. 298

RUSSELL, CHERYL. 1983. The news about Hispanics. *American Demographics*, 5 (March):15–25. 272

RUSSELL, CHERYL. 1985. The new homemakers. *American Demography*, 7:23–27. 316

RUSSELL, CHERYL. 1987. Fear of AIDS may re-create the virtuous '50s. *Wall Street Journal* (March 30):16. 490

RUSSELL, GEORGE. 1987. Rebuilding to survive. *Time* (February 16):44–45. *413*

RUSSELL, RAYMOND. 1985. *Sharing Ownership in the Workplace*. Albany: SUNY Press. *133*

RUTTER, MICHAEL. 1979. *Fifteen Thousand Hours: Secondary Schools and Their Effects on Children*. Cambridge, MA: Harvard University Press. *479*

RYDER, NORMAN B. 1965. The cohort as a concept in the study of social change. *American Sociological Review*, 30:843–861. *284*

RYFF, CAROL D. 1985. Subjective experience of life-span transition. In A. S. Rossi, Ed., *Gender and the Life Course*. New York: Aldine. *284*

RYSER, JEFFREY. 1986. Can South America's addict economies ever break free? *Business Week* (September 22):40–44. *608*

SABATELLI, RONALD M., and ERIN F. CECIL-PIGO. 1985. Relational interdependence and commitment in marriage. *Journal of Marriage and the Family*, 47:931–945. *347*

SACKS, H., E. SCHLEGLOFF, and G. JEFFERSON. 1974. A simplest systematic for the organization of turn-taking in conversation. *Language*, 50:696–735. *177*

SAGARIN, EDWARD. 1975. *Deviants and Deviance*. New York: Praeger. *192, 194,196,197*

SAHLINS, MARSHALL. 1972. *Stone Age Economics*. New York: Aldine. *73*

SAHLINS, MARSHALL, and ELMAN SERVICE, Eds. 1960. *Evolution and Culture*. Ann Arbor: University of Michigan Press. *71*

SALHOLZ, ELOISE. 1986. Feminism's identity crisis. *Newsweek* (March 31): 58–59. *323,324*

SALHOLZ, ELOISE. 1986. Too late for Prince Charming? *Newsweek* (June 2): 54–61. *335*

SALMANS, SANDRA. 1985. Man in the moon loses job at P&G. *New York Times* (April 25):31, 36. *567*

SALZMAN, PHILIP, Ed. 1971. Comparative studies of nomadism and pastoralism. *Anthropological Quarterly*, 44:104–210. *79*

SAMUELSSON, KURT. 1961. *Religion and Economic Action: A Critique of Max Weber*. Trans. E. G. French. New York: Harper Torchbooks. *386*

SANDBURG, CARL. 1956. *Prologue to The Family of Man*. E. Steicher, Ed. New York: The Museum of Modern Art. *281*

SANDAY, PEGGY REEVES. 1981. The socio-cultural context of rape: A cross-cultural study. *Journal of Social Issues*, 37:5–27. *320*

SANDERS, WILLIAM B. 1974. *The Sociologist as Detective*. New York: Praeger. *27*

SANIK, MARGARET M., and TERESA MAULDIN. 1986. Single versus two parent families: A comparison of mothers' time. *Family Relations*, 35:53–56. *363*

SANOFF, ALVIN P. 1983. Jews find new solace in the old traditions. *U.S. News & World Report* (April 4):43–44. *392*

SANOFF, ALVIN P. 1986. College sports' real scandal. *U.S. News & World Report* (September 15):62–63. *484*

SARASON, SEYMOUR B. 1977. *Work, Aging, and Social Change: Professionals and the One Life-One Career Imperative*. New York: Basic Books. *605*

SAVIN-WILLIAMS, RITCH C., and DAVID H. DEMO. 1984. Developmental change and stability in adolescent self-concept. *Developmental Psychology*, 20:1100–1110. *291*

SCARF, MAGGIE. 1976. *Body, Mind, Behavior*. Washington, DC: New Republic Book Company, Inc. *310*

SCHACHTER, STANLEY. 1959. *Psychology of Affiliation*. Stanford, CA: Stanford University Press. *103*

SCHACHTER, STANLEY, and JEROME SINGER. 1962. Cognitive, social, and physiological determinants of emotional state. *Psychological Review*, 69:379–399. *43*

SCHIFF, ROBERT L., DAVID A. ANSELL, JAMES E. SCHLOSSER, AHAMED H. IDRIS, ANN MORRISON, and STEVEN WHITMAN. 1986. Transfers to a public hospital. *New England Journal of Medicine*, 314:552–557. *499*

SCHILL, MICHAEL H., and RICHARD P. NATHAN. 1983. *Revitalizing America's Cities: Neighborhood Reinvestment and Displacement*. Albany, NY: State University of New York Press. *551*

SCHLENKER, BARRY R. 1980. *Impression Management: The Self-Concept, Social Identity, and Interpersonal Relations*. Monterey, CA: Brooks/Cole. *181*

SCHLESINGER, ARTHUR M., JR. 1986. *The Cycles of American History*. Boston: Houghton Mifflin. *576*

SCHMECK, HAROLD M., JR. 1983. U.S. panel calls for patients' right to end life. *New York Times* (March 22):1, 18. *297*

SCHMECK, HAROLD M., JR. 1985. Brain defects seen in those who repeat violent acts. *New York Times* (September 17):17, 19. *215*

SCHMECK, HAROLD M., JR. 1987. Million victims of AIDS predicted by year 2000. *New York Times* (March 4):11. *610*

SCHNEIDER, DAVID M., and KATHLEEN GOUGH. 1961. *Matrilineal Kinship*. Berkeley: University of California Press. *99,100*

SCHNEIDER, JOSEPH W. 1985. Social problems theory: The constructionist view. *Annual Review of Sociology*, 11:209–229. *500*

SCHNEIDER, KEITH. 1986. Scientific advances lead to era of food surplus around world. *New York Times* (September 9):19. *524*

SCHOFIELD, JANET WARD. 1982. *Black and White in School: Trust, Tension, or Tolerance?* New York: Praeger. *475*

SCHRECKER, ELLEN W. 1986. *No Ivory Tower: McCarthyism and the Universities*. New York: Oxford University Press. *381*

SCHREINER, TIM. 1983. Poverty plagues farmers, study says. *USA Today* (December 22):3A. *237*

SCHUMAN, FREDERICK L. 1933. *International Politics*. New York: McGraw-Hill. *381*

SCHUR, EDWIN. 1965. *Crimes Without Victims*. Englewood Cliffs, NJ: Prentice-Hall. *212*

SCHUSTER, JACK H. 1986. The faculty dilemma: A short course. *Phi Delta Kappan*, 68:275–282.

SCHUTZ, ALFRED. 1967. *Collected Papers I: The Problem of Social Reality*. The Hague: Martin Nijhoff. *35*

SCHUTZ, ALFRED. 1964. *Collected Papers, II*. A. Bodersen, Ed. The Hague: Martin Nijhoff. *35*

SCHUTZ, ALFRED. 1971. *Collected Papers*. The Hague: Martin Nijhoff. *35*

SCHWALBE, MICHAEL L. 1985. Autonomy in work and self-esteem. *The Sociological Quarterly*, 26:519–535. *418*

SCHWARTZ, JOE. 1987. Family traditions. *American Demographics*, 9 (March):

SCHWARTZ, WILLIAM. 1984. U.S. medicine "cannot do everything for everybody." *U.S. News & World Report* (June 25):71–72. *511*

SCHWARTZ, WILLIAM B. 1984. The most painful prescription. *Newsweek* (November 12):24. *504*

SCHWEINHART, LAWRENCE J., and DAVID P. WEIKART. 1985. Evidence that good early childhood programs work. *Phi Delta Kappan*, 66 (April):545–553. *9*

SCHWENDINGER, JULIA R., and HERMAN SCHWENDINGER. 1983. *Rape and Inequality*. Beverly Hills: Sage Publications. *320*

SCHWIRIAN, KENT P. 1983. Neighborhood change. *Annual Review of Sociology*, 9:83–102. *550,551*

SCIOLINO, ELAINE. 1984. American Catholics: A time for challenge. *New York Times Magazine* (November 4):40+. *391*

SCIULLI, DAVID, and DEAN GERSTEIN. 1985. Social theory and Talcott Parsons in the 1980s. *Annual Review of Sociology*, 11:396–387. *29*

SCOTT, JOAN WALLACH. 1982. The mechanization of women's work. *Scientific American*, 247 (September):167–187. *316*

SEARS, DAVID O., and DONALD R. KINDER. 1985. Whites' opposition to busing: On conceptualizing and operationalizing group conflict. *Journal of Personality and Social Psychology*, 48:1141–1147. *258*

SEARS, ROBERT R. 1970. Relation of early socialization experiences to self-concepts and gender role in middle childhood. *Child Development*, 41:267–289. *151*

SEBALD, HANS. 1986. Adolescents' shifting orientation toward parents and peers: A curvilinear trend over recent decades. *Journal of Marriage and the Family*, 48:5–13. *292*

SEEMAN, MELVIN. 1959. On the meaning of alienation. *American Sociological Review*, 24:783–791. *418*

SEIDLER, JOHN. 1986. Contested accommodation: The Catholic Church as a special case of social change. *Social Forces*, 64:847–874. *374,391*

SEITZ, VICTORIA. 1975. Integrated versus segregated school attendance and immediate recall for standard and non-standard English. *Developmental Psychology*, 11:217–223. *474*

SELIGMANN, JEAN. 1984. The date who rapes. *Newsweek* (April 9):91–92. *321*

SELIGSON, CICHELLE. 1986. Child care for the school-age child. *Phi Delta Kappan*, 67 (May):637–640. *353*

SELMAN, ROBERT L. 1980. *The Growth of Interpersonal Understanding: Developmental and Clinical Analyses*. New York: Academic Press. *290*

SERRILL, MICHAEL S. 1987. In the grip of the scourge. *Time* (February 16):58–59. *497*

SERRIN, WILLIAM. 1984. Companies widen worker role in decisions. *New York Times* (January 15):1, 12. *131,132*

SERRIN, WILLIAM. 1986. Part-time work new labor trend. *New York Times* (July 9):1, 9. *421*

SERVICE, ELMAN. 1971. *Primitive Social Organization: An Evolutionary Perspective*. New York: Random House. *595*

SEWELL, WILLIAM E. 1981. Notes on educational, occupational, and educational achievement in American society. *Phi Delta Kappan*, 62:322–325. *473*

SHABECOFF, PHILIP. 1984. Pesticide is found in food samplings. *New York Times* (January 6):1, 9. *533*

SHABECOFF, PHILIP. 1985. Toxic waste threat termed far greater than U.S. estimates. *New York Times* (March 10): 1, 15. *533*

SHABECOFF, PHILIP. 1986. Pesticide control finally tops the E.P.A.'s list of most pressing. *New York Times* (March 6):16. *516,553*

SHABECOFF, PHILIP. 1987. Man said to tax earth's systems. *New York Times* (February 15):4. *516*

SHANAS, ELEANOR. 1982. The family relations of old people. *National Forum*, LXII: 9–11. *298*

SHAW, CLIFFORD R. 1930. *Natural History of a Juvenile Career*. Chicago: University of Chicago Press. *201*

SHAW, CLIFFORD R., and HENRY McKAY. 1942. *Juvenile Delinquency in Urban Areas*. Chicago: University of Chicago Press. *201*

SHEA, JOHN C. 1984. *American Government: The Great Game of Politics*. New York: St. Martin's. *449,455*

SHEETS, KENNETH R. 1983. War over water. *U.S. News & World Report* (October 31):57–62. *532*

SHENON, PHILIP. 1986. Crime panel issues its final report. *New York Times* (April 2):1, 9. *211*

SHERIF, MUZAFER. 1936. *The Psychology of Social Norms*. New York: Harper & Row. *574*

SHERIF, MUZAFER. 1966. *In Common Predicament: Social Psychology of Intergroup Conflict and Cooperation*. Boston: Houghton Mifflin. *111–112, 265*

SHEVKY, ESHREF, and MARILYN WILLIAMS. 1949. *The Social Areas of Los Angeles*. Berkeley: University of California Press. *549*

SHIBUTANI, TAMOTSU. 1966. *Improvised News: A Sociological Study of Rumor*. Indianapolis: Bobbs-Merrill. *567*

SHIBUTANI, TAMOTSU. 1986. *Social Processes: An Introduction to Sociology*. Berkeley: University of California Press. *459,460,546,567,568,570,574, 577,589,590*

SHILS, EDWARD A., and MORRIS JANOWITZ. 1948. Cohesion and disintegration in the Wehrmacht in World War II. *Public Opinion Quarterly*, 12:280–315. *110*

SHIPLER, DAVID K. 1984. Israel's kibbutzim turn from communal ideals to needs of the individual. *New York Times* (June 27):4. *222*

SHIPLER, DAVID K. 1987. U.S. and battle against terrorism: Can a superpower be held hostage? *New York Times* (January 27):6. *579*

SHIPMAN, PAT. 1987. The myths and perturbing realities of cannibalism. *Discover*, 8 (March):70–76. *69*

SHOHAM-SALOMON, VARDA. 1985. Are schizophrenics' behaviors schizophrenic? *Journal of Abnormal Psychology*, 94:443–453. *190*

SHORTER, EDWARD. 1975. *The Making of the Modern Family*. New York: Basic Books. *350*

SHORTER, EDWARD. 1986. *Bedside Manners: The Troubled History of Doctors and Patients*. New York: Simon and Schuster. *503*

SHREVE, ANITA. 1984. The working mother as role model. *New York Times Magazine* (September 9):39–43+. *354*

SHRIBMAN, DAVID. 1987. After expensive, negative congressional races, support builds to reform candidate financing. *Wall Street Journal* (February 24):60. *449*

SILK, LEONARD. 1986. Modern views on population. *New York Times* (July 9): 26. *527*

SILK, LEONARD. 1987. Women gain, but

at a cost. *New York Times* (February 6): 30. *316*

SILVERMAN, MERVYN. 1987. Mandatory tests for AIDS? *U.S. News & World Report* (March 9):62. *490*

SIMMEL, GEORG. 1908/1955. *Conflict and the Web of Group Affiliations.* New York: The Free Press. *32,345*

SIMMEL, GEORG. 1908/1959. How is society possible. In Kurt Wolff, Ed., *Essays in Sociology, Philosophy, and Aesthetics.* New York: Harper Torchbooks. *32,345*

SIMMEL, GEORG. 1950. *The Sociology of Georg Simmel.* Kurt Wolff, Ed. and trans. New York: Free Press. *32,36*

SIMMONS, ROBERTA G., DALE A. BLYTH, EDWARD F. VAN CLEAVE, and DIANE MITSCH BUSH. 1979. Entry into early adolescence. *American Sociological Review*, 44:948–967. *292*

SIMMONS, ROBERTA G., and FLORENCE ROSENBERG. 1973. Disturbance in the self-image at adolescence. *American Sociological Review*, 38:553–568. *292*

SIMON, JULIAN L. 1981. *The Ultimate Resource.* Princeton, NJ: Princeton University Press. *525*

SIMON, JULIAN L. 1986. Flow of immigrants strengthens the USA. *USA Today* (April 3):6A. *270*

SIMON, JULIAN L., and HERMAN KAHN. 1984. *The Resourceful Earth: A Response to Global 2000.* New York: Basil Blackwell. *525*

SIMPSON, GEORGE EATON, and J. MILTON YINGER. 1972. *Racial and Cultural Minorities*, 4th ed. New York: Harper & Row. *261*

SIMPSON, RICHARD L. 1985. Social control of occupations and work. *Annual Review of Sociology*, 11:415–436. *421*

SINGER, ELEANOR. 1981. Reference groups and social evaluations. In Morris Rosenberg and Ralph H. Turner, Eds., *Social Psychology.* New York: Basic Books. *113*

SINGER, J. L., D. G. SINGER, and W. S. RAPACZYNSKI. 1984. Family patterns and television viewing as predictors of children's beliefs and aggression. *Journal of Communication*, 34:73–89. *159*

SIU, ALBERT L., FRANK A. SONNENBERG, WILLARD G. MANNING, GEORGE A. GOLDBERG, ELLYN S. BLOOMFIELD, JOSEPH P. NEWHOUSE, and ROBERT H. BROOK. 1986. Inappropriate use of hospitals in a randomized trial of health insurance plans. *New England Journal of Medicine*, 315:1259–1266. *502*

SIWOLOP, SANA. 1987. The AIDS epidemic and business. *Business Week* (March 23):122–132. *489–490*

SJOBERG, GIDEON. 1960. *The Preindustrial City.* New York: Free Press. *80, 544*

SKINNER, B. F. 1953. *Science and Human Behavior.* New York: Free Press. *146*

SKOCPOL, THEDA. 1979. *States and Social Revolution.* New York: Cambridge University Press. *51,576*

SKOCPOL, THEDA. 1980. Political response to capitalist crisis: Neo-Marxist theories of the state and the case of the New Deal. *Politics and Society*, 10:155–201. *51*

SKOCPOL, THEDA, Ed. 1984. *Vision and Method in Historical Sociology.* Cambridge: Cambridge University Press. *51*

SKOCPOL, THEDA, and EDWIN AMENTA. 1986. States and social politics. *Annual Review of Sociology*, 12:131–157. *437*

SKOLNICK, ARLENE. 1981. The family and its discontents. *Society*, 18 (January):42–47. *337*

SKRYPNEK, BERNA J., and MARK SNYDER. 1982. On the self-perpetuating nature of stereotypes about men and women. *Journal of Experimental Social Psychology*, 18:277–291. *308,309*

SLOTKIN, JAMES S. 1950. *Social Anthropology.* New York: Macmillan. *64*

SLOTKIN, JAMES S. 1955. Culture and psychopathology. *Journal of Abnormal and Social Psychology*, 51:269–275. *198*

SLOVAK, JEFFREY S. 1985. City spending, suburban demands, and fiscal exploitation: A replication and extension. *Social Forces*, 64:168–190. *557*

SMELSER, NEIL J. 1963. *Theory of Collective Behavior.* New York: Free Press. *569,570–575*

SMITH, KEVIN B. 1981. Class structure and intergenerational mobility from a Marxian perspective. *Sociological Quarterly*, 22:385–401. *246*

SMITH, NEIL. 1984. Uneven Development: *Nature, Capital and the Production of Space.* New York: Basil Blackwell. *557*

SMITH, RICHARD M., and CRAIG W. SMITH. 1981. Child rearing and single-parent fathers. *Family Relations*, 30:411–417. *364*

SMITH, TERENCE. 1984. Iran: Five years of fanaticism. *New York Times Magazine* (February 12):21+. *236*

SMITH, TOM W. 1984. America's religious mosaic. *American Demographics*, 6 (June):19–23. *390,391,392*

SNAREY, JOHN R. 1985. Cross-cultural universality of social-moral development: A critical review of Kohlbergian research. *Psychological Bulletin*, 97:202–232. *149*

SNOW, DAVID A., and RICHARD MACHALEK. 1984. The sociology of conversion. *Annual Review of Sociology*, 10:167–190. *585*

SNOW, DAVID A., E. BURKE ROCHFORD, JR., STEVEN K. WORDEN, and ROBERT D. BENFORD. 1986. Frame alignment processes, micromobilization, and movement participation. *American Sociological Review*, 51:464–481. *585*

SNOWDEN, FRANK M., JR. 1983. *Before Color Prejudice: The Ancient View of Blacks.* Cambridge, MA: Harvard University Press. *258*

SNYDER, ELDON E. 1972. Athletic dressing room slogans as folklore: A means of socialization. *International Review of Sport Sociology*, 7:89–102. *426*

SOLIS, DIANNA. 1985. From farm to farm, migrant workers struggle to survive. *Wall Street Journal* (May 15):1, 26. *237*

SOLOMON, JOLIE B. 1984. Procter & Gamble fights new rumors of link to Satanism. *Wall Street Journal* (November 8):1, 21. *567*

SOLOMON, JOLIE. 1986. Working at relaxation. *Wall Street Journal* (April 21):1D. *424*

SOLOMON, MICHAEL R. 1986. Dress for effect. *Psychology Today*, 20 (April):20–28. *170,224*

SOLOMON, ZAHAVA, MARION MIKULINCER, and STEVAN E. HOBFOLL. 1986. Effects of social support and battle intensity on loneliness and breakdown during combat. *Journal of Personality and Social Psychology*, 51:1269–1276. *111*

SOLORZANO, LUCIA. 1987. Does college cost too much? *U.S. News & World Report* (March 9):54–55. *476*

SOMMER, ROBERT. 1969. *Personal Space.* Englewood Cliffs, NJ: Prentice-Hall. *182*

SORENSEN, AAGE B. 1975. The structure of intragenerational mobility. *American Sociological Review*, 40:456–471.

243

Sorokin, Pitirim. 1937. *Social and Cultural Dynamics*. New York: Bedminister Press. 456

Sorokin, Pitirim. 1959. *Social and Cultural Mobility*. New York: Free Press. 230

Southern School News. 1954. Segregation. *Southern School News*, 1 (November):3. 383

Sowell, Thomas. 1975. *Race and Economics*. New York: David McKay Co. 261

Sowell, Thomas. 1980. Ethnic groups, prejudice and economic progress. *Wall Street Journal* (December 4):22. 261

Spanier, Graham B. 1983. Married and unmarried: Cohabitation in the United States: 1980. *Journal of Marriage and the Family*, 45:277–288. 362

Spanier, Graham B., and Linda Thompson. 1984. *Parting: The Aftermath of Separation and Divorce*. Beverly Hills: Sage. 356

Spence, Janet T., and R. L. Helmreich. 1978. *Masculinity and Femininity: Their Psychological Dimensions, Correlates, and Antecedents*. Austin: University of Texas Press. 320

Spengler, Oswald. 1918/1926. *The Decline of the West*. New York: Knopf. 596

Spradley, James P., and Brenda J. Mann. 1975. *The Cocktail Waitress*. New York: Wiley. 85–86,309,542

Sprey, Jetse. 1979. Conflict theory and the study of marriage and the family. In Wesley R. Burr, Reuben Hill, F. Ivan Nye, and Ira L. Reiss, Eds., *Contemporary Theories About the Family*, Vol. 2. New York: The Free Press. 33,345

Stagner, R. 1975. Boredom on the assembly line: Age and personality variables. *Industrial Gerontology*, 2:23–44. 419

Stamler, Jeremiah. 1985. Coronary heart disease: Doing the "right things." *New England Journal of Medicine*, 312:1053–1055. 492

Stark, David. 1986. Rethinking internal labor markets: New insights from a comparative perspective. *American Sociological Review*, 51:492–504. 422

Stark, Elizabeth. 1984. The unspeakable family secret. *Psychology Today*, 18 (May):38–46. 360

Stark, Rodney, and William S. Bainbridge. 1979. Of churches, sects, and cults: Preliminary concepts for a theory of religious movements. *Journal for the Scientific Study of Religion*, 18:117–133. 376,377

Stark, Rodney, and William S. Bainbridge. 1981. American-born sects: Initial findings. *Journal for the Scientific Study of Religion*, 20:130–149. 376

Stark, Rodney, and William S. Bainbridge. 1985. *The Future of Religion*. Berkeley: University of California Press. 380,393

Starr, Paul. 1982. *The Social Transformation of American Medicine*. New York: Basic Books. 502,503

Stearns, Linda Brewster, and John R. Logan. 1986. The racial structuring of the housing market and segregation in suburban areas. *Social Forces*, 65:28–42. 550

Stein, Andrew. 1986. Children of poverty: Crisis in New York. *New York Times Magazine* (June 8):39+. 241

Steinberg, Stephen. 1981. *The Ethnic Myth: Race, Ethnicity and Class in America*. New York: Atheneum. 277

Stephan, Cookie W., and Judy Corder. 1985. The effects of dual-career families on adolescents' sex-role attitudes, work and family plans, and choices of important others. *Journal of Marriage and the Family*, 47:921–929. 354

Stephan, G. Edward, and Douglas R. McMullin. 1982. Tolerance of sexual nonconformity. *American Sociological Review*, 47:411–415. 556

Stephens, M. W., and P. Delys. 1973. External control expectancies among disadvantaged children at preschool age. *Child Development*, 44:670–674. 474

Stephens, William N. 1963. *The Family in Cross-Cultural Perspective*. New York: Holt, Rinehart and Winston. 337,339,341

Steptoe, Sonja. 1987. Hassles and red tape destroy joy of the job for many physicians. *Wall Street Journal* (April 10):1, 12. 507

Sterba, James P. 1982. New study defends the social sciences. *New York Times* (June 22): 20. 9

Stevens, Gillian, and Gray Swicegood. 1987. The linguistic context of ethnic endogamy. *American Sociological Review*, 52:73–82. 257

Stevenson, Harold W., Shin-Ying Lee, and James W. Stigler. 1986. Mathematics achievement of Chinese, Japanese, and American children. *Science*, 231:693–699. 479

Steward, Julian H. 1955. *Theory of Cultural Change*. Urbana: University of Illinois Press. 71,595

Stewart, Sally Ann. 1985. Sex, contraception and today's single woman. *USA Today* (February 15):D–1. 327

Stinchcombe, Arthur L. 1983. *Economic Sociology*. New York: Academic Press. 421

Stith, Sandra M., and Albert J. Davis. 1984. Employed mothers and family day-care substitute caregivers: A comparative analysis of infant care. *Child Development*, 55:1340–1348. 353

Stockman, David. 1986. *The Triumph of Politics*. New York: Harper & Row. 433–434

Stokes, Randall G. 1975. Afrikaner Calvinism and economic action: The Weberian thesis in South Africa. *American Journal of Sociology*, 81:62–81. 386–387

Stokes, Randall G., and John P. Hewitt. 1976. Aligning actions. *American Sociological Review*, 41:838–849. 64

Stoller, Eleanor Palo. 1983. Parental caregiving by adult children. *Journal of Marriage and the Family*, 45:851–858. 360

Stone, C. 1982. Corporate vices and corporate virtues: Do public/private distinctions matter. *University of Pennsylvania Law Review*, 130:1441–1509. 204

Stone, Katherine. 1974. The origins of job structures in the steel industry. *The Review of Radical Economics*, 6:61–97. 130

Strasser, Herman, and Susan Randall. 1981. *An Introduction to Theories of Social Change*. London: Routledge & Kegan Paul. 590

Straus, Murray A., and Richard J. Gelles. 1986. Societal change and change in family violence from 1975 to 1985 as revealed by two national surveys. *Journal of Marriage and the Family*, 48:465–479. 359.

Strauss, Anselm L. 1975. *Chronic Illness and the Quality of Life*. St. Louis: Mosby. 491

Strauss, Anselm, and Barney Glaser. 1970. *Anguish*. San Francisco: Sociology Press. *296*

STRAUSS, ANSELM, LEONARD SCHATZ-MAN, RUE BUCHER, DANUTA EHRLICH, and MELVIN SABSHIN. 1964. *Psychiatric Ideologies and Institutions.* New York: Free Press. *130–131*

STRELNICK, A. H., ROBERT J. MASSAD, WILLIAM B. BATEMAN, and SAUNDRA D. SHEPHERD. 1986. Minority students in U.S. medical schools. *New England Journal of Medicine,* 315:67–68. *498*

STRICHARCHUK, GREGORY, and RALPH E. WINTER. 1985. Second thoughts. *Wall Street Journal* (September 16):14C. *603*

STRUBE, MICHAEL J., and LINDA S. BARBOUR. 1983. The decision to leave an abusive relationship: Economic dependence and psychological commitment. *Journal of Marriage and the Family,* 45:785–793. *359*

STRYKER, SHELDON. 1980. *Symbolic Interactionism: A Social Structural Version.* Menlo Park: CA: Benjamin/Cummings. *36,156*

STRYKER, SHELDON, and ANNE STATHAM. 1985. Symbolic interaction and role theory. In G. Lindzey and E. Aronson, Eds., *Handbook of Social Psychology.* 3rd ed. Vol. 1. New York: Random House. *35,36,169,345*

STUBBING, RICHARD A. 1986. *The Defense Game: An Insider Explores the Astonishing Realities of America's Defense Establishment.* New York: Harper & Row. *452*

STUCKERT, R. P. 1976. "Race" mixture: The black ancestry of White Americans. In P. B. Hammond, Ed., *Physical Anthropology and Archaeology.* New York: Macmillan. *255*

STUCKEY, M. FRANCINE, PAUL E. McGHEE, and NANCY J. BELL. 1982. Parent-child interaction: The influence of maternal employment. *Developmental Psychology,* 18:635–644. *353*

SUDNOW, DAVID. 1967. *Passing On: The Social Organization of Dying.* Englewood Cliffs, NJ: Prentice-Hall. *295*

SULLIVAN, WALTER. 1982. Clues to longevity in Soviet Union. *New York Times* (November 30):17, 20. *281*

SULLIVAN, SCOTT. 1986. Europe's population bomb. *Newsweek* (December 15): 52. *528*

SUMNER, WILLIAM GRAHAM. 1906. *Folkways.* Boston: Ginn & Co. *64*

SUMNER, WILLIAM GRAHAM. 1911. War.

Yale Review, 1:1–27. *457*

SUPPLE, TERRY S. 1986. The coming labor shortage. *American Demographics,* 8 (September):32–35. *602*

SURO, ROBERTO. 1986. The Vatican and dissent in America. *New York Times* (1986):9. *391*

SUSSMAN, NAM M., and HOWARD M. ROSENFELD. 1982. Influence of culture, language, and sex on conversational distance. *Journal of Personality and Social Psychology,* 42:66–74. *180*

SUTHERLAND, EDWIN H. 1939. *Principles of Criminology.* Philadelphia: Lippincott. *202*

SUTHERLAND, EDWIN H. 1949. *White-Collar Crime.* New York: The Dryden Press. *204,210*

SUTTLES, GERALD D. 1968. *The Social Order of the Slum.* Chicago: University of Chicago Press. *542*

SUTTLES, GERALD D. 1972. *The Social Construction of Communities.* Chicago: University of Chicago Press. *542*

SUTTLES, GERALD D. 1984. The cumulative texture of local urban culture. *American Journal of Sociology,* 90:283–304. *542*

SWANN, WILLIAM B., JR., and CRAIG A. HILL. 1982. When our identities are mistaken: Reaffirming self-conceptions through social interaction. *Journal of Personality and Social Psychology,* 43:59–66. *150*

SWANSON, GUY E. 1969. *The Birth of the Gods.* Ann Arbor: University of Michigan Press. *380*

SWANSON, LISA, and MARY KAY BIAGGIO. 1985. Therapeutic perspectives on father-daughter incest. *American Journal of Psychiatry,* 142:667–674. *359*

SWINGEWOOD, ALLAN. 1984. *A Short History of Sociological Thought.* New York: St. Martin's Press. *12*

SZASZ, THOMAS. 1970. *The Manufacture of Madness.* New York: Harper-Colophon. *500*

SZELYNI, IVAN. 1978. Class analysis and beyond: Further dilemmas for the new urban sociology. *Comparative Urban Research,* 6:86–96. *557*

SZYMANSKI, ALBERT. 1976. Racial discrimination and white gain. *American Sociological Review,* 41:403–414.

SZYMANSKI, ALBERT. 1978. White workers' loss from racial discrimination. *American Sociological Review,* 43:776–782. *266*

SZYMANSKI, ALBERT. 1981. *The Logic of Imperialism.* New York: Praeger. *414*

TAGLIABUE, JOHN. 1986. New terrorists: 'Kids who are trained to go out and kill.' *New York Times* (January 1):5. *582*

TAUBMAN, PHILIP. 1986. Soviet law widens private business. *New York Times* (November 20):5. *407*

TAVRIS, CAROL, and CAROLE OFFIR. 1977. *The Longest War: Sex Differences in Perspective.* New York: Harcourt Brace Jovanovich. *319*

TAWNEY, R. H. 1926. *Religion and the Rise of Capitalism.* New York: Harcourt Brace Jovanovich. *386*

TAYLOR, D. GARTH, PAUL B. SHEATSLEY, and ANDREW M. GREELEY. 1978. Attitudes toward racial integration. *Scientific American,* 238 (June):42–49. *259*

TAYLOR, FREDERICK WINSLOW. 1911. *Scientific Management.* New York: Harper & Row. *132*

TAYLOR, HUMPHREY. 1985. Healing the health care system. *Public Opinion,* 8 (August/September):16–20+. *505*

TAYLOR, RONALD A. 1984. The plague that's killing America's trees. *U.S. News & World Report* (April 23): 58–59. *533*

TAYLOR, SHELLEY E. 1986. *Health Psychology.* New York: Random House. *492,505*

TAYLOR, STAN. 1984. *Social Science and Revolutions.* New York: St. Martin's Press. *576*

TEITELBAUM, MICHAEL S., and JAY M. WINTER. 1985. *The Fear of Population Decline.* Orlando, FL: Academic Press. *528*

TEMPLE, MARK, and KENNETH POLK. 1986. A dynamic analysis of educational attainment. *Sociology of Education,* 59:79–84. *473*

TERRACE, HERBERT S. 1979. How Nim Chimpsky changed my mind. *Psychology Today,* 13 (November):65–76. *63*

TERRY, SARA. 1986. Sports fervor: part of Boston tradition. *Christian Science Monitor* (October 24):1, 6. *427*

TETLOCK, PHILIP E. 1983. Policy-makers' images of international conflict. *Journal of Social Issues,* 39:67–86. *458*

THOMAS, GEORGE M., and JOHN W. MEYER. 1984. The expansion of the state. *Annual Review of Sociology,* 10:461–482. *436*

THOMAS, MELVIN E., and MICHAEL HUGHES. 1986. The continuing significance of race: A study of race, class, and quality of life in America, 1972–1985. *American Sociological Review*, 51:830–841. 269

THOMAS, WILLIAM I. 1931. The relation of research to the social process. In *Essays on Research in the Social Sciences*. Washington, DC: The Brookings Institution. 168

THORNBERRY, TERENCE P., and MARGARET FARNWORTH. 1982. Social correlates of criminal involvement. *American Sociological Review*, 47:505–518. 214

THORNE, EMANUEL, and GILAH LANGNER. 1986. The body's value has gone up. *New York Times* (September 8): 23. 499

THRASHER, FREDERIC M. 1927. *The Gang*. Chicago: The University of Chicago Press. 201

THUROW, LESTER C. 1981. Why women are paid less than men. *New York Times* (March 8):F–2. 318

THUROW, LESTER C. 1985. Medicine versus economics. *New England Journal of Medicine*, 313:611–614. 507

TIEGER, TODD. 1980. On the biological basis of sex differences in aggression. *Child Development*, 51:943–963. 310

TIERNEY, JOHN. 1986. The population crisis revisited. *Wall Street Journal* (January 20): 14.

TILLY, CHARLES, Ed. 1978. *Historical Studies of Changing Fertility*. Princeton: Princeton University Press. 526

TILLY, CHARLES. 1978. *From Mobilization to Revolution*. Reading, MA: Addison-Wesley. 583,585

TILLY, CHARLES. 1986. *The Contentious French*. Cambridge, MA: The Belknap Press of Harvard University. 31,577,585

TIMASHEFF, NICHOLAS S. 1965. *War and Revolution*. Joseph F. Scheuer (Ed. with preface). New York: Sheed & Ward. 460

TINBERGEN, NIKO. 1954. The origin and evolution of courtship and threat display. In J. S. Huxley, A. C. Hardy, and E. B. Ford, Eds., *Evolution as a Process*. London: Allen & Unwin. 43

TITTLE, CHARLES R. 1980. *Sanctions and Social Deviance*. New York: Praeger. 215

TOENNIES, FERDINAND. 1887/1963. *Gemeinschaft und Gesellschaft*. Trans. C. P. Loomis. New York: American Book. 553–554

TOFFLER, ALVIN. 1980. *The Third Wave*. New York: Morrow. 81,610

TORREY, B. B. 1982. The lengthening of retirement. In M. W. Riley, R. P. Abeles, and M. S. Teitelbaum, Eds., *Aging from Birth to Death*, Vol. 2. Boulder, CO: Westview Press. 294

TOYNBEE, ARNOLD J. 1934/1954. *A Study of History*. 10 Vols. New York: Oxford University Press. 596–597

TRAFFORD, ABIGAIL, and PETER DWORKIN. 1986. The new world of health care. *U.S. News & World Report* (April 14):60–63. 504

TRAFFORD, ABIGAIL, and STANLEY WELLBORN. 1986. Stark fallout. *U.S. News & World Report* (May 12):18–21. 535

TRAUGOTT, MARK. 1978. Reconceiving social movements. *Social Problems*, 26:38–49. 566

TROELTSCH, ERNST. 1931. *The Social Teachings of the Christian Churches*. Trans. Olive Wyon. 2 Vols. New York: The Macmillan Company. 373

TROEN, SELWYN K. 1985. Technological development and adolescence: The early twentieth century. *Journal of Early Adolescence*, 5:429–440. 291

TROTSKY, LEON. 1932/1959. *The History of the Russian Revolution*. F. W. Dupre, Ed. New York: Doubleday. 583

TROTTER, ROBERT J. 1986. The three faces of love. *Psychology Today*, 20 (September):46–54. 348

TUMIN, MELVIN. 1953. Some principles of stratification: A critical analysis. *American Sociological Review*, 18:387–394. 227

TUMIN, MELVIN M. 1985. *Social Stratification*, 2nd ed. New York: Prentice-Hall. 228

TURKLE, SHERRY. 1984. *The Second Self: Computers and the Human Spirit*. New York: Simon and Schuster. 601

TURNBULL, COIN M. 1972. *The Mountain People*. New York: A Touchstone Book. 142–143

TURNER, JONATHAN H. 1982. *The Structure of Sociological Theory*. Homewood, IL: Dorsey. 33,41

TURNER, PAULINE H., and RICHARD M. SMITH. 1983. Single parents and day care. *Family Relations*, 32:215–226. 364

TURNER, RALPH H. 1962. Role-taking: Process versus conformity. In A. Rose, Ed., *Human Behavior and Social Processes*. Boston: Houghton

Mifflin. 96

TURNER, RALPH H. 1964. Collective behavior. In R.E.L. Faris, Ed., *Handbook of Modern Sociology*. Chicago: Rand McNally. 575

TURNER, RALPH H. 1968a. The self-conception in social interaction. In C. Gordon and K.J. Gergen, Eds., *The Self in Social Interaction*. New York: Wiley. 96,150,154

TURNER, RALPH H. 1968b. Role: Sociological aspects. In D. Sills, Ed., *International Encyclopedia of the Social Sciences*, Vol. 13. New York: Free Press. 96

TURNER, RALPH H. 1978. The role and the person. *American Journal of Sociology*, 84:1–23. 93

TURNER, RALPH H., and LEWIS M. KILLIAN. 1972. *Collective Behavior*, 2nd ed. Englewood Cliffs, NJ: Prentice-Hall. 574

TVERSKY, AMOS, and DANIEL KAHNEMAN. 1981. The framing of decisions and the psychology of choice. *Science*, 211:453–458. 48

TWADDLE, ANDREW C., and RICHARD M. HESSLER. 1977. *A Sociology of Health*. St. Louis: Mosby. 491

TYLER, WILLIAM B. 1985. The organizational structure of the school. *Annual Review of Sociology*, 11:49–73. 478

TYREE, ANDREA, MOSHE SEMYONOV, and ROBERT W. HODGE. 1979. Gaps and glissandos: Inequality, economic development and social mobility. *American Sociological Review*, 44:410–424. 245

UDRY, J. RICHARD. 1965. Structural correlates of feminine beauty in Britain and the United States. *Sociology and Social Research*, 49:330–342. 347

UHLENBERG, PETER R. 1980. Death and the family. *Journal of Family History*, 5:313–320. 350

USEEM, BERT. 1985. Disorganization and the New Mexico prison riot of 1980. *American Sociological Review*, 50:677–688. 582

USEEM, MICHAEL. 1983. *The Inner Circle*. New York: Oxford University Press. 454

U.S. NEWS & WORLD REPORT. 1984. As past events fade in memory. *U.S. News & World Report* (January 23):50–51. 590

VALENTINE, CHARLES. 1968. *Culture and Poverty*. Chicago: University of

Chicago Press. *238*

VANCE, N. SCOTT. 1984. Sport is a religion in America, controversial professor argues. *The Chronicle of Higher Education* (May 16):25–29. *381*

VAN CREVELD, MARTIN. 1982. *Fighting Power: German and U.S. Army Performance, 1939–1945*. Westport, CT: Greenwood Press. *111*

VAN DEN BERGHE, PIERRE L. 1963. Dialectic and functionalism: Toward a theoretical synthesis. *American Sociological Review*, 28:695–705. *33,230*

VAN DEN BERGHE, PIERRE L. 1981. *The Ethnic Phenomenon*. New York: Elsevier. *255*

VANDER ZANDEN, JAMES W. 1965. *Race Relations in Transition*. New York: Random House. *585*

VANDER ZANDEN, JAMES W. 1979. *Sociology*, 4th ed. New York: Wiley. *569*

VANDER ZANDEN, JAMES W. 1983. *American Minority Relations*, 4th ed. New York: Knopf. *49,233,255,581*

VANDER ZANDEN, JAMES W. 1985. *Human Development*, 3rd ed. New York: Knopf. *158,302*

VANDER ZANDEN, JAMES W. 1987. *Social Psychology*, 4th ed. New York: Random House. *49,243*

VANNEMAN, REEVE, and FRED C. PAMPEL. 1977. The American perception of class and status. *American Sociological Review*, 42:422–437. *231*

VEBLEN, THORSTEIN. 1899. *The Theory of the Leisure Class*. New York: The Viking Press. *224*

VEBLEN, THORSTEIN. 1921. *Engineers and the Price System*. New York: Viking. *126,320*

VERBA, SIDNEY, NORMAN H. NIE, and JAE-ON KIM. 1978. *Participation and Political Equality: A Seven-Nation Comparison*. New York: Cambridge University Press. *236*

VERBA, SIDNEY, and GARY ORREN. 1985. Rendering what's due: Views on income inequality. *Public Opinion*, 8 (April):48–52. *242*

VETTER, BETTY. 1986. The last two decades. *Science 86*, 7 (July):62–63. *319*

VICTOR, JEFFREY S. 1980. *Human Sexuality: A Social Psychological Approach*. Englewood Cliffs, NJ: Prentice-Hall. *327*

VINING, DANIEL R., JR. 1985. The growth of core regions in the Third World. *Scientific American*, 252 (April):42–49. *552*

VOGEL, LISE. 1983. *Marxism and the Oppression of Women*. New Brunswick, NJ: Rutgers University Press. *314*

VOLD, GEORGE B., and THOMAS J. BERNARD. 1986. *Theoretical Criminology*. New York: Oxford University Press. *199,201,583*

VON BAEYER, C. L., D. L. SHERK, and M. P. ZANNA. 1981. Impression management in the job interview: When the female applicant meets the male "chauvinist" interviewer. *Personality and Social Psychology Bulletin*, 7:45–51. *309*

WAGLEY, CHARLES, and MARVIN HARRIS. 1964. *Minorities in the New World*. New York: Columbia University Press. *257,445*

WAITE, LINDA J., GUS W. HAGGSTROM, and DAVID E. KANOUSE. 1985. The consequences for parenthood for the marital stability of young adults. *American Sociological Review*, 50: 850–857. *352*

WAITZKIN, HOWARD. 1983. *The Second Sickness: Contradictions of Capitalist Health Care*. New York: Free Press. *497*

WALDO, GORDON P., and THEODORE G. CHIRICOS. 1972. Perceived penal sanction and self-reported criminality: A neglected approach to deterrence research. *Social Problems*, 19:522–540. *215*

WALKER, HENRY A., and MARY L. FENNELL. 1986. Gender differences in role differentiation and organizational task performance. *Annual Review of Sociology*, 12:225–275. *306*

WALKER, LAWRENCE J. 1984. Sex differences in the development of moral reasoning: A critical review. *Child Development*, 55:677–691. *149*

WALL, WENDY L. 1985. Farm crisis is taking subtle toll on children in distressed families. *Wall Street Journal* (November 7):1, 20. *93*

WALLERSTEIN, IMMANUEL. 1974. *The Modern World-System: Capitalist Agriculture and the Origins of the European World Economy in the 16th Century*. New York: Academic Press. *416,460,608*

WALLERSTEIN, IMMANUEL. 1979. *The Capitalist World Economy*. New York: Cambridge University Press. *608*

WALLERSTEIN, IMMANUEL. 1980. *The Modern World-System II: Mercantilism and the Consolidation of the European World-Economy, 1600–1775*. New York: Academic Press. *416, 460,608*

WALLERSTEIN, JUDITH S. 1984. Children of divorce. 61st annual meetings of the American Orthopsychiatric Association, Toronto, April 8, 1984. *357*

WALLERSTEIN, JUDITH S., and JOAN B. KELLY. 1980. *Surviving the Breakup: How Children and Parents Cope with Divorce*. New York: Basic Books. *357*

WALLIS, ROY. 1975. *Sectarianism: Analyzes of Religious and Non-Religious Sects*. New York: Wiley. *373,377*

WALLIS, ROY. 1984. *The Elementary Forms of the New Religious Life*. London: Routledge and Kegan Paul. *376,377*

WALLIS, ROY. 1986. Figuring out cult receptivity. *Journal for the Scientific Study of Religion*, 25:494–503. *376,377*

WALLSTON, B.S., S.W. ALAGNA, B.M. DEVELLIS, and R.F. DEVELLIS. 1984. Social support and health. *Health Psychology*, 4:367–391. *495*

WALSH, DORIS L. 1986. What women want. *American Demographics*, 8 (June):60. *350*

WALSH, EDWARD J. 1981. Resource mobilization and citizen protest in communities around Three Mile Island. *Social Problems*, 29:1–21. *117*

WALSH, EDWARD J., and REX H. WARLAND. 1983. Social movement involvement in the wake of a nuclear accident. *American Sociological Review*, 48:764–780. *117*

WALSH, KENNETH T. 1984. Picking a winner: How candidates are chosen. *U.S. News & World Report* (October 8): 68–72. *450*

WALSH, MARY W., and S. KARENE WITCHER. 1986. As debt turmoil ebbs and flows in Mexico, human misery persists. *Wall Street Journal* (June 12):1, 18. *608*

WALTON, JOHN. 1976. Political economy of world urban systems: Directions for comparative research. In J. Walton and L.H. Masotti, Eds., *The City in Comparative Perspective*. New York: Wiley. *551*

WAN, THOMAS T. H., and LOIS C. GRAY. 1978. Differential access to preventive services for young children in low-income urban areas. *Journal of Health and Social Behavior*, 19:312–324. *494*

WARLICK, JENNIFER L. 1985. Why is poverty after 65 a woman's problem? *Journal of Gerontology*, 40:751–757. 299

WARNER, REBECCA L., GARY R. LEE, and JANET LEE. 1986. Social organization, spousal resources, and marital power: A cross-cultural study. *Journal of Marriage and the Family*, 48:121–128. 314

WARNER, W. LLOYD. 1949. *Democracy in Jonesville*. New York: Harper & Row. 233,234

WARNER, W. LLOYD, and PAUL S. LUNT. 1941. *The Social Life of the Modern Community*. New Haven: Yale University Press. 233

WARNER, W. LLOYD, and PAUL S. LUNT. 1942. *The Status System of a Modern Community*. New Haven: Yale University Press. 233

WARR, MARK. 1985. Fear of rape among urban women. *Social Problems*, 32:238–250. 322

WATERMAN, CHARLES. 1986. Terrorists rarely achieve main goals, but do win lesser victories. *Christian Science Monitor* (December 3):14. 582

WATKINS, BEVERLY T. 1983. When researcher becomes participant: Scholars note the risks and rewards. *The Chronicle of Higher Education* (November 2):5, 8. 50

WATKINS, LINDA M. 1986. Liberal-arts graduates' prospects in the job market grow brighter. *Wall Street Journal* (May 6):33. 23

WATT, J. MICHAEL, ROBERT A. DERZON, STEVEN C. RENN, CARL J. SCHRAMM, JAMES S. HAHN, and GEORGE D. PILLARI. The comparative economic performance of investor-owned chain and not-for-profit hospitals. *New England Journal of Medicine*, 314:89–96. 498

WATTENBERG, BEN J., and KARL ZINSMEISTER. 1986. The birth dearth: The geopolitical consequences. *Public Opinion*, 8 (December/January):7–13. 528

WATTS, AL. 1986. Breakthroughs in biotech could produce self-fertilizing plants. *Investor's Daily* (September 12):21. 524

WEBER, MAX. 1904/1958. *The Protestant Ethic and the Spirit of Capitalism*. New York: Scribner's. 385,406

WEBER, MAX. 1916/1964. *The Religion of China: Confucianism and Taoism*. New York: Macmillan. 385

WEBER, MAX. 1917/1958. *The Religion of India: The Sociology of Hinduism and Buddhism*. New York: Free Press. 385

WEBER, MAX. 1921/1968. *Economy and Society*, 3 Vols. Totowa, NJ: Bedminister Press. 438

WEBER, MAX. 1946. *The Theory of Social and Economic Organization*. A.M. Henderson and Talcott Parsons, Eds. and trans. New York: Macmillan. 124,223

WEBER, MAX. 1947. *From Max Weber: Essays in Sociology*. Hans. H. Gerth and C. Wright Mills, Eds. and trans. New York: Oxford University Press. 124

WEBSTER, MURRAY, JR., and JAMES E. DRISKELL, JR. 1983. Beauty as status. *American Journal of Sociology*, 89:140–165. 320

WEINBERG, MARTIN S. 1965. Sexual modesty, social meanings, and the nudist camp. *Social Problems*, 12:314–318. 327

WEINBERG, MARTIN S., and COLIN J. WILLIAMS. 1980. Sexual embourgeoisment? Social class and sexual activity: 1938–1970. *American Sociological Review*, 45:33–48. 236

WEINSTEIN, EUGENE, and JUDITH M. TANUR. 1976. Meanings, purposes and structural resources in social interaction. *Cornell Journal of Social Relations*, 11:105–110. 35

WEISMAN, STEVEN R. 1986. The Rajiv generation. *New York Times Magazine* (April 20):18–22+. 227

WEISS, ROBERT S. 1984. The impact of marital dissolution on income and consumption in single-parent households. *Journal of Marriage and the Family*, 46:115–127. 363

WEITZMAN, LENORE J. 1985. *The Divorce Revolution: The Unexpected Consequences for Women and Children in America*. New York: Free Press. 356,357

WELLS, KEN. 1983. The Mormon church is rich, rapidly growing and very controversial. *Wall Street Journal* (November 8):1, 16. 393

WERNER, LESLIE MAITLAND. 1986a. 13% of U.S. adults are illiterate in English, a federal study finds. *New York Times* (April 21):1, 14. 465

WESSEL, DAVID. 1986. More young doctors shun private practice, work as employees. *Wall Street Journal* (January 13):1, 15. 503

WESTOFF, CHARLES F. 1986. Fertility in the United States. *Science*, 234:554–559. 518,528

WETZEL, CHRISTOPHER G., and CHESTER A. INSKO. 1982. The similarity-attraction relationship: Is there an ideal one? *Journal of Experimental Social Psychology*, 18:253–276. 183

WHITE, GREGORY L. 1980. Physical attractiveness and courtship progress. *Journal of Personality and Social Psychology*, 39:660–668. 347

WHITE, KATHLEEN M., JOSEPH C. SPEISMAN, DORIS JACKSON, SCOTT BARTIS, and DARYL COSTOS. 1986. Intimacy maturity and its correlates in young married couples. *Journal of Personality and Social Psychology*, 50:152–162. 293

WHITE, LESLIE A. 1949. *The Science of Culture*. New York: Farrar, Straus & Cudahy. 595

WHITE, LESLIE A. 1959. *The Evolution of Culture*. New York: McGraw-Hill. 71, 595

WHITE, LYNN K., and ALAN BOOTH. 1985. The quality and stability of remarriages: The role of stepchildren. *American Sociological Review*, 50:689–698. 358

WHITE, RALPH K., and RONALD O. LIPPITT. 1960. *Autocracy and Democracy*. New York: Harper & Row. 114–115

WHITEHEAD, ALFRED NORTH. 1929. *Process and Reality*. New York: Macmillan Co. 589

WHITING, BEATRICE B. 1950. *Paiute Sorcery*. New York: Wenner-Gren Foundation. 380

WHITMAN, DAVID, and JEANNYE THORNTON. 1986. A nation apart. *U.S. News & World Report* (March 17):18–21. 239

WHITT, HUGH P., and RICHARD L. MEILE. 1985. Alignment, magnification, and snowballing: Processes in the definition of "symptoms of mental illness." *Social Forces*, 63:682–697. 207

WHITT, J. ALLEN. 1979. Toward a class-dialectical model of power: An empirical assessment of three competing models of political power. *American Sociological Review*, 44:81–100. 451

WHITT, J. ALLEN. 1982. *Urban Elites and Mass Transportation: The Dialectics of Power*. Princeton: Princeton University Press. 451,556

WHORF, BENJAMIN L. 1956. *Language*,

Thought, and Reality. Cambridge, MA: MIT Press. 63

WHYTE, MARTIN K. 1978. *The Status of Women in Preindustrial Societies*. Princeton, NJ: Princeton University Press. 315

WICKS, JERRY W., and EDWARD G. STOCKWELL. 1984. A comment on the neonatal mortality—socioeconomic status relationship. *Social Forces*, 62:1035–1039. 235

WILFORD, JOHN NOBLE. 1981. Nine percent of everyone who ever lived is alive now. *New York Times* (October 6):13. 522

WILL, GEORGE. 1986. Our schools for scandal. *Newsweek* (September 15):84. 484,485

WILLIAMS, DENNIS A. 1985. Is college worth it? *Newsweek* (April 29):66–68. 476

WILLIAMS, KIPLING, STEPHEN HARKINS, and BIBB LATANE. 1981. Identifiability as a deterrent to social loafing: Two cheering experiments. *Journal of Personality and Social Psychology*, 40:303–311. 116

WILLIAMS, LENA. 1986. Blacks debating a greater stress on self-reliance instead of aid. *New York Times* (June 15):1, 18. 261

WILLIAMS, ROBIN M., JR. 1964. *Strangers Next Door*. Englewood Cliffs, NJ: Prentice-Hall. 257

WILLIAMS, ROBIN M., JR. 1970. *American Society*, 3rd ed. New York: Knopf. 65,477

WILLIAMS, WINSTON. 1984. The shrinking of the steel industry. *New York Times* (September 23):4F. 409

WILLIE, CHARLES V. 1979. *Caste and Class Controversy*. New York: General Hall. 269

WILLIE, CHARLES V. 1984. *School Desegregation Plans that Work*. Westport, CT: Greenwood Press. 475

WILSHIRE, BRUCE. 1982. *Role Playing and Identity: The Limits of Theatre as Metaphor*. Bloomington: Indiana University Press. 169

WILSON, CRAIG. 1987. Gay bashing: Brutal AIDS backlash. *USA Today* (March 12):D–1. 329,489

WILSON, EDWARD O. 1975. *Sociobiology: A New Synthesis*. Cambridge, MA: Harvard University Press. 102,340

WILSON, EDWARD O. 1984. *Biophilia*. Cambridge, MA: Harvard University Press. 102

WILSON, FRANKLIN D. 1984. Urban ecology: Urbanization and systems of cities. *Annual Review of Sociology*, 10:283–307. 543,551,552

WILSON, FRANKLIN D. 1985. The impact of school desegregation programs on white public-school enrollment, 1968–1976. *Sociology of Education*, 58:137–153. 476

WILSON, JAMES Q. 1967. The bureaucracy problem. *The Public Interest*, 6:3–9. 127

WILSON, JAMES Q. 1983. Thinking about crime. *The Atlantic Monthly* (September):72–88.

WILSON, JAMES Q., and PHILIP J. COOK. 1985. Unemployment and crime—What is the connection? *The Public Interest*, 79:3–8. 204

WILSON, JAMES Q., and RICHARD J. HERRNSTEIN. 1985. *Crime and Human Nature*. New York: Simon and Schuster. 199

WILSON, JOHN M. 1986. Cosbys deemed white on South African TV. *Columbus Ohio Dispatch* (March 25):8B. 255

WILSON, THOMAS C. 1985. Urbanism and tolerance: A test of some hypotheses drawn from Wirth and Stouffer. *American Sociological Review*, 50:117–123. 556

WILSON, THOMAS C. 1986. Community population size and social heterogenity: An Empirical Test. *American Journal of Sociology*, 91:1154–1169. 556

WILSON, WILLIAM JULIUS. 1978. *The Declining Significance of Race*. Chicago: University of Chicago Press. 261,269

WILSON, WILLIAM JULIUS, and ROBERT APONTE. 1985. Urban Poverty. *Annual Review of Sociology*, 11:231–258. 261,269

WINCH, ROBERT F. 1958. *Mate Selection: A Study of Complementary Needs*. New York: Harper & Row. 347

WINN, EDWARD A. 1981. Looking at good schools. *Phi Delta Kappan*, 62:377–381. 480

WINN, MARIE. 1983. *Children without Childhood*. New York: Pantheon Books. 327

WIRTH, LOUIS. 1938. Urbanism as a way of life. *American Journal of Sociology*, 44:1–24. 554

WISE, PAUL H., MILTON KOTELCHUCK, MARK L. WILSON, and MARK MILLS. 1985. Racial and socioeconomic disparities in childhood mortality in Bos-ton. *New England Journal of Medicine*, 313:360–366. 235

WOLF, ERIC. 1966. *Peasants*. Englewood Cliffs, NJ: Prentice-Hall. 80

WOLF, ERIC R. 1982. *Europe and the People without History*. Berkeley: University of California Press. 609

WOLFE, DAVID A. 1985. Child-abusive parents: An empirical review and analysis. *Psychological Bulletin*, 97:462–482. 359

WOLFGANG, MARVIN E., ROBERT M. FIGLIO, and THORSTEN SELLIN. 1972. *Delinquency in a Birth Cohort*. Chicago: University of Chicago Press. 215

WOODWARD, C. VANN. 1966. *The Strange Career of Jim Crow*, 2nd rev. ed. New York: Oxford University Press. 268

WOODWARD, KENNETH L. 1984. Vows of defiance. *Newsweek* (March 19):97–100. 392

WOODWARD, KENNETH L. 1985. Islam versus the West. *Newsweek* (June 24):28–30. 385

WOODWARD, KENNETH L. 1986. From "mainline" to sideline. *Newsweek* (December 22):54–56. 390

WORK, CLEMENS P., and RONALD A. TAYLOR. 1984. Toxic chemicals: Just how real a danger. *U.S. News & World Report* (May 21):64–67. 533

World Future Society. 1986. *The Art of Forecasting*. Bethesda, MD: World Future Society. 610

WREN, CHRISTOPHER S. 1984. China defends abortion in birth control efforts. *New York Times* (July 4):4. 527,528

WRIGHT, BARBARA W. 1986. Nurses' pay—why so low? *U.S. News & World Report* (March 17):72. 506

WRIGHT, ERIK OLIN. 1978a. *Class, Crisis, and the State*. New York: Schocken Books. 246

WRIGHT, ERIK OLIN. 1978b. Race, class, and income inequality. *American Journal of Sociology*, 83:1368–1388. 245,246

WRIGHT, ERIK OLIN. 1979. *Class Structure and Income Determination*. New York: Academic Press. 224,231

WRIGHT, ERIK OLIN. 1985. *Classes*. New York: Schocken. 224,229

WRIGHT, JAMES D., and SONIA R. WRIGHT. 1976. Social class and parental values for children: A partial replication and extension of the Kohn thesis. *American Sociological Review*, 41:527–537. 157

WRIGHT, ROBIN. 1987. Eight years of Khomeini transform Iran. *Christian Science Monitor* (January 30):9. *385*

WUTHNOW, ROBERT. 1986. Religion and the social fabric. In J.F. Short, Jr., Ed., *The Social Fabric*. Beverly Hills, CA: Sage. *373,379,394*

YAMAGISHI, TOSHIO, and KAORI SATO. 1986. Motivational bases of the public goods problem. *Journal of Personality and Social Psychology*, 50:67–73. *117*

YARROW, ANDREW L. 1987. Divorce at a young age: The troubled 20's. *New York Times* (January 12):19. *356*

YELLEN, JOHN. 1985. Bushmen. *Science 85*, 6 (May):41–48. *77*

YEMMA, JOHN. 1987. Buying into America. *Christian Science Monitor* (March 10):18–19. *416*

YINGER, J. MILTON. 1957. *Religion, Society, and the Individual*. New York: The Macmillan Co. *383*

YINGER, J. MILTON. 1965. *Toward a Field Theory of Behavior*. New York: Macmillan. *383*

YINGER, J. MILTON. 1985. Ethnicity. *Annual Review of Sociology*, 11:151–180. *254,257,276*

YLLO, KERSTI, and MURRAY A. STRAUS. 1981. Interpersonal violence among married and cohabiting couples. *Family Relations*, 30:339–347. *362*

ZABLOCKI, BENJAMIN. 1980. *Alienation and Charisma: A Study of Contemporary American Communes*. New York: Free Press. *365*

ZALD, MAYER N., and JOHN D. MCCARTHY. 1979. *The Dynamics of Social Movements*. Cambridge, MA: Winthrop. *583*

ZANKER, ALFRED. 1986. Europe's immigration battles. *U.S. News & World Report* (March 31):25–27. *519*

ZAUTRA, ALEX J., ROBERT T. GUENTHER, and GEORGE M. CHARTIER. 1985. Attributions for real and hypothetical events: Their relation to self-esteem and depression. *Journal of Abnormal Psychology*, 94:530–540. *151*

ZBOROWSKI, MARK. 1952. Cultural components in responses to pain. *Journal of Social Issues*, 8:16–30. *492*

ZEITLIN, IRVING M. 1981. *Ideology and the Development of Sociological Theory*, 2nd ed. Englewood Cliffs, NJ: Prentice-Hall. *15*

ZERUBAVEL, EVIATAR. 1985. *The Seven Day Circle: The History and Meaning of the Week*. New York: The Free Press. *67*

ZETTERBERG, HANS. 1966. The secret ranking. *Journal of Marriage and the Family*, 28:134–142. *320*

ZEY-FERRELL, MARY. 1981. Criticisms of the dominant perspective on organizations. *The Sociological Quarterly*, 22:181–205. *129,130*

ZIGLI, BARBARA. 1984. Asian-Americans beat others in academic drive. *USA Today*. (April 25):1D. *276*

ZILLMAN, DOLF. 1978. Attribution and misattribution of excitatory reactions. In J. Harvey, W. Ickes, and R.F. Kidd, Eds., *New Directions in Attribution Research*, Vol. 2. Hillsdale, NJ: Erlbaum. *45*

ZIMBARDO, PHILIP G. 1969. The human choice: Individuation, reason, and order versus deindividualization, impulse, and chaos. In W. Arnold and D. Levine, Eds., *Nebraska Symposium on Motivation*, 17:237–307. *570*

ZIMBARDO, PHILIP G. 1978. Misunderstanding shyness: The counterattack. *Psychology Today*, 12 (June):17–18+. *152*

ZIMBARDO, PHILIP G., C. HANEY, and W.C. BANKS. 1973. A Pirandellian prison. *New York Times Magazine* (April 8):38–40+. *96–97*

ZIMBARDO, PHILIP G., and F.L. RUCH. 1975. *Psychology and Life*, 9th ed. Glenview, IL: Scott, Foresman. *97*

ZIMMER, JUDITH. 1984. Courting the gods of sport. *Psychology Today*, 18 (July):36–39. *372*

ZIMMERMAN, DON H. 1971. The practicalities of rule use. In Jack D. Douglas, Ed., *Understanding Everyday Life*. Chicago: Aldine. *171*

ZIMMERMAN, DON H., and D. LAWRENCE WIEDER. 1970. Ethnomethodology and the problem of order: Comment on Denzin. In J.D. Douglas, Ed., *Understanding Everyday Life*. Chicago: Aldine. *171*

ZIPP, JOHN F., RICHARD LANDERMAN, and PAUL LUEBKE, 1982. Political parties and political participation. *Social Forces*, 60:1140–1153. *236*

ZOLA, IRVING KENNETH. 1966. Culture and symptoms—An analysis of patients' presenting complaints. *American Sociological Review*, 31:615–630. *492,493,500*

ZUCKERMAN, MIRON, M.H. KERNIS, S.M. GUARNERA, J.F. MURPHY, and L. RAPPOPORT. 1983. The egocentric bias: Seeing oneself as cause and target of others' behavior. *Journal of Personality*, 51:621–630. *153*

Copyrights and Acknowledgments

Chapter 1
Figure A   From R. Alan Hedley and Susan M. Adams, "The Job Market for Bachelor Degree Holders: A Cummulation," *The American Sociologist*, 17, 1982, pp. 155–163, Table 1, p. 158.

Chapter 2
Table 2.2   "Stocks and the Big Game," January 26, 1986. Copyright 1986, *USA Today*. Reprinted with permission.

Chapter 3
Figures A-B   From John Yellan, "Bushman," *Science* 85 (May), pp. 44–45.

Figure 3.2   Chart of December 16, 1986. Copyright © 1986 by The New York Times Company. Reprinted by permission.

Chapter 4
Figure 4.1   From James P. Spradley and Brenda J. Mann, *The Cocktail Waitress*, 1975. Reprinted by permission of Random House, Inc.

Chapter 5
Table 5.3   Based on chapter 11, Preventing Group Think, from *Group Think: Psychological Studies of Policy Studies and Fiascos*, 2nd Ed. by Irving L. Janis. Copyright © 1982 by Houghton Mifflin Company. As adapted in I. H. Brandstatter, et al., *Group Decision Making*, Academic Press, 1982.

Chapter 6
Figure 6.1   From Theodosius Dobzhansky, *Mankind Evolving*, Yale University Press, 1962.

Table 6.2   Adapted from Manford H. Kuhn and Thomas S. McPartland, "An Empirical Investigation of Self-Attitudes," *American Sociological Review*, 1954.

Table 6.3   From Philip Zimbardo, *Shyness*, © 1977, Addison-Wesley Publishing Company, Inc., Reading, Massachusetts. Pg. 37 (chart). Reprinted with permission.

Figure 6.3   Chart, "Juveniles' Companion." Copyright, 1985, U.S. News & World Report. Reprinted from issue of February 18, 1985.

Chapter 7
Figure 7.3   Reprinted with permission from *Association Management* Magazine, June 1984, copyright.

Figure 7.6   From *Being Adolescent: Conflict and Growth in the Teenage Years*, by Mihaly Csikszentmihalyi and Reed Larson. Copyright © 1984 by Basic Books, Inc. Reprinted by permission of the publisher.

Chapter 8
Figure 8.1   Adapted with permission of The Free Press, a division of Macmillan, Inc. from *Social Theory and Social Structure*, Revised Edition, by Robert K. Merton. Copyright © 1949, 1957 by The Free Press, renewed 1977, 1985 by Robert K. Merton.

Chapter 10
Table 10.1   Reprinted from *Closing the Gap: Forty Years of Economic Progress for Blacks* (R-3330-00L), February 1986, The RAND Corporation, 1700 Main Street, P.O. Box 2138, Santa Monica, CA 90406-2138. Table of March 2, 1986. Copyright © 1986 by The New York Times Company. Reprinted by permission.

Figure A   From Jeffrey Albert and Marcy Eckroith-Mullins, "The Waves of Immigration to the USA," June 30, 1986. Copyright 1986, *USA Today*. Reprinted with permission.

Figure 10.2   Ten maps, "Go West, Go East." Copyright, 1986, U.S. News & World Report. Reprinted from issue of July 7, 1986.

Figure 10.3   From John Omicinski and Karen DeWitt, "Apartheid: Groups as Classified by South African Law," April 11, 1986. Copyright 1986, *USA Today*. Reprinted with permission.

Chapter 11
Table 11.1   Adapted from *Childhood and Society*, 2nd Edition, by Erik H. Erikson, by permission of W. W. Norton & Company, Inc. Copyright 1950, © 1963 by W. W. Norton & Company, Inc. Copyright renewed 1978 by Erik H. Erikson.

Figure 11.1   From Daniel J. Levinson, "Developmental Periods in Early and Middle Adulthood" in *The Seasons of Man's Life*, 1978. Reprinted by permission of Alfred A. Knopf, Inc. As it appeared in *American Psychologist* 41. Copyright 1986 by the American Psychological Association and the author.

Figure 11.2   From *Public Opinion*, February/March 1985, p. 33. Reprinted with permission of American Enterprise Institute for Public Policy Research.

Chapter 12
Table 12.1   Adapted from George P. Murdock, "Comparative Data on the Division of Labor by Sex," *Social Forces*, 1935, Vol. 15, pp. 551–553.

Figure A   Chart, "What Other Countries Do." Copyright, 1986, U.S. News & World Report. Reprinted from issue of March 10, 1986.

Table 12.2   From David B. Sugarman, Rhode Island College, and Murray A. Straus, University of New Hampshire in *Newsweek*, October 6, 1986. Reprinted by permission of the authors.

Chapter 14
Table 14.1   Reprinted from the 1986 *Britannica Book of the Year*, copyright 1986, with the permission of Encyclopaedia

Index